Twentieth-Century
Literary Criticism

Guide to Thomson Gale Literary Criticism Series

For criticism on	Consult these Thomson Gale series
Authors now living or who died after December 31, 1999	*CONTEMPORARY LITERARY CRITICISM (CLC)*
Authors who died between 1900 and 1999	*TWENTIETH-CENTURY LITERARY CRITICISM (TCLC)*
Authors who died between 1800 and 1899	*NINETEENTH-CENTURY LITERATURE CRITICISM (NCLC)*
Authors who died between 1400 and 1799	*LITERATURE CRITICISM FROM 1400 TO 1800 (LC)* *SHAKESPEAREAN CRITICISM (SC)*
Authors who died before 1400	*CLASSICAL AND MEDIEVAL LITERATURE CRITICISM (CMLC)*
Authors of books for children and young adults	*CHILDREN'S LITERATURE REVIEW (CLR)*
Dramatists	*DRAMA CRITICISM (DC)*
Poets	*POETRY CRITICISM (PC)*
Short story writers	*SHORT STORY CRITICISM (SSC)*
Literary topics and movements	*HARLEM RENAISSANCE: A GALE CRITICAL COMPANION (HR)* *THE BEAT GENERATION: A GALE CRITICAL COMPANION (BG)* *FEMINISM IN LITERATURE: A GALE CRITICAL COMPANION (FL)* *GOTHIC LITERATURE: A GALE CRITICAL COMPANION (GL)*
Asian American writers of the last two hundred years	*ASIAN AMERICAN LITERATURE (AAL)*
Black writers of the past two hundred years	*BLACK LITERATURE CRITICISM (BLC)* *BLACK LITERATURE CRITICISM SUPPLEMENT (BLCS)*
Hispanic writers of the late nineteenth and twentieth centuries	*HISPANIC LITERATURE CRITICISM (HLC)* *HISPANIC LITERATURE CRITICISM SUPPLEMENT (HLCS)*
Native North American writers and orators of the eighteenth, nineteenth, and twentieth centuries	*NATIVE NORTH AMERICAN LITERATURE (NNAL)*
Major authors from the Renaissance to the present	*WORLD LITERATURE CRITICISM, 1500 TO THE PRESENT (WLC)* *WORLD LITERATURE CRITICISM SUPPLEMENT (WLCS)*

ISSN 0276-8178

Volume 187

Twentieth-Century Literary Criticism

**Criticism of the
Works of Novelists, Poets, Playwrights,
Short Story Writers, and Other Creative Writers
Who Lived between 1900 and 1999,
from the First Published Critical
Appraisals to Current Evaluations**

**Thomas J. Schoenberg
Lawrence J. Trudeau**
Project Editors

THOMSON
GALE

Detroit • New York • San Francisco • New Haven, Conn. • Waterville, Maine • London

Twentieth-Century Literary Criticism, Vol. 187

Project Editors
Thomas J. Schoenberg and Lawrence J. Trudeau

Editorial
Kathy D. Darrow, Jeffrey W. Hunter, Jelena O. Krstović, Michelle Lee, Russel Whitaker

Data Capture
Frances Monroe, Gwen Tucker

Indexing Services
Laurie Andriot

Rights and Acquisitions
Jackie Jones, Kelly Quin, Timothy Sisler

Imaging and Multimedia
Dean Dauphinais, Robert Duncan, Leitha Etheridge-Sims, Mary Grimes, Lezlie Light, Michael Logusz, Dan Newell, Denay Wilding

Composition and Electronic Capture
Tracey L. Matthews

Manufacturing
Rhonda Dover

Associate Product Manager
Marc Cormier

LIBRARY OF CONGRESS CATALOG CARD NUMBER 76-46132

ISBN-13: 978-0-7876-8941-4
ISBN-10: 0-7876-8941-6
ISSN 0276-8178

Printed in the United States of America
10 9 8 7 6 5 4 3 2 1

Contents

Preface vii

Acknowledgments xi

Literary Criticism Series Advisory Board xiii

Preface

Since its inception *Twentieth-Century Literary Criticism* (*TCLC*) has been purchased and used by some 10,000 school, public, and college or university libraries. *TCLC* has covered more than 1000 authors, representing over 60 nationalities and nearly 50,000 titles. No other reference source has surveyed the critical response to twentieth-century authors and literature as thoroughly as *TCLC*. In the words of one reviewer, "there is nothing comparable available." *TCLC* "is a gold mine of information—dates, pseudonyms, biographical information, and criticism from books and periodicals—which many librarians would have difficulty assembling on their own."

Scope of the Series

TCLC is designed to serve as an introduction to authors who died between 1900 and 1999 and to the most significant interpretations of these author's works. Volumes published from 1978 through 1999 included authors who died between 1900 and 1960. The great poets, novelists, short story writers, playwrights, and philosophers of the period are frequently studied in high school and college literature courses. In organizing and reprinting the vast amount of critical material written on these authors, *TCLC* helps students develop valuable insight into literary history, promotes a better understanding of the texts, and sparks ideas for papers and assignments. Each entry in *TCLC* presents a comprehensive survey on an author's career or an individual work of literature and provides the user with a multiplicity of interpretations and assessments. Such variety allows students to pursue their own interests; furthermore, it fosters an awareness that literature is dynamic and responsive to many different opinions.

Every fourth volume of *TCLC* is devoted to literary topics. These topics widen the focus of the series from the individual authors to such broader subjects as literary movements, prominent themes in twentieth-century literature, literary reaction to political and historical events, significant eras in literary history, prominent literary anniversaries, and the literatures of cultures that are often overlooked by English-speaking readers.

TCLC is designed as a companion series to Thomson Gale's *Contemporary Literary Criticism*, (*CLC*) which reprints commentary on authors who died after 1999. Because of the different time periods under consideration, there is no duplication of material between *CLC* and *TCLC*.

Organization of the Book

A *TCLC* entry consists of the following elements:

- The **Author Heading** cites the name under which the author most commonly wrote, followed by birth and death dates. Also located here are any name variations under which an author wrote, including transliterated forms for authors whose native languages use nonroman alphabets. If the author wrote consistently under a pseudonym, the pseudonym is listed in the author heading and the author's actual name is given in parenthesis on the first line of the biographical and critical information. Uncertain birth or death dates are indicated by question marks. Single-work entries are preceded by a heading that consists of the most common form of the title in English translation (if applicable) and the name of its author.

- The **Introduction** contains background information that introduces the reader to the author, work, or topic that is the subject of the entry.

- The list of **Principal Works** is ordered chronologically by date of first publication and lists the most important works by the author. The genre and publication date of each work is given. In the case of foreign authors whose works have been translated into English, the English-language version of the title follows in brackets. Unless otherwise indicated, dramas are dated by first performance, not first publication. Lists of **Representative Works** by different authors appear with topic entries.

■ Reprinted **Criticism** is arranged chronologically in each entry to provide a useful perspective on changes in critical evaluation over time. The critic's name and the date of composition or publication of the critical work are given at the beginning of each piece of criticism. Unsigned criticism is preceded by the title of the source in which it originally appeared. All titles by the author featured in the text are printed in boldface type. Footnotes are reprinted at the end of each essay or excerpt. In the case of excerpted criticism, only those footnotes that pertain to the excerpted texts are included. Criticism in topic entries is arranged chronologically under a variety of subheadings to facilitate the study of different aspects of the topic.

■ A complete **Bibliographical Citation** of the original essay or book precedes each piece of criticism. Source citations in the Literary Criticism Series follow University of Chicago Press style, as outlined in *The Chicago Manual of Style,* 15th ed. (Chicago: The University of Chicago Press, 2003).

■ Critical essays are prefaced by brief **Annotations** explicating each piece.

■ An annotated bibliography of **Further Reading** appears at the end of each entry and suggests resources for additional study. In some cases, significant essays for which the editors could not obtain reprint rights are included here. Boxed material following the further reading list provides references to other biographical and critical sources on the author in series published by Thomson Gale.

Indexes

A **Cumulative Author Index** lists all of the authors that appear in a wide variety of reference sources published by Thomson Gale, including *TCLC.* A complete list of these sources is found facing the first page of the Author Index. The index also includes birth and death dates and cross references between pseudonyms and actual names.

A **Cumulative Topic Index** lists the literary themes and topics treated in *TCLC* as well as other Literature Criticism series.

A **Cumulative Nationality Index** lists all authors featured in *TCLC* by nationality, followed by the numbers of the *TCLC* volumes in which their entries appear.

An alphabetical **Title Index** accompanies each volume of *TCLC.* Listings of titles by authors covered in the given volume are followed by the author's name and the corresponding page numbers where the titles are discussed. English translations of foreign titles and variations of titles are cross-referenced to the title under which a work was originally published. Titles of novels, dramas, nonfiction books, and poetry, short story, or essay collections are printed in italics, while individual poems, short stories, and essays are printed in roman type within quotation marks.

In response to numerous suggestions from librarians, Thomson Gale also produces a paperbound edition of the *TCLC* cumulative title index. This annual cumulation, which alphabetically lists all titles reviewed in the series, is available to all customers. Additional copies of this index are available upon request. Librarians and patrons will welcome this separate index; it saves shelf space, is easy to use, and is recyclable upon receipt of the next edition.

Citing *Twentieth-Century Literary Criticism*

When citing criticism reprinted in the Literary Criticism Series, students should provide complete bibliographic information so that the cited essay can be located in the original print or electronic source. Students who quote directly from reprinted criticism may use any accepted bibliographic format, such as University of Chicago Press style or Modern Language Association (MLA) style. Both the MLA and the University of Chicago formats are acceptable and recognized as being the current standards for citations. It is important, however, to choose one format for all citations; do not mix the two formats within a list of citations.

The examples below follow recommendations for preparing a bibliography set forth in *The Chicago Manual of Style,* 15th ed. (Chicago: The University of Chicago Press, (2003); the first example pertains to material drawn from periodicals, the second to material reprinted from books:

Morrison, Jago. "Narration and Unease in Ian McEwan's Later Fiction." *Critique* 42, no. 3 (spring 2001): 253-68. Reprinted in *Twentieth-Century Literary Criticism.* Vol. 127, edited by Janet Witalec, 212-20. Detroit: Thomson Gale, 2003.

Brossard, Nicole. "Poetic Politics." In *The Politics of Poetic Form: Poetry and Public Policy,* edited by Charles Bernstein, 73-82. New York: Roof Books, 1990. Reprinted in *Twentieth-Century Literary Criticism.* Vol. 127, edited by Janet Witalec, 3-8. Detroit: Thomson Gale, 2003.

The examples below follow recommendations for preparing a works cited list set forth in the *MLA Handbook for Writers of Research Papers,* 5th ed. (New York: The Modern Language Association of America, 1999); the first example pertains to material drawn from periodicals, the second to material reprinted from books:

Morrison, Jago. "Narration and Unease in Ian McEwan's Later Fiction." *Critique* 42.3 (spring 2001): 253-68. Reprinted in *Twentieth-Century Literary Criticism.* Ed. Janet Witalec. Vol. 127. Detroit: Thomson Gale, 2003. 212-20.

Brossard, Nicole. "Poetic Politics." *The Politics of Poetic Form: Poetry and Public Policy.* Ed. Charles Bernstein. New York: Roof Books, 1990. 73-82. Reprinted in *Twentieth-Century Literary Criticism.* Ed. Janet Witalec. Vol. 127. Detroit: Thomson Gale, 2003. 3-8.

Suggestions are Welcome

Readers who wish to suggest new features, topics, or authors to appear in future volumes, or who have other suggestions or comments are cordially invited to call, write, or fax the Associate Product Manager:

Associate Product Manager, Literary Criticism Series
Thomson Gale
27500 Drake Road
Farmington Hills, MI 48331-3535
1-800-347-4253 (GALE)
Fax: 248-699-8054

Acknowledgments

The editors wish to thank the copyright holders of the criticism included in this volume and the permissions managers of many book and magazine publishing companies for assisting us in securing reproduction rights. Following is a list of the copyright holders who have granted us permission to reproduce material in this volume of *TCLC*. Every effort has been made to trace copyright, but if omissions have been made, please let us know.

COPYRIGHTED MATERIAL IN *TCLC*, VOLUME 187, WAS REPRODUCED FROM THE FOLLOWING PERIODICALS:

American Literary History, v. 9, winter, 1997. Copyright © 1997 by Oxford University Press. Republished with permission of Oxford University Press, conveyed through Copyright Clearance Center, Inc.—*The Centennial Review,* v. 29, fall, 1985. Copyright © 1985 by *The Centennial Review.* Reproduced by permission.—*Essays in Literature,* v. 17, fall, 1990. Copyright © 1990 by Western Illinois University. Reproduced by permission.—*French Forum,* v. 12, January, 1987. Copyright © 1987 by French Forum, Inc. All rights reserved. Reproduced by permission of the University of Nebraska Press.—*Frontiers: A Journal of Women Studies,* v. 8, 1984. Copyright © 1984 by Frontiers Editorial Collective. All rights reserved. Reproduced by permission of the University of Nebraska Press.—*Genre,* v. 24, spring, 1991 for "Finding out about Gender in Hammett's Detective Fiction: Generic Constraints or Transcendental Norms?" by David J. Herman. Copyright © 1991 by the University of Oklahoma. Reproduced by permission of *Genre,* the University of Oklahoma and the author.—*Hartford Studies in Literature,* v. 8, 1976. Copyright © 1976 by the University of Hartford. Reproduced by permission.—*Journal of American and Comparative Cultures,* v. 23, fall, 2000. Copyright © 2000 Basil Blackwell Ltd. Reproduced by permission of Blackwell Publishers.—*Journal of Modern Literature,* v. 27, summer, 2004. Copyright © Indiana University Press. Reproduced by permission.—*Journal of the Short Story in English,* spring, 1990. Copyright © 1990 by Presses de l'Université d'Angers. Reproduced by permission.—*Literary Imagination,* v. 2, fall, 2000. Copyright 2000, all rights reserved by the Association of Literary Scholars and Critics. Reproduced by permission.—*Modern Drama,* v. 11, February, 1969. Copyright © 1969 by the University of Toronto, Graduate Centre for Study of Drama. Reproduced by permission.—*Modern Fiction Studies,* v. 49, winter, 2003; v. 51, fall, 2005. Copyright © 2003, 2005 The Johns Hopkins University Press. Both reproduced by permission.—*Mosaic,* v. 33, March, 2000. Copyright © *Mosaic* 2000. Acknowledgment of previous publication is herewith made.—*PMLA,* v. 106, March, 1991. Copyright © 1991 by the Modern Language Association of America. Reproduced by permission of the Modern Language Association of America.—*Renascence,* v. 20, autumn, 1967. Copyright © 1967, Marquette University Press. Reproduced by permission.—*The Southern Quarterly,* v. 12, April, 1974. Copyright © 1974 by the University of Southern Mississippi. Reproduced by permission.—*Studies in American Fiction,* v. 7, autumn, 1979. Copyright © 1979 Northeastern University. Reproduced by permission.—*Studies in American Humor,* n.s., v. 4, spring-summer, 1985. Copyright © 1985 American Humor Studies Association. Reproduced by permission.—*Studies in Short Fiction,* v. 18, winter, 1981; v. 19, spring, 1982. Copyright © 1981, 1982 by *Studies in Short Fiction.* All reproduced by permission.—*Style,* v. 29, fall, 1995. Copyright © *Style,* 1995. All rights reserved. Reproduced by permission of the publisher.—*Tulsa Studies in Women's Literature,* v. 15, fall, 1996; v. 22, spring, 2003. Both reproduced by permission.—*Twentieth Century Literature,* v. 44, spring, 1998; v. 45, fall, 1999. Copyright 1998, 1999, Hofstra University Press. All reproduced by permission.—*University of Windsor Review,* v. 13, 1978. Copyright © The University of Windsor Review. Reproduced by permission.—*Yale French Studies,* 1962, 2002. Copyright © Yale French Studies 1962, 2002. All reproduced by permission.

COPYRIGHTED MATERIAL IN *TCLC*, VOLUME 187, WAS REPRODUCED FROM THE FOLLOWING BOOKS:

Blair, Walter. From "Dashiell Hammett: Themes and Techniques," in *Essays on American Literature: In Honor of Jay B. Hubbell.* Edited by Clarence Gohdes. Duke University Press, 1967. Copyright © 1967 Duke University Press. All rights reserved. Used by permission of the publisher.—Dooley, Dennis. From *Dashiell Hammett.* Frederick Ungar Publishing Co., 1984. Copyright © 1984 by Frederick Ungar Publishing Co., Inc. Republished with permission of Frederick Ungar Publishing Co., Inc., conveyed through Copyright Clearance Center, Inc.—Edenbaum, Robert I. From "The Poetics of the Private-Eye: The Novels of Dashiell Hammett," in *Tough Guy Writers of the Thirties.* Edited by David Madden. Southern Illinois University Press, 1968. Copyright © 1968 by the Board of Trustees, Southern Illinois University. All rights re-

Thomson Gale Literature Product Advisory Board

The members of the Thomson Gale Literature Product Advisory Board—reference librarians from public and academic library systems—represent a cross-section of our customer base and offer a variety of informed perspectives on both the presentation and content of our literature products. Advisory board members assess and define such quality issues as the relevance, currency, and usefulness of the author coverage, critical content, and literary topics included in our series; evaluate the layout, presentation, and general quality of our printed volumes; provide feedback on the criteria used for selecting authors and topics covered in our series; provide suggestions for potential enhancements to our series; identify any gaps in our coverage of authors or literary topics, recommending authors or topics for inclusion; analyze the appropriateness of our content and presentation for various user audiences, such as high school students, undergraduates, graduate students, librarians, and educators; and offer feedback on any proposed changes/enhancements to our series. We wish to thank the following advisors for their advice throughout the year.

Michel de Ghelderode
1898-1962

(Born Adolphe-Adhémar Martens; also wrote under pseudonym Philostène Constable) Belgian playwright, poet, and short story writer.

The following entry provides an overview of Ghelderode's life and works. For additional information on his career, see *CLC,* Volumes 6 and 11.

INTRODUCTION

Belgian playwright Michel de Ghelderode is considered an innovative and important figure in twentieth-century European literature. His dark plays, written in French, feature grotesque imagery and surreal settings, and address various themes, such as death and aging, religion, human sexuality, and the relationship between art and reality. In addition to its sources in religious and medieval drama, Ghelderode's work borrows elements from Flemish folklore, the tradition of marionette theater, and the burlesque. In this respect, it has often been compared to the paintings of the Flemish artists Hieronymus Bosch and Pieter Brueghel the Elder. Ghelderode deliberately wrote his plays to shock and confront viewers, and to challenge conventional thought. In fact, many of his works originally staged in France and Belgium scandalized audiences. Although Ghelderode's plays are performed less often than they were at the peak of his popularity after World War II, his work is still admired, particularly in academic communities throughout the world. In 1993 David B. Parsell observed that "Ghelderode's dramaturgy will continue to draw merited attention as long as actors, directors, and potential spectators return to the stage in search of stimuli and inspiration. The deliberately archaic themes and setting of Ghelderode's best plays, never timely, remain timeless in their portrayal of mankind's elemental struggle against the inevitability of death—as, to be sure, of life itself."

BIOGRAPHICAL INFORMATION

Ghelderode was born Adolphe-Adhémar Martens on April 3, 1898, in Ixelles, Belgium. His parents, Henri-Adolphe Martens, a clerk in Brussels, and Jeanne-Marie Martens were Dutch speakers who educated their children in French. Ghelderode attended the Institut St-Louis in Belgium until 1914, when he was forced to quit after contracting typhus. He was deeply affected by his illness, as well as his brother's death in World War I, and as a result of both suffered from hypochondria and suicidal tendencies during his youth. Ghelderode studied the viola briefly at the Conservatoire Royal de Bruxelles before he turned to literature and writing. His first play, *La mort regarde à la fenêtre* (*Death Looks in the Window*), was performed in April 1918 at the Théâtre de la Bonbonnière.

Ghelderode's writing career was briefly interrupted by military service from 1919 to 1921. Upon his return to civilian life, he resumed writing and took a job as a clerk in the city of Schaarbeek. During this time, Ghelderode mainly wrote fiction in French. He published all of his prose under the name Ghelderode, which he officially adopted in 1930 to emphasize his Flemish roots. In 1924 Ghelderode married Jeanne Gérard. He began to publish more of his writing, including poems under the pseudonym Philostène Constable, and restored and adapted medieval plays to be performed by marionettes. In 1925 Ghelderode published two dramatic works that foreshadowed some of his later themes: *Oude Piet,* which won a prize from La Renaissance d'Occident, and *Les vieillards* (*The Old Men*), a one-act play that Ghelderode described as a "mystical farce."

During the 1920s and 1930s Ghelderode wrote plays for the radio as well as the stage, many of which deal with issues of religion, death, and old age. Several of these early plays were produced and performed by the Vlaamsche Volkstooneel (VVT), an avant-garde Catholic theater troupe in Brussels. The group produced *La farce de la mort qui faillit trépasser* in 1925 and *Images de la vie de Saint François d'Assise* in 1927, each of which met with popular and critical success. Ghelderode also began receiving recognition in France when his play *La mort du Docteur Faust* (*The Death of Doctor Faust*) was published in 1926 and performed two years later at the Art et Action theater in Paris. In 1929 Art et Action also produced *Christophe Colomb* (*Christopher Columbus*), one of Ghelderode's best-known plays. That same year, a Dutch version of *Escurial,* a dark one-act play that explores the relationship between reality and fantasy, debuted in Brussels.

Ghelderode continued to write during World War II, and several of his plays were produced. Two of his dramas, *Hop Signor!* (1942) and *L'ecole des bouffons* (1953; *School for Buffoons*), marked his experiments with the "theater of cruelty," in which grotesque imagery is used to shock and confront audiences in an effort to destroy the false reality that clouds perception. During the Nazi occupation of Belgium, Ghelderode contributed several short works to Radio-Bruxelles. Although the pieces revealed no political affiliation, Ghelderode was charged with being a Nazi collaborator and lost his civil service job. He received a full pardon in 1949. His popularity increased during the late 1940s, particularly in France, where several of his plays were staged, including *Fastes d'enfer* (1949; *Chronicles of Hell*) and *Mademoiselle Jaïre* (1949; *Mademoiselle Jairus*), both of which won the Grand Prix des Jeunes Compagnies (Grand Prize for Young Companies) award in Paris.

By the 1950s Ghelderode had become a major literary figure in France, while his plays continued to be produced in his native Belgium. A number of his works were also staged for the first time in North and South America, as well as other parts of Europe. When Ghelderode died on April 1, 1962, he was considered one of the most influential and innovative playwrights writing in the French language.

MAJOR WORKS

In his notable early plays, Ghelderode often explored abstract concepts and experimented with the formal constraints of the theater itself. In *The Death of Doctor Faust,* he reconsidered the relationship between fantasy and reality in his retelling of the classic story of Faust. The play uses several meta-theatrical devices, including character doubling, a play-within-a-play, and complex multiple sets. In Ghelderode's version of the story, the historical figure Faust meets an actor playing the role of Faust. The two confront each other and begin fighting, and while attempting to kill his actor-counterpart, the historical Faust accidentally kills himself. In this work Ghelderode used the stage to experiment with theatrical art and to explore the psychological boundaries between reality and fantasy that reside in the minds of both actors and the audience. In one of his most anthologized plays, *Christopher Columbus,* Ghelderode reinvented the persona of the legendary explorer. He is portrayed as a bubble-blowing dreamer, rather than a visionary man, who begins his quest because he has nothing better to do. His voyage consists of a series of fantastic, anachronistic occurrences. Finally, at the end of the play, which Ghelderode categorized as a "dramatic fairy tale," Columbus becomes a statue in the new world. The drama has a distinct Anti-American sentiment, partially revealed when Columbus is criticized for being an immigrant, and not an American citizen, by the play's close.

Many critics consider the play *Magie rouge* (1934; *Red Magic*) typical of the transitional period in Ghelderode's literary career. While he had previously borrowed themes and characters from medieval literature and the Bible, during his transitional period he drew from myth and employed fantastic imagery. *Red Magic* relies on the character archetypes of the "miser" and the "alchemist" from folklore. The play explores the destructive power of greed and vengeance and portrays a morally corrupt world. The miser, Hyéronimus, is consumed by his desire to accumulate wealth. He hires Armador, a man claiming to be an alchemist, to produce gold. Concerned only with his wealth, however, the miser neglects his wife's needs and refuses to consummate their marriage. For revenge, she takes Armador as a lover, and they plot to destroy Hyéronimus. At the end of the play, the miser loses his fortune, his wife, and his freedom when he is accused of a crime that Armador committed. The conclusion of play illustrates the extent of the miser's perversion and self-delusion. Hyéronimus is so consumed by his own avarice that he falsely believes he is immortal and equal to God.

Chronicles of Hell is regarded as one of Ghelderode's most important and complex plays. The one-act drama takes place in Flanders during the burial services for Bishop Jan Eremo. The Bishop is described as a Christ-like figure who performs miracles and is drawn in sharp contrast to the sinful priest Simon Laquedeem and to the monks presiding over his funeral, whose names connote various vices. The connection between Jan Eremo and Christ is further reinforced when, toward the end of the play, the Bishop miraculously rises and accuses Laquedeem of poisoning the communion wafer that he has partially swallowed. During the confrontation, Jan Eremo threatens to kill the priest, but his mother, Vénéranda, extracts the poisoned wafer from his throat and convinces him to forgive his enemies. The Bishop dies after he submits to her request. Although much of the action in *Chronicles of Hell* is tragic, Ghelderode includes farcical elements as well and ends the play with scatological humor. The struggle between the sacred and the profane is the main theme of the play, but the resolution of that struggle remains ambiguous at the end. While some critics argue that evil triumphs at the close of the play, when Laquedeem defecates next to the Bishop's dead body, others have interpreted Jan Eremo's death as a moral victory, in which his faith remains intact.

CRITICAL RECEPTION

Critical study of Ghelderode's work has followed a pattern of neglect and rediscovery throughout the playwright's career and, especially, since his death in 1962. In Belgium, and somewhat later in France, early audiences and critics of Ghelderode's plays were often shocked by their uncompromising portrait of human depravity and sin, their treatment of religious hypocrisy, and their scatological wit. By the late 1940s and early 1950s, however, long after Ghelderode composed his major works, the Parisian theater establishment came to embrace him as an innovative and important writer. As Parsell has noted, during this period in French drama "Ghelderode's exploration of scenic and dramatic possibilities, together with his graphic contrasts of illusion and reality, helped to point new directions for antirational, 'visceral' theater, such as that proposed by Antonin Artaud." But just as suddenly as Ghelderode's fame rose on the French stage, it dissipated, as audiences and the theater establishment moved on to new writers such as Eugene Ionesco and Samuel Beckett. By the time of Ghelderode's death, his immense popularity in France had waned. Even so, his stature as a playwright of international importance began to spread outside of France and Belgium, to the United States, Great Britain, Canada, Eastern Europe, and even Latin America.

Since the 1960s Ghelderode's reputation has continued to increase. In North America Ghelderode has been regarded as an influential precursor of the Theater of the Absurd, a craftsman of theatrical form, and either a deeply religious writer or a nihilist strongly concerned with humankind's struggle to find meaning in the face of death. Scholars also have praised the playwright for his ability to deftly blend elements of folklore, religion, and medieval literature, along with a pronounced sense of romanticism. While many critics have noted the barriers to staging Ghelderode's plays, as well as the flawed and uneven quality of his total output as a playwright, most also have attested to the psychological power and dramatic precision of his writing. As Parsell asserted, "Ghelderode's plays continue to suggest possibilities for the stage, a truly open-ended performance in which text, sound, and spectacle combine to bring actors and audience into confrontation with themselves. When well-executed, the best of Ghelderode's have few peers in the domain of 'total theater,' surpassing even the wildest dreams of Artaud."

PRINCIPAL WORKS

La mort regarde à la fenêtre [*Death Looks in the Window*] (play) 1918

Le repas des fauves (play) 1919

La halte catholique (prose) 1922

L'homme sous l'uniforme (short stories) 1923

La farce de la mort qui faillit trépasser (play) 1925

Oude Piet (play) 1925

Les vieillards: Farce mystique en 1 acte [*The Old Men*] (play) 1925

La mort du Docteur Faust [*The Death of Doctor Faust*] (play) 1926

Images de la vie de Saint François d'Assise (play) 1927

Ixelles, mes amours [as Philostène Constable] (poetry) 1928

Le miracle dans le faubourg (play) 1928

Barabbas (play) 1929

Christophe Colomb [*Christopher Columbus*] (play) 1929

Escurial (play) 1929

Pantagleize (play) 1930

Trois acteurs [*Three Actors*] (play) 1931

Le cavalier bizarre (radio play) 1932

Le coeur révélateur (radio play) 1932

Le voleur d'étoiles (play) 1932

Annibal, speaker futur (radio play) 1933

Bureau ouvert de neuf à midi (radio play) 1933

Plaisir d'amour (radio play) 1933

La ronde des prisonniers (radio play) 1933

Cinq mai 1835 (radio play) 1934

Magie rouge [*Red Magic*] (play) 1934

Le mystère de la Passion de Notre-Seigneur Jésus-Christ (play) 1934

Payül au paradis (radio play) 1934

Payül champion (radio play) 1934

Payül dans le beffroi (radio play) 1934

Payül lauréat (radio play) 1934

Payül reporter (radio play) 1934

Le ménage de Caroline (play) 1935

L'Oiseau chocolat (radio play) 1937

Sire Halewyn [*Lord Halewyn*] (play) 1938

Adrian et Jusemina (play) 1939

Arc en-ciel (play) 1939

Comment l'empereur Charles devint voleur des chiens (radio play) 1939

D'un fou qui se croyait empereur (radio play) 1939

Scènes de la vie d'un bohème: Franz Schubert (radio play) 1941

Sortilèges (short stories) 1941

Hop Signor! (play) 1942

Il fiammingo (radio play) 1942

Fastes d'enfer [*Chronicles of Hell*] (play) 1949

Mademoiselle Jaïre [*Mademoiselle Jairus*] (play) 1949

Théâtre. 6 vols. (plays) 1950-82

La farce des ténébreux (play) 1952

Marie la misérable (play) 1952

La balade du Grand Macabre (play) 1953

**Le cavalier bizarre* [*The Strange Rider*] (play) 1953

L'ecole des bouffons [*School for Buffoons*] (play) 1953

Les femmes au tombeau [*The Women at the Tomb*] (play) 1953

†*Les aveugles* [*The Blind Men: In the Country of the Blind, the One-Eyed Man Is King*] (play) 1956

Le club des menteurs (play) 1957

‡*La transfiguration dans le cirque* [*Transfiguration in the Circus*] (play) 1959

Ghelderode: Seven Plays, Volume 1 (plays) 1960

§*Sortie de l'acteur* [*The Actor Makes His Exit*] (play) 1960

‖*Don Juan ou les amants chimériques* (play) 1962

Ghelderode: Seven Plays, Volume 2 (plays) 1966
#*Un soir de pitié* [*A Night of Pity*] (play) 1970
**Vénus (play) 1970
Correspondance de Michel de Ghelderode. 5 vols. [edited by Roland Beyen] (letters) 1991-98

*This work is a stage adaptation of the 1932 radio play of the same name.

†This work was originally published in 1936.

‡This work was originally published in 1928.

§This work was originally published in 1935.

||This work was originally published in 1928.

#This work was originally published in 1929.

*This work was originally published in 1927.

CRITICISM

Micheline Herz (essay date 1962)

SOURCE: Herz, Micheline. "Tragedy, Poetry and the Burlesque in Ghelderode's Theatre." *Yale French Studies* 29 (1962): 92-101.

[*In the following essay, Herz emphasizes the role of the burlesque in Ghelderode's plays, maintaining that the author uses it to underscore "man's physiological servitude" and "his wretchedness." Herz also comments on the poetic quality of Ghelderode's language.*]

At every level, including the level of appearance, Michel de Ghelderode's theatre abounds in burlesque elements. There is nothing glorious about his men, nor about his women either. However upsetting some people may find this, it is clear that Ghelderode himself, as manifested in his plays, reveled in such an atmosphere. Monsters and misshapen beings accost us at every turn. Women, apart from a few saints and other privileged creatures, tend to be fiftyish, ample as to breast and buttock, with a gash by way of a mouth and peroxide hair: typical residents of a low-grade brothel. Their names are evocative: Salivaine, Visquosine, Crême, Chose, Boule, Olympia, Aurora, Venuska, and so forth. The more or less normal creatures in this feminine galaxy (Armande in *Sortie de l'acteur* or Emmanuèle in *La Farce des ténébreux*) remind one nevertheless of Baudelaire's "Woman is the opposite of the dandy." Even those very young girls, Purmelende d'Ostrelende in *Sire Halewyn* and the living corpse Mademoiselle Jaire, cannot entirely escape the grotesquerie of woman's condition. They are Woman, young or old as circumstances require, exemplars of their sex.

Men, though treated in less summary fashion, are etched in acidly. One recalls Hiéronymus in *Magie rouge,* Videbolle, Sire Goulave in *La Balade du grand macabre,* and a whole series, in *Hop Signor, Escurial, L'Ecole des bouffons* and elsewhere, of men blind or decrepit or otherwise infirm. In conjuring up all this ugliness and, at times, poking fun at it, Ghelderode is carrying out one of the missions of the theatre as he conceives it. His aim is to deflate a number of lying myths, and one of these is the delight man takes in his own beauty. So Ghelderode stresses man's physiological servitude and harps on his wretchedness. Like Sartre and like Céline, he dwells on the intestinal aspects of these miseries. His plays smell bad. Yet these odors—which, also, are man—engender comedy, however little it may appeal to the queasy. Are we not told that la Palatine, with the aid of her husband, a nincompoop in other domains of endeavor, used to organize crepitation contests—and this was France's great century! There is much talk of fecal matter in Ghelderode's plays, to underline the fact that man is not dust alone but also dung. He would prefer to see himself as a flower or a radiant body? So much the worse for him. Whereas, if he admits the restraints imposed by his bodily functions, he ceases to be civilizedly etiolated and enrols matter in his service. And matter, even fecal, is an inexhaustible source of comedy for the robust individuality imagined by Ghelderode.

Like man's lot, the plot in which he is caught up is frequently a burlesque one. The deceived husband of *Hop Signor* dies during the hoodwinking process because he played the aristocrat, with a sword, and airs and graces that did not befit his station. The miserly Hiéronymus (*Magie rouge*) harbors the horseman Armador, who has promised to manufacture gold. But Armador steals instead of providing, and with the help of the housewife Sybilla places responsibility for a murder on Hiéronymus, who has already gone mad. This husband, who shuts up his wife with another man and marries off his doubloons so that they may multiply, is the central figure of a cruel farce in which avarice takes on hallucinatory dimensions.

Even in the more sober plays, the burlesque aspects are always present. While a father gives way to grotesque grief for his dying daughter (*Mademoiselle Jaïre*), the coffinmaker comes along to vaunt his merchandise: "For your soon-to-be-lamented daughter, I'll make a little masterpice of elegance, solidity and comfort." Or a bottle of Hollands gin consoles the three Mariekes, as they weep over the dead.

Death, in *Le Cavalier bizarre,* spares the terrified old men who await his coming and bears off a new-born child. The title character of *La Balade du grand macabre* himself dies and his victims outlive him. The author, in *Trois Acteurs, un drame,* commits suicide, and not the actor who had intended to do so. Examples could easily be multiplied.

The burlesque atmosphere allows the spectator to put up with a degree of tension that might well evaporate, if the author tried to maintain it too long. A further merit of the burlesque, in Ghelderode's eyes, is that it gives direct expression to the voice of the people, which in Greek tragedy is embodied in the chorus. He roundly declares this to be so, and refers to the Mariekes mentioned above and to the buffoons in all the plays where they appear. Even in *Barrabas* and *Marie la misérable,* his religious plays, these procedures are used. In the same strain are the "plays within a play," the processions, the lines of mourners and the speeches, to which Ghelderode sometimes turns too readily.

It is less easy to speak of a burlesque character or of burlesque psychology, since Ghelderode rejects all psychology. The dramatist, he maintains, must draw upon the wellsprings of vision or of instinct. The writer who accepts a system will sooner or later trap himself in a problem play. Jean-Jacques, the author who serves as spokesman for Ghelderode himself in *Sortie de l'acteur,* proclaims that "I have never wanted to reveal or demonstrate anything and, as long as men have been mumming, the theatre has never been known to reveal anything whatever."

The few characters who turn out well, in Michel de Ghelderode's plays, become human via their dehumanization. Like Jarry's personages, they are so untrue that they achieve a truth of their own. Nekrozotar and Videbolle, the former a divine executioner mounted on the drunkard Porprenaz, and the latter the philosopher of the kingdom and a henpecked husband, are related to Tyl Eulenspiegel. They act, like worthy representatives of legendary chronicles, in a totally unforeseeable fashion. And we accept the spectacle of Videbolle overwhelmed with blows that would kill any mortal, just as we accept the unbelievable malevolence of Videbolle's wife Salivaine, the kingdom's grey eminence. Ghelderode's more anthropomorphic heroes, among them Charles V and Barrabas, are not exempt from the hyperbole favored by this author. In that magnificent play *Le Soleil se couche* Charles V gives orders for his funeral mass, little suspecting that he is falling into the trap laid for him by his son Philip. The examination of conscience he makes, to the accompaniment of the objurgations of a talking parrot, shows him in turn as sincere and fraudulent, a believer and a skeptic, brave and cowardly, magnificent and pitiably deceived by Philip and the Holy Office.

The hero of *Barrabas* is a wild beast one cannot readily imagine associated with any kind of Christian communism. To say what Ghelderode's characters are, unavoidably one must relate what they are doing or have done. They enjoy their liberty in the midst of the incredible and the extraordinary, and this liberty appears to be gratuitous, for it is grafted much more firmly on a poetics than on any association of the characters with a world, a struggle or a passion, in which they would feel responsible for anything beyond themselves. With the sole exception of the cloistered Marie, the liberty of Ghelderode's characters revolves in a vacuum and may, in this sense, be classified as burlesque.

Ghelderode, in his *Entretiens d'Ostende,* asserts that his plays are neither clerical nor anti-clerical. "Why," he goes on to say, "don't they make me out to be a Catholic author, while they're at it, since after all I've put saints on the stage!" However that may be, his education at the hands of the "clerical gentlemen" awakened within him a sense of metaphysical anguish. At first this was stilled by the teachings of the Church, but later, as he himself expressed it, his faith "drifted" and he found himself obliged to find an answer for the problems of our human condition.

Whatever his religious feelings may have been at the time of his death, there can be no doubt that Ghelderode's guidelines are Christian. Ghelderodian man has a sense of sin. He knows that he is guilty. He is punished because he is guilty. He is capable of every "truculence," in the Latin sense of the word, and of every extravagance of behavior because, no matter what he does, he is certain to lose. His horizon is bounded by death. Thus the sense of the tragic, in Ghelderode's case, comes from the omnipresence of death. There is a lot of dying in his plays, he declares, because there is a lot of dying in life. Yet on several occasions he has let his characters protest against this bloody game. "There are three of us, and if only three of us die, it's because there's no one else."

It is, indeed, more economical to list the plays in which death has no part. They are *D'un diable qui prêcha merveilles, Le Club des menteurs, Les Vieillards, Adrian et Jusemina*—a total of four plays out of the thirty printed in the five volumes of the Gallimard edition! Death is often a medieval figure, with an eroded snubnose, who sees fit to wander among the living. In *Le Cavalier bizarre* he is described as "very taken with himself, with protruding jaw, hand on hip, scythe over shoulder, wearing white boots and wrapped in a torn cloak strewn with small silver crosses." In *Le Grand Macabre,* he resembles the disguise a student might dream up for the Beaux Arts ball. In *Escurial* the king imagines him "as a skeleton sauntering about, in monk's clothing." Death in *Christophe Colomb,* appears as a "naval officer, ageless." He is featured in the train of the Ship of Fools, along with young men wearing shrouds and women similarly attired. In *Masques Ostendais,* Death is dressed in a dirty garment covered with crosses, with a battered top hat.

In less incarnate fashion, death resolves the dilemmas confronting Doctor Faust and Sire Halewyn and Barrabas and Marie the wretched, for death alone confers peace. (The real drama for Ghelderode would be immortality, but not as Simone de Beauvoir has conceived it.) He tackles the related problem of resurrection in *Mademoiselle Jaïre* and in the religious plays. He looks on resurrection, it would seem, as a privilege reserved for the gods. Thus the attitude of Ghelderode toward death is ambivalent. He desires it because of its purity and fears it because it might funnel one into a beyond where the angels would bear a distressing similarity to cops.

He evolved, consequently, a kind of fetishism of death and brandished it, variously garbed, before the eyes of those eager to forget it. Western civilization, with its up-to-the-minute funeral rites and its painted and smiling corpses, has administered a tranquilizer to our feeling for death, and if ever Ghelderode set himself a mission, no doubt it was to remind men of how afraid they are—without overlooking the laugh that so often follows fear.

In his own way yet much as does Camus in *Caligula,* Ghelderode teaches his readers that men die and that they are not happy. But except in *Sortie de l'acteur* and *Pantagleize,* Ghelderode is on God's side—whether God exists or not. He sports death's colors no doubt because, having often been ill, he was able to become intimate with it, but also because he took great satisfaction in exorcizing it on his own account, while turning loose on other people his arsenal of Fates.

Death, finally, is also the order in which one can believe. He sometimes comes close to imagining that it's all some monstrous legpull that a jovial Creator has inflicted on us, and that serves to get the creation going again. The function of the devil, never far away from the figure of death in Ghelderode's theatre, is to restore the category of Evil and reinsert it in a cosmos beneath the blazing sun of Satan.

Love is the opium of the western world. Ghelderode goes further. Love, it is his conviction, is synonymous with lust, death's other companion on the portals of the churches. Thus eroticism is a source both of tragedy and of burlesquerie. It is tragic because it leads to nothingness, through the intermediary of sickness. Beauty, once possessed, is transmuted into a creature of the charnelhouse. But it is burlesque when baptized with the name of love and when the commentary is omitted that ". . . relates how the most azured and turtledovey amorous tale ends with the evocation of a bidet, of a bidet, Madame, were it made of gold and shaped like a heart." This is not to condemn the function that is sublimated under the name of love. The innocent Fernand d'Abcaude, in love with Azurine, is an object of ridi-

cule until he does obeisance to the cult of Azurine, now unveiled and rebaptized Putrégina. Normal pleasure, however, cannot be found in these plays, unless perhaps in the past, when the exploits of some duke are evoked. The flesh, alas, is sad and putrescent.

The couples—Marguerite Harstein and Juréal, Hiéronymus and Sybilla—are sterile. Husbands appear to derive great pleasure from leaving their wives virgins, so that they can watch them suffer. Sexuality, or lust, imprisons man and more especially, perhaps, woman, who spices it with masochism when she is young and pretty and with ravenous unsatisfied instincts when she is older. In *Hop Signor,* which Ghelderode has characterized as the drama of impotence, Marguerite compares voluptuousness to a shortened form of torture and, finally, physical satisfaction coincides with the sleep of death. Love, with Ghelderode, has monstrous dimensions. Only in the brothel is it forgivable, and Putrégina is assuredly the least morbid of all these creatures.

Chastity is a virtue because love is a trap, leading to gestures by whose burlesque character Ghelderode is obsessed. In the kind of bacchanalian revel that permeates this theatre one may, perhaps, discern the ebullition of good health. Ghelderode has denied that he is "a pornographer-industrialist specializing in bourgeois orgasms." Perhaps he specializes in more literary orgies!

The validity of Ghelderode's theater resides in its poetry. This does not appear to be so at first glance, and it was never his aim to write poetic plays. In each work there can be discovered, after careful investigation, a particular rhythm that concords with Ghelderode's vision. The words are linked in a musical sequence of cadences and leitmotifs that reinforce the overall theme. Most of his plays could readily be adapted for ballet. With him, gesture is primary and speech is subordinate to it, forming a sort of ground bass that accompanies the actors' plastic expression.

When simplicity marks this poetry or these movements performed confronted by a veritable Chaplinade (to borrow the term created by ordinary folk as in *Pantagleize* or *Le Club des menteurs,* we are by Yvan Goll). The spectator, plunged in a world that precludes direct identification, has a poetic experience of or meets as in a dream protagonists endowed with a reality that to the spectator appears absurd. This moves him. He laughs. Ghelderode admired Chaplin. And an ironic satisfaction can be gleaned from the reflection that this figure of the poet as a gentle dreamer, innocent and pure, comic yet touching, links up beyond Chaplin with the scatterbrained characters of Yiddish folklore.

This poetry has a further strain of mystery, or of magic. The world contains things that are signs, and which may awaken at any instant. Life swarms with hollow receptacles waiting to be filled and, sometimes kindly and sometimes maleficent, the forces that take them over plunge the individual if not in the religious sphere at least in the domain of the sacred. That is why puppets can represent the divine or, if one will, the essential element in human beings better than do actors of flesh and blood, whose gestures may lack the definitive or hieratic character that produces trance. And to that the spectator must be led, if the ceremony is to have its full effect.

The puppeteer, furthermore, at least in the rudimentary form of the spectacle, utilizes nothing but his own voice, dehumanized by means of a kind of whistle. There is only one mediator between author and public. The treason of language is, in this way, practically eliminated. We inhabit pure poetry, where the puppet master is God.

Clowns, puppets, buffoons and masks enrich this theatre with a poetry that is both fantastic and grotesque, realistic and allegorical, along with the "alienation" derived from a past left more or less vague. This is a specifically dramatic poetry, since the stage is needed, but in its elements it is mythical. Through allegory it can strike a didactic note, and embrace the burlesque and satirical. On a higher level, the use of puppet or clown and the availability of multiple identities, in Ghelderode's best plays, reveal a universe that transcends the one we inhabit but which we feel nevertheless belongs to us.

Thus Ghelderode's poetry, feeding on the supernatural, constitutes a kind of evocation, an incantatory art. *La Sortie de l'acteur* is concerned in part with the spell exercised by the author on his interpreter. He summons up half-extinct towns, bygone days, male and female saints. The pathetic thing about these voyages of discovery initiated by a lonely man is that they affect him too nearly. He does not always avoid psychodrama. The disharmonies that at times spoil or wreck the poetic beauty attained by Ghelderode are remarkably similar to those that sometimes irritate us in the films of Ingmar Bergman.

Michel de Ghelderode, despite his deliberately archaic and recherché vocabulary, neglected speech in favor of the visual. His world view is plastic. As a young man he haunted the art galleries, and philosophized as he looked at the canvases of the great masters of his own country: Bosch, Breughel, Teniers, Jordaens, James Ensor. "This Flemish nation in which I have my origins seems double to me. Matching its superb vitality and materialism is a preoccupation with metaphysical disquietude."

Among the friends of his maturity were the painters Jean Jacques Gailliard, Marcel Stobbaerts and others, who no doubt guided him in his scenic researches. He

was, furthermore, passionately addicted to those spectacles in which speech as such plays little part, operas, ballets, and the puppets in the vaulted cellars of Brussels. Passionately he wandered through the churches, where he admired the statues of the Virgin, and in public gardens, where he admired whatever statues were to be seen. (His book, **Mes Statues,** has been published by the Editions du Carrefour.) As to everything else that was tangible, he reacted to the spectacle of everyday life, to funeral processions, festivals, passersby.

Born in 1898, Ghelderode was inevitably affected by all the distastes manifested by the literary leaders of the closing nineteenth and early twentieth centuries, before he came under the influence of surrealism or expressionism, those movements of his own generation.

He repudiated the rationalistic humanism of the eighteenth century and, in accord with the tendencies of his masters both of painterly thought and of thought unqualified, he turned back to the ideals of the Renaissance, that savage century so like our own, with the frightening perspectives it presented to men, its unknown horizons in space and thought, its intellectual and sensual frenzies, a century in which suffering rubbed shoulders with laughter or even engendered it.— Doubtless it was this last aspect that most keenly marked the sensibility of our author.

So he set out to acquire his own manner. Despite the inspiration he found in Charles de Coster's *Ulenspiegel* and Georges Eekhoud's *Siècle de Shakespeare,* his ancestry will turn out to be more French than could at first have been anticipated. Perceptible are Rabelais, Lesage and even Léon Daudet, whose *Le Voyage de Shakespeare* was cited by Ghelderode and whose countless novels, more richly expressive than they are descriptive, have been undeservedly neglected. For all his verbal ebullience, strange personages and startling, often grotesquely cruel scenes, Daudet remains nevertheless a pamphleteer, and we should not overstress the kinship.

Ghelderode's highly charged style is sufficiently motivated by the theatrical perspective and the passions he wished to convey. But here is a sample of the way he answered journalists whose indiscreet curiosity had angered him. "You mean the hypocrites, bigots, *cagots* and *matagots* forbidden by Gargantua to cross the threshold of his Abbey of Theleme? It's altogether too kind of you, my dear colleague, to concern yourself with this clerical scum! As for me, I sh.. on them from the morning angelus to the evening angelus!"

The Word, here, is both sovereign and derelict. It is despised as a conveyor of certitudes but furbished anew with all its powers of suggestion, aristocratically, much as Louis-Ferdinand Céline did, in his own back-to-the-people vein. Pierre de Boisdeffre has actually maintained that Ghelderode wrote anti-plays! Well, yes, if the language of Céline's *Journey to the End of the Night* makes it an anti-novel. But it is no difficult matter to regard as essentially dramatic the whole weight of sensuality that is embodied and rendered visible in language. Such a utilization of language clearly engenders both poetic and burlesque elements requiring a sensitive direction that remains faithful to the author's intentions.

Michel de Ghelderode devalues the word as a bearer of meaning but reinstates it by loading it with poetry. This distrust of the word is also a distrust of the intelligence. Yet, to the extent that the burlesque expresses a certain delight in life's superabundance and that the poetic or comic elements spring from some encounter with the exaggerated and the ridiculous, in the end Ghelderode addresses himself to man's intelligence, not his sensibility.

With respect to sensibility and intelligence alike, this art has limits that the poetic afflatus cannot entirely make up for. Sometimes the mythical quality is lost, to be replaced by a symbolism of a rather shopworn kind. If modern drama is to provide a specific experience, it must present some passion involving the whole of man. Otherwise it vociferates oracularly and falls short of the universal. Confronted by man or by the created world, the dramatist must be touched by wonder, by love or its opposite. Quite certainly, in dealing with man, he must convey "something valid."

Ghelderode asserts that he loves men ". . . as they should be loved, from a certain distance, and I am just as indulgent and sympathetic toward their weaknesses as, professionally speaking, I am interested in their absurdities."

This statement seems to imply that Ghelderode himself is not always personally involved. He is fascinated by this world he has created but sometimes he remains "outside." This makes the demon of bad faith prick up his ears. Ghelderode's anti-Semitism may be explained, perhaps, as due to his preoccupation with magic. His characterizations of the children of Israel, for all that, could have found a fitting place in such publications as *Le Pilori.* In **Fastes d'enfer** Simon Laquedeem, the wandering Jew transformed into a suffragan bishop, invents a new version of ritual murder, and as the curtain descends on his scene of triumph "his visage expresses a demoniacal glee." In **Pantagleize,** Rachel Silberschatz sets out to avenge her persecuted people by persecuting others, and Pantagleize describes the projected revolution in terms already familiar to readers of *L'Action Française.* Of all the Jewish figures evoked by Ghelderode only the Judas of **Barrabas** is treated with some measure of sympathy, and in much the same way as did Léon Bloy, who recognized the metaphysical necessity of the betrayal.

The Negroes Bam-Boulas and Beni-Bouffout are blacks that have been carefully filtered through a white consciousness, and not a single cliché is missing. Might not Ghelederode's racism be one aspect of the profound attraction he feels for evil?

"Count Von Lauterbach"—that was the first literary pseudonym adopted by Adolphe Adhemar Martens. Vis-a-vis humanity his attitude was that of an aristocrat well equipped to practice the cult of the ego and with a marked predilection for magic. Far from clashing with this vaunted anarchism, a certain traditionalist outlook blended in very well with the rejection of the rational.

While all-out warfare against sentimental imbecilities may be thoroughly justified, there is a bookish quality about Ghelderode's notion of eroticism as a "seminal soup." The multiplicity of states of consciousness, and the unlimited transmutability of love and of the atmospheres it can conjure up—all that is absent from his work. For him, love is but the specter of a specter.

If love were as simple or as unabashedly sadistic as it appears in this witches' brew, its toxic properties would surely have been discovered some little while ago!

On the other hand, Michel de Ghelderode's dramatic œuvre is entirely modern in its insistence on the ambiguity of our human lot. The burlesque and the tragic remain in balance, and subsumed in a poetry whose unquestionable originality is due to a use of language devoid of all self-conscious "poetry." Yet man is man only because he is able to *declare* what he is. The modern theatre, and much of the avant-garde along with it, is perhaps all the weaker for its neglect of this basic truth. When, however, Michel de Ghelderode ventures an assertion, his thought has an undeniably reactionary ring, and leaves us dissatisfied.[1]

Note

1. Utilized in this study were the five volumes of Ghelderode's *Théâtre,* published by Gallimard, and his *Entretien de l'acteur,* published by L'Arche.

Helen Hellman (essay date autumn 1967)

SOURCE: Hellman, Helen. "*Splendors of Hell*: A Tragic Farce." *Renascence* 20, no. 1 (autumn 1967): 30-8.

[*In the following essay, Hellman acknowledges the shocking aspects of Ghelderode's* Chronicles of Hell *(here called* Splendors of Hell*) but maintains that, despite its scatological qualities and "profanation of the Mass," it is a play about faith, one in which the murdered hero "survives symbolically as the spiritual victor."*]

The play *Splendors of Hell* is interesting from a biographical point of view because its success in Paris in 1949 brought wide public attention to the Belgian playwright, Michel de Ghelderode, who until then had lived in relative obscurity. Although he had chosen the life of a recluse, this somewhat belated success, and the recognition and acclaim by an admiring group of young actors and directors in Paris amazed and delighted him. In the five or six years following the success of *Splendors of Hell,* which had won first prize in a theatrical competition, "Concours des Jeunes Compagnies," eight of his plays were produced in Paris and elsewhere in Europe.

Splendors of Hell opened in Paris at the fashionable Marigny Theater of Jean-Louis Barrault. The audience, scandalized by the scatological clowning and the apparent profanation of sacred rites, forced Jean-Louis Barrault to ring down the curtain and close the play after three nights. It then played with great success for nine months at the Théâtre des Noctambules.

Ghelderode's success prompted the publication of thirty plays in the years 1951-1957; a series of seven radio interviews in 1951, later published as *Les Entretiens d'Ostende*; and the publication of his correspondence with several of those young Paris directors in the French journal *Revue d'Histoire du Théâtre*. Since then two volumes of selected plays have appeared in English translation, and two or three have become standard works in American repertory.

Ghelderode has said remarkably little about *Splendors of Hell,* which some critics believe his most monumental and complex play. He has not commented on his intentions in writing it, nor has he discussed what some have construed as ambiguities in the play. In an interview in 1950, with *Figaro Littéraire,* he said that he never thought the play would be produced because of its violence and the Bishop's spitting up of the Host. If he had foreseen the possibility of its production, he would have made it not less violent but easier for the actors to perform. He added that for this "diabolical play, I have even received a sparging of holy water which I didn't ask for."

In the course of my exposition of this work, I shall attempt to deal with some of the play's complexities and establish the artistic function of what appears so shocking in the play, its scatological farce and profanation of the Mass. It is my belief that the play is about faith and that its murdered hero survives symbolically as the spiritual victor.

The tragedy of *Splendors of Hell* develops paradoxically in an atmosphere of wild farce and saturnalia, which liberate man's most perverse and profane possibilities. It moves into a crescendo of violence suggesting the fire and flames of the hell paintings of Bosch and Brueghel. But the most telling and revealing action is the play's dénouement in the sixteenth scene, which is a total reversal of the violence of the play up to this point. In contrast to the atmosphere of hell whose sounds are the roar of thunder, the moaning and lamenting of an invisible mob and the final diabolical laughter of the resurrected Jan in Eremo as he comes at his opponent Laquedeem with an axe, this scene takes place in total silence. Jan here reveals himself as the literal embodiment of the fool of faith, the fool in Christ.

As the old servant Veneranda, the Bishop's mother, is brought in, "the action is suddenly immobilized in space as the retributive hatchet is immobilized in air. The silence falls in the same way that thunder does—fatidically. And in this silence, this vacuum, rather, where nothing breathes—even the mob and the storm are quiet—one sees the old woman hop toward the Bishop and cry out in his face." The Bishop, despite his profound inner resistance, humbly obeys her command to pardon and absolve his enemies. He becomes like the little child, the babe to whom the mystery of salvation has been revealed. "In that hour Jesus rejoiced in spirit, and said, 'I thank thee, Oh Father, Lord of Heaven and earth, that thou hast hid these things from the wise and prudent, and hast revealed them unto babes. . . .'" He thus rejoins his savages who were closer to the divine truth in their adoration of their fetishes than the monks and priests of the church who claim to love the true God.

In his final gesture of forgiveness and submission, he dies with tears of charity and mercy. He is thus revealed as the "fool of fools," defined by Walter Kaiser in *Praisers of Folly* as the "pious Christian who emulates the folly of Christ, who accepts as Christ did, human frailty. He is a fool because, in accepting the wisdom of Christ, he rejects the wisdom of this world . . .", or in the Erasmian sense, the foolish wisdom of the false doctors and churchmen.

Jan in Eremo, or John in the Desert, is the Ghelderodian hero as the fool of faith, the thaumaturge like Christ himself, who performs the miracles of curing the plague-ridden city of Lapideopolis and finding food for the hungry. Like the other Ghelderodian heroes, he is a Silenus figure whose very humanity necessarily contains the opposing elements of angelic and demonic. After his arrival in Lapideopolis as a mysterious figure of faith who has converted savages in distant places, he accomplishes miracles in the pest-ridden city. He remains there and usurps the power of the church when he remains as Bishop with the support of the populace. His power as head of the church corrupts the force of his faith and he remains to rule over an episcopal court of monks who are in reality gross, impious buffoons. They are obscene and sacrilegious and profane the symbols of the very church they serve. Jan is in conflict and in rebellion against the institution he represents, and his resistance is confirmed in his instructions for burial. He wishes to be placed "right into the earth, without a shroud and in the graveyard of the excommunicate. . . ." He wants to remain, as he has always been, the incarnation of solitude, yet in communion with the most lowly. He is thus another form of the Silenus, whose episcopal trappings mask a spirit yearning for solitude, humility and simple faith. In his humble death, he rediscovers faith and humility and reverts to a state of unquestioning childlike obedience to his mother.

Opposed to him are the monks and priests over whom he rules. As in medieval drama, their names describe their distinctive characteristics. As the critic David Grossvogel has observed, "the symbolistic actor of the expressionists is nothing more than a renovation of the old morality figures." Jan in Eremo is the incarnation of solitude; Simon Laquedeem is the complex arch enemy of faith whose peculiarly Flemish scatological waggery is an expression of demonic forces. The name Isaac Laquedeem is one of the names for the Wandering Jew in Flanders. Simon represents also the church of Simon Peter; Carnibos is the glutton; Sodomati, the homosexual representative of the papacy. As Grossvogel remarked, Ghelderode's "monks, priests, vicars and clergymen generally are possessed by all the vices which that profoundly religious age ascribed to them while in the same breath he writes 'mystères' that reflect genuine religious transport."

Splendors of Hell was written in 1929, and can be considered Ghelderode's first really monumental play. Unlike ***School for Buffoons*** and ***Hop Signor!*** with which it has certain affinities of structure and characterization, it deals with the hero of religious faith rather than with the artist—but Folial, Juréal and Jan in Eremo are all projections of the traditional fool figure and of the author himself—the fool as *vates,* God-smitten, thaumaturge, seer and poet. They are, in Ghelderode's own words to one of his young directors, living characters who bear his stigmata.

Like ***Hop Signor!*** and ***School for Buffoons,*** it is a one-act play which had originally been conceived in three. In seventeen scenes, it suggests the continuous panorama of a medieval mystery play. Its three part structure is discernible in the development of the action and in the alterations of tone. The first seven scenes constitute the opening farce. The monks, who are the incarnation of gluttony, anger and foolishness, steal meat from the banquet table set up like the last supper for the vigil over the body of the dead bishop. They are frightened by his body which lies in state and clown among themselves as they await the arrival of Simon Laquedeem who will officiate at the burial services of the late Bishop, his rival.

In the seventh scene the tone changes when Sodomati, the papal representative, arrives. In the second group of scenes, Simon tells Sodomati the legend of the Bishop, which is also the true story of his life, or as much as is known about it. It is this part of the play, the exposition of the life of a man whom the "mob" has already canonized, which is reminiscent of the New Testament and hagiographic stories. And it is here that the character of the Bishop is created and defined, for in the play he never speaks. Jan in Eremo resembles the figure of Christ, who also performed miracles. The circumstances of Jan's birth are vague—it is rumored that he is the child of a mermaid and a monk. But Laquedeem describes them thus: "Jan in Eremo was his name. John in the desert, in memory of those sands where he was found—child of an unknown mother, child without a name—found by the monks of the Abbey of the Dunes, who had been awakened by his haunting cries. It is more than seventy years ago that he was born, John in the desert; John who was son of the sea and sand, John who used to say: 'I am solitude'—and he was!"

Just as the life of Christ is partially narrated by the evangelists and then told through his own words which reveal the events that had taken place, so, too, the legend of Jan in Eremo is recounted by his "false disciple," and the final events actually played out by Jan himself during the miraculous "resurrection." Christ, symbol of compassion and faith, was Himself forced to play the first buffoon in those moments of mockery when the crown of thorns was placed upon His head by the hypocrites and the reed placed in His hand. He knew Himself the scapegoat when He said: "For he shall be delivered unto the Gentiles and shall be mocked and spitefully entreated and spitted upon." As the body and blood of the sacrifical lamb are partaken of in continuation of the faith, Simon Laquedeem links Jan to Jesus when he rails out against the former during his struggle: "Let him not cross my path, your Jesus! . . . Wait, my people. You'll get your portion of flesh!"

The third part of the play consists of the struggle between Laquedeem and the Bishop, who rises up as if miraculously to attack his enemy. With superhuman strength he has survived and refused to swallow the poisoned host which Laquedeem had given him. He is in an agony of suffocation because of the host lodged in his throat and threatens to murder Simon. He is saved from his vengeance by Veneranda who draws the poisoned host from his throat and commands him to forgive his enemies, if he wishes forgiveness. At her command he submits to his true death.

The celebrated critic Charles de Tolnay, taking his cue from Erasmus' reference to the Silenus in *The Praise of Folly,* wrote in his study of Brueghel's drawings that these sheets on "mundane Folly are like the hermae of Silenus; they show a different face outwardly from that which is enclosed within them, that is, the truth. Their meaning becomes accessible to him who relies solely on the experience of form." So in *Splendors of Hell*, a tragedy-bouffe, the elements of farce and tragedy are often mingled, and the play's meaning in all its ambiguities is expressed in this very interplay. It begins and ends in a farce which both encloses and prefigures the tragic action, just as did *Hop Signor!,* written six years later.

The ceaseless repetition of farce in Ghelderode's plays is analogous to repetition of line and motif in Northern and Gothic art, where there is no intervention of desire for organic moderation and serenity. Wilhelm Worringer in *Form in Gothic* defines the will to form in Northern art in a remarkably illuminating passage which does much to explain why Ghelderode has been described as absolutely summing up the genius of Flanders:

> Our organically tempered sense of vitality recoils before this senseless rage of expression as from a debauch. When, however, finally yielding to compulsion, its energies flood these lifeless lines, it feels itself carried away in a strange and wonderful manner and raised to an ecstasy of movement, far outstripping any possibilities of organic movement. The pathos of movement which lies in this vitalized geometry—a prelude to the vitalized mathematics of Gothic architecture—forces our sensibility to an effort unnatural to it. When once the natural barriers of organized movement have been overthrown, there is no more holding back: again and again it is forcibly prevented from peacefully ending its course, again and again diverted into fresh complications of expression, so that tempered by all these restraints, it exerts its energy of expression to the uttermost until at last, bereft of all possibilities of natural pacification, it ends in confused, spasmodic movements, breaks off unappeased into the void or flows senselessly back upon itself.

Thus the interplay of farce and tragedy in *Splendors of Hell*, of such seemingly disparate elements as the mystic and the digestive, the divine and the scatological are repeated and expanded until the very end when the guild of butchers come to take the body of the Bishop. The play's complexities reside exactly in this interplay, in the infernal debasement of holy symbols, on the one hand, and the sublimation, on the other, of the common, the lowly and the unclean. Thus Simon Laquedeem, seized by a stomach cramp, cries out: "My belly! . . . Calvary of my belly!" Whereas Jan in Eremo uses the idols of head hunters as symbols of faith, and he is himself the patron of the guild of butchers.

The key symbol in the play is the Host, the consecrated bread which, according to Catholic dogma, contains the body, the soul and the divinity of Christ. It is here a poisoned host, representing a corrupted doctrine, and it is administered by a cleric who is physically and spiritually corrupt. The dying bishop is unable to swallow the host, just as he was unable, during his lifetime, to swallow the impure doctrine of a poisoned church. The Church was an obstruction for him in the true exercise of his faith, and he has this to say of its practitioners: "Men of the Church, my savages in adoring these lying gods were closer to the divine truth than you, the anointed, who pretend to adore the true God." The Church of which he is bishop represents also his compromise of pure subjective faith, and it is a barrier between him and the people, his communicants, who had canonized him. Real-Temblor, the arch-deacon, says as much when he reports the attitude of the populace: ". . . the people were willing to march in honor of the bishop, but without priests or sacristans, in the sole company of the giants and dragons of carnival, and all in silence and with dignity." The poisoned host remains an obstruction in his throat, which he finally spits up and rejects. As a symbol of faith, he in turn may be construed as an obstruction barring the rise to power of the auxiliary bishop, whose relief, when the obstructive bishop is removed, is expressed in the scatological farce at the end of the play.

The Host, symbol of the most exalted mystery in the Christian religion, becomes an obstruction which cannot be swallowed and absorbed, nor regurgitated or expelled. It is the cause of the Bishop's final torment, which permits him neither to live nor to die. It is also a symbol of the tragic ambiguity, conflict and hell in which he lived as ruler over a corrupt clergy.

The play opens with a parody of Christ's commandment that "except you eat the flesh of the Son of Man and drink his blood, you shall not have life in you . . . for my flesh is meat indeed; and my blood is drink indeed." This first profanation by Carnibos, the chaplain, whose spitting up of meat from the "last supper" which he had wolfed and couldn't swallow, prefigures the tragic dilemma of the Bishop, who cannot swallow the Host lodged in his throat. By analogy the Host and the meat become one, and the symbolic ritual of the Mass is reduced to its most literal action. The farce is thus a profanation of the church's most sacred ritual and an ironic comment on the suggestion of cannibalism inherent in it.

Christian symbols and events from Christ's life and the lives of the saints serve as an inspiration for the tragic action as well as the buffoonery. They are so frequently referred to that an interpretation of the play in terms of Christian myth is inescapable. Such an interpretation of the play must derive from the struggle between the two protagonists, Jan in Eremo, the thaumaturge, who represents a state of subjective faith, albeit a faith he has compromised; and Simon Laquedeem, a faithless representative of the organized Church. The first crucial episode in this conflict has taken place before the play begins, and the audience is informed about it by one of the protagonists. Laquedeem tells the secretary of the papal ambassador how he had administered final communion to the dying Bishop. He tells how the bishop had watched him like an emaciated old eagle. "That eye, full of an unspeakable hatred, missed nothing of my gestures, followed my hands. And when I offered the host, the eye shot a glance of steel at me and the lips closed tight. But when I solemnly abjured him to receive the body and the blood of the living God, the eye was extinguished and the lips unsealed. He made his communion."

The play begins with a kind of Last Supper during which the sacrament of the Eucharist, which originated with Christ's Last Supper, is burlesqued by Krakenbus and Carnibos, the meat stealer, when the former shoves a piece of meat into Carnibos' mouth. Krakenbus thus plays out the tragic offering of the poisoned host, as he says: "Open your trap? (*Puts the meat in Carnibos' mouth.*) Give thanks, worm? Thanks!" Krakenbus, the hump-backed vicar, also parodies the symbol of the nails of the cross, as he constantly crushes the feet of his fellow monks with his heel. Another parallel which may be drawn with the Last Supper of Christ is the foreknowledge of betrayal by a false disciple. Carnibos, in recounting to Sodomati the occasion of the Bishop's death, quotes the latter as having said: "The hour is coming that I know of, forestalling that hour which God has fixed, and I accept it, since he permits it to be forestalled." This is a further example of Jan's faith and submission to the Divine spirit, and his words echo those of Christ in the garden of Gethsemane: "Father, if thou be willing, remove this cup from me: nevertheless not my will but thine be done."

The Bishop Jan in Eremo, or John in the Desert, is a hero who bears an ambiguous resemblance to Christ and to John the Baptist. To begin with, there is his legendary birth: he leaves his own country and after many wanderings and a sojourn among the cannibals whom he has converted, he arrives, as if walking on the waters, to the pest-ridden city of Lapideopolis, city of stone, whose name suggests both the church of Peter and the lapidating of the Christian martyrs. Jan appears, bent under a huge cross, like Christ carrying the Cross to Calvary. But unlike Christ who dies upon the Cross, he throws his cross into the fires in which are burning the corpses of the plague-dead. The cross which Jan casts into the fire seems to purify the city; the atmosphere clears, the sick are healed, and Jan, like Christ, miraculously finds food for the hungry. This gesture may also be considered Jan's rejection of the cross, or a sacrifice to and appeasement of diabolic forces—a descent from pure subjective faith. Jan becomes the worker of objective miracles and a figure of authority in the city. Thenceforward his communion with the folk is direct, and the people become his disciples. Their love and faith sanctify him in effect. For them he has given

up subjectivity and become a part of the only institution where he can effectively use his power. By main force he becomes Bishop of Lapideopolis, resisting the official clergy and nobility which returns to the city, and commits the "imposture" which, as Laquedeem says, is later consecrated by Rome.

Jan's assumption of episcopal power puts him into the false position of representing a church he can hardly believe necessary to the adoration of divine truth. From then on he exists in a state of hell, where, as the tormented upholder of subjective faith in the divine, he rules vengefully over an episcopal court of buffoons and clowns. His revolt against the church, his inner hell are represented by the decor of hideous idols, devils, witches' masks and fetishes of the barbarians he had converted. The grotesque monks in their devilish clowning are the living expression of these bizarre images.

Although there is a certain ambiguity in the bishop's character and in the significance of his throwing down of the cross, his railing against the priests and monks seems a fairly clear indication of the nature of his tragic dilemma. In Ghelderode's vision of religion, he seems very close to the attitudes of the sixteenth century as defined by Tolnay: "The fool and rogue literature of the sixteenth century developed out of the same spiritual attitude as the universal-religious theism and the new pantheism. In religion it was the apprehension of the *one* God, who despite all the diversities of the confessions, underlies them all as the ultimate truth in each; in pantheism it was the apprehension of the one vital force, the world-soul, which lies at the basis of all Nature despite the boundless diversity of its forms."

Jan's spiritual conflict finds its external expression in his struggle with Laquedeem. The latter had been a young deacon at the time of the plague, who had stayed with the people to comfort or bury them as the situation required. But as the Bishop's auxiliary, corrupted by ambition and revolt, as an incarnation of the devil who is absolutely devoid of faith, he betrayed the Bishop when he attempted to murder him with a poisoned host, although he had betrayed him and his God long before.

In the struggle between Jan and Simon, his assistant and false disciple, Jan's condition is ambiguous. Has he been miraculously resurrected? Or is he not yet dead? "His right hand ceaselessly tries to unknot invisible bonds about his throat, and sometimes he thrusts his hand into his mouth as if trying to pull out some obstruction which is suffocating him: Inexpressible torture! . . . Is he an old man forever agonizing and asking for death? Is he a resurrected corpse, rejected by death, struggling to live again?"

Through the intervention of Veneranda, his mother, the old Bishop is enabled to spit up the poisoned host. At her command, he absolves his enemies and pardons them albeit with regret. She commands him: "Lie down, my child! And die in your tears!" He dies, relinquishing his hatred of his enemies, the hypocrites and the faithless, in obedience to her love and devotion. He dies without Communion; he has rejected the Host. But his death, in charity and merciful tears, is an expiation of his compromised faith and, at the same time, a confirmation of his faith and his communion with the folk. His wish to rest with the excommunicated outside the Church is thus granted. He is now free from the oppression of the Church which he had suffered in his lifetime, and from that crushing oppression with which Laquedeem had threatened his corpse: "We'll dress him in iron, in lead, in oak; we'll hide him in the deepest crypt, and the cathedral will rest on his bones with all its weight."

The Bishop's death had freed him from the torment of the poisoned host. His spiritual conflict is over as he dies his merciful death, which is the signal for relief and catharsis, and which clears the menacing atmosphere of storm gathering outside the palace. His death in humility and obedience has dispelled the storm, just as his arrival with the cross which he threw into the flames drove out plague and storm in its pillar of fire.

The removal of the obstructive host, the relief of the Bishop, are parodied by Laquedeem as he joyfully squats after a final attack of cramps. All the monks are purged as well, and the curtain falls as they celebrate their demoniac victory in a profane farce. It is a simple matter to see in the image of these clowning priests, leaping about in clouds of smoking incense, the inspiration of the "diableries" of Bosch and Brueghel, to whom Ghelderode frequently referred as sources of inspiration. His theatrical invention is richly permeated with the sensuousness proper to the plastic arts, an essential attribute of his theater which he discussed in *Les Entretiens d'Ostende*. Every aspect of the decor he describes for *Splendors of Hell* is the visual correlative of the action and is an expression of the play of ambiguities and paradox inherent in the tragedy-bouffe: "The wall coverings hang in rags. On the walls, hung very high, are the portraits of priests; and along the bottoms of the walls, everywhere, stand a variety of baroque objects: idols, suns, witch doctors' masks, motley devils, totems, stakes, and instruments of torture. But downstage there is a heavy table sumptuously laid with a crimson velvet cloth, silver service, and crystal glasses."

Before this table prepared for a last supper, framed by the portraits of mighty churchmen hung on torn and decayed tapestries, the low farce of the monks and the crucial struggle between Jan and Simon have taken place. The portraits hung on high constitute a typical Ghelderodian irony, whose other side is expressed by the idols, witches' masks and instruments of torture scattered about below. These diabolical images symbol-

ize at the same time the pure faith of the savages. In their grotesqueness they carry out the theme and repeat in Gothic style the bizarre and demoniac postures of the clergy.

Although *Splendors of Hell* concludes almost immediately after the death of the Bishop with the apparent triumph of the buffoons and Laquedeem, the ultimate moral victory belongs to Jan in Eremo. His lonely rebellion against hypocrisy and pharisaism, against an existence without the divine, is vindicated in his death. His tears and the absolution of his enemies suggest charity, mercy and obedience to divine will, as well as the lesson that the usurpation of worldly power does not defeat that power. In *Splendors of Hell* the buffoons, the corrupt and the damned, the hypocritical "men of the church" are in reality destroyed by ridicule and farce, while Jan in Eremo remains as a triumphant fool of faith.

Iska Fraidstern (essay date February 1969)

SOURCE: Fraidstern, Iska. "Ghelderode's *Red Magic*: Gold and the Use of the Christian Myth." *Modern Drama* 11, no. 4 (February 1969): 376-81.

[*In the following essay, Fraidstern interprets* Red Magic *as a Christian play and an ironic comedy, a work that satirizes modern people for their rejection of grace and their idolatry of money.*]

The vision of Michel de Ghelderode derives its theatrical vitality from the playwright's absorption in the anhistorical memories of the folk or the popular imagination, "about what the world was like before the appearance of homo sapiens. Through the primitive legends, poetry, and dream are revealed to us the existence of former human kinds, come from the stars and gone away again, leaving evidences in stone, astronomical, or esoteric symbols."[1] His dramatic preoccupation with the public manifestations of these archaic, frequently unconscious relics reveals an awareness of continuous human need for sacred objects, the ritual annulments of time, and the ceremonial repetition of certain exemplary gestures that demand participation in a reality greater than the limits enforced by the individual personality. Because he was haunted by physical mortality, Ghelderode became obsessed by the mortality of civilizations:

> The present is a fugitive which constantly escapes me. The past is more alive to me than this very day. I can feel the presence of the dead and their lost age more keenly than I can feel their opposites. . . . Legends of olden days, ancestral customs, the great centuries of violence . . . the brutal life and the religious wars.[2]

This cataclysmic view of history is partially conditioned by particular Flemish experience: the short reign as a commercial power at the beginning of the Renaissance, the swift decline during the fifteenth century "when Flanders staggered herself in war and danced in the orgies of the flesh,"[3] and the position of Belgium as the traditional battlefield where the forces of darkness and the angels of light contended for the soul of Europe. Ghelderode's own zest for living in spite of precarious health forced the personal recognition that the acceptance of death is the only valid hope of salvation. These widely varied perceptions coalesce to form a theater concerned with reenacting the archetypal truths present in the Christian myth. By utilizing the liturgical patterns of Christianity, stressing the Passion and Resurrection, Ghelderode can annihilate the present, inviting the spectator to enter a consecrated, timeless existence. But *Red Magic* is unusual in this regard. Unlike much of Ghelderode's work, this play uses the eschatological motifs to satirize an attitude peculiar to the modern temper—the sacralizing of money.

The other plays are clearly interested in the generalizing function of myth. In *Barabbas,* Ghelderode indicates the ecumenism of the rites surrounding the life and death of Christ by constructing a series of dramatic analogues around the figure of the thief as mock-Christ. *Miss Jairus* is a commentary on the belief that the Christian promise is a continuum with death as the bridge to a New Jerusalem. The structure of the play fuses the symbolic chronology of Christ's last year with the seasonal pattern of the vegetation myths, moving toward the necessary spring martyrdom of the god. Blandine moves through the play attempting to discover physical counterparts resembling death, waiting only for the Crucifixion to release her body. Pantagleize fulfills the Christian archetype because he completes his destiny in history in order to escape its temporal limitations, as Christ himself did. The *Chronicles of Hell* dramatizes, in a Christian context, the recurrent archetypal struggle between goodness and those demonic forces that would justify all excess. For Ghelderode, the outcome is inevitable: the Devil is enthroned as lord of this world; Christianity embodies hope in the realm outside the material present.

In these plays the symbolic pattern is redemptive. Individuals search for death, protagonists struggle for death, characters are led through secular experience to death and the life beyond time. *Red Magic,* however, is a play about the modern rejection of the idea of regeneration through death. It is an exploration of the psyche of contemporary man where the light of grace has been transformed into the mysterious glitter of gold, a false and unnatural sun. *Red Magic* concerns a successful temptation, an inversion of the Christian encounter in the wilderness, the triumph of the world, the flesh, and most especially, the devil. The title is significant because it not only describes the bloody results attendant upon the obsessive desire for money, but also presents the clue revealing the bias of the supernatural agency

that impels the action of the play. *Red Magic* is, then, an ironic comedy about human behavior after the fall. Hieronymus inexorably moves toward damnation by denying the function of death, and substitutes, instead, the desexualizing drive for the power that would make man a god.

Hieronymus moves through a satanic world of illusion—"all in this universe is nothing more than seeming"[4]—created by the devil and his minions, Armador, Sybilla, Romulus, and the Monk: virgins who are bitches; alchemy that is, in fact, counterfeiting; the promise of immortality that is the cause of death. That these characters are functions of the demonic will is made clear by the imagery of the play. The "scarlet monk," haunted by the stench of hell existing within his own body, and Romulus, the begging opportunist, are lesser imps destroyed by their own greed. Sybilla is a Lilith-figure, a succubus who is the devil's mate: "She is the lascivious, sumptuous and sordid woman dreamt about in nightmare."[5] And Armador, whose name may establish an anagrammatic link between the power of gold and the power of Satan, is depicted as the Devil himself by implication, by direct description, by ironic recognition. Romulus asserts that "the devil appears only to fools;"[6] and Hieronymus is nothing if he is not a fool. Sybilla declares passionately, "Yes, I shall follow you along the roads, across the plains, over the seas, as far as hell, which will burn less than your skin, the skin of a young devil."[7] Finally, Armador, attempting to seduce Hieronymus, tells him:

> If you betray me, you will die, die a horrible death, for I not only wield happiness in these hands, I work misery too. It is my tragic privilege to command the two elements that actuate the universe, Good and Evil . . . I have touched you. You are in my power.[8]

Alchemy, a crucial metaphor in the play, enhances the irony of these diabolically inspired misconceptions. This medieval science has an explicit spiritual content in which the purification of the metal parallels the purification of the human soul. It is a symbolic attempt to rescue nature from the consequences of the fall. To subvert the process, as does Armador, is to destroy a chance for salvation. But on a deeper level, alchemy bespeaks a commitment to lifelessness, an effort to endow gold which is in itself unproductive and non-creating with positive ritual significance.

Hieronymus is by no means a reluctant Adam. In translating all experience into possession, he willingly forfeits his humanity. The miser is concerned only with ownership. Even silence is defined as property:

> The constellations fill the sky. Who owns all these stars? I swear they burn away in sheer waste. And the moon is missing. It has been stolen. When it comes back it will have had a piece taken out of it. . . . Emp-

tiness, everywhere! All the emptiness that the room contains is mine, too. Why can't I pick it up and store it? . . . The silence that reigns in here is mine also. What can I do with it?[9]

He views his soul as an entry in an account book, "I am the owner of my soul, and such I shall remain! That is something I had forgotten in the inventory. Item, one immortal soul, ornamented with diverse virtues."[10] And in his dreams, Hieronymus recites the litany of proprietorship:

> Item . . . I own a house . . . with a ghost. . . . A bronze chest . . . in which gold pieces are breeding young. . . . A wife and her virginity. . . . I own . . . a stomach . . . and a gullet . . . that I must . . . attend to. . . .[11]

Rejecting nature, he has deflected his own physical impulses into the contents of his bronze chest. Ghelderode meant Hieronymus to be a lewd and big-bellied miser,"[12] an atypical stage figure, growing sleek and fat on sensuous dreams. Hieronymus shudders at the sun because gold has become the source of generative light in the miser's perverted cosmos:

> The moment the miser opens it [the coffer] to officiate, he is flooded with light. . . . The gold exists in its own right and burns like radium—and the miser takes on a supernatural look under this lighting. When he enters the coffer, he looks as though he has disappeared in an incandescent trap.[13]

If the universe is animated by sterility then the products of that world are barren. So his wife's supposed virginity is valued as a commodity: "No, not for anything in the world will I touch this priceless irreplaceable virginity that so few women can boast of possessing."[14] The child Hieronymus gives his wife must be a doll, not the result of intercourse between husband and wife. And his own sexuality, "A crown drops from your wallet at each spasm,"[15] is transmuted into inanimate coinage that is impotent:

> Tonight I shall mingle the male and female coins. . . . I shall marry them. Make love! Join together your golden bodies. . . . Let gold bring forth gold! . . . Conceive! Female coins, become so great that you almost burst! It is blessed, it is just, that your grand race should perpetuate itself, for yours is the domination of the world![16]

Hieronymus becomes the Devil's priest administering a black sacrament of marriage.

When alchemy enters to make his dream possible, Hieronymus is no longer concerned with possession for its own sake, but with power: "With my gold I shall buy the trinity!"[17] It is important that this change of attitude is depicted in terms of the Christian myth that he has, in fact, renounced: Romulus says ". . . in three days

the sides of the chest will burst open;"[18] and Hieronymus becomes a crazy Jesus as he immolates himself in the coffer and is resurrected with a new vision of omnipotence.

But the process that Ghelderode illustrates in the course of the play is considerably more than a delineation of the corrupting force of money. **Red Magic** is, rather, a discussion of the way man commits Original Sin in the modern world. Hieronymus desires immortality only when he believes he can acquire an endless source of wealth because accumulating money is the primary method of accomplishing deification and the continuity of self. That money is a contingent manifestation of the impulse to attain the autogenic power of God is implied in Act I and directly stated in the remainder of the play. Hieronymus rarely sleeps because

> It is only at night that each thing takes on its full value. I am double at night. Rather than lose myself in incoherent and immediately forgotten dreams, I sleep on my feet. . . . I steal time, so that I shall have more waking hours than those people who sink themselves in useless sleep.[19]

There are no clocks in his house because they tick off the minutes of human mortality. And he does not indulge in sexual intercourse because that implies self-surrender. The gold florins are his promise of immortality, his account book the path to heaven. While Hieronymus awaits the results of Armador's experiments he asserts "Men have unhealthy dreams. They dream of being more powerful than the Creator. They want to make light out of darkness."[20] After he steals the amulet, he is convinced that he is both rich and immortal. Now he can safely will his house and possessions to the church certain that "I have robbed you jackal! . . . It serves you right. . . . I am immortal!"[21] Once released from the inevitability of death, Hieronymus becomes drunk—he can now afford to yield to the demands of his appetites. When he returns from the ritual entombment in the coffer, the miser's transformation is complete. Hieronymus believes he has short-circuited the Christian pattern; he has obtained eternality without self-extinction:

> I bought the globe and all that covers it, oceans, mountains, empires, peoples, and ruins. And the seasons, storms, and creation. . . . I bought Calvary . . . Jerusalem . . . Mecca and Rome. . . . Tonight I find myself flung outside time and law. . . . This old house will have crumbled and all the monks eaten by worms, when old Hieronymus is still laughing, and he will be the last to laugh. . . . What a transformation in my substance! Here I am, hungry and thirsty, wanting to do things, to speak out loud.[22]

He kills his non-human child because he no longer needs an heir. But this emphasizes the fact that Hieronymus' sexuality is still autoerotic—he is aroused by his own incantatory speech. When he attempts to find gratification outside his own body he becomes ill. The final moments of the play are an ironic coda to the entire action. Hieronymus is vigorously proclaiming "I am like God" at the very moment he is most human: he has gradually lost his house, his wife, his gold, and he will soon lose his life.

Ghelderode, in **Red Magic,** has not departed from his concern with the ritual function of archetypal theater: he allows the old symbols to criticize a more immediate problem, the dehumanization of the modern perspective through the quest for wealth. Gold does narrow man's vision to this world; it is the appropriate motif for a moribund civilization, "the proper symbol of sublimation, both as the death of the body and as the quest for a 'higher' life which is not of the body."[23]

Notes

1. Michel de Ghelderode, "Dispatches from the Prince of Ostreland" (trans. George Haugher, *TDR* [*Tulane Drama Review*], VII [Fall, 1963], 29).

2. Samuel Draper, "An Interview with Michel de Ghelderode," *TDR,* VII (Fall, 1963), 42.

3. *Ibid.,* 42.

4. Ghelderode, "Red Magic," *Seven Plays,* vol. 2 (New York, 1964), p. 33.

5. Ghelderode, "To Directors and Actors: Letters 1948-1959," *TDR,* IX (Summer, 1965), 59.

6. Ghelderode, *Red Magic,* p. 12.

7. *Ibid.,* p. 23.

8. *Ibid.,* p. 15.

9. *Ibid.,* p. 3.

10. *Ibid.,* p. 5.

11. *Ibid.,* p. 10.

12. Ghelderode, "To Directors and Actors," p. 42.

13. *Ibid.,* p. 58.

14. Ghelderode, *Red Magic,* p. 10.

15. *Ibid.,* p. 10.

16. *Ibid.,* p. 5.

17. *Ibid.,* p. 18.

18. *Ibid.,* p. 12.

19. *Ibid.,* pp. 3-4.

20. *Ibid.,* p. 17.

21. *Ibid.,* p. 34.

22. *Ibid.,* pp. 34-35.

23. Norman O. Brown, *Life Against Death* (New York, 1959), p. 281.

Hollis T. Landrum (essay date April 1974)

SOURCE: Landrum, Hollis T. "Ghelderode's War of the Words." *Southern Quarterly* 12, no. 3 (April 1974): 273-83.

[*In the following essay, Landrum emphasizes the qualities in Ghelderode's plays, particularly his use of language and gesture, which link him to the modern Theater of the Absurd.*]

"There would almost seem to be virtue in silence, if they could only be silent."[1] Thus John Killinger describes the confused state of characters in absurdist literature. The statement is equally applicable to the characters created by Michel de Ghelderode. Although this playwright is not ordinarily identified with the theatre of the absurd, Robert Brustein comments that he comes as close as any dramatist in this century to fulfilling Artaud's request for the realization of Breughel's grotesque paintings on the stage.[2] This connection to Artaud, metaphysical spokesman for the modern theatre of the absurd, has been surprisingly glossed over by most critics of Ghelderode.

Killinger maintains that words, because of their abstractness and their loss of potency in the modern world, actually inhibit man from directly approaching reality.[3] We shall see that this attitude is one of the chief traits of Ghelderode's plays. Killinger goes on to say that by using absurd speech, most absurdists are trying to point out the absurdity of the human situation. Our real speech is absurd because it reflects the absurdness of our existence. In absurdist drama, "speech is a condemnation, for it adds to the clutter and absurdity of existence."[4] This language devaluation is the result of a general dissatisfaction with reality that was expressed by Artaud. According to Brustein, Artaud's theatre of cruelty declares war on language. Words are germs of the theatre which must be reduced into submission to the role of gesture on the stage.[5]

One reason Ghelderode has received little recognition thus far in the theatre is that some critics do not consider his drama part of the modern milieu of the theatre of existential man. Aureliu Weiss, an example of this type of critic, attacks Ghelderode, claiming that he sought no illumination, no progressive structure in his plays. Weiss further claims that there is nothing new in Ghelderode's plays and that only a few of them are worth the time to linger over.[6]

George Hauger and Martin Esslin do not attack Ghelderode, but they do separate him from the modern absurdists. Hauger classifies Ghelderode as basically an expressionist and romantic.[7] Esslin distinguishes between the theatre of the absurd and the "poetic avant-garde" of Ghelderode, which he says differs from the absurd in several minor ways. There is more emphasis on dreams and fantasy in the "poetic avant-garde"; there is also less unity, less character development, less plot, and less violence or grotesqueness. But the major difference between the two, according to Esslin, is the use of language. The "poetic avant-garde" uses poetic language consciously to set a mood: "It aspires to plays that are in effect poems, images composed of a rich web of verbal association."[8] The absurdists, on the other hand, tend "toward a radical devaluation of language, toward a poetry that is to emerge from the concrete and objectified images of the stage itself."[9] The poetry is subordinate to the action in such a structure. In this situation, "what happens on the stage transcends, and often contradicts, the words spoken by the characters."[10]

Esslin is probably correct in this distinction, but he overstates his case in regard to Ghelderode. It is true that many of Ghelderode's plays are based on lyrical flights of fancy, employing poetry to evoke a mood. Some of Ghelderode's plays, however, also contain an element of language devaluation. Perhaps he does not emphasize the devaluation to the same degree as do Ionesco or Beckett, but it is there, lurking in the poetic images themselves. One might say that Ghelderode anticipates this devaluation of language. He has not yet reached the point of denouncing language by escaping from it; he still employs language in order to attack language, which to the absurdists would appear futile as well as damaging. But even Ionesco had to utilize language in order to ridicule it. That seems to be the dilemma of the modern playwright. How does he continue to communicate when he has attacked and destroyed communication?

Despite the dilemma, most of the absurd dramatists have made non-communicative speech a central point in their drama. This is more than word play in their case; it is a reflection of the existential emptiness that these dramatists see in the world. If their plays consist of dialogue, it is anti-dialogue. Words are attacked as being only another manifestation of the absurdity of the human condition.[11]

If one examines Ghelderode's plays carefully and considers Robert Brustein's definition of existential revolt, he can perhaps grant Ghelderode's achievement among the modern dramatists. According to Brustein, existential drama is marked by subhuman characters, a mood of helplessness, and a strong tendency toward the grotesque with a degrading description of human flesh.[12] The definition is remarkably like the description of Ghelderode's plays in *The Oxford Companion to the Theatre,* in which it is pointed out that the recurrent theme of Ghelderode's plays seems to be the "agonized

appraisal of man's condition, seen as a crude and violent burlesque, where purity is engulfed by the obscene deformities of the flesh, and which ends in the eternal mystery of death."[13]

In determining whether Ghelderode belongs to an earlier tradition of the theatre or in part to the modern theatre of the absurd, one must consider first the role of words or non-words in his plays. We include non-words because of the importance they also play in absurdist drama. Killinger states that "in a world where words have become mere things, quasi-physical projectiles that clutter life and landscape, it does not seem unusual that the silent person should come to have both preternatural dignity and authority."[14] He also points out that there are a number of mutes in absurdist drama and each of them is treated with more respect than those who verbalize. It is as if the authors are saying that it is better to be a mute than the most eloquent speaker in this insane world.[15]

Ghelderode's emphasis on silence is quite clearly shown in his own life of solitude. When asked to define what he was, he referred to himself as a man who wrote all alone in a room.[16] He said later that he loved solitude for its own sake. He called it a purifying agent, and a necessary element for creation; he believed no artist could ever do anything really great except in solitude.[17] In a letter, Ghelderode writes, "I have too great a need of solitude and silence, and Paris is a sort of fascinating hell from which I always come back physically and mentally exhausted."[18] Ghelderode writes in another letter, "Do as I do: keep silent, the *silentium* of the old church."[19]

This silence is not, however, just an empty silence for Ghelderode. Inanimate and speechless objects are totally possessed with life. He states that all such objects are alive and sensitive.[20] This is particularly true of Ghelderode's interest in marionettes. His delight in them, he confesses, stems from their silence and natural reserve. He states that marionettes console him "for the cacophony of the play and the crazy glibness of the impudent creatures that theatre people most often are."[21] Ghelderode writes in a letter, "The theatre is lost the moment it speechifies, discusses, analyzes, preaches. It is out of danger when it dreams, digresses, laughs, cries, tells startling stupidities, and commits a thousand follies and atrocities. . . ."[22]

Ghelderode's silent objects thus have a language louder than words. Actualizing Artaud's philosophy of the stage as a restoring of magic to life, Ghelderode refers to the theatre as "an art of instinct."[23] He states, "For me, a theatrical work does not exist without the sensuousness proper to the plastic arts, or, in that case, exists only as a dialogue which can be read and does not call for realization on the stage."[24]

According to Ghelderode, it was painting which originally led him into the theatre.[25] He comments in a letter, "The only thing that could be useful to you is this: think of painting; this play is painting become theatre."[26] Hauger mentions that Ghelderode emphasized the visual in all of his plays. He calls them living paintings.[27] Another critic, Wellwarth, makes a similar observation. He says, "Ghelderode's theatrical sense was essentially a physical one (movement and appearance are far more important than speech in his plays) and he therefore adopted the medieval view that when man succumbs to sin his experience is reflected in his outer form."[28]

Less obvious than Ghelderode's emphasis on silence is his use of language devaluation. Ghelderode was a poet who sought a structure of poetic dialogue throughout his plays. He states at one point that he demands "a certain music in human speech."[29] Nevertheless, there is more than nice sounding language involved in poetic dialogue for Ghelderode. Musical speech is necessary to Ghelderode in order to keep language from dwindling to meaningless noise. He refers to this type of speech as "verbal incantation" and says that, without it, "the theatre disintegrates of itself, crumbles away in words, renounces its priority over other forms of literature, and disclaims its obsessional or possessional power, its marvels."[30] As he states in a letter, "Without shrieks, the theatre is merely chatter: words, words!"[31]

Thus poetry is not introduced simply because of the musical flow of the words, but in order to act as a buffer against the meaninglessness found in words used as just words. As Ruby Cohn states, "Particularly in his plays set in Christ's time or in the Flemish Middle Ages, Ghelderode energizes his drama with verbal shock."[32] It appears that Ghelderode uses poetry in order to attack language and that he amplifies the action on stage through physical movement or appearance. Ghelderode's poetry is both verbal and physical, and in each case it seems to denounce words as words.

In order, however, to discover what Ghelderode's own opinion of language is in the theatre, we must turn to his plays. We shall examine mainly four major plays of Ghelderode. These are considered his greatest achievements and illustrate his attack on language most clearly. Two other short plays will be considered briefly.

The Death of Doctor Faust, written in 1925,[33] is permeated by the confusion between art and reality. Each of the central characters has a corresponding character who is his actor. The confusion between art and reality spills over into the confusion of man himself. Man attempts an impossible task when he tries to find himself, since he is doing the looking. It is only when he acknowledges that his role is more real than himself that his search is ended. Faust admits at the end that he is only an actor who has somehow gone wrong, and when

the devil admits that he too does not exist, but only sticks to his role, the actor Faust calls him a "phrase-monger."[34]

In the prologue, Faust attacks writers, saying, "Only the ocean will speak better than they. And if someone found out, it would be a joke beyond belief."[35] What Ghelderode seems to be saying is that just as the role a man elects is more real than the man, so his words fail to reach reality because of the fact that they are only words. The writer cannot hope to capture reality; the earth will always speak more clearly because it is more natural. The man who discovers this will find it ridiculous that man should even attempt to capture the world with words. Yet Ghelderode can find no other solution; that is the problem. As the devil states in the first part of this play, "I write in forty-seven languages, but I have put my self-respect elsewhere."[36]

In **Cristopher Columbus,** written in 1927, Ghelderode comments on the man of silence as well as the man of words.[37] Ghelderode labeled this play a "dramatic fairy tale."[38] Most of the play is weak and downright boring, but the conclusion makes up for all that went before. It is outside the scope of this paper to discuss the entire meaning embodied in the closing lines of this play. For our purposes it is enough to note that the Americans fail to recognize any of the humanity of Columbus. As the American says, "In the name of America, I come to salute you, Columbus—but not the great man, only the statue."[39] Ghelderode seems to be implying here that our speeches fail to describe the true man, only the hollow form. After this sequence of speeches, the statue climbs from its pedestal and weeps, "There is nothing you can do about anything. You have to be a statue to understand."[40]

This is both irony and tragedy at the close of the play. Ghelderode had built Columbus into a truly mortal form, complete with all the doubts and foibles of a human being. At the end his humanity is destroyed, and after four hundred years his statue is more real than his own life. There is savage irony in this innocent "fairy tale." Ghelderode seems to be standing aside and mocking our modern age, replete with up-to-the-minute newscasts and modern means of analysis, none of which seems to help man reach the humanity within himself or others.

Also, Ghelderode appears to imply in the closing lines of the play that in order to truly understand, man has to be speechless and motionless, like a statue. Only when one is truly still and above or outside the movement around him can he fully comprehend the life surging around him in all directions. The irony of this is that one can never communicate his understanding to others in such a situation. Thus one is forced to moan, "There is nothing you can do about anything."[41]

A year later, Ghelderode makes an even stronger distinction between the man of words and the man of silence in his play *Barabbas.* Before the play even begins, Ghelderode emphatically points out that Barabbas is a man "who talks a great deal," whereas Jesus is one "who says nothing."[42] Thus both of the central characters are distinguished by the amount of noise they make, one continuously talking and the other continuously silent.

The difference between the two goes deeper, however, than mere words. Barabbas thinks that Jesus knows more than ordinary men even though he won't speak.[43] Hence Ghelderode suggests that the men who know more than ordinary men speak less. Barabbas, on the other hand, is in a constant state of ignorance. In the second act he carries out the wishes of the priests without knowing what he is doing. When Caiaphas asks him if he knows what is going on, Barabbas replies, "Less and less."[44] At the end of the trial by the crowd, he asks, "In that case who is being deceived?"[45] Barabbas, until that point, thought he was fooling the crowd; suddenly, he begins to realize that the only one he was fooling with his words was himself.

Ghelderode implies that words only serve to confuse their users. The men who know more than ordinary men refuse to use words. It is significant to note that the clown who imitates Jesus and manages to slay Barabbas at the end of the play repeats in several places only the line, "What did he say?"[46] It is uttered entirely out of context since no one says anything worth repeating just before this question, and the clown is never answered. These words are uttered almost as an incantation just before the clown plunges the knife into the back of the unsuspecting Barabbas. It appears, then, that Ghelderode is using this question to emphasize the confusion which exists in the words of the characters. In effect, he seems to be using the statement as a sarcastic comment rather than an actual question. The point is that although the characters seem to be making sense when they speak, their words are actually only a parody masking their own confusion. As Barabbas remarks to the prisoners in Act I, "Sometimes it's good to talk nonsense."[47]

Although Jesus is condemned because of his silence, he is condemned by a crowd which do not realize that words fail them. Words actually confuse and mask reality, but the crowd are ignorant of that fact and equate words with reality. Thus they condemn an innocent man and free the guilty one on the basis of the degree of noise each makes.

But Ghelderode does not let it rest at that. The basis of the play is the struggle of Barabbas to understand what has happened. At the very end, when he is dying, he admits that Jesus, the silent, has died for something;

while Barabbas, the talker, has died for nothing. But he calls Jesus his brother, saying that they have both been sacrificed, so they both share a common fate.[48] The difference is that there is a choice in silence and therefore a meaning for Ghelderode, but there is no choice in continuing to employ words as masks, so there is also no meaning in it.

One other point should be made here before we turn to the last major play. Crowds and background noise play a large part in *Barabbas* in that they add to the confusion of the characters. A background noise is present in most of Ghelderode's plays. It is normally composed of a crowd or a similar collective, and it is usually juxtaposed against the central character. The two best examples of this are the one act plays *Escurial* and *Chronicles of Hell.* In *Escurial,* the noise is a pack of dogs which the king eventually strangles.[49] In *Chronicles of Hell,* the noise is the howling mob that eventually breaks into the castle.[50]

These two are by no means the only instances of background noise in Ghelderode's plays. He seems anxious to parade noise and cacophony off stage to imply chaos and confusion. It is significant that in the two examples above, the noise is off stage and serves to antagonize or threaten the central characters. It is as if Ghelderode is implying that man is continuously haunted and threatened by a rabble of noise. In *Escurial,* the king laments, "My head is full of dogs and bells."[51]

The clearest example of Ghelderode's distrust of words is found in his last major play, *Pantagleize,* written the same year as *Chronicles of Hell,* 1929.[52] The entire structure of *Pantagleize* is based on irony. The names of the characters, for example, exhibit the opposite of the traits intended. Innocenti is the only figure of the play who truly knows what is happening to him. The poet's name, Blank, may be interpreted in several ways. It suggests that he speaks in blank verse and that his mind is a total blank. Ghelderode is probably making a bitter comment on modern poets through Blank. At the end of the play, during the trial, Blank confesses to be a modern poet, and the General replies, "Not content with overthrowing society, you must overthrow syntax in the bargain and sow confusion in healthy brains."[53] Blank's poetry makes no sense whatsoever, and his part in the revolution is equally cloudy.

As with Barabbas, Pantagleize is a victim of circumstances. He never comes to realize the part he is playing in the revolution and his position is entirely accidental. It is important to note that the entire action of the play is based on the misunderstanding of words. Intending only to make conversation in the beginning of the play, Pantagleize says, "What a lovely day!"[54] This phrase turns out to be the signal for the start of a revolution. Pantagleize repeats the phrase to all the revolutionaries, and they immediately assume that Pantagleize is their unknown leader. Pantagleize uses this phrase throughout the play without once realizing the consequences of what he is saying. Likewise, another innocuous phrase is the password for the government's treasure. The officials guarding the treasure are never sure when the soldiers mean to use the password or are using it literally.[55]

The very last line of the play emphasizes this irony of words. Pantagleize is dying, and he utters in a "gruesome and childish" tone, "What a lovely day."[56] The mocking use of words here is inescapable. This last phrase can be interpreted as a satiric comment on the entire play, a literal statement of fact by Pantagleize, or an ironic comment on the plight of Pantagleize. Ghelderode has based an entire play on the confusion to be found in words. Men are executed, revolutions begun, fortunes lost by the slippery use of "common" words. As Blank states, "Tonight, perhaps, I shall throw away my poet's mask and be a man among the others."[57] The use of a poet's mask could refer to the fact that Blank is an anarchist disguised as a poet in the play, or it could refer to the mask of words a poet uses to keep him from being a man among others. As Innocenti says to him, "If you could only guess for a minute what reality is like!"[58]

Ghelderode is attacking the falseness of words in this statement. Words are a mask which men use to hide from reality. Thinking their meaning is clear, men continue to exist in a state of stupidity, causing riots and calamities without knowing the slightest reason why. The farce is that the entire revolution is based on a mistake, a mistake which is fatal and thereby sad. Men play with words, hide behind them, and are finally executed by them. What is odd is that men never realize their plight. As Pantagleize says just before he is shot, "I can see less and less."[59] Apparently, no matter what his intentions, man cannot escape this mask of words as long as he employs them. If he fails to recognize the double meanings, the infinite interpretations, he is doomed by them.

All of this apparently makes a strong case for placing Ghelderode near the modern school of absurdity. His link with Artaud is inescapable, just as the existential meaninglessness in his plays is equally hard to overlook. His plays may not have consciously been designed to wage war on language, and Ghelderode would certainly deny belonging to any group of dramatists. However, his attack on words, his awe of silence, his use of the physical over the verbal, and his desire for a theatre based on instinct all seem to push Ghelderode close to the modern day absurdists. Regardless of whether we categorize him as an absurdist or a misplaced romantic, Ghelderode belongs to the present rather than to the past, and we must not make the mistake of shelving him in an antique closet and assuming that he has nothing to say about modern man. Rather than simply trying to escape the modern world, Ghelderode appears to use the past in order to show his deep existential feeling of despair of man in the twentieth century. As Wellwarth points out, "To a careful reader of his works there can be little doubt that Ghelderode is obsessed with a deep feeling of the inadequacy of the human condition."[60]

Notes

1. John Killinger, *World in Collapse* (New York: Dell, 1971), p. 100.

2. Robert Brustein, *The Theatre of Revolt* (Boston: Little, Brown, 1964), p. 376.

3. Killinger, pp. 92-93.

4. *Ibid.,* p. 100.

5. Brustein, p. 373.

6. Aureliu Weiss, "The Theatrical World of Michel de Ghelderode," *Tulane Drama Review,* VIII (Fall 1963), 60-61.

7. George Hauger, "The Plays of Ghelderode," *Tulane Drama Review,* IV (Fall 1959), 19.

8. Martin Esslin, *The Theatre of the Absurd* (Garden City, New York: Doubleday, 1961), p. 21.

9. *Ibid.*

10. *Ibid.*

11. Killinger, pp. 112-15.

12. Brustein, pp. 26-28.

13. Phyllis Hartnoll, ed., *The Oxford Companion to the Theatre,* 3rd ed. (London: Oxford University Press, 1967), p. 385.

14. *Ibid.,* p. 110.

15. *Ibid.,* pp. 110-11.

16. Michel de Ghelderode, *Seven Plays,* trans. George Hauger (New York, 1966), I, 3.

17. *Ibid.,* p. 14.

18. George Hauger, "Dispatches From the Prince of Ostrelande," *Tulane Drama Review,* VIII (Fall 1963), 26.

19. Michel de Ghelderode, "To Directors and Actors: Letters, 1948-1959," *Tulane Drama Review,* trans. Bettina Knapp, IX (Summer 1965), 53.

20. Ghelderode, *Seven Plays,* I, 24.

21. *Ibid.,* p. 23.

22. Hauger, *Tulane Drama Review,* VIII, 26.

23. Ghelderode, *Seven Plays*, I, 20.

24. *Ibid.*, p. 17.

25. *Ibid.*, p. 16.

26. Ghelderode, *Tulane Drama Review*, IX, 45.

27. Hauger, *Tulane Drama Review*, IV, 23.

28. George E. Wellwarth, "Ghelderode's Theatre of the Grotesque," *Tulane Drama Review*, VIII (Fall 1963), 21.

29. Ghelderode, *Seven Plays*, I, 9.

30. *Ibid.*, p. 11.

31. Ghelderode, *Tulane Drama Review*, IX, 56.

32. Ruby Cohn, *Currents in Contemporary Drama* (Bloomington: University of Indiana Press, 1969), pp. 56-57.

33. Hauger, *Tulane Drama Review*, IV, 30.

34. Michel de Ghelderode, *Seven Plays*, trans. George Hauger (New York, 1967), II, 142.

35. *Ibid.*, p. 101.

36. *Ibid.*, p. 105.

37. Hauger, *Tulane Drama Review*, IV, 30.

38. Ghelderode, *Seven Plays*, II, 151.

39. *Ibid.*, p. 174.

40. *Ibid.*, p. 175.

41. *Ibid.*

42. Ghelderode, *Seven Plays*, I, 50.

43. *Ibid.*, p. 70.

44. *Ibid.*, p. 88.

45. *Ibid.*, p. 92.

46. *Ibid.*, p. 122.

47. *Ibid.*, p. 61.

48. *Ibid.*, p. 123.

49. Eric Bentley, ed., *The Modern Theatre* (Garden City, N.Y.: Doubleday, 1957), V, 163-65.

50. Ghelderode, *Seven Plays*, I, 239-73.

51. Bentley, p. 165.

52. Hauger, *Tulane Drama Review*, IV, 30.

53. Ghelderode, *Seven Plays*, I, 211.

54. *Ibid.*, p. 157.

55. *Ibid.*, pp. 186-87.

56. *Ibid.*, p. 222.

57. *Ibid.*, p. 160.

58. *Ibid.*

59. *Ibid.*, p. 220.

60. Wellwarth, *Tulane Drama Review*, VIII, 22.

Gillan Farish (essay date 1978)

SOURCE: Farish, Gillan. "Michel de Ghelderode: The Theatre of the Swerving Dream." *University of Windsor Review* 13, no. 2 (1978): 5-23.

[*In the following essay, Farish regards* Chronicles of Hell *as a seminal work in Ghelderode's concern with the relationship of dream and reality, one that signaled his departure from drama based on Biblical and historical figures to one that depicts "those kinds of mystical, mysterious figures often found in fairy folktales."*]

The search for truth among the rubble of reality and the debris of dreams is not new to the theatre nor is the effort to reconstruct the past and forecast the future from totems that have survived intact among such ruins. The fascinating aspect of this search is that no matter how the artist conceives the rubble, debris and totems, the truths which emerge are original in that they are discovered again and again. Thus, although the truths that Michel de Ghelderode uncovers in his theatre are not necessarily new, the conditions of his discoveries are startling, harrowing even, and render the terms of his drama newly convincing.

As his search for the truth of reality and dream spans two decades, it is often difficult to apprehend the significance of single plays taken out of the context of his other works. Technically, his plays alter very little. He has a certain range of dramatic devices which he reuses with little variation. He relies heavily on dramatic monologue, the off-stage crowd, symbolic gestures, movements, properties and colours, and special lighting effects. He creates microdramas within his plays to intensify and expand the action. All these devices, however, acquire special meanings as Ghelderode establishes his own theatrical idioms to express his understanding of dream and reality which he develops and changes from play to play. The danger of misunderstanding Ghelderode arises when one ignores the subtle shifts which take place in the progression of his explorations and those equally subtle changes which occur in the meaning of his dramatic devices.

One play especially emerges as a pivot between the most outstanding differences in his work and marks a change in his interpretation of the experience of reality and dream. ***Chronicles of Hell*** (1929), which Ghelderode produced almost in the middle of his intensive playwriting period from 1918 to 1935, marks an important development in his art. Although the play has many characteristics of Ghelderode's theatre up to that point, **Chronicles of Hell** signals his departure from drama centered around Biblical and literary figures (Barabbas, Faust and Pantagleize) and historical figures (Christopher Columbus) to more abstract, fantastical drama based on those kinds of mystical, mysterious figures often found in fairy folktales. This shift frees Ghelderode to create major female characters who continue the search for truth between reality and dream in his later plays and gives him an entirely different perspective of the problems involved. To examine those details of dream and reality which Ghelderode sifts in his plays is to discover some truths of human existence. To trace the similarities and differences between his plays before and after **Chronicles of Hell** is to track the progression Ghelderode was making in his search for truth whose genesis is almost as fascinating as his ultimate conclusions.

Much of what happens in Ghelderode's plays involves a sleeping rather than a waking state and often results in the character's believing that he has been deluded. **Chronicles of Hell** introduces Ghelderode's audience to three terms which are unavoidable in a discussion of this aspect of his work. They are *comatose, chimera,* and *chiaroscuro.* In **Chronicles,** Simon Laquedeem describes Jan in Eremo as a "comatose, old man."[1] The comatose condition is quite common in Ghelderode's plays and takes many different forms. Sleep-walkers, zombies, catatonics, epileptics and drunkards are balanced by dreamers, visionaries and idealists who are all at different stages of realizing that the difficulty of distinguishing waking from sleeping frequently parallels the difficulty of distinguishing reality from illusion. Characters who recognize themselves as dreamers often consider that they are the victims of chimeras—impossible fantasies—that drive them to extraordinary behaviour. Ghelderode suggests that man so fears reality that he turns to the very thing that harms him—illusion—in whatever form best distracts him: inebriation, plays, spectacles, film, basic physical gratification. Further, the demand for illusion breeds unscrupulous pushers who augment man's awareness that there is a frightening chasm between reality and illusion and that one may not be in as much control of one's destiny as one thought. Ghelderode examines self will and external will in three plays which were written closely together: **Christopher Columbus, Barabbas** and **Pantagleize.**

In **Columbus** (1927), Ghelderode has the title character comment on those people who discover truth in their sleep: "They know; but they only know in their dreams, and they wake up ignorant."[2] Here the characters approach truth in the reality of dreams: their waking state confuses them; numbs them. A year later, in **Barabbas,** Ghelderode's "dreamers" become those who are sensi-

tive enough to discover the discrepancy between what appears to be and what is. More specifically, the characters discover that what they considered to be their true "selves" is often only a role played out behind an unrecognizable mask. Whereas the characters in **Columbus** have little or no control over their discovery of truth and cannot transfer their knowledge to their waking state, the characters of **Barabbas** not only contemplate the conditions of the truth about reality and illusion, they do this in their conscious waking state.

In **Barabbas,** Judas begs Christ for an explanation of what is happening:

> The kiss I gave you . . . I didn't know what I was doing, but an unknown force made me give you that kiss. Did I betray you? Yet you knew in advance that one of us would betray you. At that time you had an ineluctable expression that seemed to order me to betray you. Why did I do these things? What fate did I have to submit to?[3]

When Jocabeth, his wife, sees him, she says: "Judas! What is this horrible mask stuck on your face?"[4] Judas replies: "It is the true face, the imperishable face of Judas."[5] Judas has been cast into the role of villain, not against his will, but without his knowledge. No matter how much he protests that the mask isn't really him, no one will believe him. Finally, embittered by his position, he stops struggling to clear himself and no longer tries to understand what has happened. Ghelderode presents the issue of control through Judas: at times man is the victim of a higher volition and at times he victimizes himself by distorting his self image. More importantly, the discovery of the discrepancy between man and mask, between self reality and self illusion, causes man to question the reality and illusion of control. Whose will controls him? This question becomes an essential issue in all of Ghelderode's plays.

The following year, Ghelderode experiments with a variation of Judas's predicament in **Pantagleize** (1929) where the central character instigates a revolution, steals the national jewels, is tried for treason and executed without once becoming aware of the forces which control his behaviour. Both Judas and Pantagleize are manipulated by divine will and political wrangling respectively into roles that the former rebelled against and the latter was ignorant of. It is not surprising that in his next play, **Chronicles of Hell,** Ghelderode considers the nature of the power that forces the characters to assume roles and the power structure which results. At the bottom of this structure, Laquedeem controls the priests:

LAQUEDEEM:

> Laquedeem: Alter your faces! . . . Don't chuckle, don't get excited; assume the bearing of people overwhelmed by an infinite stupor; stick your noses out; let your arms hang down like Barbary apes after lovemak-

ing; have your eyes lustreless and full of grey water, and from time to time raise them skyward like blind men counting the stars. . . . Compose your features into this circumstantial mask, which others will imitate. . . .[6]

By commanding the priests to dissemble so, Laquedeem hopes to avoid arousing the suspicion that they were guilty of having expedited their Bishop's death struggle. However, the more the priests try to appear innocent, the more they appear demonic. Sodomati tells them:

You make unsightly grimaces like men possessed. You are the suspect priests of a people of possessed souls![7]

Ghelderode accentuates the monstrous behaviour of the priests by uncompromising chiaroscuro lighting effects. He sets the action of **Chronicles** against a brewing storm (typical of his plays) that alternately illuminates the stage and leaves it gloomy. The source of the only sustained light is "the morbid light of a stormy summer dusk."[8] The only brilliant area of the stage is the Bishop's death chamber which is "blazingly illuminated by a hundred candles."[9] It is as if Ghelderode is suggesting that death in itself may not be a journey into darkness but into illumination. By contrast, Ghelderode depicts life as a dark hell. The dark areas on stage breed perversion, cruelty and chaos. The goatish behaviour of Krakenbus and Carnibos (suggested by their stamping on each other's feet and banging their foreheads together) activates the lewdness of the priests. The inhabitants of the gloom are grotesque: they are grimacing, misshapen, disabled, immoderate or cowardly. The devil-in-chief, Simon Laquedeem, is afflicted with a spastic bowel whose flatulence parallels the rumblings of the storm outside as he nervously awaits the arrival of the Nuncio. In fact, the intensity of Laquedeem's gastro-intestinal upset leaves the audience in no doubt that the Nuncio will be able to smell out his irregular behaviour literally and well as figuratively. However, Ghelderode quickly suppresses any promise of justice by substituting a young effeminate priest, Sodomati, whose very name declares his affinity for perversion.

Having established the demonic setting and the devilish behaviour of the priests, Ghelderode then asks the audience to consider the possibility that the Bishop himself had forced the priests into such grossness:

SODOMATI:

You seem to be dreaming, Laquedeem. Are you entering into meditation when your clergy are not missing a mouthful?

LAQUEDEEM:

I was thinking about the inscrutability of the designs of Providence, the strangeness of certain destinies. . . . Somebody! whose shadow weighs on us, in whose shadow we live crushed down. Somebody. . . .

KRAKENBUS:

He was called Jan Eremo.[10]

Laquedeem considers Jan Eremo a usurper, an anti-Christ, an impostor who gave the people the illusion that he possessed Christlike powers to save them from the plague and famine which were decimating them. Having established himself, Eremo refused to yield his power to the clerics and lay rulers when they returned from fleeing these dangers. Eremo's status is ambiguous: is he an original force who poses a threat to a corrupt established order, or is he an opportunist whose sense of the theatrical and good timing brings him the power he desires? When Eremo refuses to relinquish his power, he forces the clergy to play the villain to his saviour. If they have lost their part playing good, then their hellish, perverse antics, their preoccupation with noisome bodily functions, may be the only behaviour left to them. Ghelderode is not simply criticizing the clergy in **Chronicles**; rather, he is depicting the chaos brought about by disrupting the power structure. When an individual seizes power by adopting someone else's role, he displaces everyone else in the structure.

Up to this point in the play, Ghelderode has considered only the lower regions of the power structure. Now he considers the source of power itself. To do so he creates a moment of macabre that is nearly as terrifying to the audience as it is to the priests on stage: he resurrects Eremo who like a "jerkily moving athlete"[11] has all the characteristics of a galvanized corpse. What kind of will power could (or would) force Eremo back to life in such a horrifying way? There are two alternatives: either Eremo was superhumanly tenacious of life and power, or some other force was at work on him. Here his jerky movements provide the clue. Possibly because Ghelderode was experienced in puppet theatre, the image of man the marionette appears frequently in his plays. Perhaps even more interesting than the image itself is the fact that Ghelderode's characters often simulate puppet movements; that is, they are incapable of movement, "wooden", or move frenetically with that jerkiness peculiar to puppets. Ghelderode's characters often appear afflicted with neurasthenic conditions which reduce them to zombie-like movements characteristic of the living dead and somnambulists who frequent his plays, or, conversely, propel them in spastic frenzy across the stage. Ghelderode depicted this latter state in his spider images which emerge as early as **The Death of Doctor Faust** (1925) when the title character laments: "Why go on living with all this mental mockery, this black spider in the brain?"[12] and later in **Pantagleize** through Bamboola who is described as a "tarantula, epilectic, wild Negro."[13] In neither state do the characters control their actions, and one concludes there is something sinister about an external will which would cause man to suffer paralysis or St. Vitus.

In *Chronicles of Hell,* the final image of Laquedeem squatting to evacuate his bowel, "his rabinical face expressing demonic bliss,"[14] would strongly suggest that the world has gone to the devil. At the moment when the priests are delivered from the living-dead Bishop, excrement triumphs over sacrament, leaving the audience to go home disgusted and dirty. Nevertheless, the final impression that one receives from *Chronicles* is that men are driven to perversity by their inability to withstand the cross-pressures of forces warring on a plane of existence just outside their range of apprehension. They can see manifestations of these forces in the physical world around them; they can feel themselves being shaped to some ulterior purpose; but they are denied an understanding of the experience, and, consequently, are driven mad. All Ghelderode's characters are similarly driven to make sense of experience; to distinguish reality from illusion; to be in control. These are difficult goals to attain especially as Ghelderode makes it increasingly clear that reality is illusion and illusion reality—a contradiction which one must accept if one is to understand anything.

In itself the reality of death can be an illusion. When Eremo first revives, Laquedeem cries out: "Not a genuine corpse! An impostor even in your death!"[15] Ghelderode introduces the idea that death is an illusion as early as 1926 in *Three Actors and Their Drama.* Three actors decide to end their tangled lives by committing suicide as a part of their performance in a play. However, they discover that they are so used to faking death that they are incapable of engineering their real deaths. Although the symbolism of the situation seems easy to understand, the implications inherent in the situation are not made clear until Ghelderode examines the necessity for executioners which he does in two of his last plays, *Lord Halewyn* (1934) and *Hop, Signor!* (1935). However, before he reached the state putting his characters to death, Ghelderode explored the possibilities of bringing them back from death.

In *Christopher Columbus,* Ghelderode transforms the title character into a self-commemorating statute before the audience's eyes. At the play's conclusion, the statute "comes back to life" just long enough to remark that now he understands life, he is no longer alive. Ghelderode develops the corpse-that-comes-back-to-life fully in *Miss Jairus* (1934), another of his last plays, where a young girl, Blandine, is forced back to life through the efforts of her lover and a necromancer. The catch is that Blandine is not grateful: she has been initiated into the beauty and purity of death and longs to return to that state. Blandine is visited by her male counterpart, Lazarus, who enters "draped in grey"[16] with little roots sprouting from his hands, feet and hair. These two initiates describe death joyously:

BLANDINE:

> . . . A spearhead will split the sealed skies. Dreams will be purple, bloodstained in holiness. Like bubbles to the surface we shall rise to burst. I only know these things by my dreams.

LAZARUS:

> It was the approach of that splendid solemn sadness of the immortals. You are still made from the beds of the ocean. You will pass through many forms as you go back through past time, and when you are no more than a tiny salt star, you will melt under God's tongue. Reabsorbed you will become a little vibration of the universal light. A singing atom. And you will share in God's living dream, that wheel which dreams. . . .[17]

This dialogue contains two images important to understanding Ghelderode's concept of death. In *Faust* and *Christopher Columbus,* Ghelderode presented the bubble image visually by having Faust do acrobatic tricks with a globe from his study and by having Columbus blow bubbles with a clay pipe throughout his opening monologue. Columbus discusses the significance of the image:

> I can't explain. I blow bubbles. They justify themselves and vanish. Little spheres, logical, perfect! Sphere, ideal volume, shape of my dreams, one must be like a child to understand you.[18]

To Columbus the bubble is a moment of perfection which gives him time only to appreciate it as an end in itself before it is gone. To Blandine the bubble is the moment of death which is to her a moment of perfection.

The image of the salt star melting under God's tongue leads in a different direction and helps explain another of Ghelderode's theatrical idioms; namely, the fits of choking that afflict certain characters. In *Chronicles of Hell,* Carnibos and Duvelhond choke themselves on the funeral meats set out for Eremo's wake. Considering the number of times in earlier plays that dead bodies are referred to almost instantaneously as dead meat, one might assume that the priests were, in a sense, choking on Eremo himself. This assumption is reinforced by the fact that Eremo has been choking on the host which, according to Roman Catholic dogma, *is* Christ's body. These acts of choking establish the power structure of the play: the priests choke on Eremo and Eremo chokes on God. The sacraments, the body and blood of Christ, are no comfort to them because they remind them of the noisome decay of the body which they fear and abhor. They equate death with decay. However, by *Miss Jairus,* Ghelderode's characters have progressed to the stage that those who have known death, long for it. Blandine and Lazarus can transcend decay which they accept as a condition necessary to their being reabsorbed in a mystical reversal of the communion rites where their bodies are taken under the tongue of God and restored to their cosmic state. *Chronicles* and *Jairus* reveal the characters (and possibly their creator) at different stages of apprehending the experience of death. Church ritual is of little solace to the clergy because it is only hocus-pocus against a much feared evil. Blandine understands death and accepts it because she trusts herself to die. When Lazarus remarks that: "humans in perdition clutch at the roughness and fissure of their confused reality,"[19] he is saying that man perpetuates his fear of physical death by reminding himself through his appetite for food and sex and his dwelling on the physical functions of his body that all purely physical existence must, sooner or later, be subject to decay. Perhaps, for this reason, Ghelderode turns away from the church's morbid interest in the dead Christ's body which blocks man's understanding of the illusion and reality of death. Instead, in his late plays, he turns increasingly to secular mysticism which allows him to perceive the mystery of death in a different way.

Up to this turning point in his work, Ghelderode concerned himself with the male point of view which, by necessity of the dominant position of the male, forces him to consider the issue of power and will. Enraged by the convergence of opposites which confuse them, frustrated by false goals in their search for understanding life, it is no wonder that the majority of Ghelderode's male characters are men of violence. In his first play written in 1918, Ghelderode created a peasant who brutalizes and murders his wife not realizing, perhaps, that his savage treatment of her during her pregnancy probably resulted in the simple, blind child for which he drowns her. Jan Eremo, enraged by his untimely end, tries to behead Simon Laquedeem. Lord Halewyn, rapist and murderer, is looking for his eighth victim. Peasant, bishop, lord are violent because they are impotent and they are impotent because they have confused sexual gratification and political power with their failure to gain control of their own mortality. They confuse their ability to take life with their inability to take death—especially their own. If they knew they were really seeking their own deaths, they would be horrified. When Ghelderode turns to women characters, he makes a startling discovery; unlike men, women have the capacity, by necessity of their position in life, to look upon death as the ultimate seduction and enjoy it.

Like Blandine Jairus, Lord Halewyn's eighth intended victim, Purmelende, is infatuated by the man who comes to bring her to her death:

> I heard the magic song and fell into a very lucid sleep, where all my feelings were awake and only my will was fast bound in slumber. Like all my sinning sisters I obeyed his voice, and went to him as the bird flies to the trapper's lure. I moved as light as air in a new world where snow shone bright as crystal under the stars. Souls after death must all surely pass through

that winter land. I doubted all creation, and myself. Words and thoughts no longer had meaning. I passed on, far from the beaten paths, beyond Good and Evil. . . . He was waiting for me, all ice and fire, and in his face shone a most baleful beauty, like that of a fallen archangel still glowing with the light of heaven, sweet with its odors, and yet already eloquent of Hell. I knew that I was lost and ran to him, the while his golden mouth sang songs of lust. His face shone with the light of rotting wood, and the sight of it brought tears into my eyes. I saw that he, for all his talk of bliss, was misery incarnate. I sought for tender words of consolation but none would come. I took his hands meaning to kiss them humbly.[20]

Despite her infatuation, Purmelende sees Halewyn as a man trapped by his actions and her pity for him gives her the strength to put him out of his misery. According to Purmelende's account, at the moment that Halewyn was struggling out of his coat of mail the better to seduce and murder her, she seizes his sword and beheads him. If Purmelende's audience is shocked by her account, it must be horrified by what she says next:

> She saw a man bent double, his head caught in a coat of mail, his arms imprisoned. She saw the hideous corpses and their hideous grimace. She saw the sword. Upward it whirled with a hissing sound, and I saw, for it was I who did the deed—a shrieking head bounding across the snow. I ran after it and caught it in mid-air. I wedged it between my knees and filled the gaping mouth with snow to stifle its blasphemies. And I said: "Pray to God now, my Lord, since you are dying. . . ." The head still tried to sing, though very quietly. And, since the snow could not stifle it, I pressed my mouth to its mouth, and finally they died, both head and song, together.[21]

The fact that Ghelderode had the good sense not to dramatize this scene but have Purmelende recount it does not lessen its gruesome sexuality. The sword, the head wedged between Purmelende's knees, the snow which Halewyn pierces with his sword and Purmelende crams into the blaspheming head become the erotic details of the consummation of death. Halewyn has not sought a maiden to kill, but one who will kill him so that he too can participate in death. Ghelderode seems to suggest that men desire peace and grace but resist the necessity of achieving them through death and decay. Both Blandine and Lazarus revel in the earthy smell of their decay no less than Purmelende who "breathed in the smell of rotting flesh"[22] of the seven dead girls hanging from the trees around her until she is recalled to her revulsion of decay by the sound of her own name. Which aspect of death is reality and which illusion? Is the reality of death putrefaction or peace? Should man cling to life or yield to death? The vision of death that Ghelderode projects through his snowmaidens, Blandine and Purmelende, whose very names suggest whiteness and purity, may be nothing but a dream. Both girls say that they can only know their feelings of ecstasy in dreams from which they are rudely awakened and which are shattered as easily as bubbles by the rougher, coarser reality of physical experience. It would seem that the answer to this riddle does not lie with the dream or the dreamer but with the executioner. Because many of Ghelderode's characters are afraid to yield to the seduction of death, they spend a good part of their existence looking for their executioners under the pretext of looking for love or power or happiness. Nearly all of Ghelderode's characters are killed by their conscious and unconscious flirtations with their potential executioners—a fact which he emphasizes in his last play, *Hop, Signor!,* and *Red Magic* (1931) which he wrote four years earlier.

The two plays beg to be compared: they both deal with characters who abstain from the conditions of living—sex and death—in order to gain a little control of their destinies. In both plays, these abstainers become the victims of characters who deliberately fabricate false situations which implicate the former against their will. Both plays deal with the theme of the cuckolded husband. Both deal with wives who are disillusioned with marriage. The situation of *Red Magic* is inverted in *Hop, Signor!*: in the former, the husband is a miser who is trying to abstain from life itself: from eating, drinking and making love; in the latter, the wife clings to her chastity refusing husband and suitors alike. In *Red Magic,* the miser is destroyed by his wife's passion for the sex which he has withheld from her. In *Hop, Signor!,* Ghelderode duplicates the situation in reverse. Ghelderode seems to be checking the validity of a truth he discovered in *Red Magic* by altering the variables of the conditions to that truth in *Hop, Signor!* Perhaps his caution springs from the reappearance of an earlier image, the spider, which he uses in both plays and which seems to have undergone a subtle shift in meaning that renders it infinitely more sinister than his earlier usage.

The gothic settings of both plays invite the appearance of spiders. The miser's house is haunted and built on a cemetery. The artisan's house in *Hop, Signor!* is situated in "an uncultivated garden. Among the bushes and rank weeds lie carved stones, statues of saints, bas-reliefs, capitals, pillars, sundials that make the garden look like a neglected yard or even like some forgotten cemetery."[23] Hieronymus, the miser, includes all things that fly over his land or crawl on his property in his possessions:

> I own a house with a ghost. . . . A bronze chest . . . in which gold pieces are breeding young. . . . A wife and her virginity . . . and the spiders watch over it. . . .[24]

Hieronymus's parsimony is ironic: Ghelderodian spiders do indeed watch over Sybilla's virginity, for she develops an insatiable appetite for sexual gratification.

Hieronymus doesn't want to lose control of the order he has imposed upon his life by abandoning himself to sex, yet, as he listens to Armador seducing his wife, he is seduced himself. Exciting himself with extravagant sexual fantasies, he rushes off to procure a whore with the money that Armador was supposed to be minting when he was seducing Sybilla. As in *Lord Halewyn,* eroticism ends in death: the lovers murder their two accomplices and Hieronymus, quite unjustly, is executed for the crime. This injustice invites a new consideration of the spider image. Sybilla, in her heightened sensuality says to Armador:

> Come, my ghost! Let us make love until dawn, and let us pretend we have all the abandonments, for dissembled thoughts are turning in the air like flies. I shall follow them on the wing for I too am a fly.[25]

Equally drunk on his new power, Hieronymus toasts himself:

> In your great honour, Hieronymus! I am very pleased with you! . . . Long life Hieronymus! (He laughs.) What a good joke I'm playing on death! . . . What? (He listens.) What quiet! It is as still as a spider's web. . . . (He shivers.) What is there to be afraid of? The spite of the Almighty who is angry at my powers?[26]

With his usual talent for stumbling onto a truth he'd rather not know, Hieronymus's sudden nervousness fuses the images of the spider and fly in the audience's mind. Man the fly and God the spider. Written between *Chronicles of Hell* and *Miss Jairus, Red Magic* recreates the horror of the former through the concept that God is a spider who weaves his cosmic webs the better to ensnare and devour the characters, and falls short of the latter's beauty in the concept that God melts the tiny salt stars of men under his tongue, consuming them like consecrated wafers back into the cosmos. This is not to say, however, that somewhere between *Red Magic* and *Hop, Signor!* Ghelderode mellowed and began to contemplate the relationship between man and God in beatific terms. Spider images are equally strong in *Hop, Signor!,* but in this play, Ghelderode parallels arachnid detail with human rather than cosmic reality. To emphasize this new significance of the image, Ghelderode creates two dwarves who appear "like big insects"[27] as they creep along on stilts designed to raise them "to the level of men."[28] The dwarves refer to the husband, Jureal, as "an industrious spider"[29] and are referred to themselves as "spider's seed."[30] *Hop, Signor!* seems to be a nest of spiders all weaving webs to snare the recalcitrant heroine, Margaret Harstein. This lady is very much like Hieronymus: she tries to save herself from mindless animalism to gain clarity about and hence power over her own destiny. However, like Hieronymus, Margaret is drawn into a web and devoured by the people who resent her apparent escape from the coils of physical reality.

The significant difference between the plays is mood: although **Hop, Signor!,** like many of Ghelderode's plays, comes dangerously close to melodrama, it is dead serious; **Red Magic** is farcical. However, at some point Ghelderode stops laughing and despite the comedy, Hieronymus emerges a tragic character. Not only must he choose between unstable electives (sex and money), but the criteria of good and evil, pain and pleasure fail as Hieronymus begins to question the value of his abstemious existence when he witnesses the sudden blooming of his wife. Armador says: "It is my tragic privilege to command the two elements that activate the universe, Good and Evil."[31] Although he pretends not to, Hieronymus knows that Armador is an impostor. (Could an alchemist be anything but?) Perhaps, then, good and evil are counterfeit as well. When he hears Sybilla's moaning in his cellar, he asks: "Is it with pain? Is it with pleasure? . . . The two are so alike. . . ."[32] Hieronymus is forced to reflect on the ultimate ambiguity: the nature of the volition which directs man to choose one course of action over another. He says to his "son"—a doll he makes Sybilla play with rather than give her a real child:

> Men have unhealthy dreams. They dream of being more powerful than nature, than its Creator. They want to make light out of darkness. When you grow up—if you grow up—you will be rich; but never wonder where the riches came from. Enjoy them stupidly. . . . From time to time say to yourself that your father was tortured and that he did away with his tranquillity for the happiness of his kin! . . . Sleep or I shall destroy you! . . . Do not whine Hieronymus. Be like your son, insensible and without complaint. What is taking place had to be. It is solemn. It is grotesque. It is poignant. I am no doubt very happy . . . and I feel miserable.[33]

The "child" is also an illusion "born" out of his niggardliness to give anything of himself away. Suppose his own creator is equally ungenerous: could his being, his existence, be nothing more than a figment of imagination of some stingy deity? What meaning then could sex or money have? What is left when glands and power fail? What is left to Hieronymus is death. The paradox which teases man is that the meaning to his living is in his dying. The alternative to coping with this fearful truth is to live out one's life in mindless stupor; to sleep the time away. Even the alternative is false: the terrifying reality of the illogic of dreams catches man off guard, at his most vulnerable. He can only wake again to the terrible logic of conscious reality.

Ghelderode tackles this problem through the last major character of his sustained writing period—Margaret Harstein. Piqued and humiliated by his wife's celibacy, Jureal Harstein accuses her of having lovers. Flattered by this imaginary credit, the "lovers" do little to refute the accusation, and the world accepts the unfounded charge as fact. Seeing that her husband and his priest as well as her two suitors are determined to malign her, Margaret attempts to make falsehood a reality. She becomes lascivious and tries to seduce the priest as well as the suitors. Like Hieronymus, Margaret is increasingly aware that she is the victim of seduction. With each provocative turn of the plot, she becomes enmeshed in a dream-like existence which reduces her conscious will to determine her own destiny. She acknowledges her predicament:

> There are times when each dream swerves aside and disports itself for a moment in reality before recovering itself and making off as a dream. In fact the dream never stopped. Where is the dream? Where does it begin? Where does it end? On a road where the wolves run?[34]

Fully aware of the dangers of the dream—the disorientation; the spontaneous, unwilled shifts into truth: the "wolves"—Margaret decides that these are lesser evils than the frustration of being prevented from creating a light to illuminate the darkness of waking reality. She yields to the dream and becomes increasingly somnambulant as the play progresses. Her "awakening" is her death; she refuses to "wake" again to the irritations of life. Once again Ghelderode presents the need for an executioner. Swallowed up in the executioner's cape (like Blandine in Lazarus's), she is executed, like Hieronymus, on false charges of murder and witchcraft: for the way things *appear* to be; not the way they *really* are. The world is only too ready to snatch any excuse to relieve itself of the Eremos, Hieronymuses and Margarets who challenge the "truth" that all men are at the mercy of a divine control against which they are powerless. Each of these three characters marks a progression in Ghelderode's emergent resolution of the irreconcilable forces at work on man. Eremo's angry "rejection" of physical death, his terrible "resurrection", is a just punishment for tampering with illusion to gain his power. Hieronymus is full of self-recrimination and bitterness: he resents the spite of a creator who toys with his creations, but he *resigns* himself to this fate. Only Margaret who recognizes the injustice of waking reality and illusion and the perils of dreaming reality and illusion accepts the paradox. By *yielding* to it, she alone is not defeated by it.

If in **Miss Jairus** and **Lord Halewyn,** Ghelderode created snow maidens longing for death, in **Red Magic** and **Hop, Signor!,** he creates fire men to burn away deceit and corruption. True, Amador, in the comic terms of **Red Magic,** is a false fire man: he only pretends to mint coins from Sybilla's blood. Larose is a real executioner: he knows from the outset that he will execute Margaret Harstein. Once again Ghelderode probes the problem of death—this time through his executioner. Larose is Lazarus and Armador combined. His name (which even sounds like "Lazarus") associates him with a rose tree as Lazarus is associated with a sprouting plant. Lazarus is a kind of human compost feeding living plants. Larose is the plant who feeds on the decay—the death of his victims. He scents out Margaret's readiness for her execution:

> Your flesh smells good, is in the right condition. . . .
>
> *He briskly draws near to* MARGARET *and goes around her, sniffing at her.* MARGARET *smiles, enraptured. But the executioner draws back.*[35]

Like Armador, he is the consummate lover, "a blond athlete, superbly molded in scarlet, beardless, with a nonchalant feline gait."[36] He inflames Margaret but refuses her seductive overtures knowing that the only true consummation of their relationship can occur at her moment of death in the flames of her execution. Margaret understands his affair with death and tells him so:

MARGARET:

> Could you stop the crowd shouting when the whole of your scaffold rings at the outburst? Could you stop the condemned man's shout mingling with it, so weak and all-prevailing? Well, I too shout, with this crowd and the condemned man, and you. . . .
>
> (LAROSE takes a step. MARGARET draws back.) For the executioner cries out like his victim. . . . I know, I have heard him. No one hears it. Then you go pale, you stagger imperceptibly, your gaze wanders. . . .

LAROSE:

> Be quiet! (He puts his hand over Margaret's mouth.)

MARGARET:

> And that only lasts for . . .

LAROSE (PUSHING HER AWAY):

> Madwoman! (He spits.)

MARGARET (BITTER AND SAD):

> Nice executioner . . .

LAROSE (GOING TOWARD THE STEPS):

> And on the evenings after the executions women became pregnant. Not by me, no! I spit on them. (He spits again.)

MARGARET (RUNS TO LAROSE AND PREVENTS HIM FROM GOING DOWN):

> Spit on me!

LAROSE:

> No!

MARGARET:

> Why?

LAROSE:

> Because you, Lady Margaret . . . (Pause.) Because you . . . Margaret . . . are not a woman like the others. No. In a way you were a sister. Now you are be-

coming an accomplice, for you have come across a secret that God alone knows; God who probes the loins as well as the heart.[37]

Between them, Larose and Margaret eliminate love and passion as factors in the consummation of death. When Margaret begs Larose to "deliver"[38] her from the physical sexual frustration which is consuming her, he replies: "No pretense is possible. If I begin, I finish."[39] There will be no substitution of sexual passion for death passion; there will be no *coitus interruptus mortis* for Margaret as there was for Purmelende. Although he is tempted by Margaret's sexuality, Larose refuses to participate in such a deception, explaining:

> I wasn't wanting anything. Take you away? No. Fate must lead you. Nothing is living, nothing is authentic unless fate has marked it with its indecipherable seal. Do you know that?[40]

Knowing a truth is not the same as accepting it; coping with it. Margaret has still to conquer the "animal horror"[41] which she says death awakens in her. Only when she succeeds in transcending this horror, when she falls asleep under the spell of death, does Ghelderode allow Larose to reveal the meaning of her death:

> You shall be a poisonous flower flung into the purifying fire. I shall make your death agony fruitful, and from your ashes dreadful roses shall be born.[42]

For Ghelderode it seems that the ultimate mystery occurs at the moment when Life mates with Death: an act of cosmic procreation perpetuated by the living and dying of beings who were created as fuel for the process with no regard for their individual agony. Only the perpetuation of the cosmic forces matters. To prove this point one has only to consider that there are no children in Ghelderode's plays, only puppets, dolls, dwarves and dreadful roses. There are only interrupted matings: when Blandine and Lazarus would kiss, Jacquelin interrupts them; when Halewyn would ravish Purmelende, she kills him; when Margaret would seduce Larose, he resists. Through these terms of sex (life) and death, Ghelderode depicts the human condition: at the moment when man would be seduced by life, death interferes; at the moment he would be seduced by death, life intervenes. The reality of life cancels out the illusion of death; the reality of death cancels out the illusion of life. One force seems to cancel out the other leaving man forever suspended paralysed and waiting—like the fly in the spider's web. Until man learns to accept that he is only part of forces perpetuating a larger order which for all his poor struggles he will never understand and whose truths will manifest themselves to him in elusive moments, he will never transcend the animal fear of his own mortality. He must learn to yield to Life until it is time to yield to Death; until the inexorable, irreversible momentum of the forces that make the design require him for the procreation of the universe. Small wonder that Ghelderode's final image in **Hop, Signor!** is that of a "disjointed marionette"[43] tossed in a blanket by two dwarves "rising and falling like a wounded bird faltering between earth and sky."[44] If this was the truth that Ghelderode found in the shards of reality and illusion waking or dreaming, then it is a most dreadful rose indeed.

Notes

1. *Chronicles of Hell*, 1:260.

2. *Christopher Columbus*, 2:155-6.

3. *Barabbas*, 1:64.

4. *Ibid.*, 74.

5. *Ibid.*

6. *Chronicles of Hell*, 1:248.

7. *Ibid.*, 252.

8. *Ibid.*, 238.

9. *Ibid.*, 255.

10. *Ibid.*, 256.

11. *Ibid.*, 264.

12. *Faust*, 2:101.

13. *Pantagleize*, 1:161.

14. *Chronicles*, 1:273.

15. *Ibid.*, 263.

16. *Ibid.*, 253.

17. *Ibid.*

18. *C.C.*, 2:153-4.

19. *Miss Jairus*, 2:253.

20. *Lord Halewyn*, 1:302.

21. *Ibid.*, 303.

22. *Ibid.*, 302.

23. *Hop, Signor!*, 2:51.

24. *Red Magic*, 2:10.

25. *Ibid.*, 53.

26. *Ibid.*, 36.

27. *H.,S.!*, 2:51.

28. *Ibid.*, 52.

29. *Ibid.*, 54.

30. *Ibid.*, 74.

31. *Red Magic*, 2:15.

32. *Ibid.*, 37.

33. *Ibid.*, 19.

34. *H.,S.!* 2:85.

35. *Ibid.*, 81-2.

36. *Ibid.*, 77.

37. *Ibid.*

38. *Ibid.*, 78.

39. *Ibid.*

40. *Ibid.*

41. *Ibid.*, 85.

42. *Ibid.*, 93.

43. *Ibid.*

44. *Ibid.*

Bibliography

WORKS

Ghelderode de, Michel. *Ghelderode: Seven Plays, Vol. 1* (tr. by George Hauger). New York: Hill and Wang, 1960.

————. *Ghelderode: Seven Plays, Vol. 2* (tr. by George Hauger). MacGibbon and Kee, 1966.

Chronology of Plays found in the two preceding volumes:

1918	*Piet Bouteille*
1921	*A Night of Pity*
1925	*The Death of Doctor Faust*
1926	*Three Actors and Their Drama*
1927	*Christopher Columbus*
1928	*Women at the Tomb*
	Barabbas
1929	*Pantagleize*
	Chronicles of Hell
1931	*Red Magic*
1933	*Three Blind Men*
1934	*Lord Halewyn*
	Miss Jairus
1935	*Hop, Signor!*

CRITICISM

Abel, Lionel. "Our Man in the Sixteenth Century: Michel de Ghelderode," *Tulane Drama Review*, Vol. 8, No. 1, Fall 1963.

Beyen, Roland. *Michel de Ghelderode, ou la hantise du masque*. Bruxelles: Palais des Académies, 1971.

Deberdt-Malaquais, Elisabeth. *La Quête de l'Identité dans le Théâtre de Ghelderode*, 1967.

Decock, Jean. *Le Théâtre de Michel de Ghelderode: Une Dramaturge de l'Anti-théâtre et de la Cruauté.* Paris Editions-A.-G. Nizet, 1969.

Draper, Samuel. "An Interview with Michel de Ghelderode," *TDR* [*Tulane Drama Review*], Vol. 8, No. 1, Fall 1963.

———. "Bibliography," *Modern Drama,* Vol. 8, No. 3, Winter 1965.

———. "Discovery of Ghelderode," *Commonweal,* LXXXVI, No. 7, May 1962.

———. "Infernal Theatre," *Commonweal,* LXXI, No. 10, New York, December 4, 1959.

Francis, Jean. *L'Eternal Aujourd'hui de Michel de Ghelderode.* Brussels, 1968.

Grossvogel, David. "Plight of the Comic Author and New Departures into Contemporary Comedy," *Romantic Review,* No. 45, New York, December 1954.

Guicharnaud, Jacques. *Modern French Theatre from Giroudoux to Becket.* New Haven: Yale University Press, 1961.

Hauger, George. "Dispatches from the Prince of Ostrelande," *TDR,* Vol. 8, No. 1, Fall 1963.

Pronko, Leonard, Cabell. *Avant-Garde: The Experimental Theatre in France.* Berkely and Los Angeles: University of California Press, 1962.

Weiss, Aurelui. "The Theatre of Michel de Ghelderode," *TDR,* Vol. 8, No. 1, Fall 1963.

Wellworth, George. "Michel de Ghelderode: The Theatre of the Grotesque," *TDR,* Vol. 8, No. 1, Fall 1963.

Nancy Lane (essay date January 1987)

SOURCE: Lane, Nancy. "Ghelderode's *La mort du docteur Faust* as Meta-Theater." *French Forum* 12, no. 1 (January 1987): 93-108.

[*In the following essay, Lane highlights the meta-theatrical aspects of* The Death of Doctor Faust, *calling it "arguably the most fascinating example" of self-referential drama in modern theater.*]

One of the hallmarks of twentieth-century theater has been the emergence of a type of play that foregrounds its own self-referentiality, exposing "the very process of semiotization involved in performance."[1] As semiotic studies of theater have shown, theatrical performance as a signifying system rests on the radical duplicity that inhabits the theatrical sign.[2] The conventions of naturalistic Western theater attempt to mask this process by filling the stage with objects (Antoine's famous sides of beef at the Théâtre libre, for example) or actors (Stanislavskian "method" actors, for example) endeavoring to mimic fictional entities as "realistically" as possible. Yet this type of theater is no more "realistic" than any of Beckett's most minimalist plays. In neither case can the elements of the performance be said to coincide with or resemble directly the fictional entities they perform.[3] In fact, because of the great mobility (dynamism or transformability) of the theatrical sign, naturalistic theater's attempts to deny this mobility by trying to make the world of the performance coincide with the world outside are profoundly anti-theatrical. (Auguste Renoir commented on this very point when he expressed how disappointed he had been to see "un vrai piano" on the stage the first time he was taken to the theater.)[4] What naturalistic theater tries to ignore is that *all* theatrical performance refers to itself as performance,[5] and only then to (a) the dramatic world of the performed (the play itself) and (b) the world of the spectator (locus of extra-dramatic referents). The world of the performance is the mediating ground between the other two worlds, which are separate from each other and would be closed to each other without it. (That is, it is only through performance—actual or virtual—that a spectator has access to a play as theater, rather than as a literary text.) What modern meta-theater has done is to lay bare this middle ground of the performance, "driving a dramaturgical wedge" into the middle of theatrical sign-vehicles in order to expose their fundamental dualism.[6] The importance of self-conscious theater in the twentieth century has been most widely remarked in plays by Apollinaire, Pirandello, Genet, Brecht, and Handke. Less well known, yet arguably the most fascinating example of "theater on theater" is *La Mort du docteur Faust* by the Belgian playwright Michel de Ghelderode (1898-1962).[7] It provides an excellent case study of how theater on display within the world of the performed plays off against an imbricated world of performance. Furthermore, this play at once posits and undermines extra-dramatic referents,[8] thereby pointing in a double gesture to its own theatricality, its own status as esthetically-closed world.[9]

This "tragédie pour le music-hall," composed of a prologue and three episodes, incorporates the circus, pantomime and the magic show and calls for multi-media staging—special effects, film projections and elaborate, stylized costumes and makeup. (These daunting technical problems may explain why the play has been performed rarely since its premiere at Art et Action on January 27, 1928—two years after it was published.) The play is exceedingly complex, and thoroughly meta-theatrical with regard to space and time, character and discourse: both the scenic space and the dramatic space are doubled or even tripled within each act; it is set in both the sixteenth and the twentieth centuries; and each of the characters is doubled twice—first by a play-within-a-play and then by his or her legendary counterpart. A brief synopsis will provide the basis for discussion of meta-theatrical aspects of the play. (My discussion will necessarily posit a virtual performance in which all the signs in the theatrical text [staging and verbal signs] are taken into account.)[10]

SYNOPSIS

The setting is carnival time in Flanders, both in 1550 and the "present" (a deictic meaning "1925" when the play was written). In the Prologue, set in the study of the sixteenth-century doctor, a clownish Faust proclaims in exaggerated manner his weariness with his existence and his malaise about the role he has been playing. He flees his room and Crétinus, his assistant, to escape into the carnival going on in the street outside.

Episode 1 is set in the present, in the Taverne des Quatre-Saisons. In the back of the tavern is a stage where an itinerant troupe of actors is to perform a play entitled *La Tragédie de Faust,* and in the foreground stands Diamotoruscant. He announces that he is the devil and demonstrates his powers in a series of spectacular conjurations and spells. A seventeen-year-old servant named Marguerite enters the tavern in search of "un ami," and Diamotoruscant offers to "faire le diable" if she should meet a customer named Faust. Faust does come in, expressing little surprise at finding himself transported into the twentieth century. Encouraged by Diamotoruscant, he begins his seduction of Marguerite just as the play begins on the small stage near them. This play duplicates the scene going on in the tavern, and both Faust and Diamotoruscant are indignant at the way they are being portrayed. As Diamotoruscant leaps to the stage, disrupting the performance by goading the actor playing the devil into believing that he has become the devil, Faust slips out with Marguerite.

The setting of Episode 2 represents a street in a rundown section of town. Offstage left is the interior of a cinema where a "tragique histoire d'amour" is being shown, an ironic analogue of the sordid drama (Faust's cynical seduction of a naive Marguerite) unfolding in the shabby hotel room offstage right. Waiting in the street for Faust is Diamotoruscant, who enacts yet another parody of a "love story": complaining of his inability (as a mythic figure) to find love, he plays out a comically melodramatic scene with a passing prostitute. Faust and Marguerite emerge from the hotel, and when Faust refuses to marry her, she begins to scream loud accusations of rape—just as the crowd is leaving the movie theater. They are about to set upon Faust when Diamotoruscant allows him to escape by making the crowd believe that the scene they have just witnessed is a preview of the play that will be performed at the Quatre-Saisons.

The setting of the final episode is once again divided, this time into two spaces and times. On the left side of the stage is a street where the events of the twentieth century are represented in mime and cinematic projections: outraged by Marguerite's bloody suicide, the whole city is hunting for the actor presumed guilty of her rape and responsible for her death. On the right is the sixteenth-century study of the Prologue. Seeking refuge from the angry mob, having no idea of why he has been accused, the actor who had played Faust in the tavern enters the room. Crétinus comes in and mistakes him for the doctor, and the actor's mistress, who had played Marguerite in the embedded play, soon joins them. (She has seen the actor go through the door and chooses to remain with him rather than flee, as has the actor who had played the devil.) Faust and Diamotoruscant then arrive, leading to a climactic confrontation and intense struggle between the two Fausts. Spurred on by Diamotoruscant's interventions and Marguerite's confusion about which one is her lover, each becomes increasingly unsure about who the "real" Faust is. Finally, the actor assumes the role and identity "Faust" and rushes out to be killed by the mob, and the doctor, urged on by Diamotoruscant, puts an end to both Fausts by shooting himself. As the curtain falls, Crétinus takes up both the robes and the role of his master and begins the seduction of his "Marguerite," while Diamotoruscant walks away, laughing bitterly and muttering, "Imbécile! imbécile! imbécile!" (284).

SPACE AND TIME

As Michael Issacharoff has pointed out,[11] space is perhaps the one element of theatrical performance that cannot be suppressed: "A play when enacted must take place somewhere. Its performance must occur in some real, visible space, on a stage or in an area fulfilling that purpose" (211). The "somewhere" of theatrical performance differs from the fictional space of narrative because it is ostended; as Ubersfeld says, theatrical space is the site of mimesis (155). This does not mean that any given theatrical space imitates or resembles the dramatic space it performs, as in a photograph, for example. Rather, in theater, fictional space is signified through spatial (polyphonic) media, as opposed to the single (verbal) medium of narrative. The "somewhere" of theatrical performance is defined and produced by two sets of tensions: a) the tension between the stage and the auditorium and b) the tension between theatrical space and dramatic space. Theatrical space is first of all defined in relation to the audience; the "stage" is by definition any space perceived as being the locus of "playing" as opposed to "doing," whether that space is bounded by a proscenium or not. Independently of any mimesis of concrete space, theatrical space is primarily the locus of play.[12] That is, the first reference of the stage is to its status as stage, and only then does the theatrical space of the performance acquire the capacity to represent the dramatic space of the play being performed. The tension between these two spaces constitutes the second fundamental feature of theatrical space.

Theatrical space is always polysemic, signifying both a "here" (the concrete space of the performance) and an "elsewhere" (the dramatic, fictional space of the play). Theatrical space is not directly mimetic or iconic of dramatic space, of course. The two spaces are not co-extensive, and perception of the latter is always mediated through the sign-vehicles of the former.[13]

"Illusionist" or "realistic" theater attempts to efface or at least mute the physical presence of the theatrical space in order to make the stage as transparent as possible to dramatic space. This effacement can take two forms. The first privileges the verbal signs of the text in performance; space is described rather than shown. This kind of theater (examples would include certain productions of Racine or Giraudoux by directors like Jacques Copeau and Louis Jouvet, whose aim was to make the stage "transparent") is highly "literary." The second kind of effacement is that practiced by "naturalist" theater, where the scenic space (including objects, costumes, makeup, the bodies of the actors, etc.) is constructed to resemble or mimic its dramatic counterpart. This kind of theater tries to establish a false continuity between the audience's space and the space of the play through the conceit of the "missing fourth wall' through which spectators gaze into a world that "looks just like" their own. By muting the "otherness" of theatrical media of representation, this kind of theater endeavors to deny its own status as artifice.

Meta-theater foregrounds the media of representation and therefore emphasizes the tension (or difference) between concrete space on the one hand and represented space on the other. Mimetic space dominates in this kind of theater: what is described is also shown, so that the auto-reflexivity of theatrical semiosis is highlighted.[14] Moreover, the terms used to refer to what is ostended are themselves theatrical ones. In *La Mort du docteur Faust,* space is organized into a meta-theatrical semiotic system: in each of the three episodes, stage space is identified as such through opposition to audience space, on the one hand, and offstage space on the other, mimetic space dominates while diegetic space approaches zero, and deliberately non-naturalistic media of representation emphasize the "theatricality" of the play.

Within each episode, an onstage audience space paralleling the situation of the real-world spectators is opposed to a specifically scenic space, but the relation between these two spaces is never stable. In Episode 1, the stage-within-a-stage at the rear of the tavern initially makes the interior of the tavern into an audience space inhabited by customers who will become spectators for the play-within-a-play. Before this play begins, however, Diamotoruscant adds another dimension to this straightforward configuration by putting on a show for the customers. At the beginning of the scene, Dia-

motoruscant is seated in the foreground, writing. While he explains to a cut-out figure of a waiter that he is a writer, a loudspeaker on the bar is broadcasting a series of fantastic news items: a red comet has just appeared, the emperor of India has eaten his diamonds, a prophet has been decapitated, and the newly-elected pope is a devil who has flown away on airplane wings. Angrily accusing the loudspeaker of spouting lies, Diamotoruscant leaps up to strangle it. When he slaps a woman who has attacked him, calling him a murderer, the other customers react with applause, and Diamotoruscant responds by putting on an elaborate show: he induces an epileptic fit in one of the customers (a poet) and brings to the stage all of the marvels described in the loudspeaker's broadcast. The diegetic space described in the broadcast is thus transformed into mimetic space, an indication that the world of this play is theatrical, circumscribed by a series of "stages." Furthermore, Diamotoruscant becomes the "author" of a new play, concretizing the diegesis implied by his writing (which had paralleled the loudspeaker's descriptions at the beginning of the scene). This show has the further effect of undermining the separation between stage and audience. First, reversal of stage and audience space occurs when the actor who will play the devil in *La Tragédie de Faust* leaps off the stage into the "real" audience to pluck gold coins from their ears and pockets, demonstrating to the customers in the tavern that he too can do magic tricks. Thus, theater is turned "inside out," as the onstage characters become spectators and the audience suddenly becomes the locus of play. Furthermore, the customers in the tavern themselves become unwitting "characters" in Diamotoruscant's spectacle; at first, only the woman and the poet are the "victims," and the other customers behave as spectators—passive observers of the onstage action who applaud the show and ask for more ("la fin du monde"). When Diamotoruscant complies by putting on "la fin du monde," all of the customers become "rigides et pétrifiés" (228); no longer spectators, they have become part of the play, leaving a void in the audience space to be filled by the arrival of the new audience (Marguerite and Faust).

By the time the play-within-a-play gets under way, the relationship between stage and audience has become so fluid and problematic that it is not surprising that the onstage spectators (Faust, Marguerite, and Diamotoruscant) do not remain passive observers. As we shall see, the stage merges with "the real" for Faust, who rejects the image of himself in the play and leaves the tavern with Marguerite. The other two actors then exit in disgust, and the actor whose role was the devil is left alone with Diamotoruscant, who has leaped onto the small stage to ridicule the actor's technique. Faced with Diamotoruscant's attempt to subvert scenic space, the actor tries to maintain its integrity by defending his acting skill: "Mais, vous ne m'avez pas laissé jouer! Ce rôle est un triomphe pour moi! . . . Si vous étiez quelque peu au courant de l'art dramatique, vous sauriez que je n'ai pas mon pareil!" (240). He then turns to the audience, seeking vindication: "Mesdames et Messieurs, ce n'est pas un compère, ni une scène préparée pour me permettre de me faire valoir! C'est un amateur qui a protesté contre le style du personnage que j'incarne! . . . Vous serez juges!" (241). All of the customers in the tavern are asleep, however, so the actor's speech is indirectly addressing the real-world audience in self-referential fashion. With no audience in the tavern against which the stage can define itself as such, the scenic space is no longer the locus of "playing," but of "being." Goaded on by Diamotoruscant, the actor goes mad: he *becomes* the devil, collapsing the difference between the stage and the world. Once this subversion of scenic space is achieved, Diamotoruscant awakens the customers and exits, laughing heartily at their confusion about whether they are watching a play or not: "Où sommes-nous? . . . Pourquoi sommes-nous ici? Quelle farce! Quelle tragédie? Quel est ce fou qui hurle? Il nous insulte! Rendez l'argent! Il joue très bien!" (243-44). Thus, these customers are still unwitting participants in a play-within-a-play authored by Diamotoruscant; the distinction between audience and stage which had seemed unambiguous at the outset has been undermined and even reversed.

In Episode 2, scenic space and audience space once again mirror each other and exchange places. The actions in Episode 1 unfolded and were contained within onstage interior spaces, while the exterior space of the street outside (only partially represented through the window of the tavern) functioned as a limiting horizon for the multiple scenic spaces on the inside. This configuration is turned inside out in Episode 2. "Interior" space is moved offstage, while the onstage space represents a busy street filled with passers-by throughout the act. Initially, this space (by definition, a public, neutral zone) is devoid of action and acting, in contrast to the scenic spaces offstage left and right—the cinema (partially represented onstage left by a brightly-lit marquee and some garish posters) and the hotel room (again, partially represented onstage right by a window and balcony). Diamotoruscant, waiting in the street for Faust, functions as spectator or potential spectator for the two parallel "love stories" unfolding in the wings. The cinema barker tries to lure him into the movie, describing it as "une tragique histoire d'amour où le destin joue un rôle inqualifiable. . . . Entrez, Monsieur! Une stupéfiante histoire de passion et de volupté qui finit par la mort et la damnation!" (245). The barker serves as a link between the street and the cinema ("reality" and "fiction"). His diegesis is meta-theatrical, for it describes in ironic fashion the scene going on in the hotel room as well as the entire play. Diamotoruscant catches occasional glimpses of the seduction scene going on in the hotel room when the characters appear briefly on the balcony; his one attempt to become an actor rather than a spectator (playing his own love scene with a passing prostitute) is aborted because the street is the locus of everyday, "real" life. As the action moves from the offstage space into the street, however, the street itself will become a new stage, again reversing the initial audience-to-stage relationship.

Faust and Marguerite are the first to bring their offstage drama into the street, culminating in Marguerite's loud accusations of rape. When the crowd emerges from the cinema, they are immediately confronted with this new "drama," and their remarks about the movie they have just seen provide ironic commentary for the scene taking place between Faust and Marguerite: "Triste fin! Quel film! Quels artistes! C'est la vérité! Non, c'est inventé! . . . Je préfère les films où l'on épouse!" (255). At first, these two sets of characters engage on the "real life" ground of the street, and the scene is a real one involving real passions and real crimes. Diamotoruscant intervenes, however, responding to Faust's plea for help: "Faust! Je ferai avec toi un marché infernal! Tu auras la jeunesse, la force, l'amour, la fortune. Mais . . . (*Silence.*) Cher public! La suite de ces émouvantes péripéties, vous la verrez demain soir sur le théâtre de la taverne des Quatre-Saisons où nous jouons, acteurs, talentueux, le drame, et la comédie aussi!" (256). As in the first episode, his gift is to turn "reality" into fiction, and he saves Faust from the crowd of movie-goers by turning the scene into a play, and the street into a stage. Finally, the metatheatrical ambiguity of the entire scene is once again highlighted through the barker's role as mediator between fiction and reality, as he vacillates between two possible interpretations of what he has just seen. (Diamotoruscant had earlier confided to him that he *is* the devil, and not an actor.) Closing up the cinema and preparing to leave for the evening, he pauses to speak to Diamotoruscant: "Allons! Bonsoir! (*Silence.*) Tu n'es pas le diable! Hé! Hé! Tu n'es qu'un acteur! Ton métier n'est pas plus sot que le mien! (*Silence.*) Ou alors si tu es le diable, réponds-moi!" (257).

The final episode once again plays off two spaces against each other, as the left side of the stage (the twentieth-century street outside) frames and mirrors the drama of identity and character unfolding simultaneously in the sixteenth-century study represented on the right side of the stage. Initially, the street is the locus of danger, ambiguity and *acting*, while Faust's study represents a secure refuge, locus of certainty and *being*: by entering Faust's study, the actor hopes to escape an angry mob that sees in him only the role he had played, hopes to leave the theater and enter a "real world." However, these terms will be reversed, once again as a result of Diamotoruscant's manipulations, as the study is transformed into a theater and the actor turns back to the street to confirm the reality of his new identity. By the time the actor rushes out, the street has become the stage for his death; during the confrontation between the two Fausts on the right side of the stage, an elaborate pantomime on the left portrays the townspeople's discovery of Marguerite's mutilated body and their pursuit and trial (in absentia) of the presumed criminal. First, a newsboy appears, shouting the news of the terrible crime; he is followed by the cinema barker (wearing a large question mark on his head) who reads a paper with a shocked, sympathetic expression, serving once again as a surrogate spectator, a mediator between stage and audience. Soon, the entire left side of the stage is filled with onstage spectators for the crime and trial, a reflection of the real-world spectators of **La Mort du docteur Faust.**

In this final episode, as throughout, the carnival setting emphasizes the theatricality of the entire play. Carnivalesque, exaggerated staging, using masks, elaborate costumes and projections, serves to draw the spectator's attention to the media of representation. (As we shall see, this sort of anti-naturalistic staging is particularly evident in the representation of characters.) Especially important in the final episode is the use of cinematic projections of newspaper headlines to tell the story of Marguerite's suicide and the manhunt for the actor: "UN DRAME INENARRABLE VIENT DE STUPEFIER L'OPINION. . . . UNE PROMPTE JUSTICE S'IMPOSE. . . . L'ASSASSIN PRESUME EST EN FUITE . . . LES DETECTIVES LES PLUS AVISES SONT EN ROUTE. TROUVERONT-ILS LE COUPABLE?" (273-78). As in Brechtian dramaturgy, the use of projections here inscribes the diegesis in theatrical space and heightens the audience's awareness of the fictionality of theater; the spectator is forced to recognize the duality of the theatrical sign. Along with the onstage audience, the real-world spectator becomes a "reader" of a text projected onto the stage.

Time is intimately linked to space throughout the play, as the setting is systematically doubled temporally as well as spatially. Although the play is somewhat less meta-theatrical with regard to time than plays which draw attention to their own running time (Ionesco's *Le Roi se meurt,* for example), this duality in setting emphasizes the lack of continuity between the space-time continuum of the spectator (the performance) and that of the play. Unlike time in the world of the spectator, time in the world of the play is fluid and open: when Faust enters the Quatre-Saisons in the first episode, for example, he expresses no surprise or distress about finding himself in the twentieth century: "En quel siècle sommes-nous, à propos? . . . D'ailleurs, si ça [his seduction of Marguerite] devait tourner mal, je regagnerais mon siècle! Vous comprenez, moi, j'existe ailleurs . . ." (232-34). The fluidity of dramatic time is emphasized in the final episode, where the two temporal settings are contiguous, connected to each other by the door between Faust's room and the street. Furthermore, the use of mythical figures as characters adds another meta-theatrical dimension to the representation of time. Faust and Diamotoruscant repeatedly refer to themselves as figures existing outside space and time, as ephemeral as dramatic characters. Finally, the time (as well as the place) of the play, in both centuries, is carnival, the time when acting and theater invade everyday life, providing yet another meta-theatrical frame for the play.

CHARACTER AND DISCOURSE

Even in the case (by no means the only one) where both actor and character are human, the dramatic character is always radically other with respect to the actor. In order for any play to take place, it is necessary that a tension, which I will call "vertical," separate actor from character. If actors were to be perceived as coinciding with their roles—as doing and being rather than *playing* at doing and being—no play would be performed. As long as the spectator frames the event as theater, the character acquires an absolute distance from the spectator. (Performances such as happenings or certain experiments done by the Living Theater, for example, can remain theater only up to the point where they engage the spectator directly in his own world; as soon as the represented world disappears, psycho-therapy or political action, for example, and not theater, is the result.) Whatever some actors might say, moreover, they do not disappear or become unreal while performing; their bodies and their being remain intact within the world of the performance, accessible to the spectator—we can see and hear and touch Olivier while he is performing Hamlet in our presence. The dramatic character, on the other hand, is absolutely contingent and ephemeral, signified through the words and gestures of the actor (and through the other elements that participate in the performance of any given character—makeup, costume, etc.). Unlike characters from narrative, the dramatic character always appears before us—we can see and hear (but cannot touch) Hamlet while Olivier is performing him; furthermore, each appearance of a dramatic character is unique, inextricably bound to the moment of performance.

In meta-theater, characters themselves become actors, and the tension separating actor from character is taken up by the world of the play. In traditional examples of the play-within-a-play (Corneille's *L'Illusion comique,* for example, or *Hamlet*), the two levels of the performed (outer play and inner play) are distinct, both for the spectators of the outer play and for those characters who become spectators for the inner play. For those characters who become actors in the outer play, the "otherness" of the characters they perform in the inner play poses no threat to their identity. In much of modern meta-theater, however, the distinction between the two worlds is blurred, so that the "otherness" of the dramatic character is ostended within the outer play itself. Self-conscious characters appear, and the vertical tension separating actor from character is transformed into a "horizontal" tension within the character itself—a gap between actor and role. Thus, self-conscious characters bring into the world of the play "the duality of the actor's role as stage-sign vehicle *par excellence*" (Elam 9). Foregrounding the act of representation, self-conscious characters appear ill at ease with their status as character, unsure either of who they are or of what role they are to play.

Exposing "the quotation marks that the actor assumes in representation" (Elam 9), *La Mort du docteur Faust* foregrounds exceptionally well the "otherness" of the dramatic character with regard to the actor. The mobility of the relation between actor as sign vehicle and character as signified is elaborated in the structure of the action (variations on the play-within-a-play), in the relationship of the characters to the staging signs involved in their representation, in the ontological instability they express in the dialogue, and in the way one set of dramatic characters is played off against a set of mythical counterparts, resulting in a particularly self-referential theatrical work.

The structure of *La Mort du docteur Faust* represents a variation on the normal play-within-a-play. First, *La Tragédie de Faust,* as performed in the tavern, reflects the situation in the outer play: each of the characters in the outer play has a double in the inner play who has the same name, wears the same costume, and performs the same actantial function. Unlike *Hamlet,* however, or other plays where the inner play is designed to reflect somehow on the outer play, the source (or author) of the inner play seems to be absent here. Thus, the mirroring of the outer play appears to be an impossible coincidence, blurring the status of the inner play for both sets of spectators (those on stage and those in the audience). Furthermore, the characters in the outer play do not remain detached observers, but react to and interact with the play before them, leading to its collapse. When the character "Marguerite" says to Faust in the play, "Tous les hommes sont des salauds!" (causing the character to sigh "Je n'ai pas de chance!"), Faust's reaction is "Il exagère! Tous les hommes ne sont pas des salauds! Quelle mauvaise pièce!" (236). Soon, however, the pronoun slips from the third to the first person: when Faust in the play says "Je ne suis que trop ridicule, vieillard amoureux, aux yeux de cette enfant candide!" Faust in the tavern reacts, "Mais je ne suis pas vieux!" (237), both recognizing and rejecting himself as a character. Diamotoruscant—the "real" devil—also reacts violently to the play on the stage. As the Devil in the play starts to conclude his pact with Faust, asking for his soul, Diamotoruscant leaps up, saying "Assez! C'est grotesque! Qui vous a conseillé de débiter ces foutaises?" (238). In an exchange with the actor previous to the beginning of the play-within-a-play, Diamotoruscant had already demonstrated how the devil "re-

ally acts," and the actor had gone so far as to copy his outfit in order to "modernize" his character. If the presence of an onstage audience serves to draw the real-world audience into the world of the play, then a group of alienated spectators who protest and dynamite the play they are watching, as is the case here, distances the audience even further from a dramatic world that is so self-consciously theatrical.

A second degree of meta-theater is also present in the play, for one of Diamotoruscant's functions is to serve as an implied "author" for the entire spectacle, framing the outer play in yet another level of representation. At the beginning of Episode 1, Diamotoruscant is shown writing; he tells the waiter standing next to him, "Non, garçon, je n'écris pas un roman. Voici cent mille ans que, chaque jour, prêt à mourir d'ennui, je saisis la plume" (222). Although he tells one of the actors that he is very fond of actors, he consistently dismisses the other characters in the play as mere "comédiens," thereby setting himself at a level apart from them. It is he who orchestrates the action throughout, playing the role of author and director of the play the audience is watching.

A final sort of variation on the play-within-a-play structure brings two characters in the same role face to face on the same level of representation, collapsing the inner play and the outer play into one. This occurs in the first episode between Diamotoruscant and the "devil" and in much more complex fashion at the end of the play. Not only are these characters doubled by their counterparts in the inner play, but all (except Diamotoruscant) reveal at some point in the play at least a certain amount of confusion about whether they are, in fact, characters or actors.

A second way that the gap between actor and character is emphasized is the deliberately non-naturalistic staging indicated for the play. Although Faust is to wear his traditional costume, "On ne pourra un instant le croire réel. Et s'il paraît vivant, c'est qu'il joue mal. . . . Faust déclamera et exagèrera tous ses gestes. Sa voix sera forcée. Il doit apparaître au spectateur comme un clown auquel a été confié un rôle de tragédien" (216). Diamotoruscant is to be dressed in a red monk's habit, detachable cuffs and a bowler hat. Nonrealistic media of representation are indicated for all the characters, not just the principal ones. In the Quatre-Saisons tavern, the customers have "têtes peintes, comme des mannequins," and they wear "des costumes caricaturaux et agissent comme des excentriques anglais . . ." (222). Large masks are used in the mimes, and grotesque, puppet-like characters occupy the twentieth-century street in the final episode: the cinema barker strolls by with a question mark larger than he is affixed to his head, life-sized wooden soldiers march in place, the faces of the vengeful crowd are "expressives et bariolées" (271) and the twenty-three pieces of Marguerite's dismembered body are objects to be displayed, carried on stage on a stretcher (277). By drawing attention in such fashion to the staging itself, the play subverts any attempt to view the actor as transparent sign vehicle.

The verbal signs (the dialogue) also draw attention to themselves as signs by foregrounding the "meta-linguistic" Jakobsonian function that, according to Ubersfeld (43), is muted in normal dramatic discourse. By using terms like "acteur," "comédien," "drame," "tragédie," "décor," and so on, to refer to the characters, events, and objects in the world of the play, the dialogue constantly refers to itself as dramatic discourse. Likewise, it is in the dialogue of the play that the characters draw attention to their own ontological instability. The traditional dramatic character is presumed to be "unconscious": unlike human beings, he always coincides with his role. In this play, however, as in Pirandello's theater, characters appear who are acutely self-conscious and unstable. Faust is the primary example here; his sense of self is already crumbling in the Prologue:

> Donnez-moi d'autres mots, un autre costume! . . . je ne suis pas à ma place, ni dans mon costume, ni dans mon époque! . . . Pourquoi lancer des phrases contre les cloisons? Comme un acteur! . . . Je ne suis rien, et je ne puis devenir autre chose! . . . Et cette chambre qui me paraît de plus en plus étrangère! Y ai-je réellement vécu, ou vient-elle de se dresser pour mon hallucination, comme le décor peint d'un théâtre? . . . La réalité est que j'existe, mais il est singulier que par instants je me le dise! Est-ce que j'existe, après tout? Le fait de me le dire, de m'en persuader ne le prouve pas! . . . Assez! Faust! . . . Depuis des heures, tu récites un rôle.
>
> (215-18)

At one point, he considers assuming the role of "Faust" as a way out of his dilemma: "Il me faudrait une occupation! J'ai lu dans un vieux livre qu'un homme qui, comme moi, se nommait Faust et était docteur, s'avisa un jour d'appeler le diable" (219). He dismisses this possibility immediately, however, saying that *that* Faust must have been "un niais."

In contrast to Faust, Diamotoruscant sets himself up as a "pure" character and bemoans his inability to act. In Episode 2, the barker outside the cinema mistakes him for the actor playing the role of the devil at the Quatre-Saisons. He answers, with a play on words, "Ce n'est pas moi, mais un homonyme, ou un sosie! Cependant, je fais aussi le diable! . . . Pour mon compte!" (246). He goes on to lament his immutable status as mythical character: "Je ne puis ni faiblir, ni mourir, ni espérer! Tout m'est défendu! Il m'est interdit d'aimer et de haïr! Si, au moins, j'avais le don de m'illusionner, comme les imbéciles, ou les artistes!" (248). Diamotoruscant's

one attempt to "act" in a love scene with a prostitute fails miserably, as she responds, "Pas ça! Pas comme au cinéma! Non, non, il est fou, ton type!" (251).

Diamotoruscant exploits his status as the one "stable" character to manipulate the others, exposing and widening the gap between character and actor. This conflict reaches its climax in the final episode, in the confrontation between "Faust" (the actor) and "Faust" (the character). At the beginning of the episode, the actor is convinced that he is Faust only "tous les soirs et le dimanche en matinée" (268). Doubt is immediately cast on this assumption, because he *is* Faust for Crétinus (261) and, later, even his mistress is unable to distinguish between him and the doctor. When the doctor arrives, the two characters first execute an extended "mirror" pantomime and then argue heatedly about which is the "real" Faust: responding to the doctor's assertion that *he* is "the real one, the old one," the actor says "Ce n'est pas certain, je suis Faust, aux yeux d'une foule . . ." (271). Diamotoruscant, again playing the role of "author" or "director," transforms this conflict between characters into a conflict *within* each character between "actor" (being) and "character" (role):

DIAMOTORUSCANT:

> Ah! ah! Quelle belle pièce vous jouez, qui ne trouvera pas son auteur! Vous n'avez jamais existé, ni l'un ni l'autre!

FAUST:

> Quoi? j'existe, moi, je vois, je pense, j'agis, je suis le docteur Faust!

DIAMOTORUSCANT:

> Croyez-vous?

L'ACTEUR:

> C'est entendu, il est le docteur Faust, ne nous confondons pas! Diable! tire-moi d'embarras. Nous sommes des artistes, nous avons assez joué le drame ensemble, partons! . . . moi j'existe, je veux vivre, je veux m'évader de ce costume, de cette forme. Je ne veux pas être Faust. . . .

FAUST:

> Je ne veux pas l'être non plus! J'ai menti en disant que j'étais Faust! Je suis un artiste, un acteur!

L'ACTEUR:

> Quoi?—

FAUST:

> Je suis un comédien, fourvoyé. Mon rôle était de faire l'homme supérieur, le génie. Ces livres, ces appareils, ce sont des accessoires, je sais réciter. . . .
>
> (273-74)

When the actor rushes out to his death, he has become Faust, and the doctor, now neither actor nor character, ends his existential anguish by shooting himself. Even this "murder-suicide" fails to do away with the character "Faust," however; at the end of the play, it is Crétinus who steps into the role.

Finally, the use of the Faust myth adds yet another degree of self-consciousness to the characters and to the play(s) they are in. From the beginning and throughout, the characters refer explicitly to a Faust legend that corresponds to the well-known myth. Faust shows in the Prologue that he has read this poetry, and Diamotoruscant identifies him with it when he greets him in the tavern: "Ainsi, vous êtes Faust! Qui ne vous connaîtrait? On vous a mis en roman, en pièces, en opéras . . ." (232). The legend is taken up within the world of the play itself, in *La Tragédie de Faust*. Marguerite, the young servant, has deliberately set out to mimic her legendary counterpart, and all the characters play out their own travesty of the legend. Thus, the play, in one gesture, invites the audience to identify *it* with a referent that is located outside the world of this play—the Faust legend as it figures in the literary and cultural codes of the audience. Yet, this gesture is immediately undermined every time it is made, for the play is a burlesque: Faust is a buffoon who dismisses the legend as ridiculous and out of date; the Devil wears a bowler hat and scoffs at the idea of an immortal soul; the "tragedy" put on in the tavern is aborted and turned into a comic spectacle. This double movement of inviting and denying identification with an external referent (or intertext) is a final metatheatrical twist that dramatizes the Sartrean paradox (man is what he is not, is not what he is); like human beings, these self-conscious characters in this self-referential play can never coincide with themselves.

Notes

1. Keir Elam, *Semiotics of Theatre and Drama* (London: Methuen, 1980) 9.

2. Every element of performance, because the spectator perceives it as part of performance, becomes what Elam calls a sign vehicle. (Experiments by Manfred Wekwert, as reported in Wilfried Passow's "Analysis of Theatrical Performance," *Poetics Today* 2 [1981] 241, seem "to confirm Umberto Eco's ideas [that actors become signs]. The mere appearance of a person on the stage, in their opinion, leads the spectators to consider him as a sign.") Thus, any actor or object participating in the performance is necessarily other with respect to itself. As sign-vehicle (signifier), it is linked to a dual signified, both material (that which is seen and heard as part of the world of the performance) and fictional (that which is seen and heard—not imagined—as part of the world of the play). Fur-

thermore, as sign-vehicles, the elements of the performance are unstable: both their signified and their referents may change at any moment. (These are two features of theatrical semiosis that distinguish theater from literature.)

3. Like Elam, I shall use a notion of the sign that follows Saussure more than Peirce. As Elam points out,

> ". . . even in the most literal iconic sign-functions . . . the similarity puts into play not a simple one-to-one relationship between analogous objects but a relationship necessarily mediated by the signified class or concept."
>
> (25)

> "It must be emphasized . . . that theatrical performance as a whole is symbolic, since it is only through convention that the spectator takes stage events as standing for something other than themselves. . . . [A]ll icons and indices in the theatre necessarily have a conventional basis."
>
> (27)

4. In Louis Jouvet, *Témoignages sur le théâtre* (Paris: Flammarion, 1952) 157.

5. Anne Ubersfeld emphasizes this point in her study of referents: as she says, "le théâtre est à soi-même un référent." *Lire le théâtre* (Paris: Editions Sociales, 1977) 39. As Elam puts it, "Theatrical semiosis invariably, and above all, connotes itself" (12).

6. Speaking of Brechtian theater, Elam points out how the actor's body becomes "something other than itself":

> "Brechtian epic theatre made great play with the duality of the actor's role as stage sign-vehicle *par excellence,* bound in a symbolic relationship which renders him 'transparent,' at the same time that it stresses his physical and social presence. By driving a dramaturgical wedge between the two functions, Brecht endeavored to expose the very quotation marks that the actor assumes in representation, thus allowing him to become 'opaque' as a vehicle."
>
> (9)

These "quotation marks" apply of course to all the elements of the performance—not just the human actor—in self-conscious theater; as we shall see, Ghelderode surpasses even Brecht in this respect.

7. Michel de Ghelderode, *Théâtre* (Paris: Gallimard, 1957) 5: 213-85.

8. Elam uses "referent" as the equivalent of signified ("dramatic referent"). As both Jean Alter, "From Text to Performance," *Poetics Today* 2 (1981) 113-39, and Michael Issacharoff, "Space and Reference in Drama," *Poetics Today* 2 (1981) 211-24,

point out, however, the referent is never identical to the signified and it is located outside the sign; this is the sense in which I use the term "referent." Ubersfeld's distinction between the referents of the theatrical text and those of the performance (see esp. 37-38) is an important one, but it is not pertinent to the present study, which is not directed toward the question of transformation of text into performance as such.

9. Jean Decock touches on the self-referentiality of Ghelderode's work in *Le Théâtre de Michel de Ghelderode* (Paris: Nizet, 1969), calling it "anti-théâtre" and linking it to Artaud. Yet, it is precisely this quality that makes these plays so semiotically rich—so "theatrical."

10.

> "The . . . written text may . . . be read as theater, i.e., as a graphic notation of a performance. . . . Such a reading assumes that the play was written to be performed, and hence that it should be approached as a virtual performance. . . . The totality of signs of a play thus visioned will be called the *total text* . . ."
>
> (Alter 116)

It is this "total text" I propose to read, assuming that the stage direction signs will figure in the virtual performance.

11. Issacharoff uses "dramatic space" to mean "the study of space as a semiotic system in a given play" (214), as opposed to "theater space" (architectural design) and "stage space" (the stage and set design) (212). I will use the term "theatrical space" to mean the space of the theatrical performance (including aspects of all three spatial categories established by Issacharoff), as opposed to "dramatic space," which I use to refer to fictional space in the world of the play.

12. See Ubersfeld 155. In Ch. 4 ("Le Théâtre et l'espace"), Ubersfeld makes several points pertinent to the present study: the dynamics of theatrical space are binary; the stage is defined through opposition to an audience; and everything appearing in theatrical space becomes a sign. My analysis differs from hers, however, regarding the iconicity of the theatrical sign (see note 3).

13. Issacharoff's distinction between mimetic space (that which is shown, totally or partially, on the stage) and diegetic space (space described in the dialogue) (215) is a useful one in this regard: space in the world of the play, as evoked by dialogue, may extend well beyond theatrical space.

14. See Issacharoff 216:

> "When . . . discourse is focused on mimetic space, it acquires an *indexical* function. By indexical, I mean that form of reference that is in

fact peculiar to the theater, whereby discourse may refer to a scenographic code . . . or to a costume code. . . . Semiotically, this is an instance of *one code referring to another*; the verbal is centered on the visual, or rather on the visible; the theater thus becomes auto-reflexive."

Marc Quaghebeur (essay date 2002)

SOURCE: Quaghebeur, Marc. "The Sixteenth Century: A Decisive Myth." *Yale French Studies,* 102 (2002): 115-41.

[*In the following excerpt, Quaghebeur discusses the evolution of the "myth" of Charles V and sixteenth-century Netherlands in Belgian literature, including works by Ghelderode.*]

Historical approaches to the study of a literary corpus take into account, among other things, its handling of universal and local myths as well as individual depictions of actual persons. In this respect the evocation of the sixteenth century occupies a rather privileged position in Belgian letters. In particular, the role played by someone as important as emperor Charles V in the imaginary of the country's Francophone literary production is quite remarkable, sitting as it does on the border between, on the one hand, the kind of mythologization that obtains in the case of prominent individuals who are customarily viewed as having failed in some way—as with Charles V's grandfather, Charles the Bold,—and, on the other, the indexing that occurs independently of any imaginary fabulation when a person's name is routinely used as a referent to a glorious past—as with other "successful" personages like Philip the Good in the old Netherlands and Leopold II in modern-day Belgium.

The reason behind this is that the century of Charles V (1500-1558) gave birth to two very different moments. The first was the apogee of the old Netherlands to which he gave, thanks to the Transaction of Augsbourg (1548) and the Pragmatic Sanction (1549), the means of their autonomy, including constitutions we would now refer to as federal, and a unified system of dynastic succession. On the other hand, the century also witnessed, and did so very quickly, the breakup into northern and southern Netherlands of the Circle of Burgundy, which had fulfilled both their greatness and their century-old struggle against the ambitions of France.[1] This conflict then set against each other Philip II, legitimate son of the old emperor, who had been raised in Spain, and William of Orange, a prince whom Charles V had trained in his *pays de par deça* during the last twelve years of his reign and on whose shoulder he leaned as he walked down the ancient hall of the palace of Brussels at the time of his abdication.[2]

When came the nineteenth century, with its nationalistic subspecies of romanticism, it is from the well of their memory of the sixteenth century that Belgium's literary imagination, its collective imaginary, and a significant share of its national historical investigations drew one of the myths—if not the central myth—crucial to the making of its national identity. This occurred both before and after the revolutionary days of August and September 1830, which saw Belgium spoil the Treaty of Vienna's attempt to recreate between France and Germany a space roughly equivalent to that which had been occupied by the patrimonial Estates of the seventh Duke of Burgundy.[3]

THE MYTHIFICATION OF THE SIXTEENTH CENTURY

This emergent and dynamic myth was meant to promote liberty and affirm its popular roots. Yet, it had to do so while laboring under the constraints of a necessarily manichean logic. It did, on the one hand, sometimes celebrate the Netherlands (*Pays d'en bas*) of the turn of the sixteenth century as a kind of earthly paradise.[4] Such a characterization reflected the wealth of the Netherlands, the density of their population, and their remarkable economic, political, and artistic development. The myth also made it possible for the persona of the Belgian—known as the *gueux* (beggar)—to emerge.[5] The *gueux* is a fearless and intractable rebel with a noble and generous soul. He is deprived of the means of repression and cares about the freedom of his own people. Conversely, however, the myth of the sixteenth century also conjured up, quite logically, the image of the tyrant and his henchmen. The targets of this execration are, of course, Philip II of Spain—whose reign saw the rebellion and partition of the old Netherlands—and his illustrious second-in-command, Ferdinand Alvarez de Toledo, Duke of Alba.

The reader will immediately have gathered that the figure of Charles V intersects with—and serves as a counterpoint to—this complex set of images. Not only was he the last natural prince to have been born in what is now Belgium before the birth of the future Leopold II in 1835, it was also under his reign that the old Netherlands and their symbols, the towns of Antwerp and Brussels, would know their greatest splendor.[6] At the same time, he was also the father of Philip II and the defender of that Catholic faith in whose name his son would intend to punish.

The nineteenth-century glorification of independence and the rapid and extraordinarily successful industrialization of the new Belgian state made nineteenth-century elites want to project themselves back into an earlier era, also characterized by expansionism, growth, and wealth, and of which Charles V was seen as a symbol. Needless to say, this intensified the ambiguity of this mythical figure since these same elites also tended to interpret the political and religious conflicts of the sixteenth century in light of nineteenth-century struggles for or against democratic freedoms and freedom of thought. This complex set of circumstances led people to modulate some of the emperor's features. By contrast, the image of Philip II would always be confined—unequivocally and for all Belgians—to the stock narratives and clichés of his legend.

It is equally clear that Belgians came out of this mythical reconstitution of the past looking above all like the victims of an unjust and fanatical larger foreign country. This image would be recycled freely and abundantly during World War I, sometimes by means of a simple reworking of the texts and images that had grown out of the tragedies of the sixteenth century. One of Maeterlinck's earliest writings, "Le massacre des innocents" (1886), was thus reinserted in 1916 in *Les débris de la guerre* by the man who had won the Nobel Prize for literature in 1911. The first nineteen paragraphs of the narrative have disappeared. The new version begins with the arrival of a troop of armed men, "the Spaniards," who are surrounding their leader, "an elderly man with a white beard," which is a customary description of the Duke of Alba.[7]

Spain was the Other of nineteenth-century Belgium. It was the incarnation of disaster and oppression, and of the tyranny inflicted upon a people who were only asking to live and enjoy life to the fullest and cared not a whit for the historical stakes that had entrapped them. Such representations, from which fictional texts freely drew—often by exacerbating this dualism in the most extreme manner possible—can by and large also be found in the writings of nineteenth-century historians, both Catholic and Voltairian. This overwhelming convergence between the scholar's discourse and the writer's fable demonstrates what an intense hold these representations had on the Belgian collective imaginary, traces of which it retains to this day.

As a result, the image of Spain in Belgian letters necessarily came to be dominated by the so-called "black legend," an image that pervades nineteenth-century European perceptions of the Iberian peninsula. In its specifically Belgian version, however, it was also accompanied by the celebration of Belgium as the land of milk and honey (*pays de Cocagne*), by explorations of the differences between the time of Charles V and the reign of Philip II, and by the exponential growth of the iconic figure of the *gueux*.

. . . . .

REFLECTIONS OF MYTH AND COUNTRY

One writer did take matters further. Not only did he propose several versions of the sixteenth century in many of his works, he turned it into a fantasy, to the point where it became the imaginary space of reference of his entire oeuvre and glorified a country that was somehow more real than the one in which he was living on a daily basis.

Michel de Ghelderode (1898-1962) made his entrance on the literary scene with a work dedicated to De Coster, *L'histoire comique de Keizer Karel* (1922). This work drew on the popular traditions that had been revived and distributed for centuries in the form of chapbooks. These traditions had seized on the character of the emperor and turned his life into a mock medieval epic in which it was hard to distinguish between the archetypical situations that belonged of necessity to this kind of Rabelaisian narrative and the references to authentic episodes from the life of Charles V. Ghelderode's preface to the second edition of his book (1923) makes a point of reminding the reader that "*cet empereur de farce*" might well be "the incarnation of the people themselves" and that his legend, which has wended its way alongside Ulenspiegel's, "was the only literature to which the people had access."[8]

Ghelderode's portrait of Philip II in *Escurial* (1928) stands in sharp contrast to this, but is in keeping with the mythical tradition of "black Spain." The title of the play refers to the emblematic presence of the king, who is never actually named, but who is described in very familiar ways. In *L'école des bouffons* (1942), Ghelderode brings back the character of Folial, the jester, who serves as the king's double. This time, the king is mentioned by name. However, he only intervenes by means of a letter read by the jester. The games of doubles (*dédoublements*) dear to the playwright and the ties to the sixteenth century become ever more complex.

A year later, as World War II was reaching its obvious turning point, Ghelderode wrote a play, *Le soleil se couche,* that integrated the three sides of the myth ("black Spain," *pays de Cocagne, gueux.*). This play was also a will and testament and fulfilled the author's destiny as a writer. Not only did it put together ironically the purest elements of the myth of the land of Brueghel and "black Spain," it also took up and fused all the elements that mattered to Ghelderode as a playwright. Charles V, who has retired to Yuste, and his double, Messer Ignotus (who also stands in for Ghelderode) are the central focus of the play.

In Ghelderode's play everything, starting with their respective titles, sets the emperor and the king apart. The latter's double is Fray Ramon, who is the archetypical figure of the fanatical Spanish monk. He is matched with Fray Pascual, a bawdy monk who is fascinated by the emperor and his country of origin. Fray Pascual asks Charles V whether it is true that "in his southern Netherlands, tables are as beautifully and richly set" as the table in Yuste, and if such is not the case only with princely tables. The emperor answers: "Yes, this is a land of plenty and of happiness. Master Gonorius Becanus, a doctor from Antwerp, claims that it had once been, originally, the earthly paradise. One is willing to believe it. Will it remain as the genius of its inhabitants have made it, however?"[9] Dismissing comments by Fray Ramon that herald Philip II's policies, the emperor goes on: "Was I to decimate in one fell swoop the people of the richest State the West had ever known—and from which I drew more treasures than from the Americas? I transferred it intact to my son. Indeed! I enlarged the inheritance left to me by the Grand Duke. It would be miraculous if it did not fall apart in more pious but less flexible hands than mine" (18-19). The two images that have grown out of the historical myth with which Charles V is associated are here so closely linked that they now find themselves well and truly dialectically, even consubstantially, related to one another.

The play also brings this "double people" (27) to life in a puppet show. Play within the play, it holds up a small mirror to Ulenspiegel's century. The mythical hero meets Saint Michael, emblem of the House of Burgundy and patron of the city of Brussels (not to mention patron of the name chosen for himself by the author). Having come down from his pedestal atop the town hall tower, Saint Michael tells Ulenspiegel that he has "lost his devil."[10] To which the jolly fellow responds by asking whether he would not be satisfied with a Spaniard, who could easily be found in the Palace, now that "the good genius that dwelt there," i.e., the emperor, "has departed from it" (34).

Charles V's jester makes a sudden entrance. Distraught because of the departure of "the old-fashioned knight" (36), he admits that the people of the Netherlands did recognize themselves in him. Ulenspiegel then decides to play the devil's advocate and talks about the new Caesar. The emperor finds the symposium "lively" and "natural" (37) until Ulenspiegel suggests that "Charles ruined the *Patrie* before handing it over to the foreigners" (39). Imitating Folial, the emperor refuses to remain a spectator any longer. He asserts that he was "a good father to a bad son" and that he wanted to deliver his lands from their "local *patries*" and their "outdated laws" in order to offer them "a prestigious empire" and to open "the doors of the world and of the oceans" to them (39). At this point, the jester confesses that his subjects do regret him and that his "was a grandiose reign" (40). In one of Ghelderode's signature moves, however, the devil appears at this particular juncture and asks if he has been summoned by Michael. The emperor examines the cloth structure that surrounds him. His double is projected onto it: it is the puppet master. At this point an extraordinary dialogue begins between Charles, who tosses his sword away, and his masked double, Ignotus, who comes out of the theater crushed. Ignotus later dubs and frees the emperor, in order to answer the pleas Charles is issuing "to the chimeras that pass before his eyes" (48).

In another phantasmagorical scene, Philip II is praying and following a Maid who is being led by monks to her execution. She is wearing a torn dress in which one can detect "a weave of discolored heraldic lions," i.e., an allegorical representation of the Netherlands, the *Patrie,* and Life (49). At the end of this scene, in which the real itself is brought into question, Ignotus/Ghelderode is able to give Charles V the title he had renounced when he had given up his sword: "Imperador—Verily I proclaim you" (51). The emperor now lives on for eternity, a survival he owes to the writer who had granted it to him and to whom he in turn grants the power of his own mythical aura.

This literary survival took place as Ghelderode put his pen down, just as, long ago, the emperor had laid his scepter down. Their common country, then under the Nazi heel, was going through some very dark years that would change it profoundly once again. With Ghelderode's play, however, the myth demonstrated its strength and its ability to incorporate issues pertaining to the theater and to writing. And it managed to do so in a crepuscular atmosphere. One had not witnessed such a synthesis since De Coster's *Ulenspiegel,* which had been written when people had great hopes for the future.

Historians were also focusing on this tutelary and incantatory figure of the father at the same time as Ghelderode. They included Ghislaine De Boom, author of *Charles Quint, prince des Pays-Bas* (1943), and John Bartier, who wrote a remarkable biography of Charles the Bold, Charles V's much admired ancestor. This historiographical work was pursued by and large until 1958, year of the quadricentennial of the emperor's death and of the Brussels world's fair. By contrast, as far as literature proper was concerned, the neoclassical aesthetics and the denial of the existence of anything specifically Belgian in Francophone literature that took center stage between 1945 and 1960 tended to consign to oblivion the myths of the *gueux* and the *pays de Cocagne* and to put a stop to the taking of liberties with the French language. Such distinctive features were thought to underscore too uncomfortably Belgium's difference vis-à-vis France. Only the avant-gardes, excluded from the official literary scene, rediscovered the playful attitudes and guerrilla tactics that remind us, metaphorically at least, of the *gueux* of old. They eventually came together under the banner "savage Belgium."

Notes

1. [Note from the translator: The Circle of Burgundy included the ten southern and the seven northern provinces of the Netherlands.]

2. [Note from the translator: *pays de par deça* was a quasi-official way of referring to the old Netherlands]

3. [Note from the translator: namely Charles V, who was proclaimed Duke of Burgundy in 1515.]

4. [Note from the translator: *Pays d'en bas* is an old synonym of *Pays-Bas.* It refers to all of the old Netherlands, from Arras and Luxemburg to Friesland.]

5. *Gueux* is the name supposedly given by Comte de Berlaymont to the aristocrats who had come to give a petition dealing with the Inquisition—the so-called Compromise of the Nobles—to Margaret of Parma, eldest daughter of Charles V, and regent of the Netherlands. This label, which they then chose to claim for themselves, also designates the heroes of the combats that took place later, on sea and land, against the Spanish army and eventually resulted in the independence of the northern Netherlands.

6. [Note from the translator: Charles V was born in Ghent in 1500 and died in Yuste (Spain) in 1558.]

7. Maurice Maeterlinck, *Les débris de la guerre* (Paris: Charpentier, 1916), 131.

8. Michel de Ghelderode, *L'histoire comique de Keizer Karel* (Brussels: Les Éditions du Carrefour, 1943), 13.

9. Michel de Ghelderode, *Le soleil se couche,* in *Théâtre* (Paris: Gallimard, 1979), 5:15.

10. [Note from the translator: the statue of Saint Michael that sits atop the Brussels town hall shows him standing on top of the dragon he has slain.]

FURTHER READING

Bibliography

Draper, Samuel, and Lois Alworth. "Bibliography on Michel de Ghelderode." *Modern Drama* 8, no. 3 (December 1965): 332-34.

   Bibliography of both French and English-language criticism of Ghelderode's life and work.

Biographies

Draper, Samuel. "Michel de Ghelderode: A Personal Statement." *Tulane Drama Review* 8, no. 1 (fall 1963): 33-8.

Offers a personal reminiscence of Ghelderode, whom he describes as "an affectionate, exemplary friend" and "a lovable man."

Fox, Renée C. "'Les Roses, Mademoiselle': The Universe of Michel de Ghelderode." *American Scholar* 63, no. 3 (summer 1994): 403-19.

Memoir of the author's relationship with Ghelderode, which lasted from July 1961 until Ghelderode's death in April 1962.

Parsell, David B. *Michel de Ghelderode,* New York: Twayne Publishers, 1993, 109 p.

Book-length biography and critical study of Ghelderode's life and career as a playwright.

Criticism

Abel, Lionel. "Our Man in the Sixteenth Century: Michel de Ghelderode." *Tulane Drama Review* 8, no. 1 (fall 1963): 62-71.

Disagrees with Auréliu Weiss's assessment that Ghelderode failed to confront and embrace the twentieth century in his plays, asserting that the playwright's fascination with an earlier time in history is relevant and artistically sound.

Draper, Samuel, and Michel de Ghelderode. "An Interview with Michel de Ghelderode." *Tulane Drama Review* 8, no. 1 (fall 1963): 39-50.

Conversation in which Ghelderode discusses his fascination with death, his career as a playwright, and the writers that most influenced his work.

Hauger, George. "Notes on the Plays of Michel de Ghelderode." *Tulane Drama Review* 4, no. 1 (September 1959): 19-30.

Surveys Ghelderode's plays, focusing on their highly organized and "remarkable organic form," which he locates in their common themes and pronounced visual quality.

————. "Dispatches from the Prince of Ostrelande." *Tulane Drama Review* 8, no. 1 (fall 1963): 24-32.

Provides extracts from letters Ghelderode wrote to the critic during the years of their friendship.

————. Introduction to *Michel de Ghelderode: Seven Plays, Volume 2,* translated by George Hauger, pp. ix-xi. London: MacGibbon & Kee, 1966.

Describes Ghelderode's plays as romantic, stating that their uniqueness "is largely due to the intensity of their romantic characteristics."

Hellman, Helen. "Hallucination and Cruelty in Artaud and Ghelderode." *French Review* 41, no. 1 (October 1967): 1-10.

Draws parallels between Antonin Artaud's theories of the "theatre of cruelty" and "the hallucinatory tradition in art" and Ghelderode's plays.

Knapp, Bettina. "Michel de Ghelderode's *Escurial*: The Alchemist's *Nigredo*." *Stanford French Review* 2, no. 3 (winter 1978): 405-17.

Describes *Escurial* as "an alchemical drama" and traces the manner in which Ghelderode, through the figure of his aged king, thwarts the alchemist's typical desire to transcend his base materials and achieve "the celestial sphere."

Levitt, Paul M. "Ghelderode and Puppet Theatre." *French Review* 48, no. 6 (May 1975): 973-80.

Discusses Ghelderode's attraction to puppet theater, which the critic attributes to his "dissatisfaction with living actors and his inclination toward caricature" in his plays.

Wellwarth, George E. "Ghelderode's Theatre of the Grotesque." *Tulane Drama Review* 8, no. 1 (fall 1963): 11-23.

Compares the world of Ghelderode's theater to the grotesque and fantastic paintings of Hieronymus Bosch and Pieter Breughel, maintaining that his characters' physical deformities are a reflection of the "crippling power of sin" in his plays.

Weiss, Auréliu. "The Theatrical World of Michel de Ghelderode." *Tulane Drama Review* 8, no. 1 (fall 1963): 51-61.

Derides the "fetishism" and "fanaticism" in Ghelderode's plays, which he claims limited the playwright from achieving a serious, philosophical point of view in his work.

Additional coverage of Ghelderode's life and career is contained in the following sources published by Thomson Gale: *Contemporary Authors,* **Vols. 85-88;** *Contemporary Authors New Revision Series,* **Vols. 40, 77;** *Contemporary Literary Criticism,* **Vols. 6, 11;** *Dictionary of Literary Biography,* **Vol. 321;** *DISCovering Authors Modules: Dramatists*; *Drama Criticism,* **Vol. 15;** *Encyclopedia of World Literature in the 20th Century,* **Ed. 3;** *European Writers,* **Vol. 11;** *Literature Resource Center*; **and** *Twayne's World Authors.*

Dashiell Hammett
1894-1961

(Born Samuel Dashiell Hammett) American novelist, short story writer, and screenwriter.

The following entry provides an overview of Hammett's life and works. For additional information on his career, see *CLC*, Volumes 3, 5, 10, 19, and 47.

INTRODUCTION

Dashiell Hammett is widely considered one of the most significant innovators of the "hard-boiled" detective fiction genre in America. Although he was a prolific short story writer, Hammett is best known for his cynical and often violent detective novels, including *Red Harvest* (1929), *The Maltese Falcon* (1930), and *The Glass Key* (1931). Early critics, as well as such contemporary writers as Raymond Chandler and Erle Stanley Gardner, praised Hammett's skillful characterization and unique literary style. His novels and stories, which were inspired by his own experiences as an operative for the Pinkerton Detective Agency, typically feature a tough, realistic detective grappling with issues of morality in a violent world. Present-day commentators note Hammett's immense influence on later writers of the genre, and they continue to recognize Hammett's contributions to American literature, lauding his novels as the first of the detective genre to achieve the status of literary art.

BIOGRAPHICAL INFORMATION

Hammett was born May 27, 1894, in Saint Mary's County, Maryland. He attended public school in Baltimore, where he lived with his parents, Richard and Annie Bond Hammett. In 1908 he entered the Baltimore Polytechnic Institute, but he quit after only one semester and began working at a series of jobs at various companies, including the B & O Railroad and Poe and Davies Brokerage House, until he finally became an operative for the Pinkerton National Detective Agency in 1915. In 1918, during World War I, Hammett briefly served in the U.S. Army until his health deteriorated as a result of Spanish influenza he contracted during the war; he received an honorable discharge in 1919. He returned home and resumed his employment with Pinkerton's. In May 1920 Hammett moved to Spokane, Washington, where he continued to work as an operative. He was hospitalized a few months later and diagnosed with tuberculosis. During his illness he met Josephine Dolan, a nurse at Cushman Hospital, whom he married on July 7, 1921. The couple moved to San Francisco, and Hammett returned to Pinkerton's. He participated in several well-publicized criminal investigations before he finally quit the agency and began a training course at Munson's Business College, where he studied journalism.

In 1922 Hammett began his literary career when he published his first short story, "The Parthian Shot," in the magazine *Smart Set*. Over the next few years he continued to publish stories, the most successful of which were inspired by his experiences as a detective in the Pinkerton agency. In October, 1923, Hammett published the story "Arson Plus" in *Black Mask*, a pulp magazine devoted to crime and adventure stories. The story was the first of twenty-six Hammet published in *Black Mask* that featured an operative for the Continental Detective Agency, known only as the "Continental Op." In 1926 Hammett worked briefly as an advertising manager for Samuels Jewelry Company in San Francisco, but he resigned a few months later due to his worsening health. After an eleven-month hiatus from publishing, Hammett submitted his story "The Big Knock-Over" to *Black Mask*, where it appeared in February, 1927. The magazine also published the initial sections of his first novel, *Red Harvest*, in November of that same year. Over the next seven years, Hammett published four more novels, including *The Dain Curse* (1929), *The Maltese Falcon*, *The Glass Key*, and *The Thin Man* (1934).

During the early 1930s Hammett worked on several original screenplays, most notably *City Streets* (1931) and *After the Thin Man* (1936), and lived in Hollywood, where he met and began a romantic relationship with playwright Lillian Hellman. Through much of their relationship, Hammett acted as a mentor to Hellman and greatly influenced her writing. He was also involved with several leftist political organizations and became a member of the Communist Party in the late 1930s. Though he was a vocal opponent of the war in Europe, Hammett enlisted in the U.S. Army in 1942. He was honorably discharged in 1945. He had trouble reentering civilian life and struggled with alcoholism after his release. In 1951 he was called to testify before the New York State Supreme Court in a trial that featured several Communist Party members. When he refused to testify, Hammett was sentenced to six months in prison, which he served from July to December, 1951.

After his imprisonment Hammett's popularity waned and he suffered financial difficulties, exacerbated by a federal judgment against him for tax evasion. Although he began work on an autobiographical novel, *Tulip,* which was later collected with other writings and published in *The Big Knockover* in 1966, he abandoned the project in 1953. Toward the end of his life, Hammett lived with Hellman in New York City. He died of lung cancer on January 10, 1961, and received a soldier's burial at Arlington National Cemetary.

MAJOR WORKS

Hammett's first novel, *Red Harvest,* is a violent and intricately plotted book that features a nameless detective, referred to only as the Continental Op. The Op is hired to clean up the crime-ridden city of Personville, which is called "Poisonville" by its residents. Universal corruption is an important element in the novel, and a theme to which Hammett would return in later books. When the Op arrives in town, he discovers that the business and political leaders are as corrupt as the criminals. The Op's actions are also morally and ethically questionable. He manipulates various citizens, instigates violence, and by the end of the book questions his own innocence regarding a murder. Critics praised *Red Harvest* for its stark realism and spare description and characterization, comparing it to the writings of Ernest Hemingway. The book was considered one of the first of its genre to accurately portray, rather than romanticize, the violence of its time. The novel was also noted for the hard-boiled vernacular of its dialogue. While *Red Harvest* is not explicitly political, it nonetheless offers a critique of capitalist society. Indeed, some critics, including Christopher Metress, have noted the influence of Marxist ideas in the story and have emphasized the novel's treatment of individualism. Metress has asserted that in *Red Harvest* Hammett "investigates the antagonistic relationship between residual nineteenth-century traditions of self-centered individualism and emerging twentieth-century calls for social collectivism."

Hammett's best-known novel, *The Maltese Falcon,* is the first of his longer works of fiction to assign a name to its protagonist. Sam Spade is a cynical detective who is investigating the murder of his partner. As the novel progresses, Spade becomes involved with several criminals—including the beautiful and dangerous Brigid O'Shaughnessy—each of whom are searching for a seemingly valuable artifact known as the Maltese Falcon. Hammett's characterization of Spade is considered particularly innovative. Not only does Spade act inde-

pendently of the police, he acts according to his own ideas of justice and morality, as well. At times in the novel, Spade is indistinguishable from the criminals he pursues. When he becomes sexually involved with O'Shaughnessy, he uses the opportunity to gather evidence against her, and he turns her over to the police at the end of the novel. The corruption of the law and the blurred line between good and evil are the thematic forces that drive the narrative forward. *The Maltese Falcon* has also been praised for its objective point of view, which helps to obscure Spade's true motives and creates a sense of ambiguity regarding his moral character. Through the bitter, callous characterization of Spade, as well as the terse, hard-boiled dialogue, Hammett expressed a realism that was new to the detective genre. For this reason, many critics consider *The Maltese Falcon* the first book to elevate the crime novel genre to the level of literary art.

Hammett favored his fourth novel, *The Glass Key,* over all his other works, and many critics agree that it is his finest piece of literary craftsmanship. The connection between power and corruption is the central theme of the book. Like *Red Harvest,* the novel portrays a corrupt society replete with moral ambiguities. The protagonist, Ned Beaumont, is not a detective but a criminal who, like Sam Spade, operates according to his own moral code. The plot centers on the murder of a senator's son. By the end of the novel, it is revealed that the senator murdered his son to protect his political career. The novel also explores issues of loyalty and friendship, particularly in the relationship between Beaumont and his friend Madvig, a political crime boss. While *The Glass Key* revisits familiar themes and employs stylistic techniques evident in Hammett's earlier work, including hard-boiled dialogue, objective point of view, and stark realism, many consider it Hammett's most cynical vision of a corrupt and violent society.

CRITICAL RECEPTION

In his lifetime Hammett enjoyed popularity and critical success, particularly for his realistic portrayal of morally ambiguous characters and his skillful use of hard-boiled jargon in his dialogue and narrative description. Raymond Chandler, a contemporary of Hammett, was among the first to acknowledge his role as an innovator of the hard-boiled genre. In his 1944 essay, "The Simple Act of Murder," Chandler asserted that "Hammett took murder out of the Venetian vase and dropped it into the alley." Chandler added that Hammett "gave murder back to the kind of people that commit it for reasons, not just to provide a corpse." Since the publication of Chandler's essay, Hammett's reputation as the father of the hard-boiled detective novel has been firmly established. In recent scholarship, critics have continued to examine Hammett's stylistic choices, as well as the complex moral and ethical questions raised by his stories and confronted by his characters. While some scholars consider Hammett mainly a master of the detective novel subgenre, others claim that his work deserves a permanent place in the broader mainstream of American literature, alongside such literary masters as Ernest Hemingway and William Faulkner.

PRINCIPAL WORKS

Red Harvest (novel) 1929

The Dain Curse (novel) 1929

The Maltese Falcon (novel) 1930

City Streets (screenplay) 1931

The Glass Key (novel) 1931

The Thin Man (novel) 1934

Mister Dynamite (screenplay) 1935

After the Thin Man (screenplay) 1936

Another Thin Man (screenplay) 1939

$106,000 Blood Money (short stories) 1943

Watch on the Rhine (screenplay) 1943

The Adventures of Sam Spade (short stories) 1944; republished as *They Can Only Hang You Once,* 1949

The Continental Op (short stories) 1945

The Return of the Continental Op (short stories) 1945

Hammett Homicides (short stories) 1946

Dead Yellow Women (short stories) 1947

Nightmare Town (short stories) 1948

The Creeping Siamese (short stories) 1950

Woman in the Dark (short stories) 1951

A Man Named Thin (short stories) 1962

*The Big Knockover (short stories) 1966; also published as *The Dashiell Hammett Story Omnibus,* 1966

Complete Novels (novels) 1999

Nightmare Town Stories, [edited by Kirby McCauley, Martin H. Greenberg, and Ed Gorman] (short stories) 1999

*This work contains the unfinished novel *Tulip.*

CRITICISM

Walter Blair (essay date 1967)

SOURCE: Blair, Walter. "Dashiell Hammett: Themes and Techniques." In *Essays on American Literature: In Honor of Jay B. Hubbell,* edited by Clarence Gohdes, pp. 295-306. Durham, N.C.: Duke University Press, 1967.

[*In the following essay, Blair discusses possible influences on Hammett's literary career, as well as the author's use of point of view and character description in his novels.*]

I

The influence of subliterary works (sentimental fiction and poetry, popular humor, melodrama, and the like) on literary works, or the ways literary works shape subliterature often are fascinating. Without Gothic fiction Poe and Hawthorne would have been impossible; without Scott and Dickens nineteenth-century American humor, with all its vulgarity, could not have been written. An instance is the career of Dashiell Hammett (1894-1961), writer of detective fiction. Two uncertainties furnish difficulties but add interest to a consideration of him: (1) the possibility that Hammett's writings, despite their genre, are good enough to classify not as subliterature but as literature, and (2) the impossibility of one's being sure about the precise direction of the influence—about who influenced whom. Regardless, affiliations between the detective story fictionist and some of his more reputable contemporaries, particularly Ernest Hemingway, have great interest, and in his best novel, Hammett brilliantly, and I think uniquely, adapted current techniques to his genre.

Hammett's lasting popularity and repute suggest that his work may be of more than ephemeral value. Having crowded practically all his writing into a decade, he published practically nothing after January, 1934. But between that date and his death twenty-seven years later, his novels and collected short stories sold four million copies in paperback editions; three of his novels (**Red Harvest,** 1929; **The Dain Curse,** 1929; and **The Maltese Falcon,** 1930) were collected in an **Omnibus** in 1935; and **The Complete Novels** (the three above plus **The Glass Key,** 1931, and **The Thin Man,** 1934) appeared in 1942. A few months after Hammett's death, a million copies in paperback of his various works were issued; in October, 1965, **The Novels of Dashiell Hammett** was reset and printed from new plates; in June, 1966, his **The Big Knockover: Selected Stories and Short Novels** appeared;[1] and, the following month, three of his novels (**Glass Key, Falcon, Thin Man**) were reissued in paperback editions.[2]

The nature of the critical acclaim that accompanied such successes raises the strong possibility that something more than sensational appeals was responsible. Granted, a share of these sales may well have been stimulated by portrayals of Hammett's characters in popular movies, in radio and television series, even in comic strips. But surely a good share was stimulated by Hammett's remarkable—perhaps unique—reputation.

Indicative of the nature of this is the fact that **The Maltese Falcon** went through at least fifteen printings as part of a prestigious collection, the Modern Library. Indicative, too, is the esteem in which the author was held by enthusiastic readers who belonged to a rather unusual group. Detective stories for about five decades (since World War I) were read, liked, and discussed by many professional men, political leaders, pundits, and professors. As a result, a genre of subliterature was assessed and in some instances praised by highly influential—as well as perceptive and articulate—readers. The admiration of these readers for Hammett's writings has been consistently strong and widespread. In addition, leading reviewers of mystery novels and informed historians of the genre such as Howard Haycraft and Ellery Queen, and famous practitioners such as Raymond Chandler and Erle Stanley Gardner habitually and casually—as if there were no possible question about the matter—referred to him as the greatest writer in his field, perhaps even "a genius."[3] Finally, respected literary men not as a rule much interested in mystery fiction manifested warm admiration for Hammett—Somerset Maugham, Peter Quennell, and Robert Graves of England; André Malraux and André Gide of France; and a trio of American Nobel prize winners—Sinclair Lewis, William Faulkner, and Ernest Hemingway. Quennell in 1934 correctly remarked that Hammett was almost alone among mystery writers "in being praised by writers as a serious writer and by good novelists as a master of their business."

II

Available details about Hammett's life before he began to write indicate that it provided unusual and exploitable experiences but scant training for a writing career. Born in 1894 in St. Mary's County on the eastern shore of Maryland, he attended a technical school, Baltimore Polytechnic Institute, and was a dropout from its non-literary program at thirteen. During the next several years he had a number of quite unliterary jobs—messenger, newsboy, freight clerk, timekeeper, stevedore, yardman, and machine operator. After that for eight years he was an operative for the Pinkerton Detective Agency, his chief literary exercises presumably being the writing of reports on his cases.[4] He then served during World War I as a sergeant in the ambulance corps. After emerging from the war with damaged lungs and after a period of hospitalization and a brief return to detective work, he began to make use of remembrances of his sleuthing in articles and stories.

His writings were first published early in the 1920's, some in *Pearson's Magazine,* some, unpredictably, in H. L. Mencken's *Smart Set,* most of them in a pulp mystery magazine, *Black Mask.* At first the writings attracted little attention, in part it may be because one Carroll John Daly had briefly preceded Hammett in writing what would in time be dubbed hard-boiled detective stories,[5] in part because the importance of originating this genre was not recognized or at least discussed at the time, in part because before long other writers (Gardner, for instance) began to publish similar stories. Then an editor, Joseph T. Shaw, decided that

since Hammett was "the leader in the thought that finally brought the magazine its distinctive form," he should be featured and the featuring, coupled with Hammett's outstanding talent, gave his stories pre-eminence. And when between 1929 and 1934, Hammett's five novels were published by Alfred A. Knopf and individually and collectively were enthusiastically praised far and wide, justifiably or no, he came to be known as the founder of the school.

The short stories as well as the more famous novels in time were appreciated for their innovations. For, drawing upon memories of his Pinkerton career, Hammett pictured crime and the work of a private operative (so everybody said) in a much more "real" fashion than they had been pictured before; and since the first-person narrator in many stories was a detective and since in all the stories the dialogue was largely that of dicks and criminals he used an economical vernacular style which seemed unusually lifelike.

Especially when compared with that of earlier mystery stories, Hammett's subject matter was revolutionary. From the time of their most venerable ancestor, Poe's C. Auguste Dupin, leading fictional detectives had been gentlemen and they had been erudite. In 1927, in a review of a book about one of the most exquisite and purportedly learned of such sleuths, Hammett himself scoffs at the type and at the ignorance of its portrayers about crime:

> This Philo Vance is in the Sherlock Holmes tradition. . . . He is a bore when he discusses art and philosophy, but when he switches to criminal psychology he is delightful. There is a theory that anyone who talks enough on any subject must, if only by chance, finally say something not altogether incorrect. Vance disproves this theory: he manages always, and usually ridiculously, to be wrong. His exposition of the technique employed by a gentleman shooting another gentleman who sits six feet in front of him deserves a place in a *How to be a detective by mail* course.[6]
>
> ("**Review of** *The Benson Murder Case*")

Raymond Chandler praised Hammett for doing away with the unrealities here attacked:

> Hammett gave murder back to the kind of people that commit it for reasons, not just to provide a corpse; and with the means at hand, not with hand-wrought duelling pistols, curare, and tropical fish. He put them down on paper as they are, and made them talk and think in the language they customarily used for these purposes.

The linking of matter that is "real" ("put them down on paper *as they are*") with a style that is "real" occurs in much of the praise of the detective story writer. Chandler further remarks that at its best the style "is the American language."

Anyone familiar with discussions of developments in presumably more serious American fiction during the 1920's will recognize oft-repeated concerns—with the increased "reality" of the matter and with the "Americanization" of the style. Edmund Wilson saw both in Ernest Hemingway's earliest fiction and mentioned them in a *Dial* review of it in October, 1924. "Too proud an artist to simplify in the interest of conventional pretenses," went one sentence, "he [Hemingway] is showing you what life is like." Elsewhere:

> . . . Miss Stein, Mr. Anderson, and Mr. Hemingway may now be said to form a school by themselves. The characteristic of this school is a naïveté of language, often passing into the colloquialism of the character dealt with. . . . It is a distinctively American development in prose—as opposed to more or less successful American achievements in the traditional style of English prose. . . .

After **Red Harvest** appeared in 1929, critics of Hammett frequently compared him to Hemingway. "It is doubtful," wrote Herbert Asbury in a review of that first novel, "if even Hemingway has ever written more effective dialogue. . . . The author displays a style of amazing clarity and compactness, devoid of literary frills and furbelows, and his characters speak the crisp, hard-boiled language of the underworld . . . truly, without a single false or jarring note." Gide asserted that the author's dialogues "can be compared [among American writers] only with the best in Hemingway." Peter Quennell held that the last of the novels, **The Thin Man** of 1934, provides interior evidence that Hammett admired Hemingway, since it "contains portraits, snatches of dialogue written in a terse colloquial vein—and lurid glimpses of New York drinking society, that Hemingway himself could not have improved upon."

Quennell was not alone in believing that Hemingway influenced Hammett, but a few critics wondered whether Hammett might not have influenced Hemingway. Gide said that some of Hammett's dialogues could "give pointers to Hemingway or even Faulkner." However, since both authors began to write and to publish obscurely almost simultaneously, the likelihood appears to be that neither shaped the earlier writings of the other. And by the time each had mastered his craft, the possibility of either shaping the work of the other was very small. Resemblances arose more probably because of similarities in temperament, in experiences, and in background.[7]

Not only were the two alike in picturing a world that met the post-World War I demand for "more reality" and in using a style that was "more laconic" and "more colloquial"; they were alike in other important ways. Wounded by the war and unhappy in the postwar world, both were battered by disillusionment and cynicism, and both created worlds and characters justifying their attitude. Their protagonists are forced to cope with such worlds and their inhabitants. "Hemingway's favorite characters," André Maurois has noticed, "are men who deal with death and accept its risk": the same remark of course could be made about Hammett's favorite characters. Moreover, as Joseph Haas recently remarked, "Their similarities don't end there, either. Their heroes were much alike, and we find it easy to put Sam Spade in Jake Barnes' place, or to imagine that Robert Jordan and the Continental Op[erator] could have become good friends. They all lived by that simple, sentimental code of loyalty, courage and cynicism in a world of betrayal." Many discussions of Hemingway's morality indicate that his code was a rather more complex one than Haas suggests; and so, I venture to say, was Hammett's. Interestingly, both men were accused from time to time of having no standards—probably because they both were contemptuous of many pre-World War I standards and because they both admiringly portrayed heroes who were. Oscar Handlin has said of Hammett's heroes: "Their virtues were distinctly personal—courage, dignity, and patience; and to them the hero clung for their own sake, not because the client for whom he fought had any worth. Honor to Sam Spade was conformity to a code of rules which he himself invented, a means of demonstrating his own worth against the world." The same, or something very like it, could be said of the codes of Hemingway's heroes.

Both men's lives were shaped by similar personal codes. That Hemingway's life was has been clearly demonstrated. Hammett's code compelled him at the age of forty-eight to enlist in the United States army for service in World War II and to carry out a dull assignment in the Aleutians not only with meticulous care but with gusto. Lillian Hellmann tells of another instance in 1951:

> He had made up honor early in his life and stuck with his rules, fierce in his protection of them. In 1951 he went to jail because he and two other trustees of the bail bond fund of the Civil Rights Congress refused to reveal the names of the contributors to the fund. The truth was that Hammett had never been in the office of the Committee and did not know the name of a single contributor. The night before he was to appear in court, I said, "Why don't you say that you don't know the names?" "No," he said, "I can't say that. . . . I guess it has something to do with keeping my word . . . but . . . if it were my life, I would give it for what I think democracy is and I don't let cops or judges tell me what I think democracy is."

He served a term of six months in a federal prison.

The codes of both Hemingway and Hammett related not only to their lives but also to their writing. "The great thing," remarked the former in 1932, "is to last and get your work done and see and learn and understand; and write when there is something that you know." In a late uncompleted story, **Tulip,**[8] a character obviously voicing Hammett's opinions states a similar belief that an author must write only about matters that have real significance for him. The speaker, a professional fictionist, has never written a word about some of his experiences: "Why? All I can say is that they're not for me. Maybe not yet, maybe not ever. I used to try now and then . . . but they never came out meaning very much to me."

Both authors believed strongly that harsh self-discipline was an essential to good writing. Hemingway did not go to Stockholm to receive the Nobel prize in 1954 because he refused to interrupt his writing of a novel that was going well. His manuscripts attest to the fact that, word by word, he wrote with infinite care. Lillian Hellmann testifies that, when writing a novel (*The Thin Man*), Hammett similarly let the task of composition possess him: "Life changed: the drinking stopped, the parties were over. The locking-in time had come and nothing was allowed to disturb it until the book was finished. I had never seen anybody work that way: the care for every word, the pride in the neatness of the typed page itself, the refusal for ten days or two weeks to go out even for a walk for fear something would be lost."

III

During the last few decades probably no other aspect of the technique of fiction has loomed as large in the concerns of critics and the conscious creative procedures of authors as the fictional point of view. Fictionists as different—and as influential—as Mark Twain and a bit later Henry James independently noticed the tremendous significance the choice of this had in shaping their fiction. James, and after James many leading critics, have discussed exhaustively the authors' or the narrators' insights into characters' thoughts and feelings, and the authors' or the narrators' biases and attitudes, as the narratives reveal them. Often the discussions have been very illuminating.

In about twenty-five short stories and in the first two of Hammett's novels, *Red Harvest* and *The Dain Curse,* the first-person narrator and the solver of the puzzle is an operative employed by the Continental Detective Agency. Unlike the exquisites of chiefly ratiocinative mystery stories this man (whose name is never revealed) is short, plump, and middle-aged, thus in his very ordinary appearance contrasting with a Dupin or a Sherlock Holmes. In an early story, **"The Gutting of Couffignal,"** he explains that for him his enthusiasm about his job is a strong motive:

". . . I like being a detective, like the work. And liking work makes you want to do it as well as you can. Otherwise there'd be no sense to it. . . . I don't know anything else, don't enjoy anything else, don't want to know or enjoy anything else. You can't weigh that against any sum of money. Money is good stuff. I haven't anything against it. But in the past eighteen

years I've been getting my fun out of chasing crooks and solving riddles. . . . I can't imagine a pleasanter future than twenty-some years more of it."

As Leonard Marsh has noticed, the Op's methods were accordingly different:

The conventional tale focused on the investigator's mental prowess; the later variety stressed the detective's physical engagement with the criminal . . . in [Hammett's] stories he saw crime not as a completed history to be attacked with the mind, but as a dynamic activity to be conducted with force as well as cunning . . . the Op adapts venerable investigative concepts to modern police methods. He painstakingly collects facts. He goes to the street, not to the study or the laboratory, fortified by familiarity with criminal behavior, by his wit, courage, endurance, luck. . . . He obtains information by surveillance and by questioning anyone remotely associated with crime. Finally, he often seeks help from other private operatives, from hotel and police detectives, from hired informants, from taxi drivers and railroad employees.

These techniques would be worthless, however, without the Op's ability to deduce the relevance of information and to exploit errors or weaknesses while in direct contact with his adversaries. . . .

Since action plays so large a part in the process, and since the detective's ratiocination is detailed at intervals and briefly, the narrator can (like a Twain, a Conrad, or a Hemingway) tell much of his story very concretely. Erle Stanley Gardner notices that the Continental Op stories in *Black Mask* "were told in terms of action . . . told objectively, and there was about them that peculiar attitude of aloofness and detachment which is so characteristic of the Hammett style." The same might be said of the novels in which the Continental Op appeared. And the operative's frequent concentration on the action and withholding of statements about his own reactions added mystery and suspense. Gide noticed this in **Red Harvest,** which he called "a remarkable achievement, the last word in atrocity, cynicism, and horror": "Dashiell Hammett's dialogues, in which every character is trying to deceive all the others and in which the truth slowly becomes visible through the haze of deception, can be compared only with the best in Hemingway."[9]

Even the first-person narrator's feelings and thoughts are often withheld. An outstanding instance is in Chapter XXVI of **Red Harvest,** wherein, after a drugged sleep on Dinah Brand's living room Chesterfield, the Op awakens to find himself in the dining room, his right hand holding an icepick, the sharp blade of which is buried in Dinah's left breast. "She was lying on her back, dead," he goes on. Then he tells of his actions— his examining the body, the room, the adjacent rooms, and of his departing—all without a word detailing his emotional reactions or his thoughts about the woman's death.

The Continental Op disappears after *The Dain Curse,* and the next two novels, *The Maltese Falcon* and *The Glass Key,* are told in the third person. I shall return to the *Falcon,* but here want to notice that in both books the author abjures insight into any of the characters' thoughts or feelings. What Walter R. Brooks says about *The Glass Key* is true of both: "Mr. Hammett does not show you [the characters'] thoughts, only their actions. . . ." Because not one but practically all the characters are either tight-lipped stoics or superb liars, the reader's attempts to discover what makes characters tick, what they are trying to do and how, are baffled, and the mystery is greatly augmented.

In *The Thin Man,* Hammett returns to the first-person narrator, here a former detective, Nick Charles, who is persuaded to make use of his detecting skills again. Nick is very different from the Continental Op: he is attractive, sophisticated and witty. He resembles the earlier narrator in being cynical and worldly and in being unrevealing about his emotional and intellectual responses to most people and events. In the final novel as in the first, the author therefore utilizes a fictional point of view that is well adapted to the genre which he is writing—one productive of mystery and suspense.

IV

The Maltese Falcon is generally conceded to be Hammett's best detective novel, and at least some reasons for its pre-eminence may be discovered. The fable ranges over a wide area including Russia (vaguely), Constantinople, Hongkong, Marmora (wherever that is), and San Francisco. The order in which its details are revealed is admirably managed for the puzzlement of the reader. In many of the conversations, the author shows his flair for reproducing colloquial speech. As I have said, suspense is increased because so many characters are untruthful and enigmatic.

Most important, Hammett employs a procedure which is particularly deceptive when combined with an objective dramatic narrative method. I have in mind the association of deceptive images and descriptive details with the characters. Writers of mystery novels long have employed this in representing some of their characters, e.g., in the classic representation of a humble butler who turns out to be a ruthless killer. But Hammett, in his picturing of all his leading enigmatic and deceitful characters, gives them outward aspects incongruous with their actual natures.

Joel Cairo, for instance, perfumes himself with chypre, wears many jewels, dresses carefully in fawn spats, a black derby, and yellow chamois gloves. He sucks violet pastilles. He walks with "short, mincing, bobbing steps." His hands are "soft and well cared for." He is meticulously polite. On the occasion of his first appearance, coughing apologetically and smiling nervously, this gorgeous creature pulls a pistol on the tough detective Sam Spade. And throughout the rest of the book he constantly reveals a toughness that his sissified appearance belies.

Another character whose name is "Wilmer" is constantly described as "the youth in the cap," "the kid," "the schoolboy," and "the boy." At close hand he is seen to have small features, white beardless cheeks, hazel eyes with curling lashes. This baby-faced youngster, it develops, is a sadistic gunman.

Again, there is Casper Gutman (translate "Goodman"), whose appearance—if recognized signs of character generally believed in by readers are to be trusted[10]—has the looks of a jolly, harmless, lovable fellow. For he is "a fat man . . . flabbily fat with bulbous pink cheeks and lips and chin and neck, with a great soft egg of a belly . . . and pendant cones for arms and legs." He "beams" at his visitor; he laughs heartily, his belly shaking like that of a Santa Claus, smiles benevolently, chuckles. His talk has an old-fashioned vocabulary and rhythm: "We begin well, sir. . . . Well, sir, here's to plain speaking and plain understanding. . . . You're the man for me, sir, a man cut along my own lines. . . . Well, sir, if I told you—by Gad, if I told you half!—you'd call me a liar." This jolly fat man, with his antique way of talking, is the master-mind behind the attempt to secure the falcon—a cruel, unrelenting searcher.

Then there is Brigid O'Shaughnessy, if not the heroine the chief feminine character of the narrative, who enters detective Spade's office as the book starts. Everything she does indicates that here is a shy unworldly young thing. She speaks softly through trembling lips, puts a hand to her mouth when startled, walks with "tentative steps," sits nervously on the edge of her chair, and at frequent intervals achieves the old-fashioned and all but forgotten feat of blushing. At one point, after she has "flushed slightly . . . a becoming shyness [not having] left her eyes," Spade accuses her of not being exactly the sort of person she pretends to be: "Schoolgirl manner . . . stammering and blushing and all that." Blushingly, she grants that the charge has justification. And indeed it does, for in the collection of scoundrels pictured here, the stammering, blushing Brigid is probably the most treacherous and vicious, having deceived, stolen, and murdered her way around a good part of the world.

The first paragraph in the book describes the detective with the ominous name of Spade:

> Samuel Spade's jaw was long and bony, his chin a jutting v under the more flexible v of his mouth. His nostrils curved back to make another, smaller, v. His

yellow-grey eyes were horizontal. The v *motif* was picked up again by thickish brows rising outward from twin creases above a hooked nose, and his pale brown hair grew down—from high flat temples—in a point on his forehead. He looked rather pleasantly like a blond satan.

The satanic aspects of the detective, thus introduced, recur at many intervals in the book, the feature most recurrently stressed being the yellow-grey eyes which in time, like those of Chillingworth in *The Scarlet Letter,* can hardly be mentioned without the additional statement that they are burning or blazing. Through his reading of much of the book the reader is kept in the dark as to what makes Spade tick. But as the story concludes, Spade's actions make clear that he is the only character who has integrity, who obeys a code. The outcome of Spade's investigation is the discovery not only of Brigid's distant past but also of her more recent past during which she killed Spade's partner. Despite the fact that he has fallen in love with Brigid, he determines to turn her over to the police. He tells why:

> "When a man's partner is killed he's supposed to do something about it. It doesn't make any difference what you thought of him. . . . Then it happens we were in the detective business. Well, when one of your organization gets killed it's bad business to let the killer get away with it. . . . Third, I'm a detective and expecting me to run criminals down and let them go free is like asking a dog to catch a rabbit and let it go. . . . Fourth, no matter what I wanted to do now it would be absolutely impossible for me to let you go without having myself dragged to the gallows. . . ."

His concluding reason is that he refuses to let himself be "played for a sucker," and Brigid from the start has depended upon her personal relationship to bring her release.[11] The code undoubtedly is an unusual and highly individual one—a mixture of what is admirable and what is not—which here clearly undergoes a stern test. And the technical procedures followed by the author, particularly the handling of the point of view and the attribution of deceptive physical qualities of the characters, testify that a technician of unusual skill has used this skill in telling his story.

Notes

1. Previously nine books of his short stories had been collected in paperback editions by Ellery Queen.

2. Raymond Chandler, another adept and highly praised (and a more prolific) author of detective novels, died in 1959. Since that year, he has been commemorated in a scholarly biography and a collection of his letters and articles. In 1966 nine of his books in paperback, two novels in hardcover printings, and an *Omnibus* (published in 1965) were in print.

3. "*The Maltese Falcon* may or may not be a work of genius, but. . . . Once a detective story can be as good as this, only the pedants will deny that it *could* even be better."—Howard Haycraft. "I think that of all the early pulp writers who contributed to the new format of the detective story, the word 'genius' was more applicable to Hammett than to any of the rest."—Erle Stanley Gardner.

4. Two cases on which he worked were those of Nicky Arnstein and Fatty Arbuckle.

5. Daly's pioneer creation was Private Operative Race Williams, worldly wise, hard-boiled, and laconic. "The papers," said Race, poetically, "are always either roasting me for shooting down some minor criminals or praising me for gunning out the big shots. But when you're hunting the top guy, you have to kick aside—or shoot aside—the gunman he hires. You can't make hamburgers without grinding up a little meat."

6. Review of *The Benson Murder Case, Saturday Review of Literature,* Jan. 15, 1927. Hammett also is critical of the author's manner of writing: "The book is written in the little-did-he-realize style."

7. Joseph Haas in a review of *The Big Knockover* in the Chicago *Daily News,* June 18, 1966, writes: "It seems probable that neither man was familiar with the works of the other, in those [early] years. What is likely is that their like approaches to prose were the products of two similar minds affected by comparable influences."

8. First published in *The Big Knockover* in 1966.

9. Elsewhere, soon after reading one of Hammett's novels, Gide was critical of Conrad's *Chance* because "Its finical slowness seems even more tiresome after the lively gait of Dashiell Hammett."

10. Whether science has approved or not, the lay public always has associated certain physical features with inward characteristics. As Kingsley Amis has noted, the typical siren pictured by Ian Fleming in his James Bond novels ordinarily has a wide mouth—"a supposed pointer to a sensual nature: Aristotle goes on about it." Readers of romantic fiction will recall the stock sisters, the blond, blue-eyed one who is innocent, sweet and shy, and the dark-haired, brown-eyed one who is gay, a bit more acid, and more worldly wise.

11. In a much earlier short story, "The Gutting of Couffignal," for very similar reasons the Continental Op had similarly refused to let a woman interfere with his performance of duty. Philip's ultimate refusal of Dorothy in Hemingway's *The Fifth Column* offers what seems to me to be an interesting parallel.

Robert I. Edenbaum (essay date 1968)

SOURCE: Edenbaum, Robert I. "The Poetics of the Private-Eye: The Novels of Dashiell Hammett." In *Tough Guy Writers of the Thirties,* edited by David Madden, pp. 80-103. Carbondale: Southern Illinois University Press, 1968.

[*In the following essay, Edenbaum examines Hammett's characterization of the "tough guy" hero in three of his novels:* The Maltese Falcon, Red Harvest, *and* The Dain Curse.]

> [The daemonic agent] will act as if possessed. . . . He will act part way between the human and divine spheres, touching on both, which suggests that he can be used for the model romantic hero, since romance allows its heroes both human interest and divine power. His essentially energic character will delight the reader with an appearance of unadulterated power. Like a machiavellian prince, the allegorical hero can act free of the usual moral restraints, even when he is acting morally, since he is moral only in the interests of his power over other men. This sort of action has a crude fascination for us all; it impels us to read the detective story, the western, the saga of space exploration and interplanetary travel.
>
> —Angus Fletcher, *Allegory*

Raymond Chandler, Dashiell Hammett's major successor in the tradition of the tough detective novel, Howard Haycraft, a historian of the form, and David T. Bazelon, a far from sympathetic critic, all agree that Hammett shaped the archetype and stereotype of the private-eye. Hammett's third novel, **The Maltese Falcon,** heads any list of tough guy novels of the thirties. The preeminence and popularity of that novel is not only due to its date of publication at the very start of the new decade, nor to the fact that eleven years later John Huston turned it into "the best private-eye melodrama ever made," according to James Agee (*Agee on Film*). And it is not only the vagaries of camp taste that have made Humphrey Bogart's Sam Spade a folk-hero a third of a century later. Sam Spade of **The Maltese Falcon** (1930), together with the nameless Continental Op of the earlier novels, **Red Harvest** and **The Dain Curse** (both 1929), and to a lesser extent Ned Beaumont of **The Glass Key** (1931) and Nick Charles of **The Thin Man** (1934) constitute a poetics of the tough guy hero of novel, film, and television script from 1929 to the present.

The characteristics of Hammett's "daemonic" tough guy, with significant variations in the last two novels, can be schematized as follows: he is free of sentiment, of the fear of death, of the temptations of money and sex. He is what Albert Camus calls "a man without memory," free of the burden of the past. He is capable of any action, without regard to conventional morality, and thus is apparently as amoral—or immoral—as his antagonists. His refusal to submit to the trammels which limit ordinary mortals results in a godlike immunity and independence, beyond the power of his enemies. He himself has under his control the pure power that is needed to reach goals, to answer questions and solve mysteries, to reconstruct the (possible) motivations of the guilty and innocent alike. Hammett's novels—particularly the first three, with which this essay will be primarily concerned—present a "critique" of the tough guy's freedom as well: the price he pays for his power is to be cut off behind his own self-imposed masks, in an isolation that no criminal, in a community of crime, has to face.

The Maltese Falcon is the most important of the novels in the development of the poetics of the private-eye because in it Hammett is less concerned with the intricacies of the detective story plot than with the combat between a villain(ess) who is a woman of sentiment, and who thrives on the sentiment of others, and a hero who has none and survives because he has none. As a result of that combat itself, the novel is concerned with the definition of the private-eye's "daemonic" virtue—with his invulnerability and his power—*and* with a critique of that definition.

The word "combat" has to be qualified immediately, for there can be unequal combat only when one antagonist holds all the cards and the other is always victim; when the one manipulates and the other is deceived; when the actions of the one are unpredictable and the responses of the other stock. These terms would seem to describe the villain and his victim in Gothic fiction from *The Mysteries of Udolpho* to *The Lime Twig*. But Hammett, in **The Maltese Falcon,** reverses the roles. Brigid O'Shaughnessy, the murderer of Sam Spade's partner Miles Archer, is the manipulated, the deceived, the unpredictable, finally, in a very real sense, the victim. Customarily in the detective story, the solution to the mystery—for example, the identity of the murderer—is known only to the murderer himself; terror makes everyone victim but the murderer, for only the murderer, the unpredictable element, can know what will happen next. In the first few pages of **The Maltese Falcon** Miles Archer is murdered, apparently by Floyd Thursby. Thursby is killed; that is apparently a mystery (though it takes no great imagination to settle on the young hood Wilmer as the likely culprit). The ostensible mystery, then, is why Thursby killed Archer, and why he in turn was killed. In the last pages of the novel, however, the reader (and Brigid O'Shaughnessy) discovers that he (and she) has been duped all along, for Spade has known from the moment he saw Archer's body that Brigid is the murderer. Spade himself, then, is the one person who holds the central piece of information; he is the one person who knows everything, for Brigid does not know that he knows. And though Spade is no murderer, Brigid O'Shaughnessy is his victim.

Once the reader knows, finally, that Spade has known all along that Miles Archer, with his pistol tucked inaccessibly under his arm, would not have gone up a dark alley with anyone but a girl as beautiful as Brigid, and therefore must have gone with *her,* he can make sense out of an apparently irrelevant anecdote that Spade tells Brigid early in the novel. The story, about a case Spade once worked on, concerns a man named Charles Flitcraft who had disappeared without apparent motive. The likely possibilities—as nearly always in Gothic fiction, sex and money—are eliminated beyond doubt. The mystery is cleared up when Spade finds the missing man. Flitcraft's life before his disappearance had been "a clean orderly sane responsible affair," Flitcraft himself "a man who was most comfortable in step with his surroundings." The day of his disappearance, on his way down a street, a beam had fallen from a building under construction and missed killing him by an inch. At that moment Flitcraft "felt like somebody had taken the lid off life and let him look at the works." He left his old life on the spot, for "he knew then that men died at haphazard like that, and lived only while blind chance spared them." Flitcraft spends several years living under that Dreiserian philosophy, working at a variety of jobs, until he meets another woman identical to his first wife except in face, marries her, has children identical to those by his first wife, leads a life identical to the one he had led before his black epiphany. Spade had returned to the first Mrs. Flitcraft to tell her what he had learned. Mrs. Flitcraft had not understood; Spade had no trouble understanding. Brigid O'Shaughnessy, despite her fascination with Spade's story almost against her will (she is trying to find out what he intends to do in her case) understands no more than Mrs. Flitcraft did.

Flitcraft moves from a life—and a commensurate philosophy—in which beams do not fall, to one in which beams do, back to one in which they don't. There can be no doubt which of the two Spade subscribes to: "Flitcraft *knew* then that men died at haphazard" (my emphasis). That commonplace enough naturalistic conception of the randomness of the universe is Spade's vision throughout. The contrast is of Spade's life (that of the private-eye) in which beams are expected to fall, and do fall, and that of the suburban businessman, in which they do not—or, at least, do not until they do. Since they did stop in the years between, Flitcraft merely adjusted himself back to a world where they did not. In Spade's world, of course, they never stop falling. If Brigid were acute enough—or less trammelled by conventional sentiment—she would see in the long, apparently pointless story that her appeals to Spade's sense of honor, his nobility, his integrity, and finally, his love, will not and cannot work. That essentially is what Spade is telling her through his parable. Brigid—totally unscrupulous, a murderess—should understand rather better than Mrs. Flitcraft, the bourgeois housewife. But

she doesn't. She falls back on a set of conventions that she has discarded in her own life, but which she naively assumes still hold for others'. At the end of the novel, Brigid is not merely acting her shock at Spade's refusal to shield her; that shock is as genuine as Effie Perine's at Spade for that same refusal—and as sentimental. Paradoxically, in *The Maltese Falcon* the good guy is a "blonde satan" and the villain is as innocent as she pretends to be. For that matter Gutman, Cairo, even Wilmer, are appalled by Spade, and in their inability to cope with him are as innocent as Brigid.

This reading of the Flitcraft story accounts for Spade's over-riding tone of mockery with Brigid whenever she appeals to his gallantry and loyalty based on her trust and confidence in him. His response to her talk of trust is, "You don't have to trust me . . . as long as you can persuade me to trust you." But, as we have seen, that is impossible from the very start, and Spade's saying so is a cruel joke on an unsuspecting murderer. To Brigid, Spade is "the wildest person I've ever known," "altogether unpredictable." Had she understood the Flitcraft story, she would have known that he is not unpredictable at all, but simply living by Flitcraft's vision of meaninglessness and the hard knowingness that follows from that vision. Spade is in step with his surroundings as much as Flitcraft is in step with his. Except for a brief (but important) moment at the end when he is nonplussed by Effie, Spade is never surprised by anyone's actions as Brigid is continually surprised by his. Spade several times picks up mockingly on Brigid's words "wild and unpredictable." She asks at another point what he would do if she were to tell him nothing about the history of the falcon and the quest for it; he answers that he would have no trouble knowing "what to do next." Sam Spade (cf. Humphrey Bogart) never has to hesitate about what to do next. Brigid, of course, has no idea what he will do. When a thousand dollar bill disappears from the envelope holding Gutman's "payment" to Spade, the detective takes Brigid into the bathroom and forces her to undress so that he can make sure she does not have it hidden on her person. Brigid, incredulous, responds with the appropriate clichés: "You'll be killing something." "You shouldn't have done that to me, Sam . . ." But Spade will not be stopped by "maidenly modesty," for he knows that Gutman is testing him to see what he will do. The fat man finds out; Brigid still does not, and learns only when it is too late.

The rejection of the fear of death, perhaps the most obvious characteristic of the tough guy in general, is but another aspect of the rejection of sentiment. Spade fully expects those falling beams, and thus detective work is as much a metaphor for existence as war is in *The Red Badge of Courage* or *A Farewell to Arms.* In an exchange with the driver of a rented car on its way to one unknown destination in the unending series that is the fictional detective's life, the driver comments on Miles Archer's death and on the detective business.

> "She's a tough racket. You can have it for mine."
>
> "Well [Spade answers], hack-drivers don't live forever."
>
> "Maybe that's right . . . but just the same, it'll always be a surprise to me if I don't."

The driver is a working-class Flitcraft; Spade, on the other hand, is heading towards another potential falling beam—though, in fact, the trip turns out to be a wild-goose chase planned by Gutman. And the final sentence of the dialogue—"Spade stared ahead at nothing . . ."—bears a double force.

Hammett's reversal of the trap of naturalism gives his heroes a kind of absolute power over their own destiny, a daemonic power, in Angus Fletcher's useful phrase. To stare into nothing and know it; to be as dispassionate about death as about using others—Wilmer, Cairo, *or* Brigid—as fall-guy: all this means that Spade can rob a Gutman of his ultimate weapon, the threat of death. When Gutman threatens Spade, the detective can argue that the fat man needs him alive; Gutman returns that there are other ways to get information; Spade, in his turn, insists that there is no terror without the threat of death, that he can play Gutman so that the fat man will not kill him, but that if need be he can *force* Gutman to kill him. Who but the tough guy can *make* the beam fall? In that lies the tough guy's power to set his own terms in life and death, a power that is the basis of his popularity in detective and other fiction.

To a generation of readers suckled on the violence of Mickey Spillane and Ian Fleming, it will hardly come as a shock to learn that detectives are as unscrupulous and amoral as "the enemy," as Spade calls them. In this book, though, Hammett seems to be consciously defining the nature of that unscrupulousness through Spade's relationship with Brigid, a relationship which itself becomes the major subject of **The Maltese Falcon** and itself exemplifies the terms of the detective's existence in the novel and in the fiction that ultimately derives from it. The dialogue between Sam Spade and Brigid does much of the work of developing that definition. For example, at one point Brigid says that she is afraid of two men: Joel Cairo and Spade himself. Spade answers, with his total awareness of what she means and what she is, "I can understand your being afraid of Cairo . . . He's out of your reach" (that is, because he is homosexual). And she: "And you aren't?" And he: "Not that way." Under the terms I am suggesting, this exchange must be read as follows: she says she is afraid of him; he says that that's not true because he's not out of her reach; he's right, she's not afraid of him; she should be because he *is* out of her reach. If she thinks

him unscrupulous it is because she thinks he is after her and/or her money. She "seduces" him, thinking it will make a difference, but it doesn't. As soon as he climbs out of bed in the morning he steals her key to ransack her apartment, to find further evidence of her lies, though once again the reader doesn't know what he finds until the very end. The fact that Spade does not "cash many checks for strangers," as his lawyer puts it, is the key to his survival, and it leaves him outside the pale of tenderness.

One further key to Hammett's demolition of sentiment is the all but passionless figure of Sam Spade and one further indication of the price immunity exacts is Effie Perine, the archetypal tough guy's archetypal secretary. Spade pays Effie the highest compliment of all in the classic line, "You're a damned good man, sister," but unlike many of her later peers Effie is not tough. In the course of the novel Spade baits Effie again and again by asking what her "woman's intuition" tells her about Brigid O'Shaughnessy; Effie is "for her"; "that girl is all right." The point is not simply that Effie is wrong. Even at the end, knowing that she has been wrong all along, that Brigid has murdered one of her bosses, she responds as a woman, with a woman's (from Hammett's point of view?) sentimental notions, with appalled distaste for *Spade*. The last word in the novel is Effie's. She has learned of Brigid's arrest through the newspapers; Spade returns to his office.

> Spade raised his head, grinned, and said mockingly: "So much for your woman's intuition."
>
> Her voice was queer as the expression on her face. "You did that, Sam, to her?"
>
> He nodded. "Your Sam's a detective." He looked sharply at her. He put his arm around her waist, his hand on her hip. "She did kill Miles, angel," he said gently, "offhand, like that." He snapped the fingers of his other hand.
>
> She escaped from his arm, as if it had hurt her. "Don't, please, don't touch me," she said brokenly. "I know—I know you're right. You're right. But don't touch me now—not now."

Effie's response amounts to a definition of sentiment: the impulse that tells you to pretend that what you know to be true is not true, to wish that what you know has to be, did not have to be. In the vein of the romanticism of action that becomes doing what everything sensible tells you you cannot do. You're right, you're right, but couldn't you better have been wrong? As Hammett has made sufficiently clear in the course of the book, and particularly in the final confrontation with Brigid, exactly the point about Spade—and about the tough guy in general—is that he could not have.

The confrontation of Spade and Brigid rather than the doings of Gutman, Cairo, and Wilmer, who are disposed of perfunctorily offstage, is the climax of the novel. Spade makes Brigid confess to him what, as we have seen, he has known all along—that she is Miles Archer's murderer; then he tells her, to her horror, that he is going to "send her over." His theme throughout this sequence is, "I won't play the sap for you." Though he says, "You'll never understand me" (anymore than Mrs. Flitcraft understood her husband), he goes on, in an astonishing catalogue, to tote up the balance sheet on the alternatives available to him. He ticks off the items on one side: "when a man's partner is killed he's supposed to do something about it"; "when one of your organization gets killed it's bad business to let the killer get away with it"; a detective cannot let a criminal go any more than a dog can let a rabbit go; if he lets her go, he goes to the gallows with Gutman, Cairo, and Wilmer; she would have something on him and would eventually use it; he would have something on her and eventually she couldn't stand it; she might be playing him for a sucker; he could go on "but that's enough." On the other side of the ledger is merely "the fact that maybe you love me and maybe I love you."

The tabulation of pros and cons suggests that Spade is a bookkeeper calculating the odds for getting away with breaking the law. But that is inaccurate, for his final statement demolishes his own statistics and suggests that something else is at stake: "'If that [all he has been saying] doesn't mean anything to you forget it and we'll make it this: I won't because all of me wants to—wants to say to hell with the consequences and do it—and because—God damn you—you've counted on that with me the same as you counted on that with the others.'" The rejection of sentiment as motivating force, i.e., of sentimentality, is at the heart of the characterization of Sam Spade and of the tough guy in general. It is not that Spade is incapable of human emotions—love, for example—but that apparently those emotions require the denial of what Spade knows to be true about women and about life. The sentiment Spade rejects is embodied in all three women in *The Maltese Falcon*—Brigid, Iva Archer, and Effie: murderer, bitch, and nice girl, respectively. It is in this theme itself, paradoxically, that *The Maltese Falcon* has been weakened by the passage of time. As one reads the novel now, Spade himself still retains his force; he is still a believable, even an attractive (if frightening) character. Brigid, on the contrary, is not. (Just so, Hemingway's assertion of Jake Barnes' stoical mask in *The Sun Also Rises* still works, but the attack on Robert Cohn's romanticism seems to be beating a dead horse.) And yet it is the pitting of Brigid's sentimental platitudes against Spade's mocking wise-cracks that may make this book the classic it is. This theme, too, signals a reversal in the naturalistic novel, for the tough guy in the tradition of Sam Spade can no longer be the victim of sentiment (cf., for example, Dreiser's Hurstwood or Clyde Griffith, or a Hemingway character defeated by the death of the woman he loves). On the contrary, he hedges himself so thoroughly

against betrayal that he lives in total isolation and loneliness. Spade is last seen shivering (temporarily) in revulsion as Effie Perine sends the moral slug Iva in to him. The attractions of Brigid given up to the law, the possibilities of Effie lost, Spade is left with only Iva—or an unending string of Iva's successors.

The Hammett detective most pure, most daemonic, is the Continental Op of the first two novels, his purity indicated even in his namelessness. The Op, perhaps more than Spade, is free of sentiment, of the fear of death, of a past, of the temptations of sex and money. Like Spade he is capable of anything that his opponents are in the pursuit of his goals; in *Red Harvest* he goes further than Spade ever does in his responsibility for setting criminals against one another murderously. The Op in *Red Harvest* is much like Mark Twain's mysterious stranger that corrupts Hadleyburg: the stranger drops the bag of "gold" in the laps of the townsmen and watches them scramble; and so the Op in Personville (pronounced Poisonville). Both manipulate matters with absolute assurance and absolute impunity (cf. Spade as well). In *Red Harvest* twenty-five people are killed, not counting an additional unspecified number of slaughtered hoodlums, yet the only mishaps to befall the Op are to have a hand creased by a bullet and an arm stunned by the blow of a chair leg. His powers come to seem almost supernatural, his knowledge of the forces that move men (sex and money) clairvoyance. His single-minded mission is to clean up the corruption no matter what the cost in other men's lives. The Op's own explanation of his motives—like those voiced to Gutman by Spade, a kind of personal grudge against those who have tried to get him—is not particularly convincing. It is tempting to say that the Op's apparently personal response to being picked on is the equivalent of the response of Hemingway's characters when they are picked off, but Hemingway's characters do have identifiable human emotions, whether disgust, or relief from disgust, or love; Hammett's, because of the purely external mechanistic method, do not. The superhuman is so by virtue of being all but nonhuman.

Red Harvest offers a perfect role for the Hammett private-eye. Elihu Willsson, aristocratic banker-boss of Poisonville, gives the Continental Detective Agency in the person of the Op ten thousand dollars to clean up the town because Willsson thinks the local gangsters responsible for the murder of his son. After the Op discovers that the crime was one of passion (if passion bought and sold) unrelated to the bootlegging-gambling-political corruption of the town, Willsson tries to dismiss the Op, who refuses to be dismissed, "'Your fat chief of police tried to assassinate me last night. I don't like that. I'm just mean enough to want to ruin him for it. Now I'm going to have my fun. I've got ten thousand dollars of your money to play with. I'm going to use it opening Poisonville up from Adam's apple to ankles.'" Ten thousand dollars of *your* money to play with—there is the role of invulnerable power with the most possibilities open. The Op almost seems to forget he has the money; aside from his day-to-day expenses, all he uses of it is $200.10 that he reluctantly pays Dinah Brand for information. Hammett seems to want to establish the financial freedom of his character: with ten thousand dollars in hand how can the Op be suborned? Once that immunity is established it does not matter how (or whether) the money is spent.

The Op's immunity from temptation indicates something of the allegorical nature of these novels. Rather than being amoral, they establish moral oppositions of the simplest kind: if the proletarian novel is a version of pastoral, in William Empson's witty formulation, the tough detective novel is a version of morality, with allegorical combat between the forces of good and evil, and the most obvious of object lessons. Don't be a sucker for sex (read "love"): better Spade with Iva than Spade with Brigid. Don't be a sucker for money: it leaves you wide open for the crooks *and* the cops. Myrtle Jennison (a minor character in **Red Harvest**) was once as beautiful as Dinah Brand: now she's bloated with Bright's Disease (and Dinah herself dies of an ice-pick wound). Twenty-five men, slaughtered, were once alive (**Red Harvest**). And so on.

The morality of Hammett's detectives is basically defensive, as it must be in the Gothic world posited. As I indicated earlier, in the traditional Gothic novel (and as well in the naturalistic novel in this century) corruption and evil stem from two sources of power, two kinds of end—money and sex. Innocence (virginity in the older Gothic) is eternally threatened, usually for money; sex is used to gain money, and is in turn corrupted by money. Sexual and financial power are at most equatable, at least inextricable, for it is money which makes sex purchasable and sex which makes money attainable. The Op functions as a monkish ascetic who in order to survive must stay clear of money and sex, the only real temptations. Presumably he could walk off with Elihu Willsson's ten thousand, but of course he is no more tempted to abscond than he is to seduce Dinah Brand (he is just about the only male in the novel who doesn't). He unfixes a prize-fight, lets Dinah win a pile of money, but does not himself bet. When Dinah, puzzled, questions him, he claims he was not sure his plan would work; but there is no evidence that that is anything but bluff. Dinah no more understands the Op's immunity to cash than Brigid understands Spade's to love. For Dinah, trying to get money out of the Op in exchange for the information she has on the inner workings of Poisonville, "It's not so much the money. It's the principle of the thing." The Op, refusing, parodies her with her own words: "It's not the money . . . It's the principle of the thing." Everything about Dinah, particularly her body, can be bought; nothing about the Op can be, by money or sex or sentiment. In self-defense he must be untouchable; otherwise his invulnerability would be seriously compromised.

Like Spade, the Op in his immunity from temptation becomes god-like, perhaps inseparable from a devil, his concern not a divine plan but a satanic disorder. "Plans are all right sometimes . . . And sometimes just stirring things up is all right—if you're tough enough to survive, and keep your eyes open so you'll see what you want when it comes to the top." The Op's way of unravelling the mess in Poisonville is to "experiment," in his word, to see if he can pit one set of crooks against another, when he unfixes the prizefight, for example. The result, in that case and always, is more murder and further chaos impending. Dinah Brand's irony—"So that's the way you scientific detectives work"—is Hammett's as well. The Op's metaphor makes him the same kind of godlike manipulator the naturalist novelist himself becomes in *his* experiments with the forces that move human beings to destruction. The stranger in "The Man That Corrupted Hadleyburg" may drop the bag of money in the town, but it is Mark Twain who drops the stranger there; and Hammett the Op in Poisonville. The bitter enjoyment may be Hammett's and Mark Twain's as well as their characters'.

Ultimately the Op does discover that he is paying the price for his power—his fear that he is going "blood simple like the natives." "Play with murder enough and it gets you one of two ways. It makes you sick or you get to like it," he says as he tabulates the sixteen murders to that moment. The blood gets to the Op in both ways. He finds that he cannot keep his imagination from running along murderous lines on the most common of objects; he carries an ice-pick into Dinah's living room, and Dinah asks why.

> "To show you how my mind's running. A couple of days ago, if I thought about it at all, it was as a good tool to pry off chunks of ice." I ran a finger down its half-foot of round steel blade to the needle point. "Not a bad thing to pin a man to his clothes with. That's the way I'm betting, on the level. I can't even see a mechanical cigar lighter without thinking of filling one with nitroglycerine for somebody you don't like. There's a piece of copper wire lying in the gutter in front of your house—thin, soft, and just enough to go around a neck with two ends to hold on. I had one hell of a time to keep from picking it up and stuffing it in my pocket, just in case—"
>
> "You're crazy," [Dinah says].
>
> "I know it. That's what I've been telling you. I'm going blood-simple."

Out of his head on the gin and laudanum which he takes to relieve his own morbidity, the Op wakes the next morning to find his hand around the ice-pick, buried in Dinah's breast. It is not surprising that not only the authorities but one of the other operatives sent down from San Francisco and the Op himself think he may be Dinah's murderer. If the Op, like all men, is capable of all things, then he is capable of unmotivated murder. If the calculatedly nonhuman yields to human emotion and human weakness, defenses are down; loss of control and near-destruction follow. The point would seem to be, don't let your defenses down. No one, including the detective, is exempt from the possibility of crime. Thus, in *The Dain Curse* and *The Thin Man* the murderer turns out to be an old friend of the detective; in *The Maltese Falcon* it is the girl the detective loves (or may love); in *The Glass Key* a father (and U. S. Senator) murders his own son; and in *Red Harvest* there is no one who might not be a killer—and most of them are, given those twenty-five some odd murders.

In *The Rebel* (Vintage Books) Albert Camus offers a brilliant analysis of the implications of the fear of emotion in the tough guy novel. The concomitants of the rejection of sentiment is the rejection of psychology itself and of everything that comprises the inner life in favor of the hedges themselves.

> The American novel [the tough novel of the thirties and forties, Camus explains in a note] claims to find its unity in reducing man either to elementals or to his external reactions and to his behavior. It does not choose feelings or passions to give a detailed description of . . . It rejects analysis and the search for a fundamental psychological motive that could explain and recapitulate the behavior of a character . . . Its technique consists in describing men by their outside appearances, in their most casual actions, of reproducing, without comment, everything they say down to their repetitions, and finally by acting as if men were entirely defined by their daily automatisms. On this mechanical level men, in fact, seem exactly alike, which explains this peculiar universe in which all the characters appear interchangeable, even down to their physical peculiarities. This technique is called realistic only owing to a misapprehension . . . it is perfectly obvious that this fictitious world is not attempting a reproduction, pure and simple, of reality, but the most arbitrary form of stylization. It is born of a mutilation, and of a voluntary mutilation, performed on reality. The unity thus obtained is a degraded unity, a leveling off of human beings and of the world. It would seem that for these writers it is the inner life that deprives human actions of unity and that tears people away from one another. This is a partially legitimate suspicion . . . [but] the life of the body, reduced to its essentials, paradoxically produces an abstract and gratuitous universe, continuously denied, in its turn, by reality. This type of novel, purged of interior life, in which men seem to be observed behind a pane of glass, logically ends, with its emphasis on the pathological, by giving itself as its unique subject the supposedly average man. In this way it is possible to explain the extraordinary number of "innocents" who appear in this universe. The simpleton is the ideal subject for such an enterprise since he can only be defined—and completely defined—by his behavior. He is the symbol of the despairing world in which wretched automatons live in a machine-ridden universe, which American novelists have presented as a heart-rending but sterile protest.

> (pp. 265-66)

Camus' analysis isolates both the success and the sadness of the tough novel. The success is that of the serious novel in general in that the correlation between the "voluntary mutilation" performed on reality by the author and that of the characters is complete; technique is subject matter in Hammett as much as in Joyce (though the analogy ends there). The excision of mind and emotion in tough dialogue, the understatement, the wise-guy joke-cracking cynicism—all the characteristics of Hammett's particular stylization—are matter as much as method. The sadness lies in the thinness of the world that remains and in the terror that is the common denominator of all men, who must fear all other men *and* themselves, and whose primary occupation would seem to be the development and maintenance of a reflexive self-defense. Finally, the detective's motives are as hidden as the murderer's and as indeterminable. The inner world is so thoroughly left to shift for itself (if it exists at all) that there is some question as to whether Hammett's characters *are* more than Camus' "wretched automatons"—with credits to Hollywood for the terrorless charms of Bogart, Greenstreet, *et al.*

The Dain Curse is one of the more interesting of Hammett's novels, in part because it is concerned with the implications and consequences of the mechanistic method and the mechanical world, with the difficulty of discovering, not only the motives of the actors, but the actual events that took place. As a result *The Dain Curse* is by far the most complicated of the novels. It consists of three separate plots concerning the events surrounding the drug-addict Gabrielle Leggett, events which eventually include the deaths of her father, mother, step-mother, husband, doctor, and religious "counselor," among others. In the first sequence, an apparently trivial theft of a batch of inexpensive diamonds leads to several murders and to incredible disclosures about the history of Edgar Leggett and his two wives, the Dain sisters Alice and Lily, a history that includes, for example, Alice's training of the three-year-old Gabrielle to kill Lily. In the second sequence, her father and aunt/step-mother dead, Gabrielle, a virtual prisoner in the quack Temple of the Holy Grail, is involved in another round of deaths, and the Op does battle with a man who thinks he is God and with a spirit that has weight but no solidity. In the third, after still more murders and maimings—a total of nine, plus three before the time of the novel—the Op discovers that there was, as he had suspected, a single mind behind the many criminal hands at work in all three apparently unrelated sequences of events. The man the Op has known for several years as Owen Fitzstephan is actually a Dain, a mastermind whose prime motive is—love for Gabrielle.

After the second part, the Op gives the still-unsuspected Fitzstephan his reconstruction of the events at the Temple of the Holy Grail, then adds,

> "I hope you're not trying to keep this nonsense straight in your mind. You know damned well all this didn't happen."
>
> "Then what did happen?" [Fitzstephan asks]
>
> "I don't know. I don't think anybody knows. I'm telling what I saw plus the part of what Aaronia Haldorn [the woman who runs the Temple, and, it is later disclosed, Fitzstephan's mistress and tool] told me which fits in with what I saw. To fit in with what I saw, most of it must have happened very nearly as I've told you. If you want to believe that it did, all right. I don't. I'd rather believe I saw things that weren't there."

And again the Op asks, "You actually believe what I've told you so far?" Fitzstephan says that he does, and the Op answers, "What a childish mind you've got," and starts to tell the story of Little Red Riding-Hood. In these novels there is no question of the complexity of, say, the relativity of guilt, for there is no ambiguity in human actions. As I have suggested, the allegory is fairly simple. The complexity is in the mystery of motive which results in the thorough-going ignorance that even the detective must admit to. What, finally, does move any human being—here, a criminal—to act? Put together a gaggle of the criminal and semi-criminal, the tempted and the merely self-interested, and it may be nearly as difficult to find out what happened as why. Similarly in **The Thin Man** Nora Charles is thoroughly dissatisfied with Nick's "theories" and "probablys" and "maybes" in his reconstruction of the events surrounding the death of Clyde Wynant. To the Op "details don't make much difference," details, that is, such as whether Joseph Haldorn really came to think himself God or merely thought he could fool everyone into thinking he was God. All that matters is that Joseph "saw no limit to his power." The same impossibility of determining truth recurs at the end of the novel: is Fitzstephan a sane man pretending to be a lunatic or a lunatic pretending to be sane? It's not clear whether the Op himself thinks Fitzstephan sane. That again is a detail that doesn't make much difference, especially since people are capable of anything. Fitzstephan, like Haldorn, saw no limit to his power. The exact terms of the curse are irrelevant; he is lost in any case.

In **The Dain Curse** Hammett once again explores the detective's mask by means of a woman's probing, but the Op's motives are no more susceptible to analysis than the criminals'. Gabrielle wants to know why the Op goes to the trouble of convincing her that she is not degenerate or insane, cursed by the blood of the Dains in her veins. She asks the questions the reader might ask: "Do I believe in you because you're sincere? Or because you've learned how—as a trick of your business—to make people believe in you?" The Op's response—"She might have been crazy, but she wasn't so stupid. I gave her the answer that seemed best at the time . . ."—doesn't answer the question for the reader any more than it does for the girl. *Is* it only a trick of his business or does he have a heart of gold beneath his tough exterior? Gabrielle is asking unanswerable questions, finally, because the removal of one mask only reveals another beneath. That may amount to saying that the toughness is not a mask at all, but the reality.

In their next encounter Gabrielle asks specifically why the Op went through the ugliness of supervising her withdrawal from drugs. He answers, with exaggerated tough guy surliness, "I'm twice your age, sister; an old man. I'm damned if I'll make a chump of myself by telling you why I did it, why it was neither revolting nor disgusting, why I'd do it again and be glad of the chance." By refusing to expose himself he is suggesting that he is exposing himself. Certainly his words suggest love for the girl, but he's hardly to be believed. He pretends to be hiding his sentiments under his tough manner, but it is more likely that he is pretending to pretend. Gabrielle has been the object of the "love" of a whole series of men: of the insane passion of Owen Fitzstephan and the only less insane of Joseph Haldorn, the High Priest and God of the Cult of the Holy Grail; of the petty lechery of her lawyer, Madison Andrews; and of the fumbling, well meant love of Eric Collinson, who gets himself (and nearly Gabrielle) killed as a result. This view of love as destructive force, as we have seen, is an essential part of the occasion for the tough role. The Op, like Spade, has to think himself well out of it, though the reader does not have to agree.

In the last of this series of interviews in which Gabrielle, acting as the reader's friend, tries to comprehend the Op's tough guy role, the girl accuses the detective of pretending to be in love with her during their previous talk.

> "I honestly believed in you all afternoon—and it *did* help me. I believed you until you came in just now, and then I saw—" She stopped.
>
> "Saw what?"
>
> "A monster. A nice one, an especially nice one to have around when you're in trouble, but a monster just the same, without any human foolishness like love in him, and—What's the matter? Have I said something I shouldn't?"
>
> "I don't think you should have," I said. "I'm not sure I wouldn't trade places with Fitzstephan now—if that big-eyed woman with the voice [Aaronia Haldorn] was part of the bargain."
>
> "Oh, dear!" she said.

It's tempting to take the Op at his word here, at least, and believe that he has been hurt by Gabrielle's unwittingly cruel words. But the pattern I have been developing makes it difficult to accept the Op's sensitivity about his toughness. It is more reasonable to assume that he is telling her, once again, what she wants to hear, suggesting that she is in some way unique in his life. If no sentiment whatever is involved in his actions, he *is* the monster she calls him. And, in fact, that is the case with the Op as with Sam Spade. Seen as figures in stylized romance, both men may be seen as daemons; as characters in realistic fiction they are monsters both.

The Glass Key is Hammett's least satisfactory novel, perhaps precisely because it is not allegorical Gothic romance, lacking as it does a godlike Spade or Op. It may be the case, as David T. Bazelon writing in *Commentary,* suggests, that Hammett was trying to write a book closer to a conventional novel, one in which characters are moved to action for human reasons such as loyalty and love. But Hammett's mechanistic method is unchanged and, as a result, it is still impossible to tell what is under Ned Beaumont's mask. Does Ned take the punishment he does out of loyalty to the political boss Paul Madvig, because Madvig picked him out of the gutter fifteen months earlier? Perhaps the reader's sense of propriety or decency fills in that answer, but there is no evidence that it is accurate. It can be argued, on the contrary, that Ned takes the vicious beatings, not out of loyalty but out of indifference to death (to falling beams, if you will). He "can stand anything [he's] got to stand," a gangster's sadism no more and no less than his (apparent) tuberculosis or a purely fortuitous traffic accident in a New York taxi. But "standing" punishment stoically (or suicidally) is not loyalty, not a basis for positive action; and without some clarification of motive, the sense of Ned's activities is merely muddy.

In a sequence that goes on for four brutal pages Ned tries repeatedly to escape his enemies despite being beaten after each attempt. But nothing stops him; as soon as he regains consciousness, he goes to work on the door again. It is tempting, once again, to take this behavior (which includes setting fire to the room) as motivated by loyalty, by Ned's overwhelming desire to warn Paul. But nothing of the sort is possible, for Hammett's descriptions of Ned's actions make it clear that most of his behavior—both his attempts to escape and to kill himself—are instinctual. He remembers nothing beyond his first beating, we are told. Action is determined mechanistically—or animalistically.

Ned's motives are essential to make sense of the climax of the novel when Ned allows Janet Henry, Paul's ostensible fiancée, to go off with him. His response to her "Take me with you" is hardly romantic: "Do you really want to go or are you just being hysterical? . . . It doesn't make any difference. I'll take you if you want to go." Yet there are indications earlier that Hammett wants to suggest the development of some kind of love between the two, growing out of their original mutual

dislike, a love about which Paul Madvig has no doubt. The men have a falling out when Paul accuses Ned of lying to him because of Ned's own interest in Janet; at the end of the novel, Paul is confronted with the couple going off together. The question remains whether Paul was right in the first place, whether Ned acted out of desire for the girl rather than loyalty to Paul, or for neither reason. But there is no basis for judgment, by Janet *or* the reader. Motives are once again indeterminable, but in this book it is necessary that they be determined. The result is not the richness of fruitful ambiguity but the fuzziness of inner contradiction.

The title of this novel, from a dream recounted to Ned Beaumont by Janet Henry, suggests once again the fear of unhedged emotion and thus of all human relationships despite the matching of Ned and Janet with which it ends. In the dream Janet and Ned are starving and come upon a locked house within which they can see food—and a tangle of snakes. To open the door there is a glass key; to get access to the food is to release the snakes. The fragile key breaks as the door opens, and the snakes attack: apparently to get at the heart's need is to open a Pandora's box. Given the tawdriness of the "love" relations in *The Glass Key*—Taylor Henry's unscrupulous use of Opal Madvig's love, Janet Henry's of Paul's—there is not much chance that Ned and Janet will escape the snakes ("I'll take you if you want to go"). Once again in these novels it would seem that the only safety is in not letting down your guard in the first place: do without the food and you escape the snakes.

It is perhaps significant that Ned Beaumont is not actually a detective, though he functions as one in trying to clear up the mystery of the murder of Taylor Henry. However, there is a professional detective in the novel, Jack Rumsen, who is interesting for his unHammett-like behavior; it is not Sam Spade or the Op who would say to a man trying to solve a crime, "'Fred and I are building up a nice little private-detective business here . . . A couple of years more and we'll be sitting pretty. I like you, Beaumont, but not enough to monkey with the man who runs the city.'" That modification of the private-eye character in the direction of the cynicism and timidity of self-interest prepares the way for Hammett's last novel, *The Thin Man,* published three years later. Nick Charles is the least daemonic of Hammett's heroes, but then he's only an ex-detective. However indifferent he may have been to death in the past, now he wants to be left out of danger, to be able to enjoy his wife, her wealth, and his whiskey. Nick Charles and his boozing is what happens to the Op/Spade when he gives up his role as ascetic demi-god to become husband, man of leisure, investor in futures on the stock market.

The Thin Man is perhaps less concerned with murder and the private-eye than with the people around the murder—with a wide range of social types spiritually sibling to the Alfred G. Packer of the long entry Gilbert Wynant reads in *Celebrated Criminal Cases of America*. The man-eaters Mimi, Dorothy, and Gilbert Wynant; Christian Jorgensen, Herbert Macauley, the Quinns, the Edges; as well as underworld characters like Shep Morelli and Julia Wolfe are little less cannibalistic than Packer. Nick Charles has no interest in their problems; it is his wife who drags him into the search for the missing Wynant against his will. The martini-for-breakfast cracking wise of William Powell and Myrna Loy more than anything else accounts for the popularity of **The Thin Man**. Despite Nick Charles' tough manner, Hammett's tough guy had been retired for good before this book appeared.

In Hemingway's story "In Another Country" the Italian major whose wife has just died fortuitously of a cold says, "[A man] must not marry. He cannot marry . . . If he is to lose everything, he should not place himself in a position to lose that. He should not place himself in a position to lose. He should find things he cannot lose." Knowing that, and despite that knowledge, Hemingway's characters of course always put themselves in a position to lose. They continually fall in love, knowing just how vulnerable that makes them, and they continually lose. Their hard exterior is merely a mask for the fine sensibility on a perpetual quest for good emotion. Hammett, in his best novels, literalizes the Hemingway mask and produces "monsters" who take the major's advice. The Hemingway mask is lifted every time the character is alone; he admits his own misery to himself—and to the reader—and exposes his inner life. The Hammett mask is never lifted; the Hammett character never lets you inside. Instead of the potential despair of Hemingway, Hammett gives you unimpaired control and machinelike efficiency: the tough guy refuses "to place himself in a position to lose." For all (or most) intents and purposes the inner world does not exist: the mask is the self. It is that "voluntary mutilation" of life that is the subject matter of these novels as much as Hemingway's stoical mask is of his. Hammett uses the relationships of Sam Spade with Brigid O'Shaughnessy, of the Continental Op with Dinah Brand and then with Gabrielle Leggett as proving grounds to indicate just how invulnerable his tough guys are. In each case the woman tries to find out what the man is; in each case the toughness is tested—and found not wanting. In the fantasy of detective novel readers and movie-goers who are themselves victims of a machine-ridden universe, loneliness is not too high a price to pay for invulnerability.

Steven Marcus (essay date 1974)

SOURCE: Marcus, Steven. Introduction to *The Continental Op*, by Dashiell Hammett, pp. ix-xxix. New York: Random House, 1974.

[*In the following introduction to a collection of Hammett's short stories, Marcus argues that Hammett el-evated the genre of the crime story to serious literature with his intricate, complex narrative structures that balance social and moral ambiguities and contradictions.*]

I

Dashiell Hammett—creator of such figures in the mythology of American culture as the Continental Op, Sam Spade, and the Thin Man—was born Samuel Dashiell Hammett, in St. Mary's County, Maryland, in May 1894. The family was of Scottish and French extraction, and they were Catholic. Hammett's early years were spent in Philadelphia and Baltimore, and his formal education was brought to an end at the age of fourteen, when he left high school after less than a year of attendance. His father's relative lack of success in the world seems, at least in part, to be reflected in this decision.

For the next several years Hammett worked with indifferent success and even less interest at a number of odd jobs—on the Baltimore and Ohio Railroad, in factories, at stockbrokers', and as a casual laborer. When he was about twenty he answered an advertisement in a Baltimore newspaper, and as a result, found himself employed by Pinkerton's, the most famous of American private-detective agencies. The young man had found a vocation that engaged his liveliest interests. The work was challenging, exciting, adventurous, dangerous, and humorous. It took him around the country and into and out of a large variety of walks of life, classes of society, and social and dramatic situations. These experiences were formative; their influence in his education as a writer can hardly be overestimated.

In 1918 he enlisted in the Ambulance Corps of the United States Army and was stationed near Baltimore. During his year of military service he came down with influenza, which led to the activation in him of tuberculosis. It was his first encounter with the series of lung diseases from which he was eventually to die. In 1919 he returned to his work at Pinkerton's and his travels and adventures in the service of the Agency. The active and arduous work of a private-detective agent in the field brought on another attack of tuberculosis, and he was hospitalized in 1920 and 1921 in government hospitals on the West Coast. While he was in the hospital he became involved with one of the nurses who worked there, and they were married toward the end of 1920.

Hammett was discharged from the hospital in May 1921, and he and his wife made their way along the West Coast to San Francisco. The town awakened Hammett's interest, and he went back to work there for the local branch of the Pinkerton Agency. He was to live in San Francisco for the next eight years, and the city provided him with the locale and material for a large part of his writing. Yet even as he was returning to work as a detective, other interests began to make themselves felt in him. He had conceived of the idea of becoming a writer, and was beginning to write bits of verse, small sketches from his experiences as a detective, and other pieces of apprentice work. Finally, the successful solution of a case led to his leaving the Agency. Some $200,000 in gold was missing on an Australian ship that had put into San Francisco. The Pinkerton Agency was employed by the insurance company involved to find the gold—which they believed was stashed away on the ship. Hammett and another operative were sent to search the ship, and found nothing. It was decided to send Hammett back to Australia on the ship in the belief that he might still find the missing loot. Hammett looked forward to the adventure. Just before the ship was to leave San Francisco, he made one last routine search and found the gold—it was hidden in a smokestack. He had solved the case and lost the trip to Australia. Frustrated and outdone by his own success, he handed in his resignation.

Soon after this, while working at odd jobs, Hammett began to hemorrhage again. Feeling that he had little time left to live, and that the one thing he wanted to do before he died was to write, he moved away from his family, took a cheap single room, and started to write. Sometime around here he also began to work for a local jewelry store as a writer of advertising copy. It was an odd and uncertain Bohemian existence; sometimes he lived on soup; frequently he drank too much. By the end of 1922, however, he began to break into print, with a number of small pieces in *Smart Set* and *Black Mask*. This latter, a popular pulp-fiction magazine, soon became Hammett's regular place of appearance in print, and his career and the career of the magazine traversed almost identical arcs. In October 1923 the first story in which the Continental Op appears—in his never-to-be-varied figure as anonymous narrator—was published. From then until 1930, as Hammett's writing underwent rapid and continuous development, this was the essential (though not the exclusive) form into which his fiction was cast. It was certainly the most successful, both in itself and in its appeal to a rapidly growing audience of readers. By the middle years of the 1920's Hammett was becoming known as an original talent, an innovator in a popular form of fiction, and as the central figure in a new school of writing about crime—the "hard-boiled school," as it came quickly to be called. And it was also beginning to be recognized as being within its own context the structural equivalent of what Hemingway and the writers who clustered naturally about Hemingway were doing in their kind of writing during the same period.

By 1927 Hammett was ready to work on a larger scale. He began to publish serially, in *Black Mask,* large units of fiction that were in fact quasi-independent sections of novels. After they had been published in the magazine he would revise them, and they would appear as volumes. *Red Harvest* was published as a volume in 1929, as was *The Dain Curse.* These two novels bring the Op's career to a climax (although three more short stories featuring the Op were later to appear), and Hammett was rapidly becoming both well known and affluent. In 1929 he invented Sam Spade and *The Maltese Falcon,* and became immediately famous. This was followed at once in 1930 by *The Glass Key. The Thin Man,* Hammett's last published novel, and another large success, came out in 1934.

Sometime during the late 1920's Hammett's marriage—two daughters were born of it—broke up for good. His life as a writer, as he continued to prosper, remained as intense, demanding, anarchic, and casually self-destructive as it had been in the years of his apprenticeship. On the one hand, there was a great deal of heavy drinking, there was a great deal of womanizing, and an even greater deal of compulsive and wild squandering of money. On the other hand, there were rigorous bouts of self-discipline and periods of extremely intense, ascetic, and self-denying hard work. After 1930 these latter began to diminish in frequency. Hammett had left San Francisco in 1929 and moved to New York; from there, in 1930, with the Great Depression setting deeply in, Hammett moved out to Hollywood. Warner Brothers had bought the film rights for *The Maltese Falcon,* and Hammett was offered high-paying work on a variety of film projects. It was here, one night in November, as he was coming out of a monumental drunk that had lasted for days, that he met a young woman named Lillian Hellman. The two were immediately attracted to one another, and there then began what was for both of them the most important relation in their lives. It was impassioned and tempestuous; it was often cruel and harsh and harmful; and there were times when neither was faithful to the other and when they went their own ways and lived apart. But in the end it endured; it lasted for thirty years, until his death.

By 1934 Hammett's career as a creative writer was finished. He did not know this, of course, and in 1932 in an interview, said that he was planning to write a play. That play never got written, but another one did. It was called *The Children's Hour,* and Hammett's work as a careful reader, stern schoolmaster, and relentlessly honest critic was instrumental in its realization. His connection with Lillian Hellman's career as a playwright was to remain close, intimate, and instrumental as the years went on.

During the 1930's Hammett continued to work at various kinds of writing and rewriting jobs in the movie industry. He also became involved, as did so many other writers and intellectuals of the period, in various left-wing and anti-fascist causes. He had become a Marxist; he had also committed himself to the cause of the Communist Party in America, and became a member of it probably sometime during 1937. Although he never surrendered his personal critical sense about the limitations and absurdities of many of his political associates and allies, both here and abroad, the commitment he had made was deep, and it was lasting, and he would pay for it in the end. It was characteristic of him—as both man and writer—that he was willing to pay the price.

Shortly after America entered World War II, Hammett—at the age of forty-eight—enlisted in the Army. Through some inexplicable sleight of hand and mouth he managed to persuade the Army doctors that the scars on his lungs that showed up on the X-rays were of no importance. He volunteered for overseas service and was sent to the Aleutians—where, among other things, he edited a daily newspaper for the troops. He apparently thoroughly enjoyed his tour of duty in the Army, and became a legendary character among his much younger fellow soldiers. When he was discharged from the Army in 1945, he was fifty-one, famous, and comparatively affluent. He had also developed emphysema. The adaptation of his novels and characters to movies and radio shows continued to bring in money, as did the steady sale of his novels. Times were changing, but his political loyalties were not. Neither were his drinking habits, which damaged and ravaged him until they brought him down in 1948 with the d.t.'s. From that time forward he never drank.

The Cold War was now on, the period identified with Senator Joseph McCarthy's name was taking shape, and many old scores were beginning to be paid off. In one of the numerous legal cases that characterized the period, Hammett was called to give evidence. He was asked to name the contributors to a fund (of which he was a trustee) that supplied bail for Communists and others who were brought to trial (in this particular case, a number of persons on trial had jumped bail and vanished). Hammett refused to testify, was found guilty of contempt of court, and was sentenced to six months in jail. He spent five months in various prisons and was then released. When he got out of prison he was an exhausted and very ill man.

His external troubles were by no means over. The money, which had once been so plentiful, was no longer there. He was blacklisted in Hollywood, and his radio shows had gone off the air. The government sued him for back taxes, won a judgment of $140,000 against him, and had his royalty, and all other, payments blocked. He took it all, as he had taken all that had come before, stoically and without complaint. He retired further into himself and lived a quiet and self-contained life until 1956, when his illness and weakness made it impossible to live alone. Thereafter he lived within the care and companionship of Lillian Hellman. In 1960 his lung condition worsened and became cancerous. He died on January 10, 1961. By his own wish, he was buried in Arlington National Cemetery.

He had served the nation in two World Wars. He had also served it in other ways, which were his own.

II

I was first introduced to Dashiell Hammett by Humphrey Bogart. I was twelve years old at the time, and mention the occasion because I take it to be exemplary, that I share this experience with countless others. (Earlier than this, at the very dawn of consciousness, I can recall William Powell and Myrna Loy and a small dog on a leash and an audience full of adults laughing; but that had nothing to do with Hammett or anything else as far as I was concerned.) What was striking about the event was that it was one of the first encounters I can consciously recall with the experience of moral ambiguity. Here was this detective you were supposed to like—and did like—behaving and speaking in peculiar and unexpected ways. He acted up to the cops, partly for real, partly as a ruse. He connived with crooks, for his own ends and perhaps even for some of theirs. He slept with his partner's wife, fell in love with a lady crook, and then refused to save her from the police, even though he could have. Which side was he on? Was he on any side apart from his own? And which or what side was that? The experience was not only morally ambiguous; it was morally complex and enigmatic as well. The impression it made was a lasting one.

Years later, after having read **The Maltese Falcon** and seen the movie again and then reread the novel, I could begin to understand why the impact of the film had been so memorable, much more so than that of most other movies. The director, John Huston, had had the wit to recognize the power, sharpness, integrity, and bite of Hammett's prose—particularly the dialogue—and the film script consists almost entirely of speech taken directly and without modification from the written novel. Moreover, this unusual situation is complicated still further. In selecting with notable intelligence the relevant scenes and passages from the novel, Huston had to make certain omissions. Paradoxically, however, one of the things that he chose to omit was the most important or central moment in the entire novel. It is also one of the central moments in all of Hammett's writing. I think we can make use of this oddly "lost" passage as a means of entry into Hammett's vision or imagination of the world.

It occurs as Spade is becoming involved with Brigid O'Shaughnessy in her struggle with the other thieves, and it is his way of communicating to her his sense of how the world and life go. His way is to tell her a story from his own experience. The form this story takes is that of a parable. It is a parable about a man named Flitcraft. Flitcraft was a successful, happily married, stable, and utterly respectable real-estate dealer in Tacoma. One day he went out to lunch and never returned. No reason could be found for his disappearance, and no account of it could be made. "'He went like that,' Spade said, 'like a fist when you open your hand.'"

Five years later Mrs. Flitcraft came to the agency at which Spade was working and told them that "'she had seen a man in Spokane who looked a lot like her husband.'" Spade went off to investigate and found that it was indeed Flitcraft. He had been living in Spokane for a couple of years under the name of Charles Pierce. He had a successful automobile business, a wife, a baby son, a suburban home, and usually played golf after four in the afternoon, just as he had in Tacoma. Spade and he sat down to talk the matter over. Flitcraft, Spade recounts, "had no feeling of guilt. He had left his family well provided for, and what he had done seemed to him perfectly reasonable. The only thing that bothered him was a doubt that he could make that reasonableness clear" to his interlocutor. When Flitcraft went out to lunch that day five years before in Tacoma, "'he passed an office-building that was being put up. . . . A beam or something fell eight or ten stories down and smacked the sidewalk alongside him.'" A chip of smashed sidewalk flew up and took a piece of skin off his cheek. He was otherwise unharmed. He stood there "'scared stiff,'" he told Spade, "'but he was more shocked than really frightened. He felt like somebody had taken the lid off life and let him look at the works.'"

Until that very moment Flitcraft had been "'a good citizen and a good husband and father, not by any outer compulsion, but simply because he was a man who was most comfortable in step with his surroundings. . . . The life he knew was a clean orderly sane responsible affair. Now a falling beam had shown him that life was fundamentally none of these things. . . . What disturbed him was the discovery that in sensibly ordering his affairs he had got out of step, and not into step, with life.'" By the time he had finished lunch, he had reached the decision "'that he would change his life at random by simply going away.'" He went off that afternoon, wandered around for a couple of years, then drifted back to the Northwest, "'settled in Spokane and got married. His second wife didn't look like the first, but they were more alike than they were different.'" And the same held true of his second life. Spade then moves on to his conclusion: "'He wasn't sorry for what he had done. It seemed reasonable enough to him. I don't think he even knew he had settled back into the same groove that he had jumped out of in Tacoma. But that's the part of it I always liked. He adjusted himself to beams falling, and then no more of them fell, and he adjusted himself to their not falling.'" End of parable. Brigid of course understands nothing of this, as Spade doubtless knew beforehand. Yet what he has been telling her has to do with the forces and beliefs and contingencies that guide his conduct and supply a structure to his apparently enigmatic behavior.

To begin with, we may note that such a sustained passage is not the kind of thing we ordinarily expect in a detective story or novel about crime. That it is there, and that comparable passages occur in all of Hammett's best work, clearly suggests the kind of transformation that Hammett was performing on this popular genre of writing. The transformation was in the direction of literature. And what the passage in question is about among other things is the ethical irrationality of existence, the ethical unintelligibility of the world. For Flitcraft the falling beam "had taken the lid off life and let him look at the works.'" The works are that life is inscrutable, opaque, irresponsible, and arbitrary—that human existence does not correspond in its actuality to the way we live it. For most of us live as if existence itself were ordered, ethical, and rational. As a direct result of his realization in experience that it is not, Flitcraft leaves his wife and children and goes off. He acts irrationally and at random, in accordance with the nature of existence. When after a couple of years of wandering aimlessly about he decides to establish a new life, he simply reproduces the old one he had supposedly repudiated and abandoned; that is to say, he behaves again as if life were orderly, meaningful, and rational, and "adjusts" to it. And this, with fine irony, is the part of it, Spade says, that he "'always liked,'" which means the part that he liked best. For here we come upon the unfathomable and most mysteriously irrational part of it all—how despite everything we have learned and everything we know, men will persist in behaving and trying to behave sanely, rationally, sensibly, and responsibly. And we will continue to persist even when we know that there is no logical or metaphysical, no discoverable or demonstrable reason for doing so.[1] It is this sense of sustained contradiction that is close to the center—or to one of the centers—of Hammett's work. The contradiction is not ethical alone; it is metaphysical as well. And it is not merely sustained; it is sustained with pleasure. For Hammett and Spade and the Op, the sustainment in consciousness of such contradictions is an indispensable part of their existence and of their pleasure in that existence.

That this pleasure is itself complex, ambiguous, and problematic becomes apparent as one simply describes the conditions under which it exists. And the complexity, ambiguity, and sense of the problematical are not confined to such moments of "revelation"—or set pieces—as the parable of Flitcraft. They permeate Hammett's work and act as formative elements in its structure, including its deep structure. Hammett's work went through considerable and interesting development in the course of his career for twelve years as a writer. He also wrote in a considerable variety of forms and worked out a variety of narrative devices and strategies. At the same time, his work considered as a whole reveals a remarkable kind of coherence. In order to further the understanding of that coherence, we can propose for the purposes of the present analysis to construct a kind of "ideal type" of a Hammett or Op story. Which is not to say or to imply in the least that he wrote according to a formula, but that an authentic imaginative vision lay beneath and informed the structure of his work.

Such an ideal-typical description runs as follows. The Op is called in or sent out on a case. Something has been stolen, someone is missing, some dire circumstance is impending, someone has been murdered—it doesn't matter. The Op interviews the person or persons most immediately accessible. They may be innocent or guilty—it doesn't matter; it is an indifferent circumstance. Guilty or innocent, they provide the Op with an account of what they know, of what they assert really happened. The Op begins to investigate; he compares these accounts with others that he gathers; he snoops about; he does research; he shadows people, arranges confrontations between those who want to avoid one another, and so on. What he soon discovers is that the "reality" that anyone involved will swear to is in fact itself a construction, a fabrication, a fiction, a faked and alternate reality—and that it has been gotten together before he ever arrived on the scene. And the Op's work therefore is to deconstruct, decompose, deplot and defictionalize that "reality" and to construct or reconstruct out of it a true fiction, i.e., an account of what "really" happened.

It should be quite evident that there is a reflective and coordinate relation between the activities of the Op and the activities of Hammett, the writer. Yet the depth and problematic character of this self-reflexive process begin to be revealed when we observe that the reconstruction or true fiction created and arrived at by the Op at the end of the story is no more plausible—nor is it meant to be—than the stories that have been told to him by all parties, guilty or innocent, in the course of his work. The Op may catch the real thief or collar the actual crook—that is not entirely to the point. What is to the point is that the story, account, or chain of events that the Op winds up with as "reality" is no more plausible and no less ambiguous than the stories that he meets with at the outset and later. What Hammett has done—unlike most writers of detective or crime stories before him or since—is to include as part of the contingent and dramatic consciousness of his narrative the circumstance that the work of the detective is itself a fiction-making activity, a discovery or creation by fabrication of something new in the world, or hidden, latent, potential, or as yet undeveloped within it. The typical "classical" detective story—unlike Hammett's—can be described as a formal game with certain specified rules

of transformation. What ordinarily happens is that the detective is faced with a situation of inadequate, false, misleading, and ambiguous information. And the story as a whole is an exercise in disambiguation—with the final scenes being a ratiocinative demonstration that the butler did it (or not); these scenes achieve a conclusive, reassuring clarity of explanation, wherein everything is set straight, and the game we have been party to is brought to its appropriate end. But this, as we have already seen, is not what ordinarily happens in Hammett or with the Op.

What happens is that the Op almost invariably walks into a situation that has already been elaborately fabricated or framed. And his characteristic response to his sense that he is dealing with a series of deceptions or fictions is—to use the words that he uses himself repeatedly—"to stir things up." This corresponds integrally, both as metaphor and in logical structure, to what happened in the parable of Flitcraft. When the falling beam just misses Flitcraft, "he felt like somebody had taken the lid off life." The Op lives with the uninterrupted awareness that for him the lid has been taken off life. When the lid has been lifted, the logical thing to do is to "stir things up"—which is what he does.[2] He actively undertakes to deconstruct, decompose, and thus demystify the fictional—and therefore false—reality created by the characters, crooks or not, with whom he is involved. More often than not he tries to substitute his own fictional-hypothetical representation for theirs—and this representation may also be "true" or mistaken, or both at once. In any event, his major effort is to make the fictions of others visible as fictions, inventions, concealments, falsehoods, and mystifications. When a fiction becomes visible as such, it begins to dissolve and disappear, and presumably should reveal behind it the "real" reality that was there all the time and that it was masking. Yet what happens in Hammett is that what is revealed as "reality" is a still further fiction-making activity—in the first place the Op's, and behind that yet another, the consciousness present in many of the Op stories and all the novels that Dashiell Hammett, the writer, is continually doing the same thing as the Op and all the other characters in the fiction he is creating. That is to say, he is making a fiction (in writing) in the real world; and this fiction, like the real world itself, is coherent but not necessarily rational. What one both begins and ends with, then, is a story, a narrative, a coherent yet questionable account of the world. This problematic penetrates to the bottom of Hammett's narrative imagination and shapes a number of its deeper processes—in *The Dain Curse,* for example, it is the chief topic of explicit debate that runs throughout the entire novel.

Yet Hammett's writing is still more complex and integral than this. For the unresolvable paradoxes and dilemmas that we have just been describing in terms of narrative structure and consciousness are reproduced once again in Hammett's vision and representation of society, of the social world in which the Op lives. At this point we must recall that Hammett is a writer of the 1920's and that this was the era of Prohibition. American society had in effect committed itself to a vast collective fiction. Even more, this fiction was false not merely in the sense that it was made up or did not in fact correspond to reality; it was false in the sense that it was corrupt and corrupting as well. During this period every time an American took a drink he was helping to undermine the law, and American society had covertly committed itself to what was in practice collaborative illegality.[3] There is a kind of epiphany of these circumstances in **"The Golden Horseshoe."** The Op is on a case that takes him to Tijuana. In a bar there, he reads a sign:

> Only Genuine Pre-War American and British Whiskeys Served Here

He responds by remarking that "I was trying to count how many lies could be found in those nine words, and had reached four, with promise of more," when he is interrupted by some call to action. That sign and the Op's response to it describe part of the existential character of the social world represented by Hammett.

Another part of that representation is expressed in another kind of story or idea that Hammett returned to repeatedly. The twenties were also the great period of organized crime and organized criminal gangs in America, and one of Hammett's obsessive imaginations was the notion of organized crime or gangs taking over an entire society and running it as if it were an ordinary society doing business as usual. In other words, society itself would become a fiction, concealing and belying the actuality of what was controlling it and perverting it from within. One can thus make out quite early in this native American writer a proto-Marxist critical representation of how a certain kind of society works. Actually, the point of view is pre- rather than proto-Marxist, and the social world as it is dramatized in many of these stories is Hobbesian rather than Marxist.[4] It is a world of universal warfare, the war of each against all, and of all against all. The only thing that prevents the criminal ascendancy from turning into permanent tyranny is that the crooks who take over society cannot cooperate with one another, repeatedly fall out with each other, and return to the Hobbesian anarchy out of which they have momentarily arisen. The social world as imagined by Hammett runs on a principle that is the direct opposite of that postulated by Erik Erikson as the fundamental and enabling condition for human existence. In Hammett, society and social relations are dominated by the principle of basic mistrust. As one of his detectives remarks, speaking for himself and for virtually every other character in Hammett's writing, "I trust no one."

When Hammett turns to the respectable world, the world of respectable society, of affluence and influence, of open personal and political power, he finds only more of the same. The respectability of respectable American society is as much a fiction and a fraud as the phony respectable society fabricated by the criminals. Indeed, he unwaveringly represents the world of crime as a reproduction in both structure and detail of the modern capitalist society that it depends on, preys off, and is part of. But Hammett does something even more radical than this. He not only continually juxtaposes and connects the ambiguously fictional worlds of art and of writing with the fraudulently fictional worlds of society; he connects them, juxtaposes them, and sees them in dizzying and baffling interaction. He does this in many ways and on many occasions. One of them, for example, is the Maltese Falcon itself, which turns out to be and contains within itself the history of capitalism. It is originally a piece of plunder, part of what Marx called the "primitive accumulation"; when its gold encrusted with gems is painted over, it becomes a mystified object, a commodity itself; it is a piece of property that belongs to no one—whoever possesses it does not really own it. At the same time it is another fiction, a representation or work of art—which turns out itself to be a fake, since it is made of lead. It is a *rara avis* indeed. As is the fiction in which it is created and contained, the novel by Hammett.

It is into this bottomlessly equivocal, endlessly fraudulent, and brutally acquisitive world that Hammett precipitates the Op. There is nothing glamorous about him. Short, thick-set, balding, between thirty-five and forty, he has no name, no home, no personal existence apart from his work. He is, and he regards himself as, "the hired man" of official and respectable society, who is paid so much per day to clean it up and rescue it from the crooks and thieves who are perpetually threatening to take it over. Yet what he—and the reader—just as perpetually learn is that the respectable society that employs him is itself inveterately vicious, deceitful, culpable, crooked, and degraded. How then is the Op to be preserved, to preserve himself, from being contaminated by both the world he works against and the world he is hired to work for?

To begin with, the Op lives by a code. This code consists in the first instance of the rules laid down by the Continental Agency, and they are "rather strict." The most important of them by far is that no operative in the employ of the Agency is ever allowed to take or collect part of a reward that may be attached to the solution of a case. Since he cannot directly enrich himself through his professional skills, he is saved from at least the characteristic corruption of modern society—the corruption that is connected with its fundamental acquisitive structure. At the same time, the Op is a special case of the Protestant ethic, for his entire existence is bound up in and expressed by his work, his vocation. He likes his work, and it is honest work, done as much for enjoyment and the exercise of his skills and abilities as it is for personal gain and self-sustainment. The work is something of an end in itself, and this circumstance also serves to protect him, as does his deliberate refusal to use high-class and fancy moral language about anything. The work is an end in itself and is therefore something more than work alone. As Spade says, in a passage that is the culmination of many such passages in Hammett:

> "I'm a detective and expecting me to run criminals down and then let them go free is like asking a dog to catch a rabbit and let it go. It can be done, all right, and sometimes it is done, but it's not the natural thing."

Being a detective, then, entails more than fulfilling a social function or performing a social role. Being a detective is the realization of an identity, for there are components in it which are beyond or beneath society—and cannot be touched by it—and beyond and beneath reason. There is something "natural" about it. Yet if we recall that the nature thus being expressed is that of a man-hunter, and Hammett's apt metaphor compels us to do so, and that the state of society as it is represented in Hammett's writing reminds us of the state of nature in Hobbes, we see that even here Hammett does not release his sense of the complex and the contradictory, and is making no simple-minded appeal to some benign idea of the "natural."

And indeed the Op is not finally or fully protected by his work, his job, his vocation. (We have all had to relearn with bitterness what multitudes of wickedness "doing one's job" can cover.) Max Weber has memorably remarked that "the decisive means for politics is violence." In Hammett's depiction of modern American society, violence is the decisive means indeed, along with fraud, deceit, treachery, betrayal, and general, endemic unscrupulousness. Such means are in no sense alien to Hammett's detective. As the Op says, "'detecting is a hard business, and you use whatever tools come to hand.'" In other words, there is a paradoxical tension and unceasing interplay in Hammett's stories between means and ends; relations between the two are never secure or stable. And as Max Weber further remarked, in his great essay "Politics as a Vocation": "the world is governed by demons, and he who lets himself in for . . . power and force as means, contracts with diabolic powers, and for his action it is *not* true that good can follow only from good and evil only from evil, but that often the opposite is true. Anyone who fails to see this is, indeed, a political infant." Neither Hammett nor the Op is an infant; yet no one can be so grown up and inured to experience that he can escape the consequences that attach to the deliberate use of violent and dubious means.

These consequences are of various orders. "Good" ends themselves can be transformed and perverted by the use of vicious or indiscriminate means. (I am leaving to one side those even more perplexing instances in Hammett in which the ends pursued by the Op correspond with ends desired by a corrupted yet respectable official society.) The consequences are also visible inwardly, on the inner being of the agent of such means, the Op himself. The violence begins to get to him:

> I began to throw my right fist into him.
>
> I liked that. His belly was flabby, and it got softer every time I hit it. I hit it often.

Another side of this set of irresolvable moral predicaments is revealed when we see that the Op's toughness is not merely a carapace within which feelings of tenderness and humanity can be nourished and preserved. The toughness is toughness through and through, and as the Op continues his career, and continues to live by the means he does, he tends to become more callous and less and less able to feel. At the very end, awaiting him, he knows, is the prospect of becoming like his boss, the head of the Agency, the Old Man, "with his gentle eyes behind gold spectacles and his mild smile, hiding the fact that fifty years of sleuthing had left him without any feelings at all on any subject." This is the price exacted by the use of such means in such a world; these are the consequences of living fully in a society moved by the principle of basic mistrust. "Whoever fights monsters," writes Nietzsche, "should see to it that in the process he does not become a monster. And when you look long into an abyss, the abyss also looks into you." The abyss looks into Hammett, the Old Man, and the Op.

It is through such complex devices as I have merely sketched here that Hammett was able to raise the crime story into literature. He did it over a period of ten years. Yet the strain was finally too much to bear—that shifting, entangled, and equilibrated state of contradictions out of which his creativity arose and which it expressed could no longer be sustained. His creative career ends when he is no longer able to handle the literary, social, and moral opacities, instabilities, and contradictions that characterize all his best work. His life then splits apart and goes in the two opposite directions that were implicit in his earlier, creative phase, but that the creativity held suspended and in poised yet fluid tension. His politics go in one direction; the way he made his living went in another—he became a hack writer, and then finally no writer at all. That is another story. Yet for ten years he was able to do what almost no other writer in this genre has ever done so well—he was able to really write, to construct a vision of a world in words, to know that the writing was about the real world and referred to it and was part of it; and at the same time he was able to be self-consciously aware that the whole thing was problematical and about itself and "only" writing as well. For ten years, in other words, he was a true creator of fiction.

Notes

1. It can hardly be an accident that the new name that Hammett gives to Flitcraft is that of an American philosopher—with two vowels reversed—who was deeply involved in just such speculations.

2. These homely metaphors go deep into Hammett's life. One of the few things that he could recall from his childhood past was his mother's repeated advice that a woman who wasn't good in the kitchen wasn't likely to be much good in any other room in the house.

3. Matters were even murkier than this. The Eighteenth Amendment to the Constitution was in effect from January 1920 to December 1933, nearly fourteen years. During this period Americans were forbidden under penalty of law to manufacture, sell, or transport any intoxicating liquor. At the same time no one was forbidden to buy or drink such liquor. In other words, Americans were virtually being solicited by their own laws to support an illegal trade in liquor, even while Congress was passing the Volstead Act, which was intended to prevent such a trade.

4. Again it can hardly be regarded as an accident that the name Hammett gives to the town taken over by the criminals in *Red Harvest* is "Personville"—pronounced "Poisonville." And what else is Personville except Leviathan, the "artificial man" represented by Hobbes as the image of society itself.

Bernard A. Schopen (essay date autumn 1979)

SOURCE: Schopen, Bernard A. "From Puzzles to People: The Development of the American Detective Novel." *Studies in American Fiction* 7, no. 2 (autumn 1979): 175-89.

[*In the following excerpt, Schopen traces Hammett's role in the evolution of the American detective novel, asserting that in* The Maltese Falcon *and his other novels, he "established the ambience, the basic patterns, and the central themes of the form."*]

In three rather contentious essays, Edmund Wilson once said about detective stories what F. R. Leavis said about the novels of Charles Dickens: they do not seriously engage the adult mind.[1] While it is difficult to agree with Leavis on Dickens (as, judging from his recent book on that novelist, Leavis himself discovered), it is not diffi-

cult to agree with Wilson—at least insofar as he describes the "formal" detective story as it evolved from Poe. But when Wilson proposes that Dashiell Hammett, in *The Maltese Falcon,* simply "infused the old formula of Sherlock Holmes with a certain cold underworld brutality,"[2] he demonstrates the curious critical myopia which prevents many readers of "hardboiled" detective novels from perceiving the formal singularity of these fictions. Works like *The Dain Curse* and *The Maltese Falcon, Farewell, My Lovely* and *The Long Goodbye, The Chill,* and *The Underground Man* are not detective stories: they are novels whose central characters are detectives and which employ the detective format for serious aesthetic and moral purposes. More precisely, they are American novels. They derive not from the tradition of fictional intellectual puzzles but from the novels of Cooper and Twain, Crane and Hemingway and Fitzgerald. They reside securely within the tradition of the American novel for they concern one of its central fictional figures, express its darkly enigmatic vision, and ask a question which thematically informs much of American literature.

No serious student of prose fiction has ever suggested that the detective story manifests the qualities and characteristics which constitute the generic requirements of the novel. Perhaps the most that might be insisted upon is that Conan Doyle, Dorothy Sayers, and Agatha Christie wrote "fictions in prose of a certain extent;" but E. M. Forster did not wish anyone to believe that in this ambiguous little phrase he had defined the novel. Actually, most aficionados of detective stories have taken considerable pains to distinguish the object of their affections from those prose fictions—novels—which transform the flux of human experience into meaningful moral and aesthetic structures. In two frequently cited remarks, Dorothy Sayers, surely the most sophisticated literary mind among the detective writers of the "Golden Age," focused on the essential differences. The first is general and descriptive: "For, make no mistake about it, the detective-story is part of the literature of escape, and not of expression."[3] The second is specific and proscriptive: "There is the whole difficulty of allowing real human beings into a detective story. At some point or another, either their emotions make hay of the detective interest, or the detective interest gets hold of them and makes their emotions look like pasteboard."[4] The choice must be made, that is, between people and puzzles. And the writer of detective stories must opt for the latter. In doing so, however, he must also abjure all serious moral and aesthetic considerations; since the theme of his work is simply "detection," he must abandon the attempt to create a coherent and structured narrative which develops a significant theme by presenting recognizable human characters in a thoroughly human action.

This implicit invocation of Aristotle is not gratuitous. Even a cursory review of the crucial literature on detective fiction indicates that while everyone understands that these stories cannot be classified as novels, no one seems able to construct a formal theory congenial to and descriptive of the essential characteristics of this fiction. In their attempts to create a generic foundation for their discussions, critics invariably find themselves playing Polonius. While they begin by examining detective stories, they quickly bring under their purview any fictional narrative containing a serious crime, an unsolved mystery, or a strong element of suspense; they then must attempt at once to lump together and differentiate among detective, mystery, adventure, suspense, or spy stories; they fashion complex categories like detective-thriller, gothic-suspense-mystery, and crime-adventure-romance; and ultimately they follow their own generic ingenuities into a thicket of hyphenated brambles from which they and the fiction never emerge.

Of course, the novel itself generically subsumes several types of fictional prose narratives. Nevertheless, it has certain basic requirements, among the most important of which is precisely what Dorothy Sayers in theory, and "formal" detective writers in practice, exclude from detective stories—fictional characters who demonstrate recognizably human mental and emotional qualities. All legitimate theories of the novel stress the salience of such characterization. Northrop Frye distinguishes the novel from the romance on this basis,[5] as does Richard Chase.[6] And critics who bring to the genre such antithetical assumptions as those of the Neo-Aristotelean Sheldon Sacks, who sees the novel as a "represented action,"[7] and the language analyst David Lodge, who views it as a "verbal world,"[8] still share the conviction that the novel requires, as Sacks puts it, "characters about whose fates we are made to care."[9] To suggest that the novel demands characterization consistent with human beings as they exist in life is not to insist that novels be "realistic"—whatever that may mean. It is only to require that they present to the reader fully realized characters rather than "pasteboard" silhouettes.

The fusion of "character" with the pattern of investigative action in the detective story was one of the primary objectives of those American writers who, in the twenties and thirties, began to develop a new form of detective fiction. In fact, however, such a junction had occurred long before, as Sayers herself must have been aware. *Oedipus Rex,* in which "character" and "detection" are inextricably bound with each other, and with a pattern of purposeful action, is perhaps the earliest example of the type of structure Hammett and others wished to create in their prose narratives. Joseph T. Shaw, editor of the pulp magazine *Black Mask,* in which the new stories first appeared, put forth their central theoretical premise; deliberately turning away from the detective story of "the deductive type, the crossword puzzle sort, lacking—deliberately—all other human values,"[10] they strove to fashion a form which "emphasizes character and the problems inherent in human behavior. In other words, in this new pattern, character conflict is the main theme; the ensuing crime, or its threat, is incidental."[11]

This formal conception also determined the style and tone of the new fiction. As Shaw described his editorial considerations, "we wanted simplicity for the sake of clarity, plausibility, and belief. We wanted action, but we held that action is meaningless unless it involves recognizable human character in three-dimensional form."[12] Unfortunately, what Shaw and his friends wanted they did not always get. While Shaw diligently edited the material he published, his magazine remained one of the "pulps" which purveyed "racy and adventurous" fiction to a masculine and barely literate audience. The medium through which he would transform the detective story was part of what is called "Popular Culture," and the fiction it presented had to meet the expectations of the pulp reader. In addition, the style and atmosphere of the new form appealed to writers of minimal talent. The terseness of expression, the use of street or barroom vernacular, and the physical, mental, and emotional "toughness" of the detective were easily aped and often unconsciously parodied. Meaningful action became mindless violence, succinctness a linguistic stuttering, strength of character a sophomoric bravado, and characterization a matter of black hats and white hats. In fact, hacks still produce much of the fiction in the form, as any one of the novels of Brett Halliday, Richard S. Prather, Steven Marlowe, or Mickey Spillane demonstrates. Nevertheless, the American detective novel, in the hands of its most able practitioners, succeeded in approaching what Dorothy Sayers argued the detective story could not—"the loftiest levels of literary achievement."[13] And it did so by entering the mainstream of the American novel.

In contrast to the "pure" detective story, which is written and read in most Western countries, the "hardboiled" detective novel is distinctly and exclusively an American form. While it has significantly influenced the crime, suspense, and spy stories which, in the last forty years, have proliferated through the Anglo-European world, in its classic form it has remained a product of the American literary and cultural imagination. In fact it cannot be transplanted, for the "private eye" who dominates and partially defines the form is an autochthonous American character who can come to life only in the dark alleys and mean streets of the American city. He is also the urban manifestation of a prototypical figure of both popular and serious American fiction: the frontier or cowboy hero. The pulps in which he was born featured both western and detective stories, and a hack writer named Carroll John Daly created one Race Williams, the first hardboiled private eye, by the simple expedient of taking the western hero as he had degenerated from Cooper into the popular imagination, bringing him into the city, and making him a detective. In doing so Daly began the process which was to elevate this figure through the work of serious writers back into the American novel.

Even as they appear in the most egregious forms of semi-literate entertainments, from the pulps of the twenties to the television shows and paperbacks of the seventies, both the cowboy and the private eye are manifestations of a central male figure in American literature. This character is the "man in the middle," caught between the demands of society and the dictates of his own conscience, between the moral system advocated—if not always followed—by others and the individualistic "code" which constitutes his integrity; he exists at once within and without society, and regardless of whether he attempts to remove himself from it or to enter into it and restructure its values, he is doomed to failure, isolation, or destruction. He succeeds in preserving his sense of honor only by removing himself from society—which, ironically, is the only environment in which his integrity has a significance other than the solipsistic; or he sacrifices his honor, betrays his code and himself, for the sake of the society—usually represented by a woman who offers him love—which, again ironically, assists in the destruction brought on by that betrayal. This figure and the patterns he enacts are, with admitted variations, central to the American novel. Natty Bumppo, Arthur Dimmesdale, Ahab and Pierre, Huck Finn, Merton Densher, Jake Barnes and Frederic Henry, Jay Gatsby, Quentin Compson and Joe Christmas and Ike McCaslin—all end either alone or destroyed, victims of the irresolvable conflict between the individual and his society.

Unquestionably, a similar character confronts a similar situation in the detective novels of Hammett, Raymond Chandler, and Ross MacDonald. Their private detectives, emotionally and morally estranged from their societies, lead dual lives. The inner apprehension of good and evil which constitutes the codes of Spade, Marlowe, and Archer forces them to sever all meaningful ties with their fellow men. Thus, if out of loneliness or love they try to enter the human community, they violate their integrity; but if they follow their codes, they condemn themselves to solitude. In this sense they are avatars of the central character in the American novel, the tragic victim of the dark and violent conflict between the individual and society. The adjective "tragic" is used deliberately. If most American detective novels are not formal tragedies—and some of them clearly are—they do present a pattern of tragic action. As Northorp Frye has observed, beyond the strictly generic considerations, "there is a general distinction between fictions in which the hero becomes isolated from his society and fictions in which he is incorporated into it.

This distinction is expressed by the words 'tragic' and 'comic' when they refer to aspects of plot in general. . . ."[14] And the effect of the American detective novel, as John Paterson has so accurately described it, is similar in kind if not in degree to that of tragedy:

> There is always at the end of the hardboiled novel a moment of depression when the mission is completed, the enterprise ended, as if this little victory had cost too much in terms of human suffering. But there is always, too, the notion that human dignity and human integrity have somehow been vindicated, and that this has been worthwhile.[15]

Dashiell Hammett, Raymond Chandler, and Ross MacDonald make up the "Great Tradition" of the American detective novel. They are, to use Leavis' formulation, "the major writers who count . . . in the sense that they not only change the possibilites of the art for practitioners and readers, but that they are significant in terms of the human awareness they promote; awareness of the possibilities of life."[16] The tradition obviously begins with Hammett, who, in effect, created the American detective novel. Efforts to transpose Race Williams and those of his ilk from the pulps into hardcovers had produced long fictions in prose, but Hammett's **Red Harvest** is the first that can be considered a novel. And **The Dain Curse,** which Hemingway admired, is thoroughly first-rate. But Hammett's reputation rests primarily on **The Maltese Falcon,** a novel which in itself demands that he be ranked among the important writers of the period.

As the first unmistakably great American detective novel, **The Maltese Falcon** established the ambience, the basic patterns, and the central themes of the form. Hammett's sternly Naturalistic vision renders Sam Spade's world crepuscular and savage, its inhabitants moral primitives who assume the appurtenances of civilization only to create those illusions which assist them in their rapacious pursuits. As a detective, Sam Spade thrives in this world; he so profoundly understands its nature, and has so completely removed himself from emotional contact with its denizens, that he believes nothing, trusts no one, and stalks his prey with a stolid singlemindedness which destroys or inverts the illusions created by others. Because Spade commits himself only to his profession and his inner apprehension of his duty, he can cuckold his partner without a qualm; Spade, the man, despises both Miles and Iva Archer, while Spade, the detective, finds love and fidelity irrelevant to his purpose. Aware of the treachery which attends human relations in his world, he refuses to express or act upon his feelings for others; yet he is not impervious to the value of genuine human relationships. So Spade himself embodies the basic conflict of the individual and society: as a detective he is a ruthless and successful predator in an amoral and predatory world; but as a man he is isolated by his integrity from the human community.

With the appearance of Brigid O'Shaughnessy, this conflict is transformed into dramatic action.

One pattern of action in *The Maltese Falcon* involves the "detecting" by which Spade finds his way through the labyrinth of lies to the black bird and the truth. But as Robert I. Edenbaum has observed, neither the solving of Miles Archer's murder nor the search for the falcon is central to the novel; rather, the developing relationship of Spade and Brigid "becomes the major subject of *The Maltese Falcon* and in itself exemplifies the terms of the detective's existence in the novel and in the fiction that ultimately derives from it."[17] The dramatic pattern of this relationship subsequently appeared so frequently in the hardboiled detective novel that it has become almost axiomatic that any woman to whom the detective is seriously attracted will—if she is not murdered—be revealed guilty of conspiracy, complicity, or murder itself. But in Hammett's novel something very much akin to tragic irony underlies the process by which Spade moves nearer to a genuine emotional relationship with Brigid even as he strips away her various identities and psychological costumes and exposes her guilt. So he must choose between Brigid and his integrity, although either choice results in his loss. Ultimately, he turns her over to the police because his insular integrity affords more security than the unpredictable possibilities of human relations.

During the course of the novel the Maltese Falcon itself undergoes a transformation similar to that effected by the action. As Miss Wonderly, through the alchemy of disillusion, becomes the Brigid who has murdered Miles Archer, so that "priceless" golden bird for which so many lives are paid is revealed to be a worthless lead statue. Neither Spade nor the reader ever learns if the falcon really exists. Thus, the novel raises the question which the American detective novel constantly poses: Is the falcon real, or is it, as well as the vision of human relationships founded on individual integrity and mutual fidelity, simply a dream? Since Hammett, the American private detective has always investigated the relation and distinction between illusion and reality. The detective formula is based precisely on this dichotomy, of course; but the major American detective writers use both the formula and the theme to expose the dark realities which reside in the minds and hearts of their characters, as well as within a society dedicated to the reification of the American Dream.

In *Red Harvest, The Dain Curse,* and *The Maltese Falcon,* Hammett established the protagonist, patterns, and themes of the American detective novel. And he did so in a distinctively American prose, forging a crisp spare style dominated by the precise rendering of urban American idioms and rhythms. Certainly the use of the American rather than the English language partially defines the hardboiled detective novel. As Ross MacDonald has remarked, ". . . the *Black Mask* revolution was a revolution in language as well as subject matter."[18] But Raymond Chandler, a fascinated student of the American language, has more correctly observed that this "revolution" was simply another upheaval in the continuing linguistic cataclysm in American literature which began with Whitman.

Notes

1. Edmund Wilson, "Why Do People Read Detective Stories?", "Who Cares Who Killed Roger Ackroyd?" and "'Mr. Holmes, They Were the Footprints of a Gigantic Hound!'" reprinted in his *Classics and Commercials: A Literary Chronicle of the Forties* (New York: Random House, 1962), pp. 231-37, 257-65, and 266-74.

2. Wilson, "Why Do People Read Detective Stories?" p. 235.

3. Dorothy Sayers, "The Omnibus of Crime," reprinted in Howard Haycraft, ed. *The Art of the Mystery Story* (New York: Simon and Schuster, 1946), p. 109.

4. Sayers, p. 105.

5. Northrop Frye, *Anatomy of Criticism* (Princeton: Princeton Univ. Press, 1957), pp. 304-05.

6. Richard Chase, *The American Novel and Its Tradition* (Garden City: Doubleday & Company, 1957), pp. 12-13.

7. Sheldon Sacks, *Fiction and the Shape of Belief* (Berkeley: Univ. of California Press, 1964), p. 26.

8. David Lodge, *The Language of Fiction* (New York: Columbia Univ. Press, 1967), p. 46.

9. Sacks, p. 15.

10. Joseph C. Shaw, "Introduction," in *The Hard-Boiled Omnibus: Early Stories from "Black Mask"* (New York: Simon and Schuster, 1946), p. v.

11. Shaw, p. vii.

12. Shaw, p. vi.

13. Sayers, p. 102.

14. Frye, p. 35.

15. John Paterson, "A Cosmic View of the Private Eye," *SatR,* (August 22, 1953), p. 31.

16. F. R. Leavis, *The Great Tradition* (New York: New York Univ. Press, 1963), p. 2.

17. Robert I. Edenbaum, "The Poetics of the Private Eye: The Novels of Dashiell Hammett," in David Madden, ed., *Tough Guy Writers of the Thirties* (Carbondale: Southern Illinois Univ. Press, 1968), p. 86.

18. Ross MacDonald, *On Crime Writing* (Santa Barbara: Capra Press, 1973), p. 18.

Peter Wolfe (essay date 1980)

SOURCE: Wolfe, Peter. "Fresh Mountain Gore." In *Beams Falling: The Art of Dashiell Hammett*, pp. 77-93. Bowling Green, Ohio: Bowling Green University Popular Press, 1980.

[*In the following essay, Wolfe highlights the Marxist influences in* Red Harvest.]

Hammett's first novel sends the much-traveled Op to the raw, dingy mining town of Personville, also called Poisonville and described as "an ugly city of forty thousand people, set in an ugly notch between two ugly mountains that had been all dirtied up by mining." Joe Gores has identified Personville as an amalgam of Boulder, Colorado and the Montana towns of Butte and Anaconda, the latter a copper-mining center.[1] The mountain setting harks to the old west. Hard-drinking, gun-brandishing rowdies people the city; robberies and shootouts are as commonplace as due process is unknown. But instead of riding stallions, local desperadoes roar through town in Black Marias carrying machine guns and homemade bombs. They roar through town this way nearly every day. "The city is sick from the diseases of violence, greed, and capitalist extortion," says Thompson, adding, "the people are shabby and rumpled in appearance, and dull and gray of eye."[2] The Marxist attack on free enterprise noted by Thompson carries through the whole work. Neither life nor soul is saved in **Red Harvest** (1929); nobody lives clean, works at an honest job, or plays fair if he hopes to survive. The criminals who people the action don't harm society; they constitute it. Political bosses and racketeers have already destroyed civil law, replacing it with gambling and bootlegging, graft and paid-off police. Op's victory at the end doesn't affirm community values. Personville hasn't seen these for years. The evil the Op has routed will reinstate itself because the town has nothing either to replace it or keep it at bay. Hammett doesn't describe the interference rushing into the moral vacuum. The wreckage and bloodshed described in the earlier chapters suggest a cyclical pattern of self-destruction. As **Blood Money** showed, its thirst for money and power has made the United States a nation of idolators whose predictability is only rivaled by its greed.

I

Op learns quickly that Personville's name has no basis in reality. The individual's rights are neither prized nor protected in this gloomy, vice-ridden place. Crime is the dynamic life-line joining the residents of Personville; social values all rivet on crime; the mob decides all. The pre-eminence enjoyed by mob rule makes itself felt straightaway. As in **"The Tenth Clew"** and **"A Man Called Spade,"** the detective's client dies before meeting the man he had hired to protect him. Donald Willsson, a muckraking newspaper publisher, gets shot to death on a dark, lonely street while the Op is waiting for him in his library. The next day gives Op the background of the murder. Several years ago, Willsson's father, Elihu, "the czar of Poisonville," brought thugs to town to break a workers' strike. The thugs hurt Elihu more than they helped him. After taming the striking mine workers, they entrenched themselves in the city, heretofore Elihu's private preserve:

> Old Elihu didn't know his Italian history. He won the strike, but he lost his hold on the city and the state. To beat the miners he had to let his hired thugs run wild. When the fight was over he couldn't get rid of them. . . . They had won his strike for him and they took the city for their spoils.

Unable to drive out the newly empowered hoodlums, Elihu recently turned the job over to his son. He brought Donald to Personville from Paris, where he had been studying journalism, and gave him control of the town's two newspapers, which he used to mount his reform campaigns.

The campaigns proved embarrassing, for much of Donald's civic crusading incriminated his father, and both father and son knew it. Op's visit to sick, old Elihu brings the noisy insistence from Elihu that Donald was murdered by his wife. Has Elihu something to hide? Less impressed by his bluster than by facts, Op doesn't credit the accusation. But before he has a chance to study Elihu's possible motives for murdering his son, another woman replaces Donald's widow at the center of the plot. Op learns, his second day in Personville, that Donald died just after giving a certified check for $5000 to a local woman named Dinah Brand. Dinah, who lives less than a block away from where Donald was felled, becomes Op's next witness. Described as "a soiled dove . . . a de luxe hustler, a big-league gold-digger," Dinah seems to have turned every male head she has wanted to turn in Personville. But she hardly looks or observes the life style of any town siren: The simple gray frame cottage where she lives with stringy, tubercular Don Rolff is patently middle class; her clothes are both unbecoming and unkempt; though only twenty-five or so, she has started to lose her looks, a process hastened by her carelessly applied makeup. Above all, she's totally mercenary and doesn't pretend otherwise. In a community that has shut out the female graces of gentleness and intuition, women outdo men at their own faults. Thus Op, who has asked the right questions while lowering Dinah's guard with drink, deserves credit for prying information out of her without paying.

This information doesn't define her part, if any, in the death of Donald Willsson, whose $5000 check to her was certified, meaning that payment on it couldn't have been stopped. Hoping to find fresh explanations for the certified check at the home of Donald's father, Op comes up against a more dramatic development—the discovery that Elihu has shot a prowler through the head. The development doesn't rattle him. Taking charge of the interview, he agrees to clean up Personville, but only on his own terms. Elihu must give him a free investigative hand and pay a $10,000 retainer to the Continental Detective Agency. The interview displays Op's best bargaining skills. Not only has he observed official protocol; acting quickly, he has also assessed his new assignment politically, psychologically, and morally: "These people you want taken to the cleaners were friends of yours yesterday," he tells Elihu. "Maybe they will be friends again next week. I don't care about that. But I'm not playing politics for you. I'm not hiring out to help you kick them back in line— with the job being called off then. If you want the job done you'll plank down enough money to pay for a complete job."

High-speed action follows talk, as the plot moves to a dawn raid at a bootlegger's warehouse. Accompanying the police, "a shabby, shifty-eyed crew," Op tries to make peace between the contending forces. A salvo of police bullets that bite into the wall alongside him confirms his statement that he's acting alone and gains him admission into the warehouse. Op reorders his loyalties. Even if he *had* been working for Police Chief John Noonan, the bullets Noonan's men fired at him cancelled that compact. Thus he explains to the bootlegger-gambler, Max "Whisper" Thaler, "You're to be knocked off resisting arrest, or trying to make a getaway"; cheerful, handshaking Noonan would rather execute Thaler, Dinah Brand's latest lover, than let him stand trial before a bought judge for Donald Willsson's death. What is more, the chief suspects Thaler of having killed Tim Noonan, his brother, at a lakeside lodge a year ago. But his primitive justice must wait. Thaler escapes the police stakeout easily, bribing some policemen stationed at the back of his warehouse to free him and his friends. Hammett's brief description of their flight, consisting solely of smooth-fitting one-syllable words, registers accuracy and freshness along with the quality of the sensation being recounted: "One of the blond boys drove. He knew what speed was."

The fast car pulls up in Personville's main business district, where Op names Donald Willsson's killer—a young bank clerk named Robert Albury. Recently dropped by Dinah Brand, Albury turned his frustration upon Donald, who had asked him to certify the $5000 check made out to Dinah. Op includes in the fabric of proof he weaves against Albury the fact that Donald was killed by a .32 caliber pistol, the sort favored by banks (inside information like this often enlivens the fiction of ex-detective Hammett). But his naming of the killer, normally the climax of a murder mystery, gives way to a deeper concern—that of getting even. Having been shot at by the local police, Op seeks revenge. The search both exhausts and taints him. Though brilliant and well timed, his exertions in the twenty remaining chapters of this twenty-seven-chapter novel also endanger his job and life. Nobody can afford revenge. Besides, the American city is beyond justice and redemption. Any reformer will come to grief together with his program for civic reform in the urban jungle, regardless of motives. Once the Op starts playing the lone vigilante, he can't stop, remaining in Personville even after settling his private score. His survival at the end depends as much upon luck as upon strength, skill, and sense. Luck helps him in Chapter 8, where Noonan's men fire ten bullets into his hotel room just after he goes there to turn in for the night. His luck—all ten bullets go astray—doesn't teach him prudence. Rejecting the advice to leave town, he vows once again to take on Poisonville.

But how can one man tackle the mob? The way to an answer lies in the mutual distrust and dislike the crooks feel for each other. Op will set Personville's racketeers against each other by aggravating the ill will already dividing them. His instigations allow him to dispense, rather than bring criminals to, justice. His first chance to play justicer comes with the news of a prize fight taking place locally the next night. In order to change the betting odds, he tells people that the underdog, who is secretly backed by Thaler's mob and money, will knock out the favorite in six rounds or less. Then he blackmails the favorite, who, he knows, has agreed to throw the fight, into winning. Op tightens his hold on his man. Some extra prodding at ringside between rounds of the bout convinces the favorite, who is fighting under an alias, that losing will mean being sent back to Philadelphia to stand trial in a murder case. Despite a slow count by the referee, who is also in on the fix, he knocks out the underdog in the next round. As often happens in Hammett, though, he'd have stood a better chance with the law than with the gamblers he has foiled. No sooner is he declared the winner than a knife flashes down into the ring from a balcony and lodges in his neck.

Things go badly, too, for Thaler, who lost heavily on the fight. In Chapter 14, the book's middle chapter, he is arrested as a suspect in the murder of Tim Noonan. But he is freed this same day—thanks to the best use of the convention of the dying message in all Hammett. Tim Noonan's supposed identification of Max "Whisper" Thaler as his assailant doesn't refer to Thaler at all, but to Bob MacSwain, the husband of Tim's recently castoff mistress: "Max didn't kill Noonan's brother. Tim didn't say *Max*. He tried to say *Mac Swain*, and died before he could finish," Op later tells Dinah. Thaler's release from prison, meanwhile prompts the Op to bring in two helpers from San Francisco, big, good-natured Mickey Linehan and the undersized shadow specialist from Canada, Dick Foley. Their job: to help Op drive wedges between the different gangs in town: "If we can smash things up enough—break the combination—they'll have their knives in each other's backs, doing our work for us," Op tells his helpers. But one gang has already mounted its own divide-and-conquer plot, luring a large detail of police to a remote roadhouse while it robs a big downtown bank. That the bank is owned by Op's client, Elihu, that till recently it had employed Robert Albury, Donald's killer, and that Police Chief Noonan helped get his men out of the city—these realities all tighten a high-speed, high-action novel that sometimes threatens to lurch out of control. Further unity of effect comes from an auto chase accompanied by live bullets stitching the country air. This wildness wears down the characters, though. "I can't go through with it," mutters Noonan afterward. "I'm sick of this butchering. I can't stand any more of it."

Op's reminder that Noonan's wish to avenge his brother's death started the butchering leads to one of the book's best scenes, the so-called peace conference of Chapter 19, which all the town's warweary racketeers attend in order to stop the fighting. Op attends with a different goal in mind. He wants to rid Personville of crime, rather than merely lulling it. Thompson has shown how his tactic of "stirring things up" turns the peace conference into a council of war:

> The Op's "peace conference" is at the same time the most perfect example of machiavellian policy in the novel and the most revealing about the Op himself. The conference is a gathering of all the corrupt powers in Personville. . . . All the parties are deceived in one way or another; only the Op knows the truth, and he chooses when to use it and when to distort it.[3]

"I was in a good spot if I played my hand right, and in a terrible one if I didn't," Op remarks inwardly at the conference. The judgment and decisiveness, timing and grip, he displays in the following moments reveal him a brilliant criminal psychologist. By saying things that either embarrass his hearers or make public their betrayals of each other, he sets them at one another's throats. The concentration of gangsters in a single room begets a cancer of crime, as Op had hoped and planned for. He took no great risk. As borne out in George V. Higgins's *Friends of Eddie Coyle* (1972), professional criminals lead slavishly conventional lives; both freedom and originality of choice are nearly unknown in Hammett's underworld.

The chapters following the big meeting at Elihu's mansion reek of cordite. The meeting's first casualty is Noonan, whose offstage death by gunfire comes early in Chapter 20. This death and the others that follow, though serving Op's ends, sicken his heart. Sounding a good deal like Noonan did before the peace conference, he makes us wonder if he will follow Noonan's example by getting shot. The slow tempo of Chapter 20, during which he explains his malaise to Dinah, builds suspense while smoothing the novel's pace:

> This damned burg's getting me. If I don't get away soon I'll be going blood-simple like the natives. There's been what? A dozen and a half murders since I've been here.

> * * *

> I've arranged a killing or two in my time, when they were necessary. But this is the first time I've ever got the fever. It's this damned burg. You can't go straight here.

His immersion in death goes deeper than he knows. The nervous strain building over the last several days moves him to lace his gin with laudanum, after which he reels into sleep on Dinah's Chesterfield. He wakes up after two fantastic dreams to find Dinah stabbed to death alongside him, the death weapon, an ice pick, in his hand. As the following passage shows, he seems to react neither morally nor emotionally to the death. Dinah could have been a stranger, and he could have been miles away when he heard of her death, rather than waking up in the same room with her corpse:

> She was lying on her back, dead. Her long muscular legs were stretched out toward the kitchen door. There was a run down the front of her right stocking.

> Slowly, gently, as if afraid of awakening her, I let go the ice pick, drew in my arm, and got up.

The passage has puzzled critics, Hammett's verbal irony having opened a big gap between the murder and the way the murder is reported. What must be kept in mind is that the irony serves Op's narration; Op is recounting the action of *Red Harvest,* not Hammett. Op's coolness after the discovery of Dinah's corpse hides a psychological trauma he had alluded to an hour or so before he passed out when he said, "This . . . planning death is not natural to me. It's what the place has done to me." Strong as he is, he hasn't resisted the moral corrosion exuded by Personville. How could he not be jolted by seeing Dinah dead? Her corpse tells him that he hasn't only planned a death, but that he may have also caused one. His degraded self-image having been enforced by his wild dream, he knows himself capable of murder. This knowledge he prefers to keep to himself. He affects nonchalance and buries his fears in the practical details of inspecting the house, removing his fingerprints from surfaces he may have touched, and making sure his clothes are free of bloodstains. The suspicion that he went berserk and killed Dinah forces him to muster as much self-control as he can.

In making him a murder suspect who must use an alias and limit his walking to dark streets, Dinah's death changes the flow of the action. Cawelti has yoked Op's new identity as a fugitive to changes in narrative structure:

> Hammett shifts the narrative focus from the Op as hunter to the Op as hunted. Instead of manipulator of forces and puppet-master of violence, the Op himself becomes a wanted man. . . . Such a shift is necessary to resolve the moral ambiguities of the Op's role. . . . Hammett must somehow pull his hero out of the moral dilemma created by his immersion in violence.[4]

Op's next job is to find a connection. In order to clear himself, he has to connect Dinah's death to four love letters stolen from her apartment the night she died and later found in the pocket of a freshly murdered attorney. To his surprise, the letters came from his client, Elihu Willsson. Donald never had an affaire with Dinah. Op rushes to Elihu's home, even though it is four o'clock in the morning. Elihu's role in his son's death deepens, since the lawyer Elihu hired to recover the letters may have killed Dinah while carrying out his job. Op doesn't want to incriminate the old man, though; having lost a son and a lover inside of a week, Elihu has already suffered enough. But Op doesn't want to let him off too easily, either. Now that all of his rivals have killed each other off, owing to the peace conference, the self-styled old pirate again controls Personville. What Op wants is that he get the governor's help in bringing order to the broken, exhausted city. He wants order badly enough to blackmail for it. If Elihu doesn't reorganize the mayor's office and the police department for a start, Op will publish the letters he wrote Dinah. Elihu sneers at the threat. Nor does Op want any other response in his deepest heart. He has been appealing silently to Elihu's honor and civic pride. In response to Elihu's "Publish them and be damned!" he gives up the letters and starts to leave the room. Elihu responds in kind by ignoring them. Op's silent appeal has worked; Donald's death will take on a meaning and a purpose. In what is perhaps the book's only bright moment, coming, suitably at dawn, the two men realize that they trust each other.

In keeping with the book's costive spirit, this brightness fades, as the action plays itself out in the drabness of a disused warehouse located on the fringe of town. A local thug who has only made two or three brief appearances in the action admits having killed both "Whisper" Thaler and Dinah. Then he dies of gunshot wounds. The meaning of his death? Artistically, Reno Starkey's death makes little impact because of Reno's minor role in the plot; his first appearance, in fact, following his release from jail, could be lifted from the novel without affecting plot or idea, as could his second, where he is but one of many gangsters attending the peace conference. On the other hand, his death augurs well for Personville, since the new town fathers will have one less crook tempting them with bribery and graft. The augury isn't meant to carry much force. Any happy ending imposed on *Red Harvest* would have played the work false, especially its rough, rowdy setting. Both the depravity running through *Red Harvest* and the angry vision behind it rule out happy endings.

II

Op changes more in *Red Harvest* than in any other work. In the early going, he's the complete professional—playing no wild hunches, protecting his firm, and giving away nothing in his exchanges with witnesses and client. With typical caution, he tells Chief Noonan, when asked to name Donald Willsson's killer, "I'm no good at guessing, especially when I haven't the facts." The facts come to him, though, because he knows how and where to dig for them. He also handles people well—Dinah, who gives him free information; Robert Albury, who supplies the clues Op needs to fasten Donald's murder on him; old Elihu, who thinks enough of him to pay him $10,000 to clean up Personville. A believer in plain talk, Op rejects both Elihu's man talk and his bogus appeal to social conscience:

> "I want a man to clean this pig-sty of a Poisonville for me, to smoke out the rats, little and big. It's a man's job. Are you a man?"
>
> "What's the use of getting poetic about it?" I growled. "If you've got a fairly honest piece of work to be done in my line, and you want to pay a decent price, maybe I'll take it on. But a lot of foolishness about smoking out rats and pig-pens doesn't mean anything to me."

Later, a grifter who comes to his hotel room offering to kill (the already dead) Chief Noonan for money winds up offering Op money to stay quiet. This, he rejects, as he does all bribes, bonuses, and rewards. Nor does he indulge false heroics. Realizing that fighting crime in Personville goes beyond the power of any single crime-fighter, he wires home for help. No wonder he is told, after spending less than a week in Personville, "There's no man in Personville that's got a voice big enough to talk you down."

But where Op can resist the temptations posed by easy money and male bravado, he falls prey to revenge. In his zeal to get back at Noonan for trying to kill him, he forgets to report daily to the home office, as required; he violates both company policy and civil law by dabbling in murder; he alienates his two aides from San Francisco, at least one of whom believes him Dinah's murderer. His moral degeneration is already well advanced by Chapter 15, where he says of his firm, "It's right enough for the Agency to have rules and regulations, but when you're out on a job you've got to do it the best way you can. And anybody that brings any ethics to Poisonville is going to get them all rusty. A report is no place for dirty details, anyway." Not content to bend rules, he soon begins breaking them. Thompson likens his contamination to that of the hand which becomes defiled by the pitch it has touched: "The Op has vowed to clean up a community, to act as a scourge, and we approve. Yet to accomplish the job he has had to employ the corrupt means of that world. In so doing, he has become . . . soiled."[5]

The corrupt means he has adopted are those of the traitor. Betrayal is a fact of daily life in **Red Harvest.** No relationship is immune to it; as Op proves, nobody can rise above it. "Every character," says André Gide, "is trying to deceive all the others and . . . the truth slowly becomes visible through a fog of deception."[6] Betrayal comes easily to Op, as do its uses. By making sure that the boxer "Whisper" Thaler has backed will lose, he sells out the sworn enemy of Chief Noonan, his own would-be killer. Then he turns Thaler over to Noonan because he believes Thaler killed Noonan's brother and deserves to be punished. In the next chapter, though, he helps spring Thaler from jail. He never says whether he already knew of Thaler's innocence when he set up his arrest. In a sense, it doesn't matter; justice isn't at stake. Op wants to confuse Personville's underworld, a job which includes rattling the police, but not vindicating a non-existent moral law. In the process of unnerving criminals and crooked cops, though, he also disorients himself. For most of the second half of the novel, he belongs nowhere—serving neither justice nor crime. The moral world of the loner offers little comfort or hope. The purpose he has been working for has become smudged by the means he has adopted; all is drab and annihilating. The Op of **Red Harvest** is sad and weary, haunted and self-alienated; to do his job, he has had to sacrifice both his professional and personal standards. The novel's last paragraph restores him, the self-betrayed, to the Continental, which will expose him to more lying, cheating, stealing, and killing: "I might just as well have saved the labor and sweat I had put into trying to make my reports harmless. They didn't fool the Old Man. He gave me merry hell."

Responsibility to the Continental should have stopped him from playing the footloose justicer of cowboy fiction who cleans up a troubled town. He returns to the city to be savaged by his chief and then sent out on a new case. His restoration to the brotherhood of detectives is costive, indeed. He has lost the trust of his colleagues. Both he and the Old Man know he had done wrong. But to what end? His efforts in Personville, undertaken at great moral cost to himself, have reaped dubious rewards. As the several aliases he uses during the action imply, he has grown less sure both of himself and the values his firm protects. Perhaps he has lost the moral fiber needed to beat back moral contamination. Any sleuth who goes "blood-simple" so quickly may

well doubt his mettle. Although not legally guilty, he has accepted moral blame for much of the bloodshed in Personville, especially Dinah's death.

Op's two laudanum dreams, Freudian fusions of memory, invention, and repression, describe the psyche of a man whose options are running out quickly. The dreams mirror each other. One deals with a man, the other with a woman. A chase is featured in each, one extended and one brief, one horizontal, across the land, and one vertical, to the top of a tall building. But whereas the Op searches for the woman in many cities over a long span of time, his pursuit of the man is limited to part of a Sunday morning. Both dreams end badly. Following the man to a high roof, Op loses his balance and falls to the plaza far below, his hand squeezing the man's small head. His search for the veiled woman ends less catastrophically. Worn out by his fruitless quest, he pauses to rest in a hotel lobby. Suddenly the woman comes into the lobby, marches over to him, and begins kissing him while a crowd of onlookers laugh mockingly. Any moral lesson that can be teased out of these two dreams refers more generally to the Op's stay in Personville than to his part, real or imagined, in Dinah's murder. Why bother to destroy your enemy if you destroy yourself in the process? What good is love if it ends in mockery? These questions pervade the dreams, the egg-like head of Op's victim invoking birth as strongly as the veil worn by the woman invokes death. Yet the dreams reject this symbolism while calling it forth; nearness to the widow-like veil makes for a new start, while union with the symbolic egg brings death. Reaching your goals can either embarrass you or kill you dead, the dreams suggest. Getting what you want can be worse than being denied because the prizes you strive for contain hidden dangers. These flare out when least expected; the woman Op has been seeking materializes unbidden, unannounced, and, as it turns out, unwanted. Op will learn that the satisfaction of desire kills desire and, along with it, maims the spirit. Furthermore, the grief that comes from reaching one's goals touches others. Hunter and hunted die together in Op's second dream. Having played the hunter to this point, he will soon take on the role of the hunted. Not accidentally, he wakes up to find a corpse within arm's reach, literally his own arm. Just as Marx insisted that quantitative changes lead to qualitative ones, so does Hammett show dreams edging into and overtaking consciousness.

The two dreams tone down the novel's extroversion, relating, as had been said, psychic and physical reality. They also portray the futility of goal-oriented behavior in our capitalist state, where getting what you want comes less easily than wanting what you get. Finally, they put the Op near the edge psychologically—ironically, just before he must cope with the novel's worst horror, Dinah's death. No wonder both his words and his deeds have a mechanical quality after he wakes up.

Unfortunately, he joins the walking dead for nothing. The vision put forth by *Red Harvest* is darker than that of **"Corkscrew"** or **"Nightmare Town."** Unlike Steve Threefall in **"Nightmare Town,"** he loses the girl; as has been seen, he even suspects himself of having killed her. What is more, Poisonville's future is doubtful. Though "developing into a sweet-smelling and thornless bed of roses," it may soon fester into the weedpatch of corruption it was before Op's arrival. For one thing, it has no society or morality, no ordinary peaceloving, workaday middle class, no home life, churches, or schools. Life in Personville is a battlefield of greedy impulses. Sedans speed through the streets at fifty miles an hour, their passengers firing machine guns or hurling home-made bombs. "No better symbol of the end of the frontier is available than Personville," says Robert B. Parker, "a western city, springing up on the prairie in the wake of the mines."[7] To Hammett, the end of the American frontier probably meant the culmination, or self-fulfillment, of life under capitalism. Brutal, cruel, and vicious, Personville could crush stronger souls than the Op. The novel wasn't written to deal the brave detective a defeat, but to show how capitalism maims and mangles the individual and also how unbridled freedom degenerates into chaos and the rule of force. "He was the first . . . to demonstrate the intimate links between organized crime and politics on all levels,"[8] says Jon Tuska of Hammett in *The Detective in Hollywood* (1978). Death is the price exacted for virtue in *Red Harvest*. Perhaps Op did well to go blood-simple; a corrupt life is better than none at all. The book's one virtuous character, Donald Willsson, dies. Even though he wasn't Dinah Brand's lover, the scatter effect of his father's illicit romance with her kills him. As in Dickens, virtue is ineffectual in *Red Harvest*; his father's letters cost Donald much more than the $5000 he pays for them. The letters attest to the contagion of evil, which sometimes infects and even kills the innocent and the unknowing.

The novel's poetic structure denies renewal. Free enterprise kills freedom; nobody is more badgered than Personville's criminal set, where self-reliance knows no bounds. Dawn, the time for fresh starts, fights fresh starts. Sunlight can't probe Personville's sooty cloud cover or scarred mountains. The police raid Thaler's gambling casino in Chapter 6 at dawn; the only brightness flickering over the sullen, overcast morning coming from the flash given off by the firearm blasts. Perhaps the hope associated with Charles Proctor Dawn's last name inspired Elihu to hire Dawn to recover the incriminating love letters. This Dawn serves darkness. After stealing the letters, he darkens his paymaster's hopes by keeping them. Then darkness falls on him perma-

nently when he dies for his treachery. Street names sometimes convey the moral darkness that absorbs and finally crushes lawyer Dawn. Laurel Avenue, where Donald Willsson lives, represents an oasis in a scrubland of racketeers and their rowdies. The civilized values and natural growth its well-tended greenery implies (Donald's home is built inside a hedged grassplot) have no more chance in Personville than their high-minded protector, who dies before he appears in the action.

Another ironic place name is King Street, where Thaler has his office. Thaler is no king. Nobody reigns in Personville; nobody has a clear title to power and honor. When life's prizes are open to all, the ensuing scramble for them makes everyone a potential casualty. The individualist strain in America has dwarfed the individual. The smashing of due process, i.e., the curtailment of liberty in Personville, may have prompted Hammett to set part of the action in Liberty Street. Let Thompson furnish the last moral overview of the town, and to it let us add the fact that the town's most powerful man, Elihu Willsson, is sick and bedridden most of the way. Only once, at the calamitous peace conference, is he seen out of bed. Op does well to turn down his offer to become town sheriff. An effect can have no more reality than its cause. Its richest and most influential citizen a physical wreck, Personville has little chance of a bright, safe future:

> Personville does indeed seem to be a world devoid of values. The only moral spokesman in the novel is Dan Rolff, and he is suggestively diseased and impotent. . . . The only other moral protest is heard from Dick Foley, one of the Op's detective colleagues who quits the job because he suspects the Op has committed murder. But we see this, too, as an impotent protest.[9]

III

Red Harvest has won some enthusiastic praise, W.P. Kenney terming it "a significant step forward in the American detective novel" and Tuska, with the same warmth, calling it "Hammett's profound and compelling novel of universal corruption in America."[10] In view of the novel's rampant violence, this praise seems excessive. There are too many rackets and racketeers. There are too many clashes between them. Too many bullets fly; too many bombs explode; too much blood is spilled (according to William Ruehlmann, twenty-five murders take place in the novel).[11] This brutality is numbing, not exciting. No sooner are characters introduced than they die. Like *Blood Money*, *Red Harvest* moves forward by agglomeration, not internal development. This pattern doesn't suit the book, trivializing the violence growing out of New World energy by failing to link it to characters we care about. *Red Harvest* has more data than its plot can comfortably assimilate. Nobody except Op stays alive long enough to touch our hearts. A bullet speaks more persuasively than words. But the statement it makes is also final and unanswerable.

This substitution of excess for creative energy stems from the Marxist impulse behind *Red Harvest.* The belief that capitalism destroys character and that the creed of rugged individualism destroys individuality might explain the flatness of the people in the book; Hammett's people don't relate to each other, but to the dynamics of local mob rule. Sincere political sermonizing, though, doesn't always produce good art, especially in the novel, with its traditional commitment to individuality. Politics can't explain the worries caused by the book's first-person narration. A built-in drawback of a work like *Red Harvest* is that its narrator-sleuth sometimes seems to be holding back important information in order to divulge it when his author wants it divulged. Because Op reasons often in *Red Harvest*—naming the murderers of Donald Willsson and Tim Noonan, for instance—he leaves us behind. Only after solving these murders does he confide in us. And with good reason: to have done so beforehand would have spoiled the dramatic effect gained by his revelations. There's no solution to this technical problem other than noting that it doesn't undermine Hammett's sense of fair play: Op has seen and heard no more than the reader has when he names the two murderers. But he works alone; his voice controls the action; this voice, which also controls our responses, doesn't always chime with his thoughts.

What we do hear, though, shows rare technical control, based on Hammett's refusal to give Op privileged information he can use to solve the book's first two murders. Unity both of tone and effect comes from the greed that drives all the characters—greed for power, money, and, in the Op's case, revenge. Its episodic structure doesn't disjoint the novel, Hammett controlling the rhythm of shifting loyalties as treaties form and break in Personville's criminal set. As has been seen, even Op gets drawn into the maneuvering and becomes stained by it. Hammett makes us question the depth of this stain. Does guilty self-knowledge keep the Op from staying in Personville as sheriff? Does he suspect that his moral taint will stop him from serving effectively? Perhaps Personville deserves a sheriff with more moral stamina and self-confidence. Though its citizens have little depth, they span a broad range. Hardly anybody is exhausted by his criminal impulses. Personal motives will sometimes crowd out political or financial ones, causing a good deal of inward suffering. To make Personville more realistic, Hammett includes several sorts of family relationships. Tim Noonan was having an affaire with the wife of Bob MacSwain, his murderer. Now the police chief wants to punish his brother's killer. Elihu Willsson claims his daughter-in-law killed

Donald, whose death had nothing to do with his civic reforming or his father's roughneck politics. Finally, Dinah Brand's live-in relationship with her ward, or housemate, the tubercular Dan Rolff, refers in no way to the scramble for money and power.

The enriched portrayal of human purpose created by these personal motives gains firmness from narrative structure. Hammett needs his large cast of criminal characters to convey the pervasiveness of the crime that has gripped Personville and, by extension, America. Yet he also uses the family to fend off narrative sprawl. Thus Donald's secretary is the daughter of Elihu's secretary, and Robert Albury's sister moves to Hurricane Street to watch Dinah after Robert admits having murdered Donald. Further tightening of the plot comes from Hammett's treatment of the numerous deaths. Though not restrained, *Red Harvest* could spatter the reader with more blood than it does. Given the premise that our national heritage rests on violence, the novel's gunplay and bomb-throwing can't offend anybody. But it would have raised hackles if many of the important murders—Donald's, Noonan's, Dinah's, Rolff's, and Thaler's—didn't take place out of view. No culture can be portrayed artistically if its values aren't dramatized. In *Red Harvest,* Hammett describes the pioneer creed of the right to bear arms while merely reporting the death-by-arms of his main characters. The book is violent but not spectacular or cheap.

If Hammett's good judgment doesn't redeem the novel, it nonetheless sets forth the problems faced in portraying a violent society. *Red Harvest* would be false and dishonest without its clamor, frenzied movement, and murders; Hammett barrages us with images of brutality to convey the mad, wild sensation of American city life during Prohibition. His ability to distance the brutality betokens the control and moral balance that divides art from harangue.

Notes

1. [Joe Gores, *Hammett* (New York: Ballantine, 1976)], p. 111.

2. [George J. Thompson, "The Problem of Moral Vision in Dashiell Hammett's Detective Novels," Diss., University of Connecticut, 1971], p. 7.

3. *Ibid.,* pp. 36-7.

4. [John G. Cawelti, *Adventure, Mystery, and Romance* (Chicago: University of Chicago, 1976)], pp. 171-2.

5. Thompson, pp. 38-9.

6. André Gide, "An Imaginary Interview," trans., Malcolm Cowley, *New Republic,* 7 February 1944, p. 186.

7. Robert B. Parker, "The Violent Hero, Wilderness Heritage and Urban Reality," Diss., Boston University, 1971, p. 95.

8. Jon Tuska, *The Detective in Hollywood* (Garden City, N.Y.: Doubleday, 1978), p. 159.

9. Thompson, pp. 20-1.

10. [William Patrick Kenney, "The Dashiell Hammett Tradition and the Modern Detective Novel," Diss., University of Michigan, 1964], p. 103; Tuska, p. 168.

11. [William Ruehlmann, *Saint with a Gun: The Unlawful American Private Eye* (New York: New York University, 1974)], p. 71.

Edward Margolies (essay date 1982)

SOURCE: Margolies, Edward. "Dashiell Hammett: Success as Failure." In *Which Way Did He Go?: The Private Eye in Dashiell Hammett, Raymond Chandler, Chester Himes, and Ross Macdonald*, pp. 17-31. New York: Holmes & Meier Publishers, 1982.

[*In the following excerpt, Margolies posits that one of Hammett's major contributions to the detective novel genre was making the detection process appear realistic.*]

For aficionados, Dashiell Hammett is the father of all hardboiled detectives. Masters of the genre like Raymond Chandler, Ross MacDonald, and Chester Himes pay him homage as do any number of present-day imitators. But Hammett owed something of his style and a good deal of the mythology of the private detective to one of his "pulp" predecessors, Caroll John Daly. Moreover, during the most productive years of his career, he was bound by the dictates of his editors at *Black Mask* who imposed formulas on their authors that demanded a rigorous prose style, "realistic" characters, and plenty of action. Within these limits Hammett's reputation is deserved. He wrote better than most, his narratives are more inventive, and he possessed a sense of humor. There were, however, occasions when he verged on self-parody, and toward the end of his career he had evidently begun to feel uncomfortable with his tough heroes who were cynical, unswervingly devoted to their jobs, amoral, courageous, and seemingly impervious to emotions.

Perhaps he had come to find the genre too restricting. Some of his later pieces attempt to break with formula. Shortly after the publication of his fourth novel (*The Glass Key,* 1931), Hammett wrote Lillian Hellman that he had begun work on yet another detective novel and thought, prophetically, that it would be his last. *The*

Thin Man, published in 1934, was not only Hammett's last detective novel, it was also the last major fiction he would write. Aside from a comic strip he presumably coauthored with Alex Raymond (**"Secret Agent X-9"**), a few radio scripts in the 1940s and 1950s based mainly on characters of his early fiction, and periodic journeys to Hollywood to "doctor" or to suggest stories for screenplays, Hammett's creative years had come to an end. Some time around the mid-1950s he wrote a thinly disguised autobiographical fragment, *Tulip* (published posthumously), in which the main character, Pop, a former detective story author, cries out: "Why can't I write?" Hammett died in January 1961.

Hammett's fallow years are their own mystery—especially when one contrasts them to his most fertile period, 1927 to 1930, during which he produced four novels and over seventy short stories. Perhaps his silence had something to do with the recharged social consciousness of the 1930s when a man's individual actions and his means of earning a living were reckoned to have public consequences. Heretofore Hammett's private eyes had happily served robber barons and the disagreeable rich who were willing to pay for their services. Their only principles were the standards of their profession. They could not be bribed or deterred from their obligations (as they saw them) by appeals to friendship, sentimentality, sex, or even romantic love. Like Hammett himself in his Pinkerton years, they took an almost primitive pleasure in the manhunt and the successful pursuit of criminals. They rarely questioned the morality of their profession or its political or social consequences. For instance, in one short story, **"This King Business"** (1928), Hammett's Continental Op helps to undermine a fragile Baltic republic in order to save the playboy son of his client. Such behavior on the part of Hammett's twenties heroes must have seemed the height of social irresponsibility during the early years of the Depression. In his last novel, his protagonist is a former detective, now a member of the business autocracy. As a nonprofessional he need only take a dilettantish interest in solving the crime and as a rich man he is of course pursuing his class interests in tracking down the murderer of another rich man. (Ironically, Hammett's book reviews of the late 1920s inveighed against an earlier dilettante detective, S. S. Van Dine's Philo Vance, who casually solved crimes involving persons far removed from poverty.) In *The Thin Man,* there are no characters who express the interests of the poor (mainly physical survival), except the criminals of the underworld.

Hammett's Marxism in the 1930s may also have contributed to his creative paralysis. Other writers of the Depression years evaded ideological contradictions by having their detectives criticize the rich while serving them, but Hammett did not rationalize in this fashion. The detective genre in part upholds established values by visiting fantasy punishment on its violators. If one no longer believes, what does one do? Early in their relationship, Hammett admitted to Lilliam Hellman that he had been a strikebreaker for the Pinkertons and implied he quit the detective business because an official of Anaconda Copper had asked him to kill a union organizer. Hammett refused but learned later that the organizer had been lynched anyway. One can only conjecture how Hammett reacted. Were hunter and hunted cut from the same cloth? So long as he managed to keep polarities in balance, Hammett would remain a detective. When he could not, he became a writer. The same sort of questions must have plagued him as a writer. By giving himself over to ideological commitments, he may have resolved his doubts, but in so doing he probably relinquished the kind of tensions his work required.

Some of these tensions are demonstrated in tales in which his heroes express skepticism about ever discovering truth or order. Their view of society as being inherently corrupt and unknowable is not affectation; society is ultimately a metaphor of their universe. In order to survive they betray, deceive, and kill, but the truths they ferret out very often resemble the lies they have uncovered. When Hammett reached out in these directions, he appears to be challenging formula. But whether or not he succeeded is another question.

. . . . .

Hammett's tough-guy fiction represents the marriage of two kinds of popular writing that had been developing in America since the nineteenth century: the novel of detection derived from Poe, and the western adventure derived from James Fenimore Cooper. The Poe-like puzzle element requiring some kind of intellectual effort on the part of the detective is not altogether absent in Hammett's stories, but it gives way more often than not to suspenseful episodic adventures replete with violence and danger to the hero. One of Hammett's contributions to the genre is that he rendered popular adventure more plausible by making the detection seem realistic—mental acuteness is preceded by solid plodding investigation. In **"The Girl With The Silver Eyes"** (1924), for example, the Op tracks down a missing girl by checking out bank statements, taxi trip records, railroad ticket purchases, and even weather reports. Without question Hammett brought his professional experience to bear on this kind of fiction, but he was also one of the rare pulp writers capable of conveying a feeling for character. It was not simply that he gave murder back to real murderers (to paraphrase Raymond Chandler), but he gave them style, speech, and dress. Their brutality and avarice were a part of their natures and not something grafted onto dull people to surprise the reader. Hammett had a good ear for underworld jargon.

I went gunning for Holy Joe. I knew him but didn't know where he jungled up, and didn't find out till yesterday. You was there when I came. You know about that. I had picked up a boiler and parked it over on Turk Street, for the getaway. When I got back to it, there was a copper standing close to it. I figured he might have spotted it as a hot one and was waiting to see who came for it, so I let it alone, and caught a streetcar instead, and cut for the yards. Down there I ran into a whole flock of hammer and saws and had to go overboard in China Basin. . . ."

["**Flypaper,**" 1929]

But Hammett was also proficient in rendering other people besides hoodlums. Consider, for example, the fat man, Gutman, an obviously educated mercantile type desperately anxious to possess a carved bird known as the Maltese Falcon. Hammett's description reads like Dickens.

The fat man was flabbily fat with bulbous pink cheeks and lips and chins and neck, with a great soft egg of a belly that was all his torso, and pendant cones for arms and legs. As he advanced to meet Spade all his bulbs rose and shook and fell separately with each step, in the manner of clustered soap bubbles not yet released from the pipe through which they had been blown. His eyes, made small by fat puffs around them, were dark and sleek. Dark ringlets thinly covered his broad scalp. He wore a black cutaway coat, black vest, black satin Ascot tie holding a pinkish pearl, striped grey worsted trousers, and patent-leather shoes. His voice was a throaty purr. "Ah, Mr. Spade," he said with enthusiasm and held out a hand like a fat pink star.

When the detective, Sam Spade, asks him whether he wants to talk about the bird, Gutman responds with a kind of Dickensian exuberance.

"Will we?" he asked and, "We will," he replied. His pink face was shiny with delight. "You're the man for me, sir, a man cut along my own lines. No beating about the bush, but right to the point. 'Will we talk about the black bird?' We will. I like that, sir. I like that way of doing business. Let us talk about the black bird by all means. . . ."

Unfortunately Hammett was also capable of employing the most simple-minded racial stereotypes. The bad Indians of the popular westerns often become the bad Africans, Negroes, homosexuals, and Orientals in Hammett's mythology.

The Chinese are a thorough people; if any one of them carries a gun at all, he usually carries two or three or more. . . . Once more Tai ran true to racial form. When a Chinese shoots he keeps on until his gun is empty.

["**The House on Turk Street,**" 1924]

In lieu of the monosyllabic grunts or stilted rhetoric of pulp Indians, Hammett substitutes the clever, exaggerated politeness of vaudeville Chinese:

If the Terror of Evildoers will honor one of my deplorable chairs by resting his divine body on it, I can assure him the chair shall be burned afterward, so no lesser being may use it. Or will the Prince of Thief-catchers permit me to send a servant to his palace for a chair worthy of him?

["**Dead Yellow Women,**" 1925]

In *Red Harvest,* the Op has a disturbing dream of a "brown man" who becomes a symbol of elusive evil.

I was in a strange city hunting for a man I hated. I had an open knife in my pocket and meant to kill him. . . .

The streets are full and church bells are ringing. Suddenly the Op sees him.

He was a small brown man who wore an immense sombrero. He was standing on the steps of a tall building on the far side of a wide plaza, laughing at me.

The Op chases him up miles of stairs to a roof.

My hand knocked his sombrero off, and closed on his head. It was a smooth hard round head no larger than a large egg. My fingers went all the way around it. Squeezing his head in one hand, I tried to bring the knife out of my pocket with the other.

As in the dime novels and formula westerns, perpetrators of violence (and hence objects of violence) are often dark-skinned peoples who attempt to stem the westward advance of white American civilization.

Hammett's detective, like the western hero, is an outsider who feels ambivalent about the society he is defending. For him women represent society both in its ideal aspects (domesticity and civilization) and its negative side (corruption and restraint); despite his facade of detachment and devotion to duty, he may be forced to display his anger towards women overtly:

"Stop, you idiot!" I bawled at her.

Her face laughed over her shoulder at me. She walked without haste to the door, her short skirt of grey flannel shaping itself to the calf of each gray wool stockinged leg. . . .

"Adieu!" she said softly.

And I put a bullet in the calf of her left leg.

She sat down—plump! Utter surprise stretched her white face. It was too soon for pain.

I had never shot a woman before. I felt queer about it.

["**The Gutting of Couffignal,**" 1925]

Another connection between the western hero and the detective is the almost magical role each plays in purging the community of its evil members. At least two of Hammett's short stories (**"Corkscrew,"** 1925, and **"The Farewell Murder,"** 1930) and one of his novels, *Red Harvest,* take place in remote western territory into which the Op comes as a stranger; he solves crimes, and then withdraws as would any lone ranger. Neither the Hammett detective nor the westerner regards human behavior as complicated. Most bad men and criminals act out of simple motives—avarice, fear, lust, or power. Elaborate webs of psychoanalytical theory are simply shrouds for the obvious. In *The Dain Curse,* the villain, an author who is in some respects the Op's (and Hammett's) alter ego, writes an article for the *Psychopathological Review* "condemning the hypothesis of an unconscious or subconscious mind as a snare and a delusion, a pitfall for the unwary and a set of false whiskers for the charlatan." Later the Op explains a murderer's violence as simply "dislike for being thwarted, spitefulness when trapped."

But if they are behaviorists, Hammett's characters are also idealists in their fashion. In the absence of anything else to believe in, the detectives believe in their jobs to which they gladly sacrifice themselves and even their lovers.

I pass up about twenty-five or thirty thousand of honest gain because I like being a detective, like the work. And liking work makes you want to do it as well as you can. Otherwise there'd be no sense to it. That's the fix I'm in. I don't know anything else, don't enjoy anything else. . . . You think I'm a man and you're a woman. That's wrong. I'm a manhunter and you're something that has been running in front of me. There's nothing human about it.

["**The Gutting of Couffignal**"]

Even Hammett's nondetective hero, Ned Beaumont of *The Glass Key,* an aide to a city machine boss, has created for himself a sense of identity that no amount of brutal beatings can make him relinquish. Hammett's villains are also possessed. The author-villain Fitzstephan of *The Dain Curse* weaves elaborate criminal plots not for material gain, but for the transcendent pleasures he derives from seeing them fulfilled. The evil seekers of *The Maltese Falcon* appear transported beyond mere greed; for them the Falcon is an icon they pursue as zealously as any medieval knight pursued the grail. What ultimately motivates them defies rational explanation. Many of Hammett's possessed and obsessed characters ring truer than his earth-bound materialists or ethnic stereotypes.

Hammett's humor is often larger than life and so rises above the level of the commonplace. Consider, for example, the tall-tale quality of the following collection of corpses the Op has stumbled upon.

There was the Dis-and-Dat Kid, who had crushed out of Leavenworth only two months before; Sheeny Holmes; Snohomish Shitey, supposed to have died a hero in France in 1919; L. A. Slim, from Denver, sockless and underwear-less as usual, with a thousand-dollar bill sewed in each shoulder of his coat; Spider Girrucci wearing a steel-mesh vest under his shirt and a scar from crown to chin where his brother had carved him years ago; Old Pete Best, once a congressman; Nigger Vojan, who once won $175,000 in a Chicago crap game—*Abracadabra* tattooed on him in three places; Alphabet Shorty McCoy; Tom Brooks, Alphabet Shorty's brother-in-law, who invented the Richmond razzle-dazzle and bought three hotels with the profits; Red Cudahy, who stuck up a Union Pacific train in 1924; Denny Burke; Bull McGonickle, still pale from fifteen years in Joliet; Toby the Lugs, Bull's running-mate, who used to brag about picking President Wilson's pocket in a Washington vaudeville theater; and Paddy the Mex.

["**The Big Knockover,**" 1927]

Hammett was also capable of rendering both the urban wisecrack ("She's a tough little job who probably was fired for dropping her chewing gum in the soup the last place she worked") and the banter of sophisticates:

"Whatever you're giving me [for Christmas]," she said, "I hope I don't like it."

"You'll have to keep them anyway because the man at the Aquarium said he positively cannot take them back. He said they'd already bitten the tails off the—"

[*The Thin Man*]

But Hammett is at his best when he draws together a sense of western irreverence with laconic city cynicism.

I first heard Personville called Poisonville by a red-haired mucker named Hickey Dewey in the Big Ship in Butte. He also called his shirt a shoit. I didn't think anything of what he had done to the city's name. Later I heard men who could manage their r's give it the same pronunciation. I still didn't see anything in it but the meaningless sort of humor that used to make richardsnary the thieves' word for dictionary. A few years later I went to Personville and learned better.

[*Red Harvest*]

Red Harvest is usually considered Hammett's first full length work. Set in a remote Montana mining town, the novel seems to partake of the raw western energy of its background. It is structured episodically (betraying its magazine origins once or twice), but it is always swift moving and violent, piling up at least thirty-five corpses. In some ways it modifies Daly's *Black Mask* formula. The Op, an employee of the Continental Detective Agency, is invited to Personville by a crusading newspaper editor who is murdered the night the Op arrives. The Op first clears up the killing (it was a crime of passion) and then stays on to purge the town of its all-pervading corruption. Iago-like, he manipulates each of the criminal factions that run the city—the police, the gamblers, and bootleggers—so that each sees the other as enemy. Most of them kill one another off in wild scenes of street mayhem. **Red Harvest** is a powerful adventure, but beyond the suspense lies Hammett's night-mare vision of a society completely and irreversibly immersed in evil. As the tale draws to a close the Op tells the ruthless old capitalist who owns Personville that he will have his "city back nice and clean and ready to go to the dogs again."

Hammett's second novel, **The Dain Curse** is very different from its predecessor. There are no gangs and its criticism is directed mainly against fashionable religious cults and publicity-hungry politicians. The book is divided into three loosely related novellas, each of which provides the Op with several murders to solve and a suffering heroine, Gabrielle Legge, to comfort. She fears she is cursed but needless to say she is not, for the Op discovers the external source of her trouble in the final pages. The least successful of the Hammett works, it contains many hackneyed elements: missing diamonds, missing servants, superstitious mulattoes, family curses, long-lost relatives suddenly reappearing, "ghosts," and even an escape from a desert island. The novel undoubtedly represents an attempt to break away from the hardboiled formula, but in so doing it stumbles onto a nest of romantic cliches.

What is most interesting about **The Dain Curse** is the Op's vision of an illusory universe. Each of the puzzles he confronts suggests a variety of solutions. The Op's antagonists offer up any number of false answers but he is not deceived. Yet the answers the Op asks us to believe are really no more plausible than the ones he has rejected. Further, each of his solutions leads to a deeper, more mysterious puzzle. The truth can scarcely ever be known—unless one assumes faith in the always skeptical Op.

The prime liars in Hammett's writings are women and the prime liar of all Hammett's women is Brigid O'Shaugnessy of **The Maltese Falcon.** She does not succeed in deceiving Sam Spade, Hammett's new detective hero, because liars depend on believers and Sam believes only in his job. He signals his skepticism early in the novel when he tells Brigid a story about a respectable businessman, Flitcraft, who had figured in one of his investigations. Flitcraft had been a believer in an orderly universe until one day a loose beam from an office building very nearly felled him on the sidewalk below. Flitcraft told Spade he felt as if "somebody had taken the lid off life and let him look at the works." He suddenly realized that all his assumptions about an ordered rational existence were delusions. Flitcraft therefore determined that he too would live in an arbitrary and random fashion, and he abandoned his wife and children in the process. But after a while, he unconsciously slipped back into another smug bourgeois life pattern. Spade, however, does not allow himself such an indulgence. He knows life is unpredictable and he is fearless because he has adjusted himself to the fact that death is omnipresent, which gives him great power over others who take being alive too seriously.

Despite its pulp origins, *The Maltese Falcon* reads like a traditional, well-made novel. There are fewer characters than in Hammett's other works and the plot is more centered, dealing mainly with the pursuit of the murderer of Sam's partner and the activities of an international gang of jewel thieves intent on acquiring a jeweled bird. Their account of its dismal history, reaching back centuries, reads like a metaphor of Western avarice. Fittingly, when the bird is recovered they find it is false—a fitting symbol of what its pursuers have become—predatory and perfidious. Perhaps, too, the falcon has a sadder meaning. Ross Macdonald, who named his hero, Lew Archer, after Sam Spade's murdered partner, suggests that the bird may stand "for the Holy Ghost itself, or for its absence."

The novel attempts to break with the detective formula in other ways as well. Killings take place offstage, de-emphasizing the violence, and the tale is told in the third person, unlike the stories the Op tells about himself. Sam Spade is given more of an individual existence than the Op. We see Sam's rooms, the clothes he wears, and his over-all appearance—tall, lean, blonde, and "saturnine," not unlike pictures of the young Hammett. Sam even takes Brigid to bed—a violation of the Op's principles, but unlike the Op, Spade is something of a lady's man—and on one occasion he actually gets angry when a policeman knocks him about a bit. But beneath these superficial differences, Sam possesses the same ruthless character as the Op. He is as unmoved by the threats of killers as he is by the importunities of women. Thus he can surrender Brigid to the police because, even though he loves her, his code comes first.

In Hammett's next novel, *The Glass Key,* the man-woman stuff is under better control although one is left wondering why at the end of the book the hero and a young woman decide to pack off together when they hardly know one another. Indeed why the hero does any number of things is nearly as much a puzzle as the actions of the criminal characters. The narrative revolves around Ned Beaumont, an aide and friend to a city machine boss, Paul Madvig. Madvig is threatened by a rival political organization financed by the city's leading bootlegger. He is also threatened by the scandal of an unsolved murder of a senator's son, which is doubly embarrassing because Madvig wants to marry the senator's daughter. In the course of the tale Ned Beaumont successfully confronts and defeats the opposition—like the Op, he lies, betrays, and goads his enemies to suicide and shootouts—and eventually uncovers the murderer, the senator himself. But in so doing he is brutally beaten and finds he cannot even trust his friend. In the end he severs his ties with Madvig and goes off with his girl.

One of the difficulties with the novel is that its third-person narration obscures what Ned thinks or feels. We are not sure why Ned takes his bloody beatings: Is it because of his loyalties to Madvig or because his pride is injured? He has evidently fashioned a sense of himself that others cannot touch, but we are not sure what that is. Nor do we know what he did in the past or where he will go in the future. At one juncture he appears ready to sell out Madvig—would he have?—and at another to fight with Madvig over what seems a trivial difference. Did Beaumont stage the fight to delude the enemy? The questions are never adequately answered because Hammett seldom allows us to penetrate Beaumont's shell. More the pity, since Hammett apparently intended to give a fuller portrayal of Beaumont than any of his previous heroes. He drinks considerably, he is extremely anxious about his luck (so much so that he pursues a welshing bookie to New York), and he appears to have an intense relationship with Madvig. Hammett gives him vulnerabilities that suggest inner turmoil, but we only see these from the outside.

The novel is rich in the atmosphere of the "clubhouse" where dubious businessmen, machine bosses, elected officials, and their seedier hangers-on make sordid deals, dividing and redividing power and loot. Here Hammett reveals a sure feel for the "class" psychology of some of his characters. For example, it is clear from the start that Madvig—of uncertain ethnic origin—is fascinated by the aristocratic aura that seems to him to envelop the senator and his daughter. The senator is as crooked as everyone else, but the Henrys' "respectability" and social standing blind the otherwise worldly, ambitious city boss. One wonders whether Hammett was thinking of Fitzgerald's Gatsby when he drew Madvig; like Gatsby, Madvig is caught up in a dying American dream. His success assures his failure—which might read as an epitaph for Hammett.

Some time before the book publication of *The Glass Key,* Hammett had begun work on another hardboiled novel. He evidently changed his mind about it on several occasions because *The Thin Man* (1933) is a far cry from the somber work he had begun a couple of years before. That Hammett had by now achieved some kind of respectability may be adduced from the fact that it was first serialized in the mass circulation *Redbook.* A concession Hammett evidently made to his new readership was to agree to the removal of the word "erection" which his hero may or may not have had while wrestling with one of the women in the novel. In the interests of art, presumably, the word was returned to the hard cover text.

The novel tells about the former detective, Nick Charles, and his wife Nora, of San Francisco, who are in New York for what appears to be an alcoholic vacation. Nick, who is now basking in his wife's wealth, finds himself enmeshed in an investigation of a missing inventor who had once been a client. Drawing on some of his old detective talents as well as his knowledge of the inventor's family and friends, he proceeds to solve the mystery. But Nick is no longer the hardboiled detective (if ever he had been). Instead he is slick and witty and good at repartee—which suggests Hammett's work at Hollywood studios could not have been a total loss. Nick's wife, Nora, said to have been modelled on Lillian Hellman, is equally witty and intelligent. Underlying the bright surface of *The Thin Man* prose is a comedy of manners about New York's upper-middle drinking classes near the end of Prohibition. Most of them were unhappy. The novel was a huge success and should have provided Hammett the wherewithal to write the "serious" book he had always promised himself he would do.

Which returns us once more to Hammett's creative hiatus after *The Thin Man.* Like the alcoholic Nick, he appears to have given up on the things he did best. The fierce vigor was gone and the fame and attention would now be Lillian Hellman's. Did he will this or did his successes render him impotent? Had he taken prizes his heroes would have scorned? There are mysteries about Hammett, one feels, that neither the Op nor Sam Spade would have been able to solve.

Bibliography

Red Harvest. New York: Alfred A. Knopf, 1929.

The Dain Curse. New York: Alfred A. Knopf, 1929.

The Maltese Falcon. New York: Alfred A. Knopf, 1930.

The Glass Key. New York: Alfred A. Knopf, 1931.

The Thin Man. New York: Alfred A. Knopf, 1934.

The Big Knockover, Selected Stories and Short Novels, Edited and with an introduction by Lillian Hellman. New York: Random House, 1966. Reprinted in Vintage Books Edition, 1972.

The Continental Op, Edited and with an introduction by Steven Marcus. New York: Vintage Books, 1974. Reprinted in Vintage Books Edition, 1975.

William Marling (essay date 1983)

SOURCE: Marling, William. "The Falcon and The Key." In *Dashiell Hammett,* pp. 70-98. Boston: Twayne Publishers, 1983.

[*In the following essay, Marling appraises the formal construction, character development, and leading thematic concerns of* The Maltese Falcon *and* The Glass Key.]

The Maltese Falcon

In his 1934 introduction to *The Maltese Falcon* Dashiell Hammett wrote:

If this book had been written with the help of an outline or notes or even a clearly defined plot-idea in my head I might now be able to say how it came to be written and why it took the shape it did, but all I can remember about its invention is that somewhere I had read of the peculiar rental agreement between Charles V and the Order of the Hospital of Saint John of Jerusalem, that in a short story called "The Whosis Kid" I had failed to make the most of a situation I liked, that in another called "The Gutting of Couffignal" I had been equally fortunate with an equally promising denouement, and that I thought I might have better luck with these two failures if I combined them with the Maltese lease in a longer story.

The hallmark of the best modern American novelists has been an ability to recognize in the themes and plots of early work those conflicts that can sustain even greater elaboration. Call it a sieving or a critical eye, in 1928 Dashiell Hammett had it.

Hammett had written two novels in two years, had rewritten his old stories, and he claimed to have 250,000 words—an amount equal to half of the Bible—available for publication. This work was at once recapitulative and boldly innovative. In 1925, before he wrote **"The Big Knockover"** and **"$106,000 Blood Money"** to train up to the length of the novel, he had written two stories that were good but not quite finished. In **"The Whosis Kid"** most of the action took place in the apartment of Inés Almad, an alluring foreigner who fled with the loot from a robbery. The Op was in her apartment when three former partners showed up. The "situation" that Hammett liked was the "apartment drama," in which the rising action was heightened by the physically confining space and mutual hostility of the characters. The tension built extraordinarily well while it was submerged in the dialogue, but the climax had been an ineffectual spate of bullets.

Hammett had known the advantage of tempting the hero's code with a beautiful woman since **"The Girl with the Silver Eyes."** But in **"The Gutting of Couffignal"** he attempted to increase the tension by making the Op's surrender circumstantially plausible. It failed. The Op seemed so uninvolved with the temptress that he sacrificed little in adhering to his code. In *The Maltese Falcon* Hammett clarified the archetypal traits of this femme fatale—beauty, mutability, duplicity—and involved the detective with her romantically from the first to the last chapter.

The Maltese Falcon is also given impetus by Hammett's elaborations on "classical" mystery formulas and by the reality/illusion debate that he explored in *The Dain Curse.* The use of violence to move the plot is much reduced; there are three murders, only one of them onstage. There are, however, ten important deceptions and reversals, and the detective himself is a deceiver, whose code takes shape from a parable about self-deception at the novel's core.

The detective is a new incarnation. In *The Dain Curse* Hammett seemed stumped about his hero's evolution and fell back on pure chivalric code. The hero of *The Maltese Falcon* recurs to the hero of *Red Harvest* in some traits, but in a more important way, as Hammett noted, he is an idealized vision of independence and self-reliance:

> Spade had no original. He is a dream man in the sense that he is what most of the private detectives I worked with would like to have been and what quite a few of them in their cockier moments thought they approached. For your private detective does not—or did not ten years ago when he was my colleague—want to be an erudite solver of riddles in the Sherlock Holmes manner; he wants to be a hard and shifty fellow, able to take care of himself in any situation, able to get the best of anybody he comes in contact with, whether criminal, innocent by-stander or client.[1]

Sam Spade is the hero who looks "rather pleasantly like a blond satan." From jaw to widow's peak, his face repeats a *V* motif. He is slope-shouldered, compact, and muscular, so that mien and physique together suggest an extroverted, physical man. His partner Miles Archer is a similar but less intelligent type. Their office is managed by Effie Perrine, a "lanky, sunburned girl" with a "shiny boyish face," who became Perry Mason's Della Street and every private eye's secretary afterward.

The action begins when Effie escorts into Spade's office a Miss Wonderly, really Brigid O'Shaughnessy: she asks Spade to rescue her sister from a hoodlum named Floyd Thursby, and she advances $200 for the work. Miles Archer walks in, sizes her up, and volunteers to do the job.

A 2 a.m. call from the police informs Spade that Archer has been murdered. He taxis to the scene but declines to examine the body or answer questions. "I'll bury my dead," he says. He asks Effie to call Iva Archer with the news. At home Spade is questioned by policemen Polhaus and Dundy, who have learned that he was cuckolding his partner, which makes him a suspect. They also reveal that Thursby is dead.

Miss Wonderly disappears, and has changed her name to Miss LeBlanc when Spade finds her. She only confesses her real name in the first "apartment scene," a histrionic meld of confessions, tears, and innuendos that does not fool Spade. But he agrees to help her recover a "valuable object" for an additional $500.

At the office the next day Effie ushers in Joel Cairo, who also gives Spade a retainer to help him find the object, which he identifies as the Maltese falcon. He pulls a gun on Spade, is disarmed, but repeats the trick as he leaves—all to no avail. After his contact with Cairo a man begins to shadow Spade, necessitating elaborate dodges. Brigid will not divulge details about the quest for the falcon, but, like Princess Zhukovski, offers to buy Spade's trust with her body. This disturbs Spade, who arranges a meeting between Cairo and Brigid.

Waiting for Cairo, Spade tells Brigid the story of Flitcraft. It seems like idle conversation, but it is a parable explaining, indeed forecasting, Spade's behavior. When Cairo arrives, he trades sexual insults with Brigid (he is a homosexual) until Dundy and Polhaus appear again. The police threaten to jail all three. Only Spade's brilliant improvisation, in which he persuades Cairo to play a part, prevents their arrest. Dundy again accuses Spade of Archer's murder, and punches him on the way out. Drawing on his deepest reserve of discipline, Spade refrains from striking back, but after the police and Cairo leave, he flies into a rage. The scene ends with Spade and Brigid on the way to bed, but readers are warned away from assuming paramount importance for the love interest. Spade wakes before Brigid the next morning, and searches her apartment while she sleeps.

With a clue garnered the previous night, Spade finds the man shadowing him and says he wants to see "G." When he returns to his office, Spade has a call from G., who is Casper Gutman. The shadow, a "gunsel" or kept-boy named Wilmer, escorts Spade to see Gutman. Like Effie, Wilmer has passed into the archetypal library of the detective novel. From Gutman Spade learns more about the "black bird" and those who seek it; he pretends to possess it and gives Gutman a dead-line for his participation in its recovery.

Fearing that Gutman will kill her, Brigid goes into hiding. When Spade applies himself to tracking her down, he can find no clues except a newspaper clipping about a ship due from Hong Kong called *La Paloma*. When Gutman calls and opts in, Spade learns the entire story of the falcon. Hammett embellished the history of the icon's later travels, but the data on the Hospitalers of Saint John is basically correct. They were a religious order in the Middle Ages, located on the Isle of Rhodes, and charged with providing lodging and care for pilgrims on the way to Jerusalem. They built up tremendous wealth between 1300 and the early 1500s, but were displaced by Suleiman the Magnificent and his Turkish armies in 1523. They wandered until 1530, when they gained the patronage of Charles V, who gave them four islands, including Malta (not three, as Gutman says). The actual Hospitalers were displeased by the barren islands and savage inhabitants, but delighted that the only required tribute was "simple presentation of a yearly falcon on All-Saints Day."[2] Initially they gave a live bird, but as their wealth grew they substituted jewel-encrusted statuettes.

At the finish of the history, Spade passes out—Gutman had drugged him. On waking, he finds Gutman, Wilmer, and Cairo gone. When he goes to search Cairo's room, he finds another clue leading to *La Paloma,* but is prevented from pursuing it by appointments with Polhaus and the district attorney. Then as Spade and Effie discuss the day's events at the office, Captain Jacobi of *La Paloma* enters, carrying the wrapped falcon, and falls dead at their feet.

Spade instructs Effie to phone the police while he hides the falcon. He tries to contact Gutman, but the criminals conspire to send him on a wild goose chase. Since Brigid participates in the deception, Spade is suspicious when she appears outside his door that evening. Gutman, Cairo, and Wilmer are waiting upstairs; Spade knows he is trapped. He accepts $10,000 to deliver the falcon, but insists that a "fall-guy" be given to the police for the murders. First he suggests Wilmer, then Cairo. Gutman suggests Brigid and attempts to impeach her by suggesting that she stole one of the ten $1,000 bills that she has been holding for Spade. When this ploy fails, Gutman and Cairo agree to make Wilmer the fall guy.

As dawn approaches, Spade phones Effie to retrieve and deliver the falcon. Unwrapped, it turns out to be a worthless imitation; Gutman asks for his money back, and Spade gives him all but $1,000, which he later turns over to the police. The irrepressible Gutman decides to continue his search, and Cairo joins him. As they leave Spade alerts Polhaus and Dundy, but before the criminals can be arrested Wilmer kills Gutman.

Spade urges Brigid to tell all before the police arrive. She confesses to conspiring to get the falcon, but denies involvement in Archer's murder. However all of the evidence points to her. "Miles hadn't many brains," says Spade, ". . . but he'd have gone up [the alley] with you, angel, if he was sure nobody else was up there."[3] When Brigid confesses, she attempts to force Spade's loyalty by invoking their love. In the stunning climax, Spade says that "maybe you love me and maybe I love you" but that he "won't play the sap for her." He enumerates seven reasons why, then turns her over to Polhaus and Dundy.

The novel ends on a melancholic note the next morning as Effie Perrine will have nothing to do with Spade because he has betrayed the cause of true love. Iva Archer waits outside, however, and when Effie ushers her in Spade shudders and seems resigned to an emotional wasteland.

THE IMPORTANCE OF FLITCRAFT

The rightness of the ending, as well as an understanding of Spade's earlier actions, rest on the story that he told about Flitcraft. Occurring before he goes to bed with Brigid, the parable's structural position is like that of the dream sequence in *Red Harvest* or the fight with the ghost in *The Dain Curse.* But thematically it is better integrated. Flitcraft is a reinterpretation of the character Norman Ashcraft in **"The Golden Horseshoe,"** and like other aspects of the novel he has become immortal—there are probability statistics in the insurance business known as *Flitcraft Reports.* In Hammett's first treatment, Ashcraft resents his wife's wealth and wants to prove that he can support himself independently. He moves to America, leads a scruffy life, and is in a sense reincarnated in the criminal Ed Bohannon. The fantasy of an enjoyably disreputable life available beyond the marital confines is a strong and attractive aspect of the earlier story.

In Hammett's reworking, Flitcraft is a real estate agent who leaves his office for lunch one noon and never returns. He passes a construction site and "a beam or something fell eight or ten stories down and smacked the sidewalk alongside him." Suddenly Flitcraft's eyes opened: "He felt like somebody had taken the lid off life and let him look at the works." Life was not a "clean, orderly, sane, responsible affair," he saw rather that "men died at haphazard like that, and lived only while blind chance spared them." According to Spade, "What disturbed him was the discovery that in sensibly ordering his affairs he had got out of step and not into step, with life. He said he knew before he had gone twenty feet from the fallen beam that he would never know peace again until he had adjusted himself to this new glimpse of life. . . . Life could be ended for him at random by a falling beam: he would change his life at random by simply going away."

This naturalistic conception of the universe leads Flitcraft to wander for several years, eventually marrying a woman similar to his first wife and replicating his old circumstances. Spade "always liked" this part of the story, which shows the primacy of the adaptive response: "I don't think he even knew he had settled back naturally into the same groove he had jumped out of in Tacoma. . . . He adjusted himself to beams falling, and then no more of them fell and he adjusted himself to them not falling" (*MF* [*The Maltese Falcon*], 65-67).

The moral, which Brigid misses, lies at the level of Spade's ironic appreciation rather than in Flitcraft's insight into the nature of the universe. The universe may be material and organized by chance, one may die any second; but such an insight, as Flitcraft demonstrates, does not mean that randomness constitutes a way of life. Man is above all adaptive and habitual, traits not only rationally intelligible but rather predictable. Information keeps crystallizing in a chaotic universe. Spade, for example, has found Flitcraft. Herein lies the basic irony that pervades Spade's outlook: the world may not operate rationally, but rationality is the best net with which to go hunting. The chance event—the falling beam—drives men away from cover and adaptive responses for a short time.

In telling Brigid this, Spade is explaining that his code is primary for him. It is the best adaptive response to the world in which he lives, a version of James Wright's advice to Hammett back in 1915. Spade has seen the potency of chance events—and love might be numbered among them—and he understands their relation to the patterns. Were Brigid at all perceptive about this story, she would see that each time she deceives him, Spade becomes more certain of her pattern. His "wild and unpredictable monkey-wrenches" repeatedly unseat her from romantic postures and reveal her fundamental avarice. But the uncomprehending Brigid only says "How perfectly fascinating" at the end of the Flitcraft story.

The Moral Climate of *The Maltese Falcon*

Hammett's most extraordinary fictional feat is the embodiment of this world view in the character of Sam Spade. Spade is a continuation of that interest, which Hammett expressed in **The Dain Curse,** in the deceptions that veil reality. Reality is Spade's psychological fulcrum, and yet he is more perfectly than the Op a knight of the detective code. But readers perceive him as flawed, cruel, and human, rather than as the holder of God-like powers. Hammett masks his character's power primarily by eliminating the first-person narrator, whose intimacy with the reader revealed his minor infidelities to the code and implied that he discussed his cases, a weakness alien to the entirely private personality of Spade. With a third-person point of view, the hero's person becomes more distant and independent. In addition, Hammett made Spade's code an innovation on the generic standard, a new version that allows him not only deception, but the pleasures of adultery and the rewards of betrayal. Such variations are the key mode of creativity in popular literature, allowing readers to enjoy generically or conventionally forbidden desires.

Yet Spade's code is only one of three moral climates. The reader is exposed equally to the worlds of the police and of the criminals, whose ethos Brigid shares. The exact distinctions between these worlds are blurred, and the reality/illusion question makes it clear that both Spade and the reader function, when they judge, on the basis of only some of the facts. More facts may be produced by "heaving a wild and unpredictable monkey-wrench into the works," as Spade says, but he never forgets that his facts, once linked, are still a construction of reality. As he tells his lawyer of Iva Archer's alibi, "I don't believe it or disbelieve it. . . . I don't know a damned thing about it." What counts, he explains, is that it seems "to click with most of the known facts" and "ought to hold" (*MF,* 120). Spade operates on this view of reality for the entire novel; at its end he refuses to tell Brigid whether he would have acted differently had the falcon been real and they shared its wealth.

Hammett had a bit of fun articulating Spade's world view: when Flitcraft assumes his new existence, he changes his name to Charles Pierce, a variation on Charles Sanders Peirce, the nineteenth-century American philosopher who wrote extensively about chance and probability.[4] Peirce also identified a logical process between induction and deduction called "abduction," in which the investigator accepts an event as having happened, then imagines the state of affairs that produced the situation. Its common use in detective fiction, as Hammett saw, reinforced the role of the detective as the author of reality.

The method is apropos, since the characters with whom Spade must deal live according to illusions. Most of them are greedy; they want the falcon. For some, such as Gutman, this greed is overlain with the illusion of personal quest. Others, such as Brigid, believe the world is made up of "saps," who can be manipulated by their sexual desires. All such illusions are, on the allegoric level, symbolic sins. Those of Joel Cairo, the effete criminal, and Wilmer, the homosexual gunman, have become less obvious as their characters became more stereotyped. Rhea Gutman's self-abuse is a continuation of Gabrielle Leggett's morbid self-destruction. Miles Archer, with his sartorial self-confidence, represents a traditional pride, while Effie Perrine, with her romantic conception of love, is a more simply deluded, but nonetheless erring, variation on a generic norm.

Reasoning as he does by abduction, Spade maintains his personal distance on these characters until he abduces (authors) their formative situations. He understands that everyone lives in his illusions, so he believes nothing, trusts no one, and rejects real emotional contact. Critic Bernard Schopen points out that Gutman, Cairo, Wilmer, and Brigid are moral primitives, who "create those illusions which assist them in their rapacious pursuits."[5] Most affective are those of Brigid, whose continual lies and deceptions readers excuse as long as she feigns inchoate personal emotions—claiming thus an emotional sanctity. This implication of mystery makes her character far more interesting than those of Jeanne Delano in **"The Girl with the Silver Eyes"** or the princess in **"The Gutting of Couffignal."** Yet it is the reader, not Spade, that she seduces with her sentiments. Spade merely speaks the lingua franca of each character's illusion and avoids the fate of "saps" like Archer and Thursby, who are induced to participate.

The abductive method is complicated by those properties of the formal mystery that Hammett appropriated for the structure of **The Maltese Falcon.** He had been experimenting with analytic detection in **The Dain**

Curse, and was fond of the trail of false clues that he used in **"The Tenth Clew."** The ten deceptions in *The Maltese Falcon,* according to George Thompson, begin with Brigid's representation of herself as Miss Wonderly and her portrayal of Thursby as Archer's killer. The third is Dundy's opinion that Spade murdered Archer, a view supported by new information about Spade's affair with Iva and testimony from Archer's brother. If the reader is suspicious of Spade at this point, Hammett has successfully involved him in the skeptical world view that is Spade's *modus operandi,* and the point of the Flitcraft parable. The fourth deception is Brigid's story connecting herself and Thursby to the falcon, for she says that she is the victim of the latter's greed. Later, the implication in her disappearance is that she has become the victim of foul play. The sixth deception occurs when she calls Spade for help, the seventh when the police theorize that Thursby's death is the result of underworld warfare. The wild goose chase to Burlingame is the eighth false clue, and the ninth is the $1,000 bill that Gutman palms in the final showdown. That the falcon itself is a worthless phony is the tenth and paramount deception. It suddenly illuminates the moral and spiritual emptiness of the co-conspirators, and ironically belittles their quest. It also links the nine previous deceptions in one paramount symbol of the three plot elements—the investigation of Archer's death, the mystery of the falcon, and the romance between Spade and Brigid.

The Flitcraft parable itself shines through the ten plot deceptions to illuminate the grail/quest structure in a new light. When the grail is found to be worthless, the implication is that the emotion Brigid generates is a "falling beam," discredited by her greed. But it is also true that while they seek it, the grail holds Spade and Brigid together. It represents the emptiness of sentimental emotion, but its pursuit is, paradoxically, an adaptive response, a confirming, stabilizing influence in Western society. But it no longer provides a "solution." Like so many American writers of the late twenties, Hammett sees continual emotional improvisation as the only answer. The fact that Flitcraft's life is Hammett's personal meditation on what he himself should do next makes the symbol extraordinarily compelling.

The Women in Spade's Life

There are only four women in the novel. Rhea Gutman has been discussed. The others, as Hammett indicates in **"Three Women,"** serve in one sense as the "fates." They ask questions, represent mysteries, and possess occult powers; Spade depends particularly on Effie's "female intuition." But they are also prosaic "fates," typifying three possibilities for Spade. Effie is a kind of "office wife," who is capable, dependable, and part of a team. Spade's physical intimacies with her are uncharged, innocent as a small boy's bedtime hug in the

kitchen. It is appropriate that the falcon should come to Effie and Spade, because they function psychologically as a nuclear family, and one of the subliminal features of popular entertainment is the reinforcement of tradition.

The falcon must be exposed as a fake in the presence of the second woman, Brigid, whose romantic outlook and effusive sexuality the reinforcing function rejects. Brigid's name signifies, like Gabrielle Leggett's, a touch of foreignness. As Miss Le Blanc, she recalls Blanchfleur, who nearly diverted Sir Galahad from his quest for the grail. Her beauty and sexual intensity are only one aspect of this "loathly lady"; her dark side is ingrown with lies and deceit. "I always lie," she confesses to Spade, in a scene that is her analogue to the Flitcraft parable. Although she seems to promise Spade an existence of mutual intensities, Brigid is a type not capable of bonding emotions.

Iva Archer falls between Effie and Brigid. Like Myrtle Jennison in **Red Harvest,** she serves as a cautionary example of the wages of sin: Spade's inclination is to pull the covers over her and to say "Thank you" when he is done. Yet she is Spade's lot when the novel ends, and there is something so reduced, petty, and limited in her character that it makes Spade shiver. To have Iva is to become Archer, to cuckold oneself. The irony the reader feels is that experienced when a stolen pleasure becomes a gift of ennui.

The three women are also configured to be sexually significant. As psychiatrists have pointed out, the deaths of Archer and Thursby leave Spade in possession of two women who were formerly attached to other men. There is a "fear of Oedipal victory" attached to this, of which overmuch can be made, but it undoubtedly lends tension to the plot. The sexual problem gains a third element when two of the women contrast with Effie, the "desexualized daytime mother."[6] Hammett's scheme of sexual temptation became a convention of detective fiction. Although usually there are two women, a blonde and a brunette, the detective must find the more beautiful woman guilty. He is compelled to arrest her, or in the brutal world of Micky Spillane to destroy her. "The particular terms of this sacrifice suggest the marked tendency of American fiction to depict women as potentially destructive," notes George Grella.[7] Yet artists of Hammett's rank, such as Chandler and Macdonald, have found the convention useful to more humane themes (see *The Little Sister*).

The archetype itself dates back to the Middle Ages; in pure form she is called the succubus. Heroes of the early grail romances, such as Percival, were afflicted by succubi. When Hammett calls upon this peril, however, the effect is more subtle than in a morality drama because the novel has realistic and romantic levels too.

These put the love relationship in higher relief than the quest or the question of who killed Miles Archer. Readers forget that Spade has told Brigid the story of Flitcraft, which he conceives as a warning, for he concludes, "'You don't have to trust me, anyhow, as long as you can persuade me to trust you.'" They forget that Brigid thinks she seduces Spade by warning "I am a liar. I have always been a liar."

The tension resulting from their liaison highlights the romance element in the crucial scene. The exchange of secrets seems to lock them together. Brigid has been forewarned about Spade, but she stays because, like Dinah Brand, she is hypnotized by treasure. Spade keeps close to Brigid, even when she gives him false leads and deliberately loses him, because he cannot believe that he will be as naive as Archer when Brigid reveals her ultimate allure to him.

And indeed he is not. After Spade's muscles stand out "like wales," he goes on to enumerate the reasons why he must turn her in. In the ritual of enumeration, the archetype is being summoned to unite the romantic, realistic, and allegoric levels. Surrender to emotion means surrender of self-conception, and ultimately death. "I won't because all of me wants to—wants to say to hell with the consequences and do it—and because—God damn you—you counted on that with me the same as you counted on that with the others," says Spade. To succumb is to be mortal, to see one's individuality mocked by the engulfing pattern of one's inferiors. But to suppress the almost chemical certainty of lust is to free oneself from commonness and obtain a measure of immortality. Consummation would bring a shattering confrontation with Spade's own inner emptiness and isolation—the function of "reason" here is to inform the hero that intimacy is death, which allows the mythic to predominate.

The ultimate horror that the femme fatal embodies changes with the prevailing malaise of the age. To be meaningful her threat of death through sexuality must have a current equivalent, a clear representation of death-in-life. Hammett's triumph in *The Maltese Falcon* is the way in which he develops the psychological meaning at the archetype's core on a basis of a coherent and credible intimacy. Spade's decision stuns readers because it suddenly reclaims the power that belongs to the archetypal, transcending the sentimentality with which authors usually afflict their heroes.

THE TECHNIQUE OF *THE MALTESE FALCON*

The Maltese Falcon is Dashiell Hammett's most technically adept novel. Sustaining breakneck speed through the intricacies that confront Spade is no slight accomplishment. More than usual Hammett's prose has a clipped, elided quality that gestures matter-of-factly to

the world under the reader's nose. The similarity of this style and that of Hemingway's early work is often noted, though Hemingway's terseness points to an interior world of complex, inexpressible emotions that the reader is meant to perceive.

The terseness of *The Maltese Falcon* owes not to complexity of perception, but to each word's function as an engine of plot. And few words move the action as rapidly as those in the characters' speeches. The entire novel, William Nolan writes, "is basically a series of brilliant dialogues, set in motion and bolstered by off-stage events."[8] Hammett elaborates a distinct conversational style for each character on his or her first appearance. Spade's habitual use of "Sweetheart," "Darling," and "Angel" with women establishes his character and emotional invulnerability at the outset. Just as distinctive is Brigid's first stammering, truncated line: "She swallowed and said hurriedly: 'Could you—? I thought—I—that is—'" She breaks off questions and statements before they are complete, as if overwhelmed by emotion, when she is concealing the facts. She draws her listeners into answers to incomplete questions. Gutman, Effie, Iva, Dundy, Polhaus, and Cairo have comparable conversational signatures.

Hammett also structured his characters and their moods by noting their important habits. In Sam Spade's case these became ritual, a technique that Hammett undoubtedly did notice in Hemingway's work. Most famous is Spade's habit of rolling, rerolling, lighting, and extinguishing his own Bull Durham cigarettes, according to the tenor of the talk or his own thoughts. Hammett introduces the reader to this ceremony in the first pages, after Spade learns of Archer's murder:

> Spade's thick fingers made a cigarette with deliberate care, sifting a measured quantity of tan flakes down into the curved paper, spreading the flakes slightly so that they lay equal at the ends with a slight depression in the middle, thumbs rolling the paper's inner edge down and up under the outer edge as forefingers pressed it over, thumbs and fingers sliding to the paper's cylinder ends to hold it even while tongue licked the flap, left forefinger and thumb pinching their end while right forefinger and thumb smoothed the damp seam, right forefinger and thumb twisting their end and lifting the other to Spade's mouth.
>
> (*MF*, 11-12)

The making of the cigarette, its absence, or a pause in its construction are all intended to intimate Spade's inner state. There may be sexual symbolism in the cigarette's shape, but it is more important that the ritual indicates an order beyond articulation—the detective code. Hammett changed the details of the novel in this direction in its final draft. Nolan notes, for instance, the substitution of "They shook hands ceremoniously" for "They shook hands with marked formality."[9]

Hammett refined the detective novel's handling of stereotypic characterization in *The Maltese Falcon.* Moved by their romantic interest in him, most readers forget the opening description of Spade:

> Sam Spade's jaw was long and bony, his chin a jutting V under the more flexible V of his mouth. His nostrils curved back to make another, smaller V. His yellow-grey eyes were horizontal. The V motif was picked up again by the thickish brows rising outward . . . and his pale brown hair grew down—from rather high flat temples—in a point on his forehead. He looked rather pleasantly like a blond satan.

> (*MF,* 3)

This is wit carried almost to parody, an impossible face. No one forgets the portrait of Casper Gutman, however, which harks back to Vasilije Djudakovich in **"This King Business"**:

> The fat man was flabbily fat with bulbous pink cheeks and lips and chins and neck, with a great soft egg of a belly that was all his torso, and pendant cones for arms and legs. As he advanced to meet Spade all his bulbs rose and shook and fell separately with each step, in the manner of clustered soap-bubbles not yet released from the pipe through which they had been blown.

> (*MF,* 108)

Despite his embroidery of the characters, Hammett claimed to have had real models in mind. "I followed Gutman's original in Washington," he said, "and I never remember shadowing a man who bored me so much. He was not after a jeweled falcon, of course." Hammett said "Brigid was based, in part, on a woman who came in to Pinkerton's to hire an operative to discharge her housekeeper." Nolan adds that Brigid was based also on Peggy O'Toole, the advertising artist with whom Hammett shared an office at Samuels's in San Francisco. "The Cairo character I picked up on a forgery charge in 1920," said Hammett. "Effie, the good girl, once asked me to go into the narcotic smuggling business with her in San Diego. Wilmer, the gunman was picked up in Stockton, California, a neat small smooth-faced quiet boy of perhaps twenty-one. He was serenely proud of the name the paper gave him—The Midget Bandit." He was also the character on whom Hammett had based his story "Itchy."[10]

The most notable departure from Hammett's preceding work is the lack of violence in *The Maltese Falcon.* Only one character, Captain Jacobi of *La Paloma,* dies onstage, and he is shot earlier offstage. The deaths of Archer and Thursby occur between the moments of the present action. Nor is the reader subjected to the graphic descriptions of bullet and dagger holes that Hammett had prized as recently as *The Dain Curse.* Violence is present, but psychological. An oppressing sense of closure brackets every meeting and conversation, creating a climate of emotional claustrophobia that is the diminutive of the threat of the larger world. In other words, the apartment scenes imply by their interior concentration a great external threat. As the settings increasingly become interiors, Hammett connotes more psychological peril than he could in pages of graphic violence. Violence becomes more personal as the characters become more familiar, until after the final scene between Spade and Brigid the reader feels that intimacy is its most fecund soil. Capped on the symbolic level by the falcon, this psychological violence raises the novel far above its genre.

THE DEBATE ON THE ENDING

The culmination of the tension is the confrontation between Sam and Brigid, the nature and satisfactoriness of which has been debated for some twenty years now. At first there was some contention that the end of the novel was flawed. William Kenney argued that,

> The emotional climax of the novel is surely the scene in which Spade tells Brigid of his intention to turn her over to the police. Yet this scene grows out of what has been only a minor element in the plot, the murder of Miles Archer. The novel's main action, the quest for the falcon, reaches its climax with the discovery that the bird is not genuine. There is then a structural division in the final episodes of the novel, giving the scene betwen Spade and Brigid, excellent as it is in itself, almost the air of an afterthought.

Since that time, several scholars have argued that the novel achieves its final coherence in the symbol of the falcon. One of Hammett's heirs, Ross Macdonald, voiced this view: "The black bird," he wrote, "is hollow, worthless. The reality behind appearance is a treacherous vacuum. . . . The bird's lack of value implies Hammett's final comment on the inadequacy and superficiality of Spade's life and ours. If only his bitterly inarticulate struggle for self-realization were itself more fully realized . . . Sam Spade could have become a great, indigenous tragic figure. . . . I think *The Maltese Falcon* . . . is tragedy of a new kind, deadpan tragedy." The discovery that the falcon is a fake, most scholars now agree, implies a side to the Spade-O'Shaughnessy relationship that could only be resolved in a tandem climax.[11]

The discovery of the bogus falcon should focus readers' attention on the nature of the novel's emotional world. The emotional middle distance in which Spade operates has made it difficult to ascertain his real feelings. Brigid is a habitual liar, and Hammett allows Effie to put in a word for romantic love on the last page. Few critics are willing to assert that Sam is in love with Brigid, notes George Thompson, who boldly suggests "that Hammett means us to take their relationship seriously." He argues that Hammett portrayed "a subtle rendering of Spade's growing personal anguish" in the final scene by means of the grammatical modifiers: "Spade said *tenderly*: "You angel! Well, if you get a good break you'll be out of San Quentin in twenty years. . . . He was *pale*. He said *tenderly*: "I hope to God they don't hang you, precious, by that sweet neck." Thompson argues that the lines that follow may "sound like clichés now" but that they "were a first in the 1930s, and unless our own cynicism gets in the way, what comes through here is the strength of his feeling for her."[12]

But there are as many grammatical qualifiers on the other side of the argument. Spade "smiled wolfishly," "laughed harshly," "demanded in a low, impatient voice," and "slapped her shoulder" in this scene. Most commentators agree that Spade, with great emotional effort, maintains his distance from Brigid. The issue has become: how are readers finally to judge Spade's character?

Among those sympathetic to Spade as a realistic character (though not as literally inclined as Thompson), William Nolan's argument is perhaps the most cogent:

> It would be a mistake to judge Spade as "unscrupulous" and "heartless." In the climactic sequence in which he finally turns Brigid over to the police he reveals the emotions of a man whose heart is with the woman, but whose code forbids his accepting her. Spade knows that he cannot continue to function if he breaks his personal code and goes off with Brigid—even while he admits that Miles Archer was "a louse" and that the agency is better off without him. Sam can sleep with Iva, the dead man's wife; he can bed down with his secretary (". . . his hand on her hip . . . 'Don't touch me now—not now.'") and he can spend the night with Brigid, but he must never make a permanent alliance with any of them, the good or the evil.[13]

Yet to concede that Spade acts on his code in the final scene is to admit the primacy of the code in the novel. In Robert Edenbaum's brilliant interpretation, he notes that "in the last pages of the novel . . . the reader (and Brigid O'Shaughnessy) discovers that he (and she) has been duped all along," for Spade has known from the moment he saw Archer's body that Brigid was the murderer. "Spade himself then is the one person who holds the central piece of information," writes Edenbaum; "he is the one person who knows everything, for Brigid does not know that he knows. And though Spade is no murderer, Brigid O'Shaughnessy is his victim." Edenbaum contends that "Brigid . . . is the manipulated, the deceived, the unpredictable, finally, in a very real sense, the victim." In Edenbaum's view the course of the action is "the demolition of sentiment" through the "all but passionless figure of Spade." The key to this interpretation is Edenbaum's insight that Spade is a kind of "daemonic agent," a vehicle of allegoric impulse. Those who try to redeem the sentimental level of the action have missed the point, says Edenbaum. They say

"You're right, you're right, but couldn't you better have been wrong? As Hammett made sufficiently clear . . . in the final confrontation with Brigid, exactly the point about Spade . . . is that he could not have."[14]

This interpretation gains rather than loses plausibility when considered in tandem with the final scene, in which Spade sits in his office and shivers at the prospect of meeting Iva. There is always at the end of the hard-boiled detective novel a moment of depression, when the detective reflects on the loss of a girl friend or colleague. But usually the tone implies that, rather than being defeated, he is essentially alone. This scene is Hammett's echo of that convention, but it also enforces the allegoric level that Edenbaum points out. By its nature allegory works to maintain a cultural consensus about the nature of reality and the exigency of morality. There must be human costs, and neither allegory nor its popular derivations can deny this without losing their deeper appeal. Spade's loss of Brigid and dismissal by Effie show this cost. Brigid's fate would not surprise anyone who had read **"Nelson Redline,"** Hammett's short story of 1924. In it he wrote that people "who refuse to—or for one reason or another are unable to—conduct themselves in accordance with the accepted rules—no matter how strong their justification may be, or how foolish the rules—have to be put outside." Spade must be "put outside" by Effie, in part because he put Brigid outside.

HAMMETT FINDS SUCCESS

Hammett knew as he was writing that *The Maltese Falcon* was good work, and he was thinking about how to convert it to other salable forms. He needed money to finance his planned move to New York City. On 16 June 1929 he wrote to Block, his editor at Knopf:

> I started *The Maltese Falcon* on its way to you by express last Friday, the fourteenth. I'm fairly confident that it is by far the best thing I've done so far, and I hope you'll think so too.
>
> Though I hadn't anything of the sort in mind while doing it, I think now that it could very easily be turned into a play. Will you let me know if you agree with me? I wouldn't take a chance of trying to adapt it myself, but will try to get the help of somebody who knows the theatre.
>
> Another thing: if you use THE FALCON will you go a little easy on the editing? While I wouldn't go to the stake in defense of my system of punctuation, I do rather like it and I think it goes with my system of sentence structure.[15]

The major problem that Hammett had with Block (and with his editor at *Black Mask*) was with the sex in the story. In 1929 magazines and publishing houses exercised stringent self-censorship. Cap Shaw had cut some of the sexual banter between Brigid and Joel Cairo, such as her line "The one you couldn't make," but Hammett restored it for Knopf, and Block let it stand. Shaw changed Spade's baiting of Wilmer—"How long have you been off the gooseberry lay?"—to "How long have you been off the lay?" making it more explicit in the process, he supposed, of purging the homoeroticism. But he left in "gunsel" (a boy kept by a homosexual), assuming that it meant gunman, as millions have continued to believe. The words "hell" and "damn" were permitted in both the magazine and book forms, but the all-American expletive was forbidden. Hammett got around that with the construction "The boy spoke two words, the first a short guttural verb, the second 'you.'" However, Block objected to the direct indications at the end of chapter 9 and at the beginning of chapter 10 that Sam and Brigid sleep together. Knopf's Borzoi series put itself above prurient interest. Hammett answered this criticism in a letter:

> Dear Mr. Block:
>
> I'm glad you like *The Maltese Falcon.* I'm sorry you think the to-bed and the homosexual parts of it should be changed. I should like to leave them as they are, especially since you say they "would be all right perhaps in an ordinary novel." It seems to me that the only thing that can be said against their use in a detective novel is that nobody has tried it yet. I'd like to try it.[16]

Fearful of offending readers of the series, Block held out for the changes. He was lucky that Hammett was becoming famous and was busy moving. On 31 August Hammett wrote: "OK—go ahead and change them. I don't imagine a few words difference will matter greatly, and anyway, I'll soon be on hand to do in person whatever crying is necessary."

Unlike his previous novels, *The Maltese Falcon* was immediately popular. Cap. Shaw had hyped the *Black Mask* serialization with his personal testimony—"In all of my experience I have never encountered a story as intense, as gripping or as powerful as this one . . . ," and the reviewers who had been following Hammett since *Red Harvest* could not praise it enough.[17] Walter Brooks of the *Outlook and Independent* wrote, "This is not only probably the best detective story we have ever read, it is an exceedingly well-written novel." Will Cuppy wrote in the *New York Herald Tribune* that "it would not surprise us one whit if Mr. Hammett turned out to be the Great American mystery writer." Alexander Woollcott thought the novel "the best detective story America has yet produced." Another critic said "the writing is better than Hemingway."[18]

Hammett also gained the intellectual respect that he had sought since his earlier contributions to the *Smart Set.* The *New Republic* noted that *The Maltese Falcon* was "not the tawdry gum-shoeing of the ten-cent magazine. It is the genuine presence of the myth." The aristocratic *Town & Country* devoted 1,500 words of effusive praise to the novel.

It is likely that the praise Hammett appreciated most came from fellow writers. Herbert Asbury, a reviewer, praised the novel. Hammett responded: "I can't tell you how pleased I was with your verdict on *The Maltese Falcon.*" It's the first thing I've done that was—regardless of what faults it had—the best work I was capable of at the time I was doing it."

The verdict that this is Hammett's best work has not changed. Raymond Chandler wrote that "*The Maltese Falcon* may or may not be a work of genius, but an art which is capable of it is not 'by hypothesis' incapable of anything. Once a detective story can be as good as this, only the pedants will deny that it *could* be even better." And Ross Macdonald noted "its astonishing imaginative energy persisting undiminished after more than a third of a century." *The Maltese Falcon* broke the barriers of the genre; it was, and is, a work of art.[19]

THE GLASS KEY

The writing of *The Glass Key* taxed Dashiell Hammett's creative powers and personal stamina—it was the fourth novel that he published in a thirty-two month stretch between November 1927 and June 1930. The novel began appearing in *Black Mask* in March 1930, just a few months before Hammett separated from his family and moved to the big world of New York. Unlike the sudden burst of *The Maltese Falcon* this manuscript progressed slowly. When publisher Alfred Knopf asked after it, Hammett wrote back, "*The Glass Key* is coming along slowly but not badly. I shan't leave to New York next week as I had expected but shall be there in any event by the first of October." But to a friend Hammett confided that he had been "held back thus far by laziness, drunkenness and illness."[20]

Hammett felt that the finished book was his best work, nonetheless, because "the clues were nicely placed . . . although nobody seemed to see them." Reviewers were less sanguine. David T. Bazelon, writing for *Commentary,* thought that Hammett had attempted a conventional novel, in which characters act for reasons of loyalty, passion, or power. But even on those generous grounds, he found the novel unsatisfactory: "We never know whether [the] motive in solving the murder is loyalty, job-doing or love." Other critics wrote that the novel was "Hammett's least satisfactory," and that the hero was "mechanical and his emotions were not there."[21]

The Glass Key represents some falling off from the dramatic tension and vivid characterization of *The Maltese Falcon,* but most of the critical panning of the novel can be laid to Hammett's disappointment of generic expectations. He did not do the same thing twice in his major work. It would have been difficult to improve on the tight plot, quick-sketch characters, and cascading tension of *The Maltese Falcon*; that was the end of one line of Hammett's development. Returning to his earlier, more "serious" agenda, he decided that a looser plot structure would permit more development of human conflicts, especially the question of love. In place of his former devices, he would rely on the tension inherent in "tough guy" fiction, and the crispness created by Hemingway's elliptic technique and Dos Passos's realm. The "white space" that Hemingway advocated becomes, in *The Glass Key,* the use of such clues as letters, notes, and phone calls, without an explanatory context. Hammett's use of newspaper clippings as parts of the plot indicates a generally unnoticed debt to realism. Most puzzling for his audience was that Hammett dared to demand close reading.

The World of "Tough Guy" Fiction

The setting of *The Glass Key* is Poisonville on a larger scale. Though the physical locale is not specified, the moral milieu harks back to Hammett's first novel—a vista of endemic greed, where corrupt police and politicians operate under the protection of a businessman-powerbroker who is at war with a bootlegger. The power matrix is just as corrupt, but Hammett portrays it from the inside this time. Always balancing his critiques, Hammett gives this city a few early traces of humanity. The boss provides for a foot soldier's pregnant wife and child while he is in jail, and Ned Beaumont protects the innocent Opal from the enquiries of the corrupt district attorney. But afterward Hammett paints a dark picture of society. Senator Henry, the aristocrat of the novel, is a megalomaniac, like Old Elihu, who sees his inferiors as "a lower form of animal life and none of the rules apply."[22] As in Poisonville, the rapacity of the rich is only the tip of the iceberg: everyone is on the take, even the purportedly objective newspapers. The publisher in *Red Harvest* pursued the truth, but Howard Mathews of the *Observer* toadies up to the bank that holds his mortgage and to bootlegger Shad O'Rory. Hammett underlines the failure of journalism as a moral force by juxtaposing a civic-spirited editorial with a scene in which gangsters tell Mathews what to print. The police are corrupt, of course, and District Attorney Farr is a political sycophant, prosecuting only those out of power, suppressing or refusing to investigate evidence that leads to the truth. The political system is beyond repair; Senator Henry not only raids the public treasury but murders his own son without trepidation. Even the private eye, Hammett's last just man, cannot combat this decay. When Beaumont tries to hire a detective to investigate his boss, Paul Madvig, the man refuses: "Fred and I are building up a nice little private detective business here. . . . A couple of years more and we'll be sitting pretty. I like you, Beaumont, but not enough to monkey with the man who runs the city" (*GK* [*The Glass Key*], 172).

The hero of *The Glass Key* is thus not a private eye but a political lieutenant named Ned Beaumont. Physically he resembles his creator; he is tall, lean, wears a mustache; he is a compulsive gambler at cards, dice, and horses; he is a hard drinker, suffers from tuberculosis, and is cynical and tough.

The action begins when Ned Beaumont finds the corpse of Taylor Henry, the senator's son; he takes this information to his boss, Paul Madvig, owner of the East State Construction and Contracting Company and the local political boss, who urges Beaumont to do what he can to suppress a district attorney's investigation that is sure to follow. Madvig backs the senator and wants to marry his daughter Janet. Beaumont tells Madvig he ought "to sink" the senator, but out of loyalty he keeps District Attorney Farr from proceeding.

After a tangential episode in which he goes to New York City to collect a $3,250 gambling debt, Beaumont returns to find that someone has sent anonymous letters to everyone intimate with the crime. Each contains three questions, all of which imply that Paul Madvig killed Taylor Henry. The author appears to be Opal, Paul's daughter and Taylor Henry's paramour, but Beaumont prevents any official inquiry into this matter as well.

Then Madvig's political clubhouse begins to splinter; the dividing wedge is a foot soldier named Walter Ivans, whose brother Madvig refuses to spring from jail. Ivans takes his problem to Shad O'Rory, who eliminates witnesses to the offense. When Madvig declares war on O'Rory, Beaumont objects and there is a fistfight between the two. Then O'Rory offers Beaumont $10,000 to expose Madvig in the *Observer.* In an ensuing argument, Beaumont is knocked out, wakes up in a dingy room, and is beaten every day by two of O'Rory's thugs until he escapes.

In the hospital Beaumont tells a contrite Madvig and Janet Henry how he had planned to lay a trap for O'Rory: he then struggles out of the hospital to stop the *Observer* from publishing the exposé to which he has inadvertently contributed. To do so he must confront O'Rory and Mathews at a cottage where they are holding Opal. Beaumont's rebukes and his seduction of the publisher's wife cause Mathews' suicide, but stop the publication.

After dinner at the Henrys', Beaumont interviews Janet about the murder. He discovers that the senator knew about the death before he himself found the body; he learns also that Janet is the author of the mysterious letters. Then a character named Sloss turns up with a clue, and suddenly all the evidence points to Paul Madvig. When Beaumont confronts him, Madvig makes an obviously false confession of guilt: he cannot account for

Taylor Henry's hat, a clue that Beaumont chases throughout the plot. This impasse and their rivalry for Janet lead to the second rift between the two men.

Beaumont enlists Janet's aid only when they both vow to respect the truth that their collaboration turns up. Janet solves the hat trick, and Ned eliminates the threat from Jeff, a bad guy who strangles Shad O'Rory. There is nothing to do then but confront the senator with the evidence that he killed his own son.

The senator wants to commit suicide, but Beaumont refuses him the option and turns him over to the police. "He got mad at the thought of his son interfering with his chances of being re-elected and hit him," explains Beaumont to Janet Henry. Something like mutual respect affects them, and after they inform a stoic Madvig, the pair depart for New York City.

THE CHARACTER OF NED BEAUMONT

Critics of *The Glass Key* are troubled by the character of Ned Beaumont and the "tough guy" world in which he lives, for it is difficult to uncover in either any evidence that redeems him as a human being. Beaumont is so much more cynical than Sam Spade that his motivations are unclear. He seems to exist to take punishment. Robert Edenbaum points out that the reason Beaumont takes the beating from Jeff is never clear, and that "the mask is never lifted" so that the reader can discover Beaumont's feelings. Ben Ray Redman sees only sadism and heroic drinking in Beaumont, and Philip Durham calls him close "to being an amoral character." William Kenney's comment that *The Glass Key* is "Hammett's most ambitious study of moral ambiguity," however, leads to a more productive analysis.[23]

Hammett's "ambition" consists in working the realist vein without granting his protagonist the allegorical status usually given the detective: he limits Beaumont's effectiveness in the real world. Hammett strips him of the ability to move through all social strata, of physical prowess, pinpoint markmanship, and abductive powers. Beaumont is merely an "expediter" in a corrupt political machine: all that remains of the God-like in him is a vision of how things really are, which he will express to anyone who respects truth. Lacking the ability to make things happen, to author his and the other characters' destinies, Hammett's hero must focus on his own luck, for only that will help him escape the "falling beam." In other words, Hammett tailored Beaumont to meet the 1930s, an era in which that popular vision of idealism and action common to the 1920s (and represented by the Op) could no longer be sustained. An economic bubble had burst, and with it the illusion that there were falcons to seek.

Hammett introduced his hero as a man on a losing streak. Only a year earlier, Beaumont says, Paul Madvig "picked me up out of the gutter." But he is already losing again in his gambling, only "not so long—only a month or six weeks" this time. Economic hard times reduce the world to essentials; men make "low growling noises" in their chests, and the fellow next to Beaumont seems "hawk-nosed . . . a predatory animal of forty or so." To survive, Beaumont adapts. He becomes capable of planting evidence, protecting the guilty, manipulating the law, faking alibis, and approving of Madvig's graft, because he no longer has the illusion that he stands apart from the social organism. Its diseases are his diseases; it should not surprise readers that he hates "with a dull glow that came from far beneath the surface" of his eyes (*GK*, 95, 5, 31, 83).

In this Hobbesian universe, survival can be influenced by reason and ability but it is mostly the result of luck: either the beam falls or it doesn't. When luck is bad, Beaumont says, you "might as well take your punishment and get it over with." A change in luck is what sets in motion the plot of *The Glass Key.* Beaumont wins a big bet, his bookie skips town, and he decides to hunt him down. As he explains to Madvig, "it would be the same if it was five bucks. I go two months without winning a bet and that gets me down. What good am I if my luck's gone? Then I cop, or think I do, and I'm all right again. I can take my tail out from between my legs and feel that I'm a person again and not just something that's being kicked around" (*GK*, 5, 23).

Beaumont gets his money from the bookie by threatening to frame him for the murder of Taylor Henry, a tactic unreproved by the author. This is not what counts. By taking what is his, the protagonist reverses his luck: "Ned Beaumont leaving the train that had brought him back from New York was a clear-eyed erect tall man. . . . In color and line his face was hale. His stride was long and elastic. He went nimbly up the stairs" (*GK*, 46).

The only trace of the private eye's pure power that remains in Beaumont is his ability to see the world stripped of the overlays of civility, legitimacy, and romance that blind others to its random and predatory nature. Beaumont is a private *eye*, whose vision is his sole remaining quality of allegoric status. He lives in a "large room in the old manner, light of ceiling and wide of window, with a tremendous mirror." When the reader first encounters him at home, "his feet rested in a parallelogram of late morning sun" (*GK*, 16). The age of the room connotes authenticity of vision, the emphasis on the mirror, windows, and light the actual mechanics of vision, about which Hammett had been reading. Throughout *The Glass Key* Beaumont is able to read the eyes of other men, and Hammett reveals Beaumont's own inner state by describing his eyes.

It is because Beaumont sees the world with preternatural clarity that Hammett must present scenes of shocking, seemingly gratuitous brutality. These were a staple of the tough-guy genre, of course, but they would seem extraneous if Beaumont's vision of the world did not unite them. The point is that, contrary to the fiction of the twenties, life is mostly punishment for a good number of people. When Beaumont attempts suicide rather than face continued beatings by Jeff, most critics assume that simple sadism is operating, or that the hero fails to adhere to his tough guy ethos, rather than seeing that Beaumont's collapse demythologizes brutality.

> Ned Beaumont was driven back against the wall. The back of his head struck the wall first, then his body crashed flat against the wall, and he slid down the wall to the floor. Rosy-cheeked Rusty, still holding his cards at the table, said gloomily, but without emotion: "Jesus, Jeff, you'll croak him."
>
> Jeff said: "Him?" He indicated the man at his feet by kicking him not especially hard on the thigh. "You can't croak him. He's tough. He's a tough baby. He likes this." He bent down, grasped one of the unconscious man's lapels in each hand, and dragged him to his knees. "Don't you like it baby?" he asked and, holding Ned Beaumont up on his knees with one hand, struck his face with the other fist.

Of the tough-guy character Joyce Carol Oates wrote "It is as if the world extends no further than the radius of one's desire." When the unprotected fall within that radius, they suffer. The victim has no good choices; he can only hope to get it over, and to move on, as Beaumont does when the bookie's bodyguard delivers a punishing body-blow: "He went down the stairs, loose-jointed, pallid and bare-headed. He went through the downstairs dining-room to the street and out to the curb, where he vomited. When he had vomited, he went to a taxicab that stood a dozen feet away, climbed into it, and gave the driver an address in Greenwich Village" (**GK,** 84, 32). The tough-guy world represents the diminished possibility of the heroic code in this world. The reader sensed that it took a great struggle for Sam Spade to decide that adherence to the code that kept him whole was more important than love, but the intent to survive is the only noble possibility in Beaumont's world.

The universality of this ethos highlights male behavior by reducing it. The way in which men behave toward one another has been a subject implicit in Hammett's work since **Red Harvest.** The Continental Op's male world consisted of inferiors and superiors, and few of the latter. Men existed in stratified relationships of clear authority; it was a chain of command world that mirrored the companies for which the men worked. Through most of **The Dain Curse** the same outlook prevailed, but in Quesada the Op dealt with an unranked circle of police and politicians to catch the murderer. The probing and mutual suspicion among them became the dominant male outlook in **The Maltese Falcon.** Spade's wariness, however, was directed at such flat characters as Gutman and Cairo, and only tentatively explored in his animosity toward Dundy and friendship with Polhaus. By the time of **The Glass Key,** Hammett had matured sufficiently as a creator of male characters to explore the relationship of one man to his best friend.

MALE FRIENDSHIPS

Leslie Fielder has called it the classic American literary friendship: Jim and Huck, Chingachgook and Natty Bumppo, the affection of a Noble Savage and a Faust Without Sin. Paul Madvig and Ned Beaumont move through a landscape as perverse as any created by Mark Twain, trying to retain not innocence, for that has long vanished, but a minimum of personal integrity. In stressing his sheer physical strength, his animal characteristics, Hammett makes it clear that Paul is a kind of primitive. Paul could not succeed without Ned, who sees the essential natures of things. Like Huck, Ned seems to be without past, an orphan cut off from "society" by a stigma, in this case his gambling. Only together are they an effective unit, but the respect of each for the other's ability has come to an end. "You don't talk to me like that . . . ," says Beaumont when Madvig dismisses his vision, knowing that he, in turn, is denying Paul's power.

There are two fights between Beaumont and Madvig, and the novel's conflicts and subplots are magnetized around them. After the first argument, in which Beaumont tells Madvig that he has been "outsmarted" by the senator, there is a predictable fistfight and a peace that Hammett describes with tough guy affection:

> Madvig spoke hoarsely from deep down in him. "Ned."
>
> Ned Beaumont halted. His face became paler. He did not turn around.
>
> Madvig said: "You crazy son of a bitch."
>
> Then Beaumont turned around slowly.
>
> Madvig put out an open hand and pushed Ned Beaumont's face sidewise, shoving him off balance so he had to put a foot out quickly to that side and put a hand on one of the chairs at the table.
>
> Madvig said: "I ought to knock hell out of you."
>
> Ned Beaumont grinned sheepishly and sat down on the chair he had staggered against. Madvig sat down facing him and knocked on the top of the table with his seidel.
>
> The bar-tender opened the door and put his head in.
>
> "More beer," Madvig said.
>
> (**GK,** 71-72)

The second argument occurs after Madvig makes the false confession to Taylor Henry's murder. Ned's ire is more explicable when readers understand that Madvig is tampering with the reality that informs Beaumont's vision. When his most trusted confidant lies, Beaumont, a "fixer," is bereft of his ability to repair reality. He cannot solve the mystery then without Janet Henry, whose power as a senator's daughter and a quester after truth are an aid, but do not make her a satisfactory substitute for Paul.

Madvig does not appear again until Ned and Janet have laid Taylor's murder at the senator's feet. Then Madvig appears at Beaumont's apartment to apologize and to square accounts, an intent that he carries out even when Beaumont announces that Janet is leaving with him.

> Madvig's lips parted. He looked dumbly at Ned Beaumont and as he looked the blood went out of his face again. When his face was quite bloodless he mumbled something of which only the word "luck" could be understood, turned clumsily around, went to the door, opened it, and went out, leaving it open behind him.
>
> Janet Henry looked at Ned Beaumont. He stared fixedly at the door.
>
> (*GK*, 204)

Janet is the onlooker because the central relationship of the novel is between the two men, and its demise gapes at the reader as vacantly as the empty doorway. As the world grows more complex, deceptive, and unreadable, Huck and Jim grow rare. A breach can be forgiven once, but a breach reopened is a pattern, and in Hammett's world no one stands in the path of falling beams.

BEAUMONT AND JANET HENRY

A first reading of **The Glass Key** can leave the impression that the Ned-Janet liaison, which simmers for two thirds of the novel and boils only in the finale, is of paramount importance. The novel's title, after all, comes from an exchange between the two. Each had a dream about the other. Beaumont's is short. "I was fishing," he said, "and I caught an enormous fish—a rainbow trout, but enormous—and you said you wanted to look at it and you picked it up and threw it back in the water before I could stop you" (*GK*, 169).

It is a good dream for literary purposes, illustrating the Hammett hero's continuing distrust of women. The Continental Op trusted neither Dinah Brand nor Gabrielle Leggett, but gradually he grew more sympathetic, until in **The Maltese Falcon** Spade became most involved with the woman who most deceived him. In his incarnation as Beaumont, the hero has isolated himself from women. There is a version of Dinah Brand, named Lee Wilshire, who is scheming, attractive, and tough, but who fails to move Beaumont. He could seduce a flapper named Fedink, but he goes into the bathroom and is sick instead. Courtship itself has vanished; when Opal asks, "Aren't we friends?" Beaumont's reply is that "it's hard to remember it when we're lying to each other." (*GK*, 26) This points to a new female ideal; besides emotional toughness and a poker player's ability to bluff, the heroine needs a fierce respect for the truth:

Janet Henry leaned forward in her chair. "Why don't you like me?" she asked Ned Beaumont.

"I think maybe I do," he said.

She shook her head. "You don't. I know it."

"You can't go by my manners," he told her. "They're always pretty bad."

"You don't like me," she insisted, not answering his smile, "and I want you to."

He was modest. "Why?"

(*GK*, 95)

Janet hides her emotions so effectively that Ned does not know, until a nurse tells him, that "she went out of here as near crying as anybody could without crying." But of course she *does not* cry, and Beaumont must shatter that dispassionate mask before he can allow her access to his emotions. Only when he succeeds, accusing her of being a Judith (an allusion to the biblical character who saved her people by killing her king), can Beaumont join forces with her. As he reduces her, Beaumont is "talking happily—not to her—though now and then he leaned his head over his shoulder to smile at her." She sits trembling, blanched, and silent, her femininity evident but checked by the masculine animus that attracts Beaumont. This encounter prompts the discussion of dreams. Janet's dream is much longer, and in the first telling she changes the ending.

> we were lost in a forest, you and I, tired and starving. We walked and walked till we came to a little house and we knocked on the door, but nobody answered. We tried the door. It was locked. Then we peeped through a window and inside we could see a great big table piled high with all imaginable kinds of food. But we couldn't get in through either of the windows because they had iron bars over them.

This locale is important, for Bruno Bettleheim has attested: "Since ancient times the near impenetrable forest in which we get lost has symbolized the dark, hidden, near-impenetrable world of our unconscious. If we have lost the framework which gave structure to our past life and must now find our own way to become ourselves, and have entered this wilderness with an as yet undeveloped personality, when we succeed in finding our way out we shall emerge with a much more highly developed humanity."[24] Janet's dream continues:

> Then we thought that sometimes people left their keys under door-mats and we looked and there it was. But when we opened the door we saw hundreds and hundreds of snakes on the floor where we hadn't been able to see them through the window and they all came sliding and slithering towards us. We slammed the door shut and locked it and stood there frightened to death listening to them hissing and knocking their heads against the inside of the door. Then you said that perhaps if we opened the door and hid from the snakes they'd come out and go away, so we did. . . . Then

we jumped down and ran inside and locked the door and ate and ate and I woke sitting up in bed clapping my hands and laughing.

(**GK,** 169-70)

In the novel's final scene, however, Janet adds, "I didn't tell you—the key was glass and shattered in our hands just as we got the door open, because the lock was stiff and we had to force it. . . . We couldn't lock the snakes in and they came out all over us and I woke up screaming" (**GK,** 202).

Janet's dream interprets the action of the novel, and indicates the diminished though realistic state in which Hammett leaves male-female relations. The house Janet dreams about represents the structure that she needs, the food the security of that structure. In actuality the only "key" that Ned and Janet find can unite them is a ruthless stripping away of each other's manners, illusions, and pretensions. A Freudian would say the snakes represent a male threat, and in fact this illusionless tough-guy milieu is an antifeminine world. Janet has a deep-seated, justifiable fear of life with Beaumont. When she lies about the ending of the dream, she flatters Beaumont by implying that he can put the lid back on Pandora's Box. But the dream reveals that the evil loosed cannot be vanquished. Beaumont's charges that she was a "whore" and her father a "pimp" are the *coup de grâce* in their mutual savaging. Their affection, like the glass key, "was stiff and we had to force it." The novel ends on a note of alienation as bleak as any canvas of Edward Munch. Janet watches Ned watch an empty doorway; she can only impersonate Sancho Panza to a visionary for whom quests are no longer possible. Instead of a house, they find the woods without end.

CRITICISM OF *THE GLASS KEY*

"Because it is not allegorical Gothic romance, lacking as it does a God-like Spade or Op, **The Glass Key** is Hammett's least satisfactory novel," writes Edenbaum.[25] Such a view, of course, limits Hammett's work to a genre, rather than recognizing his development as a complete writer. Seen in the progression of his work, **The Glass Key** is one of Hammett's best novels. He holds reader interest firmly while breaking free of the generic expectations that hounded him. He creates male relationships that are not merely hierarchical, and he elaborates a complex, pessimistic view of love.

Seen as a conventional novel, however, **The Glass Key** has its difficulties. There is fuzziness around the motives of the characters. "The question remains whether Paul was right in the first place, whether Ned acted out of desire for the girl rather than loyalty to Paul . . . ," Edenbaum concludes. But perhaps this is a strength. The question can be answered outside the generic limits implicit in this critic's judgment, if readers dare to see

that Beaumont has been looking out for himself all along. Hammett gives liberal clues that this is just the case. Unfortunately, few readers see how fallen the hero is. The two principal lines of plot are set in motion by Beaumont's perception that you do not get what you want if you are willing to be trumped. He sees early that Shad O'Rory will overturn Madvig's empire because Madvig is unwilling to make free use of intimidation and murder. "That the hole Shad's put you in—or don't you think he'd go that far to put you in a hole?" asks Beaumont. (**GK,** 60) Madvig's idealistic refusal to fix a jail term becomes his weakness in an opportunistic, vicious world. Nor is man at love different from man at war. When Beaumont is in the hospital, he uses his injuries to attract Janet's attention, sizing up his opportunities behind "a tight, secretive smile." When Madvig solicits advice on appropriate presents, on proper attire, Beaumont knows the field is his if he wants Janet. And when Madvig tells him to "kiss off," he telephones Janet and invites her over, "whistling tunelessly under his breath." He pours himself a drink, puts on a fresh collar and starts a fire in the fireplace. When he tells Janet that Madvig killed Taylor, which he knows to be a lie, Beaumont is simply acting as a survivor. This is Poisonville, the corruption the Op sensed would make him "blood simple" has spread throughout the social organism, and the Hammett hero is free of the illusion that he stands apart.

Notes

1. [Dashiell] Hammett, Introduction to *The Maltese Falcon* (New York, 1934), p. vii.

2. For details, see [Richard] Layman, *Shadow Man, The Life of Dashiell Hammett* (New York, 1981), pp. 110-11.

3. Hammett, *The Maltese Falcon* (New York, 1972), p. 220; hereafter cited in the text as *MF*.

4. See Layman, *Shadow Man*, p. 112, and Paul Kress, "Justice, Proof and Plausibility in Conan Doyle and Dashiell Hammett," *Occasional Review* 7 (1977): 121.

5. Bernard Schopen, "From Puzzles to People: the Development of the American Detective Novel," *Studies in American Fiction* 7, no. 2 (1979): 180.

6. S. F. Bauer, L. Balter, and W. Hunt, "The Detective Film as Myth: The Maltese Falcon and Sam Spade," *American Imago* 35 (1978): 282.

7. [George] Grella ["Murder and the Mean Streets: The Hard Boiled Detective Novel," in *Detective Fiction: Crime and Compromise,* ed. Dick Allen and David Chaco (New York, 1974)], p. 417.

8. [William] Nolan, *Dashiell Hammett, A Casebook* [Santa Barbara, Calif., 1969], p. 58.

9. Ibid., p. 63.

10. Character information, ibid., p. 59.

11. [William] Kenney, "The Dashiell Hammett Tradition and the Modern American Detective Novel" [Ph.D. dissertation, University of Michigan, 1964], p. 110; Ross MacDonald, in Nolan, *Dashiell Hammett,* p. 63.

12. [George J.] Thompson, "The Problem of Moral Vision in Dashiell Hammett's Detective Novels" [Ph.D. dissertation, University of Connecticut-Storrs, 1972], pp. 112, 115-16.

13. Nolan, *Dashiell Hammett,* p. 61.

14. Robert Edenbaum, "The Poetics of the Private-Eye: The Novels of Dashiell Hammett," in *Tough Guy Writers of the Thirties,* [ed. David Madden] (Carbondale, Ill., 1968), p. 82.

15. Hammett to Block, 16 June 1929, HRC. [Dashiell Hammett, manuscript of "Seven Pages," at the Humanities Research Center, University of Texas-Austin (hereafter this location cited as HRC).]

16. Hammett to Block, 31 August 1929, HRC.

17. Shaw, quoted in Nolan, *Dashiell Hammett,* p. 57.

18. Reviews summarized by Layman, *Shadow Man,* pp. 112-13.

19. Hammett to Asbury, 6 February 1930, HRC; Raymond Chanler, *The Simple Art of Murder* [New York, 1972], p. 17; Ross MacDonald in Nolan, *Dashiell Hammett,* p. 63.

20. Hammett to Knopf, 19 September 1929; Hammett to Asbury, 6 February 1930, HRC.

21. The citations in sequence: David T. Bazelon, *Commentary* 7 (May 1949): 471; Robert Edenbaum, "Poetics of the Private Eye," p. 99; and Phillip Durham, "The Black Mask School," in *Tough Guy Writers,* p. 71.

22. Hammett, *The Glass Key* (New York, 1972), p. 9; hereafter cited in the text as *GK.*

23. Edenbaum, "Poetics," p. 102; Durham, "School," p. 70; Kenney, "Tradition," p. 93.

24. Bruno Bettleheim, *The Uses of Enchantment* (New York: Vintage, 1977), p. 94.

25. Edenbaum, "Poetics," p. 100.

Dennis Dooley (essay date 1984)

SOURCE: Dooley, Dennis. "Dead Souls: *The Dain Curse.*" In *Dashiell Hammett,* pp. 87-98. New York: Frederick Ungar Publishing Co., 1984.

[*In the following essay, Dooley describes* The Dain Curse *as a "study in evil" that takes a "disturbing look" at "atrocity and cynicism."*]

"It does, as you put it, look like the work of one mind."

The novelist Owen Fitzstephan in *The Dain Curse*[1]

As Personville's stand-in savior the Op turns in a less-than Christ-like performance. The survivor instincts in him run too deep to accommodate martyrdom.

None of Hammett's heroes dies. But then that is in the nature of the genre to which he chose to restrict himself, or within which he was most comfortable. Whichever way you look at it, the fact is that—in marked contrast to other writers of the hard-boiled school such as Ernest Hemingway, James M. Cain, Horace McCoy, and Nathanael West—Hammett had deliberately limited himself to a type of fiction in which the main character is by definition the survivor, the one who, even if everybody else falls victim to the powers of evil, comes out on top.

Indeed, the ultimate survival of the hero is no doubt one of the satisfactions habitual readers of detective stories seek in the genre. It is something one can count on, come hell or high water. When Conan Doyle tried to kill off Sherlock Holmes the public was outraged—and not only, I suggest, because they wanted more adventures. Doyle had sinned against their deepest sense of order.

With Hammett's Op survival has become almost a theme. In **Red Harvest** he explains to Dinah Brand that it is a matter of being "tough enough to survive." And that involves not only stamina but one's very lifestyle. In **Red Harvest,** as in the earlier stories, the Op's style of talking and acting both symbolizes and abets his determination to outlast his foes.

In one memorable scene early on in the book, he has just entered a room. Suddenly he is being shot at from a dark rooftop across the street. "I looked around for something to chuck at the light globe, found a Gideon Bible and chucked it. The bulb popped apart, giving me darkness." If the Op, like his creator, is a tortured idealist who misses the presence of some kind of eternal moral principles in the world, he is also a wily pragmatist who knows that in a world of hypocrisy and evil it is sometimes not in light but in the absence of light that lies one's only chance for survival.

Darkness, oddly enough, was to become the dominant motif of Hammett's next book. The very titles of the original installments in which **The Dain Curse** first appeared between November 1928 and February 1929 in *Black Mask* reflect this preoccupation: **"Black Lives," "The Hollow Temple," "Black Honeymoon"** and **"Black Riddle."**

The Op is investigating the disappearance of some diamonds on behalf of an insurance company. As usual, he probes beyond the "obvious" solution, uncovering disconnected threads of some more mysterious goings-on. A key suspect is murdered. Then Edgar Leggett himself, the man from whom the gems were stolen, suddenly turns up dead, accompanied by a strange "suicide" note that opens the door on a sordid family history.

He is in reality, we learn, one Maurice de Mayenne, a fugitive from justice and escapee from Devil's Island who had murdered his first wife and married her sister. Within a handful of pages the Op's keen observation and habitual skepticism have exploded the dead man's story, drawing from Leggett's distraught widow Alice a second, then a third version—each more sinister than the preceding. Some twenty years before in Paris, Mayenne had married a young Englishwoman named Lily Dain, who was pregnant with his child, but secretly loving her sister Alice instead. For almost five years Alice had lusted for her sister's death—until a bizarre accident with a loaded gun in the hand of a five-year-old child ironically brought it about. In Alice Dain's final confession the story grows even more macabre. Alice, it seems, had cold-bloodedly taught the child a morbid "little game" with an unloaded pistol kept in a drawer in her parents' room.

> I would lie on Lily's bed, pretending to sleep. The child would push a chair to the chiffonier, climb up on it, take the pistol from the drawer, creep over to the bed, put the muzzle of the pistol to my head, and press the trigger. When she did it well, making little or no noise, holding the pistol correctly in her tiny hands, I would reward her with candy, cautioning her against saying anything about the game to her mother or to anyone else, as we were going to surprise her mother with it.

On that fateful day, returning home unexpectedly, Mayenne had reached the bedroom door just as little Gabrielle pulled the trigger. The traumatic memory of this monstrous incident was eventually suppressed from the consciousness of the child, who even then, says Alice, showed signs of being mentally deficient. Whether or not drugs were used at the time, the twenty-year-old girl who now stands whimpering under the venomous shower of curses by her hateful stepmother has become a dull-eyed drug addict without a shred of self-respect. She is cursed, Alice Dain Leggett tells her sister's daughter,

> with the same black soul and rotten blood that she [Lily] and I and all the Danis have had; and you're cursed with your mother's blood on your hands in babyhood; and with the twisted mind and the need for drugs that are my gift to you; and your life will be black as your mother's and mine were black; and the lives of those you touch will be black as Maurice's was black.

Within moments Alice Dain is dead, killed in a scuffle during an attempt to make her escape. And so might have ended a tale of horror, murder and frightful revelations of the sort the readers of the pulps had encountered before. But Hammett has only begun.

There is something about the three versions of the Dain family history—indeed about all that has happened—that has left the Op uneasy. "You're never satisfied until you've got two buts and an if attached to everything," an exasperated old acquaintance named Owen Fitzstephan chides him in the course of the next chapter, aptly entitled "Buts and Ifs," in which the detective worries over the "established facts" as a child would pick at a scab.

Fitzstephan, a novelist the Op had known back east ("We used to drink out of the same bottle"), serves as the Op's confidant throughout *The Dain Curse* in a series of comradely chats which usually take place over beer and supper in his landlady's basement. Together they sift through the facts and analyze the characters, often echoing each other's very phrases. Even when they are arguing, their mutual put-downs seem good-natured. The underlying similarity between a novelist's work and a detective's clearly fascinates them. "Are you—who make your living snooping—sneering at my curiosity about people and my attempts to satisfy it?" asks Fitzstephan.

> "We're different," I said. "I do mine with the object of putting people in jail, and I get paid for it, though not as much as I should."
>
> "That's not different," he said. "I do mine with the object of putting people in books, and I get paid for it, though not as much as I should."
>
> "Yeah, but what good does that do?"
>
> "God knows. What good does putting them in jail do?"

People who knew Hammett must have doubly enjoyed these exchanges since, as William F. Nolan has pointed out, the description we are given of Fitzstephan closely parallels[2]—employing some of the very words and phrases—Hammett's description of himself in a letter of the period. Fitzstephan, we are told, is "a long, lean, sorrel-haired man of thirty-two with sleepy gray eyes, a wide mouth and carelessly worn clothes; a man who pretended to be lazier than he was, would rather talk than do anything else and had a lot of what seemed to be accurate information and original ideas on any subject that happened to come up, as long as it was a little out of the ordinary."

But if Hammett the novelist allows himself to come in for a little kidding, he also takes the opportunity of this "appearance" in one of his own books to poke fun at his paunchy detective and his nose-to-the-grindstone method of forever marshaling "all the facts you can get and turn[ing] them over and over till they click."

"If that's your technic, you'll have to put up with it," Fitzstephan tells the Op. "But I'm damned if I see why I should suffer. You recited the Mayenne-Leggett-Collinson history step by step last night at least half a dozen times. You've done nothing else since breakfast this morning. I'm getting enough of it. Nobody's mysteries ought to be as tiresome as you're making this one."

"Hell," the Op comes back. "I sat up half the night after you went to bed and recited it to myself. You got to turn them over and over, my boy, until they click."

"I like the Nick Carter school better," sniffs Fitzstephan.

The novelist frowns at the detective's determination to find a more prosaic explanation for the Dain family's tragedy than some mysterious "strain in the blood." The detective dismisses the novelist's interpretation of what happened as too "literary." "I'm a novelist," says Fitzstephan. "My business is with souls and what goes on in them." In fact, it is the coexistence of a hard-headed realism with an interest in "souls and what goes on in them" in Hammett himself that makes him an interesting writer and his detective stories more truly novels than most examples of the genre. For the Op's relentless and painstaking methods—along with his poker player's knack for flushing out his opponent's hand—will uncover in the course of this, his second novel, a story of human weaknesses, jealousies, hates, lust, egotism and revenge that reveals Hammett to be a considerable student of human nature.

Like *Red Harvest, The Dain Curse* was to be a study in evil. But if the early novelette *Blood Money* and the book that followed it chronicle the Op's own sickening descent into the slough of cynicism, bringing him finally face to face with the fact of his own participation in the world's evil, *The Dain Curse* was to take an even more disturbing look (*pace* André Gide) at atrocity and cynicism. And Hammett placed at its center the most truly satanic of all his villains, the blackest and most completely cynical soul he could imagine: the novelist Owen Fitzstephan.

Indeed the sinister circumstances in which the detective continually finds himself are like bad dreams from which he cannot quite awaken—for the Op has, quite literally, become a character in a plot of Fitzstephan's making. It is the universe of some perverse, morbid god whose dark logic forever eludes one's grasp even as it teases the mind with the shadow of some obscure purpose. "It does, as you put it, look like the work of one mind," Fitzstephan finally agrees with the frustrated detective. "And a goofy one," adds the Op.

But the clues have been there from the beginning, if only we—and the Op—had been able to make the connections. The novel reread after the revelations of the last pages becomes an almost equally sinister story on a wholly different level. In the very second paragraph where the Op introduces his old friend to the reader (in a chapter ominously entitled **"Something Black"**), the detective reveals he had met him "five years before, in New York, where I was digging dirt on a chain of fake mediums who had taken a coal-and-ice dealer's widow for a hundred thousand dollars. Fitzstephan," says the Op innocently, "was plowing the same field for literary material. We became acquainted and pooled forces. I got more out of the combination than he did, since he knew the spook racket inside and out; and, with his help, I cleaned up my job in a couple of weeks."

Fewer than twenty pages later the Op is ringing the doorbell of a mysterious urban retreat known as the Temple of the Holy Grail. And another thirty pages after that, barely two into the second part of the book (**"The Temple"**), he is preparing to spend the night in the place—a night he will long if not fondly remember.

Gabrielle Leggett, with her doctor's approval, has taken refuge there with a strange couple known as the Haldorns, friends of her late parents, who have gathered a following of well-heeled society types who seem to find some solace in the druidic rites over which the Elijah-like Joseph Haldorn presides at a thirty-foot-high altar in an atrium open to the stars. The Op has been engaged by Gabrielle's guardian, an attorney named Madison Andrews, to see if his ward is all right. Andrews's skepticism concerning such mystery cults—which enjoyed a great surge of popularity on the coast during the nineteen twenties—is exceeded only by that of the Op himself. "I didn't believe in the supernatural," he says flatly. But even he, to his surprise, finds the Haldorns strangely irresistible.

"[He] looked at you and spoke to you," he tells Fitzstephan of his encounter with the white-haired prophet, "and things happened inside you. I'm not the easiest guy in the world to dazzle, I hope; but he had me going. I came damned near to believing he was God toward the last." But before that first night in the renovated six-story apartment house-cum-temple is over, the Op will experience things that seem to fall beyond the normal definition of the real: an incorporeal apparition with which he struggles desperately for his life in a tiny room, a man whom bullets pass through but cannot stop, bloody daggers and disappearing bodies, but most of all the truly spooky behavior of the young woman he has been sent to guard, who wanders the halls in a zombielike state, claiming to have murdered people and to have seen the devil.

The temple and all that goes on there—or appears to go on—is a wonderful metaphor (and Hammett, evidently sensing this, is said to have greatly expanded its role[3] and introduced it much earlier in the hardcover version of the tale) for the novel's theme: the exploitation of the need to believe. Even the curse wished on her by her dying stepmother—a continuation of the larger curse said to control the destiny of all the Dains—is embraced by poor Gabrielle, and continually urged on the bewildered detective, because at least it "explains" the monstrous series of events that seem to dog her life.

Indeed, for all the Op's casual dismissal of it as little more than "words in an angry woman's mouth," the curse seems to be slowly, relentlessly fulfilled as a series of persons close to Gabrielle one by one turn up dead under a variety of strange and often downright sinister circumstances. And the remaining threads of sanity she clings to are progressively severed as she surrenders to the morbid mysteries of the cult and the gathering darkness of despair.

But just as the Op takes obvious pleasure in exposing the temple's fakery, Hammett dispels the magical gloom that pervades the story with the hard edge of his realism. Most of Gabrielle's spooky behavior, not to mention her highly suggestive disposition, is inspired it turns out by nothing more spiritual than "a skinful of hop"—first cocaine, then morphine. Her drug habit and eventual "cold-turkey" cure at the hands of the Op are described with the clinical eye of one who had, in the employ of Pinkerton's no doubt, known his share of "hopheads" and probably seen at least one kick the habit: the attacks of sneezing and yawning, the painful sharpening of the senses as the body's system throws off its anesthetizing cargo of poison, followed by the lump in the throat and the aching in the jaws and the hollows behind the knees that signal the approach of the ordeal's end (not to mention the diminished sex drive of an addict, which plays a part in the story).

The compelling power of other popular beliefs is similarly dispelled. It is "as foolish to try to read character from the shape of ears," the Op tells Gabrielle, "as from the position of stars, tea-leaves, or spit in the sand," and "anybody who started hunting for evidence of insanity in himself would certain find plenty, because all but stupid minds [are] jumbled affairs." The "sinister" blacks and Mexican who seem at first to have some involvement in the dark work afoot turn out to be loyal servants whose "strange" ways have merely cloaked their essential innocence. Small-town law-enforcement officers bicker and covet one another's wives, men and women act in precipitous and often thoughtless ways—motivated by such eternal principles as jealousy, rage, lust and fear of exposure.

But mostly lust.

More than five decades of detective fiction, movies and television shows later, it is easy to miss the revolutionary character of Hammett's innovation in the area of motive. Gone are the bloodless villains of earlier detective fiction, monsters of greed or some vague compulsion to indulge in sly games of one-upmanship with the police. Hammett's villains—indeed the "good" characters sometimes seem to differ from the "bad" ones only in degree—are real twentieth-century adults, as earthy and lust-ridden as those in any soap opera. There "was nothing to show that her influence on people was any worse than anybody else's," the Op says of his attempt to convince Gabrielle of her normality, "it being doubtful that many people had a very good influence on those of the opposite sex." Fitzstephan may possess the elephantine ego of a Moriarity, but his rage is based on something as pedestrian—and human—as wanting a woman he cannot have.

Modern social realities such as adultery and drugs had never played so intimate a part of anyone's detective fiction—the great Sherlock's much-vaunted cocaine habit notwithstanding—as they do in Samuel Dashiell Hammett's second novel.

Oddly, it is in this novel—which Ernest Hemingway pronounced Hammett's "bloodiest to date"—that his detective hero is at his saintliest. After the agonizing self-doubts of *Red Harvest, The Dain Curse* shows the Op to be more clearly than ever on the side of the good. And it is Hammett's choice, oddly enough, of a vulnerable young woman—more genuinely innocent than any other he had created—that allows the hard-bitten Op to escape the old pattern to which he so often succumbs in the earlier stories. His hard-boiled patter is at its most transparent, his idealism the least camouflaged. And though he protests to Gabrielle that he is "only a hired man with only a hired man's interest in your troubles," the reader doesn't believe him for a moment. The Op even seems, in the last line of the story (which turns characteristically on himself), to enjoy the idea that he might have had, as he kiddingly understates it, "a refining influence" on the young lady.

"Do I believe you because you're sincere?" she asks the Op at one point, introducing a favorite theme of Hammett's (and one particularly at issue in this book). "Or because you've learned how—as a trick of your business—to make people believe in you?" "Your belief in me is built on mine in you," the Op answers her kindly. "If mine's unjustified, so is yours. So let me ask you a question first: Were you lying when you said, 'I don't want to be evil'?" "Belief" is a word that crops up often in the course of this novel. And it is her belief in him, as the Op understands only too well, that will be the key to her recovery from years of addiction.

Is it love, mere sentimentality—or something else—that motivates the Op to lead her to her cure and to stick with her through her arduous journey back from the depths of hell? Hammett avoids a straight answer. "I'm twice your age, sister; an old man," the Op barks in answer to her question. "I'm damned if I'll make a chump of myself by telling you why I did it, why it was neither revolting nor disgusting, why I'd do it again and be glad of the chance."

But a clue may lie in the next sentence out of his mouth, which chides her about parading around with her robe "hanging open." ("You ex-hopheads have to be careful about catching cold," he quickly adds, undercutting the moment again with a piece of Hammett's interesting clinical information.) But it would be unfair to suggest that his interest in her is merely carnal—though Hammett further teases us, a few pages later, when she suddenly decides he's "a monster. A nice one, an especially nice one to have around when you're in trouble, but a monster just the same, without any human foolishness like love in him, and—What's the matter? Have I said something I shouldn't?" (What has she seen—a sudden tear? a look?) After which he indirectly admits—in seriousness? in jest?—that he is drawn to her even as the monster Fitzstephan was. "Oh, dear!" is all Gabrielle can say. Though in what tone of voice we can only guess.

As a novel, *The Dain Curse* has its weaknesses. Though Hammett is said to have heavily reworked[4] the magazine material in preparing the book version and to have made many striking improvements, there is something less satisfying about the book's structure than, say, that of *Red Harvest.* The wonderfully vivid temple setting is confined almost entirely to the second quarter of the book, which subsequently jumps back and forth between the dusty gulches of the southern California coast and some fairly colorless rooms somewhere in San Francisco. Most disappointingly, the book is overly talky: We are told in the last pages—in a utilitarian kind of shorthand style—much concerning the lives of these characters that a traditional novelist would have found better ways to show.

But the story's logic is airtight, and its characters true. There are no clumsy distortions or maddening false clues such as mar many a mystery novel. No jejune switches in point of view in order to make the mystery work—such as spoil Agatha Christie's overpraised story, "Three Blind Mice" (later adapted for the stage as *The Mousetrap*), in which one moment we are inside a character's head, privy to her most intimate thoughts, and the next are not even allowed to see the mysterious person she is talking to, though we can *hear* his voice! *The Dain Curse,* by comparison, is most artfully managed. And the variations worked on the novel's theme— the exploitation of the need to believe—are positively brilliant. For just as her cruel stepmother's version (later cast in doubt) of how Gabrielle's mother died drove the gullible girl into the unprincipled clutches of the Haldorns, who further exploited her belief in her own evil

and in the operation of some sinister force in her life, so Gabrielle's ultimate deliverance was made possible by her belief that the detective sought only her good and would stand by her. But the last and most perfect stroke is the diabolical twist worked on the book's theme—a turn worthy of Fitzstephan—in its final pages.

Turned into the mangled wreck of a human being by a homemade bomb—he has lost his right arm and leg and at least half of his face—Fitzstephan had in some ways received a fitting punishment for his sins. (The shock of this development is all the greater coming as it does at a point when all but the canniest of readers must still believe in the good-natured innocence of Fitzstephan.) But the Op's—and presumably Hammett's—deeper sense of justice demanded some worse fate still for the evil genius who had brought so much misery into so many lives.

The Op finds the answer in belief. Or, to be more precise, in the exploitation of Fitzstephan's need to believe that he has succeeded in pulling off a monstrous joke on the world—having convinced both the jury and the newspapers, through his own brilliant defense, "that nobody but a lunatic" could have committed so many and such heinous crimes, and having as a result gotten off scot free to end his days, such as they are, undisturbed on an island in Puget Sound. (His helpless condition makes it unnecessary that he be kept in a mental hospital.)

The Op simply conveys the impression that he believes Fitzstephan to be actually insane. And testifies to the effect that he considers the novelist "legally entitled" to escape hanging.

> Owen Fitzstephan never spoke to me again. . . . He wanted the rest of the world, or at least the dozen who would represent the world on his jury, to think he had been crazy . . . but he didn't want me to agree with them. As a sane man who, by pretending to be a lunatic, had done as he pleased and escaped punishment, he had a joke—if you wanted to call it that—on the world. But if he was a lunatic who, ignorant of his craziness, thought he was pretending to be a lunatic, then the joke—if you wanted to call it that—was on him. And my having such a joke on him was more than his egotism could stomach.

Hammett's own ego was getting a good deal of stroking. Between the appearance of the last installment of *Red Harvest* in February 1928 and the final installment of *The Dain Curse* in February 1929, the circulation of *Black Mask* had increased, writes William F. Nolan, by 30,000.[5] Hammett was in demand. And with the publication in book form of *The Dain Curse* later in the same year his fame with an ever-growing public seemed assured.

But the popular Continental Op, that new kind of detective hero who had so captured the public's imagination, would appear in only three more stories. Hammett had outgrown him, and the possibilities the series presented. His next novel, which was to unfold in the pages of *Black Mask* over five consecutive months beginning that September, would push the detective genre to heretofore unimagined limits. Indeed, the esteemed critic Alexander Woollcott would pronounce **The Maltese Falcon** "the best detective story America has yet produced."[6] And to do what he had in mind, Hammett needed a new and rather different character.

Notes

1. Hammett, *The Dain Curse,* p. 155.

2. Nolan, *Dashiell Hammett: A Casebook,* p. 54.

3. Ibid., p. 54.

4. Ibid., p. 54.

5. Ibid., p. 55.

6. Dust jacket blurb for *The Glass Key* (New York. Alfred A. Knopf, 1931).

Bibliography

I. Works by Hammett

A. Novels

Red Harvest. New York: Alfred A. Knopf, 1929. (Vintage Books Edition, October 1972.) Dedication is to Joseph Thomas Shaw, editor of *Black Mask.*

The Dain Curse. New York: Alfred A. Knopf, 1929. (Vintage Books Edition, October 1972.) Dedication is to Albert S. Samuels, the San Francisco jeweler for whom Hammett had worked for a time.

The Maltese Falcon. New York: Alfred A. Knopf, 1930. (Vintage Books Edition, May 1972.) Dedication is to Jose, Hammett's wife.

The Glass Key. New York: Alfred A. Knopf, 1931. (Vintage Books Edition, May 1972.) Dedication is to Nell Martin, a widowed piano player and music teacher with whom Hammett went off to New York (as Ned Beaumont and Janet Henry do at the end of the novel), after leaving his wife. Said to have been Hammett's own favorite among all his books.

B. Short Fiction (in print)

The Big Knockover: Selected Stories and Short Novels by Dashiell Hammet. New York: Vintage Books, 1972. Edited and with an introduction by Lillian Hellman, which was subsequently incorporated into her book-length memoir, *An Unfinished Woman.* Includes "The Gutting of Couffignal," "Fly Paper," "The Scorched Face," "This King Business," "The Gatewood Caper," "Dead Yellow Women," "Corkscrew," *Tulip,* "The Big Knockover," and "$106,000 Blood Money."

II. Selected Works about Hammett

A. Biographical

Nolan, William F. *Hammett: A Life at the Edge.* New York: Congdon and Weed, 1983.

B. Critical

Nolan, William F. *Dashiel Hammett: A Casebook.* Santa Barbara: McNally and Loftin, 1969. Introduction by Philip Durham. Has an extensive historical bibliography of Hammett's work in various media.

Robert Shulman (essay date fall 1985)

SOURCE: Shulman, Robert. "Dashiell Hammett's Social Vision." *Centennial Review* 29, no. 4 (fall 1985): 400-19.

[*In the following essay, Shulman explores Hammett's treatment of individualism and the corruption of capitalist society in* Red Harvest, The Maltese Falcon, *and* The Glass Key.]

Dashiell Hammett has suffered from a double stigma. He writes in a popular genre academics for the most part do not take seriously. And during the Cold War his politics were dangerous, and the most promising approach to his fiction was in disrepute. These conditions are changing. We are now in a position to develop the detailed criticism that intelligent evaluation of Hammett's work must be based on.

I

As Hammett knew, *genre* is more than a set of literary conventions, and the tough-guy detective novels he wrote are no exception. *Genre* also carries a concealed social message of its own, describes in fictional form the myths of a specific social system, and prescribes for its characters a set of interrelated dilemmas, all of which can be understood for Hammet as generated by the structures and values of his unstable, acquisitive America. In **Red Harvest, The Maltese Falcon,** and **The Glass Key** Hammett also brings alive the conflicting versions of individualism that society emphasizes. Particularly in **The Maltese Falcon,** Hammett is concerned with stories and storytelling, with a market society world that systematically demands improvisation, acting, and the manipulation of appearances, people, and feelings. In 1953 Hammett testified before a House investigating committee ostensibly concerned about "pro-Communist" books in the overseas libraries run by the State Department. Hammett refused to say whether he was a Communist but he did tell the committee he thought it "was impossible to write anything without taking some sort of social stand."[1] In at least three compelling and representative novels from some twenty years earlier, Hammett had elaborated in fictional form, in a version of the detective novel *genre,* a "social stand" which reveals a brilliant and penetrating analysis of a late capitalist acquisitive society.

The Maltese Falcon is his most precise and suggestive work but Hammett gives us a general outline of his characteristic world in his first novel, *Red Harvest* (1929). In it he exposes the violence and political corruption of Poisonville, a mess brought on when the town's upper class political boss had troops come in to break a striking union. The bad elements stayed to take over his control of the town. The Hammett detective, the Continental Op, is deeply involved in the underground, anarchic chaos and violence at the same time that he restores a kind of order. Hammett, who is fascinated with subterranean, anarchic energy, gives full expression to the individualistic violence and resourcefulness of the Continental Op. The order at the end is not in the name of the law or of official society but rather of the Op's desire to get the job done and his opposition to corrupt forces much like his own energies. His individualism differs from his opponents' in that he is not after political or economic power like those who make the allegorically named "Personville" into "Poisonville." Using as his vehicle the gangland warfare of the 1920's, through the Continental Op and his opponents Hammett thus develops a suggestively mixed view of the lawlessness, violence, and energy informing the surfaces and depths of an acquisitive, individualistic society. It is the America of Hobbes's war of each against all.[2]

In the best of the two books Hammett wrote immediately after *Red Harvest,* in his most famous novel, *The Maltese Falcon* (1930), Hammett also gives his social vision its fullest expression. As Ian Watt shows in *The Rise of the Novel,* Defoe bodied forth a myth appropriate to the individualistic society of his period. Hammett, in the tradition of *Robinson Crusoe,* does the same for the American version of that society 200 years later. In *The Maltese Falcon,* Gutman, Cairo, and Brigid O'Shaughnessy ruthlessly pursue their own self-interest as they try to obtain the jeweled black bird, a Satanic embodiment of fabulous wealth. The bird is fake but the quest continues. The characters are exotic but their motives are all too familiar and their destructive results constitute a judgment on the entire enterprise of single-mindedly pursuing wealth. Much more deeply and acutely than in his earlier work and in a different mode than in his subsequent fiction, Hammett brings to a suggestive focus his concern with American individualism.

Through the motives, the dark milieu, and the structure of relations in *The Maltese Falcon,* Hammett has created a myth of early twentieth-century capitalism, a world in which self-interested entrepreneurs fiercely compete for a property whose ownership is ambiguous.[3] On the capitalistic model, contracts and the pursuit of wealth hold society together. In the novel, characters give their word, form temporary alliances, talk extensively about "trust," and do what they feel they need to in order to obtain the treasure. The literal murders are less significant than the resulting pervasive killing of human ties and relations. Because of the human isolation, betrayals, and obsessive pursuit of false goals, the novel renders a hell-on-earth, a kind of vital death-in-life that brings the outside American world to the test and that finally brought Dashiell Hammett to an independent relation with the Communist Party. In *The Maltese Falcon* Hammett has thus refined, complicated, and made much more precise the world of individualistic, Hobbesian violence, warfare, and systematic absence of trust he had imagined in *Red Harvest* and the Continental Op stories.[4]

The creator of Sam Spade was deeply critical of an acquisitive society but his social stand was independent, not doctrinaire. Sam Spade represents a different style of individualism from the other characters in *The Maltese Falcon.* He is a "blond Satan" who functions in the dark underworld and who seeks the treasure, not, however, as property but for non-material reasons.[5] Spade has his professional curiosity and his code—"I'll bury my dead"—and he pursues his objective with all of the independence, cunning, and ruthlessness of those antagonists he partly resembles. And he suffers the same alienation, intensified by the fact that he probably loves a woman he cannot trust and must turn in. Spade, moreover, betrays Archer and Iva even as Brigid betrays him: "merry-go-round" appropriately characterizes more than Chapter Twelve. Like the Continental Op and Ned Beaumont, Spade is flawed but like them his individualism is a source of moral strength as well as of alienation. As his story about Flitcraft reveals, moreover, Spade has a poetic depth of awareness about the contingency of human mortality. Spade is an ambiguous hero, tainted, mixed, and finally admirable. Much of the social drama of the novel is generated because Spade's style of individualism intersects and opposes the Gutman-Cairo-Brigid version of competitive individualism.

In a world of competing individuals, ideally contracts and the legal system are the referees and constitute the social bonds tying together the atomistic competitors. In *The Maltese Falcon* the legal system and official society are represented by the detectives, Tom Polhaus and Dundy, and the D. A., Bryan. Spade is as much at odds with them as he is with Gutman, Cairo, and Brigid. Of course he has Effie Perine and Sam Wise on his side but basically Spade is an American loner individualist, outside and opposed to both the official society and the underworld of the novel. Narrative tension results because Spade is under attack or suspicion from both sides and against powerful obstacles he must work things out for himself. Official society is almost as bad as the underworld and the law does not operate as a cohesive force, so that the sense of an atomized world is intensified.

Spade succinctly characterizes the official world and political system: "most things in San Francisco can be bought, or taken" (p. 48). Instead of examining the official world in any detail, Hammett simply takes its corruption for granted. His treatment of the underworld, however, illuminates official society, since Gutman, Cairo, and Brigid have the motives, rhetoric, and values of respectable entrepreneurs. To the extent we find these characters both more reprehensible and more fascinating than people in the "real" world, the negative judgment of the "real" world is intensified.

Joel Cairo says he heard Spade was "far too reasonable to allow other considerations to interfere with profitable business relations" (p. 44). "Reasonable" and "profitable" are key values in the world of competetive individualism, as are the "trust" and the "plain speaking and clear understanding" Gutman drinks to (p. 94). Even more important is Gutman's explicit statement of what is pervasive and implicit throughout the novel, namely, that the archetypal embodiment of property, the jeweled black bird, "is clearly the property of whoever can get ahold of it" (p. 114). The principle and its deadly results are at the heart of the system that produced the robber barons and the corporate warfare of early twentieth-century capitalism. Through Gutman and the others Hammett goes beneath the facade of capitalistic theory and exposes its predatory practices. The implicit corollary of Gutman's remark, moreover, is that the bird is valuable *because* so many people want to "get ahold of it." Thus it is "property" as "commodity." The bird is of no use to anyone (reinforced by the end of the novel where the actual object is revealed as black lead throughout), yet all the destructive energy of the novel's characters has its source in the exchange of the bird. Every time it changes hands, the value goes up.

Gutman, Cairo, and Brigid are the leading players in the serious game of exchange. They live in a world of trading, deception, expediency, risk-taking, and self-interest. These social qualities create a world that has no stability or certainty, so that the basis for uncertainty and instability is social and economic. As in *The Glass Key* the fog and darkness Spade must grope through are metaphors for a social and moral condition. By displacing his social probing, by doing it indirectly, Hammett thus creates a dark world that is vital, threatening, and deep. Through this mythic world he is able to get at conventional values and relations in a basic way, more suggestively than before or after *The Maltese Falcon.*

II

In Hammett's dark, unstable world, the most intimate ties between people are also necessarily unstable or corrupt. Hammett examines a series of love or family relations, and their characterization contributes powerfully to the novel's exposure of an acquisitive, individualistic world as a hell-on-earth or death-in-life. Immediately before he makes his most loyal associate the fall-guy, Gutman says "I feel towards Wilmer just exactly as if he were my own son'" (p. 160). So much for the ties of friendship and loyalty or the affection between a father and son. In a quite different way Cairo, with his scented handkerchiefs and effeminate manners, is in love with Wilmer. In some ways it is the most genuine love in the book but Hammett presents it as in its very nature compromised or tainted. Like other loves in the novel, moreover, it is one-sided, not reciprocated. Although Spade continually baits Wilmer as a "gunsel" (underworld slang for "homosexual"), Wilmer is totally repelled by Cairo.

But it is through the central love relation in *The Maltese Falcon* that Hammett gives his most telling treatment of the death-in-life of his acquisitive society. Spade has his suspicions of Brigid early on, as he sees through her stories and pleas, but he is compelled by her nonetheless. A relation based on deception, pretense, and sex gradually deepens without ever losing the original duplicity and without Spade's ever encountering anything more or less genuine than Brigid's beauty, vitality, and consummate skill as an actress and inventive storyteller. He is compelled but not deluded by these qualities. At first we are taken in but Spade shows his superior insight by detecting almost immediately the false notes in her speech. "'You're good,'" he tells her, "'you're very good. It's chiefly your eyes, I think, and that throb you get into your voice when you say things like 'Be generous, Mr. Spade'" (p. 32).

"Be generous"; "trust me"—these appeals to the cohesive values of generosity, sympathy, and trust recur again and again in the scenes involving Brigid and Spade. The words always remind us of the human qualities that are missing from their relation, a void that cumulatively gives their love the aura of a dance of the damned. The social vision of the novel is tragic, partly because Spade loves a woman he cannot trust, someone whose duplicity is rooted in the acquisitive motives and values of the social order. This nightmarish combination of love without trust brings into the open the painful isolation and destruction of human ties ordinarily concealed in the everyday social world.

Brigid involves Spade because she needs protection but she is only vulnerable physically, not intellectually or emotionally. She uses her femininity, variously playing the role of a rich heiress in need of help or a seductress who distracts Spade from vital questions by going to bed with him. But she is a woman who plays brilliantly in a man's hard world for the same dark stakes as the other competitors. She is one of the few women characters in American literature who are endowed with the energy, motives, and capacities of the male characters, and not at the expense of her femininity. The social criticism in the novel gains tragic force because Brigid's rich possibilities are blighted by her involvement in the world of competitive individualism. That involvement is tragically intertwined with the very promise, qualities, and achievements which both elevate and undermine her. Brigid is the most tragic figure in the underworld because her death-in-life is inseparable from a saving vitality, so that her loss suggests the price of conventional success and constitutes a judgment on an entire value system and way of life.

The dilemma Henry Adams foresaw for the twentieth-century woman was that she could play the man's game in the world of power and become as restless, mechanical, and desexualized as the American male. Or she could remain powerless but fecund. Through Brigid's restless manipulation of her own and Spade's feelings and sexuality, Hammett confirms this tragic insight. Brigid's involvement in the acquisitive world is as fatal to her relation with Spade as it is to her own inner life. She is weary with herself and the perpetual lying, acting, and improvising she nonetheless continues with astonishing persistence and vitality. Her deceptiveness, manipulation, and fluidity of identity all have social sources: they answer to the demands of the market society. Because of her brilliant acting, we never know Brigid's true feelings. Brigid may well love only the pursuit of the black bird, although Spade's intelligence, force, and personal presence are not negligible. We do know, however, that a genuine union between Brigid and Spade constitutes the most promising force of human cohesion and renewal in the world of the novel. Through the course of the book this possibility is simultaneously suggested, brought to imaginative life, and destroyed. At the end, Brigid manipulates the central value of love and loses. She ends up imprisoned, separated from Spade and the world, and under the threat of the death penalty. For his part, at the end Spade is alone and shivering. Their situation epitomizes and judges what are for Hammett the divisive realities of the market society world he has transformed into the myth of *The Maltese Falcon*.

Central to the dark, unstable world of the novel is the need to act, to invent, and to deceive. Brigid in particular has facade beneath facade, story within story, lie on top of lie, and all compelling, as she is in her resourcefulness, beauty, and sexuality. She says her name is Brigid O'Shaughnessy but she also calls herself Miss Wonderly and Miss LaBlanc. As Spade says, she has one name too many. In a fluid, unstable society, identi-

ties are also fluid. "'I'm not at all the person I pretend to be'" (p. 49), she tells Spade, and we can never be sure of the person she is. The unstable marketplace society of trading and deception is itself a world of appearances; in her rootlessness, lack of identity, and skill at manipulating appearances, Brigid is the perfect embodiment of that society.

On Hammett's vision this society demands acting and storytelling, the systematic manipulation of surfaces, feelings, and values. In her first story Brigid, a brilliant actress and storyteller, acts the part of a daughter deeply concerned about her parents and sister. In the story she invents she wants to bring the family together again; in her version Thursby is the blocking force. Brigid's story plays on and subverts the cohesive value of family love, so that from the opening scene this central unifying value exists only to be exploited and thus degraded. The full consequences appear as Hammett develops the world Brigid lives in and embodies: deceptive, acquisitive, exciting, ruthless. In this hell-like version of the market society love exists to be manipulated, as Brigid manipulates Thursby and attempts to do with Spade. In her initial story the most direct irony is that Brigid presents Thursby as a dangerous seducer, as a person exploiting love for gain, although Thursby is loyal and she is the predatory seducer exploiting Thursby's love and the reader's desire to believe in family love and a concerned, upper-class daughter and sister in distress.

Hammett, however, does not allow us the ease of simple, direct inversions. In Brigid's world it is almost impossible to tell truth from falsehood. What we have instead is a constant process of invention, improvising, of making up stories. A convention of detective fiction, the motivation of "story," checking on a "story," seeing if a "story" fits the facts, becomes in Hammett a brilliant way of playing across different codes of explanation. Thus rather than explaining events, the social values of cohesion, loyalty, and trust are revealed as so many stories told for very different ends; the personal and psychological value of a stable identity likewise becomes an effect produced by the telling of stories rather than the origin of stories; and the epistemological ground of the "facts" dissolves into a seemingly endless chain of stories about stories about stories.

Spade is as good as Brigid at the process of inventing stories. To account to the police for the fight between Cairo and Brigid he improvises a story that includes a joke within a lie within the story. Spade always has a plausible explanation—for Iva, for Cairo, for Gutman. When Cairo challenges him about his facility he asks, "'what do you want me to do? Learn to stutter?'" (p. 86). Spade gives the impression of knowing but he is groping in the dark, trying to find the truth. He bluffs, he acts as if he knows more than he does to find out something so that he can continue the baffling, dangerous process of finding out more. Brigid, apparently his ally and lover, consistently withholds, distorts, interferes. When Gutman tells his story about the missing $1,000 and Brigid tells her version, Spade brings it to the test and finds out.

For the most part, however, empirical validation is either not possible or requires Spade to penetrate a labyrinth of deceptions and obstacles. Because of the socially generated network of stories, deception, and ruthlessness, Spade does not live in a neatly patterned world where empirical truth sits fixed and quiet for the observer to discover it. Instead he and the others live in a predatory world where in order to find the truth Spade must improvise, throw a monkey-wrench in the machinery, and get out of the way if he can as the parts fly. Spade lives in a world where beams fall at random but people systematically tell stories and use any means necessary to gain what they seek. In this ruthless, acquisitive world of stories and storytelling, what counts is not the truth but whether or not the story covers most of the facts in a way people will believe.

Spade's methodological scepticism is so deep that after he sends Iva to his lawyer he is simply neutral about the story she tells. He neither believes nor disbelieves it but he thinks it will work. Even Spade, however, must sometimes act on the stories he hears. As far as we can tell, he believes Rhea Gutman but in any case he goes on a wild goose chase as a result of her drugged act and story. The handling of point of view systematically avoids the inner processes of thought and feeling. As a result we can never be certain of what Spade or Brigid think or feel. Spade periodically voices his suspicions of Brigid but until the end we do not know what his feelings are. He acts as if he cares for her; she acts as if she cares for him. To an extent both are acting, telling stories to each other, but to an extent they may also be in love. This radical uncertainty about and manipulation of basic human feelings and ties is central to Hammett's commentary on the market society.

Brigid, in an especially touching confession, says "'Oh, I'm so tired, . . . so tired of it all, of myself, of lying and thinking up lies, and of not knowing what is a lie and what is the truth'" (p. 79). Like other great actresses and storytellers, she may well be telling part of the truth but she is also manipulating Spade and she immediately goes to bed with him to keep him from finding out what he is after. We have a deep need to believe Brigid, to have her confirm our sense that systematic deception is destructive. We have a deep need to wake up from the nightmare of "not knowing what is a lie and what is the truth" because as human beings we crave the truth. Brigid is a significant modern character partly because Hammett endows her with a sensitivity to this human need and the ability simultaneously to violate it in the interests of her even deeper need to ac-

quire the falcon. Brigid's ability is uniquely personal but her motives, her weariness about her identity, her self, and her related need to deceive, to invent stories, to manipulate people, feelings, and appearances—all these are rooted in the social order she emerges from and brilliantly embodies.

As Spade shows, to survive in this painfully uncertain world a person has to make up stories systematically. Survival also calls for a disciplined control over one's feelings, for an ability sometimes to disregard, sometimes to manipulate other people's feelings, and for a final ability to read other people's stories accurately and to deny even those feelings of love which momentarily redeem the darkness of deception and self-seeking.

In Hammett's hell-like version of the market society the cohesive values of love, trust, generosity, and honesty exist almost exclusively in stories people tell to gain advantage for themselves. As in Brigid's stories, these positive values are mixed with themes of betrayal, deception, theft, and killing. The events of the novel reinforce these grimmer themes. Even casual stories further this sense of betrayal and dishonesty, of people out for themselves. A movie-house owner tells Spade a story about a cashier he suspects of theft. Iva tells her story to bring the police down on Spade. Sometimes characters believe their own stories; sometimes the stories seem accurate and we believe them, as we do the movie owner or as we believe Tom Polhaus's story about Thursby.

Although not every story is a lie, the unstable, acquisitive society of the novel generates a ruthless world of stories and storytelling, of manipulation and deception, of truth mixed with guesses mixed with half-truths and lies. For Hammett this social condition has the metaphysical consequences he has Spade develop in his story about Flitcraft. Unlike the other characters, Flitcraft comes from the ordinary world of settled commercial life. Because he comes from the straight world, his realizations are especially telling. When for no reason at all he is nearly killed by a falling beam, Flitcraft is shaken into the awareness that he lives in a world where beams fall at random. "He felt like somebody had taken the lid off life and let him look at the works" (p. 56). He comes to see that beneath its placid suburban surfaces existence is conducted under the aspect of arbitrary, unmerited death. "He knew then that men died at haphazard like that, and lived only while blind chance spared them" (p. 57). An intuitive existentialist, Flitcraft acts to get in step with existence, changes his life, and then in Spade's wry joke, Flitcraft resumes a routine identical to the one he had left. "He adjusted himself to beams falling, and then no more of them fell, and he adjusted himself to them not falling" (p. 57). Spade carefully tells a metaphysical parable that also recognizes the way ordinary people are.

Although we cannot be sure about Spade's motives in telling the story, they are probably mixed. Perhaps the story is a monkey wrench he throws in to find out how Brigid will respond. She ignores the suggestive power of the story and immediately returns to her story, to her act, trying to get Spade to trust her. She has her work cut out for her, since the man who has told the Flitcraft story has ideas about what goes on under the surfaces of things. Spade has narrated his view of existence as precisely as he can. Whatever his other motives, he wants to tell his story as clearly and accurately as he can. Unlike Brigid, who has told her story so often her manner betrays her to Spade, Spade himself "repeated a sentence slightly rearranged, as if it were important that each detail be related exactly as it had happened" (p. 54). Honesty is the final test of a style for Whitehead. As a response to a metaphysical world where beams fall at random and a social world where people ruthlessly manipulate appearances to gain advantage, the morality of style is also important to Hammett. Telling the story precisely is one of the few redeeming possibilities in the dark social and metaphysical universe Hammett imagines for his characters. The Flitcraft story, moreover, is one of the few chances Hammett gives us to glimpse what goes on inside Spade and to sense Spade's view of what goes on in the depths of things.

Brigid's story about her family and Thursby, Spade's story about Flitcraft, and Gutman's story about the Maltese falcon are the most compelling of the countless stories that give the novel its characteristic texture. Like most of the stories that form the context for the Flitcraft story, in his story Gutman narrates a tale of theft and buccaneering, of predatory robber barons on the grand scale and more recent thieves on a smaller scale, of kidnapping and ransom, of concealment, intrigue, and deception. The evidence he presents is circumstantial but his manner is authoritative and he gives his account the authenticity of an encyclopedia article on an arcane subject. He claims an "oblique" reference in a French source—"oblique to be sure, but a reference still" (p. 111). Is this valid inference or the interpretation of a man with Sir Thomas Browne's quincunx in his head? The quincunx, Brown tells us, is a five-sided figure. Once you have it in your mind, you see five-sided figures everywhere.

Gutman also claims "a clear and unmistakable statement of the facts" in an unpublished source. Maybe yes, maybe no, although why would Gutman invest a fortune and seventeen years of his life if he at least did not believe it? An eighteenth-century source vouches for the existence of the bird as among the wedding presents of King Victor Armadeus II to his wife. That seems like solid evidence but what follows is more ambiguous and depends on the evidence of "a Greek dealer named Charilaos Konstantinides [who] found it in an obscure shop" (p. 112). Do we believe the story because even a wily Greek accepts it or do we dismiss the story as the invention of a wily Greek dealer? Effie Perine's uncle in the Berkeley History Department is excited over the possibility that the story could be true "and he hopes it is" (p. 124). Effie, though, is wrong about Brigid and Uncle Ted may or may not be just as wrong about the story. Spade maintains a wary scepticism: "'that's swell,'" he tells Effie about Uncle Ted, "'as long as he doesn't get too enthusiastic to see through it if it's phony'" (p. 124).

What we know for sure is that like Uncle Ted, we also hope the story is true. In the face of all the ambiguous evidence do we accept the story finally because this tale of deception and ruthlessness in pursuit of a fabulous treasure satisfies our sense of the way things are and appeals to our desire to believe? Are we, then, like Ratliff in *The Hamlet,* the victims of a socially generated myth of buried treasure, a story that exposes the grim practices of a predatory society and, through our acceptance of the story, our own involvement in that society? Maybe yes, maybe no. We do know for sure, however, that in the novel there is one object that is under its surface exactly what it appears to be: the lead falcon Gutman chips away at to reveal black lead right through to the center. This is as certain as the fact that for Hammett Gutman's ruthless, exciting quest is deadly and leads to his death, that Brigid and Spade are separated, and that at the end Spade is alone and shivering.

III

Like any writer who has found a perfect vehicle for his vision, after *The Maltese Falcon* Hammett was faced with the problem of continuing. Unwilling simply to go over old ground, he was impelled to move away from the comprehensive myth that had allowed him to satisfy his deepest sense of social complexity within the conventions of the tough guy mystery he was at the same time elevating into serious fiction. After *Red Harvest* and *The Maltese Falcon,* moreover, Hammett could assume rather than directly expose the acquisitive individualism of his society. In *The Glass Key* (1931) he accordingly concentrates on the positive and negative features of the alienated individualism this society produces and on the moral, epistemological, and personal impact of an unstable American world.

Hammett renders this world through the sensibility of a displaced gentleman, Ned Beaumont. Beaumont has been picked up from the gutter by Paul Madvig and has an independent job as righthand man to this boss of a local political machine. "'I don't believe in anything,'" Ned Beaumont says, "'but I'm too much of a gambler not to be affected by a lot of things.'"[6] He does, however, believe in doing his job right and equally important he believes in his personal obligations to Paul Madvig. These motives impel Beaumont to probe into increasingly darker territory. Through his code of personal loyalty and his need to succeed as his own man on his own terms, Ned Beaumont also holds his personal world together and gives his life that degree of dignity and meaning it has. This precarious enterprise is rooted in the social fragmentation of his American world and in the moral individualism that is part of the American legacy along with the acquisitiveness and eroding of communal bonds that Hammett had exposed in *Red Harvest* and *The Maltese Falcon.*

Ned Beaumont's gambling is a metaphor for the uncertainty and contingency of the dark, unstable world he chooses to live in. In direct relation to the fragmentation of the social order, to maintain his sense of himself Ned Beaumont desperately needs to reverse his losing fortunes, to win at gambling, and to collect his debts, all as tokens of self-worth. For him the money is not important in itself but to lose, to fail, is even more degrading than to be cheated. Similarly, he needs to satisfy the demands of his touchy pride and he also needs to keep people at a distance emotionally to protect his easily threatened core of integrity. He cannot rely on the supports of a stable, communal society to give him a sense of self-worth.

As in an intensifying mirror Ned Beaumont's personal isolation and bad health reflect the fragmentation of the American social world of *The Glass Key.* Ned Beaumont is even more alone than Sam Spade. He is estranged from his past; except for his loyalty to Paul Madvig and his affection for Madvig's family he is cut off from those around him; and although at the end he is going to leave with Janet Henry, the conclusion enforces rather than counters the prevailing sense of isolation. On one interpretation, Ned Beaumont is caught between his love for Janet Henry and his loyalty to Paul Madvig, who for his part has been willing to sacrifice everything for her. Because of the novel's total reticence about Ned Beaumont's feelings, however, it is also possible that he does not love her at all but is leaving with her to protect his friend from an impossible involvement. In either case the ending is grim, since it severs the bond between Beaumont and Madvig, the main cohesive tie in the dislocated society of the novel. At the end Ned Beaumont has solved the mystery and won the girl but it brings no sense of fulfilment, only of loss, estrangement, and conflict with or because of his loyalty to his friend.

In his hard, unsparing way, Hammett thus gives human urgency to insights John Dewey had articulated more abstractly the year before *The Glass Key.* In a world of "impersonal and socially undirected economic forces," Dewey saw, "the significant thing is that the loyalties which once held individuals, which gave them support, direction, and unity of outlook on life have disappeared . . . It would be difficult," he observed, "to find in his-tory an epoch as lacking in solid and assured objects of belief and approved ends of action as the present." The tragedy for Beaumont, who "doesn't believe in anything," is that he either betrays or sacrifices himself to the personal loyalty that does give meaning and coherence to his life in a world in which the traditional supports are shattered. "Stability of individuality," Dewey stressed, "is dependent upon stable objects to which allegiance firmly attaches itself." But under the pressure of undirected acquisitiveness, for most contemporaries, Dewey perceived, "traditional object of loyalty have become hollow or are openly repudiated, and they drift without sure anchorage. Individuals vibrate between a past that is intellectually too empty to give stability and a present that is too diversely crowded and chaotic to afford balance or direction to ideas and emotions." Like Dewey, Hammett is sensitive to the connection between an unstable, acquisitive society and a tense, precarious individualism. "Assured and integrated individuality," Dewey knew, "is the product of definite social relationships and publically acknowledged functions."[7] In his world and Hammett's these conditions are not satisfied.

Throughout the novel social surfaces are misleading and unreliable and everyone including Ned Beaumont plays a duplicitous role. Under their patrician veneer those at the top of this world, aristocrats like Senator Henry or the newspaper owner, Howard Mathews, men who traditionally provide leadership, are shown as weak and corrupt. Concealed behind his prestige, Senator Henry is gradually revealed as the murderer. The intensity of the social dislocation is rendered and judged by the violent storm Ned Beaumont struggles through to get at the truth when he finds Opal Madvig and the gangsters and patricians who are manipulating her all hiding out together in Mathew's isolated country retreat. The aura of darkness and impenetrable uncertainty intensifies as Ned Beaumont moves deeper and deeper into a corrupt, vital world of underground violence and disorder characteristic of both patricians like Senator Henry and gangsters like Shad O'Rory.

Suggestive as it is, the scene in the storm is secondary to the one in which Beaumont pretends to sell out to Shad O'Rory. In the guise of a betrayer but actually out of loyalty to Paul Madvig, Ned Beaumont enters an enclosed region and is drugged and beaten almost lifeless but in the camp of the enemy he gains the one piece of knowledge he needs. Almost swamped by the primitive violence he is subjected to, his intellect nonetheless manages to retain its acuteness, so that the novel sustains a tension between intelligence and loyalty precariously surviving the threatening, anarchic violence at the center of this recognizably American world.

As this outline indicates, an interpretive problem in *The Glass Key* is how much emphasis to place on the social milieu, since the novel also has moral, epistemological, and psychological implications. Among the latter Hammett is especially fascinated with the undercurrents of love and irrational hostility between daughters and fathers, fathers and sons, younger women and older men, and in the topography of the self, of the drama of penetrating beneath the surface of consciousness into a dark region where vital, destructive, primitive impulses are given full play. Except in *The Maltese Falcon* Hammett slights his secondary characters, who are often stock figures. Like many twentieth-century writers, Hammett's main interest is not in conventional character development or in conventional psychological analysis. Instead, he concentrates his understated prose on elliptical insights into his central characters, their society, and the suggestively charged settings they inhabit. At his frequent best the combination of his own sense of complexity and the demands of the popular mystery story for excitement and violence but nothing too fancy in the way of intellectual analysis—this combination yields a fiction in which meaning is embodied in settings and emerges through action rather than through explicit statement or character analysis.

In Hammett the descent into the underworld, e.g., is often rendered by a literal plunge into subbasements or enclosed underground rooms where forbidden, antisocial impulses can be acted out. Throughout his work, moreover, logical connectives are withheld and meaning is conveyed through the techniques of the dream: through charged images and actions and abrupt juxtapositions and realizations intuited in advance of empirical evidence, often on the basis of strong, unarticulated feelings of love and hate. One of Hammett's major achievements is that he unpretentiously does justice to a complex of social, psychological, moral, and epistemological concerns. He also implicitly shows their interrelation, especially the connections between social and epistemological breakdown. In Hammett's work, moreover, the primitive Freudian tensions are not isolated psychological phenomena but they too reflect and intensify the pervasive sense of breakdown, as in the crucial revelation that Senator Henry, a pillar of the respectable social order, has murdered his son or that Opal Madvig has acted to incriminate her father on the mistaken belief that Madvig is the killer. As in *The Maltese Falcon* and *The Dain Curse*, Hammett is sensitive to the breakdown or perversion of primary family ties as a symptom of a larger social breakdown.

In *Red Harvest* and *The Glass Key* as in *The Maltese Falcon* Hammett's social stand also includes his probing of the dangers of sexual and emotional ties. Hammett's novels are dominated by men but in *Red Harvest* and *The Maltese Falcon* he imagines forceful, dangerous women who speak to men's fascination with and fear of sexuality. In *The Glass Key* the women characters lack the substance of Dinah Brand or her successor, Brigid O'Shaughnessy, but Opal Madvig,

Eloise Mathews, and Janet Henry continue to act as a compelling and disruptive force. In *The Glass Key,* moreover, love is either one-sided and damaging, as between Paul Madvig and Janet Henry, or it is alienating, as in the separation it causes between Madvig and Beaumont. In *The Maltese Falcon* the central bond of sexually charged love is abused and manipulated; in *The Glass Key* it is fragmenting and threatening.

The nightmares which dominate the ending of *The Glass Key* are especially charged with the threat of the fragmenting power of sexuality. Janet Henry has a nightmare of horror: in her dream the glass key breaks in the lock and because they cannot open the door she and Ned Beaumont are overwhelmed by snakes. In the waking world Beaumont does turn the key and open the door on the concealed horrors but the snakes may well overwhelm them nonetheless. Equally ominous is the suggestion of sexual threat and dislocation in the phallic images of the broken key and slithering snakes, hardly encouraging for the fulfillment of their love. The nightmare which provides the novel with its enigmatic title thus reinforces Hammett's pervasive view that sexual love is divisive, not unifying, a serious matter in a socially dislocated world.

Hammett treats sex so as to withhold systematically any sense of personal or social renewal. The tragedy for his sympathetic characters is that Hammett will not allow their lives to be fulfilled. Instead of giving us happy endings or personal fulfillments, Hammett stays true to his sense of modern life. The world his characters live in, for all its energy and their own vitality, is too fragmented and corrupt to deserve renewal, however much it needs to be transformed. Sam Spade, alone and shivering at the end of *The Maltese Falcon*; at the end of *The Glass Key,* Ned Beaumont staring fixedly at a door that leads nowhere—these are simply reminders of the way Hammett uses the tensions and failed promises of love and sexuality to underscore his social vision.

Reinforcing and reinforced by these tensions in sexual relations, in *Red Harvest, The Maltese Falcon,* and *The Glass Key* Hammett gives a negative view of the acquisitive social order and an ambivalent one of the individualistic violence, energy, and alienation that occupy much of his attention. Not only does he show the close relation between the respectable world and the underworld but also, as Steven Marcus observes, "he unwaveringly represents the world of crime as a reproduction in both structure and detail of the modern capitalist society that it depends on, preys off, and is part of."[8] It is not surprising that within a few years of *Red Harvest, The Maltese Falcon,* and *The Glass Key* Hammett had become actively engaged in the politics of the left, as if to achieve in the outside world the transformation he shows is necessary but which he refuses to imagine in his fiction.

Notes

1. Quoted in *Twentieth Century Authors, First Supplement,* ed. Stanley Kunitz (New York: H. W. Wilson, 1955), p. 408.

2. For this perception about Hobbes, see Steven Marcus, "Dashiell Hammet and the Continental Op," *Partisan Review,* 41 (1974), 373. More generally, see Frank M. Coleman, *Hobbes and America: Exploring the Constitutional Foundations* (Toronto: University of Toronto Press, 1977).

3. For narrative details on this phase of American capitalism, see Ida Tarbell, *The History of the Standard Oil Company,* 2 vols. (New York: McClure, Phillips, 1904); Gustave Myers, *History of the Great American Fortunes* (New York: Modern Library, 1910, 1936); and Theodore Dreiser's Cowperwood novels, *The Financier* (New York: Signet, 1912, 1967) and *The Titan* (New York, 1914, 1965). For analysis of the underlying principles, see C. B. Macpherson, *The Political Theory of Possessive Individualism: Hobbes to Locke* (New York: Oxford University Press, 1962).

4. Jacques Barzun and Wendell H. Taylor observe that "the tough guy story was born during the thirties and shows the Marxist coloring of its birth years," *A Catalogue of Crime* (New York: Harper, 1971) p. 11. Hammett, however, developed his social stand during the twenties. John Reilly sees *The Maltese Falcon* as embodying a populist, not a Marxist, view of society, "The Politics of Tough Guy Mysteries," *University of Dayton Review,* 10 (1973), 29, and Steven Marcus sees it as Hobbesian. These differences in terminology are not crucial. Hammett is rooted in the American grain and in the concerns of his period and he intuitively goes beneath conventional facades to what he sees as basic. Barzun and Taylor, Reilly, and Marcus seem to me more revealing about *The Maltese Falcon* than critics who stress the metaphysics or poetics of the novel. See, e.g., Robert I. Edenbaum, "The Poetics of the Private-Eye: The Novels of Dashiell Hammett" and Irving Malin, "Focus on *The Maltese Falcon,* " both in David Madden, ed. *Tough Guy Writers of the Thirties* (Carbondale, Ill.: Southern Illinois University Press, 1968), pp. 80-109.

5. Dashiell Hammett, *The Maltese Falcon* (New York: Vintage, 1930, 1972), p. 3. All other quotations will be cited in the text.

6. Dashiell Hammett, *The Glass Key* (New York: Vintage, 1931, 1972), p. 169.

7. John Dewey, *Individualism Old and New* (New York: Minton, Balch, 1930), pp. 52, 53.

8. Marcus, 373.

Christopher Metress (essay date fall 1990)

SOURCE: Metress, Christopher. "Dashiell Hammett and the Challenge of New Individualism: Rereading *Red Harvest* and *The Maltese Falcon.*" *Essays in Literature* 17, no. 2 (fall 1990): 242-60.

[*In the following essay, Metress studies the theme of individualism in* Red Harvest *and* The Maltese Falcon *and asserts that Hammett "investigates the antagonistic relationship between residual nineteenth-century traditions of self-centered individualism and emerging twentieth-century calls for social collectivism."*]

In this present reconstructive era of American literary history, Dashiell Hammett's fiction has played an invaluable role in breaking down canonical barriers and empowering marginalized popular fictions with newly recognized importance. With the initial publication of his stories and novels in the 1920s, many influential critics praised Hammett's linguistic, structural, and thematic innovations, insisting, for example, that "Hammett has something quite as definite to say, quite as decided an impetus to give the course of newness in the American tongue, as any man now writing."[1] Along with this laudatory critical reception, Hammett captured wide readership as well. Thus, Hammett long remained on the threshold between what are often considered two antithetical positions in American letters—accepted literary artist and popular storyteller. When questions of canon formation and the politics of literary history became central to the focus of many critics, Hammett emerged as a seminal figure in the reconstruction of American literary studies. Today, his place in American literature is secure, and the critical accessibility of his art has for years now encouraged perceptive reevaluations of his literary progeny in both detective and hard-boiled fictions.

But security by no means suggests consensus, and Hammett's works have engendered diverse readings. Most often, Hammett is read in light of his contributions to the detective and hard-boiled genres. Even here, though commentators agree that Hammett fathered the American detective novel and laid the foundations for hard-boiled fiction, they disagree as to exactly what it is he fathered and whether or not his offspring misread him. Recently, however, critics have been willing to consider Hammett as more than simply a master of generic formulas and a constructor of heroic archetypes. Fortunately, critics have resisted Leonard Moss's 1968 plea that Hammett "cannot through any generosity be considered a complex author. It would be fatuous to search for profound ethical, sociological, or psychological implication."[2] Instead, critics have done exactly that; they have studied Hammett for the suggestive complexities which make his fiction, unlike so much else that has won popular approval, richly rewarding.

Perhaps the most misunderstood dimension of Hammett's work is his position on individualism. We expect Hammett to be an unabashed proponent of rugged individualism, for are not the descendants of Hammett's heroes such representative individualists as Chandler's Phillip Marlowe, Spillane's Mike Hammer, Ross Macdonald's Lew Archer, and John D. MacDonald's Travis McGee? Critics have noted how the hard-boiled detective of the twentieth century is merely an urban reincarnation of the nineteenth-century apotheosis of American individualism—the cowboy. Understanding the American detective hero as the distinct progeny of the American cowboy (in the words of Leslie Fielder, the modern detective is "the cowboy adapted to life on the city streets"),[3] too many critics, however, thoughtlessly embrace the notion that writers of American detective fiction are unequivocal advocates of nineteenth-century-styled American individualism. As founder of this fiction, so the logic goes, Hammett too must be such an advocate: "If there is any Romantic element in Hammett's worldview," insists H. H. Morris, "it is the glorification of every individual, the passionate commitment to personal freedom that underlies the American myth of the frontier."[4] In her recent study of Western and hard-boiled genres, Cynthia S. Hamilton maintains that both formulas "are built around the testing and confirmation of key American values, especially individualism" and that the "theme which permeates every aspect of the master formula [supporting both Western and hard-boiled fictions] is the primacy of the individual; he is seen to be the key unit of society."[5]

Fortunately, several readers have refused to see Hammett's fiction as a glorification of this inherited frontier individualism. While it is true that Chandler, Spillane, Macdonald, and others influenced by Hammett have each embraced to some extent an ethos of rugged individualism, Hammett's fiction does not support such a doctrine. David Geherin justly asserts that "the conception of the private eye as a knight figure would be effectively developed by many later writers (notably Raymond Chandler) but it appears that Hammett wanted no part of it."[6] D. Glover concurs with Geherin's view that the individualism of Hammett's heroes is markedly different from that of his successors:

> What is interesting in the Hammett novels is the way in which . . . individualism is tempered by a kind of job-consciousness; so that although their violence is sensationalized and given a sadistic attractiveness it is never pushed completely into the world of fantasy in the way we find in, for example, the James Bond books. For the individualism of action and decision is not used to ground an illusion of total freedom—it is only relative to the job or work that the detective performs.[7]

In his seminal essay on the poetics of the private-eye, Robert Edenbaum proclaims that Hammett's novels not only temper individualism but also "present a 'critique'

of the tough guy's freedom as well: the price he pays for his power is to be cut off behind his own self-imposed masks, in an isolation that no criminal, in a community of crime, has to face."[8] Sinda Gregory goes one step further in asserting Hammett's critique of individualism by insisting that a novel like *Red Harvest* "examines the failure of both the community and the individual to maintain justice, order, and human rights."[9] In a 1985 study, Robert Shulman offers a more complex understanding of Hammett's position on individualism when he suggests that in *Red Harvest, The Maltese Falcon,* and *The Glass Key,* rather than blindly promoting a frontier brand individualism, Hammett "brings alive the conflicting versions of individualism that society emphasizes."[10]

My focus on the problem of American individualism in Hammett's fiction is markedly different from those of previous critics because it depends on understanding the socio-cultural debates over the nature and direction of individualism that dominated the first three decades of this century. If Hammett's work "brings alive conflicting versions of individualism that society emphasizes" we had better take a closer look at what those conflicting versions of individualism were before we reevaluate Hammett's own critique of individualism. What will arise from this discussion is the concept of a "new individualism" that called for a complex submission and/or allegiance of the individual's desires to those of a larger, less traditionally individualistic collective body. Like his contemporaries, Hammett struggled to reconceive the nature of American individualism, to explore the possibility of redirecting the insalubrious elements of an inherited frontier ethic into a more socially responsible new individualism. Hammett's two most important and influential novels, *Red Harvest* (1929) and *The Maltese Falcon* (1930), enact this exploration, for in them Hammett investigates the antagonistic relationship between residual nineteenth-century traditions of self-centered individualism and emerging twentieth-century calls for social collectivism.

I

Perhaps the best place to begin our discussion of this new individualism in the twentieth century is with Herbert Croly's *The Promise of American Life* (1909). Rejecting the great tradition of American individualism proclaimed by Crèvecouer, Jefferson, and Emerson, Croly expressed a central ethos of his time: "The Promise of American life is to be fulfilled—not merely by a maximum amount of economic freedom, but by a certain measure of discipline; not merely by the abundant satisfaction of individual desires, but by a large measure of individual subordination and self-denial."[11] Croly felt that "the traditional American system was breaking down" and that a twentieth-century faith in social planning needed to usurp a nineteenth-century faith in "chaotic individualism": "The experience of the last generation plainly shows that the American economic and social system cannot be allowed to take care of itself, and that the automatic harmony of the individual and the public interest, which is the essence of the Jeffersonian democratic creed, has proved to be an illusion."[12]

Croly's call for "individual subordination and self-denial" in shaping America's future continued to influence American social and political thought well into the 1910s and 1920s. Whereas in 1893 Frederick Jackson Turner could assert that frontier individualism, though it had "from the beginning promoted democracy," had "its dangers as well as its benefits,"[13] by 1917 Van Wyck Brooks, influenced by his generation's perceptions of traditional American individualism, could highlight only the unsalubrious: "Our ancestral faith in the individual and what he is able to accomplish . . . as the measure of all things has despoiled us of the instinctive human reverence for those divine resources of collective experience, religion, science, art, philosophy, the self-subordinating service of which is almost the measure of the highest happiness. In consequence of this our natural capacities have been dissipated."[14] Though rejecting the "aberrant individualism" of such "preëminent cranks" as Henry David Thoreau and Henry George, Brooks did not reject outright the concept of individualism; instead he sought a redefinition of individualism "totally different in content from the individualism of the past." For Brooks, the "old spiritual individualism" was "essentially competitive" and "gave birth to the crank, the shrill, the high-strung propounder of strange religious, the self important monopolist of truth." The new individualism, however, had "no desire to vaunt itself. . . . [I]t is not combative, it is coöperative, not opinionative but groping, not sectarian but filled with an intense, confused eagerness to identify itself with the life of the whole people."[15]

Croly, Brooks, and other political and social Progressives were seeking a balance between individual assertion and collective needs, and since the old individualism of the nineteenth century had created vast economic imbalances and had stratified social classes, a new type of individualism was sought, one which would be more amenable to collective change. Even such an "unashamed individualist" as Herbert Hoover tempered his nineteenth-century faith in individualism with a twentieth-century desire for collective social change. At the conclusion of his appropriately entitled *American Individualism* (1923), Hoover called for an adherence to individualism which seemed untouched by the Progressivist dialogue:

> Humanity has a long road to perfection, but we of America can make sure progress if we preserve our individualism, if we will preserve and stimulate the initiative of our people. . . . Progress will march if we

hold an abiding faith in the intelligence, the initiative, the character, the courage, and the divine touch in the individual. . . . We can make a social system as perfect as our generation merits and one that will be received in gratitude by our children.[16]

All this seems a far cry from Croly's proclamation a decade earlier that reformers should "understand that there must be vigorous and conscious assertion of the public as opposed to private and special interests, and that the American people must to a greater extent than they have in the past subordinate the latter to the former."[17] Throughout Hoover's book, however, we sense, as we do with Croly and Brooks, that the individualism here championed is once again being redefined, that a "new individualism" is being offered in place of an old, outdated, and inherently destructive individualism: "Salvation will not come to us out of the wreckage of individualism. What we need is steady devotion to a better, brighter, broader individualism—an individualism that carries increasing responsibility and service to our fellows. Our need is not for a way out but a way forward."[18]

A way out of individualism is exactly what many political and social philosophers of the 1920s desired. Led by Communist thinkers such as Michael Gold, many intellectuals took the Progressivist call for a new individualism of subordination and discipline one step further and demanded that Americans reject all individualism, whether old or new. By the end of the decade, the nature and role of individualism in the collective effort to reshape society was at best precarious, and individualism, however it was defined, became the central focus of many texts. The calls for self-denial and discipline in reshaping American individualism seemed to have failed, and an emerging political and social radicalism increasingly threatened to throw individualism into violent conflict with the demands of social reform. In *Individualism Old and New* (1930), John Dewey noted "a submergence of the individual," proclaimed that "individuals are confused and bewildered," and, more than a decade after Brooks, offered his own ideas "Toward a New Individualism."[19] Horace M. Kallen, in *Individualism: An American Way of Life* (1933), lamented that "Individualism [not just "rugged individualism"] is in eclipse."[20] In *The Conflict of the Individual and the Mass in the Modern World* (1932), Everett Dean Martin insisted that recent attempts to subordinate individual needs for the collective good had not created a new individual at all: "In practice the submergence of the individual in the mass, as the mass is organized to-day, divides the individual against himself. He is no longer a whole person, he counts only as he is part of some public. It is as producer, consumer, voter, subscriber—not as a person that he is of public interest."[21]

But these voices met with resistance. Many intellectuals still claimed that individualism, modified or not, continued to be a powerful and unhealthy influence in American culture. In *A Planned Society* (1932), George Soule urged that "Today more than ever we need synthesis, coördination, rational control. . . . [We are] thwarted by the dogma of absolute Liberty, by the chaos of indeterminateness, which is the natural accompaniment of planless 'freedom.' We are concerned . . . with freedom from the blind compulsions of a disorganized and unreasoned society."[22] In a 1931 editorial, the *New Republic* warned its readership that "the old recipes of 'rugged individualism' and uncontrolled competition are seen on every hand to be insufficient. Our mechanized civilization has advanced to a point where it cries out for planning and control in the interests of all—a sort of planning and control which cannot possibly be executed without encroaching on vested [individual] interests."[23]

Amidst all of this dialogue on individualism in the late 1920s and early 1930s, perhaps Dewey best expressed the importance of the issue: "The problem of constructing a new individuality consonant with the objective conditions under which we live is the deepest problem of our time. . . . So regarded, the problem is seen to be essentially that of creation of a new individualism as significant for modern conditions as the old individualism at its best was for its day and place."[24]

Red Harvest and *The Maltese Falcon* can be understood as explorations of this call for a new individualism. Each novel examines the possibility of refashioning the inherited impulses of nineteenth-century individualism into a "better, brighter, broader individualism" which seeks, either through allegiance and/or willing submission, to promote collective rather than individual needs. In *Red Harvest,* Hammett's hero initially seems to have transcended the impulses of rugged individualism, and through allegiance to the Agency he appears to have submitted his own desires to those of a collective body. The novel enacts the Op's struggle to resist the impulses of aberrant individualism and to maintain his new individualism of collective identification. In *The Maltese Falcon,* Sam Spade begins as one immersed in competitive, self-centered individualism, for he is both unwilling and unable to act out of interests other than his own. His struggle is the reverse of the Op's: he must find a way out of a maddening and destructive individualism toward a new individualism which, through "control" and "self-sacrifice," will allow him allegiance to something beyond the self. Seen as such, *Red Harvest* and *The Maltese Falcon* embody what Dewey considered the "deepest problem" of Hammett's time, for the novels explore changing and competing conceptions of old and new individualism in American culture.

II

Hammett locates his first novel in the aptly named town of Personville, Montana, a place victimized by nineteenth-century individualism run amok. As the name suggests, Personville is indeed a town of persons rather than a community, and each citizen seeks above all else to protect his or her own interests.[25] Dominating the politics and economics of Personville, old Elihu Willsson embodies the most unhealthy results of these unrestrained vested interests.

> For forty years old Elihu Willsson . . . had owned Personville, heart, soul, skin, and guts. He was president and majority stockholder of the Personville Mining Corporation, ditto of the First National Bank, owner of the *Morning Herald* and *Evening Herald,* the city's only newspapers, and at least part owner of nearly every other enterprise of any importance. Along with these pieces of property he owned a United States senator, a couple of representatives, the governor, the mayor, and most of the state legislature. Elihu Willsson was Personville, and he was almost the whole state.[26]

Eventually challenged by the labor advances of the I.W.W., old Elihu unmercifully squashes any threat of collective reforms: "Old Elihu hired gunmen, strikebreakers, national guardsmen and even parts of the regular army. . . . When the last skull had been cracked, the last rib kicked in, organized labor in Personville was a used firecracker" (7). In silencing this collective unrest, however, he surrenders most of his local control to the thugs he hired to protect his interests. As a result, Personville is ruled by four gangs that form a violent criminal network where, as critic Peter Wolfe suggests, "self-reliance knows no bounds."[27] The town's one voice of social reform, old Elihu's son Donald, is murdered before he appears in the text. A nightmare landscape of brutal self-interest, Personville is the twentieth-century apotheosis of nearly every evil associated with America's old, opportunistic individualism (note that Elihu's domination of Personville reaches back forty years, clearly identifying him and the town with the previous century). Perhaps Dinah Brand, Personville's beleaguered Siren, best articulates the town's attitude when she insists that "If a girl's got something that's worth something to somebody, she's a boob if she doesn't collect" (24).

It is down these mean streets that the Continental Op must go. Seeking the murderer of his would-be client, the Op demands that Personville "talk sense for a change" (12) and insists that "things have got to be explained" (17). As efficient as Hammett's hard-boiled prose, the Op moves about Personville with very little wasted effort, successfully pumping everyone he meets for information. Even before he solves Donald Willsson's murder, others note his skillful management and efficiency. Soon, old Elihu wants to hire him to "clean this pig-sty of Poisonville . . . to smoke out the rats, little and big" (29). When the Op asks for a ten thousand dollar retainer, old Elihu at first refuses to give so much money to a "man who's done nothing I know of but talk" (30). The Op's response, however, indicates how well he, unlike the citizens of Personville, has merged his own individuality with a larger collective body, suggesting that he has perhaps become what so many social and political philosophers of the times desired—a "new individual" seeking not self-assertion but loyalty to interests beyond his own: "When I say *me*, I mean the Continental" (30).[28] Only a short while later the Op will again assert this collective loyalty as he rejects a bribe: "The Continental's got rules against taking bonuses or rewards" (43).

Yet the Op's subordination to the rules of the Agency is not nearly as inviolate as the early sections of this novel would have us believe. When the chief of police betrays the Op and tries to have him killed, the Op loses his professional detachment. The self-denial he must maintain to perform effectively within the rules of the Agency gives way to vested self-interest. The efficient reformer can no longer subordinate his own desires and place them second to those of the Agency. After the attempt on his life, the Op no longer desires collective justice but personal revenge: "Your fat chief of police tried to assassinate me last night. I don't like that. I'm just mean enough to want to ruin him for it. Now I'm going to have my fun. I've got ten thousand dollars of your money to play with. I'm going to use it opening Poisonville up from Adam's apple to ankles" (43).[29] So much for reform.

The rest of the novel records the Op's "red harvest" of bloody revenge. The values of rational planning and cool efficiency asserted at the beginning of the novel collapse as the Op turns inward to fulfill his own violent form of frontier self-interest. We are witnessing a transformation in the Op's allegiances. The new individual who once equated his self with his Agency now reverts to the ethics of old individualism. Certainly, as Wolfe has suggested, "Responsibility to the Continental should have stopped [the Op] from playing the footloose justicer of cowboy fiction who cleans up a troubled town."[30] Unfortunately, the impulse to act from self-interest is too strong and the more independent the Op becomes from the regulations of the Agency, the more he begins to assume the guise of the cowboy justicer, except that unlike the heroic cowboy the Op "rejects his professionalism not to become the white knight who will liberate the countryside from evil and corruption but to get even."[31]

The Op's plans, once so effective, soon begin to go awry. Trying to antagonize the crime bosses, the Op "refixes" a fixed fight and, against plan, one of the fighters is murdered.[32] Soon, the Op confesses that "Plans

are all right sometimes. . . . And sometimes just stirring things up is all right—if you're tough enough to survive, and keep your eyes open so you'll see what you want when it comes to the top" (57). His loyalties altered by his lust for personal revenge, the Op no longer desires to "clean" Personville. Pursuing his self-interests, he has turned Personville into a battleground, in the process losing his social consciousness:

> Off to the north some guns popped.
>
> A group of three men passed me, shifty-eyed, walking pigeon-toed.
>
> A little farther along, another man moved all the way over to the curb to give me plenty of room to pass. I didn't know him and didn't suppose he knew me.
>
> A lone shot sounded not far away.
>
> As I reached the hotel, a battered black touring car went down the street, hitting at least fifty, crammed to the curtains with men.
>
> I grinned after it. Poisonville was beginning to boil out under the lid, and I felt so much like a native that even the memory of my very un-nice part in the boiling didn't keep me from getting twelve solid end-to-end hours of sleep.
>
> (77)

Finally, the Op rejects the demands of the Agency in favor of his own criteria: "It's right enough for the Agency to have rules and regulations, but when you're out on a job you've got to do it the best way you can" (78). When he tells two fellow operatives "don't kid yourselves that there's any law in Poisonville except what you make for yourself" (79), we can see the Op participating fully in Personville's powerful ideology of vested self-interests.[33]

Instead of being the town's efficient reformer, the Op admits that he has been "juggl[ing] death and destruction" (103). Rather than self-discipline, he must confess to having taken a less noble path: "[I could have played] legally. I could have done that. But it's easier to have them killed off, easier and surer, and, now that I'm feeling this way, more satisfying" (104). Unable to rationalize his actions, the Op confesses to Dinah that he is "going blood-simple" (104). Two surrealistic dreams preface the final movements of this otherwise intensely realistic narrative, further highlighting the irrationality which has slowly come to define the Op's experience. By the end of the novel, the reformer needs reforming. The "new individual" we saw at the beginning, the one who had merged his needs and allegiances with those of the Agency, we now find fixing up his reports "so that they would not read as if I had broken as many Agency rules, state laws and human bones as I had" (142).

The Op has become, as it were, a modern day Ahab, juggling death and destruction to satisfy the most irrational of self-centered desires—personal revenge. And, just as Ahab represented nineteenth-century individualism in destructive excess, so too does the Op represent the corruption of twentieth-century individualism, for as John Whitley proclaims, "Little in [the Op's] behavior suggests loyalty to ideals, human relations, or even abstract concepts of the law. He believes only in himself in the narrowest possible sense."[34] Fused momentarily to the reformative desires of a social agency, the Op succumbs to chaotic individualism and thus undermines the efficacy of collective action. In the end, Personville, the horrific landscape of American individualism, corrupts the Op, for "despite his code and despite being an indirect representative of law as an operative of the Continental Agency [he] becomes as lawless as the gansters and crooked politicians."[35] As Dennis Dooley maintains, we, and perhaps the Op himself, have "glimpsed a frightful truth: that in the end evil springs not merely from greed or organized crime . . . [but] from the eternal willingness of human beings to compromise their ideals and betray their nobler impulses to satisfy their baser needs."[36]

III

In *The Maltese Falcon* Hammett further explores the destructive pull of old individualism. In *Red Harvest* Hammett moves the Op from a stance of willing subordination to a posture of aberrant self-interest, and in doing so he undercuts the Op's position as the hero of the novel, a position the Op claims throughout the early chapters. The Op's failure to remain a "hero" is intimately related to his failure to resist an unhealthy individualism. The destructive threats of self-centered individualism are an even greater danger to Sam Spade. Whereas Hammett successfully suppressed two key elements of the Op's individuality—his name and specific physical description—he now positions these two elements at the very beginning of *The Maltese Falcon*:[37]

> Samuel Spade's jaw was long and bony, his chin a jutting v under the more flexible v of his mouth. His nostrils curved back to make another, smaller, v. His yellow-grey eyes were horizontal. The v motif was picked up again by thickish brows rising outward from twin creases above a hooked nose, and his pale brown hair grew down—from high flat temples—in a point on his forehead. He looked rather pleasantly like a blond satan.
>
> (295)

Compare this opening paragraph to that of *Red Harvest*:

> I first heard Personville called Poisonville by a red-haired mucker named Hickey Dewey in the Big Ship in Butte. He also called his shirt a shoit. I didn't think anything of what he had done to the city's name. Later I heard men who manage their r's give it the same pronunciation. I still didn't see anything in it but the meaningless sort of humor that used to make richardsnary

> the thieve's word for dictionary. A few years later I went to Personville and learned better.
>
> (3)

In *Red Harvest,* the focus rests on the community and we eventually see how this community of perverted self-interests manages to "poison" the reformative desires of the hero. In *The Maltese Falcon,* however, the focus begins with the individual and the "poison" exists within him, for he is "a blond satan." If the Op moves from hero to anti-hero as he succumbs to the poison of a selfish individualism, then Sam Spade, already poisoned, begins as an anti-hero.[38] Hammett's description of Spade in the introduction to the 1934 Modern Library edition of the novel attests to Spade's unhealthy self-focus: "he wants to be a hard and shifty fellow, able to take care of himself in any situation, able to get the best of anybody he comes in contact with, whether criminal, innocent by-stander or client."[39] The Op's challenge is to resist participating in the destructive individualism of Personville and to maintain his professional allegiance to the Agency. Certainly, the Op fails. Spade's challenge is to overcome his own destructive embracing of self-interest and to seek a greater collective identity.

The early chapters of *The Maltese Falcon* attest to Spade's anti-heroic posture of privileged individualism. Recall how in the opening chapters of *Red Harvest* the Op assumes an admirable stance, and, via his client Donald Willsson, is closely allied with social reform. The Op's early concerns for efficiency and justice position him well in our hearts. Not so for Spade. Whereas the Op has a client, someone he works for, Spade has a "customer" (295). Whereas the Op insists that Personville "talk sense for a change," Spade speaks "in a tone that was utterly meaningless" (304). Nearly all of Spade's early actions are self-centered, having less to do with advancing justice than with satisfying his own personal needs (recall his unwillingness to speak to Iva after Archer's murder). His secretary, Effie Perrine, warns him of the dangers of his ways, but in response Spade only reasserts his individualism:

> "You worry me," she said, seriousness returning to her face as he talked. "You always think you know what you're doing, but you're too slick for your own good, and some day you're going to find it out."
>
> He sighed mockingly and rubbed his cheek against her arm. "That's what Dundy says, but you keep Iva away from me, sweet, and I'll manage to survive the rest of my troubles." He stood up and put on his hat. "Have the *Spade & Archer* taken off the door and *Samuel Spade* put on. I'll be back in an hour, or phone you."
>
> (312-13)

Spade's individualism is explained in his often-cited story of Charles Flitcraft, whom Spade, at the time working in Seattle, was once hired to track down. Spade tells us that "Flitcraft had been a good citizen and a good husband and father, not by any outer compulsion, but simply because he was a man who was most comfortable in step with his surroundings" (335-36). One day, however, when a falling beam at a construction site nearly kills him, Flitcraft learns that he, "the good citizen-husband-father, could be wiped out between office and restaurant by the accident of a falling beam. He knew then that men died at haphazard like that, and lived only while blind chance spared them" (336). This experience gives Flitcraft a "new glimpse of life," one which leads him to the "discovery that in sensibly ordering his affairs he had gone out of step, and not into step, with life" (336). Flitcraft deserts his family and job in Tacoma, rejecting the social roles of citizen-father-husband, and, confronting absurdity for the first time, he embraces a meandering, uncommitted individualism: "He went to Seattle that afternoon . . . and from there by boat to San Francisco. For a couple of years he wandered around and then drifted by the Northwest" (336). The individualism Flitcraft embraces, however, does not endure, for soon after his drifting he settles down in Spokane and remarries. What fascinates Spade is Flitcraft's seemingly easy return to the "ordering of his affairs" after having rejected all such ordering as absurd. As Spade puts it, "He adjusted himself to beams falling, and then no more of them fell, and he adjusted himself to them not falling" (336).

Flitcraft's story serves to complement Spade's current position. Flitcraft's life before the beams begin falling is completely unlike Spade's present life: Flitcraft participated in society as citizen-father-husband, all roles that called for the subordination of self-interest to the larger collective interests of society and family. Spade has rejected all such roles, and goes so far as to mock the role of husband by committing adultery. When the beams begin to fall, Flitcraft adjusts to his new glimpse of life. Convinced of "blind chance" and life's "haphazard" nature, Flitcraft makes a path for San Francisco via Seattle, a path symbolizing a rejection of his social roles in favor of a more self-centered individualism. Flitcraft, once so unlike Spade in his acceptance of social roles, is now very much like Spade. Note that Spade too moves to San Francisco via Seattle and that doing so suggests a rejection of a collective role for a more individual stance, for Spade tells Brigid that in 1927 he was "with one of those big detective agencies in Seattle" (335). He is now, of course, on his own, first with "Spade & Archer," and then with "Samuel Spade." Flitcraft's movement away from a collective identity to a purely individual one comes full circle when he repositions himself into his social role through remarriage. Spade, however, has yet to make such a return; in fact, Spade seems to be moving farther and farther into pure individualism (i.e., "Spade & Archer" to "Samuel Spade"). Thus his fascination with Flitcraft's ability to "settle back naturally into the same groove he had jumped out of" (336) is in part a fascination with one man's ability to reassume social roles and obligations after experiencing a period of uncommitted individualism. Spade still feels what Flitcraft felt that day the beam fell. For Spade life is irrational, governed by blind chance, haphazard at best. Thus he believes in the one thing he can control and promote: his own self-interest. Faced with absurdity and chaos, Spade rejects social obligations and seeks stability by asserting his own desires and independence.

In pursuing the Maltese Falcon, Spade must confront the unhealthy effects of his rugged individualism when it is embraced by others. It is easy for Spade to promote his own self-interests while he is able to disassociate himself from others: it takes only a new paint job to remake the office door and simply a quick phone call to Effie to ward off the claims of Iva. Soon, however, Spade finds himself caught in a community where disassociation is not so easy and where self-interest is the supreme motivation of all involved. The world of Gutman, Brigid, Cairo and the ever-elusive falcon represents, as does Personville in *Red Harvest,* a community of aberrant individualists embracing an unhealthy doctrine of self-interests over the needs of others. When Gutman asks Spade whom he represents in this case and Spade indicates himself, Gutman articulates the philosophy of the micro-community to which Spade is now bound:

> "That's wonderful. I do like a man that tells you right out he's looking out for himself. Don't we all? I don't trust a man that says he's not. And the man that's telling the truth when he says he's not I distrust most of all, because he's an ass and an ass that's going contrary to the laws of nature"
>
> (365)

What Gutman here embraces, the social and economic reformers of the early twentieth century rejected outright, and the "new individual" of Croly, Brooks, Soule, and Dewey is in this world an "ass."

Supposed hero of the novel, Spade is as guilty as any in this circle of falcon-seekers. Gutman's exhortations could well be Spade's, for the detective has yet to act in any way which might indicate he thinks otherwise about "the laws of nature." At this point, the true "quest" of the novel emerges. Certainly Spade and the others seek the falcon, but, as the novel will soon bear out, that search proves to be an illusion. The real quest, the truly elusive (but not illusory) search, belongs to Spade. Repeatedly immersed in his own self-centered desires, Spade must somehow differentiate himself from his criminal associates and become the "hero" of the text. To do this, he must reshape his desires according to the demands of some system or code greater than himself. In other words, Spade must make the first move toward a "new individualism," that is, begin to merge his own identity with a larger movement or collective body. Such a move calls for self-discipline and willing subordination, two traits Spade has heretofore lacked. Spade's final confrontation with Brigid enacts his struggle to overcome the insane individualism which has dominated this novel, an insanity in which he has fully participated.

When Spade tells Brigid that he knows she killed Archer, he also tells her that he will turn her over to the police. His motivations again appear to be fully shaped by self-interest: "You're taking the fall. One of us has got to take it, after the talking those birds [Gutman and Cairo] will do. They'd hang me sure. You're likely to get a better break" (436). Here, however, we can excuse Spade's "selfishness"—the self-centeredness here does not resemble his brush-offs of Iva or his willingness to auction off his services to the highest bidder—for Brigid does indeed deserve to be turned over. Brigid, citing what they once had "been to each other," demands to know why Spade must do this to her, for, as she tells him, "Surely Mr. Archer wasn't as much to you as [I was]" (438). Spade's litany of reasons, tripartite in structure, is quite telling and deserves careful reading.[40]

In his first attempt to explain his motivations, Spade calls on the code of the detective. The reasons are worth quoting in full:

> When a man's partner is killed he's supposed to do something about it. It doesn't make any difference what you thought of him. He was your partner and you're supposed to do something about it. Then it happens we were in the detective business. Well, when one of your organization gets killed it's bad business to let the killer get away with it. It's bad all around—bad for that one organization, bad for every detective everywhere. Third, I'm a detective and expecting me to run criminals down and then let them go free is like asking a dog to catch a rabbit and let it go. It can be done, all right, and sometimes it is done, but it's not natural.
>
> (438)

Embracing the discipline of the detective code, Spade willingly subordinates his own needs to the needs of "every detective everywhere." What is "natural" here is not Gutman's insistence that all men look out for themselves; instead, professional demands and allegiances dominate any self-interests. Most critics consider these allegiances to be Spade's true motivation throughout the novel; they are thus able to excuse Spade's inexplicable moments of self-centeredness.

Should we believe, however, that Spade has been acting within this code all along?[41] If he has been, then Spade is indeed an heroic "new individual," acting always out of interests beyond his own in hopes of servicing justice. But, as Gregory notes of Spade's other actions throughout the novel, "Since the reader constantly sees Spade adopting whatever role seems most expedient, it becomes impossible for us to be certain of any of his intentions."[42] The same is true here. We would, I believe, like to think that Spade's actions have been intentionally serving a larger, collective good. Perhaps they have been, but then again, perhaps not. At best, we might be able to explain some, but not all, of Spade's actions as stemming from this collective code. The uncertainty confronting the reader here is not a fault in the novel. Instead, Hammett forces the reader to reconsider Spade's motivations and to reposition Spade's possible allegiances. We must listen further, for we feel at this moment as does Brigid: we do not fully believe that the code encompasses all of Spade's actions. His exhortation of the detective code may well be just another one of his well-devised deceptions.

Spade's second attempt to explain himself reveals a different set of motivations. Again, it is worth quoting in full:

> Fourth, no matter what I wanted to do now it would be absolutely impossible for me to let you go without having myself dragged to the gallows with the others. Next, I've no reason in God's world to think I can trust you and if I did this and got away with it you'd have something on me that you could use whenever you happened to want to. That's five reasons. The sixth would be that since I've also got something on you, I couldn't be sure you wouldn't decide to shoot a hole in *me* some day. Seventh, I don't even like the idea of thinking that there might be one chance in a hundred that you'd played me for a sucker.
>
> (438)

Most critics privilege Spade's first three reasons (all having to do with loyalty to the code) and largely ignore reasons four through seven. We should consider, however, that both sets of motivations compel Spade (whether one or the other is *more* compelling is difficult to say at this point, though the novel would seem to bear out the primacy of individual desires over professional codes).[43] In this way, Spade enacts an important tension of his generation, for he desires affiliation with a collective body while still refusing to repress the importance of his own needs. His first three reasons submerge his own individual demands; the next four reasons assert them. Spade seems split between two allegiances: the collective good and individual self-interest.

Spade's third and final explanation receives little attention but it is perhaps the most important in his development:[44] "If [all of my reasons don't] mean anything to you forget it and we'll make it this: I won't [let you go] because all of me wants to—wants to say to hell with the consequences and do it—and because—God damn you—you've counted on that with me the same as you counted on that with the others" (439). Not wanting "to play the sap," Spade discovers a way out of the insane individualism of the Gutman-Cairo-Brigid trio: self-denial. Spade knows that Brigid has been counting on him to act in his own self-interests and to cover up for the lady he loves. Spade wants to let her go and a great deal in this final scene suggests that he may indeed love her. But he will not act upon his own desires exactly because they are his own desires.

If we recall Hammett's original description of Spade looking "rather pleasantly like a blond satan," then this moment of self-imposed self-denial astounds us. Certainly this initial image of Spade as a pleasant satan conjures up for us the image of another pleasant satan, that of Milton's in the early books of *Paradise Lost.* Like Milton's Satan, Spade and his defiant individualism initially attract our sympathies. But as their narratives mature, we readers perceive the divisive ramifications of such myopic stances. Spade finally sees the implications as well and thus embraces not self-assertion but self-denial as his final posture. He is, as it were, no longer shaking his defiant fist against the heavens and fate but against himself.

At the end of *The Maltese Falcon* we know that Spade is doing the right thing and that the right thing involves a curious calculation of allegiances to both personal and professional codes. Ultimately, however, the sum of these calculations adds up to self-denial. Via this self-denial Spade begins to reshape his individualism, recalling for us the words of Herbert Croly quoted earlier in this essay: "The Promise of American life is to be fulfilled—not merely by a maximum amount of economic freedom, but by a certain measure of discipline; not merely by the abundant satisfaction of individual desires, but by a large measure of individual subordination and self-denial." Spade's decision to surrender Brigid stands as a moment of discipline for a man repeatedly described in terms suggesting not discipline but bestial ("wolfish") need for satisfaction.[45] Spade's dilemma at the conclusion of the novel enacts a dilemma of his entire generation: in moments of crisis, where do we put our allegiances, how do we protect our own self-interests without violating the demands of a larger community, how do we fuse our own needs with the needs of society and still retain our inherent American desire for self-promoting individualism?

In *Red Harvest* and *The Maltese Falcon* we witness Hammett struggling with his generation's reconception of American individualism. Just as intellectuals were calling for the refashioning of nineteenth-century individualism through efficient planning, social control, and self-denial, Hammett was investigating the possibilities of achieving and maintaining this new individualism. These investigations, however, do not supply easy answers. In *Red Harvest* Hammett portrays the failure of

new individualism, for the Op and all his allegiances to the Agency cannot withstand the pull of an old, self-seeking individualism. The lesson here seems to be that the inherited self-interest of the American landscape remains too powerful for the new allegiances to overcome. And yet in *The Maltese Falcon* Hammett reverses this movement and takes his hero from a self-indulgent individualism to a new individualism which seeks to wed collective and personal interests via self-denial. But, as John Patterson properly maintains, this movement toward a new individualism is far from triumphant: "Returned to his desk in the final scene of his career, [Spade] is in fact a bleak, lonely, and unhappy figure, without home, without love, without community, conscious perhaps that his victory is far from final and that it may have cost him far too much."[46]

The pull of old and new individualism is not resolved in these two novels, only highlighted. Hammett neither assures us of the possibility of achieving a new individualism nor does he maintain the necessary and inevitable victory of the old individualism. It has been said of detective stories that they are "wish-fulfillment fantasies designed to produce certain agreeable sensations in the reader, to foist upon him illusions he wants to entertain and which he goes to this literature to find."[47] If so, then Hammett has successfully transcended the genre, for his novels offer us profound complexities in the place of wish-fulfillments, irreconcilable realities instead of entertaining illusions. If we approach *Red Harvest* and *The Maltese Falcon* as complementary explorations of a similar dilemma, then we must face the disagreeable sensations produced by these texts when read in tandem: that is, that the refashioning of American individualism toward a more collective identity, as desirable and as necessary as it may be for the promise of American life, has been, and will always be, a painful and a precarious process.

Notes

1. William Curtis, "Some Recent Books," *Town and Country* 15 February 1930, cited in Richard Layman, *Shadow Man: The Life of Dashiell Hammett* (New York: Harcourt, 1981) 113.

2. Leonard Moss, "Hammett's Heroic Operative," *New Republic* 8 January 1968: 34.

3. Leslie Fiedler, *Love and Death in the American Novel* (New York: Criterion, 1960) 476.

4. H. H. Morris, "Dashiell Hammett in the Wasteland," *Midwest Quarterly* 19 (Winter 1978): 200-01.

5. Cynthia S. Hamilton, *Western and Hard-Boiled Detective Fiction in America: From High Noon to Midnight* (Iowa City: U of Iowa P, 1987) 1-2. To her credit, Hamilton grants Hammett a high level

of sophistication on the problem of individualism in his work. Of Hammett's novels, she writes, "Hammett appears to be caught in a philosophical 'Catch-22': competitive individualism is bad because it is divisive, but collective action is impossible because individuals are competitive. Hammett cannot get past the basic ideological assumption of the primacy of the individual, and can pose no alternative. In this respect, the later condemnation of Hammett's work as subversive must be considered wryly ironic" (32). Like Hamilton's, my focus is on Hammett's handling of complicated issues of individualism. But whereas Hamilton insists that Hammett "cannot get past the basic ideological assumption of the primacy of the individual" I would argue that Hammett is not trying to "get past" individualism but is exploring competing versions of individualism and their respective attractions and shortcomings. Any "alternative" which Hammett might pose would thus not be something outside of individualism but would be a different type of individualism. Hammett is not in the business of posing alternatives to individualism; he is, rather, interested in investigating irreconcilable and painful tensions.

6. David Geherin, *The American Private Eye: The Image in Fiction* (New York: Ungar, 1985) 21-22.

7. D. Glover, "Sociology and the Thriller: The Case of Dashiell Hammett," *Sociological Review* 27 (February 1979): 26.

8. Robert Edenbaum, "The Poetics of the Private-Eye: The Novels of Dashiell Hammett" in *Tough-Guy Writers of the 1930's,* ed. David Madden (Carbondale: Southern Illinois UP, 1968) 81.

9. Sinda Gregory, *Private Investigations: The Novels of Dashiell Hammett* (Carbondale: Southern Illinois UP, 1985) 29. Compare Gregory's statement to Hamilton's claim that in Hammett's novels the "need for self-reliance is emphasized. . . . The individual is shown to be the only source of positive social action" (31).

10. Robert Shulman, "Dashiell Hammett's Social Vision," *Centennial Review* 29 (Fall 1985): 400. Shulman opposes the individualism of the Continental Op, Sam Spade, and Ned Beaumont (a type of individualism Shulman often refers to as merely "different") to the "competitive individualism" of those whom they must confront. Though I agree with Shulman's observation that a novel like *The Maltese Falcon* "brings to a suggestive focus [Hammett's] concern with American individualism," I would suggest that the conflicting versions of individualism in such novels as *Red Harvest* and *The Maltese Falcon* are most often played out

within the hero rather than between the hero and his competitive society. Such a reading reveals not only Hammett's critique of an acquisitive capitalist culture, which most readings of his work manifest, but emphasizes Hammett's critique of his heroes as well.

11. Herbert Croly, *The Promise of American Life* (New York: Macmillan, 1909) 22.

12. Croly 25, 23, 152.

13. Frederick Jackson Turner cited in *Individualism and Conformity in the American Character,* ed. Richard Rapson (Boston: Heath, 1967) 26.

14. Van Wyck Brooks, "Toward a National Culture" in *Van Wyck Brooks: The Early Years,* ed. Claire Sprague (New York: Harper 1968) 185.

15. Brooks 186, 190, 190, 190.

16. Herbert Hoover, *American Individualism* (Garden City: Doubleday, 1922) 71-72.

17. Croly 153.

18. Hoover 66.

19. John Dewey, *Individualism Old and New* (New York: Capricorn, 1930) 51-52. See also the chapter "Toward a New Individualism" 74-100.

20. Horace M. Kallan, *Individualism: An American Way of Life* (New York: Liveright, 1933) 20.

21. Everett Dean Martin, *The Conflict of the Individual and the Mass in the Modern World* (New York: Holt, 1932) 33.

22. George Soule, *A Planned Society* (New York: Macmillan, 1932) 91-92.

23. Cited in Richard H. Pells, *Radical Visions and American Dreams: Culture and Social Thought in the Depression Years* (Middletown: Wesleyan UP, 1984) 50.

24. Dewey 31-32.

25. The town's geographical location also holds symbolic resonance. Gregory writes that Personville's "pollution, in both a physical and spiritual sense, is even more dramatic because of its geographical position; by placing the city in the West, Hammett suggests a sort of ultimate corruption: the West—the promised land whose expanse offers freedom, escape, and the realization of America's promise of opportunity and unlimited possibility—has become as 'dirtied up' as the rest of the country" (31).

26. Dashiell Hammett, *The Complete Novels of Dashiell Hammett* (New York: Knopf, 1965) 7. All further references are to this edition and are cited in parenthesis.

27. Peter Wolfe, *Beams Falling: The Art of Dashiell Hammett* (Bowling Green: Bowling Green U Popular P, 1980) 90.

28. Gregory astutely observes the importance of the Op's allegiance to the Agency: "Unlike almost all of the hard-boiled detectives who work from a small one-man office and who pride themselves on their independence (Philip Marlowe, Mike Hammer, Race Williams), the Op is part of an organization. Thus he is not a renegade maverick at odds with the police. . . . The Continental Detective Agency is, in fact, a business that approaches crime and violence with no moralistic or evangelical zeal. The Op's anonymity is reinforced by his position in such an agency" (44).

This description of the Op's unusual position in hard-boiled fiction will serve as an interesting contrast to Hammett's next creation, Sam Spade.

29. Discussing the importance of this moment, Glover observes: "It is this stubbornness which mitigates against seeing the Continental Op solely as the organization man he is and which limits the strong tendency for the detective to be reduced solely to his occupational function. Furthermore it is this irrepressible egoism which shifts the narrative towards the timeless realm of fantasy where the individual is totally superordinate and autonomous. The antinomies which the text invokes—between individual and occupation, realism and fantasy— are never ultimately resolved but provide for different modes of exposition and emphasis as the plot unfolds" (25-26).

30. Wolfe 87.

31. Gregory 50. George J. Thompson notes the Op's vengeful motives but argues differently: "The harvest of revenge promises to be red. Nowhere does the Op talk about law or justice in this vow; the matter is partly a personal one. The detective seems to represent himself more than his client, and yet his personal stand implies a social, even moral, perspective as well. The Op's emphasis is on a cleaning up, a harvesting of rottenness and corruption. The harvest image suggests a natural, if not moral, necessity for action."

32. Seeking to vindicate the Op's actions, Thompson insists the following: "Stirring things up and trying to stay tough enough to survive prove to be the Op's method throughout *Red Harvest*. In this initial case [of the fixed fight], his method is tried out: it's a pragmatic experiment, one which get results even though a man is killed in the process . . . we are not morally upset that Kid Cooper gets killed. He is not innocent, and his death is seen, though as non-legal, as poetic justice" ("The Problem of Moral Vision in Dashiell Hammett's Detective Novels, Part II: *Red Harvest* 'The Pragmatic and Moral Dilemma,'" 218).

33. In his study of popular genres, John G. Cawelti insists that "to preserve his integrity [the hard-boiled hero] must reject the public ideals and values of the society and seek to create his own personal code of ethics and his own set of values" (*Adventure, Mystery, and Romance: Formula Stories as Art and Popular Culture* [Chicago: U of Chicago P, 1976], 161). Certainly this is true of many hard-boiled heroes, but in the case of the Op it is not so. When the Op chooses to begin his vendetta against Personville, he is embracing, not rejecting, the public ideals and values of the society. Also, when the Op seeks to fashion his own personal code and set of values (codes and values free of Agency constraints) we see the dissolution of integrity, not the preservation of it, as the Op descends into the ethics of revenge. Perhaps the harshest criticism of the Op's "personal code of ethics" comes from Christopher Bentley: "Apart from his narrow and sometimes questionable professionalism, it is hard to see that the Op has any ethical code, or that his violence is any more meaningful than that it serves to keep him alive and to kill people whom he wishes to see dead."

34. John S. Whitley, "Stirring Things Up: Dashiell Hammett's Continental Op," *Journal of American Studies* 14 (Dec 1980): 449.

35. Gregory 57.

36. Dennis Dooley, *Dashiell Hammett* (New York: Ungar, 1984) 85.

37. Dooley writes: "How fitting, after six years of stories and novels featuring a nameless hero, that the first words of Hammett's new book should be the name of his detective" (99).

38. As William Ruehlman notes, "When Spade is compared to a 'blond satan' in the first paragraph, Hammett is deliberately setting him forth as a character who is a long way from being a hero" (*Saint With a Gun: The Unlawful American Private Eye* [New York: New York UP, 1974], 73).

39. Cited in Layman 106.

40. Thompson gives the most thorough reading of this confrontation, placing, as I do, great importance on all of Spade's reasons for surrendering Brigid ("The Problem of Moral Vision in Dashiell Hammett's Detective Novels, Part IV: *The Maltese Falcon* 'The Emergency of the Hero,'" *Armchair Detective* 7 (1974): 189). Though Thompson is not concerned as I am with Spade's struggle with competing versions of individualism, he recog-

nizes, as many critics fail to do, that Spade's reasons "bridge moral and professional and personal concerns" (189). In contrast to most critics, William Kenney fails to discern the indispensable importance of the Spade-Brigid confrontation to the meaning of the novel. Kenney sees the confrontation as an "afterthought" because the main action of the novel, the quest for the falcon, ends with the discovery of the fake ("The Dashiell Hammett Tradition and the Modern Detective Novel," *Dissertation,* Michigan 1964, 110 cited in Thompson, 'The Problem of Moral Vision in Dashiell Hammett's Detective Novels, Part IV: *The Maltese Falcon* 'The Emergency of the Hero,'" 179).

41. Many critics do believe that Spade has been within the code all along. For instance, William F. Nolan believes that in this scene Spade "reveals the emotions of a man whose heart is with the woman, but whose code forbids his accepting her" (*Hammett: A Life at the Edge* [New York: Congdon, 1983], 61). Edward Margolies insists that Spade "can surrender Brigid to the police because, even though he loves her, his code comes first" (*Which Way Did He Go? The Private Eye in Dashiell Hammett, Raymond Chandler, Chester Himes, and Ross Macdonald* [New York: Holmes, 1982], 30). William Marling asserts that Spade is "more perfectly than the Op a knight of the detective code" (*Dashiell Hammett* [Boston: Twayne, 1983], 76). Walter Blair concurs with the primacy of Spade's code in controlling his behavior throughout the novel: "Through his reading of much of the book the reader is kept in the dark as to what makes Spade tick. But as the story concludes, Spade's actions make clear that he is the only character who has integrity, who obeys a code" ("Dashiell Hammett: Themes and Techniques," in *Essays on American Literature in Honor of Jay Hubbell,* ed. Clarence Gohdes [Durham: Duke UP, 1967], 306).

My inclinations are more in sympathy with Hamilton, who acknowledges that "we are never told [Spade's] thoughts, only given his words and actions. Spade may have involved himself with Brigid, Gutman, and Cairo in order to solve the murders, recover the falcon and prosecute the thieves; or he may be an opportunist who finds he must turn everything over to the police in order to save himself. Some understanding of Spade is possible because the vision underlying the book is his vision, but this does not help us to interpret his actions or to place moral value on them" (132).

I feel it is not necessary to accept that Spade believes in a code; what is more important is that Spade desires to be affiliated with such a code, that he seeks, rather than believes in, allegiance to that code.

42. Gregory 105. It is interesting to note here that although Gregory suggests the impossibility of discovering Spade's intentions, she is willing to believe in Spade's professionalism: "Despite all his personal complexities and idiosyncracies, Sam Spade is, above all, a very efficient private investigator, a man who has a shrewd business sense and loyalty to and respect for his profession" (94).

43. Perhaps John Patterson is correct in asserting "that when a man has so many reasons to advance he is not really sure of any of them" ("A Cosmic View of the Private Eye," *Saturday Review* 22 August 1953: 32). Again, however, what remains important is not that we ascertain Spade's true allegiances but that we note Spade's struggle to articulate those allegiances.

44. I obviously disagree with Thompson, who feels that at this moment "Spade's diction—'If that doesn't mean anything to you forget it and we'll make it this'—certainly implies he is over-simplifying his complex reasons because he realizes all too well her inability to understand their meaning" ("The Problem of Moral Vision in Dashiell Hammett's Detective Novels, Part IV: *The Maltese Falcon* 'The Emergency of the Hero,'" 189).

Spade is not over-simplifying his motivations at this moment so that Brigid may understand him; instead, he is asserting, in a crystalized, but not an over-simplified form, his newly discovered virtue of renunciation.

45. Dooley writes: "As the novel nears its conclusion, we glimpse the animal in Spade again, looking 'hungrily from her hair to her feet and up to her eyes again.' But he denies his hunger, knowing that to satisfy it would be his undoing" (108).

46. Patterson 32.

47. William Aydelotte, "The Detective Story as Historical Source," in *Dimensions of Detective Fiction,* ed. Larry Landrum (Bowling Green: Popular P, 1976) 69.

Carl Freedman and Christopher Kendrick (essay date March 1991)

SOURCE: Freedman, Carl, and Christopher Kendrick. "Forms of Labor in Dashiell Hammett's *Red Harvest.*" *PMLA* 106, no. 2 (March 1991): 209-21.

[*In the following essay, Freedman and Kendrick consider the various forms of labor illustrated in* Red Harvest, *particularly the "linguistic or dialogic work of the Op." The critics also discuss "the decentering symbolic impersonality of dialogue itself" in the novel.*]

What kind of work does a detective do when he detects? Dashiell Hammett's most complex novel, **Red Harvest,** suggests some interesting answers. Originally published in book form in 1929, it counts as one of the first attempts—and perhaps still the greatest attempt—to forge a type of detective fiction that contrasts sharply with the classic deductive tradition most centrally identified with Sherlock Holmes. The new variety has been generally associated with the adjective *hard-boiled* and, especially during the 1920s and 1930s, with the American magazine *Black Mask*.[1] Perhaps its most obvious innovation was the abandonment of the intellectual-puzzle formula as the basis of narrative construction. Although **Red Harvest** is not without puzzles, its main interest lies elsewhere, and one can adequately summarize the text without even mentioning a "problem" of the Sherlockian type.

Red Harvest is set in Personville, also known as Poisonville, a small industrial city in the western United States. The workers at the Personville Mining Corporation, owned by Elihu Willsson, had been represented by the IWW, but the union local was crushed during a strike and the tough Wobbly leader, Bill Quint, was defeated. To beat the union, however, Elihu Willsson had enlisted the help of several gangster leaders and their thugs, and since their victory they have refused to leave and have insisted on taking a share in running the town. As the novel opens, an operative of the Continental Detective Agency has been summoned by Donald Willsson, Elihu's son and Personville's reform-minded newspaper editor. When Donald is killed before meeting with the Continental Op, Elihu himself hires the detective to "clean up" the town, that is, to remove the gangsters who have usurped much of Elihu's power and profit. The main action of the novel concerns the Op's successful efforts to carry out his charge. He consults with Bill Quint, forms a useful friendship with the community's leading courtesan, Dinah Brand, and, in general, acquires pertinent information about the structures and personalities of the town. Working his way into the highest levels of the gangster establishment, he eventually succeeds in setting the different gangs (one of which is technically the local police force) murderously against one another, with the result that the major gangster leaders are killed and their hold on the town destroyed.

Our detailed reading of **Red Harvest** centers on the term of our opening question, namely, work or labor. We argue that the narrative structure is based on several forms of labor, each autonomous and yet complexly interrelated with the others. Our greatest stress is on the linguistic or dialogic work of the Op and on the decentering symbolic impersonality of dialogue itself. We conclude by considering not only the generic composition of the novel but also its political resonances and implications.

Work in the normative capitalist sense of productive wage-labor—that is to say, economic labor—is in fact absent from the manifest text of **Red Harvest**. But its absence is strongly determinate, conditioning—while contrasting with—three other forms of labor: the political, the linguistic, and the sexual. Economic labor that is normative under capitalism may be considered a determinate absence in two different ways. In the first place, the labor of the Continental Op himself is a paradigm of the "liberated" activity that constitutes an important part of detective fiction. For detective work might almost be called a bohemian kind of labor: as work that frees the worker from the homogenized space-time of most capitalist labor and that in so doing brings the powers of the "whole man" at least potentially into play, detective work is a peculiarly nonalienated variety of labor. And it is precisely because of the atypical, nonalienated character of this labor that normative, exploited, alienated wage-labor is largely displaced by the other forms of labor that the novel's world comprises. Second, and on the level of plot, economic labor, while invisible, remains the first and most fundamental term of the novel's chain of events. The gangster establishment of Poisonville depends, after all, on the breaking of the Wobbly-led strike, and the strike itself is a consequence of the intensely alienated and exploited labor performed at the Personville Mining Corporation.[2] The nameless miners are in a certain sense the collective protagonist of the novel, but their labor is never explicitly shown—we do not even know what they mine—and, after the first chapter, is never so much as mentioned.

What *is* shown—and indeed foregrounded, since it provides much of the novel's subject matter—is what we call political labor: the various practices of administration and violence established by the uneasy coalition among the capitalist Elihu Willsson, the gangsters hired to suppress the strike, and the gangsterlike local police. This political labor is, however, itself economic, not only because it ultimately owes its being—or, at least, its municipal hegemony—to the conditions of economic production at the Personville Mining Corporation but because it is immediately based on a (mostly illegal) service economy: bootlegging, gambling, smuggling, and the loan and bail-bond business. The gangster power structure, as it quickly moves into the center of the novel, cancels the vision of class struggle conveyed by Bill Quint and replaces it with a strictly intraclass politics whose forms of power are at once more monolithic and more individualistic than those of Quint's socialism. For though the novel describes the course of a prolonged conflict between Elihu and the gangsters (between "legitimate" and "illegitimate" capitalism) in which Elihu is the ultimate victor, for the greater part of the book the gangsters and Elihu appear to be parts of a single, monolithic power bloc that is dominated and defined by the gangsters. The gangsters' murderous activities generally appear to constitute the sole form of real political power, and Elihu usually seems to be just another gangster.

At the same time, however, the gangsters' political structure is also radically individualist: their leaders must operate without the formal sanction of the state, and to retain command each must rely on the undependable personal loyalty of his own band of thugs. Hence even specifically gangster economics (e.g., bootlegging) are subordinated, in the telling, to gangster politics (e.g., gang warfare). The individualism of the gangster power structure makes for a permanent state of anarchic emergency that renders the gangsters vulnerable in a way that Elihu's capitalism never is. Whereas the position of the Personville Mining Corporation could be assaulted—and unsuccessfully at that—only by the collective action of the militantly organized working class, the actual defeat of the gangsters is triggered by the lone, chubby figure of the Continental Op (who is officially employed, not accidentally, by Elihu Willsson). His own labor, though directly political and thus indirectly economic, is in itself primarily linguistic.

For the Op's modus operandi, in **Red Harvest** as in many of Hammett's other fictions, is mainly dialogic: he "stirs things up" (in his own phrase) by making false suggestions, dispensing carefully calibrated doses of true information, and extracting verbal promises and commitments; most important, he subtly insinuates himself, primarily through his verbal style, into the criminal-political milieu of Personville as one thoroughly at home with its workings and hence capable of being a formidable ally or opponent. Thus, while the Continental Op, as the first major character in the *Black Mask* school of hard-boiled detective fiction, may be considered a paradigm of American macho, it is macho defined less as physical toughness (though he is physically tough) than as the ability to construct an authoritative rhetorical ethos—a point emphasized by his unprepossessing appearance: he stands five feet six and weighs 180 to 190 pounds.

The Op's emphatically rhetorical labor fits well with the gangster polity that he combats. His work, like the gangsters', is on the one hand apparently monolithic—inasmuch as discourse in this first-person novel presents itself as a total, pregiven system—and on the other hand individualistic, inasmuch as discourse reflects the resources of the particular speaker and readily bears the stamp of the individual stylist. Hence, although political labor and linguistic labor may seem to exist on different planes, they are homologous; and this homology is a condition for the confrontation between them that forms the novel's main conflict—that is, the Op's war against the gangsters. In addition, however, that war, and indeed the Op's very work of detecting, can be seen to mask a deeper conflict between two modes of explanation (which are two worldviews), as both political and linguistic forms of labor are revealed to serve a common repressive function. Just as the vision of gangster politics displaces the vision of class struggle glimpsed in Bill Quint's story, so the Op's rhetoric, though in fact at the service of Elihu Willsson's capitalism, appears self-subsistent and thus also effaces the socioeconomic realities of class and production. Linguistic labor is also repressive in a more obvious and direct way. If the workers at the Personville Mining Corporation are the primary economic presence in the novel, then Dinah Brand is the primary sexual presence, and sexual labor on her part bears roughly the same relation to the Op's linguistic labor that the miners' economic labor does to the gangsters' political labor. For Dinah's sexual activity and desirability largely determine the Op's procedures, since only through sex does she obtain the information and personal contacts of which the Op makes crucial (and primarily linguistic) use. Yet the reader sees no more of Dinah copulating than of the miners mining, and the Op himself has as little to do with sexuality as the gangsters do with economic production. The Op—like every male, apparently—perceives Dinah's attractions, yet sex is emphatically repressed in favor of language: they just talk.

Each of these four forms of labor, however, animates each of the other three in ways still more complex than we have thus far suggested. We can consider some of these further complexities most conveniently by examining the novel's character structure. We may begin with those characters identified primarily with labor in its economic form—Bill Quint and Elihu Willsson. Neither Quint nor Elihu, however, directly represents economic labor in its classically capitalist sense, despite the fact that they "stand for" Labor and Capital, respectively. Even Quint, the character most able to speak of and for the wage-laborers (not one of whom ever makes even a walk-on appearance), is not actually a wage-laborer himself but, evidently, a full-time official of the IWW. He arrives on the scene (from Chicago, the traditional center of American working-class militancy) when Personville is on the verge of becoming Poisonville, that is, when the municipal economy has been plunged into crisis by Elihu's reneging on his agreements with the IWW local representing the miners—in other words, when the economic is presenting itself in a transparently political form. He is thus a political laborer from the start, and so he has something in common with the main politicians of the book, the gangsters, in one of whose speakeasies he explains, for the Op and for the reader, the primarily economic matrix of the gangsters' ascension to power. And, indeed, despite the relative lucidity of his class analysis, what he describes is also the matrix of his own local position, which he views, to some extent, in rather gangsterlike terms of personal patronage and dependency: "Hell with Chi!" he tells the Op, "I run 'em here" (8). The novel also implicitly links him to the gangsters by way of his previous sexual relationship with their playmate, Dinah. Dinah, the great instrumentalist of sexual labor, uses him just as she does the gangster Whisper Thaler, for her own economic gain; finding that advance knowledge of strike activity or inactivity can be useful in planning her investments, she in effect reduces this proletarian militant to a stockbroker.

It is indeed through Dinah, who functions as a sexual "filter," that Quint is also thrown into comparison with his archenemy and opposite number in the class struggle, Elihu Willsson. Elihu's apparent gangster status (his lack of direct, unshared political control) is nowhere more neatly symbolized than in his clandestine "affair" with Dinah. With Elihu as with Quint, sex (which means Dinah) works to efface economic realities, at least symbolically, and to recast primarily economic figures in political terms. But Elihu, again like Quint, is a political worker in a more literal sense also. A legitimate capitalist who has been wont simply to "own" politicians ("a United States senator, a couple of representatives, the governor, the mayor, and most of the state legislature" [9]), he has been forced by the economic crisis in Personville to join forces with the gangster politicians in order to maintain his economic position, thus subjecting himself to their political modes and ideologies. These amount to a series of weighty but unreliable "covenants" of personal fidelity that are supported by violence and the threat of violence.

In establishing and entering the gangster polity, Elihu strips himself of much of his real political power, not only because, lacking a personal band of thugs, he is ill equipped for violence but also because the gangster covenants compromise his legitimacy. He temporarily loses the possibility of legal redress against the gangsters, since any such action would expose his own illegal complicity with them. His strictly political position is thus weak out of all proportion to his economic power, and this weakness is figured linguistically.

The two aspects of his political weakness correspond to two ways in which he is mastered by language. On the one hand, his vulnerability to gangster violence is signified by the vehement, disconnected shouting that seems to be his normal mode of oral discourse and that is also, as the Continental Op clearly discerns, a sign of physical terror. On the other hand, his legal vulnerability is signified by his relation to the various scripts and documents that appear throughout the novel: the most obviously dangerous are the records that Dinah obtains for Donald Willsson and that he has with him when he is killed, though they are useless for Donald's reforming purposes since they incriminate his father as well as the gangsters. More important, the contract that the terrified Elihu makes with the Op (and puts in writing at the Op's insistence) licenses the Op to clean up Personville by any means and thus pins Elihu to his character as legitimate capitalist, much to his own peril and against his later wishes.

Elihu, indeed, might be called a figure of the letter. Whether he is shouting stock orders and threats or signing certified checks, he is controlled by, and at the mercy of—in fact his character is projected or figured by—linguistic repositories of one kind or another, standard forms of discourse. Even his sex life enters by way of the letter. His relationship with Dinah is revealed only when his love letters to her surface in a blackmail attempt against him. Since the novel offers no other manifestation of the feeble and elderly Elihu's sexuality, sex and the letter are virtually one for him, and his sexual weakness is figured linguistically in much the same way as is his political insecurity: in sex as in politics his "legitimacy" commits and shackles him to the letter, to which he is therefore vulnerable.

Elihu, accordingly, occupies an extremely complex position regarding the various modes of labor under discussion. Linguistic labor (the form that might seem furthest removed from the economic labor that ultimately defines his place) absorbs the other three types and comes to serve as a multivalent code sending forth economic, political, and sexual messages simultaneously. But the overdeterminacy of the presiding (linguistic) code for Elihu is only a particularly telling manifestation of a system of mutual intercoding that informs character presentation in other aspects as well.

For example, intercoding makes for a curiously abstract symbolism that finds its clearest expression in the character of Dinah Brand, whose primary work is sexual. Her sexuality projects more as aura than as activity, and Dinah's defining work involves the production of sexual charisma or appeal. This appeal is conveyed not by movie-star beauty but by the apparent spontaneity of her actions or, more inclusively, by the general ambience of unrepressed openness that she makes her medium. This quality is most neatly figured by the small but blatant disorders that the Op keeps noticing in her apparel—runs in stockings, tears in dresses, and the like. Her slovenliness signifies an overabundant energy that the social forms of the gangster world cannot thoroughly contain or structure—witness the Op's remark, after Dinah's hose have run yet another time: "[Y]our legs are too big, they put too much strain on the material" (79). Dinah's runs and tears, however, not only represent her patent sensuality but also suggest (in the abstract form of surplus energy) the direct economic activity that sexual labor functions to distance and repress, to "filter" into its own terms. For Dinah's sexual labor is itself directly economic—she is after all a high-class whore—and so may be seen as a distortion of normative, productive economic labor. Hence Dinah's eruptions onto the political and linguistic scenes appear, in part, as the return of the repressed, of direct economic production. If we consider, too, that the entire gangster polity is characterized by a principle of plenitude analogous to Dinah's surplus energy, then Dinah's runs take on a further, allegorical significance: in this light, they figure the crucial weaknesses in the gangster polity (the excess of material over structure) on which the Op founds his strategy. Dinah's disarrangements are thus so many symbolic "clues," for the Op and for the reader, to the gangsters' world.

This world is, like Dinah herself, a body of vibrant energy unsanctioned by the official guarantor of bourgeois legitimacy—that is, by the letter of the law, which (thanks to the Op's linguistic machinations) eventually sweeps away the gangster polity and, with it, the opportunity for the kind of sex Dinah had practiced. But whereas the central physical activity of Dinah's sexual labor (copulation) is, like the miners' mining, never explicitly shown, the central physical activity of the gangsters' political labor (violence) is shown again and again. *Red Harvest* is, as the title suggests, an extraordinarily bloody book (the Op on one occasion is dizzied in tallying the murders that have taken place since his arrival), and this stress on violence—that is, on the political—is crucial to the novel's social vision. Since, after all, capitalism ultimately determines bourgeois legality, what could an "illegitimate" capitalism be?

Hammett at one point seems to draw a parallel between fascist Italy and gangster-dominated Personville, but the novel is not exactly "about" fascism, except in the allegorical sense we consider later. While its concrete terms may not be irrelevant to the formulation of an adequate theory of fascism, what they actually suggest is the feudalization of illicit power. The relative absence of strong, central, universalizing state power; the prominence of private and semiprivate armies; the corresponding importance of personal loyalty between master and dependent; and, above all, the way in which this highly visible, dynamic polity can overshadow economy (the reader in fact sees very little bootlegging, gambling, and the like), as the fully bourgeois politicians owned by the "real" capitalist Elihu Willsson can never overshadow him—these features of the gangster polity are all precapitalist and classically feudal. Removed from capitalist law, the gangsters temporarily appear all the stronger—is not their capacity for illicit violence a manifest sign of strength?—and they are, indeed, strong enough to rescue and then to dominate Elihu Willsson. But such dominance is unstable, because in the larger society beyond Personville full-fledged capitalism is still unchallenged and the letter of the law still operates.

One index of the gangsters' apparent strength is a mastery of discourse: contrast Max Thaler's ominous, effective whispering or Noonan's fluent Irish-cop heartiness with Elihu's wearisome vehemence. Finally, however, the gangsters are far less linguistically capable than Elihu; in other words, their political weakness as "feudalists," as less than full-fledged capitalists, is determined in part linguistically. For the kind of legal documentation to which Elihu is partially and temporarily vulnerable is ultimately fatal to them. Decisively outside the letter of the law, they are decisively vulnerable to it (though it must not be forgotten that the letter of the law itself ultimately means a capacity for greater violence—in this case, the intervention of the National Guard). Indeed, this disparity in linguistic power partly explains why the Op, the linguistic laborer, can demolish the gangsters but makes no serious attempt to overthrow Elihu, whom he seems to find equally detestable.

In fact, the Op, for all his mastery of discourse, is strictly limited by two closely related laws. First, the economic law of profit requires that the Continental Detective Agency act in the interests of its clients (and the Op, surely enough, does a good job for Elihu, returning him to undisputed control of Personville). Second, an even more striking restriction obliges the Op to operate in alliance with (if not necessarily within) the letter of bourgeois legality; thus he acts decisively only against those who have placed themselves irrevocably outside the law. This alliance points to a crucial ambiguity in the very identity of the private detective. Though he is on one level independent of the police—and hence free of certain statist constraints on the individualist or "whole man"—his entire position as a respectable entrepreneur (or an entrepreneur's loyal employee) ties him to the state and makes him function, in the last analysis, as an adjunct to the official forces of law and order. The appealing personal hostility that a Sam Spade or a Philip Marlowe displays toward the cops is thus mainly gestural. The Continental Op himself (whose own designation phonetically suggests the word *cop*) tends, in most of Hammett's fictions, to eschew even such gestures, maintaining a cautious but usually cordial relationship with the police. In *Red Harvest,* however, there is admittedly a partial vacuum where the official forces of bourgeois legality ought to be: Noonan's police are really just another private gangster army—at one point the thugs loyal to the bootlegger Pete the Finn are sworn in as new members of the force—and the Op's ultimate alliance with the National Guard is presented in extremely abstract form. Nonetheless, the Op's actions remain largely determined by his fundamental allegiance to the letter of the law.

Still, the private detective's nonofficial status does partly condition the relative autonomy that the Op enjoys vis-à-vis the written law, an autonomy expressed, symbolically and actually, by his relying more on the spoken than on the written word. The novel is in one respect almost a Platonic fable on the superiority of dialogue to document.[3] Document "doesn't know how to address the right people, and not address the wrong. And when it is ill-treated and unfairly abused it always needs its parent to come to its help, being unable to defend or help itself." The dialectician of dialogue, in contrast, deals in "words which can defend both themselves and him who planted them, words which instead of remaining barren contain a seed whence new words grow up in new characters" (Plato 521-22).

The relative defenselessness of the written word that Socrates notes in the *Phaedrus* is well illustrated by the haplessness of the newspaper editor Donald Willsson, who, with his trust in documentation, is, so to speak, the "official" reformer—or would-be reformer—of Personville. Shortly before his death, however, as if unconsciously grasping the Socratic point, he summons the help of a truly dialogic dialectician, the Continental Op. While not entirely forgoing legal and quasi-legal documentation (and, in fact, ultimately tied to it, as we have indicated), the detective realizes the need for a more supple and dialogic sort of linguistic labor. (Such is the relative absence of documentation from his world that, until the dialogic labors are complete, the Op deliberately neglects—and orders his subordinates Dick Foley and Mickey Linehan to neglect—the written reports required by their boss, the Old Man.) What he calls his "experiment" with the Cooper-Bush fight is designed in part to provide the reader with a sample of the Op's dialogic prowess. By spreading a hot tip through the town's gambling population and by a short conversation with Ike Bush, he constructs a situation in which four apparently meaningless words—"Back to Philly, Al"—can unfix a fixed boxing match and result in a man's death. The great bulk of the Op's crucial work amounts to one or another variation on "Back to Philly, Al." His dialogic achievement climaxes in the amazing "peace conference" scene, where the Op talks face-to-face with, and more adroitly than, all the gang leaders; one seed planted there, that of Noonan's death, blossoms within minutes. It is not only the substance of the Op's speech—the precisely measured bits of true and false information—that does the trick but the style as well. Much of his leverage, at the peace conference and in Poisonville generally, results from his insinuating himself into the highest levels of the gangster polity as a potentially formidable friend or foe; he is depended on, at different times, by Noonan, Thaler, and Reno, and he owes this stature not to his physical prowess but to the good impression he makes, mainly because his mastery of gangster idiom—informal, laconic, understated, oblique, amoral, enriched by an occasional striking metaphor—is superior to that of any of the actual gangsters. All this has little to do with formal structures of documentation, with letter and law, which plainly have determining power at the beginning and the end of the novel but effectively disappear through most of it, as the novel becomes absorbed in the Op's rhetorical ethos. (Indeed, the Op explicitly recognizes this disappearance when he tells his two assistants that since the gangsters "own the courts, and, besides, the courts are too slow for us now," he plans to use other, speedier methods that will result in the gangsters' having "their knives in each other's backs, doing our work for us"

[110].) One might say that the Op's dialogue becomes not only the medium in which he and (less successfully) most of the other characters live but a determining structure that lives them. While the letter of the law is suspended, dialogue is a world unto itself. And it is a world that, extending beyond the matter placed between quotation marks, encompasses the entirety of this first-person, eminently spoken novel.

The construction of this dialogic world, the detachment of the spoken word from its alliance with the letter into an autonomy that constitutes, as it were, the detective's proper homeland—this is a central accomplishment of the novel and a major end of the Op's work of detection, even though it is an end apparently only incidental to his stated goal of solving crimes or, rather, of eliminating a criminal situation. The Op's low-key version of detective macho precludes his visibly drawing any aesthetic satisfaction from the dialogic free play structuring his world and thus prevents the emergence of that aestheticist vein which typifies, for example, many of Raymond Chandler's Marlowe stories (an aestheticism, one suspects, that largely explains the professional literati's preference for Chandler over Hammett).[4] Yet a different sort of aesthetic component figures quite prominently in ***Red Harvest*** as a function of the Op's work of detecting, of his linguistic mastery: in a sense, indeed, that work is akin to artistic creation as classically defined, for it takes the Op into a realm of freedom and play in which the activity of detection appears to constitute an end in itself. The definitive entrance into this realm, and with it the surcharging of the Op's activity with immanent aesthetic value, occurs at the point where the initial puzzle (who killed Donald Willsson?) is solved and the novel opens out onto the gangster "pastoral" promised by the title. Here the contract between Elihu and the Op sets the Op down naked, as it were, in Poisonville, with $10,000 and his personal resourcefulness but with only a general goal to work toward—the destruction of the gangster polity—and, correlatively, with no specific devices at hand to implement his ends. This apparent freedom and open-endedness give the Op's detective operations their aesthetic character of play. Put another way, the reorientation and generalization of the Op's aims in the context of the entire gangster polity determine the aestheticization of detective work by bringing dialogue to the fore as both tool and medium, as both a means of achieving the Op's goal and as an end in itself, as a climate in which the Op feels truly at home.

This dual function of dialogue plays a crucial role: it marks the place where the chief contradiction in the Op's work—that between his alliance with the normative capitalist order and his apparent independence from it, between the social function and the individualist character of his activities—achieves a highly ideological resolution. For the duality of dialogue effectively resolves the split between the Op as instrument and as individualist, by absorbing it into a strictly technical unity of means and ends. Dialogue as "climate," as apparent end in itself, not only makes the Op comfortable and furnishes him with his proper habitat but also, as we have explained, empowers him in his professional capacities. It is by establishing a plausibly stable dialogic style that the Op makes things happen; dialogue as medium is a generalized tool, working in the long term to disrupt the already unstable gangster polity but serving immediate ends that are often unforeseen by the Op and the reader alike. But whether the Op is planting his effects with precision (as when he sets up Noonan during the gangster convocation) or whether, as is more often the case, he is playing things by ear, fishing for effects, he gives the impression of having a quasi-sympathetic knowledge of how his actions will affect the intricacies of the gangster establishment. So it is that this generalization of the instrumental character of the Op's labor, this foregrounding of dialogue as medium, fuses the Op's means and ends and in so doing assimilates him to the gangster world.

For the world of dialogue in which the Op is at home is virtually one with the gangster world, though the Op lives in that world with a difference. The gangster polity, structured by a tacit division of labor and by ties of personal dependence, is in effect a world of the word—of unwritten agreements—backed by violence. To preserve their hegemony, the gangsters must attempt to fix the series of agreements regulating their actions. To remain at least apparently as good as his word, each gangster chief must not only keep up his retinue of thugs but also set out for himself a dialogic terrain or register, maintaining the dialogic style that signifies self-control and power. Gangster laconicism in its various modes (as used by Whisper or Reno or even by a relative nonentity like O'Mara) acquires a ceremonial significance: it represents the ritual that symbolizes and fixes gangster relations of exchange. But this style also fixes the code of violence that is built into these relations; in gangster understatement, the more that is meant than meets the ear amounts to murderous force. Thus laconicism crystallizes within itself the tendency of the gangster kingdom to self-destruction, and the decentering effect of dialogue as medium and climate, as structural determinant of gangster activity, can only accentuate this tendency. The scene in which Reno Starkey, at the end of the novel, literally holds himself together and talks himself to death well illustrates the function of gangster style and of dialogic necessity:

> I knew he would go on talking as soon as he got himself in hand. He meant to die as he had lived, inside the same tough shell. Talking could be torture, but he wouldn't stop on that account, not while anybody was there to see him. . . . [S]itting there listening to and watching him talk himself to death wasn't pleasant.
>
> (197-98)

This last, anticlimactic interview has a medicinal effect on the Op, not only because he learns that he himself is definitely not Dinah's murderer but also because the episode, as a kind of spectacle, satiates his will to comprehend gangsterism and allows him to distance himself from the gangster community and its ethos. The spectacle thus helps him control the unnatural bloodlust and fear that the violence in Poisonville and, more important, his own participation in it inspired in him. His violent mood—his "fever," as he calls it—reaches its crest, and indeed goes out of control, in the scenes that take place in Dinah's apartment just after the "peace conference": before drugging himself into a helpless though a not necessarily harmless state, the Op informs Dinah that the whole convocation and all the resulting violence were unnecessary, since he could at this point have enlisted Elihu's aid "to swing the play [against the gangsters] legally." He has done otherwise, he explains, because "it's easier to have them killed off, easier and surer, and, now that I'm feeling this way, more satisfying" (145). Here, in the fever that threatens to assimilate him ever more deeply to gangsterism, the Op seems on the verge of losing his all-important self-control and dialogic mastery, as he unwittingly terrifies Dinah and then allows her to give him the incapacitating laudanum. The chapter that follows, in which the Op awakens from his dreams and finds himself beside Dinah's corpse, goes further toward investing him (symbolically) in gangster guise. His near unity with the gangster world is at this point so close and intense that it threatens to throw him off balance and thus to co-opt his labor. Here, then, we discover a further dimension of the ideological resolution in dialogue of the contradiction between the social function and the individualistic character of the Op's work. This resolution—that is, the Op's construction of a dialogic world that completes and overloads the gangster world—effectively replaces the conflict between the Op's freedom and the capitalist order with the more immediate conflict between the Op and the gangster polity: it is the gangster polity in its totality, as fixed and overloaded by dialogue, that threatens to take over and reinstrumentalize the Op's "unalienated" labor by destroying his freedom to make conscious play with the flexibility of dialogue.

But dialogue as medium is dangerous to the Op in what we might call its symbolic impersonality as well as in its potential for confining him to the fixity and violence of the gangster code.[5] For dialogue, as we have argued, constitutes a force in itself, a force whose effects can be seen in the gestures, the stylistic signatures, of the various characters (Elihu's vehemence, Max's ominous whisper, Dinah's casual openness). Dialogue as a massively informing and decentering structure thus appears to write the characters' lines for them and, paradoxically, almost to take on itself the attributes of the letter, of the written line, while the characters, in turn, seem to be functions of the dialogic world. (This "literal" quality of dialogue amounts to a subterranean return of the letter of the law in highly mediated form.) The Op, then, must finally guard himself against the splintering, depersonalizing tendency inherent in the dialogic world as abstract structure and symbolic Other, as well as against the violence fetish of the gangsters. At this strictly linguistic level, the Op's labors consist in maintaining a proper relation to dialogue, to the symbolic function. He prevents the linguistic alienation of his powers not by attempting directly to control dialogic free play, for there can be no question of that, but rather by rolling with the flow of dialogue, by ambiguously complying with dialogue so that it can fulfill its dual function as means and end.

Accordingly, although dialogue as structure and medium endangers the Op's equilibrium, the free play of dialogue is what preserves the unalienated and aestheticized form of his work. The Op labors, for the most part, by tapping the various energies harbored within dialogue and (through dialogue) within the gangster polity, whose structural disunity makes it susceptible to the Op's dialogic manœuvering. His modus operandi, then, is a new kind of detective procedure: it involves not the decoding of a discrete series of facts but, rather, an encoding process that activates the surplus energy inherent in his world, not deduction or ratiocination but an attempt at totalizing comprehension. This process, in which relations are to be grasped between foregrounded details and an entire social structure, defines itself against the detective process in the classic, or Sherlockian, tradition, where clues are set off from the social totality and where reason tends to be instrumentalized. The Op's detective work is hardly a "reasonable" process of that sort. It requires instead the apparently spontaneous capacity both to activate the energies present in the dialogic world and to weather the anarchic psychological and social effects that are thus set in motion: "Plans are all right sometimes," the Op explains to Dinah. "And sometimes just stirring things up is all right—if you're tough enough to survive, and keep your eyes open so you'll see what you want when it comes to the top" (79). Accordingly, the detective must live and move in the dialogic world without being subsumed by it, without losing his labor's freedom vis-à-vis the forces in this world. The Op, one might say, must consciously live his own decenteredness.

We may conclude, then, that the Op's situation typifies the limits of individualism in both form and content: not only is the Op's dialogic freedom qualified by dialogue itself as a medium and informing symbolic structure, it is also, though less urgently, compromised by the Op's ultimate political and economic ties to bourgeois legitimacy, to the letter of the law. But if the Op cannot finally be read as occupying a critical or negative position toward the normative capitalist order, the same finding is not necessarily valid for the novel as a whole, despite the natural temptation to identify the book with the character who speaks or quotes nearly its entire semantic content.

The title **Red Harvest** (perhaps the only line of the novel that is clearly *not* spoken by the Continental Op) is a pun: the harvest is both a blood-bath and the culmination of a chain of events launched by proletarian militancy. In this regard, we are bound to notice that the novel does contain an antifascist allegory of fascism,[6] if we agree to define fascism as the domination of the working class through open physical terror imposed by "respectable," though unusually reactionary, capital. Indeed, the novel can almost be read as a prophecy of the popular front (to which Hammett did adhere), for the final defeat of gangsterism ushers in the restoration of Elihu's "normal" exploitation, which is sanctioned by the liberal-democratic state. Whatever degree of radicalism one may grant to popular frontism, however, it is also true that the political vision that the novel foregrounds is not antifascist or popular-frontist or leftist in any way but, rather, anarchic and Hobbesian.[7]

In the world through which the Op moves—the "local color," as it were, of the novel—proletarian solidarity counts for little (it has, after all, been defeated before the novel begins), competition is merciless and frequently deadly, and one may constantly be thrown back exclusively on one's own resources. The prevailing lack of social trust enables the Op to set the gangsters at one another's throats and so to defeat them; but, once again, this world is to a large extent the Op's as well, and the same distrust exists between the Op and his own client, Elihu; between the Op and his own boss, the Old Man; and between the Op and his own assistant Dick (he has *some* trust in his other assistant, Mickey). In a sense, the fissure in the novel between antifascism and anarchic Hobbesianism is a matter of point of view. If one looks at the gangster polity from the outside (as Bill Quint does), it appears to be an analogue or figure of fascist power that is explicable in Marxist terms. Seen from the inside (the perspective of the Op and virtually all the other characters), the gangsters' world seems a savage, inescapable place where dog-eat-dog individualism is the only philosophy that makes sense.

The antifascist allegory of fascism is not, however, the only or the most pervasive way that **Red Harvest** stands critically opposed to capitalism. The book may be read more generally, in its formal substance, as an attack on socioeconomic relations, on the quality of social life, in the United States at the time of writing—that is, during the transitional period in which monopoly capital was beginning to be the dominant form of capital in America. The growth of monopoly capital (and of its necessary social and political concomitants, such as advertising and direct state intervention in the economic sphere) accelerates the rate at which the commodity structure penetrates into all levels of social life, into lived experience itself; and thus the reification that informs social activity and social relations is intensified and deepened in all its aspects.[8] In this light, the local-color component of the novel, the "authentic" gangster milieu, possesses a kind of conservative-radical value and takes on the poignance that is always a defining quality of local color. For what the homogenizing commodity world eradicates, as it increasingly encroaches on all areas and levels of society, are precisely the conditions of possibility—the traditional differences—that local color celebrates (it might be noted that the relative backwardness of capitalism in the western United States partly determines Hammett's use of this literary mode).

But the gangster world of **Red Harvest** may also be read as an even more direct protest against the reification imposed by the commodity world—a protest lodged through the generic slippage by which "local color" becomes "allegory of fascism," by which the gangster world, instead of remaining simply a particular local community, attains figurative status as a world unto itself. It is in this generic slippage, which is at one with the creation of the gangster world, that gangster "pastoral" comes to bear, in its essence, something like the negative imprint of the commodity world itself, inasmuch as the autonomization (and subsequent interrelation) of the various forms of labor that constitute the novel's modus operandi—the central principle of its composition—is itself previously determined by the extension of the capitalist commodity world, which, as the result of the reification and instrumentalization of social relations, is characterized by an autonomy of its various constituent activities. So it is that monopoly capitalism provides Hammett's local color with its ideological raw content, in the guise of the four discrete forms of labor that define the Op's milieu. The construction of this milieu, then, may be understood as an attack on the instrumentalization of labor enforced by the commodity structure, as an attempt to undermine reification by transforming capitalism's abstract labor into sensuously immediate activity, into activity whose relations with the total social context can be felt as if from the inside. The interdetermination of the four forms of labor (which we discussed, for instance, in connection with Elihu, whose political weakness is figured sexually and linguistically) contributes to the inherent relatedness of all activity within the gangster polity—and to the concomitant sense of feeling "at home" with one's surroundings, however murderous.

In this way, the gangster polity comes to function as a quasi-utopian figure. But it is an impossible figure from its very emergence, since the gangster world is posited precisely through the operation of the reified categories that it attempts to undermine; thus it is both a product of reification and an attack on it. (The very transforma-

tion of *Person*ville into *Poison*ville is after all a symbolically paradigmatic process of reification—one that is introduced in the novel's opening sentences and that, as the Op explains, cannot be reduced to the phonetics of gangster dialect.) This aspect of the book's utopian component is expressed, in its very impossibility, through the form taken by the elegiac-pastoral strain (alluded to in the title), which does not appear in particular passages but, rather, attaches to the entire gangster polity and thus communicates against the grain of the writing. The impossibility of this figurative utopia comes out more concretely, however, in the pastoral theme itself, the motif of abundance and plenitude. It is at this point that the attack on reification shades into the merely aesthetic, into a mute glorification of the surplus energies released by the reification of activity; and it is here, of course, that the gangster polity reveals its central weakness. It is, after all, precisely by manipulating the disunity of the gangster world, by activating the untapped and as-if-unstructured energies within it, that the Continental Op manages his work of detection and destruction. The utopian plenitude and connectedness of the gangster domain would seem, then, to confess their illusory quality as the detective work proceeds, and as it does so the essential reification of the various forms of labor in the Op's world becomes more transparent.

Thus nothing finally succeeds as a critique of the capitalist order—not the Op himself, or the antifascist allegory, or the protest against reification contained in the local-color utopia of the gangster polity. We may conclude, however, by considering the novel's actual generic composition in the same light and in a more systematic way than we have yet done. For **Red Harvest** is not only a new kind of detective novel. It contains, as it were, three novels, each a different response to the reified raw material provided by American capitalism. There is, first of all, an (unwritten) proletarian novel—more precisely, a strike novel (Bill Quint, probably, is its protagonist) dealing with the struggles of the workers of the Personville Mining Corporation. This strike novel, we may infer, attempts a radical, perhaps even a revolutionary, attack on the exploitation of labor and the consequent all-pervasive reification of life. Though it could not be written—because the strike failed—it remains a strongly determinate absence, generating the also radical but more abstract allegory of fascism; formally, that is, the failure of the strike "demotes" overt textual radicalism from novel proper to subnovelistic allegory. Accordingly, in the novel proper an important generic shift is marked in the speakeasy scene of the first chapter. There Bill Quint, as the protagonist of the strike novel, gives us a précis of that narrative and hands over to his drinking companion, the Continental Op, the role of protagonist in the novel now about to begin in earnest—namely, the *mystery* novel, the novel whose title might be "Who Killed Donald Willsson?" Here, as in any classic mystery tale, the project is to grasp and reveal a reified social totality by focusing attention on a series of discrete clues comprehensible to the superlative intelligence of the master detective. The Op, who is in fact qualified to be a Sherlockian detective, notices, for instance, as surely as Holmes or Lord Peter Wimsey or Hercule Poirot would, that a .32 is the kind of gun likely to be available to a bank clerk. Yet, as we have pointed out, *Red Harvest* is more concerned with clues of a different sort—a sort calling for construction or encoding rather than for deduction or decoding. Thus, judged by the standards of its genre, this mystery novel is both too successful and not successful enough. It is too successful because it ends prematurely; the book is little more than a quarter done when the puzzle is solved and Robert Albury is arrested for the murder of Donald Willsson. (Although the mystery novel does have a kind of afterlife in such subsequent puzzles as, Who killed Tim Noonan? and, Who killed Dinah Brand? they are not the main focus of the novel's interest, and Dinah's murder marks a particularly savage swerve from the classic mystery pattern, since the detective must number himself among the suspects.) The mystery novel is not successful enough, however, in that the confession and arrest of Albury contribute nothing to the Op's main goal, the destruction of the gangster polity. In formal terms, the book is by this point overloaded with reified clues and resonances—such as Dinah's runs and tears—that are not at all susceptible to merely deductive work.

With Albury's arrest, then, the book's generic structure again shifts, and the third and main novel of *Red Harvest* blossoms out—the adventure or gangster novel. Now the Op as decentered linguistic laborer truly comes into his own. He remains the protagonist but becomes far more a hard-boiled detective than a classic one. It is no accident that it is shortly after the arrest of Albury that he tries the Cooper-Bush experiment, his first major venture into the linguistic work of encoding and overloading the polity of Poisonville. Now he confronts the reified gangster totality through the dualities that determine his identity as a private detective—sympathetic knowledge of gangsterism and professional distance from it, bohemian individualism and ultimate bourgeois accountability. It is also at this point, as the Op becomes more and more assimilated to the gangster polity he is fighting, that the local color of *Red Harvest* comes into its own and successfully competes for our attention on the subnovelistic level, quite overshadowing the antifascist allegory. But the matter is not quite so simple. For, if the unwritten strike novel, incapable of resolving the reification of its raw material, gives way to the mystery novel, and the mystery novel, likewise incapable, gives way to the adventure novel, then how shall the adventure novel—and the whole book—end? Of course, the Op does defeat the gangsters, and by the close of the book all adventure is over, all puzzles solved. But it is just here that the strike novel and its

allegorical ghost, the story of fascism now defeated by legitimate capitalism, again make themselves felt. "Go to hell!" (188) are the Op's final words to the client whom he has returned to unshared exploitative control of Personville, which, as the Op later notes with bitter sarcasm, is now "developing into a sweet-smelling thornless bed of roses" (199).

In other words, the problem of exploitation remains, and the Continental Op's dissatisfaction at the end suggests an awareness that his own labor has inevitably been reified into an instrument wielded for the benefit of the despicable capitalist boss Elihu; indeed, Elihu's relation to the (still invisible) miners is parodically mirrored by the Op's troubles with the Old Man, which are recorded in the book's final sentence—"He gave me merry hell" (199). *Red Harvest* has left things as it found them before the strike novel, and all three novels may now be seen as moments in a larger *crisis* novel, which, attempting to resolve the crises generated by capitalist exploitation and reification, twists itself this way and that through different genres and finally must admit defeat. Reification remains, and there is no question of its resolution. But few novels—and certainly very few novels originating in the subliterary ghetto to which detective fiction has often been consigned—have made so serious and powerful an attempt to comprehend reification. Trying to comprehend reification: that is the kind of work that a detective does when he detects.

Notes

1. Most detective-fiction criticism has concerned the deductive, Sherlockian line, but there is some work on the hard-boiled variety, especially in contrast to the older type. Perhaps the single most important statement in this regard remains Raymond Chandler's great manifesto-like "The Simple Art of Murder: An Essay" (1-21). In "The Hippocratic Smile: John le Carré and the Traditions of the Detective Novel," Glenn W. Most offers some interesting and less polemical reflections on the contrast (Most and Stowe, esp. 342-53). Ken Worpole provides an excellent and more sociologically oriented account of the same matter, especially in his second chapter, "The American Connection: The Masculine Style in Popular Fiction" (29-48).

2. See Dennis Porter on Poisonville as "the typical environment of an unregulated industrial capitalism, which acknowledges no limits to the pursuit of private wealth" (197).

3. Throughout, we use the categories of dialogue and the dialogic simply to refer to spoken as opposed to written discourse; we do not intend their somewhat more technical (and currently influential) Bakhtinian sense. Though there are some affinities

between Bakhtin's concepts and our more collo-quial usage, particularly in the context of the novel (see, e.g., Bakhtin 259-422), they can hardly be detailed here.

4. See Fredric Jameson's important account of Chandler as an aesthetically self-conscious stylist. Worpole usefully comments, "Chandler's own writing, based as it was originally on a total admiration for the styles of Hammett and Hemingway, often specifically mentioned, became increasingly sophisticated and moved away from the popular and demotic. The descriptions of the settings became longer, although they were always characterized by a mordant and acerbic irony. The similes piled on top of each other, the dialogue became more consciously dry-witted and more often self-consciously studded with intellectual and literary allusions, the perorations on human weakness, civic corruption and sexual infidelity became longer. The cost of refining the genre was that it began to look towards a different readership for approval as it became more self-consciously literary and settled back again into conventional narrative forms" (44-45).

Stephen Knight suggests an additional but related reason for the highbrow tendency to prefer Chandler to Hammett: for all his apparent gritty realism, Chandler, unlike Hammett, always preserves a full-blooded romantic individualism (138).

5. Though it is not our purpose here to explicate the "symbolic order" as it figures in Lacanian psychoanalysis, our general debt to Lacan will be evident to anyone familiar with his work (see, e.g., Lacan 30-113).

6. The most explicit formulation in this regard occurs in the Op's retelling of Bill Quint's narrative: "But, said Bill Quint, old Elihu didn't know his Italian history. He won the strike, but he lost his hold on the city and the state. To beat the miners he had to let his hired thugs run wild. When the fight was over he couldn't get rid of them . . ." (9). Though the passage could easily refer to a commonplace situation in Renaissance Italy, it also accurately describes the relation that obtained between big capital in Italy and Mussolini's government after the defeat of the Italian labor and socialist movements. The Fascist party, however, was officially organized in 1919, and Mussolini seized state power three years later; since these events were relatively recent when *Red Harvest* was written, the term *history* in the above passage may seem curious. Yet, to the historically minded, like Hammett, even recent history is history, and in view of his general political formation, it is dif-ficult to believe that he was not consciously thinking of fascism. Of course, the allegory of fascism works whether or not the author explicitly meant to signal it.

7. Stephen Marcus makes this point well in one of the most insightful essays on Hammett to date. He describes the world through which the Op moves as one "of universal warfare, the war of each against all, and of all against all. The only thing that prevents the criminal ascendancy from turning into permanent tyranny is that the crooks who take over society cannot cooperate with one another, repeatedly fall out with each other, and return to the Hobbesian anarchy out of which they have momentarily arisen" (xxiii-xxiv). Though Marcus's concern is more with Hammett's short stories about the Continental Op than with *Red Harvest,* this passage is a fine account of the novel.

8. Throughout, we use the category "reification" in the classically Lukácsian sense; see Lukács 83-222.

Works Cited

Bakhtin, M. M. *The Dialogic Imagination.* Trans. Caryl Emerson and Michael Holquist. Ed. Michael Holquist. Austin: U of Texas P, 1981.

Chandler, Raymond. *The Simple Art of Murder.* New York: Ballantine, 1972.

Hammett, Dashiell. *Red Harvest.* New York: Random, 1972.

Jameson, Fredric. "On Raymond Chandler." *Southern Review* 6 (1970): 624-50.

Knight, Stephen. *Form and Ideology in Crime Fiction.* Bloomington: Indiana UP, 1980.

Lacan, Jacques. *Ecrits: A Selection.* Trans. Alan Sheridan. New York: Norton, 1977.

Lukács, Georg. *History and Class Consciousness: Studies in Marxist Dialectics.* Trans. Rodney Livingstone. Cambridge: MIT P, 1971.

Marcus, Stephen. Introduction. *The Continental Op.* By Dashiell Hammett. New York: Random, 1975.

Most, Glenn W., and William W. Stowe, eds. *The Poetics of Murder: Detective Fiction and Literary Theory.* New York: Harcourt, 1983.

Plato. *Phaedrus. The Collected Dialogues of Plato.* Ed. Edith Hamilton and Huntington Cairns. Princeton: Princeton UP, 1961.

Porter, Dennis. *The Pursuit of Crime: Art and Ideology in Detective Fiction.* New Haven: Yale UP, 1981.

Worpole, Ken. *Dockers and Detectives.* London: Verso, 1983.

David J. Herman (essay date spring 1991)

SOURCE: Herman, David J. "Finding out about Gender in Hammett's Detective Fiction: Generic Constraints or Transcendental Norms?" *Genre* 24, no. 1 (spring 1991): 1-23.

[*In the following essay, Herman explores the connection of sexuality and violence between men and women in Hammett's fiction.*]

In the violent world of Dashiell Hammett, a man's virility is, more often than not, judged by the size of his pistol. When the Whosis Kid faces down his recalcitrant French partner, for instance, "[h]is bony hands pushed his coat aside and rested where his vest bulged over the sharp corners of his hip-bones" (*CO* [*The Continental Op*] 224). In *The Maltese Falcon,* moreover, the effeminate Joel Cairo revealingly "carries a smaller gun than [the one] Thursby and Jacoby were shot with" (*MF* [*The Maltese Falcon*] 213). Hammett's treatment of Wilmer in the same novel, however, records the slippage between sign and signified that undermines this entire system of phallic correspondences. When we discover that Wilmer's "[b]lack pistols were gigantic in his small hands" (199), the discrepancy between symbol and fact becomes palpably apparent. Indeed, Sam Spade, in front of the hotel detective, draws attention to and, in effect, parodies Wilmer's effort to substitute his pistols for a phallus: "What do you let these cheap gunmen hang out in your lobby for, with their tools bulging in their clothes?" (108).[1] Later in the novel, though Wilmer's "pockets bulged more than his hands need have made them bulge" (137), Wilmer ultimately proves "impotent" in Spade's strong grip (138). But Hammett's parodic reduction of Wilmer's bulging "heaters" amounts to *self*-parody; in this rare instance Hammett attains some ironic distance from his own tendency to describe, say, Tom-Tom Carey by the way "[t]he bulge shows" when he sits down (*BK* [*The Big Knockover*] 414). In turn, this double metonymy, by which Hammett substitutes a gun for a phallus and a phallus for virility and power, finds its classic expression in **"The Big Knockover."** In that story, "Angel" Grace Cardigan, discriminating between the Op and full-blown criminals, says somewhat wistfully: "If you were a gun, I'd—. . . ." (*BK* 380).

Angel's elliptical comment raises the question of exactly where women fit into a world in which masculine sexuality is deeply bound up with the capacity for violence—a world in which masculinity itself totemically resides in pistols, sleek and explosive instruments of death. Granted, as Paul Fussell notes in *The Great War and Modern Memory,* relations between the sexes have long been figured in terms of "assaults," "attacks," and "encounters" (270). But in Hammett's fiction, violence functions not just as the vehicle but also as the tenor of the metaphoric equation between sexuality and aggression: it is not simply that figures of battle are applied to sexual experience, but that sexuality itself reduces to some sort of primordially violent energy.

In this economy of sexuality and violence, Hammett's women characters necessarily take on a highly ambivalent status. They are at once fetishized and abominated—objectified as the Other and then, because so objectified, infused with all the threatening power of the alien, the unassimilable. Because Hammett in his women characters often combines voluptuousness with viciousness, ripe sexuality with rapacious self-interest, Hammett's texts not only figure what William Marling specifies as "the Hammett succubus," but also embody in general the dynamic that de Beauvoir, in *The Second Sex,* describes as "[t]he man's hesitation between fear and desire [in his dealings with women], between the fear of being in the power of uncontrollable forces and the wish to win them over . . ." (152).[2]

In order to explain the negative, misogynistic phase of this essentially manic response to women, de Beauvoir discusses cultural traditions that encourage the Western male to see "himself as a fallen god," and to view himself as "fallen from a bright and ordered heaven into the chaotic shadows of his mother's womb"—to imagine himself as, and resent, being "imprisoned by woman in the mud of the earth" (146). Here in fact the applications of de Beauvoir's theory of misogyny overlap with those of Paul Ricoeur's theory of Evil. For if women in Hammett's fiction at some level incur the sort of metaphysical resentment that de Beauvoir associates with misogynistic thinking, Hammett's women characters also incur the equally metaphysical "dread" with which Ricoeur associates the notion of "impurity" and, by extension, the idea of Evil.

As Ricoeur says in *The Symbolism of Evil,* "[d]read of the impure is like fear, but already it faces a threat which, beyond the threat of suffering and death, aims at the diminution of existence, a loss of the personal core of one's being" (41). The dreaded object, in a macabre re-articulation of the Sublime, threatens to overwhelm and disintegrate the dreading subject.[3] By the same token, James F. Maxfield notes that "[s]exual desire is possibly the greatest threat to the Hammett hero's invulnerability" (111), and Dennis Dooley describes as a "familiar pattern" in Hammett's fiction the way "a man, in fact a series of men, [gets] exploited by a woman who has found their weak points" (38). We thus see how women in Hammett's texts become quite literally the source of an impurity that, unless contained and purged, threatens to engulf in Evil—to negate or abolish—the "personal core" or identity of the detective.[4] This inherently irrational dread of contamination does much to explain, in general, the overdetermined character of gender in Hammett's work—and *ipso facto* the violence with which Hammett's detective often responds to women. In particular, such dread helps us account for the ambivalent repugnance that the Op manifests toward Jeanne Delano, who attempts to seduce him in **"The Girl with the Silver Eyes"**: "'You're beautiful as all hell!' I shouted crazily into her face, and flung her against the door" (*CO* 176).

Yet as it turns out, the polysemousness of Hammett's own texts is precisely what lets "Evil" into Hammett's fictional world. The detective's very desire to purify himself of woman, it seems, is what most contaminates him, inscribing the dreaded object *within* the dreading subject—such that "male" and "female" cease to designate discrete entities. For by attributing androgynous features to certain of his women characters, at least in his early works, Hammett in effect blurs the differences between the sexes. In this way, Hammett, by complicating his oftentimes reductive vision of women, distends his own misogynist paradigm. Androgyny in Hammett's texts tends to neutralize, at one level, that conflict between men and women which, at another level, is one of Hammett's most abiding themes. Images of androgyny therefore make Hammett's early texts work against themselves; such images shatter that hall of mirrors in which violence replicates sexuality and sexuality, violence.

I shall turn to the issue of Hammett's later texts in a moment. But first, by abandoning the quasi-religious vocabulary ("dread," "Evil," "contamination") that I have thus far borrowed from de Beauvoir and Ricoeur, in order to align Hammett's treatment of women with the larger tradition of writing about gender, I believe that I can specify more precisely the self-divided nature of Hammett's early texts. In this connection, we need a vocabulary that, unlike de Beauvoir's and Ricoeur's, resists naturalizing or even eternalizing contingent social categories. This alternative vocabulary, I submit, will allow us to isolate one of the most interesting features Hammett's work taken as part of the *genre* of so-called hard-boiled detective fiction: namely, the way Hammett's texts make explicit, or rather formalize, the internal contradictions of the ideology they ostensibly confirm.

The ideology that I have in mind is one that ascribes a particular, and immutable, role to gender. Through this ideology, gender ceases to be merely a means by which to divide social functions—a criterion for the appropriateness for either sex of a given activity or attitude. Gender becomes instead a kind of epistemological framework, in terms of which the world itself is made intelligible. Hammett's texts thus conflate gender construed as, on the one hand, a socially useful category, and gender construed as, on the other hand, what Kant would call a transcendental condition of knowledge, a condition for our being able to know anything at all.

The upshot of Hammett's thus conflating the social with the transcendental is that, in the author's works, gender roles come to provide a sort of syntax for interpretation as such—interpretation in turn being the *raison d'être* of the detective. If a woman is almost always the crux of Hammett's mysteries, therefore, her presence is neither accidental nor a function of popular taste alone, but rather a sort of necessary constraint of the hard-boiled genre itself. In this genre, the world as a whole becomes decipherable only when looked upon from a deeply sexist vantage-point.

What I mean is that in Hammett and by extension male detective fiction generally, notions of gender in effect become interpretive axioms, syntactic laws subsisting at the same level of unquestioned generality occupied by natural laws. These axioms or laws constitute a syntax in the strict sense: they prescribe what sorts of propositions about the world are well-formed and therefore meaningful, and what sorts of propositions are ill-formed and therefore meaningless. My argument is that we can isolate pressure-points at which Hammett's interpretive syntax yields meaningful and relevant propositions about gender that do not however meet Hammett's own syntactic requirements for meaningfulness or relevance. One such proposition, crucial for my case, is that distinctions in gender are not absolute; this proposition is, as we shall see, at once implied and proscribed by Hammett's assumptions about gender. Indeed, by thus locating where Hammett's axioms of gender generate mutually incompatible claims, we are able to reverse the movement towards ideology that Hammett's own texts enact. We can demystify the transcendental pretensions of gender taken as syntax, and instead account for it as a social category with particular social uses, specific to a particular place and time.

My idea is therefore to substitute a variable for Hammett's immutable interpretive syntax, and to show how Hammett's very attempt to make gender roles constant is what plunges them into variability from the start. I contend, further, that in this connection the images of androgyny in Hammett's texts provide us with a significant analytic tool. In the first place, Hammett's androgynous images show just where the author's naturalization or rather transcendentalization of gender breaks down. Whereas the generic constraints under which Hammett operates serve to divide up experience into what should and should not be counted meaningful or important—what sorts of things should or should not be regularly factored into, say, our notion of "the feminine"—androgyny, *also* implicit within the hard-boiled genre, produces just the opposite effect. Androgyny liberates Hammett's texts from their own overrestrictive classification of what kinds of claims not just about gender, but by extension about the world itself, are in principle meaningful. In other words, images of androgyny in Hammett de-naturalize gender into a social category, and they achieve this by unmasking Hammett's own attempts to make that social category natural to the order of things.

In the second place, however, images of androgyny provide a heuristic tool to the extent that they do *not* appear in Hammett's later works—works such as *The Glass Key* and *The Thin Man.* I wish to argue that androgyny effectively drops out of Hammett's later novels because the author's interpretive syntax itself changes. Hammett's misogynistic reduction of women to a single female type, in which good and evil are indissolubly united, gives way in the later works to a broader spectrum of women characters. In *The Thin Man,* this spectrum ranges from the pathologically deceitful, and literally hysterical, Mimi Wynant to the detective's own resilient and resourceful wife, Nora Charles. Since the later Hammett can distribute positive and negative characteristics *between* different women, the author's notion of the feminine comes to include the sort of unequivocal strength and decency that Hammett formerly reserved for the masculine alone. Certain women can now be genuinely caring and helpful, just as certain others remain through and through malign and destructive. By the same token, Hammett is no longer driven toward androgyny by the exaggerated limitations he himself places on what statements can count as meaningful ones about women. The scope of claims that bear on women expands to include claims that, before, could be relevant only vis-à-vis men; and Hammett thus need no longer create *ersatz* men, androgynes, in efforts to capture with an impoverished interpretive syntax the recalcitrant complexities of gender.

We can put the matter this way: precisely because the later Hammett reincorporates into his women characters an element of contingency or variability—one woman is not by definition the same as the next—gender in the later novel ceases to do the sort of transcendental work it did in the early works. Married, Nick Charles can no longer simply assume women to be duplicitous. No longer an interpretive syntax, gender itself becomes something that needs to be constantly interpreted.

I

In "Further Notes toward a Recognition of Androgyny," Carolyn Heilbrun provides a rough, somewhat over-general formulation of what the term "androgyny" itself signifies: "a condition under which the characteristics of the sexes and the human impulses expressed by men and women are not rigidly assigned" (143). By amassing evidence from a broad range of Hammett's works, however, I wish now to work past Heilbrun's definition inductively—to arrive at a more nuanced and precise conception of how androgyny functions in Hammett's texts. First, I shall catalogue what amount to Hammett's syntactic laws of gender: those fundamental axioms about women whose permutations Hammett's male detective must master in order not just to interpret, but also to survive the world around him. I shall discuss, second, how Hammett's androgynous images disrupt this interpretive syntax; the images of androgyny suggest how survival to some extent depends on the detective's being able to permute Hammett's axioms in fundamentally incoherent ways. In the final part of my paper I shall attempt to show that Hammett's characterization of women does in fact undergo development, and that the absence of androgyny in the later works represents not an increased conservatism about gender, but rather an interpretive code according to which gender itself becomes multiple and complex. On the later Hammett's own terms, male and female no longer signify an irreducible binary opposition, but instead an unstable manifold of contingent possibilities.

Curiously, Hammett sometimes seems to lack much in the way of a descriptive vocabulary for women. In **"The Big Knockover,"** having almost perfunctorily listed Nancy Regan's blue eyes, red mouth and white teeth, and having even gone to the length of mentioning that "she had a nose," the Op says this: "Without getting steamed up over the details, she was nice" (**BK** 255). Later on, when he once more encounters Nancy, the Op again relies heavily on the banal and nondescript "nice": "I have already said that she was nice. Well, she was. And the cocky little blue hat that hid all her hair didn't handicap her niceness any tonight" (382). A moment later, the Op similarly remarks in Nancy "a blue-eyed, white-toothed smile that was—well—nice" (382). What here amounts to a kind of linguistic entropy indicates not so much Hammett's desire to avoid provocative description as a breakdown in the Op's capacity to imagine women. And for a detective whose very longevity hinges on successful sleuthing amid deceptive surfaces, the Op's inability to describe in much concrete detail the appearance of a beautiful woman suggests not simple carelessness, but rather powerful forces that inhibit and deflect the *modus operandi* of his psyche.

It is unwise, however, to conduct an argument solely in negative terms; and when we move to the descriptive vocabulary that Hammett *does* develop in connection with women, we discover a system of polarities and ironic tensions in which women at once attract and repulse, both threaten and allure.

In **"The Tenth Clew,"** for instance, Hammett in the first place ironically names Creda Dexter, whose own account of her relations with Leopold Gantvoort proves, in the end, to be far from credible. Irony also lends a double-edgedness to Hammett's descriptions of Creda's appearance and manner. On the one hand, Creda has all the sensuality and grace of a pampered cat:

> With the eyes for a guide, you discovered that she was pronouncedly feline throughout. Her every movement was the slow, smooth, sure one of a cat; and the con-

tours of her rather pretty face, the shape of her mouth, her small nose, the set of her eyes, the swelling of her brows, were all cat-like. And the effect was heightened by the way she wore her hair, which was thick and tawny.

(*CO* 18)

On the other hand, as O'Gar says to the Op: "'A sleek kitten—that dame! Rub her in the right way, and she'll purr pretty. Rub her the wrong way—and look out for the claws!'" (20). Similarly, after Creda discloses Madden Dexter's real identity, Hammett says this of Creda: "No sleek kitten, this, but a furious, spitting cat, with claws and teeth bared" (42). Granted, Hammett's use of animals as analogues for people fits him squarely into the naturalistic tradition, which, drawing from Social Darwinism, transforms the idea of survival of the fittest into a sort of mythic resource for realizing characters. Hammett's use of animals in characterizing women, however, stems not just from naturalistic but also from specifically misogynistic impulses. Perpetually oscillating between the sensual refinement and wild ferocity of a cat, Creda Dexter represents what Dennis Dooley identifies as the single female type that, with slight variations, occurs throughout Hammett's corpus: "A maddening blend of innocence and manipulation, vulnerability and villainy, sometimes she gets to him and sometimes the Op manages to keep her fixed in his cold eye" (59).

On certain occasions, in fact, women in Hammett's fiction pass from sensuality to truculence in the blink of an eye. In **"The Gutting of Couffignal,"** for example, Hammett provides this description of the Princess Zhukovski, whose instantaneous transmutation the author himself links up with traditional ways of imaging and *eo ipso* containing women:

> Her strong slender body became the body of a lean crouching animal. One hand—claw now—swept to the heavy pocket of her jacket. . . . Then before I could have blinked an eye—though my life seemed to depend on my not batting it—the wild animal had vanished. Out of it—and now I know where the writers of old fairy stories got their ideas—rose the princess again, cool and straight and tall.

(*BK* 29)

Arguably, it is these same "writers of old fairy stories" who provoke Gilbert and Gubar's comment in *The Madwoman in the Attic* that "male-engendered female figures as superficially disparate as Milton's Sin, Swift's Chloe, and Yeats's Crazy Jane have incarnated man's ambivalence not only toward female sexuality but toward their own (male) physicality" (12). Hammett's image of the bestialized-then-idealized "princess" reveals the extent to which this ambivalence informs traditional ideas of women's mutability—their radical instability and unpredictability even from one instant to the next.

On other occasions, though, as in Elvira in **"The House in Turk Street,"** a woman's sensual appeal co-exists in time with, and thus becomes indistinguishable from, the physical threat that she poses:

> Smoke-gray eyes that were set too far apart for trustworthiness—though not for beauty—laughed at me; and her red mouth laughed at me, exposing the edges of little sharp animal teeth. She was beautiful as the devil, and twice as dangerous.

(*CO* 101)

Similarly, in **"The Whosis Kid,"** Ines Almad, whom the Op portrays as "beautiful—in a wild way" (*CO* 200), derives from the sparring match between the Op and the jealous "Billie" a sadistic and nearly orgasmic pleasure: "Her eyes were shiny behind their heavy lashes, and her mouth was open to let white teeth gleam through" (212). Summing her up afterwards, the Op provides this list of characteristics, which uneasily co-exist in one and the same person: "She was an actress. She was appealing, and pathetic, and anything else that you like—including dangerous" (217).[5]

Indeed, in **"The Golden Horseshoe,"** Hammett localizes in female sexuality itself the menacing aspect that, for the detective, makes women's sensual appeal highly unsettling. Here, Hammett's descriptions of Kewpie[6] suggest how a woman's power is threatening precisely because it is hidden or latent—both figuratively and anatomically speaking. When the Op suggests to Kewpie that her lover, Ed, is going to "ditch" her, Kewpie reacts in this way:

> Her right shoulder was to me, touching my left. Her left hand flashed down under her short skirt. I pushed her shoulder forward, twisting her body sharply away from me. The knife her left hand had whipped up from her leg jabbed deep into the underside of the table. A thick-bladed knife, balanced for accurate throwing.

(*CO* 72)

Hammett in the first place emphasizes the proximity of Kewpie's "thick-bladed" knife to her genitalia, whose attraction the Op in turn registers by mentioning "her short skirt." In this way Hammett has the Op gravitate toward Kewpie sexually at the same time that she objectifies, in Freudian terms at least, some deep-seated fear of castration by women.[7] Moreover, Hammett evokes in his description of Kewpie the suggestion that women, because of the inaccessible internality that they represent to the male detective's probing mind, always have the potential to lash out like Kewpie does. For when Kewpie "slid her knife back in its hiding place under her skirt and twisted around to face me" (*CO* 73), one senses that this "hiding place" continues to haunt the wary detective, at once stimulating and defeating his attempt to interpret when and where danger may strike next. Women quite literally embody pockets of psychological and, as it were, topographical turbulence that, again and again, interrupt and deflect the detective's interpretive enterprise.

On still other occasions, however, the ironic discrepancy between the benign and malignant aspects of a single woman can be so vast as to produce tremendous cognitive dissonance; it is this dissonance that, in effect, Hammett uses to justify or at least rationalize the misogyny that informs his vision of women in general. Thus, again in **"The House in Turk Street,"** Hammett in his portrait of Mrs. Quarre plays off the nostalgia and sentimentality surrounding the image of "the mother" in contemporary or at least recent American culture.[8] Noting that Mrs. Quarre "was a very fragile little old woman, with a piece of gray knitting in one hand, and faded eyes that twinkled pleasantly behind goldrimmed spectacles" (*CO* 94), the Op goes on to record this about Mrs. Quarre and her husband: "These folks weren't made to be lied to" (94). So much does the Op wish to believe in this scene of domestic tranquillity that, when that scene is belied by the feel of a gun against the back of his neck, the Op seems to be struck by how surreal the experience is: "And looking at [the Quarres], I knew that something cold *couldn't* be against the back of my neck; a harsh voice *couldn't* have ordered me to stand up. It wasn't possible!" (*CO* 96).

Eventually, though, Hammett himself shatters all grounds for sentimentality about motherhood, because Mrs. Quarre, not only part of a crime-ring, finally presents this appearance to the Op:

> I looked at the old woman again, and found little of the friendly fragile one who had poured tea and chatted about the neighbors. This was a witch if there ever was one—a witch of the blackest, most malignant sort. Her little faded eyes were sharp with ferocity, her withered lips were taut in a wolfish snarl, and her thin body fairly quivered with hate.
>
> (*CO* 115)

In a world in which even kindly old mothers can at a moment's notice display the fierceness of a wolf, a man in approaching a woman must proceed along lines of suspicion, distrust and unremitting vigilance. Like the Op's when he is in the company of Princess Zhukovski, or Kewpie, one's life depends on one's not batting an eye in the presence of a woman.

This necessity, it is true, reappears in **"The Whosis Kid"** in a more generalized form: it is not just women, but all perceptual data that, for the sleuth, require constant interpretation, awareness uninterrupted by the smallest gap in consciousness. While struggling to discern whether the Whosis Kid's shape, in passing through a doorway, has darkened the luminous face of the watch upon which the Op has his eyes riveted, the Op describes how "I couldn't afford to blink. A foot could pass the dial while I was blinking. I couldn't afford to blink, but I had to blink. I couldn't tell whether something had passed the watch or not" (*CO* 234). In a world in which information means survival, any sign is potentially a sign of danger, and can itself dangerously mean more than one thing.

On the one hand, Hammett's emphasis on the necessity of constant interpretation may indeed reflect the sorts of generic and thematic constraints that D. A. Miller discusses in *The Novel and the Police*. Examining novels in which the police are marginalized and alternative sources of investigation and crime-solving brought to the fore, Miller describes how "[i]n the same move whereby the police are contained in a marginal pocket of representation, the work of the police is superseded by the operations of another, informal, and extralegal principle of organization and control" (3). This displacement, in turn, eventually opens up a cognitive space for novels in which the narrative techniques themselves—the meticulous recording of detail, the penetration into characters' motives and thoughts, etc.— "usurp" the power of the police (21). As Miller puts it, "[w]henever the novel censures policing power, it has already reinvented it, in *the very practice of novelistic representation*" (20). Similarly, to the extent that Hammett marginalizes and disempowers the police in his texts, he seems to reinscribe the policing function itself in the detective's consciousness, and to substitute the detective's interpretive energies for more overt and public forms of policing activity.

But on the other hand, I do not think that we can merely subsume Hammett's treatment of women under Miller's explanatory model. The threat posed by women in Hammett's texts seems to be at the very least irreducible to the threat posed by ambiguous information in general. In fact, the reverse inference seems to me more compelling: that the problem of ambiguous information is reducible to the categories in terms of which Hammett accounts for gender. This is because Hammett's assumptions about women are, *relative to the elaboration of his own plots,* a pre-given frame of reference—a syntax—within whose boundaries danger as such takes on concrete, recognizable shape. I mean that on Hammett's own terms women occupy a different order of explanation than that occupied by the male detective's threatening, naturalistic environment as a whole. Gender roles in Hammett are conceptually prior to the contingencies of experience: gender is destiny.

I think that I can substantiate these rather large claims in the following way. Granted, Hammett's women characters are part of the sometimes deadly play of signs that, on Miller's model, tends to internalize within the detective himself the tense vigilance associated with policing. But we cannot *a fortiori* explain away the threatening equivocality that Hammett ascribes to women. For in Hammett's works, women who do *not* veer back and forth between the extremes of sensual passivity and fierce aggressiveness cannot subsist; such women are, often in highly unsubtle fashion, erased from the text; and thus Hammett indirectly confers duplicity on the women who do negotiate through the treacherous circumstances and dangerous liaisons into which he leads them. Implicitly, Hammett's view is that, prior to his being able to discover anything else about a given case, the detective can know beforehand that only a "red-haired she-devil" like Elvira in **"The House in Turk Street"** could survive amid the violence that comprehends and structures male-female relationships. And as if arguing with a grotesquely foregone conclusion, Hammett proves this general interpretive rule by killing off all possible exceptions to it.

Consider Hammett's treatment of Mrs. Ashcraft in **"The Golden Horseshoe."** Although a relatively minor character, Mrs. Ashcraft is one of the most unequivocally attractive women in all of Hammett's fiction. When we first meet her, the Op describes how

> Mrs. Ashcraft received us in a drawing-room on the second floor. A tall woman of less than thirty, slimly beautiful in a gray dress. Clear was the word that best fit her; it described the blue of her eyes, the pink-white of her skin, and the light-brown of her hair.
>
> (*CO* 55)

A moment later the Op mentions how "[h]er eyes lighted up happily, but she didn't throw a fit. She wasn't that sort" (56). Indeed, the Op remarks explicitly that "I liked this Mrs. Ashcraft" (56). But in attributing such positive features to this mild and unassuming woman, it is as if Hammett is providing a *rationale* for her brutal murder:

> Mrs. Ashcraft was dead there. . . . Her body was drawn up in a little heap, from which her head hung crookedly, dangling from a neck that had been cut clean through to the bone. Her face was marked with four deep scratches from temple to chin. . . . Bedding and pajamas were soggy with the blood that the clothing piled over her had kept from drying.
>
> (*CO* 65)

Similarly, although Dinah Brand in **Red Harvest** is a prostitute, the Op achieves with her a certain straightforward intimacy; they seem to communicate well with one another. The Op and Dinah feel comfortable enough together to exchange witty repartees about Dinah's household etiquette (119). At one point, while the Op and Dinah conduct a vigil outside, "[t]he girl shivered with her cheek warm against mine" (130). Again, however, the Op's sense of connection with a woman seems to lend a kind of inexorability to that woman's brutal murder. And given the Op's troubled dreams, in which he feels embarrassed by physical contact with Dinah

(150); indeed, given the Op's uncertainty about whether or not he himself actually plunged the ice-pick into her left breast (151), Hammett suggests that violence between the sexes—whether it issues from the woman or from the man—is ineradicable because it is built into the very nature of experience. Male-female violence seems part of a tragic pattern of external circumstance precisely because, for Hammett, such violence precedes external circumstance as its immutable condition, its transcendental explanation.

II

I have thus far attempted to enumerate inductively the misogynist axioms, as it were, on which Hammett bases his model for understanding gender and, by extension, the contingencies of experience. Positively, these axioms ascribe limitless duplicity and cruelty to women; negatively, the laws imply that there cannot be, in the world as it is, a woman who has the detective's best interests at heart or who even maintains indifference towards him. But is it the case that Hammett's interpretive syntax bodes ill for any effort to rethink gender roles in non-conflictual terms? My view is, rather, that Hammett's pessimistic model tends to undermine itself from within.[9] In Hammett, the tragic necessity of violence between the sexes is undercut by the possibility that, at some fundamental level, the masculine and the feminine mirror or replicate one another. At this level, misogyny gives way to androgyny; and by blurring the boundaries between the sexes Hammett implicitly removes the basis on which men, distancing themselves from women, at times try to reduce and demean them. Indeed, through the mechanisms of androgyny, the violence that pervades relations between Hammett's men and women shows itself to be reflexive and, in effect, suicidal. Hammett's texts thus parody the misogynistic vision that simultaneously shapes and informs them.

Significantly, Hammett's representations of women prove contrary to expectations that have been built up around androgyny itself. Cynthia Secor, for instance, voices her "apprehensiveness" about the revolutionary potential of the concept by noting that "[a]ndrogyny, as the term is used in our patriarchal culture, conjures up images of the feminized male . . . and of the perfect marriage in which the female has been acquired by the male in order to complete himself. . . . There is no comparable imagistic tradition of the masculinized female" (166). Daniel A. Harris elaborates on this argument thus:

> the myth of androgyny has been created by man, and its design is the co-option, incorporation or subjugation of women: in seeking "feminine" elements with which to complete himself, the man reduces woman to merely symbolic status, plays parasite, and paradoxically demands from the creature he has thus mentally enslaved his own freedom.
>
> (172)

In Hammett, however, the image of the masculinized female occurs with much greater frequency than that of the feminized male.[10] Accordingly, Hammett's women characters do not so much "complete" their male counterparts as they are completed by them. And the interpretive crux that women constantly pose to the male detective can therefore be specified in terms that at least partially demarcate the problem at hand: women on the one hand mark the limits of the detective's identity—the threshold beyond which the detective feels compelled to ward off what threatens him—and on the other hand they remind him of his deep complicity with that by which he feels most threatened.

As before, however, I wish to translate this sort of language into somewhat less portentous and thus more useful terms. I wish to demonstrate in this connection how Hammett's works themselves de-naturalize the very categories of masculine and feminine—the brute facts of gender, so to speak—on which the author's interpretive syntax is based. As we shall see, what is controversial or constructed and what is indisputable or natural about gender roles ceases to be, on Hammett's own terms, easy to distinguish.

In the first place, it is significant that, by making the Op a short and pudgy character, Hammett brings to the fore the *size* of certain of the women he meets. Of the Princess Zhukovski in **"The Gutting of Couffignal,"** for instance, the Op observes that "[s]he was tall, I am short and thick. I had to look up to see her face . . ." (**BK** 10). Likewise, Big Flora in **"The Big Knockover,"** although her "voice was deep but not masculine" (**BK** 397), seems to have the physique of a man—and of a strong man at that:

> She stood at least five feet ten in her high-heeled slippers. They were small slippers, and I noticed that her ringless hands were small. The rest of her wasn't. She was broad-shouldered, deep-bosomed, thick-armed, with a pink throat which for all its smoothness was muscled like a wrestler's . . . and a handsome, brutal face. . . . From forehead to throat her pink skin was underlaid with smooth, thick, strong muscles.
>
> (**BK** 397)

Even Dinah Brand, who it is true seems to be "popping open" with feminine sexuality (**RH** [**Red Harvest**] 30), cuts an imposing and somewhat masculine figure when juxtaposed to the Op: "She was an inch or two taller than I, which made her about five feet eight. She had a broad-shouldered, full-breasted, round-hipped body and big muscular legs" (**RH** 30).

But it is not by size alone that Hammett suggests androgyny. In **"The Golden Horseshoe,"** Kewpie, whom the Op meets "hustling drinks" in a bar in Tijuana, appears thus: "Her short hair was brown and curly over a round, boyish face with laughing, impudent eyes" (**CO** 58). Even her grin "was as boyish as the straight look in her brown eyes" (58). Similarly, when we first meet her, Effie Perine in **The Maltese Falcon** not only has eyes that are "brown and playful in a shiny boyish face" (1); Effie also seems to have an uncommonly vivid sense of how Spade will respond to Brigid O'Shaugnessy: "'You'll want to see her anyway: she's a knockout'"(1). Passing from Spade's inner to his outer office, Effie seems to pass as well from one set of sexual possibilities to another, and she adjusts herself to conventions that constrain her to address "Miss Wonderly" with professional tact and reserve: "Will you come in . . ." (**MF** 1).

In **"The Scorched Face,"** further, Myra Banbrock meets this description:

> Myra—20 years old; 5 feet 8 inches; 150 pounds; athletic; brisk, almost masculine manner and carriage; bobbed brown hair; brown eyes; medium complexion; square face, with large chin and short nose; scar over left ear, concealed by hair; fond of horses and all outside sports.
>
> (**BK** 76)

In describing Ruth, Myra's younger sister, Hammett also mentions that Ruth is "quiet, timid, inclined to lean on her more forceful sister" (**BK** 76). Arguably, Hammett here employs the technique that, in *Swann's Way*, Proust uses to describe "beneath the mannish face" of M. Vinteuil's daughter "the finer features of a young woman in tears" (87). But whereas Proust so laminates Mlle. Vinteuil that beneath "her thick, comfortable voice" it seems "as though some elder and more sensitive sister, latent in her" were blushing at her younger sibling's "thoughtless, schoolboyish utterance" (87), Hammett in **"The Scorched Face"** objectifies masculine and feminine impulses—the animus and anima, as it were—and distributes them between the two Banbrock sisters. Thus, where Proust's method is psychological, capturing through an image or figure of speech the interior states and composite sexuality of one woman, Hammett's method is in effect allegorical, embodying in separate characters dialectically opposed psychic forces. And Hammett's allegory continues when, as the story progresses, Ruth finally shoots herself, whereas Myra, after her participation in orgies of an unspecified nature, "had none of the masculinity that had been in her photographs and description" (107)—integrating within herself, presumably, the aggressiveness and passivity once divided between her and Ruth.

We thus have at least an initial indication of the scope of androgyny in Hammett: from the author's rather vague attributions of "boyishness" to figures like Kewpie, and his ascriptions of masculine stature to figures like Big Flora, to his suggestion of a female masculinity not co-extensive with mere physical appearance, an androgyny of impulse of which androgyny of appearance is but one symptom. Certainly we might at this point undertake a more exhaustive list of the symptoms and motivations of androgyny in Hammett's corpus, as well as a thoroughgoing account of why Hammett himself apparently wants to drive a wedge between women's transgression of convention (as symptom) and women's transgression of nature (as cause). But what I wish to stress here is simply that Hammett, by describing women in a way that places them on a continuum with men, produces a series of propositions whose status is of a very special sort.

Hammett's propositions about androgyny, on the one hand, do not consist with the author's own rules for forming meaningful or relevant propositions about gender. Those rules, as I have indicated, posit an absolute antagonism of interest between men and women. Yet Hammett's female androgynes, by definition, share what on Hammett's own terms would be deemed masculine interests. Hence, if he is to avoid abrogating the rules for valid interpretation, if he is to work within the syntax that so far has allowed him to interpret and survive a hostile environment, the misogynist detective cannot afford to enter the logical space in which propositions about androgyny subsist. But on the other hand, neither can the detective afford *not* to enter this logical space, for it is the space in which interpretation itself unfolds. Simply by recording propositions about androgyny in the first place, the detective thereby includes those propositions in the domain of evidence. In turn, this domain, because it is just the set of all possible clues, thereby proves itself not only meaningful or rule-governed, but moreover relevant to the detective's particular interests. If the *misogynist* detective must in principle disallow the very possibility of androgyny, therefore, in fact the misogynist *detective* cannot disallow this possibility, on pain of closing off the avenue of evidence that he must always keep open, or else perhaps die.

To put this last point in slightly different terms: the detective belies his own misogynistic interpretive code, which he views as necessary for survival, just by including reports of evidence that destroy the very basis of misogyny, but that the detective *also* views as necessary for survival. This, I submit, is the double-bind or rather antinomy into which Hammett's own interpretive syntax leads him. And again we should take our cue from Kant: as Kant asserts in the first *Critique*, should any theoretical syntax or model lead to an antinomy of the kind that I have detailed, this very fact provides us with sufficient grounds for rejecting that theoretical model from the start.

I wish to close off my discussion by arguing that in Hammett's last two novels, *The Glass Key* and *The Thin Man,* the author does in fact circumvent what

might now be termed the antinomy of androgyny, precisely by rejecting, at least in part, his own earlier misogynistic model—a model in relation to which androgyny is, as I just suggested, at once a species of insuperable counterevidence and an inescapable consequence or corollary. In the later Hammett's treatment of women, uncontestable grounds for hating *certain* women are mitigated by equally irrefutable grounds for not hating others. As a result, Hammett's later texts imply that the detective must treat women case by case, and resist, on pain of manifest error, making any general claim about what women in essence are like.[11] Hammett's treatment of women in the later works, therefore, becomes deliberately fragmentary and particularized: it is as if each woman merits a theory in her own right. Gender no longer provides an interpretive syntax, but instead cries out for one.

Indeed, in *The Glass Key,* Hammett comes close to stating outright the view of women on which the author's later novels are premised. When Janet Henry comes to Ned Beaumont's apartment in hopes of convincing Beaumont that his friend Paul Madvig is indeed guilty of murder, and in hopes of justifying in this way her own semi-deceitful conduct toward Madvig, Hammett completes the scene in this manner:

> [Janet] sighed and stood up holding out her hand. "I'm sorry and disappointed, but we needn't be enemies, need we?"
>
> [Beaumont] rose facing her, but did not take her hand. He said: "The part of you that's tricked Paul and is trying to trick him is my enemy."
>
> She held her hand there while asking: "And the other part of me, the part that hasn't anything to do with that?"
>
> He took her hand and bowed over it.
>
> (146)

Granted, the view that a women has "parts," which sometimes consist but ill with one another, is not unique to the later Hammett. But the explicit discussion of this view by a female character herself *is* unprecedented in Hammett. We here see Hammett's fiction thematize and so transcend itself. For as Hammett himself represents them, women now have, it seems, the power to eschew enemies and establish allegiances by conscious choice, instead of being driven by some irrational mechanism that bestows upon women's every kindness, and every woman's kindness, a baleful duplicity.

I do not mean to overstate my case, however: plenty of evidence of a misogynistic interpretive scheme can be found in both *The Glass Key* and *The Thin Man.* Consider this description of Lee Wilshire in the former novel, a description that brings to mind the sort of threat associated with Kewpie's anatomy in **"The Golden**

Horseshoe": "She put a hand inside her dress and brought it out a fist. She held the fist up close to Ned Beaumont's face and opened it . . ." (18). Consider, too, Hammett's account of Eloisa Matthews, whose quasi-nymphomaniacal response to Beaumont represents at the same time a brutal disregard of her weak husband's feelings:

> [Mr. Matthews] said: "Darling, won't you come to bed? It's midnight."
>
> . . . . She did not look up from the fire until [Beaumont] had put [a drink] in her hand. When she looked up she smiled crookedly, twisting her heavily rouged exquisite thin lips sidewise. Her eyes, reflecting red light from the fire, were too bright.
>
> . . . . She lifted her glass and said, cooing: To my husband!"
>
> (125-6)

In **The Thin Man**, further, the way Miriam Nunheim and her husband settle verbal disputes suggests that violence and chaos are the invariable concomitants of marriage: "She swung her arm and let the skillet go at his head. It missed, crashing into the wall. Grease and egg-yolks made fresher stains on wall, floor, and furniture" (110). Hammett's treatment of Miriam seems calculated to warrant both Studsy Burke's later claim that "somebody could do something with that cluck if they took hold of her right," and also Shep Morelli's reply to Studsy: "[Yes,] by the throat" (158).

What is more, Hammett's treatment of Mimi Wynant in the same novel suggests how even the later Hammett, though ultimately placing in question the brute facts or rather primitive terms of a misogynist syntax, cannot wholly exorcise the misogynistic *Weltanschauung* by whose spell he remains, at the same time, profoundly fascinated. It is not only that Mimi beats her daughter Dorothy, both in private (44) and in public (164); Nick Charles also justifies his own mistrust of Mimi by telling Dorothy: "She hates men more than any woman I've every known who wasn't a Lesbian. . . . Mimi hates men—all of us—bitterly" (173). And Hammett's misogyny vis-à-vis Mimi seems to extend itself to women as a group, when Nick Charles advises the police thus:

> The chief thing . . . is not to let [Mimi] tire you out. When you catch her in a lie, she admits it and gives you another lie to take its place and, when you catch her in that one, admits it and gives you still another, and so on. Most people—*even women*—get discouraged after you've caught them in the third or fourth straight lie and fall back on either the truth or silence, but not Mimi. She keeps trying and you've got to be careful or you'll find yourself believing her, not because she seems to be telling the truth, but simply because you're tired of disbelieving her.
>
> (177, my emphasis)

In fact, when we witness Mimi's hysterical fit a moment later, Hammett uses Mimi's *physical* monstrousness to figure, as in his account of the Princess Zhukovski in **"The Gutting of Couffignal,"** women's mythic capacity to transform themselves, instantaneously, into something not only alien, but also hostile to men:

> Mimi's face was becoming purple. Her eyes protruded, glassy, senseless, enormous. Saliva bubbled and hissed between clenched teeth with her breathing, and her red throat—her whole body—was a squirming mass of veins and muscles swollen until it seemed they must burst. Her wrists were hot in my hands and sweat made them hard to hold.
>
> (186)

Are we to say, then, that the later Hammett seems to have progressed not at all past the visceral misogyny evident in his early works?

The thing to keep in mind here is that *other* women characters in the later novels do not merit the sort of treatment Hammett gives to figures like Eloise Matthews, Miriam Nunheim and Mimi Wynant. We have for instance Mrs. Madvig in **The Glass Key,** a woman whom Ned Beaumont insists on calling "Mom" (21, 107, 187). Paul's mother, in return, shows genuine affection towards Beaumont: "Her eyes were as blue and clear and young as her son's—younger than her son's when she looked up at Ned Beaumont entering the room" (21). Again, after Beaumont and Paul have exchanged words and made an irreparable split, Mrs. Madvig tries to bring about a reconciliation between the two men she seems to love equally (188). And unlike Mrs. Quarres in **"The House in Turk Street,"** Mrs. Madvig does not undergo any wolfish transmutations, but continues to exert a benign, if ineffectual, influence on affairs throughout the novel.

One could also use Opal Madvig in **The Glass Key** and Dorothy Wynant in **The Thin Man** to make a (perhaps slightly weaker) case for a change of interpretive schemes or syntaxes in Hammett's last two novels. These two women parallel one another to the extent that their youth accounts for the partly compromising situations in which they sometimes find themselves. Opal Madvig seems to be guilty of, if anything, a too-intense, somewhat misplaced idealism. After all, it is her devotion to the murdered (or else accidentally killed) Taylor Henry that prompts her to league herself with Shad O'Rory and Mr. Matthews in their smear campaign against Opal's father, Paul, whom Opal genuinely believes to have murdered Taylor. Opal, in any event, never proves herself worthy of Beaumont's distrust, and he continues to manifest toward her the same sort of candid affection he displays at the opening of the novel (24-6).

Further, Dorothy Wynant, though guilty once of lying in order to get Nora's and Nick's attention and sympathy (**TM** [**The Thin Man**], 21-22), and in general more given to the histrionic than the factual, shows herself at the same time to be up against considerable odds: her brutalization by an uncaring mother; her fear that she, like her father, may be insane (14); and an older, darker victimization at which Hammett twice hints (47, 188), but which he never reveals. Hammett's inclusion of extenuating circumstances in his treatment of Dorothy suggests that, in the author's own view, we must not be too quick to judge her. At the very least, we can make for Dorothy the same sort of negative claim that we can make for Opal, but that we could not make for the early Hammett's women characters: at no time does Dorothy pose a threat to, or exert a destructive influence on, Hammett's male detective; and yet neither does Hammett kill off these women as aberrations that prove, in grisly fashion, a misogynist rule.

But the strongest case for a global change in Hammett's interpretive syntax—a shift whose effects we can begin to register by superimposing Hammett's later on his earlier representations of women—the strongest case for such a shift can be made vis-à-vis Nora Charles, with whom the detective actually allies himself by marriage in **The Thin Man.** I might mention in passing the issue of how this novel domesticizes the genre of hard-boiled detective fiction, producing startling and unresolved tensions between sexist individualism and a sort of comic nuptial harmony. What I wish to focus on here specifically, however, are the kinds of attributes Hammett confers on Nora Charles herself.

Capable of keeping her nerve even while Shep Morelli brandishes his gun at her, and capable of maintaining interest in the serious, manly business of detection ("'Ladies usually like more color,' [the policeman] said . . . , 'kind of glamour'" [70]), Nora does not *ipso facto* exhibit androgynous features, physical or otherwise—as would have been the case were **The Thin Man** driven by the (monolithically) sexist logic of the early Hammett. Through Nora, it seems, Hammett begins to dissociate strength and seriousness from masculinity, and by extension to undo the whole nexus of assumptions according to which certain attributes remain invariably gender-specific. Or rather does Hammett's treatment of Nora initiate this transvaluation of gender only to reverse it? After all, John Guild, the official police detective assigned to the Wynant case, early on in the novel does praise Nora's poise and bravery in this way: "'Jesus,' he said, 'there's a woman with hair on her chest'" (37).

In my view, however, Hammett as it were desublimates this suggestion of Nora's androgyny in two ways. First, Hammett places the suggestion in indirect discourse and thus ascribes it to a de-privileged point of view—the view not only of a policeman, but moreover of a policeman who comically insists on informing Nick "that's a fine woman you have there" every time he

happens to see Nora. Second, Hammett phrases the suggestion in blatantly figurative terms. What the detective would have reported before in an apparently neutral observation-language—a discourse internal to the process of interpretation itself—now gets objectified in language set off by quotation marks—a discourse of limitation, bias, even farce. The early Hammett's own overrestrictive assumption that women cannot show "masculine" strength without at the same time literally being masculine—this assumption now becomes the stuff of mockery or, more precisely, self-parody.

But we need not resort to such micro-narratological analysis to see how Hammett's treatment of Nora in **The Thin Man** marks a large-scale transformation in the author's own interpretive syntax. Throughout the novel, Hammett's portrayal of Nora suggests that we cannot, as we could in the early works, make an unproblematic inference from distinctions of gender to distributions of labor—including, most importantly, *interpretive* labor. Nora constantly strains against the conventions that, within the hard-boiled genre as such, make the business of detection a specifically male enterprise. For instance, it is Nora who first sees and then points out to Nick the newspaper account of Julia Wolf's murder (9). Further, when Nora poses questions to Nick about the murder ("Do you suppose [Clyde Wynant] killed her?". . . . "Was she in love with him or was it just business?" [10-11]), Nora's discourse becomes coextensive with the discourse of interpretation itself. Hammett forces the reader here and throughout the novel to identify with Nora, whose reading-position, as it were, mirrors our own: we too must read in the interrogative mode. It is therefore characteristic of Nora that she likes solving jigsaw puzzles (133). And when Nora theorizes that Clyde Wynant is "shielding somebody else" (208)—though as it turns out she is mistaken—Nick thinks her insights important enough to mention Nora's theory to Detective Guild (228). Overall, we see that the process of interpretation takes place *between* Nora and Nick, in the give-and-take of question and answer, hypothesis and argument. Interpretive acumen ceases to be gender-specific.

Indeed, Nora provides Nick with information that he could not have obtained at all without Nora's manifest skill at observing and interpreting. We learn, for example, that Nora has feigned sleep while actually watching goings-on at the Wynant's apartment (191). In response to the other possible clues that Nora at this time also gives to Nick, Nick himself, twice, expresses a sort of admiring surprise: "Well, well" (191). Far from being congruent with distinctions of gender, therefore, the distribution of interpretive labor now seems to depend on what one happens to be in the position to hear or observe at any given time. Hammett thus reincorporates contingency into the notion of gender itself; in turn, successful interpretation requires that the male detective not prematurely exclude women's perspectives on the larger contingency of which both men and women are a part. As Nick tells Nora, in a statement no doubt meant to be patronizing, but whose irony ultimately doubles back on Hammett himself: "I don't see how any detective can hope to get along without being married to you . . ." (191-2).

One will perhaps have observed that my analysis has virtually trailed off into a discussion, *in seriatim,* of particular women in Hammett's last two novels. At the risk of appearing to rationalize a blinkered or narrowly inductive approach, however, I contend that Hammett's later treatment of women itself warrants the case-by-case procedure I have finally adopted in this paper. For in Hammett's later works, gender no longer functions (completely) as a transcendental condition for our being able to know anything at all about particular men and women. Rather, it is particular men and women with whom we are bound to concern ourselves, and whose variability from one instance to the next becomes the only thing we can assume. Not only are we to resist seeking in gender a transcendental condition for understanding the world; this need for de-transcendentalizing gender becomes, as it were, the only gender-specific assumption that we are entitled to make. In other words, by extending the concepts the later Hammett himself sets into play, we infer that any given woman deserves our special effort *not* to think of her behavior as being motivated by eternalized gender categories. I do not mean to imply that Hammett's fiction entirely lives up to the imperative of particularism that I have, for the purposes of argument, abstracted from Hammett's later texts; even **The Glass Key** and **The Thin Man,** to the extent that these texts provide grounds for misogyny at all, of course bear the pernicious impress of a sexist syntax. But I do mean to assert that, relative to the early works, Hammett's treatment of women in the late works can be mapped out along a vector of change. Whereas Hammett begins by subsuming interpretation under the rule of gender, he ends by subsuming gender, at least in part, under the rule of interpretation.

Notes

1. Note too how Wilmer stares at Spade's and the hotel detective's (phallic) neckties (108). With Hammett's description of Wilmer's hands, moreover, compare the "flaccid bluntness" of Cairo's hands (47).

2. The same dynamic, of course, is implicit in Nina Auerbach's exploration of the paradox that "[w]hile right-thinking Victorians were elevating woman into an angel, their art slithered with images of a mermaid" or else a demon (6 and *passim*). What is more, Viola Klein identifies in Freud, at what might be termed the meta-theoretical level, a similar, sometimes paradoxical

ambivalence toward women: "on the one hand the wonder at the 'enigmatic' woman, the approach to feminine psychology as a 'riddle' to be solved, and a theory which views the development of femininity as a particularly 'difficult and complicated process'; on the other hand there is contempt . . . for her inferior intellectual capacities, her greater vanity, her weaker sexual instincts, her disposition to neuroses and hysteria, and for her constitutional passivity" (84).

3. In "The Hammett Succubus," moreover, William Marling, discussing Kenneth Rayner Johnson's *The Succubus* (1979), asserts that "[t]he cause of [the protagonist's] fear is the female antagonist, the 'succubus' of the title; as in other popular novels of detection, *she threatens the protagonist's sense of discrete self*" (67, my emphasis).

4. It would be interesting in this connection, too, to consider Hammett's various statements of the detective's "code" as a sort of purifying ritual (or rather litany) aimed to dispel precisely that dread which Ricoeur associates with the fear of Evil. In "The Gutting of Couffignal," for instance, it is to a *woman,* Princess Zhukovsky, that the Op must explain his code. When the threat of contamination is greatest, it seems, the detective must ritualistically or perhaps apotropaically recite, to himself and in the face of the threatening object, the ascetic code that allows him to negotiate circumstances rife with Evil.

5. Note how Ines' and Elvira's roles in the two stories are the same: they both seduce men and then lead them on to steal from their employers either money or assets.

6. It is interesting to note that Webster's *Ninth New Collegiate Dictionary* defines "Kewpie" thus: "used for a small chubby doll with a topknot of hair."

7. Kewpie's "thick-bladed knife" also carries phallic connotations, of course. To the extent that the Op feels intensely threatened by a woman so equipped, Hammett's representation of Kewpie suggests that images of androgyny in Hammett owe much to the late nineteenth-century, "pessimistic" version of androgyny that is discussed by A. J. L. Busst. See note 9.

8. My sense of this sentimentalization of motherhood derives from a lecture given by Paul Fussell, in the fall of 1986, concerning the effects of WWI on chivalry and perceptions of motherhood.

Note too that movies of the early '30s, such as *The Public Enemy* and *Little Caesar,* rely on the image of the frail and loving, if perhaps naive, old mother. *The Public Enemy* ends with ironic (and, to the modern sensibility, comic) counterpointing between Tom Powers' return home in the form of a sort of brutalized mummy and his mother's joyous preparations upstairs in the bedroom for her son's "homecoming." Similarly, in *Little Caesar,* Joe Massera, Rico's best friend, shares a touching and nostalgic moment with his mother—a moment that, we are to assume, has something to do with Joe's abandonment of a life of crime.

9. Although, as we shall see, it does not fully account for the manifestations of androgyny in Hammett's works, A. J. L. Busst's account of "The Image of the Androgyne in the Nineteenth-Century" suggests how images of androgyny may *not* in fact undermine the pessimism that informs Hammett's view of relations between the sexes—and perhaps of the world in general. Busst describes how late in the nineteenth century the hermaphrodite symbolized generally the decay of earlier ideals, and in particular the advent of "vices" such as sadism and masochism. As Busst puts it, "a sadistic woman, in as far as she dominates her male victim, may be considered virile, since she exhibits strength . . . and her ability to indulge in her vice depends to a large extent on the male's abdication of his own virility, his masochistic willingness to be ruled—even tormented—by the female. . . . His refusal to assert himself often indicates awareness of the vanity of all action, which must accompany loss of convictions in a world without values, where good is often indistinguishable from evil" (in *Romantic Mythologies,* 56). However, as I shall explain, I believe that images of androgyny in Hammett's texts can be linked with the project of interpretation in general, such that Busst's basic opposition between "optimistic" and "pessimistic" uses of the androgyne holds valid only for androgyny taken in its narrower sense.

10. Joel Cairo in *The Maltese Falcon* is a notable exception. However, Raymond Chandler's male characters—including figures like Lindsay Mariott in *Farewell My Lovely,* Leslie Murdock in *The High Window,* and, most interestingly, Philip Marlowe himself—are in general much more aptly described as androgynous than Hammett's. Indeed, in order to get a sense of Chandler's subtlety and sophistication in this respect, one might note how, in *The Big Sleep,* Chandler figures Arthur Gwynn Geiger's androgyny by the use of significant details in descriptions of Geiger's house. Geiger, who is "like Caesar, a husband to women and a wife to men" (61), has in his house a "neat, fussy, womanish" bedroom in which "a man's brushes" rest beside "perfume on the triple-mirrored dress-

ing table" (24). Similarly, "a man's slippers" are visible "under the flounced edge of the bed cover" (24).

11. In this connection, the later Hammett's treatment of women seems to bear important resemblances to (American) philosophical pragmatism. James's and particularly Dewey's pragmatism, as Richard Rorty discusses in both *Philosophy and the Mirror of Nature* and *Consequences of Pragmatism,* also replaces the search for enduring essences with an emphasis on provisional, deliberately antisystematic explanations of the world. Note, too, the internal evidence for a pragmatist orientation in Hammett. For example, the famous story about Flitcraft in *The Maltese Falcon* concerns a man who changes his name to Charles (Sanders?) Pierce, and in *The Thin Man* we discover that Gilbert Wynant is "writing a book on Knowledge and Belief" (86). Moreover, in the latter novel's closing pages, in which Nick explains to Nora how he arrived at the conclusion that Herbert Macaulay is the culprit, Hammett seems to underwrite a basically pragmatist analysis of notions like evidence and truth.

Works Cited

Auerbach, Nina. *Woman and the Demon: The Life of a Victorian Myth.* Cambridge: Harvard UP, 1982.

Blair, Walter. "Dashiell Hammett: Themes and Techniques." In *Essays on American Literature in Honor of Jay B. Hubbell.* Ed. Clarence Gohdes. Durham: Duke UP, 1967.

Busst, A. J. L. "The Image of the Androgyne in the Nineteenth Century." In *Romantic Mythologies.* Ed. Ian Fletcher. London: Routledge and Kegan Paul, 1967.

Chandler, Raymond. *The Big Sleep.* New York: Vintage Books, 1988.

De Beauvoir, Simone. *The Second Sex.* Trans. H. M. Parshley. New York: Alfred A. Knopf, 1949.

Dooley, Dennis. *Dashiell Hammett.* New York: Frederick Ungar Publ. Co., 1984.

Eliade, Mircea. "Mephistopheles and the Androgyne, or the Mystery of the Whole." In *The Two and The One.* Trans. J. M. Cohen. London: Harvill P, 1965.

Freud, Sigmund. "Femininity." In *New Introductory Lectures on Psychoanalysis.* Trans. and Ed. James Strachey. New York: W. W. Norton and Co., 1965.

Fussell, Paul. *The Great War and Modern Memory.* London: Oxford UP, 1975.

Gilbert, Sandra M. and Susan Gubar. *The Madwoman in the Attic: The Woman Writer in the Nineteenth-Century Imagination.* New Haven: Yale UP, 1979.

Gregory, Sinda. *Private Investigations: The Novels of Dashiell Hammett.* Carbondale: Southern Illinois UP, 1985.

Hammett, Dashiell. *The Big Knockover.* Ed. Lillian Hellman. New York: Vintage Books, 1972.

——. *The Continental Op.* Ed. Stephen Marcus. New York: Vintage Books, 1974.

——. *The Glass Key.* New York: Vintage Books, 1972.

——. *The Maltese Falcon.* New York: Vintage Books, 1984.

——. *Red Harvest.* New York: Vintage Books, 1972.

——. *The Thin Man.* New York: Alfred A. Knopf, 1933.

Harris, Daniel A. "Androgyny: The Sexist Myth." *Women's Studies,* vol. 2, no. 2 (1974): 171-84.

Heilbrun, Carolyn. "Further Notes toward a Recognition of Androgyny." *Women's Studies,* vol. 2, no. 2 (1974): 143-50.

Kant, Immanuel. *Critique of Pure Reason.* Trans. Norman Kemp Smith. New York: St. Martin's Press, 1965.

Klein, Viola. *The Feminine Character: History of an Ideology.* Urbana: U. of Illinois P, 1946; 2nd ed., 1971.

Marling, William. "The Hammett Succubus." *Clues* 3 (1982): 66-75.

Maxfield, James F. "Hard-Boiled Dicks and Dangerous Females: Sex and Love in the Detective Fiction of Dashiell Hammett." *Clues* 6 (1985): 107-23.

Miller, D. A. *The Novel and the Police.* Berkeley: U of California P, 1988.

Nye, Russell. *The Unembarassed Muse: The Popular Arts in America.* New York: The Dial Press, 1970.

Proust, Marcel. *Remembrance of Things Past.* I. Trans. C. K. Scott Moncrieff. New York: Random House, 1934.

Ricoeur, Paul. *The Symbolism of Evil.* Trans. Emerson Buchanan. New York: Harper and Row, Publishers, 1967.

Rogers, Katharine M. *The Troublesome Helpmate: A History of Misogyny in Literature.* Seattle: U of Washington P, 1966.

Rorty, Richard. *Consequences of Pragmatism.* Minneapolis: U of Minnesota P, 1982.

——. *Philosophy and the Mirror of Nature.* Princeton: Princeton UP, 1979.

Secor, Cynthia. "Androgyny: An Early Reappraisal." *Women's Studies,* vol. 2, no. 2 (1974): 161-170.

Gregory Forter (essay date fall 1995)

SOURCE: Forter, Gregory. "Criminal Pleasures, Pleasurable Crime." *Style* 29, no. 3 (fall 1995): 423-40.

[*In the following essay, Forter evaluates Hammett's fiction and argues that the public's compulsion to read detective literature is derived from a "pleasurable brutality," one that is "less a pleasure in violence done to 'others' than it is joy taken in psychic self-destruction."*]

I. "I LIKED SOMEBODY BEING DEAD"

What is it in the hard-boiled novel that hooks me, binds me to it, arrests me in the tracks of an otherwise intractable desire? Where, to be precise, am I to locate the *pleasure* I take in that novel—a pleasure that is at least compulsive in that I am driven to repeat it, and that entails an interruptive thickening of a reading that might otherwise proceed too quickly, of a text we habitually characterize as thin? Taking seriously some of the commonplaces about the genre, we could open with a methodical elimination of the suspects that would please, at any rate, the classical detective. Pleasure, then—my pleasure—can hardly inhere in the hard-boiled *plot,* since plot is here, in contrast to the classical tradition, subordinated to such elements as scene, dialogue, setting, and even to some extent to character. Where the classical detective story unfolds toward a moment of epiphanic illumination, the hard-boiled novel is said to be strangely indifferent to the economy of such a movement.[1] It sacrifices the drive toward a plenitude of meaning to less teleological representational exigencies. It plays down the joys of Holmesian closure by insisting that, as Raymond Chandler famously put it, *it* is a novel we would want to keep reading even if the last chapter had been torn out. And it performs this thwarting of narrative pleasure with plots of a delinquent character that Chandler is perhaps most expert at composing: plots that, through an irresolvable complexity or a resolute poverty of suture, forever expose their very plottedness and thereby cast suspicion on their capacity to produce the end-pleasure of a positive apocalypse. The temporal ontology of the hard-boiled novel is decidedly that which Kermode calls "waiting time": a time that kills time, that wastes it by refusing to redeem it, that "shall be no more" because it exhausts itself in its unfolding and so forgoes the climactic fulfillments of a time Kermode calls "season"—of a time, that is, "charged with a meaning derived from its relation to the end" (47).

This may seem already a perverse characterization. After all, what is at issue is a *detective* novel,[2] and detective novels require crimes, which in their turn require solutions—*resolutions*—that shed light on all that has come before. We might then start to wonder how a genre so clearly geared toward closure can also be less than primarily concerned with the pleasures such closure entails. Here is at least a provisional hypothesis: in—for example—Hammett and Chandler, where crimes continue narratively to be solved and a certain resolution is no doubt achieved, such resolution is phenomenologically secondary because mystery and its apocalyptic temporality are in fact no more than "manifest" expressions of a more traumatized structure, a more dilatory temporality, *a more perverse pleasure* than those of the novels' official discourse. "The initial deception," writes Jameson of Chandler, "takes place on the level of the book as a whole, *in that it passes itself off as a murder mystery*" (143; my emphasis). And Gertrude Stein, in more elliptical fashion:

> I never was interested in cross word puzzles or any kind of puzzles but I do like detective stories. I never try to guess who has done the crime and if I did I would be sure to guess wrong but I liked somebody being dead and how it moves along and Dashiell Hammett was all that and more.
>
> (4)

"How it moves along," not "how it ends." For Stein as for Jameson, the penetration of the mystery is inessential to hard-boiled fiction, and this means again that the ending in such fiction is no longer the site of a primary delectation. "I liked somebody being dead," Stein says. Such a preference may help us already to flesh out our initial claim. It offers the disturbing but provocative suggestion that the hard-boiled *corpse*—the thing that provides the mystery and seems therefore most intimately bound to a temporality of narrative recuperation—is also and at the same time that which erodes that temporality, dysfunctionalizes pleasure, fixates us fascinatedly on a moment of brute and irrecoverable loss. To say that "I like somebody being dead" is to say that the end-pleasure of narrative meaning is replaced by a pleasure in the ravishing image of an irrepressibly murderous *violence.* And this violence is, as we'll soon see, always in these texts our own: we solicit it, call it into being, submit to it, not just as the condition but as the very convulsiveness of an utterly in(sub)ordinate enjoyment.

I want in fact to argue here that the pleasurable brutality compelling our reading is less a pleasure in violence done to "others" than it is joy taken in psychic self-destruction. When I claim, that is, to read these books because I like somebody being dead, I do not mean simply *someone else* being dead, but also and above all *myself.* I mean that the compulsive pleasure of such reading is a pleasure taken in the explosive assumption of an auto-annihilatory self-image. Hard-boiled reading is therefore best grasped through a speculative recourse to Freud, since psychoanalysis offers us terms with

which to link pleasure and destructive repetition. But it is also the case that the hard-boiled novel knows things about the enjoyments of compulsion that Freud is at pains to deny, and my account will therefore entail some revisions to psychoanalytic theories regarding the relations among pleasure, mastery, masochism, and—ultimately—masculinity and femininity. It will entail, to begin with, that we wreak a kind of violence on the explicit arguments of *Beyond the Pleasure Principle.* For that text seeks in its initial movement to *sever* compulsive repetition and pleasure in a way the hard-boiled text disallows, to connect pleasure with an act's repetition only to the extent that such repetition ceases to be compulsive. "The child cannot possibly have felt his mother's departure as something agreeable or even indifferent," writes Freud in the by-now infamous discussion of the fort-da game. "How then does his repetition of this distressing experience as a game fit in with the pleasure principle?" (9). The first answer begins as follows:

> [O]ne gets the impression that the child turned his experience [of his mother's departure] into a game from another motive. At the outset he was in a *passive* situation—he was overpowered by the experience; but, by repeating it, unpleasurable though it was, he took an *active* part. These efforts might be put down to an instinct for mastery that was acting independently of whether the memory was in itself pleasurable or not.
>
> (10; Freud's emphases)

Passivity stands to unpleasure as activity does to the (linguistic) binding of that unpleasure, and to a consequent pleasure-in-mastery: what must at all costs be outlawed by this series is the possibility of a *pleasurable compulsion,* since pleasure needs to reside with mastery if the term "perversion" is to retain its significance. A pleasurable compulsion would be a *perverse* pleasure in being unpleasurably "overpowered by the experience." It would be an enjoyment in masochistic submission to the influx of painful excitation, rather than the incipiently sadistic enjoyment to be had from subduing by binding that excitation. Since Freud is committed to a vision of pleasure that makes it correspond to "a diminution" of unbound energy (2), a repetition that declines to master such excitation, either by discharging or psychically binding it, can only for him be an abnormality. The opposition between death drive and Eros will thus turn out to require and enforce the separation of compulsion from pleasure itself.

For if—as Freud goes on to argue—the compulsion to repeat is the sign of the ego's most radically self-destructive tendencies, it cannot at the same time be pleasurable or erotic without ruining the opposition between Eros and death. If such repetition is the legible mark of the psyche's drive to unbind itself, then locating pleasure on the side of compulsion is tantamount to enabling an annihilatory eroticization of increased psychic tension that would authorize the ego's pleasure in its own unpleasurable undoing. Compulsive enjoyment is exactly this enjoyment in the implacable impulsion to self-destruction. Neither the satisfaction attaching to binding nor the satiation of complete discharge, such an enjoyment is the vexatious pleasure of a compulsively repeated embrace of psychic tension that tends ineluctably toward death. It is the pleasure of a boy resubmitting to the pain of his mother's departure for no reason other than the sheer unmitigated hell of it. It is a pleasure that, far from being masterful, resides instead in the ego's desire to repeat a past but remembered unpleasure, in order simply but self-explosively to submit to it. And it is in this compulsively pleasurable submission that the stakes of Freud's argument start to become clear. The death drive, after all, along with the compulsion to repeat that instantiates it, is meant to lie somewhere "beyond" the pleasure principle, not to inhere secretly within it. To the extent that *Beyond the Pleasure Principle* might therefore fail to separate enjoyment from compulsive repetition, it threatens to transform its intended message—"I seek (non-erotically) my own death"—into its more radically true one: "I like (take pleasure in) somebody (myself) being dead (ecstatically dying)."

And there can be little doubt that the text fails ultimately to keep these terms apart. Freud's recourse to "an instinct for *mastery*," in a passage explaining compulsive *submission,* betokens his surrender to an oxymoronic logic that portends a complete theoretical collapse. For the concept of an "instinct" has meaning only if we take seriously the entity it designates as something to which we must submit. Instincts master us, not we them. The most plausible reading, then, of an "instinct for mastery" is that I am compelled, driven, submitted to (my own) mastery, that in submitting I become master, and in mastering, I give myself up. The pleasure attendant on a will-to-mastery becomes indissociable from the Freudian scandal of a masochistically pleasurable unpleasure. What we surrender in giving ourselves over to a masterful binding of excitation, which takes pleasure only in eliminating tension, is the prior and compulsively repetitive pleasure of masochistic surrender itself, and hence the blend of pertinacity and hesitation with which Freud gives a second account of his grandson's game:

> But still another interpretation may be attempted. Throwing away the object so that it was "gone" might satisfy an impulse of the child's, which was suppressed in his actual life, to revenge himself on his mother for going away from him. In that case it would have a defiant meaning: "All right, then, go away! I don't need you. I'm sending you away myself."
>
> (10; my emphasis)

If "another interpretation may be attempted," we might well wonder why the theoretical content of that "other interpretation" resembles so closely that of the first. The movement from explanation one ("it's not masochism, it's a will-to-mastery") to explanation two ("it's *still* not masochism; it's, well, sadism") turns out to be no movement at all. The second proposition merely extends and renders explicit the aggression implicit in the "instinct for mastery" of the first. Freud's own compulsion to repeat, therefore, allows us to discover in that repetition a negative affirmation of the assertion his explanations are designed to disallow. When a footnote describes the child as staging his *own* disappearance in a mirror (9), we're entitled to see in that action what Freud tries strenuously not to see, to prevent us from seeing: that this moment marks the disruptive restaging of an originary, involuntary, and ecstatic self-abnegation that predates and predicates the pretensions of mastery and well-bound egoic control. The entire project of searching for something "beyond" the pleasure principle now comes into focus as a defense against the recognition that there is, in truth, *nothing* beyond it, and that, consequently, the compulsive submission to unpleasurable tension may be not just enjoyable, but sexual enjoyment itself.[3]

II. How to Be Dead in Style

Let us return, then, to the scene of crime, in order to reformulate our thesis. The pleasure I take in hard-boiled reading is precisely the pleasure that Freud would deny me: a pleasure in the unpleasure of increased psychic tension that might more properly be said to "take me," in that it entails my compulsory luxuriance in being violently possessed, broken, lost to myself. What does this mean? Or—more crucially—what does it look like?

One way to begin to formulate an answer is through an account of the hard-boiled style. Critics have suggested that this style is to be distinguished from that of the classical detective story because it is a language in excess, a kind of linguistic surplus that adds whole new ranges of color, affect, and consciousness.[4] I want to argue, however, that this language which seems to offer us "something extra" can best be characterized, not by what it includes, but—precisely—by what it subtracts and omits. Here is the opening of Hammett's ***The Glass Key***:

> Green dice rolled across the green table, struck the rim together, and bounced back. One stopped short holding six white spots in two equal rows uppermost. The other tumbled out to the center of the table and came to rest with a single spot on top.
>
> (3)

Language like this wreaks both epistemological and ontological havoc, disappearing in the very gesture of its emergence and unsaying as much as it says. We can stress, as critics often do, the "clipped," "bare," "sparse," "lean," "clean," "hard," or whatever stylistic indices; but clearly what is crucial is the singularly *withholding* character of a discourse that seems, at the same time, *generous*: so attentive to the minutiae of detail that it is almost forced to operate in slow-motion. The temporal distention of an event that lasts seconds mirrors in miniature the dilatory fixations of hard-boiled narrative as a whole, while simultaneously masking, beneath the strained attitude of its concentration, the informational dearth of its content. Where are we? When are we? Who is there? Who is speaking? The epistemological uncertainties of such a style give way finally to an ontological murder that is the very purpose of the hard-boiled style.

For only some of these omissions of knowledge are at last made good narrationally. Though the novel relays us, in relative coherence, along its syntagmatic chain, suturing us gradually into its "world" and binding that world in the telos of a plot that confers at least moments of mastery and control, we have come a long way from the social density of—for example—a James novel. The "where" of the main action remains unspecified, for example; the historical moment shows up only on the faces of the novel's commodities, and spatial articulations in any given scene are kept to the barest minimum. The novel's unflinching attention, therefore, to the "realities" of corruption and violence, as well as its tendency minimally to satisfy the desire to "know all" that it produces, may well betoken a certain "realism." But we need also to reckon the abrogation of that project. Hammett once wrote that "Realistic is one of those words when it comes up in conversation sensible people put on their hats and go home" (Naremore 54). For all the apparent objectivity of its vision, *The Glass Key* tends to corroborate such a sentiment—not so much because it does not "close" as because of the disturbances to the function of language effected by the particulars of its prose style. The eye of that style is too superficial in its grasp to dispel the sense that something yet remains, beyond and animating the representational field, to be seen, mastered, and understood:

> A telephone-bell, ringing close to Ned Beaumont's head, awakened him. He opened his eyes, put his feet down on the floor, turned on his side, and looked around the room. When he saw the telephone he shut his eyes and relaxed.
>
> The bell continued to ring. He groaned, opened his eyes again, and squirmed until he had freed his left arm from beneath his body. He put his left wrist close to his eyes and looked at his watch, squinting. The watch's crystal was gone and its hands had stopped at twelve minutes to twelve.
>
> (*Glass Key* 36)

The reality-effect of a passage like this results from the way it piles up nouns: what is real here is what can be nominally designated because it exists as substance.

The style therefore "works" by juxtaposing only those "things" that can be substantially grasped by the senses. If and when it highlights "qualities," these tend to be purely exterior ones, since this is a style that approximates the real by refusing to register anything but surface. It is a style that moves from object to object with a certain restless but alert rapidity; seeking to reproduce the "natural" movement of everyday consciousness, it quickly exhausts the thing that it sees, takes it in at a glance, swallows it whole and with hardly a blink. We're asked to partake of a scopic ingestion that brings things into the field of vision long enough only to abolish by registering them.

It is almost, indeed, as if the closer the hard-boiled camera "looks," the less it truly "sees"; the greater its focus on the objects it collects, the more it is forced to attenuate that linguistic dimension—the significatory—which could alone establish the reasonable grounds for any such objectal collection. Thus, while Ned Beaumont would seem to stand in some "meaningful" relation to the ringing telephone, the stopped watch, and the parts of his own body, the novel declines to make the meaning of that relation explicit. Either the point of this moment resides in its significance for *Ned,* whose consciousness presumably organizes the scene; or the objects and encounters carry some symbolic or metaphorical meaning for *readers,* but one that Ned either does not or cannot know. Whichever the case, the text appears to be "saying something." It appears to bring together its objects in the name of a legibly thematic intention. If the only way to read such a scene is nonetheless to paraphrase it, while imputing affects and motives that the text nowhere explicitly states, this is because the hard-boiled style performs the feat of *destroying* the world in the act of describing it and *banishing* signification for the sake of its own material extremity. The modernist binary of language "or" the world here gives way to a materiality that spurns both the representational and the significatory dimensions of the linguistic sign. This is a language that isolates and contains, circling its objects and breaking them off from the world, then proceeding to clobber those objects, to flatten them into emaciated thinness, to pulverize and render them astonished and mute. It is a language so committed to the arbitrary and depthless juxtaposition of objects and subjects that their coincidence in one place comes to seem no more than a colossal accident of being: they just "are," in all their brute contingency, "there together." And it is thus a language that, far from primarily satisfying the desire to see and know that it produces, epistemologically starves us instead. "To speak, and above all to write, is to fast," write Deleuze and Guattari in their book on Kafka (20).[5] When Ned Beaumont says that "all the dreams [he] ever had about food ended before [he] had a chance to do any actual eating" (179), he gives the hard-boiled version of that argument: to write is to produce a starving text, a text that starves (us); the hard-boiled novel, like the hard-boiled dream, compels a submission to the representational refusal of the realistic feast.

The eye of this style can thus "pull back" or "cut" all it wants to. It can give us belatedly the establishing shots that it at first withholds, can even try to produce a knowledge through narrational ordering of its elements. It continues, nevertheless, to enunciate with a staid and myopic parsimony. The world from its vantage is a two-dimensional affair that does not speak, a universe composed of empty clues and broken circuits, where accident has effectively absorbed essence and meaning is no more than the spartan byproduct of a predominantly material sign. All that this style can manage to do is reveal its object as an illegible *blot*. It decomposes the thing it discloses, breaks the world up in objectal fragments that have no essentially meaningful relation, so that in the light of its "objectivity" that world emerges only stupidly—darkly—*obscenely*: as an evanescent yet sticky materiality that gives rise to an interpretive recalcitrance precisely inasmuch as it is apprehended "straight."[6] Only when the text "distorts" that world with narrative, smearing it retroactively with the telos of a hermeneutical desire, does it manage to remand its objects into the custody of meaning. Narrative acts here as a fantasy structure transforming the inert signs of the desire for nothing into the meaningful objects of a desire for something. It takes the voided solidity of the world and literally rediscloses it to us, dressing it up in the significant promise of a narrational and redemptive causality. If the primary function of the detective is thus to link the world's objects by way of this causality, that function remains profoundly at odds with a style that clings to its empty secret long after the narrative secretes. That style, marshaling a logic of the missed encounter, orchestrates an impossible confrontation with a real that it always yet misses, that we can never know as such, but that it coaxes to erupt into discourse as a non-integratable objectal obscenity eroding the intentional significance of the hermeneutical code. Reading becomes a kind of trauma, interpretation a matter of unauthorized inference. The pleasure of the hard-boiled text is bound up with the pain of an interpretive dissatisfaction.

But such a pain is just part of the story. Beyond these significatory erosions and depletions, the "objectivity" of this style also entails an ontological erasure, as it refuses to open a space for interiority, affectivity—in short, for humanity itself. What makes that style above all so ghostly is its evacuation of human agency from the site of the human being, and the consequent investment of such agency in inanimate objects and the forces of nature:

> Wind-driven rain hammered tree, bush, ground, man, car with incessant blows. . . .

> Wind and rain on [the man's] back pushed him downhill towards the [light]. . . . though he stumbled often and staggered, and was tripped by obstacles underfoot, he kept his feet under him and moved nimbly enough, if erratically, towards his goal.

> Presently a path came under his feet. He turned into it, holding it partly by its sliminess under his feet, partly by the feel of the bushes whipping his face on either side, and not at all by sight. The path led him off to the left for a little distance, but then . . . brought him to the brink of a small gorge. . . .

> (**Glass Key** 123)

It would perhaps be redundant to list the preponderance of active verbs that here take Ned Beaumont for their object, or to point out the radically dehumanizing effect of the first sentence's equalizing inventory ("tree, bush, ground, man, car"). Multiplying the sites of sadistic agency, displacing subjective activity onto a rain that "hammers," obstacles that "trip," and bushes that "whip," the passage so thoroughly disperses human being across its textual landscape that it also effectively abolishes that being. Ned and his world are confused and interfused; he becomes "worldly," his world becomes human, as the relentless personification of objects marks and enforces an equally implacable objectification of the subject. The humanized object resulting from this process is no more human than the objectified subject that results on the other side. For where "humanity" ceases to coincide with a human form, the category of the human uncannily vanishes by losing all possible meaning; it may seem at first glance to lurk almost everywhere, but this is because it in fact resides, simultaneously and surely, nowhere. Human qualities survive in such a case only on the side of the "object," and they're consequently rendered utterly *in*human by the force of their spatial displacement. The human form survives, conversely, in a manner so drained of those qualities we attribute to it as to become unmistakably dehumanized.

Let us be perfectly clear, however: this displacement of subjective agency and subjection of the human to natural forces is merely the bleeding into content of an essentially *formal* necessity. It is language itself, the hard-boiled style, that first and foremost pummels human being, grinding it to a pulp and rubbing it out. The only omission indispensable to this style is the omission of the category of the human itself. The only thing it cannot abide is an affective, active, and self-conscious subject who behaves in any way *like* a subject, and we must thus insist that the entire point of its omissions and opacities is to render the human as objectal as its objects: to flatten, silence, and blind it ("not at all by sight"); to rip it away from both reference and significance; to reduce humanity to a material register that blots out the difference between people and things by making each a pulpy occasion for the objectal eruption of an unmasterable real. Ned is objectified by a style that flattens him before the objects in his world beat him up. He is objectified in style so that the reader may be traumatized, as the fictive encounter with a human form becomes a disruptive and deadly confrontation with the "stuff" that predates the emergence of the subject and that the hard-boiled style works to "embody." Sadistic agency, subjective activity, the forms of objectal use and manipulation that properly "belong" to a human intention: these are all placed on the side of the object only as a kind of representational expression of the *style's* intention to wipe out human being, both within and "without" its pulverized field. For hard-boiled discourse is a sadistic discourse that, as Bataille says of Sade, "repudiates any relation between speaker and audience"; "its purpose is the denial of humanity" (180), and in this it is in its very essence an utterly impersonal third-person language that seeks to engulf even the consciousness at its origin.[7] The hard-boiled style can belong to no one because it is characterized by an unending hostility to even the "one" who would own and utter it. It seeks above all to squash human being into states of objectal indistinction, and it therefore obliterates the enunciative "I" while also repelling all readerly entry and insisting that it speaks "to" no one. The abduction of that style by such narrating dicks as Chandler's Marlowe and Hammett's Continental Op marks their attempt to arrogate a sadistic weaponry that enables a delusional linguistic mastery in compensation for the real psychic unmanning that, as we shall see, constitutes their masculine being. In first-person narratives, hard-boiled language becomes—that is—a *fetish*: an eroticized substitute for a phallic potency that the third-person narration scorns, an instrument that erects a sadistic armor against the internal worldly seductions of a more primary masochistic unbinding. The talking dick has merely read his Freud, and he plays the fort-da game strictly by the book.

III. RETURN OF THE PRIMAL SCENE

And this language that "repudiates any relation between speaker and audience"? I may as well confess at this point that my pleasure inheres in part here: in a compulsively repeated and suicidal submission to the batterings of a *style*. The humanity denied by hard-boiled language is above all else my own. I ask for it, it gives it to me; it tracks me down, and I surrender to it. But this surrender has other dimensions as well. The representation offers a further locus of repudiated humanity, and that is the site of murder or, more properly, of the corpse. Once again, "I like somebody being dead." We might begin to suspect at this point, in the light of the arguments advanced so far, that the body here necessary

to a *narrative* pleasure serves too as an identificatory lure through which the reader is able to sustain an intolerably desirable and anti-narrational shattering of ego or self.

Geraldine Penderson-Krag has suggested the possibility of such an "identification with the victim." For her, crime stories allow the reader "a sadistic return to the primal scene," a return to that scene of parental coitus that Freud has theorized as traumatizing the (male) child who witnesses it, in part because the child "misunderstands" the sexual act as one of paternal violence toward a mother with whom he also *identifies*. The primal scene, according to this reading, is figured in detective stories by the initial murder (committed off-stage, experienced in its traces, arousing anxiety, desire, and curiosity), whose traumatic disruptions the reader is now able to bind and master through repeated readerly returns to that scene (59-62). Reading such fiction is thus once again a means for overcoming the violence of trauma. Though Penderson-Krag does not say so herself, her argument implies that the pleasure of that fiction resides in the way it helps a reader whom it addresses *as male* surmount a traumatized and unmanning identification with the "victim" of primal violence, identified as both female and maternal. And since the primal scene is here the scene of crime, the maternal victim within that scene can only be located at the site of the corpse. The male reader comes now finally to see, at the deepest unconscious level of his psyche, that *he* is not that "corpse"—not the feminine and passive recipient of an erotic paternal violation—but is himself a masculine heir to the father's sadistic legacy. Or, again, in more critical terms: the reading of crime fiction is here intended to facilitate the male subject's repudiation of a masochism that is perhaps constitutive of all subjectivity, by helping him project his desire for death onto a "feminine" object that appears in the image of a corpse.

I want both to take these arguments seriously and to move them decisively elsewhere. If, as Kaja Silverman has argued, the child's helpless *submission* to the primal moment requires we find there a "voyeurism with a difference" that is "conducive . . . of passivity and masochism" rather than mastery and sadism (171, 164); and if we accept Freud's rewriting of that moment as a *fantasy*,[8] then it follows that the child desires (fantasizes) a scenario that quite literally masters and overpowers him. The fantasy of a primal scene represents an originary wish for the traumatic effraction of the body—the ears, the eyes—and the psyche. The child is ecstatically and originally pierced by images of unmasterably scary proportions, which the infant itself calls into being. He or she conjures forth images whose very alien illegibility guarantees a traumatic submission to a scene that is also *desired*. And since it is this trauma that, according to Freud, inaugurates all subjects into sexual pleasure,[9] how can we doubt that the most enjoyable identifications in the primal scene's return would also be the most self-destroying, or that such "destruction" would entail the *male* subject's avowing the masochism he projects and calls "feminine" as finally and inexorably his own?

We cannot, I think, and thus the authorization for a hypothesis that perhaps appears somewhat extravagant. For it seems to me that, in first-person hard-boiled narratives, there are two completely different scenarios for desire and identification—a normative one featuring the detective, and a perverse or "feminizing" one starring the corpse—but that third-person narratives tend to collapse the two, absorbing the first into the second and making a certain masculine perversion as inescapable as the criminal's capture and death. First-person narratives could even be said to enforce a regime of masculine identification whose purpose is to repress the knowledge of male masochism gained by those in the third person. The enormous pathos of Chandler's (first-person) novels depends, for example, upon our enforced identification with an embattled but *impregnable* male consciousness whose cardinal imperative is, as Martin Priestman notes, *noli me tangere* (171). Marlowe retreats again and again into the rich elaborations of his interior life; he cultivates sentiment and a desire for connection only in the form of private musings designed to exclude human contact, because he knows that to touch is to *be* touched, and that to be touched is to be brutalized, psychically and physically violated, penetrated by force and by sexuality. Contact in fact becomes possible in Chandler only on condition of its extreme *neutralization*: "If I touched you," says Marlowe to Merle Davis in *The High Window,* "it was just like touching a chair or a door. It didn't mean anything" (131-32); or again in *Playback,* after one of only two sex scenes Chandler ever allows his hero, the lovers banter with each other to the tender tones of "I don't love you" and "I hate you" (78-79). Human touch becomes the stirring occasion for a self-protective and insular retreat into objectification, irony, and masculine sadism. Marlowe moves in the direction of his world only in verbal and physical assault designed to master the unending threat of a universe that unmans by brutalizing him. It is therefore no wonder that the books divide that threat rigorously between violence (perpetrated by cops, criminals, doctors), and sex (in the form of women and effeminate men). The division signals an attempt to stave off the recognition that the two are in fact one, and here we arrive at the centrality in Chandler's work of the *femme fatale* that, in the novels of Hammett, remains significantly and only tangential.[10]

For the *femme fatale* signals the eruption of a seductively excessive and dangerous pleasure. With her, the submission to sex *is* the submission to force because in fucking you—*in the very act* of fucking you—she also invariably fucks you over. What she holds out and promises as an erotically cathectable scenario is the possibility of a thrilling identification with the image of one's own death. Precisely because she refuses "to cede her desire" and so "fully assumes the death drive" (Žižek 66), the danger she poses is one of masochistic identification to the point of a self-explosive suicide, of taking as one's own a feminine and finally "frenetic enjoyment" (Laplanche 105) whose intensities are nothing short of self-annihilatory. In desiring her, the dick *desires,* period: it is a pure and non-objectal desire for what he would most like to be: dead. The femme fatale provokes, that is, a wish for the pleasurable identification with a corpse. And it is exactly to protect himself (and us) against such a wish, which figures the essential coincidence of the threat of sex and the threat of violence, that the dick so completely disappears behind the "I" of his masculine consciousness. The *body* of the detective shows up in Chandler only in order to be feminized and ravaged, and thus it seeks to make itself localizable only in its ultimate lack of locale: in its virtual and eerie withdrawal from the spaces that its investigatory quest maps. Marlowe becomes for us an identificatory possibility just to the extent that he fully identifies with his own investigative function. He remains "ideal"— an ego ideal—exactly insofar as he remains above all a private and disembodied *eye*. For in this he steers us, however circuitously, toward a vanquishing of the *femme fatale* and the narrative pleasures of solution, away from the enjoyments of *dis*solution that entail *becoming* the *femme fatale,* and he thereby enables us to keep at bay the perpetually seductive image of all those beaten, bloated, penetrated, and bruised victims of an ecstatically accepted violence.

With Hammett's **The Glass Key** everything changes. One need only teach this novel to undergraduates to grasp the profundity of the identificatory problems it poses, since what one finds in such an undertaking is an absolute *recoil* from identification. Students, as they say, "can't get into it." And they cannot because they sense that, once having gotten in, there is never any getting out. If in Chandler the dick maintains a well-cultivated sadism that facilitates an escape from suicidal identification, in Hammett's novel the "dick" is himself suicidal, an inveterate gambler and loser who insists he "can stand anything [he's] got to stand" and who demonstrates again and again, through endlessly provoked beatings, that you "Might as well take your punishment and get it over with" (6). Ned Beaumont cannot steer us toward masculine mastery and sadistic control because he remains quite madly identified with the image of his own masochistic surrender. He is, indeed, in some profound sense, the repressed unconscious of Freud's Wolf Man. His compulsive acting out of an eroticized death drive bespeaks a perverse and unyielding fixation to a literally *unmasterable* primal scene—a scene in which, identified like the Wolf Man with a "castrated" femininity, he cannot overcome that identification through a normative one with the father because he recognizes the father as castrated also "and as calling, therefore, for his sympathy" ("Infantile" 278). Ned returns us to the scene of primal trauma only to compel us to repeat and submit to it. He asks us to identify with a "feminine" pain that inheres in the image of castrative submission, and to renounce thereby a paternal function that *The Glass Key* empties of all meaningful substance. For the novel *does* empty it of substance. Paul Madvig, for example, is Ned's superior and clearly also a paternal elder, but he repeatedly turns to the younger man for advice, makes all the wrong political decisions, and remains, almost whenever we see him, impotently behind his office desk, his knowledge of the killer's identity rendered useless by his political imperatives. Indeed, wherever Paul does start brandishing about a phallic manhood, the novel quickly cuts it off, exposing it as a turgid sham. The "cyclone shot" that is "[his] kind" of "fighting" and that entails "going in [against Shad] with both hands working" (65), causes a gang war that loses him the election, and his clumsy assertions of masculine prerogative work more to repel than to attract his intended, as they lead to the immediate murder of her brother (150). The novel imagines a stubborn adherence to normative masculinity as the cause of all its woe. The more Paul tries to "act like a man" the more the novel degrades and punishes him; the closer he comes to mastering his world through the gestures of manly assertion, the farther he places the things he desires definitively out of reach. To identify with the father thus solves nothing, since it is Madvig's *excessive* identification with such manhood that *The Glass Key* codes as problematic, and that it therefore chooses to interrogate, to challenge—and, finally, to repudiate.[11]

As for the mother in this familial scenario: Ned sometimes calls *Paul's* mother "Mom," but I want to suggest, recalling the arguments of Penderson-Krag, that the truly decisive "mother" in the novel shows up as an enticing identificatory image in Ned's return to the primal scene, now restaged as the scene of primal crime:

> Ned Beaumont took his hand away from the dead man and stood up. The dead man's head rolled a little to the left, away from the curb, so that his face lay fully in the light from the corner street lamp. . . .
>
> [Ned Beaumont] was breathing through his mouth and though tiny points of sweat glistened on his hands in the light he shivered now and turned up the collar of his overcoat.
>
> He remained in the tree's shadow with one hand on the tree for perhaps half a minute. Then he straightened abruptly and began to walk towards the Log Cabin Club. . . . He . . . slackened his pace and made himself walk erect. . . .

> By the time Ned Beaumont reached the Club he had stopped breathing through his mouth. His lips were still somewhat faded. He looked at the empty automobile without pausing, climbed the Club's steps between two lanterns, and went indoors.

(14)

Here, the novel's refusal of interiority has a specific effect that we can call *indeterminacy*. The initial cold sweat; the increased rate of respiration indicated by "breathing through the mouth"; the ever more rapid movements that lead up to "erection"; the pallid lips; the sense of being so overcome that one needs support to remain standing—the bodily signs we are asked to read could obviously betoken an anxiously sexual excitation as much as they signal fear, apprehension, or a purely non-sexual trauma. The novel offers descriptive terms that suggest a sexual encounter with death, even as it declines in advance to give its assent to any interpretation at all. In reading Ned's discovery of the corpse as a playing of the primal scene, therefore, we merely read the scene in question as *The Glass Key* charges us to read it: preposterously, impossibly, by way of a claim whose very exorbitance in no way mitigates its maximal plausibility.

What must then be noted about this scene is that, through a logical extrapolation of its most radical possibilities, the father gets *abolished* except in the violence of his effects, while the mother appears in the guise of a corpse with whom Ned clearly and pleasurably *identifies*. Once again, the novel forces a collapse of two moments that Freud wants to keep distinct: The Wolf Man "seems to have assumed to begin with that the event to which he was a witness [in the primal scene] was an act of violence, but the expression of enjoyment which he saw upon his mother's face did not fit in with this; he was obliged to recognize that what he was faced by was a process of gratification" ("Infantile" 230-31). Eliding the fact that the "expression of enjoyment" when most intense is indistinguishable from that of agony, Freud equally forgets that, even on his own account, the primal scene makes no sense unless we understand it as an aggressive scenario in which the appeal of the mother's position lies in its potential for a ravished enjoyment. The Wolf Man's desire assumes "pathological" proportions because it identifies him with the mother, even after he understands her pleasure as indissociable from the violence of submissive "castration."[12] Gratification and disintegration are literally inseparable. To derive satisfaction here is the same thing as to embrace the unpleasure of a feminizing violation. And if Freud's text fails to remember this identity, *The Glass Key* never forgets it. It is almost as though, in the absence of the *femme fatale,* and because the Marlovian tactics of defense are unavailable to the third-person style, there is nothing left but for the dick himself to "assume the death drive," taking as his own the pleasurably sacrificed image he sees as the result of the father's aggressivity. Ned's identification with the corpse in this passage is both the sign of his feminization and the condition of his relentless attempts in the pages that follow to become one. His suicidal tendency to submit to pain replays an originarily perverse primal moment, in which he takes pleasure in a feminizing submission and seeks above all to recover and repeat it. The scene's abolition of the father, meanwhile, makes possible a delirious intensification of pleasure in the image of what the father can do to me: fuck me, castrate me—at the limit, kill me.

It is in the service of just such a pleasure that the novel compels us to *see* its detective. "We know that it is a psychological necessity for masochism to have witnesses," writes Reik. "The masochist does not hide his misery; he shows it to everybody, he propagates it. He seems to wish the whole world to hear him" (312). Novel of masochism that *The Glass Key* is, it declines to dissolve the male body, in Chandlerian fashion, into an investigative eye, choosing instead to specularize it in its very unmanning:

> As Ned Beaumont's arm came down the bulldog, leaping clumsily, came up to meet it. His jaws shut over Ned Beaumont's wrist. Ned Beaumont was spun to the left by the impact and he sank down on one knee with his arm close to the floor to take the dog's weight off his arm. . . .
>
> Ned Beaumont stood up. His face was pallid and damp with sweat. He looked at his torn coat-sleeve and at the blood running down his hand. His hand was trembling. . . .
>
> O'Rory stepped back and said: "Work on him."
>
> While Rusty hesitated, the apish Jeff knocked aside Ned Beaumont's upraised hand and pushed him down on the bed. "I got something to try." He scooped up Ned Beaumont's legs and tumbled them on the bed. He leaned over Ned Beaumont, his hands busy on Ned Beaumont's body.
>
> Ned Beaumont's body and arms and legs jerked convulsively and three times he groaned. . . .
>
> (86-90)

As in Chandler, this is a body that can make its way into discourse only at the price of pulverization, disintegration, and eroticized violation. The difference is that *The Glass Key* enthusiastically *embraces* that risk, making Ned Beaumont scopically available on nearly every page and subjecting him to the eroticized violation attendant upon that somatic insistence. The point is not that Marlowe never gets beat up while Beaumont does; a certain amount of bodily pain goes with the territory, and both detectives in some sense "know" it. It is just that, where the physical workovers Marlowe receives consistently give way to a more or less immediate and

complete resumption of masculine-sadistic power, *The Glass Key* prefers to defer that resumption interminably, to keep its dick on the brink of existential obliteration.

Thus, in *Farewell, My Lovely,* when the racketeers imprison Marlowe after drugging and beating him, he screams "fire" to lure his jailer and then beats him to make his escape (172-73). But when Ned Beaumont finds himself in much the same position, he tries at first to slit his throat, then *builds* a fire that almost kills him, and lastly, in the ensuing confusion, jumps in darkness from a high window that lands him in a hospital bed (91-93). Marlowe's physical escape results from an imaginary fire and is at the same time an escape *from* the physical; to vanquish both his opponents and his circumstances, he ascends to a realm of imaginative cunning that marks the re-erasure of his body from the page and the assertion, once again, of a relatively unencumbered and masculine consciousness. For Ned Beaumont the case is quite the contrary. Not only does the eye of the third-person style keep him before us as an objectified and superficial plaything whose very capacity for sadistic volition remains quite radically in question (is the fire he builds really a diversionary tactic or is it just another suicide attempt?), but the fact of his literal ignition also points to a disturbing will toward the annihilation of consciousness, a desire to become just the opposite of the Chandlerian dick: "pure" and "unsullied" *material,* a corpse displayed, with no hope of transcendence for the delectation of his antagonists' sadistic and scopic pleasure. Ned's is a body that exists to be seen and beaten, seen *to be* beaten. It is a body that is "feminized" precisely inasmuch as specularity and masochism are assigned by our culture and by the male psyche to the realm of an abhorred femininity, despite the fact that, as I have argued, they may perhaps be constitutive elements of human subjectivity itself. The fullest measure of *The Glass Key*'s subversion resides in its confronting us with just this fact. When, accordingly, Ned later encounters again "the apish Jeff," the latter no sooner lays eyes on him than he exclaims: "Well, blind Christ, if it ain't Sock-me-again Beaumont!" (185). Ned—as Jeff knows—"likes it" (88, 124). And of course, the novel demands that we like it too by coercing us into identifying with a man who identifies with the mother in the image of a corpse. Far from serving primarily as a masculine agent for the enjoyment of narrative resolutions and closures, Ned Beaumont opens up the text only to summon us to drown in it, returning us again and again, through his interminably desired undoings, to a primal and non-progressive moment of blissfully "feminine" self-destruction that staves off the narrative's ending for as long as bearable, just as the novel's incantatory repetition of his full name (Ned Beaumont, Ned Beaumont, Ned Beaumont) serves as a kind of dadaesque fixation, a retardation and erosion of developmental kernels. "Formally speaking," Deleuze writes, "masochism is a state of waiting; the masochist experiences waiting in its pure form. . . . [He] waits for pleasure as something that is bound to be late, and expects pain as the condition that will finally ensure (both physically and morally) the advent of pleasure" (*Coldness* 71). Is this not a precise phenomenological reformulation of Kermode's "waiting time," as well as of the reading experience I have been describing? Does not the narrative pleasure of **The Glass Key** come "too late," and always at the cost of an intensely expected and wished-for pain? But should we not also add, what even Deleuze seems unwilling to say,[13] that there inheres a pleasure of an exquisitely different order in thus being conned into an interminable waiting, in being brought back over and again to the transfixing nightmare of a primal and dephallicizing self-abrogation?[14]

Notes

1. The argument for the hard-boiled genre's relative lack of interest in narrative pleasure is implicit in the taxonomic descriptions of Cawelti (142) and Symons (137). See also, more recently and explicitly, Polan (324).

2. As I hope will become clear, hard-boiled fiction cannot do without the figure of the detective, for reasons having intimately to do with the erotics and libidinal politics of its form. Consequently, that fiction is to be distinguished quite rigorously from the crime novel of (say) James Cain, Patricia Highsmith, and Jim Thompson, where structurally speaking the dick is dispensable and is in practice often dispensed with.

3. My arguments concerning masochistic sexuality owe a general debt to Jean Laplanche's *Life and Death in Psychoanalysis* and, especially, Leo Bersani's *The Freudian Body*. "Sexuality," Bersani writes, is "that which is intolerable to the structured self" (38). Or, again, on the next page: "sexuality . . . could be thought of as a tautology for masochism." The relevance of such claims to my own hypotheses should by now be clear, and the remainder of this essay could even be thought as a meditation upon this "tautology" in a specifically hard-boiled context.

4. See especially Symons 124. The best discussions of hard-boiled style are in Miller, Jameson, Žižek, and Naremore.

5. My formulations in this paragraph owe a general debt to Deleuze and Guattari's book.

6. The reference here is to Lacan's discussion of the anamorphotic skull in Hans Holbein's *The Ambassadors,* lecture 7 of *Concepts* 79-90. Cf. also Žižek 90-91, 96.

7. Žižek is thus in my view mistaken when he argues that Hammett is the eccentric figure in the hard-boiled tradition who, because he wrote most of his novels in the third person, requires special treatment (62). On the contrary, and as I go on to suggest, it's precisely Hammett's third-person technique that enables his novels to speak the unconscious truth of that tradition and that consequently places him at its "center."

8. "It is impossible to suppose that these observations of coitus are of universal occurrence, so that at this point we are faced with the problem of 'primal phantasies'" ("Psychological Consequences" 186). See also "Infantile" 236.

9. Cf. "Psychological Consequences" 186: the primal "event" "may . . . act as the starting point for the child's whole sexual development."

10. Of Hammett's five completed novels, only *The Maltese Falcon* relies upon a full-blown, blame-it-on-Mame *femme fatale.*

11. For reasons of space I have limited my discussion here to *The Glass Key,* but one could equally argue that a similar repudiation of normative masculinity takes place in Hammett's *The Maltese Falcon,* despite the appearance of a more recognizably "phallic" representation.

12. "In the end there were to be found in [the Wolf Man] two contrary currents side by side, of which one abominated the idea of castration, *while the other was prepared to accept it and console itself with femininity as a compensation*" ("Infantile" 275; my emphasis).

13. "In sadism and masochism there is no mysterious link between pain and pleasure. . . . In sadism no less than in masochism, there is no direct relation to pain: pain should be regarded as an *effect* only" (*Coldness* 120-21).

14. For reasons of space, I have cut here a final section that details the passive yet virile form of masochism theorized by *The Glass Key,* and that links that paradoxical form to the political need not to succumb *completely* to the will of the phallic sadist.

Works Cited

Bataille, Georges. *Erotism: Death and Sensuality.* Trans. Mary Dalwood. San Francisco: City Lights Books, 1986.

Bersani, Leo. *The Freudian Body: Psychoanalysis and Art.* New York: Columbia UP, 1986.

Cawelti, John G. *Adventure, Mystery, and Romance: Formula Stories as Art and Popular Culture.* Chicago: U of Chicago P, 1976.

Chandler, Raymond. *Farewell, My Lovely.* 1940. New York: Vintage, 1976.

————. *The High Window.* 1943. New York: Vintage, 1976.

————. *Playback.* 1958. New York: Ballantine, 1977.

Deleuze, Gilles. *Coldness and Cruelty.* Trans. Jean McNeil. *Masochism.* New York: Zone, 1991.

Deleuze, Gilles, and Félix Guattari. *Kafka: Toward a Minor Literature.* Trans. Dana Polan. Minneapolis: U of Minnesota P, 1986.

Freud, Sigmund. *Beyond the Pleasure Principle.* 1920. Trans. James Strachey. New York: Norton, 1961.

————. "From the History of an Infantile Neurosis." 1918. *Three Case Histories.* Ed. Philip Rieff. New York: Collier, 1963. 187-316.

————. "Some Psychological Consequences of the Anatomical Distinction Between the Sexes." 1925. *Sexuality and the Psychology of Love.* Ed. Philip Rieff. New York: Collier, 1963. 183-93.

Hammett, Dashiell. *The Glass Key.* 1931. New York: Vintage, 1989.

Jameson, Fredric. "On Raymond Chandler." *Poetics of Murder: Detective Fiction and Literary Theory.* Ed. Glenn W. Most and William W. Stowe. New York: Harcourt, 1983. 123-48.

Kermode, Frank. *The Sense of an Ending.* New York: Oxford UP, 1967.

Lacan, Jacques. *The Four Fundamental Concepts of Psychoanalysis.* Ed. Jacques-Alain Miller. Trans. Alan Sheridan. New York: Norton, 1981.

Laplanche, Jean. *Life and Death in Psychoanalysis.* Trans. Jeffrey Mehlman. Baltimore: Johns Hopkins UP, 1976.

Miller, D. A. "Language of Detective Fiction, Fiction of Detective Language." *The State of the Language.* Ed. Christopher Ricks and Leonard Michaels. Berkeley: U of California P, 1990. 478-85.

Naremore, James. "Dashiell Hammett and the Poetics of Hard-Boiled Detection." *Essays on Detective Fiction.* Ed. Bernard Benstock. London: MacMillan, 1983. 49-72.

Penderson-Krag, Geraldine. "Detective Stories and the Primal Scene." *Dimensions of Detective Fiction.* Ed. Larry N. Landrum, Pat Browne, and Ray R. Browne. Bowling Green: Popular, 1976. 58-63.

Polan, Dana. *Power and Paranoia: History, Narrative, and the American Cinema, 1940-50.* New York: Columbia UP, 1986.

Priestman, Martin. *Detective Fiction and Literature.* New York: St. Martin's, 1991.

Reik, Theodor. *Masochism in Modern Man.* Trans. Margaret H. Beigel and Gertrud M. Kurth. New York: Grove, 1941.

Silverman, Kaja. *Male Subjectivity at the Margins.* New York: Routledge, 1992.

Stein, Gertrude. *Everybody's Autobiography.* New York: Vintage, 1973.

Symons, Julian. *Bloody Murder: From the Detective Story to the Crime Novel: A History.* New York: Viking, 1985.

Žižek, Slavoj. *Looking Awry: An Introduction to Jacques Lacan through Popular Culture.* Cambridge: MIT P, 1991.

Mark McGurl (essay date winter 1997)

SOURCE: McGurl, Mark. "Making 'Literature' of It: Hammett and High Culture." *American Literary History* 9, no. 4 (winter 1997): 702-17.

[*In the following essay, McGurl outlines the divide between "highbrow" and "lowbrow" culture and places Hammett's fiction between the two, asserting that "his work shows us both what modernism looks like to mass culture and what mass culture looks like to modernism."*]

> What is the thing in itself? We shall not reach the thing in itself until our thinking has first reached the thing as a thing.
>
> Martin Heidegger, "The Thing"

> The thing in itself folded itself up inside itself like you might fold a thing up to be another thing which is that thing inside in that thing.
>
> Gertrude Stein, "Portraits and Repetition"

> Then you think the dingus is worth two million?
>
> Sam Spade, *The Maltese Falcon*

1. COMMERCE AND THEOLOGY

It is often argued that culture in the late nineteenth and early twentieth centuries begins to be dispersed to either side of a "Great Divide" between modernism and mass culture, high culture and low, and though there are many different accounts of the form and function of the objects divided in this way, the values they embody or pursue are normally assumed to be strictly opposed. For Andreas Huyssen, most prominently, "modernism constituted itself through a conscious strategy of exclusion" of mass culture, to which it showed "obsessive hostility" (vii; see also Jameson 207). Lawrence Levine, similarly, speaking to the specifically American context, describes how in the late nineteenth century an elite "highbrow" culture, reacting to the shock of mass immigration, began to define itself in opposition to the "lowbrow" culture of the unruly multitude. What had been a "rich shared public culture" (9) was replaced, he argues, by a view of culture that increasingly excluded any commerce between the sacred art of the elite and the profane entertainments of the mass.

Certain period accounts of the conditions of culture, however, complicate these later accounts even as they, to a degree, confirm them. Take, for instance, Van Wyck Brooks's 1915 discussion on "'highbrow' and 'lowbrow'" (1-19), in which the analysis of this peculiarly American form of the high/low opposition makes its first sustained appearance. Brooks argues that the cultural divide these terms signify, far from a recent occurrence, has been a feature of American life since its very beginnings. Unable to merge the "steep, icy and pinnacled" (6) theology of Jonathan Edwards with the civic commercialism of Benjamin Franklin, "[h]uman nature itself in America" has ever since existed "on two irreconcilable planes, the plane of stark intellectuality and the plane of stark business" (15). For Brooks the distinction between high and low is not tied, as in Levine's account, to specific social groups. It is a division within the "American mind" as a whole, and it is a problem because it has left the task of government entirely, if covertly, in the hands of commerce. Writing 12 years later, T. S. Eliot claimed, as recent critics do, that the divergence of high and low narrative forms occurred in the early twentieth century, the result of a "dissociation of the elements of the old three-volume melodramatic novel into the various types of the modern 300-page novel." But, as Eliot's use of the term "dissociation" makes clear, the "distinction of *genre* between such-and-such a profound 'psychological' novel of today and such-and-such a masterly 'detective' novel of today" (409; see also Chinitz) is not a promising sign of the seriousness of the post-Jamesian novelist but lamentable evidence of cultural ill health.

Though the interpretive models of Huyssen or Levine might succeed in absorbing this anomaly, what remains surprising about earlier accounts of the Great Divide, from our perspective, is their effort to locate this cultural division outside the discourse of modernism itself. For Brooks and Eliot, at least, the production of a Great Divide is not an aspiration but an inheritance, a sort of curse. While in retrospect this distinction may appear a suspiciously modest denial of modernism's responsibility for, and interest in, producing cultural division, it might profit us to linger briefly on this aspect of its self-understanding. This will allow us to recover an important moment in the dialectic of early-twentieth-century modernism that has, since the consolidation and self-promotion of postmodernism as a discourse of recovery from modernist elitism, received little attention; it will also allow us to draw renewed attention to the

intimacy between modernism's preoccupation with literary form—in particular with the text's status as a thing, or object—and the "materialistic" mass culture it purportedly rejected.[1] The following pages read an important strand of American modernism not as aspiring to *produce* a Great Divide between high and low—that is, to distance itself from mass culture—but as *responding* to a divide that seemed to have a vestigially religious significance.

This response to a divide between high and low, between theology and civic commercialism, simultaneously intensifies the text's claims to both "materiality" and "spirituality," as though the two might thus be made to signify the same thing. A model for this approach can be found in Edgar Allan Poe's detective fiction. Poe was deeply embedded in the mass culture of the mid nineteenth century; however, it is not an accident, I think, that he became the guiding spirit of French Symbolism, whose apparent hostility to unholy mass culture is so striking (see Jonathan Elmer's *Reading at the Social Limit: Affect, Mass Culture, and Edgar Allan Poe* [1995]). Though the detective story serves for Eliot as an emblem of the contemporary low genre, it has functioned under this guise as a privileged site in modern culture for the negotiation of the high and low, especially when these terms mark an opposition between theology and civic practicality, as they do for Brooks. To the degree that the detective genre is defined by its engagement with *policing,* it partakes of the larger discursive project of realist narrative of making individuals accountable to social norms and to the law, as D. A. Miller has shown in *The Novel and the Police* (1988). One might however balance this view with that of Gertrude Stein, who in the essay "What Are Master-Pieces and Why Are There So Few of Them" (1936) speaks of the asocial masterpiece and the detective story in virtually the same breath:

> In real life people are interested in the crime more than they are in detection . . . but in the story it is the detection that holds the interest, . . . it is another function that has very little to do with human nature that makes the detection interesting. And so always it is true that the master-piece has nothing to do with human nature or with identity, it has to do . . . with a thing in itself and not in relation. The moment it is in relation it is common knowledge and anybody can feel and know it and it is not a master-piece.
>
> (149)

This version of the detective story, which turns the genre inward, instead of to the outward production of "common knowledge," runs directly counter to policing, or what Stein calls "governing," which "has completely to do with identity but has nothing to do with master-pieces" (153). For Stein the philosophical purity of detective fiction serves "God," not "Mammon." Indeed, her account can be seen to link detective fiction to the long tradition of the Christian mystery, which addresses the unbridgeable distance of God from "human nature." The detective story genre thus could be said to inhabit the very breach between the high and low, the theological and the practical described by Brooks. If for Brooks the problem with "poetry" in his divided nation is that it is "hidden away, too inaccessible, too intangible, too unreal in fact ever to be brought into the open" (15), Poe's purloined letter responds rather precisely to this problem of intangibility and invisibility. Turned inside out and hidden in plain view, Poe's letter admits, indeed asserts, its presence as a physical object in social space. At the same time, it suggests that a text's higher truth is not available on its surface as empirical, or "common," knowledge. In this way, Poe's text offers a model of the social relations of a certain kind of modernist text. Advertising both its physical availability and its spiritual difficulty, this text seeks to serve "God and Mammon" at once.

This search, however, does not necessarily succeed, as we shall see in Dashiell Hammett's *The Maltese Falcon* (1930), which recalls "The Purloined Letter" (1845)—as well as subsequent "crime novels" such as Nathaniel Hawthorne's *The Scarlet Letter* (1850), Wilkie Collins's *The Moonstone* (1868), and Henry James's *The Golden Bowl* (1904)—in proposing a characteristically symbolist analogy between an object in the novel and the object that is the novel itself.[2] This recursive gesture, which enfolds a version of the text in the social world it imagines, enables the text's interrogation of its own social function. As a result, Hammett ultimately recognizes his failure to merge the high and low, and this sense of failure is, as we shall see, important.[3] But Hammett's deep involvement with these problems is confirmed not only by the ambiguous nature of his chosen genre but also by his peculiar status with respect to early-twentieth-century literary institutions, whose complexity has not, I think, been adequately addressed. For while Hammett's career begins in the pulp serials, most notably in *Black Mask,* it takes him rather quickly into the literary institutions of the "smart set," where his work functions not so much to exemplify the low as to represent and interrogate the mechanisms of distinction that generate this abject category in the first place. Admired by such as André Gide, André Malraux, and Stein, Hammett's fiction echoes the more obviously elite modernism whose central texts he appreciated and discussed even as he continued to sell his work to the pulp audience. His work shows us both what modernism looks like to mass culture and what mass culture looks like to modernism, without canceling the relative autonomy of these two discourses.

Hammett's own sense of the complexity of his position and his frank aspiration to produce high art emerges in a letter he wrote to Blanche Knopf upon being taken up by this highly respected publisher in 1928, after six years of publishing in the pulps: "I'm one of the few . . . people moderately literate who take the detective story seriously. I don't mean that I necessarily take my own or anybody else's seriously—but the detective story as a form. Some day some body's going to make 'literature' of it, . . . and I'm selfish enough to have my hopes, however slight the evident justification may be" (qtd. in Johnson 72). To be published by Knopf was for Hammett a badge of distinction, a sign that his work had somewhat departed the grubby milieu of the serials where his sleuth, as he once put it, had "degenerated into a meal-ticket" (qtd. in Johnson 53). Here the fragments he published in pulp would be bound together and presented whole by a publisher as famous for the beauty and high production values of its books as for its importation of serious European modernism into America.[4] Hammett would now rub shoulders with the likes of André Gide, whose novel *Les Faux-Monnayeurs* (1925) Knopf had published in 1927 as *The Counterfeiters.* For his part Gide would claim, to Hammett's satisfaction, that the greatest American writers of the time were William Faulkner and Hammett (Johnson 12).

Hammett's statement of high purpose to Blanche Knopf, however, suggests the inadequacy of the idea either that Hammett's work unambiguously partakes of "literature" or that, in the manner of our recent postmodernist populism, Hammett simply saw through the insidious Great Divide. The distinction between high and low retains an obvious force, where the relation of Hammett's actual work to an ideal "form" of the detective story is managed in the affective register of "seriousness." My contention here, pressing this idea further, will be that the problem of Hammett's ambiguous place in early-twentieth-century cultural hierarchies, which he hoped to overcome by taking his genre seriously, paradoxically reveals itself in his habitual lack of seriousness with respect to the ontological status of his own representations. In this he echoes the critique of stable, or popular, symbolism by the rigorously hermetic Symbolists, and by their self-conscious heirs such as Eliot.

Hammett's problem with representation becomes explicit at the very end of his career. In the penultimate paragraph of the unfinished novel *Tulip* (1952), the Hammett-like narrator looks back to the time when he was still a productive professional writer and observes that "representations seemed to me—at least they seem now, and I suppose I must have had some inkling of the same opinion then—devices of the old and tired, or older and more tired, to ease up, like conscious symbolism, or graven images. If you are tired you ought to rest, I think, and not try to fool yourself or your customers with colored bubbles" (347). Thus Hammett attributes the sudden collapse of his productivity after *The Thin Man* (1934) to a fundamental, indeed theological, disappointment with his craft. He is disappointed with its inability to transcend the fallen forms of representation—its failure simply to *be* rather than *mean*. This critique of representation takes the form of a kind of ritual murder in the early novels, where what are murdered are not so much persons as representations of persons. The murder of these representations expresses, for one thing, a deep uneasiness with what most saw as the popular novel's fundamental appeal. In her critique of the debased "bestseller," *Fiction and the Reading Public* (1932), Q. D. Leavis disdains the naive mass reader precisely for his "confusion of fiction with life" (60), and for his "co-operat[ing] to persuade himself that he is in contact with 'real people'" who might be his friends (59).[5]

Hammett's "murder" of his own representations enables him to negotiate the relation of high to low, at once distancing himself from his popular work and figuring an image of "literature" and its "timeless" spiritual value as its unrealized aspiration. Through Hammett's *The Dain Curse* (1929), I will show the operation of this ritual murder, a project perhaps most fully realized in *The Maltese Falcon*. In the context of *The Dain Curse*, we can see that the grail-like statuette revealed at the end of Hammett's third novel to be an enameled fake—that is, a species of "colored bubble" or counterfeit coin—is a figure for the failed aspiration to the status of "literature," or, more precisely, for the unity of matter and spirit, of commerce and theology, that "literature" had come for Hammett to represent.

2. MURDERING REPRESENTATION

Hammett liked the word *dingus*. In his writings of the period from 1924 to 1952, "dingus" signifies, variously, a magician's prop, a typewriter, a short story, a novel, and an elusive artifact—the black bird better known as the Maltese Falcon. It also signifies a funny-looking portable seat used by hunters; though this usage of *dingus,* unlike the others, has nothing directly to do with writing, perhaps it emphasizes, by associating those that do with portable chairs, how curious Hammett thought the things of writing to be.

For "thing" is what *dingus,* related by way of Dutch to the German *Ding,* more or less means. Like *whatchamacallit, thingamajig, gizmo,* and *doodad, dingus* acts as a linguistic placeholder, a way of noting the thingly quality of some thing whose adequate designation is unknown, avoided, or caught on the tip of the tongue. At the same time, saying "dingus" rather than simply "thing" makes fun of the process of naming, feigns catching it mid-stride, before thing and noun are fused: once upon a time, "dingus" seems to say, words like pot-holder or parrot or plasma, or pen or pencil or paper, may have sounded equally awkward. Like *gizmo,* however, *dingus* calls attention as much to the peculiarity of the thing not named as to the speaker's inability

to name it. *Dingus* is not merely a place-holder or parody of naming, but the beginnings of a bemused or a mildly contemptuous specification.

For instance when Hammett, in correspondence with his editor at Knopf, said of his recently revised novel *The Dain Curse* "the dingus is still undoubtedly rather complicated" (qtd. in Layman 103), he no doubt had the words *novel* and *book* at his command. By recourse to the phallic diminutive "dingus," he diffidently deprived the thing he had just revised of a small portion of its dignity. But what for Hammett makes a short story or novel or black falcon a dingus? These literary dinguses share a proximity, for Hammett, to the problem of conceiving the artifact he produces as *one* thing at all. In other words, dingus *is* complication, in the root sense of *thing* as the product of combination or of a "folding together." Insofar as an artifact is seen as a plurality, it becomes difficult for Hammett to think of it as a thing after all, for he will trouble the movement—*e pluribus unum*—in which what is conceivable as a number of things is also conceivable as one thing. Calling his literary artifact a "dingus," then, at once draws attention to and questions the artifact's status as an individual thing.

Take, for instance, *The Dain Curse.* It had originally been published serially in four issues of *Black Mask* and, according to Knopf editor Harry Block, still fell "too definitely into three sections" as a novel (qtd. in Johnson 74). These three sections no doubt endure as the three "Parts" of the published book—the first two corresponding more or less to the first two magazine segments, the last being a combination of the last two magazine segments. Still bearing the traces of its serial origins, it needed, Block thought, a "connecting thread" (qtd. in Johnson 74).

Block's aspirations for *The Dain Curse* are familiar enough: a demand for unity in any artistic project has been one of the more common demands of prescriptive aesthetics. In the case of *The Dain Curse,* however, the editor's prescription of unity is thematized in the central question driving the novel, namely, whether the "theory that there [is] some connecting link" (39) in a number of murders—note the similarity between "connecting link" and Block's "connecting thread"—will hold up to scrutiny. Hammett's unnamed detective the Continental Op, who has "stopped believing in accidents" (138), thinks it will, and the question then becomes what "connecting link" he will uncover. The "Dain curse" is adduced by several characters to explain as supernatural the common source of a number of murders that occur in the vicinity of Gabrielle Leggett, whose mother was a Dain. The Continental Op sets himself the task of finding a more "tangible, logical and jailable answer than any curse" (188), namely, a human being, one body and "one mind" with a "system that he likes, and sticks to" (169).

This "one mind," as it turns out, belongs to Hugh Fitzstephen, a novelist who looks conspicuously like Hammett did. Such coy self-reflexivity suggests a familiar analogy between the author who presides over his created world, endowing it with coherent intention, and the will of God Himself. That the answer to the question Whodunit? in *The Dain Curse* is the author does, however, reinforce the notion that the novel interrogates the possibility of its own unity. Form and theme converge in *The Dain Curse,* since the potential unity the novel ponders is conspicuously its own. Its possibility hinges on the ability to map to a single person the novel's discrete parts—conceivable now either formally as "sections" of the book or thematically as its numerous murders. Appropriately enough, this person is both a murderer and a novelist. When at the end of part I the Op says "we [at the Agency] wrote *Discontinued* at the bottom of the Leggett record" (66), the question of continuity that would bother Block is inscribed, indeed italicized, in the pages of the novel itself. When a few sentences later the Op is told that "the Leggett matter is active again" (67) because someone else has been murdered, this announces at once the continuation of the Leggett record, the continuation of the novel *The Dain Curse,* and the renewed search for the single person who forces both of these narratives onward.

But can either the Op, or the text itself, find this single person? A conversation between the Op and the novelist Fitzstephen—the former concerned with realities, the latter with representations—suggests that discovering this unity will be difficult:

> "Are you—who [as a detective] make your living snooping—sneering at my curiosity about people and my attempts to satisfy it?"
>
> "We're different," I said. "I do mine with the object of putting people in jail, and I get paid for it, though not as much as I should."
>
> "That's not different," he said. "I do mine with the object of putting people in books, and I get paid for it, though not as much as I should."
>
> "Yeah, but what good does that do?"
>
> "God knows. What good does putting them in jail do?"
>
> "Relieves congestion," I said. "Put enough people in jail and cities wouldn't have traffic problems."
>
> (22)

For all the apparent similarities between the "snooping" detective and the "curious" novelist, then, "putting people in books" only makes flesh into representations which, as the Op would say, are not "jailable." So even if the Op succeeds in jailing the single body responsible for the murders, the novel itself only ambiguously succeeds in locating the individual author/murderer that will guarantee its own unity.

The convergence of the formal and the thematic in *The Dain Curse* is held, that is, in a state of incompletion. Fitzstephen may be the origin of the murders in the book, but as he tells the Op, in court the "number of my crimes will be to my advantage, on the theory that nobody but a lunatic could have committed so many. And won't they be many? I'll produce crimes and crimes, dating from the cradle" (220). The Op (to Fitzstephen's dismay) does in fact think the novelist is a lunatic. The sheer number of the novelist's crimes makes the category of intentionality useless for the Op, and the body that is sent to the prison-psychiatric hospital will not have the status of a responsible, intending subject. The (moral) unconsciousness implied by Fitzstephen's insanity, then, mirrors his necessary unconsciousness of the formal problems in the novel of which he is a part. Only a representation of an author, he may not be held responsible for resolving its formal pluralities.

Beyond the Op's grasp, the real author is present in the world of the novel only as phantom, something like the "writhing"—or is that "writing"?—"indescribable thing" who appears to the Op in a chapter entitled, pointedly enough, "God." This chapter tells of the Op's adventures in the temple of the "Holy Grail Cult" run by the novelist Fitzstephen:

> Not more than three feet away, there in the black room, a pale bright thing like a body, but not like flesh, stood writhing before me. . . . Its feet—it had feet, but I don't know what their shape was. They had no shape, just as the thing's legs and torso, arms and hands, head and face, had no shape, no fixed form. They writhed, swelling and contracting, stretching and shrinking. . . . The legs were now one leg like a twisting pedestal, and then three, and then two. No feature or member ever stopped twisting, quivering, writhing long enough for its average outline, its proper shape, to be seen. The thing was a thing like a man who floated above the floor. . . .
>
> (92-93)

Whether this figure signifies the author-god, evident in the novel in the form of the shifting effects of his cause, or the unreality of fictional character as such (What are these beings in books but a kind of ghost?), or the disunity of the novel itself—the dingus, as Hammett would put it—is still undoubtedly rather complicated. In the more practical terms of editors and authors, the unresolved problem of the unity of the novel reveals itself in Hammett's criticism, upon receiving last galley proofs, of Block's editorial efforts: "I had my hands full . . . trying to make it look like all the work of the same writer" (qtd. in Johnson 77).

What is fascinating about this problem, the problem of multiplicity, is how faithfully it is mirrored in the criticism surrounding Hammett's first two novels. Widespread opinion held that they were, like the writhing ghost itself, almost too chaotic to comprehend. And what is curious about these judgments is the ambiguity they evince with respect to the source of the chaos. About Hammett's first novel, **Red Harvest** (1929), for instance, there was considerable uncertainty as to whether this chaos resulted from its excessive number of murders or its excessive number of characters. **Red Harvest** was at first to be called "Poisonville," a pun on the name of the crowded city of Personville and suggestive at the same time of a novel problematically inhabited by many characters. So, too, Donald Willsson, the captain of industry who "was Personville," who "owned Personville heart, soul, skin and guts" (8), is a single person inhabited by many. The task of the Op will be, in a sense, to cure this individual of the poisonous social occupation of his identity.[6] One reviewer, who seems to be bothered more by the novel's number of murders than by its "crowd of characters," is canny enough to see the necessarily intimate or economic relation of the two: "There has been in detective stories a decided increase in the number of murders deemed necessary to complete the story. Such an appetite will certainly be glutted in **Red Harvest.** It is crowded with characters—it had to be to supply material for the murders—the action moves dizzily and when it is all over, the reader wonders just what it was all about" (Layman 97). Only numerous characters can "supply material" for numerous murders. Since they are necessarily coincident, it is often unclear which of the two is really at issue. Immediately after complaining that **The Dain Curse** falls "too definitely into three sections," Block, like this dizzied critic, complains about the "violence" that "is piled on a bit thick" and about its "immense number of characters, which is so great as to create confusion" (qtd. in Johnson 74). Blanche Knopf finds about **Red Harvest** that "so many killings on a page . . . make the reader doubt the story, and instead of the continued suspense and feeling of horror, the interest slackens" (qtd. in Johnson 70). Knopf, however, only repeats the Op's observation *within* the novel of an excess of killing: "[T]here's been what? A dozen and a half murders since I've been here. Donald Willsson; Ike Bush; the four wops at Cedar Hill . . . [etc.]. That's sixteen of them in less than a week, and more coming up . . ." (154). Hammett himself, roughly when he was assuring Blanche Knopf that removing a few murders from **Red Harvest** would "relieve the congestion" of killing, was making the Continental Op in **The Dain Curse** claim with the same phrasing that the value of his profession is to "relieve [the] congestion" of persons in cities.

What are we to make of this odd convergence of bothersome pluralities? I am suggesting here that Hammett's problem with many-ness is a symptom of his uneasiness with his place as an author in a commercial culture Henry James had characterized by its "multiplication, multiplication of everything . . . multiplication with a vengeance" (qtd. in Levine 171). He must serve, as an author of popular fiction, the multitude, a reversal of authority Hammett, typical of his time, found disturbing. For Stein, for example, the very idea of a social relation between writer and audience, which forces the writer to hear not him- or herself but "what the audience hears one say" (147), disables her pursuit of the lofty thing-in-itself. This notion can put a surprising spin on the question of Hammett's style. Indeed, rejecting the notion that the famed Hemingwayesque sparseness of his prose represents the language of the common "man on the street," Hammett once averred that the language of the street is in fact "not only excessively complicated and repetitious, but almost purposeless in its lack of coherence," while "[s]implicity and clarity . . . are the most elusive and difficult of literary accomplishments" (qtd. in Johnson 54-55; see also Marling 116-18). Hammett suggests here that he intended the sparseness of his prose to resist the incoherence of the man on the street for whom he nonetheless wrote. Similarly, producing many characters represents the many, while murdering them symbolically resists the imposition of a social relation between writer and audience. In this construction the purer realm of "literature" is not so much realized in the work as produced as the work's timeless negative image, an uninhabited, asocial space.

I believe we should read the pursuit of the graillike statuette in **The Maltese Falcon,** an object centuries old but now lost, in this context. For the falcon's very pricelessness suggests that its value, if realized, would transcend the logic of exchange. When Sam Spade asks Gutman what the "maximum" value of the "dingus" might be, Gutman refuses "to guess": "You'd think me crazy. I don't know. There's no telling how high it could go, sir, and that's the one and only truth about it" (130). It is probably no accident that the novel that produces an image of "timeless" value is precisely the novel of Hammett's upon which literary history begins, though tentatively, to confer the status of "literature." **The Maltese Falcon** has relatively few characters, and its small number of murders all occur offstage, so to speak. Its formal unity, as one biographer puts it, "[makes] no concession to magazine publication" (Layman 107) and, like that of the grail itself, resists periodicity as such, or "timely" social history.[7] **The Maltese Falcon** as novel aspires to the absolute value, or unity, of the Maltese Falcon as object.[8]

But, notoriously, the object actually acquired in the novel turns out to be a fake, not the real thing. And this suggests, first, that the falcon remains merely a commodity, trapped in the logic of commodity fetishism as described by Marx. In this familiar account the commodity provokes, but never truly satisfies, a desire for the existential plenitude it represents. Thus Spade says to Gutman, demanding payment for his services even though the falcon has turned out to be fake: "You got your dingus. It's your hard luck, not mine, that it wasn't what you wanted" (203). This counterfeit continues Hammett's distinction between the "colored bubbles" he produces in his fiction and the transcendental thing to which he aspires, and which no accumulation of riches won by his writing can buy for him.[9] The sarcasm Hammett heaps upon the novelist Fitzstephen's Holy Grail Cult in *The Dain Curse* could in this context be read as a measure of his sense that the time of a legitimate theological culture has passed and that the obvious religious preoccupations of his own work as a novelist can only unfold in the similarly debased form of the dingus.[10]

Predictably, then, *The Maltese Falcon,* a study in narrative economy, ultimately collapses back into the multiplicity so evident in the earlier novels. When the treacherous Brigid O'Shaughnessy begs Sam Spade to admit that he loves her, he does so, but only to state the impotence of his love in the face of the sheer multiplicity of practical reasons she should be hanged, which Spade proceeds to list. His seventh reason is a question of odds, since he does not "even like the idea of thinking that there might be one chance in a hundred that" he is being "played . . . for a sucker." His last reason is the "eighth—but that's enough. . . . Maybe some of them are important. I won't argue about that. But look at the number of them" (214).

This confession of failure to find the One is precisely what in retrospect will make Hammett appear so much the shadow modernist, the producer of "literature." Indeed, even as for Hammett access to high-culture institutions meant the unification of his serial fragments in the form of the beautiful Knopf book, for T. S. Eliot the hermetic "heap of broken images" (38) of "The Waste Land" (1922) had become the proper form of modern poetry. In the context of elite modernism, that is, something like the chaos of Hammett's first two novels, so bothersome to his editors and critics, will be revalued as a sign of modernism's critique of romantic unities and traditional forms. Without denying the obvious differences between the two texts, then, we can see the degree to which protocols of reading determine what is normally asserted to be a quality inherent in the object itself. In Eliot's case the high-culture reader could be asked to supply, as an erudite hermeneut, the spectral unity of "The Waste Land"'s fragments. The comparatively "low" Hammett, speaking to the many, was required to make sense.

Inspired, he tells us, by his reading of Jessie Weston's analysis in *From Ritual to Romance* of the grail legend, which Weston argues had its origins in ancient rites surrounding the harvest, Eliot figures London life in "The Waste Land" as a bleak urban desert, deprived of spiritual nourishment. In the Unreal City of his poem, "A crowd flowed over the London Bridge, so many, / I had not thought death had undone so many" (39)—an image that in a sense looks forward to the carnage, the "red harvest," of the many characters of Personville. And while Hammett declined to pursue the project of Christian cultural renewal that Eliot would take up in later years, Lillian Hellman gives evidence that Hammett was reading "The Waste Land" around the time he wrote *The Maltese Falcon* (we know as well that Eliot was a fan of "low" detective fiction). Both works make conspicuous use of the "timeless" value of the Holy Grail as a measure of the inauthenticity of the merely "representational" culture in which they are produced and which in turn produces them, not as single artifacts able to do work of God and Mammon at once but as two seemingly different kinds of object.[11]

In later years, it is true, Eliot became less concerned to champion the necessary pleasures of the popular, as he had in the essay "Wilkie Collins and Dickens"—less concerned to figure the dissociation of the high and low as the unfortunate rupture of a single thing. Increasingly, he became the impassioned spokesman for elite culture that he is now remembered to have been. The cultural-hierarchical complexities his later career presents are worth pondering, however, since even as he began to speak in the unambiguous accents of privilege he was raised to the status of popular modernist icon, departing the rarefied milieu of the little magazines to appear, in 1950, on the cover of *Time.* "No one thinks of me as a poet any more," Eliot would lament, "but as a celebrity" (qtd. in Gordon 192). This irony is in many ways reciprocal to that in the career of the low modernist Hammett, the self-appointed beacon of "literature" flashing from the mire of the social mass. Perhaps we could say, then, that in the convergence of Eliot and Hammett—each lamenting the absence of the grail, the cure for a divided culture—we begin to see, if not finally to solve, the true mystery of the relation of mass culture to modernism.

Notes

1. Modernist novelists in particular, as the occasional best-seller status of such as F. Scott Fitzgerald, Ernest Hemingway, and even Gertrude Stein attests, never lost sight of this genre's traditional intimacy with the idea, if not always the fact, of the mass audience. On the cultural-institutional specificity of the modernist novel, see Berman 41-42.

2. For philosophical implications of symbolist self-inclusion, see Irwin.

3. The pervasiveness of modernism's sense of failure in merging the high and low has no doubt encouraged postmodernism to rewrite this failure as modernism's aspiration.

4. "I liked the look of those . . . books," Willa Cather would write, explaining why she began to publish with Knopf. "Every publisher nowadays tries to make his books look interesting (jacket, cover, type, make-up), but . . . it was Alfred Knopf who set the fashion" (10). This fashion became widespread enough that historians of the publishing industry now refer to the late 1920s and '30s as a golden age of the American book.

5. By contrast Leavis would champion the highbrow novelist, who, if he "'creates' character at all[,] is apt to produce personalities that do not obey the literary agent's rule ('The principal characters must be likeable. They must be human'), that do not lend themselves to [such] fantas[ies of friendship]" (60).

6. Two other titles Hammett pondered for what eventually became *Red Harvest*—"The Seventeenth Murder" and "Murder Plus"—would have indicated the mathematical sublimity of this bloody project.

7. About high literature's resistance to time, Gertrude Stein observes that "the word timely as used in our speech is very interesting but you can any one can see that it has nothing to do with a masterpiece. . . . The word timely tells that masterpieces have nothing to do with time" (153).

8. In *The Maltese Falcon* Hammett for the first time in his career uses third person narration, which allows Hammett to present his named detective, Sam Spade, as a visible body, an object. Thus are we told that "the steep, rounded slope of [Spade's] shoulders made his body seem almost conical—no broader than it was thick" (4), which suggests the ontological intimacy of the object that Samuel Spade is, the object that he as an author-figure pursues, and the object, in this case named after an object, which is the novel itself. The novel's quest, no less than Gide's in *The Counterfeiters* to include its own authorship, is thus a quest for the reconstituted unity of author and book in the transcendental object that Stein describes as serving God: "Now serving god for a writer who is writing is writing anything directly, it makes no difference what it is but it must be direct, the relation between the thing done and the doer must be direct. In this way there is completion" (38-39).

9. On these grounds I would dispute James Naremore's claim that Hammett "managed to reconcile some of the deepest contradictions in his culture" (49).

10. Thus Hammett traces a constitutive lack at the center of individual identity—like that in the account of Jacques Lacan—to its origins in the social and historical realm, where in dialectical turn it is seen to produce the constitutive discrepancy internal to the individual representation. In this Hammett appears precursive, in some respects of the Marxism of Fredric Jameson, who similarly reads modern culture as a sort of fall into market relations (see Jameson 285).

11. The transposition of the high/low division from the "American mind" to the realm of objects themselves is perhaps the most important and ultimately disabling legacy of modernism's failure to merge the high and low in a single object. As John Guillory, following Pierre Bourdieu, demonstrates in *Cultural Capital: The Problem of Library Canon Formation* (1993), what we mean by "highness" is best understood not as a quality of certain objects but as a privileged *relation* to knowledge. The modernist texts I have been examining here had the virtue at least of partly recognizing this fact, though they tended to understand it not as an outrage but as an opportunity: an opportunity to produce social distinctions within the "common" space of mass culture.

Works Cited

Berman, Art. *Preface to Modernism.* Urbana: U Illinois P, 1994.

Brooks, Van Wyck. "America's Coming-of-Age." *America's Coming-of-Age.* Rev. ed. Garden City: Anchor-Doubleday, 1958. 1-88.

Cather, Willa. "Portrait of the Publisher as a Young Man." *Alfred A. Knopf: Quarter Century.* By Cather et al. [Norwood]: Plimpton, 1940. 9-16.

Chinitz, David. "T. S. Eliot and the Great Divide." *PMLA* 110 (1995): 236-47.

Eliot, T. S. *Selected Essays.* New ed. 1964. New York: Harcourt, 1967.

———. "The Waste Land." *The Complete Poems and Plays, 1909-1950.* San Diego: Harcourt, 1980. 37-55.

Gordon, Lyndall. *Eliot's New Life.* Oxford: Oxford UP, 1988.

Hammett, Dashiell. *The Dain Curse.* 1929. New York: Vintage, 1989.

———. *The Maltese Falcon.* 1930. New York: Vintage, 1989.

———. *Red Harvest.* 1929. New York: Vintage, 1989.

———. *Tulip. The Big Knockover: Selected Stories and Short Novels.* Ed. Lillian Hellman. 1966. New York: Vintage, 1989.

Huyssen, Andreas. *After the Great Divide: Modernism, Mass Culture, Post-modernism.* Bloomington: Indiana UP, 1986.

Irwin, John T. *The Mystery to a Solution: Poe, Borges, and the Analytic Detective Story.* Baltimore: Johns Hopkins UP, 1994.

Jameson, Fredric. *The Political Unconscious: Narrative as a Socially Symbolic Act.* Ithaca: Cornell UP, 1981.

Johnson, Diane. *Dashiell Hammett: A Life.* New York: Random, 1983.

Layman, Richard. *Shadow Man: The Life of Dashiell Hammett.* New York: Harcourt, 1981.

Leavis, Q. D. *Fiction and the Reading Public.* 1932. New York: Russell, 1965.

Levine, Lawrence W. *Highbrow/Lowbrow: The Emergence of Cultural Hierarchy in America.* Cambridge: Harvard UP, 1988.

Marling, William. *The American Roman Noir: Hammett, Cain, and Chandler.* Athens: U of Georgia P, 1995.

Naremore, James. "Dashiell Hammett and the Poetics of Hard-Boiled Detection." *Art in Crime Writing: Essays on Detective Fiction.* Ed. Bernard Benstock. New York: St. Martin's, 1983. 49-72.

Stein, Gertrude. *Writings and Lectures 1911-1945.* Ed. Patricia Meyerowitz. London: Owen, 1967.

John Walker (essay date spring 1998)

SOURCE: Walker, John. "City Jungles and Expressionist Reifications from Brecht to Hammett." *Twentieth Century Literature* 44, no. 1 (spring 1998): 119-33.

[*In the following essay, Walker argues that Hammett's work "reproduces the model of human relations exhibited in expressionist drama," such as that developed by Bertolt Brecht in his play* Jungle of Cities.]

The subject of expressionism, that tortured mutilation of congealed panic and anxiety, emanates its strongest contours when cast against the background of the modern urban landscape. The noisy and unpredictable machinery of the metropolis confronts the subject as an alien force that continuously threatens any vestige of individual autonomy. The harsh juxtaposition of wounded subjectivity with the chaos of commerce, the cacophony of technologies, and the utterly inhuman industrial backgrounds exhibits the dissolution of social community into scattered and disconnected fragments. In the midst of the most developed concentration of the forces of technological achievement and civilized social organization, the isolated and alienated character of the modern subject comes most prominently to the surface.

The urban zone of expressionism is a monolithic entity that antagonizes and annihilates the isolated energies of the subject. Walter Benjamin refers to "the impenetrable obscurity of mass existence" (*Baudelaire* 64) in which the individual is dissolved into the mob. The city itself figures as the anthropomorphic subject of many modernist endeavors, from Fritz Lang's *Metropolis* to Alexander Döblin's quasi-expressionist *Berlin Alexanderplatz,* which depicts a protagonist entirely constructed from the assembled rhythms, ideologies, and fragments of information imposed on subjectivity by the monolith metropolis. In the cityscapes of George Grosz and Otto Dix, the geography of the city resembles the infernal regions of Hieronymous Bosch, where each individual is consigned to a particular torment and compelled to replicate mechanically a specific and pointless task in utter isolation from the swarming multitudes on all sides.

Modern literatures unite the paradoxical vision of the urban landscape as technological anti-utopia with the metaphor of the primeval jungle. Metropolitan technologies contribute to an atmosphere of noise, light, and sudden violence whose obscure origins and unpredictable concatenations conjure visions of jungle environments. The arbitrary violence and apparent lawlessness of city life create an atmosphere of anarchy that recalls social configurations of tribal warfare. Economic imperatives that set individuals in hostile competition replicate primeval conditions where survival is based on a struggle against all others.

The conflation of city and jungle corresponds to a similar conflation of machine and animal. The total mechanization of activity and the subsequent death of inner life experienced by the subject of modern labor is represented by analogies to inanimate mechanical processes or to the unreflective instinctual violence of the savage beast. The absence of civilized responses of sympathy and social conscience, made obsolete by market imperatives of total competition, engender a sense of identity with the amoral extravagances of the animal kingdom.

American gangster and detective literatures fully incorporate the urban mythos of expressionism; the *noir* genre is based on the exploration of the underside and the unconscious of the city and its geography. *Noir* film and the detective story of the 1920s and 30s do not merely adopt the landscape of the expressionist scene, but further assimilate and develop expressionist atmospheres, techniques, and theoretical orientations. These genres intersect most prominently in films like Fritz Lang's *M* and the works of German emigrant Otto Preminger. The expressionist resonances in Dashiell Hammett's work are so pronounced that direct citations from the movement can be clearly identified.

The urban jungle mythos that serves as the background for expressionism and *noir* is elaborated in Bertolt Brecht's *Jungle of Cities,* composed in 1924. Brecht constructs a gigantic Chicago of mythic proportions, a metaphysical projection of Chicago in its distorted and transfigured essence in which the audience is instructed to concentrate on the expressionist agon: "concern yourself with the human element, evaluate the antagonists' fighting spirit impartially and concentrate your interest on the showdown" (12).

While Brecht was careful to distance himself theoretically from expressionism, the aesthetic resonances of the movement abound in his work. *Jungle of Cities* dramatizes a vast retinue of expressionist styles and techniques: Hyperbole, distortion, caricature, and mechanization all modulate characteristic expressionist themes of domestic conflict and a revolt against reification and economic determination.

Brecht utilizes the telegraphic fragments of speech and compacted phrases of expressionist dialogue. His protagonist, in the midst of conflict and apropos of nothing, suddenly gazes idly out the window and intones, "Ninety-four degrees in the shade. Traffic, noise from the Milwaukee bridge. A morning, like any other" (16). The Salvation Army Officer recites an inventory of commodities as if a section from a menu had been cut out and pasted into the dialogue: "Cherry Flip, Cherry Brandy, Gin Fizz, Whiskey Sour, Golden Slipper, Manhattan Cocktail . . . and, the specialty of this bar: Eggnog. This alone consists of the following . . ." (76). These montaged fragments of discourse are mixed with blunt colloquialisms punctuated by extended lyrical monologues.

Brecht's arrangements of scenes recall the *stationendrama* model of expressionist theater. Certain scenes are arranged as a series of vignettes from isolated stage areas where self-sufficient minidramas or parables are enacted. Scene 5 alternates between the separate dramas going on in a bedroom, a hallway, and a saloon. These seemingly arbitrary arrangements undermine conventional aesthetic models of harmonious transition and organic totality, and instead exhibit an organizational principle based on mechanization and dissonance.

The pronounced mechanization of character and discourse is exemplified by the sudden appearance and staccato monologue of The Man in scene 8:

> I've got three minutes to give you some information, and you've got two minutes to act on it. This is it: half an hour ago, Police Headquarters received a letter from one of the state prisons. It is signed by a certain George Garga, and he incriminates you on several counts. The patrol wagon will be here in five minutes. You owe me a thousand bucks.
>
> (Brecht 70)

He is paid and immediately disappears in the manner of an automaton. He comes from nowhere and vanishes into nowhere. His totally disinterested attitude, his pre-

fabricated speech and its precise price tag testify to the administrative zeal and bureaucratic efficiency that not only dictate business affairs and legal relations but thoroughly permeate the consciousness and experience of the economic subject in the modern urban environment.

This expressionist trademark of objectification of character by function can be seen in the list of cast members, which includes The Worm, The Baboon, and The Snubnose. These characters are the magnified perversion of their economic functions; the mutilations imposed on the personality are externalized and projected in the form of caricature.

Expressionist distortions of nature or the urban landscape are precipitated by the projection of wounded subjectivity onto the external world. The assault of urban conditions on the senses of the individual is often characterized by the experience of claustrophobia. Hence Marie complains of the intrusive pressure of the sky against her body. On the shores of Lake Michigan, the only scene outside of the city in the drama, she fails to experience a sense of comfort from the pastoral scene, and instead observes, "Those trees—they look as if they were covered with human shit. . . . And the sky's so close you could touch it, and what do I care for it" (Brecht 57). Her projected anxiety transforms her environment into a sinister and oppressive monstrosity.

The antagonist Shlink embodies the fully dehumanized being. From poor migrant beginnings, he rose to the position of owner of a timber industry, and the economic exploitations entailed in that rise have reduced him to an empty and dehumanized replicant. He explains, "don't expect any words out of my mouth. All I have in my mouth is teeth" (Brecht 41). His lack of words testifies to the absence of any modicum of humanity capable of expression; there is nothing left of him but material. Shlink's understanding of his condition is based on a corporealization of interiority: He projects his inner state onto his skin and thereby recognizes it as part of his own displaced body. He explains to Marie:

> my body's gone numb, it affects even my skin. You know, in its natural state human skin is too thin for this world. So men take care to see it grows thicker. There would be nothing wrong with the method, if only you could stop it from growing.
>
> (43)

The dehumanization necessitated by economic objectification colonizes all other spheres of personal life as well, and the doomed attempt to mediate between objectifying economic activity and human emotional relations reconfigures subjectivity as a form of schizophrenia.

Shlink tells Marie about his skin to explain why he is incapable of love. He has no emotional surplus to give her, and the only value she can have for him is market value. Her exclamation "They're selling me!" (53) demonstrates the painful awareness of her own objectification in a capitalist economy where prostitution is universalized and desire is bought and sold on the market. Her only consolation for this awareness is in a masochistic identification with her commodity function as prostitute, and she thereby demands to be paid for love from Shlink.

The stake wagered on the metaphysical battle of Shlink and Garga is whether or not there is any way out of reification. When Garga refuses to sell his opinion in the opening scene, he affirms that there is some sphere of his existence that remains self-determined and is therefore not for sale. Shlink's response that "Your opinion is immaterial too—except that I want to buy it" (14) refutes the prospect of a sphere of existence that is not reducible to quantifiable exchange value.

As Shlink demonstrates the power of his position by buying off Garga's family, mistress, and job, Garga revolts by stripping off his clothes and running amok. This archetypically expressionistic response to moral conflict is reminiscent of the Cashier in *From Morning to Midnight,* who performs a similar flight from signifying systems. Intoxicated by the heat of conflict and the suspense of his sudden catastrophic awakening, Garga quotes Rimbaud and raves expressionistically: "And that—is freedom. . . . I have no knowledge of metaphysics, I do not understand the laws, I have no moral sense, I am an animal" (21). He equates his freedom with the abolition of his inherited civilization and a renewed identification with the primeval beast. He responds to the challenge of urban economic demands by abandoning morality and culture, and reverting to animal instincts. Karl Marx refers to the alienation of labor as a process whereby "What is animal becomes human and what is human becomes animal" (137). Garga embodies this transposition through a reversion to the uninhibited instinctual activity of the wild beast.

Shlink circumvents this strategy by converting Garga into an exploiter and thus reintegrating him into economic determinations. In order to wage conflict, Garga must objectify himself; as an object he in turn objectifies others and thereby enters into complicity with cycles of reification. Confronted with the apparent ubiquity of these cycles, he expresses his awareness to his mother in terms that do not permit a satisfactory resolution:

> We aren't free. It starts with coffee in the morning, and blows for being such a bad monkey, and mother's tears are salt to season the children's meal: and she washes their little shirts in her sweat, and you are all taken care of and safe, safe, until the Ice Age comes, while the root grows right through your heart. And when he's grown up, and wants to do something, wants to go the whole hog, what does he find out? He'll find he's already been consecrated, paid for, stamped and sold at a good price, so he isn't even free to go and drown himself!
>
> (35)

Family life and the maternal relation, ideologically conceived as zones of refuge from economic determinations, are here represented as thoroughly permeated by the paralyzing processes of reification. Even suicide is figured as a prefabricated gesture already inscribed within these ubiquitous cycles.

Yet human beings cannot be entirely obliterated: The individual retains a ghost of vanquished humanity even in urban environments of totalizing objectification. The Salvation Army Officer's lament—"People are too durable, that's their main trouble . . . they last too long" (77)—is confirmed by his failure to die even after shooting himself in the head. These remnants of humanity, distorted beyond recognition by economic dehumanization, come to the surface and reemerge in immeasurably disfigured forms: Love and affection are thereby transformed into sadism and masochism. This is the psychological mechanism implied by the frontier code that motivates the love/hate ambivalence in Shlink and Garga's relations. The objective impossibility of benevolent human contact in an atmosphere of total alienation compels them to seek contact through hatred, conflict, and antagonism.

The tableau for the staging of their final showdown is in the gravel pits on the edge of town. The industrial wasteland thus replaces the prairie as the site for the isolated male confrontation in the new world. Shlink concedes the inevitable stalemate of their attempt at engagement by emphasizing the impossibility of transversing the utter isolation that separates human beings:

> I've been watching animals: and love, or the warmth given off by bodies moving in close to each other, that is the only mercy shown to us in the darkness. But the coupling of organs is all, it doesn't make up for the divisions caused by speech. . . . And the generations stare coldly into each other's eyes. If you cram a ship's hold full of human bodies, so it almost bursts—there will be such loneliness in that ship that they'll all freeze to death.
>
> (83)

Spatial proximity is described as a condition that paradoxically increases spiritual separation, and the metaphor of the ship's hold suggests an analogy to the claustrophobic conditions of modern urban arrangements. Shlink proceeds to invoke the vision of the primeval jungle as a utopian counterpart to the emotional death of the subject of civilization: "The forest! That's where mankind comes from, from right here. Hairy, with ape's mouths, good animals who knew how to live. It was all so easy. They just tore each other to pieces" (83). Far from the cheerful pastoral utopias of harmony with nature envisioned by the Enlightenment, Shlink projects a utopia of anarchic and bestial violence. Characteristic of expressionist reverie, the deepest desire of wounded subjectivity is found in atavistic frenzies of destruction; existence is validated exclusively by moments of highest passion and fiercest energy.

The detective fiction of Dashiell Hammett reproduces the model of human relations exhibited in expressionist drama and developed in Brecht's *Jungle*: The antagonists are stripped of individual characteristics and reduced to a deformed though imperishable human essence. Against the backdrop of a bleak and brutal chaos ruled by utterly immoral forces, they face each other in their respective moral isolation, locked in deadly opposition.

The urban zone of the crime novel appropriates the jungle metaphor of the expressionist metropolis by representing the modern city as an arena of anarchic violence where individuals are set against each other in hostile conflict. George Grella observes that "the gangster novel (like many American detective stories) seems a kind of urban pastoral" (187). The gangster novel functions as a meditation on the landscape of the modern city.

The mythic vision of the American landscape, both urban and rural, has always held a great fascination for European projections of absolute alienation and moral solitude. Brecht and Kafka, among many others, utilized this mythic territory as the background for their modernist fictions. André Gide remarks that "the American cities and countryside must offer a foretaste of hell" (qtd. in Madden xxvi). In the proportions of mythic America, one confronts the realities of Europe by gazing on them in magnified form. Hammett's work performs this same optical demonstration for the natives: By defamiliarizing conditions that have become ideologically obscured by processes of habituation, the horror of those conditions is made manifest.

Hammett's *Red Harvest* presents the modern city as a zone of tribal warfare where legally justified structures of authority cannot be distinguished from illegal hierarchies of gang rule. These anarchic conditions are indicated as the direct result of the antagonistic competition imposed on social relations by capitalist economies. The protagonist's client, Elihu Willsson, has exercised the iron rule of capital over the town for 40 years as baron of the banks and newspapers. This perfect collusion of the interests of capital and the production of ideology does not prevent a mass uprising of the mine workers, and Willsson hires armed mobs to bust the labor unions. By the beginning of the novel, the mobs have shattered the unions and are fighting among themselves to divide up the town, compelling Willsson to call on the Continental Detective Agency to secure his interests.

In Carl Freedman and Christopher Kendrick's article, "Forms of Labor in Dashiell Hammett's *Red Harvest*," the resulting social conditions in the town are described as an analogy to fascist Italy in terms of a "feudalization of illicit power" (213). With reference to Benjamin, they observe that "The individualism of the gangster power structure makes for a permanent state of anarchic emergency" (210). The ceaseless cycles of violent retribution among conflicting gangs are assimilated by the populace as the normalized environment of urban life, and economic survival is predicated on a strategic alliance with superior firepower.

Hammett's town, with characteristic lack of subtlety, is appropriately named "Personville" (pronounced by the locals as "Poisonville"), an almost direct citation of expressionist abstraction of place into general category. Hammett's description of the town could serve as stage directions for the backdrop of the expressionist metropolis:

> the smelters whose brick stacks stuck up tall against a gloomy mountain to the south had yellow-smoked everything into uniform dinginess. The result was an ugly city of forty thousand people, set in an ugly notch between two ugly mountains that had been all dirtied up by mining. Spread over this was a grimy sky that looked as if it had come out of the smelter's stacks.
>
> (*Red Harvest* 4)

Nature is hereby reified as a waste product of labor, and the claustrophobia imposed by this industrial sky contrasts to the metaphorical transposition of the jungle onto the activity within the city.

With characteristic expressionist condensation, Hammett's protagonist is named "the Op": a two-letter abbreviation of his economic function as Continental Operative. After noting the infernal character of Personville, the Op spots three caricatures of policemen, unshaved, unbuttoned, and smoking cigars while directing traffic, and he immediately deciphers the absence of legitimized authority in the town. "Don't kid yourselves that there's any law in Poisonville" (*Red Harvest* 111), he explains later to his recently arrived assistants.

The Op internalizes and absorbs the anarchy of the urban environment and embarks on a strategy based on the provocation of violence and antagonisms among rival gangs in the effort to have them destroy each other in the process. He explains to his ally, the junky-prostitute Dinah Brand, that he could have accomplished his ends through legal means, "But it's easier to have them killed off, easier and surer, and, now that I'm feeling this way, more satisfying" (**Red Harvest** 145). He derives sadistic pleasure from the replication of the cycles of violence, and he describes his desensitized condition with the same corporealization of interiority as Brecht's Shlink: "I've got hard skin all over what's left of my soul" (145). He identifies the encroaching metropolis as the source of the violent fever that penetrates his subjectivity like a disease: "It's this damned town. Poisonville is right. It's poisoned me" (145). The smothered condition of his soul seeks cathartic release in violent agitation, and he refers to the pleasure experienced from this release as an intoxication.

The Op internalizes and replicates the violence of his environment in the manner of a machine, yet his delirium precipitates a regression to animal instincts. This paradoxical conflation of machine and animal serves as the principle of characterization that motivates the inhabitants of the urban pastoral. In "The Poetics of the Private-Eye," Robert Edenbaum observes that in Hammett's novels, "Action is determined mechanistically—or animalistically" (100). The apparent ease with which Edenbaum equates mechanical and animal determinations reflects the instability of these categories in Hammett's narration.

In *The Rebel*, Albert Camus reads the American crime narrative as an aesthetic that operates "as if men were entirely defined by their daily automatisms. On this mechanical level men, in fact, seem exactly alike, which explains this peculiar universe in which all the characters appear interchangeable, even down to their physical peculiarities" (265). Camus refers to these characters as "the symbol of the despairing world in which wretched automatons live in a machine-ridden universe" (266). The totalizing mechanization of behavior in the crime narrative testifies to the violence done to subjectivity by the encroaching technologies of modern urban conditions.

Despite Camus's disparaging view of the crime novel, he perceives what most commentators on the genre have missed: "This technique is called realistic only owing to a misapprehension. . . . It is born of a mutilation, and of a voluntary mutilation, performed on reality" (265). The conventional circumscription of Hammett's fiction within a tradition of American realism totally disregards all characteristic components of his style and theoretical orientation. Hammett's use of abstraction, mechanization, and caricature dismantle realist conventions by mutilating the subject of representation into defamiliarized form.

The perfectly prefabricated automatisms of Hammett's subjects contrasts to a reified animation of the technological object. Automobiles dart about and weapons dis-

charge as if operating according to their own independent volition. The cigarette ashes on Sam Spade's desk come to life and twitch and crawl about in the breeze. These anthropomorphisms testify to the fetishized character of objects in an urban environment of totalizing reification.

Hammett's generally sparse descriptions are based on a rigorous condensation of the subject, which is reconfigured as congealed abstraction. In **"The Farewell Murder,"** the Op describes a house in terms of a mutilated conglomeration of geometric figures; the intensely asymmetrical arrangement of converging diagonal lines reads like a stage setting for *Caligari*:

> Take a flock of squat cones of various sizes, round off the points bluntly, mash them together with the largest one somewhere near the center, the others grouped around it in not too strict accordance with their sizes, adjust the whole collection to agree with the slopes of a hilltop, and you would have a model of the Kavalov house.
>
> (278)

The Op's observations disdain attention to referential detail. Instead they enact a narrative compression of the scene that approximates an expressionist model of prose: His subject is transformed into a generic abstraction that is consequently mutilated into idiosyncratic form. Hammett's prose here undermines realist conventions by emphasizing the discursive construction of the image and directing attention towards the artificiality of the descriptive act.

Hammett's narration reduces the subject to economic function or idiosyncratic trait, and then distorts and magnifies this feature to subsume the entire individual. Physical characteristics are contorted into cartoon proportions and arranged surrealist configurations. In **"The Golden Horseshoe"** the Op spots a stranger in the bar and describes him as "A tall, rawboned man with wide shoulders, out of which a long, skinny, yellow neck rose to support a little round head. His eyes were black shoe-buttons stuck close together at the top of a little mashed nose" (72). This absurd collage of distorted features and incongruous objects has more in common with dada caricature than realism.

The description of Willsson in **Red Harvest** could refer to one of Grosz's sinister portraits: "The short-clipped hair on his round pink skull was like silver in the light. . . . His mouth and chin were horizontal lines" (135). Hammett's characters are drawn with a mark and a dash: reduced to compact visual signifiers and geometries of abstracted essence. The description of Sam Spade that opens **The Maltese Falcon** evokes a similar geometry of personal characteristics:

> Samuel Spade's jaw was long and bony, his chin a jutting v under the more flexible v of his mouth. His nostrils curved back to make another, smaller, v. His

yellow-grey eyes were horizontal. The *v motif* was picked up again by thickish brows rising outward from twin creases above a hooked nose, and his pale brown hair grew down—from high flat temples—in a point on his forehead. He looked rather pleasantly like a blond Satan.

(3)

The alphabetical figure is stamped on Spade's face like a typographical collage; individuality is dissolved into typology. Hammett's relentless abstraction of character responds to the increasingly abstract conditions imposed by pervasive modern bureaucracies, which are inscribed as a visual signifier on the subject's body.

The nickname, partially necessitated to maintain anonymity in the city crowd, reconfigures subjectivity as caricature. Hammett's novels are populated by characters identified according to the conspicuously deformed physical characteristic: the Thin Man, the Fat Man, Big Chin, or Chinless Jerry. In *Red Harvest,* the villains Whisper and the Voice are named according to their discursive capacities. The Dis an' Dat Kid and the Whosis Kid are reduced to cartoon parodies of their namelessness. The Op's boss is simply the Old Man, an abstract typology that suggests the presence of authority in the colloquial reference to the father.

The notoriously compact prose for which the crime novel is famous necessitates a narrative contraction of action into brief staccato segments. These segments tend to focus on the sharply delineated visual image, and the action unfolds like a montage of snapshots.

> A curtain whipped loose in the rain.
>
> Out of the opening came pale fire-streaks. The bitter voice of a small-caliber pistol. Seven times.
>
> The Whosis Kid's wet hat floated off his head—a slow balloon-like rising.

("Whosis Kid" 189)

Hammett substitutes the empty hat in the place of the Kid, which defies gravity and floats off as if under its own power. The intense objectification of images recalls expressionist contractions of the subject, and the fragmented pace of the unfolding scene imitates expressionist rhythms of sudden shocks and abrupt pauses. Human beings are carefully subtracted from the scene, whereas the pistol is invested with the power of speech, and inanimate objects like the curtain and the hat seem to be animated with independent volition.

As the Op walks into a boxing arena in *Red Harvest,* he gives an atomic inventory of the scene in four sentences, one word each: "Smoke. Stink. Heat. Noise" (69). This intensified brevity recalls the telegraphic conventions of expressionism. One of the Op's colleagues speaks exclusively in miniaturized fragments of infor-

mation. He reports his activities in the manner of a speaking machine: "Spot two. Out three-thirty, office to Willsson's. Mickey. Five. Home. Busy. Kept plant. Off three, seven. Nothing yet" (132). The Op then flaunts his semiotic prowess by translating the meaning of these prefabricated signifiers for the benefit of the reader. Hammett parodies this convention in a section from *The Dain Curse,* where the Op objects to the verbosity of a friend who responds, "Tell me what's up while I try to find one-syllable words for you" (20).

The brevity of dialogue and description in Hammett makes his novels almost appropriate to stage production. Sometimes he dispenses with description entirely, and large sections of his books (particularly *The Thin Man*) are composed exclusively of character dialogue and monologue. The extended monologues, often confessions or case histories, can be highly idiosyncratic in their use of colloquialisms and regional slang. At other times they are simply journalese, speech stripped down to the delivery of commodified fragments of information. In *Red Harvest,* some nameless detective informs the Op, "'Donald Willsson, Esquire, publisher of the *Morning* and *Evening Heralds,* was found in Hurricane Street a little while ago, shot very dead by parties unknown,' he recited in a rapid singsong" (7). The detective's mechanical voice confirms what his speech has already made clear: He is an automaton capable of replicating prefabricated speech patterns devoid of human inflection or digression.

The Op is located in San Francisco, an appropriate city for the gothic atmospheres of Hammett's scenery. The fog hangs low, and figures are obscured like ghosts wandering in and out of the darkness. In **"The Big Knockover,"** the shadows themselves are personified, speak and vanish. The Op is often performing the function of the shadow, tailing unsuspecting nomads of the city. During pursuits, Hammett inserts precise geographies of the city streets, reminiscent of Döblin's insertion of urban topographies in *Berlin Alexanderplatz.*

Hammett's interiors, perfectly appropriated by *noir* film, are defined by their angular composition and harsh dark and light contrast. A typical interior is described in **"The House on Turk Street"**:

> the hall was lighted with the glow that filtered through the glass from the street lights. The stairway leading to the second-story threw a triangular shadow across part of the hall—a shadow that was black enough for any purpose. I crouched low in this three-cornered slice of night, and waited.

(109)

This highly expressionistic scenography suggests the anthropomorphic character of darkness that seeks to penetrate the interior. The unstable demarcation of inside and outside dramatizes the threat posed to urban interiors by the external forces of crime and darkness. The Op as the morally ambivalent figure who crosses that boundary is significantly attracted to the darkness in which he seeks refuge and the cover of invisibility.

The Op's invisibility constitutes the foremost characteristic of his wavering and mutable identity. His capacity as detective consists mainly in his ability to disappear into the background or transform his personality to deceive his antagonists. He is presented without preexisting personal relationships or familial antecedents. Just as he busily removes all traces of his presence before leaving the scene of a crime, he is constantly erasing his identity in personal relationships.

The absence of stable identity in Hammett's work corresponds to an epistemological uncertainty concerning the nature of being. The anthropomorphic character of objects suggests a capacity for mutability that undermines the potential for a fixed essence. The symbol for this epistemological emptiness is the Maltese falcon: the priceless artifact of historical significance that motivates a global pursuit and inspires a murderous determination in all those attempting to take it into possession. At the conclusion of the novel, the falcon turns out to be counterfeit: an empty projection of the fictions imposed on it by imagination.

The verbal reticence of so many of Hammett's figures can be partially ascribed to a conviction that the act of signification is a philosophically futile process that does nothing to alter the fundamental emptiness of significd phenomena. The Op's customary reliance on tautological utterances reflects a conscious inability to construct an authentic discursive response. After hearing the impassioned confession of a murderous bank clerk struggling to understand his own motives, the Op reflects, "I couldn't find anything to say except something meaningless, like: 'Things happen that way'" (***Red Harvest*** 57-58).

The emptiness of signification in Hammett's work negates the possibility of satisfactory closure to the mysteries and puzzles conjured up in his narratives. The conclusions of his novels are always vaguely unsettling because the final solutions seem like false constructions and shed suspicion on the inventive powers of the detective. ***The Thin Man*** concludes with a highly conjectural and somewhat preposterous explanation of events by the protagonist, who concedes that his hypothetical resolution is based on speculation. The last word of the book belongs to his wife, Nora, who responds, "That may be, but it's all pretty unsatisfactory" (180). This is a startling concluding note for a genre conventionally based on the expectation of definitive resolution and stable closure.

How does a detective operate in an epistemologically uncertain universe in which there is no stable truth be-hind the deceptive illusions on the surface? The Op responds by abandoning the chimerical search for concealed master narratives and instead scrambles signification by inventing falsehoods and projecting them onto phenomena. The Op's most important talent thus becomes his capacity for discursive intervention as a means of generating conflict. Unlike most detective figures, he rarely resorts to physical coercion, but rather relies on his ability to spread rumor and create subversive alliances and antagonisms. He walks into a boxing ring in ***Red Harvest,*** and merely by the utterance of the phrase "Back to Philly, Al" (72)—which conceals a false threat of reprisal against one of the fighters—he manages to unfix the fight and provoke a series of murders and conflicts among rival gangs. He routinely fixes false alibis for himself and manufactures evidence against others. In **"The Golden Horseshoe,"** unable to sustain a conviction due to lack of evidence, he invents a false crime to hang a criminal for a murder he didn't commit.

The Op's illicit tactics of detection suggest the profound moral ambivalence of his identity and activity. The diabolical character of Hammett's protagonists is reinforced by the visual analogy of Spade to Satan in the first paragraph of ***The Maltese Falcon.*** Edenbaum refers to the Op's method as "not a divine plan but a satanic disorder" (92). The subversive potential to collapse systems of signification places these characters in opposition to the reified administrative structures that dominate and determine their environment.

In ***Red Harvest,*** the Op explains his twisted methodology to Dinah Brand: "Plans are all right sometimes . . . and sometimes just stirring things up is all right—if you're tough enough to survive, and keep your eyes open so you'll see what you want when it comes to the top" (79). Freedman and Kendrick translate this strategy as "the apparently spontaneous capacity both to activate the energies present in the dialogic world and to weather the anarchic psychological and social effects that are thus set in motion" (217). The Op works to short-circuit the machinery of social relations through an expenditure of surplus energy; his liberating function is his destructive capacity for dismantling systems of signification and discursive alliances and preserving himself in the process of their collapse.

Hammett's detectives operate as agents of sabotage in the manner of Benjamin's "Destructive Character": "For destroying rejuvenates in clearing away the traces of our own age; it cheers because everything cleared away means to the destroyer a complete reduction, indeed eradication, of his own condition" (*Reflections* 301). This reduction and eradication is performed by the narrative as well, which obliterates referential capacities through a relentless application of dissonant aesthetic maneuvers designed to dismantle narrative content. The utopian aspect of this narrative is achieved by the momentary liberation from ossified discursive reifications.

Freedman and Kendrick contrast modes of detection in Hammett with conventional detective narration by explaining that "it involves not the decoding of a discrete series of facts but, rather, an encoding process that activates the surplus energy inherent in his world" (217). It is within this encoding process that the Op enacts his rebellion against instrumental reason. By imposing his own creative narrative on the world, he constructs a utopian moment that evades the administrative imperatives of his work. He momentarily defies the mechanisms that otherwise determine his reified function, and gives his labor the aesthetic character of play.

Works Cited

Benjamin, Walter. *Charles Baudelaire: A Lyric Poet in the Era of High Capitalism*. Trans. Harry Zohn. Thetford, Norfolk: Thetford, 1985.

———. *Reflections*. Trans. Edmund Jephcott. New York: Schocken, 1986.

Brecht, Bertolt. *Jungle of Cities*. Trans. Anselm Hollo. New York: Grove, 1966.

Camus, Albert. *The Rebel*. Trans. Anthony Bower. New York: Vintage, 1956.

Edenbaum, Robert I. "The Poetics of the Private-Eye: The Novels of Dashiell Hammett." *Tough Guy Writers of the Thirties*. Ed. David Madden. Carbondale: Southern Illinois UP, 1968.

Freedman, Carl, and Christopher Kendrick. "Forms of Labor in Dashiell Hammett's *Red Harvest*." *Publications of the Modern Language Association* 106 (1991): 209-21.

Grella, George. "The Gangster Novel: The Urban Pastoral." *Tough Guy Writers of the Thirties*. Ed. David Madden. Carbondale: Southern Illinois UP, 1968.

Hammett, Dashiell. "The Big Knockover." *The Big Knockover*. New York: Vintage, 1989.

———. *The Dain Curse*. New York: Vintage, 1989.

———. "The Farewell Murder." *The Continental Op*. Ed. Steven Marcus. New York: Vintage, 1975.

———. "The Golden Horseshoe." *The Continental Op*.

———. "The House on Turk Street." *The Continental Op*.

———. *The Maltese Falcon*. New York: Vintage, 1972.

———. *Red Harvest*. New York: Vintage, 1972.

———. *The Thin Man*. New York: Vintage, 1972.

———. "The Whosis Kid." *The Continental Op*.

Madden, David, ed. Introd. *Tough Guy Writers of the Thirties*. Carbondale: Southern Illinois UP, 1968.

Marx, Karl. "Economico-Philosophical Manuscripts of 1844." *The Portable Karl Marx*. Ed. and trans. Eugene Kamenka. Kingsport: Viking Penguin, 1983.

Carl D. Malmgren (essay date fall 1999)

SOURCE: Malmgren, Carl D. "The Crime of the Sign: Dashiell Hammett's Detective Fiction." *Twentieth Century Literature* 45, no. 3 (fall 1999): 371-84.

[*In the following essay, Malmgren analyzes* Red Harvest, *contending that in this novel Hammett's vision of reality "derives in large part from his subversion of basic frames of intelligibility, including the frame that allows the art of fiction, language itself."*]

> Hammett took murder out of the Venetian vase and dropped it into the alley.
>
> —Raymond Chandler 234

In 1941 Howard Haycraft wrote a literary history called *Murder for Pleasure: The Life and Times of the Detective Story*. In it he celebrated what he termed the Golden Age of Detective Fiction, and he singled out certain people as masters of the "classic detective story"— Christie, Sayers, and Bentley, among others. In December 1944, in an essay in the *Atlantic Monthly* called "The Simple Art of Murder," Raymond Chandler issued a broadside against Haycraft's primarily British tradition. This narrative form, Chandler claimed, fails to provide, among other things, "lively characters, sharp dialogue, a sense of pace and an acute use of observed detail" (225). The murders in these stories are implausibly motivated, the plots completely artificial, and the characters pathetically two-dimensional, "puppets and cardboard lovers and papier mâché villains and detectives of exquisite and impossible gentility" (232). The authors of this fiction are ignorant of the "facts of life" (228), "too little aware of what goes on in the world" (231).

As the last quotes suggest, Chandler is accusing the writers of Haycraft's Golden Age of failing to be true to the real world: "if the writers of this fiction wrote about the kind of murders that happen," he says, "they would also have to write about the authentic flavor of life as it is lived" (231). Chandler goes on to single out Dashiell Hammett as the person who rescued the genre by bringing it back to the real world. Hammett, he says, "tried to write realistic mystery fiction" (233).

John Cawelti, a leading critic of detective fiction, qualifies Chandler's claims, insisting that Hammett's novels are not necessarily more realistic. Rather, they "embody a powerful vision of life in the hard-boiled detective formula" (163). Another critic remarks that Hammett "adapted to the genre a new and more exciting set of literary conventions better suited to the time and place" (Porter 130). While I grant that Chandler's arguments are partisan and naive, and that Hammett's "realism" is every bit as conventional as Christie's,[1] I would like to take Chandler at his word and to investigate the "real world" of Hammett's fiction and, by extension, the world of American detective fiction. By looking closely at Hammett's fiction, especially *Red Harvest,* his first novel (1929), I propose to demonstrate that his "powerful vision of life" derives in large part from his subversion of basic frames of intelligibility, including the frame that allows the art of fiction, language itself.

Chandler uses the synecdoche "mean streets" to define Hammett's world, and various critics have characterized those streets in some detail.[2] The world "implied in Hammett's works, and fully articulated in Chandler and MacDonald," says George Grella, "is an urban chaos, devoid of spiritual and moral values, pervaded by viciousness and random savagery" (110). The world of *Red Harvest* is representative. The novel takes place in a western mining town named Personville, which has been owned for 40 years by an industrial capitalist: "Elihu Willson was Personville, and he was almost the whole state" (9). Willson controls congressmen, city officials, and the police, but at the opening of the novel, his control of the town is in jeopardy. In order to break a strike by the mineworkers, he called in thugs connected with the mob. After brutally suppressing the strike, the gangsters refused to leave and took over the town, occupying its offices and businesses. At the time of the Continental Op's arrival, an uneasy peace prevails in a thoroughly corrupt town, as rival gangster factions run different operations. The police are bought off casually; they even supply getaway cars for criminals. At one point in the narrative, criminals are let out of jail in order to commit a midday bank robbery; they later use their incarceration as an unimpeachable alibi. In short, the world of the novel is thoroughly dishonest. As one critic notes, "In *Red Harvest* we never meet an honest businessman or an honest policeman, and the only lawyer is a blackmailer" (Bentley 67).

When the Op first strolls about the city, he says "most of its builders had gone in for gaudiness" (3-4). The Op chooses an appropriate noun to describe the world of detective fiction, a world where a cheap and thin veneer of glamour conceals a shabby or seedy reality, where "a gleaming and deceptive facade" hides "empty modernity, corruption, and death" (Cawelti 141). In order to strip away this facade, we need to look back at Chandler's description of realism in detective fiction:

> The realist in murder writes of a world in which gangsters can rule nations and almost rule cities, in which hotels and apartment houses and celebrated restaurants are owned by men who made their money out of brothels, in which a screen star can be the fingerman for a mob, and the nice man down the hall is a boss of the numbers racket; a world where a judge with a cellar full of bootleg liquor can send a man to jail for having a pint in his pocket, where the mayor of your town may have condoned murder as an instrument of money-making, where no man can walk down a dark street in safety because law and order are things we talk about but refrain from practising.
>
> (236)

In the "real world" of Hammett's fiction, gangsters wield political power, people are not what they pretend to be, justice is not served, and law and order are polite fictions. "It is not a very fragrant world," Chandler notes in an understatement, "but it is the world you live in" (236).

As Chandler's description makes clear, one of most salient characteristics of this world is the chasm between appearance and reality, a chasm exacerbated by wholesale role-playing and pretense. In a rare moment of honesty, Brigid O'Shaughnassey tells Sam Spade in *The Maltese Falcon,* "I'm not at all the sort of person I pretend to be" (55). For once she is telling the truth, but using it to serve a lie. The point is that her line could be spoken by most of Hammett's characters. In *Red Harvest,* for example, Chief of Police Noonan adopts a bluff and hearty role with the Op; he's always glad to see the Op (92) and continually expresses concern about his welfare (62) even while he is engineering two attempts to assassinate him. The Op himself carries a walletful of false IDs. Trying to pick up information after arriving in Personville, the Op runs into union boss Bill Quint and plays the garrulous stranger:

> I dug out my card case and ran through the collection of credentials I had picked up here and there by one means or another. The red card was the one I wanted. It identified me as Henry F. Neill, A. B. seaman, member in good standing of the Industrial Workers of the World. There wasn't a word of truth in it.
>
> (7)

The Op, blatantly masquerading as A(ble) B(odied) seaman, is indeed the ABC man, able to construct an identity made of letters in a moment. The Op argues that role-playing is required in his profession, that it enables him to get the job done. But the impersonations of detective fiction are not only ubiquitous and overdone; they can also be entirely gratuitous. The first sentence of the Hammett short story **"They Can Only Hang You Once,"** for example, is: "Samuel Spade said, 'My name is Ronald Ames.'" This entry line is entirely appropriate, since everyone else in the story is acting, but there is little reason for Spade's misrepresentation, since no one in the house he is calling on knows who he is.

One of the most egregious examples of misleading appearances occurs in **"The House in Turk Street."** While conducting a routine investigation, the Op encounters a sweet old couple, the Quarres. The Op soon figures out that this couple knows nothing about his case, but he lingers in the homey atmosphere. It turns out, of course, that the couple are ringleaders of a criminal gang (not in any way connected to the Op's investigation), and the next thing the Op feels is a gun pressed against his neck. The woman's last appearance in the story, just before she catches a hailstorm of bullets, highlights the gap between appearance and reality:

> I looked at the old woman again, and found little of the friendly fragile one who had poured tea and chatted about the neighbors. This was a witch if there ever was one—a witch of the blackest, most malignant sort. Her faded eyes were sharp with ferocity, her withered lips were taut in a wolfish snarl, and her thin body fairly quivered with hate.
>
> (106)

The same kind of metamorphosis occurs in the first part of **The Dain Curse,** when Alice Dain Leggatt is transformed, in an instant, from "Betty Crocker" to "Ma Barker." With radical transformations such as these, Hammett begins to call into question the idea that most things are what they seem to be. In Hammett that is just not the case, and naively succumbing to such common-sensical ideas can be downright dangerous.

In fact, the Op inhabits a world so histrionic, so unstable, so fluid that role-playing sometimes creates a kind of flickering half-reality. False appearances manufacture unreal realities. A case in point is the notorious seduction scene in **"The Girl with the Silver Eyes,"** in which the eponymous character tries to persuade the Op not to take her to jail:

> "Little fat detective whose name I don't know"—her voice had a tired huskiness in it, and a tired mockery— "you think that I am playing a part, don't you? You think that I am playing for liberty. Perhaps I am."

She continues in this vein, reciting the story of her lurid sexual past, teasing the Op, all the while undermining his firm purchase on the situation: "But because you do none of these things, because you are a wooden block of a man," she wheedles, "I find myself wanting you. Would I tell you this, little fat detective, if I were playing a game?" (*Continental Op* 148-50). That final question, balanced between mockery and self-conscious surrender, acts out the ontological precariousness of the Op's world. When she falls into his arms at the end of the siren song, no one—Op, girl, reader—can be sure if she is acting or not. The Op is forced to impose a kind of certainty on the situation by insisting that everything she has told him is a lie and by trying, almost hysterically, to punch holes in her story.

The same kind of ontological confusion occurs again and again between Brigid O'Shaughnassey and Sam Spade in **The Maltese Falcon.** Early on she makes the

following "confession" to Sam Spade during a harsh grilling: "Oh, I'm so tired," she blurts out, "so tired of it all, of myself, of lying, and thinking up lies, and of not knowing what is a lie and what is the truth" (89). There is just no way to tell if this too is part of her act, her ongoing seduction of Spade, but it works, because she reaches out to touch Spade and they fall into bed together. Analyzing the final encounter between Spade and O'Shaughnassey, Robert Shulman notes, "He acts as if he cares for her; she acts as if she cares for him. To an extent both are acting, telling stories to each other, but to an extent they may also be in love" (409). In a world of nonstop role-playing, it is often impossible to distinguish between acting and being. This confusion of appearance and reality opens up in Hammett's world a zone of cognitive indeterminacy.

Throughout Hammett's fiction runs the fear that nothing can be taken at face value, nothing is what it appears to be—a fear that culminates in a suspicion not only of individual people but also of the social order itself. In **Red Harvest,** Hammett gives full play to this suspicion. The mean streets of Personville are the stage for a massive fiction, where gangsters masquerade as businessmen, capitalists contract with criminals, and no one can tell the difference between them. The arrival of the Op can be seen as the addition of another player, someone ready to ad-lib his own script.

CHANDLER'S KNIGHT AND HAMMETT'S OPERATIVE

> But down these mean streets a man must go who is not himself mean, who is neither tarnished nor afraid. The detective in this story must be such a man. He is the hero, he is everything.
>
> —Raymond Chandler 237

As noted above, Chandler praised Hammett for getting it right, for bringing detective fiction back to the "real world." But Chandler and other detective writers who followed Hammett were not entirely comfortable with Hammett's "dark, unstable world" (Shulman 405), a world in which all values seem undermined, a world apparently without center or anchor. Chandler himself found a way to counterbalance the situation, to reground the world of detective fiction: in his fiction, the detective is heroized, converted into a latter-day knight (Marlowe = Mallory), a locus of value. Chandler's knight is "a man of honor, by instinct, by inevitability, without thought of it, and certainly without saying it. He must be the best man in his world and a good enough man for any world" (Chandler 237). Chandler's detective serves as lawmaker, supplying his anarchic world with a valid code of behavior, creating a kind of "absolute value" (Knight 287). Detective fiction after Chandler follows his lead, articulates an ethos of the individual, the private "I," and reinforces a popular American view, namely that justice finally depends more on the individual than on society.

At first look Hammett's detective seems to fit in with this scheme. In all the stories featuring him, he remains nameless, simply "the Continental Operative," an agent wholly identified with his agency: "When I say *me*," he tells Elihu Willson, "I mean the Continental" (41). The Operative is, his "name" tells us, simply his function, a worker, with "no commitment, personal or social, beyond the accomplishment of his job" (Willett 11). A basic part of that function is to adhere to his agency's code, which stipulates, for one thing, that agents cannot profit from their cases. Near the beginning of **Red Harvest,** Willson tries to buy the Op off; the Op rebuffs him, citing the Continental's rules against taking bonuses or rewards (59). In another story, the detective articulates his basic credo to a client:

> Now I'm a detective because I happen to like the work. . . . And liking work makes you want to do it as well as you can. Otherwise there'd be no sense to it. That's the fix I am in. I don't know anything else, don't enjoy anything else, don't want to know or enjoy anything else. You can't weigh that against any sum of money.
>
> (*Big Knockover* 50-51)

Since the Op remains completely silent about his private life, he apparently has no life outside his work. The nearest thing to a personal relationship for the Op involves the father figure he serves, the Old Man, the head of the agency, whose "fifty years of sleuthing had left him without any feelings at all on any subject" (**Big Knockover** 99). The Operative is thus detached, principled, dedicated—in short, the perfect professional.

Only not in "Poisonville." Near the end of the novel, the Op makes a rambling confession to Dinah Brand: "Poisonville is right. It's poisoned me" (145). Something does happen to the usually unflappable Op in the town; he does become infected, caught up in its schemes and practices. In Personville, violence is the basic means to selfish ends, and its inhabitants play out the Hobbesian war of all against all (Marcus 19). The Op manipulates and exacerbates this state of affairs, time and again "just stirring things up" (79, 178). In so doing, he becomes an active, involved, interested participant in the "red harvest" and thereby relinquishes his claim as locus of value.[3] "Cleaning up the town" becomes for him a euphemism for systematically eliminating its various players. The Op "declares war on Poisonville" (62), and his intervention results in a full-scale shooting war that ends only when all the major players, except Willson and the Op, are eliminated.

Since the Op is solely concerned with "cleaning up the town," he "is quickly drawn into the expanding circle of violence in Personville and eventually becomes himself an agent of this violence" (Gregory 37). But this is not the full measure of the extent to which Personville

has infected the Op. He does not simply participate in the wholesale slaughter; he masterminds it. He sets up the relatively innocent prize-fighter Ike Bush and then makes no comment at all when Ike gets a knife in the neck. Working with Sheriff Noonan, he fingers Whisper Thaler for Noonan's brother's murder even though he knows Whisper is innocent, and even though Noonan has double-crossed him and tried to murder him twice. Supposedly acting as peacemaker at the council of war, the Op goads the participants into a subsequent orgy of bloodletting. Several hours later, when he wakes up with his hand on an icepick sticking in the heart of the woman he is supposedly emotionally involved with, the Op methodically cleans up all traces of himself and walks out of the door.

Inevitably the question becomes how to account for the Op's active role in the bloodletting that he catalyzes in Personville. He himself tries to point the finger elsewhere, suggesting in one place that Dinah Brand is responsible; she has been "stirring up murderous notions" in her boyfriends, including apparently the Op (147). In general, though, he lays it off on the gap between theory and practice: "It's right enough for the Agency to have rules and regulations," he tells his coworker Mickey Linehan, "but when you're out on a job you've got to do it the best way you can" (109). Where the job is concerned, the end, no matter how suspect, justifies the means, no matter how bloody.

A more compelling explanation of the Op's participation in the red harvest has been offered by Sinda Gregory, who holds the "system" responsible. By insisting on the "moral neutrality" that produces efficiency and gets the job done, the Continental Detective Agency inevitably dehumanizes its agents, turns them into mere operatives:

> Although the Op seems most disturbed by his failure to live up to his code, clearly what Hammett finds more dangerous is the code itself, which allows men to subordinate moral responsibility to an allegiance to an abstract, self-devised system. . . . The Op depends on the strictness of his code to rationalize his actions and emotionless responses to situations; by obeying rules and regulations, he is freed from moral responsibilities and ethical choices that inevitably arise with any complex dilemma.
>
> (54)

Gregory's strong reading thus indicts the agency itself, and by extension the system that produced the agency, for "its refusal to consider human morality or man's responsibility to others" (55). Such a reading, however, tends to exculpate the Op, who becomes a cog in the works, simply carrying out his assignment. And as Christopher Bentley points out, it also misreads the true nature of the Op's professionalism and whitewashes his relation to the agency: The Op's "loyalty to his employers and to his work has no moral dimension, and is merely pride in a job that gives meaning to his life, providing acceptable outlets for his violence and need for power" (56). For the Op, a job is just that.

Gregory's reading does not finally explain the excessiveness of the Op's behavior, the blood lust that consumes him. The Op himself suggests that there is a more personal motive here—namely, revenge. He has been forced to declare war to get back at the "fat chief of police" who "tried to assassinate" him, not once but twice (60, see also 62-63). But as Robert Edenbaum notes, "the Op's own explanation of his motives . . . is not particularly convincing" (90). For one thing, this supposedly personal motive leads to highly impersonal behaviors. If the Op is simply trying to get even, then he goes about it in a coldly calculated, indirect way, much of the time conspiring with the chief of police, the very man he wants revenge on. At the same time he implicates relatively innocent bystanders such as Ike Bush. And he continues his war even after the chief's death.

In general, these explanations fail to satisfy. As Bentley concludes, "the Op's motives remain fundamentally unclear" (62). Indeed, most of the Op's behavior is ultimately unfathomable. There are no motives, public or private, social or antisocial, to explain what happens to him. Nor should this surprise readers. Gregory is right to argue that with the Op, Hammett has given us "a character whose motives, actions, and values are as complex and ambiguous as the world in which he operates" (48). That world is mean and unpredictable, and there is no satisfactory explanation for its "ethical unintelligibility" (Marcus 14). The same kind of unintelligibility characterizes the Op's entire stay in "Poisonville." We don't know how to react to what he's doing while he's doing it, or what he has "accomplished" when he's done, when control of the town reverts to Willson because the Op has eliminated all of Willson's rivals. The Op comes to town to perform an operation, to rid the body social of its disease. Trying to get something done, he works by expedience; the Operative becomes the operator. Later he is infected by a kind of blood lust, becoming "blood simple" (146). The Operative becomes the operated, a bloodthirsty machine. In Hammett's fallen world, we all fall down. But as the slide in signifiers above suggests—from operative to operator to operated—that lapsarian state affects language as well.

HAMMETT'S MEAN-INGLESS STREETS

The realist in murder writes of a world . . . where no man can walk down a dark street in safety because law and order are things we talk about but refrain from practising.

—Raymond Chandler 236

Hammett makes it clear in **Red Harvest** that the acts of social rupture he is recording have begun to affect the sign, creating a rift between signifier and signified. At one point in the narrative Dinah Brand urges the Op not to mention killing, because she is afraid of the word. The Op chides her for the childishness that makes her confuse words with deeds: "You think if nothing's said about it, maybe none of the God only knows how many people in town who might want to will kill you. That's silly" (148). Unlike Dinah Brand, most of the other people in the Op's world labor under no such misconception. They are very much aware that Personville's lawlessness infects language itself, with the result that most speech acts are highly suspect.

They are aware, for example, that there is no necessary correspondence between words and deeds. The most typical action in **Red Harvest** is the double-cross, to say one thing and do something else. Sheriff Noonan spends much of the novel double-crossing Whisper Thaler. Dinah Brand systematically double-crosses most of her admirers. In this world basic words no longer mean what they used to. Promises are made and routinely broken; truces are called only to be violated. Waving the white flag of surrender, Pete the Finn emerges from his wrecked headquarters, hands on head. The sender has faith in his sign; the receiver ignores it. Pete the Finn is greeted by an insult, four bullets in the face and body, and laughter from an onlooker (182). These and other crimes go unsolved or unpunished, in large part because all the perpetrators have alibis, which they invent casually and trade freely. Whisper Thaler has a group of hoods who regularly provide him with an alibi. Reno Starkey gives the Op an alibi for a crime that he himself has committed, the murder of Dinah Brand.

In Personville everyone has a story and seems anxious to share it with the Op. Unfortunately for the Op, most of these stories are misrepresentations or even complete fabrications. At one point the Op abruptly breaks off an interview because he knows his informant would only lie to him (28). After boozily rehearsing the history of her relation with Donald Willson, Dinah Brand challenges the Op to figure out "which part of the story I told you is true" (37). The Op himself is confident that "I looked most honest when I was lying" (156). In passages of dialogue, he sometimes replaces the tag "I said" with "I lied," as if to show that while he carries on his masquerade in Personville he is at least playing square with the readers.

As the above quotes suggest, the Op frequently makes references to the acts of storytelling and conversation, to saying and meaning. **Red Harvest** is a talky novel, composed in great part of dialogue, much of which is metalinguistic; it talks about talk itself. "You talked too much, son," the Op says, when he fingers the bank clerk Albury for the murder of Donald Willson: "That's a way you amateur criminals have. You've always got to overdo the frank and open business" (55). When ex-cop McSwain offers to do "things" to move the operation along, the Op asks bluntly, "You want to stool-pigeon for me?" McSwain shoots back, "There's no sense in a man picking out the worst name he can find for everything" (89). It's appropriate that the mayhem in the novel ends with the Op listening to the last of the gangsters, Reno Starkey, "talk himself to death" (198).

In a world of nonstop talkers, the Op himself is a man of few words; his partner sarcastically complains, "You're going to ruin yourself some time telling people too much" (194). The Op also has a keen ear for linguistic mumbo jumbo or rhetorical gas, a talent he uses most frequently with Elihu Willson, the client continually manipulating words to get what he wants. The following exchange between the two is typical:

> "You're a great talker," [Willson] said. "I know that. A two-fisted, you-be-damned man with your words. But have you got anything else? Have you got the guts to match your gall? Or is it just the language you've got?"
>
> There was no use in trying to get along with the old boy. I scowled and reminded him:
>
> "Didn't I tell you not to bother me unless you wanted to talk sense for a change?"
>
> "You did, my lad." There was a foolish sort of triumph in his voice. "And I'll talk you your sense. I want a man to clean this pig-sty of a poisonville for me, to smoke out the rats, little and big. It's a man's job. Are you a man?"
>
> "What's the use of getting poetic about it?" I growled. "If you've got a fairly honest piece of work to be done in my line, and you want to pay a decent price, maybe I'll take it on. But a lot of foolishness about smoking rats and pig-pens doesn't mean anything to me."
>
> "All right. I want Personville emptied of its crooks and grafters. Is that plain enough language for you?"
>
> (39)

Even at the end of this exchange, Willson is only apparently using "plain language" since he obviously exempts himself from his charge, and he is the biggest crook of all. Later the Op responds in a similar no-nonsense way to the pontifications of the shyster lawyer Charles Proctor Dawn.

But even the Op succumbs to the linguistic evasions that affect discourse in Personville. The Op describes the aftermath of a particularly bloody evening as follows: "I felt so much like a native that even the memory of my very un-nice part in the boiling didn't keep me from getting twelve solid end-to-end hours of sleep" (108). Here the Op goes "native" and uses euphemistic language of the clumsiest kind—"my very un-nice part"—to gloss over his involvement in the massacre. When he later tells Mickey Linehan that in Personville

the end justifies the means, his line of argument is undercut by Linehan's response, itself an example of the plain talking that the Op supposedly values: "What kind of crimes have you got for us to pull?" (109-10). And the Op's multiple attempts to excuse his actions in the city finally seem "overcooked." Regardless of whom or what he is blaming—the woman Dinah Brand; Noonan, the chief of police; the assignment; the "damned burg" (142)—his protestations come across as self-serving, suspect, themselves products of the rhetorical effluence that infects Personville.

At one point Dinah Brand equates language with money, insisting that the latter is the only language she speaks (31). Brand's throw-away line actually passes over a profound resemblance. Jean-Joseph Goux remarks that money metaphors haunt discussions of language and "betray an awareness, as yet veiled and embryonic, of the correspondence between the mode of economic exchange and the mode of signifying exchange" (96). Both money and words, Goux argues, are abstract "general equivalents" with no necessary connection to the values (economic or semantic) that they substitute for. Under the system of capitalism, money is the privileged medium of exchange, and "commodities are universally evaluated only through the detour of *specie*—that is, through signs, masks, representations" (38). In the world of the 1920s, where the U.S. Treasury is printing more and more greenbacks, each of which is, as a result, more abstracted from the real labor-value it supposedly represents, this kind of specie, paper money, would be revealing its specious nature. Brand may prefer money to language, but in Hammett's world both of them are undergoing an extended period of inflation that undermines their value. It's all paper money and paper language.[4]

Critics have noted that Hammett's is a disturbing world in which behavior is unpredictable, motivation obscure, and evaluation suspect. But equally disturbing is the fact that language has succumbed to a process of erosion, that the lack of motivation has begun to infect the words we speak. Words are becoming arbitrary counters whose real value is unknown. Language, like behavior, begins to reveal its arbitrary nature. The basis of Hammett's unsettling power lies in the fact that he records a historical process of uncoupling, the unzipping of the relation between outer signs and inner meanings, between words and deeds—in short, between the signifier and the signified. Hammett's world is in the process of losing the consolation, certitude, or stability provided by grounds. This subversion of foundations lies at the heart of Hammett's detective fiction, informing the cognitive, ethical, and linguistic unintelligibility that characterizes it.

Chandler claims that Hammett's brand of detective fiction provides better models of the world, that it faces up to and records "the seamy side of things" (234). But that unsavory world, we have seen, is one in which there is no stable or secure relation between signifiers and signifieds. Hammett is finally much more skeptical than Chandler about the ability of language to reflect reality, to capture reality in a satisfactory way; and he makes that skepticism clear in **Red Harvest**. The experiences recorded in Hammett's detective fiction inevitably subvert the whole idea of valid models, insofar as a model is itself a sign vehicle presupposing a motivated relation between signifier and signified. The vision of his detective fiction, in other words, undermines the reality claims of its proponents. What Hammett's fiction finally records is not the "real world" but rather the beginning of the fall of language from motivation to non-motivation, from identity to difference, from presence to absence.

But even in Hammett there is resistance to this lapsarian state. When Dinah Brand asks the Op why he didn't eliminate Whisper Thaler when he had the chance, his reply is curious: "'Sorry,' I said, *meaning it*" (148, emphasis added). That the Op is sorry that he did not cold-bloodedly murder someone reveals much about his state of mind. But, the dialogue tag insists, he is *truly* sorry. In **Red Harvest** readers are immersed in a world in which honesty can never be taken for granted, in which the enunciation goes to some lengths to inform them that something is true, that something is finally "meant." But that enunciation exists, in the form of the novel itself. When the case is over, the Op submits to the agency a doctored report, full of lies: "I spent most of my week in Ogden trying to fix up my reports so they would not read as if I had broken as many Agency rules, state laws and human bones as I had" (198). He may lie to the Old Man; he doesn't lie to the reader. His narrative can be seen as a last-ditch attempt to "come clean" in the cleaning-up process—not to erase the red stain but to acknowledge his complicity with it.

Narrating his story for the reader, the Op implicitly promises to tell all. In so doing he establishes a convention that detective fiction picks up on, a commitment to the truth of the enunciation. The narrator of detective fiction cannot and does not break faith with the reader because his narration is the last, best, and only ground. This is finally why, for those who come after Hammett, that narration and the voice that renders it become so important; they represent an affirmation of signification, an assertion of mastery and control over a world otherwise unanchored. For Chandler and others, the style (of the enunciation) is indeed the man. Hammett, for his part, is true enough to his vision to call a spade a spade and show just what that means to the ground(s) we tend to take for granted.

Notes

1. Barzun and Taylor say: "There is no warrant for the commonly held belief that the tough detective tale yields a greater truth than the gentler classical form and marks a forward step toward the 'real novel'" (9). They go on to enumerate (and make fun of) the conventions and motifs of detective fiction (9-11). For an extended discussion of the difference between Hammett's *detective* fiction and Christie's *mystery* fiction, see Malmgren.

2. See, for example, Cawelti, esp. 139-61, and Grella.

3. Metress says: "While it is true that Chandler, Spillane, MacDonald, and others influenced by Hammett have each embraced to some extent an ethos of rugged individualism, Hammett's fiction does not support such a doctrine" (243).

4. For a skeptical view of language and communication in *The Maltese Falcon*, see Hall.

Works Cited

Barzun, Jacques, and Wendell H. Taylor. Introductory. *A Catalogue of Crime*. New York: Harper, 1971. 3-21.

Bentley, Christopher. "Radical Anger: Dashiell Hammett's *Red Harvest*." *American Crime Fiction: Studies in the Genre*. Ed. Brian Docherty. New York: St. Martin's, 1988. 54-70.

Cawelti, John. *Adventure, Mystery, and Romance: Formula Stories as Art and Popular Culture*. Chicago: U of Chicago P, 1976.

Chandler, Raymond. "The Simple Art of Murder." *The Art of the Mystery Story*. Ed. Howard Haycraft. New York: Carrol, 1985. 222-37.

Edenbaum, Robert I. "The Poetics of the Private Eye: The Novels of Dashiell Hammett." *Tough Guy Writers of the Thirties*. Ed. David Madden. Carbondale: Southern Illinois UP, 1968. 80-103.

Goux, Jean-Joseph. *Symbolic Economies: After Marx and Freud*. Trans. Jennifer Curtiss Gage. Ithaca: Cornell UP, 1990.

Gregory, Sinda. *Private Investigations: The Novels of Dashiell Hammett*. Carbondale: Southern Illinois UP, 1985.

Grella, George. "The Hard-Boiled Detective Novel." *Detective Fiction: A Collection of Critical Essays*. Ed. Robin W. Winks. Englewood Cliffs: Prentice, 1980. 103-20.

Hall, Jasmine Yong. "Jameson, Genre, and Gumshoes: *The Maltese Falcon* as Inverted Romance." *The Cunning Craft: Original Essays on Detective Fiction and Contemporary Literary Theory*. Ed. Ronald G. Walker and June M. Frazer. Macomb: Yeast, 1990. 109-19.

Hammett, Dashiell. *The Big Knockover and Other Stories*. Harmondsworth: Penguin, 1986.

———. *The Continental Op*. London: Picador, 1984.

————. "The House in Turk Street." *The Continental Op*. Ed. Steven Marcus. London: Picador, 1975. 90-119.

————. *The Maltese Falcon*. 1930. New York: Vintage, 1989.

————. *Red Harvest*. 1929. New York: Vintage, 1972.

————. "They Can Only Hang You Once." *Fiction 100*. 4th ed. Ed. James H. Pickering. New York: Macmillan, 1985. 462-69.

Haycraft, Howard. *Murder for Pleasure: The Life and Times of the Detective Story*. 1941. New York: Biblo, 1974.

Knight, Stephen. *Form and Ideology in Crime Fiction*. Bloomington: Indiana UP, 1980.

Malmgren, Carl D. "Anatomy of Murder: Mystery, Detective, and Crime Fiction." *Journal of Popular Culture* 30.4 (Spring 1997): 115-36.

Marcus, Steven. Introduction. *The Continental Op*. London: Picador, 1975. 7-23.

Metress, Christopher. "Dashiell Hammett and the Challenge of the New Individualism: Rereading *Red Harvest* and *The Maltese Falcon*." *Essays in Literature* 17.2 (Fall 1990): 242-60.

Porter, Dennis. *The Pursuit of Crime: Art and Ideology in Detective Fiction*. New Haven: Yale UP, 1981.

Shulman, Robert. "Dashiell Hammett's Social Vision." *The Centenniel Review* 29.4 (Fall 1985): 400-19.

Willett, Ralph. *Hard-Boiled Detective Fiction*. British Association for American Studies Pamphlet 23. Keele: Keele UP, 1992.

Brian Cooper and Margueritte Murphy (essay date March 2000)

SOURCE: Cooper, Brian, and Margueritte Murphy. "Taking Chances: Speculation and Games of Detection in Dashiell Hammett's *Red Harvest*." *Mosaic* 33, no. 1 (March 2000): 145-60.

[*In the following essay, Cooper and Murphy study* Red Harvest *to demonstrate the affinities between game theory in the field of economics and the strategies of "clue-detection" in detective fiction.*]

Especially in the wake of New Historicism, considerations of the economic and the political have come to dominate literary analysis. As important as the work of Marxist theorists Louis Althusser, Fredric Jameson and Terry Eagleton has been in laying the groundwork for much of this analysis, there has also been growing interest in economic thought outside the Marxist tradition.

Much of the thrust of such work is critical, interrogating the foundations and assumptions of classical and neoclassical economics and the relationship between these discourses and aesthetic and cultural discourses. John Guillory's analysis of discourses of value, including the convergence of aesthetics and political economy in the work of Adam Smith (300-17), Mary Poovey's discussion of the trace of aesthetics in classical political economy, and Regenia Gagnier's work on the neoclassical marginalists and late 19th-century aestheticism are noteworthy examples of scholarship which goes beyond inquiry into literary text and economic context to consider literary and aesthetic writings and economics as comparable and interrelated discursive structures.

It is in the spirit of such inquiry that we turn to the consideration of detective fiction and game theory, a means of economic modeling which has become part of the basic tool-kit of mainstream economics. As a representation of risk-taking in literature, the detective plot is nearly emblematic. It involves danger, calculations, and constant gambles as the detective, playing a cat-and-mouse game with criminals, "wins" by proving the better strategist. Much of the pleasure of reading detective fiction lies in witnessing the detective "playing" the game of clue-detection and strategic manipulation of opponents, and winning. Our particular focus, Dashiell Hammett's **Red Harvest** (1929), in line with much detective fiction, is rife with strategizing, second-guessing, anticipations of opponents' moves, and the wins going to whomever can outwit the opponent, usually the detective himself. Indeed, references to "play" appear repeatedly in **Red Harvest** as they do often in the lingo employed by hard-boiled detectives.

Such strategic games are prominent in game theory as well. Developed by mathematicians, game theory offers a systematic analysis of strategic behavior, or interaction, between rational "players" (individuals or groups) in a "game." A game describes a list of players, a set of actions or strategies available to players in the game, and the outcomes contingent upon their actions. In a game, each player's thoughts and actions anticipate and depend upon what other players may think and do, and all players are concerned with furthering their interests. References to literary works and how literary characters try to determine the intentions of other characters, and act strategically to gain certain ends, crop up frequently in game theoretic analyses (Brams, "Game Theory and Literature" and *Theory of Moves*; Dixit and Nalebuff). In fact, in the pioneering work on game theory, *Theory of Games and Economic Behavior* (1944) by John von Neumann and Oskar Morgenstern, an episode from *The Adventures of Sherlock Holmes* appears as an illustration of one kind of game (176-78). Thus the analysis of detective plotting using game theory was adumbrated decades ago.

The structural similarities between the discourses are revelatory: parallels between game theory and detective plotting illuminate a modernist impulse in which the "rational" subject makes decisions faced with some degree of uncertainty, and thereby develops a strategy of control over uncertainty. Likewise, both game theory and the genre of detective fiction purport to domesticate irrationality by similar strategies of control: both discourses interpret and recuperate irruptions of irrationality (for instance, financial crises for economists, the criminal act or evil for writers of detective fiction) as rational strategizing, thus displacing irrational outcomes onto a grid of complex, but ultimately explicable strategic behavior.

In this essay, we will look at strategies of detection in **Red Harvest** and their affinities to some of the themes of contemporary game theoretic analyses in economics. It is a commonplace of **Red Harvest** criticism that the novel serves as a critique of capitalism. Steven Marcus observes that generally Hammett does not differentiate strongly between the criminal world and the use of political and economic power by "respectable" people (199). Curiously critics agree that the novel offers no attractive alternative to the current system, socialist or otherwise, but disagree on whether a Marxist reading is appropriate since in 1929 Hammett had not yet affiliated himself openly with leftist politics. So, while Peter Wolfe sees **Red Harvest** as a "Marxist attack on free enterprise" (77), and Dennis Porter describes the setting as "the alienated product of human labor on the level of a total environment" (197), Christopher Bentley concludes that Hammett's attitude in the novel is one of "an angry observer" of an unredeemable world (68), and William Marling notes that the politics of **Red Harvest** here include an "accommodation to late Progressivism" since Hammett ignores the collusion of the mines and the railroads contemporary to the writing of the novel, and treats reforming newspapers somewhat favorably (111).

But the ideology of the author need not, and indeed rarely does, dictate the choice of critical tools applied to the work. In their Marxian analysis of **Red Harvest,** Carl Freedman and Christopher Kendrick do not directly address the question of Hammett's own political sympathies. They argue instead that within the context of the novel, the detective's linguistic labor triumphs and subsumes other forms of labor in a narrative driven by the forces of monopoly capitalism. They maintain, however, that this triumph is hollow in that the detective's dissatisfaction at the end signals a perception that even his linguistic labor has been "reified into an instrument wielded for the benefit of the despicable capitalist boss Elihu" (220). We, too, find a critique of capitalism in **Red Harvest,** but will suggest ways in which the detective's plotting and the economic activity represented in the novel are both species of gaming. As a game, the detective's "linguistic labor" is strategic in creating and undoing a set of conspiracies. All the elements central to the detective's speculative strategies are salient features of game theoretic models: the presence of incomplete information, uncertainty and risk, the constant negotiations and renegotiations, the need to establish trust, credibility, and cooperation, the (in)ability to enforce contracts and the (in)ability to punish deviations from agreements through threats and reprisals, the key roles of learning and deception, rationality and irrationality, and the lack of a unitary subject.

Thus, game theory proffers a more nuanced economic model for analyzing the strategizing which creates and attempts to control the uncertainty of the characters in **Red Harvest.** This mode of analysis offers insights into Hammett's critique of the workings of capital in bargaining and speculation, a matter that Freedman and Kendrick's focus on the typology of labor in the novel misses.

From such analysis, we will move to consider the broader epistemic assumptions underlying both game theory and detective plotting. Rational strategies and solutions are crucial to both. While the history of game theory's application in the social sciences has been a move towards greater formalization, as if to overdetermine the rational solutions the theory has posited from the start (Cudd), developments in the field have eroded the hold of rationality in economic theory. The novel signals the implosion of a similarly overdetermined rationality when the detective, the hyperrational agent, intentionally drugs himself, passes out, and awakens to the charge of murder.

The plot of **Red Harvest** implies from the beginning that capitalism in America is involved in a deadly game in which self-interested strategizing rules, without ethical or legal restraint. At the opening of the novel, the detective, the Continental Op, arrives in Personville, tagged Poisonville, summoned by Donald Willsson, publisher of the local newspapers. Willsson is murdered before he can meet with the Op. His father, Elihu Willsson, owns not only the mines that give employment to the town but the bank, the newspapers, and some part of "nearly every other enterprise of any importance" (8). Prior to the start of the novel's action, Elihu has broken a miners' strike by bringing in help from organized crime. After the strike, the criminals decide to stay, and Elihu, unable to break publicly with men whose aid he sought during the strike, loses control over his town. When Elihu himself is threatened in his own bedroom by a thug with a blackjack, he panics and hires the Op to clean up the town. The fee is ten thousand dollars and Elihu agrees to give the Op free rein in Poisonville.

The Op accomplishes his task through an intricate game of playing the crooks (including Elihu) off one another through talk, disrupting the fragile alliances based on pecuniary interests and the threat of reprisal, violent and otherwise. The main gang leaders are Lew Yard, a loan shark and money launderer, Pete the Finn, a bootlegger, Max "Whisper" Thaler, an aptly named gambler ("thaler" is a variant of "taler," the German root of "dollar"), and Noonan, the chief of police. As Freedman and Kendrick argue, the novel demonstrates the strategic value of the Op's use of the spoken as opposed to the written word, as he sets the gangsters against one another (214-17). Yet the written word serves as an enforceable contract, unlike the verbal promises made, revised, and broken throughout the course of the book. The Op gets his original agreement with Elihu in writing and immediately sends it along with Elihu's check to the agency's office in San Francisco. Knowing that Elihu will back down on the agreement once the immediate scare has passed, the Op uses the existence of the check and the written contract at crucial points in the story to force Elihu to stick to the original terms of their bargain, and let the Op do as he pleases.

The contractual struggles between the Op and Elihu are an example of the principal-agent model in economics, a class of problems that has been extensively studied using game theoretic analyses. In the principal-agent problem, one person, the agent, acts on behalf of another person, the principal. The agent may act against the interests or desires of her or his employer in favor of her or his own interests (a typical case is a board of directors not working hard enough to obtain an adequate return for shareholders). Bargaining analyses have illuminated how contracts between principals and agents can be structured to better monitor the performance of agents, and more closely align their interests with those of their principals (Zeckhauser). In this case, however, a fearful Elihu has given the Op the contractual authority to use whatever means necessary to do the job.

Contracts are also taken to be always renegotiable and never totally enforceable in game theoretic literature. In fact, each meeting between the Op and Elihu begins with Elihu attempting to renegotiate the terms of their contract. The meetings, however, always end with a reaffirmation of the original agreement. That the Op can defy Elihu's wishes and operate as he pleases demonstrates both the Op's bargaining skills and the weakness of Elihu's bargaining position. Elihu could break the contract by going to court, but abstains from doing so because it would entail a public airing of evidence, something that could only hurt the old man. Ironically, the detective himself sees no point in any public revelation of the criminal activities—the criminals virtually own the law and the courts through Noonan and Elihu, who very soon turns on the Op—but instead works to incite a bloodbath. He enforces Elihu's contract with

the agency to put in play what game theorists would term the criminals' own contract enforcement mechanism, violence—thus the title, **Red Harvest.** It is a harvest, too, of the consequences of suppressing the Wobbly-sponsored or "red" strike with paid thugs, and so the title shows Hammett toying with "his readers' expectations of leftist worker violence," according to Dennis Dooley (77).

The Op also negotiates with Dinah Brand, a gangster's moll, "[a] soiled dove [. . .] a deluxe hustler, a big-league gold-digger" (22), whose actions are central to the plot of the novel and to the plotting of the Continental Op. Dinah is also preeminently an economic agent. As Freedman and Kendrick point out, she is a sexual worker, although we see none of this activity. Rather we see her live up to her reputation as "thoroughly mercenary" (27) through her bargaining and speculative activities. She sells information about the powerful men of Personville, in each instance negotiating a price, a process to which she brings a number of strategies. She is also the character in the novel most involved in gambling in the conventional sense: calculating odds, making bets, and anticipating monetary gains.

Dinah's role as information broker puts her at risk. The Op seeks information from Dinah first because Donald Willsson was seen coming from her house when he was shot and killed. This visit itself involved the sale of information. Willsson gave Dinah a certified check for five thousand dollars in return for evidence on the criminal activities of Personville's powerful thugs, documents he sought in his campaign to clean up the town through newspaper exposure. Dinah, calculating that Donald Willsson would not use the information because it incriminated his father, demanded a certified check or cash, so he could not stop payment and pull out of the agreement.

According to her account, Willsson was hesitant to pay her price, but she pretended he had a competitor for the information, and gave him a deadline, which he met. As she put it, "he hadn't been around much, so he fell for it" (37). In game theoretic terms, she practiced deception and manufactured competition to improve her bargaining position. Yet, in demanding cash or a certified check, she, in effect, "signaled" that there was something wrong with her information; why would the publisher renege on the deal, especially if he hoped to get more evidence of criminal activity from her in the future? But, as a neophyte bargainer and poor analyst of strategy, he paid the high, non-refundable price demanded by the seller.

All this information comes to the Op in the context of his first conversation with Dinah. Immediately we see the Op's superior strategic skills. He will not negotiate a price for her information, but instead, demonstrates how her risk-free strategy has backfired. Dinah took a calculated gamble that the documents she sold would be of no use to Donald Willsson. If she had been right, the information would have remained secret, and she would not have had to fear reprisal from any "friends" or lovers also incriminated. But she did not count on the information actually falling into the hands of one of the criminals. The Op informs Dinah (through half-truths) that she herself is being targeted as the murderer by Noonan, the police chief, who now possesses the documents she sold that detail his own involvement in illegal activities. The Op literally offers her "safety" as he seeks to discover the true murderer and thus free Dinah from suspicion. At this point, Dinah proposes a drink, and after emptying a bottle of gin, she, not he, loosens up and "spills" the information he wants for free.

Thus, where Dinah was clearly the superior strategist in the first bargaining agreement with Donald Willsson, the Op wins this game both by insinuating a threatening scenario that she does not see through and by holding his liquor better. The second factor signals an important vulnerability of the strategic player: the possibility of the loss of clear-headed rationality. The Op's greatest slip comes later when he loses consciousness after (intentionally) imbibing laudanum-laced gin fixed by Dinah. He awakes as a suspect in Dinah's ice-pick murder, a suspicion he himself holds until he discovers the actual murderer, Reno Starker, and hears him confess. Certainly the weakening or loss of rationality figured by drink and drugs is synecdochic for the crisis at the heart of hyper-rational strategic analysis: its own implosion into the irrational. Witness Sherlock Holmes's seven per cent solution of cocaine that he relies on to get him through mental boredom between cases. The impulse on the part of the Op to seek relief through laudanum may appear reasonable: all the Op wants is a good night's sleep. But in this instance he ignores the obvious perils of his choice, uncharacteristically taking a risk without foreseeing or estimating its repercussions.

In his choice to embrace the unconscious, the Op puts his whole enterprise of rationality in jeopardy and precipitates unforeseen and uncontrollable irrational action. Reno recounts how the detective's stupefaction contributes to Dinah's death and the suspicion that the Op committed the murder. Reno meets with Dinah at her house, and, though he does not know of the Op's presence, fears a trap. He struggles with Dinah while trying to "slap the truth out of her," and stabs her after hearing a man's (the Op's) feet hitting the floor in another room. Reno recalls: "You [the Op] gallop out, coked to the edges, charging at the whole world with both eyes shut. She tumbles into you. You go down, roll around till your hand hits the butt of the pick. Holding on to that, you go to sleep, peaceful as she is" (215). The Op liter-

ally does not know where he is or see what he is doing. Yet he acts, and awakes to find himself the prime suspect for her murder.

The irruption of the irrational into the game is a theme common to both the detective's strategic games and games of financial speculation. Dinah Brand plays the stock market, and bets on races and prize-fights; indeed, when we first see her, she is sitting at a table strewn with papers, "financial service bulletins, stock and bond market forecasts" alongside "a racing chart" (31). It is clear that for Dinah, as for most characters in this novel, there is little difference between legal and illegal speculation. Dinah, for example, made a profit on the stock market through information gained from a lover, the Wobbly leader, Bill Quint, about the timing of the beginning and ending of the miner's strike, a patent use of insider information. The speculative risk in this case is a double risk: she earns a death threat from Quint for her betrayal.

For Dinah, all talk is speculative. It is expensive talk, contrary to what game theorists call "cheap talk," or talk devoid of meaning. Information is a commodity which Dinah and other characters attempt to exchange for money. The novel's logic of exchange, however, demonstrates the instability and indeterminacy of the value of information. It is not clear how much her information is worth to any particular person at any point in time in the narrative, as we see in this exchange between the Op and Dinah:

> I [the Op] said: "You were saying you'd work with me if there was a cut of the Willsson money in it for you. There is."
>
> "How much?"
>
> "Whatever you earn. Whatever what you do is worth."
>
> "That's uncertain."
>
> "So's your help, so far as I know."
>
> (84)

Information's value is contingent, determined as the uncertain outcome of the "work" people do, and bargaining over the worth of that labor.

But money too is just a convention, its value determined by trust that its worth will remain stable over time. The recurrent figure of the runs in Dinah's stockings—she complains, "Every day—runs, runs, runs!" (33)—is a metonym for this instability of money. The runs represent rents in the (logic of) the fabric of capital. These are literally speculative runs—we almost always see her in disarray, with tears in her stockings which she buys and replaces daily, betting, trusting as it were, that this time the structure, the stockings, will hold. If the logic of political economy is to represent the operations of the economy (or capital) as a stable, rational grid, this grid is undone, even in its normal operations, by the instability of money as accounting measure and by its speculative function.

The Op remarks, noting another in Dinah's series of stocking runs, "Your legs are too big [. . .]. They put too much strain on the material" (84). Freedman and Kendrick read Dinah's runs and the "strain" that her legs put on "the material" as figurative for her sexual energy, itself a distortion of the economic labor that the action of the novel displaces, and the "strain" on the gangsters' organization, in other words, as energies from within the gangster world that its structures cannot contain (213). But Dinah's body, the erotic center of the novel, is also a metonym of speculative desire, straining the market structures that would contain it. Dinah embodies the libidinal intensity driving speculation. Object and subject of desire, Dinah is fully caught up in the circulation of tips and secrets, Personville's hottest commodities. As she puts it, "If a girl's got something that's worth, something to somebody, she's a boob if she doesn't collect" (35).

The fixed fight is the episode in the novel where the reader sees Dinah most clearly affected by the fever of gambling and speculation. Whisper, after trying to dissuade the Op from his clean-up Poisonville campaign, unwittingly unleashes a speculative run by "whispering" to the Op information about what the Op takes to be a "straight tip"—"telling me any bet on the main event would be good if its maker remembered that Kid Cooper would probably knock Ike Bush out in the sixth round" (69). The Op decides to circulate this tip in this town of "only some forty thousand inhabitants" (70), thus driving down the odds. Contrary to their purely economic interests, the townspeople pass along the tip in order to prove themselves insiders: as rational calculators of odds, they should see that such information would have a direct and negative impact on their anticipated gains when they place their own bets.

The Op then learns information that allows him to "uncook" the fight by threatening Ike Bush with disclosure of his criminal identity. The Op gives Dinah the counter-tip, and, gripped by the desire to win big, she calculates her chances and bets, despite the danger that such winnings may appear to Whisper as evidence of betrayal. Timing is everything:

> "Everybody in town seems to know Bush is going to dive," I said. "I saw a hundred put on Cooper at four to one a few minutes ago." I leaned past Rolff and put my mouth close to where the gray fur collar hid the girl's ear, whispering: "The dive is off. Better copper your bets while there's time."
>
> Her big bloodshot eyes went wide and dark with anxiety, greed, curiosity, suspicion.

> "You mean it?" she asked huskily.
>
> "Yeah."
>
> She chewed her reddened lips, frowned, asked:
>
> "Where'd you get it?"
>
> I wouldn't say. She chewed her mouth some more and asked:
>
> "Is Max on?"
>
> "I haven't seen him. Is he here?"
>
> "I suppose so," she said absent-mindedly, a distant look in her eyes.
>
> Her lips moved as if she were counting to herself.
>
> I said: "Take it or leave it, but it's a gut."
>
> She leaned forward to look sharply into my eyes, clicked her teeth together, opened her bag, and dragged out a roll of bills the size of a coffee can. Part of the roll she pushed at Rolff.
>
> "Here, Dan, get it down on Bush. You've got an hour anyway to look over the odds."
>
> Rolff took the money and went off on his errand. I took his seat. She put a hand on my forearm and said:
>
> "Christ help you if you've made me drop that dough."
>
> (75)

As a rational economic agent, Dinah calculated her potential winnings, based on the odds, but her heightened excitement is apparent in the look in her eyes, in the huskiness in her voice, and in the chewing of her "reddened lips." She is aware of the danger to herself if Max (Whisper) is not in on the tip, but takes that risk in the frenzy of the sure bet. (We might even say that here the Op usurps Max's "whispering" role, displacing him as Dinah's closest ally.) While one might protest that this is not a true gamble, that she acts on insider information, she does take a gamble in deciding whose information to trust. This circumstance epitomizes how strategic risk-taking dominates in the criminal world of this novel. Although Dinah does not know the whole story, the fight is, in fact, decided by which side is able to put the most persuasive pressure on the boxer at the crucial moment. Hammett does not leave his readers with any true foreknowledge of the outcome either; as the fight proceeds, it seems that Ike Bush (a.k.a. Al Kennedy) has forgotten the Op's threat until the Op yells "Back to Philly, Al" (77), and others join in for the fun of it.

The Op describes this episode in retrospect as an "experiment." In "uncooking" the fight, he sets in motion the latent energies of the novel's criminal forces. The Op sees the hold that Whisper's reputation has on the general populace through the circulation of "whispers" and what enforces that hold—swift revenge for transgression: a knife flashes through the air, instantly killing Bush in the ring, a sign of Whisper's power for all to see. The Op is learning the rules of play in Poisonville, the characters of the players, and what their preferred strategies are. He is also learning about Dinah, her loyalties (or lack thereof), her weaknesses, her price.

After the fight, Dinah breaks with Whisper and proposes selling more information to the Op. Typically, Dinah's "money talk" puts into play and into jeopardy not just her own credibility but every character's physical security. Every conversation threatens to unleash events resulting in death. If speculative fever mobilizes the play of desire, it mobilizes as well anxiety over the possibility of blood letting and blood fever, the pleasure murder engenders, a true death drive. This becomes clear in the chapter entitled "—$200.10—" where nervous haggling between Dinah and the Op sets the price at which she will turn over Whisper.

The Op exploits the blood fever by keying on Noonan's weariness of the mayhem to arrange a peace conference. The conference itself is portrayed as a deadly game, with the players seated around Willsson's library table with poker faces. In the Op's estimate, "I was in a good spot if I played my hand right, and in a terrible one if I didn't" (148). At the conference, the Op's carefully selected words initiate the undoing of the gangs' coalitions, and Noonan is gunned down immediately after the meeting breaks up. The Op's strategy works, yet he expresses the fear that he himself has caught the blood fever (154) for by playing his "hand" he had a hand in any consequent murders. This sickness, which Dinah Brand warns will lead to "a nervous breakdown" (158), has led him to reject an alternative solution, an earlier end to the game:

> I could have gone to him [Elihu] this afternoon and showed him that I had them ruined. He'd have listened to reason. He'd have come over to my side, have given me the support I needed to swing the play legally. I could have done that. But it's easier to have them killed off, easier and surer, and, now that I'm feeling this way, more satisfying.
>
> (157)

This alternative solution is less easy, less efficient. It is, nonetheless, a rational solution. Without going into a full-blown review of the literature, we note that for some classes of evolutionary games players are more likely to survive by playing slightly less-efficient strategies. The Op's preferred solution, more cold-blooded and calculated to be a more efficient use of Elihu's funds, is also more satisfying. Death eliminates uncertainty, the true random element that eludes analysis in economics. But death is also the preferred enforcement mechanism of the criminal gangs. The atavistic dissolution of the self, succumbing to "blood fever" or going "blood simple" and becoming just like the criminals

"getting a rear out of planning deaths" (157), is exactly what unsettles the Op and leads him to embrace the unconscious through the amnesia-inducing laudanum. Sinda Gregory's insight is relevant here: Hammett endows the Op with the efficiency, moral neutrality, and allegiance to his job that is typical of the hard-boiled detective, but also highlights the destructive consequences of this ethic, creating an irony that the Op himself fully and painfully perceives (48).

The Op takes the laudanum in a scene that parodies the ideology of separate spheres ("Honey, I'm home. Work is killing me, it's murder out there. Fix me a drink, will ya?"). Dinah's home is hardly a haven safe from the competition of the marketplace; rather, it's the base of her business operations, and the site of an earlier fatal shootout. Nor does Dinah initially play the part of the dutiful housewife to the Op's hardworking husband. When he asks, "Haven't you got any gin? Or do you like making me ask for it?" she replies with a tart "You know where it is" (154). When she finally does become anxious, it is for both the Op's mental state and for her own safety. But her domestic ministrations to the Op set in motion the action of the unconscious that results not in her security but in her death.

The surrender of the rational strategist to the unconscious in **Red Harvest** parallels the threat to the logic of political economy latent in speculative markets. Economists have attempted to domesticate the irrational in theories of speculative behavior precisely by taming the atavistic behavior (Bagehot's "herd mentality" or Keynes's "animal spirits") which mobilize the destructive capacities of capital. Financial market analyses have both redescribed financial crises—where, like the action of the novel, the convention of money is called into question and a nervous breakdown occurs—as the logical outcome of rational processes (Kyle; Abolafia and Kilduf), and assumed that day-to-day irrationality on the part of traders or "noise" guides the market even as there is underlying (annual) stability, that is, a tight correlation between a company's stock performance and real world performance in the long run (Kreps). It is possible that anxiety about such "noise" drives innovation in game theory, and that it is similar to the anxiety that is figured in the drink and drugs that release the Op temporarily from his highly risky, hyper-rational game.

Jean-François Lyotard's characterization of financial crises in *Libidinal Economy* as evidence of desire's ubiquity and violence is a more satisfactory representation of the underlying psychology of currency speculation, panics and crises than conventional economic narratives (Cooper and Murphy). Lyotard also berates political economy for dissimulating the singular quality of each economic exchange, with its libidinal excess that political economy cannot account for in every sense of the word. This championing of singularities over the explanatory systems of mainstream economists suits the profile of gambling as economic event well. Von Neumann and Morgenstern demonstrate that the apparent irrationality of the gambler's bluff, overstating or understating your hand in poker, can serve a strategic end (it pays to mislead the other player), and can be analyzed quantitatively (186-219). Bluffing plays a large role in the novel. Yet there is no predictive value for a single gamble: each bet constitutes a single event governed by uncertainty (chance, or true randomness) rather than probabilistic risk, which governs a series of events, and where players can assign odds to the possible outcomes. And even where the bets are repeated again and again, and outcomes can be assigned odds, the gambles, like Dinah's speculation in stock(ing)s, are taken more for the sake of their libidinal charge than for any real economic gain.

Interestingly, this randomness links the risk-taking lifestyle of Dinah Brand to the Op's methodology as a detective. Incredulous that the Op did not bet on the fight with his insider information, Dinah asks him about other motives for "uncooking" the fight. It is at this point that he calls it an "experiment," and goes on to explain his expectations:

> "Plans are all right sometimes," I said. "And sometimes just stirring things up is all right—if you're tough enough to survive, and keep your eyes open so you'll see what you want when it comes to the top."
>
> (85)

So the Op has gambled as well; his campaign to clean up Poisonville is a series of calculated risks.

But chance is the great repressed "explanation" in *Red Harvest.* The famous "beam falling" parable of *The Maltese Falcon* is relevant here: a man, barely missed by a falling beam from a construction site, realizes the power of blind chance, flees his staid life with his wife and children in Tacoma, Washington, but soon forgets what he learned and returns to the same life with another woman in another town, Spokane (62-64). Sam Spade, like the Op, is adept at anticipating "falling beams," but he knows that he can't foresee all of them. He also knows that ordinary people will soon forget the moral lessons of near disaster. At the end of *Red Harvest,* despite the success of the Op's clean-up, we are left with the impression that this narrative is ultimately a circular one, that Personville will soon revert to Poisonville when new players move in to take over the old players' roles. In a sense, the Op was Personville's "falling beam," who happened to come into town at the right moment and "stir things up." But in a world of random chance-taking and the unbridled speculation of capitalism, no narrative of progress is credible.

In concluding, we might note that the reader not only witnesses a game in *Red Harvest,* but also plays one in deciphering clues along with the Op. Certainly this sort

of game is more marked in traditional detective stories like Conan Doyle's or Agatha Christie's. (For a general discussion of the author-reader dynamic in the detective story as a game, see Suits.) Yet in witnessing the stratagems of the "hard-boiled" detective, the reader is disciplined in forms of rational, strategic thought. The reader is also exposed to the confusion and lacunae that an increasingly complicated and sophisticated game produce. Bernard Williams captures well how knowledge diminishes as information accumulates in describing the history of criminal conspiracy in post-war France:

> The baroque structure of these intrigues, in which an agent might act to create the impression that a second agent was acting so as to create the impression that the first agent was engaged in a conspiracy (for instance, that one), must surely have resulted in a situation in which no one really understood what anyone was doing; and this lack of understanding will also have affected the situation to be understood. Since such a situation is structured by the agents' intentions, and their intentions are conditioned by their increasingly confused grasp of others' intentions, there comes a point at which there is no truth of the matter about what they are doing.
>
> (4-5)

Or, as the Op's assistant, the wise-cracking Mickey, puts it when the Op gives him his assignment:

> "After I take this Finnish gent," Mickey said, "what do I do with him? I don't want to brag about how dumb I am, but this job is plain as astronomy to me. I understand everything about it except what you have done and why, and what you're trying to do and how."
>
> (118)

Yet we would also like to make the larger point that these striking parallels between plotting and its satisfactions in detective fiction and game theoretic analysis are more than coincidental. They represent a mode of thought that is peculiarly attractive to the contemporary mind: a winning strategy reliant on a clear, comprehensible model of rationality. Game theory in the last few decades has tackled more and more complex strategic analysis through increasing mathematical formalism, which assumes ever-expanding notions of rationality (Aumann). Some game theoretic solutions, however, have postmodern aspects such as indeterminacy (outcomes in which there are multiple equilibria or no equilibrium), nonunitary subjects, and subjects whose irrationality is the outcome of rational decision-making. And the proliferation of game theoretic solutions has occasioned a partial abandonment of economic postulates of rationality, purposeful behavior and equilibrium, a fundamental shift which is discomfiting to those economists who appreciate the metanarrative of general equilibrium theory (the specific set of conditions under which all markets clear simultaneously) (Kreps). In a sense, the "field" is betting on rationality to circumscribe the irrational, but this too is an ongoing "game."

Works Cited

Abolafia, Mitchel Y., and Martin Kilduf. "Enacting market crisis: the social construction of a speculative bubble." *Administrative Science Quarterly* 33 (June 1988): 177-93.

Aumann, Robert J. "What is game theory trying to accomplish?" *Frontiers of economics.* Eds. Kenneth J. Arrow and Seppo Honkapohja. Oxford: Blackwell: 1985. 28-76.

Brams, Steven J. "Game Theory and Literature." *Games and Economic Behavior* 6 (1994): 32-54.

Bentley, Christopher. "Radical Anger: Dashiell Hammett's *Red Harvest.*" *American Crime Fiction: Studies in the Genre.* Ed. Brian Docherty. London: Macmillan, 1988. 54-70.

Cooper, Brian P., and Margueritte S. Murphy. "'Libidinal economics': Lyotard and accounting for the unaccountable." *The New Economic Criticism: Studies at the intersection of literature and economics.* Eds. Martha Woodmansee and Mark Osteen. London: Routledge, 1999. 229-41.

Cudd, Ann E. "Game Theory and the History of Ideas about Rationality: An Introductory Survey." *Economics and Philosophy* 9 (1993): 101-33.

Dixit, Avinash K., and Barry J. Nalebuff. *Thinking Strategically: The Competitive Edge in Business, Politics, and Everyday Life.* New York: Norton, 1991.

Dooley, Dennis. *Dashiell Hammett.* New York: Ungar, 1984.

Freedman, Carl, and Christopher Kendrick. "Forms of Labor in Dashiell Hammett's *Red Harvest.*" *PMLA* 106 (1991): 209-21.

Gagnier, Regenia. "On the Insatiability of Human Wants: Economic and Aesthetic Man." *Victorian Studies* 36 (1993): 125-53.

Gregory, Sinda. *Private Investigations: The Novels of Dashiell Hammett.* Carbondale: Southern Illinois UP, 1985.

Guillory, John. *Cultural Capital: The Problem of Literary Canon Formation.* Chicago: U of Chicago P, 1993.

Hammett, Dashiell. *The Maltese Falcon.* 1930. New York: Vintage, 1992.

——. *Red Harvest.* 1929. New York: Vintage, 1989.

Kreps, David M. "Economics—The Current Position." *Daedalus* 126.1 (1997): 59-85.

Kyle, Albert S. "Informed speculation with imperfect competition." *Review of Economic Studies* 56 (July 1989): 317-55.

Lyotard, Jean-François. *Libidinal Economy.* 1974. Trans. Iain Hamilton Grant. Bloomington: Indiana UP, 1993.

Marcus, Steven. "Dashiell Hammett and the Continental Op." *Partisan Review* 41 (1974): 366-377. Rpt. in *The Critical Response to Dashiell Hammett.* Ed. Christopher Metress. Westport, CT: Greenwood, 1994. 194-202.

Marling, William. *The American Roman Noir: Hammett, Cain, and Chandler.* Athens, GA: U of Georgia P, 1995.

Poovey, Mary. "Aesthetics and Political Economy in the Eighteenth Century: The Place of Gender in the Social Constitution of Knowledge." *Aesthetics and Ideology.* Ed. George Levine. New Brunswick, NJ: Rutgers UP, 1994. 79-105.

Porter, Dennis. *The Pursuit of Crime: Art and Ideology in Detective Fiction.* New Haven: Yale UP, 1981.

Suits, Bernard. "The Detective Story: A Case Study of Games in Literature." *Canadian Review of Comparative Literature* 12.2 (1985): 200-19.

Von Neumann, John, and Oskar Morgenstern. *Theory of Games and Economic Behavior.* 1953. 3rd ed. Princeton: Princeton UP, 1980.

Williams, Bernard. "Formal Structures and Social Reality." *Trust: Making and Breaking Cooperative Relations.* Ed. Diego Gambetta. Oxford: Blackwell, 1988. 3-13.

Wolfe, Peter. *Beams Falling: The Art of Dashiell Hammett.* Bowling Green, OH: Bowling Green U Popular P, 1980.

John T. Irwin (essay date fall 2000)

SOURCE: Irwin, John T. "Unless the Threat of Death Is behind Them: Hammett's *The Maltese Falcon.*" *Literary Imagination* 2, no. 3 (fall 2000): 341-74.

[*In the following essay, Irwin draws connections between the story of Flitcraft in* The Maltese Falcon, *Nathaniel Hawthorne's short story "Wakefield," and the Book of Job from the Old Testament.*]

Over the last ten or fifteen years I have reread Dashiell Hammett's **The Maltese Falcon** at least once, sometimes twice, a year and accompanied each rereading with a viewing of John Huston's film version of the novel. Some readers may dismiss this yearly or twice-yearly rereading of the same book as either boring or silly, or merely obsessive-compulsive. I hope to find on examination that it is neither boring nor silly, and though I may accept "obsessive-compulsive," I reject the "merely."

Of course, I can account in part for my returning again and again to *The Maltese Falcon* on the practical grounds that I was using the book to work on a long narrative poem, begun in 1981 and finished in 1997, called *Just Let Me Say This About That*. It was written in blank verse, and given its subject matter, I wanted its diction to be as colloquial and American, as hard-nosed, energetic, and unsentimental as I could make it. So I re-read *The Maltese Falcon* periodically to remind myself of the kind of idiomatic, knowing, skeptical sound I wanted the poem to have, and I found that whenever I'd been working on the blank verse for a long time and the cadences and diction of Wordsworth's *Prelude* or Marlowe's dramas had begun to creep in, reading Hammett's prose washed them away quick. So there's part of the reason for my going back continually to the book, but only the smaller part. The bigger one's not so quickly nor so easily described.

Let me start that description by saying that for me *The Maltese Falcon* is the emotional and intellectual equivalent of comfort food, that particular dish or meal each one of us has that's always appetizing and familiar and that serves to console or reassure us when we're low or sick or suffer some reversal. It's a work so intelligent, with dialogue so witty and a view of life so worldly-wise, presented with such formal economy and flawless pacing, and yet such fun to read, that it continually serves to renew my belief in the principle that art and brains can transform just about anything, no matter how lowly or unpromising that thing might seem, into something intelligent, moving, and worthy, indeed, that art and brains could translate a pulp genre into the big leagues with one book. It has always seemed to me somehow appropriate that in the same decade in which Hammett demonstrated the high-art possibilities of the hard-boiled detective genre with the publication of *The Maltese Falcon* (1930), his friend William Faulkner demonstrated that the gothic detective genre, founded by Poe in the Dupin stories, was capable of being translated into the very highest realms of literary art, accomplishing this with the publication of *Absalom, Absalom!* (1936), the story of two amateur detectives puzzling over the facts of a very old murder, trying to solve the mystery of why a man killed his best friend and half-brother. And in what follows I hope to show why it does not seem to me at all inappropriate to mention Hammett's achievement in the same breath with Faulkner's.

* * *

Most critics of *The Maltese Falcon* and most readers who have read it more than once have sensed the importance for the novel's overall meaning of the story of Flitcraft that Sam Spade tells Brigid O'Shaughnessy at the start of Chapter 7, tells her, ostensibly as a way of killing time, while they wait in Spade's apartment for Joel Cairo to show up. The story of Flitcraft, a little over a thousand words in length, is usually treated by critics as a parable, as Spade's way of obliquely telling Brigid, with whom he is becoming romantically involved at this point, his view of life and the world, of telling her the sort of person he is.

According to Spade, Flitcraft, a successful businessman in Tacoma, left his office one day to have lunch and never came back, he vanished "like a fist when you open your hand."[1] Flitcraft was happily married, had two young children, a thriving real estate business, owned his own home, had a new Packard, "and the rest of the appurtenances of successful American living" (64). (One can imagine Hammett slyly relishing that last phrase as if it had been copied from an ad for some new appliance that aimed to become the next criterion of successful American living. Hammett had, of course, worked for a while in the 1920s as the advertising manager for a jewelry store.) At the time of his disappearance, Flitcraft was worth about two hundred thousand dollars, and while his affairs were in order, there were still enough loose ends to suggest that he hadn't planned to disappear. Indeed, he had called a friend that morning and made a date to play golf at four that afternoon.

Spade became involved in the Flitcraft case about five years later. He was working for a large detective agency in Seattle when Mrs. Flitcraft hired the agency to send someone to investigate a man she had seen in Spokane who looked a lot like her husband. Spade was sent, found Flitcraft, who had changed his name to Charles Pierce, and found as well that Flitcraft now owned his own automobile business, had a wife and baby son, owned his home in a Spokane suburb, "and usually got away to play golf after four in the afternoon during the season" (65). Spade interviewed Flitcraft and found that he had "no feeling of guilt," since he had "left his first family well provided for" (65). But Flitcraft was concerned that he wouldn't be able to make the "reasonableness" of what he'd done "clear to Spade" (65).

It seems that on the day he'd disappeared Flitcraft had been going to lunch when he walked past a new building that was being built and a steel beam had fallen and hit the sidewalk so close to him that a chip from the sidewalk flew up and scratched his cheek. More shocked than frightened, Flitcraft said that "he felt like somebody had taken the lid off life and let him look at the works" (66):

> Flitcraft had been a good citizen and a good husband and father, not by any outer compulsion, but simply because he was a man who was most comfortable in step with his surroundings. . . . The life he knew was a clean orderly sane responsible affair. Now a falling beam had shown him that life was fundamentally none of these things. . . . He knew then that men died at haphazard like that, and lived only while blind chance

spared them. . . . What disturbed him was the discovery that in sensibly ordering his affairs he had got out of step, not into step, with life.

(66)

Flitcraft immediately decided that he had to adjust himself "to this new glimpse of life," and that if life "could be ended for him at random by a falling beam," then "he would change his life at random by simply going away" (66). He left that afternoon for Seattle, took a boat to San Francisco, then wandered around for a couple of years before drifting back to the Northwest. He settled in Spokane and got married again: "His second wife didn't look like the first, but they were more alike than they were different. You know, the kind of women that play fair games of golf and bridge and like new salad-recipes" (67). Spade's final comment on the story is

> I don't think he even knew he had settled back naturally into the same groove he had jumped out of in Tacoma. But that's the part of it I always liked. He adjusted himself to beams falling, and then no more of them fell, and he adjusted himself to them not falling.

(67)

And thus as abruptly as the story began, it ends, with Spade's listener, Brigid, remarking, "How perfectly fascinating" (67). (One can imagine her saying these words in the same tone that Arte Johnson on the old *Laugh-In* show used when he turned to the camera and in a heavy German accent beneath a coal-scuttle helmet, remarked, "Interesting, v-e-r-y interesting"—that tone of meaningful meaninglessness that conveys "It may mean the world to you, but it's chopped liver to me.") In fact, Hammett suggests that Brigid's inability to grasp the meaning of Flitcraft's story is somehow gender-related. Flitcraft had originally agreed to talk to Spade in order to explain his actions and make their "reasonableness explicit" (66). Spade says of that explanation: "I got it all right, . . . but Mrs. Flitcraft never did. She thought it was silly. Maybe it was" (66). At any rate, the first Mrs. Flitcraft wanted a divorce "after the trick he had played on her—the way she looked at it" (66). So it's not just Brigid that doesn't get Flitcraft's story, it's the first Mrs. Flitcraft as well.

Now, clearly, one of the structural purposes of Flitcraft's story in the novel, this tale that Spade tells Brigid while they are alone together in his apartment waiting for Joel Cairo to arrive, is that it foreshadows the novel's final scene between Spade and Brigid in which they are again alone together in his apartment, this time waiting for the police to arrive, and Spade explains to her in great detail why he is going to turn her in for Miles Archer's murder. Needless to say, Brigid doesn't grasp that explanation either. At one point in the scene, Spade tells her that if she gets a break, she'll only serve

twenty years and he'll wait for her, but if she doesn't, they'll hang her and he'll always remember her, and Brigid says, "Don't, Sam, don't say that even in fun. Oh, you frightened me for a moment! I really thought you—You know you do such wild and unpredictable things that—" (223). To which Spade replies, "Don't be silly. You're taking the fall" (223).

Brigid's comment that Spade does "such wild and unpredictable things" is meant to remind us of a similar exchange between the two in that earlier scene at Spade's apartment. After Spade finishes the story of Flitcraft, Joel Cairo arrives and gets into an argument with Brigid that turns violent just as the police show up at Spade's door. Leaving Brigid in the living room holding a gun on Cairo, Spade stalls the police, telling them they can't come in without a search warrant. But when the sounds of a scuffle in the living room and Cairo's cries for help create probable cause, the police go in, and Spade, in order to keep the cops from "pulling the whole lot of them in" (79), manufactures an incredible story that the scuffle and the call for help were part of an elaborate gag to razz the cops. By sheer bravado and the craziness of the story, Spade makes the cops uncertain enough about whether they're being kidded that finally they leave, taking Cairo with them. At this point, Brigid tells Spade, "You're absolutely the wildest person I've ever known," adding a bit later, "You're altogether unpredictable" (85-87). The phrase "wild and unpredictable" is applied to Spade three more times during the course of this scene, culminating with Spade's remark that if Brigid won't tell him what she knows about the case, then his "way of learning is to heave a wild and unpredictable monkey-wrench into the machinery. It's all right with me, if you're sure none of the flying pieces will hurt you" (90).

So it's clear that when Brigid, in that final scene where Spade tells her he's going to turn her over to the police, thinks he's joking and says, "You know you do such wild and unpredictable things," the phrase comes bearing a load of freight that leads directly back to the story of Flitcraft. For the story that Spade tells Brigid at the start of that earlier scene in the apartment is essentially a tale about a man who has learned from a close brush with accidental death that life is not "a clean orderly sane responsible affair," is "fundamentally none of these things," that men live "only while blind chance" spares them. And Flitcraft's response to "this new glimpse of life" is to match his behavior to it, like to like: the random unpredictability of an individual's behavior responding to haphazardness of life's events as a way, in Flitcraft's words, of getting "into step with life." The parable of Flitcraft presents, in effect, a rationale for doing "wild and unpredictable things," and just so that the reader won't miss the connection between Flitcraft's behavior and Spade's, Hammett links the two with an image. Just as Flitcraft says that the falling beam which almost killed him sent "a piece of the sidewalk" flying up to cut his cheek, so Spade tells Brigid that if he has to heave "a wild and unpredictable monkey-wrench into the machinery" in order to learn what's going on, she may be hurt by "the flying pieces."

From a flying "piece of the sidewalk" to "flying pieces" of machinery seems like a short step, though the images are separated by twenty-five pages of text, but before we assume we know what this linking of Flitcraft's revelation about life with Spade's unpredictable actions means, we should look more closely at what Flitcraft's encounter with the falling beam actually teaches him. What the accident demonstrates is that there is no necessary connection between, on the one hand, the way a man leads his life and, on the other, the time and manner of his death. As a successful businessman, Flitcraft sees that being a good citizen-husband-father, leading an "orderly sane responsible" life, has bought him nothing, no assurance either about longevity of years or about an appropriately dignified, honored, and loving end. Had he been hit by the beam, he would have died a very young man with a wife and two small children, died senselessly and horribly in a city street surrounded by strangers. What he learns is the difference between life-as-being and life-as-having, between what one is and what one owns, between life as the simple persistence of individual consciousness in time and life as the accumulation of people, property, habits, whatnot, by an individual during the course of his existence. And Flitcraft's response to this traumatic event reminds us of the kind of response Freud described as occurring in children's play when youngsters attempt to master a trauma by reenacting it as a game.

According to Freud, the child is originally in "a *passive* situation" as regards the trauma, he experiences it as something beyond his control, something he must helplessly endure, and thus he is "overpowered by the experience." But, "by repeating it, unpleasurable though it was, as a game," he takes "an *active* part;" in voluntarily initiating the repetition he achieves a kind of mastery of the trauma by switching from a passive to an active role in relation to it.[2] And this is precisely what Flitcraft does. In response to the falling beam, the trauma of almost losing his life-as-being, Flitcraft voluntarily reenacts the event by losing, by actively giving up, his life-as-having. He leaves all those people, things, and habits that had previously constituted his life. He symbolically replays his own death and thus seems to regain active control of his own fate.

* * *

I have gone to some length emphasizing the circumscribed character of the lesson Flitcraft learned from the falling beam (i.e., that there is no necessary relationship between the way a man lives his life and the time and manner of his death) precisely because this rigorously delimited sense of the event's significance serves both to explain the ease with which Flitcraft, once beams no longer fell, settled back into a life so much like the one he left, but also to combat an influential reading of the Flitcraft episode that in effect sees it as an *ur*-existentialist fable—an interpretation that to my mind overstates the falling beam's lesson. The origin of this interpretation seems to be Steven Marcus' 1974 essay "Dashiell Hammett and the Continental Op" in which, as part of a discussion of Hammett's Continental Op stories, Marcus gives a reading of the Flitcraft tale, a story he calls "the most important or central moment" in *The Maltese Falcon* and "one of the central moments in all of Hammett's writing."[3] After briefly summarizing the Flitcraft episode, Marcus concludes that what it "is about among other things is the ethical irrationality of existence, the ethical unintelligibility of the world," and that what Flitcraft learns from the incident of the falling beam is "that life is inscrutable, opaque, irresponsible, and arbitrary—that human existence does not correspond in its actuality to the way we live it" (196). One gets the sense from Marcus that this must have been a load-bearing beam indeed. He says that Flitcraft, in responding to this new insight by leaving his wife and children, "acts irrationally and at random, in accordance with the nature of existence" (196). Yet to act at random, to act in an unpredictable manner, is not necessarily to act irrationally. Indeed, the whole point of Flitcraft's telling Spade his story is that he wants to make clear to him the "reasonableness" of his actions. But Marcus goes on to comment on Flitcraft's falling back into his old way of life a few years later that

> here we come upon the unfathomable and the most mysteriously irrational part of it all—how despite everything we have learned and everything we know, men will persist in behaving and trying to behave sanely, rationally, sensibly, and responsibly. And we will continue to persist even when we know there is no logical or metaphysical, no discoverable or demonstrable reason for doing so. It is this sense of sustained contradiction that is close to the center—or to one of the centers—of Hammett's work. The contradiction is not ethical alone; it is metaphysical as well. And it is not merely sustained; it is sustained with pleasure.
>
> (196)

So it's not just Flitcraft's sudden leaving of his previous life that's irrational but also his returning to a similar life two years later. In trying to account for Marcus' reading of the Flitcraft episode, one is left with the sense that his interpretation resulted from a backpressure of the film on the novel. Marcus begins his essay by telling us that he was first introduced to *The Maltese Falcon* at the age of twelve when he saw the John Huston film and that it was only years later after he'd read and reread the book and reseen the movie that he "could begin to understand why the impact of the film had been so memorable":

> The director, John Huston, had had the wit to recognize the power, sharpness, integrity, and bite of Hammett's prose—particularly the dialogue—and the film script consists almost entirely of speech taken directly and without modification from the written novel. . . . Huston had to make certain omissions. Paradoxically, however, one of the things that he chose to omit was the most important or central moment in the entire novel. It is also one of the central moments in all of Hammett's writing. I think we can make use of this oddly "lost" passage as a means of entry into Hammett's vision or imagination of the world.

(194)

The omitted passage is, of course, the story of Flitcraft, and the reasoning implicit in Marcus' argument is that since the Flitcraft episode is central to the novel and, indeed, to all Hammett's writing, because it expresses parabolically his "vision or imagination of the world," the episode's world-view pervades the entire book, coloring the dialogue to which Huston's film is so faithful. The omitted Flitcraft episode is, then, the hidden center around which the visible memorableness of the movie orbits, and though Marcus ostensibly sets out to explain the film's memorableness in terms of the novel's world-view, he in fact ends up interpreting Flitcraft's story in terms of a pre-existing sense of what constitutes the film's memorableness, its place in cultural and in film history.

As we know, Huston's **The Maltese Falcon** was one of the first—and certainly the first great—examples of *film noir*, a genre originally described and named by French film critics at the end of World War II. As the well-known story goes, the French hadn't been able to get new American movies during the years of the war and the German occupation, and then suddenly with the peace, there was an influx into French theaters of American films made between 1940-45, among which was a type of film whose scripts were based on the hard-boiled fiction of writers like Hammett, Chandler, and Cain and whose visual style and subject matter, as distinct from the pre-war American films the French were used to, had substantially darkened. Indeed, one of these critics, Jean Pierre Chartier, titled his 1946 article in *Revue du Cinéma* "The Americans Are Making Dark Films Too,"[4] the "too" clearly evoking the author's sense that this dark subject matter had already been a staple of such pre-war French films as Marcel Carne's *Quai des Brumes, Hôtel du Nord,* and *Le Jour Se Lève,* Julien Duvivier's *Pepe le Moko,* and Sacha Guitry's *Le Roman d'un tricheur.* And clearly what these critics responded to in this new genre of American films was a world-view that could be assimilated to the most influential contemporary French thought, the existentialist philosophy and literature of Sartre and Camus. For hadn't Camus once said that the book that was "both the inspiration and the model" for *The Stranger* was James M. Cain's *The Postman Always Rings Twice*? (At least that's what it says in the blurb on the back of my paperback edition of Cain's novel. Of course, whether or not Camus actually said this is of no interest to me because that's not the point. Rather, the point is this characteristic strategy, illustrated by the paperback blurb, of trying to give hard-boiled detective fiction an intellectual and aesthetic cachet by associating it with existentialism and Camus, which is to say, this strategy of trying to establish the seriousness of some aspect of American popular culture by showing that the French take it seriously, the same ploy that would have us believe that Jerry Lewis is a comic genius because the French made him a member of the Legion of Honor or that Mickey Rourke is a great actor because he's all the rage in Paris.)

At the very start, then, in the very critiques that identified and named the genre, *film noir* had been associated with existentialism, and as this association became a commonplace of subsequent discussions of the genre, it exercised a retrospective influence on critical readings of the hard-boiled detective novels from which many of the films were adapted. In a 1976 article in *Sight and Sound* entitled "No Way Out: Existential Motifs in the Film Noir," Robert Porfirio, discussing Huston's **Maltese Falcon,** says "the film's one unfortunate omission is the Flitcraft parable Spade tells Brigid O'Shaughnessy, for this is our only chance to peep into Spade's interior life. And what it reveals is that Spade is by nature an existentialist, with a strong conception of the randomness of existence."[5] In that same year Charles Gregory writing in the *Journal of Popular Film* characterizes the world-view of *film noir* by citing the Flitcraft story, which he paraphrases at some length, and comments "French critics have admired Spade's anecdote for its 'existential' nature, proving Hammett's philosophic grasp of a world ruled by chance rather than Divine Order. . . . Steven Marcus has noted in his introduction to some Continental Op stories that this passage means that 'life is inscrutable, opaque, irresponsible, and arbitrary.'"[6]

But it seems to me an enormous, and ultimately unjustifiable, leap to go from a tale illustrating that there's no necessary connection between the way one leads one's life and the time and manner of one's death to a reading that finds life to be inscrutable, opaque, irresponsible, and arbitrary, particularly since the conclusion of Flitcraft's story is his ending up voluntarily leading the same kind of life he had previously abandoned. Indeed, I've evoked at some length this backpressure of *film noir* criticism on the interpretation of hard-boiled detective fiction precisely because I want to free the Flitcraft episode, and thus Hammett's novel as a whole, from this retrospective existentialist overlay, a frame of reference that reduces the real complexity of the Flitcraft story and diminishes the richness of the novel whose world-view it informs.

* * *

Part of the appeal of Flitcraft's adventure for me is that it belongs to a much older and more interesting tradition than that provided by existentialism. To begin with, it has always reminded me of one of Hawthorne's best short works, the 1835 tale "Wakefield," about a man who,

> under the pretence of going a journey, took lodgings in the next street to his own house, and there, unheard of by his wife or friends, and without the shadow of a reason for such self-banishment, dwelt upwards of twenty years. During that period, he beheld his home every day, and frequently the forlorn Mrs. Wakefield. And after so great a gap in his matrimonial felicity— when his death was reckoned certain, his estate settled, his name dismissed from memory, and his wife long, long ago, resigned to her autumnal widowhood—he entered the door one evening, quietly, as from a day's absence, and became a loving spouse till death.[7]

One sees immediately the structural resemblance between Wakefield and Flitcraft, two men who leave a former life suddenly for no reason apparent to those left behind, and then after an absence of two or twenty years return, either to that former life or to its equivalent. And what for me gives these stories their peculiar power is that they both seem to be modern reworkings of the story of Job. Which is to say that Job, Wakefield, and Flitcraft are all men who lose their "lives" without losing their life, men who either are deprived of or voluntarily give up their life-as-having while retaining their life-as-being and who in one way or another ultimately recover the former, with some recognition of the difference between the two accruing to the readers of their stories if not to the men themselves. Examining the similarities and differences among the three stories will make clear what gives the Flitcraft episode its special quality and how the significance of that episode pervades the whole novel.

Like the Flitcraft episode, the story of Job is concerned with the sudden, apparently undeserved reversal of fortune that can be suffered by a good man, but where such a reversal is only threatened in the case of Flitcraft (a close brush with a falling beam) and its cause explained by the random nature of accidents, it is actually endured by Job, who loses his possessions, sons and daughters, health, and peace of mind, and its cause explained as the will of God. Which is to say that God has permitted Satan to test his servant Job, who "was perfect and upright," who "feared God, and eschewed evil" (Job 1:1), because Satan had said that Job's rectitude was merely a function of how greatly he had been blessed with the good things of life. So God allows Satan to remove all Job's possessions (offspring, wealth, health, tranquillity), but with the specific stipulation that he not kill him, in order to prove that Job, no matter how much he suffers, will remain faithful, that he will not, as Satan had predicted, curse God to his face.

Clearly, in Flitcraft's case, it makes sense to explain a single close encounter with a falling beam (which can instantly wipe out all Flitcraft is and has) by invoking the random, haphazard component of existence, but in the case of Job, such an explanation is ruled out by the sheer number and frequency of the disasters befalling the same man, indeed, so many that they can't be random and coincidental, they must be intentional, meaningful. But such a scenario necessarily raises the further question of what kind of intention or will, what kind of meaning, can lie behind bad things happening to good people. The Job story is, then, front-loaded by the repetitive nature of its hero's sufferings for an explanation involving intention rather than chance. This is not to say that God willed this good man's sufferings but rather that his will permitted Satan to test his servant, presumably knowing that Job would remain faithful through his trials and gain even greater favor in the eyes of the Lord. Thus, at the conclusion of the narrative, God speaks out of a whirlwind, rebukes the false comforters, and makes "the latter end of Job's life" more blessed than the beginning, giving him seven sons and three daughters to replace those that were lost and returning his herds of sheep, camels, oxen, and she-asses but doubling their numbers. Job is further blessed with a long life, living to see "his sons, and his sons' sons, even four generations" (Job 42:16).

Granted, the Book of Job as we have it seems to be the work of more than one author, with various parts written at different periods. The book's prologue (chapters 1 and 2: the dialogue of God and Satan, and the disasters that Satan inflicts on Job) and its epilogue (chapter 42: the restoration of God's blessings and prolongation of Job's life in which to enjoy those blessings) are both written from an omniscient viewpoint, with the writer knowing both what goes on in heaven and in the mind of God. In contrast, the large middle portion of the narrative (chapters 3 through 41: the dialogue of Job and his comforters, and the concluding statement by God from the whirlwind) is written from a limited viewpoint associated with Job. Given the book's various authors, compilers, or revisers, it is not surprising that the work, in terms of its overall meaning, often seems at cross-purposes with itself. The long middle section is a text illustrating patience in adversity as personified by Job and evoking, in the dialogue of Job and his three false comforters and in God's closing statement, that it is pointless, indeed, presumptuous, for man to inquire into the ways of God, to try to puzzle out, for example, why bad things happen to good people. Yet this moral is clearly undercut by the prologue which provides just such an explanation in the story of God's allowing Satan to test his servant's rectitude. Even more puzzling is the epilogue in which Job gets back all he'd lost and then some, for if the point of the dialogue between God and Satan at the start of the book had been, on the one hand, Satan's assertion that Job worshipped God only because God had showered him with blessings and built a "hedge about him, and about his house" (Job 1:10) and, on the other hand, God's rejoinder that Job would remain faithful even if he lost all he had, then certainly this ending seems to undermine that point. For Satan could argue that Job only remains faithful to God because he knows he will ultimately have all his blessings restored, that is, that the necessary connection between conduct and rewards, between worshipful service and God's blessings, is still intact, even though it may be delayed for a while in the case of Job's trials, and that thus Job continues to worship God only because he has expectations of some return. Satan might then propose that the only true test of Job's motives would be for God to break absolutely the necessary connection between conduct and rewards by letting Satan not only deprive Job of his life-as-having but also of his life-as-being. But that is, as we noted, the one thing God specifically forbids Satan from doing, for the overall point of the book as it now exists is to reaffirm the long-term link between one's behavior and one's desserts.

The Old Testament has, of course, no clearly defined notion of a blessed afterlife. God and the angels are in heaven, and on occasion, room is made there for exceptional persons such as Elijah and Enoch. But because the Old Testament isn't so much interested in the survival of individuals in the next world as in the survival of a people in this one, its notion of every person's fate at death is that they descend to a place of darkness called *sheol,* similar to the classical underworld of shades. Lacking the sense of a commonly available blessed afterlife, the Book of Job must make the link between conduct and compensation visible *within* its hero's lifetime, unlike the New Testament where the notion of personal immortality allows Job's two-part trajectory (first, patience and faithfulness in adversity; second, ultimate compensation) to be distributed on either side of death and thereby to define the difference between this life and the next. The Book of Job gives a further indication of its lack of interest in the fate of individuals in the detail of Job's ten children's sudden death and their subsequent compensatory replacement by ten new children. The impersonality of this ten-for-ten reimbursement speaks volumes. Interestingly enough, the story of Flitcraft exhibits in its modern way as little interest in the notion of compensation in the next world for behavior in this one as does the Book of Job in its Old Testament way. Flitcraft never considers any form of metaphysical response to the perceived injustice of a good life ending in a random, premature death. Indeed, one can imagine him agreeing with Brigid O'Shaughnessy's remark, "I'm not heroic. I don't think there's anything worse than death" (39).

Considering the relationship of the stories of Job and Flitcraft, we can see that in the case of Job it is precisely the *repetitive* nature of the disasters which befall him that mark them as intentional and meaningful (that "half-credence in the supernatural" caused "by *coincidences* of so seemingly marvelous a character that, as *mere* coincidences, the intellect has been unable to receive them," as Poe says[8]) and that it is the *singular,* the one-shot, nature of the event that befalls Flitcraft (the falling beam) which marks it as random and meaningless. Now we should note in this regard that Job, Flitcraft, and Wakefield are all married men and that Job and Flitcraft both have families and have enjoyed success in their work (in Wakefield's case, no mention is made of children or of any kind of employment). Which is simply to say that all three have a settled domestic existence and that two of them have successful lives beyond the family. They are men who have settled into a routine in their lives: Wakefield is described as "a man of habits" (77); indeed, so unremarkable had been Wakefield's life up to the point he left, says the narrator, that no one who knew him "could have anticipated" (76) this "very singular step" (77). While Spade says that Flitcraft's "habits for months" before his disappearance "could be accounted for too thoroughly to justify any suspicion of secret vices, or even of another woman in his life" (64). And he adds that Flitcraft had reestablished this same habitual lifestyle in his new incarnation, even down to the detail of his usually getting away "to play golf after four in the afternoon during the season" (65).

What I would draw attention to here is the difference between the repetitive, habitual, or routine character of Flitcraft's life and the singular character of the event that befalls him (the falling beam) in order to point out that this event is not strictly speaking "singular," not something that could only happen once to Flitcraft and never again. For of course, as long as the falling beam didn't hit Flitcraft and kill him, beams could theoretically fall on the sidewalk near Flitcraft every day as he goes to lunch. What the *exceptional* occurrence of the falling beam in fact stands for in Flitcraft's story is the most important, absolutely singular event that can occur in his or anyone's life after their birth, the only life-encompassing event that can't be repeated, one's own death. And this is clearly why Flitcraft's response to this random event, his decision to get himself "into step with life" by matching the random component in existence with a random component in his own behavior by suddenly leaving his life of settled habits, doesn't work. For if the actual singular event that that random occurrence stands for is Flitcraft's own death, then by the very nature of its singularity, it can't be incorporated into a rule of living, can't be domesticated into anything that, like a rule, presumes the possibility of repetition. One might think of it by analogy with the way that mathematicians use the word "singularity" to refer to the center of that theoretical phenomenon known as a black hole, i.e., an object whose mass is so great that it captures its own radiation and at whose center the mathematics of quantum mechanics, the known laws of physics that describe the rest of the universe, break down, and where time and space as we know them cease to exist. We each have our own personal black hole coming at some point in our lives, and there is no actual way of matching any sort of human behavior, short of suicide, to the reality of that one-and-only, once-and-for-all event. One can respond to an associative evocation (such as the falling beam) of that real singularity by a symbolic action (Flitcraft's abrupt leaving of his life-as-having), but whether one interprets Flitcraft's sudden departure as a psychological move that aims to master a traumatic event passively suffered by transforming it into something actively replayed in symbolic form, thus metaphorically reasserting one's control over one's own fate, or whether as a philosophical move that existentially enacts the primacy of life-as-being over life-as-having, no symbolic, that is, no repetitive, action can ever truly replicate the non-repetitive essence of that event: there exists no way of putting one's life "into step," as Flitcraft says, with something that has no second step. And so Flitcraft's solution of suddenly leaving his old life and wandering around for two years (a wandering that doubtless represents a series of sudden, random leavetakings attempting to replicate the first one) falls of its own weight, for if one's own death is an unrepeatable event, then sudden violent evocations of the possibility of one's own death are an only slightly-less-frequent occurrence and, given the singularity of the former and the rarity of the latter, neither are worth trying to make the basis of a design for living.

If Flitcraft's subsequent adjustment of his life to the fact of no more beams falling involves his settling "back naturally into the same groove he had jumped out of in Tacoma," then this same recapturing of the central character by repetition, after an initial instance of extraordinary behavior, is acted out in "Wakefield." Hawthorne refers to Wakefield's sudden disappearance as "this very singular step" (77) and speaks of "the singularity of his situation" (79) in dissevering "himself from the world" by giving "up his place and privileges with living men, without being admitted among the dead," characterizing Wakefield's as the "unprecedented fate to retain his original share of human sympathies, and to be still involved in human interests, while he had lost his reciprocal influence on them" (79). Certainly this language of "singularity" and of the "unprecedented" evokes Wakefield's sudden leaving of his life-as-having as an exceptional figure of the singularity of his own

death, but what distinguishes Wakefield's fate from Flitcraft's is that after his disappearance Wakefield continues to haunt his old surroundings. He constructs his new existence around the very absence that his departure has created in his home and marriage. Having abruptly left a domestic routine, he establishes another routine in watching over that empty place which had once been his: "We must leave him, for ten years or so, to haunt around his house, without once crossing the threshold, and to be faithful to his wife, with all the affection of which his heart is capable, while he is slowly fading out of hers. Long since, he had lost the perception of singularity in his conduct" (78). Which is to say that what had started as a "very singular step," in terms of both its oddness and its random, unpremeditated quality, soon becomes through its prolongation something unremarkable, just another habit for this "man of habits" (77).

If when a man dies he "shall return no more to his house, neither shall his place know him any more" (Job 7:10), as the Book of Job says, then when Wakefield on the spur of the moment decides one evening to return to *his* home after a twenty-year absence, Hawthorne seems to echo Job when he thunders, "Stay, Wakefield! Would you go to the sole home that is left you? Then step into your grave!" (80). And I would argue that there is yet another Jobean reference that has been present all along in the name of the tale's central character, for Wakefield's name has always seemed to me to be an allusion to Goldsmith's *The Vicar of Wakefield,* a novel that, in its story of Mr. Primrose's many trials patiently endured and the ultimate restoration of his lost blessings (including a daughter he had thought was dead), has long been acknowledged as based on Job.

Where Hammett gives us a reason for Flitcraft's disappearance, Hawthorne leaves the motive for Wakefield's departure and twenty-year absence a matter of conjecture to the end. He focuses instead on the effect that stepping out of one's accustomed place can have: "Amid the seeming confusion of our mysterious world, individuals are so nicely adjusted to a system, and systems to one another and to a whole, that, by stepping aside for a moment, a man exposes himself to a fearful risk of losing his place forever. Like Wakefield, he may become, as it were, the Outcast of the Universe" (80). And yet it may be precisely that sense of "a fearful risk" which is the key to understanding Wakefield's actions. Hawthorne tells us that Wakefield's character is compounded of "a quiet selfishness," a "peculiar sort of vanity," a "disposition to craft," and "a little strangeness" (76). And one can easily imagine that an individual at once selfish, vain, crafty, and strange, who has been immersed for some years in a habitual domestic existence, might well feel the perverse attraction of this "fearful risk," feel his vanity, craftiness, and peculiarity drawn suddenly and irresistibly toward an action precisely because it is the one thing *he should not do,* the one thing that, precisely because it is opposed to his best interests, represents a supreme test of the self's freedom and perhaps of its cleverness as well. Such a risky manipulation of the conditions of one's own exist-ence might well appeal to Wakefield as a means of dem-onstrating that he is a creature of habit not out of neces-sity but out of free choice, of demonstrating this by suddenly choosing to step out of his domestic routine with the vain self-assurance that only he would be crafty enough to do so and still be able to resume his former life at will. My reading of Wakefield's possible motives for his sudden departure and prolonged absence has clearly been influenced by Poe's explication, in his 1845 tale "The Imp of the Perverse," of that basic, primitive psychological component he calls *perverse-ness.* Yet in failing to provide a definite interpretation of Wakefield's motives while at the same encouraging the reader to speculate, Hawthorne in effect authorizes each reader to make an interpretation of his own, and this, combined with Hawthorne's frequent rhetorical warnings to Wakefield during the course of the tale that his sudden departure from home and his continued ab-sence are actions directly opposed to his own best inter-ests and his further suggestion that these actions are without any discernible purpose, points us toward that psychological principle through whose promptings, as Poe says, "we act without comprehensible object," a principle in which "the assurance of the wrong or error of any action is often the one unconquerable *force* that impels us to its prosecution" (*Collected Works* 2: 1220-21).

* * *

All of which brings us to a final question: if, as I have suggested, "Wakefield" and the Book of Job are the al-lusive backgrounds for Flitcraft's story, then how does a reading of the Flitcraft story in this context alter or enrich our reading of Hammett's novel? Let me start with the book's central eponymous object and note that the Maltese falcon has a dual significance in the book, in part because there seem to be two falcons. On the one hand, there is the fantastic golden, jewel-encrusted statue that Gutman says was sent by the Order of the Hospital of St. John of Jerusalem to the Emperor Charles V in 1531 as tribute to show that, even though Charles had given the island to the Order, "Malta was still under Spain," a statue that is hijacked on the way to Charles V by "a famous admiral of buccaneers" (*The Maltese Falcon* 129) and thus launched on an obscure four-hundred-year trajectory through the hands of vari-ous possessors, some of whom do and some of whom don't know what the object is. But what we must keep in mind is that no one in the novel has ever actually seen this object (not even Gutman). Its existence has simply been deduced by Gutman from examining his-torical documents. On the other hand, there is the actual

foot-high statue of a falcon made of lead and coated with black enamel, a fake that Cairo and Gutman con-clude was produced by the Russian general, Kemidov, when Gutman's attempt to buy the statue from him in Istanbul alerted the Russian to its true value. And while the former statue is the one Gutman and Spade are seeking, it is the latter they end up with.

What becomes clear as Gutman discusses the original Maltese falcon with Spade is that its value is a function not just of its material (gold and precious jewels) and workmanship (crafted by Turkish slaves in the castle of St. Angelo) but of its uniqueness (dare I say its singularity) and its historical provenance, as an art dealer would say. When Gutman asks Spade if he has "any conception of how much money can be made out of that black bird," Spade says no, but adds that if Gut-man tells him what it is, he'll figure out the profits. To which Gutman replies, "'You couldn't do it, sir. No-body could do it who hadn't a world of experience with things of that sort, and'—he paused impressively—'there aren't any other things of that sort'" (112). So at the start Hammett codes the golden bird as singular, and in the very next exchange he associates it with death. Gutman asks Spade if he really doesn't know what the black bird is, and Spade says, "I know what it's supposed to look like. I know the value in life you people put on it" (112). And of course, before the novel is done, four people will have been murdered, and two more will be facing a possible death penalty for murder. Indeed, it is precisely the ambiguity of the statue's sig-nification, in part a function of there being two falcons, that Hammett intends to make use of, for while the golden bird is coded as unique and associated with death, thus capable of serving as a figure for the singu-larity of one's own death, it is also coded as long-lived, as an object whose historical longevity, whose ability to survive its creators and all its subsequent possessors, makes it capable, like other objects of this sort, such as the pyramids, of serving as a figure of immortality.

It would not, of course, be the first time in English lit-erature that a bird simultaneously evoked death and im-mortality, as any reader of Keats' "Ode to a Nightin-gale" knows. When Keats contemplates the impersonal species-longevity of the bird and its song compared to the uniqueness of his own song and his personal mor-tality, he exclaims, "Thou wast not born for death, im-mortal Bird!" And it certainly wouldn't be the first time in American literature that a black bird, as the falcon is frequently referred to in the novel, was associated with death, as any reader of the inventor of the detective genre's most famous poem knows.

So we have a novel whose characters are pursuing the golden statue of a bird, a statue whose existence may be nothing more than the interpretive dream of the ob-sessive Gutman, a putative object that serves as a figure at once of the singularity of one's own death and of the traditional golden dream of the great good thing associated with that singularity in the Christian West, the dream of personal immortality after death, of being given back one's life after losing one's life. And what these characters actually find is a leaden statue of a bird with a string of violent deaths in its wake. But of course a falcon is a bird of prey and thus already associated with death. And does one really need to invoke Shakespearean imagery to establish "lead" and "the leaden" as common evocations of death? Or, on the other hand, cite the fact that since gold has no oxide and thus doesn't corrupt when buried, it has traditionally functioned as a figure of immortality? No, I think it is sufficient at this point to note that *The Maltese Falcon* plays itself out as a quest for possession of a golden possibility that ends with possession of a leaden singularity, a pursuit that is an ironic enough, not to say a cynical enough, inversion of the quest-romance structure underlying hard-boiled detective fiction to satisfy even the most hard-boiled reader.

But there's more. Looking again at the scene in Spade's apartment where he tells Brigid the story of Flitcraft, we realize that this tale of an explained disappearance, whose central figure was found to be still alive, corresponds to a tale Brigid had told Spade earlier in her own apartment about an unexplained disappearance, in which the missing person was presumed to be dead. Responding to Spade's question about Floyd Thursby, her protector and the supposed killer of Miles Archer, Brigid says that she met him in the Orient:"There was a story in Hong Kong that he had come out there, to the Orient, as bodyguard to a gambler who had to leave the States, and that the gambler had since disappeared. They said Floyd knew about his disappearing. I don't know. I do know that he always went heavily armed . . ." (39). When Spade asks her if she's in physical danger, she says yes and adds, "I'm not heroic. I don't think there's anything worse than death" (39). It's a line that resonates through the entire novel, evoking not only Brigid's worldview but that of most of the other characters as well. For if nothing is worse than death, if death is a total loss of everything one has or is (as it seems to be for Flitcraft, for example), then human conduct, no longer restrained by the hope or fear of an afterlife, is governed only by the kinds of rewards and punishments that can be assessed in this world and by the kind of limited human means that exist for judging that conduct.

But there is something else in Brigid's remark as well, for certainly Hammett intends for the reader to hear this comment, made by an American woman in the 1920s, as both an echo, and repudiation, of a moral dictum from an earlier era, the dictum that for a woman forcible sexual violation was "a fate worse than death," a fate to be resisted at the cost of one's life if necessary.

And certainly Hammett further intends that on a second reading of the novel we should grasp the deeper point of this echo, understand that though a certain type of conventionally moral woman might consider forced sexual intercourse as a fate worse than death, for Brigid, who thinks there's no fate worse than death, sexual intercourse, in fact or in prospect, becomes a means of deflecting or delivering death to someone else (as when she sexually entices Miles Archer up a dark alley to put a bullet through his heart) or of manipulating men to do her bidding (as when she tells Spade that she doesn't have enough money if she has to bid for his loyalty, then asks provocatively "Can I buy you with my body?" [59]). The answer, of course, is yes—temporarily. But her echoic invocation of an older morality regarding women's virtue also functions as an ironic underlining of the role of helpless female she plays with Spade, a role Spade characterizes as her "schoolgirl manner, stammering and blushing and all that" (57). After Spade tells Brigid the Flitcraft story in his apartment before Cairo arrives, Brigid tries again to convince Spade that he should trust her completely because she trusts him completely, as evidenced by her coming to his apartment: "I don't have to tell you how utterly at a disadvantage you'll have me, with him here, if you choose. . . . And you know I'd never have placed myself in this position if I hadn't trusted you completely" (67). To which Spade succinctly replies, "That again!" and then goes on to explain, "You don't have to trust me, anyhow, as long as you can persuade me to trust you" (67).

But perhaps the fullest resonance of Brigid's remark that there isn't anything worse than death only comes in those concluding scenes at Spade's apartment when Gutman, Cairo, and Wilmer Cook take Spade prisoner at gunpoint after Brigid has led him into a trap, comes as that distinction between life-as-being and life-as-having (which is part of the point of the Flitcraft story) resurfaces in one of the most intriguing moments of the novel.

Though held at gunpoint, Spade begins bargaining with Gutman about the black bird, demanding not only the money Gutman had promised him but also a fall guy for the police to pin the murders on. When Spade suggests they give the police Wilmer, Gutman at first rejects the notion, saying "I feel towards Wilmer just exactly as if he were my own son" (187). Spade then suggests they give the police Cairo, and Cairo, who at the beginning of the bargaining had warned Spade that "though you may have the falcon yet we certainly have you" (183), flies into a rage and says, "You seem to forget that you are not in a position to insist on anything" (192). To which Spade replies, "If you kill me, how are you going to get the bird? And if I know you can't afford to kill me till you have it, how are you going to scare me into giving it to you?" (193). When Gutman points out that "there are other means of persuasion besides killing and threatening to kill," Spade says, "Sure, . . . but they're not much good unless the threat of death is behind them to hold the victim down. See what I mean? If you try anything I don't like I won't stand for it. I'll make it a matter of your having to call it off or kill me, knowing you can't afford to kill me" (193). Gutman affably warns Spade that such situations require delicate judgment on both sides since men may forget "in the heat of action where their best interest lies and let their emotions carry them away" (193). To which Spade just as affably replies, "That's the trick, from my side, . . . to make my play strong enough that it ties you up, but yet not make you mad enough to bump me off against your better judgment" (193).

It is one of the most intelligent exchanges in a novel noted for the quality of its dialogue, and certainly from the reader's viewpoint part of the force of this exchange derives from its structural resemblance to the Flitcraft story. Consider the similarity of the two situations: Flitcraft confronts the real possibility of his own violent death in the incident of the falling beam, while Spade confronts the same possibility in being captured by three armed men who he knows have killed before. Flitcraft responds to this possibility with a typical psychological move: he splits the endangered object (his life) in two and then separating his life-as-being from his life-as-having he voluntarily sacrifices the latter either as a philosophical gesture to reassert control of his own destiny or as a psychological defense mechanism to master a trauma, a reply that, as Flitcraft eventually learns, doesn't work as a rule of life.

Spade, on the other hand, responds to the possibility of his own death not by any symbolic action but by trying to manipulate that death's real singularity, manipulate it through another being/having distinction. Cairo says that though Spade *has* the falcon, they most certainly *have* him, but Spade demonstrates that their *having* him (and thus the falcon) depends entirely on their willingness and ability to exercise an ultimate sanction over his *being,* a sanction which, if exercised, will make his being and their having vanish together. It is precisely the real possibility of his own death (and the loss with it of the secret of the falcon's whereabouts) that Spade wields like a weapon when he tells Gutman that he will certainly make it a matter of their having to kill him if they try to extract the information through torture. Convinced by their conversation of Spade's willingness to take this risk, Gutman agrees to make Wilmer the fall guy, telling Wilmer, in a kind of Jobean postscript to this dialogue of having and being, "Well, Wilmer, I'm sorry indeed to lose you, and I want you to know that I couldn't be any fonder of you if you were my own son; but—well, by Gad!—if you lose a son it's possible to get another—and there's only one Maltese falcon" (204).

Though at first glance the obvious difference between Flitcraft's and Spade's cases would seem to be the type of death each confronts (for Flitcraft random and accidental, for Spade intentional), yet in describing the type of death Spade risks, Hammett makes clear that to some extent it too would be accidental, that while Gutman and his associates simply intend to learn from Spade the whereabouts of the falcon, they might accidentally kill him in the heat of action. Thus the types of death Flitcraft and Spade confront differ as an accident at random (any number of variables could have altered the time and position of Flitcraft and the falling beam in relation to one another) differs from a work-related accident, and also by the fact that there is enough human agency involved in the death Spade is threatened with that Spade's reasoning with his captors allows him to avoid this death, allows him the kind of negotiation denied to Flitcraft and the falling beam.

There is in the novel, of course, one death whose randomness resembles to some extent that of the death which almost befell Flitcraft—Miles Archer's. Brigid kills Archer with a gun she had borrowed from Floyd Thursby, her former protector, in order to get rid of Thursby by pinning Archer's murder on him. But as Spade makes clear in his climactic conversation with Brigid, since all she'd needed was a murder victim that could be plausibly linked to Thursby, any number of people could have been the possible victim, including Spade if he, instead of Archer, had volunteered to shadow Brigid and Thursby that evening. It is the element of haphazardness in Miles Archer's death, then, that accounts for the ultimate appropriateness of Spade's telling the story of Flitcraft's brush with random death to Archer's killer, for as Spade also makes clear in that final conversation with Brigid, he has suspected she was Archer's killer from the moment the police told him the physical circumstances of the murder. He tells Brigid that Archer had had "too many years' experience as a detective to be caught like that by a man he was shadowing. Up a blind alley with his gun tucked away on his hip and his overcoat buttoned . . . but he'd've gone up there with you, angel, . . . and then you could've stood close to him in the dark and put a hole in him" (220).

Which brings us to the core of that climactic conversation between Spade and Brigid and to the central moral dilemma facing Spade in the novel, the fact that he has allowed himself to become sexually involved, even perhaps to fall in love, with a woman he believes is a murderer. This involvement with Brigid is the last instance I want to examine of the way that the story of Flitcraft, with its allusive background in "Wakefield" and the Book of Job, informs the novel as a whole.

There is this curious asymmetry about the stories of Job, Wakefield, and Flitcraft: all three men have wives, but where Wakefield and Flitcraft leave their wives

(Wakefield for twenty years, Flitcraft for good) as part of giving up their life-as-having, Job does not lose *his* wife when he's deprived of his blessings. Job's wife survives to comfort him with the words, "Dost thou still retain thine integrity? curse God, and die" (Job 2:9). Indeed, it has always seemed to me part of the Jewish humor of the Book of Job that it is not the death of his wife but her survival that its author means for us to number among Job's trials. Similarly, there seems to be no great bond of affection between Wakefield and his wife or between Flitcraft and his first wife. Wakefield leaves his spouse without hinting what he intends to do and returns twenty years later without a word of explanation, while Flitcraft, says Spade, "had no feeling of guilt" (65) for what he'd done: "He loved his family, he said, as much as he supposed was usual, but knew he was leaving them adequately provided for, and his love for them was not of the sort to make absence painful" (66).

I would say that the ease, not to say the apparent callousness, with which Flitcraft leaves his wife and family is related, on the one hand, to Wakefield's cavalier treatment of his wife and, on the other, to Spade's behavior with Brigid. For if, as we have suggested, Spade, on the basis of the physical description of the crime scene, had strongly suspected from the very beginning that Brigid killed Miles Archer, then his becoming sexually, if not romantically, involved with her suggests that he knew their liaison had a brief life span built into it from the start, and for precisely those reasons that he gives Brigid in their final conversation. Depending on how you count, there are seven or eight reasons Spade rehearses for "sending her over," and at least two of these are crucial. He says that "no matter what I wanted to do now it would be absolutely impossible for me to let you go without having myself dragged to the gallows with the others," and further that if he did let her go, then she'd have something on him and he'd have something on her, and "I couldn't be sure you wouldn't decide to shoot a hole in *me* some day" (226-27).

Spade understands that what could easily result, one way or the other, from his continuing their affair is his own death. But when Spade had first told Brigid that he was turning her in for reasons he must have known all along, she says, "You've been playing with me? Only pretending you cared—to trap me? You didn't care at all? You didn't—don't—l-love me?" To which he replies, "I think I do. What of it?" (223-24). And then after enumerating all the reasons for sending her over, he says, "Now on the other side we've got what? All we've got is the fact that maybe you love me and maybe I love you," and when she objects that he must know whether he loves her or not, he says, "I don't. It's easy enough to be nuts about you. . . . But I don't know what that amounts to. Does anybody ever? But suppose I do? What of it? Maybe next month I won't. I've been

through it before—when it lasted that long. Then what? Then I'll think I played the sap. And if I did it and got sent over then I'd be sure I was the sap. Well, if I send you over I'll be sorry as hell—I'll have some rotten nights—but that'll pass" (227). If Spade's point is that this too shall pass away, then we can see here the dark side of repetition, the side expressed not by Job but by Ecclesiastes: the sense that if repetition in the case of Flitcraft, Wakefield, and Job equates with a kind of domestic routine whose attributes are comfort and safety and the familiar (Flitcraft is said to be "a man who was most comfortable in step with his surroundings. He had been raised that way. The people he knew were like that. The life he knew was a clean orderly sane responsible affair" [66]), then the other side of such a settled, predictable life may well be a feeling of senseless repetition, of a universal existential boredom (what Stevens called "the celestial ennui of apartments"), the sense that if there is no once-and-for-all in life (short of one's own death), then there is nothing that's supremely valuable, nothing whose worth isn't continually eroded by endless repetition or instantiation, what one might call the Jake-it's-Chinatown syndrome or the dark side of Kant's mathematical sublime. And thus one might see in an exceptional event (such as the pursuit of a fabulous statue that may or may not exist, or a short-term love affair with an attractive and dangerous woman that might or might not result in one's own death) a figurative evocation of that ultimate singularity, similar to the one provided by the falling beam in Flitcraft's case, see that such an exceptional event (a once-in-a-lifetime adventure or an affair that's too hot not to cool down) has meaning and value in a life only by means of a constitutive opposition with all that is routine, repetitive, familiar, and humdrum. When Gutman tells Spade the history of the Maltese falcon, he begins by saying, "This is going to be the most astounding thing you've ever heard of, sir, and I say that knowing that a man of your caliber in your profession must have known some astounding things in his time" (127). The pursuit of the Maltese falcon is evoked, then, by Gutman as an extraordinary event even in the life of a professional detective. Which may be true enough, though to judge the detective business from what we know of Spade's work both with Spade & Archer and with the big detective agency in Seattle that sent him looking for Flitcraft, that business amounts essentially to tail jobs, tracking down missing persons, and divorce work—fairly routine. Indeed, the only time Spade, during the course of the exceptional case of the Maltese falcon, recounts something from his own working life that struck him as extraordinary, it's the story of Flitcraft.

And here is perhaps the full meaning of the structural link in the novel between, on the one hand, Flitcraft's random-action response to his new view of life-as-random-event (in the wake of the falling beam) and, on the other, Spade's method of "wild and unpredictable" behavior as a "way of learning" (90) what's going on. For while Flitcraft's random-action response may be a temporary psychological or philosophical reply to "a new glimpse of life," it cannot be prolonged. And since Spade knows this, because he knows Flitcraft's whole story and has apparently understood it better than Flitcraft himself has (i.e., understood the meaning of his ultimate return to a domestic environment and to a workaday world), he employs this random-action response, this "wild and unpredictable" behavior, as simply a professional ploy, a psychological tool to disrupt his opponents' settled plans and keep his enemies off balance—a method that must be only occasionally and unpredictably applied, since random action loses its psychological effect, its force as a ploy, if it becomes expected and routine.

If, then, the case of the Maltese falcon is the great adventure of Spade's career as a detective (as it is most certainly the best detective novel of Hammett's career as an author) and if his affair with the beautiful, sensuous murderess Brigid is the most exciting and memorable liaison in his life, then his decision both to complete the case and end the affair by "sending over" Brigid for Archer's murder is essentially the decision to choose repetition over singularity (as figured by the exceptional), to choose life over death (the death he knows could easily have resulted if the affair had continued), or more exactly, to choose *his* life, and thus allow himself to be recaptured by repetition.

Because the ending of the film version of **The Maltese Falcon** is so visually striking and so memorable (the closing of the elevator's grated door, so like the door of a prison cell, in front of Brigid's face in close-up as she stands next to Lieutenant Dundy, then the closing of the grated, translucent glass door as the elevator descends into darkness, like the fall through the trapdoor of a scaffold, as Tom Polhaus and Spade, carrying the falcon, descend the stairs of the scaffold) people often forget that that isn't the way the book ends. The final scene in the novel takes place the next morning when Spade comes into his office and finds his secretary Effie Perrine sitting in his chair reading the newspaper account of the case. She asks him, "Is that—what the papers have—right?" When he says yes, and adds, "So much for your woman's intuition," referring to her earlier belief in Brigid, Effie asks, "You did that, Sam, to her?"

> He nodded. "Your Sam's a detective." He looked sharply at her. He put his arm around her waist, his hand on her hip. "She did kill Miles, angel," he said gently, "offhand, like that." He snapped his fingers.
>
> She escaped from his arm as if it had hurt her. "Don't, please, don't touch me," she said brokenly. "I know—I know you're right. You're right. But don't touch me now—not now." Spade's face became pale as his col-

lar. The corridor-door's knob rattled. Effie Perrine turned quickly and went into the outer office, shutting the door behind her. When she came in again she shut it behind her. She said in a small flat voice: "Iva is here."

> Spade, looking at his desk, nodded almost imperceptibly. "Yes," he said, and shivered. "Well, send her in."

(239)

Iva, of course, is Miles Archer's widow, with whom Spade had been having an adulterous affair before the start of the novel and of whom he had grown tired and begun to avoid by the time Archer was killed. During the earlier part of the novel, Iva had repeatedly sought out Spade, expecting that with her husband's death their liaison would lead to a more permanent union, indeed, even asking Spade at one point if *he* had killed Miles so that they could be together. And now with the extraordinary case of the Maltese falcon and the affair with Brigid over, repetition recaptures Spade in both the professional and the personal spheres: he returns to work at his office the next morning, and his former lover walks back into his life—Spade's shiver of revulsion suggesting that, *faute de mieux,* he will resume their liaison.

Job's wife, who had told him to curse God and die, is still there waiting around when Job's blessings are restored; Wakefield returns to his wife after twenty years; Flitcraft takes a second wife "who didn't look like the first, but they were more alike than they were different" (67); and Spade ends up with Iva, the woman with whom he'd been involved at the beginning. Are these mere coincidences, or are they somehow related to that recurring situation in **The Maltese Falcon** of Spade telling parabolic stories or giving elaborate explanations that both reveal his inner life and account for his actions only to have those stories and explanations not be understood by the women who hear them. Flitcraft had originally been concerned that he could make the reasonableness of what he had done clear to Spade, and Spade says, "I got it all right, . . . but Mrs. Flitcraft never did" (65). And neither does Brigid when Spade tells her Flitcraft's story, any more than she understands Spade's explanation of why he must send her over for Miles Archer's murder:

> "Listen. This isn't a damned bit of good. You'll never understand me, but I'll try once more and then we'll give it up. Listen. When a man's partner is killed he's supposed to do something about it. It doesn't make any difference what you thought of him. He was your partner and you're supposed to do something about it. Then it happens we're in the detective business. Well, when one of your organization gets killed it's bad business to let the killer get away with it. . . . Third, I'm a detective and expecting me to run criminals down and then let them go is like asking a dog to catch a rabbit and let it go. It can be done, all right, and sometimes it is

done, but it's not the natural thing. The only way I could have let you go was by letting Gutman and Cairo and the kid go. That's—"

"You're not serious," she said. "You don't expect me to think that these things you're saying are sufficient reason for sending me to the—"

"Wait till I'm through and then you can talk . . ."

(226)

Spade interposes here a new third term into the opposition between life-as-being and life-as-having, which is to say, life-as-doing. He tells Brigid in effect that for him what he is is what he does, not what he has. He says, "I'm a detective," just as on the morning after turning Brigid over to the police, when Effie asks, "You did that, Sam, to her?" he says, "Your Sam's a detective." And though Effie knows he's right, she, like Brigid, doesn't seem to understand—either doesn't understand or doesn't want to face what she does understand: that for Spade, perhaps for any man, no merely personal relationship can ever be as important for him as his work, as what he does and thus what he is. Indeed, Spade even claims that what a man does can become so much a part of his nature that it's almost an instinctive reflex, like a dog catching rabbits, and that though one can on occasion act against that reflex, "it's not the natural thing."

In Spade's view a man may *have* a wife and family like Flitcraft, may be "a good citizen and a good husband and father," but *being* a husband and father is not what he *is*. His wife and family are part of his life-as-having, but his work is the practical embodiment of his life-as-being. When Flitcraft decides to stop wandering around, decides that random action can't be a rule of life, he returns, in effect, to steady work. And Spade makes clear the priorities involved in that return: "He had been living in Spokane for a couple of years as Charles—that was his first name—Pierce. He had an automobile business that was netting him twenty or twenty-five thousand a year, a wife, a baby son, owned his own home in Spokane, and usually got away to play golf after four in the afternoon during the season" (65). It is, in effect, simply the successful businessman's return to success, selling cars in Spokane this time rather than real estate in Tacoma, a work success that permits his reestablishment of a second wife and family, home and lifestyle, that, in its impersonal substitution for the first wife and family and "the rest of the appurtenances of successful American living," makes Job's ruthless substitution of ten new children for the ten Job lost seem like child's play—no pun intended. Though Hawthorne tells us nothing about what Wakefield does for a living (whether he has a profession or a business) and nothing about how he supports himself during the twenty years he surreptitiously keeps watch over his home and wife, he does tell us something about Wakefield's character, i.e.,

the fact that he had "a peculiar sort of vanity" coupled with "a disposition to craft," that tends to resonate with something in Spade's character as evoked by Effie Perrine's remark to Spade, "You always think you know what you're doing, but you're too slick for your own good, and some day you're going to find it out" (29) and evoked again later in a conversation between Lieutenant Dundy and Spade when the former says, "'It'd pay you to play along with us a little, Spade. You've got away with this and you've got away with that, but you can't keep it up forever.' 'Stop me when you can,' Spade replied arrogantly" (73). As we noted earlier, there is about Wakefield's twenty-year escapade not only the perverse sense that it is a thing done precisely because it is in his own worst interests but also the sense that part of its attraction for him is his feeling that only he would be clever enough, adept enough to manipulate his life this way and pull it off. And something of that same quality is at the core of Spade's character as well: the pro's sense that what he is is what he knows how to do and that his success in wielding his knowledge and ability makes him to some degree a law unto himself.

In that same vein, any event that could have occurred to Flitcraft that still left him in possession of his faculties (i.e., his self-consciousness and thus his unique personality), whatever possessions it might have deprived him of, could never have affected what he was, his ability to work and succeed and thus his ability to reconstitute his life-as-having. And this sense that no merely personal relationship can ever be as important to a man as his work or profession is presented in that final conversation between Spade and Brigid as the opposition between a professional commitment and a personal one, between what one owes to one's business partner as opposed to one's bed partner, to Miles Archer but not to Brigid O'Shaughnessy. Indeed, you don't even have to like or respect your business partner, you only have to have made a professional commitment to him, for then to let a merely personal commitment override that professional one is, as Spade says, "bad business . . . It's bad all around—bad for that one organization, bad for every detective everywhere" (226).

Now I don't claim that this sense—that what a man *does* (and thus, *is*) takes precedence over any mere personal relationship he may *have*—is something *peculiarly* American, but I do claim that it is *typically* American and that the delineation of this sense has created some of the central moments in some of the most characteristic works of twentieth-century American literature: from Gatsby's famous remark (after the failure of his quest to recover Daisy from Tom and thus confirm that through his own brains and work, he has bested Tom's inherited wealth), the remark he makes after realizing that Daisy might in fact have loved Tom at some point in their marriage, that this momentary betrayal on

Daisy's part was "At any rate . . . just personal";[9] to Spade's story of Flitcraft and his subsequent explanation of why one owes more to a partner than to a lover; and on to *The Death of a Salesman* where Willie Loman's wife and sons are left in the wake of what it takes for a salesman not just to be liked but to be well liked.

It is this deep American secret (that most men know, all women suspect, and some women can't accept, which is to say, don't understand, don't see why something that is of primary importance to them might be of secondary importance to their partners) that on one level animates the novel. Hence the incomprehension exhibited in turn by the first Mrs. Flitcraft, by Brigid O'Shaughnessy, and finally by Effie Perrine in that final scene of the novel when Sam puts his arm around her waist and she escapes "from his arm as if it had hurt her," saying "Don't, please, don't touch me. . . . You're right. But don't touch me now—not now" (229). Effie has seen how little personal relationships mean to Sam, and she is disturbed because she wonders what she herself means to Sam. But she shouldn't have worried because as far as Spade is concerned she doesn't have a personal relationship with him, no matter what she may think is her due after her years of faithful service as his secretary. She has only a professional relationship, she is one of his organization and thus covered by that same sense of responsibility that Spade says he owed his dead partner Miles Archer. Or as Spade says to Effie earlier in the novel when he leaves her alone in his office with the body of Captain Jacobi to wait for the police and tell them an edited version of the truth, "You're a damned good man, sister" (167).

* * *

These seem to me to be some of the things going on in *The Maltese Falcon,* some of the matters at issue in the book's evocation of the interplay among the repetitive (ordinary daily routine), the exceptional (an event like Flitcraft's falling beam or Spade's extraordinary case of the Maltese falcon or his love affair with Brigid), and the singular (one's own death) in any life, an evocation that speaks not only to questions the novel shares with works like Job and "Wakefield" but also to its own exceptional place and the place of its genre in the routine lives of twentieth-century Americans. For in the lives of many readers hard-boiled detective fiction has served for decades now as precisely that vicarious experience of the exceptional (in its character as a figure of the singular) that releases readers temporarily from the humdrum and routine of their own lives and then returns them to their lives with a renewed appreciation of the pleasures of the humdrum and the routine. And *The Maltese Falcon,* the best of the hard-boiled detective novels, in making, as it were, a self-reflexive gesture toward its genre by thematizing the interplay among the

repetitive, the exceptional, and the singular, makes us see that the ceaseless repetition which constitutes the very stuff of our lives only means in a constitutive opposition with the possibility of the exceptional on the one hand and the certainty of the singular on the other, makes us see that what keeps the ceaseless repetition of life from becoming empty and meaningless, from boring us to death, is the possibility of the exceptional, and that what gives life its weight, its seriousness, is that sense of the once-and-for-all that flows from the certainty of the singular. It is not so much that "death is the mother of beauty," as Stevens says, as that death is the mother of meaning and value, that, to alter Spade's statement slightly, when it comes to meaning and value "they're not much good unless the threat of death is behind them."

And so at least once a year I reread this hard-boiled novel about repetition, though I also try to reread Job and Ecclesiastes at least once a year as well, but *The Maltese Falcon* has this big advantage over the other two: that I can accompany each rereading of the novel with a re-viewing of the John Huston film, a movie that holds as honored a place in the history of film as that which Hammett's novel deserves to hold in the history of twentieth-century fiction.

Notes

1. Dashiell Hammett, *The Maltese Falcon* (New York, 1972), p. 64. All subsequent quotations from *The Maltese Falcon* are taken from this edition.

2. Sigmund Freud, *Beyond the Pleasure Principle,* trans. James Strachey (New York, 1972), p. 35.

3. Steven Marcus, "Dashiell Hammett and the Continental Op" in *The Critical Response to Dashiell Hammett,* ed. Christopher Metress (Westport, 1994), p. 194. All subsequent quotations from Marcus are taken from this edition.

4. Jean Pierre Chartier, "The Americans Are Making Dark Films Too" in *Perspectives on Film Noir,* ed. R. Barton Palmer (New York, 1996), pp. 25-27.

5. Robert G. Porfirio, "No Way Out: Existential Motifs in the Film Noir" in Palmer, *Perspectives on Film Noir,* p. 120.

6. Charles Gregory, "Living Life Sideways" in Palmer, *Perspectives on Film Noir,* p. 155.

7. Nathaniel Hawthorne, *The Complete Short Stories of Nathaniel Hawthorne* (Garden City, 1959), p. 75. All subsequent quotations from "Wakefield" are taken from this edition.

8. Edgar Allan Poe, *Collected Works of Edgar Allan Poe,* 3 vols., ed. Thomas Ollive Mabbott (Cambridge, MA, 1978), 2:723. All subsequent quotations from Poe are taken from this edition.

9. F. Scott Fitzgerald, *The Great Gatsby* (New York, 1953), p. 152.

Christopher T. Raczkowski (essay date winter 2003)

SOURCE: Raczkowski, Christopher T. "From Modernity's Detection to Modernist Detectives: Narrative Vision in the Work of Allan Pinkerton and Dashiell Hammett." *Modern Fiction Studies* 49, no. 4 (winter 2003): 629-59.

[*In the following essay, Raczkowski compares the portraits of Pinkerton detectives in founder Allan Pinkerton's memoirs and Hammett's fiction, asserting that "a critical shift becomes apparent in how vision is narratively constructed" in Hammett's works.*]

If we compare Allan Pinkerton's post-Civil War memoirs of his Pinkerton National Detective Agency with the Prohibition Era detective fiction of ex-Pinkerton detective Dashiell Hammett, a critical shift becomes apparent in how vision is narratively constructed. In his various "Detective Memoirs" from the 1870s and 1880s, Pinkerton articulates and frankly promotes a systematized network of fully professionalized detectives whose vision makes crime and criminals visible to the State. Such a nationwide techno-bureaucratic surveillance—the first of its kind in the United States—was underwritten by an ocular-centric positivism that pervaded American intellectual cultures from the mid-century.[1] Forty years after Pinkerton's last memoir, Dashiell Hammett rewrote the detective's sight as a vexed affair, reformulating the detective's vision as both embodied and perceptually limited to exteriority and surface. In these short stories and novels, Hammett refuses the epistemological priority of vision expressed in Pinkerton's memoirs and epitomized in Pinkerton's self-designed corporate logo, the "Pinkerton Eye". Hammett's refusal of the rational, scientific, technocratic gaze transformed the detective from an instrument of American political and economic modernity to a literary modernist agent for the critique of modernity.

Hammett's place as a modernist is best formulated in terms of his prolonged literary engagement with the problem of vision.[2] Recent theoretical work by Martin Jay, Douglas Mao, and Karen Jacobs situates a crisis of vision and epistemology at the center of literary modernism's cultural project. Influenced by fin de siècle discourses of Marxism and psychoanalysis, modernists experienced broad disillusionment with a visually oriented enlightenment rationality and its aesthetic offspring: literary realism. Rapidly evolving and expanding institutions of social surveillance and documentation made the coercive power of the disembodied observer increasingly onerous to society.[3] Simultaneous with these new strategies of social seeing, new forms of visibility emerged in the twentieth century. The evolving modern visual world at the turn of the century—characterized by what Karen Jacobs calls the "growing dominance of the image"—was given its distinctive form by a burgeoning North American commodity culture. New technologies made it possible for mechanically reproduced images to saturate social space, mediating even the most intimate aspects of people's lives (Jacobs 2). The twentieth century's crisis of visuality—in terms of both vision and visibility—led literary modernists to interrogate the relationship of viewing subject to object viewed and to reconsider the epistemological limits of narrative constructions of the visible.[4] Put differently, we might say that seeing was not knowing for Anglo-American literary modernists (at least not in the conventional sense of seeing or knowing). The exploration and maintenance of a divide between seeing and knowing may well be one of modernism's most characteristic narrative postures. It also marks modernism's most decisive departure from the aesthetic project of nineteenth-century literary realism in America.[5]

Among the elite Anglo-American modernists preoccupied with the question of vision, Gertrude Stein was a consistent, vocal supporter of Dashiell Hammett's fiction. She described Hammett as "one of the best contemporary American writers," and during her 1935 return visit to the United States, she singled him out as one of only two people that she wished to meet in America (qtd. in Nolan 152).[6] Stein's abiding admiration for Hammett acknowledges their similar critiques of epistemological foundationalism and a strong aesthetic commitment to exteriority. In *Everybody's Autobiography*, Stein writes, "I do like detective stories. I never try to guess who has done the crime . . . but I like somebody being dead and how it moves along and Dashiell Hammitt [sic] was all that and more" (xxii-xxiii). It is not the elaborate unraveling of a mystery that Stein values: she never tries to guess who the murderer is. Instead, Stein's interest lies in how the traumatic uncertainty of the crime affects the surface of social relations: "how it moves along." Such an explanation is supported by and expanded in Stein's occasional writing about crime and detective fiction. In "American Crimes and Why They Matter," for example, Stein explains, "Everybody remembers a crime when nobody finds out anything about who did it and particularly where the person mixed up with it goes on living . . . it is most interesting if you do not know the answer at all" (102-03). Hammett's "interest" for Stein lies in the guarded, epistemological uncertainty of his fiction. No doubt, this is a remarkable technical accomplishment in a genre whose narrative arc depends so heavily on the gradual revelation of an "answer" to the crime—what Barthes has referred to as teleological narrative's elaborate "striptease" (10). Not only do lingering doubts and uncertainty disturb the epistemological coziness of solutions within Hammett's fictions, but Hammett formulates this uncertainty on the level of structure as a limit to narrative vision. Rejecting the penetrative, "scientific" vision of the Pinkerton Detective and literary realism's third-person omniscient narrating overseer, Hammett typically constructs a visual world of surfaces and exteriority—a type of vision where motivation, desire, and identity remain largely invisible to the viewing subject. Such constructions of narrative vision are closely allied to the experimental techniques of Gertrude Stein. As the narrator of Stein's 1933 detective novel, *Blood on the Dining-Room Floor,* approvingly explains, "That is the way to see a thing, from the outside" (19).

"THE EYE THAT NEVER SLEEPS"

The curious Chicago pedestrian of 1855 stopping to examine the new office building at 89 Washington Street might well have been alarmed to find a giant disembodied eye looking back. This staring eye, emblazoned on a wooden sign with the ominous words "We Never Sleep" printed across the bottom, advertises a powerful and apparently relentless scrutiny. In its relationship with the viewing pedestrian, the sign organizes what Martin Jay has described as the menacing "God's Eye view" of Rousseauist social philosophy (91).[7] The unlucky subject is caught in the sight of the Father and made to feel, individually, his own transparency to the surveillance of god; or in the case of the pedestrian on Washington Street, the somewhat less austere but still intimidating surveillance of "Pinkerton and Co.," the new detective agency of Allan Pinkerton.

My interest in the appearance of Pinkerton's Eye as it stares down on Chicago pedestrians at mid-century is twofold: as a type of Foucauldian "panoptic eye," the sign announces the emergence of the modern techniques of social surveillance, and as "private eye," it announces the emergence of a new literature about this surveillance. Pinkerton was both the author of the first systemic, nation-wide surveillance network in America and the author of seventeen memoirs narrating that surveillance whose popular success did much to inspire a dime detective novel industry that mushroomed in the second half of the century.

It is difficult to imagine, but when Pinkerton first opened his Agency, there was no official state or municipal police force in Chicago. The city still used a largely volunteer-based constable and night watch system for law enforcement. In fact, only a few large American cities in 1855 had a public police force in any recognizably modern sense of the word (Morn 26). While such policing was adequate to the small, relatively isolated communities they served, dramatic changes in the socioeconomic structure of the nation put an end to their usefulness. New manufacturing technologies and the development of a transcontinental railroad and telegraph system, as well as the new corporate monopoly forms of capital accumulation at mid-century all contributed to the emergence of a national marketplace.[8] With limited resources, jurisdiction, and manpower, existing police systems could not meet a national economy's demands for the secure transfer of capital and labor across a vast continent. Nor did the answer seem to lie with the federal government, where attempts to institute a national police force encountered an American public's long-standing suspicion of the relation between concentrated power and tyranny. In 1855, however, Allan Pinkerton circumvented popular distrust of centralized policing authority by creating a private police that was contracted, very lucratively, by a consortium of six Midwestern railroads to protect their lines—the Michigan Central, the Michigan Southern and Northern Indiana, the Chicago and Galena Union, the Chicago and Rock Island, the Chicago Burlington and Quincy, and the Illinois Central. Together, the consortium's railroads represented almost three thousand miles of track (MacKay 77). As a consequence of the Agency's success, many of the domestic policing powers that Americans feared granting to the federal government were granted, by default, to an unregulated private business; Pinkerton's agents had no jurisdictional restrictions, were able to give testimony in court, and were subject only to the Agency's supervision. Under such fertile conditions, Pinkerton's Agency grew rapidly in size and power in these early years, contracting with local, state, and federal, as well as international, governments.

Significantly, the Midwestern railroads that hired Pinkerton were not motivated by the threat of masked bandits waiting in the hills (although there was enough of that), but by fear of the uniformed employees on the train. The railroad consortium hired Pinkerton primarily to protect them from theft by the engineers, conductors, ticket-takers, and other employees working on trains far from the disciplinary mechanisms of the company's offices.[9] Foremost among the thefts committed was the pocketing of train fares; on some of the consortium's railroads, this reached as high as 50 percent of the fares (Morn 46). Confronted with the impossibility of anything close to comprehensive surveillance by a handful of employees over a railroad spanning several thousand miles, Pinkerton's agents watched the trains invisibly, as it were, by posing as passengers or disguising themselves as engineers or other railroad employees. Pinkerton would then promote the invisible presence of disguised agents on the railroads by submitting accounts of the Agency's successes for publication in newspapers. Like Jeremy Bentham before him—architect of the "Panopticon" and a founder of British Utilitarianism—Allan Pinkerton understood that the perception of being watched was more important than the watching; people who believe they are being watched will internalize the disciplinary gaze regardless of anyone watching. Pinkerton's innovative approach to the problem of unruly railroad labor was cost-effective and immensely successful. The results spoke for themselves: fare theft on the Midwestern consortium's various railroads decreased by as much as 40 percent (Morn 46). The deepening conflict between organized capital and organized labor in the post-Civil War era only increased the Pinkerton Agency's value to capital. At a time when the cultural meaning of corporations was still in solution, Pinkerton participated in the hegemonic struggle over the significance and legitimacy of new corporate social and economic forms. In his memoirs, lectures, public appearances, and interviews, Pinkerton idealized the rationality and social virtue of corporate structures, equated corporate policy to democracy in economics—which then needed defending from foreign-born socialism— and repeatedly attempted to strike identifications between his agency and the corporations he served. Meanwhile, as the head of the nation's largest private police, Pinkerton exercised coercive power over organized labor and other more obstinate threats to corporate authority through surveillance, intimidation, and—not infrequently—violent force. Pinkerton's corporate industrial clients did not overlook the value of such services, and already by 1860 they enriched "Pinkerton and Co." sufficiently enough for Allan Pinkerton to accurately rename it the "Pinkerton National Detective Agency," with regional offices connecting up the continent. After having contracted as a military secret service with the US Army during the Civil War, Pinkerton's Agency became the single most powerful criminal investigation organization in the United States; according to many historians, it functioned as a de facto national police.[10]

In 1870, following a minor stroke, Pinkerton left the Agency to his son's management and undertook a literary campaign promoting the detective's work. Between the years of 1874 and 1884, with the help of what could only have been a small army of ghostwriters, he authored over seventeen detective memoirs. While varied in form and effect, the texts share some signal traits. Typically, Pinkerton's memoirs begin with some form of promise to the reader that his memoirs transparently represent the events they narrate—promises that "[n]o tint or coloring of the imagination has given a deeper touch to the action of the story" (*The Burglar's Fate* v). The compulsion to establish the truth of the events narrated and the transparency of their representation is critical to understanding Pinkerton's project. Beyond advertising the agency, the principle purpose of the memoirs was to reformulate the detective's vision as rational and scientific over and against an earlier romantic formulation of the detective. In much the same way that American realism's central promoter, William Dean Howells, instrumentalizes the "romanticistic" or "neoromantic" novel as a foundational negative term upon which to construct his "realist novel," so does Pinker-

ton draw on the "romantic" detective as a foundational negative term against which to define his Pinkerton Detective.

In the writing of both, the romantic figures as a kind of geographic, temporal, and political dislocation to which Howells's realism or Pinkerton's detective narrative acts as a corrective: it is a remnant of the Old World, simultaneously irrational, feminized, and anti-American. As an editor for *Harper's Monthly*, Howells contended that popular romanticist novels represented contemporary, vulgarized—and highly sensationalist—distortions of a romantic movement that "grew out of the political, social, and even economical conditions [in Europe] at the close of the eighteenth century." In its day, it was "noble and beautiful," but to revisit the romantic in Howells's modern America is to pose a politically dangerous anachronism: "Romanticism belonged to a disappointed and bewildered age, which turned its face from the future, and dreamed out a faery realm in the past; and we cannot have its spirit back because this is the age of hopeful striving . . . when the recognition of all the facts in the honest daylight about us is the service which humanity demands of the humanities" ("Editor's Study" 158). The realist novelist who observes society in "the honest daylight" and the Pinkerton detective who reports his findings with "no tint or coloring of the imagination" both implement a gaze that promises clarity, reason, and truth against the antisocial opacity and melodrama of popular romantic narrative. More than a decade before Howells fought his "realism war" against the neoromantic novel in the editorial pages of *Harper's Monthly*, Pinkerton railed against what he described as the "halo of romance" that covered the "disreputable" old world Parisian Corps Detectif and Bow Street Runner; the Pinkerton detective, he continually reminds us, is an "American detective [who] stands out in pure relief from all such associations" (*Thirty Years* 15-16).

It is safe to assume that the threat of "romanticism" for Howells and popular "romanticized" detective fiction for Pinkerton was exaggerated by their general popularity with the reading public. For Howells, this meant strong competition from what he saw as cynical, irrelevant, sentimental fiction, the continued popular success of which seems to have kept the realist ranks rather thin; American realism was never a colossal marketplace success (Budd 37). Meanwhile, Pinkerton had to contend with flamboyant dime detectives such as Old Sleuth—a popular literary hero inspired, ironically enough, by Pinkerton's exploits. To Pinkerton's perpetual chagrin, these popular cheap format fictions glamorized and made mysterious the detective figure Pinkerton wished ardently to professionalize and make respectable (Morn 82). In *Strikers, Communists, Tramps and Detectives* and *Thirty Years a Detective*, Pinkerton painstakingly details the rationally bureaucratic, methodical, bourgeois activities of his agents, but such attempts to effect a mutual identification with the bourgeois industrialists he worked for were continually undermined by the proliferation of cheap, romantic dime detectives. In 1884, Pinkerton's son, William, claimed that this cheap format "yellow back" literature was responsible for the flood of "romantics" who were weakening the detective profession (Morn 82).[11]

And yet, Pinkerton did strive for literary effects in his memoirs; they are interspersed with allusions to respectable literary figures from John Burroughs, John Bunyan, and Sir Walter Scott to Charles Dickens and Lord Byron. Such consciously literary aims are also apparent in the generous use of what might be called lyrical set pieces in the narratives—self-contained poetic rhapsodies on the beauty of a country road, a hillock, a woman's foot. The high culture cachet of the memoirs was important enough to Pinkerton that he refused lucrative offers to publish them in popular dime novel and story paper formats, and even trademarked his name against low culture appropriations (Denning 144; Morn 82). The full importance of the literary campaign to Pinkerton's social project can only be understood, however, if we consider that before Pinkerton established his Agency, the primary antecedents of the detective in America were almost entirely literary ones.[12] The immensely successful American publication of Eugène François Vidocq's memoirs in 1832, and Edgar Allen Poe's Dupin stories of the 1840s predate any significant appearance of extra-literary detectives in North America (which may suggest why Poe leaves his detective in Paris).

The detective formed by the Pinkerton Agency and articulated in the memoirs presents a strategic departure from the literary detectives that preceded him in the American popular imagination (principally Vidocq and Dupin). Pinkerton ardently worked to professionalize and make respectable the detective that Vidocq had presented to American audiences as a flamboyant, mysterious, ex-master criminal; the resilience of Vidocq's portrait of the detective drove Pinkerton to distraction. On the other hand, Pinkerton shares with Poe's Dupin a similar commitment to Enlightenment values of sight and knowledge. The critical difference is that Pinkerton's vision has less to do with an exaggerated faith in causal reasoning from visual sense data than with faith in the rational organization of seeing bodies. In other words, vision in the Pinkerton memoirs and agency is thoroughly bureaucratized, structurally complementing the client corporations his agency served. Indeed, borrowing from the late-nineteenth-century rhetoric of "rationalized" managerial policy, Pinkerton referred to individual detectives in his intricately hierarchized system as "agents" whose anonymous looking is organized on the behalf of and made meaningful by their "Principal," Allan Pinkerton (Morn 53). Each agent was strictly regulated by Agency procedural rules, codes of conduct, chain-of-command, and an elaborate system of written reports and internal surveillance. In such a regimented system, vision is not in the service of individual acts of highhanded logical deduction from crime scene clues, but multiplied and organized as surveillance over suspected criminals. Just watch your suspects closely and long enough, the Pinkerton memoirs seem to tell us, and they will expose their hidden guilt directly to your eyes.[13] Finally, Pinkerton's bureaucratized vision exceeds the limited individual sight of the Vidocq or Poe detective and at times it even exceeds individual consciousness.

In his 1877 memoir, *The Molly Maguires and the Detective,* Pinkerton describes the three-year infiltration and investigation of a secret Irish labor organization, the Molly Maguires, by his agent, James McParlan. Franklyn B. Gowen, the president of both the Philadelphia and Reading Railroad Company and the Philadelphia and Reading Coal and Iron Company, hired the Pinkerton Agency to investigate the purported role of the Molly Maguires in a series of crimes committed against his company's property and personnel in the Pennsylvania anthracite region: specifically, the dynamiting of a railroad track and a series of beatings and murders of company managers over the preceding decade. The memoir's account of the investigation—still considered the most valuable primary source for the study of this prominent event in nineteenth-century race and labor history—reveals the transcendental qualities of Pinkerton's Eye/I. While we are informed that Pinkerton remains stationary at the Agency's Chicago Headquarters, he provides such detailed and intimate knowledge of the events, sights, and spaces comprising McParlan's experience that Pinkerton's presence is fully implied. Narrative insights to the unspoken thoughts of McParlan contribute to an eerie feeling that McParlan is more a host for Pinkerton's seeing and consciousness than for his own. Meanwhile, Pinkerton's vision, directed outwards from McParlan to the social world of the miners, makes visible the motivation of the transparent miner/criminals. Here is an alternative to the classical "detective as individual genius": Pinkerton as a "Bureaucratized Eye" whose hierarchized vision, disseminated through a host of anonymous agents—themselves referred to as "Pinkertons" or "Pinks" in common usage—permeates late-nineteenth-century American social order and makes it visible. In effect, Pinkerton's transition from the first-person of the introduction and conclusion to the third-person omniscient narration of the narrative proper identifies the narrative vision of Pinkerton with the third-person omniscient narrator of nineteenth-century American realism.

In Howells's *A Hazard of New Fortunes,* the acquisition of a suitably objective, adequately distanced viewing perspective becomes one of the novel's central narrative conflicts. While the novel responds most immediately to the contemporaneous New York street car strikes of 1889 and the Haymarket Riot of 1886, it is also deeply informed by the Great Strikes of 1877.[14] In his memoir accounts of these last strikes, Pinkerton struggles mightily with the problem of seeing the upheaval of striking masses that exploded along the railroads of the Baltimore and Ohio and spread across the nation. "It was everywhere; it was nowhere," Pinkerton laments. Mobile, amorphous, and impossible to predict, Pinkerton refers to the strikes of 1877 as "The Great Terror" because they cannot be "located, fixed, or given boundaries" (*Strikers* 14). Howells's *A Hazard of New Fortunes* rehearses a similar visual problem through Basil March's attempts to report on the streetcar strikes for his magazine, *Every Other Week.* Like the Great Strikes for Pinkerton, Basil has trouble seeing the conflict; he's either too soon or too late. One of his colleagues quips, "I can't get any show at them: haven't seen a brickbat shied or a club swung yet"—and March eventually begins to "doubt whether there were any such outbreaks" (408, 411).[15]

When March finally encounters the strike firsthand, he is briefly overtaken by a frightening loss of perspective or, more precisely, the frightening acquisition of an *involved* perspective. Recognizing that he was being watched by the police, March "began to feel like populace; but he struggled with himself and regained his character of 'philosophical observer'" (412). Through this trompe l'oeil, March abstracts himself once again from the scene he dangerously occupies and ascends into the event's narrative framework as an unattached observer. From such a "philosophical" distance, the streetcar strike can be narrated as "something that happened several centuries ago; De Foe's Plague of London style" (409). When March proceeds in this Olympian vein to witness the death of Dryfoos's altruistic son at the hands of the strike police, however, Howells undercuts the impossible security and pretense to objectivity that March's posture assumes. Despite such critiques, the third-person omniscient narrative structure of *A Hazard of New Fortunes* endorses the visual posture of the philosophical observer on the level of form as the only perspective that can adequately "see" the totality of the fragmented society. In this sense, March's refusal of Fulkerson's suggestion that they find a striker to "write up" a firsthand account of the streetcar strike for the magazine must be recognized simultaneously as Howells's refusal: both the fictional magazine, *Every Other Week,* and the fiction that contains it, *A Hazard of New Fortunes,* discount the explanatory authority of the embodied observer's limited perspective.

In his account of the nationwide labor strikes of 1877, Pinkerton authorizes his seeing of the strikes in terms similar to Basil March above. Pinkerton's physical absence from the scene in *Strikers, Communists, Tramps*

and the Detective—underwritten by his paradoxical presence through his agents—guarantees the perspective-less and therefore limitless quality of his seeing. Following the legal fiction of his client corporations, Pinkerton might be said to incorporate himself in this memoir. Not an embodied, individual detective observer, Pinkerton describes himself as the organizing "principle" behind a system of observation. Dismissing popular newspaper accounts that emplotted him as a Vidocq-inspired individual hero, Pinkerton attributed his success instead to rational administration and efficient bureaucracy: "an extensive and perfected detective system has made this work easy for me" (*Strikers* ix-x). Howellsian realist or Pinkertonian detective, both posit a disembodied observer and an abiding faith in a social project that aims at making America visible to itself through the exercise of a visually centered reason. Hammett would approach the problem from a crucible where neither reflective philosophy nor scientific, systematic techniques could guarantee the authority of vision for knowledge.[16]

"Philo Vance / Needs a Kick in the Pance"

As a Pinkerton agent for close to seven years in the Agency's Baltimore and San Francisco Offices, Dashiell Hammett looked in on many of the explosive loci of twentieth-century America's shifting modernity. Besides working as a Pinkerton detective for the defense in the notorious Fatty Arbuckle trial, Hammett also claimed to have worked as a detective in the service of mine officials at the Anaconda Copper Strike led by the Industrial Workers of the World (IWW) when labor organizer Frank Little was castrated and lynched by anti-labor vigilantes. According to Paul Buhle's *Encyclopedia of the American Left,* the Frank Little episode left Hammett embittered with the Pinkerton Agency and responsive to Marxist critique. Politically, if not professionally then, Hammett's adoption of Pinkerton's detective memoir form was a complicated one. Initially, Hammett had attempted a more traditional "literary" writing career with poetry, criticism, and short stories contributed to H. L. Mencken's and George Jean Nathan's important *Smart Set.*[17] Under their guidance, though, he was gradually directed toward more lucrative work in *Black Mask,* one of a number of cheap format "pulps" operated by Mencken and Nathan—along with the more luridly titled *Saucy Stories* and *La Parisienne*—in order to fund the critically admired but fiscally embarrassed *Smart Set* (Goulart 23-24). Hammett never recorded his feelings about this shift in literary fortunes, but given his financial desperation in 1923— virtually unemployable as a result of chronic bouts of tuberculosis caught during an ill-fated stint as an army ambulance driver in 1918—it seems doubtful that his relationship with *Black Mask* was other than a source of relief, if not celebration.

The field of American popular detective fiction that Hammett encountered in the twenties, however, was heavily influenced by Conan Doyle and the British tradition of "drawing-room mysteries." From 1926 to 1939, William Huntington Wright's "Philo Vance" novels, written under the pseudonym of S. S. Van Dine, presided over the literary detective marketplace, outselling all competition. Wright's highly formalized novels of detection—replete with a list of characters, maps of crime scenes, and drawings of critical evidence—record the investigative virtuosity of Philo Vance, an erudite New York aristocrat and amateur detective. Vance even has his own admiring Watson-like narrator to dote on his genius, but that is where the obvious comparisons with Doyle end. When in *The "Canary" Murder Case,* Vance states plainly, "If you could distinguish between rationality and irrationality . . . you'd be a god," he effects a distinct break with a Holmesian tradition of detective fiction that posited absolute explanatory authority to the detective's rational method (160). While this critique of rationality marks quite an advance over reductive tendencies in Doyle, a substitution takes place in Wright's novels that allows him to introduce a different type of idealized explanatory authority. Vance refers to this technique in *The "Canary" Murder Case* as putting the suspects under "the psychological microscope, as it were" (312). According to Van Dine, his Watson-like narrator, Vance exercises an expert psychological gaze that penetrates to the "hidden truth beneath misleading exteriors" (*Bishop* 8). Wright's rejection of the epistemological certainty of Holmesian ratiocination then is premised on its substitution with the (qualified) epistemological certainty of an expert psychological vision penetrating the criminal psychoses of his suspects.[18]

For his detractors (Ogden Nash once punned "Philo Vance / Needs a Kick in the Pance" [183]), Vance appeared an insufferable know-it-all who dropped his g's for affect, quoted Cato the Elder, and made extravagant use of his French and Italian phrase books. The first-person narrated Continental Op stories, the fruit of Hammett's work for *Black Mask,* allowed Hammett to intervene on the psychological positivism of Philo Vance's vision as well as the exquisitely bourgeois—almost aristocratic—sensibilities that support Vance's viewing posture. Meanwhile, Hammett's colleagues at *Black Mask*—Caroll John Daly, Raol Whitfield, Paul Cain, and Frederick Lewis Nebel—shared in the proletarian politics of Hammett's grim social vision and evoked similar despair about the possibility of justice in the modern social world of their fictions, but none shared Hammett's rigorous skepticism of the detective's production of knowledge. Together, these class-based ideological and antifoundationalist epistemological concerns structured Hammett's critique of the emergent social surveillance project initiated by his former employer, Allan Pinkerton.

Hammett's Continental Op stories are narrated by an anonymous, short, stout, middle-aged detective in the employ of the Continental Agency. This fictional, nationwide detective agency resembles Pinkerton's in a number of important details. Random House's 1966 compilation of Hammett's Continental Op stories, *The Big Knockover,* iconically refers to this identification in its cover art. The disembodied Pinkerton Eye is directly alluded to and revised here, only its gaze is averted, contextualized—albeit abstractly against the checkerboard and coffin—and its visual field is limited.[19] In the stories collected there, Pinkerton's magisterial organizing presence emerges in the figure of the "Old Man," the Op's superior and supervisor whose "gentle eyes behind gold spectacles and his mild smile, [hide] the fact that fifty years of sleuthing had left him without any feelings at all on any subject" ("Scorched Face" 91). The Pinkerton Agency's use of strict codes, daily reports, and internal overseeing are evident in the Continental Agency's regulation of its operatives' activities. The Continental Agency also serves the same bourgeois industrialist clientele as the Pinkerton Agency and retains the same quasi-official status with the criminal and legal institutions of the State.

Nonetheless, Pinkerton would have been scandalized by Hammett's accounts of the incoherence and limits of the Agency's visual operations. The surveillance network described by Pinkerton indulges a visual fantasy where he positions himself in his office as in a panoptic tower, watching his agents as they watch the Agency's social objects. Pinkerton describes his position in an 1872 letter to a friend:

> I occupy a Building about thirty-six feet by ninety-five feet. It is fitted up most beautifully. The first floor is my "Preventive Watch," we now have nearly eighty men and probably by the end of the year we shall have a hundred . . . and over all is an Eye. The all-seeing Eye under which are the words "We Never Sleep." . . . as one of the forces goes to bed, another one gets up. Everything is in motion and the Eye is looking after them all the time. . . . The next farthest away, where all is quiet, is my office. There I survey everything that is going on, everything must come under my supervision.
>
> (qtd. in Morn 65)

Aside from communicating the Agency's vigorous growth in the 1870s, the letter gives us a detailed look at the internal workings of Pinkerton's surveillance apparatus. The Eye that Pinkerton writes of is, of course, the trademarked emblem of the Pinkerton Eye replete with its insomniac's promise and reproduced on lampshades and murals throughout the Agency's offices. Sitting at his desk, looking up at the Pinkerton Eye emblazoned on the lamp above him along with the words "We Never Sleep," the Pinkerton agent faced more than an admonition not to sleep at his desk. Just as those pedestrians who first encountered the sign on Washington Street, the Pinkerton agent finds himself caught in the gaze of Pinkerton's Eye. Its discrete placement at each level of the office serves as a reminder to Pinkerton employees at every rank of the organization that they are a conduit for a gaze in which they are also caught; it reminds them, as Pinkerton explains to his correspondent, that "the Eye is looking after them all the time." Administering this central gaze, Pinkerton stands over everyone on the building's top floor, from which he "survey[s] everything that is going on, everything must come under my supervision." In *Discipline and Punish,* Foucault writes of the prison cells at Mettray, on the walls of which are written in black letters: "God sees you" (294). What do the words beneath the Pinkerton Eye—"We Never Sleep"—signify if not a secular translation of Mettray's promise/threat of an omnipresent surveillance?—a threat in which Pinkerton fantastically adopts the viewing posture of God.[20]

In Hammett's first novel, his 1929 *Red Harvest,* the vulnerability of the Agency's surveillance is thematized.[21] The prehistory to the novel provides the occasion of the title. Just prior to the Op's arrival in Personville—the mining town that stages the novel's action—there had been a lengthy and very violent IWW-led labor strike.[22] In the process of defeating the strike, Personville's aged industrialist and political boss Elihu Willsson unwittingly surrendered his control of the city to the gangsters he paid to subdue the strikers. Willsson then hired the Continental Agency to investigate the murder of his son, primarily because he believed—incorrectly—that the investigation would simultaneously destroy his new political adversaries. As the narrative unfolds, it becomes apparent that the visual economy imagined by Hammett in *Red Harvest* is quite different than the orderly surveillance machine imagined by Pinkerton. Not only do subjects dissemble before the surveillance of the Continental Agency in Hammett's text (authoring their own visuality), but the agents themselves dissemble before each other and the Old Man. The Op routinely falsifies his daily reports to the Old Man; as he explains to the agents who are sent in part to check up on him and whom he in turn deceives, "a report is no place for dirty details" (118). The surveillance Hammett reveals in his Continental Op stories is obviously not unidirectional, and the patriarchal Old Man menacing us from the center of the system is limited and vulnerable to our impostures.

The Old Man at the center of Hammett's Continental Agency, relative to Pinkerton above, finds himself in a decidedly humble position. Indeed, the Continental Op stories as a whole might accurately be described as a chronicle of old men in crisis. A quick look at the stories anthologized in *The Big Knockover* reveals a phalanx of "old gentlemen"—industrialists, politicians, and bankers—who took their "profits from the world with both hands in their younger days," but now require the Agency's protection ("Gutting" 4). With very few exceptions, the stories collected in *The Big Knockover* narrate the Continental Detective Agency's service to a bourgeois patriarchy imperiled by reckless daughters and ambitious criminals. In these stories, the well-fed old men are neither able to justify their social power—they are universally characterized as an avaricious, duplicitous, violent and ill-tempered lot—nor defend that social power effectively against the gender and class-based threats that challenge them. Rebellious daughters undermine patriarchal authority in the stories **"Fly Paper," "The Scorched Face"** and **"The Gatewood Caper."** And Hammett sketches nothing short of a proletarian revolution in the large-scale criminal operation (involving over two hundred mainly Irish, Italian and Mexican criminals) against the San Francisco financial district described in **"The Big Knockover"** and **"$106,000 Blood Money."** Meanwhile, **"The Gutting of Couffignal"** describes the same old men threatened again, only this time from a residual monarchist threat of immigrant White Russians who attempt to seize control of a small resort island of retired capitalists, and **"This King Business"** narrates revolutions manipulated in Muravia in order to bring back the prodigal son and heir of an old-line American family. Virtually everywhere we look in Hammett's short fiction, bourgeois patriarchy needs defending. Where Pinkerton's memoirs sing the virtue and virility of the bourgeois capitalist, Hammett intones something closer to a funeral march. Even the Continental Agency's intimidating Old Man is finally an old man defending old men, for he too is vulnerable. Unlike Pinkerton's portrait of his agency, the Continental Agency's surveillance is neither seamless nor totally efficient, and as a result the Old Man at the center of the Continental Agency may see a lot, but he does not see everything, and this is critical.

Pinkerton's epistemological assumptions about vision were inspired, no doubt, by what now might be called an "optimistic empiricism" generally seen as characteristic of nineteenth-century America's relationship with Enlightenment thought: that if vision and reason could make knowable the latent structures of meaning that organize the natural world as Darwin seemed to do, then the same vision and reason could be applied to reveal latent structures of meaning in the social world—as the new nineteenth-century social sciences now promised. One of Pinkerton's most important innovations was his use of photography to produce an extensive archive of "mug shots" of all criminals and suspects investigated by the Agency to accompany the written reports. The sociological and ethnographic foundation to this photographic project is established in memoirs that classify and document an invisible menace of ethnic and class others to Pinkerton's largely middle-class readers. In *Criminal Reminiscences,* Pinkerton puts his sociological ambition bluntly to the reader: "The position which I occupy gives me an unusual opportunity to see life from the underside, and the worst as well as the best phases of human conduct are forced upon my notice, until they become, by second nature, a matter for study" (282). Such rhetoric and methodology should remind us that Pinkerton's visual project developed almost simultaneously with the science of sociology in America; the American Social Sciences Foundation was founded in 1865, five years after Pinkerton's officially became a "national" detective agency. The table of contents of *Professional Thieves and the Detective* reveals Pinkerton's surprisingly elaborate taxonomies of crime and criminals. The production of this social knowledge is the reward, Pinkerton goes on to explain, of a "system of minute examination" extended across a culture through agents whose "investigations have been fully and regularly reported to me." Through this extended vision, Pinkerton can "penetrate into the mysteries of the [criminal's] operations" (*Thirty Years* 19). In Pinkerton's memoirs, then, he is a detective in the etymologically most accurate sense. According to the *Oxford Dictionary of English Etymology,* "detective" comes from the French word "de-tegere," meaning "to uncover, or expose the secret of." Because "tegere" derives from the French word for "thatch," it would be more accurate to say "un-roof."[23] In Pinkerton then, the Agency's vision is primarily de-tective; it lifts the roof to expose hidden interiors to a viewing agent, whose invisible sightlines penetrate the object's mysteries. Such an uncovering of true essence is fundamental to most definitions of the detective's sight. In his social history of the American criminal justice system, *Crime and Punishment in American History,* Lawrence M. Friedman historicizes the nineteenth-century appearance of the detective and the detective narrative as a compensatory response to a culture's new mobility: "Both reflect a fluid, restless mobile social system, with endless possibilities for false identity, mysterious origins, strange secrets. The detective . . . cuts through to the hidden core . . . peel[s] away the outer covering . . . reveal[s] the underlying reality" (207). The invasive—and decidedly violent—verbs Friedman employs to describe the detective's vision are typical of most accounts of the detective's vision, past or present: in the vast majority of his incarnations, the detective is understood to use his vision to dominate the object viewed.

In this sense, Hammett's are not detective fictions at all; vision does not "cut" or "peel" or otherwise penetrate into the object's interior. In Hammett's fiction, sight is limited to the surface, exteriority; it remains on the "thatch roof." Consider the description of Sam Spade's first encounter with Casper Gutman, in Hammett's third and perhaps most influential novel, his 1930 *The Maltese Falcon*:

> A fat man came to meet him. The fat man was flabbily fat with bulbous pink cheeks and lips and neck, with a great soft egg of a belly that was all his torso and pen-

dant cones for arms and legs. As he advanced to meet Spade all his bulbs rose and shook and fell separately, in the manner of clustered soap bubbles not yet released from the pipe through which they had been blown.

(104)

The narrative's vision of Gutman above has more to do with the physics of surface tension than psychology; characters are living surfaces of so much matter, energy, motion, and force. Psychological depth, introspection, and interiority are not visible to the detective's sightlines or, therefore, the narrative's vision. In this instance, Hammett's metaphor entails the radical implication that there is nothing other than surface to observe. Nor do the remarkably eloquent object/clues of classical detective fiction reveal anything beyond their thingness in Hammett. Routine searches of apartments, people, and crime scenes in Hammett seldom reveal anything resembling a traditional detective's clue; indeed, such seemingly random lists of objects are striking precisely because they remain mute in a narrative frame where such objects are expected most to signify, to speak some meaning. Objects are not mere containers to be opened by a visually centered reason. In Hammett's later work, particularly the novels, this hypothesis takes on growing weight and is repeatedly reformulated. The eponymous statuette of Hammett's *Maltese Falcon* stands over all his fiction as an iconic meditation on depthless surface. The Falcon, the object of desire that fuels the narrative, is covered in a black lacquer that—finally being penetrated in the novel's conclusion—is found to conceal no hidden wealth of precious metals and gems, but further layers of dense, soft, black lead: meaningless black surface layered over meaningless black surface.

Compared with Pinkerton's ambitious formulations of vision, Hammett's are humble indeed. Vision neither unveils concealed truths nor does it establish the transcendental perspective of Pinkerton's disembodied eye. When the Op declares, "This damned burg is getting to me," he speaks for the involvement of all Hammett's observers in the social world they observe (*Red Harvest* 154). And yet, Hammett does not devalue vision, but revalues it. The phenomenological priority of sight is upheld in Hammett, but it is situated with the other senses. And so, in *Red Harvest,* a boxing match is described: "Smoke. Stink. Heat. Noise" (74). When the Op announces in the first line of this same novel, "I first heard Personville called Poisonville by a red-haired mucker named Hickey Dewey in the Big Ship in Butte," the importance of the ear, in particular, is heard in Hammett's prose (3). As with the previous description of Gutman, Hammett emphasizes the conscious artistry of descriptive language through poetic techniques of alliteration, assonance, and meter. Consequently, the ear qualifies the eye in Hammett by drawing attention to the absence of an artless language for the observer to reflect the observed. Hammett's response to naïve realist claims for the transparent representation of the real—claims that underwrote Pinkerton's project—is bluntly expressed by the narrator of his unfinished final novel, **Tulip**: "Realistic is one of those words when it comes into a discussion, sensible people leave the room" (327).

When, at the beginning of **The Maltese Falcon,** Spade refuses the police's offer to view the corpse and crime scene of his murdered partner, it becomes clear that knowledge has a diminished reliance on vision in Hammett's fiction. His simple assertion that "You've seen him. You'd see everything I could" (401), does not discount the value of seeing but unseats it from the singular authority it tends to hold for producing truth in Pinkerton's memoirs and throughout the classical detective genre. While there are exceptions, especially in his earlier short fiction, Hammett's detectives do not detect in the sense that they uncover the truth of the crime so much as they might be said to cover over the corpse, the crime scene, the objects of the investigation with an explanation that never truly fits, but fits more satisfactorily than the competing explanations. In his work on Hammett, Steven Marcus describes this investigative technique as one where the detective "actively undertakes to deconstruct, decompose and thus de-mystify the fictional—and therefore false—reality created by the characters [in their narrative accounts of what happened]. . . . More often than not he tries to substitute his own fictional-hypothetical representation for theirs" (xxi). In this fashion, Hammett's narratives are concerned with the constructed-ness of knowledge and the unavailability of any foundationalist concept of truth. The conclusion of **The Thin Man** exemplifies the lingering epistemological uncertainty of solutions characteristic of Hammett's novels. After Nick's involved, heavily qualified explanation of the murder of Clyde Wynant, Nora's response is the novel's deflationary final line: "That may be . . . but it's all pretty unsatisfactory."[24]

As against Pinkerton's conception of vision, Hammett's fiction insists that vision does not provide direct access to an independently existing truth, but that truth is produced by and within a specific social context for its usefulness. The solutions that simultaneously offer the greatest aesthetic coherence—that "seem to click with most of the known facts," as Sam Spade expresses it in **The Maltese Falcon**—and practical benefit for the key players work as the truth of the crime in Hammett's fiction; think here of the accounting columns Spade rhetorically maintains when he explains to Brigid his reasons for sending her over (115). This type of antifoundationalism finds a counterpart with William James's antifoundationalism. In his 1907 lecture "Pragmatism's Conception of Truth," James argues that "Truth lives . . . for the most part on a credit system.

Our thoughts and beliefs pass, so long as nothing challenges them, just as banknotes pass so long as nobody refuses them." While what James refers to as the "cash value" of truth resides on a verification somewhere down the line by somebody, still James explains, "indirectly or only potentially verifying processes may be true as well" (100). Hammett acknowledges the socially maintained character of truth and knowledge in his fiction, but insists upon the material character of James's economic and financial metaphors as a critique of the institutional and economic pressures that influence the production of truth in class society, pressures that remain oddly invisible to James. In a society where power is determined by unequally distributed wealth, Hammett tells us, those with the most wealth have the greatest ability to define truth and establish knowledge. However, even as the influence of capital weighs in on the legal and criminal institutions of the State, there is still an unsettling arbitrariness to the process. As Nick Charles explains it to Nora in **The Thin Man,**

> You find someone you think did the murder, and you think he's guilty and put his picture all over the newspapers, and the District Attorney builds up the best theory he can on what information you've got and meanwhile you pick up additional details here and there and people recognize his picture in the paper—as well as people who'd think he was innocent if you hadn't arrested him—come in and tell you things about him and presently you've got him sitting on the electric chair.
>
> (195)

While the legal system is not a mere fiction managed from above by the captains of industry—Hammett's is not a paranoid universe—still, the resources required to make the system run result in an unequal distribution of justice that favors the wealthy. Repeatedly in Hammett's fictions, the detective's vision and explanatory authority are so much labor-rendered directly to the Agency's well-heeled clients—the well-fed old men—or to the State that protects their interests, a dynamic that contributes to the almost routinely anticlimactic conclusions of Hammett's fiction.

"THE SITUATION OF OUR TIME / SURROUNDS US LIKE A BAFFLING CRIME"

If we consider the detective and literary line from Pinkerton to Hammett, a dramatic shift occurs in the detective writer's relationship to the object. Pinkerton's project in 1850 supports and is in turn supported by an emergent American economic and scientific modernity whose relationship to the object has been described frequently by twentieth-century critics as one of commercial and/or scientific domination: in terms of ownership, commodification, knowledge, and control. On this point I should add that Pinkerton's detective narratives are almost entirely concerned with crimes of theft; there are no murder investigations here, just the return of commodity objects to their legitimate owner. In both Vidocq and Poe, Pinkerton's two major literary antecedents, murder was given frequent narrative treatment. For the relentlessly optimistic Pinkerton, however, murder seems to have been too sordid an affair. Likely, murder did not coordinate with Pinkerton's reformulation of the detective as a bourgeois professional; it worked at cross-purposes with the identification he wished to strike with his staid, respectable clients. When Pinkerton places the criminals into legal custody and returns the stolen goods to his clients, there is a full and satisfying business exchange. The guilty are punished and the world as it existed before the crime is reinstituted. A symbolic economy of debt and compensation is established that would please the most accountant-minded reader. Compared to this, murder is a sloppy affair.

The narratives of classic detective fiction, like those of Pinkerton's memoirs, depend on the recovery of the prefallen social world before the crime. This balancing of accounts is only possible because the corpse exists abstractly as the chief signifier of a formal puzzle. Murders tend to happen offstage, seem oddly nonviolent, even aestheticized, and when the puzzle is solved, it is as if the corpse never existed. The "sporting" treatment of a corpse in classic detective fiction—formalized in the London Detective Club's rules of "fair play"—encourages the reader to compete with the narrative's detective, who is frequently an amateur, to reach a solution to the crime. Classic detective fiction thus opposes what I like to think of as an aesthetic of "professional realism" in Pinkerton's memoirs. Had he lived long enough to encounter it, Allan Pinkerton would likely have viewed classic detective fiction's treatment of murder as both unreal (highly formalist) and bad for business (devalues the detective's labor as something anyone could do). Pinkerton's professional realism, on the other hand, had no way of representing murder without threatening either the memoir's stated commitment to realism or Pinkerton's ardent professionalism. Treated as something other than a formal puzzle, murder always generates surplus meaning, something left over that does not fit easily into the very tidy epistemological universe presented in Pinkerton's memoirs. It rends the social fabric in such a fashion that it can never be restitched as it existed before the crime, while revealing limits to the knowledge produced by the scientific, detached observer.

Where Pinkerton embraces a modernity that elevates the knowing subject over his object—and in doing so consolidates the social authority of his client corporations—Hammett's fiction yields to the object. The objects found in Hammett's writing are best understood as what Douglas Mao describes as Anglo-American modernism's "solid objects": they are impenetrable to a visually centered reason, radically other, nonself, contingent in a world where subjectivity and human consciousness threaten to absorb every thing (4).[25] The force of the intellectual currents generated by Marx and Freud in the twentieth century, Mao argues, deeply troubled the Enlightenment subject's cognizance of her object: indicated the difficulty, if not the impossibility of understanding the object as other than "commodity" or "symbol" respectively. Here Hammett's aesthetic commitment to exteriority and critique of a Cartesian visual posture reveal his engagement of literary modernism's central problem: how to narratively represent the integrity of the object world—what Mao terms its "solidness"—without subordinating it to consciousness (the self) or instrumentality (power). Hammett's representational strategy, crystallized in **The Maltese Falcon**'s titular statuette, is to repeatedly tell us that the object's surface conceals no hidden treasure—epistemological, psychological, or otherwise—for a grasping subjectivity. These "cold" aesthetic commitments—temperature here measuring the gap for epistemology between subject and object—explain the cachet that Hammett's fiction garnered with contemporary modernists from Robert Graves to Andre Gide and Gertrude Stein. Communicating modernism's crisis of vision and epistemology to a popular audience, Hammett also communicated to an audience of literary modernists a popular crime and detective genre's capacity for critique of vision. A considerable number of elite Anglo-American literary modernists, such as William Faulkner, Gertrude Stein, and Vladimir Nabokov, wrote detective fiction in Hammett's wake. Still others, including T. S. Eliot, Ford Maddox Ford, Graham Greene, and W. H. Auden, expressed their abiding interest in detective fiction through criticism and reviews.[26]

Indeed, Auden used popular detective narrative as an extended metaphor for the experience of modernity in "Part I" of his long poem, *New Years Letter (January 1, 1940).* "The situation of our time," Auden writes,

> Surrounds us like a baffling crime.
> There lies the body half-undressed,
> We all had reason to detest,
> And all are suspects and involved.

> (271-72)

The political and cultural crisis of modernity—convulsed in a second bloody World War in 1940—constitutes a "baffling crime" in need of detection. But the crisis is simultaneously a crisis of detection; there is no innocent place from which to investigate the crime according to the poem; "all are suspects," and furthermore, the means of investigating may itself be constitutive of the disaster. Not only does the crime "make nonsense of our laws," but in the act of investigating,

our equipment all the time
Extends the area of the crime
Until the guilt is everywhere.

(272)

Located between a "baffling crime" and an investigation that "extends the area of the crime," Auden's detective/poet/narrator in *New Year's Letter* is caught in the same double bind as Hammett's fictional detective. Conceptualizing modernity as a "baffling crime," Auden calls attention to the modernist work of detective fiction, as well as the detective work of modernism. Elite modernist interest in detective narrative reflects more than just the marketplace profitability of detective and crime fiction. It underscores—explicitly in Auden's poem above—detective and crime fiction's engagements with modernist concerns about (or sense of crisis in) vision and epistemology; especially as visual practices and ideologies impact society through the legal and criminal apparatuses of the state that vie for explanatory authority around the genre's many corpses.

And yet, the corpse that provides occasion for all five of Hammett's novels also marks the limit of this fiction. The corpse as object provides the fertile, dialectic tension fundamental to Hammett's aesthetic project. Against Hammett's preoccupation with the mute contingency of the object, the corpse as object generates structural demands for its narrative representation or voicing. Within the social world of Hammett's fiction, such demands are produced by the criminal/legal institutions of the state that insist upon the representation of the corpse in a satisfactory explanatory narrative. Hammett, as author, faces a similar—and similarly material—demand from a detective genre institution of publishers, booksellers, reviewers, and readers that insist upon the detective narrative's aesthetic closure in a revelatory solution. As I have already suggested, Hammett's representational strategy is to yield to the contingency of the object through an aesthetic vision privileging exteriority and the production of solutions that are themselves expressly contingent, if legally binding. Nowhere are the implications of this aesthetic more apparent than in Hammett's treatment of the hardboiled novel's femme fatale. In Hammett's **Maltese Falcon,** Brigid O'Shaugnessy, who may be one of the first femme fatales in hardboiled literature, is physically searched and revealed as the murderer, but there is no un-masking or dis-covering in the epistemological sense: neither the exact details of the murder, Brigid's motivations, nor her desires are made visible by the activities of the detective or the narrative. In effect, she remains at the novel's conclusion as unknowable or impenetrable to the reader as to the detective who investigates her. This opens up an ethical dimension to Hammett's cold narrative aesthetic. As what Mary Anne Doane calls a "figure of epistemological trauma," the femme fatale typically serves the male detective as "something which

must be aggressively revealed, unmasked, discovered," as a site for staging masculine domination and mastery (3). The violence that Doane points out in traditional detective narrative's visual posture is the violence signified by the etymological root of detection ("to un-roof"). Hammett counters this model of seeing and knowing with one limited to exteriority. And so the Falcon's black lacquer surface only covers further layers of dense, soft lead, and "Brigid" is only the latest in a series of names—from Miss Wonderly, to Miss LeBlanc, and finally Brigid O'Shaugnessy—that threaten to go on indefinitely.[27] In both cases, the investigation reveals no hidden depth, discovers no secreted essence or identity.

Hammett's detective shares with certain elite modernist writers a refusal to function as the subject of a revelatory, scientific gaze so thoroughly implicated in the crimes of modernity. And by this I mean the forms of violence associated with the neutral, disembodied observer's domination of the object: the modern emergence of new social scientific projects diagnosing otherness and a disciplinary social surveillance. The qualified, limited surface vision of Hammett's detectives disrupts a techno-bureaucratic surveillance formulated in Pinkerton's memoirs. The visual circuit established by this system constitutes individuals as subjects of a gaze that simultaneously produces them as its object. The *non serviam* of Hammett's fiction is rendered structurally through a narrative strategy that defuses the priority of the eye for knowledge; the interior contents or essence of Sam Spade, for example, remain as invisible to the narrative vision of **The Maltese Falcon** as Brigid O'Shaughnessy's. On the level of content, the detective protagonist's refusal to participate as a subject of the penetrative gaze coincides with his unavailability as an object to a narrative gaze. Ultimately, Hammett's detectives serve neither as subject nor object of a disciplinary, Pinkertonian gaze.

But finally, this is not enough. Hammett implicitly announces his weariness with the detective genre in his last completed novel. Returning to the first-person perspective of his earlier Continental Op fictions, Hammett's acerbic **The Thin Man** is narrated by a functioning alcoholic and retired detective, Nick Charles, who grudgingly undertakes the investigation of a former client's murder. To make matters worse, the corpse that propels the investigation appears to be Hammett's own.[28] The amplified misanthropy of this last novel, with its thematic and metaphorical reflection on the 1874 cannibalism trial of Alfred "The Man Eater" G. Packer and the painstaking interrogation of the detective's final tentative solution mark a culmination of the narrative trajectories staked out in his earlier detective fictions. They also quite clearly express his exhaustion with detective narrative. However, Hammett abandoned the detective genre at his peril. In the unfinished, loosely autobiographical novel **Tulip**, the productive tension—

between subjectivity as contagion and objectivity as impenetrable—snaps entirely in the absence of the generic structure of the detective novel. Without the formal demands of the institutions of the State and genre, there is no warrant to speak on behalf of mute object: it is to take too much license, to risk too much with too little to gain. And so, Hammett announces something like his full yielding to the object in the silence that follows the unfinished manuscript's final line. Hammett writes: "But representations seemed to me—at least they seem now, and I suppose I must have had some inkling of the same opinion then, devices of the old and tired, or older and more tired—to ease up, like conscious symbolism, or graven images. If you are tired you ought to rest, I think, and not try to fool yourself and your customers with colored bubbles" (348).

Notes

1. I am greatly indebted here to Martin Jay's *Downcast Eyes* for its detailed account of the evolution and modern crisis of European philosophical and aesthetic ocular-centrism.

2. It is also notable that the material production and distribution of Hammett's fiction took place in a broadly modernist literary system. Alfred and Blanche Knopf, critical figures in the history of modernism in America, published all five of Hammett's novels. The advertisements, reviews, and other promotional material organized around Hammett's novels tended to emphasize their art and literariness. In *The World* and other newspapers, Knopf used advertisements that simply declared of Hammett's 1930 *Maltese Falcon*: "Better than Hemingway" (Mellon 106). Six months later, *The Maltese Falcon* was chosen for publication, along with a reprint of *The Sun Also Rises,* by no less an institution of American literary modernism than the Modern Library. Meanwhile, writers from Knopf's stable of authors—including W. Somerset Maugham, Carl Van Doran, and Walter Brooks—joined in the promotional chorus. Among these Knopf authors, Robert Graves announced Hammett's *Red Harvest* "an acknowledged literary landmark" (qtd. in Nolan 80), and Andre Gide argued that Hammett "could give pointers to Hemingway or even Faulkner" (qtd. in Metress 3). In 1932, Hammett was even engaged for a lecture tour by W. Colston Leigh, the lecture agent of Sherwood Anderson, Harry Elmer Barnes, and Stuart Chase. What this should suggest to us is that Hammett's novels were materially produced and distributed, professionally received, reviewed, and evaluated within a modernist cultural field.

3. While it was not until the mid-1930s that J. Edgar Hoover's "war on crime" propelled him and his FBI to national prominence, it is worth noting here that he was first appointed director of the Bureau of Investigation (later renamed the FBI) in 1924, within a year of the publishing of Hammett's first Continental Op story. (Ironically enough, Hoover, whose Bureau kept a file on Hammett from the early 1930s, was an avowed fan of the comic strip "X-9," a comic that Hammett started in 1934 for the Hearst chain [Powers 13]).

4. Hammett understood the crisis of vision in specifically philosophical terms from an early point in his career. In an unpublished typed manuscript entitled "The Boundaries of Science and Philosophy," Hammett argues that there is no purified, scientific seeing: "Science can neither assert nor deny that any *thing* is white. Philosophy can neither assert nor deny that anything is *white. Thing* belongs to philosophy, *white* to science, and neither has an equivalent in the world of the other. You must put science and philosophy together to get that entity, the *white thing.*" For Hammett, philosophy organizes the relationship of the viewing subject to the object viewed; it organizes perception. Without it, there are no "things." Science is concerned with the sensual properties of what philosophy provides as an object, its "whiteness." But because the "surrounding, contrasting, extra-visual area of non-white gives you your percept of white," a truly scientific viewing of only the object itself is impossible (3).

5. I am not suggesting that nineteenth-century American realists blithely assumed that the author's function was simply to translate the visible world into a legible world. If Howells's literary criticism tends to simplify the texts' relationship to the visible world—and it certainly does—his novels can suggest a much more complicated relation.

6. The other was Charlie Chaplin.

7. Our hypothetical pedestrian might also have had a relationship with Pinkerton's disembodied eye vis-à-vis New England Puritanism, a transplanted cultural tradition of some influence in mid-century Chicago. It was common in early colonial era churches like the Old Ship Meeting House in Hingham, MA, to have a single large eye emblazoned on the pulpit—its lone ornament—looking out with the minister over the gathered congregation. The eye produced a gaze supplementary to the minister's. If the minister momentarily averted his eyes from the congregation, the unblinking eye on the pulpit did not. At the same time, it reminded the congregation that the minister's gaze was in the service of a still more powerful gaze; an austere observer who saw the Puritan subject's every move and from whose disciplinary vision no interior thought or desire could be concealed.

Here is an appropriate antecedent to the secular eye Pinkerton positioned over mid-nineteenth-century America.

8. Howard gives a condensed history of the radical social changes that occurred between the Civil War and World War I that my account here condenses further.

9. While involved in various high profile cases with "master criminals," the subjects of most of Pinkerton's memoirs, the Pinkerton Detective Agency depended on much less publicized—and much less popular—industrial policing contracts for the profitability of the Agency, which continue to this date. Currently, the Agency specializes in investigating copyright infringements of genetically copyrighted seeds on the behalf of Monsanto and other large agribusiness concerns.

10. See, for example, Johnston, Morn, Lucas, and Denning.

11. While overdetermined, the threat of the romantic for these contemporary male writers and social commentators was imbricated by a threat of the feminine—an assertion maintained in Bell's influential study of realism. In Pinkerton as with Howells, the familiar binaries of structural gender ideologies are lined up in their appropriate columns. Both define their realist project's struggle with romanticism in a gendered rhetoric that pits reason against emotion, science against fancy, work against play, order against chaos, objective against subjective. Such an emphatic formulation of traditional Western sexist axiology is probably symptomatic of their mutual professional anxiety. Howells—as a male novelist in a profession perceived as the domain of women in the nineteenth century—and Pinkerton—as the primary figure of a not yet established detective profession—inhabited subjectivities whose cultural status was as yet undetermined and vulnerable to an anxiety that they expressed in gendered terms. Both subscribed to a rigid and seemingly unassailable formulation of "professional respectability" that was codified in the rhetoric of masculinity.

12. Both Lucas and Morn have found evidence of some businesses that advertised in newspapers as "detectives" in Boston and New York before 1850, but they were so few in number and so limited in scope—primarily warehouse guards—that they seem to have had little to no command on either Pinkerton's or the popular imagination.

13. It is worth noting Pinkerton's abiding interest in phrenology on this point, a science that would guarantee the efficacy of Pinkerton's visual project.

14. Almost alone among prominent literary figures, Howells defied popular opinion and courageously defended the radicals summarily arrested after the 1887 Haymarket bombing. Six years later, Governor John P. Altgeld granted a full pardon to the accused and publicly denounced the Pinkerton Agency for instigating the strikers to violence.

15. The cultural memory of the Great Strikes underwrites the structural dynamics of Howells's streetcar strikes in terms of their frightening mobility and shifting form, and establishes for his novel the imaginative proximity of an apocalyptic nationwide class war that haunts the narrative. This becomes especially apparent in the climactic dinner party scene that precipitates the novel's tragic ending. At this banquet, the magazine's capitalist owner, Dryfoos, is pitted against Basil March's old German socialist tutor, Lindau. General debate about economics and politics leads ineluctably backward in time to an argument about the "great railroad strikes of 1877"—including the violent role of Pinkerton detectives in quashing organized labor—before Lindau storms out and resigns from the magazine (341-42).

16. By the third decade of the twentieth century, the ocular-centric social projects of Pinkerton's surveillance apparatus and Howellsian realism were everywhere in crisis. John Dos Passos's *42nd Parallel*, the first installment of his *U.S.A.* trilogy, crystallizes the disillusionment that such visionary projects encountered in the early twentieth century. The holistic, unifying view of society promised by realism's third person omniscient observer is cut-up and fragmented into multiple narrators, refracted through experimental "camera eye" and "news reel" narrative lenses. And the surveillance that promised a well organized social order safe *for* middle-class business and leisure in Pinkerton's memoirs emerges as a pervasive, coercive, disciplinary mechanism *over* society in Dos Passos. The *42nd Parallel* is littered with references to detectives—there are three in the first twenty pages alone—who seem to be everywhere looking in on labor strikes and political rallies, lurking in hotels and tenements, patrolling stockyards and debutante balls alike.

17. *Smart Set* is the slick literary magazine that launched the careers of a number of elite American literary modernists, including F. Scott Fitzgerald.

18. In *The "Canary" Murder Case*, Vance's suspects make this easy for Vance by wearing their insides on the outside. The features of Dr. Lundquist's cranium provide Vance's phrenologically informed gaze with enough information for Vance to accurately read his homicidal intentions.

19. In its latest incarnation, the Pinkerton Eye has come to resemble the eye represented on the cover of the 1966 Random House edition of *The Big Knockover*: an abstract eye whose gaze—represented as a ray emitting from its cornea—is focused away from the viewer.

20. In both instances, the efficiency of a surveillance that is internalized by the surveilled subject is the ultimate goal: the production of a subject who surveils himself. Pinkerton's description of his Chicago office presents a microcosmic formulation of the new technology of power Foucault theorizes in *Discipline and Punish* and that the Agency puts at the disposal of its customers: a surveillance whose presence/power—ideally—could be felt on the social body in the absence of any*body* actually watching.

21. This is a consistent theme throughout Hammett's Continental Op fiction.

22. The specifics of the locale and the labor strike provided by Hammett in the novel have led many critics to read Personville as a metaphor for Butte, Montana, the site of the two-year-long IWW strike at the Anaconda Copper Mine that Hammett attended as a Pinkerton Detective in the early twenties. This seems to me an unnecessary literalization of a place—"Personville"—whose name announces its status as an open signifier for any of the North American industrial cities plagued by violent clashes between labor and capital in that decade.

23. I first encountered this etymology in Lucas's *The Big Trouble,* only his interpretation is one that stresses the detective's connection to medieval Christian European myths about Satan, who was believed to possess the ability to peer into people's houses while flying overhead. My interest is in its implications for the epistemological work of the detective rather than the moral and mythic implications of the etymology that interests Lucas.

24. In addition to *The Thin Man,* there is a lingering uncertainty to the solutions of each of Hammett's five novels, sometimes understated, sometimes openly discussed among the characters. The solution to Dinah Brand's murder in *Red Harvest* is presented by a gangster in what the Op described as his final act of self-dramatizing. Its easy acceptance by the Op and those involved is a consequence of its convenience and mutual benefit; and that it does not challenge anyone's credulity. *The Dain Curse* features a chapter titled "Buts and Ifs" dedicated to a dialogue between the Op and the novelist, Owen Fitzstephan, about the epistemological sloppiness of detection. In the penultimate chapter of *The Maltese Falcon*, Spade reconstructs the scene of his partner's murder, but when challenged about the details of the murder, he concedes, "But [its] exact enough" (578). *The Glass Key* may be an exception to this rule, but it's also the novel where the murder plot is structurally the least important and receives the least attention.

25. Diane Johnson's narrative strategies in *Dashiell Hammett: A Life* are distressingly antithetical to Hammett's narrative strategies as I have been discussing them. Incorporating the omniscient viewing posture that Hammett rejected in his own fiction, Johnson unveils for her readers the thoughts, desires, motives, and fears of her seemingly transparent historical subjects. Johnson even seems to imply that Hammett's "minor" status as an author is a consequence of his failure to provide the psychological depth for his fictional characters that she provides for the "characters" in her biography.

26. The number of Anglo-American literary modernists indirectly engaging detective fiction's major narrative structures and signifiers would be enormous: from Hemingway's "The Killers" (1927) and Wyndam Lewis's *Snooty Baronet* (1930) to Fitzgerald's *The Great Gatsby* and Nella Larsen's *Passing* (1929), published by Knopf in the same year as *Red Harvest*. The production of corpses and their explanation is a critical feature of the literary modernist landscape.

27. While the shift in names from Wonderly and LeBlanc to O'Shaugnessy reveals a suspicious shift into unprivileged ethnicity, the novel gives us no reason to believe that the final O'Shaugnessy has any determinant priority over the other names in the series.

28. Hammett's physical description of the murdered "thin man," Clyde Wynant, provides the reader with a remarkably accurate self-portrait of the author: "Tall—over six feet—and one of the thinnest men I've ever seen. He must be about fifty now, and his hair was almost white when I knew him. Usually needs a haircut, ragged brindle mustache, bites his fingernails" (11).

The literary portrait's similarity to Hammett is reinforced by Hammett's appearance on the cover of Knopf's first edition of the novel, seemingly as the eponymous Thin Man.

Works Cited

Auden, W. H. *New Years Letter (January 1, 1940). The Collected Poetry of W. H. Auden.* New York: Random, 1945. 265-316.

Barthes, Roland. *The Pleasure of the Text.* Trans. Richard Miller. New York: Noonday, 1975.

Bell, Michael Davit. *The Problem of American Literary Realism: Studies in the Cultural History of a Literary Idea.* Chicago: U of Chicago P, 1993.

Budd, Louis J. "The American Background." *The Cambridge Companion to American Realism and Naturalism.* Ed. Donald Pizer. New York: Cambridge UP, 1995. 21-46.

Denning, Michael. *Mechanic Accents: Dime Novels and Working Class Literature in America.* New York: Verso, 1998.

"Detective." *The Oxford Dictionary of English Etymology.* 1969.

Doane, Mary Anne. *Femme Fatales: Feminism, Film Theory, Psychoanalysis.* New York: Routledge, 1991.

Dos Passos, John. *U.S.A.: I. The 42nd Parallel, II. Nineteen Nineteen, III. The Big Money.* New York: Modern Library, 1930-37.

Foucault, *Discipline and Punish: The Birth of the Prison.* Trans. Alan Sheridan. New York: Vintage, 1979.

Friedman, Lawrence M. *Crime and Punishment in American History.* New York: Basic, 1993.

Goulart, Ron. *The Dime Detectives.* New York: Mysterious, 1988.

"The Grandest Enterprise Under God." *The West.* Turner Broadcasting System, 1996.

Hammett, Dashiell. *The Big Knockover: Selected Short Stories and Short Novels.* New York: Vintage, 1989.

———. "The Boundaries of Science and Philosophy." Ms. Ransom Lib. U of Texas, Austin.

———. *The Continental Op Stories.* New York: Vintage, 1975.

———. *The Dain Curse.* New York: Vintage, 1989.

———. *The Glass Key.* New York: Vintage, 1989.

———. "The Gutting of Couffignal." Hammett, *Big Knockover* 3-37.

———. *The Maltese Falcon.* New York: Vintage, 1992.

———. *Red Harvest.* New York: Vintage, 1992.

———. "The Scorched Face." Hammett, *Big Knockover* 74-114.

———. *The Thin Man.* New York: Vintage, 1992.

———. *Tulip.* Hammett, *Big Knockover* 301-48.

"Hammett, Dashiell." *Encyclopedia of the American Left.* 2nd ed. 1998.

Haycraft, Howard. *Murder for Pleasure; the Life and Times of the Detective Story.* New York: Biblo, 1968.

Hellman, Lillian. Introduction. Hammett, *Big Knockover v-xxiii.*

Howard, June. *Form and History in American Literary Naturalism.* Chapel Hill: U of North Carolina P, 1985.

Howells, William Dean. "The Editor's Study." *W. D. Howells as Critic.* Ed. Edwin H. Cady. Boston: Routledge, 1973. 157-60.

———. *A Hazard of New Fortunes.* Bloomington: Indiana UP, 1976.

Jacobs, Karen. *The Eye's Mind: Literary Modernism and Visual Culture.* Ithaca: Cornell UP, 2001.

James, William. "Pragmatism's Conception of Truth." *Pragmatism and The Meaning of Truth.* Cambridge: Harvard UP, 1978. 95-113.

Jay, Martin. *Downcast Eyes: The Denigration of Vision in Twentieth Century French Thought.* Berkley: U of California P, 1994.

Johnson, Diane. *Dashiell Hammett: A Life.* New York: Columbine, 1985.

Johnston, Les. *The Rebirth of Private Policing.* New York: Routledge, 1992.

Lucas, J. Anthony. *The Big Trouble: A Murder in a Small Western Town Sets Off a Struggle for the Soul of America.* New York: Simon, 1997.

MacKay, James. *Allan Pinkerton: The First Private Eye.* New York: Wiley, 1996.

Mao, Douglas *Solid Objects: Modernism and the Test of Production.* Princeton: Princeton UP, 1998.

Marcus, Steven. Introduction. *The Continental Op Stories.* New York: Vintage, 1975. vii-xxix.

Mellon, Joan. *Hellman and Hammett: The Legendary Passion of Lillian Hellman and Dashiell Hammett.* New York: Harper, 1996.

Metress, Christopher, ed. *Critical Response to Dashiell Hammett.* Westport, Conn.: Greenwood, 1994.

Morn, Frank. *The Eye that Never Sleeps: A History of the Pinkerton National Detective Agency.* Bloomington: Indiana UP, 1982.

Nash, Ogden. "Random Observations: Literary." *The New Yorker Book of Verse: An Anthology of Poems First Published in the New Yorker, 1925-1935.* New York: Harcourt, 1935. 183.

Nolan, William F. *Hammett: A Life at the Edge.* New York: Congdon, 1983.

Pinkerton, Alan. Introduction. *The Burglar's Fate and the Detective.* New York: Dillingham, 1883. v-vi.

———. *Criminal Reminiscences and Detective Sketches.* New York: Carleton, 1879.

————. *The Molly Maguires and the Detectives.* New York: Dillingham, 1877.

————. *Professional Thieves and the Detective.* New York: Carleton, 1880.

————. *Strikers, Communists, Tramps and the Detective.* New York: Carleton, 1878.

————. *Thirty Years a Detective: A Thorough and Comprehensive Expose of Criminal Practices all Grades and Classes.* New York: Carleton, 1884.

Powers, Richard Gid. *G-men: Hoover's FBI in American Popular Culture.* Carbondale: Southern Illinois UP, 1983.

Stein, Gertrude. "American Crimes and Why They Matter." *How Writing is Written.* Ed. Robert Barlett Haas. New York: Black Sparrow, 1974. 100-05.

————. *Blood on the Dining Room Floor.* New York: Black Lizard Crime, 1994.

————. *Everybody's Autobiography.* Cambridge: Exact Change, 1993.

Van Dine, S. S. [William Huntington Wright]. *A Philo Vance Week-End, Containing Three Mystery Novels. The "Canary" Murder Case; The Greene Murder Case; The Bishop Murder Case.* New York: Grosset, 1929.

Dean DeFino (essay date summer 2004)

SOURCE: DeFino, Dean. "Lead Birds and Falling Beams." *Journal of Modern Literature* 27, no. 4 (summer 2004): 73-81.

[*In the following essay, DeFino discusses the concept of redemption in Hammett's work.*]

> Images are not arguments, rarely even lead to proof, but the mind craves them, and, of late more than ever, the keenest experimenters find twenty images better than one, especially if contradictory; since the human mind has already learned to deal in contradictions.
>
> —Henry Adams, *The Education of Henry Adams* (1907)

> But that's the part of it I always liked. He adjusted himself to beams falling, and then no more of them fell, and he adjusted himself to them not falling.
>
> —Sam Spade in *The Maltese Falcon* (1930)

In his oft-cited essay, "The Simple Art of Murder," hard-boiled fiction writer Raymond Chandler argues that, by removing the puzzle-game intrigues of the classic detective form and imbuing it with "realism"— where murder is committed for reasons, and people talk and act as real people do—hard-boiled innovators like Dashiell Hammett and, by implication, Chandler him-self created a style that brought this generic form to a new level of artistic substance. One might easily quibble over Chandler's hierarchizing "art" over "not-art," but his remarks are interesting for the way they make that distinction. At the very end of the essay, after describing the various merits of "realism" over puzzle games and murder-mysteries-cum-comedies-of-manners, he says, "In everything that can be called art there is a quality of redemption" (237). Surely readers of the classic detective story would not be surprised to read such a statement from the pen of, say, a Dorothy Sayers or a Ronald Knox, whose own cant runs to the theological and whose puzzle stories represent a putting-back-in-order. The detective's role, for them, is to make order of chaos: a spirit central to the whole issue of redemption. As W. H. Auden argues in his essay, "The Guilty Vicarage," "the detective story addict indulges the fantasy of being restored to the Garden of Eden": a recovery of innocence displaced by the criminal act (24). But for Chandler, who writes of a corrupt world peopled by corrupt beings and whose stories resolve themselves in far more confusions than answers, this idea of "redemption" seems incongruous. Here we will consider what that incongruity reveals about the structure and/or meaning of what Chandler calls "realism."

Though redemption simply means "buying back," it is a term mired in theological implications. Redemption is the essential function of eschatology. The dominant Western model is Christianity, which defines human existence as a passage from the Fall to the Last Judgment. Think of a circle inscribed by a line. The circle is eternity, a Paradise-absolute without beginning or end. The line is Fallen existence, the curse of original sin, the thread of time and space from birth to death that connects lost Eden to the salvation of Heaven. Physically speaking, we proceed along this line in one direction only: towards annihilation. But Christ promises to reconnect the line at the posterior end, to announce the resurrection (the nullification of death) in the Last Judgment and the *possibility* of recovering eternity in the future. He "buys back" eternity for mankind *in the future*. What is somewhat confusing about the system is that it conceives of the future in terms of the past, because Christ restores an eternity that is always there. So the models of the redeemed world all borrow from images of the past: a New Eden or New Jerusalem that consummates the promise of the past.[1]

As I said, the classic detective story models itself on this eschatology. The detective enters the scene of the crime *after* the fact and, through a feat of analysis, constructs a chain of effects and causes back to the source of the crime—mode and motive—which, while not annulling the deed (the body is still dead), gives the reader a sense of intellectual control over it. The story redeems that sense of order and control by (fictionally) exposing its logic, its cause-and-effect chain, how one thing leads to another. Hence the form's popularity: it constructs a logical discourse from seeming chaos— disparate bits of evidence, cryptic clues—through an objective scientific method. Of course this method is an illusion, a fiction, but the reader abides or, as Auden puts it, "escapes into" this fiction because he or she desires the sense of control and the *possibility* of order on which the story is predicated. In fact it is just this sense of unreality and game playing—"spillikins in the parlor," as Chandler puts it ("Simple Art" 236)—that attracts readers to the classic story. From a distance, with a critical pseudo-scientific eye, he or she can observe the foulest atrocities without blinking and draw from the most gruesome details grinning affirmation that they are "on the right track." Their heroes are odd looking (obese Nero Wolfe, Professor Van Dusen with the tiny body and the size-eight head) and eccentric (Auguste Dupin enshrouding himself in continual darkness, Philo Vance affecting strange accents), with habits that run from the quaint (Miss Marples' constant knitting) to the corrupting (Sherlock Holmes' addiction to cocaine), but these features only attest to their genius (like the unkempt scientist with the tangled explosion of hair) and their charm. Readers of the classic detective story do not want to nurse Holmes back from his addiction or chastise Wolfe for his absurd eating habits, since these are the charms against which their own wits define the challenge of the story, which is solving the puzzle before these extraordinary analysts do.

That the classic whodunit achieved its height of popularity in the period between the First and Second World Wars should come as little surprise, then, considering the sense of escape or objective control it offered in the age of Einstein's General Theory of Relativity, Heisenberg's Uncertainty Principle, the Scopes trial, and the Big Bang theory. It was a period where traditional values, essentialisms and idealisms constantly found themselves threatened, where the "progress" of enlightened scientific and philosophical discourse seemed to hit a wall and even the objective laws of physics gave way to probability equations. The first "modern" war fought with the technology of the industrial age seemed to fulfill historian Henry Adams' prophesy of a generation before, that the power modern man harnessed would outstrip its servitude and destroy us. The new emblems of that power were the bomb and the machine gun, which left much of Europe in physical and economic ruins. Considering the heavy damage done to Great Britain in that war, it isn't surprising so many writers turned their gaze back to the genre that Conan Doyle had popularized in the nation's Victorian ascendency, looking for some source of redemption. England became the center of the classic detective story's "Golden Age,"—a title appropriate to their larger eschatological aims—creating writers' guilds and societies like the famous London Detection Club to publish criticism and rules of fair play to respond to the burgeoning reading

public's demand for more fictions. America, too, though it fared much better in the war (leaving the nation in a stronger geopolitical position than it had previously known), embraced an ultra-conservatism once the war had ended. The 1920s, which history remembers as "The Roaring Twenties" and "The Jazz Age," began on a sober note, with the institution of Prohibition on the first day of 1920 and the seizure of 4000 suspected radicals in the Palmer Raids on the second. An age of confusion bred paranoid intolerance, and Warren G. Harding won himself the presidency by appealing to grass-roots White Anglo-Saxon values and an Edenic sense of homogeneity and social tranquility with the campaign slogan, "Return to Normalcy." Here native authors like S. S. Van Dine and John Dickson Carr found an audience for their puzzle stories and effete genius detectives, modeled on the British parlor murders of the Christies and Sayers and Chestertons.

But no amount of mystery fiction can disguise reality. By the time Harding died in office in 1923, the various scandals within his administration and the incorporation of organized crime around the bootlegging business had all but undermined any possibility of "normalcy," even if anyone were able to define such a thing. Out of this profound sense of cultural schizophrenia, out of the collision between redemptive ideals and corrupted realities, came literature that scrutinized not only the scars of war and the growing pains of modernity, but also the illusions of redemption that consumed figures in this landscape. Witnessing the devastation of European civilization, T. S. Eliot resurrected Tiresias, blind prophet of ancient Greece, in the modern wasteland, where he attempts to read meaning from "a heap of broken images," like so many tea leaves: neither much use to a blind man (*Waste Land* 30). In America, F. Scott Fitzgerald studied a gangster's redemptive gaze on a former lover's green dock light, which to him held the promise of "the orgiastic future" (*Great Gatsby* 182).

Out of this time a new form of detective story emerged, called "hard-boiled" for the laconic, unsentimental way it describes the corruption and violence that infiltrated the culture at every level. It did not strain a retrospective glance upon some objective image of innocence, nor offer its reader a sense of controlling chaos. Rather, it made a study of that chaos—the corruption, the degradation, the violence—and the illusions of order that grow out of it. Like any detective fiction, hard-boiled has a keen interest in the past, only it inverts its significance. Where the classic detective story uses the image of the past as an ordering or idealizing structure—the image of redemption—hard-boiled deals with the damning effects of the past on the present, a sense of being bound by what we once were. It is a theme one is likely to find in *any* hard-boiled story. Dashiell Hammett's **Red Harvest** (1929) and **The Glass Key** (1931) chart the results of a history of political corruption, while

The Dain Curse (1929) and *The Thin Man* (1933) are structured around family histories and *The Maltese Falcon* (1930) traces the history of a black statuette from 16th century Spain to San Francisco in the 1920s. A similar list might be made from Raymond Chandler's or Ross Macdonald's novels. Critics of the hard-boiled genre have not been insensitive to the qualities it shares with Greek tragedy, where an attempt to defy fate leads one right into it. Chandler himself lists art's qualities of redemption as "pure tragedy, if it is high tragedy," "pity and irony," and "the raucous laughter of the strong man": tragedy, drama, comedy. But if the form revisits the three classical modes of narrative, it does so with a difference. Where classical tragedy pictures the tragic, ironic, and sometimes comic fall of great men to desperate lows, hard-boiled pictures only common men. Among them is a new sort of hero, himself common, but a strong man, "a man of honor" by instinct, and "a man fit for adventure." Like Oedipus, he has "a range of awareness that startles you," but that belongs to him by right, "because it belongs to the world he lives in" ("Simple Art" 237). If he is extraordinary, it is only because he is *more* of a man than others around him. And the tragedy/drama/comedy in which he participates is of people not unlike himself: common, entangled in piteous and ironic existential crises that occasion the bitter laughter of strong men.

One such strong man is detective Sam Spade, who in Hammett's *The Maltese Falcon* tells the somewhat laughable story of a common man so piteously and unwittingly tangled. The story appears early in the novel and concerns a man named Flitcraft, whom Spade had been hired to find some years earlier. Flitcraft had disappeared and was presumed by wife and family gone for good, until a mutual acquaintance spotted him in a nearby city. He had changed his name to Charles Pierce, but Spade tracks him down without too much difficulty. When he does, Flitcraft offers an extraordinary explanation for his disappearance. He had been walking from work to lunch one afternoon when a steel beam fell from a construction site and narrowly missed hitting him. The accident struck him as a revelation of the nature of existence: "He felt like someone had lifted the lid off of life and let him look at the works" (63). What he saw was the randomness against which all the order in his life was a mere flitting shade. "He knew then that men died at haphazard like that, and lived only while blind chance spared them" (64). In order to get into step with the randomness, he resolved to abandon family and job and wander the world. But before long, and without knowing it, Flitcraft had settled down into a life very much like the one he had left. Spade comments that this is the part he "always liked": "He adjusted himself to beams falling, and then no more of them fell, and he adjusted himself to them not falling" (64).

The Flitcraft story has been the subject of intense critical scrutiny (most notably in Peter Wolfe's 1980 book-length study of Hammett entitled *Beams Falling*), much of which identifies Spade's tale as the cipher to Hammett's oeuvre, and perhaps hard-boiled fiction in general. It is about the illusions of order, and how they reveal and conceal themselves. In *Dashiell Hammett: A Daughter Remembers,* Jo Hammett recalls the particular delight her father took in the story, "as if it were a gift he had received that was just right. As a boy he had wanted to find the Ultimate Truth—how the world operated. And here it was. There was no system except blind chance. Beams falling." But the Flitcraft story is more than just an existential joke. It inverts of the myth of redemption perpetuated by the typical whodunit, where models of the past give meaning to present hopes. In it the objective continuity of myth is transformed into the habit of order, and the backdrop of eternity that circumscribes redemptive myth is replaced by chaos. Flitcraft attempts to make meaning of this event by objectifying or idealizing it, by holding it at a distance. He tells the story to Spade because it takes on meaning in the telling, it becomes intelligible. Flitcraft assures Spade that he just wants to make its "reasonableness clear," at the same time flattering himself that he understands what that "reasonableness" is (63). He imagines himself transformed from "flit-craft" or surface-skimmer to a "piercer" who breaks through the surface appearance of things. But Spade uncovers the deeper irony of Flitcraft's self-deceit.[2] Where Flitcraft conceives of meaning as the circumscription of the unknown into the known, an act of cause-and-effect historiography not unlike the genius detective's, Spade reads that meaning on the gap between revealed chaos and the specificity of perception. Flitcraft fixes meaning on the beam, itself. It becomes an emblem of chaos, an ideal posing as memory and fact. But Flitcraft misses the point. It is not the beam itself that signifies meaning, but its juxtaposition to ever-present chaos, which makes it impossible to predict what the beam—ordinarily a symbol of structure and surety—will do. The action of the beam falling is a function of its significance, the immediate truth that the beam is *not* the fixture of stability it is supposed to be, but a collapsing structure losing its ordinary meaning. The event's significance is subjective, contingent on the immediate relationship between the beam and chaotic forces. But in the absence of a falling beam and its subjective significance as an event, the event recedes into memory. In the widening gap between perceiver and perceived—between Flitcraft and event—it takes on the sort of objective value that the origins of crime do in the classic detective story.

Hammett, perhaps more than any other hard-boiled writer, takes on the pretenses of the classic detective story—its sense of objective truth and narrative consistency. If one theme lies at the center of hard-boiled detective fiction, it is the instability of these objective values in a post-Einsteinian world, where "truth" is merely the currency of the moment. *The Maltese Falcon,* for instance, constantly negotiates the value of a story. It opens with a woman calling herself Wonderly offering Spade and his partner Miles Archer two hundred dollars to find a sister who had run away with a man named Thursby, but before ten pages have gone by, both Archer and Thursby have been murdered and "Miss Wonderly" has disappeared. When she reappears three chapters later, her name is Brigid O'Shaughnessy, and she is being hunted by "dangerous men" whom she has betrayed in a business arrangement concerning a valuable black enamel bird. Spade learns this pages later from one of these men, an effeminate Levantine named Joel Cairo, and confronts Brigid. She offers Spade apologies, which he sloughs off ("We didn't believe your story," Spade tells her. "We believed your two hundred dollars"), and five hundred dollars more in protection money, but when Cairo promises Spade a bounty of five thousand for the recovery of the "ornament," Brigid fears she is losing his loyalty and offers Spade her body.

Nowhere is this sense of narrative currency more apparent than in the story of the title object, which is told by its sole archivist, treasure hunter Caspar Gutman. His "history" describes the gold bejewelled gift of a wealthy order of 16th century knights to the King of Spain in gratitude for his generous gift of the island of Malta, which, after his own seventeen-year pursuit, has led him to Sam Spade. Gutman's story poses two questions. First, who, and by what right, possesses the falcon? Is it the one who can hold tightest to it, the one who can make the most of it, or the King of Spain? Second, what makes the falcon valuable, its weight in gold or its legacy? In the end the bird that they have been chasing turns out to be lead: either a "replica," as Gutman claims, or the object of a larger historical hoax. But by so resolving the matter, the novel hardly mocks or derides the value of the object *as such.* On the contrary, it asks the more disturbing question: is value really just a myth with no object? If the lead bird is a joke, it is of the most serious sort. As Chandler puts it, "It is not funny that a man should be killed, but it is sometimes funny that he should be killed for so little, and that his death should be the coin of what we call civilization" ("Simple Art" 237). It is the kind of joke to make the strong man laugh, just as he laughed at Flitcraft: not to mock but to call attention to the ever-widening gap between perceiver and perceived by which "meaning" is made, where the "coin of what we call civilization"—in this case, the black bird—has no gold standard at all.

In Hammett's second novel, *The Dain Curse,* he investigates a number of murders circumscribed by a curse of insanity inherited by female descendants of the Dain family. It borrows elements of the gothic mystery, the potboiler, and the drawing-room puzzle story to frame a tale of brutal violence, drug addiction, cultic ritual and a web of revenge plots. It is as close to a direct parody of the classic form as any in hard-boiled fiction, and as such one of Hammett's least accessible stories, because the laconism of hard-boiled makes such an irregular fit with the more expository elements of the classic form. Readers of the classic story are put off by its brutal frankness, and most fans of hard-boiled are confused by its baroque absurd plot and still more absurd characters. But Hammett mitigates this confusion by including a running dialogue between the detective, the Continental Op from 36 earlier stories and Hammett's first novel, *Red Harvest,* and Owen Fitzstephan, a former acquaintance of the Op's and a fiction writer. Throughout the novel, the two debate their relative positions on the case at hand. The Op takes the hard-boiled line, that things are almost never as they seem and that any statement should be qualified with "a but or an if." Fitzstephan takes the novelistic/aesthetic view, where "truth" is the revelation of order, a position that mimics such classic detectives as Sherlock Holmes and Philo Vance. Fitzstephan is interested in the psychological basis of the case and in the way certain details reflect a "poetic necessity." First and foremost among these is the curse itself, which Fitzstephan insists gives structure and meaning to the series of murders, but which the Op takes for nothing more than "words in an angry woman's mouth": a cruel hoax perpetrated by an elder aunt to destroy her niece (*Dain Curse* 64). It is the sort of subject we expect to see in gothic detective fiction: the presence of some supernatural or preternatural force that it is the job of the detective to explain away.[3] The resolution of the crime is directly connected to proving the hoax of the curse. But Hammett plays matters a bit differently.

Though his detective never takes the curse seriously *as such,* still he is forced to deal with the effects of the curse on the main female character: young Gabrielle Dain Leggett, whose aunt has so convinced her of its viability that she has taken to cultic religious practices, morphine addiction, and the belief that she is responsible—directly or indirectly—for all of the crimes that occur in the story. Expressing her belief that insanity has finally taken hold of her, the detective explains:

> Nobody thinks clearly, no matter what they pretend. Thinking's a dizzy business, a matter of catching as many of those foggy glimpses as you can and fitting them together the best way you can. That's why people hang on so tight to their beliefs and opinions; because, compared to the haphazard way in which they're arrived at, even the goofiest opinion seems wonderfully sane, and self-evident. And if you let it get away from you, then you've got to dive back into that foggy muddle to wrangle yourself out another to take its place.

(181)

Here the Op describes the same illusion of cognition that muddles Flitcraft: the habit of order that grows out of the need for meaning. The curse shows the extent to which we demand a certain sense of order or coherence; so much so that we are willing to take damnation upon ourselves. The theme of the past damning the present again emerges, only here the Op emphasizes the *constructedness* of that past: how it is our mind's repulsion from the task of diving back into "that foggy muddle," that chaos of contradictory meanings, which forces us to cling to "even the goofiest opinions." That said, Gabrielle's acceptance of the curse reveals its own contradictions, just as Flitcraft's story describes the *impossibility* of getting into step with randomness. What Gabrielle takes for her insanity is, in fact, her realization of the gap between reality and perception, which makes her in the judgment of the Op "tougher, saner, and cooler than normal" (182).

But while the detective is finally able to convince Gabrielle that no curse corrupts her, the text as a whole does not so easily dispose of it. When the Op exposes Fitzstephan himself as the murderer, the writer claims his own Dain heritage and enters a plea of insanity, which the court accepts. The curse no more dissipates than the avarice of Gutman and Cairo when they discover that the falcon they have been pursuing is a fake: a "replica" they call it, assuming still that an original exists. The myths no more disappear than the desire to be transported by them. But Hammett's commentary in all of this is pointed. Though Fitzstephan escapes legal justice by endorsing the curse, much as he has throughout the novel to throw the Op off his trail, he is undone by it in two ways. First, he is brutally mangled by a bomb he planted in a final act of terrorism, a victim of his own crimes. Second, his claim of insanity prevents the novelist from sharing his plot to destroy the Dain family with the world. He who creates the fictions succumbs to them, both in body and in mind. His attempts to make "meaning" only highlight his folly. With *The Maltese Falcon,* Hammett pushes these considerations still further by undermining—rather, focusing—the source of myth's currency. Where Eden and the Dain curse acquire value through an implied cultural consent, the story of the Maltese falcon *as such* is known to only two persons: Gutman, who has carried the story with him over a seventeen-year quest and, when Gutman tells him, Spade himself. The reader, too, is left in the dark as to what it is or means until almost three-quarters of the way through the novel. It figures as the central "mystery" in the text. Yet Gutman has built quite a retinue around him, of loyal minions like his bodyguard Wilmer, of thieves like Brigid and Thursby, and of cowards like Cairo. Their motivation? Money, plain and simple. They know nothing of the value or nature of the bird but what Gutman has told them in his silence, yet that is enough to compel them to acts of murder and treachery. They do not need the past to give

them meaning: wealth is its own reward. Nor does Spade, who negotiates his services not against the mythic value of the bird—which he finds highly suspect—but on what it will bring him at the moment. He knows, as Gutman's associates do, how currency shifts.[4] But if the story questions the values of the past, it does so only to revisit that past in the present. When the falcon, whose value Gutman measures by a Golden Age standard, turns out to be lead, each of the characters finds themselves back where they began: looking for a bird whose value no one can substantiate, and for a partner's murderer.

In the last few pages, Spade attempts to make an account of his feelings for Brigid: on one side, the reasons why he should turn Brigid over to the police for Miles' murder, and on the other, reasons he should not. But it is not the equation—which grossly disfavors Brigid—that sways him. Rather, it is his belief that she has been playing him for a sap, that she has counted on his desire for her all along and used it to manipulate him. Spade sees himself falling into Flitcraft's trap: of seeing the world circumscribed by a single image. For Flitcraft it is the falling beam, which comes to mean "freedom," or "truth," but which in fact only means his commitment to habit. For Spade it is the image of a woman, which looks like "love" within the context of the fantasy he might construct around her, but which is in fact poison, because she will destroy him. By forcing Spade and the other characters to revisit their motivations, Hammett in no way means to clarify or put back into order. On the contrary, he wants to show how the actions of the story only serve to further degrade the characters, to confront them with their baser natures without giving them recourse to any others, to allow demons of the past to show themselves. The story does not resolve, but dissolves.

Having given some consideration to how and why hard-boiled detective fiction—or Hammett's version of it—critiques or calls attention to the gaps between perception and reality, I will shift attention to how the text constructs its *own* meaning. To answer this question, I want to look at another scene towards the end of *The Maltese Falcon,* where Spade himself takes possession of the bird. The bird has been shipped on a slow boat from Hong Kong, and when it finally arrives Brigid has it delivered directly to Spade for safekeeping. It is perhaps the *only* moment in the text when Spade is genuinely excited. In fact, he's so beside himself that he fails to notice he is stepping on the hand of the dead deliveryman—shot on his way to Spade's office—and that he is squeezing his secretary so hard around the waist that she squeals in pain. It is a moment of exaltation. He tears away the bird's newspaper and excelsior wrapping and perches it on his desk, then laughs and puts his hand down on the bird. The narrator remarks, "His widespread fingers had ownership in their grip"

(159). Why does Spade laugh? Is it the raucous laughter of the strong man realizing the existential joke? And why the gesture of ownership? Significantly, Spade is the first of all the characters in the text to ever lay a hand on the bird. Brigid and Thursby had only glanced at it, and Cairo not at all. So there is a sense of discovery and laying claim in the gesture: claiming ownership to the central figure of meaning in the whole text, the object around which the rest of the story constructs itself. He possesses the amulet of meaning, and so controls the story. He is now in a position to put all that he has learned to use, to consummate the negotiated parts of the story into his own cohesive narrative, in short, to perform the role we associate with detective. With this difference: Spade knows that what information he has is a collection of arbitrated fictions, a string of lies that might be brought into some sort of order, but that require the bargaining power of the falcon to achieve order. In the classic model of the detective story, the bird serves as the motive that makes sense of the rest. But if Gutman operates like a classic detective, constructing a "history" that gives existence to the mythic Maltese falcon, which *only* appears in the story as myth, Spade moves in the opposite direction. He starts with the bird, and from it makes the story, complete with murderer/fall guy (Gutman's bodyguard, Wilmer), motive (jealous rage) and weapons. The others are forced to accept his version of things because 1) he holds the bird and 2) he is the one who will stay behind to pitch the story. Even when the bird turns out to be a "fake," he still holds the cards because they have nothing to rely on but his discretion to keep them out of jail.

In effect, Spade has reversed the entire structure of the detective story, and of its eschatology of redemption in general. Where the classic story moves towards, and lays faith in, an objective signification of value in some ideal from the past, be it a myth of gold or a Golden Age, the hard-boiled story moves out of the mythic signifiers of the past—black birds, family curses—toward subjective meaning in the present. As in the Flitcraft story, meaning is created by the instability of the objective frame of reference, where the object—the falling beam, the lead bird—undermines its perceived value—stability, wealth. As with objects, so with language. Words do not *mean* until they are given a context, a position in relation to other words or to wordlessness. Our eyes perceive billions of bits of information every second, but we construct meaning from those bits only when the image they configure *differentiates* itself.

In Chandler's essay, he speaks of the style that Hammett developed out of the American language, one that "had no overtones, left no echo, evoked no image beyond a distant hill," but with which Hammett "wrote scenes that seemed never to have been written before" ("Simple Art" 235). Hammett's originality, Chandler argues, is in his ability to *diffuse* the traditional, the stable connotations in language and setting, to create something that doesn't rely upon the habits of myth or the gold standard of a Golden Age for meaning, but begins again *in the present.*[5] And here we begin to understand what Chandler meant by "redemption": not the recovery of the past in the future, but the buying back of the present *in the very act* of invention.

Notes

1. Christian eschatology has had a profound influence on the intellectual, as well as the spiritual, history of the North American continent since its designation as a "New World": an opportunity to bring all the progress of humanity to bear on a place unstained by all of its errors and degradations. When the Puritan forefathers spoke of establishing a city of God cut out of the wilderness, they described it as a "New Jerusalem," referring to the city of Christ's elect after the Last Judgment. Similar echoes ring through such political slogans as the "New Deal" (*i.e.*: New Covenant) and the "New Frontier." Each of these participates in the sense of a world to reflect the one *to come.*

2. Sam Spade's name is itself a cue to the means and merits of the uncovering. He is named for a digging tool, a Biblical prophet and judge, and the author himself, Samuel Dashiell Hammett.

3. Poe's "Murders in the Rue Morgue" does away immediately with "preternatural" suppositions, as does Doyle's *Hound of the Baskervilles* and hundreds of other stories that might be cited.

4. The themes of valuation and currency in *The Maltese Falcon* are also significant to the moment of the novel's publication, in the second year of the Great Depression, and as Hammett's mature engagement with Marxism and left-wing ideology was beginning to manifest itself in activism.

5. Though I speak only of the normative values of myth here, it is with an understanding that, within those normative values are areas of inquiry. But those areas only open up when we *re*consider them—reread, rethink: that is, bring them into the present.

Works Cited

Adams, Henry. *The Education of Henry Adams.* Ed. Ernest Samuels. Boston: Houghton Mifflin, 1973.

Auden, W[ystan] H[ugh]. "The Guilty Vicarage." *Harper's Magazine* 196:1176 (1948). 406-12.

Chandler, Raymond. "The Simple Art of Murder." 1944. *The Art of the Mystery Story.* Ed. Howard Haycraft. New York: Simon and Schuster, 1946. 222-37.

Eliot, T[homas] S[tearns]. *The Waste Land.* 1922. *The Waste Land and Other Poems.* New York: Harcourt Brace Jovanovich, 1934. 25-54.

Fitzgerald, F[rancis] Scott. *The Great Gatsby.* 1925. New York: Charles Scribner's Sons, 1953.

Hammett, Dashiell. *The Dain Curse.* 1929. New York: Random House, 1989.

———. *The Maltese Falcon.* 1930. New York: Random House, 1992.

———. *Red Harvest.* 1929. New York: Random House, 1992.

Hammett, Jo. *Dashiell Hammett: A Daughter Remembers.* New York: Carroll & Graf, 2001.

Wolfe, Peter. *Beams Falling: The Art of Dashiell Hammett.* Bowling Green: Popular Press, 1980.

Thomas Heise (essay date fall 2005)

SOURCE: Heise, Thomas. "'Going Blood-Simple Like the Natives': Contagious Urban Spaces and Modern Power in Dashiell Hammett's *Red Harvest.*" *Modern Fiction Studies* 51, no. 3 (fall 2005): 485-512.

[*In the following essay, Heise investigates issues of crime, violence, and the law in* Red Harvest.]

> In the great city the poor, the vicious, and the delinquent, crushed together in an unhealthful and contagious intimacy, breed in and in soul and body, so that it has often occurred to me that those long genealogies of the Jukes and the tribes of Ishmael would not show such a persistent and distressing uniformity of vice, crime, and poverty unless they were peculiarly fit for the environment in which they are condemned to exist.
>
> —Robert Park, Ernest Burgess, and Roderick McKenzie, *The City*

> "ARE YOUR FINGER PRINTS ON FILE? How J. Edgar Hoover's F.B.I. Can Help You Protect Yourself and Your Family"
>
> —Headline from the cover of *Feds* magazine, Sept. 1937

Dashiell Hammett's 1929 novel, **Red Harvest,** ends with an appeal to the forces of federal law, the professional and bureaucratic "white-collar soldiers" (134) of national law enforcement that historically in the 1920s and 1930s took over much of the terrain once patrolled by the private detective. The ending surprises because it apparently signifies that Hammett's hero, the anonymous Continental Op, has failed in the job he was hired to perform, namely, to rid the working-class city of Personville (called Poisonville by its residents)—"an ugly city of forty thousand people, set in an ugly notch between ugly mountains that had been all dirtied up by mining"—of the criminal elements of its organized, ethnic underworld (3). In one of his final acts in the service of his client, the Op informs him that the dire situation in the city necessitates the intervention of an authority greater than that which the Op alone can provide:

> You're going to tell the governor that your city police have got out of hand, what with bootleggers sworn in as officers, and so on. You're going to ask him for help—the national guard would be best. I don't know how various ruckuses around town have come out, but I do know that the big boys—the ones you were afraid of—are dead. The ones that had too much on you for you to stand up to them. There are plenty of busy young men working like hell right now, trying to get into the dead men's shoes. The more, the better. They'll make it easier for the white-collar soldiers to take hold while everything is disorganized. . . . Then you'll have your city back, all nice and clean and ready to go to the dogs again.
>
> (134)

Originally summoned to Personville by Donald Willsson, the editor of the local *Herald,* a civic reformer, and "a lousy liberal" who functions as the novel's spokesperson for the bourgeois values of fairness and transparency in government, the Op quickly finds himself working instead for Donald's corrupt father, Elihu (21). Before the novel begins, Donald's efforts to expose the roots of civic corruption lead him directly to his father—a nineteenth-century industrial magnate determined to hold on to power in the ruthlessly competitive world of twentieth-century capitalism—and lead indirectly to his (Donald's) murder on the day the Op arrives to meet him.[1] Instead of returning to his San Francisco office, the Op remains in town, commissioned now by Elihu, purportedly to clean the city of the gangs of bootleggers and gamblers that once were—like the mining company, the bank, the press, and the majority of elected officials—firmly under his control. As the I.W.W. union leader Bill Quint recounts it, these criminals initially were hired by Elihu from the ranks of "gunmen, strike-breakers, national guardsmen and even parts of the regular army" to violently beat down a union action at his mine in 1921, but stayed on after the strike, eventually taking "the city for their spoils" (7). The Op's pledge to Elihu to wipe out the city's Irish and Italian thugs—and in the process, to stamp out the illegal working-class pleasures of drinking and gambling—comprises the bulk of Hammett's tightly woven narrative. With the intention of "stirring things up" (57), he embarks on a relentless crusade to infiltrate and double-cross members of the city's corrupt police force and its criminal underworld by monitoring the poolrooms and speakeasies where they socialize, then setting them at war with each other until the last of them is killed off. By the end of Hammett's short novel, the Op has rigged a boxing match, participated in shootouts both with and against the police, is framed for the murder of the femme fatale Dinah Brand, helps destroy stashes of illegal alcohol, drinks a great deal of gin, and then returns back to San Francisco. If by the conclusion organized crime is vanquished in Personville, so too are the criminalized pleasures of working-class life. As if a rotten Elsinore, the city is subjected by the Op to a sacrificial bloodbath and to the imposition of an oppressive authority from the outside, "white-collar soldiers" (134), who place the blue-collar city "under martial law," replacing the detective who, back in the safe confines of his office, is thankful that he himself "was no longer officially a criminal" (142).

This essay argues that the American hardboiled narrative emerges in the midst of a profound shift in the study and prosecution of urban crime. Before the mid-1920s there was no national police force in America, nor any systematic accounting of nationwide trends in crime. Law enforcement was conducted at the municipal level by local police departments and private detective agencies—many of which provided the most rudimentary training, and many of which were corrupt and brutal, little more than an extension of the power of local political bosses. The methods and theories of law enforcement changed drastically in the 1920s and early 1930s. Along with the emergence of the hardboiled narrative in this period came an unprecedented federal and state intervention into the roots of criminality, a confluence of disciplinary and penal forces that sought to bring the origin of crime under new scientific examination and which, in the process, brought the spatiality and sociality of working-class life in the city under intensive scrutiny. In the 1920s, poor and working-class urban spaces were seen as the point of origin and dispersion of sensationalized new formations of deviancy. Most worrying for law enforcement and for urban sociologists (especially those associated with the Chicago School) was the development under Prohibition of syndicated criminality—criminal networks founded on extortion, racketeering, corruption, violence, and codes of loyalty and secrecy that defined organized criminal activity in the period.[2] The study and prosecution of underworld crime, this essay will show, gave license to sociological experts and to a new, professionally trained federal police force to intervene into the sociality of the ethnic and working-class inner city.

There is "an ill-defined yet wide-spread feeling . . . that one is not secure in his life and his good, that the police have failed in their task of protection, and that all forms of crime are steadily mounting," the *Uniform Crime Reporting* manual alarmingly stated in 1929, the same year **Red Harvest** was published (Committee on Uniform Crime Records 17). The juridical and discursive response to this growing "wide-spread feeling" amounted to nothing less than an epochal shift in the 1920s and 1930s in the study of deviancy and criminality, a move away from the crude Lombrosian theories that argued for the genetic predispositions for crime and toward newer theories that stressed the influence of en-

vironmental factors in the formation of the criminal subject. This shift was announced perhaps nowhere more clearly than in *The City,* the collaborative study by the influential Chicago School of Sociology's leading researchers Robert Park, Ernest Burgess, and Roderick McKenzie: "In the great city, the poor, the vicious, and the delinquent [are] crushed together in an unhealthful and contagious intimacy" (45). This "contagious intimacy" could only lead, the study predicted, to crime, vice, and "the disintegration of the moral order" (Park, Burgess, and McKenzie 25). Contemporaneous with the Chicago School's socio-scientific studies of criminal spaces was a revolution in scientific policing inaugurated with J. Edgar Hoover's appointment as Director of the Bureau of Investigation in 1924.[3] As Claire Bond Potter has shown, Hoover's bureaucratic reforms converted a corrupt and disgraced department—which had been run by a former private detective—into a highly professional, "white-collar," national police force comprised of educated, middle-class officers governed by "a strict code of conduct," along with "a heavy reliance on the acquisition and sorting of information, and a system of uniform investigative procedures" (35). When the mammoth 1931 *Report on the Causes of Crime* declared in simple but sweeping language that "general delinquency results not from any racial disposition toward crime, but from the influence of the social environment," Lombrosian presumptions regarding the origins of crime seemed to be overturned once and for all in favor of the scientific study of environmental factors (US National Commission lvii). Theories that linked culture and space to crime were the new dominant episteme. With these theories would come an invasive monitoring of the "delinquent" urban spaces where crime was imagined to be produced and reproduced, planned and perpetrated.

The stated impetus for the 1920s' and 1930s' socio-scientific investigations of the linkages between crime and urban life was to understand delinquency and to quell the gangland violence orchestrated by organized criminal factions in large metropolitan centers. Prominent among the decade's many sociological studies of criminal urban spaces were *The City* by Park, Burgess, and McKenzie and *Delinquency Areas* by Clifford Shaw. More straightforwardly legal and juridical studies, such as the landmark *Illinois Crime Survey, Report on the Causes of Crime* by the US National Commission on Law Observance and Enforcement, and the US Department of Justice's *Uniform Crime Reports,* which tracked crime rates nationwide for the first time, also played an important role in the formation of a discourse on urban criminality in the years between the two world wars. The actual scope of the period's crime reports and new federal law enforcement tactics were in truth much wider than their purportedly narrow focus on delinquency and organized crime. They represent, I argue, a campaign to control the uses of urban space by surveying and criminalizing the sociality of nonnormative populations.[4] Such is the hitherto underappreciated discursive context of the American hardboiled crime novel of the 1920s and 1930s, which, unlike the so-called Golden Age genteel mysteries of Conan Doyle, Agatha Christie, and Ellery Queen, is noted for its naturalistic presentation of violence, its urban setting, and its representation of the milieu of poor, ethnic, and working-class Americans and of the criminal who is a product of these socially, economically, and spatially marginalized relations.[5] If the official studies of crime were ostensibly a response to the highly publicized crime waves of the period, so too was the contemporaneous hardboiled novel, which investigated an urban milieu roiled by murder, assault, deception, and moral corruption. From its inception in the 1920s, the hardboiled novel used organized crime as a pretext for a study of "delinquent" urban spaces—speak-easies, poolrooms, gambling parlors, empty warehouses, and dark streets. Widely considered to be the first work to master the genre's developing formulas, styles, and themes, Hammett's *Red Harvest* is an ideal site for interrogating the means by which the genre at its beginnings managed the tensions of its historical moment.[6]

Through its narrative of detection, *Red Harvest* dramatizes the massive bureaucratic intervention to monitor the poor and working-class urban terrain—the "breeding places of delinquency and crime" (US National Commission lxviii)—a project that Foucault argues authorizes a "generalized policing," "a means of perpetual surveillance of the population . . . that makes it possible to supervise . . . the whole social field" (281).[7] Hammett's narrative maps out urban space, plotting a social geography of criminality that substantiates the "ill-defined yet wide-spread feeling . . . that the police have failed in their task of protection, and that all forms of crime are steadily mounting." Yet *Red Harvest,* I will show, also narratively embodies the explosive aggression that inheres not in crime, but in the operations of law itself, the violent supplement undergirding the scientific study of crime in the period. Hammett details—through the figure of the detective—the methods by which law organizes urban space by suppressing underworld criminality, policing working-class leisure and crushing industrial labor action. While "no longer officially a criminal," the Op is, Hammett suggests, guilty of transgressions that are startling and manifold.

To argue that *Red Harvest* investigates the relays between modern power and the working-class city with irony and ambivalence is to be guilty of wild understatement. Historically, the breaking of strikes was performed by lower-middle-class detectives, a fact that Hammett himself learned when in 1917, as a Pinkerton, he was approached by vigilantes who promised to pay him thousands of dollars if he agreed to help murder an I.W.W. union leader in Butte, Montana, an offer he im-

mediately declined. *Red Harvest*'s similar founding moment of violence is the brutal suppression of labor, a moment that sets the stage for the optic lens of the Op to survey Personville's urban criminality, leading thus to the internecine war among Elihu's competitors for power and money. In eliminating them, the lower-middle-class detective strengthens the position of the text's *ur*-criminal, the savage capitalist whose politics are as dirty as his mines. Additionally, in clearing the way for the intervention of a national police force that will impose "martial law," Hammett's Op lays the groundwork for his own occupational obsolescence. At *Red Harvest*'s end, the lone detective is replaced by a professional, bureaucratic army. Importantly, *Red Harvest* refuses to critique explicitly the violent techniques of power or to make ethical distinctions between the sites upon which power is exercised, but instead presents its reader with a narrative of power in action, one in which the line between law and crime is so blurred as to be erased altogether. Hammett's hardboiled novel is a contested terrain profoundly marked by its discursive moment and by a competing array of social anxieties—over crime, justice, class relations, and urban life—which it tries to manage. Though entangled with the scientific discourses of penality, *Red Harvest* ultimately destabilizes the discursively produced definitions of criminality, while confirming the contention made by the official literature on crime that urban criminality is an effect of poor, ethnic, and working-class spaces and social relations.

With nearly two dozen murders in under 150 pages, *Red Harvest* is an exceptionally bloody book, even by the standards of the typical hardboiled narrative patterned around the surveillance and often, revengeful murder of dangerous, nonnormative subjects. The Op, a modern version of the frontier Indian-killer that Richard Slotkin has examined in *Gunfighter Nation,* orchestrates by the novel's end a "'savage war' . . . in which one side or the other attempts to destroy its enemy root and branch" (Slotkin 12). If Slotkin sees the hardboiled detective as a twentieth-century incarnation of this prototypical American figure who is reimagined for the new urban jungle, then Steve Marcus, in his study of Hammett's work, sees him as participant in a world of "universal warfare" where "the war of each against all, and of all against all" is a condition of life. "The only thing that prevents the criminal ascendancy from turning into permanent tyranny," Marcus posits about Hammett's work, "is that the crooks who take over society cannot cooperate with one another, repeatedly fall out with each other, and return to . . . Hobbesian anarchy" (205). What Marcus sees as a descent into anarchy, Slotkin views as a stage leading to an eventual "*regeneration through violence*" (12), a caustic cleansing of Personville's corrupted social body that the Op achieves by triggering a war between the city's ethnic gangsters.

Broadly speaking, scholars of the hardboiled genre—such as Slotkin and Marcus—have characterized it as ideologically conservative, both in its surface representation of the twentieth-century city as chaotic and in need of policing, and in its deep formal structures—notably, the reifying tendencies of its prose realism, the heroic individualism of its protagonists, and the deterministic nature of its plots, which invariably end with the triumph of law and order.[8] Such arguments falter though when applied to Hammett's *Red Harvest.* While Hammett's world is one of pervasive warfare, the lawlessness that the text represents stems not from universal, ahistorical, or atavistic forces. But instead in *Red Harvest,* violence and disorder are an effect of the direct imposition of law. As Hammett's Prohibition-era narrative shows, the crimes of gambling and alcohol distribution and consumption are presented as de rigueur, victimless activities that in the absence of outside authority and in the presence of a corrupt police force have become a part of the fabric of everyday social life in the working-class city. Modes of entertainment that had been criminalized nationally, could be, the text implies, transacted openly without fear of legal retribution in Personville. While violence—in the form of labor-related strife—is part of the city's recent history before the Op's arrival, this earlier incident of bloodshed was perpetrated by strikebreakers acting in the name of law and order and hence stands as part of the text's representation of law's brutal repression of working-class life and culture. Though by no means idyllic, Hammett's grimy Personville was apparently a relatively peaceful city until the Op makes his entrance. Only when he arrives does the killing begin in earnest.

Hammett's first-person narrative opens with the Op stepping foot into Personville, having been sent out to the mountain city by his office, a thinly disguised version of the Pinkerton agency that employed Hammett in the years before he began professionally writing.[9] The Pinkertons, Slotkin writes, were "the largest provider of investigative and protective services in the United States between 1858 and 1898." Noted for their brutality and cunning, they were "the only instrument of police power to function throughout the nation," that is, until the creation of Hoover's white-collar police force in the 1920s (Slotkin 139).[10] Before Hoover assumed stewardship of the Bureau of Investigation, it was led by William Burns, himself a former private detective. As Potter notes, under Burns's leadership the Bureau's reputation plummeted. Its tactics were slipshod and its agents repeatedly were tied to political corruption, favoritism, graft, and the "widespread abuse of Prohibition laws" (Potter 10). "The disgraced Burns," Potter writes, "became the symbol of an amateur past that was being replaced by professionalism," namely the "rigorous training, dress regulations, [and] internal inspections," that Hoover imposed, rules that transformed the Bureau, making its "federal agents recognizable as professionals in any group of law officers," and thus ushering in "a new era in federal enforcement" premised on what she calls "scientific policing" (35). Under Hoover, the ragtag Bureau was turned into a "scientifically trained national police force" (Potter 12), one versed in the collection of fingerprints, lie detector tests, and in the compilation of statistics that could be marshaled into profiles in criminality.[11] The internal history of the Bureau of Investigation emblematizes the emergence more generally of the scientific study of the interrelations of criminality and urban space that aimed to bring large parts of the citizenry under the scrutiny of an interventionist state. Published in the midst of this new discourse and new practices, *Red Harvest* narrativizes these historical shifts, representing as it does a passing of the torch as the detective and the "police [who] have got out of hand" give way to the new "federal agent."

When the Op first arrives in Personville, he drops his bags off and immediately goes "out to look at the city" (3), thus beginning his campaign to map its social geography of criminality, which will take him—as it did the urban sociologists of the Chicago School in the 1920s and 1930s—to the city's working-class spaces. Killing time until he is to meet Donald Willsson, he rides a street car though the town, hopping off upon noticing "[t]hirty or forty men and a sprinkling of women" gathered in front of City Hall (5). Thus initiates a program of social surveillance that involves linking each observed subject to a particular type of urban space that reveals his or her position in the city's class structure. As Hammett's narrative moves forward, it enforces the associations between class, space, and criminality with increasing intensity. The Op is no Hoover acolyte, but a private dick who works by intuition and strength. Yet as he "looks at the city" (Hammett 3), he does so with an eye for collecting and sorting information about class and criminality with "the prospect of discovering patterns of regularity in its apparent confusion" (Park, Burgess, and McKenzie viii), a goal the Op, Hoover, and the Chicago School's sociologists all shared. As the Op scans the crowd in this opening scene, he is not yet aware that a murder has occurred, yet he still studies it, taking in visual information from which he creates a composite that equals a cross-section of the urban citizenry, the city's "whole social field." He looks not so much for an individual suspect, but instead looks suspiciously at each and every individual who may prove to be a criminal: "There were men from mines and smelters still in their working clothes, gaudy boys from pool rooms and dance halls, sleek men with slick pale faces, men with the dull look of respectable husbands, a few just as respectable and dull women, and some ladies of the night" (5). Here working-class male laborers from the mines, young "delinquent" boys from the rough and tumble world of pool rooms and dancehalls, middle-class men accompanying women whose primary site of activity are the private spaces of bourgeois domesticity, and prostitutes negotiating the city's public streets are gathered to receive news of Donald Willsson's death. At the intersection of murder and law, the text draws together representative urban types from the city's disparate spaces, creating a lineup in which the citizenry, its sartorial codes, and its spaces of work and pleasure are anatomized.

Soon after the scene in front of City Hall, Hammett places his Op in the services of Elihu, who hires him to rid the city of the bootleggers and gamblers who, by opportunistically exploiting demands in the market caused by the criminalization of working-class leisure, have enriched themselves in a challenge to Elihu's hegemony. Positioning himself as a Progressive-era social reformer with a gun, the Op promises him "a good job of city-cleaning" (43). From this moment forward, *Red Harvest*'s narrative focuses the Op's investigation exclusively on the city's working-class spaces, which are not simply the text's setting, but are where the text contends the social relations of organized underworld criminality are shaped and produced. In this manner, *Red Harvest* bears the impress of its historical moment, which saw, along with an increased scientific sophistication in the study of crime, a shift away from outdated theories that argued that deviancy was biologically determined. From the second half of the nineteenth century to the early years of the twentieth, the most influential theorist of the origins of crime was criminal-anthropologist Cesare Lombroso, who professed that some individuals were born criminal and that visible traces of their innate criminality could be discerned in the anatomical aberrations of their faces and bodies. What constituted deformity was aligned closely with the features of eastern Europeans and Africans who, under Lombroso's taxonomy, became permanently categorized as the criminal classes. Viewed in its time as the most advanced scientific methodology in crime studies, by the 1930s Lombroso's theory was seen for what it was: the latest version of an older, racist, moral philosophy that superstitiously believed that the inward disposition of a person was reflected in his or her face. Park and his fellow researchers argued for a different focus: "It is probably the breaking down of local attachments and the weakening of the restraints and inhibitions of the primary group, under the influence of the urban environment, which are largely responsible for the increase of vice and crime in great cities" (Park, Burgess, and McKenzie 25). The mass migrations and accelerated urbanism of the early twentieth century changed the face of American cities and altered the disposition of the urban citizenry who were forced to experience hyperstimulation, anonymity, and the "shock of . . . new contacts" (Park, Burgess, and McKenzie 40). The cacophonous urban environment resulted in the unleashing of "vagrant and suppressed impulses, passions, and ideals," which eroded "the dominant moral order" and led to the sensationalized urban crime waves of the 1920s and 1930s (Park, Burgess, and McKenzie 43).

Though the studies by the sociologists of the Chicago School and their associates were theoretically concerned with the effects of the urban environment in general on crime, in practice their investigations took them almost exclusively to the working-class, ethnic neighborhoods populated by new immigrants. As a result, their findings often ended up indicting the same populations that were stigmatized by earlier theories of criminality. In *The City*, for instance, they referred to "[t]emperament and social contagion" of "the poor, the vicious, the criminal," making no effort to distinguish between them. The possibility of a widespread "unhealthful and contagious intimacy" lent "special importance to the[ir] segregation" (Park, Burgess, and McKenzie 45). Shaw's *Delinquency Areas*—a massive survey of sixty thousand adult and juvenile offenders in Chicago—reinforced these observations with scientific rigor. "[L]ittle systematic effort has been made to study delinquency from the point of view of its relation to the social situation in which it occurs," Shaw began, promising that "this volume represents a preliminary step" in an emerging field (ix). Shaw's project aimed to bring all of Chicago under surveillance, plotting as it did incidents of crime block by block by using over thirty distribution, rate, radial, and zone maps, which it supplemented by statistical analysis and first-person narrative accounts by anonymous, self-described underworld criminals. In the "zone in transition" and "the zone of workingmen's homes"—interstitial areas undergoing great change—Shaw claimed to have found the highest percentage of the city's crime on a per capita basis (18, 19). In these inner city spaces, he wrote, one discovers "poverty, desertion, bad housing," "areas of first immigrant settlement," "Little Sicily, the Ghetto, the Black Belt," "pleasure seeking Bohemians . . . professional criminals," and a space "where play is crime" (18, 19). These poor, immigrant, and working-class neighborhoods were subject to systemic "social disorganization," that resulted, Shaw argued, from a deteriorating physical infrastructure and the continual "influx of foreign national and racial groups" (205). In the inner-city slum, Shaw charged, the harshness and anonymity of life gave birth to a criminally oriented value system, which was then passed from generation to generation, actively in the form of gang recruitment, and passively—as if a kind of communicable social disease—through the daily practices and traditions of its immigrant, poor, and working-class residents. The rundown ethnic neighborhood deformed its residents, who were in turn treated as the source of urban blight. Or as Park, Burgess, and McKenzie wrote, "the poor, the vicious, the criminal were peculiarly fit for the environment in which they are condemned to exist" (45).

Far from being confined to an elite circle of academic crime scholars, the findings of the new urban sociologists influenced the practices of state and law federal enforcement and, more indirectly, as Morris Janowitz contended, "the American literary scene" (vii). The 1931 national *Report on the Causes of Crime,* for instance, drew conclusions similar to Park, Burgess, and McKenzie, and Shaw: "poor housing conditions," "a marked absence of the home-owning class," "a largely foreign population of inferior social status," and "unwholesome types of recreation" were the roots of nonnormative social behaviors that, if left untreated, formed the basis of the social activities of organized criminal gangs whose members were often comprised of former young delinquents (US National Commission lv). Two years prior, the report *Organized Crime in Chicago*—part of the *Illinois Crime Survey,* then the most far-reaching study of criminal justice in America—observed, "It is a noticeable fact that in these less favored areas, in these abiding places of the transients and of the 'downs and outs,' and of the newly arrived immigrant, are to be found the breeding place of gangs, of the Mafia, and of the professional criminal" (Landesco 5).

Tellingly, the *Organized Crime in Chicago* report cast its disciplinary net much wider than the narrow scope of its titular subject as it sought "the application of business methods and scientific procedure" to "deal with the crime problem in detail" (281). Laying out a far-reaching role for the social science expert, *Organized Crime in Chicago* asserts, "If we would control crime in Chicago, we must control the thoughts and the aspirations and the ambitions of youth and the moral and social atmosphere and outlook of the districts and localities where our criminals are trained and nurtured" (Landesco 7). The report's exploration of the social relations of Chicago's organized criminal leaders—Mont Tennes, John Torrio, and Al Capone (all of whom seem to have been employed as models for **Red Harvest***'s* gamblers and bootleggers)—soon gives way to the text's "real" concern, the disciplining of the urban space of the city's poor, working-class, immigrant, and African American populations, who represent a potentially politically radicalizing element in the urban fabric. "There are reasons," the survey announced, "why there are more murders and assaults and more race and gang conflicts in Chicago than there are in any European capital. In Europe, the races are segregated into nations and states and principalities" (Landesco 3). For the authors of the *Illinois Crime Survey,* the fence of American urban apartheid had too many openings.

This purported study of "organized, underworld criminality" goes on to argue that the "thousands of Negroes [who] have come to us from the rural centers of the south" turn to crime because their "natural home is in the field and not in the streets and congested quarters of a great city" where they "lack the guardianship and advice of their white masters and friends" (Landesco 5). Certain urban spaces—or urbanness in general—were "naturally" less amenable to certain populations—"Negroes," but also Italians, Irish, and Jews—and more amenable to others. Criminal subjects were no longer "born criminal," but were instead bred in the "breeding places of delinquency and crime." "[A]tempts to control crime" were only "makeshifts" until the "sociological sciences secure[d] a more fundamental understanding of the forces moulding human nature and society." "The science of criminology," the report cautioned, "is only in its beginnings" (Landesco 283). A year later, criminology gained what it needed to qualify as a science: the ability to quantify its observations. In 1930, the National Division of Identification and Information of the Bureau of Investigation was commissioned by J. Edgar Hoover to "collect and compile" and publish "crime statistics" in the *Uniform Crime Reports* (1). The *UCR* helped nationalize and standardize definitions of criminal offenses, whose "geographic distribution . . . and periodic fluctuation" it mapped city by city, state by state, bringing into focus, for the first time, a portrait of crime in America (US Dept. of Justice 1, 2).[12]

The hardboiled crime novel, like the sociological urban ethnographies of the 1920s and 1930s, is a study of poor, immigrant, and working-class social relations through the lens of criminality. Sidney L. Harring, in *Policing a Class Society,* historicizes the intersection of crime and urban space in ways that elucidate the hardboiled novel's depiction of criminalized sociality that these studies aimed to uncover. The late-nineteenth- and early-twentieth-century city, Harring writes, was represented in the middle-class imaginary as a space that was increasingly "dark, unknowable . . . [and] working-class" (153).[13] "Within one generation," he notes, "large cities had been transformed from comfortable, secure, homogenous small towns to sprawling, diverse conglomerates full of unfamiliar people. Large crowds of foreigners gathered on corners all over town, spoke strange languages . . . hung out in saloons, shops, and vacant lots, and exhibited strange customs and beliefs" (153). In this atmosphere, middle-class reformers, urban sociologists, and representatives of manufacturing and commercial interests combined forces to regulate the spaces of working-class leisure—especially the saloon—which were thought to dissipate workers' energies into nonproductive consumption, to undermine middle-class social and religious mores, and to "inflame radical tendencies" among the working class (155). The primary site of working-class and immigrant socializing, the saloon cashed checks, made loans, collected mail for itinerant workers, and served as a meeting place for unions and labor-affiliated political organizations. Under the auspices of enforcing Prohibition, the surveillance of saloons, pool rooms, dancehalls, and clubhouses, places where "play is crime," was officially legitimized. But the law did not merely observe these places, it produced them. Prohibition created new physical spaces in the city that were designed solely for the clandestine manufacture, storage, distribution, and consumption of alcohol. The policing of these spaces created, in turn, an underworld of organized criminal networks on the municipal, and eventually, national level. In a Möbius strip of repression and production, the law produced a "dark, unknowable" underworld of the city which, as Foucault contends, the discursive and penal forces of law could "place in full light and . . . organize as a relatively enclosed, but penetrable, milieu" (276).

Red Harvest's representation of the city mirrors that of Harring's portrayal of it in the anxiety-ridden bourgeois mind. Attempting to penetrate the city's criminal milieu, the Op navigates its working-class, delinquent spaces: the "pool rooms, cigar stores, speakeasies, soft drink joints, and . . . street corners—wherever I found a man or two loafing" (47).[14] The spaces of working-class and immigrant leisure and underworld criminality are conflated in Hammett's text. In these spaces, the Op seeks Personville's organized crime factions' leaders, whom the text ethnically inscribes: among them are the gambler Max "Whisper" Thaler, "a small dark young man" with a "little dark head" (36, 46); the bootlegger Pete the Finn, whose underlings are "dagoes" (84), "swarthy foreign-looking men in laborers' clothes" (82); the fencer Lew Yard; the bootlegger and saloon owner Reno Starkey; the Irish police chief Noonan, his Lieutenant McGraw; Bob MacSwain, a former police detective and now "a sap and a cheap crook" (58); and the "foreigners" who run the department's own bootlegging operations (113). Sean McCann, in *Gumshoe America,* calls Personville "a fantastically cosmopolitan underworld," rightly noting that it "draws no racial distinctions." "Its members associate along commercial lines," McCann states, "rather than ethnic ones, and this criminal world includes 'old stock' Americans as well as new arrivals" (80). McCann's observations comport with official disciplinary studies of crime decades earlier, which found that in the urban spaces that produced the city's preponderance of crime—"Little Sicily, the Ghetto, the Black Belt"—"[t]he relative rates of delinquents . . . remained more or less constant over a period of 20 years," despite the fact that "the nationality composition of the population changed almost completely in this interval" (US National Commission lvii). Space, not race, led to crime, though the spaces of crime—or one should say, criminalized spaces—consistently proved to be poor, ethnic, and racialized.

In the first third of Hammett's narrative, the Op's survey of space ranges from the "pool rooms" to the "street corners" and finally to the "lunch counter[s]," places where money exchanges hands for information circulating through an informal but efficient social network. He

does so in order to strategically infiltrate working-class centers for the distribution of information in an attempt to disrupt the city's underworld of organized gambling, classified by the *Report on the Causes of Crime* as one of the more "unwholesome types of recreation" (lv). "I don't like the way Poisonville has treated me," the Op reveals, and so he begins his secret campaign to "even up" (45). He begins by "spreading" the news that in an approaching boxing match the favored fighter, Ike Bush, is to take "a dive in the sixth" (47). "My spreading technique was something like this: 'Got a match? . . . Thanks . . . Going to the fights tonight?,'" the Op says, passing himself off as a local by mimicking working-class male reticence (47). "I looked most honest when I was lying," he later professes in a moment of ironic self-disclosure (112).

As he forges his way through the working-class milieu, the Op sets in motion what he labels, in a conversation with the erotically charged Dinah Brand, "an experiment," a moment when the novel parodically acknowledges the discursive context that has shaped its representation of crime (47). "What's your idea of how to go about purifying our village?" she asks tauntingly. Knowing full well that the Op's methodology is not "scientific procedure," but simply "stirring things up," she goes on to say, "So that's the way you scientific detectives work" (57). Before the bout begins, the Op arranges the final pieces of his "experiment" by secretly reversing course and threatening Bush that if he does not win, he will escort him back to Philadelphia, where the boxer is wanted on criminal charges. Accordingly Bush emerges victorious, but only to be killed by a knife that is thrown from the crowd into "the nape of Bush's neck" (53). The Op is wholly unconcerned: "That was only an experiment—just to see what would happen," he says (57). The other results of his social experimentation are a near riot, a financial hit to Max Thaler, and apparently great losses to the working-class men duped by the Op's advice. The homosocial space of the boxing arena, with its "Smoke. Stink. Heat. Noise," is one of the sites of the illegal working-class leisure that the text places under scrutiny. In what is perhaps the Op's most significant observation of the event, he notes that "most of the population seemed to be on hand" (50).

In the scenes following the fight, the Op and Dinah Brand drink a "couple of hookers of gin" and discuss the corruption in the city's police department. Brand, whose alluring sex appeal has led men to buy her favors (she is in many senses of the word, a brand), stands at the center of the city's networks of gossip. She reveals to the Op that the ex-police detective Bob MacSwain—"a big good-looking Irishman" who is now "[a] small-time grifter" (58, 61)—was involved two years ago in the cover-up of the murder of Tim Noonan, the brother of the police chief. Both Brand and Chief

Noonan think Max Thaler shot Tim in a love dispute over another woman, but the Op soon discovers his murderer was MacSwain. As he sets off to find Mac-Swain, he again perfunctorily comments, "I went out to hunt. . . . I did the pool rooms, cigar stores, speakcasies, looking around first, then asking cautious questions" (62). The near-identical repetition of language from the prior scene before the boxing match signifies his rote surveillance of working-class male space. Upon apprehending MacSwain, the Op hauls him into Noonan's office where the two corrupt cops confront each other. Hoping to spark a war between Noonan and Max Thaler, the Op does not reveal that MacSwain is his brother's real killer, but instead leads him to believe that MacSwain was merely involved in an attempt to make the death look like a suicide. Instead of arresting him for accessory to a murder, Noonan savagely beats him, threatens to kill him, and then sends him down to the cellar where "the wrecking crew" tortures him (66). In this case, Hammett's narrative leads directly from the working-class "pool rooms, cigar stores, speakeasies" to the center of the local criminal justice system where punishment is administered in a manner that is itself criminal.

In addition to these sites, Hammett's narrative takes the reader through other spaces in Personville's social landscape, into what Shaw in *Delinquency Areas* termed the down and out "zone in transition" and "the zone of workingmen's homes" (18, 19). **Red Harvest** escorts the reader into Brand's "disorderly, cluttered up" apartment (22), into a "Ronney Street rooming house" (109), and into cheap hotels with "narrow front doors . . . and shabby stairs leading up to second-story offices" with "dirty day-book register[s]" on their counters (49). It directs the reader down "a dark street not far from the center of town" (33) where Thaler's gambling "joint" is concealed by a "cigar store" (34), and out into a dilapidated warehouse district where Finn and Starkey manufacture and store their alcohol. As the Op moves through these underworld spaces, he employs methods common to detective and criminal both, at one point falsely identifying himself as a "member in good standing of the Industrial Workers of the World" (6) and at another acting "so excessively secretive" that he is asked by a woman, "You aren't a bootlegger, are you?" "I let her get whatever she could out of a grin" is the Op's response (4). The Op trespasses into the spaces where the report *Organized Crime in Chicago* contended "criminals are trained and nurtured" (7). Here he learns underworld mores, practices—the value of deception, the dangers of pride—and the social relations of criminality that he redeploys in destructive ways.

But what is peculiar about **Red Harvest**'s portrait of working-class spaces is how little labor and socializing the text actually represents. Carl Freedman and Christopher Kendrick, in "Forms of Labor in Dashiell Hammett's **Red Harvest**," make a similar observation, noting for instance that the labor of the text's nameless miners "is never explicitly shown . . . and, after the first chapter, is never so much as mentioned" (13). McCann as well comments that it is "as if Personville had no inhabitants except thieves and corrupt officials" (79). While committed to depicting the infrastructure of working-class sociality, Hammett's novel largely represents these spaces as vacant forms, devoid of the manifestations of everyday life that the text implies forms the fabric of this blue-collar city. This city of forty thousand is—with the exception of a couple of crowds and an anonymous waiter, bartender, and restaurant customer or two—empty of people who are not underworld criminals. The effect is not to lessen the extent to which **Red Harvest** is a narrative of detection centered in working-class life, but is rather to heighten the sense of working class life as criminal. Emptying Personville of manifestations of ordinary labor, Hammett's narrative fills the city's spaces with an organized, underworld criminality that is presented as indigenous to working-class and immigrant life. This is why the Op in the end must call in the "white-collar soldiers" to impose martial law even though the leaders and minions of the city's organized criminal underworld have been killed off. Who are these federal officers going to police, if not the working-class and immigrant men whose appetite for prohibited leisure activities sustained the illicit syndicates of organized criminality in the first place?

Midway through the narrative, the Op becomes less an observer of the urban working-class scene—less of a "scientific detective"—and more of a direct catalyst for violence. Or more accurately, he unleashes the violent undercurrent implicit in his nefarious study of Personville's social mores. "I've got to have a wedge," he says, "that can be put between [the city's criminal leaders]. . . . If we can smash things up enough—break the combination—they'll have their knives in each other's backs" (78). To "break the combination" is to shatter the network of shared social practices, languages, or counterhegemonic cultural customs that form a protective membrane against upperworld intrusions into the hermetic relations of socially and spatially marginalized or criminalized populations. In Park, Burgess, and McKenzie's study of the city, they posited that in the dilapidated centers of the great metropolises where life was characterized by "mobility" and by the "number and intensity of stimulations [that] tends inevitably to confuse and to demoralize the person," alternative or "deviant" criminal cultures developed to compensate for the breakdown of "social control" and "moral order" (59). In Shaw's *Delinquency Areas,* the anonymous, petty underworld figure Case #5 brought their theory into the practice of everyday life. In Shaw's study, Case #5 relates how in Chicago's "flophouses" and "cheap hashhouses" he "brushed shoulders with crooks and gunmen of the underworld" (128). In the slums of Chicago, Shaw's unnamed subject found a spatially and socially marginalized world composed of "[m]en of all nationalities and races . . . a 'brotherhood' whose object was mutual pity and sympathy," a sphere held together by a code of loyalty and secrecy that "was unbreakable." "To violate this code by 'squalking'" to the police was, Case #5 discloses, "an unpardonable sin" (128). In Hammett's novel, the Op circumnavigates through Personville's criminal milieu, seeking not so much to decode it, but to break it. The more progressive social reformers of the 1920s and 1930s endeavored—at least on paper—to move the ethnic and immigrant citizenry of the city away from what they viewed as tribal loyalties and brotherhoods, so as to integrate them into national social and political institutions. The goals of Hammett's Op are not nearly so high-minded. As he tells Elihu near the end of his crusade, now that "everything is disorganized," the conditions are ripe "for white-collar soldiers to take hold" and reorganize the city under an oppressive authority whose presence will benefit, first and foremost, the brutal Elihu. In this manner, **Red Harvest** dramatically embodies a major project of early-twentieth-century progressive social reform, while simultaneously casting doubt upon it, suggesting that its ultimate beneficiary may be the industrial capitalist who reaps the profit of a cowed and disciplined citizenry.

The Op gains the confidence of Personville's working-class citizenry and criminal leaders by offering up false information at some points—such as when he impersonates a union member—and withholding it at others—such as when he lets linger the impression that he himself is a bootlegger. He secures entry into this world too by speaking its tough, staccato, pragmatic language: "Give me the straight of it. I only need that to pop the job," he demands of Thaler (36). By enacting the practices of this criminal milieu—participating in shootouts, showing his skill with his gun—he gains its trust. After Thaler sees the Op shoot a man, he tells him, "You dropped Big Nick . . . I'll take a chance on you" (37). Once he has earned the loyalty of Thaler, Noonan, Starkey, Elihu, and others, he gathers the rivaling bands together for what he ironically calls a "peace conference" in which he skillfully turns the "delegates" against each other (97). Violent infighting, he declares, is "no good for business," though an internecine war is exactly what he seeks (100). "We won't get anywhere unless everybody comes clean," he announces, and then begins to narrate a misleading version of events regarding recent murders (primarily that of Tim Noonan) and recent police raids. The Op's conference breaks any remaining loyalties, an act that precipitates the bloody slaughter that consumes the remainder of the text in the red harvest of its title. At the conference, Elihu claims that he wants an end to the slaughter, but the Op soon turns the city into a grim abattoir.

In the late 1920s and early 1930s, the "ill-defined yet widespread feeling . . . that all forms of crime are steadily mounting" (US Committee on Uniform Crime Records 17) and the sense that "the present disturbing conditions" were in need of "ultimate relief" (US National Commission xvi) led to calls for a coordinated, scientifically organized campaign of aggressive policing. In **Red Harvest** and in the hardboiled novel more generally, these social anxieties were dramatized and ironized in narratives that presented the enforcer of law not as the tonic to violence, but as its leading instigator. In Hammett's novel, the "ill-defined . . . feeling" becomes quantifiable by a mounting body count. The flow of the crime wave that the Op's presence unleashes largely moves along the pathways devoted to the manufacture, storage, and consumption of alcohol. From the city's ramshackle warehouse district to its speakeasies, the Op follows its scent, leaving a trail of working-class and immigrant corpses behind him. He participates in a raid on Finn's warehouse that leaves "four dead bodies . . . swarthy foreign-looking men in laborers' clothes . . . practically shot to pieces" and the building "ankle-deep with booze" (82). At Reno's speakeasy, "The Silver Arrow," where "[y]ou can get away with anything . . . so long as you don't get noisy," the Op stumbles upon a shootout, an effect of the war he has triggered between the rival gangs (89). Later, he watches "[m]en . . . being led, dragged, carried, from pool room to wagon" as police officers in cahoots with Finn arrest Whisper's and Thaler's henchmen (122). In the narrative's final chapter, the Op surveys "the street . . . hunting for buildings that looked like deserted warehouses" (137). Here he discovers both more murder—"a battered face . . . of the useless, characterless sort that goes well with park benches"—and a cache of Canadian Club "branded Perfection Maple Syrup" (138). In Hammett's novel, the down and out—the "sort that goes well with park benches"—and underworld crime are awash in alcohol that spills everywhere like blood.

As the death count piles up in **Red Harvest,** even the crooked Chief Noonan cries, "I'm getting sick of this killing. . . . I'm sick of this butchering. I can't stand it anymore" (95, 96). The Op, on the other hand, is not sickened but disturbingly invigorated by murder: "I've arranged a killing or two in my time, when they were necessary. But this is the first time I've ever got the fever. . . . It makes you sick, or you get to like it" (102). The feverish contagion of murder is contracted, the text makes clear, by prolonged dwelling in the urban sphere: "This damned burg's getting to me," the Op divulges (102). Hammett's narrative bears out Park, Burgess, and McKenzie's fear of the city's "unhealthful and contagious intimacy" (45). "If I don't get away soon," the Op worries, "I'll be going blood-simple like the natives" (102). When he is in the city, he behaves like one of them; what Park, Burgess, and McKenzie labeled the "vagrant and suppressed impulses [and] passions" are elicited from the Op by his proximity to "the poor, the vicious, and the delinquent" (Park, Burgess, and McKenzie 43, 45). Before the Op escapes Personville, almost all of the text's minor and major characters are gunned down in a violent flourish. Noonan himself is "shot to hell" by Thaler (101). The speakeasy owner Reno kills "the bitch" Dinah Brand with an ice pick and tries to pin it on the Op. He knocks off Lew Yard too, then murders Finn after dynamiting his headquarters. In a fitting ending, Thaler and Reno shoot each other, their bodies hauled away, the Op wryly observes on the very last page, by a "tired looking ambulance crew" (142).

Red Harvest—along with the hundreds of other pulp novels and magazines published yearly in the 1920s and 1930s for an estimated readership of ten million—ultimately chooses violence over urban sociology, reformist politics, and the progressive journalism embodied by Donald Willsson as the best weapon in fighting crime (Smith 19). Hammett's hero's ultimate answer to Brand's question of how he plans "to go about purifying our village" is, by the novel's end, to wash Personville in blood until it is "all nice and clean" (57, 134). The line between law and crime is deliberately rubbed out by Hammett, who consistently figures the detective as the most violent, bloodthirsty presence in a city where municipal reform is made synonymous with the expunging of immigrants and criminalized working-class culture. The inability of newspaper exposés to uproot urban crime in the 1920s and the 1930s is what led, in part, to the period's sociological studies of criminality. In arguing for "the application of business methods and scientific procedure," these studies were calling into question the efficacy of reform-minded journalism. *Organized Crime in Chicago* made this point clear by classifying "the many exposures of vice, gambling, bootlegging, and graft, and . . . [the] series of earnest and determined civic crusades that have been launched against the rule of the underworld" all "failure[s]" (Landesco 278, 279). The hardboiled novel makes a similar assessment in its portrayal of newspaper journalism as ineffectual, bourgeois, and effete. The "newspapers were good for nothing except to hash things up so nobody could unhash them again," the Op says as he finishes the job Donald Willsson was unable to complete (123). Yet as quickly produced and widely circulated responses to news headlines, the hardboiled novel itself functioned as a sensational exposé of crime, a fitting role given that crime literature developed out of the nineteenth-century broadsheet.[15]

When Herbert Asbury, author of *The Gangs of New York: An Informal History of the Underworld* (1928), favorably reviewed *Red Harvest* in 1929, he declared, "It reads like the latest news from Chicago" (1). Asbury undoubtedly had in mind the late 1920s newspaper exposés of bootlegging and gangland murder, rather than the news offered by *Delinquency Areas* and the *Illinois Crime Survey,* both of which had taken Chicago as their privileged (or infamous) site of study. Suffering at the hands of successive and competing organized criminal factions and pervasive political corruption, Chicago in the 1920s emerged in the national imaginary as a symbol of rampant urban violence in a wide-open town. The criminologists and crime historians, Dennis Kenney and James Finckenauer estimate that by the mid-1920s there were "10,000 professional criminals . . . at work in Chicago" (130). Others speculate that upwards of sixty percent of Chicago's police department was actively engaged in bootlegging (Panek 99). Much like the crime wave in *Red Harvest,* Chicago's crime wave between 1923 and 1926 was triggered by renewed efforts to suppress the illicit circuit of profit in prohibited alcohol. The law and order campaign of Mayor William Dever—who had ousted the publicly corrupt administration of William Thompson—sparked Chicago's infamous beer wars, which in the end left 365 dead. "Where the Thompson administration," Kenney and Finckenauer recall, "had permitted an occasional gun battle, full-scale guerrilla warfare now existed" (126). In retrospect, *Red Harvest*'s appeal to the new methods of federal law enforcement proved to be prescient. The arrest of Al Capone in 1931 was obtained not through a shoot-out, but by a careful review of his income tax statements. The collecting and sorting of information won out over sheer brute force. The final demise of the most publicly visible aspects of Chicago's organized crime came in 1933 with Repeal, which relegalized the production of alcohol and placed it under the jurisdiction of the states, which began intensely regulating and taxing its distribution and consumption for their own profits.

While for Asbury *Red Harvest* represented all the latest news about bourgeois crime-fighting tactics in Chicago, for Hammett's working-class reader the text's red mountain town of Personville most likely would have called to mind the aforementioned traumatic repression of union workers in Butte, Montana, a decade earlier. Understanding the possible receptions of *Red Harvest*—or of the hardboiled novel more generally—is essential for detailing the way in which its representation of modern power was consumed by different readers. In its conflation of working-class space with organized crime, *Red Harvest* reveals its commitment to bourgeois law, but it simultaneously problematizes this commitment by foregrounding the fundamental, explosive violence that is produced by the law's repression of working-class life. The hardboiled detective novel's fraught relationship to class and power originates in the historically contested relations that the profession of private detection had to negotiate. Recruited from the ranks of the working class, private detectives—especially during America's bloodiest years of labor strife from 1880-1930—regularly were hired by railroads, factories, and mining companies to break strikes through violence and intimidation or to infiltrate unions and destroy them from within. As Harring recounts it, striking workers were denounced repeatedly as "criminals" and "viewed as part of the criminal classes," a fact that reveals how power has historically deployed and shifted the category and definition of criminality to suit its own ends (143). Of all the detective agencies responsible for crushing unions, none was more effective than the Pinkerton Detective Agency, which for years had employed Hammett as an agent. Pinkerton's agents had helped fight dozens of strikes, most notably the McCormick strike of 1885, the Homestead strike of 1892, and the Pullman strike of 1894. As a Pinkerton assigned in 1917 to disrupt the union activities of the I.W.W. in Butte, Hammett had been offered five thousand dollars to murder strike leader Frank Little, which he refused to do. Little was subsequently lynched by masked vigilantes widely suspected to be Pinkerton detectives.[16] The incident arguably was a turning pointing for Hammett who for the rest of his life devoted himself to leftist causes.

The parallel moment in *Red Harvest*—the breaking of the I.W.W. strike at Elihu's mine—transpires before the narrative even begins, but overshadows everything that follows. "The strike lasted eight months. . . . When the last skull had been cracked, the last rib kicked in, organized labor in Personville was a used firecracker," Bill Quint says (7). For Hammett's working-class readers in 1929, the "strikebreakers" and hired "gunmen" certainly would have been understood to be former private detectives.[17] In *Red Harvest,* the original offer of five thousand dollars to murder Frank Little is reimagined as ten thousand dollars to kill off the men who lynched him. Published in a year that saw 921 strikes involving more than 288,000 workers (Peterson 21), *Red Harvest* can be read, and undoubtedly was read by some of its working-class readers, as a revenge narrative in which one representative of law rights a historic wrong by orchestrating a war between other representatives of law who are guilty of the text's original crime, the violent destruction of Personville's I.W.W. union.[18] In this light, *Red Harvest* becomes a narrative of a "'savage war'" between private cops (Slotkin 12), rather than between various factions of the city's underworld.

Under different circumstances, the war in *Red Harvest*'s frontier city might have led to what Slotkin calls a *"regeneration through violence"* and the birth of an uncorrupted democratic sphere (12). But Hammett's cynical novel forestalls this utopian possibility. Much like the bureaucratic and scientific interventions in the 1920s, Hammett's narrative moves through the spaces in the urban field that had been labeled the "breeding places" of the criminal underworld and reinforces the impression that in these spaces originates a modality of life that is criminal and contagious. But unlike these discourses, Hammett's text destabilizes what constitutes criminal behavior both "in its individual and organized forms" (Landesco 283). If at the text's very end the Op's juridical status is—negatively formulated—"no longer officially a criminal," then it remains unanswered what his positive status is. Is he a free and legal, law-abiding subject? Is he officially a representative of law and unofficially a criminal? And for that matter, has the

law produced both the organized urban criminality he suppresses and the criminal methods by which he stamps out crime to make the city "all nice and clean"? The text also blurs the definition of what does and doesn't constitute organized criminality. Certainly the network established by *Red Harvest*'s bootleggers and gamblers is organized and criminal, but historically the definition of organized crime would have included the strike tactics of the text's I.W.W. workers who were, Bill Quint remembers, "advised the old sabotage racket, staying on the job and gumming things up from the inside" as part of their struggle against Elihu (7). For its part, the nationwide agency for which the Op works is based on a historical model that possessed a laundry list of offenses rivaling that of the era's organized crime networks. And yet this list pales when compared against the harassment and intimidation perpetrated by the Bureau of Investigation under its scientific manager, J. Edgar Hoover.

Ultimately the Op works for the person who can afford to pay for his services, Elihu, the text's industrial capitalist. Hence the first-person narrative the Op voices serves his interests. As Freedman and Kendrick observe, the Op is in the end obligated both to "the economic law of profit [which] requires that the Continental Detective Agency act in the interests of its clients" and to "the letter of bourgeois legality" (18). The Op "breaks" the strikebreakers and returns to Elihu a broken city that is purged of underworld criminals, but also free of the networks that had produced the city's alcohol. In the end, it remains unclear whether Elihu will exploit these new openings in the market and become further enriched by establishing himself as Personville's source of criminalized working-class pleasure or whether he'll suppress production of alcohol so as to extract greater efficiency from his unionless workers. In circulating a dire portrait of the plight of the urban working class, *Red Harvest* does not vindicate the forces of industrial capitalism that emerge victorious from its narrative. Rather, the news that it brings to its reader is the extent to which industrial capitalism is undergirded by the law's organized and systematic repression of the activities of working-class production and consumption. The crimes committed by Hammett's private detective disclose the violence of law, but also work to eliminate the working-class and ethnic criminality that impedes the efforts of the text's bourgeois character to amass capital. In disclosing this truth, *Red Harvest* erases the distinction between law and criminality that was vital to the legitimization of the moralistic bourgeois sociology of the 1920s and 1930s and that continues to be vital to the bourgeois accumulation that the law seeks to advance. In an era when the official discourse of criminology repeatedly singled out the poor and working-class neighborhoods of the city as the source of crime, Hammett's text implies that the whole city will "go to the dogs again" if the true origins of crime—systemic political corruption, economic exploitation, state-sponsored violence—are not uncovered. The absence of this kind of investigation in *Red Har-*

vest suggests that the roots of crime will remain a mystery, one which will go unsolved by the city's new "white-collar soldiers."

Notes

1. As it turns out, Donald was murdered by Robert Albury, a poor assistant bank clerk in love with the femme fatale Dinah Brand. Albury spies Donald entering her apartment one night. Mistakenly suspecting that Donald is another of Brand's lovers and humiliated over his inability to compete with a wealthier man for her affections, Albury shoots him. The narrative thread surrounding Willsson and Albury comes to a quick finish—the Op solves the murder within the first third of the novel—and primarily serves to dramatize the class tensions that structure and destroy all personal relationships in the city. These tensions are magnified, if still implicit, in the largely unspoken agon between Donald and his villainous father, Elihu.

2. The phenomenon of organized criminal gangs is perhaps as old as urban culture itself. But prior to Prohibition, the territoriality of urban gangs tended to be narrowly circumscribed by neighborhood. While criminologists differ over the constituent features that define "organized crime," most view the phenomenon as a process or an activity, rather than a fixed, localizable entity. In a definition broad enough to account for historical changes in the patterns of organized criminality, Peter A. Lupsha singles out its central attributes as a sustained interaction by a group of individuals, who employ violence or the threat of violence and corruption of public officials in order secure a long-term accumulation of capital through the exploitation of market disparities between supply and demand that are created by government over- or under-regulation (33, 34).

3. What is today known as the FBI grew out of the Bureau of Investigation (1908-34), which was renamed in 1934 as the Division of Investigation and which, in 1935, assumed its current denomination. For an excellent history of the transformations in federal law enforcement, see Claire Bond Potter's *War on Crime: Bandits, G-Men, and the Politics of Mass Culture.*

4. Municipal police departments were first organized and professionalized with the massive influx of immigrants to urban centers in the mid to late nineteenth century. The campaign to discipline the use of urban space by nonnormative populations in the early twentieth century included harassment of gay and lesbian populations in places such as New York's Greenwich Village in the 1910s and the infiltration and disruption of the organizing efforts of communists and radical (usually immigrant) unionists during World War I. As Potter notes, the public image of the Bureau of Investigation in the 1920s was that of "a disgraced unit of Red-baiters" (3). Upon his promotion to Director, J. Edgar Hoover transformed the Bureau of Investigation by replacing the overtly brutal suppression of political dissent with more scientific methods, which consisted primarily of collecting information on radicals.

5. In addition to Hammett's *Red Harvest,* the period saw the publication of dozens of other hardboiled novels, including W. R. Burnett's *Little Caesar* (1929), Carroll John Daly's *The Hidden Hand* (1929) and *The Tag Murders* (1930), and Paul Cain's *Fast One* (1932).

6. Published in 1929, *Red Harvest* is not the first hardboiled crime story. That honor belongs to Carroll John Daly's "The False Burton Combs" (1922).

7. Foucault goes on to state that "[d]elinquency functions as a political observatory" (281). Describing how delinquency produces this observatory, Foucault remarks that "[p]olice surveillance provides the prison with offenders, which the prison transforms into delinquents, the targets and auxiliaries of police supervisions, which regularly send back a certain number of them to prison" (282). I argue that the study of organized crime in the 1920s and 1930s was, for all intents and purposes, a study of poor, immigrant, and working-class men and women who were labeled delinquent populations.

8. Dennis Porter argues that the "mission" of the detective novel "involves the celebration of the repressive state apparatus or at least of that important element of it formed by the police" (121). Along similar lines, Ernest Mandel contends that "bourgeois ideology['s] . . . privileged expression in the field of literature is the crime story" (109). While recognizing its conservatism, the recent critical engagements by Erin Smith and Sean McCann have presented a more nuanced portrait of the hardboiled genre's politics.

9. Since Hammett's first-person novel begins with the Op's arrival, the narrative is tainted from the start by his presence. But what Personville was like before the Op can be discerned in the way illegal drinking and gambling are represented as aspects of everyday life. The relative peace of Personville is implied too by the Police Chief's nauseated reaction to the crime wave the Op unleashes.

10. Ward Churchill and Jim Vander Wall note that the Department of Justice frequently retained personnel from the Pinkerton agency until Congress prohibited the practice in 1892 (17).

11. In 1930, the Bureau launched a campaign to fingerprint all Americans, which it advertised on the cover of the magazine *Feds* with banners that

asked "ARE YOUR FINGER PRINTS ON FILE? How J. Edgar Hoover's F.B.I. Can Help You Protect Yourself and Your Family"; see Churchill and Wall (11, 25, 27). By 1974, the Division of Identification and Information had gathered the prints of approximately 159,000,000 Americans. By the 1920s, the General Intelligence Division had assembled 450,000 personal files on Americans, a collection that had grown to approximately 20 million by the 1980s.

12. See Daniel Bell's *The End of Ideology* for an analysis of what he terms "the myth of crime waves" (151). Bell convincingly argues that the *UCR* consistently inflated its crime statistics by, among other things, using older census figures for the basis of calculating per capita rates of current criminal offenses.

13. Harring's study investigates the historical role of the police in the regulation and repression of working-class culture. Hardly a neutral arbiter of justice, the police, he argues, are an ideological state apparatus that serves to protect and advance bourgeois interests through the unique position afforded them, namely, the legitimate use of violence and coercion. Wishing to avoid a crude instrumentalist notion of state power, though, Harring contends the tensions within police departments between working-class, immigrant officers and their duty to uphold bourgeois interests (such as to protect property from striking workers), make the police department a site of class struggle as well as an instrument against the struggles of the working class.

14. David E. Ruth reinforces Harring's claims about the anxiety experienced by the white, middle class living in the midst of rapid demographic, social, and economic change in urban America. Ruth writes,

> Especially in the first two decades of the new century, middle-class men and women combined professional organization with political and social activism to impose their vision of order on the apparent chaos of the new urban, industrial society. These progressives marshaled bureaucratic organization, expert management, and the creed of efficiency to construct social institutions that would regulate otherwise dangerous urban phenomena: huge corporations, impersonal markets, and unprecedented concentrations of workers and immigrants. Issues that commanded middle-class attention—from public health, to the assimilation of immigrants, to housing, labor, and civil-service reform—were pieces of the era's most challenging puzzle. How to live in the city?
>
> (6-7)

15. In *Discipline and Punish,* Foucault theorizes that law produces the criminal subject who in turn produces not only crime, but "an enormous mass of 'crime stories'" (286).

16. See Diane Johnson's biography of Hammett (esp. 20, 21); see also Churchill and Vander Wall (19).

17. In tracing the genealogy of the hardboiled detective to the frontier Indian-killer, Slotkin suggests that "In the 'detective story' the 'man who knows Indians' is replaced by a 'man who knows strikers'" (126). Slotkin goes on to argue that the hardboiled detective figure was often based on the real-life actions of Pinkerton detectives. Given Hammett's years of experience as a Pinkerton, this is almost certainly the case in *Red Harvest*. Pinkerton was a writer too, the author of *The Mollie Maguires and the Detectives* (1877) and *Strikers, Communists, Tramps and Detectives* (1877). Of the former Slotkin comments, it was "a pattern-setter for the genre: it follows a clear narrative line and centers on the adventures of a single heroic detective whose persona is carefully built up as a model of the anti-labor detective as hero" (141).

18. For an early record of strikes in America in the 1910s, see Jay Lovestone's 1923 study, *The Government Strikebreaker: A Study of the Role of the Government in the Recent Industrial Crisis.* For a historical account of the use of police officers as strikebreakers, see Sidney Harring's *Policing a Class Society: The Experience of American Cities, 1865-1915* (esp. 101-48).

Works Cited

Asbury, Herbert. Rev. of *Red Harvest,* by Dashiell Hammett. *The Critical Response to Dashiell Hammett.* Ed. Chris Metress. Westport, CT: Greenwood, 1994. 1-2.

Bell, Daniel. *The End of Ideology: On the Exhaustion of Political Ideas in the Fifties.* New York: Free P, 1967.

Churchill, Ward, and Jim Vander Wall. *Agents of Repression: The FBI's Secret Wars Against the Black Panther Party and the American Indian Movement.* 1988. Cambridge, MA: South End, 2002.

Committee on Uniform Crime Records, International Assoc. of Chiefs of Police. *Uniform Crime Reporting: A Complete Manual for Police.* New York: Little and Ives, 1929.

Foucault, Michel. *Discipline and Punish: The Birth of the Prison.* Trans. Alan Sheridan. New York: Vintage, 1979.

Freedman, Carl, and Christopher Kendrick. "Forms of Labor in Dashiell Hammett's *Red Harvest.*" *The Critical Response to Dashiell Hammett.* Ed. Christopher Metress. Westport, CT: Greenwood, 1994. 12-30.

Hammett, Dashiell. *Red Harvest.* 1929. *Five Complete Novels.* New York: Wings Books, 1965. 3-142.

Harring, Sidney L. *Policing a Class Society: The Experience of American Cities, 1865-1915.* New Brunswick: Rutgers UP, 1983.

Illinois Assoc. for Criminal Justice. *Illinois Crime Survey.* Chicago: Assoc. for Criminal Justice and the Chicago Crime Commission, 1929.

Janowitz, Morris. Introduction. *The City.* By Robert E. Park, Ernest W. Burgess, and Roderick D. McKenzie. Chicago: U of Chicago P, 1967. vii-x.

Johnson, Diane. *Dashiell Hammett: A Life.* New York: Fawcett, 1983.

Kenney, Dennis, and James Finckenauer. *Organized Crime in America.* Belmont, CA: Wadsworth, 1995.

Landesco, John. *Organized Crime in Chicago: Part III of the Illinois Crime Survey.* 1929. Chicago: U of Chicago P, 1968.

Lovestone, Jay. *The Government Strikebreaker: A Study of the Role of the Government in the Recent Industrial Crisis.* New York: Workers Party of America, 1923.

Lupsha, Peter A. "Organized Crime in the United States." *Organized Crime: A Global Perspective.* Ed. Robert J. Kelly. New York: Rowman, 1986. 32-58.

Mandel, Ernest. *Delightful Murder: A Social History of the Crime Story.* Minneapolis: U of Minnesota P, 1986.

Marcus, Steve. "Dashiell Hammett." *The Poetics of Murder: Detective Fiction and Literary Theory.* Ed. Glenn W. Most and William W. Stowe. San Diego: Harcourt, 1983. 197-209.

McCann, Sean. *Gumshoe America: Hard-boiled Crime Fiction and the Rise and Fall of New Deal Liberalism.* Durham: Duke UP, 2000.

Panck, LeRoy Lad. *Probable Cause: Crime Fiction in America.* Bowling Green, OH: Bowling Green State U Popular P, 1990.

Park, Robert E., Ernest W. Burgess, and Roderick D. McKenzie. *The City.* 1925. Chicago: U of Chicago P, 1967.

Peterson, Florence. *Strikes in the United States: 1880-1936.* Bureau of Labor Statistics, Department of Labor, Bulletin No. 651. Washington, DC: GPO, 1937.

Porter, Dennis. *The Pursuit of Crime: Art and Ideology in Detective Fiction.* New Haven: Yale UP, 1981.

Potter, Claire Bond. *War on Crime: Bandits, G-Men, and the Politics of Mass Culture.* New Brunswick: Rutgers UP, 1998.

Ruth, David E. *Inventing the Public Enemy: The Gangster in American Culture, 1918-1934.* Chicago: U of Chicago P, 1996.

Shaw, Clifford R. *Delinquency Areas: A Study of the Geographic Distribution of School Truants, Juvenile Delinquents, and Adult Offenders in Chicago.* Chicago: U of Chicago P, 1929.

Slotkin, Richard. *Gunfighter Nation: The Myth of the Frontier in Twentieth-Century America.* New York: Atheneum, 1992.

Smith, Erin A. *Hardboiled: Working-Class Readers and Pulp Magazines.* Philadelphia: Temple UP, 2000.

United States. Dept. of Justice. Bureau of Investigation. *Uniform Crime Reports.* Washington, DC: GPO, 1930.

———. US National Commission on Law Observance and Enforcement. *Report on the Causes of Crime: Volume I and II.* Washington, DC: GPO, 1931.

FURTHER READING

Bibliography

Layman, Richard. *Dashiell Hammett: A Descriptive Bibliography,* Pittsburgh: University of Pittsburgh Press, 1979, 185 p.

A descriptive bibliography of the works of Dashiell Hammett.

Biographies

Hammett, Jo. *Dashiell Hammett: A Daughter Remembers,* edited by Richard Layman with Julie M. Rivett, New York: Carroll & Graf Publishers, 2001, 172 p.

A memoir from the perspective of Dashiell Hammett's daughter.

Hellman, Lillian. Introduction to *The Dashiell Hammett Story Omnibus,* by Dashiell Hammett, pp. vii-xxi. London: Cassell, 1966.

In an introduction to a collection of Hammett's stories, Hellman recalls moments in the life of the author.

Layman, Richard. *Shadow Man: The Life of Dashiell Hammett,* New York: Harcourt Brace Jovanovich, 1981, 285 p.

A book-length biography of Dashiell Hammett.

Mellen, Joan. *Hellman and Hammett: The Legendary Passion of Lillian Hellman and Dashiell Hammett,* New York: HarperCollins Publishers, 1996, 572 p.

A book-length study of the personal and professional relationship between Lillian Hellman and Dashiell Hammett.

Nolan, William F. *Hammett: A Life at the Edge,* New York: Congdon & Weed, Inc., 1983, 276 p.

A book-length biography of Dashiell Hammett that includes some of his letters, interviews, public statements, and memoirs.

Skinner, Robert E. "Introduction: In the Tradition of Hammett, Chandler, and Macdonald." In *The Hard-Boiled Explicator: A Guide to the Study of Dashiell Hammett, Raymond Chandler, and Ross Macdonald,* pp. 1-24. Metuchen, N.J.: Scarecrow Press, 1985.

Recounts biographical details from Hammett's life.

Criticism

Burelbach, Frederick M. "Symbolic Naming in *The Maltese Falcon.*" *Literary Onomastics Studies* 6 (1979): 226-45.

Investigates the "multiple and ironic meanings" of character names in *The Maltese Falcon.*

Gale, Robert L. *A Dashiell Hammett Companion,* Westport, Conn.: Greenwood Press, 2000, 317 p.

References characters and provides summaries of the novels and short fiction of Dashiell Hammett.

Gregory, Sinda. *"The Thin Man*: The Detective and the Comedy of Manners." In *Private Investigations: The Novels of Dashiell Hammett,* pp. 148-73. Carbondale: Southern Illinois University Press, 1985.

Addresses differences in tone, characterization, and plot development between *The Thin Man* and Hammett's earlier novels.

Guetti, James. "Aggressive Reading: Detective Fiction and Realistic Narrative." *Raritan* 2, no. 1 (summer 1982): 133-54.

Analyzes Hammett's prose style and demonstrates how it involves the reader in the detection process.

Marling, William. "Dashiell Hammett: Copywriter." In *The American Roman Noir: Hammett, Cain, and Chandler,* pp. 93-147. Athens: University of Georgia Press, 1995.

Demonstrates how *Red Harvest* and *The Maltese Falcon* reflect the historical and social atmosphere, as well as the aesthetic trends, of the 1920s and 1930s.

Nolan, William F. "Behind the *Mask*: Dashiell Hammett." In *The Black Mask Boys: Masters in the Hard-Boiled School of Detective Fiction,* pp. 75-93. New York: William Morrow and Company, Inc., 1985.

Discusses Hammett's influence on the detective genre and his association during the 1920s and 1930s with *Black Mask,* a magazine devoted to the publication of hard-boiled detective fiction.

———. Introduction to *Nightmare Town Stories,* by Dashiell Hammett, edited by Kirby McCauley, Martin H. Greenberg, and Ed Gorman, pp. vii-xvii. New York: Alfred A. Knopf, 1999.

Asserts that in his tales written mostly for *Black Mask* Hammett "launched a new style of detective fiction in America: bitter, tough, and unsentimental, reflecting the violence of the time."

Panek, LeRoy Lad. "Making the Continental Op." In *Reading Early Hammett: A Critical Study of the Fiction Prior to* The Maltese Falcon, pp. 69-120. Jefferson, N.C.: McFarland & Company, Inc., Publishers, 2004.

Chronicles the development and significant characteristics of Hammett's detective hero, the Continental Op.

Pierpont, Claudia Roth. "Tough Guy: The Mystery of Dashiell Hammett." *New Yorker* 77, no. 47 (February 11 2002): 66-75.

Recounts events from Hammett's life and his literary achievements.

Skenazy, Paul. *The New Wild West: The Urban Mysteries of Dashiell Hammett and Raymond Chandler,* Boise, Idaho: Boise State University, 1982, 52 p.

Explores Hammett's development of character and plot in his novels, particularly *Red Harvest, The Glass Key,* and *The Maltese Falcon.*

Additional coverage of Hammett's life and career is contained in the following sources published by Thomson Gale: *American Writers Supplement,* **Vol. 4;** *Authors and Artists for Young Adults,* **Vol. 59;** *Authors in the News,* **Vol. 1;** *Beacham's Encyclopedia of Popular Fiction: Biography & Resources,* **Vol. 2;** *Concise Dictionary of American Literary Biography: 1929-1941; Contemporary Authors,* **Vols. 81-84;** *Contemporary Authors New Revision Series,* **Vol. 42;** *Contemporary Literary Criticism,* **Vols. 3, 5, 10, 19, 47;** *Dictionary of Literary Biography,* **Vols. 226, 280;** *Dictionary of Literary Biography Documentary Series,* **Vol. 6;** *Dictionary of Literary Biography Yearbook,* **1996;** *DISCovering Authors 3.0; Encyclopedia of World Literature in the 20th Century,* **Ed. 3;** *Literature and Its Times,* **Vol. 3;** *Literature Resource Center; Major 20th-Century Writers,* **Eds. 1, 2;** *Major 21st-Century Writers; Modern American Literature,* **Ed. 5;** *Mystery and Suspense Writers; Novels for Students,* **Vol. 21;** *Reference Guide to American Literature,* **Ed. 4;** *Reference Guide to Short Fiction,* **Ed. 2;** *St. James Guide to Crime & Mystery Writers,* **Vol. 4;** *Short Story Criticism,* **Vol. 17;** **and** *Twayne's United States Authors.*

Shirley Jackson
1919?-1965

American novelist, short story writer, children's writer, playwright, and nonfiction writer.

The following entry provides an overview of Jackson's life and works. For additional information on her career, see *CLC,* Volumes 11, 60, and 87.

INTRODUCTION

Although she wrote in various forms and styles, Shirley Jackson is remembered today primarily as a leading contributor to the modern gothic genre in contemporary fiction. She is best known for her short story "The Lottery," a widely anthologized work that explores the darker aspects of human nature. Much of Jackson's "gothic" fiction, which has been praised for its spare, unadorned style, deals with deep psychological issues such as isolation and prejudice, and borrows elements from the traditional gothic horror formula. Recent scholarship, however, has focused on both the versatility and complexity of Jackson's fiction. In an essay written in 2005, James Egan argued that "to examine the interacting narrative structures in Jackson's work is to discover how expertly she manipulates rhetorical and genre conventions to achieve rich thematic permutations and tonal effects, ranging from domestically comic scenarios like those of Jean Kerr and Erma Bombeck; to mainstream, conventional satires of manners such as Sinclair Lewis might have written; to the metaphysically fantastic idioms of Nathanael West and Franz Kafka."

BIOGRAPHICAL INFORMATION

Jackson was born December 14, 1919, in San Francisco, California (though some accounts give her birth year as 1916). She spent much of her childhood, however, in Burlingame, California, with her parents, Leslie Hardie and Geraldine Bugbee Jackson. She developed an interest in writing at an early age and kept journals and wrote poetry throughout her childhood. In the early 1930s, Jackson's family moved to Rochester, New York, and in 1934, Jackson enrolled in the University of Rochester. Although she withdrew from the university after two years in order to devote her time to writing, she later returned to college and attended Syracuse University from 1938 to 1940. During her college years, she continued writing and was published in various campus

magazines. Jackson also met Stanley Edgar Hyman at Syracuse, and together they founded a campus magazine called *The Spectre.* They married after graduation, in 1940, and moved to New York City. Jackson's first national publication occurred in 1941, when her short story "My Life with R. H. Macy" was published in *The New Republic.* She lived in New York City for five years and continued writing and publishing short stories. In 1945, Jackson and her family moved to Bennington, Vermont, where Hyman had been given a teaching position. In 1948, Jackson's most famous short story, "The Lottery," was published in the *New Yorker.* That same year, she published her first novel, *The Road through the Wall.* In 1949, she published her first short story collection, *The Lottery; or, The Adventures of James Harris.*

During the 1950s, Jackson continued writing short stories and published several novels, including *Hangsaman* (1951) and *The Bird's Nest* (1954), as well as *The Witchcraft of Salem Village* (1956), a book for children. Though much of her serious fiction explores darker themes, Jackson also wrote humorous sketches for publication in various women's magazines, including *Good Housekeeping* and *Mademoiselle.* Some of these sketches were later collected and published in *Life among the Savages* (1953) and *Raising Demons* (1957). During the late 1950s and early 1960s, Jackson wrote two of her most acclaimed novels, *The Haunting of Hill House* (1959) and her last complete novel, *We Have Always Lived in the Castle* (1962), which was nominated for the National Book Award. During her writing career, Jackson suffered from numerous health problems and anxiety. She remained active, however, in the last years of her life, traveling and presenting lectures at writer's conferences and colleges. Jackson died of heart failure at the age of forty-six, on August 8, 1965. An unfinished novel, *Come along with Me,* and three lectures, including "Biography of a Story" and "Notes for a Young Writer," which discuss the art of writing, were published posthumously together in 1968.

MAJOR WORKS

Loneliness and alienation are predominant themes in *The Haunting of Hill House.* In the novel, research participants gather at the allegedly haunted "Hill House" to take part in a psychological study conducted by Dr. Montague. Among the participants is Eleanor Vance, a shy, lonely woman with strong psychic abilities. Although the house fills Eleanor with a sense of foreboding, she is also drawn to it, partly out of a desire to belong somewhere. The other participants, like many of Jackson's characters, are only superficially kind and eventually reveal their self-centeredness. The theme of isolation becomes more pronounced as the novel progresses; by the story's end, Eleanor is completely alienated from the other characters. Jackson also explores the process of mental and emotional disintegration through her characterization of Eleanor. The spirits that haunt the house concentrate their efforts on Eleanor because she is the most vulnerable member of the group. The combination of the supernatural events and her own feelings of guilt culminate in her complete mental breakdown, as she retreats from reality through the course of the book.

Jackson explores the familiar themes of isolation and female victimization in *We Have Always Lived in the Castle,* which some critics consider her finest novel. The novel revolves around two sisters, Constance and Merricat, who are surviving members of the Blackwood family, four of whom died from arsenic poisoning. The sisters are regarded with suspicion and contempt in the community, despite the fact that Constance was acquitted of killing her family. Jackson wrote the novel in first-person narrative form, from the perspective of Merricat, who is revealed as the actual murderer. The book has often been praised for its sympathetic portrayal of the mentally disturbed Merricat, who cannot accurately perceive right and wrong and therefore lives in a kind of innocence. A fierce loyalty exists between the two sisters, despite Constance's suspicions of her sister's guilt, and the community's capacity for hatred is drawn in sharp contrast to their devotion. When the house burns down at the end of the story, neighbors who have come to extinguish the fire are tempted to further vandalize the dwelling. The alienation of the two sisters is complete at the end of the novel, when they barricade themselves in the kitchen. Jackson justifies their dependence on one another by illustrating the inhospitable world that surrounds them.

Many critics consider "The Lottery," which was later collected with other short stories in *The Lottery; or, The Adventures of James Harris,* Jackson's masterpiece and the culminating articulation of her most important themes as a writer. The tranquil and small-town setting belies a history of brutality for the townspeople, who participate in an annual ritualistic sacrifice of a member of their community, chosen through a lottery system. Among the most striking features of the story is the tension between the surface congeniality of the townspeople and their latent ability to commit violence. The incongruity is accentuated by Jackson's spare writing style and neutral narrative tone. While some critics have interpreted the events of the story as a critique of

capitalist society, others have emphasized the feminist subtext and its negative portrayal of a patriarchal social system. Many have also noted the story's commentary on ritual and tradition, as well as society's need for a scapegoat through which it can purge its own sins by a sacrificial act. Many of the other stories collected in *The Lottery; or, The Adventures of James Harris,* including "The Witch," "The Renegade," and "Pillar of Salt," illustrate the prejudices that govern human behavior, as well as humankind's capacity for evil and violence.

CRITICAL RECEPTION

While Jackson's first novel, *The Road through the Wall,* received moderate praise when it was published in 1948, it wasn't until "The Lottery" appeared in the *New Yorker* later that same year that her reputation was established. The story's bleak depiction of humankind's evil nature prompted intense reaction from readers and critics alike. The *New Yorker* received hundreds of outraged letters and phone calls from readers who were bewildered by the story's meaning, though a number of reviewers lauded Jackson for her ability to blur the lines between reality and fantasy, and for her deft interweaving of religious symbolism in the narrative. Despite the notoriety of "The Lottery," many critics regard *The Haunting of Hill House* as Jackson's most accomplished work. Here, commentators agree, Jackson successfully fused a tale of supernatural terror with a critique of female submission to the domestic ideal. As Bernice M. Murphy asserted, "The book has all the familiar trappings of the traditional haunted house tale . . . but the real horror lies perhaps in the fact that a lonely, unmarried woman like Eleanor is so out of place in a society that can only project one particular path for a young woman—that of wife and mother—that she becomes the perfect victim."

Despite the overt feminist subtext running through several of Jackson's novels, feminist scholars—and the literary community in general—gradually lost interest in Jackson's work in the decades following her death in 1965. In his 2003 study, Darryl Hattenhauer attributed this neglect to the changing tastes of feminist critics, stating that in the twenty years after Jackson's death, "American feminists privileged realism over postmodernism, and looked for role models rather than victims." Other commentators tended to regard Jackson primarily as an entertainer and a storyteller, a writer who could spin a dark yarn or humor her audience with comical renditions of the mundane, but whose writing did not merit serious critical attention. In recent years, scholars have offered a decidedly different assessment of Jackson's contributions as an artist. According to Hattenhauer, "Jackson's reputation should be restored to the lofty position it occupied during her life. The main rea-

son for this recuperation is that her writing is more varied and complex than critics have realized. She deserves recuperation not for her few works that readers
have simplified as horror. Rather, she should be included with many of the other canonical writers of her
time for many of the same reasons they are: she excels
in a number of forms and themes." Ranging from dark
and pessimistic to comically ordinary, Jackson's gift for
storytelling, as well as her nuanced treatment of character, has both delighted and perplexed readers for nearly
half a century. As her husband and noted literary critic
Stanley Edgar Hyman concluded, "I think that the future will find [Jackson's] powerful visions of suffering
and inhumanity increasingly significant and meaningful,
and that Shirley Jackson's work is among that small
body of literature produced in our time that seems apt
to survive."

PRINCIPAL WORKS

The Road through the Wall (novel) 1948
The Lottery; or, The Adventures of James Harris (short
   stories) 1949; also published as *The Lottery and
   Other Stories*, 1991
Hangsaman (novel) 1951
Life among the Savages (nonfiction) 1953
The Bird's Nest (novel) 1954
The Witchcraft of Salem Village (juvenilia) 1956
Raising Demons (nonfiction) 1957
The Sundial (novel) 1958
The Bad Children: A Play in One Act for Bad Children
   (play) 1959
The Haunting of Hill House (novel) 1959
We Have Always Lived in the Castle (novel) 1962
9 Magic Wishes (juvenilia) 1963
Famous Sally (juvenilia) 1966
The Magic of Shirley Jackson [edited by Stanley Edgar
   Hyman] (short stories and novels) 1966
*Come along with Me: Part of a Novel, Sixteen Stories,
   and Three Lectures* [edited by Stanley Edgar Hy-
   man] (unfinished novel, short stories, and lectures)
   1968
Just an Ordinary Day [edited by Laurence Jackson Hy-
   man and Sarah Hyman] (short stories) 1996
Shirley Jackson Collected Short Stories (short stories)
   2001

CRITICISM

Stanley Edgar Hyman (essay date 1966)

SOURCE: Hyman, Stanley Edgar, ed. Preface to *The
Magic of Shirley Jackson,* edited by Stanley Edgar Hyman, pp. vii-ix. New York: Farrar, Straus and Giroux,
1966.

[*In the following essay, Hyman, who was both a literary critic and husband to Shirley Jackson, offers a brief
but intimate exploration of his wife's fiction.*]

People often expressed surprise at the difference between Shirley Jackson's appearance and manner, and
the violent and terrifying nature of her fiction. Thus
many of the obituaries played up the contrast between a
"motherly-looking" woman, gentle and humorous, and
that "chillingly horrifying short story 'The Lottery'"
and similar works. When Shirley Jackson, who was my
wife, published two light-hearted volumes about the
spirited doings of our children, *Life Among the Savages* and *Raising Demons,* it seemed to surprise people
that the author of her grim and disturbing fiction should
be a wife and mother at all, let alone a gay and apparently happy one.

This seems to me to be the most elementary misunderstanding of what a writer is and how a writer works, on
the order of expecting Herman Melville to be a big
white whale. Shirley Jackson, like many writers, worked
in a number of forms and styles, and she exploited each
of them as fully as she could. When she wrote a novel
about the disintegration of a personality, *The Bird's
Nest,* it was fittingly macabre and chilling; when she
wrote a funny account of **"My Life with R. H. Macy,"**
it was fittingly uproarious. Everything she wrote was
written with absolute seriousness and integrity, with all
the craft she could muster; nothing was ever careless or
dashed off; but she did not believe that a serious purpose necessarily required a serious tone.

Shirley Jackson wrote in a variety of forms and styles
because she was, like everyone else, a complex human
being, confronting the world in many different roles and
moods. She tried to express as much of herself as possible in her work, and to express each aspect as fully
and purely as possible. While she wanted the fullest
self-expression consistent with the limits of literary
form, at the same time she wanted the widest possible
audience for that self-expression; she wanted, in short,
a public, sales, "success." For her entire adult life she
regarded herself as a professional writer, one who made
a living by the craft of writing, and as she did not see
that vocation as incompatible with being a wife and
mother, so she did not see her dedication to art as incompatible with producing art in salable forms. In this,
as in other respects, she was curiously old-fashioned.

Despite a fair degree of popularity—reviews of her
books were generally enthusiastic, reprints and foreign
publications were numerous, and her last two novels,
The Haunting of Hill House and *We Have Always
Lived in the Castle,* became modest best-sellers—Shirley Jackson's work and its nature and purpose have
been very little understood. Her fierce visions of dissociation and madness, of alienation and withdrawal, of
cruelty and terror, have been taken to be personal, even
neurotic, fantasies. Quite the reverse: they are a sensitive and faithful anatomy of our times, fitting symbols
for our distressing world of the concentration camp and
the Bomb. She was always proud that the Union of
South Africa banned **"The Lottery,"** and she felt that
they at least understood the story.

Shirley Jackson's own preferred reading was Jane Austen or Samuel Richardson. She rarely read, and did not much enjoy, Kafka and the other writers to whom she is usually compared. But she was far too honest to try to write like Miss Austen or Richardson in our fragmented and fragmenting times. If the source of her images was personal or neurotic, she transformed those images into meaningful general symbols; if she used the resources of supernatural terror, it was to provide metaphors for the all-too-real terrors of the natural. Obituary references to her in such terms as the "Virginia Werewolf of seance-fiction writers" show a considerable obliviousness to her meanings and purposes.

In her short and busy life—she died peacefully of heart failure during a nap in her forty-sixth year—Shirley Jackson nevertheless managed to publish quite a few short stories and twelve books: six novels, a volume of stories, two fictionalized memoirs, and three juveniles, one of them a play. At the time of her death she was at work on a new novel, savagely comic in tone, and a fantasy book for children. After the first years, when several interviews and radio appearances failed to satisfy her, she consistently refused to be interviewed, to explain or promote her work in any fashion, or to take public stands and be a pundit of the Sunday supplements. She believed that her books would speak for her clearly enough over the years, and I share her belief. The only exception she made to this vow of silence was a willingness, even an eagerness, to lecture about the craft of fiction at colleges and writers' conferences, where she could assume an audience with some serious interest in such matters. She was reluctant to publish those lectures, for a variety of reasons, but they include some of the few sensible and useful words I know on that impossible subject—what fiction is and how it gets made—and I believe that those lectures should and will be published.

For all her popularity, Shirley Jackson won surprisingly little recognition. She received no awards or prizes, grants or fellowships; her name was often omitted from lists on which it clearly belonged, or which it should have led. She saw these honors go to inferior writers, or to writers who were no writers, without bitterness, but with the wry amusement which was her habitual attitude toward her own life and career. Those few contemporary writers whose work she valued almost without exception knew her work in turn and valued it, and she was content with the approbation of her fellow craftsmen—in this as in so many respects she was the purest of professionals. I think that the future will find her powerful visions of suffering and inhumanity increasingly significant and meaningful, and that Shirley Jackson's work is among that small body of literature produced in our time that seems apt to survive. That thought, too, she would have found wryly amusing.

Lenemaja Friedman (essay date 1975)

SOURCE: Friedman, Lenemaja. "Overview." In *Shirley Jackson*, pp. 155-61. Boston: Twayne Publishers, 1975.

[*In the following essay, Friedman provides an overview of Jackson's work, highlighting the unusual characteristics of her fiction as well as her unique literary style.*]

I PRINCIPLES OF AND FOR A WRITER

Among Miss Jackson's non-fiction works are the essays about the craft of writing. These are significant to this study in that they embody the principles around which Miss Jackson formed her own works. Each rule is one that applies to her own stories. Three of the lectures, presented earlier at college and writers' conferences, are included in the anthology *Come Along With Me*. Of these, **"Experience and Fiction"** later appeared in the January, 1969, issue of *The Writer*. As the title implies, all experience counts for something; the writer regards the events of his life as a potential source for stories. These events may have to be manipulated and shaped, for true experiences as such seldom make good fiction. Along with this realization, she indicates several specific truths about fiction writing: ". . . no scene and no character can be allowed to wander off by itself; there must be some furthering of the story in every sentence, and even the most fleeting background characters must partake of the story in some way; they must be characters peculiar to *this* story and no other."[1]

Miss Jackson practices what she preaches, for her background characters are individuals. Mr. and Mrs. Dudley in *The Haunting of Hill House* are good examples, for they appear as eccentric as the old house of which they are caretakers. In the short story form, following this advice is more difficult, but such characters as the housekeeper in **"The Rock"** and the storekeepers in **"Home," "Renegade,"** and **"The Summer People"**—who are sources of important advice or information—show that Miss Jackson uses her characters to advantage. They are also appropriate to the surroundings in which she places them.

A second point Miss Jackson makes is that "people in stories are called characters because that is what they are. They are not real people. Therefore the writer should not try to transfer real people literally to his pages of fiction. He does not need pages and pages of description. A person in a story is identified through small things—little gestures, turns of speech, automatic reactions. . . ." (209). In the same way, Mrs. Dudley is remembered for her automatic responses to the visitors at Hill House. It should be noted that, even in the autobiographical family tales, the characters and events are heightened and shaped to conform to Miss Jackson's purposes.

Thereafter, Miss Jackson gives several instances of experiences she used in the process of creating stories. One of these is her account of how she happened to write *The Haunting of Hill House*; another is the family interview with the income-tax man, which she turned into a short story; and another involved the night that all of the family, including herself, became ill with the grippe, one of her funniest stories. This particular lecture ends with her acknowledgment of a letter from a lady in Indiana who wanted to earn some extra money. The lady, who asked where Miss Jackson got her ideas for stories and stated that she, herself, could "never make up anything good," had apparently never considered shaping her own experiences.

Another of Miss Jackson's favorite lectures is entitled **"Biography of a Story,"** and it was given in conjunction with a reading of **"The Lottery."** She presents a history of the famous short story and then a detailed account of the public reactions to it, including excerpts of letters from all over the world. The third of the lectures included in the anthology, **"Notes for a Young Writer,"** was originally intended as a stimulus for her daughter Sally; but she again cites principles exhibited in her own works. Among the "do's" and "don't's" she warns: the reader will willingly suspend disbelief for a time, but he will not suspend reason: a story is an uneasy bargain with the reader. The author's objective is to play fair and to keep the reader interested—his role is to keep reading. The writer has the right to assume that the reader will accept the story on the author's terms, but the story must have a surface tension that can be stretched but not shattered.

The story should move as naturally and easily as possible without any unnecessary side trips. The writer must *always* make the duller parts of his story work for him: "the necessary passage of time, the necessary movement must not stop the story dead, but must push it forward" (245). The writer must describe only what is necessary; his "coloring words, particularly adjectives and adverbs, must be used where they will do the most good." As has been observed previously, she, herself, uses adjectives sparingly and makes excellent use of strong nouns and verbs.) "Inanimate objects," she states, "are best described in use or motion" (246). The writer must use a great deal of economy in written speech, and he must spend time listening to people talking, noting the patterns of speech reflected in the speaking. A writer's characters must be consistent—in speech and action. Also, the would-be writer must remember that he is living in a world of people, and he must think in terms of concrete rather than abstract nouns.

He must realize that the beginning and ending of a story belong together and that the ending is implicit in the beginning. For instance, the first line of **"The Beautiful Stranger,"** which reads: "What might be called the first intimation of strangeness occurred at the railroad station," foreshadows the ending in which Margaret has lost all sense of reality and no longer knows where she is. But even **"The Lottery,"** which begins with a pleasant summer day, shows traces of tension within a few lines; and the reader (looking back) can see that the ending, surprise though it may be, has been adequately planned from the beginning.

A portrait artist selects his materials carefully; he mixes here, blends there, and focuses always on the evolving subject on his canvas; and what he chooses to include in his scheme tells much about him as an individual. In the same way, Miss Jackson has chosen to include the specific subjects that are the most meaningful to her as an artist, and her themes and the characters of her special world represent evil cloaked in seeming good; prejudice and hypocrisy, the character whose mind escapes the bounds of reality; the suspense and terror of the helpless protagonist-victim; and loneliness and frustration.

II Characteristics

The subjects she has *ignored* in presenting her material, however, may also be significant in revealing the characteristics of her work. For example, the major characters in her stories are rarely elderly; they tend to be young, often teen-agers or persons in early middle age. In *Road Through the Wall*, the focus is on the fourteen- and fifteen-year-olds of Pepper Street; in *Hangsaman*, the schizoid Natalie is seventeen and just entering college; in *The Bird's Nest*, the multiple personality of Elizabeth is in her early twenties; in *The Haunting of Hill House*, the psychic researchers are in their late twenties and early thirties; in *The Sundial*, although Mrs. Halloran is a main character, the younger persons in the household receive equal emphasis—Gloria, Maryjane, Julia, Arabella, and the ten-year-old Fancy who is to become Mrs. Halloran's heir; in *We Have Always Lived in the Castle*, Merricat is eighteen and Constance is twenty-eight. In the short stories, also, except for those cases of kind, harmless-looking grandmothers with benevolent exteriors and warped interiors, most of the protagonists are "youngish."

One sees these people most often in isolation; and, aside from the instances of social interaction that reveal prejudice, one observes them in their loneliness. They are single people; and discounting the brief glimpse into the unhappy married state of the families of *Road Through the Wall*, Miss Jackson does not deal with marital relationships. Her heroines are unmarried; and, while the early-"thirtyish" ladies in her stories may suffer from sexual frustrations (about which nothing is said), no one in all of the stories has a love affair. One finds in them no love scenes and no sexual deviates; in fact, Miss Jackson avoids sex altogether.

The characters are often concerned, instead, with establishing their own identity. The teen-agers on Pepper Street in *Road Through the Wall* are vying for attention and recognition, and rivalry also exists among the families—the Robertses, the Martins, and the Donalds—because each wants to be important in the eyes of the community. In *Hangsaman,* Natalie struggles with her insecurities; she wants to be appreciated for what she is, but the resultant Tony-Natalie conflict almost destroys her. In *The Bird's Nest,* the multiple personalities of Elizabeth fight for control until she at last becomes well and discovers who she is, thereby making friends with the past. Eleanor's stay at Hill House involves the process of seeking her own identity and her desperate need to belong somewhere; and the narrative ends with her desire to join the spirits of the house. Mrs. Halloran in *The Sundial,* after playing foully for her supremacy in the household, seeks to establish herself as a queen. Her desire is to reign over the family, but each of the other characters strives to maintain his own dignity and pride. Merricat eliminates her family, outmaneuvers Charles, and becomes her sister's protectress before she feels secure and free to be herself, not realizing that they are now doomed.

As stated previously, the Jackson world is set apart from the usual world. In the psychological stories, the reader is carried through the convolutions of the protagonist's mind—a detour from normal everyday events. In *We Have Always Lived in the Castle,* the isolation is both physical and mental. The Blackwoods are isolated from the rest of the community, but Merricat with her psychotic nature is also isolated from the normal understanding of others. The remaining novels, too, involve groups that are outside the pale of ordinary living; for example, *The Road Through the Wall* has its own milieu in Pepper Street, which the reader sees, on the one hand, as typical, but, on the other, as the very special environment of a closed society. The would-be survivors in the Halloran mansion cling together as they prepare to live in the new world, since they alone seem to have been chosen to see it; and Dr. Montague's people, isolated in Hill House, experience contact with the spirit world.

Because few close, meaningful relationships exist among her fictional people, her characters experience no deep emotions except those of fear and anxiety; no strong love; no strong anger, jealousy, or hate. The most violent moments of hatred are found in *The Bird's Nest* when two of the multiple personalities of Elizabeth battle in one scene to dominate each other and in *We Have Always Lived in the Castle* in which Merricat has in the past hated her family and now vaguely (in a psychotic state) hates the villagers, who are on the periphery of the scene. She hates and fears Charles, but the moment that the object of her hatred is removed, she is in a euphoric state, knowing that she is safe, that

no outside forces will take Constance away from her. Her relationship with Constance is closer than that of any other characters; and, because they feel secure in each other, Constance and Merricat are prepared to withstand the terrors of the outside world. The vague hatred that other characters feel appears often in the form of prejudice, like that of the villagers for the Blackwoods or of the Pepper Street families for the one Jewish family on the block. This hatred is a chronic illness in a society in which there is more hate than love.

Miss Jackson avoids ugliness or grisly realistic details of unpleasantness. When death occurs, which is seldom, it happens offstage as in *Road Through the Wall,* or is disposed of in a sentence or two as in *The Haunting of Hill House* when Eleanor crashes into the tree and as in *The Sundial* when Orianna Halloran is found lying at the bottom of the stairs. The body is carried off to rest beside the sundial on the lawn, but no unpleasant details are given. At the end of **"The Lottery,"** the reader discovers with horror what is about to happen; but the story ends with the casting of the first stones. Miss Jackson prefers to leave the sordid details to the reader's imagination.

Again one notes that there is a lack of religion or of reference to God in Miss Jackson's work: the characters struggle against loneliness, insanity, or the hatred of others, but they never call upon God for aid. God is nonexistent. Even in *The Sundial* the would-be voyagers do not see or anticipate a supernatural being. Mrs. Halloran is to be supreme ruler, and she does not intend to take orders from anyone. Fanny's father acts as a comic-ominous being who hovers about somewhere in space but has no specific authority. Only the domain of spirits manifests itself in the presence of ghosts. Beyond this manifestation, the hereafter is a big nothing, which, if not polluted already, will soon be so by contact with humans.

Many of Miss Jackson's people, the villains, lack sensitivity and an awareness of the needs of others; and, because of this lack, they intentionally or unintentionally inflict pain. Since these people are not grotesques but ordinary human beings, the discovery of evil beneath the seeming good is especially terrifying, as in **"The Lottery."** The outward grotesques are those characters who have ceased to function normally, having been trapped in a world of shadows, such as Mrs. Montague in **"Island,"** or Elizabeth in *The Bird's Nest*; but they are in most cases sympathetic if vulnerable persons.

Because Miss Jackson does not concentrate on love, on sexual relationships, or on broad social problems, her fiction differs from the popular, usual fictional fare of the day; nor does her work have any kinship to the so-called modern Gothic novels. Instead, her sphere is that of the individual involved in good and evil; therefore, her work resembles more that of a modern Hawthorne or Edgar Allan Poe. Her family tales, so different from the rest of her work, revolve around the humor that arises from the problems of daily living; and they resemble other such family chronicles as Jean Kerr's *Please Don't Eat the Daisies* or the stories of Betty MacDonald.

III ACHIEVEMENT

Delightful as Miss Jackson's humor is, and touches of it are found throughout her fiction, it is not for the family chronicles that she will be remembered although the story **"Charles"** has become a favorite with anthologists. Her most effective tale is still **"The Lottery"**; but, even if she had not written **"The Lottery,"** she would still be an important writer. Her greatest strengths are in the expert handling of humor, mystery, ambiguity, and suspense. Her wit and imagination have created off-beat and original stories. Her characters are authentic, if often strange, people; and, as the critics point out, her prose style is excellent. Why? Because her style is admirably suited to the purposes of the storyteller: she does not write long, unwieldy sentences cluttered with abstract nouns or long metaphorical passages of description; her thoughts and sentiments are not muddied through endless philosophical meanderings; there is no attempt at affectation or fussiness. Instead, she chooses a simple, unadorned direct, clear manner of speaking to her reader. Her lines flow evenly, smoothly, and have a distinct rhythm. She shows a meticulousness in word choice and a deft manipulation of words; she has a poet's ear. She has, also, an excellent sense of timing with a punch line, but more often, her sense of fun creeps into the lines and takes the reader by surprise. Her wit and imagination add sparkle to her prose.

Miss Jackson is not, however, a major writer; and the reason she will not be considered one is that she saw herself primarily as an entertainer, as an expert storyteller and craftsman. She has insights to share with her readers; but her handling of the material—the surprise twists, the preoccupation with mystery and fantasy, her avoidance of strong passions, her versatility, and her sense of sheer fun—may not be the attributes of the more serious writer who wishes to come to grips with the strong passions of ordinary people in a workaday world, who prefers to deal directly with the essential problems of love, death, war, disease, poverty, and insanity in its most ugly aspects. Even with **"The Lottery"** one wonders if Miss Jackson may have chosen the situation for its shock value. The message is, nevertheless, effective; and the story is superb, regardless of the intent of the author. Despite the lack of critical attention, her books continue to be popular with those people who are sensitive, imaginative, and fun-loving; and perhaps, in the long run, that popularity will be what counts.

Note

1. "Experience and Fiction," *Come Along With Me*, p. 208.

Selected Bibliography

PRIMARY SOURCES

1. NOVELS

The Road Through the Wall. New York: Farrar, Straus and Company, 1948.

Hangsaman. New York: Farrar, Straus and Company, 1951.

The Bird's Nest. New York: Farrar, Straus and Young, 1954.

The Sundial. New York: Farrar, Straus and Company, 1958.

The Haunting of Hill House. New York: Viking Press, 1959.

We Have Always Lived in the Castle. New York: Viking Press, 1962.

4. SHORT STORY COLLECTIONS

The Lottery, or The Adventures of James Harris. New York: Farrar, Straus and Company, 1949.

Come Along With Me. Ed. Stanley Edgar Hyman. New York: The Viking Press, 1968.

6. ARTICLES

"Experience and Fiction." *The Writer,* 82, 1 (January, 1969), 9-14, 45. (Excerpted from *Come Along With Me.*)

7. SHORT STORIES

"The Lottery." *The New Yorker,* XXIV (June 26, 1948), 25-28.

"Charles." *Mademoiselle,* XXXVI (July, 1948), 87, 114.

"Renegade." *Harper's,* CXCVII (November, 1948), 37-43.

"The Summer People." *Charm,* LXXIII, 1 (September, 1950), 108-109, 193-97.

"The Island." *New Mexico Quarterly Review,* XX, 3 (1950), 294 ff.

"Home." *Ladies' Home Journal,* LXXXII, 8 (August, 1965), 64, 116-118.

Steven K. Hoffman (essay date 1976)

SOURCE: Hoffman, Steven K. "Individuation and Character Development in the Fiction of Shirley Jackson." *Hartford Studies in Literature* 8, no. 3 (1976): 190-208.

[*In the following essay, Hoffman applies Carl Jung's theory of individuation to Shirley Jackson's fiction, including the collections* The Haunting of Hill House, The Bird's Nest, *and* We Have Always Lived in the Castle.]

Although Shirley Jackson produced in a fairly short writing career a dozen books and over one hundred short stories and sketches, critics have chosen, for the most part, to ignore her. She is best remembered as a writer of a modern form of the Goth horror story with Freudian—and Kafkaesque—overtones. Having read Miss Jackson widely, however, one is able to see beyond her skillful development of mood and atmosphere, of a nature best described as eerie or comically supernatural, to a pattern similar to that of the *Bildungsroman*. It seems that Miss Jackson does not merely offer an object lesson in the creation of suspense, but makes significant comments on the modern world and the age-old problem of the development of the self in a world that not only is not hospitable to individual development, but one which at times seems to actively combat the blossoming of the personality. Jackson's tales and novels all involve a basic struggle, that of the developing personality against external and internal forces that would arrest growth. It is this stress on the struggle for self that makes a comparison with Jung's process of individuation fruitful both as an organizing technique, and as a mark of the author's universality.

Stanley Edgar Hyman, the noted critic, has laid the basis for a new look at his wife's importance with the statement, "If the source of her images was personal or neurotic, she transformed these images into meaningful general symbols: if she used the resources of supernatural terror, it was to provide metaphors for the all-too-real terrors of the natural."[1] Compare this with C. G. Jung's remarks on literary creation:

> Should it chance that the conscious and purposeful manner of production with all its apparent consciousness of intention is nevertheless a mere subjective illusion of the poet, then his work will also possess the same symbolical qualities, passing into the indefinable and thus transcending contemporary consciousness.[2]

It appears that Jackson's work lays claim to greater notice than has been hitherto afforded it.

In employing Jung and the mythic method in an analysis of the work of any writer, one runs a great risk of overemphasizing the symbolic content of his or her writing. Hyman himself accepts the ritual and mythic approach of Jung with some reservations. Still, with Jung's claim that "the presentation of experience in symbolic form [is] the earliest and still most direct and immediate form of human expression,"[3] Hyman would most certainly agree:

> Our arts may not rival the flowering of Greece any more than our coins do, but to the extent that they can furnish us with meaningful and moving symbols they can bring mana back into a culture sadly deficient in it, and may yet save us where eagle and bison failed.[4]

It seems then that it is from her husband's researches into myth that Shirley Jackson may have evolved the ritual and symbolic mode of approach to life in the modern world that runs throughout her writing. It also may be that her use of the magical and the supernatural is an attempt to restore "mana . . . into a culture sadly deficient in it."

While Jung's theories of the collective unconscious may not appeal to Stanley Edgar Hyman, and do not, in fact, manifest themselves in the work of his wife, it seems Hyman's interest in the Jungian dynamism and process of human individation is of considerable importance. The process of human individuation and its attendant archetypes seem to be the operative principle in the writings of Shirley Jackson. There are strong parallels between Jung's conception of individuation and Jackson's idea of character development:

> Becoming a single, homogeneous being, and, in so far as "individuality" embraces our innermost, last and incomparable uniqueness, it also implies becoming one's own self. We could therefore translate individuation as "coming to selfhood" or "self-realization".[5]

In so maturing it is necessary to "break down the barriers and walls which the ego has erected between itself and the surrounding world,"[6] and also to come to terms with the unconscious strata, whether they be collective (Jungian) or personal (Freudian). The developed personality would then be in mediate relation between the conscious and the unconscious. At this point "the personality is released from emotional and intellectual entanglements. A unity of one's whole nature is experienced which is felt as a liberation."[7]

In the Jungian scheme of individuation, as reflected in Jackson, the development of the personality proceeds through a series of archetypal situations. The process initiates with a feeling of dissatisfaction with a self bound to situations (both internal and external) not of one's own making. At the point where this old center of the psyche is most untenable (the dangerous moment), the individual breaks ties with the past, identifies the separation of the self into the realms of conscious and unconscious, and moves to a new center which takes in elements of both. Along the way two major archetypes, the shadow and the animus/anima, must be encountered and objectified. Once the new center is reached, the individual is essentially reborn and the accouterments of the psyche are of his own creation. In Jackson the new, independent center is rarely reached, either because the risks involved in abandoning the old ways are too great or because society actively prevents the character from self-development. The Jackson character, usually a young girl coming of age, or an older woman verging on spinsterhood, attempts to expand outwardly, and is most often rebuffed by an indifferent or even hostile world.

In her Jungian analysis of the works of T. S. Eliot, Elizabeth Drew traces the beginnings of the individuation process "to those who have reached a dead end in the field of conscious adaptation to external experience without however achieving any sense of fulfillment" (Drew, 64). Jung places the start of the process squarely on the inadequate ego which "seems to arise in the first place from the collision between the somatic factor and the environment, and, once established as a subject, it goes on developing from further collisions with the outer world and the inner."[8] The pre-individuated individual most often has not taken the unconscious into account, and reacts only to the outer world. The dominant motif at this stage of dissatisfaction is the dominating mother figure, and, as adapted by Jackson, the house, garden, or room. The author establishes a character in a sheltered setting and develops the first pangs of uneasiness.

In a number of her works Jackson portrays a person or group of persons totally dominated by a tangible mother figure or the semi-conscious memory (and corresponding guilt feelings) of the mother. Miss Jackson's mother figure is the "terrible mother," the enslaver, the spinner of illusion. *The Sundial* mother, Mrs. Orianna Halloran, an absolute tyrant over her domain, is the probably murderer of her only son. Her reign is so dominating that one character is moved to say, "the path [out] gets narrower all the time" (p. 29). Mrs. Halloran controls all aspects of the lives of her family and guests, and even sets herself up as a monarch of the prospective survivors of an impending apocalypse. She stands for stifling and rigid order. "I want to know that I am bringing with me into that clean world a family neat, prepossessing, and well groomed" (p. 326). Under her control the other members of the sheltered community can only ineffectually bicker among themselves, but the hint of dissatisfaction with the 'queen' is firmly established.

In *The Haunting of Hill House* and *The Bird's Nest* the major characters, Eleanor Vance and Elizabeth Richmond, are dominated by a dead, grasping mother figure who, although no longer tangibly present, is the major influence in their lives. Eleanor Vance, living, in her mid-thirties, with a sister and brother-in-law, had cared for a sick mother for most of her adult life, and bears, for a momentary lapse in attention, the guilt for her parent's death. Dissatisfied with a confining and tedious life, she goes on a ghost hunt sponsored by a student of the occult, but carries with her the maternal bonds. Elizabeth Richmond, residing with an aunt and working at an unfulfilling, routine museum secretarial job, is also under the spell of a deceased mother whose memory causes the character to split into four separate personalities, all influenced by the mother image. If Elizabeth is to come to terms with her warring alter egos, she must first deal effectively with the ever-present mother.

At this stage of the individuation process Jackson employs as the primary image the enclosed house, room, or walled estate. The Halloran estate is enclosed by a wall. Similarly, Blackwood, the feudal manor of *We Have Always Lived in the Castle,* is completely surrounded by walls with a single gate for escape. Elizabeth Richmond is identified with a small office in the museum, and it is only when a wall is removed by construction work that she begins the personality split that will eventually establish her as an individual. In *Hangsaman* the college room of Natalie Waite is almost devoid of furnishings, those which are present having been borrowed from home and serve to connect her with the past. The enclosure motif, traditionally associated with the mother imago, also functions as a "representative of the different layers of the psyche."[9] Thus the general atmosphere of the enclosure is significant as an indication of the internal conditions of the characters. In these works the prevailing aura is one of solid, but gloomy and depressing domiciles. The corresponding personalities are also fairly secure, but generally morose, lacking any of the ease and cheer that one might expect from a satisfactory center of self.

The mother-dominated, enclosed existence of the typical Jackson character points to the need for some kind of escape from the "closed room [which] . . . may be symbolic of virginity . . . and also other kinds of non-communication" (Cirlot, 262). The prevailing features of the characters fit comfortably into Cirlot's analytical mode. They all suffer from a kind of psychic virginity, bound to the past, limited in experience, and almost desperate for a wider source of acquaintance. It is this drive that Jung considers essential to the individuation process. An individual must feel dissatisfied with his physical, social, and psychic surroundings in order for him to move toward a new center of self. Intimately related to this pre-individuated personality is a firmly established persona which takes into account the internal and external environment, and through which the character deals with the world.

Jung views the persona as

> a complicated system of relations between individual consciousness and society, fittingly enough a kind of mask, designed on the one hand to make a definite impression upon others, and, on the other, to conceal the true nature of the individual
>
> (Jung, *Two Essays on Analytical Psychology,* 190)

Elizabeth Richmond faces the world, and herself, as a museum piece, exhibiting a "self-imposed stupidity." The title character in the short story **"Elizabeth,"** a middle-aged career girl in a dead-end job, leads a life of dulling routine, but plays the part of a moderately successful and efficient publishing agent in order to hide that part of her which yearns for affection and advancement. To deal with the problems of a confining persona, domineering mother figure, and stultifying existence "man must distinguish what he is and how he appears" (Jung, *Two Essays on Analytical Psychology*, 192). None of these characters have yet approached this problem of appearance and reality. Before the development of an independent personality can be achieved, the individual must recognize the unacceptability of the old center, and move towards a break for the new. Along the way she must deal with two major archetypes, the shadow and the animus.

In her discussion of Eliot, Elizabeth Drew summarizes the role of the shadow:

> The poet sees himself inescapably identified with his environment, and any power of choice or movement towards action of any kind seems utterly paralysed. It is a condition which Jung, as well as Eliot, characterizes symbolically as the meeting with the shadow. To Jung it is the confrontation with our own inner "darkness" which means "bitter shock," though it is the indispensable prerequisite of every renewal of the spirit.
>
> (Drew, 92)

To deal with the shadow one must both confront it squarely and recognize its origins. In Jackson the shadow functions both internally and externally. It is operative in the individual characters and ominously pervades the entire social fabric.

The personal manifestation of the shadow is most evident in *Hangsaman.*

Natalie Waite's alter ego, Tony, functions as her shadow. Tony, who may or may not be a separate character, is, in effect, the dark side of Natalie's personality. Where Natalie is insecure and given to childhood fantasies, Tony is an ebullient thief, liar, and temptress. When Tony offers adventure and romance, it is tinged with evil. In the final section of the novel Natalie is forced to face her shadow objectively. Instead of repressing or falling victim to the evil in her personality, Natalie Waite recognizes its existence and rejects its allure.

Elizabeth Richmond also experiences her shadow in the form of one of her four personalities, Betsy. Emerging first in a psychiatric counselling session, Betsy is described as "the shadow of the grinning fiend" (p. 192). Like Tony, Betsy is the destructive essence in the personality, wanton, insolent, and coarse, who takes on the identity of the archly evil Rosalita or Lilith. Again, the crucial action for Elizabeth is to recognize and conquer her evil side.

> Someone had contrived a closed room where Betsy was to perform all the most private acts of her life for a space of time depending upon herself, in whatever order she chose, at her own expense.
>
> (p. 232)

Thus the emergence of the shadow enables Elizabeth to eventually escape its influence.

A situation in which the shadow is repressed, resulting in the failure to individuate the personality, occurs in *We Have Always Lived in the Castle.* Here Constance Blackwood has assumed guilt for the murder of her parents which rightfully belongs to her sister, Merricat. The memory and public shame stemming from the mass killing has prevented Constance from developing her personality in society at large, but rather has kept her a prisoner on the Blackwood estate. At the crucial point in her battle with the shadow, the fire in the house, Constance is moved to objectify the evil and place the blame in its proper perspective. Unfortunately, Merricat has emerged as the ascendant personality, and Constance must retract her statement and resume once again the burden of guilt for the crime. She not only remains unindividuated, but loses all interest in becoming an independent entity.

The shadow figure in Jackson also appears externally in the form of modern society. One critic seems to sense this and credits Miss Jackson with finding "commonplace details coexisting with poisonous events and the deadly supernatural possibilities that agitate the commonplace."[10] Another sees her as a moralist detecting "cruel and lustful conduct not far beneath the surface in those who count themselves normal and respectable."[11] No better example can be found than Jackson's best known piece of fiction, **"The Lottery."** Here, through a ritual of blood sacrifice, the author symbolizes the inherent hate and brutality of which society is capable. Likewise, *We Have Always Lived in the Castle* presents a view of a world "so mean and small . . . so lacking in love and understanding, that we soon came to share Merricat's distaste and . . . approve of the castle-dwellers' self imposed isolation."[12] The same villagers who offer aid and condolences to the two sisters are the ones who lead the pillaging of Blackwood. Thus one cannot help feeling that the dark side merely lies dormant, waiting for another conflagration to rear its ugly visage. In order to undergo self-development the characters must deal both with the personal shadow and that of society.

The animus/anima archetype is yet another stage that must be passed on the way toward the integrated personality. This archetype appears usually as a contrasexual projection, stemming from a contra-sexual imprint on the unconscious. A woman (and since Miss Jackson deals mostly with women the discussion will be limited to the animus) will project her masculine tendencies upon a male or assert masculine characteristics in her own demeanor. The masculine imprint usually manifests itself as the will to power and an opinionated personality. To pass the animus stage one must objectify the effects of the animus, recognize the projection, and accept the latent masculine tendencies in the personality. The animus is often associated with the Freudian concept of the father figure.

Natalie Waite deals with the animus in the form of her own father, and her surrogate father, Professor Arthur Langdon. In a similar manner Eleanor Vance faces the animus in the person of the explorer of the occult, Dr. Montague. Mr. Waite fulfills all the requirements for an animus figure. He is knowledgeable, but also opinionated, petty, and carping. Natalie breaks with her father when she realizes that "it seemed that perhaps her father was trying to cure his failures in [her]" (p. 210). She also is not long taken with Arthur Langdon, who, after an initial infatuation, emerges as the same sort of person as Mr. Waite, domineering and hyper-critical. Eleanor Vance sees a father figure in Montague, but her attraction is dashed with the arrival of the domineering, boorish Mrs. Montague. Eleanor then turns to the ghostly incarnation of Hugh Crain, the late master of Hill House, for her father-lover. Unlike Natalie, she is not able to objectify her feelings for the man or his house, and is totally dominated by both.

The Bess part of Elizabeth Richmond's personality functions as her animus. Bess also is opinionated and is the most powerful of the four selves. It is the Bess persona who is concerned most with the financial and practical side of Elizabeth's plight, and becomes locked in a death struggle with the shadow, Betsy. Elizabeth, in the person of the individuated Victoria Morgan, defeats the challenge of her animus in much the same way that she deals with the shadow. She is able to identify the sources and effects of the animus archetype in her personality, and, in that manner, escape domination and emerge as an independent self.

A third type of animus appearance in the work of Shirley Jackson emerges in three stories **"The Daemon Lover," "Elizabeth,"** and **"The Tooth"**. In all three a romanticized and perhaps entirely illusory lover becomes the hope for salvation. The female character of **"The Daemon Lover,"** nearing middle age, searches for a real or imagined suitor and becomes enmeshed in her fantasy. Similarly, the heroine of **"The Tooth"** escapes a deadening and unsatisfactory routine with a fairy prince whose existence is, at best, speculative. Finally, **"Elizabeth,"** also trapped in an unfulfilling life, compensates with the memory of a high school sweetheart whom she invests with a full set of romantic credentials. All three characters fall victim to illusion and fantasy through their failure to identify the animus, and it is this failure that prevents them from approaching the real problem, the integration of their personalities. The fantasy world they choose is a flimsy substitute for the more difficult soul searching necessary to achieve a new psychic center.

Returning again to Drew, one finds the dangerous moment, "in which the decision takes place between annihilation and new life," a "hovering between the possibility of permanent distortion or of the total arrest of growth on the one hand, and the possibility of fertility rising from spiritual renewal on the other" (Drew, 93). It is at this point that one must make a decisive and potentially dangerous choice. The individual

> cannot bring herself to this decision [to leave the infantile past and venture into a strange new world with all its unforeseen possibilities] which would tear aside all sentimental attachments to childhood, to father and mother, and yet it must be taken if she wishes to follow the call of her individual destiny.
>
> (Drew, 99)

Shirley Jackson employs the dangerous moment as the turning point in the action. Natalie Waite experiences her dark night of the soul in the forest, confronting her shadow. She is left with three viable choices: returning the dependence on her parents and home; being overwhelmed; or overcoming the shadow and achieving a whole and independent personality. The third choice, although the best, is by far the most difficult since it includes all of the dangers of complete independence. Natalie, however, opts for this and rejects the shadow's appeal, "One is one and all alone and evermore shall be so; 'I will not,' said Natalie, and ripped herself away. She wants me, Natalie thought with incredulity, and said again, aloud, 'I will not'" (p. 274).

Constance Blackwood faces her moment of decision in *We Have Always Lived in the Castle.* With the arrival of spring and the visit of her cousin Charles, Constance moves toward the possibility of abandoning her self-imposed imprisonment and going out into society. She actually reaches the point where the decision to escape has been made, but her shadow, in the person of her sister, Merricat, and external evil, the riotous townspeople, force her back to the safety of the family home. Constance re-assumes her isolation following the fire, only now it is far deeper, and, as the author leads us to believe, probably permanent. Her dangerous moment has been reached, but she has neither the courage or the strength to forge a new personality.

The achievement of the new center, the integrated self, is a process fraught with difficulties and dangers.

> Through her active participation the patient merges herself in the unconscious processes, and she gains possession of them by allowing them to possess her. In this way she joins the conscious to the unconscious.
>
> (Jung, *Two Essays in Analytical Psychology,* 221)

One must then not only intellectually grasp the unconscious, but actively experience it. The whole process leads to the establishment of the self. "When this has established itself the center of the personality has been shifted from the ego to a hypothetical point of equilibrium between the individual conscious and the collective psyche" (Drew, 13). The achievement of the new center results in the separation of a single being from the group along with the development of fidelity to the law of one's own being.

For Shirley Jackson the achievement of the new center is rare, and, once achieved, a great deal of effort is needed to make it a comfortable mode of being. The crucial point, however, is the achievement itself. Guy Davenport, commenting on Miss Jackson's last novel, unfinished at her death, recognizes the crux of her writing:

> This last novel, for instance, was clearly to have been about the escape of a captured spirit into a different life that would turn out, as so often before in Shirley Jackson's tales, to be a deeper loneliness but one more tolerable because it is at least in one's own terms and by one's own choice. Only things haunted by our own touch are worth having, our hell is to live with things haunted by another's hands.[13]

The new center can indeed be lonely, but it is also the source of a great deal of pride and self-assurance. Natalie Waite, in achieving an independent personality, recognizes the projections and threats stemming from her unconscious, and is also dominated by them at times. She emerges however with a new sense of self, "She had defeated her own enemy, she thought, and she would never be required to fight again" (p. 276). "As she had never been before, she was now alone, and grownup, and powerful, and not at all afraid" (p. 280). Jackson's use of the hanged man in her title suggests such a rebirth into a more exalted sphere of existence.

Elizabeth Richmond emerges from the battle with her alter-egos, without the assurance of Natalie, but with the pride to say, as Victoria Morgan, "I know who I am" (p. 276). She is at a point from which she can never return to the past, "Each life asks the devouring of other lives for its continuance; the radical aspect of ritual sacrifice" (p. 273). The blood ritual theme is also found in the liberation of the members of the Halloran household in *The Sundial.* It is not enough merely to survive the apocalypse and enter the new world, supposedly cleansed of their sins. They must first deal with the domineering matriarch, Orianna Halloran. Her murder, strikingly similar to that of her son which gained her ascendance in the beginning, releases the other survivors from the bickering and petty jealousies that had characterized the group, and they are able to face the new world, if not totally free from fear, at least with the sense of personal freedom.

It would not be an accurate reading of Shirley Jackson to end an analysis of her works on a note of successful individuation. The large majority of her characters fail to establish the new center and either lapse into fantasy or the drudgery of the old life. Jung's description of the unintegrated personality aptly summarizes Jackson's failures:

> An individual is infantile because he has freed himself insufficiently, or not at all, from his childish environment and his adaptation to his parents, with the result that he has a false reaction to the world: on the one hand he acts towards his parents like a child, always demanding love and immediate emotional rewards, while on the other hand he is so identified with his parents through his close ties with them that he behaves like his father or his mother. He is incapable of living his own life and finding the character that belongs to him.

(Jung, *Symbols of Transformation,* 274)

Constance Blackwood is unable to come to terms with either the internal or external shadow and regresses into her own psychic prison, symbolized by the cave-like maternal home she inhabits with her sister. Eleanor Vance, powerless to deal with society or her internal, guilt-ridden world, loses herself in the supernatural, exchanging the guilt surrounding the death of her mother for the ghostly womb that is Hill House. For those who fail to integrate their personalities, the fantasy world offers an attractive haven. Clara Spencer in **"The Tooth"** succeeds in breaking ties with the past, but turns instead to a dream world where she could run "barefoot through hot sand." Elizabeth, in the story of the same name, takes the same path by imagining "a gallant dark man" and a world of "sunlight, a warm garden, green lawns". To be sure, a necessary stage in the individuation process involves a recognition of fantasy, and even domination by it, but this is only a stage toward the development of the new center of self. Most of Shirley Jackson's characters reach the fantasy stage and are unwilling or unable to proceed further.

The works of Shirley Jackson have, at their base, significant statements on the modern world and the perennial problem of the developing self. Through her skillful depiction of young girls, and not-so-young women, fighting the world and themselves for a comfortable and independent existence, Miss Jackson has created fiction, if not the equal of that of Faulkner and Fitzgerald, at least deserving of a ranking in the second tier of modern American writers. With the application of Jung's process of individuation, hitherto unexpected complexities in her work come to light that underline her skill in the creation of character, and the universality of her subject matter. One can imagine that critics, allured (or perhaps repelled) by her interest in the creation of atmosphere, and emphasis on the strange and the supernatural, have neglected to delve further to explore the patterns of personal development that are, in effect, the crux of her fiction.

Notes

1. Stanley Edgar Hyman, ed., *The Magic of Shirley Jackson* (New York, 1966), p. 1.

2. Carl Gustav Jung, *Contributions to Analytical Psychology,* trans. by H. G. and Cary F. Baines (New York, 1963), p. 240.

3. Elizabeth Drew, *T. S. Eliot—The Design of His Poetry* [A Jungian Study] (New York, 1949), p. 3. Hereafter referred to as "Drew" plus page reference.

4. Stanley Edgar Hyman, "The Symbols of Folk Culture," in *The Promised End* (Cleveland, 1963), p. 277.

5. Carl Gustav Jung, *Two Essays on Analytical Psychology,* trans. by RFC Hull, The Bollingen Series XX, Vol. VII (New York, 1953), p. 171.

6. Josef Goldbrunner, *Individuation* (London, 1955), p. 122.

7. *Ibid.,* p. 145.

8. Carl Gustav Jung, *AION—Researches Into the Phenomenology of the Self,* trans, by RFC Hull, The Bollingen Series XX, Vol. IX (Princeton Univ Press, 1968), p. 5.

9. J. E. Cirlot, *A Dictionary of Symbols,* trans. by Jack Cage (New York, 1962), p. 207. Hereafter referred to as "Cirlot" plus page reference.

10. Geoffrey Wolff, "Shirley Jackson's 'Magic Style'," review of *The Magic of Shirley Jackson,* ed. by Stanley Edgar Hyman, in *The New Leader,* September 9, 1968, p. 18.

11. *Obituary*: Shirley Jackson, *The New York Times,* August 10, 1965, p. 29.

12. Stuart C. Woodruff, "The Real Horror Elsewhere: Shirley Jackson's Last Novel," *Southwest Review,* LII (Spring 1967), 153.

13. Guy Davenport, "Dark Psychological Weather," review of *Come Along With Me,* ed. by Stanley Edgar Hyman, in the *New York Times Book Review,* September 15, 1968, p. 4.

Dennis M. Welch (essay date winter 1981)

SOURCE: Welch, Dennis M. "Manipulation in Shirley Jackson's 'Seven Types of Ambiguity'." *Studies in Short Fiction* 18, no. 1 (winter 1981): 27-31.

[*In the following essay, Welch explores Jackson's use of ambiguity as a narrative technique in her short story "Seven Types of Ambiguity."*]

Despite the literary reverberations suggested by its title, "Seven Types of Ambiguity" has evoked very little critical discussion. Lenemaja Friedman, author of the only book-length study of Shirley Jackson, says that the story deals with an "injury" to a "teen-age boy by the man he aided."[1] In the instructor's manual for *Studies in the Short Story,* Virgil Scott says essentially the same thing,

adding that the story follows the Shirley Jackson "formula" of, first, portraying people who seem to be decent and kind, then revealing their pettiness and cruelty, and finally returning ironically to decency and humane behavior.[2] Formulaic or not, Jackson's stories do depict human nature as deceitful, often hypocritically so, and hence ambiguity, ruses, and fictional reversals are not uncommon in them. Witness, for example, the hypocrisy of the smiling, seemingly good-natured Miss Strangeworth in **"The Possibility of Evil"** and of the blind man and his supposed wife in **"On the House,"** where they cheat a retail clerk out of a bottle of brandy which he offered them at a discount, thinking they were newly married.

Both Friedman and Scott are aware of irony and ambiguity in **"Seven Types of Ambiguity."** But they neglect Jackson's other fictional techniques, in particular, a possible ruse in the story and a subtle ambiguity based on the ruse and suggested by the story's title. One of the seven types of ambiguity that William Empson talks about in his book "occurs when the two meanings, . . . the two values of the ambiguity, are the two opposite meanings defined by the context. . . ."[3] While the situation in Jackson's story suggests that the teen-age boy is deprived of a valued book by an older man (both appearing to be patrons in the same bookstore), I think that many details imply an opposite meaning, namely, that the young man in a ruse with the store owner plays a humorous game of manipulation whereby they get an ignorant customer to buy a hard-to-sell book which he will never read. Jackson presents the teen-ager and the bookstore owner, Mr. Harris, with such details and with such attentiveness, word choice, and timing in relation to the customer that the game of manipulation becomes clear. Granted, there are no *direct* clues as to the game. But just as there are no direct clues in Jackson's **"Daemon Lover"** as to whether the lover is a real man or a phantom, so there are no such clues as to the collusion between the teen-ager and Mr. Harris—clues that would surely destroy a subtle and comic ambiguity.

That the young man in Harris's shop seems to be more than a mere customer is suggested by his name, Mr. Clark, a name that implies both scholarliness and salesmanship and links him to Harris, who is also a "salesclerk."[4] As a matter of fact, according to Harris, Clark "'knows where the books in the basement are as well as'" Harris does (p. 213). It is possible that the young man knows the basement well by being a frequent visitor to the shop, but its basement is said to be "enormous": "it stretched in long rows of books off into dimness . . . with books lined in tall bookcases along the walls, and books standing in piles on the floor" (p. 209). A relationship different from the usual one between a buyer and a seller appears to exist between Clark and Harris since the former does not seem to be much of a cash customer and the latter is a rather thrifty book dealer (p. 209). Finally, more than a customer/ dealer relationship appears to exist between these two, for Clark quite literally takes over the sale of books to the older man, asking him how much he is willing to spend, suggesting specific sets of books to him, and writing down the authors and prices with "a pencil and a pocket memorandum from his coat pocket" (p. 214).

Other details, especially those involving attentiveness, imply a tacit, if not working, interrelationship between Clark and Harris. For example, when the older man and his wife enter the bookstore upstairs and speak with the clerk up there, "both Mr. Harris and the boy listened" from the basement (p. 210). It is perfectly natural for Harris to take an interest in the arrival of some customers, but for Clark to divert his attention from the book in his hands in order to listen and then to shelve the book, "still listening" to the customers upstairs (p. 210), seems a bit more than idle regard. Indeed, the young man listens more than casually, for he hears the man's wife mention later in a "soft voice" that she wants a copy of *Jane Eyre* and he remembers, in accord with Harris's suggestion, to include not just the one novel but a whole collection of Brontës among the man's purchases (pp. 212, 214). Perhaps the reason why Clark left the light on where he was apparently looking at books was not so much that he left his hat and gloves there but that he heard the man express an interest in "sets of books," which happen to be near the place where the boy seemed to be browsing (p. 213).

After the customer admits his ignorance of books, which he is determined to buy, Clark and Harris, knowing that a sizeable sale is all but wrapped up, select and time their words and expressions in order to get him to buy an additional book, which has probably sat around the store for some time and is ridiculously inappropriate for him. Thus, immediately after the customer asks for the store owner's help in the selection of books, Clark comes up and, "as though unwilling" to do so, interrupts the conversation between him and Harris and asks for "'another look at the Empson,'" which Harris, interestingly enough, keeps in a "glass-doored book-case . . . behind his desk" (p. 211). If Clark, who is quite perceptive, wants the Empson book for himself, I do not think that he would request to see it in front of the older man and risk having his already established interest in buying books focused on that one. Upon the teenager's request, Harris hands the book to him with much attention focused on it and the "big man": "'Here it is,' he [Harris] said, 'you'll have it read through before you buy it at this rate.' He smiled at the big man and his wife. 'Some day he's going to come in and buy that book . . . and I'm going to go out of business from shock'" (p. 211). Harris's words are those of either an annoyed salesman or a collaborator with Clark. I think of Harris as the latter, for if he were really irked with Clark's free-loading, he would not allow the young

man to interrupt so easily what appears to be a big sale in progress—unless something else that has perhaps sat around for a long time can be sold to the determined buyer.

Clark and Harris's manipulation continues as they listen to the customer talk. When he emphasizes that the books he buys "'look nice,'" the young man interrupts again, returning the Empson to Harris with the words: "'It still *looks* good'" (p. 212; italics mine). Immediately after putting the book back in the glass-doored case, Harris refers to it as "'pretty scarce, that book'"—a reference that is superfluous for Clark, who refers to it as such later (p. 214), but may be calculated to attract further the man's interest in the book. Indeed, no sooner does Harris refer to the Empson as scarce than the customer asks "curiously" what its title is (p. 212). The young man tells him and then says twice that it is a "'good book'" (p. 212)—the kind the man first asked for when he entered the basement ("'good books'"). If Clark wants the Empson for himself, I do not think that he would refer to it so favorably, echoing the words of both the customer and Harris.

When the "big man" tells how much he is willing to spend, the teen-ager laughs briefly. Like Harris's smile, Clark's laugh coincides ambiguously with both the sense of ease in this manipulation and the carefreeness of the man, who "'never thought'" he would see the day when he would "'just walk into a bookstore and buy up all the books'" that he "'always wanted to read'" (p. 213). "'It's a good feeling,'" the young man adds supportively as if he has done the same thing before, although he claims that he has been trying to buy the Empson "'for quite a while.'" For what appears as his first try, Clark is a fairly good salesman. Smoothly combining the wife's request for a copy of *Jane Eyre* with Harris's suggestion of a whole set of Brontës, he says to the man: "'Your wife was interested in the Brontës. . . . Here's a very good set'" (pp. 213, 214). The young man also recognizes that the wife would probably like a set of Austen's works too and that her husband, who has worked hard all his life, would get more enjoyment out of Meredith and Thackeray than Carlyle. With the stories by Meredith and Thackeray the man is "'going to have a fine time,'" as Clark says encouragingly (p. 214). Little doubt is there that the teen-ager recognizes the customer's lack of reading and hence does not load him (i. e., his new book shelf) up with more than there is room for. The sets of Meredith, Thackeray, Dickens, the Brontës, and Austen "'ought to hold him for a while,'" as Clark remarks (p. 215).

Knowing that the man has become interested in the Empson book, Clark refers to it again before leaving the store. And like a good salesman pitting potential buyers against each other, Harris says that he will "'try to keep it around'" but that he "'can't promise to hold it'" (p. 215). Playing on the man's obvious envy of Clark's education, Harris subtly encourages him to deprive the young man of the book without feeling guilty. Thus, according to the store owner, Clark "'sure wants that book,'" but when the man asks if the boy will "'ever buy it'" Harris is, of course, doubtful (p. 216). For "a minute" the customer and the shopkeeper seem to forget about the Empson book. But Harris's involvement in the manipulation becomes quite clear when the man asks for "'another look at that book,'" which he has *not* yet looked at personally, and the storekeeper, who is not looking at him, seems to know exactly what book he is referring to: "'The Empson?'" (p. 216). The customer frowns while looking at the book but asks to buy it anyway, and Harris adds it "quickly" into the list (p. 216), assuring the man's wife that he has "'bought a lot of very pleasant reading'" (p. 216). It is perhaps with the enjoyment of success and ambiguity in his words that Harris reminds the man and his wife to "'Watch the bottom step'" when they are about to ascend the stairs (p. 217). As he cautioned earlier, "'There's one more than people think'" (p. 210).

To interpret Jackson's story as suggested in this essay may be only to sympathize with the cynical delight of this reader. The humor implied in this interpretation is dependent on one of the seven types of ambiguity (according to Empson), namely, ambiguity as "full contradiction," for which there is abundant evidence in the text. Because I believe that Jackson's story is intentionally ambiguous, I do not insist on my reading alone. I conclude only with a thought from Empson himself: ". . . the way in which opposites can be stated so as to satisfy a wide variety of people, for a great number of degrees of interpretation, is the most important thing about the communication of the arts."[5]

Notes

1. Lenemaja Friedman, *Shirley Jackson* (Boston: Twayne Publishers, 1975), p. 59.

2. Virgil Scott, *Instructor's Manual* for *Studies in the Short Story,* alternate ed. (New York: Holt, Rinehart and Winston, 1971), pp. 47-48.

3. William Empson, *Seven Types of Ambiguity* (London: Chatto and Windus, 1947), p. 192.

4. Shirley Jackson, "Seven Types of Ambiguity," in *The Lottery or, The Adventures of James Harris* (New York: Farrar, Straus and Cudahy, 1949), pp. 211, 209. All subsequent references to and quotations from the story are indicated by page number(s) in parentheses.

5. Empson, p. 221. To paraphrase a more fashionable critic, Wolfgang Iser, the "chief value" of literature is the indeterminacy of its meaning and its availability for multiple interpretations ("Indeterminacy and the Reader's Response in Prose Fiction," in *Aspects of Narrative,* ed. J. Hillis Miller [New York: Columbia University Press, 1971], pp. 1-46).

Richard Pascal (essay date spring 1982)

SOURCE: Pascal, Richard. "'Farther than Samarkand': The Escape Theme in Shirley Jackson's 'The Tooth'." *Studies in Short Fiction* 19, no. 2 (spring 1982): 133-39.

[*In the following essay, Pascal maintains that the theme of escape is central to Jackson's short story "The Tooth" and also appears in many of her other stories, including "A Day in the Jungle" and "I Know Who I Love."*]

To attentive readers of Shirley Jackson's work, it came as no surprise to discover that the novel she was working on at the time of her death was to be about a middle-class woman who has abandoned her lifelong home town and former identity. "I erased my old name and took my initials off everything, and I got on the train and left,"[1] says the heroine of **Come Along With Me,** articulating the desire felt by many other Jackson protagonists to liberate themselves from communal and domestic obligations and referents. For the best-selling authoress of **Life Among the Savages** and **Raising Demons,** those sprightly autobiographical chronicles which reassuringly make light of the anxieties of bourgeois domestic life, the fantasy of running away from it all was a constant fictional preoccupation. In her stories and novels she explores with remarkable skill and insight the impulse to escape from the familial universe which her non-fiction implicitly celebrates. In this as in many other respects, the best of her fiction is deserving of wider critical interest than it has hitherto received. My objective in this discussion is to examine the escape theme in one of the most fascinating stories, **"The Tooth,"** and to offer by way of introduction some suggestions about Jackson's treatment of it elsewhere and its relevance to other concerns apparent throughout her work.[2]

Prominent among the latter is the conception of the small communal group which is bound together less by love and respect than by fear, guilt, and dumb tradition. In story after story the small town or neighborhood is depicted as a nexus of sanctioned intrigue against whatever is individual, different, or alien, and in which the ties that bind may also strangle. In **"The Lottery,"** even the individualism of valuing one's own life is ritualistically and horrifyingly exorcised by the community. In **"The Summer People,"** two vacationers from the city who stay on in a small resort community past the traditional Labor Day leavetaking discover that that tradition is to the townsfolk a taboo, the breaking of which entails forfeiture of normal services and amenities and leads, ultimately, to dark hostility. Sometimes the communal group is simply the family, oppressively nuclear. Elsa Dayton in **"A Day in the Jungle"** leaves her home and husband because they represent a life of stifling quotidian regularity; marriage has been for her a succession of "hideous unprivate months" (**CAWM** [**Come Along With Me**], 130). Catharine Vincent in **"I Know Who I Love,"** leaving home as a young woman, ceases immediately to think about her nagging parents, and does so only "dutifully" (**CAWM,** 48) after they have died. The sense of duty, inspired not by love or deep moral awareness, but by anxiety and insecurity, is to the family in Jackson's fiction what custom is to the small community: a bonding mechanism whose primary function is to ensure cohesiveness.

Opposed to the regulated world of the small group is the realm of freedom and self-centeredness represented, usually, by the city. To those in recoil from the confines of the small group, the city stands as a glistening dream of freedom in which communally inculcated patters of self-abnegating behavior do not hold. Thus Elsa, during her day in the "jungle" of the downtown area to which she has fled from her suburban home, is "very much aware of the fact that for the first time she moved knowingly and of choice through a free world" (**CAWM,** 130). Such freedom, not merely to do what one likes, but to create a life and a self of one's own, is the promise which the city seems to hold. Yet the inverse of the freedom to create a new self is the destruction of the old, which the city also seems to portend. In **"Pillar of Salt,"** the impression of things crumbling is continually with Margaret during her visit to New York, and she suspects that the disintegrating buildings, streets, and vehicles are symptomatic of the city's effect on people: it is the place where they "come apart."[3] At the end of the story she is utterly panicked by the swarming anonymity of the crowds on the streets outside, and at not being noticed familiarly. Similarly, Elsa Dayton's fears of accidental injury during her day downtown really amount to an insecurity about her ability to hold the jungle of an unfamiliar world at bay. Without the constant external verification of identity which the small community provides, the self may seem to lose its reality and the world may crumble crazily.

These, then, are the two realms between which many of Shirley Jackson's heroines gravitate. In the family or town or neighborhood the ties may chafe, but they do hold you together; in the city there are no ties, and *you* must hold you together—assuming there is a "you" which can exist independently, out of familiar context. Some of the most interesting moments in Jackson's fiction are those in which the flight from familiarity to the realm of strangeness and freedom causes a character's sense of identity to weaken or even vanish. Such experiences of fundamental tremors in the self's sense of who it is aren't easily explicable as schizoid disturbances or breakdowns, a line of analysis which assumes a pre-existent central self to feel disturbed or break down. What seems to fascinate Shirley Jackson most is the possibility that behind the self which we ordinarily assume to be irrevocably engrained, if not preordained, there is nothing immutably necessary which we can call our own: it is, for her, an idea which is both frightening *and* alluring.

In **"The Tooth,"** Clara Spencer, a middle-class housewife, boards an evening bus for New York from the small town which is her home. The reason for the overnight journey is that she must see a dentist about a severe flareup of a toothache which she has suffered from intermittently for years. Just prior to her departure, she complains to her husband of feeling "'so *funny*,'" and he expresses concern that there might be something seriously wrong with her. To this she responds uneasily, "'It's just a *toothache* . . . nothing very serious about a *toothache*,'" and the reason for her unease is hinted at a moment later when, after shivering at the suggestion that the tooth might have to be pulled, she says, "'I just feel as if I were all tooth. Nothing else'" (**MSJ** [**The Magic of Shirley Jackson**], 121). On the bus she feels "closed in alone with the toothache" (**MSJ,** 125), and later, in the dentist's office, her tooth seems to her to be "the only part of her to have any identity" (**MSJ,** 128). When told by the dentist that she must go to an extractionist, the questions she wants to ask him (though she refrains) are "What about me? or, How far down do the roots go?" He replies to her spoken question, "'What will they do?'" but also, in a sense, to the imagined ones, by saying "'They'll take that tooth out . . . Should have been done years ago'" (**MSJ,** 129).

In retrospect, then, her husband's earlier assertion that she has been having that same toothache off and on for as long as he has known her indicates clearly that the tooth represents the deeply rooted lifetime-old self inculcated by the domestically oriented small community, and further implies that she was never happy being that self. From their parting conversation at the bus station, we are given an impression of the life-style which the community instills. The talk is all of plans and duties, not of love or personal wishes, and the nearest her husband comes to a declaration of affection is this:

> 'You know, Clara,' he made his voice very weighty, as though if he spoke more seriously his words would carry more conviction and be therefore more comforting, 'you know, I'm glad you're going down to New York to have Zimmerman take care of this. I'd never forgive myself it it turned out to be something serious and I let you go to this butcher up here.'

> (**MSJ,** 121)

Their relationship is a somberly moral connection in which the important gratification is not erotic or emotional, just the satisfaction derived from knowing that one's weighty obligations have been discharged with impeccable conscientiousness. Once launched on her journey Clara never thinks of her husband or children, and what she and he are really concerned about in their farewell conversation is mutual reinforcement of faith in the mores of the family and the small community.

For Clara, the reinforcement is insufficient. Shortly after boarding the bus she is chatting with the bus driver without fully understanding why, "except that it was late at night and people isolated together in some strange bus had to be more friendly and communicative than at other times" (*MSJ,* 123). Faced with a universe of motion and darkness and armed only with the isolated self, Clara feels the Jackson "city experience" immediately upon departure from home. The world of structured familial and communal relationships seems very fragile to her as, sitting toward the back of the bus, she senses that "only the thin thread of lights along the ceiling of the bus held them together, brought the back of the bus where she sat along with the front of the bus where the driver sat" (*MSJ,* 125).

But sitting next to her then is "Jim," a stranger who, she is foggily aware, assists her in the roadside restaurants where the bus stops periodically, and who offers her his shoulder upon which to rest her head while she dozes. She is also dimly conscious of strange things he is telling her, about a beautiful island "farther than Samarkand" (*MSJ,* 124). Jim is clearly fantastic, a creation of Clara's overstrained mind. This is implied throughout the story: in a restaurant, for example, she asks him "'What do you want?'" (*MSJ,* 126), and he points to a cup of coffee and a sandwich *she* then consumes; without having been told, he knows that she is going to see a dentist; when he leaves her in New York she does not see him go, even though she is watching very carefully; and at the end of the story, thinking she is running hand in hand with him "barefoot through hot sand," she doesn't notice the tellingly "curious glances" (*MSJ,* 136) of pedestrians passing by on the city sidewalk. A substitute for and alternative to not just her husband, but the entire domestic society which she has left behind, he provides guidance just when she feels most disorientingly apart from other people. As a creature of her imagination he is really an aspect of herself, of course, and for her to follow his directions and hearken to his seductive verbal travelog is to tell herself what to do and what to want.[4] But so used is she to thinking of the "Clara" identity as her very self that she cannot consciously assume proprietorship of her egocentric impulses, and so she must objectify them and render them somewhat distant in a dream figure.

In essence, it is the realm of passive, ego-centripetal wish-fulfillment, the world of pleasant dreams, that Clara seems to yearn for. The combined effects of codeine, whiskey, a sleeping pill, and lack of food have propelled her into a state of dreamlike altered consciousness, making her feel comfortable about "being carried along without effort of her own" (*MSJ,* 125). In the course of her drugged journey of enchantment, she doesn't quite have the *ultimate* dream, but, as it were, dreams of having it. The land "farther than Samarkand" described by "Jim" represents that ultimate dream, and its appeal is that it inverts the basic values and features of the tightly strictured communal group. This is apparent from the very nature of the place, which seems to be a tropic isle with an ambiance of lazy, unfocussed eroticism, in sharp contrast to the world of sterile matrimonial devotion which Clara has just left. More deeply, though, it is its asocial quality which is most alluring about the faraway land. There, there are voices and songs but, it would seem, no other people—or, at least, none who impress themselves upon one's attention. Similarly, life there is characterized by guiltless, recumbent passivity: "'Nothing to do all day but lie under the trees'" (*MSJ,* 125). When there is nothing to do, consequences are impossible, and so too are responsibility and decisiveness.

Ironically, however, when the enchantment is at its deepest and she is most passive, a new power of determination is liberated within her. Her state of dreamlike consciousness reaches its peak during the extraction as a result of the anaesthetic she has been given:

> First of all things get so far away, she thought, remember this. And remember the metallic sound and taste of all of it. And the outrage.
>
> And then the whirling music, the ringing confusedly loud music that went on and on, around and around, and she was running as fast as she could down a long horribly clear hallway with doors on both sides and at the end of the hallway was Jim, holding out his hands and laughing, and calling something she could never hear because of the loud music, and she was running and then she said, 'I'm not afraid,' and someone from the door next to her took her arm and pulled her through and the world widened alarmingly until it would never stop and then it stopped with the head of the dentist looking down at her and the window dropped into place in front of her and the nurse holding her arm.
>
> 'Why did you pull me back?' she asked, and her mouth was full of blood. 'I wanted to go on.'
>
> (*MSJ,* 131-132)

Clara's commands to herself to remember her sensations during the initial phase of the operation and her subsequent cry of "I'm not afraid," reveal that she is finally making an effort to embrace her mental and emotional life at its deepest level and to accept the consequences, hazards, and indignities of that commitment. In the midst of the disorienting whirl of unstructured mental and physical sensations, the figure of Jim reappears to provide guiding direction. It is still a dream at the end of that hallway, of course, as is made clear when she feels herself being pulled back into the world of waking reality which widens beyond the scope of control of her isolated ego. But the bravery and dignity of Clara's avowal that she wanted to go on cannot be attributed dismissively to an inability to face the alarming breadth of reality unaided by the wishful imagination. Jackson's careful rendering of the experience stresses that the difference between inability and unwillingness in this regard is not altogether meaningful or clear, and that Clara is admirably aware on some level of having chosen her own fate. Thus, moments after the operation, this exchange takes place:

> 'God has given me blood to drink,' she said to the nurse, and the nurse said, 'Don't rinse your mouth or it won't clot.'
>
> (*MSJ,* 132)

She is willing to drink the blood in her mouth as an act of expiation, though more in payment than atonement, for the sin of choosing to live for herself. But the nurse misses the deeper implication of her words and seems, sanely proffering formulaic advice, shallow and automaton-like by comparison.

Subsequently, in the crowded Ladies' Room, Clara seems more self-sufficient and can cope almost calmly with the loss of her previous identity. With only a "slight stinging shock" she realizes that she has no idea which of the several faces reflected in the mirror is hers, and that "no one was familiar in the group, no one smiled at her or looked at her with recognition" (*MSJ,* 134). It is an extreme of the Jackson "city experience" of enswarming anonymity and loss of the identity-sustaining familiar context. Yet Clara's response is merely a "queer numbness in her throat" (*MSJ,* 134). On discovering which of the faces is hers, her reaction is only sullenness at not having a chance to "take" one of the pretty ones, and she immediately sets about letting her hair down, applying rouge to her pallid cheeks, and drawing "an emphatic rosy mouth" on her lips (*MSJ,* 136). The old Clara would never have done those things, not simply because they bespeak sexual self-awareness and narcissism, but even more so because they are done with such emphatic determination to seize control of self and circumstance. She proceeds to stride "purposefully" to the elevator (*MSJ,* 136), as the neurotically driven old Clara would never have done, to seek a lover the old Clara would never have admitted to herself that she desired, much less sought. When "Jim" appears out of the crowd to take her hand, she remembers that she has lost her bottle of pain-killing codeine pills and left in the Ladies' Room a slip of paper containing the nurse's instructions for alleviating painful aftereffects of the extraction. But neither is needed, for the real pain

she has suffered throughout her life was the result of being forced to maintain her old identity, and its absence seems an anodyne. Jim is a fantasy and she may be insane, but there is nonetheless a "happily ever after" ring to the story's ending: "her hand in Jim's and her hair down on her shoulders, she ran barefoot through hot sand" (*MSJ,* 136).

It should be noted, in conclusion, that Shirley Jackson intended the figure of "Jim" to be associated with James Harris, the "daemon lover" of Child Ballad 243, who entices a married woman to abandon her family and run away with him on a voyage which, she realizes too late, is destined for hell.[5] Thus some readers might be tempted to regard the story as a sort of Freudian version of the morality tale contained in the old ballad: the sin of feeling solipsistically happy and free, it might seem, is punished by the damnation of madness. Certainly the story's ending, while hardly moralistic, has the thrust of a cautionary warning about the consequences of succumbing to the seductive murmurings of that "daemon lover," one's wishful imagination. Yet even as the warning is imparted, the lure of the fantasy world is powerfully felt, and it is far from clear that the passing pedestrians who walk upon what they know to be the sidewalk are wiser or happier than Clara, running barefoot through imagined sand. Jackson's careful suspension of judgement at the end helps to explain why **"The Tooth"** is an oddly more unsettling story than a straightforward Freudian line of analysis would allow: she refuses to assume unblinkingly the value and desirability of the "reality principle," of remaining aware of things, people, and events as they objectively are (or are generally understood to be). It is, in her fictional universe, the small communal group which champions that principle, discouraging individual gratification in favor of duty and, necessarily therefore, instilling intense awareness of reality as sternly independent of the wishful self. But if self-gratification replaces communal responsibility as the supreme and guiding value for the individual, the world of private fantasy, or of reality as colored by personal desires, may come to seem a superior kind of reality. Rarely concerned with the moral implications of the quest for self-gratification and pure personal freedom, for Shirley Jackson the intriguing considerations tend to be strategic: whether and how the self can make good its escape, and what the rewards and consequences might be. She knows very well that running away with the daemon lover may mean going to hell. But she knows equally well why so many individuals thrill to his talk of a land "farther than Samarkand."

Notes

1. Shirley Jackson, *Come Along With Me: Part of a Novel, Sixteen Stories, and Three Lectures,* ed. Stanley Edgar Hyman (New York: Viking, 1968),

p. 4. References to this volume will henceforth be incorporated into the text, where it will be designated as "*CAWM*"

2. Book reviews aside, critical works on Shirley Jackson amount to a comparative handful. To date there has been one book about her, Lenemaja Friedman's *Shirley Jackson,* Twayne's United States Authors Series No. 253 (New York: Twayne, 1975). Friedman offers a bibliography of secondary sources, but, as she says, many of these contain "only a sentence or two, and none very helpful" (Friedman, pp. 170-171). Readers interested in criticism of Jackson should supplement Friedman's list with the following: Stewart C. Woodruff, "The Real Horror Elsewhere: Shirley Jackson's Last Novel," *Southwest Review,* 52 (Spring 1967), 156-162; Robert L. Kelly, "Jackson's 'The Witch': A Satanic Gem," *English Journal,* 60 (December 1971), 1204-1208; Helen E. Nebeker, "'The Lottery': Symbolic Tour de Force," *American Literature,* 46 (March 1974), 100-107; Steven K. Hoffman, "Individuation and Character Development in the Work of Shirley Jackson," *Hartford Studies in Literature,* 8 (1976), 190-208; John G. Park, "The Possibility of Evil: A Key to Shirley Jackson's Fiction," *Studies in Short Fiction,* 15 (1978), 320-323, and "Waiting for the End: Shirley Jackson's *The Sundial,*" *Critique,* 19, No. 3 (1978), 74-88. Even much of the best of her work, however, remains unexplored. Friedman and Hoffman are the only commentators who discuss "The Tooth," for example, and they do so only briefly and superficially.

3. Shirley Jackson, *The Magic of Shirley Jackson,* ed. Stanley Edgar Hyman (New York: Farrar, Straus, and Giroux, 1966), p. 35. References to this volume will henceforth be incorporated into the text, where it will be designated as "*MSJ.*"

4. In this qualified sense I agree with Hoffman, who sees Jim as a "contra-sexual projection of Clara's mind." He also regards Jim as a Jungian "animus" figure, however, an interpretation which I find rather forced. Whatever else Jim may represent, it is not "the will to power and an opinionated personality," which are, Hoffman says, the characteristics manifested by the animus. See Hoffman, pp. 200-201.

5. A portion of that ballad was included in the collection of stories in which "The Tooth" first appeared, and the Jim Harris character recurs through several of the other stories contained therein. See Shirley Jackson, *The Lottery* (1949; rpt. New York: Avon, 1960), p. 222.

Lynette Carpenter (essay date 1984)

SOURCE: Carpenter, Lynette. "The Establishment and Preservation of Female Power in Shirley Jackson's *We Have Always Lived in the Castle.*" *Frontiers: A Journal of Women Studies* 8, no. 1 (1984): 32-8.

[*In the following essay, Carpenter contends that Jackson's last novel,* We Have Always Lived in the Castle, *includes her "most radical statement on the causes and consequences of female victimization and alienation, a theme that runs throughout her work."*]

When Mary Katherine Blackwood, at the age of twelve, poisoned her family by putting arsenic in the sugar, she was careful not to endanger her sister Constance, whom she calls "the most precious person in my world, always."[1] Now, six years later, with everyone dead but the invalid and feeble-minded Uncle Julian, Constance has become head of the Blackwood family, which consists of Constance, Mary Katherine (affectionately called Merricat by her sister), Uncle Julian, and Jonas the cat. When the events at the beginning of Mary Katherine's narrative take place, they live in seclusion in the Blackwood house, surrounded by extensive Blackwood property, barricaded against the intrusion of the outside world. They might have continued to live contentedly enough, had their neighbors allowed it. But female self-sufficiency, Jackson suggests, specifically women's forceful establishment of power over their own lives, threatens a society in which men hold primary power and leads inevitably to confrontation.

Jackson's portrayal of the institution of patriarchy and its terrifying power over women predates by more than five years Kate Millett's introduction of the terminology of contemporary feminist criticism in *Sexual Politics.* Her rendering of a modern confrontation between witches and witchhunters anticipates by more than ten years the writings of Andrea Dworkin and Mary Daly on the gynocide of the witchhunt as one patriarchal response to female rebellion.[2] Jackson's last completed novel and a best seller, **We Have Always Lived in the Castle** is her most radical statement on the causes and consequences of female victimization and alienation, a theme that runs throughout her work. The novel may represent a personal culmination for Jackson, who suffered a nervous breakdown shortly after its publication in 1962; her journal from that period records longings for "freedom and security," "self-control," and "refuge" that echo the novel's central concern with the self-determination of women in a safe environment.[3]

When the book opens, masculine authority has already suffered a decisive defeat at the hands of Mary Katherine Blackwood, its narrator (although the identity of the poisoner is not revealed or confirmed until the climactic scene much later): the poisoning has resulted in a transfer of power from Blackwood men to Blackwood women. The motive for the poisoning is not clear at first, but we are given clues in the characterizations of the victims throughout the narrative. Of the men, the most clearly drawn figure is John Blackwood, father of Merricat and Constance and head of the Blackwood family. A redoubtable patriarch, he was a man of property who, as Uncle Julian relates, "took pride in his table, his family, his position in the world" (p. 47). He gave sparingly and grudgingly of his wealth and viewed all such transactions as financial investments to be taken down in his notebook, where, according to Merricat, "he used to record the names of people who owed him money, and people who ought, he thought, to do favors for him" (p. 77). When he quarreled with his wife the night before their deaths, Uncle Julian assumed the quarrel was about money (p. 32). In short, John Blackwood's power in his family and his community derived not only from his gender but also from his material wealth. Six years after his death, Merricat says of the villagers, "I knew they talked about the money hidden in our house, as though it were great heaps of golden coins" (p. 9).

A financial failure, John's brother Julian was dependent on his brother's charity and subject to his authority. In a society that values masculine authority and the accumulation of private wealth and defines that accumulation as a male responsibility and prerogative, Uncle Julian was twice victimized by expectations he could not fulfill. He is perhaps the Blackwood man who most deserved to survive the assault, yet his continuing denial of Merricat's existence serves as a reminder of her former status in the Blackwood family and of her especial invisibility to the Blackwood men. Both legally and symbolically he must be rendered powerless (in/valid) in order to ensure the empowerment of Constance and Merricat. His invalid state no doubt confirms the general belief that financial failure for men leads to powerlessness, dependency, emasculation. The heir to the Blackwood money and property was ten-year-old Thomas, Constance and Merricat's younger brother, who, according to Uncle Julian, "possessed many of his father's more forceful traits of character" (p. 48). It was no accident that Thomas used the most sugar.

Of Julian's wife very little is said; she may or may not have been an undeserving but unavoidable victim. Constance and Merricat's mother, on the other hand, emerges as the primary keeper of the Blackwood possessions, a woman obsessively tidy and aloof. Her snobbery, inherited by her daughters, later ensures their seclusion: "Our mother disliked the sight of anyone who wanted to walking past our front door, and when our father brought her to live in the Blackwood house, one of the first things he had to do was close off the path and fence in the entire Blackwood property" (p. 26). Like Blackwood wives before her, she added her share of material goods to the Blackwood family wealth. But in one important respect she broke with the tradition of the Blackwood women: she was a bad cook. Although she made her obligatory contribution to the cellar legacy of the Blackwood women—her six jars of apple jelly crowded by "jars of jam made by great-grandmothers, . . . and pickles made by great-aunts and vegetables put up by our grandmother" (p. 60)—she left the cooking and gardening to Constance. To the visiting Mrs. Wright's question about Mrs. Blackwood's cooking, Uncle Julian replies with a shudder, "I personally preferred to chance the arsenic" (p. 50). Mrs. Blackwood's indifference to the kitchen and garden not only sets her apart from her daughters but violates the creative tradition of the Blackwood women, whose accumulated preserves Merricat calls "a poem" (p. 54).

Functioning as the family preservers, the Blackwood women, cleaners and dusters of Blackwood property, lavished attention on a different kind of preserves, burying the fruits of their creative labor beneath the accumulated wealth of their dowries and other Blackwood acquisitions. What property they brought to the Blackwood house became Blackwood property, by law or tradition passed from father to son rather than from mother to daughter, as Merricat suggests by her comment on the Rochester house: "Our mother had been born there and by rights it should have belonged to Constance" (p. 4). While her daughters appear to value objects as artifacts from the domestic history of the Blackwood women (a respect they do not afford masculine possessions), Mrs. Blackwood deviated from her female predecessors and from her daughters in valuing the objects over the foodstuffs, the teacups over the tea itself. This attitude aligns her with the Blackwood men, whose highest regard is reserved for money, a thing of no intrinsic value. Obsessed with the preservation of order in her drawing room, she had not allowed her daughters to enjoy its beauty (pp. 33-34), making it a monument to Blackwood physical wealth and spiritual desiccation.

The Blackwood family exploited its women if they were docile and dismissed them if they were not. Mary Katherine, the middle child who was neither a useful daughter nor a male heir, had no appropriate function in the family and was frequently dismissed from its presence for her rebellion against its laws. On the day of the poisoning she had been sent to her room without supper, as Constance reports with a smile: "Merricat was always in disgrace. I used to go up the back stairs with a tray of dinner for her after my father had left the dining room. She was a wicked, disobedient child" (pp. 48-49). Constance's reminiscence suggests whom Merricat disobeyed, whose will she opposed. Six years after the fall of the Blackwood patriarch, she is still being dismissed by the surviving male member of her family, Uncle Julian, who insists that she is dead.

Merricat's raging rebellion, culminating in her overthrow of the Blackwood patriarchy, established Constance as the head of the Blackwood family and the sisters' mutual affection as its binding force. At first glance, theirs may appear to be a relationship between opposites—Constance, the domestic, traditional, even unimaginative one, and Merricat, the unrestrained, creative, imaginative one.[4] Yet Merricat's self-imposed rules and her insistence on routine reveal an obsession with order, just as Constance's skill at growing and preparing food reveals her creativity. Although Merricat's rules do not allow her to prepare food, she helps Constance in the kitchen and garden. Merricat's knowledge of poisonous plants, upon which she bases much of her claim to magical power, comes from Constance.

This shared knowledge, passed from sister to sister, is only one manifestation of a deeper bond between the two women, a bond that has ultimately united them against the Blackwood patriarchal power structure. Constance herself had been a victim of that structure; as elder daughter, she was the unpaid, unrecognized family servant. The smile with which she reports her sister's disobedience suggests her sympathy. In revealing deadly secrets to Merricat, Constance empowered her sister to use them and therefore shares responsibility for the deaths that followed. Yet her complicity was more direct, according to the account Uncle Julian gives Mrs. Wright: "It was Constance who saw them dying around her like flies—I do beg your pardon—and never called a doctor until it was too late. She washed the sugar bowl" (pp. 52-53). Constance herself purchased the arsenic—"to kill rats," she explains, with another smile for Merricat (p. 52). The general belief that Constance was the poisoner both underscores Merricat's invisibility to a society that has no place for her and points to Constance's actual guilt. She not only protected her sister by destroying evidence; she aided her by waiting to call the doctor. Uncle Julian adds, "She told the police those people deserved to die" (p. 53), a comment suggesting that, whatever her ambivalence later, the docile, constant Constance shared her sister's rage and outrage.

Having vanquished one patriarchy, the women are confronted with another in the form of a village controlled by men, by other fathers. Although Constance has been acquitted of murder, the two women must remain vigilant against the encroachment of hostile villagers. Merricat explains, "The people of the village have always hated us" (p. 6), but the sisters are more vulnerable now that they no longer have the protection of the Blackwood men; the town's hostility has become overt, expressed, active. The original source of that hostility was the Blackwood economic and social self-sufficiency, a self-sufficiency underscored by the Blackwood sisters' survival. Villager Jim Donell complains of "the way they live up in their fine old private estate, with their fences and their private path and their stylish way of living" (p. 19). That this conflict can now be viewed in terms of sexual politics is suggested by Merricat's description of the village power structure: "In this village the men stayed young and did the gossiping and the women aged with grey evil weariness and stood silently waiting for the men to get up and come home" (p. 4). In such a society, the Blackwood wealth might be an affront, but Blackwood wealth in the hands of women is a travesty. Initially, the village women in general are silent, weary noncombatants in the struggle between the male villagers and the Blackwood sisters. When Merricat imagines the village children learning the rhyme with which they taunt her, she thinks not of their mothers but of their fathers, "Jim Donell and Dunham and dirty Harris leading regular drills of their children" (p. 22).

The parallel between a witchhunt and the attempt to purge the village of the Blackwood sisters is suggested first by Merricat's own experiments with magic. When she tells us in the third sentence of her narrative, "I have often thought that with any luck at all I could have been born a werewolf" (p. 1), she expresses a longing for power that is one of her chief characteristics. Her magic words and charms constitute attempts to gain power over a world in which, first as the second girl child in a patriarchal family and then as a grown woman in a patriarchal society, she is essentially powerless. Elizabeth Janeway has written, "The witch role permits the woman to imagine that she can exercise some sort of power, even if it is evil power."[5] With any luck at all, Merricat could have been a "real" witch, but her magic is largely ineffectual. What power she has derives from the knowledge she has gained from Constance about plants and their properties. This knowledge links Constance with the countless women healers of the past who were persecuted and executed as witches.

The familiarity of those women with the curative properties of plants presupposes other deadlier knowledge. In her 1921 classic, *The Witch-Cult in Western Europe,* Margaret Alice Murray asserts, "The society of witches had a very creditable knowledge of the art of poisoning."[6] It is also interesting to note that at least one writer, William Dufty, has argued that the Church persecuted witches as healers for speaking out against sugar at a time when the Church had an economic interest in the prosperity of the new sugar industry—a further link to Constance, on whose habit of refusing sugar Merricat depends to save her life at the time of the poisoning.[7]

Jackson, whose works include *The Witchcraft of Salem Village* (1956), owned an extensive collection on witchcraft and demonology. She would certainly have known the major sources, including the now infamous *Malleus Maleficarum* (1486), or Hammer of Witches, used for over 200 years as a guide to the identification and punishment of witches.[8] Its authors' fear of female power is particularly evident in their attention to the threat of actual or perceived castration. These anxieties about male sexual impotence suggest anxieties about male political impotence as well. The Church fathers were threatened by female indomitability and by the followers attracted by women who lived outside the regime of the Church and the familial social unit it controlled.

Thus, significantly, Merricat and Constance are seen as witches because they choose to live outside the boundaries of patriarchal society, because they choose to live with women rather than with men, and because they have challenged masculine power directly by the poisoning. The invalid Uncle Julian survives as a reminder to the patriarchal village of the two women's choice and of their ability to act on that choice. Their only other male companion, the black cat Jonas, completes the popular image of two witch sisters with their feline consort, the Devil in disguise.

If the primary source of the village's hostility is not simply Blackwood self-sufficiency but female self-sufficiency, then the most logical attack would be an undermining of the relationship between the two women. In fact, the beginning of the final assault on the Blackwood women is marked by a visit from Helen Clarke, who, as self-proclaimed friend of Constance, bears a revealing message to her, "It's spring, you're young, you're lovely, you have a right to be happy. Come back into the world" (p. 38). Several unspoken premises lie behind this piece of advice, not the least ludicrous of which is the assumption that the world, or in this case the village, could make Constance happy. Of course, Helen Clarke also assumes that Constance is not happy living with her sister, indeed could not be happy living with a woman when she is young and lovely enough to attract a man. Ultimately, she tempts Constance with the illusion of romantic happiness upon which the continuation of masculine dominance so heavily depends, and Constance is tempted because she forgets or discounts her own past experience. Her choice and Merricat's of celibacy or homosexuality (the latter an option made less explicit here than in other Jackson novels), their replacement of heterosexual romance with sisterhood as their central emotional bond, makes them less vulnerable to sexual coercion by men and keeps their fortunes out of men's hands. Constance's marriage would not only disrupt the relationship between the sisters but would also bring them and their wealth back into the realm of masculine control and restore patrilineal inheritance. That a woman initiates the assault suggests the degree to which village women have come to collude with men in the perpetuation of women's oppression.

Helen Clarke's visit prepares the way for the arrival of Cousin Charles Blackwood, Merricat's archrival, who aspires to be the new Blackwood patriarch, a pretender both to family position and to the family fortune. Appropriately, as Constance tells Merricat, "he looks like Father" (p. 82); his face exposes him to Merricat as "one of the bad ones" (p. 79). Charles is the son of Arthur, the only Blackwood to be more acquisitive and less generous than Constance and Merricat's father. And he immediately begins to acquire things: Father's room, Father's place at the table, Father's gold watch chain, Father's clothes. If, as Merricat tells Constance, "Charles is a ghost" (p. 99), she recognizes immediately whose ghost he is. His presence causes a series of confrontations between the values of the Blackwood women and the values of the Blackwood men. He cannot understand, for example, Constance and Merricat's disregard for gold and money, the legacy of the Blackwood men; what Constance and Merricat value most is the legacy of the Blackwood women—Dresden figurines, dishes brought to the house by generations of Blackwood brides, preserves made lovingly by generations of Blackwood wives. Charles reintroduces the notions of punishment and competition into a house where they have not been invoked for years. He accords Uncle Julian no respect. Having dismissed Uncle Julian as inconsequential, he attempts to enlist the sympathies of the only other male member of the household, Jonas.

The village men, who have always hated Blackwoods before, form an alliance with Charles because he embodies their means of destroying the Blackwood women. Following him to the village one day, Merricat watches him sit down on the benches with the men who are her worst tormentors: "If I went into the village shopping again Charles would be one of the men who watched me going past" (p. 118). The men's acceptance of Charles is a recognition that his family name is not as important as his gender. Their friendship signals approval of his plan to restore Blackwood wealth to masculine control.

To Merricat's horror, Charles' campaign begins to succeed, and the relationship between the two sisters changes:

> She [Constance] was increasingly cross with me when I wanted Charles to leave; always before Constance had listened and smiled and only been angry when Jonas and I had been wicked but now she frowned at me often, as though I somehow looked different to her.
>
> (p. 114)

To masculine eyes, Merricat does look different—not imaginative, independent, and interesting, but eccentric, rebellious, and dangerous. Under Charles' influence, Constance experiences shifts in vision and begins to talk and act strangely:

> "We should have been living like other people. You should . . ." She stopped and waved her hands helplessly. "You should have boy friends," she said finally,

and then began to laugh because she sounded funny even to herself.

(pp. 118-19)

Besieged by Charles, Constance takes on maternal guilt for depriving her sister of a "normal" life, while recognizing that her sister would find, indeed has found, a "normal" life intolerable. For her part, Merricat clearly perceives the source of the threat to their relationship and does not allow herself to be used against her sister, saying, "Constance needed guarding more than ever before and if I became angry and looked aside she might very well be lost" (p. 115).

Merricat's stubborn resistance to Charles leads to a cataclysmic confrontation between the forces of the male power structure and the forces of female self-sufficiency. The scene is richly symbolic. Still seething because of Charles' attempt to assert a fatherly authority over her, Merricat discovers a family heirloom, a saucer from her great-grandmother's dowry, being used as an ashtray in her father's bedroom, now Charles' room. She says, "I brushed the saucer and the pipe off the table into the wastebasket and they fell softly onto the newspapers he had brought into the house" (p. 145). Her act literally sparks a conflagration as two symbols of masculinity, the pipe and the newspaper, begin to burn.

That Merricat herself starts the fire complicates the symbolic reading of this scene as a witch burning. It is the only point in Jackson's novel when the reader is asked to believe that Merricat's perceptions are limited, inadequate. She does not seem to be aware of what she has done. From her perspective, she has disposed of Charles' pipe and newspapers, which in turn have started a fire; they are to blame, not she. The sentence following her description of her actions reads, "I was wondering about my eyes; one of my eyes—the left— saw everything golden and yellow and orange, and the other saw shades of blue and grey and green" (p. 145). Although the reader might suspect that Merricat is intelligent enough to know a fire when she sees one, she does not clarify the passage by identifying what she saw. When Charles and Constance later smell smoke and Constance remembers Charles' pipe, Merricat responds, "Would it start a fire?" (p. 147), suggesting that she is not aware of the situation, unless her true motive is to disrupt Charles' relationship with Constance by blaming him. Yet, although she might wish to destroy Charles' (and her father's) room, she could hardly wish to destroy the house that she and Constance love so dearly, again unless she believes the sacrifice necessary to repudiate the material heritage of the Blackwood men and to exorcise her father's ghost.

The fire brings the villagers and the fire fighters; Jim Donell, the village spokesman and Merricat's greatest enemy next to Charles, is their chief. The firemen put out the fire, despite one woman's exhortations to "let it burn" (p. 152). His duty done, however, Jim Donell carefully removes his fire hat and leads an assault on the house:

> While everyone watched, he took up a rock. In complete silence he turned slowly and then raised his arm and smashed the rock through one of the great tall windows of our mother's drawing room. A wall of laughter rose and grew behind him and then, first the boys on the steps and then the other men and at last the children, they moved like a wave at our house.

(pp. 153-54)

The mob stones the house as an extension of the two women who live in it and strongly identify with it. The scene recalls other stonings, including the ancient practice of stoning witches and the fictional stoning in Jackson's own fable about a sacrifice ritual, **"The Lottery."** The villagers attempt to destroy the women by destroying the house, focusing their energies on the drawing room and the kitchen, special domains of the Blackwood women; they leave Charles to struggle with the family safe, protector of the monetary legacy of the Blackwood men. Their rage is directed at those objects most precious to Constance and Merricat, the dishes and silverware contributed by Blackwood grandmothers, great-grandmothers, aunts, and great-aunts, and at the foodstuffs that Constance holds sacred. Adding insult to injury, they leave the house a mess when it has only just been tidied, a severe blow to Constance. They verbally abuse and physically threaten the two sisters, who are saved, ironically, by Uncle Julian's death. The crowd leaves not out of respect for the sisters but out of respect for Uncle Julian, whom they perceive to have been the sisters' last surviving victim. Defeated, Charles leaves as well.

The confrontation of the fire scene is necessary to prove to Constance what Merricat has always believed—that heterosexual romance is a dangerous illusion, that patriarchy is an inherently destructive institution, and that no compromise is possible. Just as Constance has always felt a responsibility to take care of Merricat, to be a kind of mother to her, so Merricat has always felt a responsibility to protect Constance from an outside world her sister has not clearly understood, a world of hatred and violence. To Merricat, the overthrow of the Blackwood patriarchy six years before had been an act not merely of vengeance but of self-preservation; banished from the family's presence one too many times, she was in very real danger of disappearing altogether. Now, with renewed conviction, Constance and Merricat turn their backs on the outside world, barricading themselves inside the ruined house. There are no more compromises: they do not answer the voices that call to them; they do not allow Helen Clarke in for tea. Dishes and silverware have been broken or bent in the onslaught, sugar has been spilt, but the preserves of the Blackwood women stand undisturbed in the cellar, emblems of the sisters' survival. Ironically, they also retain possession of the safe, a bitter reminder to Charles and the villagers that their survival constitutes a victory not only in their own terms but also in those of the village men.

When the offerings of food begin to arrive from the villagers, the accompanying notes express regret and shame for individual acts of destruction, but the scene evokes other scenes of ritualistic food offerings to ancient deities. Fear seems a more likely motive than genuine regret, especially as tales about the house and its two invisible occupants spread throughout the village. Women speak in hushed voices on the front lawn and frighten their children with stories of the sisters' penchant for eating little girls and boys. The sisters' perceived power has grown since the fire: after all, they are two witches who have survived a burning and a stoning.

At the same time, the food offerings establish a new relationship between the Blackwood women and the women of the village, perhaps recalling that deities can be simultaneously loved and feared. In this matter, the village women seem able to assert themselves, as the sisters imagine: "We thought that the men came home from work and the women had the baskets ready for them to carry over" (p. 204). Constance handles the food lovingly and speculates on the circumstances of its preparation:

> Everything's still warm. . . . She must have baked them right after dinner so he could bring them right over. I wonder if she made two pies, one for the house. She wrapped everything while it was still warm and told him to bring it over.
>
> (p. 203)

The sisters come to know the village women by their distinctive culinary traits, and the food becomes a means of communication, its careful preparation a sign that the women feel more than fear toward the rebellious Blackwood sisters.

Readers and critics have struggled to explain the effect the *We Have Always Lived in the Castle* has on them. The *Time* reviewer wrote, "The book manages the ironic miracle of convincing the reader that a house inhabited by a lunatic, a poisoner, and a pyromaniac is a world more rich in sympathy, love, and subtlety than the real world outside."[9] Many readers express discomfort at being made to identify with a madwoman, but is Merricat mad? If paranoia depends upon delusion, Merricat is not paranoid because the hostility she perceives in the villagers is real. Like most of Jackson's protagonists, she seems young for her age, but immaturity is not madness.

Perhaps the aspect of Merricat's character that is most difficult to accept, however, is the violence. Early in the book, the violence of Merricat's fantasies is horrifying; while confronting hostile villagers in the grocery store, she says, "I would have liked to come into the grocery some morning and see them all, even the Elberts and the children, lying there crying with the pain and dying" (p. 12). The villagers' hostility, although misdirected if they believe the poisoner to be Constance and not Merricat, might at first seem a justifiable response to a daughter's particularly cruel murder of four members of her family. Readers' sympathy with Merricat remains uneasy, even though they may feel, as Stuart Woodruff has suggested, that "parricide on such a scale is certainly regrettable, but the real horror in Miss Jackson's novel originates elsewhere."[10] Yet the villagers' own violence invalidates once and for all their moral judgment of the sisters and indicates that the poisoning is only one violent action in a world where violence threatens to erupt at any moment, a world familiar to readers of Jackson's fiction. Thus Merricat's belief that she is literally embattled is confirmed, and her rage against the villagers is justified. Within the context of feminist psychology, rage is the most appropriate response to oppression. In Jackson's time as now, it was also the most dangerous, the most likely to be labeled madness and treated by institutionalization.

Merricat's rage against her family and the murders that resulted from it are less justifiable on the basis of the scant information her narrative provides; apart from sketchy descriptions of the victims and their treatment of Merricat, the reader has only Constance's word that "those people deserved to die" (p. 53). Because the danger to Merricat in this case seems to be one of psychological or emotional violence rather than physical violence, many readers feel uncomfortable with her response. Ihab Hassan has written that the novel addresses "the human ambivalences of guilt and atonement, love and hate, health and psychosis."[11] By identifying Charles with Father and with the villagers, Jackson relates physical and psychological violence; both can destroy human beings.

Jackson died in 1965 before the current resurgence of feminism and its accompanying new body of feminist theory, including psychological theory. But she studied psychology in college and often wrote psychological studies of women in her fiction. The typical Jackson protagonist is a social misfit, a young woman not beautiful enough, charming enough, or articulate enough to get along with other people—like Merricat, a woman with no recognized place in society. In the early sixties, Jackson herself fell victim to attacks of severe anxiety and depression. Shortly after publication of *We Have Always Lived in the Castle,* the woman known to neighbors and friends as a tireless family chauffeur, an energetic cook and hostess, an active PTA mother, and a model faculty wife retreated into seclusion and underwent psychiatric treatment.[12] A letter from family friend Howard Nemerov during this period suggests that Jackson's illness was publicly attributed to the strain of success when *Castle* was nominated for a National Book Award. To her parents, Jackson wrote that her illness had been building for eight years.[13]

From the perspective of current feminist criticism, it is difficult to read biographer Lenemaja Friedman's account of Jackson's numerous domestic and literary achievements without wondering how she sustained her sanity as long as she did. Many of her literary predecessors have recorded the special difficulties faced by women who aspire to be great writers. Jackson's own journal from the period of her illness is revealing. She writes of insecurity and anxiety, but also often of her status as a professional writer. Not a journal keeper by nature, she kept it at her psychoanalyst's suggestion, even though she "always hated stream of consciousness" (Dec. 2). Yet she finds her journal therapeutic and hopes that it will help her with her fiction, once commenting, "writing is the way out writing is the way out writing is the way out" (Dec. 3), and "there is a calm which begins to come" (Dec. 3). She claims that she writes surreptitiously, fearful of censure from her husband, the distinguished literary critic Stanley Edgar Hyman: "there is literally no telling him what i am doing. i think he would regard me as a criminal waster of time, and self-indulgent besides" (Dec. 3). A few sentences later, she observes more succinctly, "i feel i am cheating stanley because i should be writing stories for money" (Dec. 3). Still further on, she comments, "this is the most satisfying writing i have ever done" (Dec. 3). The picture of Jackson that emerges from these lines is one of a dedicated writer who is concerned because the writing she now enjoys most is not sufficiently remunerative to fulfill her husband's expectations and to remove the stigma of "criminality" from her act of "self-indulgence." Whether or not this concern represented a fair assessment of Hyman's views, the anxiety was real to Jackson.

Like her female protagonists before Constance and Merricat, Jackson expresses a strong sense of inferiority, asking, "why am i less, why am i inferior, why am i put down?" (Dec. 18). Although the terminology suggests that some person or persons are acting against her, she often represents her "problem" or "obsession" as "imaginary" (Dec. 2): "it isn't real. it is a huge cloud of looming nothingness triggered off by small events" (Feb. 7). Earlier she writes, "the troubles i dwell on are closer to fiction than to real life" (Dec. 2), but later in the same entry she reflects on the vital connection between her life and her fiction:

> insecure, uncontrolled, i wrote of neuroses and fear and i think all my books laid end to end would be one long documentation of anxiety. if i am cured and well and

oh glorious alive then my books should be different. who wants to write about anxiety from a place of safety? althougy [sic] i suppose i would never be entirely safe since i cannot completely reconstruct my mind.

(Dec. 2)

Jackson is implying either that she projects her own unrealistic fears in her fiction as if they were real, or that all of her female protagonists are neurotics whose problems can be cured by reconstructing their own minds. The latter contradicts her own fictional accounts of female victimization, often by men—from the psychological oppression of domineering fathers (portrayed in *Hangsaman* [1951] and *The Sundial* [1958]) to the sexual abuse by a mother's boyfriend that helps to precipitate Elizabeth's multiple personalities in *The Bird's Nest* (1954). And surely none of these portrayals of female oppression is unrealistic, whatever fantastic or fabulistic qualities the narrative itself may demonstrate. The attack on the Blackwood house is the most dramatic example of male violence against women in the Jackson canon since the stoning of Jessie Hutchinson in "**The Lottery**" (1948).[14] In the earlier story, the victim is female presumably by chance; the implications of *We Have Always Lived in the Castle* are darker, surely more unsettling personally for a woman writer sensitive to oppression, one known to call herself "the only practicing witch in New England."[15]

The journal reiterates a longing for safety and security in the context of personal liberation, and it emphasizes Jackson's desire to be alone: "i look forward every now and then to freedom and security (and i do mean security by myself)" (Dec. 2). She describes "the glorious world of the future" when she will be "alone. safe" (Dec. 3), and her aspirations:

> to be separate, to be alone, to *stand* and *walk* alone, not to be different and weak and helpless and degraded (now that word again; if there has been a refrain that word is part of it) and shut out. not shut out, shutting out.

(Dec. 3)

The correction in the last line again suggests a conflict between her own perception that she is being victimized and the belief, perhaps supported by her psychological studies and her psychoanalyst, that her fears are unfounded.[16] Contemporary feminists might well question whether a male psychoanalyst in the early 1960's could have understood the kind of psychological danger Jackson perceived (not only to herself, but to all her female characters) in masculine control over women's lives.

The solution Jackson proposes in *We Have Always Lived in the Castle* is a self-contained community of women, however small—one that shuts out the violence of the surrounding patriarchal society but accepts the support of its women. Jackson must have known that such a fantasy was more permissible in fiction than in reality.

Jackson's mental health improved in the final years of her life. At the time of her fatal heart attack in 1965, she was working on a new book. From the surviving fragment, it appears to be the "happy book" she looked forward to in her journal, but it was not about "husbands and wives" as she had speculated (Dec. 2). In it, a middle-aged woman buries her husband, picks a city at random, and sets off alone to make a new life for herself, with a new name of her own invention.

Notes

1. Shirley Jackson, *We Have Always Lived in the Castle* (New York: Viking, 1962), p. 28. All further references are to this edition of the text.

2. See Kate Millett, *Sexual Politics* (Garden City, N.Y.: Doubleday, 1970); Andrea Dworkin, *Woman Hating* (New York: E. P. Dutton, 1974); and Mary Daly, *Gyn/Ecology: The Metaethics of Radical Feminism* (Boston: Beacon, 1978).

3. All journal quotations are from undated journal pages (in the Library of Congress) headed only by the month and day, by which I will subsequently refer to them. This one is headed "Dec. 2." From internal evidence, I would date the journal from 1963.

4. I am indebted to a student, James Bradbury, for his discussion in a paper of the differences between the two sisters.

5. Elizabeth Janeway, *Man's World, Woman's Place: A Study in Social Mythology* (New York: William Morrow, 1971), p. 129.

6. Margaret Alice Murray, *The Witch-Cult of Western Europe* (1921; rpt. Oxford: Clarendon Press, 1971), p. 279.

7. William Dufty, *Sugar Blues* (New York: Warner Books, 1975), p. 31.

8. Henricus Institoris, *Malleus Maleficarum*, trans. and ed. Montague Summers (London: Pushkin, 1948).

9. *Time*, September 21, 1962, p. 94.

10. S. C. Woodruff, "The Real Horror Elsewhere," *Southwest Review*, 52 (Spring 1967), 152.

11. Ihab Hassan, *New York Herald Tribune Book Review*, September 23, 1962, p. 5.

12. See Lenemaja Friedman's account in *Shirley Jackson* (Boston: Twayne, 1975), pp. 26-43.

13. All manuscripts referred to here are in the Jackson and Hyman collections, Library of Congress. The letter from Nemerov is in the Hyman collection (uncatalogued), dated January 23, 1963; Jackson's letter to her parents (in the Jackson collection) is only dated 1963 (I would place it around April).

14. Although women participate in the stoning, the authority who presides over the lottery is Mr. Summers.

15. Friedman, p. 33.

16. My colleague Ellen Peel has suggested that these lines may instead record a desire for solitude and the power to enforce it, to shut others out. She read this essay in draft and made a number of helpful suggestions, as did Heather Arden.

Anne LeCroy (essay date spring-summer 1985)

SOURCE: LeCroy, Anne. "The Different Humor of Shirley Jackson: *Life Among the Savages* and *Raising Demons*." *Studies in American Humor* n.s., 4, nos. 1-2 (spring-summer 1985): 62-73.

[*In the following essay, LeCroy emphasizes Jackson's humorous tone and style, specifically as it appears in her autobiographical "family books,"* Life Among the Savages *and* Raising Demons.]

In an essay titled "Humor and Gender Roles," Nancy Walker discusses the "domestic" humor of several American woman writers of the 1940s and 1950s, among them Shirley Jackson, who wrote "with a strong suggestion of dark humor or self-satire (Walker 98-99). She makes brief acknowledgment of Jackson's two "family" bio-fictions (which every library I have access to classifies as non-fiction or biography). She also notes that Jackson, successful novelist and prolific writer of short story and essay, must have managed her combination of career and marriage with more efficiency than her books seem to suggest. The bulk of the essay, however, concentrates on Betty McDonald, Jean Kerr, Mary McCarthy, and Phyllis McGinley, with special emphasis on McDonald.

Perhaps the reason for this is that McDonald, almost continually self-deprecating and emphasizing the "wife" and "I-try-so-hard-but-I'm-just-not-up-to-expectations" element of her farm life gives strong support to Walker's thesis that the humorous writers she is discussing provide background for Freidan's explosive *Feminine Mystique* arguments of the 1950s. Jackson has not the episodic tongue-in-cheek attitude of Kerr nor the dark humorous tones of McCarthy, nor the cheery domesticated cover-ups of McGinley's suburban poetic meditations about life along the Westchester commuter circuit. Furthermore, the work of Shirley Jackson does not permit classification, unless in a very superficial way that might require much Procrustean tailoring, with the more recent school of humorous writers: Erma Bombeck, Judith Viorst, Theresa Bloomingdale, Shirley Lueth, Nancy Stahl—journal feature and paperback best-sellers of the late 1960s to the present. These are overall representative of the style and approach of Jean Kerr. They deal with the domestic scene primarily in an episodic, not a chronological form; their stories (or essays) are generally short, not more than six or seven pages at the longest, tailored to be magazine or newspaper column features in syndicate. The perceptive reader is aware that these women are not the average housewife-mother figures in the split level, though the accounts they present are undeniably funny and often quite realistic reports of domestic crises and situations.

Shirley Jackson's family sagas also reflect on crises and situations in domestic life, interaction with husband and children, teachers, merchants, and the rest of the daily round. As a result, she may have been classed with the other women writers; this may also be the reason that little critical study has been made of the family stories. The bulk of critical writing on Jackson has centered on the gothic and the psychological novels, and on her most famous short story, **"The Lottery."** Lenemaja Friedman remarks: "very little has been written about Shirley Jackson; . . . comments are often limited to a sentence or two" (170). This is especially clear in relation to her family stories. Friedman's bibliography lists six short reviews of *Life Among the Savages* (1953), all but one favorable, but none claiming any sort of special excellence in the work. *Raising Demons* (1957) stirred a modest set of reviews—five—with one defining the book as "a shrewd and witty social document as well as a beguiling family chronicle" (Friedman 176). Since Jackson's death in 1965, aside from obituary comments and the introductions to the two collections issued by her husband, Friedman finds no further article or criticism on her writing, and my own searches have produced nothing other than Friedman's book. The most recent books analyzing American humor do not include her as a humorous writer, although in her lifetime "her gift for casual humorous storytelling gained many readers . . . her funny family tales sold well" (Friedman 29). Of course, one could discourse at length on the standard literary observation that humorous writing, while often immediately best-selling, does not usually remain so. The continuing popularity of a Thurber or a Twain, outside even the academic and scholarly study of their work, is a rare phenomenon. Jackson, when she is remembered and read, is best remembered for **"The Lottery,"** widely anthologized, and *The Haunting of Hill House,* probably because of its being made into a film, *The Haunting,* which still is shown on late night television. A check among my acquaintances who are addicted to such writers as Bombeck, Lueth, Viorst, *et al* has produced only one who shares with me the enjoyment of Jackson's family books. Both of us are more readily and happily caught up by her humor than by that of her contemporary and more recent peers in the humorous domestic field. She is "different," and I hope to explain why I think so.

In an interview she said, "fifty percent of my life is spent washing and dressing children, cooking, washing dishes and clothes, and mending . . . writing is great fun and I love it" (Breit 15). She seems also to have enjoyed the family life and the result was the ten family short stories published between 1949 and 1952, later expanded into *Life Among the Savages.* Eleven more such stories became the nucleus of *Raising Demons.*

Readers who see her as the writer of gothic, occult, or psychological novels and stories, may lose sight of a persistent humorous strain in most of her writing or see it as totally macabre. Closer reading, however, will show that, from her earliest published work, humor was an intrinsic part of her style and tone: light, warmly funny episodes, wry looks at human nature, witty and realistic-sounding conversations pierce even the foreboding atmosphere of Hill House and the violent undertone of *We Have Always Lived in the Castle* or **"The Lottery."** But I wish in the remainder of the discussion to concentrate on the two family books.

Both are expansions of and chronological ordering of the earlier, single stories tracing the family activities from the time Mother, Father, and two children moved from New York to a white-columned old house in Vermont, through the addition of two more children and the move to a second, much larger house, ending as Laurie and Jannie, the older children, enter their teens. The family picture follows the actual experiences of Jackson, her husband Stanley Edgar Hyman, Laurance, Joanne, Sarah, and Barry living in a small town in Vermont where Hyman taught at Bennington (as did Shirley on an occasional basis) and both wrote extensively. The incidents she narrates really did happen, though she may at times slightly alter details and do some moderate exaggerating. The reader seems to be following the family almost on a day-to-day basis, so smooth are the transitions from one chapter to the next. Natural and credible situations develop, colored by a keen spirit of fun apparent in familiar family happenings: the son's first weeks of school; the daughter's attempts to neaten up the family in accord with a favorite teacher's rather eccentric ideas of dress and behavior; a trip to the city with two small, restless children; the birth of the third child. She pokes fun at herself, her husband, and children "in the clear, unadorned, conversational style" (Friedman 70) of a chatty letter writer sharing the ups and downs of her home life with an old friend. Her animal participants—dogs and cats—feature in several crises, sometimes showing a natural superiority to a human involved. There is the episode of Father and the air gun. He planned to shoot a large rat that was in the cellar:

> For the better part of a Sunday morning he crouched dangerously at the open cellar door, waiting for the rat to show his whiskers, which the rat was kind enough not to do. Our two excellent cats were also inside, sitting complacently and with some professional interest behind my husband.
>
> (Jackson *LAS* [*Life Among the Savages*] 403)

Shortly afterward, one of the cats caught a chipmunk which was not cooperative and got loose in the house, climbing a potted plant on the kitchen window. Subsequently, the husband tried to get a bead on it with the gun while Ninki went to fetch the second cat, Shax, "who is extraordinarily lazy and never catches his own chipmunks, but at least a cat, and preferable, Ninki saw clearly, to a man with a gun." As the chipmunk swayed back and forth on the plant, with cats on either side batting at it, events climaxed:

> All of this happened so quickly that I believe—unless I prefer to move out I have no choice but to believe—that my husband pressed the trigger of the gun without really meaning to . . . missed the chipmunk and the cats and hit the window. The crash sent the cats, chipmunk, and Nimrod himself in all directions—the cats under the table, the chipmunk, with rare presence of mind, out the broken window, and my husband, with even rarer presence of mind, back to the dining room and to his seat at the table.
>
> (*LAS* 405)

The end of the gun experiences came when Ninki, later in the week, caught a bat—a full-grown and horribly active bat—which managed to escape and land on the blanket under which the narrator was hiding. In mortal fear of bats, and of a husband who had the air gun aimed at the bat, she reports:

> I do not know what the official world's record might be for getting out from under a blanket, flying across the room, opening a door and a screen door, and getting outside on the front porch with both doors shut behind you, but if it is more than four seconds I broke it.
>
> (*LAS* 406)

Inside, the husband and Ninki are snarling at each other; there are crashes and sounds of shots. Then all is quiet. The cat has the bat for supper, having outsped the gun pellet. "I was just getting ready to aim and she passed me and passed the pellet just as the pellet hit the wall." the husband reports. Shortly thereafter Ninki "came out the dining room, nodded contemptuously at my husband, glanced at me and, with a grin at the air gun, got into my husband's chair and went to sleep on his paper." Can anyone speak more definitively of the occasional triumph of the cat over the human owner?

The pervasive conversational tone of the two books, exemplified in this brief excerpt from one episode, is evident from the opening paragraph of *Life Among the Savages*:

> Our house is old, and noisy, and full. When we moved into it we had two children and about five thousand books; . . . we also own assorted beds and tables and chairs and rocking horses and lamps and dolls and ship models and paint brushes and literally thousands of socks. This is the way of life my husband and I have fallen into, inadvertently, as though we had fallen into a well and decided that since there was no way out we might as well stay there and set up a chair and a desk and a light of some kind; even though this *is* our way of life, and the only one we know, it is occasionally bewildering, and perhaps even inexplicable to the sort of person who does not have the swift, accurate conviction that he is going to step on a broken celluloid doll in the dark.
>
> (*LAS* 385)

As she reflects on the paraphernalia of living—sandwich bags, typewriters, little wheels off things—it is easy to reflect with her on one's own "little wheels off things" which, when one cleans them out occasionally and is starting to live without them, seem to reappear and fill up even more space. The house they have acquired, following frustrating search of a variety of real estate offerings that "would be just the thing" if the new resident put in plumbing, a new furnace, a driveway up a long hill, or was willing to pay $50,000.

> It was a good old house, after all. Our cats slept on the rocking chair, our friends came to call. We accustomed ourselves to trading at certain stores and we bought our cheese locally and we found a doctor and a dog.
>
> (*LAS* 396)

She moves easily into the famous anecdote of "Charles," the mischievous boy in Laurie's class on whom there is daily report to the family: he is teaching little girls bad words, hitting the teacher, being fresh to teacher's friend, yelling during nap time, and hitting smaller boys.

> Within the third week of school Charles was an institution in our family; Jannie was being a Charles when she cried all afternoon; Laurie was being a Charles when he filled his wagon with mud and pulled it through the kitchen; even my husband was a Charles when he caught his elbow in the telephone cord and pulled telephone, ashtray, and a bowl full of flowers off the table. . . .
>
> (*LAS* 401)

Later Charles seems to reform, actually help with passing crayons and papers, with an occasional fall from grace. Eager to find out all about Charles from the teacher, the narrator attends the first Parent-Teacher get together and maneuvers to meet the young woman.

"We're all so interested in Laurie," the teacher says, admitting that there was a little trouble in adjusting for the first week or so.

"Laurie usually adjusts very quickly," I said. "I suppose this time it was Charles' influence."

"Charles?"

"Yes," I said, laughing. "You must have your hands full in that kindergarten with Charles."

"Charles?" she said. "We don't have any Charles in the kindergarten."

(*LAS* 402-3)

The whole question of Charles was at once dropped at home and became, without discussion, a forbidden topic. Throughout both books the children participate actively in various episodes, often being as highly creative as Laurie was in the invention of "Charles." Their conversation sounds natural and changes naturally as they grow older. For a time, for example, Sally uses language to "magic" things, talking open the door of the refrigerator and casting spells on Laurie's shoelaces. To entertain Sally, Jannie tells stories about a lion eaten by a bus or a boy eaten by a bicycle. Grown up a bit, Sally creates the magic world of "Pudge" where she and Barry spend afternoons beyond the big oak tree in the back yard and Barry wins mighty victories with his "srop" ("sword," as Sally translates it). They share a language understood only by themselves.

Although she is a highly individual child, Sally's birth was realistic enough.

"A what?" said Jannie.

"What for" said Laurie.

Thus the account of the third baby is introduced, "the easiest baby and the funniest, because you have been there before and you know."

Sentimental people keep insisting that women go on to have a third baby because they love babies, and cynical people seem to maintain that a woman with two active healthy children around the house will do anything for ten quiet days in the hospital; my own position is somewhere between the two, but I acknowledge that it inclines somewhat toward the latter.

(*LAS* 421)

The morning the baby makes its imminent arrival known is at first rather routine. As Jackson recollects "I was doing everything the way I had a thousand times before . . . and everything seemed to be moving along handsomely." She was heating coffee in the frying pan—a broad shallow container will heat quickly, "though I admit it *looked* funny," as the family came down to breakfast.

My husband asked politely, "May I help you with breakfast?"

"No, indeed," I said. I stopped to catch my breath and smiled reassuringly. "I feel so well," I said.

"Would you be offended," he said, still very politely, "if I took this egg out of my glass?"

(*LAS* 423)

Things move to a climax. There is a trip to the hospital with a very nervous taxi driver, registration with the desk clerk who insists on putting down occupation "housewife," instead of "writer" and questions the legitimacy of the baby. Following contacts with nurses recovering from some party the night before, the doctor who is jovial and self-confidently wanders off to the coffee shop, and the husband, who is unceremoniously shooed from the room, Sarah is born. It all seems very familiar, somehow, whether the reader has had three children or only one. Again there is the feeling, "she could have been writing my experience almost exactly."

The night everyone had grippe, later in the book, cannot be condensed into any sort of paraphrase. It has the cumulative, growing chaos of a Thurber family tale that the reader can enjoy only through Shirley Jackson's telling of the events: moving from bed to bed, carrying glasses, onion rolls, blankets, the Baby's suitcase of discarded decks of cards. Even the dog is involved in the game of musical beds. At the end there is a mystery.

The puzzle is, of course, what became of the blanket from Sally's bed? I took it off her crib and put it on the bottom half of the double-decker, but the dog did not have it when he woke up, and neither did any of the other beds. It was a blue-patterned patchwork quilt, and has not been seen since, and I would most particularly like to know where it got to. As I say, we are very short of blankets.

(*LAS* 471)

The reader is sorely tempted to go back over the story again and try to solve the mystery.

On a rare occasion when her husband must go to New York, the mother is left to face a car that suddenly refuses to start and a furnace that will not turn on. The day is spent in telephone calls to repairmen and plumbers—all of whom seem to be at a convention—and a desperate search for money to pay the plumber who does come.

Mr. Anderson always operates on a strictly cash basis; there is a rumor about him, implicitly believed by me, that if he is not paid immediately he goes right back downstairs and breaks the furnace again.

(*LAS* 480)

Miss Jackson's humor most frequently stems from her comprehension of the everyday nuances and working of the average family—the role of the mother and the helpless frustration mothers often feel at observing the inexplicable behavior of their children.

When Laurie and his bike are struck by a car, she does not make much of her shock feelings about the accident; she does present a highly believable conversation during Laurie's recovery period when he seeks to know all the gory details and is terribly upset because she did not keep his bloody T-shirt for him. Later she ponders:

> Sometimes in my capacity as mother, I find myself sitting open-mouthed and terrified before my own children, little individual creatures moving solidly along their own paths and yet in some manner vividly reminiscent of a past which my husband and I know we have never communicated to them. . . .
>
> (*LAS* 489)

Possibly it is this sense of reminiscence that makes her so skilled at presenting their quirks, their speech patterns, their varied personalities so successfully and realistically. She never seems to be manipulating their activities just to make a funny story.

The house becomes too small for all the books, boots, hockey sticks, skates, a vast coin collection, and all the other impedimenta of nine years' residence. It is almost through working of fate that the village grapevine decides the best house for them to move into is a bigger house in town, formerly a four-apartment dwelling with appalling wall paper in all the rooms but plenty of space and a large barn. Following predictions of bankruptcy and the poorhouse by her husband, she becomes first involved with moving arrangements and later with a very independent storage company. They spend a somewhat disorganized summer in the house of a friend on a lake seventy miles away where Laurie suddenly becomes addicted to horses.

Back in the new house, their furniture finally retrieved from Mr. Cobb's storage and put in place, they find that the plumbing needs extensive repair, the furnace is in bad shape, and the roof must have new shingles. Her reflection has a familiar ring:

> When we bought the house, my husband and I had both assumed, upon the candid statement of the real estate agent, that the only thing defective about the property was the left-hand gatepost leaning off at a rakish angle. The roof, the plumbing, the furnace, the wiring, the foundations—all of these, we believed innocently, were new, newly repaired, or so solid that not even an earthquake could shake them.
>
> (*RD* [*Raising Demons*] 580)

She describes the extensive repair and refurbishing operations as background for the family birthdays: on Sally's, men were sanding the floors; on Jannie's, much of the furniture was being reupholstered; when Barry's birthday arrived, the plumbing was under repair.

> When they were repairing the plumbing in the bathroom downstairs . . . they had taken out the bathtub and put it in the study where my husband fell into it one night when he couldn't sleep and went downstairs to get a book.
>
> (*RD* 582)

An invitation to spend a weekend with an old college friend arrives at a critical moment when the narrator has just decided that her fondest dream would be for the doctor to drop in casually, take one look at her and exclaim that she is desperately ill and must be put in the hospital. Her husband urges her to make the visit—he can handle everything. Preparations for the trip, however, involve more details, telephone calls, arrangements, and list-makings than would have seemed necessary to prepare for D-day. She writes a detailed agenda for her husband, covering such matters as who is spending the night with whom, what to fix for meals, and how to handle emergencies (foreseeable ones). When she returns, after a moderately pleasant weekend, the house is empty and quiet, except for a note stirring gently on the coffee table:

> SUNDAY, it said. Barry and/or dog ate all directions. Have taken all children incl. Barry to hamburger stand for dinner, movies. Barry fond of movies, went yesterday too, also fr.fr. potatoes. Don't wait up for us. Casserole on kitchen table, cats not fed. Milkman left two dozen eggs. Jannie says six jellybeans is not plenty. Leave front door unlocked. Jar in refrigerator labeled Mayonnaise was mayonnaise.
>
> (*RD* 588)

In the second book Barry, the youngest, plays a feature role. One reviewer found him "an engaging young two-year-old with a distinct personality" (Jones 45). Jannie dresses him in costume jewelry and ribbons. Sally sings to him to make him dance. Laurie directs his behavior in fatherly tones. And his name is a very fluid element:

> Barry was clearly too formal a name, and we took to calling him B. B was too short, however, and he became Mr. B., then Mr. Beetle, and finally Mr. Beekman. He stayed Mr. Beekman until he was almost ready for nursery school, then came around full circle, moving back to Mr. B, then B., and, at last, to Barry again. . . . Thus dancing, and decked in ribbons, Beekman walked instead of creeping, and learned to drink from a cup.
>
> (*RD* 588)

Expenses continue to mount. Following a minor accident with the old car, which leaves it with smashed nose, one headlight hanging crooked, they maneuver Father into purchase of a new station wagon ("bankruptcy in style" he predicts) and acquire a car seat with gearshift and steering wheel for Beekman-Barry. He manipulates the gearshift and wheel with such abandon and skillful maneuvering "as to earn himself the title of Mad-Dog Beekman" (*RD* 604).

While Jannie is seeking to develop herself into the ideal lady, Sally is living with magic and the world of "Pudge," and Beekman is dancing through the days, Laurie develops an interest in Little League (his mother is an avid sidelines fan) and learns to play trumpet.

Mother resists, but an unexpected incident changes things—and brings a few more expenditures. The old refrigerator suddenly fills the house with an appalling odor which the repairman is certain is gas escaping, fatal to all if the house is not vacated and the appliance carted off. The ensuing days bring in not only a shiny new refrigerator, but a dishwasher and a new kitchen floor. Father is too much in shock even to mutter "bankruptcy." A little later, Laurie asks innocently whether his mother knows anything about the sodium bisulphite from his chemistry set. He had put it in a pan on the kitchen radiator and cannot find it. With a sudden insight, she requests that he not tell his father about the loss just yet, and buys his silence with promise of trumpet lessons.

Following a family trip to New York, by no means uneventful, with Barry excited about taking his bear, Sally assuring everyone that New York doesn't really exist—people just think it does—the family settles back into the routine of father teaching, mother learning to be a faculty wife, and the children directing the purchase of a new dog. The purchase is necessitated by the sudden invasion of some very assertive mice, with which the cat Gato refuses to deal. One episode will give the picture:

> I went into the kitchen about eleven o'clock to make my husband a cold potroast sandwich and when I reached for the light cord a mouse ran down my arm and my husband had to come into the kitchen and lead me out. Gato, who had been sleeping on the waffle iron, arose in great indignation and went upstairs to sleep on Jannie's doll bed, after several pointed remarks about people who kept decent cats awake all night with their mice.

> (*RD* 714)

When another mouse is discovered eating salted peanuts in the dining room, Gato, who has been sleeping in the oven, stalks upstairs and spends the rest of the day sulking in Sally's toy box. Then Toby, the dog, does arrive; attempts to help him make peace with Gato assume a Summit situation, until the day of another Thurberlike episode involving the entire family, Yain, another cat, a large grey cat, Gato, Toby, and the puppy someone has given Sally. The conclusion is the acquisition of another puppy to add to the menagerie.

Like the first book, the second ends with the Christmas Eve decorating of the tree. The family has settled down, shaded by the tree and watching the fall of snow outside the lighted windows.

> "Say," my husband said to Sally in a low voice, "how about that package hidden in the kitchen?"

> "Mice," Sally said firmly, "full of mice."

> "Listen," Laurie said in my ear, "suppose he doesn't like it, after all? I mean, suppose he doesn't *like* it?"

> "Don't worry about that," I said, "it's just beautiful."

> Barry climbed up into his father's lap to look further at the tree and his father bent and whispered in his ear. "What package?" said Barry, turning.

> "Careful," said Laurie, warningly.

> "Don't tell," Sally said.

> Barry chuckled. "An elephant," he said.

> Jannie sang "Hark, the Herald Angels Sing," Laurie took out cartons to stack on the back porch until we took the tree down again, Sally sat cross-legged on the floor watching the tree. Suddenly Sally and Barry spoke at once.

> "Last Christmas—" Sally said.

> "Next Christmas—" Barry said.

Were Shirley Jackson as episodic a writer as some of the undeniably excellent women humorists mentioned earlier, it would be much easier to balance quoted material and paraphrase with comment. The flavor of Erma Bombeck or Judith Viorst or Nancy Stahl can be tasted by the reader through short quotes and classification of the various topics they deal with in matters of family life. It is not really possible to present the full flavor of Shirley Jackson's humor that way. Because her stories are longer and link frequently to one another, the real quality of her humor can be discovered only by reading the work itself. Professional critics have been inclined to discount her talents as a humorist, Friedman points out (68). They forget, I think, that humor in fictionalized biography is a hard element to handle; it is either overdone to the point of ennui or oversentimentalized, or based too much on "in jokes" that lose their meaning with the passage of time. Shirley Jackson handles such humor with success, perhaps occasionally becoming sentimental, as in the Christmas scene, but overall with the quality that might rank her with Thurber or Twain when she is at her best, which is most of the time.

Works Cited

Breit, Harvey. "A Talk with Miss Jackson." *New York Times Book Review* 26 June 1949: 15.

Friedman, Lenamaja. *Shirley Jackson.* Boston: Twayne, 1975.

Jackson, Shirley. *Come Along with Me.* Ed. Stanley E. Hyman. New York: Viking Press, 1968.

Jackson, Shirley. *Life Among the Savages* and *Raising Demons.* In *The Magic of Shirley Jackson.* Ed. Stanley E. Hyman. New York: Farrar, Straus, Giroux, 1965, 1966.

Jones, J. C. "Writer as Mother." *Saturday Review* 40 (19 January 1957): 45.

Walker, Nancy. "Humor and Gender Roles." *American Quarterly* 37 (Spring 1985): 98-113.

Danielle Schaub (essay date spring 1990)

SOURCE: Schaub, Danielle. "Shirley Jackson's Use of Symbols in 'The Lottery'." *Journal of the Short Story in English,* no. 14 (spring 1990): 79-86.

[*In the following essay, Schaub relates Jackson's symbolic use of numbers, names, and objects to the role of tradition in her story "The Lottery."*]

At mid morning on a late June day a peaceful village crowd gathers on the square for the annual lottery. The procedures have been handed down over generations with little change. While in the harmless process of drawing lots the villagers reveal their excitement. Suddenly, when the winner is selected, the innocent game turns out to be a horrifying sacrifice: the winner is stoned to death for the welfare of the community. Such is the limited picture that could be given of Shirley Jackson's « **The Lottery** » if symbols were overlooked.

Most critics are puzzled by the final shock, its purpose and effect: they feel they are « only (left) shaken up » with « a sense of an unclosed gap ».[1] In fact their major concern seems to be with the anthropological allusions to the rituals of the summer solstice. Seymour Lainoff claims that « anthropology provides the chief symbol »[2] so that the lottery is to be understood as a « modern representation of the primitive annual scapegoat rite ».[3] Brooks and Warren explain that the story reveals « the all-too-human tendency to seize upon a scapegoat »[4] which Virgil Scott voices as « the human tendency to'punish' innocent and often accidentally chosen victims for our sins ».[5] If these comments are to the point they nevertheless do not disclose how the remarkable reversal of expectations is anticipated. True Helen E. Nebeker throws light on the author's « symbolic tour de force »[6] but then only partially. Indeed she focuses on the underlying theme—the role of tradition in man's life—but fails to consider the symbolism prevailing in the main theme—man's recurrent need of a victim. Yet symbols are Jackson's major device in her tightly-knit handling of both themes.

Although ominous symbolic details prepare for the tragic outcome the reader's attention is skilfully distracted.[7] With her conventional title Jackson misleads the reader into thinking that the story is merely a fable or a fairy tale.[8] The description of the pastoral-like setting implies an idyllic atmosphere. Besides, the lively, decent and friendly population lives as harmoniously as a close community can possibly do. Since the ceremony is official and causes much excitement its true nature is not examined, the more so as it is associated with other pleasant social occasions. No reason then for tradition to be questioned or to be given up. And indeed very little has changed: the original chips of wood may well have been replaced by slips of paper, the present box

may be made with some pieces of the preceding one, the former initial recital may no longer be performed but the core of the ritual has remained unchanged. In such a tradition-abiding community there seems little point for the reader to doubt the ceremony's benevolence. Mrs Hutchinson's late arrival therefore merely seems to single her out and to cast a favourable light on her: she has almost forgotten about the lottery because, as a perfect housewife, she would not leave her dishes in the sink. Nobody in the crowd seems to mind. As a good-humoured wife and mother she joins her husband and children while the crowd shows the friendliest feelings. The reader is thus made to sympathise not only with her but also with the rest of the population before the actual drawing of lots. After the first round, when the Hutchinsons are selected, Tessie seems to object but is gently rebuked so that little attention is paid to her apparently inexplicable objections. The second round determines the winner in the selected family: all have blank slips of paper except Tessie who has a black spot on hers. As she does not react at all when the main official urges his folks to finish the ceremony quickly the event is felt as thoroughly natural and in keeping with the general harmony. Then, suddenly, without apparent break, the reader is thrust into a symbolic realm: with no warning Tessie is stoned by all the villagers including her youngest child Davy. Taken at their face value the cold description of seemingly inoffensive and habitual circumstances, the banal structure and narration contrast with the abrupt ending. The shock is thus inevitably enhanced, the more so as the villagers' relaxed attitudes and lively speech do not prepare the reader for the gory outcome. Clearly the pastoral setting, commonplace characterisation, familiar down-to-earth vocabulary, impersonal and unimaginative style, detached point of view and plain chronological structure, all contribute to mislead the reader.

Yet, all along tension should be felt as several allusions to the villagers' nervousness are made. The talk about giving up tradition, Mrs Hutchinson's emotional outburst, the increasing rhythm also point—even if indirectly—to the unhappy issue. Moreover the author's recurrent use of symbols stresses the duality of things and beings,[9] which paves the way for the final horrendous revelation. Nothing—as a careful analysis of symbols reveals—is left to chance: tension lies at the heart of the story. Most numbers, colours, objects, stars, surnames in the text are ambivalent.[10] Their ambivalence corroborates the message of the story, namely that first-hand impressions may well be deceptive: on the surface, things are smooth; deep down, reality is cruder. The usually positive value of any symbol is to be counterbalanced by its hidden or less well-known negative value so as to have a clearer picture of the text. Its richness and quality result from the mixture of opposite values. Instead of a straightforward account of small-town life, the reader gets a fuller picture of Life with its inescapable conjunction of opposites.

Tension is already present in the description of the setting and in the atmosphere. Like a Janus figure the sun is felt throughout as an ambiguous presence. Its generative heat associated with youth, vitality and fertility heals and restores, but come Midsummer and its scorching heat leads to the poisoning, burning madness of the solstice rite. The sun will provide better crops but only at the cost of the ritual murder of an innocent villager. Besides, the ambivalent character of the rite is stressed by the profusely blossoming flowers. By their very nature they symbolise beauty as well as point to the transitory stages of the vegetal cycle. They suggest not only virtue, goodness and purity but also temptation and deceit. As such they are part of pleasant occasions but also of distressing functions—as a last tribute paid at a funeral, Tessie's for example. The green grass too reveals the discrepancy between the character's appearance and deeds. Indeed, on the one hand, green denotes fertility, peace, balance, harmony, freshness, youth: these qualities, at first sight, seem to fit the description of the population. But, on the other hand, green implies ignorance, unripeness, inexperience—the very characteristics attributed to pagan sacrifices.[11] Significantly too, prior to the insane murder of Tessie Hutchinson, the villagers gather in the square. As the square stands for firmness and stability, organisation and construction, it is the source of order.[12] No wonder then that traditions are perpetuated in the square, particularly those regulating the material stability of the community. And if stability is to be gained at the expense of one villager no one need to worry: the existence of the square justifies such injustice provided it serves the group. So the setting and atmosphere prefigure the ritual killing or confirm the villagers' rights and obligations to perform such a function.

If the setting and atmosphere reveal the dramatic denouement, so does the symbolic use of numbers.[13] That they are not chosen at random is made obvious in the choice of the 27th of June as the date for the Midsummer solstice ceremony. Indeed according to Frazer[14] fertility rites take place on Midsummer Eve (that is the 23rd of June) or on Midsummer Day (that is the 24th of June). One may wonder at this point which line of the cabalistic tradition Shirley Jackson follows.[15] Indeed as 27 is not a primary number it has to be fused by mystic addition ($2 + 7 = 9$) or by succession (2, then 7), or else to be considered the result of multiplications (either 3^3 or 3×9).[16] Now 9 is a multiple of 3, so the symbolic value attached to 3 is increased, namely completeness, perfection and fertility, and the end of a cycle (death) before the return to unity.[17] So whether 27 is fused or merely the result of a multiplication it reveals the transitoriness of life. As a consequence it alludes to the im-

minent death that awaits any outcast who prevents the community from being a tightly-knit group. Once the outcast is dead unity is restored and fertility secured. That symbolism fits the story is also true when 27 is interpreted as fused by succession. The number 27 would then reduce its conflict (as symbolised by the number 2) to its solution (as symbolised by the number 7).[18] As 2 stands for the conjunction of opposites, such as life and death, man and woman, good and evil,[19] and 7 for perfect completion of a cycle,[20] the perfect solution is to grant death to either man or woman. Indeed a complete cycle implies decay or death so its perfect completion is closely linked with the death of a man or a woman. This is further emphasised in the twice-drawn lots. Furthermore by the use of the number 2 Shirley Jackson stresses the all-so-human conjunction of opposites.[21] Man is not just good or evil but both. Since all human beings are dual there must be a way to determine which group in the population will provide a victim. The population is made of the elementary nucleus 3, namely children, men and women.[22] As the elementary nucleus is self-sufficient the solution to its problem, in this case the selection of a victim for the material welfare of the community, lies within. And whenever there is a choice of three the magic solution is offered by the third choice.[23] Therefore in « The Lottery » it is within the third group presented to the readers (the women) that a victim will be chosen. The whole ceremony must take place between 10 and 12 o'clock. By 10 o'clock on the 27th of June the community has fallen from its high position of perfection. By 12, salvation, holiness and perfection are restored so that the community shares with the number 12 in the inner unity and harmony of all matters.[24] So by decoding the numbers used by Jackson the full implications of the fertility rite can be fathomed.

Such is certainly the case with the objects connected with the ritual. The black wooden box, the three-legged stool, the slips of paper for drawing lots combine the idea of death and rebirth, unexpected destructiveness and fertility.[25] The outcome of the lottery could be anticipated from the sheer repetition of the adjective 'black'—the colour for death, mourning, punishment, penitence in western civilisation. The black box used to draw lots and the slip of paper with a black dot marking out the 'winner' are mentioned too frequently to be coincidental. Like Pandora's box and its unexpected, excessive and destructive gifts, the wooden box is associated with the vegetal cycle, with death followed by rebirth. The three-legged stool too participates in the cycle of fertility and is considered a divine object bringing all solutions.[26] By allowing the lottery to take place, that is by supporting the box, the stool helps marking out the martyr. The negative connotations ascribed to the preceding objects may well escape the reader but the ominous collecting of stones cannot be overlooked. Stones are indeed the universal symbol for punishment and martyrdom: they can only be part of a morbid ceremony. Consequently the marked emphasis on the objects related to the lottery can only but confirm that the lottery is a death-bringing ritual.

The villagers' fear of changing either the course of the lottery or the ritualistic objects discloses to what extent they are caught in the web of tradition. Even the pervading tension of their lives will not help change matters. This need surprise nobody as their surnames are symbolic of the overall duality which has governed their lives for generations. They are all friendly commonplace villagers who are capable of the most atrocious deeds. Most of their surnames reflect their gentility, their humanity. Indeed all but four names[27] refer to past renowned men who have contributed to the welfare of humanity or to the world's cultural heritage.[28] Their names obviously clash with their baffling potential destructiveness. Death is even announced in the very surname or characteristics of the two officials who conduct the ceremony. Mr Summers is indeed the head of the coal business in which capacity he has close contacts with the Underworld. His childlessness and marital disharmony are both outward signs of his morbid role.[29] None but Mr Graves could best assist Mr Summers to preserve the ceremony. To crown it all the Delacroix are singled out as the most fervent participants in the ritualistic killing: Dickie is said to stack up masses of stones in advance while Mrs Delacroix is seen picking up a huge stone and hurrying on whole-heartedly to stone her friend. The latter's surname is strikingly indicative of her fate as it refers to Anne Hutchinson. a seventeenth-century American religious enthusiast who founded the Puritan colony of Rhode Island. She had new theological views which opposed her to other ministers. After a local trial banished her she was tried before the Boston Church and formally excommunicated.[30] The parallelism between her story and Tessie's is clear: to her excommunication meant spiritual death just as to Tessie being cast out from the group implies death. The symbolic use of names thus reveals that human nature is an unaccountable mixture of the creative and the destructive: normal people can turn out to be real monsters capable of the worst atrocities.

Despite its apparently conventional start and artless narration the story, with its shift from realism to symbolism, brings about a striking shock and the sudden realisation that appearances are deceptive. The unexpected awe-inspiring contrast between man's appearance and deeds as well as the abrupt ending after a crime that allows no hope force the reader to ponder over human habits and more specifically over man's need of a scapegoat. He becomes conscious that he too may be a victim or a persecutor if he resorts unquestioningly to tradition as a line of conduct. This newly acquired awareness then prompts him to be suspicious of any systematic line of conduct, arbitrary deeds and sterile

habits of mind. In this respect the victim's first and last words throw light on man's contradictory attitudes: at first Tessie's forgetfulness—possibly a premonitory sign of her imminent death—does not result from her questioning the ritual; in the end her cry words her sudden awareness of human irrationality and injustice. Her case is universal: man's awareness of absurd habits of mind always comes too late, that is when victimised and no longer in a position to change things.

Notes

1. Robert B. Heilman, *Modern Short Stories: A Critical Anthology* (Westport, Conn.: Greenwood Press, 1974), p. 385.

2. Seymour Lainoff, « Jackson's 'The Lottery' », *Explicator* 12, n° 5 (March 1954), item 34.

3. *Ibid.*

4. Cleanth Brook and Robert Penn Warren, *Understanding Fiction* (Englewood Cliffs, New Jersey: Prentice-Hall, 1971), p. 74.

5. Virgil Scott, *Studies in the Short Story,* Instructor's Manual (New York: Norton, 1968), p. 20.

6. Helen E. Nebeker, « The Lottery: Symbolic Tour de Force », *American Literature* 46, n° 1 (March 1974), 100-107. Her analysis is based on religious symbolism.

7. Heilman is convinced that « the symbolic intention of the story (should) have been made clear » (op. cit., p. 385) immediately. But then the actual meaning and effect of the story would have been lessened and the reader would quickly forget the message.

8. Even Brooks and Warren compare « The Lottery » to a fable or a parable (op. cit., pp. 72-74).

9. Although Brooks and Warren mention that the « author's point in general has to do with the awful doubleness of the human spirit » (op. cit., p. 76) they do not comment on the use of symbols denoting it.

10. For all interpretations of symbols see Jean Chevalier and Alain Gheerbrant, *Dictionnaire des symboles* (Paris: Seghers, 1973), J.E. Cirlot, *A Dictionary of Symbols* (London and Henley: Routledge and Kegan Paul, 1978) and Ad de Vries, *Dictionary of Symbols* (Amsterdam and London: North-Routledge and Kegan Paul, 1978). Where necessary, further references will be given in the course of the interpretation of symbols.

11. Frédéric Portal, *Des Couleurs symboliques, dans l'Antiquité, le Moyen Age et les Temps Modernes* (Paris: Treutel and Würtz, 1937).

12. Enel, *La Langue sacrée* (Paris: A. Michel, 1932).

13. [See note 10.]

14. James G. Frazer, *The Golden Bough: A Study in Magic and Religion* (London: Macmillan, 1900), vol. 3, p. 266.

15. [See note 10.]

16. Papus, *La Science des nombres* (Paris: A. Michel, 1934).

17. Papus, *Traité méthodique de science occulte* (Paris: G. Carré, 1891).

18. [See note 17.]

19. Marius Schneider, *La danza de espadas y la tarantela* (Barcelona: Emece, 1946).

20. [See note 17.]

21. Marc Saunier, *La Légende des symboles philosophiques, religieux et maçonniques,* 2nd edition (Paris: E. Sansot, 1911).

22. L. Paneth, *Zahlensymbolik im Bewusstsein* (Zürich: Rascher, 1952).

23. [See note 22.]

24. These are Harburt, Overdyke, Summers and Zanini.

25. [See note 10.]

26. [See note 22.]

27. [See note 24.]

28. A detailed list of the historical allusions would add little to this point. Suffice it to say that the past counterpart of the villagers were renowned painters, poets, playwrights, actors, storytellers, ministers, legislators, governors, architects, surgeons, pathologists, physicians, botanists, etc.

29. Scott sees in Summers « the appropriate leader of the rite » (op. cit., p. 20) as his barenness and unhappiness predispose him « to shift the burden of his pains and sorrows to another, who will suffer them in his stead » (this he quotes from *The Golden Bough,* p. 1). The main official's name also evokes the pervading duality: at its start the summer brings perfection and light but come its scorching heart or harvest and it refers to death. So with his very surname he points to the inevitable decline of beauty.

30. Winnifred King Rugg, *Unafraid: The Life of Anne Hutchinson* (Boston and New York: Houghton and Miflin, 1930), pp. 221-226.

Judie Newman (essay date 1990)

SOURCE: Newman, Judie. "Shirley Jackson and the Reproduction of Mothering: *The Haunting of Hill House.*" In *American Horror Fiction: From Brockden Brown to Stephen King,* edited by Brian Docherty, pp. 120-34. London: Macmillan, 1990.

[*In the following essay, Newman applies "feminist psychoanalytic theory" to a reading of* The Haunting of Hill House, *exploring the ways in which both "the pleasures and the terrors of the text" derive from Jackson's treatment of the mother-daughter relationship in the novel.*]

One of the most enduring mysteries of horror fiction consists in its exploitation of the attractions of fear. Why, one may ask, should a reader seek out the experience of being terrified, particularly by horror fiction, which adds abhorrence, loathing and physical repulsion to the purer emotions of terror evoked by the supernatural tale? For H. P. Lovecraft[1] the answer lay in the human fear of the unknown. Freud,[2] however, developed a different hypothesis, describing the experience of the 'uncanny' (*unheimlich*) as that class of the frightening which leads back to what is known of old and long-familiar. Observing that *heimlich* (familiar, homely) is the opposite of *unheimlich,* Freud recognises the temptation to equate the uncanny with fear of the unknown. Yet he noted that *heimlich* also means 'concealed', 'private', 'secret', as the home is an area withdrawn from the eyes of strangers. In Freud's argument, therefore, the experience of the uncanny arises either when primitive animistic beliefs, previously surmounted, seem once more to be confirmed (Shirley Jackson's **'The Lottery'** is a case in point) or when infantile complexes, formerly repressed, are revived (a theory which brings *The Haunting of Hill House* into sharp focus). For Freud, various forms of ego disturbance involve regression to a period when the ego had not marked itself off sharply from the external world and from other people. In the context of a discussion of ghosts and doubles, Freud cites Otto Rank's description of the double as originally an insurance against the destruction of the ego, an energetic denial of the power of death. (In this sense the 'immortal soul' may be considered as the first double of the body.) The idea of doubling as preservation against extinction therefore springs from the unbounded self-love of the child. When this stage of primitive narcissism is surmounted, however, the double reverses its aspect, and, from being an assurance of immortality, becomes the uncanny harbinger of death and a thing of terror. Since Freud considered art as an organised activity of sublimation, providing the reader with pleasures 'under wraps', it is tempting to argue that the horror tale actively eliminates and exorcises our fears by allowing them to be relegated to the imaginary realm of fiction.[3] Rosemary Jackson, however, has indicated the case for the fantastic as a potentially subversive reversal of cultural formation, disruptive of conventional distinctions between the real and the unreal.[4] Arguably, although Shirley Jackson builds her horrors on the basis of the *heimlich* and of repressed infantile complexes, in the process she subverts the Freudian paradigm, both of art as sublimation, and in broader psychoanalytic terms. In this connection, new developments in psychoanalytic theory offer fresh insights into Jackson's work.

Recent feminist psychoanalytic theorists[5] have set out to revise the Freudian account of psychosexual differences, which bases gender, anatomically, on possession or lack of the phallus. In the Freudian paradigm, the male achieves adulthood by passing through the Oedipus complex, which fear of castration by the father induces him to overcome. Fear facilitates acceptance of the incest prohibition, promoting the formation of the superego, which thereafter polices desire in accordance with adult social norms. In a parallel development, the female discovers the lack of the phallus, sees herself as castrated, recognises her mother as similarly inferior, and therefore abandons her attachment to the mother to form the Oedipal relation with the father, which is the necessary precursor of adult heterosexual relationships—always the Freudian goal. Feminist analysts, however, have shifted the focus from the Oedipal to the pre-Oedipal stage, tracing the influence of gender on identity to the dynamics of the mother-infant bond. Nancy Chodorow in *The Reproduction of Mothering* offers a persuasive analysis of early infant development in these terms. Because children first experience the social and cognitive world as continuous with themselves, the mother is not seen as a separate person with separate interests. In this brief period of immunity from individuality, the experience of fusion with the mother, of mother as world, is both seductive and terrifying. Unity is bliss; yet it entails total dependence and loss of self. In contrast the father does not pose the original threat to basic ego integrity, and is perceived from the beginning as separate. Thus, the male fear of women may originate as terror of maternal omnipotence in consequence of the early dependence on the mother, and may be generalised to all women (in images such as the witch, the vampire and the Terrible Mother[6]) since it is tied up with the assertion of gender. Boys define themselves as masculine by difference from, not by relation to, their mothers. Girls, however, in defining themselves as female, experience themselves as resembling their mothers, so that the experience of attachment fuses with the process of identity formation. Girls therefore learn to see themselves as partially continuous with their mothers, whereas boys learn very early about difference and separateness. Male development therefore

entails more emphatic individuation, and more defensive firming of experienced ego boundaries, whereas women persist in defining themselves relationally, creating fluid, permeable ego boundaries, and locating their sense of self in the ability to make and maintain affiliations. Female gender identity is therefore threatened by separation, and shaped throughout life by the fluctuations of symbiosis and detachment from the mother. Girls may also fear material omnipotence and struggle to free themselves, idealising the father as their most available ally. Daughterly individuation may be inhibited by paternal absence and by over-closeness to mothers, who tend to view their daughters as extensions of themselves. Conversely, coldness on the mother's part may prevent the loosening of the emotional bond because of the unappeased nature of the child's love. In maturity women may form close personal relationships with other women to recapture some aspects of the fractured mother-daughter bond. Alternatively they may reproduce the primary attachment, by themselves bearing children, thus initiating the cycle once more, as the exclusive symbiotic relation of the mother's own infancy is re-created. Mothering therefore involves a double identification for women in which they take both parts of the pre-Oedipal relation, as mother and as child. Fictions of development reflect this psychological structure. Recent reformulations of the female *Bildungsroman*[7] have drawn attention to the frequency with which such fictions end in deaths (Maggie Tulliver, Rachel Vinrace, Edna Pontellier) understandable less as developmental failures than as refusals to accept an adulthood which denies female desires and values. In addition, a persistent, if recessive, narrative concern with the story of mothers and daughters often exists in the background to a dominant romance or courtship plot.

An exploration of *The Haunting of Hill House* in the light of feminist psychoanalytic theory reveals that the source of both the pleasures and the terrors of the text springs from the dynamics of the mother-daughter relation with its attendant motifs of psychic annihilation, reabsorption by the mother, vexed individuation, dissolution of individual ego boundaries, terror of separation and the attempted reproduction of the symbiotic bond through close female friendship. Eleanor Vance, the central protagonist, is mother-dominated. On her father's death the adolescent Eleanor was associated with an outbreak of poltergeist activity, in which her family home was repeatedly showered with stones. The event invites comparison with **'The Lottery',** in which the victim of the stoning, Tessie Hutchinson, is not only a mother, but a mother who sees her daughter as so much an extension of herself that she attempts to improve her own chances of survival by involving Eva in the fatal draw. Eleanor clearly resented her recently dead mother, whom she nursed for eleven years: 'the only person in the world she genuinely hated, now that her mother was dead, was her sister' (p. 9).[8] Initially her excursion to Hill House to participate in Dr Montague's study of psychic phenomena appears as an opportunity for psychological liberation, the first steps towards autonomy. The trip begins with a small act of assertion against the mother-image. When Eleanor's sister refuses to allow her to use their shared car ('I am sure Mother would have agreed with me, Eleanor'—p. 14), Eleanor reacts by simply stealing it, in the process knocking over an angry old woman who is clearly associated with the 'cross old lady' (p. 10) whom she had nursed for so long. Once *en route* Eleanor is haunted by the refrain 'Journeys end in lovers meeting', suggesting (as the *carpe diem* theme of the song confirms) that Eleanor's goal is the realisation of heterosexual desires.

Eleanor's fantasies on the journey, however, imply that her primary emotional relation remains with her mother. In imagination she dreams up several 'homes', based on houses on her route. In the first, 'a little dainty old lady took care of me' (p. 19), bringing trays of tea and wine 'for my health's sake'. The fantasy reveals just how much Eleanor herself wishes to be mothered. In the preceding period, as nurse to a sick mother, Eleanor may be said to have 'mothered' her own mother, losing her youth in the process. A second fantasy centres upon a hollow square of poisonous oleanders, which seem to Eleanor to be 'guarding something' (p. 20). Since the oleanders enclose only an empty centre, Eleanor promptly supplies a mother to occupy it, constructing an enthralling fairy world in which 'the queen waits, weeping, for the princess to return' (p. 21). Though she swiftly revises this daydream of mother-daughter reunion, into a more conventional fantasy of courtship by a handsome prince, she remains much preoccupied with images of protected spaces and magic enclosures, of a home in which *she* could be mothered and greeted as a long-lost child. A subsequent incident reinforces this impression. Pausing for lunch, Eleanor observes a little girl who refuses to drink her milk because it is not in the familiar cup, patterned with stars, which she uses at home. Despite material persuasion, the child resists, forcing her mother to yield. The small tableau emphasises both the child's potential independence and resistance to the mother, and the attractions of the familiar home world, here associated with mother's milk and starry containment. Eleanor empathises with the little girl's narcissistic desires: 'insist on your cup of stars; once they have trapped you into being like everyone else you will never see your cup of stars again' (p. 22). Eleanor's final fantasy home, a cottage hidden behind oleanders, 'buried in a garden' (p. 23), is entirely secluded from the world. Taken together, her fantasies suggest her ambivalent individuation and the lure of a magic mother-world. They form a striking contrast to the reality of Hillsdale, a tangled mess of dirty houses and crooked streets. For all its ugliness, however,

Eleanor deliberately delays there over coffee. Despite her reiterated refrain 'In delay there lies no plenty', Eleanor is not quite so eager to reach her goal and realise her desires as she thinks. Another scene of enforced delay, negotiating with a surly caretaker at the gates of Hill House, further retards her progress. The emphasis here on locked gates, guards against entry, a tortuous access road, and the general difficulty in locating the house reinforces the impression of its desirability as *heimlich*, secret, a home kept away from the eyes of others.

Entry to this protected enclave provokes, however, a response which underlines the consonance of the familiar and the uncanny: childish terror. Afraid that she will cry 'like a child sobbing and wailing' (p. 34), tiptoeing around apprehensively, Eleanor feels like 'a small creature swallowed whole by a monster' which 'feels my tiny little movements inside' (p. 38). The intra-uterine fantasy immediately associates Hill House with an engulfing mother. Eleanor's fellow guest, Theo, reacts in opposite terms, characterising the two women as Babes in the Woods (abandoned by parents) and comparing the experience to the first day at boarding-school or camp. The vulnerable continuity between fear of engulfment and fear of separation is indicated in the women's response to the threat. Reminiscing about their childhoods, they eagerly associate themselves through fancied family resemblances, until Theo announces that theirs is an indissoluble relationship: 'Would you let them separate us now? Now that we've found out we're cousins?' (p. 49). Yet on the arrival of the remaining guests, Luke and Dr Montague, Theo's assertion of female strength through attachment is swiftly replaced as the four establish their identities, in playfully exaggerated form, through separation and differentiation: 'You are Theodora because *I* am Eleanor'; 'I have no beard so *he* must be Dr Montague' (pp. 53-4). Fantasy selves are then elaborated. Luke introduces himself as a bullfighter; Eleanor poses as an artist's model, living an 'abandoned' life while moving from garret to garret; Theo describes herself as a lord's daughter, masquerading as an ordinary mortal in the clothes of her maid, in order to escape a parental plot of forced marriage. Interestingly, though both women characterise themselves as homeless, Eleanor converts homelessness into an image of abandonment, Theo into active escape from an oppressive parent by asserting a different identity. For Eleanor, however, identity remains elusive. In envisaging herself as an artist's model she acquiesces in a self-image created by a controlling other.

Introductions over, the foursome make a preliminary exploration of Hill House which confirms its character as an ambivalent maternal enclave. Comfortable, its menu excellent, the house has 'a reputation for insistent hospitality' (p. 59), and is distinguished by inwardness and enclosure. Labyrinthine in layout, its concentric circles of rooms, some entirely internal and window-less, make access to the outside world problematic. Doors close automatically on its occupants, who are further confused by its architectural peculiarities. In Hill House every apparent right-angle is a fraction off, all these tiny aberrations of measurement adding up to a large overall distortion, which upsets the inhabitants' sense of balance. An encircling verandah obscures awareness of the distortion. While this structure mirrors the conventional twisted line of Gothic (in plot as in architecture), baffling the reader's sense of direction and threatening to lead at any point out of one world and into another, it also emphasises an internalised entrapment which threatens reason and balance. Luke is in no doubt as to the house's identity: 'It's all so motherly. Everything so soft. Everything so padded. Great embracing chairs and sofas which turn out to be hard and unwelcoming when you sit down, and reject you at once—' (p. 174). The ambivalent suggestions here of maternal comfort and maternal rejection invite comparison with *The Sundial,* in which the labyrinthine connection between mother as security and mother as trap is foregrounded in a physical maze, to which only Aunt Fanny knows the key. The pattern of the maze is built upon her mother's name, Anna, so that, by turning right, left, left, right, then left, right, right, left, the centre is reached. As long as the mother's name is remembered, Fanny is secure in 'the maze I grew up in',⁹ despite the activities of the matriarch, Orianna, the murderess of her own child.

Paradoxically, the doctor's history reveals that Hill House is actually notable for an absence of mothers. The first Mrs Crain died in a carriage accident in the drive, the second in a fall, the third in Europe of consumption. Since Hugh Crain's two daughters were therefore brought up without a mother, the house is simultaneously associated with mothering and with motherlessness. Later the older of the two daughters took possession of the house, dying there amidst accusations that her young companion had neglected her. The latter, persecuted by the younger sister's attempts to regain the house, eventually hanged herself. The history of the house therefore provides a psychic configuration not unlike Eleanor's own, which also involves a dead mother, two warring sisters, and a neglected old lady. Eleanor later accuses herself: 'It was my fault my mother died. She knocked on the wall and called me and called me and I never woke up' (p. 177). On learning the history of the house, however, Eleanor empathises with the unmothered girls and the companion. Eleanor has been both mother and child. On the one hand she detests the mother's dominance, resenting the loss of her own youth in the forced assumption of the 'mothering' role. On the other, she feels guilt at not having mothered adequately. Both images are internalised so that Eleanor is haunted by guilt as a mother over the neglected child within herself.

As a result two rooms in Hill House are of special significance to her—the library and the nursery, the one associated with the mother, the other with the unmothered child. Eleanor is quite incapable of entering the library: '"I can't go in there." . . . She backed away, overwhelmed with the cold air of mould and earth which rushed at her. "My mother—"' (p. 88). Eleanor's mother had forced her to read love stories aloud to her each afternoon, hence the library's supulchral associations. The library is also the point of access to the tower, where the companion hanged herself. Theo jokes, 'I suppose she had some sentimental attachment to the tower; what a nice word "attachment" is in that context' (p. 88). If attachments can be linked with annihilation and wilful surrender of the self, their absence can be equally damaging. The nursery of the unmothered girls is marked by a cold spot at its entrance 'like the doorway of a tomb' (p. 101). On its wall is painted a frieze of animals which appear as if trapped or dying. Ironically Dr Montague describes this area of cold nurturance as 'the heart of the house' (p. 101).

The stage is now set for the first appearance of the 'ghost', which occurs at the heart of Jackson's novel, almost exactly at its centre. Eleanor's internalisation of both the 'unmothered child' and the 'neglected mother' images is reflected in the double mother-child nature of the haunting. Awakening, Eleanor at first thinks that her mother is calling and knocking on the wall. In fact a tremendous pounding noise, beginning close to the nursery door, accompanied by a wave of cold, has disturbed her. The violence of the phenomenon suggests a force strong enough to threaten the boundaries of the ego; amidst deafening crashes it very nearly smashes in the door. Nevertheless, Eleanor's first reaction is relief that it is *not* her mother, but 'only a noise' (p. 108). Indeed, she sees it as 'like something children do, not mothers knocking against the wall for help' (p. 108). The ghost now undergoes a metamorphosis, its vehement demands yielding to an insidious seductive appeal. The doorknob is 'fondled', amidst 'little pattings' 'small seeking sounds', 'little sticky sounds' (p. 111). The relentless emphasis on smallness and the affectionate pattings suggest a child. Eleanor and Theo, huddled together in fear, have also been reduced to 'a couple of lost children' (p. 111). Importantly, the haunting is limited to the women. (The men, outside chasing a mysterious dog, hear nothing.) Alarmed, Dr Montague draws the conclusion that 'the intention is, somehow, to separate us' (p. 114). Eleanor, however, argues that 'it wanted to consume us, take us into itself, make us a part of the house' (p. 117). The threat which the men perceive in terms of separation is understood by both women in terms of fusion and engulfment. In the light of this identification of the haunting with the reassertion of the ambivalent mother-daughter bond, it is unsurprising that Eleanor awakens next day with a renewed feeling of happiness, a fresh appetite and the urge to sing and dance. When Dr Montague argues for the reality of the haunting, given the presence of independent witnesses, Eleanor cheerfully suggests the possibility that 'all three of you are in my imagination' (p. 118). The doctor's warning that this way madness lies—a state which would welcome Hill House in a 'sisterly embrace' (p. 118)—points to an incipient narcissism in Eleanor which would make self and world conterminous once more, assimilating all to the subjective imagination.

Initially Eleanor responds to the threat of ego dissolution by a strategic attachment to Theo, quickly forming a close friendship in which more than one reader has detected lesbian content (as the film version also implied). A similar uncertainty besets the reader of **Hangsaman**: is Natalie's mysterious friend Tony real, imaginary, supernatural, a double or a lesbian lover? Since Natalie is always terrified of being alone with *her* mother, the attachment may be read as the result of the projection of the symbiotic bond onto an alter ego. Similarly Eleanor fosters autonomy by division, creating in Theo a double as insurance against the destruction of her own self, and as simultaneous confirmation of relational identity. Several incidents in the novel make sense only in these terms. On her first evening at Hill House, Eleanor revels in her own individuality, contemplating her feet in new red shoes: 'What a complete and separate thing I am . . . individually an I, possessed of attributes belonging only to me' (p. 72). In contrast she regards her hands as ugly and dirty, misshapen by years of laundering her mother's soiled linen. Theo, telling Eleanor teasingly that she disliked 'women of no colour' (p. 99), paints Eleanor's toenails red in celebration of her emergent independence. Unlike the highly individuated Theo, Eleanor is drab, mousy, with a tendency to merge into her surroundings. Theo's subsequent casual comment that Eleanor's feet are dirty provokes a violent emotional reaction, for Eleanor cannot cope with the clash between colour and grime, between individuation and association with the mother. The sight of her feet now fills her with an immediate sense of helpless dependence: 'I don't like to feel helpless. My mother—' (p. 99). In what follows Eleanor fluctuates ambivalently between an antagonistic and an associative relation to Theo.

When a second apparent manifestation occurs (the message 'HELP ELEANOR COME HOME' chalked in the hall) Eleanor both revels and recoils. On the one hand the message expresses her own desire for home. On the other, she is anxious at being identified by name. *Her* identity is targeted; she has been 'singled out' (p. 124) and separated from the group. Indeed, the message also effectively divides Eleanor and Theo, sparking a quarrel when each accuses the other of writing it. Eleanor's outburst reveals both her own suppressed need for attention, and her projection of the childish identity onto Theo: 'You think *I* like the idea that I'm the centre of attention? *I'm* not the spoiled baby after all' (p. 124). Separate identity is thus both desired and rejected. When the message is reinscribed on Theo's walls, and her clothes smeared with a substance which may be paint or blood, Theo immediately accuses Eleanor, who views the 'bloody chamber' with smiling satisfaction, admitting that it reminds her of Theo applying red polish (p. 131). The reader puzzles as to whether the hauntings are supernatural or caused by Eleanor, thus drawing attention to the central question of the novel—the degree of Eleanor's independent agency. Eleanor's apparent hostility is double-edged. Scrubbing the colour off Theo, she feels uncontrollable loathing for her polluted alter ego, who is 'filthy with the stuff', 'beastly and soiled and dirty' (p. 132). Watching her, Eleanor thinks, 'I would like to batter her with rocks' (p. 133). The conjunction of the two images of enforced laundering and of stoning indicates Eleanor's hostility to the mother, and to the mother within herself. The destruction of Theo's clothes, however, suggests an attempt to destroy an independent identity (the reader recalls Theo's previous fantasy of disguise), rendering Theo colourless and bringing the women into close association. Theo now has to share Eleanor's clothes and bedroom. As she comments, 'We're going to be practically twins' (p. 133). The entire sequence culminates in an admission from Eleanor of her own fear of disintegration. Contemplating Theo, dressed in Eleanor's sweater and therefore presenting an alternative self-image in which narcissism and self-hate are almost equally involved, Eleanor expresses her desire to return to a state of primal unity:

> There's only one of me, and it's all I've got. I hate seeing myself dissolve and slip and separate so that I'm living in one half, my mind, and I see the other half of me helpless . . . and I could stand any of it if I could only surrender.
>
> (p. 134)

Forming a close relation with Theo, constituting Theo as 'other half', are strategies which culminate disastrously in the replication rather than the repudiation of the symbiotic bond, and a desire to surrender autonomy altogether.

In consequence, the subsequent 'haunting' is quite different in character, and limited to Eleanor. In the night Eleanor appears to hear a voice in Theo's empty room: 'It is a child', 'I won't let anyone hurt a child' (p. 136). While the voice babbles, Eleanor tries but fails to speak; only when it pauses is she able to cry out. It thus appears to emanate from her. Indeed, Eleanor recognises its screams from her own nightmares. Throughout the scene Eleanor has been holding Theo's hand for reassurance, clutching it so hard that she can feel the 'fine bones' (p. 137) of the fingers. On coming to consciousness (it has all been a dream) she discovers Theo sitting apart in her own bed, and shrieks, 'Whose hand was I holding?' (p. 137). The juxtaposition of a skeletal dead hand, first as reassurance then as terror, with a child's voice screaming is consonant with Eleanor's deepening neurosis. Although she adopts a mothering role ('I won't let anyone hurt a child') the penalty is to be associated with a form of security which is also a horror, with the mother as death to the self.

In desperation Eleanor makes a last attempt to establish identity outwith the mother-daughter bond. But when she solicits a confidence from Luke, in a bid for a special token of affection, his response horrifies her: '"I never had a mother." The shock was enormous. Is *that* all he thinks of me' (p. 139). Luke's subsequent comment, that he had always wanted a mother to make him grow up, prompts Eleanor's acid reply, 'Why don't you grow up by yourself?' (p. 140), indicating her impatience with a courtship model which provides no escape from the dynamics of the original relationship. That night, when Theo teases Eleanor about Luke, the women are the victims of another haunting while they are following a path through the grounds. Ostensibly squabbling over Luke, they are described in terms which suggest the persistence of a more primary bond. Each is 'achingly aware of the other' (p. 145) as they skirt around an 'open question'. The language suggests that they are trembling on the brink, *not* of an open quarrel, but of mutual seduction: 'walking side by side in the most extreme intimacy of expectation; their feinting and hesitation done with, they could only wait passively for resolution. Each knew, almost within a breath, what the other was thinking, (p. 146).

As they draw closer, arm in arm again, the path unrolls before them through a suddenly 'colourless' (p. 147) landscape, in an 'annihilation of whiteness'. Ahead there appears a ghostly tableau of a family picnic, in a garden full of rich colour, 'thickly green' grass (p. 148), red, orange and yellow flowers, beneath a bright blue sky. Theo's immediate response is to run ahead, screaming, 'Don't look back', placing colourlessness behind her, along with the risk of annihilation in a symbiotic relationship. Eleanor, however, her development definitively arrested, collapses, feeling 'time, as she had always known time, stop' (p. 149). The haunting foreshadows the outcome of their relationship. When Eleanor announces her intention of accompanying Theo to her home, Theo rejects her once and for all, impatient with what she perceives as a schoolgirl crush, 'as though I were the games mistress' (p. 177). As Eleanor's identity founders, Theo's is secured: her clothes are now restored to their original condition.

The image of the two women trampling the 'happy family' vignette under foot also foregrounds the insufficiencies of the Oedipal model, a point which is generalised by Luke's discovery of a book, composed by Hugh Crain for his daughter. Ostensibly a series of moral lessons, with illustrations of Heaven, Hell, the seven deadly sins, the book purports to guide the child in the paths of righteousness, threatening her with various terrible fates, and offering the reward of reunion in her Father's arms in Heaven 'joined together hereafter in unending bliss' (p. 143). The erotic content of the offer is fully revealed in the obscenity of Crain's accompanying illustration to 'Lust'. The pretence of guiding the child's moral development is actually an excuse to indulge in sensation, transgressing in the guise of moral admonition. Jackson thus explodes both the Freudian view of the father as former of the superego, and of art as an activity of sublimation, replacing instinctual gratifications. Here, far from being the basis of psychic ascension, the Oedipal model is an alibi for male self-indulgence, and a legitimation of patriarchal tyranny. Importantly, Crain has cut up several other books to form his own, so that his individual text draws upon all the resources available in the cultural formation of the female subject.

The arrival of Dr Montague's wife, a conventional spiritualist, measures the distance between fashionable psychic explanations and more radical theories of the psyche. The parodic Mrs Montague is primarily notable for the bookishness of her images of psychic phenomena, most of which are drawn from obvious sources.[10] Thus, receiving a spirit message via 'planchette' from a mysterious nun, she promptly conjures up a monk and extrapolates to a heterosexual courtship model, broken vows and the nun walled up alive. Although a long correspondence in *The Times* in 1939 failed to establish evidence of any such immurement, nuns remain the most common of reported apparitions,[11] their popularity possibly the result of the recognition that the repression of female desires is a source of psychic disturbance (as in *Villette*). 'Planchette' also produces the words 'Elena', 'Mother', 'Child', 'Lost', 'Home', endlessly repeated. As a result of botched introductions Mrs Montague takes Theo for Eleanor, and passes the message to the former. The suggestion lingers that Eleanor's bid for independent identity has failed, and that she is locked into psychic repetition.

It is therefore appropriate that the next haunting repeats the features of the others (Theo remarks on the ghost's exhausted repertoire—p. 166). Noisy knockings are followed by a 'caressing touch' (p. 168) 'feeling intimately and softly', 'fondling' and 'wheedling' at the door, and by a babbling both inside and outside Eleanor's head. For Eleanor, the distinction between self and world is collapsing: 'I am disappearing inch by inch into this house, I am going apart a little bit at a time' (p. 168). As Eleanor resists dissolution, so the house shakes and threatens to fall, until she surrenders: 'I will relinquish my possession of this self of mine, abdicate. . . . "I'll come," she said' (p. 170). Instantly all is quiet, and the chapter ends with Theo's joke 'Come along, baby. Theo will wash your face for you and make you all neat for breakfast' (p. 171). Eleanor has thus given up all hope of mature individuation, welcoming the role of child.

From this point on, only Eleanor is haunted, by ghostly footsteps and a welcoming embrace (p. 178), and by a child's voice at the empty centre of the parlour singing, 'Go in and out the windows' (p. 189)—a singing-game which replaces the earlier refrain. In surrendering to the child within, Eleanor finally becomes herself the haunter, assuming the attenuated identity of the ghost. Rising by night, she thinks 'Mother', and when a voice replies 'Come along' (p. 190) she runs to the nursery, to find the cold spot gone, darts in and out of the encircling verandah, and continues the childish game by pounding on the others' doors. Around her the house is 'protected and warm' (p. 193), its layout entirely familiar. Ego dissolution has become primal bliss. Hearing Luke's voice, she recognises that of all those present she would least like *him* to catch her, and flees from male pursuit into the library, now 'deliciously fondly warm' (p. 193), its rotten spiral staircase perceived not as a danger but as a means of escape. Though in fact Eleanor is caught in a spiral of fatal repetition, moving towards complete annihilation, she is exultant: 'I have broken the spell of Hill House and somehow come inside. I am home' (p. 194). Eleanor has transferred her 'crush' to the house, described by Luke as 'a mother house, a housemother, a headmistress, a housemistress' (p. 176), and now becomes entirely conterminous with her chosen world, alive to sounds and movements in all its many rooms. Unsurprisingly, when Dr Montague excludes her from his experiment, Eleanor finds separation unthinkable and accelerates her car into a tree in the driveway. Her last thoughts reveal a fatal connection between female self-assertion and annihilation: 'I am really doing it, I am doing this all by myself, now, at last; this is me, I am really really really doing it by myself' (p. 205). In the second before collision her last lucid thought is '*Why* am I doing this?' Feminist psychoanalytics offers an answer which is oddly confirmed in the conclusion. The novel closes with a repetition, almost without alteration, of its own original paragraph, as the cycle of creation closes only to begin once more.

If, by repressing desire, human beings condemn themselves to repeat it, the appeal of Jackson's work to both male and female readers is secure. Just as each individual 'haunting' derives its horrors from the fear of regression to infantile complexes, specifically of fusion with the mother, so the general features of Jackson's fiction are comprehensible in terms of the reproduction of mothering. The anticipation of revisionist psychoanalytics in the reformulation of the sources of horror may also be traced in *The Bird's Nest,* which attributes Elizabeth Richmond's breakdown to her motherlessness; in the murdered child of *The Road through the Wall*; in the murderous and eventually murdered mother of *The Sundial,* and in Jackson's own fascination with the Lizzie Borden case, which looms behind the acquitted murderess, Harriet Stuart, of *The Sundial* and the unconvicted Merricat (*We Have Always Lived in the Castle*), who poisons the rest of her family in order to establish the symbiotic bond with her sister. It would be impertinent, not to say impossible, to speculate on the influence of Jackson's own experience of mothering on her fiction. She was herself a devoted mother of four children, as her two humorous chronicles of family life reveal. Interestingly, the titles of these celebrations of maternal experience, *Raising Demons* and *Life among the Savages,* immediately suggest works of horror fiction.

Notes

1. H. P. Lovecraft, *Supernatural Horror in Literature* (New York: Dover, 1973).

2. 'The Uncanny', in *The Standard Edition of the Complete Psychological Works of Sigmund Freud,* ed. James Strachey, vol. XVII (London: Hogarth Press, 1955).

3. See Peter Penzoldt, *The Supernatural in Fiction* (London: Peter Nevill, 1952).

4. Rosemary Jackson, *Fantasy: The Literature of Subversion* (London: Methuen, 1981).

5. See Nancy Chodorow, *The Reproduction of Mothering* (Berkeley, Calif.: University of California Press, 1978); Carol Gilligan, *In a Different Voice: Psychological Theory and Women's Development* (Cambridge, Mass.: Harvard University Press, 1982); Jean Baker Miller, *Towards a New Psychology of Women* (London: Allen Lane, 1978).

6. A motif traced, in Jungian terms, in Jackson's work by Steven K. Hoffman, in 'Individuation and Character Development in the Fiction of Shirley Jackson', *Hartford Studies in Literature*, 8 (1976) 190-208.

7. Elizabeth Abel, Marianne Hirsch and Elizabeth Langland (eds), *The Voyage In: Fictions of Female Development* (Hanover, NH: University Press of New England, 1983).

8. Page references in parentheses relate to Shirley Jackson, *The Haunting of Hill House* (London: Michael Joseph, 1960).

9. Shirley Jackson, *The Sundial* (New York: Penguin, 1986) p. 109.

10. Mrs Montague's discoveries recall the worst excesses of the ghost hunter, at Borley Rectory in Essex. See Harry Price, *The Most Haunted House in England: Ten Years Investigation of Borley Rec-*

tory (London: Longmans, Green, 1940) and *The End of Borley Rectory* (London: George G. Harrap, 1946). Jackson refers to Borley in the text (p. 101). Though an examination of Jackson's sources would run to another essay, it is worth noting that almost all the psychic phenomena are drawn from the above work, including a haunted Blue Room, a cold spot, the girl in the tower, the nun and monk, immurement, the digging-up of an old well (proposed by Mrs Montague), messages on walls and from planchette, nightly crashings and patterings at doors, and investigation by a team of psychic researchers. Jackson described her book as originating in an account of nineteenth-century psychic researchers, almost certainly those of Ballechin House, also referred to in the text (p. 8). See A. Goodrich Freer and John, Marquess of Bute, *The Alleged Haunting of Ballechin House* (London: George Redway, 1899).

11. See Peter Underwood, *Dictionary of the Occult and Supernatural* (London: George G. Harrap, 1978) p. 147.

Karen J. Hall (essay date 1993)

SOURCE: Hall, Karen J. "Sisters in Collusion: Safety and Revolt in Shirley Jackson's *We Have Always Lived in the Castle.*" In *The Significance of Sibling Relationships in Literature,* edited by JoAnna Stephens Mink and Janet Doubler Ward, pp. 110-19. Bowling Green, Ohio: Bowling Green State University Popular Press, 1993.

[*In the following essay, Hall interprets the behavior of the two female protagonists in Jackson's novel* We Have Always Lived in the Castle *as being symptomatic of patriarchal abuse.*]

> She understood that telling what you remembered, and writing down what had happened to you when you were young were radical acts of personal history that would force the rewriting of social history.
>
> Louise DeSalvo, *Virginia Woolf*

> And for a minute we stood very still, pressed together by the feeling of people all around us.
>
> Shirley Jackson, *We Have Always Lived in the Castle*

In the first paragraph of Shirley Jackson's *We Have Always Lived in the Castle,* the narrator introduces herself as Mary Katherine Blackwood, known affectionately as Merricat, an 18-year-old who lives with her sister, Constance. With any luck, she says, she would have been a werewolf "because the two middle fingers on both [her] hands are the same length" (1). She dislikes washing herself, dogs and noise; she likes her sister Constance, Richard Plantagenet, and *Amanita phalloides,* the death-cup mushroom. Everyone else in her family is dead.

As the plot unfolds we learn that Merricat and Constance live with their invalid uncle, Julian, that the rest of the family died of arsenic poisoning, that Constance stood trial for the murders but was acquitted for lack of evidence, and that there is a change in the air. Cousin Charles Blackwood embodies this change and will appear on the scene and attempt to transmogrify himself into the dead patriarch John Blackwood until Merricat frightens him away by setting fire to the Blackwood ancestral home. We also learn that Merricat, not Constance, killed her family by putting arsenic in the sugar bowl, and that Constance knew what her sister had done but remained silent for six years.

Castle is a complex and violent novel which has been relegated to the realm of juvenile fiction where its core of physical and psychic pain and its transgressive forces have been reinscribed, silenced and made safe for adolescent female readers. My goal as a reader is to untangle the psychological horror story told in *Castle* by borrowing the assumptions of theorists who are contesting the categorical boundaries and definitions of evidence and experience, and the discourse of the current recovery movement.[1] To this end, I read Merricat's and Constance's behaviors and actions in the novel as symptoms of the aftereffects of sexual abuse. I then theorize their behaviors as feminist interventions against the patriarchy which violates and oppresses them.

Uncle Julian has the most recognizable symptoms of trauma—on the night of the family murders, he consumed enough arsenic to leave him crippled and confined to a wheelchair. Julian is the only character in the novel who has a discourse available to him which allows him to say, "I am a survivor" (45). Julian is also the only character who has symptoms which a doctor can diagnose and treat. The way Julian copes with his trauma, however, suggests that rather than acting as a point of closure, the trauma which occurred on the night of the poisoning acts as a point of departure which explains the anxieties, rituals and behaviors the surviving Blackwoods manifest.

Despite Julian's ability to name and classify his victimhood, he is unable to reassure himself that the family murders really did take place. When Helen Clarke tells Julian at tea that he must forget about that night and put his morbid thoughts away, Julian turns to Constance to ask, "'Didn't it really happen?'" and when Charles refuses to discuss the murders with him, he again asks Constance, "'It *did* happen?'"—both times touching his fingers to his mouth as if searching for a trace of the arsenic (46, 95). Julian is obsessed with the murders and makes their study his life's work (43). His life is a ritualized, compulsive pattern of days in which he rises from sleep to eat, nap and study his notes of the events of the family's final day. Julian's obsessive compulsive behavior and his inability to believe in or even to remember his own victimization suggests that the Blackwood house was a dangerous place even before the murders.

To say that the family lacked closeness is an understatement. Mrs. Blackwood refused to cook or to garden or to nurture any living thing, jobs which all Blackwood women had traditionally made a show of fulfilling. She was intent on keeping a private home where the only visitors were people of the proper class. She trained her daughters to clean the house thoroughly, especially her drawing room which she could not bear to see untidy; for this reason she never allowed her daughters to come in the room, except of course to clean (34).

The only descriptions we get of John Blackwood come from Merricat, who says that her father kept a small notebook where he listed the people who owed him money or whom he felt owed him favors, and from Julian who remembers that he was inconsiderate on the last morning, whistling and waking his wife, Dorothy, who was still sleeping (67), that he was stingy, and that he was dishonest (121). Julian also remembers that John Blackwood was very fond of his person, "given to adorning himself, and not overly clean" (113). Julian's most descriptive recollection of his brother labels the most likely perpetrator of violence in the Blackwood home narcissistic and dirty.

This description of the Blackwood family corresponds to the portrait Louise DeSalvo paints of an incestuous family. Relying on Judith Herman and Lisa Hirschman's work, *Father-daughter Incest,* DeSalvo claims that incest is not a deviance from the ethics of family care, but is "a logical outgrowth of how the patriarchal family is organized" (8). One of the key players in such a family is a father who maintains despotic paternal rule (DeSalvo 9). This is a reasonable description of John Blackwood, a vain man who readers are told asserts power over his brother and sister-in-law by always making Julian and Dorothy aware that they are guests in his home, who meddles in and mediates family arguments which do not immediately concern him, who keeps thorough accounts of his finances, including debts of social obligation, and who maintains his status as much through his accumulation of personal possessions as through the power he asserts over his family and within his class.

Before the murders, Constance was in charge of all the family's cooking. Julian tells the inquisitive visitor Lucille Wright that the family "relied upon Constance for various small delicacies which only she could provide" (48). Mrs. Wright comments that Constance should not have been doing all the cooking. Julian replies, "Well, of course, there is the root of our trouble" (50). Mrs. Wright feels Constance was an unfit family cook because of her vast knowledge of poisons, but Julian knows that Constance's cooking is quite safe; what is not safe is the fact that, following the pattern of many incestuous homes, Mrs. Blackwood was a disinterested, absent mother, which left Constance to stand in for Mrs. Blackwood in the kitchen.

Many incest survivors develop eating disorders in an attempt to regain control over their bodies—control of the shape of their bodies, control of what can and cannot enter their bodies, and, by mediating a fine line between starvation and nourishment, survivors control who will punish their bodies. Although Merricat does not manifest what we may recognize as an eating disorder, food is a mystified, powerful substance for her. She has an extremely complex set of rules for what food she can and cannot touch, and she refuses to eat in front of people. Constance enables these behaviors. She feeds Merricat alone in the kitchen after meals are over or guests have left, she does not force Merricat to touch foods or kitchenware she does not want to touch, and she takes special car in the preparation of Merricat's meals. Most of all, Constance does not challenge Merricat's systems; she doesn't punish Merricat, make fun of her, or expect her to behave differently.

E. Sue Blume suggests in her work *Secret Survivors* that more women than men manifest eating disorders because women have "primary responsibility for providing food for those around them" (151). Food has long been an overdetermined signifier of power for Blackwood women. Generations of Blackwood women leave traces of their lives and nurturing abilities by filling the basement of the Blackwood ancestral home with their preserved foodstuffs. The script which stipulates that Blackwood women are responsible for maintaining the family through food production pre-exists Constance, and she is forced to assume this responsibility before she reaches adulthood, much, I suspect, as she is forced to assume responsibility for her father's sexual desires before she is an adult. Thus, it is no wonder that the majority of rules Merricat creates involve the preparation and eating of food or that the weapon she uses against her family is food. Merricat transforms the substance they force Constance to nurture them with into a poison, and she chooses to poison the sugar specifically—a food witches believed was unhealthy (Carpenter 34), a food Constance refuses to allow into her body, and, perhaps most importantly, a food their younger brother Thomas, the heir to the Blackwood fortune and a privileged son who "possessed many of his father's more forceful traits of character" (48), eats in excessive amounts.

Unlike Constance who assumes the role of the responsible child, the little parent of the dysfunctional family,

Merricat is the child who manifests her symptoms by abreacting a number of psychosomatic symptoms when she feels threatened or frightened.[2] She claims that she cannot see color in the village, that everything is a dull gray, and when Constance begins to be converted into "one of them" by Cousin Charles, even Constance looks gray (88). Merricat feels chilled and shivers when she is approached by villagers, when she first sees Charles outside the house, and when Constance whistles the tune John Blackwood whistled on the morning of the last day of his life. Whenever Merricat panics, she feels as though she cannot breathe. When she fears Constance will leave her, she feels tied with wire and cannot breathe (39); when she first sees Charles, she cannot breathe (79); when Charles first stands in their kitchen, Merricat "was held tight, wound round with wire, [she] couldn't breathe, and [she] had to run" (82); and the thought of her father's ring around her finger made her feel tied tight (111). Each time Merricat's surroundings trigger her fears and she panics, she feels the sensation that she is bound and cannot breathe. Merricat is describing what sounds like a body memory, a physical sensation the body remembers but the mind has no narrative for. Ellen Bass and Laura Davis state that such memories are stored in survivors' bodies "and it is possible to physically re-experience the terror of the abuse" (74-75). The sensation of being strangled or being unable to catch one's breath is common among survivors of abuse, and I feel it is significant that one of Merricat's memories is linked directly to her father his ring, and a possession which symbolizes union with him.

A further symptom of Merricat's earlier abuse is her ability to split when she feels threatened. Splitting is a coping mechanism common among survivors of sexual abuse:

> In its milder form, you live exclusively on the mental level, in your thoughts, and aren't fully present. At its most extreme, you literally leave your body. This feat, which some yogis work for decades to achieve, comes naturally to children during severe trauma. They cannot physically run away, so they leave their bodies.
>
> (Bass and Davis 209-10)

At the grocery store Merricat stops in the doorway "feeling around inside myself for some thought to make me safe" (13). Moments later during her confrontation with Jim Donell in Stella's diner, Merricat distances herself by watching her hands rip her napkin into tiny pieces and making a rule for herself that whenever she sees tiny scraps of paper she will be kinder to Julian (17). As Merricat leaves the diner and Donell's cruel laughter, she thinks to herself, "I liked my house on the moon, and I put a fireplace in it and a garden outside" (21). The moon is Merricat's safe place, a world a winged horse carries her to when she is threatened,

punished or afraid. As Merricat passes the Harris' house and the Harris boys taunt her, she pretends she does not speak their language, "on the moon we spoke a soft, liquid tongue and sang in the starlight, looking down on the dead dried world," and she thinks to herself that it is strange to be inside herself, "hiding very far inside but [still able] to hear them and see them from the corner of my eye" (23).

Merricat thinks and talks about the moon a great deal more once Cousin Charles arrives. Charles threatens her safety by transgressing the boundaries of his role as guest and as cousin by desiring to marry Constance. Merricat is well practiced at thinking herself out of her body and into a place of safety, so well practiced that as her burned out house is invaded by violent villagers she thinks, "I am on the moon . . . please let me be on the moon" (154). Merricat is able to dissociate during all of this violence yet still be present enough to protect herself and Constance from the villagers and escape to the safety of the woods. And it is to Merricat's safe place that Constance and Merricat retreat after the fire, "We are on the moon at last," and Constance replies, "I'm glad to be here . . . Thank you for bringing me" (165).

Critics who claim Merricat is crazy refer most frequently to her violent desires to act out rather than to her frequent breaks with reality. Even before readers find out Merricat poisoned her family, we see her imagine all the customers in the grocery store falling over, writhing in pain and dying while she steps over them to help herself to the groceries she needs. Merricat asserts that she was never sorry when she had thoughts like this; she only wished they would come true (12). She wishes she could see the Harris boys lying dead on the ground (23), and even the thought of Charles' big white face, a face which looks very much like John Blackwood's, makes her want "to beat at him until he went away . . . to stamp on him after he was dead, and see him lying on the grass" (116).

Even more disturbing than Merricat's desires are the scenes where she carries them out. Worried that Constance may venture outside their home, Merricat goes into the kitchen and smashes their best milk pitcher (39). Furious that Charles will not leave the house even after she has politely asked him to, Merricat carries all the furnishings out of his bedroom, pulls down the curtains, and dumps twigs and dirt and water in his bed. These acts are symbolic, indeed; in a more contemporary novel Merricat would no doubt have defecated in Charles' bed.[3] What provokes her most violent and confrontational rages, however, is the threat of punishment. On the night of the murders, Merricat had been sent to her room without dinner for bad behavior, and on the night when she sets fire to the house, Charles has threatened to punish her for making his room filthy.

As Charles rants about the filth in his room, he completely collapses into the identity of John Blackwood. Even Julian confuses him with the dead patriarch and says to Charles, "You are a very selfish man, John, perhaps even a scoundrel, and overly fond of the world's goods; I sometimes wonder, John, if you are every bit the gentleman" (134). Merricat calls Charles an evil ghost and Julian, once he recognizes him as his nephew, not his brother, calls him a bastard. Charles says the house is a crazy house. Readers have a perspective which allows them to see the "craziness" of the present scene and its striking, and for Merricat and Julian, confusing, resemblance to the crazy house of the past in which John Blackwood often stood in the kitchen and yelled just as Charles yells now.

Merricat's reaction to Charles' insistence that she be punished is intense. She stands in the kitchen doorway shivering, shrieks at him, "Punish me? You mean send me to bed without my dinner?" and then flees the house in search of safety. She then goes to the summerhouse, a wild, abandoned ugly place the family never used because it was damp and mold grew on everything. Here she sits and fantasizes that she is at the dinner table surrounded by a loving family. Everyone is extending themselves to her, offering her presents, saying they love her, vowing never to punish her, and even ordering her brother to give her his dinner (139). This wish fulfilling fantasy suggests that at least a part of Merricat's trauma involved neglect and fear of abandonment. Merricat is not the only character who recognizes these fears; Julian believes that Merricat literally died of neglect six years ago in an orphanage (135), and, on the morning after the fire while their house stands in ruins, Constance's primary concern is that Merricat has missed her dinner (165).

Charles calls up a wealth of Merricat's childhood memories. She can run away to a safe place and create a fantasy script where her memories are rewritten, but she must return to the house for her dinner, and Charles is unwilling to forget the mess this wild child has made in his room. When Merricat enters the house, she can hear Charles' voice in the dining room droning on about his need to punish her. Past and present again conflate for Merricat. She climbs the stairs, goes into Charles' room, and, in an act of erasure, throws his lit pipe and smoldering ashes into the garbage. Lynette Carpenter argues that this is the only point in the novel where readers are asked to believe that Merricat's perceptions are "limited" and "inadequate" (35). Merricat's perceptions are not limited, I would argue, but because she feels threatened by Charles, her altered ability to perceive colors is a return of the psychosomatic symptom we have seen her exhibit before. I would also argue Merricat is splitting when she goes into Charles' room. Because she is confusing the present with the past, it is not the 18-year-old Merricat who throws a burning pipe onto newspapers without understanding the consequences. Merricat is acting out rage against John Blackwood and Charles Blackwood simultaneously, and though the narrative may offer scant material evidence for why her rage is so intense, there is more than enough symptomatic evidence to suggest that Merricat has reason to be angry. Alice Miller points out in her book, *Thou Shalt Not Be Aware,* that rage is "an appropriate reaction to cruelty" (qtd. in DeSalvo 6) despite its frequent misinterpretation as a sign of mental imbalance, and Merricat's aftereffects extensively document her experience of cruelty.

Merricat's and Constance's behaviors are reasonable. Before the fire Constance fulfilled a maternal role. She was the sibling who accepted full responsibility for her father's abuse, for her own victimization, and for the results of Merricat's rages. Constance represses her father's abuse and Merricat acts out. She is the container of the sisters' unspoken rage, the signifier of a violent household. Their characters are distinct, but they collude in their silence and the boundaries between them blur. When Julian tells Mrs. Wright the stories of the poisoning, Constance admits that she bought the arsenic to kill rats, and as she says this she turns to Merricat and smiles (52). Merricat and Constance also share a glance during a conversation about their family's murder which suggests to Merricat that Constance was as full of merriment as she was (44). Constance cleans the sugar bowl before the police arrive, waits to call the doctor, and confesses to Merricat's crime, telling the police "those people deserved to die" (53). In quiet but revealing ways, Constance is able to collude with her sister and to share Merricat's rage.

Merricat and Constance strive to erase the abusive patriarchal power structure they live under. For six years that power structure is weakened enough to allow the sisters to live in safety. But there were Blackwood men who lived outside their house whom the arsenic-poisoned sugar could not reach, and Charles' penetration of their space makes action necessary. Charles' power to convert Constance into a phallic mother is as dangerous as living with his big white face is disturbing. Constance is easily swayed by Charles and the familiar order he represents. Shortly after Charles has established himself in the castle, Constance takes up the refrain that she hasn't been doing her duty (114), that she and Merricat and Julian should be living "normal lives" (118), and that the situation they are now living in is all her fault; this "was her new way of thinking" (131) and it demonstrates how quickly Constance is reabsorbed into the phallic patriarchal structure where Charles' prerogatives (which are always on the brink of collapsing into John Blackwood's) rule the house and her obligations and responsibilities enable him. Before Constance is irretrievably lost, Merricat must erase Charles.

Neither of Merricat's acts of erasure are simple inversions of the patriarchal order. In the first instance, she and Constance collude to turn Constance's obligation to nourish the family against them and they kill all of the dangerous participants of the phallic order. Constance and Merricat manipulate feminine obligations rather than usurp masculine power. James Egan argues in his essay, "Sanctuary: Shirley Jackson's Domestic and Fantastic Parables," that Constance and Merricat are unable to create a better world. He claims that they create a nihilistic, inescapable Gothic maze, an endless procession of destructive illusions and that a "'family' more bizarre and monstrous than the one Merricat poisoned [has] risen to take its place, a mutated family, without parents, which cannot rise above distorted emotional relationships" (23). Egan's interpretation of the family Constance and Merricat establish is not entirely inaccurate, though his definition of family sounds frighteningly similar to current ultra-conservative definitions of the family unit. Erasing the dangerous presence of John Blackwood, the perpetrator of violence sanctioned by the patriarchal family, provides no guarantee that Constance and Merricat will be able to establish healthy emotional relationships. Their obsessive compulsive behaviors will not magically disappear. And though they arc frcc of John Blackwood's violcncc, thcy rcalizc that they are unable to control all forces which may harm them. Merricat checks the locks on the doors approximately 30 times in this short novel, checks the fence line enclosing their property every Wednesday, buries magical safeguards on the property which she checks every Sunday, and realizes Charles' presence must be erased immediately upon his arrival.

Merricat's second act of erasure like her first is instinctive. Only a week after his arrival, Merricat intuits that this erasure of the patriarchal order must be more complete than the first, and just as she and Constance manipulated their feminine obligations rather than attempting to usurp masculine power the first time, Merricat again attempts to rid the house of the patriarchal order by turning it against itself. Merricat claims that the fire belongs to Charles; it is not her rage or wrongdoing but his own carelessness and evil which is responsible for the fire which burns the Blackwood home, and also gets rid of Charles and enables the sisters to sever all ties with the outside world.

When Julian dies in the panic caused by the fire, the sisters no longer need to invite Dr. Levy into their home. Though he returns once to threaten and coerce these two errant daughters, Merricat and Constance will never again have to admit this powerful enforcer of the patriarchy into their castle. The dining room which stood as a memorial to the family who died in it, the stately living room in which Mrs. Blackwood held court, the attic where trunks of their clothes were stored (clothes which Merricat dressed up in every Thursday), and the bed-rooms where Merricat and Constance slept are all gone, either burned away by the fire or closed off for all time. Also changed forever is the pattern of Merricat's and Constance's days. They no longer clean the house on Fridays as Mrs. Blackwood taught them to, they do not admit their parents' friends into the house for tea, and they no longer have reason to go to their father's safe in his study for money. Life on the moon truly is a new life for the sisters.

But even after an apocalyptic fire, all traces of the patriarchal order are not gone. The sisters use the remnants of wedding china and silver, and though Constance has never seen it used and does not know what Blackwood woman brought the china and silver into the house, both sisters know patriarchal enforcement of heterosexuality and laws of inheritance are responsible for its presence in their castle (178). Merricat continues to assert control by creating food rules: "[u]sually I ate fruit and vegetables still moist from the ground and the air, but I disliked eating anything while it was still dirty with the ash from our burned house." All the food from the garden now must be washed first and even then Merricat thought the smoke from the fire would always be in the ground where their food grew, that the Blackwood ancestral home would always penetrate what she relied on for sustenance (196). And locks are still a necessity in this new world because the sisters are aware that people are still watching them.

Despite their attempts to erase the patriarchal order, Constance and Merricat can never be completely free of its abusive structure. Traces of John Blackwood's world exist inside their secure locks, and outside on their lawn villagers come and stare at the burned out house. The castle and the sisters have been reinscribed into the patriarchal structure as haunted, monstrous beings. Strangers frighten each other with stories and discipline their children with frightening lies about Constance and Merricat:

> "They'd hold you down and make you eat candy full of poison; I heard that dozens of bad little boys have gone too near that house and never been seen again. They catch little boys and they—"
>
> "Shh. *Honestly*, Ethel."
>
> "Do they like little girls?" The other child drew near.
>
> "They hate little boys and little girls. The difference is, they *eat* little girls."
>
> (206-07 Jackson's italics)

Women cannot live self-sufficiently under the law of the father, nor are they supposed to transgress his law. Constance and Merricat must be represented in a way which will serve a function in the patriarchal system; they become witches, monsters used to frighten children by day and adults by night back into the boundaries of acceptable, obedient behavior.

Merricat tells Constance that life on the moon "'is not quite as [she] supposed it would be.'" Constance replies, "'It is a very happy place, though'" (195), and Merricat echoes this sentiment in the final line of the novel, "'Oh, Constance,' I said, 'we are so happy'" (214). Merricat desires a safe home. This in itself is a transgression against patriarchal structures, but because Merricat's resistance is motivated by her personal experience of trauma, her actions are not necessarily transformative. Safety means containment in the castle and containment means watching without being heard. When Helen Clarke and her husband come back to the castle to bring Merricat and Constance back to the world outside, Merricat wants to laugh out loud but does not (189). When Charles returns to their castle to try to talk to the sisters or at least get a picture of them that he can sell to a newspaper, Constance finally sees Charles as Merricat has seen him all along: as "a ghost and a demon, one of the strangers" (209). Constance smiles unpleasantly, and both sisters restrain their laughter until Charles finally leaves, which is not soon enough for Merricat. She "did not know whether Constance was going to be able to contain herself until he got down the steps and safely into the car" (211). Merricat is afraid Constance will not be able to hold back her laughter and her rage until Charles is gone. If Merricat and Constance felt free enough to laugh or if they could leave their home as Ruthie and Sylvie do in Marilynne Robinson's novel, *Housekeeping,* perhaps my reading of the novel would feel more satisfying and liberating, but because Merricat and Constance accept safety in containment, their resistance against the patriarchal order is readily contained. Collusive sisterhood is only truly powerful when sisters remain in motion and allow each other to laugh out loud, and when sisterhood extends beyond the boundaries of our families or origin, uniting us in politically transgressive struggle.

Notes

1. See Joan W. Scott, "The Evidence of Experience," *Critical Inquiry* 17 (1991): 773-797, and the two special issues of *Critical Inquiry* entitled, "Questions of Evidence," 17.4 and 18.1 (1991).

2. A number of works on adult children of dysfunctional families include descriptions of the roles children assume. I have relied on Claudia Black's book, *Double Duty: Help for the Adult Child who is also Gay or Lesbian* (New York: Ballantine, 1990) 15-23 for my description here of the responsible child and the child who acts out.

3. For more on the way anthropologists have explained the politics of dirt for contemporary literary critics, see Mary Douglas *Purity and Danger* (London: Ark Paperbacks, 1966).

Works Cited

Bass, Ellen and Laura Davis. *The Courage to Heal: A Guide for Women Survivors of Child Sexual Abuse.* New York: Harper and Row, 1988.

Black, Claudia. *Double Duty: Help for the Adult Child who is also Gay or Lesbian.* New York: Ballantine, 1990.

Blume, E. Sue. *Secret Survivors: Uncovering Incest and its Aftereffects in Women.* New York: Ballantine, 1990.

Carpenter, Lynette. "The Establishment and Preservation of Female Power in Shirley Jackson's *We Have Always Lived in the Castle.*" *Frontiers* 8.1 (1984): 32-38.

DeSalvo, Louise. *Virginia Woolf: The Impact of Childhood Sexual Abuse on Her Life and Work.* New York: Ballantine, 1989.

Egan, James. "Sanctuary: Shirley Jackson's Domestic and Fantastic Parables." *Studies in Weird Fiction* 6 (1989): 15-24.

Hoffman, Steven K. "Individuation and Character Development in the Fiction of Shirley Jackson." *Hartford Studies in Literature* 8.3 (1976): 190-208.

Jackson Shirley. *We Have Always Lived in the Castle.* New York: Penguin, 1962.

Parks, John G. "Chambers of Yearning: Shirley Jackson's Use of the Gothic." *Twentieth Century Literature.* 30.1 (1984): 15-29.

———. "'The Possibility of Evil': A Key to Shirley Jackson's Fiction." *Studies in Short Fiction* 15.3 (1978): 320-23.

Scott, Joan W. "The Evidence of Experience." *Critical Inquiry* 17 (1991): 773-97.

Woodruff, Stuart C. "The Real Horror Elsewhere: Shirley Jackson's Last Novel." *Southwest Review* 52.2 (1967): 152-62.

Roberta Rubenstein (essay date fall 1996)

SOURCE: Rubenstein, Roberta. "House Mothers and Haunted Daughters: Shirley Jackson and Female Gothic." *Tulsa Studies in Women's Literature* 15, no. 2 (fall 1996): 309-31.

[*In the following essay, Rubenstein situates Jackson's fiction within the "Female Gothic" genre, emphasizing in particular the nature of mother/daughter relationships in* Hangsaman, The Bird's Nest, The Sundial, *and* We Have Always Lived in the Castle.]

Although for many readers, Shirley Jackson is indelibly linked with her chilling and universally anthologized short story **"The Lottery,"** her oeuvre (six novels, with a seventh left unfinished at her death, and over a hundred short stories) deserves wider recognition for its emotionally resonant literary representations of the psychology of family relationships. I explore here the ways in which Jackson's fiction demonstrates her increasingly masterful, and also increasingly Gothic, representations of the primitive and powerful emotional bonds that constitute the ambivalent attachment between mothers and daughters in particular.[1] I situate this discussion within several contexts: Shirley Jackson's life, feminist and object-relations psychology,[2] and the conventions of Gothic narrative—specifically the pattern of characteristics identified as Female Gothic.

These contexts intersect in several pairs of strongly marked elements that occur in tension throughout Jackson's oeuvre; I identify these pairs as *inside/outside, mother/self, home/lost,* and *"eat or be eaten."* "Inside/outside" signifies the fluid emotional boundaries that occur as an infant progressively distinguishes itself from her/his environment during the formation of identity.[3] The tensions between "mother/self" and between "home/lost" connote a young child's ambivalent desires and fears: both to remain merged with the mother (who becomes emotionally identified with "home") and to separate from her, with the attendant danger of being "lost."[4] "Eat or be eaten" suggests the literal and figurative correspondences between consuming and being consumed or incorporated.[5] Psychoanalytically, a female's anxieties about food and body image suggest that her body is (or once was) a battleground in the struggle for autonomy in the face of what she may experience as her mother's consuming criticism, possessiveness, or withholding of love. Moreover, food involves a transition across boundaries as it is transformed from "outside" to "inside" the self by the act of consumption; less literally, incorporation may signal a predatory "consume or be consumed" relationship, as indeed exists between several mother-daughter pairs in Jackson's fiction.

The author's biography confirms that issues in her personal life resonate with these narratively expressed motifs in her fiction. Though of course biography cannot (and should not) be used uncritically to explain literary texts, it is nonetheless instructive to acknowledge some of the sources of Jackson's narrative preoccupations within their psychological and social contexts. According to the author's remarks about and correspondence with her mother as well as other evidence supplied by her biographer, tensions between daughter and mother originated early in the author's life and were not resolved by the time of her premature death of a heart attack at the age of forty-six. As Judy Oppenheimer determines in her account of Jackson's life, Geraldine Jackson's attitude toward her daughter was a deeply disconfirming one from the very beginning: Shirley "was not the daughter her mother wanted; that much

was clear from the start."[6] Throughout her life, Shirley was distressed by her mother's profound insensitivity to her actual personality, combined with persistent attempts to control her unconventionality. By contrast, Shirley's father seems to have been a figure on the margins of her life who corroborated his wife's conventional expectations for their daughter.

For much of her life, Jackson was significantly overweight, even obese, a fact that her mother never accepted and tried repeatedly to alter through disparaging remarks and disapproving actions: "Years after Shirley had left home, married, and given birth to her own children, her mother still sent her corsets in the mail, trying foolishly but persistently to rein in the overgrown creature she had somehow, unbelievably produced" (Oppenheimer, p. 14).[7] Indicative of Geraldine Jackson's preoccupation with her daughter's size and physical appearance, her letters to Shirley were punctuated with such comments as "Glad you're dieting." "Excess weight is hard on the heart." "You should get down to normal weight. Try non-fat milk" (Oppenheimer, p. 161). Soon after the publication of Jackson's last novel, *We Have Always Lived in the Castle,* her mother responded to the publicity picture of the by-then obese Shirley by writing, "Why oh why do you allow the magazines to print such awful pictures of you? . . . I have been so sad all morning about what you have allowed yourself to look like" (Oppenheimer, pp. 245-46).

Jackson's relationships with her own four children, particularly her two daughters, duplicated some of the ambivalence she experienced in her relationship with her mother. A deeply committed and involved mother, she was also "emotional and erratic. . . . Her moods and her anxieties colored the children's days; her demands, both surface and subterranean, often confused and upset them. No one could be more loving; no one could be meaner" (Oppenheimer, p. 199). She saw her children not only "as individuals, but . . . as mirrors . . . reflecting her various parts. With time, this would be refined into only two rays—Joanne and Sally, her daughters" (Oppenheimer, p. 163). Like Shirley with her own mother, her first daughter, Joanne, felt "from a very young age, that 'I was not the daughter she wanted. . . . I was too conventional'" (Oppenheimer, p. 201). Jackson's second daughter, Sarah (Sally), was much more like Shirley herself: volatile, impetuous, unconventional. As a young child, Sarah's "wildness, her arguments, her maverick ways . . . were the very things that made Shirley identify so strongly with her" (Oppenheimer, p. 200).

Virtually all of Jackson's longer narratives and a significant number of her short stories demonstrate a preoccupation with family relationships, if not also with problematic mother-daughter relationships, ambiguous houses, and eating or incorporation. Her family chronicles, *Life Among the Savages* (1953) and *Raising Demons* (1956), are wryly comic explorations of her experiences as a mother of four lively children; yet their droll tone is belied by the title words, underscoring the "savage" and "demonic" elements that laced Jackson's vision of family. While in the domestic comedies the doting if unorthodox mother regards her children, albeit genially, as savages and demons, in a number of her short stories and in most of her longer fiction, Jackson represents her own far darker relational anxieties from not only maternal but a filial perspective.

As Joan Wylie Hall observes of Jackson's oeuvre of over 110 stories, the short fiction frequently focuses on "imperiled females" and "divided" or "anxious" women:[8] "Whether her mood was comic or serious, Jackson often wrote of ordinary characters typically women in their twenties and thirties—who become enmeshed in extraordinary situations that either free them or, more often, trap them."[9] In the longer narratives, the central female characters, typically at the pivotal age between childhood and womanhood, are particularly anxious and ambivalent about their relationships with their mothers. In the first two novels, the mother is invasively present in the daughter's life; in each of the four succeeding novels, the mother is dead but no less powerfully present. In fact, the mother's absence becomes a haunting presence that bears directly on the daughter's difficult struggle to achieve selfhood as well as to express her unacknowledged rage or her sense of precariousness in the world.

Jackson's choice of the Gothic genre—for her last three novels in particular—is especially appropriate, given the psychological issues that dominated her own life. Gothic narratives pivot upon anxieties about selfhood and entrapment, represented through bizarre or exaggerated events that may or may not be explained as manifestations of the (typically) female central character's troubled imagination.[10] More specifically, Jackson's later narratives contain distinct elements of the type of Gothic narrative that has been termed "Female Gothic."[11] Claire Kahane identifies the characteristics of traditional Gothic narratives, including "an imprisoning structure" within which the protagonist, "typically a young woman whose mother has died, is compelled to seek out the center of a mystery, while vague and usually sexual threats to her person from some powerful male figure hover on the periphery of her consciousness" (p. 334). Kahane notes that critical approaches to Gothic narratives characteristically emphasize an underlying oedipal or incestuous struggle between a powerless daughter and an erotically powerful father or other male figure (p. 335). She proposes, instead, that the central feature of Female Gothic is not an oedipal conflict but, implicitly, a preoedipal one,[12] embodied in the daughter's search for/fear of "the spectral presence of a dead-

undead mother, archaic and all-encompassing, a ghost signifying the problematics of femininity which the heroine must confront" (p. 336). Thus, in these narratives authored by women and focusing on female protagonists, traditional elements of the Gothic genre are elaborated in particular ways, notably through the central character's troubled identification with her good/bad/dead/mad mother, whom she ambivalently seeks to kill/merge with; and her imprisonment in a house that, mirroring her disturbed imaginings, expresses her ambivalent experience of entrapment and longing for protection.

Events that pivot on an unstable, threatening, or anxious relationship between mother and daughter, as well as concerns about food and nurturance or body image, are present from the beginning of Jackson's fiction and become increasingly central in succeeding short stories and longer narratives. In the interest of focus, I shall briefly mention aspects of several stories and early novels that either anticipate or exhibit these central preoccupations and will then concentrate on the later novels, which most vividly represent within Gothic narrative frameworks the psychological oppositions I have suggested above.

In an early story, **"I Know Who I Love"** (1946), a daughter attempts to come to terms with the emptiness of her life and her feelings about her parents, who had demanded too much filial compliance. Catherine's widowed mother, who lives with her until her death, responds to her dutiful nurturance with contemptuous disregard, expressing her feelings with comments such as "You always were an ungrateful, spoiled child."[13] Catherine replies, "You eat, don't you? . . . *Some*thing must make me take care of you and feed you."[14]

Another of Jackson's early stories and her early novels focus not on the mother-daughter relationship but on a woman's progressive estrangement from herself and her domestic surroundings. In **"The Beautiful Stranger"** (1946), a young woman initially believes that her husband has been replaced by an imposter, a "beautiful stranger." Ultimately, when she returns after a shopping trip in town, she cannot even recognize her own home. The estranged environment and self assume a different expression in Jackson's first novel, **The Road Through the Wall** (1948): an apparently benign suburban neighborhood is exposed as a hypocritical—indeed, terrifying—place in which two children die, shockingly, by murder and suicide. Harriet Merriam, one of two adolescent girls who figure among the novel's many characters, is overweight while her best friend is skinny; observing herself as others see her, Harriet acknowledges "a gross, a revolting series of huge mountains, a fat fat fat girl."[15] Natalie Waite, the emotionally unstable adolescent protagonist of Jackson's second novel, **Hangsaman** (1951), also inhabits an estranged environment. She hears secret voices, in particular the voice of a police detective who interrogates her about a murder committed in her house. Natalie also struggles with anxieties about her parents and her body image. Her mother induces powerful guilt in her for the family sacrifices made in order for her to attend college, while her bombastic father also exerts a consuming role in her emotional life. A writer himself, he alternately praises and disparages her written efforts, even sharply critiquing her letters home from college.[16]

During her first year away from home, Natalie's apprehensions increase: she begins to eat more and becomes preoccupied with her weight (her surname, Waite, is a homonym of "weight"), and at the same time she fears the annihilation of her self, thinking about "when [she] would be dead."[17] In her loneliness and self-doubt, she fantasizes a secret female companion named Tony, who may be understood as her braver, more self-sufficient alter ego. At one point late in the novel, Natalie's emotional disorientation is externalized as she becomes literally lost. Wandering in confusion in a forest near the college, she briefly considers suicide and wishes that her mother would "come to take [her] home" (p. 276). Eventually she masters her fears, asserting to herself—in words that sound rather hollow, given the anxieties that shape her story—that she is "now alone and grown up, and powerful, and not at all afraid" (*Hangsaman,* p. 280).

Jackson represents filial anxiety, ambivalence, and anger, as well as the consuming aspect of maternal power, with greater psychological and narrative complexity in her middle novels, *The Bird's Nest* (1954) and *The Sundial* (1958). In *The Bird's Nest,* Elizabeth Richmond's mother has been dead for four years before the narrative commences. Nineteen-year-old Elizabeth—who shares her mother's name and is thus implicitly identified with her—lives with her mother's sister, the jealous and tyrannical Aunt Morgen, who regards her deceased sister as a "brutal, unprincipled, drunken, vice-ridden beast."[18] Veiled references in the narrative suggest that Elizabeth's mother was herself a victim of an abusive lover who may also have abused Elizabeth as a child. Other details imply that Elizabeth contributed directly to her mother's death through a physical attack precipitated by anger at maternal neglect, the circumstances of which she cannot remember. As a manifestation of both the estranged environment and the emotional disarray that ultimately fragment Elizabeth's inner life, the museum where she works begins to collapse on its foundations: "It is not proven that Elizabeth's personal equilibrium was set off balance by the slant of the office floor, nor could it be proven that it was Elizabeth who pushed the building off its foundations, but it is undeniable that they began to slip at about the same time" (p. 150). In her fictional representation of what is currently termed multiple personality disorder,[19] Jackson persuasively portrays the disintegration of Elizabeth's personality into four distinct and partial "selves," which act out either excessive concern with good behavior or the guilt and rage she feels toward her unavailable mother—feelings that the previously undissociated Elizabeth has repressed.

The unresolved question that occupies the subtext of *The Bird's Nest* is whether Elizabeth in fact killed her mother or only imagined it, either as the wish to annihilate her or the fear that she might have done so. Jackson splits the daughter's feelings towards the mother not only psychologically—the four fragmentary personas into which Elizabeth disintegrates—but narratively: between Elizabeth, whose unresolved grief and longing for her absent mother as well as her unacknowledged guilt concerning her contributory role in her mother's death, precipitate her personality fragmentation, and Aunt Morgen, who "enjoyed every minute of [her sister's death]" (p. 311)—that is, who celebrated the death that Elizabeth could not. Ultimately, through the intervention of a pointedly named psychiatrist, Dr. Victor Wright, Elizabeth achieves reintegration into a single self, but that recovery is not without cost. At the novel's conclusion, the "nuclear family" is ironically reconstituted with the tyrannical Aunt Morgen as mother, the equivocal Dr. Wright as father, and Elizabeth—divested of the name she shared with her mother and renamed "Morgen Victoria" by the new "parents" who have assumed possession of her—as the reintegrated but psychologically diminished, compliant daughter.

As expressed in this narrative, Jackson's solution to the problem of personal integration within the social realm illuminates the predatory element she identified within family relationships. In a view that invites comparison with the law of the jungle—"eat or be eaten"—Dr. Wright of *The Bird's Nest* dryly concludes that "each life . . . asks the devouring of other lives for its own continuance; the radical aspect of ritual sacrifice . . . its great step ahead, was in organization; *sharing* the victim was so eminently practical" (p. 378, emphasis in original). In Jackson's final novels, not only sacrifice but incorporation and consumption become both literal and figurative as the expression of connection—or, more accurately, disconnection—between mothers and daughters.

In *The Sundial,* the Female Gothic sensibility is elaborated through a daughter's ambivalent relation to both (dead) parents. The visionary Fanny Halloran believes she has received a revelation of the end of the world from her deceased father's spirit. All but one of the other occupants of the Halloran country estate enter into Fanny's fantasy, longing for a benevolent being who will lead them into the promised land suggested by her apocalyptic vision; collectively, they reinforce her conviction of the world's imminent annihilation. The exception is Fanny's sister-in-law Orianna, a Halloran by marriage only, whom the others regard distrustfully as a predatory mother who pushed her own son down a flight of stairs to his death. Orianna (Mrs. Halloran) functions in the story as Fanny's dark double; seizing power over the credulous lodgers who await the apocalypse, she establishes herself as the house mother or "queen," even fashioning a crown to signify her authority.

The Sundial is the first of Jackson's novels to represent the precariousness of female selfhood through the image of a house that becomes the daughter's fortress against a threatening and hostile world outside its boundaries. (Several of Jackson's short stories also feature distinctly Gothic houses, including those described in **"The Visit"** [1950] and **"The Little House"** [1962].) Psychologically, the house embodies the legacy of the all-powerful parents lodged within an insecurely developed self. In Fanny Halloran, the ego's precarious but heavily defended boundary between what exists "inside" and "outside" the self is expressed through her father's message of incipient danger from the external world: the Halloran estate is "distinguished from the rest of the world by a stone wall . . . so that all inside the wall was Halloran, all outside was not."[20] Additionally, the regressive dimension of Fanny's orientation to the world is signaled by her apartment in the attic of the house, a retreat that she maintains as a virtual shrine to her childhood and to her since-deceased parents.

Like Natalie Waite of *Hangsman,* Fanny Halloran briefly becomes literally what she is psychologically: a lost child who longs for reunion with her mother. Though it is her father whose spiritual presence fuels her apocalyptic fantasies, it is her mother whose image she invokes when she is in distress. Wandering in a maze on the estate grounds, she recalls that, as a child, "I used to come along this path pretending I was lost and could never go home again" (*The Sundial,* p. 88). Reaching the center of the maze and discovering that she is indeed lost, she thinks, "mother, mother" (p. 89) before she finds her way out of the maze and experiences her first "revelation." The image of the mother is thus split between the "good mother" for whom the daughter longs—protective and idealized, but absent—and the "bad mother"—the predatory and tyrannical Mrs. Halloran.[21] In order for Fanny and the other occupants of the house to enact their collective fantasy of apocalypse and the regressive desire for escape from the world, they must annihilate the woman who usurps the maternal role—Fanny's nemesis, Orianna Halloran. Though the world does not come to an end by the conclusion of *The Sundial,* the "bad mother" does: in an event that reproduces her own earlier murderous act against her son, Mrs. Halloran is apparently pushed down a flight of stairs to her death by one of her followers. One observer unrepentantly remarks, "Live by the sword, die by the sword" (p. 187).

The tensions between inside/outside, mother/self, and/or home/lost persist not only through her early stories and novels but throughout her oeuvre. Two late stories elaborate on the psychological estrangement of mother and daughter and the impossibility of the daughter's returning home. In **"Louisa, Please Come Home"** (1960), nineteen-year-old Louisa ran away from home two years earlier, changing her name and relishing her freedom from her family. Once a year her mother makes an emotional plea for her return in a radio message. Louisa finally decides, "Maybe I did want to go home. Maybe all that time I had been secretly waiting for a chance to get back" (*Come Along with Me,* p. 165). When she ultimately returns, no one in her family recognizes her. They all believe she is an imposter—in fact, one less convincing than others who have shown up to claim the reward for her return. Louisa acknowledges that "maybe once my mother had looked in my face and seen there nothing of Louisa, but only the long careful concentration I had put into being Lois Taylor, there was never any chance of my looking like Louisa again" (p. 168). The story ends ironically with the mother who has failed to acknowledge her true daughter imploring once again on the radio: "Louisa . . . please come home. . . . Your mother and father love you and will never forget you" (pp. 169-70).

In **"The Bus"** (1965), the narrator reveals early in the story—ostensibly referring to the poor bus service that the elderly traveler, Miss Harper, deplores—that "getting away from home was bad enough . . . but getting home always seemed very close to impossible" (*Come Along with Me,* p. 180). Miss Harper is let off the bus in the rain and darkness, only to discover that the driver has, as she phrases it, "put me off . . . at the wrong stop and I can't seem to find my way home" (p. 187). Lost, wet, and bedraggled, she gets a ride to a roadhouse converted from an old mansion that oddly reminds her of her childhood home. When she opens the closet in the bedroom where she expects to sleep, the toys frighten her by coming alive. In a plea that implicitly reverberates throughout much of Jackson's fiction, she screams, "Mommy, Mommy" (p. 191). Awaking from her nightmare, she finds herself still on the bus. As the earlier sequence of events uncannily repeats itself, the driver proceeds to let Miss Harper off at the place she has just dreamed about, declaring as she exits, "This is as far as you go" (p. 192).

The bus driver's darkly resonant comment suggests the coherence within Jackson's shorter and longer Gothic fiction, sustained through images of "home" (an emotional space) and houses (which often function as the material manifestation of that space) that typically captivate their female occupants or seekers in both appealing and threatening senses. As Jackson identified the ambivalent tension in her work, in an unsent letter written late in her career, "I have always loved to use fear, to take it and comprehend it and make it work. . . . I delight in what I fear" (Oppenheimer, pp. 233-34).

In Jackson's two final novels, the Gothic pleasure-in-fear that she acknowledged as a driving force in her fiction blends with preoedipal preoccupations to dramatize explicitly not only the ambivalence of the mother-daughter relationship but its figurative expression in consuming houses or other representations of incorporation. In the 1959 novel *The Haunting of Hill House* (a paradigmatic Female Gothic text, according to Kahane), the mother is dead and the daughter is confined within a house that functions figuratively as the externalized maternal body, simultaneously seductive and threatening. The daughter, Eleanor Vance, is drawn to Hill House as a participant in the study of occult phenomena. As Kahane observes,

> from the very beginning the house itself is presented as
> . . . a maternal antagonist . . . [that singles] out
> Eleanor as its destined inhabitant. . . . Jackson dislocates [readers] in typical Gothic fashion by locating
> [us] in Eleanor's point of view, confusing outside and
> inside, reality and illusion, so that [we] cannot clearly
> discern the acts of the house—the supernatural—from
> Eleanor's own disordered acts—the natural. But
> whether the agency of the house is inside Eleanor's
> mind or outside it, in either location it clearly functions
> as a powerful maternal imago.
>
> (p. 341)

While Kahane valuably highlights the Female Gothic elements of the narrative, I want to complicate her reading by suggesting that the confusion between inside and outside that structures this novel (and also *We Have Always Lived in the Castle*) is additionally represented through food as literal and symbolic substance. In both narratives, food signals both desire and fear: both the longing for sustenance and the predatory "consume or be consumed" relationship between mother and daughter. Moreover, in these final novels, tensions between opposing elements introduced in the earlier narratives—inside/outside, mother/self, and home/lost—overlap and converge to achieve their fullest representation. For Eleanor Vance of *The Haunting of Hill House,* the mother's death precipitates the daughter's existential homelessness and her literally annihilating experience of being lost: the loss of the self.

Early in the narrative, Eleanor stops at a country restaurant for lunch en route to Hill House for the first time; there she observes a young child who refuses her milk because it is not served in the familiar "cup of stars"[22] from which she is accustomed to drink at home. Eleanor appropriates the image of the child's magical milk cup

with its suggestive sense of the mother's absent and idealized nourishment. The very fact that Eleanor never possessed such a cup but makes it hers in imagination, referring to it several times, betrays her distance from and longing for maternal nurturance. However, when Eleanor mentions her recently deceased invalid mother, the association with nourishment is negative. As she explains to Theodora, the other young woman of the group who becomes her confidante, "In my mother's house the kitchen was dark and narrow, and nothing you cooked there ever had any taste or color" (p. 111). The cook who provides food for the guests at Hill House, Mrs. Dudley, prepares delectable dishes, yet is the antithesis of a nurturing figure, utterly mechanical in her insistence on a rigid and undeviating schedule of meals.[23]

Even before the "hauntings" begin, Eleanor is seductively drawn into the house while feeling as if she is being consumed by it, "like a small creature swallowed whole by a monster" (p. 42). When the first manifestation occurs—terrifyingly loud pounding on her door in the night—Eleanor believes it is her dead mother knocking (p. 127). Later she admits her guilt about the circumstances of her mother's death: "She knocked on the wall and called me . . . and I never woke up" (p. 212). For Theodora, the manifestation of knocking suggested someone trying "to get in and eat us" (p. 133); in Eleanor's words, "The sense was that it wanted to consume us, take us into itself, make us a part of the house" (p. 139). As Eleanor is progressively incorporated—and infantilized—by the malign powers of Hill House, she feels as if she is quite literally being consumed: "I am disappearing inch by inch into this house, I am going apart a little bit at a time . . ." (pp. 201-02). The walls of Hill House exude messages intended specifically for Eleanor: "HELP ELEANOR COME HOME" (p. 146). Later the newly arrived Mrs. Montague attempts to communicate with spirits through her "planchette" (Ouija board), which repeatedly produces the words "mother," "child," "lost," and "home" (pp. 192-93).

The meaning of "home" is deeply ironic, and Hill House is indeed both enticing and devouring mother:[24] Eleanor, acknowledging its powerful attraction, *chooses* to "relinquish my possession of this self of mine, abdicate, give over willingly what I never wanted at all; whatever it wants of me it can have" (p. 204). Ultimately, the haunted Eleanor is destroyed by her own ambivalent submission to maternal domination.[25] Of all of Jackson's protagonists, she is most literally consumed by the entrapping/embracing house that overpowers her even as she submits almost joyfully to it. Her assertion, "I am home, I am home . . ." (p. 232), paired with her conviction that she cannot leave Hill House because "I haven't any [other] home" to return to (p. 239), vividly exemplifies the convergence of desire and fear in the oppositions inside/outside, mother/self, and home/lost. By the novel's end, Eleanor is dead, having crashed her car into a tree just outside the house in a gesture that may be understood as a suicidal sacrifice to the embracing/consuming mother/house.[26]

In each of Jackson's final novels, the daughter struggles with the powerful presence of her mother's absence, along with her ambivalent wish/fear, expressed as "eat or be eaten": either she is the source of her mother's annihilation or her mother is the source of hers. The association between literal and psychological incorporation that originates in the (female) preoedipal attachment and is narratively represented in Jackson's own transformations of Female Gothic culminate in the author's final completed novel[27] through the further elaboration of the several opposing motifs that I have traced thus far.

The question of death or murder that typically lingers at the edge of awareness in Gothic narratives depends in **We Have Always Lived in the Castle** not on whether one occurred—several did—or even why, but on what follows from the perpetrator's efforts to contain her guilt. Six years before the narrative present, when Mary Katherine (Merricat) Blackwood was twelve, she had laced the sugar bowl with arsenic, an action that resulted in the deaths of both of her parents as well as her brother and her aunt. The villagers presumed (and still presume) that the actual murderer was her older sister Constance. Although a trial in the town had ultimately acquitted Constance, both Blackwood sisters are still ostracized by the villagers. The two young women continue to reside in the Blackwood family mansion with their father's brother, Uncle Julian, the only other survivor of the mass murder, who is paralyzed, delusional, and dependent on Constance's ministrations as chief cook and homemaker. As a result of her reputation in the village as a murderer, Constance is literally housebound; periodically, Merricat goes to the village, as if running a gauntlet, on essential household errands, including the purchase of groceries. The trio of surviving occupants of the Blackwood family thus functions as an ironic nuclear family: an incapacitated and dependent male figure, a housebound maternal figure who soothes anxieties and provides literal and figurative nurture, and a child who lives in a fantasy world sustained by magical thinking.

The brilliance of Jackson's narrative arises from her success at presenting the story from Merricat Blackwood's skewed perspective as the guiltless murderer who neither accepts responsibility nor feels remorse for her extreme action in the past. Jackson simultaneously represents the daughter's inner division and externalizes her ambivalent emotional relationship to the mother by splitting her into two separate characters: the saintly Constance and the "wicked" Merricat. Although on the literal level their relationship functions convincingly as a reciprocally affectionate sibling bond, psychologically

it mirrors an idealized mother-daughter attachment, fantasized from the younger female's (Merricat's) perspective. The appropriately named Constance, six years older, is good enough to have accepted responsibility for the monstrous crime Merricat committed against their family. Thus while the "daughter" is narratively split into separate "good" and "bad" parts (Constance and Merricat), within Merricat herself the internalized "mother" is also split: between the "bad" parent whom she killed and the "good" mother whose place is assumed by her saintly older sister. If one understands Constance psychologically not only as the idealized maternal figure for whom the daughter longs but also as a projection of the idealized "good" aspect within the daughter herself, then the "wicked" aspect (the murderous, angry Merricat) is threatened by the loss of both her "good" mother and her "good" self.[28] Each time the possibility arises that Constance might leave the claustrophobic world of Blackwood House—might go "outside"—Merricat feels emotionally imperiled or "chilled."[29]

The question of evil that pervades most Gothic narratives, and Jackson's later narratives, is ambiguously refracted in **We Have Always Lived in the Castle**: is Merricat Blackwood the source or the victim of the malice she feels around her? Locating evil in the external world rather than within herself, Merricat constructs a protective fantasy world defined by arbitrary magical talismans, taboos, and rituals that she feels compelled to observe. The reader, privy to Merricat's thoughts and feelings as the sole narrative voice but also to her blurring of inside and outside, can never ascertain whether her skewed vision of the world is the cause or the result of her murderous deed six years before. However, through her exaggerated childish vision, we can discern the intensity of her (and Jackson's) psychological preoccupations.

In Female Gothic narratives, houses and mansions function figuratively as maternal spaces: "the maternal blackness to which every Gothic heroine is fatefully drawn [which encompasses] the mysteries of identity and the temptation to lose it by merging with a mother imago who threatens all boundaries between self and other" (Kahane, p. 340). The few times that Merricat refers directly to her deceased mother early in the novel establish her filial ambivalence. The sight of the house where her mother was born fills her with anxiety: "I could not bear to think of our mother being born there" (p. 7). Her uneasiness is a screen for anxiety concerning her own literal birthplace—the "maternal blackness" of her mother's body.

On the evening of the fateful dinner at which Merricat's parents, brother, and aunt died by poison, Merricat had been "sent to bed without her supper" (p. 48) for reasons not explained, although Constance reveals years later to one of the infrequent guests at Blackwood House that her younger sister was a "wicked, disobedient child" (p. 49). Constance had frequently carried a tray of food up the back stairs for Merricat when she was barred from the family meal in the dining room. The affectionate attachment between the sisters is mutual. Since childhood, Merricat has idealized Constance as a young child idealizes not a sibling but the emotionally primitive, fantasied "good" mother with whom she is partially merged: "When I was small I thought Constance was a fairy princess. . . . She was the most precious person in my world, always" (p. 28). Constance is explicitly identified with nurturance, not only emotionally but literally. As Merricat phrases it, "food of any kind was precious to Constance, and she always touched food-stuffs with quiet respect" (p. 29). She enjoys reading cookbooks, preserves vegetables, and prepares meals for her reconfigured family as she had done before her parents' deaths. Though Merricat "bring[s] home food," she is "not allowed" to prepare it (p. 29); through magical thinking and ritual, she sets rules (as if imposed by someone other than herself), dictating restrictions on her actions as a way to order her world.

The most powerful magical metaphor—and object-relations issue—governing Merricat's vision of the world is her attempt to maintain and control the unstable boundary between "inside" and "outside" in order to defend her conviction that destructive evil exists apart from, not within, herself. The Blackwood mansion is her fortress, and she repeatedly attempts to secure its boundaries. Thus, although Merricat leaves the house and fenced-in grounds on occasional errands, the mere suggestion that Constance might "after all this time of refusing and denying . . . go outside" (pp. 39-40) produces great anxiety and dread ("chill") in Merricat, provoking her attempts to control her surrogate mother's actions through symbolic magic. In one particularly resonant instance, when two curious women from the village are having tea with the sisters, she deliberately smashes her mother's best milk pitcher, leaving the pieces "on the floor so Constance would see them" (p. 39) and bringing another pitcher of milk to the drawing room.

The more serious assault on Merricat's defensive castle is a "demon-ghost" (p. 127): an opportunistic cousin, Charles Blackwood, whose greatest threat is not his interest in the Blackwood money (which he believes is hidden in the house) but the prospect that he will take Constance away. Despite Merricat's efforts to secure the boundary between inside and outside, Charles penetrates the barrier and enters the house. Persevering as if in male sexual penetration of female space, he is "the first one who had ever gotten inside and Constance had let him in" (p. 82). Merricat's "wall of safety . . . crack[s]" (p. 83), and the "inside" becomes even less secure when Constance entrusts Charles with a key to the gates. Charles threatens not only to usurp but also to reproduce the original Blackwood family by assuming the role of the patriarchal father,[30] appropriating Constance as the submissive wife/mother, and punitively controlling the "child's" behavior—a configuration that threatens Merricat because it dangerously mimics the emotional reality of her childhood.

Because Charles radically threatens the defensive but precarious order of her world, Merricat wishes his death in a variety of ways, including magical incorporation, with her mother-surrogate's collaboration. As she suggests to Constance, "I was thinking that you might make a gingerbread man, and I could name him Charles and eat him" (p. 109). Alternatively, identifying Charles with her father, Merricat believes that she can destroy the interloper by magically controlling objects that belonged to John Blackwood. Nonetheless, Constance, under Charles's influence, begins to dream of a more traditional life and to question their prolonged isolation from the world. While she regards as merely "silly" Merricat's increasingly desperate actions to protect her from Charles's presence, Charles demands that Merricat's unacceptable behavior be punished. She responds, "Punish me? You mean send me to bed without my dinner?" (p. 137).

The anticipated punishment prescribed by the "disobedient child" herself—withholding of food—suggests a crucial link to Merricat's earlier life, as she unconsciously reproduces the structure of her earlier experience of punitive rejection by her family.[31] The withholding of food as a form of punishment may reflect emotional dynamics in Jackson's own family life, from both maternal and filial perspectives. As Oppenheimer writes, her daughter Sally "could drive Shirley around the bend faster than any other kid in the house—and once went an entire year without seeing the end of a meal because she was sent to her room long before dessert every single night" (p. 135). In the novel, Merricat retreats to a decaying summer house located on the Blackwood property, where she constructs a conversation from her childhood as a soothing magical antidote to the threat represented by Charles's malign presence "inside" her world. Her deceased parents are revised as adoring, even worshipful, rather than rejecting:

> "Mary Katherine, we love you."
>
> "You must never be punished. Lucy, you are to see to it that our most loved daughter Mary Katherine is never punished."
>
> "Mary Katherine would never allow herself to do anything wrong; there is never any need to punish her."
>
> "I have heard, Lucy, of disobedient children being sent to their beds without dinner as a punishment. That must not be permitted with our Mary Katherine."
>
> "I quite agree, my dear. Mary Katherine must never be punished. *Must never be sent to bed without her dinner.*

Mary Katherine will never allow herself to do anything inviting punishment."

"Our beloved, our dearest Mary Katherine must be guarded and cherished. Thomas, give your sister your dinner; *she would like more to eat.*"

(p. 139, emphasis added)

This fantasied conversation is critical to an understanding of Merricat's inner world, for it emphasizes the emotional resonances between love (or its withholding) and food.

Although Merricat's banishment from the family table was apparently initiated by her father with her mother's acquiescence, it is specifically maternal affection whose withdrawal Merricat seeks to reverse through her consuming attachment to her older sister. Constance, untouched by the poison since she never uses sugar (the association between sugar and poison is not without irony), is the one person who, through unconditional love, can neutralize the inner deprivation that shapes Merricat's relation to the world. No wonder Merricat feels compelled to do all within her power to restore the security of her "castle" and to expel the man who threatens its idealized maternal order.

Prohibited by her own codes from handling food, Merricat chooses another form of consumption: fire. Brushing Charles's still-smoldering pipe into a wastebasket filled with newspapers, she intends for the fire to remain magically "inside" her father's room, "belonging entirely to Charles" (p. 148). However, in endeavoring to destroy the father-rival alone, Merricat inevitably facilitates consumption of part of the mother as well (the protective space of the house). Local firefighters attempt to extinguish the fire that spreads through the Blackwood mansion, while vindictive villagers urge them to let it burn. In a chilling detail reminiscent of Jackson's classic story, **"The Lottery,"** the fire chief, having fulfilled his professional duty, removes the hat bearing his official insignia and tosses a rock at the house, unleashing a public stoning by the vengeful onlookers.

Following the stoning of the house, Merricat conveys her beloved Constance to her secret lair on the estate grounds. Together with her mother-surrogate in that safe shelter "on the moon"—her term for an idealized magical sanctuary—Merricat admits to Constance that she would like to

"put death in all [the villagers'] food and watch them die."

. . . "The way you did before?" Constance asked.

It had never been spoken of between us, not once in six years.

"Yes," I said after a minute, "the way I did before."

(p. 161)

After Merricat verbalizes her culpability for the murders six years earlier, she expresses a poignant fantasy that the irrevocable events she has precipitated might be undone; this is the closest she ever comes to remorse for her prior actions.

Perhaps the fire had destroyed everything and we would go back tomorrow and find that the past six years had been burned and they were waiting for us, sitting around the dining-room table waiting for Constance to bring them their dinner . . . perhaps the fire might be persuaded to reverse itself and abandon our house and destroy the village instead. . . . Perhaps the village was really a great game board, with the squares neatly marked out, and I had been moved past the square which read "Fire; return to Start," and was now on the last few squares, with only one move to go to reach home.

(p. 164)

Though the Blackwood mansion, now bereft of its roof, becomes "a castle, turreted and open to the sky" (p. 177), the maternal presence still reigns silently: Lucy Blackwood's face "look[ed] down on us graciously" from her portrait "while her drawing room lay destroyed around her" (p. 174). As if to propitiate the dead mother whose house/space has been seriously compromised, Constance places beneath her portrait a Dresden figurine that has escaped destruction; the sisters close the door to their mother's favorite room, figuratively entombing her image and the world over which she had presided, and "never [open] it afterwards" (p. 176). Constance, undeterred by the demolished household, calmly reestablishes order and resumes her nurturant role, salvaging the most important room in the house, the kitchen, which has been ransacked by spiteful pillagers, in order to prepare meals for Merricat and herself amid the shards.

The self-abnegating Constance also blames herself for the destruction, the indirect result of her temptation to accept Charles Blackwood's vision of her. Assuring Merricat that "somehow it was all my fault" (p. 174), she once again absolves Merricat of guilt and responsibility for her destructive actions. One might ask, at this or other points in the narrative, how are we to understand what motivates Constance? If Merricat embodies the principles of infantile impulsive anger and selfish action, Constance is her complementary double, representing a selfless, idealized maternal love whose virtue is its own reward. In a sense, the two young women are "two halves of the same person"—in fact, two aspects of Shirley Jackson herself, as well as representations of her two daughters and of her ambivalent relationships with them (Oppenheimer, p. 233).[32]

The house fire that Merricat initiates, like the murders she had perpetrated before, radically transforms her world. However, rather than being expelled from the magical maternal space as she had been as a child, Merricat succeeds in permanently ejecting the patriarchs, Charles Blackwood (who leaves) and Uncle Julian (who dies in the fire), while consolidating her merger with her "good mother," Constance. Absolved of guilt and forgiven for her "wicked" actions both past and present by the mother-surrogate who loves her unconditionally, she succeeds in sustaining her regressive fantasy, incorporating Constance into her emotionally primitive magical world. She is confident enough of the durability of that world to observe of the repentant villagers outside her castle, "Poor strangers. . . . They have so much to be afraid of" (p. 214). Speaking as the good daughter gratifyingly merged with her good mother, Merricat declares in the narrative's final line, "Oh, Constance . . . we are so happy" (p. 214).

Merricat's ironic comment about strangers who have much to fear is illuminated by an observation Jackson made concerning the emotional reality that fed her characters' psychology. In an unsent letter, she commented,

> We are afraid of being someone else and doing the things someone else wants us to do and of being taken and used by someone else, some other guilt-ridden conscience that lives on and on in our minds, something we build ourselves and never recognize, but this is fear, not a named sin. Then it is fear itself, *fear of self* that I am writing about . . . fear and guilt and their destruction of identity.
>
>   (ellipsis in Oppenheimer, p. 233; emphasis added)[33]

Although Jackson was referring specifically to the Blackwood sisters of *We Have Always Lived in the Castle,* her comments clarify the link between her other mother-haunted narratives and central issues within her own life. Much of her fiction derives its power from the emotional truth and energy of her lifelong defensive struggle against a consuming mother (not simply Geraldine Jackson but the universally fantasied internal image of "mother"), which may in turn have led to her troubled relationships with her own two daughters and to her excessive consumption of food and drink. Additionally and poignantly, for an author who made emotionally resonant houses the central image of her later fiction, Jackson was virtually consumed by her own house: she developed agoraphobia several years before her death. During an especially difficult period, "she was unable to leave the house . . . unable, for much of the time, even to leave her bedroom" (Oppenheimer, p. 247).

Jackson's narratives refract and transform some of her own idiosyncratic emotional history; at the same time, they illuminate a darker aspect of the ambivalent mother-daughter relationship in general, amplified through the devices of Female Gothic narrative structure. In several of Jackson's stories and virtually all of her novels, a woman's troubled relation to her mother (whether alive or dead) and/or to a house or to "home" produces anxieties about the world that coincide with a central element in Female Gothic narratives, "fear of self."[34] One source of that emotional predicament is the tension between desire and fear that originates as the (female) infant negotiates the unstable boundaries between inside and outside, "goodness" and "badness," *self* and *(m)other*[35] during the process of establishing selfhood; its residues persist within and influence the self into adulthood and (for women) motherhood.

Thus the fusion of the ideas of mother and home—the "mother house . . . housemother" (*The Haunting of Hill House,* p. 211) that looms so large in Jackson's later fiction—may be understood as the materialized specter/structure of anxiety that haunts and even paralyzes the daughter as she struggles with her confusion concerning "inside" and "outside." That dilemma is expressed through her ambivalent desires: on the one hand, to leave home to become an autonomous self and, on the other, to remain an unindividuated child within its protective—but also consuming—enclosure. Indeed, in Jackson's fiction, the daughter's conflict is embodied as both the temptation and the torment of her wish/fear to return "home" and to her mother and of not knowing whether she is lost or saved when she finds herself either stranded far from home or "inside the house, with the door shut behind . . ." (*We Have Always Lived in the Castle,* p. 142).

Notes

1. As Adrienne Rich has phrased it,

   > "Few women growing up in patriarchal society can feel mothered enough; the power of our mothers, whatever their love for us and their struggles on our behalf, is too restricted. And it is the mother through whom patriarchy early teaches the small female her proper expectations."
   >
   >   (*Of Woman Born: Motherhood as Experience and Institution* (New York: Bantam, 1977), p. 246)

   Several critics have specifically highlighted Jackson's protofeminist impulses by focusing on her representations of female characters who are oppressed within patriarchy. Lynette Carpenter considers the impact of patriarchy not only on Jackson's female characters but on her own situation as a woman writer, in "Domestic Comedy, Black Comedy, and Real Life: Shirley Jackson, A Woman Writer," in *Faith of a (Woman) Writer,* ed. Alice Kessler-Harris and William McBrien (New York and Westport, Connecticut: Greenwood Press, 1988), pp. 143-48. See also feminist readings of individual novels: Carpenter, "The Establishment and Preservation of Female Power in Shirley Jackson's *We Have Always Lived in the Castle,*" *Frontiers,* VIII, No. 1 (1984), 31-38; Tricia Lootens, "'Whose Hand Was I Holding?' Familial and Sexual Politics in Shirley Jackson's *The Haunting of Hill House*," in *Haunting the House of Fiction: Feminist Perspectives on Ghost Stories by American Women*, ed. Carpenter and Wendy K. Kolmar (Knoxville: University of Tennessee Press, 1991), pp. 166-92; and Judie Newman, "Shirley Jackson and the Reproduction of Mothering: *The Haunting of Hill House*," in *American Horror Fiction: From Brockden Brown to Stephen King* (New York: St. Martin's Press, 1990), pp. 120-34.

Besides the 1988 biography of Shirley Jackson by Judy Oppenheimer, the only book-length studies of her work are Lenemaja Friedman's *Shirley Jackson* (Boston: Twayne/G.K. Hall, 1975) and Joan Wylie Hall's *Shirley Jackson: A Study of the Short Fiction* (New York: Twayne, 1993). Most scholarly essays on Jackson's work focus on individual stories—especially "The Lottery"—or novels. Those most pertinent to my own approach (in addition to those listed above) include Stuart C. Woodruff's "The Real Horror Elsewhere: Shirley Jackson's Last Novel," *Southwest Review*, 52, No. 2 (1967), 152-62; Steven K. Hoffman's "Individuation and Character Development in the Fiction of Shirley Jackson," *Hartford Studies in Literature*, 8, No. 3 (1976), 190-208; John G. Parks's "The Possibility of Evil: A Key to Shirley Jackson's Fiction," *Studies in Short Fiction*, 15, No. 3 (1978), 320-23; Parks's "Waiting for the End: Shirley Jackson's *The Sundial*," *Critique*, 29, No. 3 (1978), 74-88; Parks's "Chambers of Yearning: Shirley Jackson's Use of the Gothic," *Twentieth Century Literature*, 30, No. 1 (1984), 15-29; and James Egan's "Sanctuary: Shirley Jackson's Domestic and Fantastic Parables," *Studies in Weird Fiction*, 6, No. 1 (1989), 15-24.

Several collections of essays on detective and horror fiction contain discussions of one or two of Jackson's novels: Mary Kittredge's "The Other Side of Magic: A Few Remarks about Shirley Jackson," in *Discovering Modern Horror Fiction I*, ed. Darrell Schweitzer (Mercer Island, Washington: Starmont, 1985), pp. 3-12; Jack Sullivan's "Shirley Jackson," in *Supernatural Fiction Writers: Fantasy and Horror*, ed. E. F. Bleiler (New York: Scribners, 1985), pp. 1031-36; and Carol Cleveland's "Shirley Jackson," in *Then There Were Nine . . . .: More Women of Mystery*, ed. Jane S. Bakerman (Bowling Green, Ohio: Popular Press, 1985), pp. 199-219.

2. In contrast to classical Freudian psychoanalytic theory, which focuses primarily on instinctual drives, object-relations psychology focuses primarily on the individual's relationships with others in his/her external world; see Jay R. Greenberg and Stephen A. Mitchell, *Object Relations in Psychoanalytic Theory* (Cambridge: Harvard University Press, 1983), p. 20. However, within this broad context, a number of different, even incompatible, perspectives exist in place of a unitary theory. As Greenberg and Mitchell define this group of approaches within the larger context of psychoanalytic theory, the term "object relations"

> "designates theories, or aspects of theories, concerned with exploring the relationship between real, external people and internal images and residues of relations with them, and the significance of these residues for psychic functioning."

> (p. 12)

Nancy Chodorow was among the first feminist scholars to use object relations theory to revise Freud's position concerning early mother-infant relations by focusing on significant differences between female and male experiences. See *The Reproduction of Mothering: Psychoanalysis and the Sociology of Gender* (Berkeley: University of California Press, 1978).

3. Psychoanalytically, the determination of what constitutes "inside" and "outside" is problematic. As Roy Schafer phrases the problem,

> "how is one to understand the inside or outside location of an object? Inside of what? Outside of what? It can only be inside or outside the subjective self . . . [which] comprises a variety of changing, more or less organized and overlapping selves . . . the self-as-agent (the 'I'), the self-as-object (the 'me'), and the self-as-place (for which no pronoun is specific). These selves are not synonymous or necessarily congruent."

> (*Aspects of Internalization* (New York: International Universities Press, Inc., 1968), pp. 79-80)

4. In an object-relations context,

> "merging with another person is essentially a primary-process phenomenon. It condenses representations of the total subjective self and the object. In the subject's experience, it is as if there were only one person, not two."

> (Schafer, pp. 151-52)

Moreover,

> "a person's early relation to her or his mother leads to a preoccupation with issues of primary intimacy and merging. On one psychological level, all people who have experienced primary love and primary identification have some aspect of self that wants to recreate these experiences."

However, "fear of fusion may overwhelm the attraction to it, and fear of loss of a love object may make the experience of love too risky."

> (Chodorow, pp. 78-79)

5. Incorporation refers to the idea in object-relations psychology that

> "one has taken a part or all of another person (or creature or thing) into one's self corporeally, and, further, that this taking in is the basis of certain novel, disturbing, and/or gratifying sensations, impulses, feelings, and actions of one's own and of correlated changes in one's experience of the environment . . . incorporation may be said to indicate a de-emphasis of the boundaries between the inner and outer worlds."
>
> (Schafer, pp. 20-21)

Additionally, "the wish to incorporate an object [or person] is usually the wish to eat it in a sucking or biting fashion . . ." (Schafer, p. 121).

6. Judy Oppenheimer, *Private Demons: The Life of Shirley Jackson* (New York: Fawcett Columbine, 1988), p. 11. Subsequent references will be cited parenthetically in the text.

7. According to Susie Orbach, who first theorized the sources of eating disorders from a feminist perspective in the 1970s, female obesity and overeating may be understood as

> "a symbolic rejection of the limitations of women's role, an adaptation that many women use in the burdensome attempt to pursue their individual lives within the proscriptions of their social function."

Furthermore,

> "women are prepared for this life of inequality by other women who themselves suffer its limitations—their mothers. The feminist perspective reveals that compulsive eating is . . . an expression of the complex relationships between mothers and daughters."
>
> (*Fat is a Feminist Issue* (New York: Paddington Press, 1978), p. 26)

More recently, Susan Bordo has illuminated the relationship between consumption and consumer capitalism as regulator of desire. In that context,

> "the obese and anorectic are . . . disturbing partly because they embody resistance to cultural norms. . . . In the case of the obese, in particular, what is perceived as their defiant rebellion against normalization appears to be a source of the hostility they inspire."
>
> ("Reading the Slender Body," *Unbearable Weight: Feminism, Western Culture, and the Body* (Berkeley: University of California Press, 1993), p. 203)

8. Hall, *Shirley Jackson: A Study of the Short Fiction,* pp. xiv, 25, 27.

9. Hall, p. xii.

10. See Eve Kosofsky Sedgwick's valuable discussion of the structure and conventions of Gothic narratives in *The Coherence of Gothic Conventions* (New York and London: Methuen, 1986).

11. See Ellen Moers, *Literary Women* (Garden City, New York: Doubleday, 1976), pp. 90-110, and Claire Kahane, "The Gothic Mirror," in *The (M)other Tongue: Essays in Feminist Psychoanalytic Interpretation,* ed. Shirley Nelson Garner, Kahane, and Madelon Sprengnether (Ithaca: Cornell University Press, 1985), pp. 334-51, esp. p. 334. Subsequent references will be cited parenthetically in the text.

12. "Preoedipal" refers to the early developmental period before gender identity is established by a child at about the age of three. As Chodorow describes this phase,

> "The content of a girl's attachment to her mother differs from a boy's precisely in that it is not at this time oedipal (sexualized, focused on possession, which means focused on someone clearly different and opposite). The preoedipal attachment of daughter to mother continues to be concerned with early mother-infant relational issues. It sustains the mother-infant exclusivity and the intensity, ambivalence, and boundary confusion of the child still preoccupied with issues of dependence and individuation."
>
> (Chodorow, p. 97)

13. Years after Jackson published this story, during the last year of her life, her mother wrote in a letter, "You were always a wilful child" (Oppenheimer, p. 14).

14. Jackson, "I Know Who I Love," in *Come Along with Me,* ed. Stanley Edgar Hyman (New York: The Viking Press, 1968), p. 51. Subsequent references to stories in this collection will be cited parentheticaly in the text.

15. Jackson, *The Road Through the Wall* (New York: Farrar, Straus and Co., 1948), p. 264.

16. Fathers, both living and dead, figure in several of Jackson's later novels as well. My intent here is not to disregard their presence but to emphasize the central tension within the mother-daughter relationship.

17. Jackson, *Hangsaman* (New York: Farrar, Straus and Young, 1951), p. 130. Subsequent references will be cited parenthetically in the text.

18. Jackson, *The Bird's Nest,* in *The Magic of Shirley Jackson,* ed. Hyman (New York: Farrar, Straus and Giroux, 1966), p. 307. Subsequent references will be cited parenthetically in the text.

19. Interestingly, *The Bird's Nest* antedates by three years the publication of the more widely known nonfictional case history, *The Three Faces of Eve,* by Corbett Thigpen and Hervey M. Cleckley (New York: McGraw-Hill, 1957).

20. Jackson, *The Sundial* (New York: Ace Books, 1958), p. 11. Subsequent references will be cited parenthetically in the text. Sedgwick identifies as

a central convention of Gothic narratives the focus on spatial topography: "what's inside, what's outside, and what separates them" (p. 12). See also note 3 above.

21. Melanie Klein—a central, although controversial, analyst and formulator of object-relations theory—proposed that in the very earliest stage of psychological development, an infant's primitive wishes and fears become split between pleasurable and terrible experiences of the mother (as presumed from the infant's essentially undifferentiated perspective): the "good mother" who provides nurture and the "bad mother" who withholds gratification. As Thomas Ogden outlines Klein's position on this primitive mechanism of emotional division,

> "Splitting allows the infant, child, or adult to love safely and hate safely by establishing discontinuity between loved and feared aspects of self and object."
>
> (*The Matrix of the Mind: Object Relations and the Psychoanalytic Dialogue* (Northvale, New Jersey: Jason Aronson, Inc., 1986), p. 65

The residue of this primitive split may persist into adult object relations. See also notes 28 and 32 below.

22. Jackson, *The Haunting of Hill House* (New York: Viking Penguin, 1984), p. 21. Subsequent references will be cited parenthetically in the text.

23. Although this cannot be biographically confirmed, one may speculate that as an infant Shirley Jackson was probably fed, like others of her generation, according to the principles of child-rearing of her mother's generation: on a rigid schedule unrelated to the infant's own desires.

24. Lootens, who has traced the evolution of the novel through several drafts, observes that

> "Hill House is the original womb/tomb, with all the comforts of home. There are good beds, excellent cooking, companionship; and nothing to do but die in a house that does not want you . . . but that does not want to let you go."
>
> (p. 176)

Kahane describes the house as "protector, lover, and destroyer" (p. 342).

25. Newman also explores the ambivalent mother-daughter bond that structures Eleanor's emotional reality, although she draws somewhat different conclusions from mine. In her view, Eleanor

> "detests the mother's dominance, resenting the loss of her own youth in the forced assumption of the 'mothering' role. . . . [She also] feels guilt at not having mothered adequately. Both

images are internalized so that Eleanor is haunted by guilt as a mother over the neglected child within herself."
>
> (p. 126)

26. Interestingly, shortly before Jackson began to write *The Haunting of Hill House,* she wrote a one-act play for her children's school, "a variation on *Hansel and Gretel*" titled *The Bad Children* (Oppenheimer, p. 222). Defending her unorthodox revision of the fairy tale—it is the children who are wicked, not the witch—she noted in an unpublished lecture that she "resented violently the fact that Hansel and Gretel eat the witch's house and never get punished for it" (Oppenheimer, p. 222). In the play, the children are "horrible" brats (p. 222) who deserve what they get; in *The Haunting of Hill House,* it is instead the house itself that is "horrible." Moreover, rather than the children consuming the house, as in the fairy tale, in the novel the house consumes the childlike Eleanor.

27. Jackson's unfinished and posthumously published novel, *Come Along with Me,* consists of only thirty pages, so one can only speculate on the direction it would have taken if completed. Although lighter in tone than her other novels, it retains several suggestive links to the recurring emotional issues I suggest here. The narrative opens with the first-person narrator's comment, "I always believe in eating when I can" (p. 3). Forty-four years old, the speaker has sold her house after her husband's death; having "erased [her] old name" (p. 4), she seeks a new life and a new "place to go" (p. 3) to practice her clairvoyant powers. As she considers names for the new identity she intends to establish, she confesses, "what is really more frightening than being without a name, nothing to call yourself, nothing to say when they ask you who you are?" (p. 9). Eventually, she decides she will be Angela Motorman. She takes a room in a rooming house, repeatedly stressing the room's perfect squareness. The Gothic element seems to be directed toward a more comic vein: as Angela explains her vocation, "I dabble in the supernatural. Traffic with spirits. Seances, messages, psychiatric advice, that kind of thing" (p. 12).

28. As Ogden explains Melanie Klein's theoretical perspective on the splitting of the object (mother),

> "one achieves safety in relation to internal danger by magically placing the danger outside of oneself; one protects oneself against persecutory objects by acquiring a greater army of good objects; *one projects an endangered aspect of self by magically transforming another person into a repository for that aspect of self, thus preserving oneself in the form of another with whom one maintains a connection of identity (projective identification).*"
>
> (p. 76, my emphasis)

29. Jackson, *We Have Always Lived in the Castle* (New York: Viking Press, 1962), pp. 38-39. Subsequent references will be cited parenthetically in the text.

30. Carpenter focuses on Jackson's "portrayal of the institution of patriarchy and its terrifying power over women" in *We Have Always Lived in the Castle*. In her view, Charles Blackwood "reintroduces the [patriarchal] notions of punishment and competition into a house where they have not been invoked for years" (pp. 32, 35).

31. Jean Wyatt notes that feminist object-relations psychology

> "accounts for women's compulsion to perpetuate the structures of their own oppression: unconscious desire becomes enmeshed with the setting of their earliest experiences of satisfaction (or frustration) in the nuclear family; so desire always moves them (unconsciously) to reconstruct in their adult lives the patterns of their original family life."
>
> *Reconstructing Desire: The Role of the Unconscious in Women's Reading and Writing* (Chapel Hill: University of North Carolina Press, 1990), p. 9)

Chodorow also explores the blurred boundaries between inside and outside and between mother and (female) self.

32. Jackson

> "quite consciously [split] herself into the two characters, Merricat and Constance, and at the same time [modeled] them directly after her daughters."
>
> (Oppenheimer, p. 234)

33. Unsent letter from Shirley Jackson to Howard Nemerov, circa 1960, quoted in Oppenheimer, p. 233.

34. Jackson's phrase anticipates Moers's observations concerning the relationship between Gothic narratives and female anxieties. As Moers phrased it,

> "Despair is hardly the exclusive province of any one sex or class in our age, but to give *visual* form to the *fear of self,* to hold anxiety up to the Gothic mirror of the imagination, may well be more common in the writings of women than of men."
>
> (p. 107; the first emphasis is Moers's, the second is mine)

35. In a somewhat different context, Madelon Sprengnether usefully distinguishes between "mother" as "a fantasy of plenitude" and "(m)other" as a sign for "the otherness contained in the figure of mother" or as "that which cannot be appropriated by the child's or infant's desire and hence signals

a condition of division or loss," in "(M)other Eve: Some Revisions of the Fall in Fiction by Contemporary Women Writers," in *Feminism and Psychoanalysis,* ed. Richard Feldstein and Judith Roof (Ithaca and London: Cornell University Press, 1989), p. 300, n. 5.

Barbara Levy (essay date 1997)

SOURCE: Levy, Barbara. "Shirley Jackson: 'In the country of the story, the writer is King.'" In *Ladies Laughing: Wit as Control in Contemporary American Women Writers,* pp. 51-70. Amsterdam: Gordon and Breach Publishers, 1997.

[*In the following essay, Levy reviews Jackson's career, from her "witty" autobiographies to her more "serious" literary endeavors, such as* Hangsaman, The Bird's Nest, *and* We Have Always Lived in the Castle.]

In 1962, Shirley Jackson opened **"Notes for a Young Writer,"** written originally for her younger daughter Sally, with this royal proclamation.[1] She was forty-six years old and the mother of four. Sally was fourteen and had an older sister and brother, Joanne seventeen, Laurence twenty, and one younger brother, eleven-year-old Barry. Sally was the one Jackson felt had a mind most like her own and the one who, supposedly, wanted to be a writer. But Sally seemed to have had so much encouragement at so early an age it could not have been clear to her whether she genuinely wanted to write or whether she was simply being groomed, even pushed into it by a mother who recognized her daughter's talents from the outset. Jackson's story **"The Intoxicated"** describes a teenager who thinks and speaks exactly like Sally, although it was written before her daughter born. The story prompted family and friends to claim that Shirley Jackson conceived of her daughter's original mind even *before* she was born.[2]

Actually, both Sally's parents showed an interest in her writing. Shirley Jackson, her successful fiction-writer mother, insisted she write ten pages a night, although she did not have to show anyone what she wrote. Meanwhile her father, Stanley Edgar Hyman, corrected her writing like the professor and literary critic he was—looking for grammar and logic errors. "Between them," Sally said to Jackson's biographer, "I didn't stand a chance" (264). When Sally was only sixteen, she had a story published in *Gentleman's Quarterly,* sold to the magazine by Shirley's agent, Carol Brandt. But when Sally was only seventeen, her mother died, unexpectedly, during a nap on a "hot stuffy Sunday afternoon in August" (268). And Sally has not written since (264).

WRITING TECHNIQUES TO CONTROL YOUR
AUDIENCE

The fact that these notes were written for a promising young talent who turned away from a writing career in no way invalidates them. Shirley Jackson recognized their value outside of her home circle and used them at writing conferences during her last three years of life. They are not only clear and clever but absolutely above-board on the issue of control. Jackson knew that every effective writer has techniques to manipulate her audience, and decided to let her fourteen-year-old daughter privy to some of hers. She would have to keep her readers interested and play fair, Jackson explained, by not asking more of their imaginations than they could reasonably grant. The readers will be able to suspend reason and agree that there really is a Land of Oz, for example, but not that it can be seen from their windows. But then,

> for as long as the story does go on you are the boss. You have the right to assume that the reader will accept the story on your own terms. You have the right to assume that the reader, however lazy, will exert some small intelligence while he is reading.
>
> (**"Notes,"** 234)

That last sentence does not sound quite so patronizing in context, since Jackson goes on to say that her daughter need not describe everything, that she "need only describe one gardener to imply that the castle is well stocked with servants" (235).

Jackson is well aware of the control she has over her readers, over how she can sneak up on them, affect the speed at which they read, and help them digest complicated passages. Easy sections, simple clear paragraphs, provide "benches for the reader to sit down upon," a phrase she attributes to another writer, whose name she has forgotten. On these benches, "the poor reader who had struggled through the complex maze of ideas for several pages could rest gratefully" (241). But sometimes the rest is a set-up:

> If you would like him to rest for a minute so you can sneak up behind him and sandbag him, let him have a little peaceful description, or perhaps a little something funny to smile over, or a little moment of superiority.
>
> (**"Notes,"** 241)

The idea that the writer might have the ability and the desire to affect the speed at which her text can be read is, at first, surprising, and, on reflection, obvious:

> And if you want your reader to go faster and faster make your writing go faster and faster: "The room was dark. The windows were shaded, the furniture invisible. The door was shut and yet from somewhere, some small hidden precious casket of light buried deep in the darkness of the room, a spark came, moving in mad colored circles up and down, around and in and out and over and under and lighting everything it saw." (Those adjectives are unspeakable in every sense of the word, and wholly unnecessary; this is an example, not a model.) If you want your reader to go slower and

slower make your writing go slower and slower: "After a wild rush of water and noise the fountain was at last turned off and the water was gone. Only one drop hung poised and then fell, and fell with a small musical touch. Now it rang. Now."

> (**"Notes,"** 241)

Another technical strategy Jackson revealed to her daughter that seems so obvious in hindsight involves what she calls conversation, and reviewers usually call dialogue. When a writer is praised for realistic and convincing dialogue, the critic, duped along with the general reader, often claims the writer has a good ear for how people really talk. But, according to Jackson, convincing written dialogue has little to do with the way people really talk. Jackson explains that you mustn't let your characters speak the way real people talk because "the way people usually talk is extremely dull" (236). Of course she is right. Listen to the way people repeat, stumble, hesitate. The writer's trick is to convince the reader that the characters *sound* like real people talking, even though they speak with far more economy of speech, with far more thought given to the choice and effect of their words. Characters usually use short sentences, but if they have to tell a long story, do so "only in the most carefully stylized and rhythmic language" (237). If you are not convinced that Jackson is correct about the high degree of stylization in written conversation, just

> . . . look at some written conversation that seems perfectly smooth and plausible and natural on the page, and then try reading it aloud; what looks right on the page frequently sounds very literary indeed when read aloud; remember that you are writing to be read silently.
>
> (**"Notes,"** 237)

The following, from Jackson's last fragment of a novel, **Come Along With Me,** where Angela Motorman (age and size both forty-four) is explaining a little about herself to the woman in whose home she plans to rent a room, is a good example of the economy of written conversation:

> "I've just buried my husband," I said.
>
> "I've just buried mine," she said.
>
> "Isn't it a relief?" I said.
>
> "What?" she said.
>
> "It was a very sad occasion," I said.
>
> "You're right," she said, "It's a relief."
>
> (**Come Along With Me,** 10-11)

The fact that Jackson is writing these notes to nurture her daughter's writing efforts must have awakened memories of the very different reception her own childhood writing received. Her mother was interested in the social graces and did not know how to handle her intelligent, strong-willed, overweight bookworm of a daughter, except to criticize her appearance constantly (Opp. 24). The most intense part of young Shirley's day was spent privately in her bedroom, writing. In an unpublished piece written at Syracuse University between 1937 and 1940, which Oppenheimer, her biographer, found in the Library of Congress Jackson collection (after her death, Jackson's husband donated forty-two boxes of her scrapbooks, diaries, letters, and journals to the Library of Congress), Jackson tried to write about a painful part of her childhood, putting herself in the third person:

> Every day all the way home from school she would think about going into her room and closing the door. She would think about her desk and the sunlight coming into the room and being alone with her desk and writing . . . She would touch her pocket to make sure that the key to her desk was safe.

> (Opp. 23)

But one day she came home and found her grandmother reading the papers she had locked in the desk:

> She opened the door of her room quietly; there was no need to let them know she was home. When she opened her door she saw her grandmother at the desk; the desk was open and her grandmother was reading the papers from the desk. . . . She stood in the doorway watching and finally she said "You mean it doesn't lock any more? My desk doesn't lock?"

> (Opp. 23, Ellipsis Jackson's)

This brazen invasion of privacy, practiced by her mother as well as her grandmother, so enraged Jackson that before leaving home permanently she openly burned every page of her childhood writing (24). If she couldn't control the invasion, she could at least destroy what had been invaded. Nor did she forget this experience. As an adult, she never once went through any of her children's papers (24).

CONTROLLING ONE'S ENVIRONMENT WITH WITTY FICTION

As an adult, Jackson tried to control unpleasant events with a lighter touch. In 1958, at forty-two, she wrote a lecture in an enchantingly good-humored vein which she called **"Experience and Fiction."**[3] The lecture opens with a whimsical anecdote from her life, an anecdote which appeared in a different form in her autobiography, *Raising Demons.*[4] The anecdote involves her old refrigerator, whose door always stuck in damp weather. Her daughter Sally, after watching her mother struggling one rainy morning, suggests she use magic to unstick it. Here the lecture parts company with the version in her autobiography. In the autobiographical version, Jackson allows Sally to use magic until the whole door comes off in her husband's hands.

("'Jeekers,' Sally said, eyes wide. 'I went and unstuck the wrong side'" 649.) In the lecture version, she points out that Sally's suggestion need not be taken so literally. Jackson goes to her typewriter and writes the version that appeared in *Raising Demons.* She then sells the story to a magazine and buys a new refrigerator with the money received. The point? According to Jackson, looking for a lead-in for her lecture, this anecdote illustrates "the practical application of magic" and also answers the question she is posing for herself in the talk: "where do stories come from?" (195).

In all probability, neither version of the refrigerator story is precisely what happened, since both versions were edited when fictionalized. All fiction comes from life, according to Jackson, but has to be reworked:

> . . . the genesis of any fictional work has to be human experience. This translation of experience into fiction is not a mystic one. It is, I think, part recognition and part analysis. A bald description of an incident is hardly fiction, but the same incident, carefully taken apart, examined as to emotional and balanced structure, and then carefully reassembled in the most effective form, slanted and polished and weighed, may very well be a short story.

> (**"Exp. & Fict."** [**"Experience and Fiction"**] 196)

Fiction, then, improves on the experience by reshaping it, giving it a form, a point, granting it what Ephron referred to as the illusion of having an intelligence at the center—the writer herself. Jackson's lecture quarrels "with the statement that this event cannot be improved upon because that is the way it really happened" (199). According to Jackson, there is nothing sacred about reality. Fiction is always preferable:

> It is much easier, I find, to write a story than to cope competently with the millions of daily trials and irritations that turn up in an ordinary house and it helps a good deal—particularly with children around—if you can see them through a flattering veil of fiction. It has always been a comfort to me to make stories out of things that happen, things like moving, and kittens, and Christmas concerts at the grade school, and broken bicycles. It is easier, as Sally said, to magic the refrigerator than it is to wrench at the door.

> (**"Exp. & Fict."** 203)

The lecture goes on to illustrate the psychological control and comfort fiction afforded Jackson the day the local IRS representative came to audit their tax return. While her husband was sealed up in the study with the tax man, Jackson sat down to defend herself the only way she knew how—at her typewriter. She began straightforwardly enough, intending to write a letter to the government protesting such harassment of law-abiding citizens. But "she could not resist a few words of description" and, before she knew it, the letter turned into a story. When the interview was over, she "was well along in a story about a quietly lunatic investigation" (204). In her lecture, she could not resist adding that the income-tax man stopped by her typewriter on his way out and, recalling she was a writer, asked her where writers got their ideas. This last ironic twist seals the event in such vintage Jackson style that it is hard to believe the conversation actually took place. But it could have, and if life were as polished and pointed as fiction, it would have. Nevertheless, a version of the tax man story does appear in **Raising Demons,** which proves to skeptics that she really did, at least, turn the tax man's visit into a story, and, simultaneously, turn a situation where she and her husband were the victims of the IRS into one where she could pull all the strings.

Controlling Fear: Jackson's "Serious" Writing

Jackson was aware of the therapeutic value of her writing. During her last years, 1962-65, she was consciously using her writing, along with therapy, to combat the fears that had developed into a full-blown breakdown. But she had been aware of the way writing controlled her fears before that. We know that she began lecturing at the Suffield Writer's Conference in the summer of 1956. So even though the lecture notes which Oppenheimer uncovered and included in her biography are undated, they were most likely written in the late fifties. A comment in one of these lectures reveals her personal awareness of the therapeutic value of her writing, although it is presented as a generalization useful for all writers:

> The very nicest thing about being a writer is that you can afford to indulge yourself endlessly with oddness, and nobody can really do anything about it, so long as you keep writing and kind of using it up, as it were. All you have to do—and watch this carefully, please—is keep writing. So long as you write it away regularly nothing can really hurt you.
>
> (Opp. 211)

What Jackson feared would hurt her most was loss of control. She was afraid of losing control of her own words, which implied losing control of herself, of her identity. In an unsent letter to the poet Howard Nemerov, who taught at Bennington College with her husband, Jackson tried to put this fear of words *into* words. The unsent letter began in anger and ended in fear. What prompted her outburst was a misinterpretation of an earlier novel, **Hangsaman,**[5] in an English publication called *Sex Variant Woman in Literature.* Jackson's novel was referred to as "an eerie novel about lesbians" (Opp. 232). But Jackson had not meant Natalie and Tony, the two female characters in **Hangsaman,** to be lesbians, any more than she intended a lesbian reading of the two female characters she was currently creating (Merricat and Constance in **We Have Always Lived in the Castle**). In **Hangsaman** she had been trying to rep-

resent two warring psyches within the same person. In the letter to Nemerov, Jackson said she was writing about the "ambivalence of the spirit, or the mind, not the sex" (233). She was writing of the fear of a word, but the word she feared was not "lesbianism." The word she feared was "fear," fear of losing control to a stronger conscience which would destroy what she thought of as herself:

> We are afraid of being someone else and doing the things someone else wants us to do and of being taken and used by someone else, some other guilt-ridden conscience that lives on and on in our minds, something we build ourselves and never recognize, but this is fear, not a named sin. Then it is fear itself I am writing about . . . fear and guilt and their destruction of identity. . . . Why am I so afraid?
>
> So here I am. I am frightened by a word. I am frightened by a word because it tells me I am frightened. But I have always loved to use fear, to take it and comprehend it and make it work and consolidate a situation where I was afraid and take it whole and work it from there . . . I delight in what I fear.
>
> (Opp. 233, Ellipses Jackson's)

Jackson's articulation of what she fears elucidates nearly all of her so-called "thrillers." In **Hangsaman,** Natalie nearly succumbs to the will of Tony, who is no more than a second guilt-ridden conscience living in Natalie's own mind ("some other guilt-ridden conscience that lives on and on in our minds, something we build ourselves and never recognize"). Natalie is guilt-ridden by the fact that she has no friends, that her father thinks she is so wonderful, but she knows the truth: that she is isolated, friendless, unhappy, and ashamed. But the novel is actually a triumph of Natalie's healthier conscience, which escapes the efforts of the second guilt-ridden conscience to commit suicide. Natalie ends up escaping from Tony and a dark, damp, deserted wood and hitching a ride to the edge of her college campus, which she reenters alone but alive.

The Bird's Nest is another variation on the theme of absorption into another's conscience.[6] Unable to deal with the reality surrounding her mother's death, Elizabeth has become fragmented into four incomplete personalities. The novel follows her struggles back to one reintegrated whole. But Jackson teases us with the fear of absorption by making each fragmented personality feel complete, whenever each is able to gain control and surface. Towards the end of the treatment, each worries about the fact that she will be lost or dead when the whole person is cured. One of the personalities tries to explain her worries to her Aunt Morgen:

> "He said, the doctor, that when I was cured it would be that all of us, Betsy and Beth and all, were all back together. He said I was one of them. Not myself, just one more of them. He said he was going to put us all back together into one person."

"So? . . . Why not wait and see what happens?" Morgan suggested, inspired.

"Look," Elizabeth turned and looked at her. "I'm just one of them, one *part*. I think and I feel and I talk and I walk and I look at things and I hear things and I eat and I take baths—. . . But I do it all with *my* mind." Elizabeth spoke very slowly, feeling her way. "What he's going to have when he's through is a new Elizabeth Richmond with *her* mind. *She* will think and eat and hear and walk and take baths. Not me. I'll maybe be a part of her, but I won't know it—*she* will."

"I don't get it," said Morgen.

"Well," said Elizabeth, "when *she* does all the thinking and knowing, won't I be . . . dead?"

(Bird's Nest, 333)

"Fear of being someone else and doing the things someone else wants us to do," Jackson's words in her unsent letter to Nemerov, aptly describes the frightening touches in this novel.

The Haunting of Hill House can and has been read as a struggle between Eleanor and a haunted house, but the plot is more understandable if we recognize that Eleanor's struggles are also against that other guilt-ridden conscience "living on and on" within her own mind.[7] Eleanor feels guilty over her mother's death. She is certain that her dying mother had knocked on the wall and called for her medicine, as usual, but that she had not awakened as usual. (If Eleanor had not awakened, a rational, non guilt-ridden person might ask, how can she be certain that her mother had called?) Eleanor is also guilty and ashamed because she is thirty-two, unmarried, alone, has wasted eleven years caring for her invalid mother, is more relieved over her mother's death than sorry, has taken the car she and her sister own jointly (against her sister's wishes), and is now having rather a good time at Hill House. She is there by invitation, which means she belongs somewhere for the first time in her life. Since we can all manage to feel guilty over joy as well as misery, we all live in constant danger of absorption by that other guilt-ridden conscience living in our own minds, as Jackson well knew. In this novel Jackson chose to have Eleanor succumb to that second conscience, which drives her into a tree to her death: "*Why* am I doing this? Why am I doing this? Why don't they stop me?" blurts Eleanor's primary conscience, aware to the end (246).

We Have Always Lived in the Castle presents the confrontation even more obscurely.[8] It describes the struggle between the joint conscience of two sisters, Merricat and Constance, where our sympathies are directed, and the threatening group conscience of the townsfolk. Because the girls keep their "castle" (really a large estate), albeit in a battered and mostly burnt condition, and because the townfolk guiltily slink up one by one to the house under cover of night with offerings of food to atone for their attack, this novel reads like a triumph.

Triumphant or not, it was writing this novel that helped destroy the balance in Jackson's mind, turning her from a clever functioning writer into a severely troubled woman who was afraid to leave her bedroom. For this tale of two sisters isolating themselves from hostile and evil townsfolk came very close to voicing Jackson's own fears of her position in Bennington, Vermont, as Oppenheimer observes (233-237). Jackson had many other stresses at the time: Stanley had fallen in love with another woman, Jackson's role as a mother had become less demanding with the two eldest children away at school, she was suffering from colitis, and she had been taking amphetamines and tranquilizers since a doctor began the cycle over ten years before to help her lose weight (Opp. 238-241).

Unable to quiet the fears writing this novel had awakened, Jackson grew unable to leave home: "I have written myself into the house" she wrote to a friend (Opp. 237). She admitted to others that she had, in fact, written into the novel what it was like for her in North Bennington, where she was taunted by the villagers on her daily walks to the grocery store (Opp. 234). By Thanksgiving of 1962, Jackson refused to leave her bedroom. After staying indoors for three months, she agreed to see a psychiatrist. But it was to be three years before she began another novel. Twenty-nine pages of text were completed when she died in 1965 at age forty-nine.

Probably her most masterful use of fear, the story that was banned in South Africa, the one for which she is best known, is **"The Lottery."** Rather than approach this as the cynical exposure of the evil in human nature (a perfectly valid if overused approach), it is more interesting to approach it from Jackson's love of using fear, from her constant need to control it, to "use it up," as she put it. All her life, Jackson played with fear, prodded it the way you would a sore tooth. The fears she played with were both private: the fear of being swallowed by that second guilt-ridden conscience; and social: the fear of rejection, isolation, and persecution. She learned to frame these fears within the safe confines of a plot. All she need do to stay sane was to redirect her feeling of annihilation, rejection, or persecution into a plot which justified such fears. By doing so, by putting her fears into the story, Jackson was able to contain her paranoid feelings against the townsfolk in Bennington, Vermont. She was able to control her suspicions that the grocer would just as soon stone her as sell her a pork chop. Within the confines of the plot, such hostility would feel impersonal. It was not anything Shirley Jackson deserved, nor was it anything Tess Hutchinson had done, to merit being blackballed. **"The Lottery"** was illustrating how that other side of human nature, that other "guilt-ridden conscience," could take over en masse and control the more civilized everyday conscience under which we usually operate.

Even little Davy Hutchinson was given a few pebbles to throw at his mother.

CONTROLLING FEAR: JACKSON'S WITTY AUTOBIOGRAPHIES

I am reluctant to write that Shirley Jackson was misunderstood. She was, but my saying so suggests that I, alone, understand her, which would set myself up on a pompous, precarious, and doomed critical podium. While I do not claim to understand *everything* about Shirley Jackson's writing, I can make one important observation: her witty autobiographies and her so-called supernatural horror tales are not so far apart as everyone has assumed. Hovering over all reviews of her work is always the question of how the same person who wrote **"The Lottery"** could come up with the warm family autobiographical stories of *Life Among the Savages* and *Raising Demons*. The book critic for *Time* magazine, reviewing *We Have Always Lived in the Castle,* one of Jackson's last publications, had a wonderful time presenting the division:

> Shirley Jackson is a kind of Virginia Werewoolf among the seance-fiction writers. By day, amiably disguised as an embattled mother, she devotes her artful talents to the real-life confusions of the four small children (*Life Among the Savages, Raising Demons*) in her Vermont household. But when shadows fall and the little ones are safely tucked in, Author Jackson pulls down the deadly nightshade and is off. With exquisite subtlety she then explores a dark world (*The Lottery, Hangsaman, The Haunting of Hill House*) in which the usual brooding old houses, fetishes, poisons, poltergeists and psychotic females take on new dimensions of chill and dementia under her black-magical writing skill and infra-red feminine sensibility.
>
> (21 Sept. 1962: 93)

The split was presented in her obituary in *The New York Times* so straight-forwardly that it seems pedestrian by contrast, despite its adjective-overload:

> Shirley Jackson wrote in two styles. She could describe the delights and turmoils of ordinary domestic life with detached hilarity; and she could with cryptic symbolism, write a tenebrous horror story in the Gothic mold in which abnormal behavior seemed perilously ordinary.
>
> (10 Aug. 1965: 29)

Her husband skirted the issue by showing a patronizing, critical grudge against the naïveté of people who raise the question in the first place:

> People often expressed surprise at the difference between Shirley Jackson's appearance and manner, and the violent and terrifying nature of her fiction. Thus, many of the obituaries played up the contrast between a "motherly looking" woman, gentle and humorous, and that "chillingly horrifying" short story **"The Lottery"** and other works. When Shirley Jackson, who was my wife, published two lighthearted volumes about the spirited doings of our children, . . . it seemed to surprise people that she should be a wife and mother at all, let alone a gay and apparently happy one. This seems to me to be the most elementary misunderstanding of what a writer is and how a writer works, on the order of expecting Herman Melville to be a white whale.[9]

Hyman is upholding the notion of Art for Art's sake, the study of the corpus divorced from the person, as if there were no connection between what a person writes about and what that person needs to write about, no connection between who you are and what issues you are struggling with. His wife knew better than that, as all her words on the act of writing show.

A few critics *were* able to admit they did not understand her "gothic" or "supernatural" tales. These novels have never seemed particularly gothic to me, for while they do contain castle-like estates, these estates are filled with quirky characters rather than the cardboard counts, villains, and maidens of gothic thrillers. Nor do they deal precisely with the supernatural. For Jackson, the supernatural is mainly a way to express the subconscious, an observation made by Isaac Bashevis Singer, an admirer of Jackson's work (Opp. 228). And her fiction is at least as psychological as it is supernatural. It is difficult to know how to refer to these novels. I am calling them "serious" only to separate them from the lighthearted wit of the autobiographies. But the serious fiction is filled with (indeed, saved by) witty observations. And while the autobiographies are obviously meant to be witty, it does not follow that they are therefore frivolous. It is simply that they allow the reader to feel comfortable because they allow him to think he knows what is going on. Since he can then feel superior, he tends to write them off as lightweight. Jackson's serious fiction, on the other hand, is never written off, even when it is not understood. Confusion, in fact, tends to inspire awe. The less the critic understands, the more highly does he praise. Edmund Fuller starts his review of *The Haunting of Hill House* with rare honesty:

> This review of Shirley Jackson's new novel properly begins with the confession that I am not sure of anything about it except its almost unflagging interest.[10]

Ihab Hassan felt the same way about *We Have Always Lived in the Castle,* but he veiled his perplexity beneath a literary-sounding generalization:

> I have always felt that some writers should be read and never reviewed. Their talent is haunting and utterly oblique: their mastery of their craft seems complete. Even before reading Shirley Jackson's latest novel, I would have thought her case to be clear; she is of that company. And now Miss Jackson has made it even more difficult for a reviewer to seem pertinent: all he can do is bestow praise.[11]

But such humility, as well as such praise, was saved for the serious fiction. No one feels her witty autobiographical pieces deserve equal respect. Even Lenemaja Friedman, author of one of the two books that exist on Jackson to date (the other is Oppenheimer's biography), who devotes her last brief chapter to the family chronicles, makes this clear in a telling aside:

> She must have had tremendous resources of energy, for it was during these years, the 1950s, when her children were growing up that her literary output was the greatest: at least forty-four short stories were published during this decade (many of these, however, are the family-based stories for the women's magazines);[12]

Even her husband felt defensive about the image his wife projected in the autobiographies. When she granted a rare interview to Harvey Breit, playing up her cozy mothering role as well as the restful, non-physical side of writing, declaring "It's the only way I can get to sit down," Stanley would not take it silently.[13] He wrote a sarcastic little note to her which Oppenheimer tells us she saved in her **"Lottery"** scrapbook:

> dear neat detached miss jackson . . . writin? taint nothin but fun!!! neatly tucking a wisp of grey hair in place . . . d'ruther be raisin my passel of kids but since they laid henry off at the mill . . . flouring her apron with careworn hands . . . n'poppin blueberry pies in the oven . . . neatly detaching her goddamn head . . . shucks . . . yessir yessiree yesirreeindeedee!
>
> (Opp. 141)

Despite her husband's mockery, there was probably a serious motivation for the persona she created in her witty family sagas. The serious fiction is coping, or trying to cope, with fear by rechanneling it into plots. But Jackson is also combating fear in her witty autobiographies. In these, she is combating fear by distancing it, rather than rechanneling it. Between herself and her fears she places four children, one large but cozy house, any number of cats, a large cowardly dog, little wheels off things, a husband in his den, homemade brownies, inept maids, and terribly funny insights about it all:

> Our house is old, and noisy, and full. When we moved into it we had two children and about five thousand books; I expect when we finally overflow and move out again we will have perhaps twenty children and easily half a million books; we also own assorted beds and tables and chairs and rocking horses and lamps and doll dresses and ship models and paint brushes and literally thousands of socks. This is the way of life my husband and I have fallen into, inadvertently, as though we had fallen into a well and decided that since there was no way out we might as well stay there and set up a chair and a light of some kind;[14]

In about 98% of her two witty autobiographies, *Life Among the Savages* and *Raising Demons*, Jackson keeps a safe distance between herself and her fears. She presents herself as the wise, warm mother threading her way through her children's devious but demanding egos, her house's cantankerous furnace, and the daily meals and laundry.[15] But occasionally that distance shortens, giving us a fleeting glimpse of what her wit is keeping at bay. Even the popular story of Laurie's initial experience in kindergarten (which is often anthologized separately as "Charles") is but a cute rendition of what is, in fact, a difficult child. He not only bit, swore, and kicked a teacher, he had the panache to create a cover story to cover his misdeeds. The whole class stayed after school to keep Charles company, Laurie told his mother. But in this chapter Jackson's "wise mother" mask is so firmly in place that we are not at all disturbed by the fact that her eldest is what is usually called a problem child. Indeed, the self-centeredness of all her children is always so cleverly portrayed, and her mother's mask is always so firmly in place that we are not even disturbed by the story of Sally refusing to give the policeman her penny to put in the parking meter so her mother won't get a ticket. She tells him he can have her shilling, not her penny, but only if he promises "not to ask little girls for money ever again."[16]

But Jackson's mask slips somewhat in *Raising Demons* when she describes Sally's excursions into magic. One day Sally and her baby brother Barry disappear for a few hours, and her two older children try to reassure her they are safe with "Pudge," the ruler of an underground magic kingdom. The next morning she finds a large tub of spring flowers on her back porch with a thank-you note from Pudge. Since this is supposed to be autobiography, Jackson may not be playing fair, may be asking more than her reader could possibly grant. Sally's dealings with magic are never given an explanation, but left hanging in that murky area of the inexplicable which is not far from fear.

The other occasion in her autobiography when fear draws a little closer is when Jackson presents herself as a faculty wife. Her brilliant acerbic wit is sustained throughout the anecdote:

> I was not bitter about being a faculty wife, very much, although it did occur to me once or twice that young men who were apt to go on and become college teachers someday ought to be required to show some clearly distinguishable characteristic, or perhaps even wear some large kind of identifying badge, for the protection of innocent young girls who might in that case go on to be the contented wives of furniture repairmen or disc jockeys or even car salesmen. The way it is now, almost any girl is apt to find herself hardening slowly into a faculty wife when all she actually thought she was doing was just getting married.
>
> (*Raising Demons*, 639)

But her wit, however bright, cannot eradicate the disturbing facts beneath the surface cleverness: many of the students *were* young, beautiful, and idolatrous, while

Jackson *was* older, fatter, and no longer infatuated by her husband, and her husband *did* love the adulation, not to mention the young nubile bodies, of his students.

These sections afford glimpses into a world that is not the safe, warm, and loving one Jackson is operating in for most of her two memoirs. Her children's self-centeredness suggests the self-absorbed world in which the adolescent Natalie was enmeshed (*Hangsaman*), the faculty wife's fears are similar to the fear of being forever left out of love which is eating away at Eleanor (*The Haunting of Hill House*), while Sally's adventures link up with the inexplicable parts of life expressed by the supernatural in all Jackson's serious novels.

Conversely, there are many witty touches in the serious fiction, as well as countless evocations of the cozy domestic safety which dominates the autobiographies. Although I have never cared for gothic tales, or tales of the supernatural, science fiction, or mystery, the intelligent, wry, domestic tone in all of Jackson's fiction lifts it into a category of its own. A brief tribute to her in *Newsweek* made a similar observation:

> In her art, as in her life, Shirley Jackson, who died last week at 45 [sic], was an absolute original. She belonged to no literary movement and was a member of no "school." She listened to her own voice, kept her own counsel, isolated herself from all fashionable intellectual and literary currents. She was not an urban, or existential, or "new," or "anti-"novelist. She was unique.

> (23 Aug. 1956: 83B)

By mingling wit and domestic detail with the inexplicable and fearful, Jackson has shortened the gap between her witty and her serious writing. Her wit also makes the serious fiction more acceptable. Many of the characters have sardonic sides which serve to ease a skeptical reader into the story. Mrs. Halloran, in *The Sundial*, is one such character. Although she goes along with her sister-in-law's vision of the end of the world (if Aunt Fanny proves to be right, Mrs. Halloran plans to be the queen in their new utopia), she is aware of Aunt Fanny's shortcomings, as well as the humor of their situation. Aunt Fanny has started to replace the library books with survival supplies:

> but Mrs. Halloran, looking in some surprise on a carton of cans of peaches, asked Aunt Fanny, "Surely we are entering a land of milk and honey? Must we take our own lunch?

> (*The Sundial*, 95)

Familiar domestic tensions add a comfortable touch. The doctor who is running the experiment at Hill House turns out to be a henpecked husband, and, though Eleanor has psychic abilities, she also has a dominating married sister who treats her like a servant. When

Eleanor sets out for Hill House in their jointly-owned car, which she took despite her sister's objections, she becomes somewhat freed from her usual timid personality. Passing a tiny cottage en route to Hill House, she dares to daydream, to imagine a possible alternate life for herself inside:

> No one would find me there, either, behind all those roses, and just to make sure I would plant oleanders by the road. I will light a fire in the cool evenings and toast apples at my own hearth. I will raise white cats and sew white curtains and sometimes come out of my door to go to the store to buy cinnamon and tea and thread. People will come to me to have their fortunes told, and I will brew love potions for sad maidens; I will have a robin . . .

> (*Hill House*, 22-23)

All the cozy domestic details, the cinnamon and tea and thread, make her sudden urge to hide ("No one would find me there, either"), and to establish herself as a kindly witch for young maidens, that much easier to accept. Moreover, the emotional motivation behind Eleanor's daydream has been carefully established. In her dream she hides from those who have been powerful enough to hurt her in the past and enjoys a skill which will draw harmless and powerless people to her in the future. Above all, she will be safe, with her cats, her curtains, her toasted apples—safe, useful, and maybe even loved. And Jackson has presented the daydream to us with her own unique, wry, domestically-informed wit.

WIT AS CONTROL IN JACKSON'S PRIVATE LIFE

Jackson's biographer spoke to an old friend of Stanley Edgar Hyman's about the marital relationship. Frank Orenstein, whose friendship with Stanley went back to their high school days, had this to say:

> He was the czar, but she was the real ruler. It was her house, her rule. Stanley was probably smarter than anybody, but he didn't have the quick wit—and I think that was part of what evened up the balance.

> (Opp. 179)

It was her quick wit that had impressed Stanley from the start. What first brought Shirley to Stanley's attention was a piece she had written for *The Threshold*, a magazine published by her creative writing class at Syracuse University in 1938 (Opp. 61). And wit remained important in their relationship. "They were big fans of each other," recalls their eldest son, Laurence, thinking of their wonderful family dinners (Opp. 198). "Both of them were total suckers for anything slapstick," remarked Barry, the younger son. Their elder daughter, Joanne, recalled one of her mother's most memorable dinner table performances, the night she did an impression of a drunken goldfish (Opp. 198).

The more ominous side to Jackson's wit was her interest in witchcraft. After her death, no one was willing to take a definite position as to whether Jackson was serious about being a witch. She did fill her home with books on witchcraft, with charms, and cats. A hedged reference to her witchcraft abilities crept into *The New York Times* Obituary:

> In that connection [to the subject of witchcraft], Brenden Gil, the critic, who was a friend of Miss Jackson, said yesterday that she had considered herself responsible for an accident to an enemy by having fashioned a wax figure of him that had a broken leg.
>
> (10 Aug. 1965: 29)

Even if the controlling aspect of witchcraft *did* appeal to Jackson, she undoubtedly knew that any show of interest, let alone declaration of belief, would provoke scorn. She usually packaged her public allusions in an acceptable form: "I have always been interested in witchcraft and superstition but never had much traffic with ghosts" she said in one of her writing lectures.[17] Her language makes the observation that much more palatable. The phrase "never had much traffic with ghosts" mocks the whole enterprise and suggests that her interest in witchcraft is purely intellectual. That is, in fact, what her brother believed: "She studied it like you'd study history," he told Oppenheimer, "I always thought it was a little tongue-in-cheek" (37).

But if we accept her brother's version, what do we make of her eldest son's comment that "my mother believed strongly and firmly in the supernatural. She believed it and was very tuned in to it, perhaps more than she cared to be" (Opp. 37). Or how do we react to Jackson's more candid words uncovered by Oppenheimer in the draft version for another writing lecture: "No one can get into a novel about a haunted house without hitting the subject of reality head-on; either I have to believe in ghosts, which I do, or I have to write another kind of novel altogether" (226).

Her tarot readings were reputed to be so accurate that several of her friends nervously refused to let her tell them their fortunes. After the family moved to Vermont in 1945, she never had fewer than six cats at a time. A friend of her elder daughter recalled a dinner when a grey cat jumped on Shirley Jackson's shoulder and seemed to whisper in her ear, at which point Jackson announced that the cat had told her a poem—which she then repeated. Joanne reported another light side to her witchcraft. She kept all the small kitchen tools crammed in one drawer. When she wanted one, she would slam the drawer shut, call out the desired utensil's name, and open the drawer. According to Joanne, it would always be on top (Opp. 189).

Still, these intriguing details are hardly conclusive proof that Jackson considered herself a witch. We probably have to settle for ambiguity. Harriet Fels, wife of the president of Bennington College and friend of Jackson, summed up the ambiguity nicely: "She would allude to witchcraft. She acted as if she believed in it on the one hand, but it was a game on the other hand. She wasn't above stricking pins in dolls, it was a real thing—but she treated it in conversation as a game" (Opp. 189).

According to Oppenheimer, everyone knew Jackson had the tools of magic in her home—her books, devices, and amulets were in plain sight. But she wouldn't even tell her children whether or not she practiced magic in earnest:

> "When she was asked, she would say nothing about whether she did or didn't," said Laurence. She could joke—or seem to joke—about being a witch, she could allude to certain charms and spells in passing, but the actual practice of magic was very private and real to her, something she felt strongly should be hidden from the outside world. "I wouldn't want to violate any secrets," Laurence said.

While Laurence's comments suggest he believed her to be in earnest, Barry, her younger son, offered the explanation I quoted in my introduction, which leads away from the question of belief and back to the relationship between witchcraft, writing, and control:

> She realized that the only tools the magician needs are in the head. You make the world, you decide what your name is, your role, decide what people are going to think of you by your own force of will. And that's real magic in the real world.
>
> (Opp. 190)

This, as Oppenheimer observes, is "not unlike writing itself" (190).

While Jackson's wit could put her in complete control in her fiction ("for as long as the story does go on you are the boss"), it could never function quite so effectively in daily life. Stanley Edgar Hyman had his own agenda, and an active participation in parenting or household duties was not on it. He was the professor and literary critic. Their den was always called Stanley's study, however many best sellers Shirley wrote in it (Opp. 170). What *was* on his agenda, however, was sexual promiscuity. Also, Jackson's difficult relationship with her parents could never be resolved, however many competent pictures she drew of her life for her mother in her letters home. Sally, commenting to Jackson's biographer on her mother's breakdown, assessed the question of her mother's mental control succinctly, if bitterly:

> She got the four kids and the big house and the smart husband and she went crazy anyway. And I think she felt really bad. She felt bad that the books weren't enough therapy, that writing a book every year or two didn't keep her sane. Because she put her guts into it. But it wasn't enough.
>
> (Opp. 248)

Sally is Jackson's daughter, and was only seventeen when her mother died. Her bitterness is understandable. But what can never be determined is the degree to which Jackson's writing had helped keep her fears at bay. Toward the end of her life, Jackson worried about what she would be able to write about were she to be cured of her anxieties. Oppenheimer quotes from her last journal, kept while she was in therapy:

> If I am cured and well and oh glorious alive then my books should be different. Who wants to write about anxiety from a place of safety? Although I suppose I would never be entirely safe since I cannot completely reconstruct my mind. But what conflict is there to write about then? I keep thinking vaguely of novels about husbands and wives . . . but I do not really think this is my kind of thing. Perhaps a funny book. A happy book. There's room for it and I could do it.

(Opp. 258)

Jackson had begun **Come Along With Me** when she died of cardiac arrest in August of 1965. She seemed to be recovering from her breakdown, but too little of the novel was written (only twenty-nine pages) to be certain about where she was planning to take it. Still, it begins like one more vintage Jackson, with Angela Motorman a choice blend of the supernatural and homey, her voice saturated with Jackson's wit. I like to think that the border between the unknown and the comfortably known *was,* in fact, Jackson's "place of safety" and I take the fact that she had begun this novel with her usual droll blend of the two as a sign that she had come to appreciate her unique vantage point on life before she died.

Notes

1. Shirley Jackson, "Notes for a Young Writer," *Come Along With Me; Part of a novel, sixteen stories, and three lectures,* ed. Stanley Edgar Hyman (NY: Viking, 1968) 234-243.

2. Judy Oppenheimer, *Private Demons: The Life of Shirley Jackson* (NY: Putnam, 1988) 121. Oppenheimer's bibliography was invaluable for this chapter and will be cited parenthetically, abbreviated Opp.

3. Shirley Jackson, "Experience and Fiction," *Come Along With Me,* 195-204.

4. Shirley Jackson, *Raising Demons,* 1957, rpt. in *The Magic of Shirley Jackson.* ed. Stanley Edgar Hyman (NY: Farrar, Straus, and Giroux, 1965) 533-753.

5. Shirley Jackson, *Hangsaman* (NY: Farrar, Straus, and Young, 1951).

6. Shirley Jackson, *The Bird's Nest,* 1954, rpt. in *The Magic of Shirley Jackson,* 147-380.

7. Shirley Jackson, *The Haunting of Hill House* (1959; NY: Viking Penguin, 1987).

8. Shirley Jackson, *We Have Always Lived in the Castle* (1962; NY: Viking Penguin, 1984).

9. Stanley Edgar Hyman, "Shirley Jackson: 1919-1965," *Sat Eve Post* 18 Dec. 1965: 63. Jackson was actually born in 1916, according to Oppenheimer. Hyman was the one born in 1919, but upheld the fiction they were the same age into her death.

10. *The New York Times Book Review* 10 Oct. 1959: 4.

11. *The New York Times Book Review* 23 Sept. 1962: 5.

12. Lenemaja Friedman, *Shirley Jackson* (Boston: Twayne, 1975) 31.

13. *The New York Times Book Review* 26 June 1949: 15.

14. Shirley Jackson, *Life Among The Savages,* 1953 rpt. in *The Magic of Shirley Jackson,* 385.

15. Walker cites *Life Among the Savages* as an example of a woman's double text—the wise warm mother is part of the "official" text, but there is also a subtler "unofficial" one. See *A Very Serious Thing* (Minneapolis: Univ. of Minn. Press, 1988) 31.

16. Jackson, *Raising Demons,* 612.

17. Jackson, "Experience and Fiction," *Come Along With Me,* 202.

Richard Pascal (essay date fall 2000)

SOURCE: Pascal, Richard. "New World Miniatures: Shirley Jackson's *The Sundial* and Postwar American Society." *Journal of American and Comparative Cultures* 23, no. 3 (fall 2000): 99-111.

[*In the following essay, Pascal analyses what he describes as the postwar "sociocultural features" of Jackson's novel* The Sundial.]

> [The American home] must be a home built and loved upon new world, and not the old world, ideas and principles.
>
> A.J. Downing, *The Architecture of Country Houses,* 1850

"'We are in a pocket of time,'" claims a character in Shirley Jackson's 1958 novel *The Sundial,* "'a tiny segment of time suddenly pinpointed by a celestial eye'" (45). It is a preposterously oracular utterance delivered by a dithery and slightly deranged figure, yet it hints at an aspect of Jackson's undervalued text that has hitherto escaped the notice of even those few commentators who have directed their attention towards it.[1] *The Sundial,* which focuses upon a handful of people who wait together at a country estate in expectation of a prophesied new world to be born from the destruction of the old, aspires to *be* that celestial eye, pinpointing sociocultural features of its own postwar "pocket of time," calling attention to their origins in the nineteenth and early twentieth centuries, and locating them within the even older historical context of one of America's foundation myths. Like most of Jackson's fictions, it is a narrative that adheres tenuously to basic conventions of naturalistic realism, deploying contrariwise just enough traces of uncanniness to caution against complete skepticism about the intrusion of the paranormal into the domain of the ordinary. Unlike most, however, it openly essays to comment upon contemporary social issues and delusions and to pronounce upon their implications for the nation.

In this sense the novel is, to borrow Sacvan Bercovitch's famous phrase, Shirley Jackson's American Jeremiad, and in one obvious way, it announces itself as such: the "celestial eye" is also a stentorian voice from the heavens that speaks its displeasure with what it has descried.[2] The narrative voice, though generally more satirically speculative than authoritative, is similarly condemnatory and portentous with regard to contemporary social arrangements. The text's critique, however, is grounded in historical particularity, and encompasses several closely related aspects of American social life in the postwar period: (1) the accelerated relocation of the middle class segments of the population from urban centers to smaller, neo-traditional communities; (2) anxieties about challenges to the dominant patriarchal ideologies of domesticity and gender; (3) disruptive effects of self-seeking individualism within the nuclear family; and most broadly, (4) the imminent prospect of a society fissured by the triumph of childish solipsism as a national ideal. As is consonant with one of the predominant social obsessions of the initial phase of the post-nuclear era, the prospect of widespread annihilation, possibly to be followed by utopian renewal, precipitates all of the action in *The Sundial* and dominates the minds of the characters. Yet even though its shadow is all but palpable throughout, the bomb is never mentioned, a decisive indication that atomic anxiety is not the basic source of the apocalyptic mentality that pervades the characters' thoughts. That obsession is traced, rather, to two venerable American traditions: the socially sanctioned impulse to retreat to "American miniatures," or small, exclusive enclaves of communal, familial, and individual sanctuary from the claims of the larger social universe; and the nation's perennial fascination with the promise of some vague but fervently dreamt of communal fulfillment implicit in its originat-

ing image of itself as a New World. The former, as the text in various ways implies, began to gain hold in the nineteenth century and has accelerated in the 1950s; and the latter, it suggests, is a construct that derives from Elizabethan imperial aspirations which supplanted a still older, and less holistic, European notion of "world." Miniaturist projects are linked with (even as they are dissociated from) utopian New World imaginings in that they represent, ostensibly, attainable scaled down versions of what was originally a dream of global magnitude and comprehensiveness. And their failure in the postwar era to deliver even the diminished and oppositional alternative site of worldly fulfillment that they had come to signify, tantalizingly, has issued into a widespread receptivity to apocalyptic fantasies of a world cleansed by horrible destruction into originative, pre-cultural freshness.

SUBURBANIZATION AND THE AMERICAN MINIATURE

Set in a small town that is figured as an anachronistic relic of a largely bygone America, and concerned with the struggles of a rich family and its hangers-on over an inheritance of redoubtable proportions, *The Sundial* must have seemed far removed from the lives and concerns of the postwar middle class readers who presumably comprised its intended and actual audiences. In these and some other respects its trappings brazenly replicate those of the early English Gothic tradition as exemplified by the novels of Walpole, Reeve, and Radcliffe. In constructing feudal pasts cleansed of any threat of social disorder, those fictions signalled a desire to retreat into a tidily controllable new *old* world—modern ideological assumptions comfortingly in hand. Their antique facades were, in this sense, as pointedly ungenuine as Walpole's own lovingly fabricated miniature "castle" in the suburbs, Strawberry Hill. Jackson's narrative ransacks these older texts in order to stage an updated version of the discursive camouflage act that defined Gothicism as a modern mode from the very outset. Its fancifully incorporated borrowings are less a summons to imaginative escapism—although they certainly inveigle the reader with that option—than indicators of the modern middle class impulse to retreat into communities and domestic sites that simulate a past expunged of uncertainty.

More specifically, they function as subtle reminders of the early correlation between the development of the Gothic mode and the emergence of the suburban movement in that proto-America, England. In this regard, of course, it is particularly significant that the estate in *The Sundial* is likened to Walpole's actual castle—which was, of course, his actual replicated castle—rather than to his more famous fictional one, Otranto (188-89). The effect of this and other Gothic analogs in the novel is to foreground, by way of exaggeration and parody, a similar though historically more recent and local obsession with fictitious pastness. For the text construes as a native near equivalent to the romanticized feudalism of English Gothic fiction the idealized era of the American small town, in which class relations are entirely static and the possession of house and land constitutes an ineluctably secure hedge against social and financial disruption. Americans, as is well known, like to imagine themselves as constituting a large and mighty nation. Yet conversely, many also like to imagine the site of the "true" America as being rural and parochial. But though the image of the small country town basking in somnolent pastoral stability is the basic model for the nationally venerated small social unit, the social actuality in modern times has been somewhat different. For more than a century, though most spectacularly after the Second World War, the major demographic shift in the United States has been the migration from the cities to outlying semi-rural residential areas. The phenomenon is of course widely referred to as "suburbanization," a term which, in stressing such communities' subordinate relationship with cities, has tended to obscure one of its most fundamental aspects. Just as Strawberry Hill was a make-believe medieval estate, modern suburbs are make-believe small towns of a bygone era—even when, as has often been the case, the "suburb" is an old town that has in effect been subsumed within the commuting range of a relatively nearby urban unit.

In a percipient study of the suburban movement published in the same year that the *The Sundial* appeared, Robert C. Wood argued that the middle class flight to both planned suburbs and pre-existing towns had been a retreat to more or less fabricated versions of a mythic small community he astutely termed "the American miniature" (53). Wood employed that term because he wished to encapsulate the small town paradigm that underlies and haunts diverse varieties of suburban community, and to suggest as well that the fundamental reason for its power over the national imagination is that it is taken to signify the essence of the American social structure. As we'll see, when applied to Jackson's novel it can be refined so as to comprehend progressively even smaller communities—the home, the family, and ultimately that polity of one, the self. Each of these, the text suggests, is also a miniature "world," and frustrations encountered in one such sphere may inspire emigration to another that is smaller and more controllable. But the most important point to take into account initially in thinking about *The Sundial* in this context is that the town that is sketched lightly therein does not represent in any simple sense the surviving remnant of an older American way of life that it is taken to be, by its inhabitants as well as by visitors. It is situated only nine miles away from the nearest city, a negligible distance in the automotive age. And while the time frame for the narrative is the contemporary period, the text

compels awareness that the process of "suburbanizing" the area had been initiated well before the story's opening by the very family that sought in it the enclave of pastoral timelessness signified by the timepiece of pre-industrial devising that gives the novel its title. The estate that seems so entrenched within the traditional configuration of the old-fashioned town was built in the relatively recent past by an exurbanite migrant, referred to throughout the text as "the first Mr. Halloran." This figure, the deceased father of two of the adult characters inhabiting the estate in the 1950s, brought his family to the town early in the century, during the period in which, according to social historians, the first significant wave of middle class migrations to suburban areas occurred.[3]

Mr. Halloran was apparently so rich that his construction of an elaborate private estate in rural surroundings might seem to bear little resemblance to the middle class suburban flights of the book's time, rather establishing him as an imitator of Nineteenth Century American plutocrats like Cornelius Vanderbilt, with his famously gaudy mansion on the pastoral cliffs of the Hudson. But the point is that the conspicuous consumption of the Vanderbilts and their ilk actually operated as a source of inspiration for much of the rest of the populace. As Susman and Griffin have noted, the ideal of suburban life that began to take hold in America late in the last century, initially "a fantasy fulfilled only for the wealthy . . . continued to be a dream, however, for less well-to-do Americans" (21). Thus a Mr. Halloran, once his fortune had been secured, would have assumed the status of a culture hero who had enacted on a particularly grand scale the exurbanizing project that in more modest forms had become by the 1950s an available alternative even for those of fairly ordinary means. It is and has always been inherently a dream of wealth, but of wealth in the service of social idealism on a personal level—of funding fully, that is, a private domain of the self that is also patriotic display.

It follows then that what he attempted in the building of the mansion is only partially indicated by his choice of an old fashioned town for its setting; it was also, and perhaps primarily, the estate itself that was to be his American miniature. He was, we are told,

> a man who, in the astonishment of finding himself suddenly extremely wealthy, could think of nothing better to do with his money than set up his own world. His belief about the house . . . was that it should contain everything. The other world, the one the Hallorans were leaving behind, was to be plundered ruthlessly for objects of beauty to go in and around Mr. Halloran's house; infinite were the delights to be prepared for its inhabitants.
>
> (11)

The retreat from the city to the suburbanized town thus involved yet a further withdrawal into a domestic site immured against an outside world regarded as deflatingly or threateningly other. Mr. Halloran was not an immigrant seeking affiliation within the pre-established community, but a colonizer, carving out a personal empire within a space that has been transformed, through the power of brute wealth, into virgin land. And this, the novel implies, has been modern America's twist on the traditional valorization of the small community: to a large degree, relocation to a suburban site has signified disaffiliation, virtual secession, from larger social units, including even the local community itself which has become, in the words of Kenneth T. Jackson, "a mass of small, private islands" (280). The initial stage of the middle class withdrawal into domestic spaces that are discrete to the point of isolation dates back to the latter half of the nineteenth century. It was during that period, Jackson also notes, that the home "came to represent the individual himself," and "the new ideal was no longer to be part of a close community, but to have a self-contained unit, a private wonderland walled off from the rest of the world" (52, 58). That this ideal was intrinsically a *social* one—not only, that is, in the obvious sense that even superficially "personal" ideals must to some degree be socially instilled, but in that it was regarded as a communally salutary and even patriotic aspiration—is a distinctive irony of American social history. As Dolores Hayden has commented, "the dream house is a uniquely American form because for the first time in history, a civilization has created a utopian ideal based on the house rather than the city or the nation" (18).

For Mr. Halloran's descendants and their cohabitants, the estate he built in his own image continues to wall out much of the world he wished to abandon. To none, however, is it an entirely personal realm, as is evident from the tendency of several to fashion for themselves pretend spaces, personal miniatures, in which solipsistic control is absolute. Mrs. Halloran, for example, the founder's daughter-in-law and successor as tyrannical ruler of the estate (with implications that we will examine shortly), is inclined to fantasize about "a little, small house" of her own, deep in the woods:

> I will sit in the one chair or I will lie on the soft rug by the fire, and no one will talk to me, and no one will hear me; there will be only one of everything—one cup, one plate, one spoon, one knife. Deep in the forest I am living in my little house and no one can ever find me.
>
> (113)

The keynotes here are singularity, rusticity, and diminutiveness: it is another, more extreme version of a miniature world, particularly revealing in that it is the fantasy of someone who has attained control over a far grander actual home than the one she loves to imagine. Another character, Aunt Fanny, has actually constructed within the larger house her ideal miniature site, a carefully re-

stored semblance of the apartment in which she passed her childhood. This area she refers to as her "doll house," a formulation that encompasses, both metaphorically and metonymically, all of the miniature worlds under scrutiny in the novel.

Those connections are established most emphatically by the prominence accorded an actual doll house possessed by the ten-year-old granddaughter of Mrs. Halloran and great-niece of Aunt Fanny. Fancy, who has been lavishly indulged by well-off relations, regards her exquisitely equipped doll house as a toy version of the Halloran household to which she is the heiress apparent. "'When my grandmother dies,'" she says, "'I am going to smash my doll house. I won't need it any more'" (22), suggesting less that the things of childhood will be discarded in pursuit of an adult relationship to the world than that the "real" house will be a scaled-up version of the toy, the fantasy model. Only the toy is literally "miniature," but the estate is analogously a fabrication of the larger "world left behind," rendered safely insular and amenable to the unrestricted play of the proprietary ego. The defining aspect of the miniaturist project, in other words, is not diminutiveness as such, but totalizing sham of the kind that Walpole pioneered with the home at Strawberry Hill to which he once referred as his "toy castle."[4] And the simulation, the toy-like aspect, must be openly evident to at least some degree, for it is the signal that nothing excessive, nothing disturbing to fantasy, will be permitted.

THE CHALLENGE TO PATRIARCHY

On the basis of what has been argued thus far, it would appear that the novel envisions a postwar social world that is essentially an expanded version of the middle class suburban culture which began to emerge in the previous century. This is certainly the impression conveyed by its presentation of the ethos informing the contemporary miniaturist project in the respects hitherto considered. There is, however, one seeming discontinuity between the social climate of the period in which the first Mr. Halloran lived and that experienced by his mid-century heirs: gender relations are no longer securely in alignment with a patriarchal model. Matriarchy is now threatening to subvert or even invert the traditional (im)balance of power between the sexes, with implications for familial and social structures that are profoundly disquieting—so much so that it is because of the challenge to patriarchy that apocalypse comes to seem imminent, and perhaps even desirable.

To understand why this is imagined to be so, it is necessary to observe first of all that the impression of "discontinuity" is deceptive in that, as the text indicates, patriarchal ideology had for a long time contained within itself the basis for that challenge. Conventionally, since the early nineteenth century, the private domestic sphere ("home") and the public arena of production and exchange ("world") had been regarded as gendered spaces, female and male respectively (Cott 64-74). By the first Mr. Halloran's era, however, the home was "woman's sphere" only in a formal sense. The estate was from its inception his brain child and ego-projection; his wife, who had no say in the decision to relocate from their urban home, lived in it for only three months and then sickened and died. The point is that the female domain, to which had been ascribed at least a modicum of social power in the first half of the nineteenth century, was later separated and distinguished from the larger world only to be regarded as an inseparable and undistinguished aspect of the male ego. The first Mrs. Halloran, then, was only another of the objects of beauty plundered from the world left behind. That she contracted a fatal affliction in a dwelling far warmer than the family's "bleak and uncomfortable" (175) city apartment signifies clearly that her illness was a form of the malaise suffered by many affluent married women during the era that was the focus of Charlotte Perkins Gilman's famous story "The Yellow Wallpaper" (1892).

By mid-century the estate has become a living space dominated by the presence of females, approximating what "home" in the nineteenth century and "suburbia" in the mid-twentieth were often held to be.[5] The important difference, however, is that in the contemporary era the women really are threatening preeminence, the still dominant patriarchal social norm notwithstanding. It is at the story's opening that the inversion of the traditionally gendered power structure has come to pass decisively. The "second" Mrs. Halloran, wife of the original Mr. Halloran's son, has assumed control of the estate because her son Lionel, the rightful heir, has recently died in shady circumstances in which she herself may well have literally had a hand—he either fell or was pushed down a flight of stairs. Her husband, the owner, is still alive, but only feebly and ineffectually, and the only other male living at the Estate is her kept lover, Essex. The other residents, who include, in addition to Aunt Fanny, the widow of the deceased Lionel, her ten-year old daughter Fancy, and Fancy's tutor, Miss Ogilvie, are all female. As the story progresses, newcomers, mostly women, arrive to stay indefinitely, making the preponderance of females even more pronounced. The one male addition is a fortune hunter who has been picked up by Aunt Fanny to serve as the slightly ridiculous object of her schoolgirlish romantic fantasies. (Strikingly, the only two active men in the household are regarded as objects plundered from the outside world for the delight of female inhabitants.)

The accession of the imperious Halloran daughter-in-law to full command indicates most decisively that a female-oriented regime has been installed, and, as the ruler of the estate is apparently the most powerful figure in the adjacent town, it is a development that sig-

nals at least the possibility of a radical transformation of the gender hierarchy in American communal life. But although the new order is clearly gynocracy of a sort, it is no less a tyranny than was the system it has supplanted. The second Mrs. Halloran's given name, "Orianna," indicates that she is constructed as a monarch-mother, a "matriarch," as it incorporates the name of the wife of the founder, "Anna," and it was also one of the literary sobriquets of Queen Elizabeth I.[6] Correspondingly, Mrs. Halloran's primary desire is to rule the household, not to share power with its denizens, much less love and serve them as a conventional mother theoretically would. The inhabitants are, on the contrary, considered by her to be quite dispensable, untidy presences within her commandingly personal premises. On the day of Lionel's funeral she announces to the others that the recent "change"—her own son's sudden death, that is!—"'has been both refreshing and agreeable,'" and has convinced her of the necessity of a "housecleaning," by which innocuous-sounding term borrowed from the reassuring rhetoric of domesticity she means the summary dismissal of most of them (17).

The figure of Mrs. Halloran therefore does not signal a brave new world of nurturing femaleness or gender equality, but rather conjures up that most fearsome spectre of postwar social mythology, the domineering mother. The period is now remembered as one in which most American women were severely oppressed in many ways. They were, of course, but what is sometimes factored out of our latter day impression is that many contemporary commentaries saw the society as being deeply threatened by insidious maternal power. In *Modern Woman: The Lost Sex,* a particularly influential 1947 work by two psychiatrists, it was soberly alleged that via motherhood, "women are the principal transmitting media of the disordered emotions that today are so widely spread throughout the world and are reflected in the statistics of social disorder." (This certainly wasn't true of all mothers, the "study" went on to stress—only "40 to 50 per cent" of them!) And "just what have these women done to their sons? They have stripped them of their male powers—that is, they have castrated them" (Lundberg and Farnham, 23, 305, 319). Philip Wylie's *Generation of Vipers,* another pervasive influence in the postwar period, asserted that "when the mothers built up their pyramid of perquisite and required reverence in order to get at the checkbook . . . they donned the breeches of Uncle Sam," in the course of a tantrum-like jeremiad that climaxes in a histrionic unveiling: "I give you mom. I give you the destroying mother" (200, 203). *The Sundial,* wryly responsive to the ideological temper of its time, gave it a mom who has allegedly destroyed her own son in order to get at his checkbook and don his breeches. The intent is clearly to satirize the era's paranoia over what Wylie mirthlessly dubbed "Momism." Yet traces of that widespread anxiety of the 1950s are also discernible in the narrative; Mrs. Halloran and what she represents, it is stressed, will not be easy to live with.[7]

In any case, hers is a matriarchy that has not yet sealed its position securely. The degree to which her newly established dominance constitutes a turbulent disruption of the patriarchal social order is signaled by the events leading up to Aunt Fanny's initial premonition of an apocalyptic transformation in the near future. On the morning following the day of Lionel Halloran's funeral, when she goes for a walk with Fancy in the garden, the grounds of the estate and everything upon them still reflect in her mind the domineering personality of the first Mr. Halloran. Images of containment, orderliness, and control abound, pompously signifying the enslavement of all that is spontaneous or natural. The water that runs through fountains and pools, for example, though it clothes in sensuous transparency the curvaceous body of a marble nymph, eventually becomes "twisted and trapped and forced down, pushed underground to run secretly" (30). The grounds feature a number of such pieces of ersatz classical statuary—fauns, nymphs, and satyrs that hint at disturbing, socially disapproved modes of sexuality but which, frozen in marble and relegated to a discourse of the ornamental, celebrate bourgeois money's triumph over desire's powerful mischief. In the "present" of the narrative, however, it seems that Mr. Halloran's posthumous imposition of order may be coming undone. The hedges have grown "almost wild," darkening the pathways, and Aunt Fanny remarks that her father would not have tolerated such disrepair (24). Eventually she loses her way and experiences a state of delirium in which surroundings familiar since childhood turn invasive. Lost in a mist evidently more mental than actual, she stumbles and clutches "the long marble thigh" of a tall male figure that stands "soberly on his pedestal," and as her hysteria heightens, she finds herself dodging "a marble embrace" and turns away from "a marble mouth reaching for her throat" (28). With her emotional stability in peril, she then experiences a restorative frigidity provoked by the reassuring fearfulness of her father's voice calling her name, and subsequently, "with nothing but ice to clothe her," discipline of a sort is restored to Aunt Fanny's mind (31).

The Freudian implications of this spell of panic-stricken passion in the garden are readily apparent. The impingement of transgressive eroticism into the strictly ruled domain of the father, with as its object the very figure of the patriarch (or at least a close approximation), has initiated the return in frighteningly grotesque forms of what has long been repressed; and only the complete refiguring of the father as a deifically huge but ethereal voice safely de-eroticises him and endows him with the power to subdue the demon of sexual desire. But the episode also invites a sociopolitical reading: Aunt Fanny's passion in the garden has been provoked by a radical disturbance within the public order of the estate.

That her sexual anxieties have not simmered to the surface until the day after Lionel's funeral, which is to say not until there is no longer a male heir apparent, is telling. Even more significant, however, is the gist of the prophecy: in its foretelling of widespread destruction, the voice reclaims the family, the house, and in effect the future, in the name of patriarchy.

> "When the sky is fair again the children will be safe; the father comes to his children who will be saved. Tell them in the house that they will be saved. Do not let them leave the house; say to them: Do not fear, the father will guard the children. Go into your father's house and say these things."
>
> (32)

The others in the household, their awareness of the neurotically troubled soul of the messenger notwithstanding, find themselves tacitly accepting the apocalyptic portent of the prophecy because Aunt Fanny's proclamation of it in the drawing room is spectacularly reinforced by the brief appearance of a "small brightly-banded snake" that is instantly regarded as an emissary of the first Mr. Halloran. That this evidently harmless animal which departs quickly upon being discovered elicits a cowed response from all present is an indication of patriarchy's resilience in the face of the female challenge to its dominance. Egregiously phallic to the point of silliness, the snake represents, so to speak, mystified male power demystified—power which the text respects for the efficacy with which it commands awe from otherwise sensible (or at least secular-minded) people, but which is also mocked for its incongruous pretensions, in its pretty diminutiveness, to huge importance and venerability.

On one level the target of Jackson's satire is nothing less than the patriarchal basis of the dominant religious tradition of the Western world. The awe-inspiring voice in the garden is clearly a reworking of the Yahweh of *Genesis,* and the imagery, diction, and apocalyptic portent of the voice's prophecies conjure up the fulminating poetry of the *Book of Revelation.* But in the America of the mid-twentieth century, the text implies, religion is not a powerful social influence. Its diminished prestige is hinted at with the appearance of some members of a doomsday cult that calls itself the "True Believers," who truly believe that the although the end of the world is imminent, a select few will be saved and taken to Saturn in flying saucers.[8] Yet although traditional religious forms no longer provide spiritual sustenance, other than in degenerate versions to handfuls of credulous crackpots, their commanding deity, the all-powerful father, lingers ghostlike within contemporary society's superficially secular myths and values. That the ideology of domesticity is as haunted by father-worship even in the 1950s as it was in the first Mr. Halloran's time is slyly indicated by the phrasing of one of Aunt Fanny's interpretative assertions concerning the thrust of the revelations. "'Wrong is wrong and right is right and Father knows best'" (111), she says, revealing with those final three words that like many of her compatriots she must often have watched—devotedly, so to speak—the highly acclaimed television domestic melodrama of that name which starred Robert Young as the benign yet firm patriarch of an archetypally perfect middle-class American family.[9]

NUCLEAR MONSTERS

The reference to that popular program calls attention to another of *The Sundial*'s disturbing concerns. While it is a text that registers in its treatment of one woman's unwomanly aspiration to supremacy postwar society's nervousness about the subversion of the traditional gender hierarchy, its own anxiety is more pronounced with regard to perceived rifts in the structure of the family. From its earliest paragraphs the novel signals that relations between the various family members are coldly Machiavellian at best, and in some cases even gleefully vindictive. Upon returning from her husband's funeral the "young" Mrs. Halloran says to her daughter "'Fancy dear, would you like to see Granny drop dead on the doorstep?'"; and Fancy blithely replies "'Yes, mother,'" and a moment later asks "'Shall I push her? . . . Like she pushed my daddy?'" (3). It is a scandalous, even heretical opening for a narrative of the time. The 1950s, as Lynn Spigel has observed, "was a decade that invested an enormous amount of cultural capital in the ability to form a family and live out a set of highly structured gender and generational roles" (2). The period's veneration of family life was evident not only in numerous popular printed and screened narratives, but in such diverse cultural phenomena as newly coined phrases that highlighted the centricity of the family ("family-size carton," "family room," "family car") and the 1958 American National Exhibition in Moscow which displayed to the enemy as proof of the superiority of its social system a model American home that highlighted the private life of the family (Marling 278; May 17-18; Susman and Griffin 22).

And "family" almost invariably designated the nuclear unit: parents and one or more children inhabiting the same household. In this regard it may seem odd that in the contemporary period the Halloran estate houses various blood relations as well as diverse visitors, but no complete nuclear group. It is soon made clear, however, that the nuclear model was from the start the fundamental Halloran paradigm, for the extended household headed by Mrs. Halloran has accrued from three successive nuclear units, the most recent of which has only just been rendered incomplete. In its presentation of the problematic ethos informing contemporary family life, *The Sundial* yet again links a venerated mid-twentieth century social ideal back to a nineteenth cen-

tury origin, and suggests that it contained within itself from the start seeds of its own potential undoing. Recent scholarship has demonstrated persuasively that, contrary to a still widely held belief, the nuclear family was not a development of the post-industrial era; nonetheless, the nineteenth century marked a decline in the importance of extended networks of kinship relations, as well as an erosion of the practical preconditions for actively maintaining them. The nuclear unit came then to be regarded not merely as the fundamental building block of the larger society that the "family values" rhetoric of some twentieth century politicians alludes to, but also, and contrariwise, as a sort of counter-society.[10] It is quietly significant therefore that no grandparents for the first generation of Halloran children are mentioned, and that the uncle and cousins to whom Lionel refers at one point have been only distant relations. Clearly the Halloran family in those years was turning inward, isolating itself from its kinship network even as it walled out the larger society.

By the contemporary period, some longterm effects of years and years of rigidly imposed familial exclusiveness, effects that are ironically corrosive of nuclear integrity, are becoming apparent. Aggressive individualism and solipsistic defensiveness belie the weak pantomime of warmth and togetherness enacted in the Halloran household. The nuclear ideal has bred and nurtured grotesquely involuted social misfits like the first generation siblings, or else rapacious, self-aggrandizing monsters like Mrs. Halloran and her granddaughter. Neither Aunt Fanny nor her brother seems ever to have been capable of dealing with the outside world effectively. Aunt Fanny, in particular, seems trapped within the nuclear paradigm. She has developed the habit of periodically repairing to the area of the house in which she has laboriously replicated the domestic environment of her early childhood, there to pass the time perusing an old family photo album.

> "Some day I will be with my mother," Aunt Fanny would think, turning the pages, "I am with her in this book, no one can separate us *here*. Some day we will all be together again."

> (177)

Staticity and isolation thus define the true family. It is not a communal group that grows and diversifies over time, or that radiates outward beyond the immediate household, but one that resembles a photograph, a spatio-temporal moment from the past frozen into an image that is non-contiguous, and miniature.

Similarly, Mrs. Halloran's monstrous ways are promoted by the nuclear ideal. There is, as suggested by the earlier discussion of 1950's "momism," an ironic aptness about the younger daughter-in-law's reference to her as an "unmotherly monster" (20); in that era it was often alleged that the essence of motherhood was, so to speak, to depart monstrously from the essence of motherhood. But the text also implies that the nuclear family itself nurtures such tyrannical powermongering, by inculcating in family members a cult of reverence for the head of the household so intensively that envious aspirations to royal prerogative must inevitably be implanted in the souls of some. The absolute sovereignty over her domestic domain that Mrs. Halloran desires obsessively is signified by the crown that she insists, ridiculously, upon bestowing upon herself. Yet the self-absorption of even such an imperious ego as hers is also, within a claustrophobically familial context, a necessary *defensive* stance. In her dream of a miniature home of her own, she casts herself as a sympathetic refiguring of the witch in the story of Hansel and Gretel who justifiably resists the vandalism of the two children who want to eat her house. The children bear strong resemblances to Essex and a seventeen-year old woman named Gloria (a later arrival at the estate); but they are also imagined as her own offspring, and she, having trapped them in the cupboards, sits in monstrously insular serenity in front of her home, "hearing them call pitifully to her from inside" (115).

Those children possessed of such importunate chewing egos instantiate yet another sort of family monster hungry for imperious selfhood that harrowed the postwar America's fantasies of idyllic domesticity: the figure of the spoiled child. Families, it seemed to some contemporary observers, might be conceding to children an imbalance of power that constituted a threat to the ideal of harmonious family life. William H. Chafe has noted that in popular images "this 'new' family was run by children. Filiality had taken the place of both patriarchy and matriarchy" (123). Numerous situation comedies in the electronic and print media focussed upon rebellious and mischievous offspring, and if in most such narratives the self-willed and anarchic behavior of the young was regarded indulgently and as a source of reassuring laughter, in many an undertone of anxiety is also discernible.

Shirley Jackson's own highly successful semiautobiographical chronicles of sunny family life, published in popular magazines, and subsequently in best-selling book collections with the insinuating titles *Life Among the Savages* and *Raising Demons,* are prime examples. It is telling also that the now familiar (if slightly dated) phrase "juvenile delinquency" entered common usage in this era. The most unnerving aspect of that term was that it frequently connoted subversion from within the social stronghold of middle class domesticity; the juvenile delinquents that postwar America worried about were less often alienated youths from underprivileged backgrounds than kids from "nice" families, as is indi-

cated by the popularity of such narratives as William Marsh's novel, *The Bad Seed,* and Nicholas Ray's film, *Rebel without a Cause.*[11]

The opening of *The Sundial,* as we have seen, confronts the reader with a ten-year-old from a nice family who imagines herself capable of murdering her grandmother and is chillingly blithe about admitting to that capacity. The threat that she represents, not merely to Mrs. Halloran but to the idea of the sanctity of the family, is suggested by a lengthy, superficially digressive discussion of the town's "enshrined murderess," who had killed her parents and two younger brothers not long before the original Halloran family moved to the estate. The incident is overtly based on the famous case of Lizzie Borden of Fall River, Massachusetts, who was accused of the brutal murders of her father and stepmother in 1892. That Borden was 32 years old when the killings occurred is not mentioned in the jingle that appeared in the public domain not long after the grotesque event ("Lizzie Borden took an axe / And gave her mother forty whacks / And when she saw what she had done / She gave her father forty-one"), possibly because to imagine them as the work of an adult might dilute the titillating sense of sacrilege evoked by the thought of a child, especially a daughter, deviating spectacularly from the loving dependency that is her allotted role within the family structure (Spiering 5). Borden's fictitious counterpart in *The Sundial,* in any case, represents a similar recasting of the historical record into a myth about generational subversion from within the family, for "Harriet Stuart" was only "a young-looking fifteen" when the act occurred—and she killed her siblings as well as her parents (78).

INSULAR EGOTISM: THE ULTIMATE MINIATURE

Harriet Stuart's latter day alter ego eventually does murder her grandmother—or so it appears—and in precisely the same way as the latter is believed to have killed her son. In this, as in other respects, there is a significant congruency between the two characters. In Fancy, Mrs. Halloran sees her own future, or rather, a means of commodifying it: "'Fancy is mine, too, now,'" she says on the day of the funeral, adding "'some day everything I have will belong to Fancy, and I think to keep Fancy with me'" (20). Fancy, too, regards herself as, in a sense, the "future" Mrs. Halloran. On that same day she says, "'When my grandmother dies, no one can stop the house and everything from being mine'" (21), and similar comments are voiced by her on several subsequent occasions. However, what links the two most closely, and makes Mrs. Halloran seem at times rather childish and Fancy uncannily adult, is not merely the possessive impulse that they have in common. All of the other characters display at least some degree of avarice, but these two are held out as revealingly extreme in that their possessiveness seems not so much materialistic as egoistic at base. It is Fancy who is most taken with the idea of the crown that Mrs. Halloran insists—childishly—upon wearing. At an enormous garden party given by her grandmother for the townspeople on the eve of the day of apocalypse, Fancy asks, "'When can I have your crown?,'" to which Mrs. Halloran replies, after turning slowly to look at her, "'When I am dead'" (221, 222). They appear to understand one another perfectly: the world can have but one queen, one omnipotent ego. And it is not long after that the body of Mrs. Halloran is found by the others at the foot of the staircase, whereupon Fancy's coldly opportunistic response is to exclaim, "'My crown!'" and bolt down the stairs to claim it (238).

Fancy's climactic attempt to usurp the position of regal supremacy originally claimed by her grandmother carries to a logical end point the "miniaturist" tendency that is a dominant concern throughout the text and, as argued earlier, a recurrent force in American social history in the modern era. Beyond the small community, beyond the family, and beyond the household, and underlying the appeal of all of these as alternative social worlds, there is the most secure and self-gratifying miniature of all: the make-believe realm created by "fancy," the narcissistic childish imagination that desires no restrictions upon its playful power. In *The Sundial* the spectre of the inward-looking ego actively condensing and refashioning experience into a fantasy module that offers a controllable alternative to the larger world recurs often, and it is construed as being inherently childish. What is at stake in the struggle between Mrs. Halloran and Fancy is in this respect essentially the same as the house for which the dream siblings and the dream witch compete: pure candy, childish abandon, the pleasurable power to subsume otherness within the world of self.

And childish imperialism of this sort isn't some perverse inclination restricted to the strange individuals who have clustered together within the walls of the Halloran estate. The world beyond those walls, Gloria tells Fancy, "'isn't real,'" and her elaboration seems less the independent assessment of a bright seventeen-year old than an authorially ventriloquized commentary influenced by such contemporary social commentators as William H. Whyte and David Reisman:[12]

> "It's real inside here, *we're* real, but what is outside is like it's made of cardboard, or plastic, or something. *Nothing* out there is real. Everything is made out of something else, and everything is made to look like something else, and it all comes apart in your hands. The people aren't real, they're nothing but endless copies of each other, all looking just alike, like paper dolls, and they live in houses full of artificial things and eat imitation food."

> "My doll house," Fancy said, amused.

(185-86)

Intuitively at least, Fancy comprehends the gist here: the conformist, commercially and politically engineered postwar society is an endlessly mimetic fantasy, a vast public doll house. As such, it is to be evaded if at all possible—but in favor of what? "'I wouldn't like being a doll in a doll house,'" Gloria goes on to say, a sentiment that sums up the defensive rationale for withdrawing into one's own fantasy constructs, which are at least more personalized, and enable a degree of agency for the self. When the external social world is a substanceless sham—when "'the only real people left any more are the shadows on the television screens'" (186)—the miniature domain of the insular self, further populated (if at all) only by a severely restricted group of others, may offer some measures of autonomy, security, and, to the extent that the concept retains any credible referential significance, "reality." Such, at least, is Gloria's hope, rather forlornly expressed.

New World Miniatures

And such, in the view of the novel, is the state of the American nation at midcentury. As a narrative in which various notions of a "world" are repeatedly summoned, and in which much of the action gravitates toward the prospect of exiting from one world and beginning afresh in a new one, *The Sundial* ends teasingly, on the eve of what may or may not be the beginning of the apocalyptic transformation. Neither climactic nor resoundingly the opposite, its bleary denouement is the perfect unsatisfying termination of a text that has delighted in dangling before the reader a variety of miniature worlds in which the self may aspire to rest secure and reign supreme. As these are shown to be substanceless and more or less solipsistic, it is not surprising that the anticipated new world is progressively revealed to be only the sum of various characters' subjective projections upon the prospect of it—a sum that does not add up to a cohesive or coherent whole. For Aunt Fanny, it will be a fresh new Eden, with no moral prohibitions or inhibitions; for Mrs. Halloran it will be much the same as the present, a small social universe that she will rule autocratically and puritanically; and Gloria has several visions, all of which she conjures up while gazing absorbedly into a mirror. Ironically it is left to the one actual child in the group to call attention to the narcissism and delusiveness of the millennialist expectations of the others. Fancy, who despite her regal yearnings hasn't yet felt sufficiently disappointed by the ego abashing ways of the larger world to wish to see it obliterated, points out to Gloria that as the supposed new world will be inhabited by the same old unhappy people who have failed to appreciate the present one, an Eden that will suit all is unlikely. It will inevitably incorporate, she stresses, the very frustrations, frictions, and disappointments that inspired it: "'you all want the whole world to be changed to *you* will be different,'" she says, "'but I don't suppose people get changed any by just a new world. And anyway, that world isn't any more real than this one'" (165).

Fancy may understand her hard words in this instance to be directed at the "you all" who inhabit the Halloran estate, but the text's encouragement to the reader to understand a wider reference has been set in place by a series of earlier invocations of that key phrase, "new world." Thus construed, her criticism of her housemates becomes *The Sundial*'s address to its American reading audience, one of several indications that the millennialist expectations and miniaturist projects that entrance the characters in this narrative, and everything associated with them, are endemic to the national character. Hinted at here is the strange irony of American social history mentioned earlier: the socially sanctioned belief in the prospect of a "world" that is radically "new" has, particularly in the postindustrial era, encouraged middle class Americans to think small, and to look inward, which is also to look backward. Globally scaled futuristic visions have degenerated into mere nostalgic projections of a cosmetically improved old self.

That the nation's originating desire for a "new world" remains influential even in the 1950s is made clear by the text's construction of Mrs. Halloran as a latter day incarnation of Elizabeth I. For Elizabeth was not only the most powerful queen in the history of Britain, and thus, as suggested above, a fitting model for Mrs. Halloran's pretensions to matriarchal might; she was also the monarch who presided over England's initial entry into the Americas. This the text reminds us of in an early incident wherein Mrs. Halloran—"Orianna"—stands before the sundial in the garden and "caressingly" touches part of the inscription on it, the word "world" (46-47). The scene draws its significance from its mimicry of yet another Elizabethan referent, the late sixteenth century "Armada Portrait," in which the queen of the nation that was poised for dominance in the wake of its defeat of the Spanish fleet is depicted as fingering lightly a globe of the world placed prominently just to her right.[13] Like her namesake, Jackson's Orianna, too, wills to exert possessive sovereignty over a miniature model of a world that is to be recast, made "new," in homage to her.

But be that new world the Halloran estate, her dream house in the woods, or the future as transformed by apocalypse, residual traces of the world beyond imagining, the world of contingent actuality, will perpetually intrude, defying the efforts of even the most imperious self to exclude, replace, or colonize it. Fancy is right: there is a "this" world that will always be the measure of all fantasized new ones in that they will all, upon being tested, be reabsorbed into it. Early on in the narrative the reader's attention is directed to a quizzical inscription on the sundial, taken from Chaucer's "Knight's Tale":

Intruding purposefully upon the entire scene, an inevitable focus, was the sundial, set badly off center and reading WHAT IS THIS WORLD?

(13)

"An inevitable focus . . . set badly off center": the oxymoron subtly insinuates the futile effort of the individual subject to impose egocentricity—globally proportioned, totalizing pattern—upon actuality in all its intrusive eccentricity and asymmetry. "What is this world?" is in this sense a rhetorical question: the only possible answer, one that defeats all notions of global comprehensiveness, is "This world is what." But that non-answer itself admits of a lived response that modern society has largely lost sight of. Slightly farther along, the quotation in bold face is augmented by the lines that follow in the original Chaucer text (44):

"What is this world?" Essex said quietly, "What asketh man to have? Now with his love, now in his colde grave, Allone, with-outen any companye."

(14)

In the context of *The Sundial* the somber wisdom of these words from another cultural milieu is made to seem both anachronistic and pointed—the first, because they suggest that in Chaucer's time, but no longer in the present, it was possible to conceive of the self in "this world" as desirous beyond all else of ego-transcending social intercourse, of love and "companye"; and the second, because they foreshadow contemporary society's valorization of miniature worlds of subjectivity and link them with the chill solipsism of that single truly exclusive miniature world of selfhood, the grave. "'I dislike it,'" Mrs. Halloran says of the Chaucer passage (14), and her response is clearly not an aesthetic judgement. She has taken the point—which is also the text's point, as refracted through the Chaucerian fragment—and, with a childlike imperiousness that is as characteristic of Shirley Jackson's America as it is of her, chosen to reject it.

Notes

1. The only extended study is John G. Parks's "Waiting for the End: Shirley Jackson's *The Sundial*." More general commentaries on Jackson's work or aspects of it that devote some attention to *The Sundial* include Lenemaja Friedman, James Egan, S. T. Joshi, and Roberta Rubenstein.

2. The allusion is of course to Sacvan Bercovitch's famous phrase. Readers familiar with *The American Jeremiad* may object that *The Sundial*, in the reading presented in this study, does not conform to Bercovitch's conception of the "American Jeremiad" as a discourse that "simultaneously [laments] a declension and [celebrates] a national dream" (180); as will be seen, virtually nothing

American is celebrated in Jackson's text, though much is lamented. Nonetheless, it seems to me legitimate and useful to invoke Bercovitch's term if it is remembered that it contains within it an oppositional sub-category, that of the American "anti-jeremiad," or a discourse that involves "the denunciation of all ideals, sacred and secular, on the grounds that America is a lie" (191).

3. The text does not specify the precise year or decade when the Hallorans relocated; but the story is clearly set in the 1950s (several references to television confirm this), and as one of the Halloran siblings, Aunt Fanny, is said to be 48 years old at the start of the narrative, it is apparent that the family moved to the estate in the first or second decade of the century.

The earliest stirrings of suburbanization in the United States date back to the nineteenth century, when improved methods of public transport first created the possibility of rapid and efficient daily travel between urban centers and outlying districts. Suburban relocation was nonetheless almost exclusively a prerogative for the very well off at that time, and as Margaret Marsh has observed, the critical elements of the ideological impetus for such a move did not coalesce until late in the century, well after the actual technology facilitating it was in place. Only then, it appears, did the notion that it was in the best interests of the family to locate the home outside the city in a "country" environment become sufficiently dominant to initiate a small trend (15-16). Not until the decade following World War I did suburbanization become a "demographic process of magnitude for the first time," however (Donaldson 35); by 1930, the suburban population of American cities was 45 per cent as large as the central-city population (Palen 50). And as is well known, it was in the period after World War II that the movement, curtailed for awhile by the Depression and World War II, accelerated so enormously as, in the words of one historian, to "rip apart and remake the texture of social life in America." In the 1950s, suburbs grew six times faster than cities; and by the end of the decade, one out of four Americans lived in them (Chafe 117; Diggins 181-83).

An abbreviated summary of the suburban movement in America cannot adequately register the nuances and permutations that scholarly researchers call attention to, or gesture more than briefly towards those aspects of it that are often debated; as Donaldson points out, homogenizing generalizations tend invariably to break down under scrutiny, because there are "suburbs and suburbs" (51). For our purposes here, however, such problems of definition are tangential, for *The Sundial* is less

concerned to represent or comment upon the actual natures of various suburban social structures than to explore the mythic formulation that almost invariably shimmers within what Palen has called the "marvelous vague agreement" that the term "suburb" is self-defining: the image of a reconstituted small town as the ideal (8). Wood is one of numerous commentators to take note of the recurrence of the small town paradigm in suburban social planning and the ideology informing it. (See, for other examples, Fischer and Jackson 280-304; Rowe 120; and Baldassore, 47.)

4. Quoted in Lewis, xi. For a detailed description of *Strawberry Hill,* see Fothergill 41-42.

5. Scott Donaldson, writing in 1969, noted that "the observation about matriarchy in the suburbs has been made so often that it threatens to become axiomatic" (122). (See also Dobriner 18; Kenneth Jackson 243; and Palen 163.)

6. For the significance of "Orianna" in Elizabethan literature, see Drabble 719. *The Sundial* incorporates a number of corroborating references to Elizabethan England—Mrs. Willow's older daughter is named "Arabella," for example, and Elizabeth had a courtier named "Essex"—in order to ensure, presumably, that the allusion does not go unremarked.

7. James Egan suggests that the character represents "a monstrous parody of the nurturing mother" (20). The contention here, however, is that something more complex is insinuated: Jackson's figure both reflects and parodies the widely prevalent social nightmare of the domineering mother, which itself inadvertently parodied the era's venerated image of saintly motherhood by way of grotesque inversion. On the pervasive influence of *Modern Woman: The Lost Sex* and *A Generation of Vipers,* see Marsh 185; Palen 84; and Strickland and Ambrose 536-37.

8. It was undoubtedly a widely publicized such cult of the early '50s that gave Jackson the idea for the flying saucer "believers." See the 1956 study *When Prophecy Fails* by Festinger, et al.

9. For an excellent discussion of the patriarchal ideology informing *Father Knows Best,* and the implications of the program's enormous popularity, see Leibman, especially 87-89; 120-26. In the light of the earlier discussion of the significance of the miniaturist ideal in suburban ideology, it is useful to relay also Lynn Spigel's observation that the family home in *Father Knows Best* was represented "as if it were a public spectacle, a monument commemorating the values of the ideal American town" (131).

10. On the increased significance of the nuclear family in the post-industrial era, especially its function as an oppositional miniature society, see Davis 16 and Demos 5, 31.

11. *The Bad Seed,* which quickly metamorphosed into equally successful stage and screen versions, featured an innocent seeming eight-year-old murderess who may well have been, along with Lizzie Borden (see below), Jackson's inspiration for the character of Fancy. Its sociological significance as an indication of the postwar period's anxiety about child-rearing and juvenile delinquency, and its importance as a precedent for later and more extreme "child as monster" films, is discussed insightfully by Kathy Merlock Jackson 112-14, 137-54; and by Strickland and Ambrose 561-66.

12. Gloria's brief diatribe is still more reminiscent of John Keats's *The Crack in the Picture Window* (1956), a best-selling attack on suburban conformity. (With regard to that text, it may be of some significance that the Halloran mansion contains a picture window that shatters [112].) My reason for alluding to Riesman's *The Lonely Crowd* (1950) and Whyte's *The Organization Man* (1954) is that these are now the most well remembered social critiques of middle class life of a period in which such "state of the nation" commentaries proliferated and were popular. (Wylie's *A Generation of Vipers* also falls into this category.)

13. A reproduction of the painting can be found in Strong 43-45, or accessed at http://tudor.simplenet.com/elizabeth/armadalarge.jpg.

Works Cited

Baldassare, Mark. *Trouble in Paradise: The Suburban Transformation in America.* New York: Columbia UP, 1986.

Bercovitch, Sacvan. *The American Jeremiad.* Madison: U of Wisconsin P, 1978.

Chafe, William. *The Unfinished Journey: America since World War II.* New York: Oxford UP, 1986.

Chaucer, Geoffrey. *The Works of Geoffrey Chaucer.* Ed. F. N. Robinson. 2nd ed. Boston: Houghton, 1957.

Cott, Nancy F. *The Bonds of Womanhood: "Woman's Sphere" in New England, 1780-1835.* New Haven: Yale UP, 1977.

Davis, David Brion. "The American Family and Boundaries in Historical Perspective." *The American Family: Dying or Developing?.* Ed. David Reiss and Howard A. Hoffman. New York: Plenum Press, 1979. 13-41.

Demos, John. *Past, Present, and Personal: The Family and the Life Course in American History.* New York: Oxford UP, 1986.

Diggins, John Patrick. *The Proud Decades: America in War and Peace, 1941-1960.* New York: Norton, 1988.

Dobriner, William M. *Class in Suburbia.* New Jersey: Prentice-Hall, 1963.

Donaldson, Scott. *The Suburban Myth.* New York: Columbia UP, 1969.

Drabble, Margaret, ed. *The Oxford Companion to English Literature, Fifth Edition.* Oxford: Oxford UP, 1985.

Egan, James. "Sanctuary: Shirley Jackson's Domestic and Fantastic Parables." *Studies in Weird Fiction* 6 (Fall 1989): 15-24.

Festinger, Leon, Henry W. Riecken, and Stanley Schachter. *When Prophecy Fails.* Minneapolis: U of Minnesota P, 1956.

Fothergill, Brian. *The Strawberry Hill Set: Horace Walpole and His Circle.* London: Faber and Faber, 1983.

Friedman, Lenemaja. *Shirley Jackson.* Boston: Twayne/G. K. Hall, 1975.

Hayden, Dolores. *Redesigning the American Dream: The Future of Housing, Work, and Family Life.* New York: Norton, 1986.

Jackson, Kathy Merlock. *Images of Children in American Film: A Sociocultural Analysis.* Metuchen: Scarecrow Press, 1986.

Jackson, Kenneth T. *Crabgrass Frontier: The Suburbanization of the United States.* New York: Oxford UP, 1985.

Jackson, Shirley. *The Sundial.* New York: Farrar, Straus, and Cudahy, 1958.

Joshi, S. T. "Shirley Jackson: Domestic Horror." *Studies in Weird Fiction* 14 (1992): 9-28.

Lewis, W. S. Introduction. *The Castle of Otranto: A Gothic Story.* By Horace Walpole. London: Oxford UP, 1964.

Leibman, Nina C. *Living Room Lectures: The Fifties Family in Film and Television.* Austin: U of Texas P, 1995.

Lundberg, Ferdinand, and Marynia F. Farnham. *Modern Woman: The Lost Sex.* New York: Harper, 1947.

Marling, Karal Ann. *As Seen on TV: The Visual Culture of Everyday Life in the 1950s.* Cambridge: Harvard UP, 1994.

Marsh, Margaret. *Suburban Lives.* New Brunswick: Rutgers UP, 1990.

May, Elaine Tyler. *Homeward Bound.* New York: Basic Books, 1988.

Palen, J. John. *The Suburbs.* New York: McGraw-Hill, 1995.

Parks, John G. "Waiting for the End: Shirley Jackson's *The Sundial.*" *Critique* XIX, No. 3 (1978): 74-88.

Rowe, Peter G. *Making a Middle Landscape.* Cambridge: MIT P, 1991.

Rubenstein, Roberta. "House Mothers and Haunted Daughters: Shirley Jackson and Female Gothic." *Tulsa Studies in Women's Literature* 15.2 (Fall 1996): 309-31.

Spiering, Frank. *Lizzie.* New York: Random House, 1985.

Spigel, Lynn. *Make Room for TV: Television and the Family Ideal in Postwar America.* Chicago: U of Chicago P, 1992.

Strickland, Charles E., and Andrew M. Ambrose. "The Changing Worlds of Children, 1945-1963." *American Childhood: A Research Guide and Historical Handbook.* Ed. Joseph M. Hawes and N. Ray Hines. Westport: Greenwood Press, 1985. 533-85.

Strong, Roy. *The Cult of Elizabeth: Elizabethan Portraiture and Pageantry.* n.p. [London?]: Thames and Hudson, 1977.

Susman, Warren, and Edward Griffin. "Did Success Spoil the United States?: Dual Representations in Postwar America." *Recasting America: Culture and Politics in the Age of the Cold War.* Ed. Lary May. Chicago: U of Chicago P, 1989. 19-37.

Wood, Robert C. *Suburbia: Its People and Their Politics.* Boston: Houghton-Mifflin, 1958.

Wylie, Philip. *A Generation of Vipers.* New York: Rinehart, 1942.

Honor McKitrick Wallace (essay date spring 2003)

SOURCE: Wallace, Honor McKitrick. "'The Hero is Married and Ascends the Throne': The Economics of Narrative End in Shirley Jackson's *We Have Always Lived in the Castle.*" *Tulsa Studies in Women's Literature* 22, no. 1 (spring 2003): 173-91.

[*In the following essay, Wallace underscores Jackson's treatment of economic exchange and erotic desire in her novel* We Have Always Lived in the Castle.]

The quotation in my title, from Vladimir Propp's *Morphology of the Folktale,* is a classic ending not only of Russian folktales but also of many traditional novels: the hero gets the girl and settles down in relative material comfort, if not outright wealth.[1] For Propp, the hero's reward is "the princess and her father": as Teresa de Lauretis explains, Propp's "intimate connection be-tween the functions of the princess and her father in folk narratives derives from her historical role in dynastic succession, the transfer of power from one ruler to another."[2] The kingdom is transmitted through the body of the princess, a textbook example of traffic in women. But the conflation of the princess, her father, and his lands further implies that the erotic and the economic are conjoined and that the traditional ending Propp describes fulfills both the hero's sexual and material desires. The connection of the erotic and the economic raises the question of whether psychoanalytic theories of narrative, with their primarily erotic emphasis, can explain the role of material acquisition in narrative—a question further compounded by what this connection might mean for a specifically female protagonist. On the one hand, she might, even in her own stories, function as the erotic and (mediated) economic reward for the hero's labors; on the other, she herself might receive such rewards. In the pages that follow, I derive a theory of economic desire from psychoanalytic theories of erotic narrative desire and then explore the female protagonist's relation to economic desire, describing how such desire operates in the marriage plot. I then look at ways female protagonists claim economic desire for their own, examining Shirley Jackson's *We Have Always Lived in the Castle* and looking more briefly at other woman-authored novels. I argue that such claims profoundly rework economic and narrative paradigms in order for the female protagonist to receive a material reward—a throne, if not a princess—as the end of her narrative.

In *The Pleasures of Babel: Contemporary American Literature and Theory,* Jay Clayton points out that economic theories of narrative desire, along with other kinds of desire, play no role in much of narrative theory, which chooses to focus on erotic models informed by psychoanalysis. But while Clayton suggests that the erotic emphasis "follows its own economy of pleasure,"[3] economic desire as I develop it here receives much of its force from its connection to the psychoanalytic. By this I do not mean that material reward in narrative serves as a mere symbol of successfully negotiated psychoanalytic tensions. Rather, the economic is produced by the erotic and is bound up with it.

Judith Roof argues in *Come As You Are: Sexuality and Narrative* that narrative production shores up, and is in turn produced by, desires that can be configured both as erotic and as economic. Thus, "the connection between human heterosexual reproduction and capitalist production provides an irresistible merger of family and state, life and livelihood, heterosexual order and profit whose formative presence and naturalized reiterations govern the conceptions, forms, logic, and operation of narrative."[4] She establishes a link between the erotic (at least the heterosexual erotic) and the economic (at least the capitalist economic) as they produce and are produced by narrative. Roof's link, however, is metaphoric and operates causally only in the abstract (in that we think about family, economics, and narrative in the same ways because their ideologies support each other). Her link is limited also by its emphasis on capitalism. How, for instance, would the connections Roof mentions intersect in the precapitalist folk tales Propp describes? I argue that the connection between these two factors is manifested—and should be examined—not only formally but also materially.

If, as Peter Brooks argues in *Reading for the Plot: Design and Intention in Narrative,* narrative is motivated by the working out of death drives, material production is necessary as testament to the ego.[5] In negotiating death drives, the ego leaves a material trace behind. When confronting Sigmund Freud's explanation of death drives, Luce Irigaray suggests in *Speculum of the Other Woman* that a man "build[s] up his ego" "in order to use his life to ward off death for as long as it takes to choose a death."[6] Irigaray adds that "if this ego is to be valuable, some 'mirror' is needed to reassure it and re-insure it of its value. Woman will be the foundation of this specular duplication, giving man back 'his' image" (p. 54). In narrative terms, the need to confirm the building of one's own ego ("raising his own tomb" as Irigaray describes it, p. 54) constitutes a legacy: the working through of narrative desire that entails leaving a monument to oneself behind. As Roof's connection between sexual reproduction and economic production suggests, this legacy might take the form of offspring (or the potential for offspring) or of economic achievement. When, then, the hero "is married and ascends the throne," he prepares for (re)production—prepares to establish a testament to his ego and its narrative.

But the female protagonist relates to the notion of legacy differently from the male hero. Freud's explanation of the "work of death" in *Beyond the Pleasure Principle* and Brooks's narrative elaboration in *Reading for the Plot* are, as critics have noted, particularly masculine understandings of desire. As Irigaray asks when she confronts Freud, "is working out the death drives limited to men only?" (p. 53), or is this model of narrative closed to a woman? If she does not carry out "the work of death," what structures her narrative? The narrative paradigm that sets up the death drive and its work as a propulsion system operating according to Brooks's description cannot be accessed by women. In Irigaray's critical rereading of the Freudian paradigm, women do not experience ardent desire that is ultimately sublimated by submitting to the work of death; instead, "by suppressing her drives, by pacifying and making them passive, she will function as a pledge and reward for the 'total reduction of tension.' By the 'free flow of energy' in coitus, she will function as a promise of the libido's evanescence, just as in her role as 'wife' she will be assigned to maintain coital homeostasis,

'constancy.' To guarantee that the drives are bound in/by marriage" (p. 53). Furthermore, Irigaray argues,

> by maintaining the subject-object polarity in sexual activity, woman will provide man with an outlet for that "primary masochism" which is dangerous and even life-threatening for the "psychic" as well as the "organic" self. . . . Freud states that this "primary" or "erogenous" masochism will be reserved to the woman and that both her "constitution" and "social rules" will forbid her any sadistic way to work out these masochistic death drives. She can only "turn them around" or "turn them inward." . . . Secondary masochism added to primary masochism—this is apparently the "destiny" of the death drives in woman, and they survive only because of their unalterably sexuate nature, through the erotization of this "masochism."
>
> (p. 54)

If women characters cannot follow Freud's narrative pattern of desire, it is because they are already destined to sublimate desire through sacrifice and have, moreover, been taught to like it. Thus, a female character confirms the male legacy and testifies to his working out of death drives, rather than producing her own legacy.

The most obvious way for a woman to participate in the production of conventional narrative is through *re*production. Indeed, the heroine's role in the marriage plot of conventional narratives prefigures that "accomplishment." Rachel Brownstein argues that a heroine demonstrates her worth by choosing the right man; in other words, she participates in reproduction by determining her mate,[7] but as de Lauretis explains, even that participation is illusory. Describing the process of female maturation as a "journey" (making the female a hero in her own life), de Lauretis explains that "the end of the girl's journey, if successful, will bring her to the place where the boy will find her. . . . For the boy has been promised, by the social contract he has entered into at his Oedipal phase, that he will find woman waiting at the end of *his* journey" (p. 133). The heroine, insofar as she is involved in the marriage plot, finds that her narrative is not, finally, about her: "thus the itinerary of the female's journey, mapped from the very start on the territory of her own body . . . is guided by a compass pointing not to reproduction as the fulfillment of *her* biological destiny, but more exactly to the fulfillment of the promise made to 'the little man,' [i.e., the man as a child] of his social contract, *his* biological and affective destiny—and to the fulfillment of his desire" (p. 133). While Elizabeth's "journey" in Jane Austen's *Pride and Prejudice* certainly leads to the joys of love and character reformed, she also figures as Darcy's reward for his reform, and, as far as the material dynamics of the plot go, she is ensured continued social existence via her status as mistress of Pemberley and, presumably, mother to the Darcy heirs.

If, then, reproductive accomplishment is a testament to the hero rather than the heroine, what about productive accomplishment—what can the female protagonist achieve economically? If the social structures of the oedipal process and of marriage ensure her erotic marginalization, the economic structures of capitalism also limit her options.

Under capitalism, of course, emphasis is moved from land to capitalist exchange of commodities. Karl Marx tells us that because "the exchange of commodities breaks through all local and personal bonds inseparable from direct barter, and develops the circulation of the products of social labor; . . . it develops a whole network of social relations spontaneous in their growth and entirely beyond the control of the actors."[8] Since those social relations are at bottom economic relations, imagining an economic position outside that system is difficult. To succeed in capitalism is to succeed within a system, to enroll in production and in economic relations with other producers and the hegemony that guides them. Despite Horatio Alger stories stressing the role of individual will in achieving capitalist rewards and despite the implication of such stories that one can choose success and freely pursue it, the networked nature of capital precludes autonomy on the part of the producer. While it may be possible to imagine a precapitalist situation in which the participants of a given economic microcosm worked and lived in relative independence from prevailing economic relations, to imagine such isolation today is rather more difficult. Indeed, this imagined system may be just that—imagined: a fantasy for our times, an escapist dream allowing us to play (but only play) with the idea of "living off the land."

But even as fantasy, fictions of economic independence have their function. A fantasized precapitalist past is one of the possible articulations of "romantic anticapitalism" discussed by Robert Sayre and Michael Löwy (who also identify feminism, however, as a form of romantic anticapitalism). They argue that "the romantic vision takes a moment of the real past in which the negative traits of capitalism were lacking or were attenuated, and in which human values crushed under capitalism existed still, and *transforms it into a utopia*."[9] Just as feminist scholar Rachel Blau DuPlessis speculates that "romance as a mode may be historically activated: when middle-class women lose economic power in the transition from precapitalist economies and are dispossessed of certain functions, the romance script may be a compensatory social and narrative practice,"[10] narratives in which the female protagonist achieves economic self-sufficiency act as a fantasized compensation for the way capitalism fixes subjects, particularly female subjects, into place.

In this quest for self-sufficiency, for what might be described as a type of economic stasis, perhaps even a lyric economic mode, the female protagonist works out new relations to capital and to land. But because economic achievement involves her in modes of production and because narrative traditionally tries to achieve a state of rest that nevertheless assures production, the end of her story is fraught with ideological implications. The nature of her story's end, her status as a producer, and the question of whether she simply reiterates the patriarchal, heterosexual, and capitalist ideology of conventional narrative make determining the extent of her achievement difficult.

Certainly, one ingredient in the female protagonist's attainment of economic self-sufficiency is space, in the form of land and/or a house, that she can claim for herself. Land and houses allow characters relative independence from capitalist economic relations. They enable a fantasy of self-sufficiency, the sense that one can survive simply by cultivating one's garden. The importance of personal space may at first appear problematic, however, given the way property figures in conventional narratives. For instance, Brownstein, noting that finding a home is a goal in all of Austen's novels save *Emma,* points out that "the heroine's story is always . . . about defining and being defined by a space, about finding a space of one's own. Austen's novels are about attaining the external correlative (husband, social position, house) that makes inner potential real" (p. 95). The female hero's achievement of a space of her own, seen in this light, does not seem quite so radical. Further, de Lauretis argues, the space to which narrative directs itself is already inscribed as feminine and thus reinforces gender difference; she quotes Jurij Lotman who says that "closed space *can be interpreted* as 'a cave,' 'the grave,' 'a house,' 'woman'" (p. 118). Here the domestic space is where the male hero ends up, or it is the heroine's reward for marrying the right man.[11] In either case, attainment of land and house shores up Brownstein's "materialistic society based on the preservation of private property through monogamy" (p. 43). But this association between land/house and the end (both in the sense of a goal and of termination) of narrative hardly subverts the capitalist paradigm. Surely such subversion requires more than a change in the hero's gender or a rejection of the marriage plot. The female protagonist, then, must redefine her relationship to capital and yet attain a space of her own over the course of her narrative.

One key difference between the female hero's attainment of property and property's role in conventional narrative is the way property fits in with production. In the latter case, of course, private property is preserved through matrimony, and it also enables further production, inasmuch as it is tied to reproduction and to the economic potential of future generations. As Roof explains,

> while the "natural" events that seem to account for narrative's shape . . . appear to be natural, they are in fact

not only reproductions of the quintessentially natural-ized "biological function" of human reproduction, they are also metaphors of capitalist relations of production. The connection between reproduction and production occurs in their common appeal to a productive joinder. Where in human reproduction male and female come together to produce offspring, in capitalist production capital and labor come together to generate products.

(p. xvii)

In narratives of the traditional heroine, house and land are the sites and economic guarantors of further production. If, however, house and land do not enter into production or enter into it in a way that subverts capitalist production, the traditional narrative end may hold new possibilities, new answers for what desires motivate female characters.

Even if the ideological implications of house and land as the heroine's rewards for proper participation in a capitalist system can be subverted, there remains de Lauretis's critique of what Lotman describes as "closed space": the feminization of the notion of house as the end point of narrative. Indeed, as we shall see, female protagonists can enact a sort of revised domesticity in their relations to the property they achieve by/as the end of their stories: the spaces in which the the female protagonist's narrative terminates are often distinctly feminized, even in excess of Lotman's paradigm—not merely associated with the feminine, the spaces bear the imprint of traditionally feminine activity, such as cooking or decorating. Admittedly, the subversive potential of the female protagonist's narrative in relation to capital, joinder, and gender difference is threatened if that narrative follows and reinforces the gender mark-ings of the most traditional narratives. But the feminization of the end space may occur in such a way that economic relations and (re)production are redefined or enlisted in a cause other than that of capitalist production: in essence, so that the feminized end space takes on utopic connotations and creates systems of relations that are independent of the capitalist paradigm. Such a utopic configuration of the end space is by definition a fantasy, an imagining of new economic structures, and whether that fantasy adequately subverts the actual capitalist system in which the text itself is produced and consumed remains to be seen.

In Shirley Jackson's *We Have Always Lived in the Castle* (1962), Merricat and Constance must free themselves from the property they have inherited and from the social and economic networks that constrain and threaten them. Littered with the remnants of patriarchal wealth, the castle grounds create a persistence of the Law of the Father with all its attendant woes. The Blackwood money, the Blackwood land, and hence the Blackwood daughters are all marked by Constance and Merricat's father and his wealth. Despite the anchoring

that wealth provides (Merricat comments that "we always had a solid foundation of stable possessions"), it often seems to do more harm than good.[12] While wealth ensures the regular companionship of other well-off members of the community, it separates the girls from the largely poor village and creates hostility towards them among the villagers. Moreover, money's mere presence threatens to reinstitute the marriage plot, inso-far as Constance is sought, not merely for her beauty, but for her possessions. Such a plot resolution would reduce Constance to a mere stand-in for her dead father, recalling Propp's formulation of the princess and her father as the twinned objects of heroic quest.[13] Thus, the Blackwood fortune threatens to transform Merricat's tale, and accordingly the novel, into the adventure of Cousin Charles, who goes forth in search of Constance's hand, her father's fortune, and indeed his identity (Uncle Julian constantly confuses Charles with his dead brother John, and Charles covets and occasionally even wears John's effects). As Merricat notes, "he already had our father's bedroom, after all, and our father's watch and his gold chain and his signet ring"—in short, Charles has taken over the father's erotic space and the symbols of authority (p. 120).

But Merricat's narration undoes the fairy tale because she endeavors to demonstrate that Charles is a "ghost" (p. 88) or a "demon" (p. 120) rather than a knight in shining armor. Interestingly, Merricat's narrative also places her in the role of Propp's hero, questing after the princess Constance: "when I was small," Merricat con-fides, "I thought Constance was a fairy princess" (p. 28). The difference between Charles's forestalled heroic narrative and Merricat's is what acquisition of the princess means: whether closure is founded on a union dedi-cated to the reproduction of capital and life or whether a different set of desires is answered by the story's end.

If the Blackwood sisters and their castle are marked by their father's economic legacy, moreover, they also have access to an alternate economy, one that may inform Merricat's quest to live happily ever after with her sis-ter "on the moon" (p. 63). This "economy" returns the word to its original meaning of household management in that it is almost entirely domestic. Like any fairy-tale castle, the Blackwood manor has a treasure room, but in it, rather than gold and gems, the legacy of the "Blackwood women" waits: "there were jars of jam made by great-grandmothers, with labels in thin pale writing, almost unreadable by now, and pickles made by great aunts and vegetables put up by our grand-mother, and even our mother had left behind her six jars of apple jelly" (p. 60). Constance adds to this store: as Merricat teases her, "you bury food the way I bury treasure" (p. 61). But while Constance's rationale for preserving food follows the capitalist logic of produc-tion and consumption—"the food comes from the ground and can't stay there and rot; *some*thing has to be done with it"—the jars of food actually enter into a specifically lyric stasis, in that they "stood side by side in our cellar and would stand there forever, a poem by the Blackwood women" and, moreover, cannot be consumed (p. 61). With the exception of the most recent products, the food has turned lethal.

As Merricat reveals by comparing Constance's food preservation with her own "treasure," both sisters are engaged in an ongoing stockpiling of worthless objects. This activity implies exactly the sort of economy and domesticity that removes the objects of exchange from the market. In part, the purposelessness of the sisters' activities allows slippage of the very notion of worth. Thus, when Charles reacts with outrage to Merricat nailing the gold watch chain to a tree, Constance answers "it's not important" (p. 112). While Charles "mourn[s]" over the chain and catalogues the ways to enter such objects into economic circulation—"I could have worn it; what a hell of a way to treat a valuable thing. We could have sold it"—the sisters read the object differently. Constance sees it as a toy for "silly Merricat," while Merricat sees it as a talisman against Charles and his plans to reenlist the household in the system of production (p. 112). Likewise, Constance's putting-by of food becomes a signifier not of consumption, but rather of the "poem" the Blackwood women create, the matrilinear legacy of inedible food that anchors Constance in her sense of herself as caretaker. Both sisters develop alternative value systems to the economic standards implied by their father's fortune, with Constance establishing value in domestic terms and Merricat in magical symbolism.

If the sisters have enabled a slippage of the worth of what Charles calls "valuable thing[s]," that slippage is only partial, however, and they remain tied to conventional economic relations insofar as their accumulation of objects turns on occasion into economic exchange—clearly so in their use of money. The first episode Merricat narrates is, after all, a shopping trip during which she exchanges money, noting that "the people of the village disliked the fact that we always had plenty of money to pay for whatever we wanted; we had taken our money out of the bank, of course, and I knew they talked about the money hidden in our house" (p. 9). The Blackwood money, out of sight and no longer reproducing itself through the bank, nevertheless still circulates in the village. Moreover, Constance's domestic economy is implicated in the patriarchal Blackwood ethos; the "poem" created by generations of Blackwood women is absorbed by the patriarch's name and house: "as soon as a new Blackwood wife moved in, a place was found for her belongings, and so our house was built up with layers of Blackwood property weighting it, and keeping it steady against the world" (p. 2). Just as killing off the father did not fully abort the marriage plot, the interrogation of economic worth conducted

through Constance and Merricat's "economies" can only be partial.

Only partial, that is, until the break with the village becomes explicit. A fire redefines what the Blackwood "castle" signifies. Though the evening before, the house is a symbol of security for Merricat—"the roof pointed firmly against the sky, and the walls met one another compactly, and the windows shone darkly; it was a good house. . . . I wanted to be inside the house, with the door shut behind me" (p. 142)—after the fire, with its top gone, "the house ended above the kitchen doorway in a nightmare of black and twisted wood" (p. 167). Moreover, as Merricat notes, "it seemed that all the wealth and hidden treasure of our house had been found out and soiled" (p. 168). Significantly, this "treasure" is in the form of domestic goods associated with the Blackwood women, including "silverware that had been in the house for generations of Blackwood wives" and "tablecloths and napkins hemmed by Blackwood women" (p. 167). The house's security and contents have been violently redefined, and this thus establishes new relations to material goods.

Deprived of its masculine "roof pointed firmly against the sky," the house no longer serves as testament to Blackwood prominence or as a storage place for the lineage of goods brought to it by Blackwood women. Instead, it is restructured to fit the sisters' more modest needs. Space must be redefined, reorganized with Constance's kitchen as the center. The parts of the house that remain, yet are marked by the old order, are excluded from the sisters' new space. Thus, their mother's drawing room, once a site of social exchange and status ("our mother had always been pleased when people admired her drawing room") is shut off from view and use as the sisters "closed the . . . door behind [them] and never opened it afterwards" (p. 176). Merricat sleeps in the kitchen, and the sisters spend "a good deal of time at the front door" watching the strangers come by (p. 205). The visual dynamics of the house have also been shifted. While once the house was for looking at, an ostentatious public symbol of the Blackwood opulence, now, despite the many gawkers, the house is mysterious, hidden behind boarded-up windows and climbing vines, and the sisters are the only ones who can see it. As Merricat explains, "we had new landmarks in our house, just as we had a new pattern for our days. The crooked, broken-off fragment which was all that was left of our lovely stairway was something we passed every day and came to know as intimately as we had once known the stairs themselves. The boards across the kitchen windows were ours, and part of our house, and we loved them. We were very happy" (p. 212). If the house once served as John Blackwood's legacy, a testament to his reportedly considerable ego, it serves the sisters quite differently, as something occluded and thus testament to nothing as well as the necessary, protective space in which the sisters can meet all their desires.

Likewise, the dynamic between the sisters and the villagers and with it their economic relations have been altered. Obviously, the sisters' money no longer circulates in the village and hence disappears from the text altogether (with the exception of Charles's brief reference to it). Then, too, Merricat revises her approach to her "treasures," discovering, "I was not allowed to bury anything more" (p. 205). The sole economic relation remaining between the castle and the village follows the feudal custom of tribute rather than any logic of capitalist exchange. Though Constance describes the villagers' habit of leaving food on the doorstep as "the biggest church supper they ever had" (p. 204), she misunderstands the dynamic, which is founded not on charity but on guilt and fear. Because the villagers believe the girls have malevolent power (a power that ultimately derives from the hidden space the sisters create since the more mysterious they become, the more the villagers fear them) they offer gifts to avert misfortune and punishment. Thus paradoxically, the more thoroughly Merricat barricades the house and ensures their isolation, the more their influence reaches into the village. This relation is not one of production; the sisters' consumption of the food is tied to psychic, not economic exchange.

The sisters achieve a narrative, therefore, that allows them to escape the logic of reproduction. Constance is no longer available for the marriage plots laid by their wealthy friends or their greedy cousin, and in fact the logic of the novel's conclusion in bringing together two women who live, at least according to Merricat, happily ever after subverts and parodies the marriage plot.[14] Instead of husband and wife, marriage as the proper happy ending, we have here what Roof describes as "too many girls" (p. 80), the excess of sameness that shuts down the possibility of production. (While I do not assume that Constance and Merricat's union is a lesbian one, it clearly defies heterosexual narrative norms; the suggestion of incest further violates such norms and communicates sameness.) Thus Jackson establishes the end of linearity, of legacy, of forward progression. In short, the girls have attained a perfect lyric state untainted by the remnants of narrative, the intrusions of the outside world, or the necessity of economic exchange and production.

The economic revisions carried out in *We Have Always Lived in the Castle* are certainly not attained by most female protagonists. As I suggested earlier, too often the end of a woman's story matches her elided role in Propp's formulation: she becomes the unspoken object that the hero marries, the physical reflection of his story. Nevertheless, the emphasis I place here on the reworking of economic and narrative paradigms sheds light on a number of endings of woman-authored narratives.

Consider, for example, the conclusion of Marilynne Robinson's *Housekeeping* (1980). Under Sylvie's care, the space of the home is redefined; the parlor becomes cluttered and dirty because, as Ruth explains, "we had simply ceased to consider that room as a parlor, since . . . no one ever came to call. Who would think of dusting or sweeping the cobwebs down in a room used for the storage of cans and newspapers—things utterly without value."[15] Eventually, Sylvie and Ruth attempt to burn the house in order to defy legacy, to leave no "relics to be pawed and sorted and parceled out," and to learn a new kind of economic existence as vagabonds on the fringes of capitalism (p. 209). In Toni Morrison's *Paradise* (1997), the women of the Convent establish an economically independent community but then go even further, transcending (in one of the "two editions of the official story") materiality itself, as they "took other shapes and disappeared into thin air."[16] In each of these novels, as in *We Have Always Lived in the Castle,* female economic independence provokes violence from the community, but each novel also suggests escape from those communities. Less dramatically, but nevertheless significantly, more traditional novels such as *Jane Eyre,* with its suggestion that the wife will support the husband economically, suggest (admittedly vexed) reworkings of economic paradigms. Thinking through the economic implications of the conclusion of the female protagonist's narrative may, then, demonstrate subversion not only of reproductive narrative tropes, but also of capitalist economic structures.

But before my claims for such narratives grow too bold, we must examine the ideological function of their form as well as their content. In these and other similar narratives, traditional notions of closure are disrupted, as the logic of the marriage plot, heterosexual pairing and reproduction, capitalist success stories, and imperatives of production is interrogated. At the same time, however, one must question the success of such interrogations, the extent to which the abiding presence of closure itself reins in their subversive potential. The conclusion of the narrative of female economic independence is both unsettled and unsettling: it mirrors traditional narrative ends too closely for comfort, yet disrupts those ends even as it mimics them. In its movement towards closure, it deploys a structure of meaning and suggests some sort of final word on the subject—but establishing what that final word is proves to be an especially tricky business.

In gesturing towards home, rest, and the cessation of narrative in favor of the lyric, narratives such as Merricat's formulate what Brooks refers to as "those shaping ends that, terminating the dynamic process of reading, promise to bestow meaning and significance on the beginning and the middle" (p. 19), holding out the hope that some lesson can be learned from the quest. Yet that very gesture, by virtue of its form, is ideologically charged. Positing an end in such a traditional manner, these narratives suggest the possibility of totalization, subscribing to Brooks's gloss on Walter Benjamin that "only the end can finally determine meaning, close the sentence as a signifying totality" (p. 22). While Brooks does not fully explore the implications of this "signifying totality," others have exposed the ideological work of narrative closure. D. A. Miller, for instance, posits a "central tension in the traditional novelistic enterprise, namely, as discomfort with the processes and implications of narrative itself," suggesting that closure calls an ideological halt to the destabilizing forces of the "narratable" (a halt, as I will explain below, that can never be complete).[17] Roof is even more explicit in her analysis of the ideology of closure. "What is really at stake in the ends of narratives," she argues, is "the impossible, amplified totality of complete joinder and cessation of desire that are perpetually denied in favor of the seeds of another story" (p. 5). One's story must come to an end so that the larger, ideological story can go on: "reproduction in its promise of continuity also signals individual discontinuity or death; and the deaths of individuals enable the continuation of a group liable to excessive production" (p. 21). The pleasure of closure is thus the pleasure of renunciation of desire in the service of ideology—what Slavoj Žižek in *The Sublime Object of Ideology* refers to as "ideological renunciation," an enjoyment of form for its own sake.[18] Sensitive to how ideology and form map their pleasures onto each other (or are ultimately the same pleasure), Roof argues that "our comfort in the end is produced by a cause/effect logic where the end promises an ultimate result" (p. 7) and that "reflecting finally a belief that meaning can be had at all, the fact of an end appears to give us a sense of mastery over what we can identify as a complete unit" (p. 8). Roof shares Miller's distrust of the end but ultimately concedes its logic: "criticism relating the parts to the whole also tends to focus on the end, not as a subject of, but as a precondition to criticism, even while the parts themselves are equally important. But if an emphasis on the end is a product of the ideologies by which the story is formed in the first place, it is difficult to find meaning in the rest of the story without reference to the end" (pp. 13-14).

Clearly, to let the body of the female protagonist's narrative speak for itself against its end is insufficient; the interaction between the end and the middle, the comforting ideological gesture, and the unsettling subversive content must be carefully explored. The fact that a story restores equilibrium in the manner of traditional narrative might render it (despite whatever problematic moments may exist) traditional. Existing as they do in the half-light of tradition and subversion of that tradition, and presenting as they do vexed solutions to the problems of economic, psychoanalytic, and narrative desire, such narratives must be cautiously examined.

First, then, we must decide how happy the happy endings of these novels are. If they are success stories of sorts—successful articulations of female desire and action—the fulfillment of that desire must be evaluated. Second, assuming happiness is achieved in these conclusions, we must determine to what extent it results from collusion with traditional structures rather than escape from them. Certainly, psychoanalytic desire is conceived of as unfulfillable, insofar as that which is desired is metonymically linked in an endless chain—the object of desire is never what will actually answer the desire. When Brooks speaks of the fulfillment of narrative desire, he resorts ultimately to the death of desire, in that the desiring subject ceases to exist. But my discussion of desire has emphasized, in apparent paradox, the fulfillment of desire and the continuing existence of the desiring subject. One possible resolution to this paradox is the shift to a different kind of desire; hence I address an economic, rather than erotic, fulfillment. It might be argued that economic desire, in contrast to the desires addressed by psychoanalysis, operates differently and can be fulfilled.

Not according to Žižek, however, who links psychoanalytic and capitalist desire, implying that such a distinction is impossible since both types of desire operate according to an endlessly progressive logic. Like psychoanalytic desire, economic desire, at least within capitalism, resists fulfillment, continually moving through a metonymic chain, propelled by the excess that covers its fundamental lack. Thus, economic "pleasure," or what Žižek refers to as "surplus-enjoyment,"

> is not a surplus which simply attaches itself to some "normal," fundamental enjoyment, because *enjoyment as such emerges only in this surplus,* because it is constitutively an "excess." If we subtract the surplus we lose enjoyment itself, just as capitalism, which can survive only by incessantly revolutionizing its own material conditions, ceases to exist if it "stays the same," if it achieves internal balance.
>
> (p. 52)

Here the connection between the logic of capitalist production and heterosexual reproduction finds both confirmation and expansion; both economic and psychoanalytic desire are driven relentlessly forward by excessive production covering a lack. Hence, Žižek asks, "is not the paradoxical topology of the movement of capital, the fundamental blockage which resolves and reproduces itself through frenetic activity . . . precisely that of the Lacanian *objet petit a,* of the leftover which embodies the fundamental, constitutive lack?" (p. 53). According to this argument, economic desire within capitalism cannot be sated, and to speak of economic stability and self-sufficiency as the answer to such desire is to speak of a fantasy that contradicts desire's very structure.

But some of the novels examined above suggest the possibility of escaping the capitalist system. If Žižek's "surplus-enjoyment" is a function of capitalism, can the female protagonist evade the necessity of surplus by rejecting any role within the network of capitalist economic relations? Merricat is a good example of such escape, in that she arrives at an economic state untouched by capitalist relations. Merricat and Constance operate, as I have previously suggested, according to a feudal model, and indeed Žižek is most illuminating here due to his commentary on Marx's distinction between feudalism and capitalism. In the former, "relations between people are mystified, mediated through a web of ideological beliefs and superstitions" (p. 34), while in the latter, the relations between people are replaced by relations between objects, so that "the crucial social relations, those of production, are no longer immediately transparent in the form of the interpersonal relations of domination and servitude . . . they disguise themselves—to use Marx's accurate formula—'under the shape of social relations between things, between the products of labor'" (p. 26). Merricat's narrative reverses Marx's passage from feudalism to capitalism: while formerly the relationships between the sisters and the village have been described as relations between things (money for food as well as envy of class status and material wealth), after the fire the connection becomes, to use Žižek's phrase, "mystified," as the villagers' fear and superstition combine to create a fantasy of the sisters as witches, requiring ritualistic tribute that just happens to take material form. Here one might argue that Merricat stages a successful retreat from capitalism, that she ends in a space in which economic desire can escape the insistent forward drive of capitalist production and thus achieve equilibrium and fulfillment.

That said, the environment that permits the backwards movement to feudalism is itself already a fantasy of backwardness.[19] The castle and its surroundings are not located historically or geographically and indeed seem steeped in a vague timelessness; although Merricat notes that "all of the village was of a piece, a time, and a style" (p. 9), she never pinpoints the attributes of that style, except to comment on its "ugliness" (pp. 8-9). The villagers, in particular, seem unconnected to anything that might be identified as the networks of national, let alone global, capitalist exchange, and the very existence of their town seems to Merricat to be arbitrary, created not by economic progress but by a sort of aesthetic fantasy: "the houses and the stores seemed to have been set up in contemptuous haste to provide shelter for the drab and the unpleasant, and the Rochester house and the Blackwood house had been brought here perhaps accidentally from some far lovely country where people lived with grace. Perhaps the fine houses had been captured . . . and were held prisoner in the village" (p. 9). Thus, Merricat's regression from capitalism to feudalism is predicated upon an economic environment that already operates independently of advanced capitalism—predicated upon an isolation that allows the superstitious development of alternate economic patterns. The fantasy of feudal economic relations exists in an already fantasized space outside of the networks of capitalism.

Then too, although Merricat professes repeatedly that she is "very happy," her claim must be examined in light of the fact that she is a grossly unreliable narrator. That she evidently has a pathology that leads her to kill her family, that she is obsessed with her sister Constance, and that she believes in magic words and charms might lead the reader to doubt what she says, particularly her insistence that Constance too is "very happy." Even if we can take Merricat's word that she is happy—there is nothing in the text to suggest otherwise—we still must question the function of such happiness. Given the gap that Merricat's pathology has presumably established between her and her reader, can her narrative tell us anything other than the lengths to which an insane woman will go to satisfy her obsessions? Is the success of Merricat's narrative any different from the failure of a narrative such as Djuna Barnes's *Nightwood,* in which the protagonist's challenge to masculine structures of desire leads inevitably to madness?[20]

I argue, however, that despite the insanity in both narratives, the happiness of the endings is qualitatively different. In *Nightwood,* Robin's insanity is inarticulate, degraded, and animalistic; such insanity can only communicate the breakdown of communication itself. In contrast, Merricat's madness is oddly empowering, a warped model of what can (if perhaps not should) be achieved once one claims one's own desires and forges an identity accordingly. Although the reader may not want to emulate Merricat's quest, he or she can still see in it the successful subversion of many elements of traditional narrative and thus an alternative to conventionally happy endings.

But again, if on the level of content the troubled or imperfectly happy endings of these narratives subversively highlight the jarring intersection between female freedom and systems (such as capitalism) that restrain women, on the formal level the very notion of a happy ending may subvert the subversion. When Roof traces the structural implications of the work of writers largely considered both thematically and formally radical, such as Monique Wittig, she repeatedly finds that any potentially subversive gestures, any attempts to escape heterosexual and capitalist ideologies are ultimately subsumed by "the same old story" (p. 130) and the imposition of joinder, linearity, and closure. Narrative is a structuring device that inevitably establishes priorities, hierarchies, and thus values; as Brooks reminds us, "narrative demarcates, encloses, establishes limits, orders" (p. 4).

Accordingly, Roof demonstrates how subversive content always falls prey to ordered narrative form. For instance, she points out that coming out stories replicate the oedipal dramas of identity and the coming together of binary opposites that, respectively, create and reproduce the terms of heterosexual reproduction. If, Roof argues, "the lesbian character's visibility is the end product of a narrative struggle between inner and outer that results in knowledge about sexual truth and identity, then coming out stories embody the same reproductive narrative trajectory as dominant cultural stories" (p. 106). Even when subversive content leads to formal experimentation, like the radical disruptions of the *Bildungsroman* enacted in lesbian coming out stories, narrative structure and its imperative to organize according to heteroideological principles have their way with the story. For this reason, a text such as Wittig's *Les Guérillères,* despite the construction of a lesbian utopia and incorporation of ostensibly non-narrative elements—such as the lengthy listing of women's names—is eventually undercut by what Roof describes as Wittig's "very traditional reliance upon the originary existence of a subject outside of ideology" (p. 131). What Roof claims about the lesbian coming out story might be even more applicable to the narratives of female economic independence (the novels I mention often make no explicitly radical challenge to heterosexuality, though they can certainly be read queerly):

> Coming out stories provide a way for the female who refuses her sexual role to nonetheless function in narrative and in the world; heteronarrative's emphasis on identity exhibits and contains her desire and the very moment the lesbian's self-affirmation would presumably free her from heterosexual expectations. The coming out story is, thus, a story of sequestration, comforting and exultant on one level, but robbed of or trading away its really disturbing potential to mess up heterosexual systems.
>
> (p. 107)

Like the self-outed lesbian, the economically independent female protagonist, by following the narrative trajectory of the *Bildungsroman* and by adhering to the significance of individual identity, may limit her narrative's subversive potential.

Moreover, as Roof argues, "the similarity between the logics of narrative and Western ideologies of gender partly explains the real difficulty of establishing a female protagonist who is not somehow recuperated by the narrative; narrative logic, combined with entrenched gender ideologies, works more or less invisibly against her" (p. 63). Ultimately, the pervasive effects of these logics lead Roof to despair of ever subverting structures of capitalist production and heterosexual reproduction: "To combat heteroideology would mean thinking out-side the system altogether, changing conceptions of time, cause and effect, and knowledge. To effect such a change will take more than narrative or a consciousness thereof" (pp. 186-87). Although Roof continues to hope for the subversion of narrative patterns, she only vaguely sketches on what principles such opposition can work.

All this might tempt us to despair of ever subverting the narrative of reproduction, suggesting that any narrative with closure (and therefore, perhaps, any narrative) is simply another instance of conventional understandings of gender difference, linearity, and ideological conformity. Nonetheless, one way out of this narrative bind is to question what might be *too* much emphasis on closure. As Miller charges, "once the ending is enshrined as an all-embracing cause in which the elements of a narrative find their ultimate justification, it is difficult for analysis to assert anything short of total coherence. One is barred even from suspecting possible discontinuities between closure and the narrative moment preceding it, not to mention possible contradictions and ambiguities within closure itself" (p. xiii). In contrast to this emphasis on the ending, Miller argues "not that novels do not 'build' toward closure, but that they are never fully or finally governed by it" (p. xiv). Perhaps rather than isolating the formal movement of closure and elevating it above other movements within the text as a whole, we can focus instead on the relations between the middle (and even the beginning) and the end. This is not to imply that Roof in any way ignores how the middle of a narrative connects to its end. Her thesis in fact is that "patterns in narrative that have never counted because they did not lead to closure or production" (p. 187) are a vital part of the narrative "middle" insofar as the "metaphorically perverse" element, that which defies heterosexual logic, "both threatens to short-circuit and leads toward a satisfying, very heterosexual closure" (p. xxxiv). But if Miller's contention is valid, Roof's assertion of the primacy of closure leads her to overlook the ways in which such moments articulate a resistance (Miller refers to an "instability" and an "uneasiness," pp. x, xiv) that the ending cannot ever completely silence and cannot negate simply as a matter of textual pragmatics—the middle has existed, has been read, has articulated powerful possible alternatives to even the most orderly of narrative finales. Perhaps the subversion of the female protagonist's narrative should not be sought solely in the ending, particularly not solely in the form of the ending, but instead be looked for in the tensions generated by the middle that always—as long as we suspend closure's primacy—destabilizes the ending. The female protagonist's reward, whether erotic or economic, a princess or a throne, must be read in the context of the subversive middle actions for which she is being rewarded.

Notes

1. Vladimir Propp, *Morphology of the Folktale,* 2nd ed., trans: Laurence Scott, rev. and ed. Louis Wagner (Austin: University of Texas Press, 1968), p. 63.

2. Teresa de Lauretis, *Alice Doesn't: Feminism, Semiotics, Cinema* (Bloomington: Indiana University Press, 1984), p. 113. Subsequent references will be cited parenthetically in the text.

3. Jay Clayton, *The Pleasures of Babel: Contemporary American Literature and Theory* (New York: Oxford University Press, 1993), p. 63.

4. Judith Roof, *Come As You Are: Sexuality and Narrative* (New York: Columbia University Press, 1996), p. xvii. Subsequent references will be cited parenthetically in the text.

5. Peter Brooks, *Reading for the Plot: Design and Intention in Narrative* (New York: Alfred A. Knopf, 1984).

6. Luce Irigaray, *Speculum of the Other Woman,* trans. Gillian C. Gill. (Ithaca: Cornell University Press, 1985), p. 54. Subsequent references will be cited parenthetically in the text.

7. Rachel M. Brownstein, *Becoming a Heroine: Reading about Women in Novels* (New York: Viking Press, 1982). Subsequent references will be cited parenthetically in the text.

8. Karl Marx, *Capital: A Critique of Political Economy,* Vol. I (New York: The Modern Library, 1906), p. 126.

9. Robert Sayre and Michael Löwy, "Figures of Romantic Anticapitalism," in *Spirits of Fire: English Romantic Writers and Contemporary Historical Methods,* ed. G. A. Rosso and Daniel P. Watkins (Rutherford, New Jersey: Fairleigh Dickinson University Press; London and Toronto: Associated University Press, 1990), p. 34.

10. Rachel Blau DuPlessis, *Writing beyond the Ending: Narrative Strategies of Twentieth-Century Women Writers* (Bloomington: Indiana University Press, 1985), p. 2.

11. See too Irigaray's description of "the meaning of [man's] work[s]: the endless construction of a number of substitutes for his prenatal home" in which home, and even home building, are mapped onto the womb, in *An Ethics of Sexual Difference,* trans. Carolyn Burke and Gillian C. Gill (Ithaca: Cornell University Press, 1993, 1984), p. 11.

12. Shirley Jackson, *We Have Always Lived in the Castle* (New York: Penguin Books, 1962), p. 2. Subsequent references will be cited parenthetically in the text.

13. See also de Lauretis's gloss of this comment, quoted at the beginning of this essay.

14. Merricat's unreliability as a narrator, of course, casts doubt on whether Constance is as satisfied as she by the narration's conclusion. But the narrative (that is, the story as told rather than the "real" events upon which it is based—the *szujet* rather than the *fabula*) is simply reinforced by the identification with her own views that Merricat assumes on her sister's part. Far from the coming together of binary opposites, Merricat's narration establishes a sameness, the marriage of two perfectly identifying minds.

15. Marilynne Robinson, *Housekeeping* (New York: Noonday Press, 1980), p. 180. Subsequent references will be cited parenthetically in the text.

16. Toni Morrison, *Paradise* (New York: Alfred A. Knopf, 1997), p. 296.

17. D. A. Miller, *Narrative and Its Discontents: Problems of Closure in the Traditional Novel* (Princeton: Princeton University Press, 1981), p. x.

18. Slavoj Žižek, *The Sublime Object of Ideology* (London and New York: Verso, 1989), p. 84. Subsequent references will be cited parenthetically in the text.

19. Because Žižek also uses the word "fantasy" (p. 30), I want to distinguish my use of the term from his. Žižek suggests that the "ideological fantasy" (p. 30) is the "overlooked, unconscious illusion" (p. 33) that "structur[es] our real, effective relationship to reality" (pp. 32-33), while I am using "fantasy" in the broader sense of that which breaks with historical and/or scientific reality.

20. Djuna Barnes, *Nightwood* (New York: The Modern Library, 2000).

Darryl Hattenhauer (essay date 2003)

SOURCE: Hattenhauer, Darryl. "*The Road Through the Wall.*" In *Shirley Jackson's American Gothic,* pp. 83-97. Albany: State University of New York Press, 2003.

[*In the following essay, Hattenhauer explicates Jackson's first novel,* The Road through the Wall, *highlighting such themes as dissociation, the search for self, and ritual sacrifice in the work.*]

The Road Through the Wall, Shirley Jackson's first novel, appeared early in 1948 before the *New Yorker* published **"The Lottery"** and a year before her first anthology, *The Lottery or, The Adventures of James Har-*

ris. Of all of her novels, this one comes closest to expressing her political themes about gender, ethnicity, and class explicitly. And its form owes more to modernist realism than do her others. Its episodic plot makes it a composite novel—it reads a little like a short story cycle. This discontinuous quality arises not only from the episodic plot but also from the dizzying array of characters, none of whom is readily identifiable as the protagonist. And the matching array of family households creates a setting that frustrates spatial orientation. As such, this debut volume is solidly modernist and does not give strong hints of the complex forms to come. Nonetheless, this novel evinces concern with language in subject formation and interpellation, destabilizes narrative reliability a little, and lacks clear plot resolution.

The characters most relevant to this study are the protagonist, Harriet Merriam, and her friend Marilyn Perlman. At thirteen, Marilyn is a bookish loner. However, she does not withdraw; rather, she is shunned. She is the object of anti-Semitism. Marilyn is not just the only moral exemplar in this novel but the only moral exemplar in any of Jackson's novels. She is both forgiving and yet the only character to defend not only herself but others. When one of Marilyn's tormentors, Harriet, later befriends her because Harriet cannot get any other friends, Marilyn forgives her. But when Harriet again rejects her for being Jewish, Marilyn calls her a "big fat slob" (221). Similarly, Marilyn sticks up for Frederica when the children harass the new proletarian in the neighborhood.

As with Jackson, Harriet Merriam's quandary is her attachment to her father. Both Jackson and Harriet are traces of Cathy, but they have no Nelly to help them. James H. Kavanagh describes the Brontean situation from which Jackson and Harriet arise:

> Nelly . . . enacts a "progressive" quasi-analytic project of tearing Cathy out of the Imaginary—that is, out of an attachment to the desiring Father (itself . . . a transference of the attachment to the enveloping Mother). This incestuous obsession with the Father *is* in the realm of morbidity, closure and self-absorption/consumption, the realm of the pre-oedipal and the pre-linguistic, of the womb and the tomb.
>
> (48-49)

Similar to Cathy and Jackson, Harriet is also enveloped by her mother. When the neighborhood girls write childish love letters to the neighborhood boys, Mrs. Merriam takes it upon herself to prevent Harriet and the neighborhood girls from writing any more "filthy" letters (207). Mrs. Merriam makes Harriet destroy not only her letters but everything else she has written, not just her diaries but her notebooks: "She and her mother stood religiously by the furnace and put Harriet's diaries and letters and notebooks into the fire one by one" (42).[1]

Their sadomasochism—and their denial of it—surfaces when the mother follows this cruelty with lavish forgiveness and Harriet responds with gratitude: "Warmly Harriet smiled at her mother, and thought how pleasant it always was after these scenes . . ." (44).

Yet Mrs. Merriam (her first name is Josephine; Jackson's mother was named Geraldine, perhaps the origin of the many androgynous names that Jackson gives her many phallic women) does not want her daughter to cease writing. In fact, Mrs. Merriam requires her daughter to write for two hours every day. Mrs. Merriam just wants her to write so innocently and childishly that her daughter's only production could be a pale, sanitized parody of the most pale and sanitized genre, sentimental literature, with even the implications of romantic love expunged. And Harriet agrees to show her textual reproduction to her mother. Mrs. Merriam will also read and write with her, but in conjunction with the proper domestic activity of teaching her how to cook. Mrs. Merriam's aggressive insistence on neutered domesticity emerges in her opinion that her husband, the picture of feminization, is nonetheless not feminized enough. She accuses him of "coarseness" and tells her daughter, "Never marry a man who is *inelegant,* Harriet; I can tell you it brings nothing but sorrow" (76). Part of her sorrow is that she endorses so much of the Law that she imagines herself resisting.

Harriet is victimized not only *by* her mother but also *as* her mother; that is, she fears becoming like her. Pat Macpherson believes that matrophobia is a central issue for women of Jackson's era: "Encountering the fear of becoming one's mother is the central experience of female adolescence, in my book, and denying-while-projecting the fear and hatred of mothers the central experience of the American middle class in the 1950s" (59).[2] The difficulty for Harriet lies in object relations. As Nancy Chodorow has argued, oedipal males can separate from the mother more easily than girls can because the separation will reward the males with a substitute, another female. But for oedipal girls, the separation is more difficult because it is more threatening: they must displace the original object of their desire and replace it with a displacement of the father.[3] The response to the oedipal situation by adopting a gendered position necessarily interpolates the subject, including Harriet. The displacement of the imaginary maternal object exemplifies the Marxist dictum that ideology arises from an imaginary relation to the real conditions of existence.

Alienated by her feminized father and masculine mother, Harriet becomes somewhat dissociative. She wants to accept a Chinese man's invitation for her and her friend Virginia Donald to come to tea, but her interpellation leaves her anxious about such an encounter with the Other. Ambivalent, she and Virginia accept the invitation, but then they do not keep it. When they happen to run into him again, he invites them again, and this time they go. He is supremely polite; they are supremely condescending. When they find out that the luxurious apartment he has taken them to is not his own, that he is only a servant, they leave contemptuously. Later, Harriet keeps secret the scandalous fact that she visited a Chinese man, but tells Marilyn (an ethnic minority) that Virginia "goes around with Chinks" (137). When Harriet remembers how she had taken part with a group of girls who harassed Marilyn Perlman, she thinks not of the victim's suffering but of her own image as "dirty and fat and overbearing" (24). And when she awakes the morning after learning of three-year-old Caroline Desmond's murder, she again thinks not of the victim but of Lillian telling her that she is fat and ugly. As with some of Jackson's other victims, Harriet is not improved by her suffering. As such, she is one of the least admirable of the many antiheroes of the era—another divided subject alienated from both self and others.[4] In the end, Harriet neither marries nor moves out on her own. After her mother dies, she stays single and lives with her father. As such, she can neither conform nor individuate.

But the quest for the self misstates the matter. Although Lenemaja Friedman asserts that Jackson's characters are bent on "establishing their own identity" (158) the fact is that in Jackson's characterization, the self does not constitute the self. Rather, history does. Jackson's characters do not try to formulate a self as much as they try to cope with the self that history gives them. Her fiction represents not self-creating individuals but rather the constituting of subjects. It might even be accurate to say that in many instances, a Jackson character is not just a subject but several subjects. For example, history has made Harriet by turns a friend of Marilyn's and an anti-Semite, attached to, and alienated from, her mother, attached to, and alienated from, her father, narcissistic and alienated from herself. In other words her mind has a mind of its own—or rather several. Harriet does not make her mind up; history makes her mind up. The ability of her mind(s) to do anything is always already conditioned. Her mind is more of an effect than a cause. Her behavior is more a response than a choice. As Patricia Waugh puts it, "Our confidence that we are the source of our beliefs and values is an illusion" (55).

This dissociativeness also describes Jackson's male characters. As a more pathological adolescent than Holden Caulfield, Tod Donald is largely dissociated from simple logic and basic ethics. For example, after snooping through the Desmonds' home, he sees Marilyn Perlman in a vacant rental—all the privacy of it gone—and asks as superciliously as Mrs. Merriam,

"What are *you* doing in other people's houses?" (87). He does not choose; he just acts with little or no thinking in his stunted consciousness:

> Tod Donald rarely did anything voluntarily, or with planning, or even with intent acknowledged to himself; he found himself doing one thing, and then he found himself doing another, and that, as he saw it, was the way one lived along, never deciding, never helping. When he found himself one afternoon walking down Pepper Street nearly at the Desmond driveway, . . . it never occurred to him to slip into the Desmond yard; and once there, . . . his mind did not encompass the notion of stepping into the Desmond house, nor did it suggest to him, once in, that he had no right to be there.
>
> (89-90)[5]

In this field of changing matrices of subject positions, Jackson figures her ensemble cast as refractions of each other through doubling. Doubling appears in the arrangement of the houses. Starting at the east end of Pepper Street, doubles line up across the street from each other: the two vacant lots; the Roberts and Donald households with a boy named James in each one; the Byrnes' barely middle-class rental and the house that is perpetually changing impoverished renters, that itself will house two single mothers, each with two daughters, and that is doubled again by being next door to the Donalds' rental; the two old spinsters, Mrs. Mack and Mrs. Fielding; the two wealthiest families, the Desmonds and the Merriams, the latter of whom share a lot with the Martins; and the two houses that face Cortez Road, the Desmonds' and the Martins'.

Names are also paired. Like the two boys named James, two girls have similar names: Marilyn and Mary. Two boys have androgynous names: James Roberts is called Jamie, and Patrick Byrne is called Pat. And the Terrel girls each have an androgynous name, Frederica and Beverley.

Doubles occur in many other ways. There are two houses where poor families live, the Martins and the Williamses. Mr. Desmond and Mrs. Byrne each read a mystery story. Mrs. Roberts and Harriet Merriam are both obese. There are two old spinsters, Mrs. Fielding and Mrs. Mack. That pair is doubled by another aged female double, the two grandmothers, both of them poor, one Williams and one Martin. Lillian twice calls Mrs. Roberts "coarse" (237) and Mrs. Merriam complains of her husband's "coarseness" (76). Two boys appear older and more mature than they really are, Patrick Byrne and James Donald. Patrick Byrne and Artie Roberts agree on descriptors that classify their fathers as twins of insufferableness. These same two boys exploit Tod by feigning friendship to get him to buy them things. Two girls, Virginia Donald and Hallie Martin, do the same to Beverley. Harriet's bosom buddy is Virginia, but then they become enemies; Harriet's best friend is Marilyn, but then they too become enemies.

Scapegoating also comes in twos. The neighbors discriminate against four pairs: the two ethnic minorities, the Chinese servant and the Perlmans; the two religious minorities, the Jewish Perlmans and the Catholic Byrnes (the Chinese man's religion does not surface); the two waitresses, Mrs. Williams and Mrs. Martin; and the two teenage temptresses, Helen Williams and Hester (who of course is a double of Hester Prynne); and the two spinsters, Mrs. Fielding and Mrs. Mack. Two boys, Tod and Artie, are hated by their fathers. Two die, Tod and Caroline; he is scapegoated, and in turn does the same to her. She appears while he studies his reflection; she is his mirror opposite—a female TODdler pampered by DOTing parents.[6] The formation of these subjects through metonymic interpellation necessarily involves language. Harriet's mother tries to forestall Harriet's contact with the "filthy" Other (temptress girls like Helen and tempting boys like James Donald) by controlling her writing. But this intervention requires Harriet to dissociate herself from herself. It also requires that the mother and daughter to both deny that dissociation. Harriet not only has to burn the love letters, but also diaries and even notebooks labeled "Moods," "Poems," "Daydreams," and "Me" (18-19). The importance of writing in her identity surfaces when she tells her father, "Mostly I'm a writer" (128). Like Jackson, the most important activity to her was reading and writing alone in her room. Harriet Merriam even bears the last name of a dictionary.

Also like Jackson, Harriet's favorite reading—the narratives that inserted her into the social text, or failed to—was sentimental fiction. She says her favorite novels are Louisa May Alcott's *Little Women* and *Jo's Boys*. When the Williamses have moved out, she hopes that the new renters will be like something out of Alcott: "Perhaps one of the new girls who would live in the house—they would be like in *Little Women*, and Harriet's friend would be Jo (or just possibly Beth, and they could die together, patiently)—would love and esteem Harriet, and some day their friendship would be a literary legend . . ." (134-35). Later, when Marilyn Perlman introduces her to the notion of reincarnation, Harriet thinks she might be Jo March (152). When she and Marilyn write down what each thinks she will be when she grows up, Harriet writes that she will be a famous writer who is desired by many men but never marries. She is half right. Becoming a spinster living with her widower father, she fits the matrix of her mother's discourse control: she is gendered a feminine heterosexual but is limited in her ability to affirm that identity by virtue of being bound to her father's apron strings.

Marilyn's written vision of herself is that she will be powerful and that everyone will obey her. Oppressed in the discursive matrix of ethnic and religious discrimination, her desire is to compensate for the threat not only to her autonomy, but also, in 1936, to the threat to her survival. Marilyn likes *Vanity Fair* and *Pendennis* and says she remembers Pantaloon, Rhodomont, Scaramouche, Pierrot, and Harlequin from a previous life. Like Harriet and Jackson, then, she has been decentered from her safe reference point in the pre-industrial past.

Mr. Desmond hopes to interpellate his son through the canon. He says he wants his son to read Homer and Chaucer to him someday. Similarly, he imagines extending a discursive helping hand to the neighborhood children through sanctioned texts. He plans to enlist them in a new model army of thespians in a production of Shakespeare, preferably *Romeo and Juliet*, starring his son, of course. But the plan fizzles when Mrs. Desmond (who snubs Mrs. Perlman) says they would have to exclude Marilyn so as to avoid embarrassing her with the anti-Semitic passages. Likewise, she says they would have to exclude the proletarian Martins because Hallie is too young, and so it would be discriminatory to invite any other Martins. Moreover, they would exclude the servant, Hester, because she is not from the neighborhood. After excluding these Others, they are left with too few players, so they scrap the idea rather than sully their home and the texts. Besides, the official texts are not the real texts. While Mr. Desmond arranges his reading list of classics for his son, Mr. Desmond reads a mystery and his son reads a comic book.

Texts also interpellate other characters. When the neighborhood is looking for Tod to question him about the murder, Tod's brother James hears the sacrificial lamb and exclaims, "Christ!" (261). Tod also recalls other victims from other enabling texts. After Caroline is killed, Tod apparently falls asleep nearby with his head against the wall, recalling Bartleby's very literal subject position at the end of Herman Melville's parable of walls and Pierre's death with his head against the wall. Prior textual interpellations facilitate Tod's persecution and suicide. The police officer questioning him is intimidating because the interrogator's display of writing makes the police officer a metonymic displacement of prior threatening authority figures, not just the school superintendent (who would write down notes about Tod's mental incapacities) but other vicious officials like the dentist and doctor (who would write down notes about his physical faults). The narrator states twice that the police officer questions Tod while referring to information on a "piece of paper" (262). Even the interrogator's wielding of his pencil threatens Tod (perhaps reminding him of a medical or dental instrument): "He leaned forward and pointed his pencil toward Tod. . . ." When the inquisitor gathers all of his papers together with finality, Tod responds by regressing to prior textual anxiety: "Tod gasped; once he had been caught copying from his book in an exam." When the cop finds him hanging, he does not try to revive him; rather, he just scrutinizes him while "flipping his thumbnail across the edge of the papers he still held in his hand" (263).

Other neighbors also attempt to use text as power. When six-year-old Mildred Williams moves, nine-year-old Hallie Martin loses the only girl in the neighborhood between three and twelve. To stop time from eroding their friendship, she does what even many adults do. She tries to solve the problem by writing letters. Twice Hallie says, "Write to me" (85). Mildred's mother also desires to defeat time, in her case by losing track of it. When she moves, she leaves the calendar hanging on the wall. Tod's father also uses text to facilitate denial, but whereas Mrs. Williams's calendar is an absence of something necessary, Mr. Donald's is a presence of something unnecessary. While the neighborhood is crawling with people looking for his son to arrest him for rape and murder, Mr. Donald sits in his easy chair reading. Hester resists her marginality by inserting two others into cartoons. She names Harriet "Crazy Cat" and Artie "Popeye" (140). For the retarded Beverley, the function of text is the relief of boredom. When Frederica tells her about the murder, Beverley says twice, "Tell it again" (270). It is fitting that this textually rendered setting is Pepper Street, a name that is almost a homonym of "paper."

As the textuality is decentered, so the narrative point of view is destabilized. The third-person narrator is seemingly reliable and consistent. But three traits qualify that reliability and consistency. First, the limited omniscience necessarily qualifies the reliability. By staying outside of most characters' interiors most of the time, the narrator does not know all of the characters' thoughts and so, of course, cannot report them. Usually these absences are relatively unimportant. For example, when the narrator reports that Mrs. Fielding sold the furniture of the previous occupant of her house, the narrator does not know who that resident was: "Miss Fielding had gradually sold . . . most of the furniture she had been encumbered with at the death of whoever had preceded Miss Fielding in this quiet life . . ." (166). Similarly, the narrator does not know what thoughts Helen might have about her harassment of Marilyn and can only speculate what, if any, those thoughts might be: "Perhaps Helen Williams, if she thought of it, remembered *her*self as friendly and teasing" (24-25).

But sometimes the narrator's claim of ignorance seems feigned. For example, by implication the narrator claims not to know if anyone other than the children has ever explored the woods bordering the neighborhood: "A heavily wooded section [was] probably unexplored except by the Pepper Street children . . ." (10). Yet all of this land has necessarily been surveyed and plotted by and for property owners and public officials. Elsewhere narratorial authority is clearly ironic. For example, the narrator says that when Mrs. Desmond snubbed Mrs. Perlman on the street, she did so "almost certainly not intentionally" (24). But context clues show that Mrs. Desmond was, indeed, acting intentionally.

Sometimes the unreliable focalization works with the destabilizing of character. For example, Tod's guilt or innocence would be decidable if the narrator focalized more thoroughly on Tod's thoughts. In the limited views of his interior, no thoughts of having killed her appear, not even indirectly.

If the destabilizing narrative point of view enables the decentered characterization, then that destabilizing of the focalization's authority also serves the plot resolution's indeterminacy. By speculating unauthoritatively that after the estate was broken into parcels "perhaps small boys with stones" intruded, the narrator foreshadows Caroline's death but does not suggest its agent (185). There are many such foreshadowings that implicate Tod, but do so undecidably. First, of course, is that his name in German means "dead." Next he throws stones at a group of girls. Then at the Desmonds home, he crushes a yellow blossom. When he eavesdrops on Hester and his brother, just before she rejects Tod, he is leaning against a stone: "Tod . . . felt the cold rough stone of the porch against his shoulder" (130). Right after Caroline disappears, he anxiously tries to sell his bicycle. And when he is lurking behind the brick wall, he twice fears that a brick will fall on him. And there is the possibility he might have fallen asleep with his head against the wall. All of these foreshadowings create the expectation that the plot will continue to be unified through a decidable resolution.

But after his suicide, doubts appear. Mr. Perlman says that Tod was too small to lift the murder weapon. But when Mr. Perlman says that Tod would not have come home, Mr. Perlman applies notions about the unified subject to a fragmented one. Mr. Merriam says that Tod had no blood on his clothes. But he could have changed, and the narrator might not know that or might know and not report it. On the other hand, to say that Tod would have changed his clothes is again to expect behavior of a less destabilized subject. Pat Byrne thinks Caroline's death was accidental, that she fell and Tod panicked. Even so, the implication of sexual assault remains. Mrs. Merriam no doubt expresses the feeling of many of the characters that the absence of a confession or suicide note does not really frustrate their reader expectation. She says that his suicide is "as good as a confession" (267). Others blame outside agitators. At any rate, there is no decidable end.

Thus Jackson undermines traditional plot. She has written a detective story that exposes the detective story; she frustrates the genre that relies most on the expectation of rational explanation. And what is more proto-postmodern, there is no epiphany. This plot is not a continuous one of the successful quest into the outside world and retrieval of a boon. Rather it is a contiguous, metonymic plot of the struggle in the inner world resulting in dissolution and fragmentation. Marianne Hirsch explains, "The plot of inner development traces a discontinuous, circular path which, rather than moving forward, culminates in a return to origins, thereby distinguishing itself from the traditional plot outlines of the *Bildungsroman*" (26). Indeed, the plot makes this composite novel seem more like a short story cycle because the proliferation of characters fragments the plot, making it hard to identify the main characters. There is not one protagonist but several. Although Harriet is on stage a little more than Tod Donald and Marilyn Perlman, her struggles are no more significant than theirs (or even those of the Terrels, the Williamses, Hester, or Artie Roberts, all of whom are misfits for sometimes differing and sometimes comparable reasons). As a result, the subplots are not readily distinguishable from the main plot. Thus Jackson's ending, or the lack thereof, undermines the realist definition of plot and the realist definition of reality. As Fredric Jameson says, "our satisfaction with the completeness of plot is . . . a kind of satisfaction with society as well" (1: 9). Many reviewers objected to Jackson's use of nonrealist form to pursue social criticism. But unlike traditional Marxists of the time, who insisted on social realism, she anticipates recent Marxism because she critiques the dominant culture's social formations by departing somewhat from the dominant culture's reigning forms of representation.

Yet in Jackson's proto-postmodern representations, the phenomenal world as a profusion of confusion still points to an underlying system that is determinate. In other words, her sense is that the absurd plethora of signification nonetheless lies on a largely (though not totally) decidable foundation. Whereas some poststructuralists would later claim that there is nothing outside the text, for Jackson there is a whole lot outside the text. For Jackson, just because she is decentered does not mean the universe is. Indeed, her aporias as well as the world's reveal not just more contiguity but continuity. The destruction of the wall (which restrains the middle class from aping the aristocracy by encroaching on the estate) repeats the recurring moment in the disruptive spread of the middle class. When the narrator says "Once the wall was broken into, the fields of the estate, the sacred enclosed place which harbored the main house, the garages, the tennis courts and the terraced gardens as well as Mr. Martin's greenhouses, would be exposed to intrusions from the outside world," the "would" suggests a future predictably repeating the past (185). Similarly the narrator implies an inevitability to the decay of the neighborhood: "Eventually, of course, it was more and more degraded . . ." (181).

The determinacy surfaces more clearly: "Their lives were quietly *governed* for them by a mysterious faraway force" (italics added). The neighborhood originated in the financial power plays of that "force": "Its very paving had been laid down by men now far away,

planned by someone in an office building . . ." (178). Those decisions from the past recur in the three occurrences (in 151 words) of the root word "govern," underscoring the economic base of politics. According to Jackson, the "unseen *governors*" are "the prices in a distant town, regulated by minds and hungers in a town even farther away, all the possessions which depended on someone in another place, someone who controlled words and paper and ink, who could by the changing of a word on paper influence the very texture of the ground" (italics added 178-79). As ever in Jackson, she explicitly textualizes power.

Characteristically for Jackson's fiction, the specifics of production emerge:

> The very chair on which Mr. Desmond sat in the evenings belonged to him only on sufferance; it had belonged first to someone who made it, in turn *governed* by someone who planned it, and Mr. Desmond, although he did not know it, had chosen it because it had been presented to him as completely choosable.
>
> (italics added 179)

With illusions of individualism and self-determination, the residents of Pepper Street think they are exercising choice by registering their behavior in words: "They possessed it with statements like 'good place to live,' and 'when I decide to move.' Consequently any change on Pepper Street was beyond their control." The change that comes, the suburbanization of the estate that brings down the wall, issues from an anonymous businessperson and elderly female landowner who "from the depths of their private unowned lives, made a decision with the words and paper . . ." (180). The successful WASPs experience their predetermined status as their just reward for their own efforts, not as a result of their privileged position at the start of the game. But the ethnic minorities should not be blind to the predetermining limits on their status: the narrator says that John Desmond, Bradley Ransom-Jones, Michael Roberts, and Susannah Fielding "thought of their invulnerability as justice; Mr. Myron Perlman and possibly Mr. William Byrne . . . would have been optimistic if they thought of it as anything less than fate" (3).

Jackson deflates the either/or of cyclic versus linear history. She affirms both in a dialectical synthesis: the circular and the linear combine like the spiral that binds a notebook. The cycles are repetition of moral failure. The abstract line pointing straight as a pencil consists of those cycles. In the prison house of history, Jackson subscribes to the Gothic's historicism, in which the past interpenetrates the present. The interpenetration that keeps Tod's past in his present and that will keep Harriet's past in her present is the eternal return of the repressed that is structured metonymically. William Patrick Day is right when he says that in Gothic, "the past is the place from which all evil and corruption flows . . ." (96).

But he is not entirely right. For in the long run, the Gothic is a trace of the middle class' eventual desire to appropriate for itself what it originally abjured in the upper class: unnecessary affluence. The middle class will ultimately preserve the goal of excess in part by preserving one of the means: affirming family connections. One of Gothic's recurrent anxieties, as Chris Baldick notes, is "the decline and extinction of the old family line" (xviii).[7] Most of the families in this novel want to displace the pre-industrial estate by appropriating it (by breaking through the wall and appropriating the estate). In so doing, they affirm the values of the past. In this process of conservative revolution, the home becomes a place for revitalizing the cult of domesticity (and for Jackson, a place for exposing it). This location of women's interpellation, the sphere of domesticity, is ostensibly separate from the marketplace. Never discussing what they do for a living, the male characters maintain the opposition of domesticity and power. Even if Harriet married, exchanging one home for another and one man for another, she would still be harried. The Gothic exposes the home as a repressive location for the policing of gender roles. The separation of public and private spheres restrains women from escaping domesticity. However, this separation also mystifies the fact that to leave the home for the marketplace is not necessarily to repudiate capitalism but also to endorse it somewhat. The domestic sphere is always already interpellated into the marketplace. The victimized, the subjugated, and the feminized are not necessarily purified, are not a new saving remnant innocent of history.

The walls of the home are doubled at the end of Pepper Street by the wall that encloses the estate. When the matriarch owning the estate sells off part of it for a new housing development, the destruction of part of the wall to let Pepper Street extend farther west initiates a breakdown in the neighborhood rules. The first thing that happens after workers begin destroying the wall is that Mrs. Perlman has the temerity to undermine anti-Semitism by paying a friendly visit to Mrs. Merriam. When Mrs. Merriam learns that her daughter is friends with a Jew, she not only forbids Harriet to play with her anymore but also insists that Harriet tell Marilyn Perlman that they must end their friendship because Marilyn is a Jew. Harriet does so willingly, seeing nothing wrong in her mother's policing of the ethnicity line. Next Mr. Roberts and Mrs. Martin go through the hole in the wall apparently for a romantic encounter. Ultimately, Caroline's body is found there. This decline appears to be fated: "Once the wall was broken into, the . . . estate . . . would be exposed to intrusions from the outside world . . ." (185). The demolition of the wall signals the repressive desublimation of Eros and Thanatos. Sigmund Freud's metaphor for repression was the building of a wall. Evil breaks out of the home and out of the subject simultaneously.

In the best analysis of *The Road Through the Wall*, Joan Wylie Hall shows that this novel figures California as a lost Eden ("Fallen"). Indeed, the estate that the Pepper Streeters violate is a lost Eden. That friend of Jackson's who said that California "was her Eden," her "lost paradise," was right (Oppenheimer 18). Living in a house designed by her grandfather, Jackson grew up, like Harriet, close to a large estate appropriately named "Newcastle." For her, Samuel Richardson's texts figure the illusory innocence she lost when she moved as an adolescent to the East at the start of the Great Depression. David Daiches says that for Richardson, Eden "is no garden but an estate" (15).

Yet for the mature, fallen Jackson, the American Eden is consonant with what David W. Noble calls "the eternal Adam in the new world garden." For Jackson as for Noble, Adam is in fact forever postlapsarian and the new world garden a type of the old world garden. According to Kate Ferguson Ellis,

> The Gothic fall leaves Satan in control of a walled Eden, where he can stay as long as its walls conceal the crime that allows him to be there. The fall in the Gothic world, then, in line with the tradition of the spotless regainer of paradise set in motion by Richardson, happens to a virginal place, not to a virginal person. The Gothic landscape is in this respect very much like the world through whose manifold dangers Pamela and Evelina make their way; only a heroine who does not fall can emerge from her trial-filled journey to make herself a home. By having the villain violate the Garden rather than the heroine, we can have an "angel" for the "house" in the process of reconstitution, and at the same time provide her with some real evil over which to triumph.
>
> (44)

But for Jackson, all subjects are fallen, and evil violates not only the garden but everything in it. There is no saving remnant, and no place of grace. In fact, it is the very quest for paradise that exacerbates human depravity. What Tony Tanner says about John Hawkes is also true of Jackson: "Evil is in part summoned up by the dreams of innocence . . ." (213).

If Jackson treats America's sacred myths as, in Lauren Berlant's terms, *national fantasy,* she also treats America's rituals as witchcraft. For her close friend, Kenneth Burke, and her husband, who were both leading scholars in ritual and myth criticism, ritual gives the master narrative its structure. For Burke, the structure underlying literature derives from ritual, in this case the breaking of a hymen. The neighborhood ritualizes the breaking of the wall with a suburban version of carnival, with normally staid adults getting drunk, flirting with minors, and becoming aggressive. Michael Holquist says that for Bakhtin, "carnival, like the novel, is a *means for displaying otherness*" (89). During this repressive desublimation (such as it is) Tod Donald and Caroline Desmond disappear. As the neighbors search for them, pondering what has happened and fearing the worst, they wonder if the carnival has been comic or tragic: "Either it was a great climactic festival over nothing, . . . or else it was . . . a tragedy." These de-centered subjects, with all of their denial and projection and displacement, have arranged an ostensibly purpo-sive celebration of the wall's demolition, yet this cel-ebration might be a "festival over nothing" (253). They unconsciously intend to ritualize nothingness. For Burke (and for Jackson) this aporia between conscious intent and unconscious intent—that the mind is of two minds about everything—is normative. Burke's understanding of literature and ritual assumes that the bicameral mind is normative. For Burke (and for Jackson) ritual is comic because it totalizes (and does so through self-interest), but also tragic because it sacrifices.

One kind of sacrifice is the scapegoat. The old, the poor, the minority, and the female are classic examples of scapegoats, Others on whom the dominant culture projects its Otherness. Originally, ritualized sacrificial scapegoating ostensibly resulted in rebirth, as it ostensi-bly does in **"The Lottery."** But increasingly in proto-postmodernism, the redemptive results are at best quali-fied. Scapegoating also serves what David W. Noble calls the central myth of America as a new Eden: "time-lessness" *(Eternal)*. In such rituals as human sacrifice, time stops. A scapegoat like Tod (or whoever the killer is) can project his Otherness and scapegoat to someone else, and can do so to a love object—can combine Eros and Thanatos. Love can be perverted into ritual sacri-fice because to stop time is to preserve the love object. A recurring theme in Jackson is that scapegoating sur-faces in children almost as soon as they enter the Sym-bolic. But it seems to be innocent, even comic, because it emerges in games. For example, the children's game on Pepper Street called "tin-tin" contains an early step in scapegoating, the pleasurable play of victimization: "The first resisting victim in each game became the next 'It'" (139). And in a foreshadowing of the murder and pursuit, the children play tag and hide-and-seek ac-cording to "some ancient ritual of capture and pursuit" (38). But the rituals quickly become hollow. Like the ritual in **"The Lottery,"** some of the ritual has been lost: "The entire introductory ritual had lost its meaning and probably its accompanying dance" (138). Similarly, Marilyn and Harriet ritualize their friendship by each writing down her respective future and then hiding the paper in a pit and, finally, shaking hands over it: "'Rest here, all my hopes and dreams,' Marilyn said, and Har-riet, a little embarrassed, said, 'A curse be on whoever touches these papers'" (155). Just as the adults do not know if their carnival is comic or tragic, these girls do not know their friendship from a hole in the ground: "The hole in the ground was so special a symbol of their new and enduring friendship" (150), a friendship

that will not last the summer when Harriet conveys her anti-Semitic marching orders. A more lasting ceremony is the purification ritual that sacrifices Harriet's voice by burning her writings.

For Jackson, the dominant culture's rituals and myths were, as Richard Slotkin would later call them, "regen-eration through violence." With figurations of witch-craft, she subverts the privileging of the dominant cul-ture and collapses the opposition between its mythology and those of Others. Her brother said that for her, witch-craft was a field of study. As the logical extension of Burke and Hyman's interrogations, she studied demon-ology and represented demonizing in scapegoat rituals. But she also knew that demonizing was an increasingly Western ritual. In Greek, Hebrew, and Norse myth, de-mons could be either good or evil. As Angus Fletcher states, "Ancient myth and religion recognized many mild and beneficent daemons, the *eudaimoniai*" (39-40). She did not take demons or witchcraft literally any more than she did recent myths of a new Eden. Rather she used a broader definition of myth—included its Other—to subvert it. As Guy Davenport says, Jackson enables "motifs and fables as ancient as our civilization itself to show through" ("Dark" 4). Her poses as a witch were playful and calculating.

To defamiliarize her readers from their myths, she does what Fredric Jameson notes about one of the seminal figures in mythology; she exposes contradictions in so-cial formation: "For Levi-Strauss, myth is a narrative process whereby tribal society seeks an imaginary solu-tion, a resolution by way of figural thinking, to a real social contradiction . . ." (2:77). She thereby figures ritual myth as fantasy and witchcraft to develop what she said is her recurring theme: "an insistence on the uncontrolled, unobserved wickedness of human behav-ior" (Oppenheimer 125).

For Jackson, then, the metanarrative of the dominant culture is not the modernist metanarrative of society resting on a base of mythic veracity. In that regard, she uses Burke, Malamud, and Hyman against themselves, undermining the myth of myth by showing it as witch-craft. As such, she anticipates such postmodernists as Barth, Vonnegut, and Pynchon, who figure myth as de-lusion. For Jackson, myth is not the base; it is still on the epiphenomenal level. Moreover, myth does not en-code truth. It encodes ideology. Apologists for myth are interpellated into it. Although necessarily containing contradictions of her own, Jackson uses Gothic and witchcraft not to invent formal solutions to social con-tradictions but as subversive fictional strategies to ex-pose them. Class, the home, the subject, and the mind—all of these conflict with each other. She reinserts myths of American innocence into sentimental literature, even if she likes Richardson, because her mind has a mind of its own.

Notes

1. In "Why Can't They Tell You Why?" Purdy creates a similar scene. A mother forces her son to throw into the furnace the only pictures—the only representations of any kind—of the dead father he must somehow grow up to emulate.

2. Pat Macpherson shows that Esther Greenwood in *The Bell Jar* (Sylvia Plath wanted to be the next Shirley Jackson) was matrophobic. Whereas Greenwood hates and fears her mother for being feminized, Jackson hated and feared hers for being phallic. Strictly speaking, matrophobia is not necessarily misogynist, since it is not femaleness that is the immediate object of the hatred. On the other hand, of course, "female" as a signified can metonymically displace both "feminized" and "phallic."

3. As Claire Kahane puts it,

> "While boys can use their maleness to differentiate themselves from an engulfing maternal-female presence, girls are locked into a mother-daughter confusion of identity by virtue of their gender, encouraged in that confusion by the tendency of mothers to see daughters as duplicates of themselves and to reflect that vision
>
> ("Maternal" 243)

4. Manfred Putz describes the origin and result of this process:

> Being given over, in whatever modified form, to the world, to society, to an antagonistic "other" that demands servitude and restrains freedom, the self remains in the circumference of alienated existence. Accepting this state and agreeing to a part reconciliation with the very powers that threaten to dominate it, the self agrees to even more than the abolition of its autonomy. It makes alienation the ultimate condition of its existence.
>
> (39)

This definition of alienation by absorption into the Other is essentially Lacanian.

5. Tod's alienation, originating in pre-oedipal object relations, proceeds by means of contiguous, metonymic associations. Patricia Waugh describes this phenomenon as follows:

> "The infant becomes human through *absence* and the creation of *desire* rather than presence and the discovery of satisfaction. Desire cannot be satisfied."
>
> (55)

Compare with Putz in note 4.

6. William Patrick Day explains how the encounter with the Other desublimates the repressed, giving rise to scapegoating as a way of self-recrimination through projection:

> "The figure of the double transforms the self-Other relationship into a self-self relationship. . . . The other resolves itself into a version of the self, a fragmentation and externalization of identity that destroys the self as fully and as surely as the overt attacks of its nemesis."
>
> (20)

Jackson's characters, then, resemble Flannery O'Connor's: both authors use doubles obsessively (as will Plath in *The Bell Jar,* whose protagonist is even writing a paper on doubles).

7. A legitimate anxiety figured in this text is the fear of households limited to the nuclear family. And small ones at that: these families average fewer than two children. As such, in these confining households, although they are neither architecturally Gothic nor holding people under a descending pendulum, most of these children are confined in various ways, especially psychologically. On the other hand, Jackson in her own life exemplifies the anxiety of having one's parents too near.

Works Cited

Baldick, Chris, ed. *The Oxford Book of Gothic Tales.* New York: Oxford UP, 1992.

Berlant, Lauren. *The Anatomy of National Fantasy: Hawthorne, Utopia, and Everyday Life.* Chicago: U of Chicago P, 1991.

Chodorow Nancy. *The Reproduction of Mothering: Psychoanalysis and the Sociology of Gender.* Berkeley: U of California P, 1978.

Daiches, David. "Samuel Richardson." *Twentieth-Century Interpretations of* Pamela. Ed. Rosemary Cowler. Englewood Cliffs, NJ: Prentice, 1969. 14-25.

Davenport, Guy. "Dark Psychological Weather." Rev. of *Come Along with Me: Part of a Novel, Sixteen Stories, and Three Lectures,* by Shirley Jackson. Ed. Stanley Edgar Hyman. *New York Times Book Review* 15 Sept. 1968: 4.

Day, William Patrick. *In the Circles of Fear and Desire: A Study of Gothic Fantasy.* Chicago: U of Chicago P, 1985.

Ellis, Kate Ferguson. *The Contested Castle: Gothic Novels and the Subversion of Domestic Ideology.* Urbana: U of Illinois P, 1989.

Fletcher, Angus. *Allegory: The Theory of a Symbolic Mode.* Ithaca: Cornell UP, 1964.

Friedman, Lenemaja. *Shirley Jackson.* Boston: Twayne, 1975.

Hall, Joan Wylie. "Fallen Eden in Shirley Jackson's *The Road Through the Wall.*" *Renaissance* 46 (1994): 261-70.

Hirsch, Marianne. "Spiritual *Bildung*: The Beautiful Soul as Paradigm." *The Voyage In: Fictions of Female Development*. Ed. Elizabeth Abel, Marianne Hirsch, and Elizabeth Langland. Hanover, NH: UP of New England for Dartmouth College, 1983. 23-48.

Holquist, Michael. *Dialogism: Bakhtin and His World*. London: Routledge, 1990.

Jackson, Shirley. *The Lottery or, The Adventures of James Harris*. New York: Farrar, 1949.

———. *The Road Through the Wall*. New York: Farrar, 1948.

———. *Shirley Jackson Reads "The Lottery."* Folkways Recording #9728.

Jameson, Fredric. *The Ideologies of Theory: Essays 1971-1986*. 2 vols. Minneapolis: U of Minnesota P, 1988.

Kahane, Claire. "The Maternal Legacy: The Grotesque Tradition in Flannery O'Connor's Female Gothic." Fleenor 232-56.

Kavanagh, James H. *Emily Brontë*. London: Basil Blackwell, 1985.

Macpherson, Pat. *Reflecting on The Bell Jar*. London: Routledge, 1991.

Noble, David W. *The Eternal Adam and the New World Garden: The Central Myth in the American Novel Since 1830*. New York: Braziller, 1968.

Oppenheimer, Judy. *Private Demons: The Life of Shirley Jackson*. New York: Putnam's, 1988.

Plath, Sylvia. *The Bell Jar*. London: Faber and Faber, 1963.

Putz, Manfred. *The Story of Identity: American Fiction of the Sixties*. Munich: Wilhelm Fink Verlag, 1987.

Slotkin, Richard. *Regeneration through Violence: The Mythology of the American Frontier*. Middletown, Conn.: Wesleyan UP, 1973.

Tanner, Tony. *City of Words: American Fiction 1950-1970*. New York: Harper, 1971.

Waugh, Patricia. *Feminine Fictions: Revisiting the Post-modern*. London: Routledge, 1989.

James Egan (essay date 2005)

SOURCE: Egan, James. "Comic-Satiric-Fantastic-Gothic: Interactive Modes in Shirley Jackson's Narratives." In *Shirley Jackson: Essays on the Literary Legacy*, edited by Bernice M. Murphy, pp. 34-51. Jefferson, N.C.: McFarland & Company, 2005.

[In the following essay, Egan argues that Jackson's fiction cannot be classified by one particular literary genre but rather contains various combinations of comic, satiric, fantastic, and gothic modes.]

Critical reaction to Shirley Jackson's work has divided itself into several familiar, appropriate camps. Recently her fantastic mode has been linked with the weird tradition of H.P. Lovecraft and Ramsey Campbell, and her adaptations of "female gothic" have been contextualized more carefully than they had been earlier (Joshi 13; Rubinstein 311). Ample attention has been paid to Jackson's comedy and satire, where the range of response has been wide, with S.T. Joshi calling Jackson a "horrific satirist" and Carol Cleveland pointing to Jackson's "scathing moral analysis of American society," while Nancy Walker traces her relationship to "women's humor . . . [and its] critique of American culture" (Joshi 49; Cleveland 199; Walker 35). This analysis has been locally quite sensitive to Jackson; yet, when one assesses the scholarship as a whole, it is apparent that an unintended but definite compartmentalization of her writing has occurred. In this essay I want to move toward a renewed sense of the sophisticated totality of the Jackson canon, a body of material where the whole often exceeds the sum of its parts, by proposing that her most subtly crafted fictions draw upon interactive narrative modes. As a first step, it will be necessary to characterize the primary structures: the comic, the satiric, the fantastic, and the gothic. To examine interacting narrative structures in Jackson's work is to discover how expertly she manipulates rhetorical and genre conventions to achieve rich thematic permutations and tonal effects ranging from domestically comic scenarios like those of Jean Kerr and Erma Bombeck; to mainstream, conventional satires of manners such as Sinclair Lewis might have written; to the metaphysically fantastic idioms of Nathanael West and Franz Kafka.

I

The primary sources for the study of Jackson's comic mode are the family chronicles, **Life Among the Savages** (1953) and **Raising Demons** (1957), where comic parameters and their attendant devices are fully established. In the domestic tales, Jackson simultaneously develops and undercuts, or at least qualifies, a normative environment. Several core strategies and circumstances can be identified, one of which appears in the following passage from **Life Among the Savages**:

> Ninki's [one of the family cats] supper, a full-grown and horribly active bat, was sweeping magnificently down the length of the living room. For a minute I watched it with my mouth open and then, still yelling, buried my head under the blanket. . . .
>
> "Is it on the *blanket*?" I insisted hysterically, "On *Me*?" I do not know what the official world's record might be for getting out from under a blanket, flying across the room, opening a door and a screen door, and getting outside onto a porch with both doors closed behind you, but if it is more than about four seconds I broke it.

[406]

Frenetic physical movement, exaggerated into a type of slapstick, defines this scene. Jackson achieves comedy by playing off of rapid movement and confusion, all of which has been juxtaposed, for burlesque or lowering effect, with the bat's "sweeping magnificently down the length of the living room." In her domestic writings, farcical slapstick and nearly-falling-down movement seem omnipresent, so much so that the normative environment itself appears haphazard, topsy-turvy, on the verge of collision. The cumulative effect of repetition and magnification of such domestic detail qualifies as comic—a narrative environment has been undercut but not presented as malignant or aggressive. Because *Life Among the Savages* and *Raising Demons* have as their main characters the narrator's young and adolescent children, she need only reproduce some of the familiar activities of children to create another tonality of comedy. The "Baby-Ate-a-Spider Episode" would be a typical instance:

> Sally peered at me curiously through the bars of her crib and grinned, showing her four teeth. "What did you eat?" I demanded. "What do you have in your mouth?" Laurie shouted triumphantly. "A spider," he said. "She ate a spider." I forced the baby's mouth open; it was empty. "Did she *swallow* it?" "Why?" Jannie asked, wide-eyed. "Will it make her sick?" "*Jannie* gave it to her," Laurie said. "*Laurie* found it," Jannie said. "But she ate it herself," Laurie said hastily.

> [*LS* [*Life Among the Savages*] 436]

We notice discrepancy: an anxious mother and curious, inventive children, whose innocence melts into mischief as they quickly transfer blame to one another with a rapid succession of one-liners. The scene appears chaotic, with no two characters in complete agreement, a sort of verbal collision, yet one without apparent damage to the baby, her siblings, or the beleaguered mother. Nonsense conversations, many of them at the dinner table, are frequent in both domestic collections, and they parallel the cross-purposed dialogue of the spider tale.

Miscellaneous tactics supplement the compounded clutter, confusion, and mistaken identity that are the mainstays of Jackson's comic mode. Lists and inventories are part of the narrator's housekeeping ritual, a ritual well represented by her habit of "picking things up":

> Every time I picked up something I put it down again somewhere else where it belonged better than it did in the place I found it. Nine times out of ten I did not notice what I was picking up or where I put it until sometime later when someone in the family needed it; then, when Sally said where were her crayons I could answer at once: kitchen windowsill, left.

> [*RD* [*Raising Demons*] 726]

The order presumably involved in this process of categorizing and redistributing proves inseparable from the

disorder it intends to control, yet the process works, perhaps very well; an improbability that sets the comic tenor of the episode.

The last example brings to the foreground the most important comic tactic of Jackson's domestic works, the device that unifies and coordinates the others: the role of the narrator. Anne Lecroy has called attention to the "pervasive conversational tone" of *Life Among the Savages* and *Raising Demons* (66). Jackson achieves that conversational tone primarily through the use of the first-person narrator, who characterizes herself as fallible and ordinary, to say the least:

> I am not of a mechanical turn of mind. I am wholeheartedly afraid of fuses and motorcycles and floor plugs and lightning rods and electric drills and large animals and most particularly of furnaces. Laboriously, over the space of years of married life, my husband has taught me to use such hazardous appliances as a toaster and an electric coffee pot, but no one is ever going to get me to go down cellar and fool around with a furnace.

> [*LS* 475]

As in this passage, the narrator invariably seems self-effacing, even inept (having taken a long time to learn how to use a toaster), and prone to burlesque her own weaknesses by exaggerating them. She resolutely forgives the errors and shortcomings of her family because they are part and parcel of her own. Generally, the narrator conveys what Morton Gurewitch describes as the "comic rhythm," the affirmation of life (15). In contemporary theory, comedy involves "rebirth or transcendent reconciliation or . . . social harmony," of which Jackson's domestics provide frequent illustrations (Gurewitch 17). Consider the freshly repaired house the family will rent for several years in Vermont, after nervously moving from New York:

> [The house] had been literally scraped clean, down to the wood in the walls. Mr. Fielding had put on new wallpaper, rich with great gorgeous patterns, the windows had been washed, the pillars straightened, the broken step repaired, and a cheerful man in the kitchen was putting the last touches of glittering white paint to the new shelving.

> [*LS* 394]

The house becomes a metaphor of security, warmth, welcome and nurturing, the dominant themes of *Life Among the Savages* and *Raising Demons*. The repair presents a legitimate cause for celebration, a happy ending. In the comedies, the normative world is reassuringly predictable, the family a closed, protective circle. Fallibility in this environment has been widely distributed enough to be normalized, while clutter, confusion, mishaps of communication, or periodic bouts of discomfort are the greatest threats to family harmony.

II

Jackson's satires are very much the opposite of her domestic tales, a relentless, unnerving display of disharmony. Some of the rhetorical strategies and devices of the comic mode reappear in the satires. Like the comedies, the satires diminish the normative, yet in a profoundly harsher fashion, along different thematic lines. The definition of satire in this essay draws upon several components, both formalist and neo-formalist. The most essential quality would be the "systematic exploitation, with aggressive intent, of what are, or are made to seem, deviations within the norm within a context" (Nichols 27). The norms implicit in satiric assessment may be treated as vantage points from which to evaluate the satiric portrayal; they are derived from the "general attitudes which most readers [presumably] share" (Nichols 26). Satire, of course, can be direct or insinuated. Several reductive strategies, primarily invective, caricature, burlesque, and irony, have long been associated with the medium. Formalist criticism of the 1960s isolated the primary characteristics of satiric fictions (one of which will be discussed in some detail) "through which the satirist conveys his subject matter: the corruption of an ideal and the behavior of fools, knaves, dupes, and the like" (Paulson 9). Dustin Griffin's recent evaluation of satire as a rhetoric of "inquiry and provocation" that teases "readers with the play of 'contraries,'" rather than as a medium that presupposes "a world of clear standards and boundaries," would allow for the flexibility generally absent from formalist criteria (4, 60, 35). Jackson's satires are the epicenter of the darkest, most misogynistic themes readers have found in her canon. Surely "human cruelty and the precariousness of life" are significant satiric concerns, along with the "pointless violence and general inhumanity in [human] lives" (Sullivan 1031; Friedman 64).

Jackson's satiric temperament manifests itself early and seems especially active during the 1940s. Her centerpiece is *The Road Through the Wall* (1948), a display of the full range of rhetorical devices and fictions of diminution at Jackson's command. The novel studies the manners and mores of selected residents, young and old, of Pepper Street, a small community in Cabrillo, California, in 1936. From the outset, the reader can easily discern that the narrator aims to expose the malaise and menace that infect many of the street's inhabitants at the same time that she details their everyday routines, concentrating on a core group of families and individuals (the Donalds, the Perlmans, the Byrnes, the Merriams, Mrs. Mack, Miss Fielding, and several others) and their occasional social gatherings, the play habits of their children, their parenting styles, and their attitudes toward gender roles, social status, marriage, and jobs. *The Road Through the Wall* reads as a twentieth century *novel* of manners, wherein Jackson determines Pepper Street's identity through the sum total of its occupants' behaviors, behaviors that are moral and ethical measuring devices for their incidental successes and their far more frequent failures, which are exposed by the narrator's satiric strategies.

Many of her most effective means of diminution are rhetorical forms of denunciation, whether direct, literal attacks by the narrator or subtle combinations of omission, association, or understatement meant to expose a deficiency. Describing the Donald home, the narrator observes that it was "made of bricks put together in a square, ample enough for Mr. and Mrs. Donald and their three children, and pretentious enough for Mr. Donald's wife and daughter to feel at home" (8). Again describing Mrs. Donald, the narrator notes "her whole naïve childishness [which was] a deliberate denial of the years of experience she had had and Virginia [her daughter] was still entitled to" (142). Such characterizations as "pretentious" and "childishness" leave no doubt of the narrator's disdain for what she describes. Jackson's invective often turns on a careful arrangement of language that suggests as much as it denotes, for example, her hostile description of Mrs. Merriam: "She sat in the long light living room with the basket of sewing on the floor beside her, unaware that with her tall thin body silhouetted against the big window, and her narrow severe head bent slightly to the sewing, she looked bleak and menacing" (14). Here, terms such as "bleak and menacing," and especially the combinations of three ("tall thin body," "narrow severe head") not only diminish Mrs. Merriam literally and directly, but implicitly compare her to an unpleasantly angular bird (14). In these instances, Jackson's plain, precise style intensifies her attack, often epitomizing characters in a word or phrase, and sometimes diminishing them in several ways simultaneously. Particularly at the verbal level of satire, the third-person narrator becomes a powerful means of conveying the narrative's doubt, skepticism, or lack of sympathy for the normative world of Pepper Street. Invariably the narrator appears distant, cool, detached and censorious, emphatically distant from what she narrates, not complicit in or forgiving of the events under scrutiny.

A second level of attack, more fictively intricate than invective and overt denunciation, employs a range of devices long associated with the mode of satire. Some of these (for example, burlesque and blaming while ostensibly praising) are used in isolation, while others are extended into scenes of disclosure. *The Road Through the Wall* contains Jackson's best specimens of caricature, the satiric device of accentuating through repetition or exaggeration of a specific flaw, as in this description of Mrs. Desmond:

> She was ungenerous because her family had been poor before she married Mr. Desmond, she was unsympathetic because no one had ever required any sensitivity

of her, she was gracious because her mother before her had been gracious and because her daughter Caroline must in her turn learn to be womanly and ladylike. Mrs. Desmond was neither intelligent nor unintelligent, because thinking and all its allied attributes were completely outside her schedule for life; her values did not include mind, and nothing she intended ever required more than money.

[84]

Mrs. Desmond has been shrunken satirically into a one-dimensional, unreflective automaton, a creature of habit, without the humanizing qualities of sympathy and generosity, without the need for "mind" and the bothersome complications that thinking would involve (Test 265; Dentith 2-38). Jackson's characterization of Miss Fielding provides a fuller version of the way she sketches Mrs. Desmond. Miss Fielding, the narrator reports,

> For more years than she could remember . . . had been following herself along a well-defined path, around the circle of hours that make a day. . . . Sometimes it seemed, even, that Miss Fielding's long convalescence from birth would culminate in sufficient strength for her to die without effort. . . . [After she died], the Pepper Street house would snap back to its original purpose as a dwelling for the living.

[134-35]

Miss Fielding's hollow, comatose life is a caricature of the life of a normal, emotionally and socially interactive human being. The metaphor of convalescence implies that all of Miss Fielding's energy has been incorporated into her systematic withdrawal from life, into recovering from the illness of being born, until she has managed to exist without actually living.

Satiric irony qualifies as Jackson's sharpest weapon for laying bare the menace and malice of Pepper Street, and satiric irony in turn permeates the most effective trope in the novel, a trope described by Alvin Kernan as the "mob tendency." Examining the mob scene at the conclusion of Nathanael West's *The Day of the Locust* (1939), Kernan theorizes that mobs in satire characteristically pursue and destroy victims, often in search of "compensation" or "fun" (71-73). Kernan's definition of this pervasive satiric fiction localizes Ronald Paulson's claim that satire resonates with violence of all sorts, violence which represents an outburst of energy, the "chaos of uncontrol" (17-20). Jackson shapes her own version of this fiction into a powerful indictment of the hypocrisy, sadism, and "general inhumanity" (Friedman 64) of Pepper Street's inhabitants, young and old.

The first usage occurs early in the story, when a group of Marilyn Perlman's "friends" surrounds her:

> Helen laughed, "Maybe you have two Christmases," she said. She turned around to the other girls, to Harriet, and said, "Marilyn has *two* Christmases. One of her own and one she gets in on with us."

"I don't get it," one of the girls said, and the one edging toward the door said, "Come *on*."

"Marilyn knows what I mean," Helen said.

It was the feeling of having them all around her that bothered Marilyn . . .

[23]

Marilyn, a Jew, has been beset by a mob of "friends" intent on harassing her about the fact that Jews have a Christmas tradition separate from that of Christians. The mob does not intend physical violence, but psychological: they want to humiliate, to let Marilyn know that, as a minority, she merely "gets in on" the Christian holiday. Perhaps, in Kernan's view, this mob of girls seeks merely "fun" or "compensation," but the fact that their predatory, encircling pleasure will come at Marilyn's expense denigrates them even as they try to denigrate her. Marilyn's unfortunate partner in victimization by mobs is Tod Donald, singled out for special attention by his family at the dinner table, and by other children in the neighborhood:

> Tod was on his own front lawn. "I ate a whole mince pie once," he said, giggling. According to neighborhood ethics, there was only one person who could lead the attack on Tod on his own land. His sister turned slowly to look at him and then back to the other children. "He never does anything really," she said.
>
> "You never did it," Helen said. "Your sister says so."
>
> "I did so," Tod began weakly, but Mary Byrne said, "I don't believe you could eat even one piece of mince pie."
>
> "Even a piece as big as an ant," Hallie Martin said. Having nine-year-old Hallie join in against him was the lowest indignity.

[42-43]

Like Marilyn, Tod has been encircled, again verbally, by a mob intent on ridiculing and humiliating him, feeding off of his innocent insecurity. When these acts of childish mockery mark Tod as a victim, they simultaneously discredit his cruel tormentors. Even after he commits suicide, Tod continues to be harassed by a mob, this time metaphorically. The Pepper Street neighborhood as a whole becomes the largest group of all arrayed against him, as gossip and rumor abound, all of it assuming Tod's guilt. "[Tod] was always strange" becomes the community-mob's epitaph for him, as it slowly devours Tod's reputation.

While the narrative structures of *Life Among the Savages* and *Raising Demons* are essentially comic and those of *The Road Through the Wall* essentially satiric, Jackson achieves narrative intricacy and thematic complication by mixing these modes. In *Life Among the Savages,* the narrator's underscoring of the flaws in Mrs. Skinner, Jannie's know-it-all teacher (498-502) would qualify as satire, along with the presentation of the anti-intellectual Mrs. Ferrier in *Raising Demons* (543). In both episodes, the narrator maintains a judgmental distance between herself, her family and the outsiders, two women guilty of intellectual pretension and overreaching, flaws which the narrator does not participate in or condone. *The Road Through the Wall*, moreover, contains several comic characters and events, especially those involving the elderly Mrs. Mack and her discussions with her dog (98-101) and the eccentric friendship of Miss Fielding and Mr. Donald, whose "conversations" are revealed as the antidialogues of two individuals "given to talking to themselves" (165). Neither Mrs. Mack and her dog nor Miss Fielding and Mr. Donald appear to have any topics in common, and Miss Fielding and Mr. Donald are both immune to the oversights and indifference of each other, so that their attempted interaction registers as foolish and ultimately harmless when measured against the prejudicial, predatory interactions that are the norm in *The Road Through the Wall*. By mixing comedy and satire, Jackson achieves a more nuanced story line, which allows for fine distinctions between comic and satiric behavior. The typically subtle movement of the narrative from comedy to satire and back again often occurs, as S.T. Joshi has claimed, with a minimum of verbal alteration (20), thereby demonstrating Jackson's mastery of narrative craft, her precise control of character, action, setting, and descriptive detail.

III

An equally significant narrative interaction, quite apart from these satiric-comic overlaps, occurs when Jackson links the satiric mode we have just considered to the fantastic mode in several of its manifestations. Though fantasy has been subject to many codifications over the past quarter-century, the major definitions currently in play all involve what Kathryn Hume and Eric Rabkin have called a departure from the conventional, "armchair world" of the "normative" (Hume 8-25; Rabkin 13, 16), whether that departure involves a violation of the "reader's conceptions of natural laws" (Heller 43) or a "direct reversal of ground rules" (Rabkin 14). Virtually all postmodern criticism of fantasy incorporates Tzvetan Todorov's notion of the fantastic as "that hesitation experienced by a person who knows only the laws of nature, confronting an apparently supernatural event" (25), as well as his classification of fantastic themes: "a special causality, pan-determinism; multiplication of the personality; collapse of the limit between subject and object; and lastly, the transformation of time and space" (120). The narrative bridging of the satiric and the fantastic that will form the basis of the following discussion of Jackson's fiction has been made very generally in contemporary scholarship, and more

specifically by Eric Rabkin, who proposes that satire is "inherently fantastic," locating several points of intersection between the two modes (18-22).

In **"The Renegade"** (1948) the fantastic serves as a device for clarifying and gradually intensifying the satiric subtext. The narrative predicament of **"The Renegade"** is that Mrs. Walpole's presumably gentle dog, Lady, has been accused of killing the neighbors' chickens. That the narrator wishes to challenge the values of the normative can be inferred from the first report Mrs. Walpole gets of Lady's alleged crimes, an "early morning call":

> "Do you have a dog? Brown-and-black hound?"
>
> . . . "Yes. . . ." Mrs. Walpole said shortly, "I own a dog. Why?"
>
> "He's been killing my chickens." The voice sounded satisfied now; Mrs. Walpole had been cornered.
>
> [71]

The ambivalence embedded in this question, of whether Mrs. Walpole qualifies as "irritable" and "short," perhaps unduly defensive (she answers the phone "forbiddingly"), or whether the neighbor qualifies as cruelly "satisfied," appears to be resolved by the story's fantastic complications. As soon as the warning about a chicken-killing dog on the loose has been sounded, the rural community considers Lady the culprit, not allowing for the possibility of mistaken identity. Fantastic elaborations occur when the narrator recounts the growing enthusiasm for punishing the offender and the sadistic ingenuity beneath that enthusiasm. At first, simple, fathomable remedies are proposed, such as tying Lady with a "good stout chain," but more exotic suggestions soon prevail, displacing the realistic with the incredible. Mr. White's remedy constitutes an example:

> "You get a dead chicken and tie it around the dog's neck, so he can't shake it loose, see?"
>
> . . . "See, when he can't shake it loose at first he tries to play with it and then it starts to bother him, see, and then he tries to roll it off and it won't come and then he tries to bite it off and it won't come and then when he sees it won't come he thinks he's never gonna get rid of it, see, and then he gets scared. . . ."
>
> "But the dog," Mrs. Walpole said . . . "How long do we have to leave it around her neck?"
>
> "Well," Mr. White said with enthusiasm, "I guess you leave it on until it gets ripe enough to fall off by itself. See, the head . . ."
>
> [77]

Mr. Shepherd, finally, advises that thick nails be pounded into Lady's collar and that she be turned loose "where there are chickens" (83). Then, when Lady has been made to chase the chickens, the owner pulls on the rope, and "The spikes cut her head off" (83). That this suggestion has been relayed from Mr. Shepherd to Mrs. Walpole by her own children magnifies its macabre effects. One could object that each of these homespun solutions might be possible and would not, therefore, be fantastic according to Todorov's definition, yet their crescendo arrangement from practical and mundane to bizarre and lethal suggests that Jackson deliberately transgresses the plausible and the mimetic in order to intensify the satiric effort of **"The Renegade,"** to disclose the perverse, blighted imaginations of Mrs. Walpole's neighbors. The gruesome torments seem to delight those who propose them, as though punishing the chicken-killing suspect were a means to another, darker, end.

"Pillar of Salt" (1948) incorporates the fantastic in a manner more compatible with postmodern understanding of the concept yet for narrative purposes similar to those of **"The Renegade."** New York City, the vacation environment of Brad and Margaret, a New Hampshire couple, is aggressively undercut, satirized in several ways, by descriptive details, images, and events. As she shops, Margaret begins to "picture" New Yorkers:

> She had a picture of small children in the city dressed like their parents, following along with a miniature mechanical civilization, toy cash registers in larger and larger sizes that eased them into the real thing, millions of clattering jerking small imitations that prepared them nicely for taking over the large useless toys their parents lived by.
>
> [242]

The images of children and their noisy toys, a deployment of the widespread satiric trope of the robotic, conflate the mechanical and the spiritual, in the process reducing parents to bad imitations of their children, but without the excuse of childhood to justify their "useless toys." If the exterior of the city is unlovely, the attitudes of its inhabitants are coarse and insensitive, as Margaret discovers when mentioning to one of her hosts that a leg had washed up on the beach near the host's home:

> [Margaret and Brad] went back to their host and hostess, talking about the leg, and their host apologized, as though he had been guilty of a breach of taste in allowing his guests to come [upon] a human leg; their hostess said with interest, "There was an arm washed up in Bensonhurst . . ."
>
> [247]

Sympathy for the owners of the arm and leg seems absent from the reaction of the host and hostess, but the hostess does manage to develop "interest" in the "arm [that] washed up in Bensonhurst."

The fantastic enters **"Pillar of Salt"** in a series of impressions that internalize for Margaret the decay of New York, and allow her to apprehend the city psycho-

logically. She reaches beyond space and time to "feel" the entropic dissolution of New York, noticing some unusual developments: "She stopped suddenly when it seemed to her that the windowsill she had just passed had soundlessly crumbled and fallen into fine sand" (249). Another unnerving experience becomes the counterpoint to Margaret's perceptions of quiet, material decay:

> A crowd of people formed around her suddenly; they had come off a bus and were crossing here, and she had a sudden feeling of being jammed in the center and forced out into the street when all of them moved as one with the light changing, and she elbowed her way desperately out of the crowd and went off to lean against a building and wait.
>
> [251]

This image of the feverish, chaotic energy of the crowd recalls the satiric trope of the mob, which seems to encircle and crush its victims. Margaret imagines that she has been "jammed . . . and forced" by design, captured and hurried off against her will by something as conspicuous and animated as the forces of entropy she had perceived in the crumbling sandstone were inconspicuous and inanimate. **"Pillar of Salt"** enacts very effectively the moment of hesitation Todorov equates with the fantastic. On the one hand, Margaret senses that time and motion have become frenzied. "It went too fast," she says of an elevator (250), and "they all go by too fast," of a crowd (251). On the other, she witnesses evidence of the entropic dissolution of everyday objects, evidence normally very slow to unfold. All of the above might be explained as panic attacks, threatening but psychologically plausible, culminating in the paranoia of the story's final paragraph. But another possibility remains; that Margaret has been able to internalize and apprehend emotionally the deterioration, plasticity, and callousness that constitute the mimetic exterior of New York, described satirically by the narrator. Her fantastic perception metamorphoses the aggressive crowds of New York into the satiric trope of the chaotic, engulfing, predatory mob. In effect, the fantastic elements of **"Pillar of Salt"** reinforce the satiric-mimetic elements, intensifying and personalizing the entropic meltdown of the city.

One of Jackson's most concise, adept narrative mixtures of the satiric and the fantastic, **"The Witch"** (1949), again uses this mixture to undercut the normative, but in a more subtle, understated fashion than **"Pillar of Salt"** did. While a mother and her young son journey on a train, the evidently bored child searches for entertainment even as his mother placates and pacifies him. When the boy complains, "How far do we have to go?" his mother answers with a familiar parental refrain, "Not much longer now" (63). When the boy exclaims that he has seen "a big old ugly old bad old witch outside," his mother answers dismissively, "Fine" (64). As the conversation between the child and the man who enters the compartment shifts to the murder and dismemberment of the man's sister, the mother intervenes, demanding that the stranger leave. After the man exits, she tries to assert the normative: "He was just teasing," the mother said, "Just *teasing*" (67). The narrative implies, however, that a darkly fantastic rendering of these events is available, a hint reinforced by the ending: "Prob'ly he was a witch," recalls the boy. As a possible record of a fantastic intervention, **"The Witch"** contains several chilling alternatives: that the stranger's account of the murder and dismemberment of his sister was not an *ad absurdum* exercise in teasing a child and mocking his imaginative excesses, but a literal event; that the laughter the stranger shares with the child has one connotation for the boy and a far more ominous one for him. The normative point of view, represented by the mother, cannot allow for the option of the horrific, the terrifyingly fantastic invading the everyday world, an option that her placating rhetoric quickly dismisses. The story's implication that the boy's version of what happened (the stranger really was a witch) might have validity undercuts the narrow, conventional, normative sort of adult thinking that disallows the possibility of witches. The fantastic reading of the story's actions reinforces the child's version of them. Rather than merging to reinforce a perspective as they do in **"Pillar of Salt,"** fantastic and mimetic narratives in **"The Witch"** remain disjunctive, yet with the same overall effect of satiric disclosure.

IV

The final illustrations of interactive narrative structures to be considered are taken from the portion of Jackson's fiction most commonly characterized as gothic, **"The Bus"** (1965) and *The Haunting of Hill House* (1959). Each develops unique narrative variations resulting from fundamental revisions in the normative world. Because **"The Bus"** and *Hill House* are set in gothic environments, the works contain qualities best described as parodic, both metaphysically and narratively. William Day has shown that "Gothic fantasy is . . . an anticonventional vision of reality . . . a parody of other narratives and conceptions of the world" (4). In brief, the gothic world may be interpreted as a naturally monstrous universe, one that subverts the "cosmological visions" lying behind both romance and realism (Day 8). Since Jackson's deployment of these conventions in **"The Bus"** and *Hill House* and her articulation of an intricately parodic normative environment build on metamorphosis and regression, the comic and satiric narrative patterns we have been examining undergo substantial modifications, into extraordinary combinations. In particular, the gothic normative sharpens Jackson's irony and intensifies her vision of a flattened, empty world.

She develops **"The Bus"** around the gothic trope of a circular voyage, a journey with no ending and no exit, which maroons characters "in an eternal present, without connections in any direction in time or space" (Heller 169; Malin 126; Botting 14). As the story opens, the elderly Miss Harper returns home on a bus from an unspecified location on a dark, drenching night. Given the range of gothic features apparent throughout the tale, darkness here has a quality both literal and metaphorical. What the narrator presents as the normative setting in **"The Bus"** seems diminished in several ways, by strategies recalling those Jackson used to describe the blighted urban settings in **"Pillar of Salt."** When Miss Harper buys her ticket, "the old man at the other end of the counter [puts] down his paper and [gives] her a look of hatred" (180). Nor does she fare especially well on the bus itself:

> "Look lady," [the bus driver] was saying, "I'm not an alarm clock." "Wake up and get off the bus."
>
> . . . "This is as far as you go. You got a ticket to here. You've arrived."
>
> [182]

After Miss Harper exits into a thunderstorm at Ricket's Landing, she begs a ride with two young, unsympathetic men annoyed by her dishevelled condition: "Get in," the young man says, and, "My God, you're wet" (184). Not only are her escorts vaguely threatening, which she learns when she threatens to report the bus driver for letting her off at the wrong stop, they are also dull:

> "I've never heard of Ricket's Landing," Miss Harper said. "I can't imagine how he came to put me off there."
>
> "Maybe someone else was supposed to get off there and he thought it was you by mistake." This deduction seemed to tax the young man's mind to the utmost, because he said, "See, someone else might of been supposed to get off instead of you."
>
> [185]

She eventually arrives at an old house that has been converted into a bar and grill, populated by "perhaps a dozen young people, resembling the two who had brought Miss Harper here, all looking oddly alike" (187).

Though the looming menace of Miss Harper's plight cannot be overlooked, her own flaws do not escape the narrator's eye either. When Miss Harper orders her bus ticket, she does so "sharply" (180), and nothing she does early on dispels the initial impression of her as peevish, complaining, a fault-finder very easily agitated. No matter her temperament, Miss Harper soon discovers that she has entered the dark world of the fantastic, a discovery that coincides with her growing belief that the ramshackle bar and grill is actually her childhood home, now badly deteriorated, a home complete with a closet full of her old toys:

> The inside of the closet was all alive; a small doll ran madly from side to side, the animals paraded solemnly down the gangplank of Noah's ark. . . . The noise was louder and louder, and then Miss Harper realized that they were all looking at her hatefully and moving toward her.

[191]

When the sentient toys move closer, Miss Harper screams, then suddenly wakes. She has apparently fallen asleep on the bus and has had a nightmare. After she wakes, she is dropped off at an ominously familiar location: "Ricket's Landing" (192).

The dark allegory embedded in the ostensibly real events of **"The Bus"** contains an explanation of the satiric diminishment of all the main characters, an explanation substantially different from the patterns of reduction at work in Jackson's non-gothic tales. As Joan Wylie Hall has noticed, the bus driver recalls the ferryman to the underworld in classical mythology (67). Following Hall's cue, one might easily conclude that the two men in the truck assume the role of Miss Harper's courtiers/guards, who take her to her destination/prison, a gothic building/nightmare world. The catch-phrase greeting of the "hostess"/warden Belle now assumes telling connotations: "'Hell, you say,' the woman said at last. Her voice was surprisingly soft. 'Hell you say'" (187). Assuming that Jackson expected to describe Miss Harper's journey in **"The Bus"** as a descent into the nether world with its personalized horrors and circular wanderings, a world whose inhabitants are themselves darkened, the satiric diminution noted earlier takes on a narrative appropriateness, and the fantastic scenarios of the story an ironic function: to clarify rather than to obscure the setting. In the netherworld, these bizarre events might seem realistic and normative indeed. The metaphysical terror of **"The Bus"** lingers no matter how the reader construes Miss Harper's weaknesses. If she is judged worthy of her destination, then she has denied her past crimes and hidden them from her immediate perception; but she will meet these crimes again in hell, as the scene with the advancing, vigilante-like toys suggests. If, alternatively, we consider her not to be truly damnable, a Kafka-like predicament, an unknowable disconnection between crime and punishment, confronts us.

Comic and satiric narrative strands also occur in Jackson's gothic masterpiece, *The Haunting of Hill House,* with their specific connotations again charged by the novel's parodic normative setting. The opening paragraph clarifies the environment within which the various functions of satire and comedy must be evaluated:

"Hill House, not sane, stood by itself against its hills, holding darkness within. . . . Silence lay steadily against the wood and stone of Hill House, and whatever walked there, walked alone" (3). Within this metaphysically distorted place, two major species of comic and satiric expression can be located, the first of which is caricature, familiar from its appearance in **Road Through the Wall** in Jackson's treatments of Mrs. Desmond and Miss Fielding. Caricature appears in two complementary forms, first the obsessive Mrs. Dudley, whose robotic, mechanical repetitiveness sounds like a dull refrain throughout the novel, in such ritualistic forms as "In the night. . . . In the dark" (45), or "I set dinner on the sideboard at six o'clock" (48). If Mrs. Dudley is laconic, her opposite number, Mrs. Montague, plays the compulsive babbler, rude, intrusive, intent on dominating any conversation she enters. Jackson carefully sets Mrs. Montague's boasts that she can freely access the spirit world against her obliviousness of the aggressive supernatural phenomena that terrify the other guests. Clearly, folly, pretentiousness, and other defects are disclosed in the behavior of these two characters, defects which could be, arguably, either satiric or comic. I would argue that the caricatures are comic when measured against the ominous, mocking universe of Hill House, whose darkness turns ridiculous actions that might seem satiric in a realistic, nongothic setting into comic, silly, relief-giving distractions from the overbearing intensity of the menace about to engulf Eleanor. Such caricatures should be read as farce, a movement away from menace and toward harmless folly.

Another species of undercutting in Hill House, different in technique and intention, likewise attempts to confront the darkness by speaking a parodic version of its own language (Test 121-25; Nichols 53). This dialogue with Hill House itself can be attributed primarily to Theodora, with occasional choric accomplishment from Luke. Theodora replies to Eleanor's fear that "[Mrs. Dudley] probably watches every move we make, anyway; it's probably part of what she agreed to" (48) with an impertinent question:

> "Agreed to with whom, I wonder? Count Dracula."
>
> . . . "I think he spends all his week ends here; I swear I saw bats in the woodwork downstairs."

[48]

After one of the manifestations of preternatural cold in the house, Eleanor jokes that she had considered writing to her sister to explain what a "perfectly *splendid*" time she was having. Theodora proposes some amendments: "You really must plan to bring the whole family next summer. . . ." "We sleep under blankets every night. . . ." "The air is so bracing, particularly in the upstairs hall . . ." (152). What Theodora does in these passages and frequently throughout *Hill House* functions as a strategy of satiric attack, replete with such conventional mechanisms as irony, burlesque, and sarcasm. Yet it is a strategy apart from what Jackson typically employs, and adapted to the gothic normative space. Theodora attempts to fend off Hill House somewhat paradoxically, by seeming to accept its operating premises (those of the gothic universe, themselves reversed), and then reversing them, diminishing Hill House's own nature and identity by *ad absurdum* over-application and misapplication. She does so in an attempt to achieve distance and control in what amount to systematic gestures of contempt and defiance, "teasing" the house with its own devices by speaking its "language." However, when she echoes the gothic language of Hill House in a parodic, deflating way, Theodora achieves another satiric effect, that of a curse, a form of invective associated with satire's possible origins as a component of primitive tribal ritual (Elliott 286-92). On one level, then, her attack burlesques and exaggerates gothic storytelling conventions and ground rules, and on another, she denounces and aims invective at Hill House, cursing it in an idiom the house will surely recognize.

V

As we have seen, the predominant narrative structures in Shirley Jackson's work are the comic, satiric, fantastic, and gothic, while her most intricate stories typically derive from combinations of these modes. S.T. Joshi has argued for the unity of the Jackson canon, a unity so well orchestrated that "distinctions about genre and classification become arbitrary and meaningless" (13). In contrast, this essay argues that a modal analysis allows for, at the least, a more detailed awareness of her narrative tendencies and habits and the variations she plays upon recurring structures, as well as a specific familiarity with her craft and control as a maker of fiction. It seems apparent that Jackson's four favored narrative patterns draw upon distinct yet overlapping rhetorical devices and tactics. *Life Among the Savages* and *Raising Demons* have been identified as the most fully developed comic statements, with several distinguishing features: a flawed but redemptive normative setting consisting of the magnification of the daily activities of family life; the snowballing effect of minor problems; frantic, slapstick physical movement, often resulting in collisions, literal and figurative; identity-confusions, jumbled language, and miscellaneous mix-ups; a first-person narrator eager to confess and exemplify her own fallibility. If *Life Among the Savages* and *Raising Demons* amount to domestic comedies of manners for Shirley Jackson, *The Road Through the Wall* reads as a satire of manners. Like her comedies, Jackson's social satire presupposes a flawed setting, but her satiric tactics (principally invective, irony, caricature, and the fiction of the mob) expose an environment

blighted by selfishness, hypocrisy, aggressive viciousness, and insidious betrayal. A distant third-person narrator reveals these defects both directly and by insinuation, making no apologies for the failures uncovered, and in fact portraying them as menacing, ugly, and corrosive. While the mood and tenor of Jackson's comedies connote reconciliation, closure, and bonding, the mood and tenor of her satires connote agony, alienation, and anti-closure.

For the most part, her fantastic tales may be explained by the criteria of Todorov and other postmodern theorists: conditions of hesitation between natural and supernatural causality, reversals of ground rules, transformations of time and space. Jackson's gothic narratives represent the extension of these same axioms and procedures into a setting where darkness is normative. Her comic, satiric, fantastic, and gothic structures are sufficiently distinct to qualify as separate and independent. However, this essay has proposed that if critical assessment were to rest simply at the point of definition, Joshi's objections to "arbitrary and meaningless" placement into categories might be valid: the nomenclature could become self-absorbed and limiting. Narrative categorization should, instead, serve as a precondition for appreciating some of Shirley Jackson's most sophisticated, subtly crafted fictions, those in which comic, satiric, fantastic and gothic elements are made to interact, to define, qualify, complicate, intensify, and resolve one another; to engineer reversals and double-reversals and posit complex ironies; and ultimately to shape a unique, authentic signature.

Works Cited

Botting, Fred. *Gothic*. London and New York: Routledge, 1996.

Cleveland, Carol. "Shirley Jackson." In *And Then There Were Nine . . . More Women of Mystery*. Ed. Jane S. Bakerman. Bowling Green, Ohio: Popular Press, 1985, 199-219.

Day, William Patrick. *In the Circles of Fear and Desire: A Study of Gothic Fantasy*. Chicago and London: University of Chicago Press, 1985.

Dentith, Simon. *Parody*. London and New York: Routledge, 2000.

Elliott, Robert C. *The Power of Satire: Magic, Ritual, Art*. Princeton: Princeton University Press, 1960.

Friedman, Lenemaja. *Shirley Jackson*. Boston: Twayne, 1975.

Griffin, Dustin. *Satire: A Critical Reintroduction*. Lexington: University Press of Kentucky, 1994.

Gurewitch, Morton. *Comedy: The Irrational Vision*. Ithaca and London: Cornell University Press, 1975.

Hall, Joan Wylie. *Shirley Jackson: A Study of the Short Fiction.* New York: Twayne, 1993.

Heller, Terry. *The Delights of Terror: An Aesthetics of the Tale of Terror.* Urbana and Chicago: University of Illinois Press, 1987.

Hume, Kathyrn. *Fantasy and Mimesis.* New York and London: Methuen, 1984.

Jackson, Shirley. "The Bus." In *Come Along With Me.* Ed. Stanley Edgar Hyman. New York: The Viking Press, 1968, 180-92.

————. *The Haunting of Hill House.* 1959. New York: Penguin, 1984.

————. *Life Among the Savages.* 1953. In *The Magic of Shirley Jackson.* Ed. Stanley Edgar Hyman. New York: Farrar, Straus, and Giroux, 1966, 383-530.

————. "Pillar of Salt." *The Lottery, or The Adventures of James Harris.* New York: Farrar, Straus, and Company, 1949, 235-53.

————. *Raising Demons.* 1957. In *The Magic of Shirley Jackson,* 533-753.

————. "The Renegade." In *The Lottery,* 69-83.

————. *The Road Through the Wall.* 1948. New York: Popular Library, 1976.

————. "The Witch." In *The Lottery,* 63-67.

Joshi, S.T. *The Modern Weird Tale.* Jefferson, N.C.: McFarland, 2001.

Kernan, Alvin B. *The Plot of Satire.* New Haven and London: Yale University Press, 1965.

Lecroy, Anne. "The Different Humor of Shirley Jackson." *Studies in American Humor* 4.1-2 (1985): 62-73.

Malin, Irving. *New American Gothic.* Carbondale: Southern Illinois University Press, 1962.

Nichols, James W. *Insinuation: The Tactics of English Satire.* The Hague and Paris: Mouton, 1971.

Paulson, Ronald. *The Fictions of Satire.* Baltimore: The Johns Hopkins University Press, 1967.

Rabkin, Eric S. *The Fantastic in Literature.* Princeton: Princeton University Press, 1976.

Rubinstein, Roberta. "House Mothers and Haunted Daughters: Shirley Jackson and Female Gothic." *Tulsa Studies in Women's Literature* 15.2 (1996): 309-31.

Sullivan, Jack. "Shirley Jackson." In *Supernatural Fiction Writers: Fantasy and Horror.* New York: Scribner's, 1985, 1031-36.

Todorov, Tzvetan. *The Fantastic: A Structural Approach to a Literary Genre.* Trans. Richard Howard. Cleveland: Case Western Reserve University Press, 1973.

Test, George A. *Satire: Spirit and Art.* Tampa: University of South Florida Press, 1991.

Walker, Nancy A. *A Very Serious Thing: Women's Humor and American Culture.* Minneapolis: University of Minnesota Press, 1988.

FURTHER READING

Bibliographies

Herrick, Casey. "Shirley Jackson's 'The Lottery'." *Bulletin of Bibliography* 46, no. 2 (June 1989): 120-21.

A bibliography of criticism of Jackson's "The Lottery," which Herrick offers as a supplement to Robert S. Phillips's 1966 publication of "Shirley Jackson: A Chronology and a Supplementary Checklist."

Phillips, Robert S. "Shirley Jackson: A Chronology and a Supplementary Checklist." *The Papers of the Bibliographical Society of America* 60 (1966): 203-13.

A comprehensive bibliography of Jackson's works, which includes a list of biographies and critical reviews as well as a chronology of her life.

Biography

Oppenheimer, Judy. *Private Demons: The Life of Shirley Jackson,* New York: G. P. Putnam's Sons, 1988, 304 p.

Highly regarded biography of Jackson that provides a detailed account of her life as a writer, wife, and mother.

Criticism

Crowley, John W. "Ernest Hemingway by Shirley Jackson. Introduction: Shirley Jackson on Ernest Hemingway: A Recovered Term Paper." *Syracuse University Library Associates Courier* 31 (1996): 33-50.

A critical introduction plus the reprint of the full text of Jackson's 1940 college term paper on Ernest Hemingway.

Hall, Joan Wylie. *Shirley Jackson: A Study of the Short Fiction,* New York: Twayne Publishers, 1993, 204 p.

Includes a critical survey of Jackson's short fiction.

————. "Fallen Eden in Shirley Jackson's *The Road Through the Wall.*" *Renascence* 46, no. 4 (summer 1994): 261-70.

Posits that the theme of a lost or fallen Eden is central to Jackson's novel *The Road through the Wall,* as well her short story "Dorothy and My Grandmother and the Sailors."

Lootens, Tricia. "'Whose Hand Was I Holding?': Familial and Sexual Politics in Shirley Jackson's *The Haunting of Hill House*." In *Haunting the House of Fiction: Feminist Perspectives on Ghost Stories by American Women,* edited by Lynette Carpenter and Wendy K. Kolmar, pp. 166-92. Knoxville: The University of Tennessee Press, 1991.

> Maintains that "one of the most terrifying aspects" of *The Haunting of Hill House* is the story's intimacy, as Jackson devises a book of haunting based on the characters' familial and erotic illusions and their struggles with their own "most intimate fears."

McGrath, Patrick. Introduction to *The Lottery and Other Stories,* by Shirley Jackson, pp. xi-xvi. New York: The Modern Library, 2000.

> Identifies displacement as a central theme in Jackson's stories, including "Like Mother Used to Make," "Pillar of Salt," "The Renegade," "Flower Garden," and "The Lottery."

Parks, John G. "Waiting for the End: Shirley Jackson's *The Sundial*." *Critique* 19, no. 3 (1978): 74-88.

> Classifies Jackson's *The Sundial* as a work of new American gothic and explores the way in which the novel "parodies the apocalyptic imagination while portraying it."

Williams, Richard H. "A Critique of the Sampling Plan Used in Shirley Jackson's 'The Lottery'." *Journal of Modern Literature* 7, no. 3 (September 1979): 543-44.

> Details the problems with Jackson's two-stage "sampling plan" in her short story "The Lottery."

Additional coverage of Jackson's life and career is contained in the following sources published by Thomson Gale: *American Writers Supplement,* Vol. 9; *Authors and Artists for Young Adults,* Vol. 9; *Beacham's Encyclopedia of Popular Fiction: Biography & Resources,* Vol. 2; *Concise Dictionary of American Literary Biography: 1941-1968; Contemporary Authors,* Vols. 1-4R, 25-28R; *Contemporary Authors New Revision Series,* Vols. 4, 52; *Contemporary Literary Criticism,* Vols. 11, 60, 87; *Dictionary of Literary Biography,* Vols. 6, 234; *DISCovering Authors; DISCovering Authors: Canadian Edition; DISCovering Authors Modules: Most-studied Authors; DISCovering Authors 3.0; Exploring Short Stories; Literature and Its Times,* Vol. 4; *Literature Resource Center; Major 20th-Century Writers,* Ed. 2; *Major 21st-Century Writers; Modern American Literature,* Ed. 5; *Reference Guide to American Literature,* Ed. 4; *Reference Guide to Short Fiction,* Ed. 2; *St. James Guide to Horror, Ghost & Gothic Writers; Science Fiction, Fantasy, and Horror Writers; Short Stories for Students,* Vol. 1; *Short Story Criticism,* Vols. 9, 39; *Something About the Author,* Vol. 2; *Supernatural Fiction Writers,* Eds. 1, 2; and *World Literature Criticism,* Vol. 3.

How to Use This Index

The main references

> **Calvino, Italo**
> 1923-1985 .... CLC **5, 8, 11, 22, 33, 39,**
> **73;** SSC **3, 48**

list all author entries in the following Thomson Gale Literary Criticism series:

AAL = *Asian American Literature*
BG = *The Beat Generation: A Gale Critical Companion*
BLC = *Black Literature Criticism*
BLCS = *Black Literature Criticism Supplement*
CLC = *Contemporary Literary Criticism*
CLR = *Children's Literature Review*
CMLC = *Classical and Medieval Literature Criticism*
DC = *Drama Criticism*
FL – *Feminism in Literature: A Gale Critical Companion*
GL = *Gothic Literature: A Gale Critical Companion*
HLC = *Hispanic Literature Criticism*
HLCS = *Hispanic Literature Criticism Supplement*
HR = *Harlem Renaissance: A Gale Critical Companion*
LC = *Literature Criticism from 1400 to 1800*
NCLC = *Nineteenth-Century Literature Criticism*
NNAL = *Native North American Literature*
PC = *Poetry Criticism*
SSC = *Short Story Criticism*
TCLC = *Twentieth-Century Literary Criticism*
WLC = *World Literature Criticism, 1500 to the Present*
WLCS = *World Literature Criticism Supplement*

The cross-references

> See also CA 85-88, 116; CANR 23, 61;
> DAM NOV; DLB 196; EW 13; MTCW 1, 2;
> RGSF 2; RGWL 2; SFW 4; SSFS 12

list all author entries in the following Thomson Gale biographical and literary sources:

AAYA = *Authors & Artists for Young Adults*
AFAW = *African American Writers*
AFW = *African Writers*
AITN = *Authors in the News*
AMW = *American Writers*
AMWR = *American Writers Retrospective Supplement*
AMWS = *American Writers Supplement*
ANW = *American Nature Writers*
AW = *Ancient Writers*
BEST = *Bestsellers*
BPFB = *Beacham's Encyclopedia of Popular Fiction: Biography and Resources*
BRW = *British Writers*
BRWS = *British Writers Supplement*
BW = *Black Writers*
BYA = *Beacham's Guide to Literature for Young Adults*
CA = *Contemporary Authors*
CAAS = *Contemporary Authors Autobiography Series*
CABS = *Contemporary Authors Bibliographical Series*
CAD = *Contemporary American Dramatists*
CANR = *Contemporary Authors New Revision Series*
CAP = *Contemporary Authors Permanent Series*
CBD = *Contemporary British Dramatists*
CCA = *Contemporary Canadian Authors*
CD = *Contemporary Dramatists*
CDALB = *Concise Dictionary of American Literary Biography*

CDALBS = *Concise Dictionary of American Literary Biography Supplement*
CDBLB = *Concise Dictionary of British Literary Biography*
CMW = *St. James Guide to Crime & Mystery Writers*
CN = *Contemporary Novelists*
CP = *Contemporary Poets*
CPW = *Contemporary Popular Writers*
CSW = *Contemporary Southern Writers*
CWD = *Contemporary Women Dramatists*
CWP = *Contemporary Women Poets*
CWRI = *St. James Guide to Children's Writers*
CWW = *Contemporary World Writers*
DA = *DISCovering Authors*
DA3 = *DISCovering Authors 3.0*
DAB = *DISCovering Authors: British Edition*
DAC = *DISCovering Authors: Canadian Edition*
DAM = *DISCovering Authors: Modules*
   DRAM: *Dramatists Module;* ***MST:*** *Most-studied Authors Module;*
   MULT: *Multicultural Authors Module;* ***NOV:*** *Novelists Module;*
   POET: *Poets Module;* ***POP:*** *Popular Fiction and Genre Authors Module*
DFS = *Drama for Students*
DLB = *Dictionary of Literary Biography*
DLBD = *Dictionary of Literary Biography Documentary Series*
DLBY = *Dictionary of Literary Biography Yearbook*
DNFS = *Literature of Developing Nations for Students*
EFS = *Epics for Students*
EXPN = *Exploring Novels*
EXPP = *Exploring Poetry*
EXPS = *Exploring Short Stories*
EW = *European Writers*
FANT = *St. James Guide to Fantasy Writers*
FW = *Feminist Writers*
GFL = *Guide to French Literature,* Beginnings to 1789, 1798 to the Present
GLL = *Gay and Lesbian Literature*
HGG = *St. James Guide to Horror, Ghost & Gothic Writers*
HW = *Hispanic Writers*
IDFW = *International Dictionary of Films and Filmmakers: Writers and Production Artists*
IDTP = *International Dictionary of Theatre: Playwrights*
LAIT = *Literature and Its Times*
LAW = *Latin American Writers*
JRDA = *Junior DISCovering Authors*
MAICYA = *Major Authors and Illustrators for Children and Young Adults*
MAICYAS = *Major Authors and Illustrators for Children and Young Adults Supplement*
MAWW = *Modern American Women Writers*
MJW = *Modern Japanese Writers*
MTCW = *Major 20th-Century Writers*
NCFS = *Nonfiction Classics for Students*
NFS = *Novels for Students*
PAB = *Poets: American and British*
PFS = *Poetry for Students*
RGAL = *Reference Guide to American Literature*
RGEL = *Reference Guide to English Literature*
RGSF = *Reference Guide to Short Fiction*
RGWL = *Reference Guide to World Literature*
RHW = *Twentieth-Century Romance and Historical Writers*
SAAS = *Something about the Author Autobiography Series*
SATA = *Something about the Author*
SFW = *St. James Guide to Science Fiction Writers*
SSFS = *Short Stories for Students*
TCWW = *Twentieth-Century Western Writers*
WLIT = *World Literature and Its Times*
WP = *World Poets*
YABC = *Yesterday's Authors of Books for Children*
YAW = *St. James Guide to Young Adult Writers*

Literary Criticism Series
Cumulative Author Index

Bakhtin, M. M.
    See Bakhtin, Mikhail Mikhailovich
Bakhtin, Mikhail
    See Bakhtin, Mikhail Mikhailovich
Bakhtin, Mikhail Mikhailovich
    1895-1975 .... **CLC 83; TCLC 160**
    See also CA 128; 113; DLB 242; EWL 3
Bakshi, Ralph 1938(?)- .... **CLC 26**
    See also CA 112; 138; IDFW 3
Bakunin, Mikhail (Alexandrovich)
    1814-1876 .... **NCLC 25, 58**
    See also DLB 277
Baldwin, James 1924-1987 ... **BLC 1; CLC 1,**
    2, 3, 4, 5, 8, 13, 15, 17, 42, 50, 67, 90,
    127; DC 1; SSC 10, 33; WLC 1
    See also AAYA 4, 34; AFAW 1, 2; AMWR
    2; AMWS 1; BPFB 1; BW 1; CA 1-4R;
    124; CABS 1; CAD; CANR 3, 24;
    CDALB 1941-1968; CN 1, 2, 3, 4; CPW;
    DA; DA3; DAB; DAC; DAM MST,
    MULT, NOV, POP; DFS 11, 15; DLB 2,
    7, 33, 249, 278; DLBY 1987; EWL 3;
    EXPS; LAIT 5; MAL 5; MTCW 1, 2;
    MTFW 2005; NCFS 4; NFS 4; RGAL 4;
    RGSF 2; SATA 9; SATA-Obit 54; SSFS
    2, 18; TUS
Baldwin, William c. 1515-1563 .... **LC 113**
    See also DLB 132
Bale, John 1495-1563 .... **LC 62**
    See also DLB 132; RGEL 2; TEA
Ball, Hugo 1886-1927 .... **TCLC 104**
Ballard, J.G. 1930- .... **CLC 3, 6, 14, 36, 137;**
    SSC 1, 53
    See also AAYA 3, 52; BRWS 5; CA 5 8R;
    CANR 15, 39, 65, 107, 133; CN 1, 2, 3,
    4, 5, 6, 7; DA3; DAM NOV, POP; DLB
    14, 207, 261, 319; EWL 3; HGG; MTCW
    1, 2; MTFW 2005; NFS 8; RGEL 2;
    RGSF 2; SATA 93; SCFW 1, 2; SFW 4
Balmont, Konstantin (Dmitriyevich)
    1867-1943 .... **TCLC 11**
    See also CA 109; 155; DLB 295; EWL 3
Baltausis, Vincas 1847-1910
    See Mikszath, Kalman
Balzac, Honore de 1799-1850 ... **NCLC 5, 35,**
    53, 153; SSC 5, 59; WLC 1
    See also DA; DA3; DAB; DAC; DAM
    MST, NOV; DLB 119; EW 5; GFL 1789
    to the Present; LMFS 1; RGSF 2; RGWL
    2, 3; SSFS 10; SUFW; TWA
Bambara, Toni Cade 1939-1995 .... **BLC 1;**
    CLC 19, 88; SSC 35; TCLC 116;
    WLCS
    See also AAYA 5, 49; AFAW 2; AMWS 11;
    BW 2, 3; BYA 12, 14; CA 29-32R; 150;
    CANR 24, 49, 81; CDALBS; DA; DA3;
    DAC; DAM MST, MULT; DLB 38, 218;
    EXPS; MAL 5; MTCW 1, 2; MTFW
    2005; RGAL 4; RGSF 2; SATA 112; SSFS
    4, 7, 12, 21
Bamdad, A.
    See Shamlu, Ahmad
Bamdad, Alef
    See Shamlu, Ahmad
Banat, D. R.
    See Bradbury, Ray
Bancroft, Laura
    See Baum, L(yman) Frank
Banim, John 1798-1842 .... **NCLC 13**
    See also DLB 116, 158, 159; RGEL 2
Banim, Michael 1796-1874 .... **NCLC 13**
    See also DLB 158, 159
Banjo, The
    See Paterson, A(ndrew) B(arton)
Banks, Iain
    See Banks, Iain M.
    See also BRWS 11

Banks, Iain M. 1954- .... **CLC 34**
    See Banks, Iain
    See also CA 123; 128; CANR 61, 106; DLB
    194, 261; EWL 3; HGG; INT CA-128;
    MTFW 2005; SFW 4
Banks, Lynne Reid .... **CLC 23**
    See Reid Banks, Lynne
    See also AAYA 6; BYA 7; CLR 86; CN 4,
    5, 6
Banks, Russell 1940- . **CLC 37, 72, 187; SSC**
    42
    See also AAYA 45; AMWS 5; CA 65-68;
    CAAS 15; CANR 19, 52, 73, 118; CN 4,
    5, 6, 7; DLB 130, 278; EWL 3; MAL 5;
    MTCW 2; MTFW 2005; NFS 13
Banville, John 1945- .... **CLC 46, 118, 224**
    See also CA 117; 128; CANR 104, 150; CN
    4, 5, 6, 7; DLB 14, 271, 326; INT CA-
    128
Banville, Theodore (Faullain) de
    1832-1891 .... **NCLC 9**
    See also DLB 217; GFL 1789 to the Present
Baraka, Amiri 1934- .... **BLC 1; CLC 1, 2, 3,**
    5, 10, 14, 33, 115, 213; DC 6; PC 4;
    WLCS
    See Jones, LeRoi
    See also AAYA 63; AFAW 1, 2; AMWS 2;
    BW 2, 3; CA 21-24R; CABS 3; CAD;
    CANR 27, 38, 61, 133; CD 3, 5, 6;
    CDALB 1941-1968; CP 4, 5, 6, 7; CWP;
    DA; DA3; DAC; DAM MST, MULT,
    POET, POP; DFS 3, 11, 16; DLB 5, 7,
    16, 38; DLBD 8; EWL 3; MAL 5; MTCW
    1, 2; MTFW 2005; PFS 9; RGAL 4;
    TCLE 1:1; TUS; WP
Baratynsky, Evgenii Abramovich
    1800-1844 .... **NCLC 103**
    See also DLB 205
Barbauld, Anna Laetitia
    1743-1825 .... **NCLC 50**
    See also DLB 107, 109, 142, 158; RGEL 2
Barbellion, W. N. P. .... **TCLC 24**
    See Cummings, Bruce F(rederick)
Barber, Benjamin R. 1939- .... **CLC 141**
    See also CA 29-32R; CANR 12, 32, 64, 119
Barbera, Jack (Vincent) 1945- .... **CLC 44**
    See also CA 110; CANR 45
Barbey d'Aurevilly, Jules-Amedee
    1808-1889 .... **NCLC 1; SSC 17**
    See also DLB 119; GFL 1789 to the Present
Barbour, John c. 1316-1395 .... **CMLC 33**
    See also DLB 146
Barbusse, Henri 1873-1935 .... **TCLC 5**
    See also CA 105; 154; DLB 65; EWL 3;
    RGWL 2, 3
Barclay, Alexander c. 1475-1552 .... **LC 109**
    See also DLB 132
Barclay, Bill
    See Moorcock, Michael
Barclay, William Ewert
    See Moorcock, Michael
Barea, Arturo 1897-1957 .... **TCLC 14**
    See also CA 111; 201
Barfoot, Joan 1946- .... **CLC 18**
    See also CA 105; CANR 141
Barham, Richard Harris
    1788-1845 .... **NCLC 77**
    See also DLB 159
Baring, Maurice 1874-1945 .... **TCLC 8**
    See also CA 105; 168; DLB 34; HGG
Baring-Gould, Sabine 1834-1924 ... **TCLC 88**
    See also DLB 156, 190
Barker, Clive 1952- .... **CLC 52, 205; SSC 53**
    See also AAYA 10, 54; BEST 90:3; BPFB
    1; CA 121; 129; CANR 71, 111, 133;
    CPW; DA3; DAM POP; DLB 261; HGG;
    INT CA-129; MTCW 1, 2; MTFW 2005;
    SUFW 2

Barker, George Granville
    1913-1991 .... **CLC 8, 48**
    See also CA 9-12R; 135; CANR 7, 38; CP
    1, 2, 3, 4, 5; DAM POET; DLB 20; EWL
    3; MTCW 1
Barker, Harley Granville
    See Granville-Barker, Harley
    See also DLB 10
Barker, Howard 1946- .... **CLC 37**
    See also CA 102; CBD; CD 5, 6; DLB 13,
    233
Barker, Jane 1652-1732 .... **LC 42, 82**
    See also DLB 39, 131
Barker, Pat 1943- .... **CLC 32, 94, 146**
    See also BRWS 4; CA 117; 122; CANR 50,
    101, 148; CN 6, 7; DLB 271, 326; INT
    CA-122
Barker, Patricia
    See Barker, Pat
Barlach, Ernst (Heinrich)
    1870-1938 .... **TCLC 84**
    See also CA 178; DLB 56, 118; EWL 3
Barlow, Joel 1754-1812 .... **NCLC 23**
    See also AMWS 2; DLB 37, RGAL 4
Barnard, Mary (Ethel) 1909- .... **CLC 48**
    See also CA 21-22; CAP 2; CP 1
Barnes, Djuna 1892-1982 .... **CLC 3, 4, 8, 11,**
    29, 127; SSC 3
    See Steptoe, Lydia
    See also AMWS 3; CA 9-12R; 107; CAD;
    CANR 16, 55; CN 1, 2, 3; CWD; DLB 4,
    9, 45; EWL 3; GLL 1; MAL 5; MTCW 1,
    2; MTFW 2005; RGAL 4; TCLE 1:1;
    TUS
Barnes, Jim 1933- .... **NNAL**
    See also CA 108, 175; CAAE 175; CAAS
    28; DLB 175
Barnes, Julian 1946- .... **CLC 42, 141**
    See also BRWS 4; CA 102; CANR 19, 54,
    115, 137; CN 4, 5, 6, 7; DAB; DLB 194;
    DLBY 1993; EWL 3; MTCW 2; MTFW
    2005; SSFS 24
Barnes, Julian Patrick
    See Barnes, Julian
Barnes, Peter 1931-2004 .... **CLC 5, 56**
    See also CA 65-68; 230; CAAS 12; CANR
    33, 34, 64, 113; CBD; CD 5, 6; DFS 6;
    DLB 13, 233; MTCW 1
Barnes, William 1801-1886 .... **NCLC 75**
    See also DLB 32
Baroja, Pio 1872-1956 .... **HLC 1; TCLC 8**
    See also CA 104; 247; EW 9
Baroja y Nessi, Pio
    See Baroja, Pio
Baron, David
    See Pinter, Harold
Baron Corvo
    See Rolfe, Frederick (William Serafino Aus-
    tin Lewis Mary)
Barondess, Sue K(aufman)
    1926-1977 .... **CLC 8**
    See Kaufman, Sue
    See also CA 1-4R; 69-72; CANR 1
Baron de Teive
    See Pessoa, Fernando (Antonio Nogueira)
Baroness Von S.
    See Zangwill, Israel
Barres, (Auguste-)Maurice
    1862-1923 .... **TCLC 47**
    See also CA 164; DLB 123; GFL 1789 to
    the Present
Barreto, Afonso Henrique de Lima
    See Lima Barreto, Afonso Henrique de
Barrett, Andrea 1954- .... **CLC 150**
    See also CA 156; CANR 92; CN 7; SSFS
    24

Beecher, Catharine Esther
    1800-1878 .... NCLC **30**
    See also DLB 1, 243
Beecher, John 1904-1980 .... CLC **6**
    See also AITN 1; CA 5-8R; 105; CANR 8;
    CP 1, 2, 3
Beer, Johann 1655-1700 .... LC **5**
    See also DLB 168
Beer, Patricia 1924- .... CLC **58**
    See also CA 61-64; 183; CANR 13, 46; CP
    1, 2, 3, 4, 5, 6; CWP; DLB 40; FW
Beerbohm, Max
    See Beerbohm, (Henry) Max(imilian)
Beerbohm, (Henry) Max(imilian)
    1872-1956 .... TCLC **1, 24**
    See also BRWS 2; CA 104; 154; CANR 79;
    DLB 34, 100; FANT; MTCW 2
Beer-Hofmann, Richard
    1866-1945 .... TCLC **60**
    See also CA 160; DLB 81
Beg, Shemus
    See Stephens, James
Begiebing, Robert J(ohn) 1946- .... CLC **70**
    See also CA 122; CANR 40, 88
Begley, Louis 1933- .... CLC **197**
    See also CA 140; CANR 98; DLB 299;
    RGHL; TCLE 1:1
Behan, Brendan (Francis)
    1923-1964 .... CLC **1, 8, 11, 15, 79**
    See also BRWS 2; CA 73-76; CANR 33,
    121; CBD; CDBLB 1945-1960; DAM
    DRAM; DFS 7; DLB 13, 233; EWL 3;
    MTCW 1, 2
Behn, Aphra 1640(?)-1689 .. DC **4**; LC **1, 30,
    42, 135**; PC **13**; WLC **1**
    See also BRWS 3; DA; DA3; DAB; DAC;
    DAM DRAM, MST, NOV, POET; DFS
    16; DLB 39, 80, 131; FW; TEA; WLIT 3
Behrman, S(amuel) N(athaniel)
    1893-1973 .... CLC **40**
    See also CA 13-16; 45-48; CAD; CAP 1;
    DLB 7, 44; IDFW 3; MAL 5; RGAL 4
Bekederemo, J. P. Clark
    See Clark Bekederemo, J.P.
    See also CD 6
Belasco, David 1853-1931 .... TCLC **3**
    See also CA 104; 168; DLB 7; MAL 5;
    RGAL 4
Belcheva, Elisaveta Lyubomirova
    1893-1991 .... CLC **10**
    See Bagryana, Elisaveta
Beldone, Phil "Cheech"
    See Ellison, Harlan
Beleno
    See Azuela, Mariano
Belinski, Vissarion Grigoryevich
    1811-1848 .... NCLC **5**
    See also DLB 198
Belitt, Ben 1911- .... CLC **22**
    See also CA 13-16R; CAAS 4; CANR 7,
    77; CP 1, 2, 3, 4, 5, 6; DLB 5
Belknap, Jeremy 1744-1798 .... LC **115**
    See also DLB 30, 37
Bell, Gertrude (Margaret Lowthian)
    1868-1926 .... TCLC **67**
    See also CA 167; CANR 110; DLB 174
Bell, J. Freeman
    See Zangwill, Israel
Bell, James Madison 1826-1902 .... BLC **1**;
    TCLC **43**
    See also BW 1; CA 122; 124; DAM MULT;
    DLB 50
Bell, Madison Smartt 1957- ..... CLC **41, 102,
    223**
    See also AMWS 10; BPFB 1; CA 111; 183;
    CAAE 183; CANR 28, 54, 73, 134; CN
    5, 6, 7; CSW; DLB 218, 278; MTCW 2;
    MTFW 2005

Bell, Marvin (Hartley) 1937- .... CLC **8, 31**
    See also CA 21-24R; CAAS 14; CANR 59,
    102; CP 1, 2, 3, 4, 5, 6, 7; DAM POET;
    DLB 5; MAL 5; MTCW 1
Bell, W. L. D.
    See Mencken, H(enry) L(ouis)
Bellamy, Atwood C.
    See Mencken, H(enry) L(ouis)
Bellamy, Edward 1850-1898 ..... NCLC **4, 86,
    147**
    See also DLB 12; NFS 15; RGAL 4; SFW
    4
Belli, Gioconda 1948- .... HLCS **1**
    See also CA 152; CANR 143; CWW 2;
    DLB 290; EWL 3; RGWL 3
Bellin, Edward J.
    See Kuttner, Henry
Bello, Andres 1781-1865 .... NCLC **131**
    See also LAW
**Belloc, (Joseph) Hilaire (Pierre Sebastien
    Rene Swanton)** 1870-1953 .... PC **24**;
    TCLC **7, 18**
    See also CA 106; 152; CLR 102; CWRI 5;
    DAM POET; DLB 19, 100, 141, 174;
    EWL 3; MTCW 2; MTFW 2005; SATA
    112; WCH; YABC 1
Belloc, Joseph Peter Rene Hilaire
    See Belloc, (Joseph) Hilaire (Pierre Sebas-
    tien Rene Swanton)
Belloc, Joseph Pierre Hilaire
    See Belloc, (Joseph) Hilaire (Pierre Sebas-
    tien Rene Swanton)
Belloc, M. A.
    See Lowndes, Marie Adelaide (Belloc)
Belloc-Lowndes, Mrs.
    See Lowndes, Marie Adelaide (Belloc)
Bellow, Saul 1915-2005 ...... CLC **1, 2, 3, 6, 8,
    10, 13, 15, 25, 33, 34, 63, 79, 190, 200**;
    SSC **14**; WLC **1**
    See also AITN 2; AMW; AMWC 2; AMWR
    2; BEST 89:3; BPFB 1; CA 5-8R; 238;
    CABS 1; CANR 29, 53, 95, 132; CDALB
    1941-1968; CN 1, 2, 3, 4, 5, 6, 7; DA;
    DA3; DAB; DAC; DAM MST, NOV,
    POP; DLB 2, 28, 299, 329; DLBD 3;
    DLBY 1982; EWL 3; MAL 5; MTCW 1,
    2; MTFW 2005; NFS 4, 14; RGAL 4;
    RGHL; RGSF 2; SSFS 12, 22; TUS
Belser, Reimond Karel Maria de 1929-
    See Ruyslinck, Ward
    See also CA 152
Bely, Andrey .... PC **11**; TCLC **7**
    See Bugayev, Boris Nikolayevich
    See also DLB 295; EW 9; EWL 3
Belyi, Andrei
    See Bugayev, Boris Nikolayevich
    See also RGWL 2, 3
Bembo, Pietro 1470-1547 .... LC **79**
    See also RGWL 2, 3
Benary, Margot
    See Benary-Isbert, Margot
Benary-Isbert, Margot 1889-1979 .... CLC **12**
    See also CA 5-8R; 89-92; CANR 4, 72;
    CLR 12; MAICYA 1, 2; SATA 2; SATA-
    Obit 21
Benavente (y Martinez), Jacinto
    1866-1954 .... DC **26**; HLCS **1**; TCLC **3**
    See also CA 106; 131; CANR 81; DAM
    DRAM, MULT; DLB 329; EWL 3; GLL
    2; HW 1, 2; MTCW 1, 2
Benchley, Peter 1940-2006 .... CLC **4, 8**
    See also AAYA 14; AITN 2; BPFB 1; CA
    17-20R; 248; CANR 12, 35, 66, 115;
    CPW; DAM NOV, POP; HGG; MTCW 1,
    2; MTFW 2005; SATA 3, 89, 164
Benchley, Peter Bradford
    See Benchley, Peter

Benchley, Robert (Charles)
    1889-1945 .... TCLC **1, 55**
    See also CA 105; 153; DLB 11; MAL 5;
    RGAL 4
Benda, Julien 1867-1956 .... TCLC **60**
    See also CA 120; 154; GFL 1789 to the
    Present
Benedict, Ruth 1887-1948 .... TCLC **60**
    See also CA 158; CANR 146; DLB 246
Benedict, Ruth Fulton
    See Benedict, Ruth
Benedikt, Michael 1935- .... CLC **4, 14**
    See also CA 13-16R; CANR 7; CP 1, 2, 3,
    4, 5, 6, 7; DLB 5
Benet, Juan 1927-1993 .... CLC **28**
    See also CA 143; EWL 3
Benet, Stephen Vincent 1898-1943 ..... PC **64**;
    SSC **10, 86**; TCLC **7**
    See also AMWS 11; CA 104; 152; DA3;
    DAM POET; DLB 4, 48, 102, 249, 284;
    DLBY 1997; EWL 3; HGG; MAL 5;
    MTCW 2; MTFW 2005; RGAL 4; RGSF
    2; SSFS 22; SUFW; WP; YABC 1
Benet, William Rose 1886-1950 ...... TCLC **28**
    See also CA 118; 152; DAM POET; DLB
    45; RGAL 4
Benford, Gregory (Albert) 1941- ..... CLC **52**
    See also BPFB 1; CA 69-72; 175; CAAE
    175; CAAS 27; CANR 12, 24, 49, 95,
    134; CN 7; CSW; DLBY 1982; MTFW
    2005; SCFW 2; SFW 4
Bengtsson, Frans (Gunnar)
    1894-1954 .... TCLC **48**
    See also CA 170; EWL 3
Benjamin, David
    See Slavitt, David R(ytman)
Benjamin, Lois
    See Gould, Lois
Benjamin, Walter 1892-1940 .... TCLC **39**
    See also CA 164; DLB 242; EW 11; EWL
    3
Ben Jelloun, Tahar 1944-
    See Jelloun, Tahar ben
    See also CA 135; CWW 2; EWL 3; RGWL
    3; WLIT 2
Benn, Gottfried 1886-1956 .. PC **35**; TCLC **3**
    See also CA 106; 153; DLB 56; EWL 3;
    RGWL 2, 3
Bennett, Alan 1934- .... CLC **45, 77**
    See also BRWS 8; CA 103; CANR 35, 55,
    106, 157; CBD; CD 5, 6; DAB; DAM
    MST; DLB 310; MTCW 1, 2; MTFW
    2005
Bennett, (Enoch) Arnold
    1867-1931 .... TCLC **5, 20**
    See also BRW 6; CA 106; 155; CDBLB
    1890-1914; DLB 10, 34, 98, 135; EWL 3;
    MTCW 2
Bennett, Elizabeth
    See Mitchell, Margaret (Munnerlyn)
Bennett, George Harold 1930-
    See Bennett, Hal
    See also BW 1; CA 97-100; CANR 87
Bennett, Gwendolyn B. 1902-1981 .... HR **1:2**
    See also BW 1; CA 125; DLB 51; WP
Bennett, Hal .... CLC **5**
    See Bennett, George Harold
    See also CAAS 13; DLB 33
Bennett, Jay 1912- .... CLC **35**
    See also AAYA 10; CA 69-72; CANR 11,
    42, 79; JRDA; SAAS 4; SATA 41, 87;
    SATA-Brief 27; WYA; YAW
Bennett, Louise 1919-2006 .. BLC **1**; CLC **28**
    See also BW 2, 3; CA 151; CDWLB 3; CP
    1, 2, 3, 4, 5, 6, 7; DAM MULT; DLB 117;
    EWL 3
Bennett-Coverley, Louise
    See Bennett, Louise

Bodel, Jean 1167(?)-1210 .... **CMLC 28**
Bodenheim, Maxwell 1892-1954 .... **TCLC 44**
See also CA 110; 187; DLB 9, 45; MAL 5; RGAL 4
Bodenheimer, Maxwell
See Bodenheim, Maxwell
Bodker, Cecil 1927-
See Bodker, Cecil
Bodker, Cecil 1927- .... **CLC 21**
See also CA 73-76; CANR 13, 44, 111; CLR 23; MAICYA 1, 2; SATA 14, 133
Boell, Heinrich (Theodor)
1917-1985 ..... **CLC 2, 3, 6, 9, 11, 15, 27, 32, 72; SSC 23; TCLC 185; WLC 1**
See Boll, Heinrich (Theodor)
See also CA 21-24R; 116; CANR 24; DA; DA3; DAB; DAC; DAM MST, NOV; DLB 69; DLBY 1985; MTCW 1, 2; MTFW 2005; SSFS 20; TWA
Boerne, Alfred
See Doeblin, Alfred
Boethius c. 480-c. 524 .... **CMLC 15**
See also DLB 115; RGWL 2, 3; WLIT 8
Boff, Leonardo (Genezio Darci)
1938- .... **CLC 70; HLC 1**
See also CA 150; DAM MULT; HW 2
Bogan, Louise 1897-1970 .... **CLC 4, 39, 46, 93; PC 12**
See also AMWS 3; CA 73-76; 25-28R; CANR 33, 82; CP 1; DAM POET; DLB 45, 169; EWL 3; MAL 5; MBL; MTCW 1, 2; PFS 21; RGAL 4
Bogarde, Dirk
See Van Den Bogarde, Derek Jules Gaspard Ulric Niven
See also DLB 14
Bogosian, Eric 1953- .... **CLC 45, 141**
See also CA 138; CAD; CANR 102, 148; CD 5, 6
Bograd, Larry 1953- .... **CLC 35**
See also CA 93-96; CANR 57; SAAS 21; SATA 33, 89; WYA
Boiardo, Matteo Maria 1441-1494 .... **LC 6**
Boileau-Despreaux, Nicolas 1636-1711 . **LC 3**
See also DLB 268; EW 3; GFL Beginnings to 1789; RGWL 2, 3
Boissard, Maurice
See Leautaud, Paul
Bojer, Johan 1872-1959 .... **TCLC 64**
See also CA 189; EWL 3
Bok, Edward W(illiam)
1863-1930 .... **TCLC 101**
See also CA 217; DLB 91; DLBD 16
Boker, George Henry 1823-1890 . **NCLC 125**
See also RGAL 4
Boland, Eavan 1944- ... **CLC 40, 67, 113; PC 58**
See also BRWS 5; CA 143, 207; CAAE 207; CANR 61; CP 1, 6, 7; CWP; DAM POET; DLB 40; FW; MTCW 2; MTFW 2005; PFS 12, 22
Boll, Heinrich (Theodor)
See Boell, Heinrich (Theodor)
See also BPFB 1; CDWLB 2; DLB 329; EW 13; EWL 3; RGHL; RGSF 2; RGWL 2, 3
Bolt, Lee
See Faust, Frederick (Schiller)
Bolt, Robert (Oxton) 1924-1995 ...... **CLC 14; TCLC 175**
See also CA 17-20R; 147; CANR 35, 67; CBD; DAM DRAM; DFS 2; DLB 13, 233; EWL 3; LAIT 1; MTCW 1
Bombal, Maria Luisa 1910-1980 .... **HLCS 1; SSC 37**
See also CA 127; CANR 72; EWL 3; HW 1; LAW; RGSF 2
Bombet, Louis-Alexandre-Cesar
See Stendhal

Bomkauf
See Kaufman, Bob (Garnell)
Bonaventura .... **NCLC 35**
See also DLB 90
Bonaventure 1217(?)-1274 .... **CMLC 79**
See also DLB 115; LMFS 1
Bond, Edward 1934- .... **CLC 4, 6, 13, 23**
See also AAYA 50; BRWS 1; CA 25-28R; CANR 38, 67, 106; CBD; CD 5, 6; DAM DRAM; DFS 3, 8; DLB 13, 310; EWL 3; MTCW 1
Bonham, Frank 1914-1989 .... **CLC 12**
See also AAYA 1, 70; BYA 1, 3; CA 9-12R; CANR 4, 36; JRDA; MAICYA 1, 2; SAAS 3; SATA 1, 49; SATA-Obit 62; TCWW 1, 2; YAW
Bonnefoy, Yves 1923- . **CLC 9, 15, 58; PC 58**
See also CA 85-88; CANR 33, 75, 97, 136; CWW 2; DAM MST, POET; DLB 258; EWL 3; GFL 1789 to the Present; MTCW 1, 2; MTFW 2005
Bonner, Marita . **HR 1:2; PC 72; TCLC 179**
See Occomy, Marita (Odette) Bonner
Bonnin, Gertrude 1876-1938 .... **NNAL**
See Zitkala-Sa
See also CA 150; DAM MULT
Bontemps, Arna(ud Wendell)
1902-1973 .. **BLC 1; CLC 1, 18; HR 1:2**
See also BW 1; CA 1-4R; 41-44R; CANR 4, 35; CLR 6; CP 1; CWRI 5; DA3; DAM MULT, NOV, POET; DLB 48, 51; JRDA; MAICYA 1, 2; MAL 5; MTCW 1, 2; SATA 2, 44; SATA-Obit 24; WCH; WP
Boot, William
See Stoppard, Tom
Booth, Martin 1944-2004 .... **CLC 13**
See also CA 93-96; 188; 223; CAAE 188; CAAS 2; CANR 92; CP 1, 2, 3, 4
Booth, Philip 1925- .... **CLC 23**
See also CA 5-8R; CANR 5, 88; CP 1, 2, 3, 4, 5, 6, 7; DLBY 1982
Booth, Wayne C. 1921-2005 .... **CLC 24**
See also CA 1-4R; 244; CAAS 5; CANR 3, 43, 117; DLB 67
Booth, Wayne Clayson
See Booth, Wayne C.
Borchert, Wolfgang 1921-1947 .... **TCLC 5**
See also CA 104; 188; DLB 69, 124; EWL 3
Borel, Petrus 1809-1859 .... **NCLC 41**
See also DLB 119; GFL 1789 to the Present
Borges, Jorge Luis 1899-1986 ... **CLC 1, 2, 3, 4, 6, 8, 9, 10, 13, 19, 44, 48, 83; HLC 1; PC 22, 32; SSC 4, 41; TCLC 109; WLC 1**
See also AAYA 26; BPFB 1; CA 21-24R; CANR 19, 33, 75, 105, 133; CDWLB 3; DA; DA3; DAB; DAC; DAM MST, MULT; DLB 113, 283; DLBY 1986; DNFS 1, 2; EWL 3; HW 1, 2; LAW; LMFS 2; MSW; MTCW 1, 2; MTFW 2005; RGHL; RGSF 2; RGWL 2, 3; SFW 4; SSFS 17; TWA; WLIT 1
Borowski, Tadeusz 1922-1951 .... **SSC 48; TCLC 9**
See also CA 106; 154; CDWLB 4; DLB 215; EWL 3; RGHL; RGSF 2; RGWL 3; SSFS 13
Borrow, George (Henry)
1803-1881 .... **NCLC 9**
See also BRWS 5; DLB 21, 55, 166
Bosch (Gavino), Juan 1909-2001 ..... **HLCS 1**
See also CA 151; 204; DAM MST, MULT; DLB 145; HW 1, 2
Bosman, Herman Charles
1905-1951 .... **TCLC 49**
See Malan, Herman
See also CA 160; DLB 225; RGSF 2

Bosschere, Jean de 1878(?)-1953 ... **TCLC 19**
See also CA 115; 186
Boswell, James 1740-1795 ... **LC 4, 50; WLC 1**
See also BRW 3; CDBLB 1660-1789; DA; DAB; DAC; DAM MST; DLB 104, 142; TEA; WLIT 3
Bottomley, Gordon 1874-1948 ..... **TCLC 107**
See also CA 120; 192; DLB 10
Bottoms, David 1949- .... **CLC 53**
See also CA 105; CANR 22; CSW; DLB 120; DLBY 1983
Boucicault, Dion 1820-1890 .... **NCLC 41**
Boucolon, Maryse
See Conde, Maryse
Bourdieu, Pierre 1930-2002 .... **CLC 198**
See also CA 130; 204
Bourget, Paul (Charles Joseph)
1852-1935 .... **TCLC 12**
See also CA 107; 196; DLB 123; GFL 1789 to the Present
Bourjaily, Vance (Nye) 1922- .... **CLC 8, 62**
See also CA 1-4R; CAAS 1; CANR 2, 72; CN 1, 2, 3, 4, 5, 6, 7; DLB 2, 143; MAL 5
Bourne, Randolph S(illiman)
1886-1918 .... **TCLC 16**
See also AMW; CA 117; 155; DLB 63; MAL 5
Bova, Ben 1932- .... **CLC 45**
See also AAYA 16; CA 5-8R; CAAS 18; CANR 11, 56, 94, 111, 157; CLR 3, 96; DLBY 1981; INT CANR-11; MAICYA 1, 2; MTCW 1; SATA 6, 68, 133; SFW 4
Bowen, Elizabeth (Dorothea Cole)
1899-1973 . **CLC 1, 3, 6, 11, 15, 22, 118; SSC 3, 28, 66; TCLC 148**
See also BRWS 2; CA 17-18; 41-44R; CANR 35, 105; CAP 2; CDBLB 1945-1960; CN 1; DA3; DAM NOV; DLB 15, 162; EWL 3; EXPS; FW; HGG; MTCW 1, 2; MTFW 2005; NFS 13; RGSF 2; SSFS 5, 22; SUFW 1; TEA; WLIT 4
Bowering, George 1935- .... **CLC 15, 47**
See also CA 21-24R; CAAS 16; CANR 10; CN 7; CP 1, 2, 3, 4, 5, 6, 7; DLB 53
Bowering, Marilyn R(uthe) 1949- .... **CLC 32**
See also CA 101; CANR 49; CP 4, 5, 6, 7; CWP
Bowers, Edgar 1924-2000 .... **CLC 9**
See also CA 5-8R; 188; CANR 24; CP 1, 2, 3, 4, 5, 6, 7; CSW; DLB 5
Bowers, Mrs. J. Milton 1842-1914
See Bierce, Ambrose (Gwinett)
Bowie, David .... **CLC 17**
See Jones, David Robert
Bowles, Jane (Sydney) 1917-1973 ..... **CLC 3, 68**
See Bowles, Jane Auer
See also CA 19-20; 41-44R; CAP 2; CN 1; MAL 5
Bowles, Jane Auer
See Bowles, Jane (Sydney)
See also EWL 3
Bowles, Paul 1910-1999 ..... **CLC 1, 2, 19, 53; SSC 3**
See also AMWS 4; CA 1-4R; 186; CAAS 1; CANR 1, 19, 50, 75; CN 1, 2, 3, 4, 5, 6; DA3; DLB 5, 6, 218; EWL 3; MAL 5; MTCW 1, 2; MTFW 2005; RGAL 4; SSFS 17
Bowles, William Lisle 1762-1850 . **NCLC 103**
See also DLB 93
Box, Edgar
See Vidal, Gore
See also GLL 1
Boyd, James 1888-1944 .... **TCLC 115**
See also CA 186; DLB 9; DLBD 16; RGAL 4; RHW

Boyd, Nancy
See Millay, Edna St. Vincent
See also GLL 1

Boyd, Thomas (Alexander)
1898-1935 .... **TCLC 111**
See also CA 111; 183; DLB 9; DLBD 16, 316

Boyd, William (Andrew Murray)
1952- .... **CLC 28, 53, 70**
See also CA 114; 120; CANR 51, 71, 131; CN 4, 5, 6, 7; DLB 231

Boyesen, Hjalmar Hjorth
1848-1895 .... **NCLC 135**
See also DLB 12, 71; DLBD 13; RGAL 4

Boyle, Kay 1902-1992 .... **CLC 1, 5, 19, 58, 121; SSC 5**
See also CA 13-16R; 140; CAAS 1; CANR 29, 61, 110; CN 1, 2, 3, 4, 5; CP 1, 2, 3, 4; DLB 4, 9, 48, 86; DLBY 1993; EWL 3; MAL 5; MTCW 1, 2; MTFW 2005; RGAL 4; RGSF 2; SSFS 10, 13, 14

Boyle, Mark
See Kienzle, William X.

Boyle, Patrick 1905-1982 .... **CLC 19**
See also CA 127

Boyle, T. C.
See Boyle, T. Coraghessan
See also AMWS 8

Boyle, T. Coraghessan 1948- ..... **CLC 36, 55, 90; SSC 16**
See Boyle, T. C.
See also AAYA 47; BEST 90:4; BPFB 1; CA 120; CANR 44, 76, 89, 132; CN 6, 7; CPW; DA3; DAM POP; DLB 218, 278; DLBY 1986; EWL 3; MAL 5; MTCW 2; MTFW 2005, SSFS 13, 19

Boz
See Dickens, Charles (John Huffam)

Brackenridge, Hugh Henry
1748-1816 .... **NCLC 7**
See also DLB 11, 37; RGAL 4

Bradbury, Edward P.
See Moorcock, Michael
See also MTCW 2

Bradbury, Malcolm (Stanley)
1932-2000 .... **CLC 32, 61**
See also CA 1-4R; CANR 1, 33, 91, 98, 137; CN 1, 2, 3, 4, 5, 6, 7; CP 1; DA3; DAM NOV; DLB 14, 207; EWL 3; MTCW 1, 2; MTFW 2005

Bradbury, Ray 1920- ... **CLC 1, 3, 10, 15, 42, 98; SSC 29, 53; WLC 1**
See also AAYA 15; AITN 1, 2; AMWS 4; BPFB 1; BYA 4, 5, 11; CA 1-4R; CANR 2, 30, 75, 125; CDALB 1968-1988; CN 1, 2, 3, 4, 5, 6, 7; CPW; DA; DA3; DAB; DAC; DAM MST, NOV, POP; DLB 2, 8; EXPN; EXPS; HGG; LAIT 3, 5; LATS 1:2; LMFS 2; MAL 5; MTCW 1, 2; MTFW 2005; NFS 1, 22; RGAL 4; RGSF 2; SATA 11, 64, 123; SCFW 1, 2; SFW 1, 2; SSFS 1, 20; SUFW 1, 2; TUS; YAW

Braddon, Mary Elizabeth
1837-1915 .... **TCLC 111**
See also BRWS 8; CA 108; 179; CMW 4; DLB 18, 70, 156; HGG

Bradfield, Scott 1955- .... **SSC 65**
See also CA 147; CANR 90; HGG; SUFW 2

Bradfield, Scott Michael
See Bradfield, Scott

Bradford, Gamaliel 1863-1932 .... **TCLC 36**
See also CA 160; DLB 17

Bradford, William 1590-1657 .... **LC 64**
See also DLB 24, 30; RGAL 4

Bradley, David (Henry), Jr. 1950- .... **BLC 1; CLC 23, 118**
See also BW 1, 3; CA 104; CANR 26, 81; CN 4, 5, 6, 7; DAM MULT; DLB 33

Bradley, John Ed 1958- .... **CLC 55**
See also CA 139; CANR 99; CN 6, 7; CSW

Bradley, John Edmund, Jr.
See Bradley, John Ed

Bradley, Marion Zimmer
1930-1999 .... **CLC 30**
See Chapman, Lee; Dexter, John; Gardner, Miriam; Ives, Morgan; Rivers, Elfrida
See also AAYA 40; BPFB 1; CA 57-60; 185; CAAS 10; CANR 7, 31, 51, 75, 107; CPW; DA3; DAM POP; DLB 8; FANT; FW; MTCW 1, 2; MTFW 2005; SATA 90, 139; SATA-Obit 116; SFW 4; SUFW 2; YAW

Bradshaw, John 1933- .... **CLC 70**
See also CA 138; CANR 61

Bradstreet, Anne 1612(?)-1672 .... **LC 4, 30, 130; PC 10**
See also AMWS 1; CDALB 1640-1865; DA; DA3; DAC; DAM MST, POET; DLB 24; EXPP; FW; PFS 6; RGAL 4; TUS; WP

Brady, Joan 1939- .... **CLC 86**
See also CA 141

Bragg, Melvyn 1939- .... **CLC 10**
See also BEST 89:3; CA 57-60; CANR 10, 48, 89; CN 1, 2, 3, 4, 5, 6, 7; DLB 14, 271; RHW

Brahe, Tycho 1546-1601 .... **LC 45**
See also DLB 300

Braine, John (Gerard) 1922-1986 . **CLC 1, 3, 41**
See also CA 1-4R; 120; CANR 1, 33; CDBLB 1945-1960; CN 1, 2, 3, 4; DLB 15; DLBY 1986; EWL 3; MTCW 1

Braithwaite, William Stanley (Beaumont)
1878-1962 .... **BLC 1; HR 1:2; PC 52**
See also BW 1; CA 125; DAM MULT; DLB 50, 54; MAL 5

Bramah, Ernest 1868-1942 .... **TCLC 72**
See also CA 156; CMW 4; DLB 70; FANT

Brammer, Billy Lee
See Brammer, William

Brammer, William 1929-1978 .... **CLC 31**
See also CA 235; 77-80

Brancati, Vitaliano 1907-1954 .... **TCLC 12**
See also CA 109; DLB 264; EWL 3

Brancato, Robin F(idler) 1936- .... **CLC 35**
See also AAYA 9, 68; BYA 6; CA 69-72; CANR 11, 45; CLR 32; JRDA; MAICYA 2; MAICYAS 1; SAAS 9; SATA 97; WYA; YAW

Brand, Dionne 1953- .... **CLC 192**
See also BW 2; CA 143; CANR 143; CWP

Brand, Max
See Faust, Frederick (Schiller)
See also BPFB 1; TCWW 1, 2

Brand, Millen 1906-1980 .... **CLC 7**
See also CA 21-24R; 97-100; CANR 72

Branden, Barbara .... **CLC 44**
See also CA 148

Brandes, Georg (Morris Cohen)
1842-1927 .... **TCLC 10**
See also CA 105; 189; DLB 300

Brandys, Kazimierz 1916-2000 .... **CLC 62**
See also CA 239; EWL 3

Branley, Franklyn M(ansfield)
1915-2002 .... **CLC 21**
See also CA 33-36R; 207; CANR 14, 39; CLR 13; MAICYA 1, 2; SAAS 16; SATA 4, 68, 136

Brant, Beth (E.) 1941- .... **NNAL**
See also CA 144; FW

Brant, Sebastian 1457-1521 .... **LC 112**
See also DLB 179; RGWL 2, 3

Brathwaite, Edward Kamau
1930- .... **BLCS; CLC 11; PC 56**
See also BRWS 12; BW 2, 3; CA 25-28R; CANR 11, 26, 47, 107; CDWLB 3; CP 1, 2, 3, 4, 5, 6, 7; DAM POET; DLB 125; EWL 3

Brathwaite, Kamau
See Brathwaite, Edward Kamau

Brautigan, Richard (Gary)
1935-1984 .... **CLC 1, 3, 5, 9, 12, 34, 42; TCLC 133**
See also BPFB 1; CA 53-56; 113; CANR 34; CN 1, 2, 3; CP 1, 2, 3, 4; DA3; DAM NOV; DLB 2, 5, 206; DLBY 1980, 1984; FANT; MAL 5; MTCW 1; RGAL 4; SATA 56

Brave Bird, Mary .... **NNAL**
See Crow Dog, Mary

Braverman, Kate 1950- .... **CLC 67**
See also CA 89-92; CANR 141

Brecht, (Eugen) Bertolt (Friedrich)
1898-1956 ..... **DC 3; TCLC 1, 6, 13, 35, 169; WLC 1**
See also CA 104; 133; CANR 62; CDWLB 2; DA; DA3; DAB; DAC; DAM DRAM, MST; DFS 4, 5, 9; DLB 56, 124; EW 11; EWL 3; IDTP; MTCW 1, 2; MTFW 2005; RGHL; RGWL 2, 3; TWA

Brecht, Eugen Berthold Friedrich
See Brecht, (Eugen) Bertolt (Friedrich)

Bremer, Fredrika 1801-1865 .... **NCLC 11**
See also DLB 254

Brennan, Christopher John
1870-1932 .... **TCLC 17**
See also CA 117; 188; DLB 230; EWL 3

Brennan, Maeve 1917-1993 ... **CLC 5; TCLC 124**
See also CA 81-84; CANR 72, 100

Brenner, Jozef 1887-1919
See Csath, Geza
See also CA 240

Brent, Linda
See Jacobs, Harriet A(nn)

Brentano, Clemens (Maria)
1778-1842 .... **NCLC 1**
See also DLB 90; RGWL 2, 3

Brent of Bin Bin
See Franklin, (Stella Maria Sarah) Miles (Lampe)

Brenton, Howard 1942- .... **CLC 31**
See also CA 69-72; CANR 33, 67; CBD; CD 5, 6; DLB 13; MTCW 1

Breslin, James 1930-
See Breslin, Jimmy
See also CA 73-76; CANR 31, 75, 139; DAM NOV; MTCW 1, 2; MTFW 2005

Breslin, Jimmy .... **CLC 4, 43**
See Breslin, James
See also AITN 1; DLB 185; MTCW 2

Bresson, Robert 1901(?)-1999 .... **CLC 16**
See also CA 110; 187; CANR 49

Breton, Andre 1896-1966 .. **CLC 2, 9, 15, 54; PC 15**
See also CA 19-20; 25-28R; CANR 40, 60; CAP 2; DLB 65, 258; EW 11; EWL 3; GFL 1789 to the Present; LMFS 2; MTCW 1, 2; MTFW 2005; RGWL 2, 3; TWA; WP

Breton, Nicholas c. 1554-c. 1626 .... **LC 133**
See also DLB 136

Breytenbach, Breyten 1939(?)- .. **CLC 23, 37, 126**
See also CA 113; 129; CANR 61, 122; CWW 2; DAM POET; DLB 225; EWL 3

Bridgers, Sue Ellen 1942- .... **CLC 26**
See also AAYA 8, 49; BYA 7, 8; CA 65-68; CANR 11, 36; CLR 18; DLB 52; JRDA; MAICYA 1, 2; SAAS 1; SATA 22, 90; SATA-Essay 109; WYA; YAW

Bridges, Robert (Seymour)
1844-1930 .... **PC 28; TCLC 1**
See also BRW 6; CA 104; 152; CDBLB
1890-1914; DAM POET; DLB 19, 98

Bridie, James .... **TCLC 3**
See Mavor, Osborne Henry
See also DLB 10; EWL 3

Brin, David 1950- .... **CLC 34**
See also AAYA 21; CA 102; CANR 24, 70,
125, 127; INT CANR-24; SATA 65;
SCFW 2; SFW 4

Brink, Andre 1935- .... **CLC 18, 36, 106**
See also AFW; BRWS 6; CA 104; CANR
39, 62, 109, 133; CN 4, 5, 6, 7; DLB 225;
EWL 3; INT CA-103; LATS 1:2; MTCW
1, 2; MTFW 2005; WLIT 2

Brinsmead, H. F.
See Brinsmead, H(esba) F(ay)

Brinsmead, H. F(ay)
See Brinsmead, H(esba) F(ay)

Brinsmead, H(esba) F(ay) 1922- ...... **CLC 21**
See also CA 21-24R; CANR 10; CLR 47;
CWRI 5; MAICYA 1, 2; SAAS 5; SATA
18, 78

Brittain, Vera (Mary) 1893(?)-1970 . **CLC 23**
See also BRWS 10; CA 13-16; 25-28R;
CANR 58; CAP 1; DLB 191; FW; MTCW
1, 2

Broch, Hermann 1886-1951 .... **TCLC 20**
See also CA 117; 211; CDWLB 2; DLB 85,
124; EW 10; EWL 3; RGWL 2, 3

Brock, Rose
See Hansen, Joseph
See also GLL 1

Brod, Max 1884-1968 .... **TCLC 115**
See also CA 5-8R; 25-28R; CANR 7; DLB
81; EWL 3

Brodkey, Harold (Roy) 1930-1996 .. **CLC 56;**
TCLC 123
See also CA 111; 151; CANR 71; CN 4, 5,
6; DLB 130

Brodsky, Iosif Alexandrovich 1940-1996
See Brodsky, Joseph
See also AITN 1; CA 41-44R; 151; CANR
37, 106; DA3; DAM POET; MTCW 1, 2;
MTFW 2005; RGWL 2, 3

Brodsky, Joseph . **CLC 4, 6, 13, 36, 100; PC**
9
See Brodsky, Iosif Alexandrovich
See also AAYA 71; AMWS 8; CWW 2;
DLB 285, 329; EWL 3; MTCW 1

Brodsky, Michael 1948- .... **CLC 19**
See also CA 102; CANR 18, 41, 58, 147;
DLB 244

Brodsky, Michael Mark
See Brodsky, Michael

Brodzki, Bella .... **CLC 65**

Brome, Richard 1590(?)-1652 .... **LC 61**
See also BRWS 10; DLB 58

Bromell, Henry 1947- .... **CLC 5**
See also CA 53-56; CANR 9, 115, 116

Bromfield, Louis (Brucker)
1896-1956 .... **TCLC 11**
See also CA 107; 155; DLB 4, 9, 86; RGAL
4; RHW

Broner, E(sther) M(asserman)
1930- .... **CLC 19**
See also CA 17-20R; CANR 8, 25, 72; CN
4, 5, 6; DLB 28

Bronk, William (M.) 1918-1999 .... **CLC 10**
See also CA 89-92; 177; CANR 23; CP 3,
4, 5, 6, 7; DLB 165

Bronstein, Lev Davidovich
See Trotsky, Leon

Bronte, Anne
See Bronte, Anne

Bronte, Anne 1820-1849 ..... **NCLC 4, 71, 102**
See also BRW 5; BRWR 1; DA3; DLB 21,
199; TEA

Bronte, (Patrick) Branwell
1817-1848 .... **NCLC 109**

Bronte, Charlotte
See Bronte, Charlotte

Bronte, Charlotte 1816-1855 ...... **NCLC 3, 8,**
33, 58, 105, 155; WLC 1
See also AAYA 17; BRW 5; BRWC 2;
BRWR 1; BYA 2; CDBLB 1832-1890;
DA; DA3; DAB; DAC; DAM MST, NOV;
DLB 21, 159, 199; EXPN; FL 1:2; GL 2;
LAIT 2; NFS 4; TEA; WLIT 4

Bronte, Emily
See Bronte, Emily (Jane)

Bronte, Emily (Jane) 1818-1848 ... **NCLC 16,**
35, 165; PC 8; WLC 1
See also AAYA 17; BPFB 1; BRW 5;
BRWC 1; BRWR 1; BYA 3; CDBLB
1832-1890; DA; DA3; DAB; DAC; DAM
MST, NOV, POET; DLB 21, 32, 199;
EXPN; FL 1:2; GL 2; LAIT 1; TEA;
WLIT 3

Brontes
See Bronte, Anne; Bronte, Charlotte; Bronte,
Emily (Jane)

Brooke, Frances 1724-1789 .... **LC 6, 48**
See also DLB 39, 99

Brooke, Henry 1703(?)-1783 .... **LC 1**
See also DLB 39

Brooke, Rupert (Chawner)
1887-1915 .. **PC 24; TCLC 2, 7; WLC 1**
See also BRWS 3; CA 104; 132; CANR 61;
CDBLB 1914-1945; DA; DAB; DAC;
DAM MST, POET; DLB 19, 216; EXPP;
GLL 2; MTCW 1, 2; MTFW 2005; PFS
7; TEA

Brooke-Haven, P.
See Wodehouse, P(elham) G(renville)

Brooke-Rose, Christine 1926(?)- ..... **CLC 40,**
184
See also BRWS 4; CA 13-16R; CANR 58,
118; CN 1, 2, 3, 4, 5, 6, 7; DLB 14, 231;
EWL 3; SFW 4

Brookner, Anita 1928- .. **CLC 32, 34, 51, 136**
See also BRWS 4; CA 114; 120; CANR 37,
56, 87, 130; CN 4, 5, 6, 7; CPW; DA3;
DAB; DAM POP; DLB 194, 326; DLBY
1987; EWL 3; MTCW 1, 2; MTFW 2005;
NFS 23; TEA

Brooks, Cleanth 1906-1994 . **CLC 24, 86, 110**
See also AMWS 14; CA 17-20R; 145;
CANR 33, 35; CSW; DLB 63; DLBY
1994; EWL 3; INT CANR-35; MAL 5;
MTCW 1, 2; MTFW 2005

Brooks, George
See Baum, L(yman) Frank

Brooks, Gwendolyn 1917-2000 .... **BLC 1;**
CLC 1, 2, 4, 5, 15, 49, 125; PC 7;
WLC 1
See also AAYA 20; AFAW 1, 2; AITN 1;
AMWS 3; BW 2, 3; CA 1-4R; 190; CANR
1, 27, 52, 75, 132; CDALB 1941-1968;
CLR 27; CP 1, 2, 3, 4, 5, 6, 7; CWP; DA;
DA3; DAC; DAM MST, MULT, POET;
DLB 5, 76, 165; EWL 3; EXPP; FL 1:5;
MAL 5; MBL; MTCW 1, 2; MTFW 2005;
PFS 1, 2, 4, 6; RGAL 4; SATA 6; SATA-
Obit 123; TUS; WP

Brooks, Mel 1926-
See Kaminsky, Melvin
See also CA 65-68; CANR 16; DFS 21

Brooks, Peter (Preston) 1938- .... **CLC 34**
See also CA 45-48; CANR 1, 107

Brooks, Van Wyck 1886-1963 .... **CLC 29**
See also AMW; CA 1-4R; CANR 6; DLB
45, 63, 103; MAL 5; TUS

Brophy, Brigid (Antonia)
1929-1995 .... **CLC 6, 11, 29, 105**
See also CA 5-8R; 149; CAAS 4; CANR
25, 53; CBD; CN 1, 2, 3, 4, 5, 6; CWD;
DA3; DLB 14, 271; EWL 3; MTCW 1, 2

Brosman, Catharine Savage 1934- ..... **CLC 9**
See also CA 61-64; CANR 21, 46, 149

Brossard, Nicole 1943- .... **CLC 115, 169**
See also CA 122; CAAS 16; CANR 140;
CCA 1; CWP; CWW 2; DLB 53; EWL 3;
FW; GLL 2; RGWL 3

Brother Antoninus
See Everson, William (Oliver)

Brothers Grimm
See Grimm, Jacob Ludwig Karl; Grimm,
Wilhelm Karl

The Brothers Quay
See Quay, Stephen; Quay, Timothy

Broughton, T(homas) Alan 1936- ..... **CLC 19**
See also CA 45-48; CANR 2, 23, 48, 111

Broumas, Olga 1949- .... **CLC 10, 73**
See also CA 85-88; CANR 20, 69, 110; CP
5, 6, 7; CWP; GLL 2

Broun, Heywood 1888-1939 .... **TCLC 104**
See also DLB 29, 171

Brown, Alan 1950- .... **CLC 99**
See also CA 156

Brown, Charles Brockden
1771-1810 .... **NCLC 22, 74, 122**
See also AMWS 1; CDALB 1640-1865;
DLB 37, 59, 73; FW; GL 2; HGG; LMFS
1; RGAL 4; TUS

Brown, Christy 1932-1981 .... **CLC 63**
See also BYA 13; CA 105; 104; CANR 72;
DLB 14

Brown, Claude 1937-2002 ... **BLC 1; CLC 30**
See also AAYA 7; BW 1, 3; CA 73-76; 205;
CANR 81; DAM MULT

Brown, Dan 1964- .... **CLC 209**
See also AAYA 55; CA 217; MTFW 2005

Brown, Dee 1908-2002 .... **CLC 18, 47**
See also AAYA 30; CA 13-16R; 212; CAAS
6; CANR 11, 45, 60, 150; CPW; CSW;
DA3; DAM POP; DLBY 1980; LAIT 2;
MTCW 1, 2; MTFW 2005; NCFS 5;
SATA 5, 110; SATA-Obit 141; TCWW 1,
2

Brown, Dee Alexander
See Brown, Dee

Brown, George
See Wertmueller, Lina

Brown, George Douglas
1869-1902 .... **TCLC 28**
See Douglas, George
See also CA 162

Brown, George Mackay 1921-1996 ... **CLC 5,**
48, 100
See also BRWS 6; CA 21-24R; 151; CAAS
6; CANR 12, 37, 67; CN 1, 2, 3, 4, 5, 6;
CP 1, 2, 3, 4, 5, 6; DLB 14, 27, 139, 271;
MTCW 1; RGSF 2; SATA 35

Brown, (William) Larry 1951-2004 . **CLC 73**
See also CA 130; 134; 233; CANR 117,
145; CSW; DLB 234; INT CA-134

Brown, Moses
See Barrett, William (Christopher)

Brown, Rita Mae 1944- .... **CLC 18, 43, 79**
See also BPFB 1; CA 45-48; CANR 2, 11,
35, 62, 95, 138; CN 5, 6, 7; CPW; CSW;
DA3; DAM NOV, POP; FW; INT CANR-
11; MAL 5; MTCW 1, 2; MTFW 2005;
NFS 9; RGAL 4; TUS

Brown, Roderick (Langmere) Haig-
See Haig-Brown, Roderick (Langmere)

Brown, Rosellen 1939- .... **CLC 32, 170**
See also CA 77-80; CAAS 10; CANR 14,
44, 98; CN 6, 7

Brown, Sterling Allen 1901-1989 ...... **BLC 1;**
CLC 1, 23, 59; HR 1:2; PC 55
See also AFAW 1, 2; BW 1, 3; CA 85-88;
127; CANR 26; CP 3, 4; DA3; DAM
MULT, POET; DLB 48, 51, 63; MAL 5;
MTCW 1, 2; MTFW 2005; RGAL 4; WP

Brown, Will
See Ainsworth, William Harrison
Brown, William Hill 1765-1793 .... **LC 93**
See also DLB 37
Brown, William Wells 1815-1884 ...... **BLC 1;
DC 1; NCLC 2, 89**
See also DAM MULT; DLB 3, 50, 183,
248; RGAL 4
Browne, (Clyde) Jackson 1948(?)- ... **CLC 21**
See also CA 120
Browne, Sir Thomas 1605-1682 .... **LC 111**
See also BRW 2; DLB 151
Browning, Robert 1812-1889 . **NCLC 19, 79;
PC 2, 61; WLCS**
See also BRW 4; BRWC 2; BRWR 2; CD-
BLB 1832-1890; CLR 97; DA; DA3;
DAB; DAC; DAM MST, POET; DLB 32,
163; EXPP; LATS 1:1; PAB; PFS 1, 15;
RGEL 2; TEA; WLIT 4; WP; YABC 1
Browning, Tod 1882-1962 .... **CLC 16**
See also CA 141; 117
Brownmiller, Susan 1935- .... **CLC 159**
See also CA 103; CANR 35, 75, 137; DAM
NOV; FW; MTCW 1, 2; MTFW 2005
Brownson, Orestes Augustus
1803-1876 .... **NCLC 50**
See also DLB 1, 59, 73, 243
Bruccoli, Matthew J(oseph) 1931- ... **CLC 34**
See also CA 9-12R; CANR 7, 87; DLB 103
Bruce, Lenny .... **CLC 21**
See Schneider, Leonard Alfred
Bruchac, Joseph 1942- .... **NNAL**
See also AAYA 19; CA 33-36R; CANR 13,
47, 75, 94, 137; CLR 46; CWRI 5; DAM
MULT; JRDA; MAICYA 2; MAICYAS 1;
MTCW 2; MTFW 2005; SATA 42, 89,
131, 172
Bruin, John
See Brutus, Dennis
Brulard, Henri
See Stendhal
Brulls, Christian
See Simenon, Georges (Jacques Christian)
Brunetto Latini c. 1220-1294 .... **CMLC 73**
Brunner, John (Kilian Houston)
1934-1995 .... **CLC 8, 10**
See also CA 1-4R; 149; CAAS 8; CANR 2,
37; CPW; DAM POP; DLB 261; MTCW
1, 2; SCFW 1, 2; SFW 4
Bruno, Giordano 1548-1600 .... **LC 27**
See also RGWL 2, 3
Brutus, Dennis 1924- ... **BLC 1; CLC 43; PC
24**
See also AFW; BW 2, 3; CA 49-52; CAAS
14; CANR 2, 27, 42, 81; CDWLB 3; CP
1, 2, 3, 4, 5, 6, 7; DAM MULT, POET;
DLB 117, 225; EWL 3
Bryan, C(ourtlandt) D(ixon) B(arnes)
1936- .... **CLC 29**
See also CA 73-76; CANR 13, 68; DLB
185; INT CANR-13
Bryan, Michael
See Moore, Brian
See also CCA 1
Bryan, William Jennings
1860-1925 .... **TCLC 99**
See also DLB 303
Bryant, William Cullen 1794-1878 . **NCLC 6,
46; PC 20**
See also AMWS 1; CDALB 1640-1865;
DA; DAB; DAC; DAM MST, POET;
DLB 3, 43, 59, 189, 250; EXPP; PAB;
RGAL 4; TUS
Bryusov, Valery Yakovlevich
1873-1924 .... **TCLC 10**
See also CA 107; 155; EWL 3; SFW 4

Buchan, John 1875-1940 .... **TCLC 41**
See also CA 108; 145; CMW 4; DAB;
DAM POP; DLB 34, 70, 156; HGG;
MSW; MTCW 2; RGEL 2; RHW; YABC
2
Buchanan, George 1506-1582 .... **LC 4**
See also DLB 132
Buchanan, Robert 1841-1901 .... **TCLC 107**
See also CA 179; DLB 18, 35
Buchheim, Lothar-Guenther 1918- .... **CLC 6**
See also CA 85-88
Buchner, (Karl) Georg
1813-1837 .... **NCLC 26, 146**
See also CDWLB 2; DLB 133; EW 6;
RGSF 2; RGWL 2, 3; TWA
Buchwald, Art 1925- .... **CLC 33**
See also AITN 1; CA 5-8R; CANR 21, 67,
107; MTCW 1, 2; SATA 10
Buchwald, Arthur
See Buchwald, Art
Buck, Pearl S(ydenstricker)
1892-1973 .... **CLC 7, 11, 18, 127**
See also AAYA 42; AITN 1; AMWS 2;
BPFB 1; CA 1-4R; 41-44R; CANR 1, 34;
CDALBS; CN 1; DA; DA3; DAB; DAC;
DAM MST, NOV; DLB 9, 102, 329; EWL
3; LAIT 3; MAL 5; MTCW 1, 2; MTFW
2005; RGAL 4; RHW; SATA 1, 25; TUS
Buckler, Ernest 1908-1984 .... **CLC 13**
See also CA 11-12; 114; CAP 1; CCA 1;
CN 1, 2, 3; DAC; DAM MST; DLB 68;
SATA 47
Buckley, Christopher 1952- .... **CLC 165**
See also CA 139; CANR 119
Buckley, Christopher Taylor
See Buckley, Christopher
Buckley, Vincent (Thomas)
1925-1988 .... **CLC 57**
See also CA 101; CP 1, 2, 3, 4; DLB 289
Buckley, William F., Jr. 1925- ..... **CLC 7, 18,
37**
See also AITN 1; BPFB 1; CA 1-4R; CANR
1, 24, 53, 93, 133; CMW 4; CPW; DA3;
DAM POP; DLB 137; DLBY 1980; INT
CANR-24; MTCW 1, 2; MTFW 2005;
TUS
Buechner, Frederick 1926- ..... **CLC 2, 4, 6, 9**
See also AMWS 12; BPFB 1; CA 13-16R;
CANR 11, 39, 64, 114, 138; CN 1, 2, 3,
4, 5, 6, 7; DAM NOV; DLBY 1980; INT
CANR-11; MAL 5; MTCW 1, 2; MTFW
2005; TCLE 1:1
Buell, John (Edward) 1927- .... **CLC 10**
See also CA 1-4R; CANR 71; DLB 53
Buero Vallejo, Antonio 1916-2000 ... **CLC 15,
46, 139, 226; DC 18**
See also CA 106; 189; CANR 24, 49, 75;
CWW 2; DFS 11; EWL 3; HW 1; MTCW
1, 2
Bufalino, Gesualdo 1920-1996 .... **CLC 74**
See also CA 209; CWW 2; DLB 196
Bugayev, Boris Nikolayevich
1880-1934 .... **PC 11; TCLC 7**
See Bely, Andrey; Belyi, Andrei
See also CA 104; 165; MTCW 2; MTFW
2005
Bukowski, Charles 1920-1994 ... **CLC 2, 5, 9,
41, 82, 108; PC 18; SSC 45**
See also CA 17-20R; 144; CANR 40, 62,
105; CN 4, 5; CP 1, 2, 3, 4, 5; CPW; DA3;
DAM NOV, POET; DLB 5, 130, 169;
EWL 3; MAL 5; MTCW 1, 2; MTFW
2005
Bulgakov, Mikhail 1891-1940 .... **SSC 18;
TCLC 2, 16, 159**
See also BPFB 1; CA 105; 152; DAM
DRAM, NOV; DLB 272; EWL 3; MTCW
2; MTFW 2005; NFS 8; RGSF 2; RGWL
2, 3; SFW 4; TWA

Bulgakov, Mikhail Afanasevich
See Bulgakov, Mikhail
Bulgya, Alexander Alexandrovich
1901-1956 .... **TCLC 53**
See Fadeev, Aleksandr Aleksandrovich;
Fadeev, Alexandr Alexandrovich; Fadeyev,
Alexander
See also CA 117; 181
Bullins, Ed 1935- ... **BLC 1; CLC 1, 5, 7; DC
6**
See also BW 2, 3; CA 49-52; CAAS 16;
CAD; CANR 24, 46, 73, 134; CD 5, 6;
DAM, MULT; DLB 7, 38, 249;
EWL 3; MAL 5; MTCW 1, 2; MTFW
2005; RGAL 4
Bulosan, Carlos 1911-1956 .... **AAL**
See also CA 216; DLB 312; RGAL 4
**Bulwer-Lytton, Edward (George Earle
Lytton)** 1803-1873 .... **NCLC 1, 45**
See also DLB 21; RGEL 2; SFW 4; SUFW
1; TEA
Bunin, Ivan
See Bunin, Ivan Alexeyevich
Bunin, Ivan Alekseevich
See Bunin, Ivan Alexeyevich
Bunin, Ivan Alexeyevich 1870-1953 ... **SSC 5;
TCLC 6**
See also CA 104; DLB 317, 329; EWL 3;
RGSF 2; RGWL 2, 3; TWA
Bunting, Basil 1900-1985 ...... **CLC 10, 39, 47**
See also BRWS 7; CA 53-56; 115; CANR
7; CP 1, 2, 3, 4; DAM POET; DLB 20;
EWL 3; RGEL 2
Bunuel, Luis 1900-1983 ... **CLC 16, 80; HLC
1**
See also CA 101; 110; CANR 32, 77; DAM
MULT; HW 1
Bunyan, John 1628-1688 .. **LC 4, 69; WLC 1**
See also BRW 2; BYA 5; CDBLB 1660-
1789; DA; DAB; DAC; DAM MST; DLB
39; RGEL 2; TEA; WCH; WLIT 3
Buravsky, Alexandr .... **CLC 59**
Burckhardt, Jacob (Christoph)
1818-1897 .... **NCLC 49**
See also EW 6
Burford, Eleanor
See Hibbert, Eleanor Alice Burford
Burgess, Anthony . **CLC 1, 2, 4, 5, 8, 10, 13,
15, 22, 40, 62, 81, 94**
See Wilson, John (Anthony) Burgess
See also AAYA 25; AITN 1; BRWS 1; CD-
BLB 1960 to Present; CN 1, 2, 3, 4, 5;
DAB; DLB 14, 194, 261; DLBY 1998;
EWL 3; RGEL 2; RHW; SFW 4; YAW
Burke, Edmund 1729(?)-1797 .... **LC 7, 36;
WLC 1**
See also BRW 3; DA; DA3; DAB; DAC;
DAM MST; DLB 104, 252; RGEL 2;
TEA
Burke, Kenneth (Duva) 1897-1993 ... **CLC 2,
24**
See also AMW; CA 5-8R; 143; CANR 39,
74, 136; CN 1, 2; CP 1, 2, 3, 4, 5; DLB
45, 63; EWL 3; MAL 5; MTCW 1, 2;
MTFW 2005; RGAL 4
Burke, Leda
See Garnett, David
Burke, Ralph
See Silverberg, Robert
Burke, Thomas 1886-1945 .... **TCLC 63**
See also CA 113; 155; CMW 4; DLB 197
Burney, Fanny 1752-1840 .... **NCLC 12, 54,
107**
See also BRWS 3; DLB 39; FL 1:2; NFS
16; RGEL 2; TEA
Burney, Frances
See Burney, Fanny

Callimachus c. 305B.C.-c.
240B.C. .... **CMLC 18**
See also AW 1; DLB 176; RGWL 2, 3
Calvin, Jean
See Calvin, John
See also DLB 327; GFL Beginnings to 1789
Calvin, John 1509-1564 .... **LC 37**
See Calvin, Jean
Calvino, Italo 1923-1985 .... **CLC 5, 8, 11, 22,
33, 39, 73; SSC 3, 48; TCLC 183**
See also AAYA 58; CA 85-88; 116; CANR
23, 61, 132; DAM NOV; DLB 196; EW
13; EWL 3; MTCW 1, 2; MTFW 2005;
RGHL; RGSF 2; RGWL 2, 3; SFW 4;
SSFS 12; WLIT 7
Camara Laye
See Laye, Camara
See also EWL 3
Camden, William 1551-1623 .... **LC 77**
See also DLB 172
Cameron, Carey 1952- .... **CLC 59**
See also CA 135
Cameron, Peter 1959- .... **CLC 44**
See also AMWS 12; CA 125; CANR 50,
117; DLB 234; GLL 2
Camoens, Luis Vaz de 1524(?)-1580
See Camoes, Luis de
See also EW 2
Camoes, Luis de 1524(?)-1580 . **HLCS 1; LC
62; PC 31**
See Camoens, Luis Vaz de
See also DLB 287; RGWL 2, 3
Campana, Dino 1885-1932 .... **TCLC 20**
See also CA 117; 246; DLB 114; EWL 3
Campanella, Tommaso 1568-1639 .... **LC 32**
See also RGWL 2, 3
Campbell, John W(ood, Jr.)
1910-1971 .... **CLC 32**
See also CA 21-22; 29-32R; CANR 34;
CAP 2; DLB 8; MTCW 1; SCFW 1, 2;
SFW 4
Campbell, Joseph 1904-1987 .... **CLC 69;
TCLC 140**
See also AAYA 3, 66; BEST 89:2; CA 1-4R;
124; CANR 3, 28, 61, 107; DA3; MTCW
1, 2
Campbell, Maria 1940- .... **CLC 85; NNAL**
See also CA 102; CANR 54; CCA 1; DAC
Campbell, (John) Ramsey 1946- ..... **CLC 42;
SSC 19**
See also AAYA 51; CA 57-60; 228; CAAE
228; CANR 7, 102; DLB 261; HGG; INT
CANR-7; SUFW 1, 2
Campbell, (Ignatius) Roy (Dunnachie)
1901-1957 .... **TCLC 5**
See also AFW; CA 104; 155; DLB 20, 225;
EWL 3; MTCW 2; RGEL 2
Campbell, Thomas 1777-1844 .... **NCLC 19**
See also DLB 93, 144; RGEL 2
Campbell, Wilfred .... **TCLC 9**
See Campbell, William
Campbell, William 1858(?)-1918
See Campbell, Wilfred
See also CA 106; DLB 92
Campbell, William Edward March
1893-1954
See March, William
See also CA 108
Campion, Jane 1954- .... **CLC 95, 229**
See also AAYA 33; CA 138; CANR 87
Campion, Thomas 1567-1620 .... **LC 78**
See also CDBLB Before 1660; DAM POET;
DLB 58, 172; RGEL 2
Camus, Albert 1913-1960 ...... **CLC 1, 2, 4, 9,
11, 14, 32, 63, 69, 124; DC 2; SSC 9,
76; WLC 1**
See also AAYA 36; AFW; BPFB 1; CA 89-
92; CANR 131; DA; DA3; DAB; DAC;
DAM DRAM, MST, NOV; DLB 72, 321,

329; EW 13; EWL 3; EXPN; EXPS; GFL
1789 to the Present; LATS 1:2; LMFS 2;
MTCW 1, 2; MTFW 2005; NFS 6, 16;
RGHL; RGSF 2; RGWL 2, 3; SSFS 4;
TWA
Canby, Vincent 1924-2000 .... **CLC 13**
See also CA 81-84; 191
Cancale
See Desnos, Robert
Canetti, Elias 1905-1994 .. **CLC 3, 14, 25, 75,
86; TCLC 157**
See also CA 21-24R; 146; CANR 23, 61,
79; CDWLB 2; CWW 2; DA3; DLB 85,
124, 329; EW 12; EWL 3; MTCW 1, 2;
MTFW 2005; RGWL 2, 3; TWA
Canfield, Dorothea F.
See Fisher, Dorothy (Frances) Canfield
Canfield, Dorothea Frances
See Fisher, Dorothy (Frances) Canfield
Canfield, Dorothy
See Fisher, Dorothy (Frances) Canfield
Canin, Ethan 1960- .... **CLC 55; SSC 70**
See also CA 131; 135; MAL 5
Cankar, Ivan 1876-1918 .... **TCLC 105**
See also CDWLB 4; DLB 147; EWL 3
Cannon, Curt
See Hunter, Evan
Cao, Lan 1961- .... **CLC 109**
See also CA 165
Cape, Judith
See Page, P(atricia) K(athleen)
See also CCA 1
Capek, Karel 1890-1938 .... **DC 1; SSC 36;
TCLC 6, 37; WLC 1**
See also CA 104; 140; CDWLB 4; DA;
DA3; DAB; DAC; DAM DRAM, MST,
NOV; DFS 7, 11; DLB 215; EW 10; EWL
3; MTCW 2; MTFW 2005; RGSF 2;
RGWL 2, 3; SCFW 1, 2; SFW 4
Capella, Martianus fl. 4th cent. - .. **CMLC 84**
Capote, Truman 1924-1984 . **CLC 1, 3, 8, 13,
19, 34, 38, 58; SSC 2, 47, 93; TCLC
164; WLC 1**
See also AAYA 61; AMWS 3; BPFB 1; CA
5-8R; 113; CANR 18, 62; CDALB 1941-
1968; CN 1, 2, 3; CPW; DA; DA3; DAB;
DAC; DAM MST, NOV, POP; DLB 2,
185, 227; DLBY 1980, 1984; EWL 3;
EXPS; GLL 1; LAIT 3; MAL 5; MTCW
1, 2; MTFW 2005; NCFS 2; RGAL 4;
RGSF 2; SATA 91; SSFS 2; TUS
Capra, Frank 1897-1991 .... **CLC 16**
See also AAYA 52; CA 61-64; 135
Caputo, Philip 1941- .... **CLC 32**
See also AAYA 60; CA 73-76; CANR 40,
135; YAW
Caragiale, Ion Luca 1852-1912 ...... **TCLC 76**
See also CA 157
Card, Orson Scott 1951- .... **CLC 44, 47, 50**
See also AAYA 11, 42; BPFB 1; BYA 5, 8;
CA 102; CANR 27, 47, 73, 102, 106, 133;
CLR 116; CPW; DA3; DAM POP; FANT;
INT CANR-27; MTCW 1, 2; MTFW
2005; NFS 5; SATA 83, 127; SCFW 2;
SFW 4; SUFW 2; YAW
Cardenal, Ernesto 1925- .... **CLC 31, 161;
HLC 1; PC 22**
See also CA 49-52; CANR 2, 32, 66, 138;
CWW 2; DAM MULT, POET; DLB 290;
EWL 3; HW 1, 2; LAWS 1; MTCW 1, 2;
MTFW 2005; RGWL 2, 3
Cardinal, Marie 1929-2001 .... **CLC 189**
See also CA 177; CWW 2; DLB 83; FW
Cardozo, Benjamin N(athan)
1870-1938 .... **TCLC 65**
See also CA 117; 164

Carducci, Giosue (Alessandro Giuseppe)
1835-1907 .... **PC 46; TCLC 32**
See also CA 163; DLB 329; EW 7; RGWL
2, 3
Carew, Thomas 1595(?)-1640 . **LC 13; PC 29**
See also BRW 2; DLB 126; PAB; RGEL 2
Carey, Ernestine Gilbreth
1908-2006 .... **CLC 17**
See also CA 5-8R; CANR 71; SATA 2
Carey, Peter 1943- ...... **CLC 40, 55, 96, 183**
See also BRWS 12; CA 123; 127; CANR
53, 76, 117, 157; CN 4, 5, 6, 7; DLB 289,
326; EWL 3; INT CA-127; MTCW 1, 2;
MTFW 2005; RGSF 2; SATA 94
Carleton, William 1794-1869 .... **NCLC 3**
See also DLB 159; RGEL 2; RGSF 2
Carlisle, Henry (Coffin) 1926- .... **CLC 33**
See also CA 13-16R; CANR 15, 85
Carlsen, Chris
See Holdstock, Robert P.
Carlson, Ron 1947- .... **CLC 54**
See also CA 105, 189; CAAE 189; CANR
27, 155; DLB 244
Carlson, Ronald F.
See Carlson, Ron
Carlyle, Thomas 1795 1881 ..... **NCLC 22, 70**
See also BRW 4; CDBLB 1789-1832; DA;
DAB; DAC; DAM MST; DLB 55, 144,
254; RGEL 2; TEA
Carman, (William) Bliss 1861-1929 ... **PC 34;
TCLC 7**
See also CA 104; 152; DAC; DLB 92;
RGEL 2
Carnegie, Dale 1888-1955 .... **TCLC 53**
See also CA 218
Carossa, Hans 1878-1956 .... **TCLC 48**
See also CA 170; DLB 66; EWL 3
Carpenter, Don(ald Richard)
1931-1995 .... **CLC 41**
See also CA 45-48; 149; CANR 1, 71
Carpenter, Edward 1844-1929 .... **TCLC 88**
See also CA 163; GLL 1
Carpenter, John (Howard) 1948- ..... **CLC 161**
See also AAYA 2; CA 134; SATA 58
Carpenter, Johnny
See Carpenter, John (Howard)
Carpentier (y Valmont), Alejo
1904-1980 . **CLC 8, 11, 38, 110; HLC 1;
SSC 35**
See also CA 65-68; 97-100; CANR 11, 70;
CDWLB 3; DAM MULT; DLB 113; EWL
3; HW 1, 2; LAW; LMFS 2; RGSF 2;
RGWL 2, 3; WLIT 1
Carr, Caleb 1955- .... **CLC 86**
See also CA 147; CANR 73, 134; DA3
Carr, Emily 1871-1945 .... **TCLC 32**
See also CA 159; DLB 68; FW; GLL 2
Carr, John Dickson 1906-1977 .... **CLC 3**
See Fairbairn, Roger
See also CA 49-52; 69-72; CANR 3, 33,
60; CMW 4; DLB 306; MSW; MTCW 1,
2
Carr, Philippa
See Hibbert, Eleanor Alice Burford
Carr, Virginia Spencer 1929- .... **CLC 34**
See also CA 61-64; DLB 111
Carrere, Emmanuel 1957- .... **CLC 89**
See also CA 200
Carrier, Roch 1937- .... **CLC 13, 78**
See also CA 130; CANR 61, 152; CCA 1;
DAC; DAM MST; DLB 53; SATA 105,
166
Carroll, James Dennis
See Carroll, Jim
Carroll, James P. 1943(?)- .... **CLC 38**
See also CA 81-84; CANR 73, 139; MTCW
2; MTFW 2005

Carroll, Jim 1951- .... **CLC 35, 143**
See also AAYA 17; CA 45-48; CANR 42,
115; NCFS 5

Carroll, Lewis ...... **NCLC 2, 53, 139; PC 18,
74; WLC 1**
See Dodgson, Charles L(utwidge)
See also AAYA 39; BRW 5; BYA 5, 13; CD-
BLB 1832-1890; CLR 2, 18, 108; DLB
18, 163, 178; DLBY 1998; EXPN; EXPP;
FANT; JRDA; LAIT 1; NFS 7; PFS 11;
RGEL 2; SUFW 1; TEA; WCH

Carroll, Paul Vincent 1900-1968 ...... **CLC 10**
See also CA 9-12R; 25-28R; DLB 10; EWL
3; RGEL 2

Carruth, Hayden 1921- ..... **CLC 4, 7, 10, 18,
84; PC 10**
See also AMWS 16; CA 9-12R; CANR 4,
38, 59, 110; CP 1, 2, 3, 4, 5, 6, 7; DLB 5,
165; INT CANR-4; MTCW 1, 2; MTFW
2005; SATA 47

Carson, Anne 1950- .... **CLC 185; PC 64**
See also AMWS 12; CA 203; CP 7; DLB
193; PFS 18; TCLE 1:1

Carson, Ciaran 1948- .... **CLC 201**
See also CA 112; 153; CANR 113; CP 6, 7

Carson, Rachel
See Carson, Rachel Louise
See also AAYA 49; DLB 275

Carson, Rachel Louise 1907-1964 .... **CLC 71**
See Carson, Rachel
See also AMWS 9; ANW; CA 77-80; CANR
35; DA3; DAM POP; FW; LAIT 4; MAL
5; MTCW 1, 2; MTFW 2005; NCFS 1;
SATA 23

Carter, Angela (Olive) 1940-1992 ...... **CLC 5,
41, 76; SSC 13, 85; TCLC 139**
See also BRWS 3; CA 53-56; 136; CANR
12, 36, 61, 106; CN 3, 4, 5; DA3; DLB
14, 207, 261, 319; EXPS; FANT; FW; GL
2; MTCW 1, 2; MTFW 2005; RGSF 2;
SATA 66; SATA-Obit 70; SFW 4; SSFS
4, 12; SUFW 2; WLIT 4

Carter, Nick
See Smith, Martin Cruz

Carver, Raymond 1938-1988 ..... **CLC 22, 36,
53, 55, 126; PC 54; SSC 8, 51**
See also AAYA 44; AMWS 3; BPFB 1; CA
33-36R; 126; CANR 17, 34, 61, 103; CN
4; CPW; DA3; DAM NOV; DLB 130;
DLBY 1984, 1988; EWL 3; MAL 5;
MTCW 1, 2; MTFW 2005; PFS 17;
RGAL 4; RGSF 2; SSFS 3, 6, 12, 13, 23;
TCLE 1:1; TCWW 2; TUS

Cary, Elizabeth, Lady Falkland
1585-1639 .... **LC 30**

Cary, (Arthur) Joyce (Lunel)
1888-1957 .... **TCLC 1, 29**
See also BRW 7; CA 104; 164; CDBLB
1914-1945; DLB 15, 100; EWL 3; MTCW
2; RGEL 2; TEA

Casal, Julian del 1863-1893 .... **NCLC 131**
See also DLB 283; LAW

Casanova, Giacomo
See Casanova de Seingalt, Giovanni Jacopo
See also WLIT 7

Casanova de Seingalt, Giovanni Jacopo
1725-1798 .... **LC 13**
See Casanova, Giacomo

Casares, Adolfo Bioy
See Bioy Casares, Adolfo
See also RGSF 2

Casas, Bartolome de las 1474-1566
See Las Casas, Bartolome de
See also WLIT 1

Casely-Hayford, J(oseph) E(phraim)
1866-1903 .... **BLC 1; TCLC 24**
See also BW 2; CA 123; 152; DAM MULT

Casey, John (Dudley) 1939- .... **CLC 59**
See also BEST 90:2; CA 69-72; CANR 23,
100

Casey, Michael 1947- .... **CLC 2**
See also CA 65-68; CANR 109; CP 2, 3;
DLB 5

Casey, Patrick
See Thurman, Wallace (Henry)

Casey, Warren (Peter) 1935-1988 .... **CLC 12**
See also CA 101; 127; INT CA-101

Casona, Alejandro .... **CLC 49**
See Alvarez, Alejandro Rodriguez
See also EWL 3

Cassavetes, John 1929-1989 .... **CLC 20**
See also CA 85-88; 127; CANR 82

Cassian, Nina 1924- .... **PC 17**
See also CWP; CWW 2

Cassill, R(onald) V(erlin)
1919-2002 .... **CLC 4, 23**
See also CA 9-12R; 208; CAAS 1; CANR
7, 45; CN 1, 2, 3, 4, 5, 6, 7; DLB 6, 218;
DLBY 2002

Cassiodorus, Flavius Magnus c. 490(?)-c.
583(?) .... **CMLC 43**

Cassirer, Ernst 1874-1945 .... **TCLC 61**
See also CA 157

Cassity, (Allen) Turner 1929 .... **CLC 6, 42**
See also CA 17-20R; 223; CAAE 223;
CAAS 8; CANR 11; CSW; DLB 105

Castaneda, Carlos (Cesar Aranha)
1931(?)-1998 .... **CLC 12, 119**
See also CA 25-28R; CANR 32, 66, 105;
DNFS 1; HW 1; MTCW 1

Castedo, Elena 1937- .... **CLC 65**
See also CA 132

Castedo-Ellerman, Elena
See Castedo, Elena

Castellanos, Rosario 1925-1974 .... **CLC 66;
HLC 1; SSC 39, 68**
See also CA 131; 53-56; CANR 58; CD-
WLB 3; DAM MULT; DLB 113, 290;
EWL 3; FW; HW 1; LAW; MTCW 2;
MTFW 2005; RGSF 2; RGWL 2, 3

Castelvetro, Lodovico 1505-1571 .... **LC 12**

Castiglione, Baldassare 1478-1529 ...... **LC 12**
See Castiglione, Baldesar
See also LMFS 1; RGWL 2, 3

Castiglione, Baldesar
See Castiglione, Baldassare
See also EW 2; WLIT 7

Castillo, Ana 1953- .... **CLC 151**
See also AAYA 42; CA 131; CANR 51, 86,
128; CWP; DLB 122, 227; DNFS 2; FW;
HW 1; LLW; PFS 21

Castle, Robert
See Hamilton, Edmond

Castro (Ruz), Fidel 1926(?)- .... **HLC 1**
See also CA 110; 129; CANR 81; DAM
MULT; HW 2

Castro, Guillen de 1569-1631 .... **LC 19**

Castro, Rosalia de 1837-1885 ... **NCLC 3, 78;
PC 41**
See also DAM MULT

Cather, Willa (Sibert) 1873-1947 . **SSC 2, 50;
TCLC 1, 11, 31, 99, 132, 152; WLC 1**
See also AAYA 24; AMW; AMWC 1;
AMWR 1; BPFB 1; CA 104; 128; CDALB
1865-1917; CLR 98; DA; DA3; DAB;
DAC; DAM MST, NOV; DLB 9, 54, 78,
256; DLBD 1; EWL 3; EXPN; EXPS; FL
1:5; LAIT 3; LATS 1:1; MAL 5; MBL;
MTCW 1, 2; MTFW 2005; NFS 2, 19;
RGAL 4; RGSF 2; RHW; SATA 30; SSFS
2, 7, 16; TCWW 1, 2; TUS

Catherine II
See Catherine the Great
See also DLB 150

Catherine the Great 1729-1796 .... **LC 69**
See Catherine II

Cato, Marcus Porcius
234B.C.-149B.C. .... **CMLC 21**
See Cato the Elder

Cato, Marcus Porcius, the Elder
See Cato, Marcus Porcius

Cato the Elder
See Cato, Marcus Porcius
See also DLB 211

Catton, (Charles) Bruce 1899-1978 . **CLC 35**
See also AITN 1; CA 5-8R; 81-84; CANR
7, 74; DLB 17; MTCW 2; MTFW 2005;
SATA 2; SATA-Obit 24

Catullus c. 84B.C.-54B.C. .... **CMLC 18**
See also AW 2; CDWLB 1; DLB 211;
RGWL 2, 3; WLIT 8

Cauldwell, Frank
See King, Francis (Henry)

Caunitz, William J. 1933-1996 .... **CLC 34**
See also BEST 89:3; CA 125; 130; 152;
CANR 73; INT CA-130

Causley, Charles (Stanley)
1917-2003 .... **CLC 7**
See also CA 9-12R; 223; CANR 5, 35, 94;
CLR 30; CP 1, 2, 3, 4, 5; CWRI 5; DLB
27; MTCW 1; SATA 3, 66; SATA-Obit
149

Caute, (John) David 1936- .... **CLC 29**
See also CA 1-4R; CAAS 4; CANR 1, 33,
64, 120; CBD; CD 5, 6; CN 1, 2, 3, 4, 5,
6, 7; DAM NOV; DLB 14, 231

Cavafy, C(onstantine) P(eter) .... **PC 36;
TCLC 2, 7**
See Kavafis, Konstantinos Petrou
See also CA 148; DA3; DAM POET; EW
8; EWL 3; MTCW 2; PFS 19; RGWL 2,
3; WP

Cavalcanti, Guido c. 1250-c.
1300 .... **CMLC 54**
See also RGWL 2, 3; WLIT 7

Cavallo, Evelyn
See Spark, Muriel

Cavanna, Betty .... **CLC 12**
See Harrison, Elizabeth (Allen) Cavanna
See also JRDA; MAICYA 1; SAAS 4;
SATA 1, 30

Cavendish, Margaret Lucas
1623-1673 .... **LC 30, 132**
See also DLB 131, 252, 281; RGEL 2

Caxton, William 1421(?)-1491(?) .... **LC 17**
See also DLB 170

Cayer, D. M.
See Duffy, Maureen (Patricia)

Cayrol, Jean 1911-2005 .... **CLC 11**
See also CA 89-92; 236; DLB 83; EWL 3

Cela (y Trulock), Camilo Jose
See Cela, Camilo Jose
See also CWW 2

Cela, Camilo Jose 1916-2002 .... **CLC 4, 13,
59, 122; HLC 1; SSC 71**
See Cela (y Trulock), Camilo Jose
See also BEST 90:2; CA 21-24R; 206;
CAAS 10; CANR 21, 32, 76, 139; DAM
MULT; DLB 322; DLBY 1989; EW 13;
EWL 3; HW 1; MTCW 1, 2; MTFW
2005; RGSF 2; RGWL 2, 3

Celan, Paul .... **CLC 10, 19, 53, 82; PC 10**
See Antschel, Paul
See also CDWLB 2; DLB 69; EWL 3;
RGHL; RGWL 2, 3

Celine, Louis-Ferdinand .. **CLC 1, 3, 4, 7, 9,
15, 47, 124**
See Destouches, Louis-Ferdinand
See also DLB 72; EW 11; EWL 3; GFL
1789 to the Present; RGWL 2, 3

Cellini, Benvenuto 1500-1571 .... **LC 7**
See also WLIT 7

Cendrars, Blaise .... **CLC 18, 106**
See Sauser-Hall, Frederic
See also DLB 258; EWL 3; GFL 1789 to
the Present; RGWL 2, 3; WP

Centlivre, Susanna 1669(?)-1723 .... **DC 25; LC 65**
See also DLB 84; RGEL 2

Cernuda (y Bidon), Luis
1902-1963 .... **CLC 54; PC 62**
See also CA 131; 89-92; DAM POET; DLB 134; EWL 3; GLL 1; HW 1; RGWL 2, 3

Cervantes, Lorna Dee 1954- ..... **HLCS 1; PC 35**
See also CA 131; CANR 80; CP 7; CWP; DLB 82; EXPP; HW 1; LLW

Cervantes (Saavedra), Miguel de
1547-1616 .... **HLCS; LC 6, 23, 93; SSC 12; WLC 1**
See also AAYA 56; BYA 1, 14; DA; DAB; DAC; DAM MST, NOV; EW 2; LAIT 1; LATS 1:1; LMFS 1; NFS 8; RGSF 2; RGWL 2, 3; TWA

Cesaire, Aime 1913- ..... **BLC 1; CLC 19, 32, 112; DC 22; PC 25**
See also BW 2, 3; CA 65-68; CANR 24, 43, 81; CWW 2; DA3; DAM MULT, POET; DLB 321; EWL 3; GFL 1789 to the Present; MTCW 1, 2; MTFW 2005; WP

Chabon, Michael 1963- ... **CLC 55, 149; SSC 59**
See also AAYA 45; AMWS 11; CA 139; CANR 57, 96, 127, 138; DLB 278; MAL 5; MTFW 2005; SATA 145

Chabrol, Claude 1930- .... **CLC 16**
See also CA 110

Chairil Anwar
See Anwar, Chairil
See also EWL 3

Challans, Mary 1905-1983
See Renault, Mary
See also CA 81-84; 111; CANR 74; DA3; MTCW 2; MTFW 2005; SATA 23; SATA-Obit 36; TEA

Challis, George
See Faust, Frederick (Schiller)

Chambers, Aidan 1934- .... **CLC 35**
See also AAYA 27; CA 25-28R; CANR 12, 31, 58, 116; JRDA; MAICYA 1, 2; SAAS 12; SATA 1, 69, 108, 171; WYA; YAW

Chambers, James 1948-
See Cliff, Jimmy
See also CA 124

Chambers, Jessie
See Lawrence, D(avid) H(erbert Richards)
See also GLL 1

Chambers, Robert W(illiam)
1865-1933 .... **SSC 92; TCLC 41**
See also CA 165; DLB 202; HGG; SATA 107; SUFW 1

Chambers, (David) Whittaker
1901-1961 .... **TCLC 129**
See also CA 89-92; DLB 303

Chamisso, Adelbert von
1781-1838 .... **NCLC 82**
See also DLB 90; RGWL 2, 3; SUFW 1

Chance, James T.
See Carpenter, John (Howard)

Chance, John T.
See Carpenter, John (Howard)

Chandler, Raymond (Thornton)
1888-1959 .... **SSC 23; TCLC 1, 7, 179**
See also AAYA 25; AMWC 4; AMWS 4; BPFB 1; CA 104; 129; CANR 60, 107; CDALB 1929-1941; CMW 4; DA3; DLB 226, 253; DLBD 6; EWL 3; MAL 5; MSW; MTCW 1, 2; MTFW 2005; NFS 17; RGAL 4; TUS

Chang, Diana 1934- .... **AAL**
See also CA 228; CWP; DLB 312; EXPP

Chang, Eileen 1920-1995 .... **AAL; SSC 28; TCLC 184**
See Chang Ai-Ling; Zhang Ailing
See also CA 166

Chang, Jung 1952- .... **CLC 71**
See also CA 142

Chang Ai-Ling
See Chang, Eileen
See also EWL 3

Channing, William Ellery
1780-1842 .... **NCLC 17**
See also DLB 1, 59, 235; RGAL 4

Chao, Patricia 1955- .... **CLC 119**
See also CA 163; CANR 155

Chaplin, Charles Spencer
1889-1977 .... **CLC 16**
See Chaplin, Charlie
See also CA 81-84; 73-76

Chaplin, Charlie
See Chaplin, Charles Spencer
See also AAYA 61; DLB 44

Chapman, George 1559(?)-1634 . **DC 19; LC 22, 116**
See also BRW 1; DAM DRAM; DLB 62, 121; LMFS 1; RGEL 2

Chapman, Graham 1941-1989 .... **CLC 21**
See Monty Python
See also CA 116; 129; CANR 35, 95

Chapman, John Jay 1862-1933 .... **TCLC 7**
See also AMWS 14; CA 104; 191

Chapman, Lee
See Bradley, Marion Zimmer
See also GLL 1

Chapman, Walker
See Silverberg, Robert

Chappell, Fred (Davis) 1936 .... **CLC 40, 78, 162**
See also CA 5-8R, 198; CAAE 198; CAAS 4; CANR 8, 33, 67, 110; CN 6; CP 6, 7; CSW; DLB 6, 105; HGG

Char, Rene(-Emile) 1907-1988 .... **CLC 9, 11, 14, 55; PC 56**
See also CA 13-16R; 124; CANR 32; DAM POET; DLB 258; EWL 3; GFL 1789 to the Present; MTCW 1, 2; RGWL 2, 3

Charby, Jay
See Ellison, Harlan

Chardin, Pierre Teilhard de
See Teilhard de Chardin, (Marie Joseph) Pierre

Chariton fl. 1st cent. (?)- .... **CMLC 49**

Charlemagne 742-814 .... **CMLC 37**

Charles I 1600-1649 .... **LC 13**

Charriere, Isabelle de 1740-1805 .. **NCLC 66**
See also DLB 313

Chartier, Alain c. 1392-1430 .... **LC 94**
See also DLB 208

Chartier, Emile-Auguste
See Alain

Charyn, Jerome 1937- .... **CLC 5, 8, 18**
See also CA 5-8R; CAAS 1; CANR 7, 61, 101; CMW 4; CN 1, 2, 3, 4, 5, 6, 7; DLBY 1983; MTCW 1

Chase, Adam
See Marlowe, Stephen

Chase, Mary (Coyle) 1907-1981 .... **DC 1**
See also CA 77-80; 105; CAD; CWD; DFS 11; DLB 228; SATA 17; SATA-Obit 29

Chase, Mary Ellen 1887-1973 .... **CLC 2; TCLC 124**
See also CA 13-16; 41-44R; CAP 1; SATA 10

Chase, Nicholas
See Hyde, Anthony
See also CCA 1

Chateaubriand, Francois Rene de
1768-1848 .... **NCLC 3, 134**
See also DLB 119; EW 5; GFL 1789 to the Present; RGWL 2, 3; TWA

Chatelet, Gabrielle-Emilie Du
See du Chatelet, Emilie
See also DLB 313

Chatterje, Sarat Chandra 1876-1936(?)
See Chatterji, Saratchandra
See also CA 109

Chatterji, Bankim Chandra
1838-1894 .... **NCLC 19**

Chatterji, Saratchandra .... **TCLC 13**
See Chatterje, Sarat Chandra
See also CA 186; EWL 3

Chatterton, Thomas 1752-1770 .... **LC 3, 54**
See also DAM POET; DLB 109; RGEL 2

Chatwin, (Charles) Bruce
1940-1989 .... **CLC 28, 57, 59**
See also AAYA 4; BEST 90:1; BRWS 4; CA 85-88; 127; CPW; DAM POP; DLB 194, 204; EWL 3; MTFW 2005

Chaucer, Daniel
See Ford, Ford Madox
See also RHW

Chaucer, Geoffrey 1340(?)-1400 .. **LC 17, 56; PC 19, 58; WLCS**
See also BRW 1; BRWC 1; BRWR 2; CD-BLB Before 1660; DA; DA3; DAB; DAC; DAM MST, POET; DLB 146; LAIT 1; PAB; PFS 14; RGEL 2; TEA; WLIT 3; WP

Chavez, Denise 1948- .... **HLC 1**
See also CA 131; CANR 56, 81, 137; DAM MULT; DLB 122; FW; HW 1; LLW; MAL 5; MTCW 2; MTFW 2005

Chaviaras, Strates 1935-
See Haviaras, Stratis
See also CA 105

Chayefsky, Paddy .... **CLC 23**
See Chayefsky, Sidney
See also CAD; DLB 7, 44; DLBY 1981; RGAL 4

Chayefsky, Sidney 1923-1981
See Chayefsky, Paddy
See also CA 9-12R; 104; CANR 18; DAM DRAM

Chedid, Andree 1920- .... **CLC 47**
See also CA 145; CANR 95; EWL 3

Cheever, John 1912-1982 ..... **CLC 3, 7, 8, 11, 15, 25, 64; SSC 1, 38, 57; WLC 2**
See also AAYA 65; AMWS 1; BPFB 1; CA 5-8R; 106; CABS 1; CANR 5, 27, 76; CDALB 1941-1968; CN 1, 2, 3; CPW; DA; DA3; DAB; DAC; DAM MST, NOV, POP; DLB 2, 102, 227; DLBY 1980, 1982; EWL 3; EXPS; INT CANR-5; MAL 5; MTCW 1, 2; MTFW 2005; RGAL 4; RGSF 2; SSFS 2, 14; TUS

Cheever, Susan 1943- .... **CLC 18, 48**
See also CA 103; CANR 27, 51, 92, 157; DLBY 1982; INT CANR-27

Chekhonte, Antosha
See Chekhov, Anton (Pavlovich)

Chekhov, Anton (Pavlovich)
1860-1904 .... **DC 9; SSC 2, 28, 41, 51, 85; TCLC 3, 10, 31, 55, 96, 163; WLC 2**
See also AAYA 68; BYA 14; CA 104; 124; DA; DA3; DAB; DAC; DAM DRAM, MST; DFS 1, 5, 10, 12; DLB 277; EW 7; EWL 3; EXPS; LAIT 3; LATS 1:1; RGSF 2; RGWL 2, 3; SATA 90; SSFS 5, 13, 14; TWA

Cheney, Lynne V. 1941- .... **CLC 70**
See also CA 89-92; CANR 58, 117; SATA 152

Chernyshevsky, Nikolai Gavrilovich
See Chernyshevsky, Nikolay Gavrilovich
See also DLB 238

Chernyshevsky, Nikolay Gavrilovich
1828-1889 .... **NCLC 1**
See Chernyshevsky, Nikolai Gavrilovich

Cherry, Carolyn Janice .... **CLC 35**
See Cherryh, C.J.
See also AAYA 24; BPFB 1; DLBY 1980; FANT; SATA 93; SCFW 2; SFW 4; YAW

Cherryh, C.J. 1942-
See Cherry, Carolyn Janice
See also CA 65-68; CANR 10, 147; SATA 172

Chesnutt, Charles W(addell)
1858-1932 .... **BLC 1; SSC 7, 54; TCLC 5, 39**
See also AFAW 1, 2; AMWS 14; BW 1, 3; CA 106; 125; CANR 76; DAM MULT; DLB 12, 50, 78; EWL 3; MAL 5; MTCW 1, 2; MTFW 2005; RGAL 4; RGSF 2; SSFS 11

Chester, Alfred 1929(?)-1971 .... **CLC 49**
See also CA 196; 33-36R; DLB 130; MAL 5

Chesterton, G(ilbert) K(eith)
1874-1936 . **PC 28; SSC 1, 46; TCLC 1, 6, 64**
See also AAYA 57; BRW 6; CA 104; 132; CANR 73, 131; CDBLB 1914-1945; CMW 4; DAM NOV, POET; DLB 10, 19, 34, 70, 98, 149, 178; EWL 3; FANT; MSW; MTCW 1, 2; MTFW 2005; RGEL 2; RGSF 2; SATA 27; SUFW 1

Chettle, Henry 1560-1607(?) .... **LC 112**
See also DLB 136; RGEL 2

Chiang, Pin-chin 1904-1986
See Ding Ling
See also CA 118

Chief Joseph 1840-1904 .... **NNAL**
See also CA 152; DA3; DAM MULT

Chief Seattle 1786(?)-1866 .... **NNAL**
See also DA3; DAM MULT

Ch'ien, Chung-shu 1910-1998 .... **CLC 22**
See Qian Zhongshu
See also CA 130; CANR 73; MTCW 1, 2

Chikamatsu Monzaemon 1653-1724 ... **LC 66**
See also RGWL 2, 3

Child, Francis James 1825-1896 . **NCLC 173**
See also DLB 1, 64, 235

Child, L. Maria
See Child, Lydia Maria

Child, Lydia Maria 1802-1880 .. **NCLC 6, 73**
See also DLB 1, 74, 243; RGAL 4; SATA 67

Child, Mrs.
See Child, Lydia Maria

Child, Philip 1898-1978 .... **CLC 19, 68**
See also CA 13-14; CAP 1; CP 1; DLB 68; RHW; SATA 47

Childers, (Robert) Erskine
1870-1922 .... **TCLC 65**
See also CA 113; 153; DLB 70

Childress, Alice 1920-1994 . **BLC 1; CLC 12, 15, 86, 96; DC 4; TCLC 116**
See also AAYA 8; BW 2, 3; BYA 2; CA 45-48; 146; CAD; CANR 3, 27, 50, 74; CLR 14; CWD; DA3; DAM DRAM, MULT, NOV; DFS 2, 8, 14; DLB 7, 38, 249; JRDA; LAIT 5; MAICYA 1, 2; MAICYAS 1; MAL 5; MTCW 1, 2; MTFW 2005; RGAL 4; SATA 7, 48, 81; TUS; WYA; YAW

Chin, Frank (Chew, Jr.) 1940- .... **AAL; CLC 135; DC 7**
See also CA 33-36R; CAD; CANR 71; CD 5, 6; DAM MULT; DLB 206, 312; LAIT 5; RGAL 4

Chin, Marilyn (Mei Ling) 1955- .... **PC 40**
See also CA 129; CANR 70, 113; CWP; DLB 312

Chislett, (Margaret) Anne 1943- ...... **CLC 34**
See also CA 151

Chitty, Thomas Willes 1926- .... **CLC 11**
See Hinde, Thomas
See also CA 5-8R; CN 7

Chivers, Thomas Holley
1809-1858 .... **NCLC 49**
See also DLB 3, 248; RGAL 4

Choi, Susan 1969- .... **CLC 119**
See also CA 223

Chomette, Rene Lucien 1898-1981
See Clair, Rene
See also CA 103

Chomsky, Avram Noam
See Chomsky, Noam

Chomsky, Noam 1928- .... **CLC 132**
See also CA 17-20R; CANR 28, 62, 110, 132; DA3; DLB 246; MTCW 1, 2; MTFW 2005

Chona, Maria 1845(?)-1936 .... **NNAL**
See also CA 144

Chopin, Kate .... **SSC 8, 68; TCLC 127; WLCS**
See Chopin, Katherine
See also AAYA 33; AMWR 2; AMWS 1; BYA 11, 15; CDALB 1865-1917; DA; DAB; DLB 12, 78; EXPN; EXPS; FL 1:3; FW; LAIT 3; MAL 5; MBL; NFS 3; RGAL 4; RGSF 2; SSFS 2, 13, 17; TUS

Chopin, Katherine 1851-1904
See Chopin, Kate
See also CA 104; 122; DA3; DAC; DAM MST, NOV

Chretien de Troyes c. 12th cent. - . **CMLC 10**
See also DLB 208; EW 1; RGWL 2, 3; TWA

Christie
See Ichikawa, Kon

Christie, Agatha (Mary Clarissa)
1890-1976 .. **CLC 1, 6, 8, 12, 39, 48, 110**
See also AAYA 9; AITN 1, 2; BPFB 1; BRWS 2; CA 17-20R; 61-64; CANR 10, 37, 108; CBD; CDBLB 1914-1945; CMW 4; CN 1, 2; CPW; CWD; DA3; DAB; DAC; DAM NOV; DFS 2; DLB 13, 77, 245; MSW; MTCW 1, 2; MTFW 2005; NFS 8; RGEL 2; RHW; SATA 36; TEA; YAW

Christie, Philippa .... **CLC 21**
See Pearce, Philippa
See also BYA 5; CANR 109; CLR 9; DLB 161; MAICYA 1; SATA 1, 67, 129

Christine de Pisan
See Christine de Pizan
See also FW

Christine de Pizan 1365(?)-1431(?) ...... **LC 9, 130; PC 68**
See Christine de Pisan; de Pizan, Christine
See also DLB 208; FL 1:1; RGWL 2, 3

Chuang Tzu c. 369B.C.-c.
286B.C. .... **CMLC 57**

Chubb, Elmer
See Masters, Edgar Lee

Chulkov, Mikhail Dmitrievich
1743-1792 .... **LC 2**
See also DLB 150

Churchill, Caryl 1938- .... **CLC 31, 55, 157; DC 5**
See Churchill, Chick
See also BRWS 4; CA 102; CANR 22, 46, 108; CBD; CD 6; CWD; DFS 12, 16; DLB 13, 310; EWL 3; FW; MTCW 1; RGEL 2

Churchill, Charles 1731-1764 .... **LC 3**
See also DLB 109; RGEL 2

Churchill, Chick
See Churchill, Caryl
See also CD 5

Churchill, Sir Winston (Leonard Spencer)
1874-1965 .... **TCLC 113**
See also BRW 6; CA 97-100; CDBLB 1890-1914; DA3; DLB 100, 329; DLBD 16; LAIT 4; MTCW 1, 2

Chute, Carolyn 1947- .... **CLC 39**
See also CA 123; CANR 135; CN 7

Ciardi, John (Anthony) 1916-1986 . **CLC 10, 40, 44, 129; PC 69**
See also CA 5-8R; 118; CAAS 2; CANR 5, 33; CLR 19; CP 1, 2, 3, 4; CWRI 5; DAM POET; DLB 5; DLBY 1986; INT CANR-5; MAICYA 1, 2; MAL 5; MTCW 1, 2; MTFW 2005; RGAL 4; SAAS 26; SATA 1, 65; SATA-Obit 46

Cibber, Colley 1671-1757 .... **LC 66**
See also DLB 84; RGEL 2

Cicero, Marcus Tullius
106B.C.-43B.C. .... **CMLC 3, 81**
See also AW 1; CDWLB 1; DLB 211; RGWL 2, 3; WLIT 8

Cimino, Michael 1943- .... **CLC 16**
See also CA 105

Cioran, E(mil) M. 1911-1995 .... **CLC 64**
See also CA 25-28R; 149; CANR 91; DLB 220; EWL 3

Cisneros, Sandra 1954- .... **CLC 69, 118, 193; HLC 1; PC 52; SSC 32, 72**
See also AAYA 9, 53; AMWS 7; CA 131; CANR 64, 118; CN 7; CWP; DA3; DAM MULT; DLB 122, 152; EWL 3; EXPN; FL 1:5; FW; HW 1, 2; LAIT 5; LATS 1:2; LLW; MAICYA 2; MAL 5; MTCW 2; MTFW 2005; NFS 2; PFS 19; RGAL 4; RGSF 2; SSFS 3, 13; WLIT 1; YAW

Cixous, Helene 1937- .... **CLC 92**
See also CA 126; CANR 55, 123; CWW 2; DLB 83, 242; EWL 3; FL 1:5; FW; GLL 2; MTCW 1, 2; MTFW 2005; TWA

Clair, Rene .... **CLC 20**
See Chomette, Rene Lucien

Clampitt, Amy 1920-1994 ..... **CLC 32; PC 19**
See also AMWS 9; CA 110; 146; CANR 29, 79; CP 4, 5; DLB 105; MAL 5

Clancy, Thomas L., Jr. 1947-
See Clancy, Tom
See also CA 125; 131; CANR 62, 105; DA3; INT CA-131; MTCW 1, 2; MTFW 2005

Clancy, Tom .... **CLC 45, 112**
See Clancy, Thomas L., Jr.
See also AAYA 9, 51; BEST 89:1, 90:1; BPFB 1; BYA 10, 11; CANR 132; CMW 4; CPW; DAM NOV, POP; DLB 227

Clare, John 1793-1864 .. **NCLC 9, 86; PC 23**
See also BRWS 11; DAB; DAM POET; DLB 55, 96; RGEL 2

Clarin
See Alas (y Urena), Leopoldo (Enrique Garcia)

Clark, Al C.
See Goines, Donald

Clark, Brian (Robert)
See Clark, (Robert) Brian
See also CD 6

Clark, (Robert) Brian 1932- .... **CLC 29**
See Clark, Brian (Robert)
See also CA 41-44R; CANR 67; CBD; CD 5

Clark, Curt
See Westlake, Donald E.

Clark, Eleanor 1913-1996 .... **CLC 5, 19**
See also CA 9-12R; 151; CANR 41; CN 1, 2, 3, 4, 5, 6; DLB 6

Clark, J. P.
See Clark Bekederemo, J.P.
See also CDWLB 3; DLB 117

Clark, John Pepper
See Clark Bekederemo, J.P.
See also AFW; CD 5; CP 1, 2, 3, 4, 5, 6, 7; RGEL 2

Clark, Kenneth (Mackenzie)
1903-1983 .... **TCLC 147**
See also CA 93-96; 109; CANR 36; MTCW 1, 2; MTFW 2005

Collier, Jeremy 1650-1726 .... **LC 6**

Collier, John 1901-1980 . **SSC 19; TCLC 127**
See also CA 65-68; 97-100; CANR 10; CN
1, 2; DLB 77, 255; FANT; SUFW 1

Collier, Mary 1690-1762 .... **LC 86**
See also DLB 95

Collingwood, R(obin) G(eorge)
1889(?)-1943 .... **TCLC 67**
See also CA 117; 155; DLB 262

Collins, Billy 1941- .... **PC 68**
See also AAYA 64; CA 151; CANR 92; CP
7; MTFW 2005; PFS 18

Collins, Hunt
See Hunter, Evan

Collins, Linda 1931- .... **CLC 44**
See also CA 125

Collins, Tom
See Furphy, Joseph
See also RGEL 2

Collins, (William) Wilkie
1824-1889 .... **NCLC 1, 18, 93; SSC 93**
See also BRWS 6; CDBLB 1832-1890;
CMW 4; DLB 18, 70, 159; GL 2; MSW;
RGEL 2; RGSF 2; SUFW 1; WLIT 4

Collins, William 1721-1759 ...... **LC 4, 40; PC
72**
See also BRW 3; DAM POET; DLB 109;
RGEL 2

Collodi, Carlo .... **NCLC 54**
See Lorenzini, Carlo
See also CLR 5, 120; WCH; WLIT 7

Colman, George
See Glassco, John

Colman, George, the Elder
1732-1794 .... **LC 98**
See also RGEL 2

Colonna, Vittoria 1492-1547 .... **LC 71**
See also RGWL 2, 3

Colt, Winchester Remington
See Hubbard, L. Ron

Colter, Cyrus J. 1910-2002 .... **CLC 58**
See also BW 1; CA 65-68; 205; CANR 10,
66; CN 2, 3, 4, 5, 6; DLB 33

Colton, James
See Hansen, Joseph
See also GLL 1

Colum, Padraic 1881-1972 .... **CLC 28**
See also BYA 4; CA 73-76; 33-36R; CANR
35; CLR 36; CP 1; CWRI 5; DLB 19;
MAICYA 1, 2; MTCW 1; RGEL 2; SATA
15; WCH

Colvin, James
See Moorcock, Michael

Colwin, Laurie (E.) 1944-1992 .... **CLC 5, 13,
23, 84**
See also CA 89-92; 139; CANR 20, 46;
DLB 218; DLBY 1980; MTCW 1

Comfort, Alex(ander) 1920-2000 .... **CLC 7**
See also CA 1-4R; 190; CANR 1, 45; CN
1, 2, 3, 4; CP 1, 2, 3, 4, 5, 6, 7; DAM
POP; MTCW 2

Comfort, Montgomery
See Campbell, (John) Ramsey

Compton-Burnett, I(vy)
1892(?)-1969 .... **CLC 1, 3, 10, 15, 34;
TCLC 180**
See also BRW 7; CA 1-4R; 25-28R; CANR
4; DAM NOV; DLB 36; EWL 3; MTCW
1, 2; RGEL 2

Comstock, Anthony 1844-1915 ...... **TCLC 13**
See also CA 110; 169

Comte, Auguste 1798-1857 .... **NCLC 54**

Conan Doyle, Arthur
See Doyle, Sir Arthur Conan
See also BPFB 1; BYA 4, 5, 11

Conde (Abellan), Carmen
1901-1996 .... **HLCS 1**
See also CA 177; CWW 2; DLB 108; EWL
3; HW 2

Conde, Maryse 1937- ..... **BLCS; CLC 52, 92**
See also BW 2, 3; CA 110, 190; CAAE 190;
CANR 30, 53, 76; CWW 2; DAM MULT;
EWL 3; MTCW 2; MTFW 2005

Condillac, Etienne Bonnot de
1714-1780 .... **LC 26**
See also DLB 313

Condon, Richard (Thomas)
1915-1996 .... **CLC 4, 6, 8, 10, 45, 100**
See also BEST 90:3; BPFB 1; CA 1-4R;
151; CAAS 1; CANR 2, 23; CMW 4; CN
1, 2, 3, 4, 5, 6; DAM NOV; INT CANR-
23; MAL 5; MTCW 1, 2

Condorcet .... **LC 104**
See Condorcet, marquis de Marie-Jean-
Antoine-Nicolas Caritat
See also GFL Beginnings to 1789

Condorcet, marquis de
Marie-Jean-Antoine-Nicolas Caritat
1743-1794
See Condorcet
See also DLB 313

Confucius 551B.C.-479B.C. .... **CMLC 19, 65;
WLCS**
See also DA; DA3; DAB; DAC; DAM
MST

Congreve, William 1670-1729 ... **DC 2; LC 5,
21; WLC 2**
See also BRW 2; CDBLB 1660-1789; DA;
DAB; DAC; DAM DRAM, MST, POET;
DFS 15; DLB 39, 84; RGEL 2; WLIT 3

Conley, Robert J(ackson) 1940- .... **NNAL**
See also CA 41-44R; CANR 15, 34, 45, 96;
DAM MULT; TCWW 2

Connell, Evan S., Jr. 1924- .... **CLC 4, 6, 45**
See also AAYA 7; AMWS 14; CA 1-4R;
CAAS 2; CANR 2, 39, 76, 97, 140; CN
1, 2, 3, 4, 5, 6; DAM NOV; DLB 2;
DLBY 1981; MAL 5; MTCW 1, 2;
MTFW 2005

Connelly, Marc(us Cook) 1890-1980 . **CLC 7**
See also CA 85-88; 102; CAD; CANR 30;
DFS 12; DLB 7; DLBY 1980; MAL 5;
RGAL 4; SATA-Obit 25

Connor, Ralph .... **TCLC 31**
See Gordon, Charles William
See also DLB 92; TCWW 1, 2

Conrad, Joseph 1857-1924 ..... **SSC 9, 67, 69,
71; TCLC 1, 6, 13, 25, 43, 57; WLC 2**
See also AAYA 26; BPFB 1; BRW 6;
BRWC 1; BRWR 2; BYA 2; CA 104; 131;
CANR 60; CDBLB 1890-1914; DA; DA3;
DAB; DAC; DAM MST, NOV; DLB 10,
34, 98, 156; EWL 3; EXPN; EXPS; LAIT
2; LATS 1:1; LMFS 1; MTCW 1, 2;
MTFW 2005; NFS 2, 16; RGEL 2; RGSF
2; SATA 27; SSFS 1, 12; TEA; WLIT 4

Conrad, Robert Arnold
See Hart, Moss

Conroy, Pat 1945- .... **CLC 30, 74**
See also AAYA 8, 52; AITN 1; BPFB 1;
CA 85-88; CANR 24, 53, 129; CN 7;
CPW; CSW; DA3; DAM NOV, POP;
DLB 6; LAIT 5; MAL 5; MTCW 1, 2;
MTFW 2005

Constant (de Rebecque), (Henri) Benjamin
1767-1830 .... **NCLC 6**
See also DLB 119; EW 4; GFL 1789 to the
Present

Conway, Jill K(er) 1934- .... **CLC 152**
See also CA 130; CANR 94

Conybeare, Charles Augustus
See Eliot, T(homas) S(tearns)

Cook, Michael 1933-1994 .... **CLC 58**
See also CA 93-96; CANR 68; DLB 53

Cook, Robin 1940- .... **CLC 14**
See also AAYA 32; BEST 90:2; BPFB 1;
CA 108; 111; CANR 41, 90, 109; CPW;
DA3; DAM POP; HGG; INT CA-111

Cook, Roy
See Silverberg, Robert

Cooke, Elizabeth 1948- .... **CLC 55**
See also CA 129

Cooke, John Esten 1830-1886 .... **NCLC 5**
See also DLB 3, 248; RGAL 4

Cooke, John Estes
See Baum, L(yman) Frank

Cooke, M. E.
See Creasey, John

Cooke, Margaret
See Creasey, John

Cooke, Rose Terry 1827-1892 ...... **NCLC 110**
See also DLB 12, 74

Cook-Lynn, Elizabeth 1930- .... **CLC 93;
NNAL**
See also CA 133; DAM MULT; DLB 175

Cooney, Ray .... **CLC 62**
See also CBD

Cooper, Anthony Ashley 1671-1713 .. **LC 107**
See also DLB 101

Cooper, Dennis 1953- .... **CLC 203**
See also CA 133; CANR 72, 86; GLL 1;
HGG

Cooper, Douglas 1960- .... **CLC 86**

Cooper, Henry St. John
See Creasey, John

Cooper, J. California (?)- .... **CLC 56**
See also AAYA 12; BW 1; CA 125; CANR
55; DAM MULT; DLB 212

Cooper, James Fenimore
1789-1851 .... **NCLC 1, 27, 54**
See also AAYA 22; AMW; BPFB 1;
CDALB 1640-1865; CLR 105; DA3;
DLB 3, 183, 250, 254; LAIT 1; NFS 9;
RGAL 4; SATA 19; TUS; WCH

Cooper, Susan Fenimore
1813-1894 .... **NCLC 129**
See also ANW; DLB 239, 254

Coover, Robert 1932- .. **CLC 3, 7, 15, 32, 46,
87, 161; SSC 15**
See also AMWS 5; BPFB 1; CA 45-48;
CANR 3, 37, 58, 115; CN 1, 2, 3, 4, 5, 6,
7; DAM NOV; DLB 2, 227; DLBY 1981;
EWL 3; MAL 5; MTCW 1, 2; MTFW
2005; RGAL 4; RGSF 2

Copeland, Stewart (Armstrong)
1952- .... **CLC 26**

Copernicus, Nicolaus 1473-1543 .... **LC 45**

Coppard, A(lfred) E(dgar)
1878-1957 .... **SSC 21; TCLC 5**
See also BRWS 8; CA 114; 167; DLB 162;
EWL 3; HGG; RGEL 2; RGSF 2; SUFW
1; YABC 1

Coppee, Francois 1842-1908 .... **TCLC 25**
See also CA 170; DLB 217

Coppola, Francis Ford 1939- ... **CLC 16, 126**
See also AAYA 39; CA 77-80; CANR 40,
78; DLB 44

Copway, George 1818-1869 .... **NNAL**
See also DAM MULT; DLB 175, 183

Corbiere, Tristan 1845-1875 .... **NCLC 43**
See also DLB 217; GFL 1789 to the Present

Corcoran, Barbara (Asenath)
1911- .... **CLC 17**
See also AAYA 14; CA 21-24R; 191; CAAE
191; CAAS 2; CANR 11, 28, 48; CLR
50; DLB 52; JRDA; MAICYA 2; MAIC-
YAS 1; RHW; SAAS 20; SATA 3, 77;
SATA-Essay 125

Cordelier, Maurice
See Giraudoux, Jean(-Hippolyte)

Corelli, Marie .... **TCLC 51**
See Mackay, Mary
See also DLB 34, 156; RGEL 2; SUFW 1

Damas, Leon-Gontran 1912-1978 .... **CLC 84**
 See also BW 1; CA 125; 73-76; EWL 3
Dana, Richard Henry Sr.
 1787-1879 .... **NCLC 53**
Daniel, Samuel 1562(?)-1619 .... **LC 24**
 See also DLB 62; RGEL 2
Daniels, Brett
 See Adler, Renata
Dannay, Frederic 1905-1982 .... **CLC 11**
 See Queen, Ellery
 See also CA 1-4R; 107; CANR 1, 39; CMW
 4; DAM POP; DLB 137; MTCW 1
D'Annunzio, Gabriele 1863-1938 ... **TCLC 6,
 40**
 See also CA 104; 155; EW 8; EWL 3;
 RGWL 2, 3; TWA; WLIT 7
Danois, N. le
 See Gourmont, Remy(-Marie-Charles) de
Dante 1265-1321 .... **CMLC 3, 18, 39, 70; PC
 21; WLCS**
 See Alighieri, Dante
 See also DA; DA3; DAB; DAC; DAM
 MST, POET; EFS 1; EW 1; LAIT 1;
 RGWL 2, 3; TWA; WP
d'Antibes, Germain
 See Simenon, Georges (Jacques Christian)
Danticat, Edwidge 1969- ... **CLC 94, 139, 228**
 See also AAYA 29; CA 152, 192; CAAE
 192; CANR 73, 129; CN 7; DNFS 1;
 EXPS; LATS 1:2; MTCW 2; MTFW
 2005; SSFS 1; YAW
Danvers, Dennis 1947- .... **CLC 70**
Danziger, Paula 1944-2004 .... **CLC 21**
 See also AAYA 4, 36; BYA 6, 7, 14; CA
 112; 115; 229; CANR 37, 132; CLR 20;
 JRDA; MAICYA 1, 2; MTFW 2005;
 SATA 36, 63, 102, 149; SATA-Brief 30;
 SATA-Obit 155; WYA; YAW
Da Ponte, Lorenzo 1749-1838 .... **NCLC 50**
d'Aragona, Tullia 1510(?)-1556 .... **LC 121**
Dario, Ruben 1867-1916 .... **HLC 1; PC 15;
 TCLC 4**
 See also CA 131; CANR 81; DAM MULT;
 DLB 290, EWL 3; HW 1, 2; LAW;
 MTCW 1, 2; MTFW 2005; RGWL 2, 3
Darley, George 1795-1846 .... **NCLC 2**
 See also DLB 96; RGEL 2
Darrow, Clarence (Seward)
 1857-1938 .... **TCLC 81**
 See also CA 164; DLB 303
Darwin, Charles 1809-1882 .... **NCLC 57**
 See also BRWS 7; DLB 57, 166; LATS 1:1;
 RGEL 2; TEA; WLIT 4
Darwin, Erasmus 1731-1802 .... **NCLC 106**
 See also DLB 93; RGEL 2
Daryush, Elizabeth 1887-1977 ...... **CLC 6, 19**
 See also CA 49-52; CANR 3, 81; DLB 20
Das, Kamala 1934- .... **CLC 191; PC 43**
 See also CA 101; CANR 27, 59; CP 1, 2, 3,
 4, 5, 6, 7; CWP; DLB 323; FW
Dasgupta, Surendranath
 1887-1952 .... **TCLC 81**
 See also CA 157
**Dashwood, Edmee Elizabeth Monica de la
 Pasture** 1890-1943
 See Delafield, E. M.
 See also CA 119; 154
da Silva, Antonio Jose
 1705-1739 .... **NCLC 114**
Daudet, (Louis Marie) Alphonse
 1840-1897 .... **NCLC 1**
 See also DLB 123; GFL 1789 to the Present;
 RGSF 2
Daudet, Alphonse Marie Leon
 1867-1942 .... **SSC 94**
 See also CA 217

d'Aulnoy, Marie-Catherine c.
 1650-1705 .... **LC 100**
Daumal, Rene 1908-1944 .... **TCLC 14**
 See also CA 114; 247; EWL 3
Davenant, William 1606-1668 .... **LC 13**
 See also DLB 58, 126; RGEL 2
Davenport, Guy (Mattison, Jr.)
 1927-2005 .... **CLC 6, 14, 38; SSC 16**
 See also CA 33-36R; 235; CANR 23, 73;
 CN 3, 4, 5, 6; CSW; DLB 130
David, Robert
 See Nezval, Vitezslav
Davidson, Avram (James) 1923-1993
 See Queen, Ellery
 See also CA 101; 171; CANR 26; DLB 8;
 FANT; SFW 4; SUFW 1, 2
Davidson, Donald (Grady)
 1893-1968 .... **CLC 2, 13, 19**
 See also CA 5-8R; 25-28R; CANR 4, 84;
 DLB 45
Davidson, Hugh
 See Hamilton, Edmond
Davidson, John 1857-1909 .... **TCLC 24**
 See also CA 118; 217; DLB 19; RGEL 2
Davidson, Sara 1943- .... **CLC 9**
 See also CA 81-84; CANR 44, 68; DLB
 185
Davie, Donald (Alfred) 1922-1995 .... **CLC 5,
 8, 10, 31; PC 29**
 See also BRWS 6; CA 1-4R; 149; CAAS 3;
 CANR 1, 44; CP 1, 2, 3, 4, 5, 6; DLB 27;
 MTCW 1; RGEL 2
Davie, Elspeth 1918-1995 .... **SSC 52**
 See also CA 120; 126; 150; CANR 141;
 DLB 139
Davies, Ray(mond Douglas) 1944- ... **CLC 21**
 See also CA 116; 146; CANR 92
Davies, Rhys 1901-1978 .... **CLC 23**
 See also CA 9-12R; 81-84; CANR 4; CN 1,
 2; DLB 139, 191
Davies, Robertson 1913-1995 .. **CLC 2, 7, 13,
 25, 42, 75, 91; WLC 2**
 See Davies, William Robertson; March-
 banks, Samuel
 See also BEST 89:2; BPFB 1; CA 33-36R;
 150; CANR 17, 42, 103; CN 1, 2, 3, 4, 5,
 6; CPW; DA; DA3; DAB; DAC; DAM
 MST, NOV, POP; DLB 68; EWL 3; HGG;
 INT CANR-17; MTCW 1, 2; MTFW
 2005; RGEL 2; TWA
Davies, Sir John 1569-1626 .... **LC 85**
 See also DLB 172
Davies, Walter C.
 See Kornbluth, C(yril) M.
Davies, William Henry 1871-1940 ... **TCLC 5**
 See also BRWS 11; CA 104; 179; DLB 19,
 174; EWL 3; RGEL 2
Da Vinci, Leonardo 1452-1519 ..... **LC 12, 57,
 60**
 See also AAYA 40
Davis, Angela (Yvonne) 1944- .... **CLC 77**
 See also BW 2, 3; CA 57-60; CANR 10,
 81; CSW; DA3; DAM MULT; FW
Davis, B. Lynch
 See Bioy Casares, Adolfo; Borges, Jorge
 Luis
Davis, Frank Marshall 1905-1987 ...... **BLC 1**
 See also BW 2, 3; CA 125; 123; CANR 42,
 80; DAM MULT; DLB 51
Davis, Gordon
 See Hunt, E(verette) Howard, (Jr.)
Davis, H(arold) L(enoir) 1896-1960 . **CLC 49**
 See also ANW; CA 178; 89-92; DLB 9,
 206; SATA 114; TCWW 1, 2
Davis, Hart
 See Poniatowska, Elena
Davis, Natalie Zemon 1928- .... **CLC 204**
 See also CA 53-56; CANR 58, 100

Davis, Rebecca (Blaine) Harding
 1831-1910 .... **SSC 38; TCLC 6**
 See also AMWS 16; CA 104; 179; DLB 74,
 239; FW; NFS 14; RGAL 4; TUS
Davis, Richard Harding
 1864-1916 .... **TCLC 24**
 See also CA 114; 179; DLB 12, 23, 78, 79,
 189; DLBD 13; RGAL 4
Davison, Frank Dalby 1893-1970 ..... **CLC 15**
 See also CA 217; 116; DLB 260
Davison, Lawrence H.
 See Lawrence, D(avid) H(erbert Richards)
Davison, Peter (Hubert) 1928-2004 . **CLC 28**
 See also CA 9-12R; 234; CAAS 4; CANR
 3, 43, 84; CP 1, 2, 3, 4, 5, 6, 7; DLB 5
Davys, Mary 1674-1732 .... **LC 1, 46**
 See also DLB 39
Dawson, (Guy) Fielding (Lewis)
 1930-2002 .... **CLC 6**
 See also CA 85-88; 202; CANR 108; DLB
 130; DLBY 2002
Dawson, Peter
 See Faust, Frederick (Schiller)
 See also TCWW 1, 2
Day, Clarence (Shepard, Jr.)
 1874 1935 .... **TCLC 25**
 See also CA 108; 199; DLB 11
Day, John 1574(?)-1640(?) .... **LC 70**
 See also DLB 62, 170; RGEL 2
Day, Thomas 1748-1789 .... **LC 1**
 See also DLB 39; YABC 1
Day Lewis, C(ecil) 1904-1972 . **CLC 1, 6, 10;
 PC 11**
 See Blake, Nicholas; Lewis, C. Day
 See also BRWS 3; CA 13-16; 33-36R;
 CANR 34; CAP 1; CP 1; CWRI 5; DAM
 POET; DLB 15, 20; EWL 3; MTCW 1, 2;
 RGEL 2
Dazai Osamu .... **SSC 41; TCLC 11**
 See Tsushima, Shuji
 See also CA 164; DLB 182; EWL 3; MJW;
 RGSF 2; RGWL 2, 3; TWA
de Andrade, Carlos Drummond
 See Drummond de Andrade, Carlos
de Andrade, Mario 1892(?)-1945
 See Andrade, Mario de
 See also CA 178; HW 2
Deane, Norman
 See Creasey, John
Deane, Seamus (Francis) 1940- ...... **CLC 122**
 See also CA 118; CANR 42
de Beauvoir, Simone
 See Beauvoir, Simone de
de Beer, P.
 See Bosman, Herman Charles
De Botton, Alain 1969- .... **CLC 203**
 See also CA 159; CANR 96
de Brissac, Malcolm
 See Dickinson, Peter (Malcolm de Brissac)
de Campos, Alvaro
 See Pessoa, Fernando (Antonio Nogueira)
de Chardin, Pierre Teilhard
 See Teilhard de Chardin, (Marie Joseph)
 Pierre
de Crenne, Helisenne c. 1510-c.
 1560 .... **LC 113**
Dee, John 1527-1608 .... **LC 20**
 See also DLB 136, 213
Deer, Sandra 1940- .... **CLC 45**
 See also CA 186
De Ferrari, Gabriella 1941- .... **CLC 65**
 See also CA 146
de Filippo, Eduardo 1900-1984 ... **TCLC 127**
 See also CA 132; 114; EWL 3; MTCW 1;
 RGWL 2, 3

Ford, Richard 1944- .... **CLC 46, 99, 205**
See also AMWS 5; CA 69-72; CANR 11, 47, 86, 128; CN 5, 6, 7; CSW; DLB 227; EWL 3; MAL 5; MTCW 2; MTFW 2005; RGAL 4; RGSF 2

Ford, Webster
See Masters, Edgar Lee

Foreman, Richard 1937- .... **CLC 50**
See also CA 65-68; CAD; CANR 32, 63, 143; CD 5, 6

Forester, C(ecil) S(cott) 1899-1966 . **CLC 35; TCLC 152**
See also CA 73-76; 25-28R; CANR 83; DLB 191; RGEL 2; RHW; SATA 13

Forez
See Mauriac, Francois (Charles)

Forman, James
See Forman, James D(ouglas)

Forman, James D(ouglas) 1932- .... **CLC 21**
See also AAYA 17; CA 9-12R; CANR 4, 19, 42; JRDA; MAICYA 1, 2; SATA 8, 70; YAW

Forman, Milos 1932- .... **CLC 164**
See also AAYA 63; CA 109

Fornes, Maria Irene 1930- .... **CLC 39, 61, 187; DC 10; HLCS 1**
See also CA 25-28R; CAD; CANR 28, 81; CD 5, 6; CWD; DLB 7; HW 1, 2; INT CANR-28; LLW; MAL 5; MTCW 1; RGAL 4

Forrest, Leon (Richard)
1937-1997 .... **BLCS; CLC 4**
See also AFAW 2; BW 2; CA 89-92; 162; CAAS 7; CANR 25, 52, 87; CN 4, 5, 6; DLB 33

Forster, E(dward) M(organ)
1879-1970 ...... **CLC 1, 2, 3, 4, 9, 10, 13, 15, 22, 45, 77; SSC 27, 96; TCLC 125; WLC 2**
See also AAYA 2, 37; BRW 6; BRWR 2; BYA 12; CA 13-14; 25-28R; CANR 45; CAP 1; CDBLB 1914-1945; DA; DA3; DAB; DAC; DAM MST, NOV; DLB 34, 98, 162, 178, 195; DLBD 10; EWL 3; EXPN; LAIT 3; LMFS 1; MTCW 1, 2; MTFW 2005; NCFS 1; NFS 3, 10, 11; RGEL 2; RGSF 1; SATA 57; SUFW 1; TEA; WLIT 4

Forster, John 1812-1876 .... **NCLC 11**
See also DLB 144, 184

Forster, Margaret 1938- .... **CLC 149**
See also CA 133; CANR 62, 115; CN 4, 5, 6, 7; DLB 155, 271

Forsyth, Frederick 1938- .... **CLC 2, 5, 36**
See also BEST 89:4; CA 85-88; CANR 38, 62, 115, 137; CMW 4; CN 3, 4, 5, 6, 7; CPW; DAM NOV, POP; DLB 87; MTCW 1, 2; MTFW 2005

Forten, Charlotte L. 1837-1914 .... **BLC 2; TCLC 16**
See Grimke, Charlotte L(ottie) Forten
See also DLB 50, 239

Fortinbras
See Grieg, (Johan) Nordahl (Brun)

Foscolo, Ugo 1778-1827 .... **NCLC 8, 97**
See also EW 5; WLIT 7

Fosse, Bob 1927-1987
See Fosse, Robert L.
See also CA 110; 123

Fosse, Robert L. .... **CLC 20**
See Fosse, Bob

Foster, Hannah Webster
1758-1840 .... **NCLC 99**
See also DLB 37, 200; RGAL 4

Foster, Stephen Collins
1826-1864 .... **NCLC 26**
See also RGAL 4

Foucault, Michel 1926-1984 . **CLC 31, 34, 69**
See also CA 105; 113; CANR 34; DLB 242; EW 13; EWL 3; GFL 1789 to the Present; GLL 1; LMFS 2; MTCW 1, 2; TWA

Fouque, Friedrich (Heinrich Karl) de la Motte 1777-1843 .... **NCLC 2**
See also DLB 90; RGWL 2, 3; SUFW 1

Fourier, Charles 1772-1837 .... **NCLC 51**

Fournier, Henri-Alban 1886-1914
See Alain-Fournier
See also CA 104; 179

Fournier, Pierre 1916-1997 .... **CLC 11**
See Gascar, Pierre
See also CA 89-92; CANR 16, 40

Fowles, John 1926-2005 .... **CLC 1, 2, 3, 4, 6, 9, 10, 15, 33, 87; SSC 33**
See also BPFB 1; BRWS 1; CA 5-8R; 245; CANR 25, 71, 103; CDBLB 1960 to Present; CN 1, 2, 3, 4, 5, 6, 7; DA3; DAB; DAC; DAM MST; DLB 14, 139, 207; EWL 3; HGG; MTCW 1, 2; MTFW 2005; NFS 21; RGEL 2; RHW; SATA 22; SATA-Obit 171; TEA; WLIT 4

Fowles, John Robert
See Fowles, John

Fox, Paula 1923- .... **CLC 2, 8, 121**
See also AAYA 3, 37; BYA 3, 8; CA 73-76; CANR 20, 36, 62, 105; CLR 1, 44, 96; DLB 52; JRDA; MAICYA 1, 2; MTCW 1; NFS 12; SATA 17, 60, 120, 167; WYA; YAW

Fox, William Price (Jr.) 1926- .... **CLC 22**
See also CA 17-20R; CAAS 19; CANR 11, 142; CSW; DLB 2; DLBY 1981

Foxe, John 1517(?)-1587 .... **LC 14**
See also DLB 132

Frame, Janet .. **CLC 2, 3, 6, 22, 66, 96; SSC 29**
See Clutha, Janet Paterson Frame
See also CN 1, 2, 3, 4, 5, 6, 7; CP 2, 3, 4; CWP; EWL 3; RGEL 2; RGSF 2; TWA

France, Anatole .... **TCLC 9**
See Thibault, Jacques Anatole Francois
See also DLB 123, 330; EWL 3; GFL 1789 to the Present; RGWL 2, 3; SUFW 1

Francis, Claude .... **CLC 50**
See also CA 192

Francis, Dick
See Francis, Richard Stanley
See also CN 2, 3, 4, 5, 6

Francis, Richard Stanley 1920- ... **CLC 2, 22, 42, 102**
See Francis, Dick
See also AAYA 5, 21; BEST 89:3; BPFB 1; CA 5-8R; CANR 9, 42, 68, 100, 141; CD-BLB 1960 to Present; CMW 4; CN 7; DA3; DAM POP; DLB 87; INT CANR-9; MSW; MTCW 1, 2; MTFW 2005

Francis, Robert (Churchill)
1901-1987 .... **CLC 15; PC 34**
See also AMWS 9; CA 1-4R; 123; CANR 1; CP 1, 2, 3, 4; EXPP; PFS 12; TCLE 1:1

Francis, Lord Jeffrey
See Jeffrey, Francis
See also DLB 107

Frank, Anne(lies Marie)
1929-1945 .... **TCLC 17; WLC 2**
See also AAYA 12; BYA 1; CA 113; 133; CANR 68; CLR 101; DA; DA3; DAB; DAC; DAM MST; LAIT 4; MAICYA 2; MAICYAS 1; MTCW 1, 2; MTFW 2005; NCFS 2; RGHL; SATA 87; SATA-Brief 42; WYA; YAW

Frank, Bruno 1887-1945 .... **TCLC 81**
See also CA 189; DLB 118; EWL 3

Frank, Elizabeth 1945- .... **CLC 39**
See also CA 121; 126; CANR 78, 150; INT CA-126

Frankl, Viktor E(mil) 1905-1997 ...... **CLC 93**
See also CA 65-68; 161; RGHL

Franklin, Benjamin
See Hasek, Jaroslav (Matej Frantisek)

Franklin, Benjamin 1706-1790 .. **LC 25, 134; WLCS**
See also AMW; CDALB 1640-1865; DA; DA3; DAB; DAC; DAM MST; DLB 24, 43, 73, 183; LAIT 1; RGAL 4; TUS

Franklin, (Stella Maria Sarah) Miles (Lampe) 1879-1954 .... **TCLC 7**
See also CA 104; 164; DLB 230; FW; MTCW 2; RGEL 2; TWA

Franzen, Jonathan 1959- .... **CLC 202**
See also AAYA 65; CA 129; CANR 105

Fraser, Antonia 1932- .... **CLC 32, 107**
See also AAYA 57; CA 85-88; CANR 44, 65, 119; CMW; DLB 276; MTCW 1, 2; MTFW 2005; SATA-Brief 32

Fraser, George MacDonald 1925- ...... **CLC 7**
See also AAYA 48; CA 45-48, 180; CAAE 180; CANR 2, 48, 74; MTCW 2; RHW

Fraser, Sylvia 1935- .... **CLC 64**
See also CA 45-48; CANR 1, 16, 60; CCA 1

Frayn, Michael 1933- .... **CLC 3, 7, 31, 47, 176; DC 27**
See also AAYA 69; BRWC 2; BRWS 7; CA 5-8R; CANR 30, 69, 114, 133; CBD; CD 5, 6; CN 1, 2, 3, 4, 5, 6, 7; DAM DRAM, NOV; DFS 22; DLB 13, 14, 194, 245; FANT; MTCW 1, 2; MTFW 2005; SFW 4

Fraze, Candida (Merrill) 1945- .... **CLC 50**
See also CA 126

Frazer, Andrew
See Marlowe, Stephen

Frazer, J(ames) G(eorge)
1854-1941 .... **TCLC 32**
See also BRWS 3; CA 118; NCFS 5

Frazer, Robert Caine
See Creasey, John

Frazer, Sir James George
See Frazer, J(ames) G(eorge)

Frazier, Charles 1950- .... **CLC 109, 224**
See also AAYA 34; CA 161; CANR 126; CSW; DLB 292; MTFW 2005

Frazier, Ian 1951- .... **CLC 46**
See also CA 130; CANR 54, 93

Frederic, Harold 1856-1898 ... **NCLC 10, 175**
See also AMW; DLB 12, 23; DLBD 13; MAL 5; NFS 22; RGAL 4

Frederick, John
See Faust, Frederick (Schiller)
See also TCWW 2

Frederick the Great 1712-1786 .... **LC 14**

Fredro, Aleksander 1793-1876 .... **NCLC 8**

Freeling, Nicolas 1927-2003 .... **CLC 38**
See also CA 49-52; 218; CAAS 12; CANR 1, 17, 50, 84; CMW 4; CN 1, 2, 3, 4, 5, 6; DLB 87

Freeman, Douglas Southall
1886-1953 .... **TCLC 11**
See also CA 109; 195; DLB 17; DLBD 17

Freeman, Judith 1946- .... **CLC 55**
See also CA 148; CANR 120; DLB 256

Freeman, Mary E(leanor) Wilkins
1852-1930 .... **SSC 1, 47; TCLC 9**
See also CA 106; 177; DLB 12, 78, 221; EXPS; FW; HGG; MBL; RGAL 4; RGSF 2; SSFS 4, 8; SUFW 1; TUS

Freeman, R(ichard) Austin
1862-1943 .... **TCLC 21**
See also CA 113; CANR 84; CMW 4; DLB 70

French, Albert 1943- .... **CLC 86**
See also BW 3; CA 167

French, Antonia
See Kureishi, Hanif

French, Marilyn 1929- .. **CLC 10, 18, 60, 177**
See also BPFB 1; CA 69-72; CANR 3, 31, 134; CN 5, 6, 7; CPW; DAM DRAM, NOV, POP; FL 1:5; FW; INT CANR-31; MTCW 1, 2; MTFW 2005
French, Paul
See Asimov, Isaac
Freneau, Philip Morin 1752-1832 .. **NCLC 1, 111**
See also AMWS 2; DLB 37, 43; RGAL 4
Freud, Sigmund 1856-1939 .... **TCLC 52**
See also CA 115; 133; CANR 69; DLB 296; EW 8; EWL 3; LATS 1:1; MTCW 1, 2; MTFW 2005; NCFS 3; TWA
Freytag, Gustav 1816-1895 .... **NCLC 109**
See also DLB 129
Friedan, Betty 1921-2006 .... **CLC 74**
See also CA 65-68; 248; CANR 18, 45, 74; DLB 246; FW; MTCW 1, 2; MTFW 2005; NCFS 5
Friedan, Betty Naomi
See Friedan, Betty
Friedlander, Saul 1932- .... **CLC 90**
See also CA 117; 130; CANR 72; RGHL
Friedman, B(ernard) H(arper)
1926- .... **CLC 7**
See also CA 1-4R; CANR 3, 48
Friedman, Bruce Jay 1930- ...... **CLC 3, 5, 56**
See also CA 9-12R; CAD; CANR 25, 52, 101; CD 5, 6; CN 1, 2, 3, 4, 5, 6, 7; DLB 2, 28, 244; INT CANR-25; MAL 5; SSFS 18
Friel, Brian 1929- .... **CLC 5, 42, 59, 115; DC 8; SSC 76**
See also BRWS 5; CA 21-24R; CANR 33, 69, 131; CBD; CD 5, 6; DFS 11; DLB 13, 319; EWL 3; MTCW 1; RGEL 2; TEA
Friis-Baastad, Babbis Ellinor
1921-1970 .... **CLC 12**
See also CA 17-20R; 134; SATA 7
Frisch, Max 1911-1991 ...... **CLC 3, 9, 14, 18, 32, 44; TCLC 121**
See also CA 85-88; 134; CANR 32, 74; CDWLB 2; DAM DRAM, NOV; DLB 69, 124; EW 13; EWL 3; MTCW 1, 2; MTFW 2005; RGHL; RGWL 2, 3
Fromentin, Eugene (Samuel Auguste)
1820-1876 .... **NCLC 10, 125**
See also DLB 123; GFL 1789 to the Present
Frost, Frederick
See Faust, Frederick (Schiller)
Frost, Robert 1874-1963 . **CLC 1, 3, 4, 9, 10, 13, 15, 26, 34, 44; PC 1, 39, 71; WLC 2**
See also AAYA 21; AMW; AMWR 1; CA 89-92; CANR 33; CDALB 1917-1929; CLR 67; DA; DA3; DAB; DAC; DAM MST, POET; DLB 54, 284; DLBD 7; EWL 3; EXPP; MAL 5; MTCW 1, 2; MTFW 2005; PAB; PFS 1, 2, 3, 4, 5, 6, 7, 10, 13; RGAL 4; SATA 14; TUS; WP; WYA
Frost, Robert Lee
See Frost, Robert
Froude, James Anthony
1818-1894 .... **NCLC 43**
See also DLB 18, 57, 144
Froy, Herald
See Waterhouse, Keith (Spencer)
Fry, Christopher 1907-2005 ... **CLC 2, 10, 14**
See also BRWS 3; CA 17-20R; 240; CAAS 23; CANR 9, 30, 74, 132; CBD; CD 5, 6; CP 1, 2, 3, 4, 5, 6, 7; DAM DRAM; DLB 13; EWL 3; MTCW 1, 2; MTFW 2005; RGEL 2; SATA 66; TEA
Frye, (Herman) Northrop
1912-1991 .... **CLC 24, 70; TCLC 165**
See also CA 5-8R; 133; CANR 8, 37; DLB 67, 68, 246; EWL 3; MTCW 1, 2; MTFW 2005; RGAL 4; TWA

Fuchs, Daniel 1909-1993 .... **CLC 8, 22**
See also CA 81-84; 142; CAAS 5; CANR 40; CN 1, 2, 3, 4, 5; DLB 9, 26, 28; DLBY 1993; MAL 5
Fuchs, Daniel 1934- .... **CLC 34**
See also CA 37-40R; CANR 14, 48
Fuentes, Carlos 1928- .. **CLC 3, 8, 10, 13, 22, 41, 60, 113; HLC 1; SSC 24; WLC 2**
See also AAYA 4, 45; AITN 2; BPFB 1; CA 69-72; CANR 10, 32, 68, 104, 138; CDWLB 3; CWW 2; DA; DA3; DAB; DAC; DAM MST, MULT, NOV; DLB 113; DNFS 2; EWL 3; HW 1, 2; LAIT 3; LATS 1:2; LAW; LAWS 1; LMFS 2; MTCW 1, 2; MTFW 2005; NFS 8; RGSF 2; RGWL 2, 3; TWA; WLIT 1
Fuentes, Gregorio Lopez y
See Lopez y Fuentes, Gregorio
Fuertes, Gloria 1918-1998 .... **PC 27**
See also CA 178; 180; DLB 108; HW 2; SATA 115
Fugard, (Harold) Athol 1932- . **CLC 5, 9, 14, 25, 40, 80, 211; DC 3**
See also AAYA 17; AFW; CA 85-88; CANR 32, 54, 118; CD 5, 6; DAM DRAM; DFS 3, 6, 10; DLB 225; DNFS 1, 2; EWL 3; LATS 1:2; MTCW 1; MTFW 2005; RGEL 2; WLIT 2
Fugard, Sheila 1932- .... **CLC 48**
See also CA 125
Fujiwara no Teika 1162-1241 .... **CMLC 73**
See also DLB 203
Fukuyama, Francis 1952- .... **CLC 131**
See also CA 140; CANR 72, 125
Fuller, Charles (H.), (Jr.) 1939- .... **BLC 2; CLC 25; DC 1**
See also BW 2; CA 108; 112; CAD; CANR 87; CD 5, 6; DAM DRAM, MULT; DFS 8; DLB 38, 266; EWL 3; INT CA-112; MAL 5; MTCW 1
Fuller, Henry Blake 1857-1929 .... **TCLC 103**
See also CA 108; 177; DLB 12; RGAL 4
Fuller, John (Leopold) 1937- .... **CLC 62**
See also CA 21-24R; CANR 9, 44; CP 1, 2, 3, 4, 5, 6, 7; DLB 40
Fuller, Margaret
See Ossoli, Sarah Margaret (Fuller)
See also AMWS 2; DLB 183, 223, 239; FL 1:3
Fuller, Roy (Broadbent) 1912-1991 ... **CLC 4, 28**
See also BRWS 7; CA 5-8R; 135; CAAS 10; CANR 53, 83; CN 1, 2, 3, 4, 5; CP 1, 2, 3, 4, 5; CWRI 5; DLB 15, 20; EWL 3; RGEL 2; SATA 87
Fuller, Sarah Margaret
See Ossoli, Sarah Margaret (Fuller)
Fuller, Sarah Margaret
See Ossoli, Sarah Margaret (Fuller)
See also DLB 1, 59, 73
Fuller, Thomas 1608-1661 .... **LC 111**
See also DLB 151
Fulton, Alice 1952- .... **CLC 52**
See also CA 116; CANR 57, 88; CP 5, 6, 7; CWP; DLB 193
Furphy, Joseph 1843-1912 .... **TCLC 25**
See Collins, Tom
See also CA 163; DLB 230; EWL 3; RGEL 2
Fuson, Robert H(enderson) 1927- .... **CLC 70**
See also CA 89-92; CANR 103
Fussell, Paul 1924- .... **CLC 74**
See also BEST 90:1; CA 17-20R; CANR 8, 21, 35, 69, 135; INT CANR-21; MTCW 1, 2; MTFW 2005
Futabatei, Shimei 1864-1909 .... **TCLC 44**
See Futabatei Shimei
See also CA 162; MJW

Futabatei Shimei
See Futabatei, Shimei
See also DLB 180; EWL 3
Futrelle, Jacques 1875-1912 .... **TCLC 19**
See also CA 113; 155; CMW 4
Gaboriau, Emile 1835-1873 .... **NCLC 14**
See also CMW 4; MSW
Gadda, Carlo Emilio 1893-1973 ...... **CLC 11; TCLC 144**
See also CA 89-92; DLB 177; EWL 3; WLIT 7
Gaddis, William 1922-1998 ... **CLC 1, 3, 6, 8, 10, 19, 43, 86**
See also AMWS 4; BPFB 1; CA 17-20R; 172; CANR 21, 48, 148; CN 1, 2, 3, 4, 5, 6; DLB 2, 278; EWL 3; MAL 5; MTCW 1, 2; MTFW 2005; RGAL 4
Gaelique, Moruen le
See Jacob, (Cyprien-)Max
Gage, Walter
See Inge, William (Motter)
Gaiman, Neil 1960- .... **CLC 195**
See also AAYA 19, 42; CA 133; CANR 81, 129; CLR 109; DLB 261; HGG; MTFW 2005; SATA 85, 146; SFW 4; SUFW 2
Gaiman, Neil Richard
See Gaiman, Neil
Gaines, Ernest J. 1933- .. **BLC 2; CLC 3, 11, 18, 86, 181; SSC 68**
See also AAYA 18; AFAW 1, 2; AITN 1; BPFB 2; BW 2, 3; BYA 6; CA 9-12R; CANR 6, 24, 42, 75, 126; CDALB 1968-1988; CLR 62; CN 1, 2, 3, 4, 5, 6, 7; CSW; DA3; DAM MULT; DLB 2, 33, 152; DLBY 1980; EWL 3; EXPN; LAIT 5; LATS 1:2; MAL 5; MTCW 1, 2; MTFW 2005; NFS 5, 7, 16; RGAL 4; RGSF 2; RHW; SATA 86; SSFS 5; YAW
Gaitskill, Mary 1954- .... **CLC 69**
See also CA 128; CANR 61, 152; DLB 244; TCLE 1:1
Gaitskill, Mary Lawrence
See Gaitskill, Mary
Gaius Suetonius Tranquillus
See Suetonius
Galdos, Benito Perez
See Perez Galdos, Benito
See also EW 7
Gale, Zona 1874-1938 .... **TCLC 7**
See also CA 105; 153; CANR 84; DAM DRAM; DFS 17; DLB 9, 78, 228; RGAL 4
Galeano, Eduardo (Hughes) 1940- . **CLC 72; HLCS 1**
See also CA 29-32R; CANR 13, 32, 100; HW 1
Galiano, Juan Valera y Alcala
See Valera y Alcala-Galiano, Juan
Galilei, Galileo 1564-1642 .... **LC 45**
Gallagher, Tess 1943- .... **CLC 18, 63; PC 9**
See also CA 106; CP 3, 4, 5, 6, 7; CWP; DAM POET; DLB 120, 212, 244; PFS 16
Gallant, Mavis 1922- ..... **CLC 7, 18, 38, 172; SSC 5, 78**
See also CA 69-72; CANR 29, 69, 117; CCA 1; CN 1, 2, 3, 4, 5, 6, 7; DAC; DAM MST; DLB 53; EWL 3; MTCW 1, 2; MTFW 2005; RGEL 2; RGSF 2
Gallant, Roy A(rthur) 1924- .... **CLC 17**
See also CA 5-8R; CANR 4, 29, 54, 117; CLR 30; MAICYA 1, 2; SATA 4, 68, 110
Gallico, Paul (William) 1897-1976 ..... **CLC 2**
See also AITN 1; CA 5-8R; 69-72; CANR 23; CN 1, 2; DLB 9, 171; FANT; MAICYA 1, 2; SATA 13
Gallo, Max Louis 1932- .... **CLC 95**
See also CA 85-88
Gallois, Lucien
See Desnos, Robert

Gallup, Ralph
See Whitemore, Hugh (John)
Galsworthy, John 1867-1933 .... **SSC 22;**
TCLC 1, 45; WLC 2
See also BRW 6; CA 104; 141; CANR 75;
CDBLB 1890-1914; DA; DA3; DAB;
DAC; DAM DRAM, MST, NOV; DLB
10, 34, 98, 162, 330; DLBD 16; EWL 3;
MTCW 2; RGEL 2; SSFS 3; TEA
Galt, John 1779-1839 .... **NCLC 1, 110**
See also DLB 99, 116, 159; RGEL 2; RGSF
2
Galvin, James 1951- .... **CLC 38**
See also CA 108; CANR 26
Gamboa, Federico 1864-1939 .... **TCLC 36**
See also CA 167; HW 2; LAW
Gandhi, M. K.
See Gandhi, Mohandas Karamchand
Gandhi, Mahatma
See Gandhi, Mohandas Karamchand
Gandhi, Mohandas Karamchand
1869-1948 .... **TCLC 59**
See also CA 121; 132; DA3; DAM MULT;
DLB 323; MTCW 1, 2
Gann, Ernest Kellogg 1910-1991 ..... **CLC 23**
See also AITN 1; BPFB 2; CA 1-4R; 136;
CANR 1, 83; RHW
Gao Xingjian 1940- .... **CLC 167**
See Xingjian, Gao
See also MTFW 2005
Garber, Eric 1943(?)-
See Holleran, Andrew
See also CANR 89
Garcia, Cristina 1958- .... **CLC 76**
See also AMWS 11; CA 141; CANR 73,
130; CN 7; DLB 292; DNFS 1; EWL 3;
HW 2; LLW; MTFW 2005
Garcia Lorca, Federico 1898-1936 ...... **DC 2;**
HLC 2; PC 3; TCLC 1, 7, 49, 181;
WLC 2
See Lorca, Federico Garcia
See also AAYA 46; CA 104; 131; CANR
81; DA; DA3; DAB; DAC; DAM DRAM,
MST, MULT, POET; DFS 4, 10; DLB
108; EWL 3; HW 1, 2; LATS 1:2; MTCW
1, 2; MTFW 2005; TWA
Garcia Marquez, Gabriel 1928- .... **CLC 2, 3,**
8, 10, 15, 27, 47, 55, 68, 170; HLC 1;
SSC 8, 83; WLC 3
See also AAYA 3, 33; BEST 89:1, 90:4;
BPFB 2; BYA 12, 16; CA 33-36R; CANR
10, 28, 50, 75, 82, 128; CDWLB 3; CPW;
CWW 2; DA; DA3; DAB; DAC; DAM
MST, MULT, NOV, POP; DLB 113, 330;
DNFS 1, 2; EWL 3; EXPN; EXPS; HW
1, 2; LAIT 2; LATS 1:2; LAW; LAWS 1;
LMFS 2; MTCW 1, 2; MTFW 2005;
NCFS 3; NFS 1, 5, 10; RGSF 2; RGWL
2, 3; SSFS 1, 6, 16, 21; TWA; WLIT 1
Garcia Marquez, Gabriel Jose
See Garcia Marquez, Gabriel
Garcilaso de la Vega, El Inca
1539-1616 .... **HLCS 1; LC 127**
See also DLB 318; LAW
Gard, Janice
See Latham, Jean Lee
Gard, Roger Martin du
See Martin du Gard, Roger
Gardam, Jane (Mary) 1928- .... **CLC 43**
See also CA 49-52; CANR 2, 18, 33, 54,
106; CLR 12; DLB 14, 161, 231; MAI-
CYA 1, 2; MTCW 1; SAAS 9; SATA 39,
76, 130; SATA-Brief 28; YAW
Gardner, Herb(ert George)
1934-2003 .... **CLC 44**
See also CA 149; 220; CAD; CANR 119;
CD 5, 6; DFS 18, 20

Gardner, John, Jr. 1933-1982 ... **CLC 2, 3, 5,**
7, 8, 10, 18, 28, 34; SSC 7
See also AAYA 45; AITN 1; AMWS 6;
BPFB 2; CA 65-68; 107; CANR 33, 73;
CDALBS; CN 2, 3; CPW; DA3; DAM
NOV, POP; DLB 2; DLBY 1982; EWL 3;
FANT; LATS 1:2; MAL 5; MTCW 1, 2;
MTFW 2005; NFS 3; RGAL 4; RGSF 2;
SATA 40; SATA-Obit 31; SSFS 8
Gardner, John (Edmund) 1926- .... **CLC 30**
See also CA 103; CANR 15, 69, 127; CMW
4; CPW; DAM POP; MTCW 1
Gardner, Miriam
See Bradley, Marion Zimmer
See also GLL 1
Gardner, Noel
See Kuttner, Henry
Gardons, S. S.
See Snodgrass, W.D.
Garfield, Leon 1921-1996 .... **CLC 12**
See also AAYA 8, 69; BYA 1, 3; CA 17-
20R; 152; CANR 38, 41, 78; CLR 21;
DLB 161; JRDA; MAICYA 1, 2; MAIC-
YAS 1; SATA 1, 32, 76; SATA-Obit 90;
TEA; WYA; YAW
Garland, (Hannibal) Hamlin
1860-1940 .... **SSC 18; TCLC 3**
See also CA 104; DLB 12, 71, 78, 186;
MAL 5; RGAL 4; RGSF 2; TCWW 1, 2
Garneau, (Hector de) Saint-Denys
1912-1943 .... **TCLC 13**
See also CA 111; DLB 88
Garner, Alan 1934- .... **CLC 17**
See also AAYA 18; BYA 3, 5; CA 73-76,
178; CAAE 178; CANR 15, 64, 134; CLR
20; CPW; DAB; DAM POP; DLB 161,
261; FANT; MAICYA 1, 2; MTCW 1, 2;
MTFW 2005; SATA 18, 69; SATA-Essay
108; SUFW 1, 2; YAW
Garner, Hugh 1913-1979 .... **CLC 13**
See Warwick, Jarvis
See also CA 69-72; CANR 31; CCA 1; CN
1, 2; DLB 68
Garnett, David 1892-1981 .... **CLC 3**
See also CA 5-8R; 103; CANR 17, 79; CN
1, 2; DLB 34; FANT; MTCW 2; RGEL 2;
SFW 4; SUFW 1
Garnier, Robert c. 1545-1590 .... **LC 119**
See also DLB 327; GFL Beginnings to 1789
Garrett, George (Palmer, Jr.) 1929- . **CLC 3,**
11, 51; SSC 30
See also AMWS 7; BPFB 2; CA 1-4R; 202;
CAAE 202; CAAS 5; CANR 1, 42, 67,
109; CN 1, 2, 3, 4, 5, 6, 7; CP 1, 2, 3, 4,
5, 6, 7; CSW; DLB 2, 5, 130, 152; DLBY
1983
Garrick, David 1717-1779 .... **LC 15**
See also DAM DRAM; DLB 84, 213;
RGEL 2
Garrigue, Jean 1914-1972 .... **CLC 2, 8**
See also CA 5-8R; 37-40R; CANR 20; CP
1; MAL 5
Garrison, Frederick
See Sinclair, Upton
Garrison, William Lloyd
1805-1879 .... **NCLC 149**
See also CDALB 1640-1865; DLB 1, 43,
235
Garro, Elena 1920(?)-1998 .. **HLCS 1; TCLC**
153
See also CA 131; 169; CWW 2; DLB 145;
EWL 3; HW 1; LAWS 1; WLIT 1
Garth, Will
See Hamilton, Edmond; Kuttner, Henry
Garvey, Marcus (Moziah, Jr.)
1887-1940 ... **BLC 2; HR 1:2; TCLC 41**
See also BW 1; CA 120; 124; CANR 79;
DAM MULT

Gary, Romain .... **CLC 25**
See Kacew, Romain
See also DLB 83, 299; RGHL
Gascar, Pierre .... **CLC 11**
See Fournier, Pierre
See also EWL 3; RGHL
Gascoigne, George 1539-1577 .... **LC 108**
See also DLB 136; RGEL 2
Gascoyne, David (Emery)
1916-2001 .... **CLC 45**
See also CA 65-68; 200; CANR 10, 28, 54;
CP 1, 2, 3, 4, 5, 6, 7; DLB 20; MTCW 1;
RGEL 2
Gaskell, Elizabeth Cleghorn
1810-1865 .... **NCLC 5, 70, 97, 137; SSC**
25, 97
See also BRW 5; CDBLB 1832-1890; DAB;
DAM MST; DLB 21, 144, 159; RGEL 2;
RGSF 2; TEA
Gass, William H. 1924- . **CLC 1, 2, 8, 11, 15,**
39, 132; SSC 12
See also AMWS 6; CA 17-20R; CANR 30,
71, 100; CN 1, 2, 3, 4, 5, 6, 7; DLB 2,
227; EWL 3; MAL 5; MTCW 1, 2;
MTFW 2005; RGAL 4
Gassendi, Pierre 1592-1655 .... **LC 54**
See also GFL Beginnings to 1789
Gasset, Jose Ortega y
See Ortega y Gasset, Jose
Gates, Henry Louis, Jr. 1950- .. **BLCS; CLC**
65
See also BW 2, 3; CA 109; CANR 25, 53,
75, 125; CSW; DA3; DAM MULT; DLB
67; EWL 3; MAL 5; MTCW 2; MTFW
2005; RGAL 4
Gatos, Stephanie
See Katz, Steve
Gautier, Theophile 1811-1872 .. **NCLC 1, 59;**
PC 18; SSC 20
See also DAM POET; DLB 119; EW 6;
GFL 1789 to the Present; RGWL 2, 3;
SUFW; TWA
Gay, John 1685-1732 .... **LC 49**
See also BRW 3; DAM DRAM; DLB 84,
95; RGEL 2; WLIT 3
Gay, Oliver
See Gogarty, Oliver St. John
Gay, Peter 1923- .... **CLC 158**
See also CA 13-16R; CANR 18, 41, 77,
147; INT CANR-18; RGHL
Gay, Peter Jack
See Gay, Peter
Gaye, Marvin (Pentz, Jr.)
1939-1984 .... **CLC 26**
See also CA 195; 112
Gebler, Carlo 1954- .... **CLC 39**
See also CA 119; 133; CANR 96; DLB 271
Gee, Maggie 1948- .... **CLC 57**
See also CA 130; CANR 125; CN 4, 5, 6,
7; DLB 207; MTFW 2005
Gee, Maurice 1931- .... **CLC 29**
See also AAYA 42; CA 97-100; CANR 67,
123; CLR 56; CN 2, 3, 4, 5, 6, 7; CWRI
5; EWL 3; MAICYA 2; RGSF 2; SATA
46, 101
Gee, Maurice Gough
See Gee, Maurice
Geiogamah, Hanay 1945- .... **NNAL**
See also CA 153; DAM MULT; DLB 175
Gelbart, Larry
See Gelbart, Larry (Simon)
See also CAD; CD 5, 6
Gelbart, Larry (Simon) 1928- .... **CLC 21, 61**
See Gelbart, Larry
See also CA 73-76; CANR 45, 94
Gelber, Jack 1932-2003 ...... **CLC 1, 6, 14, 79**
See also CA 1-4R; 216; CAD; CANR 2;
DLB 7, 228; MAL 5

Gellhorn, Martha (Ellis)
    1908-1998 .... CLC 14, 60
    See also CA 77-80; 164; CANR 44; CN 1,
        2, 3, 4, 5, 6 7; DLBY 1982, 1998
Genet, Jean 1910-1986 .. CLC 1, 2, 5, 10, 14,
        44, 46; DC 25; TCLC 128
    See also CA 13-16R; CANR 18; DA3;
        DAM DRAM; DFS 10; DLB 72, 321;
        DLBY 1986; EW 13; EWL 3; GFL 1789
        to the Present; GLL 1; LMFS 2; MTCW
        1, 2; MTFW 2005; RGWL 2, 3; TWA
Genlis, Stephanie-Felicite Ducrest
    1746-1830 .... NCLC 166
    See also DLB 313
Gent, Peter 1942- .... CLC 29
    See also AITN 1; CA 89-92; DLBY 1982
Gentile, Giovanni 1875-1944 .... TCLC 96
    See also CA 119
Gentlewoman in New England, A
    See Bradstreet, Anne
Gentlewoman in Those Parts, A
    See Bradstreet, Anne
Geoffrey of Monmouth c.
    1100-1155 .... CMLC 44
    See also DLB 146; TEA
George, Jean
    See George, Jean Craighead
George, Jean Craighead 1919- .... CLC 35
    See also AAYA 8, 69; BYA 2, 4; CA 5-8R;
        CANR 25; CLR 1; 80; DLB 52; JRDA;
        MAICYA 1, 2; SATA 2, 68, 124, 170;
        WYA; YAW
George, Stefan (Anton) 1868-1933 . TCLC 2,
        14
    See also CA 104; 193; EW 8; EWL 3
Georges, Georges Martin
    See Simenon, Georges (Jacques Christian)
Gerald of Wales c. 1146-c. 1223 ... CMLC 60
Gerhardi, William Alexander
    See Gerhardie, William Alexander
Gerhardie, William Alexander
    1895-1977 .... CLC 5
    See also CA 25-28R; 73-76; CANR 18; CN
        1, 2; DLB 36; RGEL 2
Gerson, Jean 1363-1429 .... LC 77
    See also DLB 208
Gersonides 1288-1344 .... CMLC 49
    See also DLB 115
Gerstler, Amy 1956- .... CLC 70
    See also CA 146; CANR 99
Gertler, T. .... CLC 34
    See also CA 116; 121
Gertsen, Aleksandr Ivanovich
    See Herzen, Aleksandr Ivanovich
Ghalib .... NCLC 39, 78
    See Ghalib, Asadullah Khan
Ghalib, Asadullah Khan 1797-1869
    See Ghalib
    See also DAM POET; RGWL 2, 3
Ghelderode, Michel de 1898-1962 ..... CLC 6,
        11; DC 15; TCLC 187
    See also CA 85-88; CANR 40, 77; DAM
        DRAM; DLB 321; EW 11; EWL 3; TWA
Ghiselin, Brewster 1903-2001 .... CLC 23
    See also CA 13-16R; CAAS 10; CANR 13;
        CP 1, 2, 3, 4, 5, 6, 7
Ghose, Aurabinda 1872-1950 .... TCLC 63
    See Ghose, Aurobindo
    See also CA 163
Ghose, Aurobindo
    See Ghose, Aurabinda
    See also EWL 3
Ghose, Zulfikar 1935- .... CLC 42, 200
    See also CA 65-68; CANR 67; CN 1, 2, 3,
        4, 5, 6, 7; CP 1, 2, 3, 4, 5, 6, 7; DLB 323;
        EWL 3
Ghosh, Amitav 1956- .... CLC 44, 153
    See also CA 147; CANR 80; CN 6, 7; DLB
        323; WWE 1

Giacosa, Giuseppe 1847-1906 .... TCLC 7
    See also CA 104
Gibb, Lee
    See Waterhouse, Keith (Spencer)
Gibbon, Edward 1737-1794 .... LC 97
    See also BRW 3; DLB 104; RGEL 2
Gibbon, Lewis Grassic .... TCLC 4
    See Mitchell, James Leslie
    See also RGEL 2
Gibbons, Kaye 1960- .... CLC 50, 88, 145
    See also AAYA 34; AMWS 10; CA 151;
        CANR 75, 127; CN 7; CSW; DA3; DAM
        POP; DLB 292; MTCW 2; MTFW 2005;
        NFS 3; RGAL 4; SATA 117
Gibran, Kahlil 1883-1931 . PC 9; TCLC 1, 9
    See also CA 104; 150; DA3; DAM POET,
        POP; EWL 3; MTCW 2; WLIT 6
Gibran, Khalil
    See Gibran, Kahlil
Gibson, Mel 1956- .... CLC 215
Gibson, William 1914- .... CLC 23
    See also CA 9-12R; CAD; CANR 9, 42, 75,
        125; CD 5, 6; DA; DAB; DAC; DAM
        DRAM, MST; DFS 2; DLB 7; LAIT 2;
        MAL 5; MTCW 2; MTFW 2005; SATA
        66; YAW
Gibson, William 1948- .... CLC 39, 63, 186,
        192; SSC 52
    See also AAYA 12, 59; AMWS 16; BPFB
        2; CA 126; 133; CANR 52, 90, 106; CN
        6, 7; CPW; DA3; DAM POP; DLB 251;
        MTCW 2; MTFW 2005; SCFW 2; SFW 4
Gide, Andre (Paul Guillaume)
    1869-1951 ...... SSC 13; TCLC 5, 12, 36,
        177; WLC 3
    See also CA 104; 124; DA; DA3; DAB;
        DAC; DAM MST, NOV; DLB 65, 321,
        330; EW 8; EWL 3; GFL 1789 to the
        Present; MTCW 1, 2; MTFW 2005; NFS
        21; RGSF 2; RGWL 2, 3; TWA
Gifford, Barry (Colby) 1946- .... CLC 34
    See also CA 65-68; CANR 9, 30, 40, 90
Gilbert, Frank
    See De Voto, Bernard (Augustine)
Gilbert, W(illiam) S(chwenck)
    1836-1911 .... TCLC 3
    See also CA 104; 173; DAM DRAM, POET;
        RGEL 2; SATA 36
Gilbert of Poitiers c. 1085-1154 .... CMLC 85
Gilbreth, Frank B(unker), Jr.
    1911-2001 .... CLC 17
    See also CA 9-12R; SATA 2
Gilchrist, Ellen (Louise) 1935- .. CLC 34, 48,
        143; SSC 14, 63
    See also BPFB 2; CA 113; 116; CANR 41,
        61, 104; CN 4, 5, 6, 7; CPW; CSW; DAM
        POP; DLB 130; EWL 3; EXPS; MTCW
        1, 2; MTFW 2005; RGAL 4; RGSF 2;
        SSFS 9
Giles, Molly 1942- .... CLC 39
    See also CA 126; CANR 98
Gill, Eric .... TCLC 85
    See Gill, (Arthur) Eric (Rowton Peter
        Joseph)
Gill, (Arthur) Eric (Rowton Peter Joseph)
    1882-1940
    See Gill, Eric
    See also CA 120; DLB 98
Gill, Patrick
    See Creasey, John
Gillette, Douglas .... CLC 70
Gilliam, Terry 1940- .... CLC 21, 141
    See Monty Python
    See also AAYA 19, 59; CA 108; 113; CANR
        35; INT CA-113
Gilliam, Terry Vance
    See Gilliam, Terry
Gillian, Jerry
    See Gilliam, Terry

Gilliatt, Penelope (Ann Douglass)
    1932-1993 .... CLC 2, 10, 13, 53
    See also AITN 2; CA 13-16R; 141; CANR
        49; CN 1, 2, 3, 4, 5; DLB 14
Gilligan, Carol 1936- .... CLC 208
    See also CA 142; CANR 121; FW
Gilman, Charlotte (Anna) Perkins (Stetson)
    1860-1935 ...... SSC 13, 62; TCLC 9, 37,
        117
    See also AMWS 11; BYA 11; CA 106; 150;
        DLB 221; EXPS; FL 1:5; FW; HGG;
        LAIT 2; MBL; MTCW 2; MTFW 2005;
        RGAL 4; RGSF 2; SFW 4; SSFS 1, 18
Gilmour, David 1946- .... CLC 35
Gilpin, William 1724-1804 .... NCLC 30
Gilray, J. D.
    See Mencken, H(enry) L(ouis)
Gilroy, Frank D(aniel) 1925- .... CLC 2
    See also CA 81-84; CAD; CANR 32, 64,
        86; CD 5, 6; DFS 17; DLB 7
Gilstrap, John 1957(?)- .... CLC 99
    See also AAYA 67; CA 160; CANR 101
Ginsberg, Allen 1926-1997 .... CLC 1, 2, 3, 4,
        6, 13, 36, 69, 109; PC 4, 47; TCLC
        120; WLC 3
    See also AAYA 33; AITN 1; AMWC 1;
        AMWS 2; BG 1:2; CA 1-4R; 157; CANR
        2, 41, 63, 95; CDALB 1941-1968; CP 1,
        2, 3, 4, 5, 6; DA; DA3; DAB; DAC; DAM
        MST, POET; DLB 5, 16, 169, 237; EWL
        3; GLL 1; LMFS 2; MAL 5; MTCW 1, 2;
        MTFW 2005; PAB; PFS 5; RGAL 4;
        TUS; WP
Ginzburg, Eugenia .... CLC 59
    See Ginzburg, Evgeniia
Ginzburg, Evgeniia 1904-1977
    See Ginzburg, Eugenia
    See also DLB 302
Ginzburg, Natalia 1916-1991 .... CLC 5, 11,
        54, 70; SSC 65; TCLC 156
    See also CA 85-88; 135; CANR 33; DFS
        14; DLB 177; EW 13; EWL 3; MTCW 1,
        2; MTFW 2005; RGHL; RGWL 2, 3
Giono, Jean 1895-1970 .... CLC 4, 11; TCLC
        124
    See also CA 45-48; 29-32R; CANR 2, 35;
        DLB 72, 321; EWL 3; GFL 1789 to the
        Present; MTCW 1; RGWL 2, 3
Giovanni, Nikki 1943- ...... BLC 2; CLC 2, 4,
        19, 64, 117; PC 19; WLCS
    See also AAYA 22; AITN 1; BW 2, 3; CA
        29-32R; CAAS 6; CANR 18, 41, 60, 91,
        130; CDALBS; CLR 6, 73; CP 2, 3, 4, 5,
        6, 7; CSW; CWP; CWRI 5; DA; DA3;
        DAB; DAC; DAM MST, MULT, POET;
        DLB 5, 41; EWL 3; EXPP; INT CANR-
        18; MAICYA 1, 2; MAL 5; MTCW 1, 2;
        MTFW 2005; PFS 17; RGAL 4; SATA
        24, 107; TUS; YAW
Giovene, Andrea 1904-1998 .... CLC 7
    See also CA 85-88
Gippius, Zinaida (Nikolaevna) 1869-1945
    See Hippius, Zinaida (Nikolaevna)
    See also CA 106; 212
Giraudoux, Jean(-Hippolyte)
    1882-1944 .... TCLC 2, 7
    See also CA 104; 196; DAM DRAM; DLB
        65, 321; EW 9; EWL 3; GFL 1789 to the
        Present; RGWL 2, 3; TWA
Gironella, Jose Maria (Pous)
    1917-2003 .... CLC 11
    See also CA 101; 212; EWL 3; RGWL 2, 3
Gissing, George (Robert)
    1857-1903 ...... SSC 37; TCLC 3, 24, 47
    See also BRW 5; CA 105; 167; DLB 18,
        135, 184; RGEL 2; TEA
Gitlin, Todd 1943- .... CLC 201
    See also CA 29-32R; CANR 25, 50, 88
Giurlani, Aldo
    See Palazzeschi, Aldo

Gladkov, Fedor Vasil'evich
See Gladkov, Fyodor (Vasilyevich)
See also DLB 272
Gladkov, Fyodor (Vasilyevich)
1883-1958 .... **TCLC 27**
See Gladkov, Fedor Vasil'evich
Scc also CA 170; EWL 3
Glancy, Diane 1941- .... **CLC 210; NNAL**
See also CA 136, 225; CAAE 225; CAAS
24; CANR 87; DLB 175
Glanville, Brian (Lester) 1931- .... **CLC 6**
See also CA 5-8R; CAAS 9; CANR 3, 70;
CN 1, 2, 3, 4, 5, 6, 7; DLB 15, 139; SATA
42
Glasgow, Ellen (Anderson Gholson)
1873-1945 .... **SSC 34; TCLC 2, 7**
See also AMW; CA 104; 164; DLB 9, 12;
MAL 5; MBL; MTCW 2; MTFW 2005;
RGAL 4; RHW; SSFS 9; TUS
Glaspell, Susan 1882(?)-1948 ..... **DC 10; SSC
41; TCLC 55, 175**
See also AMWS 3; CA 110; 154; DFS 8,
18; DLB 7, 9, 78, 228; MBL; RGAL 4;
SSFS 3; TCWW 2; TUS; YABC 2
Glassco, John 1909-1981 .... **CLC 9**
See also CA 13-16R; 102; CANR 15; CN
1, 2; CP 1, 2, 3; DLB 68
Glasscock, Amnesia
See Steinbeck, John (Ernst)
Glasser, Ronald J. 1940(?)- .... **CLC 37**
See also CA 209
Glassman, Joyce
See Johnson, Joyce
Gleick, James (W.) 1954- .... **CLC 147**
See also CA 131; 137; CANR 97; INT CA-
137
Glendinning, Victoria 1937- .... **CLC 50**
See also CA 120; 127; CANR 59, 89; DLB
155
Glissant, Edouard (Mathieu)
1928- .... **CLC 10, 68**
See also CA 153; CANR 111; CWW 2;
DAM MULT; EWL 3; RGWL 3
Gloag, Julian 1930- .... **CLC 40**
See also AITN 1; CA 65-68; CANR 10, 70;
CN 1, 2, 3, 4, 5, 6
Glowacki, Aleksander
See Prus, Boleslaw
Gluck, Louise 1943- .... **CLC 7, 22, 44, 81,
160; PC 16**
See also AMWS 5; CA 33-36R; CANR 40,
69, 108, 133; CP 1, 2, 3, 4, 5, 6, 7; CWP;
DA3; DAM POET; DLB 5; MAL 5;
MTCW 2; MTFW 2005; PFS 5, 15;
RGAL 4; TCLE 1:1
Glyn, Elinor 1864-1943 .... **TCLC 72**
See also DLB 153; RHW
Gobineau, Joseph-Arthur
1816-1882 .... **NCLC 17**
See also DLB 123; GFL 1789 to the Present
Godard, Jean-Luc 1930- .... **CLC 20**
See also CA 93-96
Godden, (Margaret) Rumer
1907-1998 .... **CLC 53**
See also AAYA 6; BPFB 2; BYA 2, 5; CA
5-8R; 172; CANR 4, 27, 36, 55, 80; CLR
20; CN 1, 2, 3, 4, 5, 6; CWRI 5; DLB
161; MAICYA 1, 2; RHW; SAAS 12;
SATA 3, 36; SATA-Obit 109; TEA
Godoy Alcayaga, Lucila 1899-1957 .. **HLC 2;
PC 32; TCLC 2**
See Mistral, Gabriela
See also BW 2; CA 104; 131; CANR 81;
DAM MULT; DNFS; HW 1, 2; MTCW 1,
2; MTFW 2005

Godwin, Gail 1937- ...... **CLC 5, 8, 22, 31, 69,
125**
See also BPFB 2; CA 29-32R; CANR 15,
43, 69, 132; CN 3, 4, 5, 6, 7; CPW; CSW;
DA3; DAM POP; DLB 6, 234; INT
CANR-15; MAL 5; MTCW 1, 2; MTFW
2005
Godwin, Gail Kathleen
See Godwin, Gail
Godwin, William 1756-1836 .. **NCLC 14, 130**
See also CDBLB 1789-1832; CMW 4; DLB
39, 104, 142, 158, 163, 262; GL 2; HGG;
RGEL 2
Goebbels, Josef
See Goebbels, (Paul) Joseph
Goebbels, (Paul) Joseph
1897-1945 .... **TCLC 68**
See also CA 115; 148
Goebbels, Joseph Paul
See Goebbels, (Paul) Joseph
Goethe, Johann Wolfgang von
1749-1832 . **DC 20; NCLC 4, 22, 34, 90,
154; PC 5; SSC 38; WLC 3**
See also CDWLB 2; DA; DA3; DAB;
DAC; DAM DRAM, MST, POET; DLB
94; EW 5; GL 2; LATS 1; LMFS 1:1;
RGWL 2, 3; TWA
Gogarty, Oliver St. John
1878-1957 .... **TCLC 15**
See also CA 109; 150; DLB 15, 19; RGEL
2
Gogol, Nikolai (Vasilyevich)
1809-1852 .... **DC 1; NCLC 5, 15, 31,
162; SSC 4, 29, 52; WLC 3**
See also DA; DAB; DAC; DAM DRAM,
MST; DFS 12; DLB 198; EW 6; EXPS;
RGSF 2; RGWL 2, 3; SSFS 7; TWA
Goines, Donald 1937(?)-1974 ... **BLC 2; CLC
80**
See also AITN 1; BW 1, 3; CA 124; 114;
CANR 82; CMW 4; DA3; DAM MULT,
POP; DLB 33
Gold, Herbert 1924- ... **CLC 4, 7, 14, 42, 152**
See also CA 9-12R; CANR 17, 45, 125; CN
1, 2, 3, 4, 5, 6, 7; DLB 2; DLBY 1981;
MAL 5
Goldbarth, Albert 1948- .... **CLC 5, 38**
See also AMWS 12; CA 53-56; CANR 6,
40; CP 3, 4, 5, 6, 7; DLB 120
Goldberg, Anatol 1910-1982 .... **CLC 34**
See also CA 131; 117
Goldemberg, Isaac 1945- .... **CLC 52**
See also CA 69-72; CAAS 12; CANR 11,
32; EWL 3; HW 1; WLIT 1
Golding, Arthur 1536-1606 .... **LC 101**
See also DLB 136
Golding, William 1911-1993 . **CLC 1, 2, 3, 8,
10, 17, 27, 58, 81; WLC 3**
See also AAYA 5, 44; BPFB 2; BRWR 1;
BRWS 1; BYA 2; CA 5-8R; 141; CANR
13, 33, 54; CD 5; CDBLB 1945-1960;
CLR 94; CN 1, 2, 3, 4; DA; DA3; DAB;
DAC; DAM MST, NOV; DLB 15, 100,
255, 326, 330; EWL 3; EXPN; HGG;
LAIT 4; MTCW 1, 2; MTFW 2005; NFS
2; RGEL 2; RHW; SFW 4; TEA; WLIT
4; YAW
Goldman, Emma 1869-1940 .... **TCLC 13**
See also CA 110; 150; DLB 221; FW;
RGAL 4; TUS
Goldman, Francisco 1954- .... **CLC 76**
See also CA 162
Goldman, William 1931- .... **CLC 1, 48**
See also BPFB 2; CA 9-12R; CANR 29,
69, 106; CN 1, 2, 3, 4, 5, 6, 7; DLB 44;
FANT; IDFW 3, 4
Goldman, William W.
See Goldman, William
Goldmann, Lucien 1913-1970 .... **CLC 24**
See also CA 25-28; CAP 2

Goldoni, Carlo 1707-1793 .... **LC 4**
See also DAM DRAM; EW 4; RGWL 2, 3;
WLIT 7
Goldsberry, Steven 1949- .... **CLC 34**
See also CA 131
Goldsmith, Oliver 1730-1774 .... **DC 8; LC 2,
48, 122; WLC 3**
See also BRW 3; CDBLB 1660-1789; DA;
DAB; DAC; DAM DRAM, MST, NOV,
POET; DFS 1; DLB 39, 89, 104, 109, 142;
IDTP; RGEL 2; SATA 26; TEA; WLIT 3
Goldsmith, Peter
See Priestley, J(ohn) B(oynton)
Gombrowicz, Witold 1904-1969 .... **CLC 4, 7,
11, 49**
See also CA 19-20; 25-28R; CANR 105;
CAP 2; CDWLB 4; DAM DRAM; DLB
215; EW 12; EWL 3; RGWL 2, 3; TWA
Gomez de Avellaneda, Gertrudis
1814-1873 .... **NCLC 111**
See also LAW
Gomez de la Serna, Ramon
1888-1963 .... **CLC 9**
See also CA 153; 116; CANR 79; EWL 3;
HW 1, 2
Goncharov, Ivan Alexandrovich
1812-1891 .... **NCLC 1, 63**
See also DLB 238; EW 6; RGWL 2, 3
Goncourt, Edmond (Louis Antoine Huot) de
1822-1896 .... **NCLC 7**
See also DLB 123; EW 7; GFL 1789 to the
Present; RGWL 2, 3
Goncourt, Jules (Alfred Huot) de
1830-1870 .... **NCLC 7**
Scc also DLB 123; EW 7; GFL 1789 to the
Present; RGWL 2, 3
Gongora (y Argote), Luis de
1561-1627 .... **LC 72**
See also RGWL 2, 3
Gontier, Fernande 19(?)- .... **CLC 50**
Gonzalez Martinez, Enrique
Scc Gonzalez Martinez, Enrique
See also DLB 290
Gonzalez Martinez, Enrique
1871-1952 .... **TCLC 72**
See Gonzalez Martinez, Enrique
See also CA 166; CANR 81; EWL 3; HW
1, 2
Goodison, Lorna 1947- .... **PC 36**
See also CA 142; CANR 88; CP 5, 6, 7;
CWP; DLB 157; EWL 3
Goodman, Paul 1911-1972 ...... **CLC 1, 2, 4, 7**
See also CA 19-20; 37-40R; CAD; CANR
34; CAP 2; CN 1; DLB 130, 246; MAL
5; MTCW 1; RGAL 4
GoodWeather, Harley
See King, Thomas
Googe, Barnabe 1540-1594 .... **LC 94**
See also DLB 132; RGEL 2
Gordimer, Nadine 1923- ...... **CLC 3, 5, 7, 10,
18, 33, 51, 70, 123, 160, 161; SSC 17,
80; WLCS**
See also AAYA 39; AFW; BRWS 2; CA
5-8R; CANR 3, 28, 56, 88, 131; CN 1, 2,
3, 4, 5, 6, 7; DA; DA3; DAB; DAC; DAM
MST, NOV; DLB 225, 326, 330; EWL 3;
EXPS; INT CANR-28; LATS 1:2; MTCW
1, 2; MTFW 2005; NFS 4; RGEL 2;
RGSF 2; SSFS 2, 14, 19; TWA; WLIT 2;
YAW
Gordon, Adam Lindsay
1833-1870 .... **NCLC 21**
See also DLB 230
Gordon, Caroline 1895-1981 . **CLC 6, 13, 29,
83; SSC 15**
See also AMW; CA 11-12; 103; CANR 36;
CAP 1; CN 1; DLB 4, 9, 102; DLBD
17; DLBY 1981; EWL 3; MAL 5; MTCW
1, 2; MTFW 2005; RGAL 4; RGSF 2

Gordon, Charles William 1860-1937
See Connor, Ralph
See also CA 109

Gordon, Mary 1949- .. CLC 13, 22, 128, 216;
SSC 59
See also AMWS 4; BPFB 2; CA 102;
CANR 44, 92, 154; CN 4, 5, 6, 7; DLB 6;
DLBY 1981; FW; INT CA-102; MAL 5;
MTCW 1

Gordon, Mary Catherine
See Gordon, Mary

Gordon, N. J.
See Bosman, Herman Charles

Gordon, Sol 1923- .... CLC 26
See also CA 53-56; CANR 4; SATA 11

Gordone, Charles 1925-1995 .. CLC 1, 4; DC
8
See also BW 1, 3; CA 93-96, 180; 150;
CAAE 180; CAD; CANR 55; DAM
DRAM; DLB 7; INT CA-93-96; MTCW
1

Gore, Catherine 1800-1861 .... NCLC 65
See also DLB 116; RGEL 2

Gorenko, Anna Andreevna
See Akhmatova, Anna

Gorky, Maxim .... SSC 28; TCLC 8; WLC 3
See Peshkov, Alexei Maximovich
See also DAB; DFS 9; DLB 295; EW 8;
EWL 3; TWA

Goryan, Sirak
See Saroyan, William

Gosse, Edmund (William)
1849-1928 .... TCLC 28
See also CA 117; DLB 57, 144, 184; RGEL
2

Gotlieb, Phyllis (Fay Bloom) 1926- .. CLC 18
See also CA 13-16R; CANR 7, 135; CN 7;
CP 1, 2, 3, 4; DLB 88, 251; SFW 4

Gottesman, S. D.
See Kornbluth, C(yril) M.; Pohl, Frederik

Gottfried von Strassburg fl. c.
1170-1215 .... CMLC 10
See also CDWLB 2; DLB 138; EW 1;
RGWL 2, 3

Gotthelf, Jeremias 1797-1854 .... NCLC 117
See also DLB 133; RGWL 2, 3

Gottschalk, Laura Riding
See Jackson, Laura (Riding)

Gould, Lois 1932(?)-2002 .... CLC 4, 10
See also CA 77-80; 208; CANR 29; MTCW
1

Gould, Stephen Jay 1941-2002 .... CLC 163
See also AAYA 26; BEST 90:2; CA 77-80;
205; CANR 10, 27, 56, 75, 125; CPW;
INT CANR-27; MTCW 1, 2; MTFW 2005

Gourmont, Remy(-Marie-Charles) de
1858-1915 .... TCLC 17
See also CA 109; 150; GFL 1789 to the
Present; MTCW 2

Gournay, Marie le Jars de
See de Gournay, Marie le Jars

Govier, Katherine 1948- .... CLC 51
See also CA 101; CANR 18, 40, 128; CCA
1

Gower, John c. 1330-1408 .... LC 76; PC 59
See also BRW 1; DLB 146; RGEL 2

Goyen, (Charles) William
1915-1983 .... CLC 5, 8, 14, 40
See also AITN 2; CA 5-8R; 110; CANR 6,
71; CN 1, 2, 3; DLB 2, 218; DLBY 1983;
EWL 3; INT CANR-6; MAL 5

Goytisolo, Juan 1931- .... CLC 5, 10, 23, 133;
HLC 1
See also CA 85-88; CANR 32, 61, 131;
CWW 2; DAM MULT; DLB 322; EWL
3; GLL 2; HW 1, 2; MTCW 1, 2; MTFW
2005

Gozzano, Guido 1883-1916 .... PC 10
See also CA 154; DLB 114; EWL 3

Gozzi, (Conte) Carlo 1720-1806 .... NCLC 23

Grabbe, Christian Dietrich
1801-1836 .... NCLC 2
See also DLB 133; RGWL 2, 3

Grace, Patricia Frances 1937- .... CLC 56
See also CA 176; CANR 118; CN 4, 5, 6,
7; EWL 3; RGSF 2

Gracian y Morales, Baltasar
1601-1658 .... LC 15

Gracq, Julien .... CLC 11, 48
See Poirier, Louis
See also CWW 2; DLB 83; GFL 1789 to
the Present

Grade, Chaim 1910-1982 .... CLC 10
See also CA 93-96; 107; EWL 3; RGHL

Graduate of Oxford, A
See Ruskin, John

Grafton, Garth
See Duncan, Sara Jeannette

Grafton, Sue 1940- .... CLC 163
See also AAYA 11, 49; BEST 90:3; CA 108;
CANR 31, 55, 111, 134; CMW 4; CPW;
CSW; DA3; DAM POP; DLB 226; FW;
MSW; MTFW 2005

Graham, John
See Phillips, David Graham

Graham, Jorie 1950- .... CLC 48, 118; PC 59
See also AAYA 67; CA 111; CANR 63, 118;
CP 4, 5, 6, 7; CWP; DLB 120; EWL 3;
MTFW 2005; PFS 10, 17; TCLE 1:1

Graham, R(obert) B(ontine) Cunninghame
See Cunninghame Graham, Robert
(Gallnigad) Bontine
See also DLB 98, 135, 174; RGEL 2; RGSF
2

Graham, Robert
See Haldeman, Joe

Graham, Tom
See Lewis, (Harry) Sinclair

Graham, W(illiam) S(idney)
1918-1986 .... CLC 29
See also BRWS 7; CA 73-76; 118; CP 1, 2,
3, 4; DLB 20; RGEL 2

Graham, Winston (Mawdsley)
1910-2003 .... CLC 23
See also CA 49-52; 218; CANR 2, 22, 45,
66; CMW 4; CN 1, 2, 3, 4, 5, 6, 7; DLB
77; RHW

Grahame, Kenneth 1859-1932 ...... TCLC 64,
136
See also BYA 5; CA 108; 136; CANR 80;
CLR 5; CWRI 5; DA3; DAB; DLB 34,
141, 178; FANT; MAICYA 1, 2; MTCW
2; NFS 20; RGEL 2; SATA 100; TEA;
WCH; YABC 1

Granger, Darius John
See Marlowe, Stephen

Granin, Daniil 1918- .... CLC 59
See also DLB 302

Granovsky, Timofei Nikolaevich
1813-1855 .... NCLC 75
See also DLB 198

Grant, Skeeter
See Spiegelman, Art

Granville-Barker, Harley
1877-1946 .... TCLC 2
See Barker, Harley Granville
See also CA 104; 204; DAM DRAM;
RGEL 2

Granzotto, Gianni
See Granzotto, Giovanni Battista

Granzotto, Giovanni Battista
1914-1985 .... CLC 70
See also CA 166

Grass, Guenter
See Grass, Gunter
See also CWW 2; DLB 330; RGHL

Grass, Gunter 1927- .. CLC 1, 2, 4, 6, 11, 15,
22, 32, 49, 88, 207; WLC 3
See Grass, Guenter
See also BPFB 2; CA 13-16R; CANR 20,
75, 93, 133; CDWLB 2; DA; DA3; DAB;
DAC; DAM MST, NOV; DLB 75, 124;
EW 13; EWL 3; MTCW 1, 2; MTFW
2005; RGWL 2, 3; TWA

Grass, Gunter Wilhelm
See Grass, Gunter

Gratton, Thomas
See Hulme, T(homas) E(rnest)

Grau, Shirley Ann 1929- .... CLC 4, 9, 146;
SSC 15
See also CA 89-92; CANR 22, 69; CN 1, 2,
3, 4, 5, 6, 7; CSW; DLB 2, 218; INT CA-
89-92; CANR-22; MTCW 1

Gravel, Fern
See Hall, James Norman

Graver, Elizabeth 1964- .... CLC 70
See also CA 135; CANR 71, 129

Graves, Richard Perceval
1895-1985 .... CLC 44
See also CA 65-68; CANR 9, 26, 51

Graves, Robert 1895-1985 ... CLC 1, 2, 6, 11,
39, 44, 45; PC 6
See also BPFB 2; BRW 7; BYA 4; CA 5-8R;
117; CANR 5, 36; CDBLB 1914-1945;
CN 1, 2, 3; CP 1, 2, 3; DA3; DAB;
DAC; DAM MST, POET; DLB 20, 100,
191; DLBD 18; DLBY 1985; EWL 3;
LATS 1:1; MTCW 1, 2; MTFW 2005;
NCFS 2; NFS 21; RGEL 2; RHW; SATA
45; TEA

Graves, Valerie
See Bradley, Marion Zimmer

Gray, Alasdair 1934- .... CLC 41
See also BRWS 9; CA 126; CANR 47, 69,
106, 140; CN 4, 5, 6, 7; DLB 194, 261,
319; HGG; INT CA-126; MTCW 1, 2;
MTFW 2005; RGSF 2; SUFW 2

Gray, Amlin 1946- .... CLC 29
See also CA 138

Gray, Francine du Plessix 1930- ..... CLC 22,
153
See also BEST 90:3; CA 61-64; CAAS 2;
CANR 11, 33, 75, 81; DAM NOV; INT
CANR-11; MTCW 1, 2; MTFW 2005

Gray, John (Henry) 1866-1934 ...... TCLC 19
See also CA 119; 162; RGEL 2

Gray, John Lee
See Jakes, John

Gray, Simon (James Holliday)
1936- .... CLC 9, 14, 36
See also AITN 1; CA 21-24R; CAAS 3;
CANR 32, 69; CBD; CD 5, 6; CN 1, 2, 3;
DLB 13; EWL 3; MTCW 1; RGEL 2

Gray, Spalding 1941-2004 .... CLC 49, 112;
DC 7
See also AAYA 62; CA 128; 225; CAD;
CANR 74, 138; CD 5, 6; CPW; DAM
POP; MTCW 2; MTFW 2005

Gray, Thomas 1716-1771 .... LC 4, 40; PC 2;
WLC 3
See also BRW 3; CDBLB 1660-1789; DA;
DA3; DAB; DAC; DAM MST; DLB 109;
EXPP; PAB; PFS 9; RGEL 2; TEA; WP

Grayson, David
See Baker, Ray Stannard

Grayson, Richard (A.) 1951- .... CLC 38
See also CA 85-88; 210; CAAE 210; CANR
14, 31, 57; DLB 234

Greeley, Andrew M. 1928- .... CLC 28
See also BPFB 2; CA 5-8R; CAAS 7;
CANR 7, 43, 69, 104, 136; CMW 4;
CPW; DA3; DAM POP; MTCW 1, 2;
MTFW 2005

Horkheimer, Max 1895-1973 .... **TCLC 132**
   See also CA 216; 41-44R; DLB 296
Horn, Peter
   See Kuttner, Henry
Horne, Frank (Smith) 1899-1974 ...... **HR 1:2**
   See also BW 1; CA 125; 53-56; DLB 51;
   WP
Horne, Richard Henry Hengist
   1802(?)-1884 .... **NCLC 127**
   See also DLB 32; SATA 29
Hornem, Horace Esq.
   See Byron, George Gordon (Noel)
Horney, Karen (Clementine Theodore
   Danielsen) 1885-1952 .... **TCLC 71**
   See also CA 114; 165; DLB 246; FW
Hornung, E(rnest) W(illiam)
   1866-1921 .... **TCLC 59**
   See also CA 108; 160; CMW 4; DLB 70
Horovitz, Israel (Arthur) 1939- .... **CLC 56**
   See also CA 33-36R; CAD; CANR 46, 59;
   CD 5, 6; DAM DRAM; DLB 7; MAL 5
Horton, George Moses
   1797(?)-1883(?) .... **NCLC 87**
   See also DLB 50
Horvath, odon von 1901-1938
   See von Horvath, Odon
   See also EWL 3
Horvath, Oedoen von -1938
   See von Horvath, Odon
Horwitz, Julius 1920-1986 .... **CLC 14**
   See also CA 9-12R; 119; CANR 12
Horwitz, Ronald
   See Harwood, Ronald
Hospital, Janette Turner 1942- .... **CLC 42,
   145**
   See also CA 108; CANR 48; CN 5, 6, 7;
   DLB 325; DLBY 2002; RGSF 2
Hostos, E. M. de
   See Hostos (y Bonilla), Eugenio Maria de
Hostos, Eugenio M. de
   See Hostos (y Bonilla), Eugenio Maria de
Hostos, Eugenio Maria
   See Hostos (y Bonilla), Eugenio Maria de
Hostos (y Bonilla), Eugenio Maria de
   1839-1903 .... **TCLC 24**
   See also CA 123; 131; HW 1
Houdini
   See Lovecraft, H. P.
Houellebecq, Michel 1958- .... **CLC 179**
   See also CA 185; CANR 140; MTFW 2005
Hougan, Carolyn 1943- .... **CLC 34**
   See also CA 139
Household, Geoffrey (Edward West)
   1900-1988 .... **CLC 11**
   See also CA 77-80; 126; CANR 58; CMW
   4; CN 1, 2, 3, 4; DLB 87; SATA 14;
   SATA-Obit 59
Housman, A(lfred) E(dward)
   1859-1936 .... **PC 2, 43; TCLC 1, 10;
   WLCS**
   See also AAYA 66; BRW 6; CA 104; 125;
   DA; DA3; DAB; DAC; DAM MST,
   POET; DLB 19, 284; EWL 3; EXPP;
   MTCW 1, 2; MTFW 2005; PAB; PFS 4,
   7; RGEL 2; TEA; WP
Housman, Laurence 1865-1959 .... **TCLC 7**
   See also CA 106; 155; DLB 10; FANT;
   RGEL 2; SATA 25
Houston, Jeanne Wakatsuki 1934- .... **AAL**
   See also AAYA 49; CA 103, 232; CAAE
   232; CAAS 16; CANR 29, 123; LAIT 4;
   SATA 78, 168; SATA-Essay 168
Howard, Elizabeth Jane 1923- ..... **CLC 7, 29**
   See also BRWS 11; CA 5-8R; CANR 8, 62,
   146; CN 1, 2, 3, 4, 5, 6, 7

Howard, Maureen 1930- .... **CLC 5, 14, 46,
   151**
   See also CA 53-56; CANR 31, 75, 140; CN
   4, 5, 6, 7; DLBY 1983; INT CANR-31;
   MTCW 1, 2; MTFW 2005
Howard, Richard 1929- .... **CLC 7, 10, 47**
   See also AITN 1; CA 85-88; CANR 25, 80,
   154; CP 1, 2, 3, 4, 5, 6, 7; DLB 5; INT
   CANR-25; MAL 5
Howard, Robert E 1906-1936 .... **TCLC 8**
   See also BPFB 2; BYA 5; CA 105; 157;
   CANR 155; FANT; SUFW 1; TCWW 1,
   2
Howard, Robert Ervin
   See Howard, Robert E
Howard, Warren F.
   See Pohl, Frederik
Howe, Fanny (Quincy) 1940- .... **CLC 47**
   See also CA 117, 187; CAAE 187; CAAS
   27; CANR 70, 116; CP 6, 7; CWP; SATA-
   Brief 52
Howe, Irving 1920-1993 .... **CLC 85**
   See also AMWS 6; CA 9-12R; 141; CANR
   21, 50; DLB 67; EWL 3; MAL 5; MTCW
   1, 2; MTFW 2005
Howe, Julia Ward 1819-1910 .... **TCLC 21**
   See also CA 117; 191; DLB 1, 189, 235;
   FW
Howe, Susan 1937- .... **CLC 72, 152; PC 54**
   See also AMWS 4; CA 160; CP 5, 6, 7;
   CWP; DLB 120; FW; RGAL 4
Howe, Tina 1937- .... **CLC 48**
   See also CA 109; CAD; CANR 125; CD 5,
   6; CWD
Howell, James 1594(?)-1666 .... **LC 13**
   See also DLB 151
Howells, W. D.
   See Howells, William Dean
Howells, William D.
   See Howells, William Dean
Howells, William Dean 1837-1920 ... **SSC 36;
   TCLC 7, 17, 41**
   See also AMW; CA 104; 134; CDALB
   1865-1917; DLB 12, 64, 74, 79, 189;
   LMFS 1; MAL 5; MTCW 2; RGAL 4;
   TUS
Howes, Barbara 1914-1996 .... **CLC 15**
   See also CA 9-12R; 151; CAAS 3; CANR
   53; CP 1, 2, 3, 4, 5, 6; SATA 5; TCLE 1:1
Hrabal, Bohumil 1914-1997 ...... **CLC 13, 67;
   TCLC 155**
   See also CA 106; 156; CAAS 12; CANR
   57; CWW 2; DLB 232; EWL 3; RGSF 2
Hrabanus Maurus 776(?)-856 .... **CMLC 78**
   See also DLB 148
Hrotsvit of Gandersheim c. 935-c.
   1000 .... **CMLC 29**
   See also DLB 148
Hsi, Chu 1130-1200 .... **CMLC 42**
Hsun, Lu
   See Lu Hsun
Hubbard, L. Ron 1911-1986 .... **CLC 43**
   See also AAYA 64; CA 77-80; 118; CANR
   52; CPW; DA3; DAM POP; FANT;
   MTCW 2; MTFW 2005; SFW 4
Hubbard, Lafayette Ronald
   See Hubbard, L. Ron
Huch, Ricarda (Octavia)
   1864-1947 .... **TCLC 13**
   See also CA 111; 189; DLB 66; EWL 3
Huddle, David 1942- .... **CLC 49**
   See also CA 57-60; CAAS 20; CANR 89;
   DLB 130
Hudson, Jeffrey
   See Crichton, Michael
Hudson, W(illiam) H(enry)
   1841-1922 .... **TCLC 29**
   See also CA 115; 190; DLB 98, 153, 174;
   RGEL 2; SATA 35

Hueffer, Ford Madox
   See Ford, Ford Madox
Hughart, Barry 1934- .... **CLC 39**
   See also CA 137; FANT; SFW 4; SUFW 2
Hughes, Colin
   See Creasey, John
Hughes, David (John) 1930-2005 ..... **CLC 48**
   See also CA 116; 129; 238; CN 4, 5, 6, 7;
   DLB 14
Hughes, Edward James
   See Hughes, Ted
   See also DA3; DAM MST, POET
Hughes, (James Mercer) Langston
   1902-1967 ..... **BLC 2; CLC 1, 5, 10, 15,
   35, 44, 108; DC 3; HR 1:2; PC 1, 53;
   SSC 6, 90; WLC 3**
   See also AAYA 12; AFAW 1, 2; AMWR 1;
   AMWS 1; BW 1, 3; CA 1-4R; 25-28R;
   CANR 1, 34, 82; CDALB 1929-1941;
   CLR 17; DA; DA3; DAB; DAC; DAM
   DRAM, MST, MULT, POET; DFS 6, 18;
   DLB 4, 7, 48, 51, 86, 228, 315; EWL 3;
   EXPP; EXPS; JRDA; LAIT 3; LMFS 2;
   MAICYA 1, 2; MAL 5; MTCW 1, 2;
   MTFW 2005; NFS 21; PAB; PFS 1, 3, 6,
   10, 15; RGAL 4; RGSF 2; SATA 4, 33;
   SSFS 4, 7; TUS; WCH; WP; YAW
Hughes, Richard (Arthur Warren)
   1900-1976 .... **CLC 1, 11**
   See also CA 5-8R; 65-68; CANR 4; CN 1,
   2; DAM NOV; DLB 15, 161; EWL 3;
   MTCW 1; RGEL 2; SATA 8; SATA-Obit
   25
Hughes, Ted 1930-1998 . **CLC 2, 4, 9, 14, 37,
   119; PC 7**
   See Hughes, Edward James
   See also BRWC 2; BRWR 2; BRWS 1; CA
   1-4R; 171; CANR 1, 33, 66, 108; CLR 3;
   CP 1, 2, 3, 4, 5, 6; DAB; DAC; DLB 40,
   161; EWL 3; EXPP; MAICYA 1, 2;
   MTCW 1, 2; MTFW 2005; PAB; PFS 4,
   19; RGEL 2; SATA 49; SATA-Brief 27;
   SATA-Obit 107; TEA; YAW
Hugo, Richard
   See Huch, Ricarda (Octavia)
Hugo, Richard F(ranklin)
   1923-1982 .... **CLC 6, 18, 32; PC 68**
   See also AMWS 6; CA 49-52; 108; CANR
   3; CP 1, 2, 3; DAM POET; DLB 5, 206;
   EWL 3; MAL 5; PFS 17; RGAL 4
Hugo, Victor (Marie) 1802-1885 .... **NCLC 3,
   10, 21, 161; PC 17; WLC 3**
   See also AAYA 28; DA; DA3; DAB; DAC;
   DAM DRAM, MST, NOV, POET; DLB
   119, 192, 217; EFS 2; EW 6; EXPN; GFL
   1789 to the Present; LAIT 1, 2; NFS 5,
   20; RGWL 2, 3; SATA 47; TWA
Huidobro, Vicente
   See Huidobro Fernandez, Vicente Garcia
   See also DLB 283; EWL 3; LAW
Huidobro Fernandez, Vicente Garcia
   1893-1948 .... **TCLC 31**
   See Huidobro, Vicente
   See also CA 131; HW 1
Hulme, Keri 1947- .... **CLC 39, 130**
   See also CA 125; CANR 69; CN 4, 5, 6, 7;
   CP 6, 7; CWP; DLB 326; EWL 3; FW;
   INT CA-125; NFS 24
Hulme, T(homas) E(rnest)
   1883-1917 .... **TCLC 21**
   See also BRWS 6; CA 117; 203; DLB 19
Humboldt, Alexander von
   1769-1859 .... **NCLC 170**
   See also DLB 90
Humboldt, Wilhelm von
   1767-1835 .... **NCLC 134**
   See also DLB 90
Hume, David 1711-1776 .... **LC 7, 56**
   See also BRWS 3; DLB 104, 252; LMFS 1;
   TEA

Jean Paul 1763-1825 .... **NCLC 7**
Jefferies, (John) Richard
   1848-1887 .... **NCLC 47**
   See also DLB 98, 141; RGEL 2; SATA 16;
   SFW 4
Jeffers, (John) Robinson 1887-1962 .. **CLC 2,**
   3, 11, 15, 54; PC 17; WLC 3
   See also AMWS 2; CA 85-88; CANR 35;
   CDALB 1917-1929; DA; DAC; DAM
   MST, POET; DLB 45, 212; EWL 3; MAL
   5; MTCW 1, 2; MTFW 2005; PAB; PFS
   3, 4; RGAL 4
Jefferson, Janet
   See Mencken, H(enry) L(ouis)
Jefferson, Thomas 1743-1826 . **NCLC 11, 103**
   See also AAYA 54; ANW; CDALB 1640-
   1865; DA3; DLB 31, 183; LAIT 1; RGAL
   4
Jeffrey, Francis 1773-1850 .... **NCLC 33**
   See Francis, Lord Jeffrey
Jelakowitch, Ivan
   See Heijermans, Herman
Jelinek, Elfriede 1946- .... **CLC 169**
   See also AAYA 68; CA 154; DLB 85, 330;
   FW
Jellicoe, (Patricia) Ann 1927- .... **CLC 27**
   See also CA 85-88; CBD; CD 5, 6; CWD;
   CWRI 5; DLB 13, 233; FW
Jelloun, Tahar ben 1944- .... **CLC 180**
   See Ben Jelloun, Tahar
   See also CA 162; CANR 100
Jemyma
   See Holley, Marietta
Jen, Gish .... **AAL; CLC 70, 198**
   See Jen, Lillian
   See also AMWC 2; CN 7; DLB 312
Jen, Lillian 1955-
   See Jen, Gish
   See also CA 135; CANR 89, 130
Jenkins, (John) Robin 1912- .... **CLC 52**
   See also CA 1-4R; CANR 1, 135; CN 1, 2,
   3, 4, 5, 6, 7; DLB 14, 271
Jennings, Elizabeth (Joan)
   1926-2001 .... **CLC 5, 14, 131**
   See also BRWS 5; CA 61-64; 200; CAAS
   5; CANR 8, 39, 66, 127; CP 1, 2, 3, 4, 5,
   6, 7; CWP; DLB 27; EWL 3; MTCW 1;
   SATA 66
Jennings, Waylon 1937-2002 .... **CLC 21**
Jensen, Johannes V(ilhelm)
   1873-1950 .... **TCLC 41**
   See also CA 170; DLB 214, 330; EWL 3;
   RGWL 3
Jensen, Laura (Linnea) 1948- .... **CLC 37**
   See also CA 103
Jerome, Saint 345-420 .... **CMLC 30**
   See also RGWL 3
Jerome, Jerome K(lapka)
   1859-1927 .... **TCLC 23**
   See also CA 119; 177; DLB 10, 34, 135;
   RGEL 2
Jerrold, Douglas William
   1803-1857 .... **NCLC 2**
   See also DLB 158, 159; RGEL 2
Jewett, (Theodora) Sarah Orne
   1849-1909 .... **SSC 6, 44; TCLC 1, 22**
   See also AMW; AMWC 2; AMWR 2; CA
   108; 127; CANR 71; DLB 12, 74, 221;
   EXPS; FL 1:3; FW; MAL 5; MBL; NFS
   15; RGAL 4; RGSF 2; SATA 15; SSFS 4
Jewsbury, Geraldine (Endsor)
   1812-1880 .... **NCLC 22**
   See also DLB 21
Jhabvala, Ruth Prawer 1927- . **CLC 4, 8, 29,**
   94, 138; SSC 91
   See also BRWS 5; CA 1-4R; CANR 2, 29,
   51, 74, 91, 128; CN 1, 2, 3, 4, 5, 6, 7;
   DAB; DAM NOV; DLB 139, 194, 323,

326; EWL 3; IDFW 3, 4; INT CANR-29;
   MTCW 1, 2; MTFW 2005; RGSF 2;
   RGWL 2; RHW; TEA
Jibran, Kahlil
   See Gibran, Kahlil
Jibran, Khalil
   See Gibran, Kahlil
Jiles, Paulette 1943- .... **CLC 13, 58**
   See also CA 101; CANR 70, 124; CP 5;
   CWP
Jimenez (Mantecon), Juan Ramon
   1881-1958 .... **HLC 1; PC 7; TCLC 4,**
   183
   See also CA 104; 131; CANR 74; DAM
   MULT, POET; DLB 134, 330; EW 9;
   EWL 3; HW 1; MTCW 1, 2; MTFW
   2005; RGWL 2, 3
Jimenez, Ramon
   See Jimenez (Mantecon), Juan Ramon
Jimenez Mantecon, Juan
   See Jimenez (Mantecon), Juan Ramon
Jin, Ba 1904-2005
   See Pa Chin
   See also CA 244; CWW 2; DLB 328
Jin, Xuefei
   See Ha Jin
Jodelle, Etienne 1532-1573 .... **LC 119**
   See also DLB 327; GFL Beginnings to 1789
Joel, Billy .... **CLC 26**
   See Joel, William Martin
Joel, William Martin 1949-
   See Joel, Billy
   See also CA 108
John, Saint 10(?)-100 .... **CMLC 27, 63**
John of Salisbury c. 1115-1180 ..... **CMLC 63**
John of the Cross, St. 1542-1591 .... **LC 18**
   See also RGWL 2, 3
John Paul II, Pope 1920-2005 .... **CLC 128**
   See also CA 106; 133; 238
Johnson, B(ryan) S(tanley William)
   1933-1973 .... **CLC 6, 9**
   See also CA 9-12R; 53-56; CANR 9; CN 1;
   CP 1, 2; DLB 14, 40; EWL 3; RGEL 2
Johnson, Benjamin F., of Boone
   See Riley, James Whitcomb
Johnson, Charles (Richard) 1948- .... **BLC 2;**
   CLC 7, 51, 65, 163
   See also AFAW 2; AMWS 6; BW 2, 3; CA
   116; CAAS 18; CANR 42, 66, 82, 129;
   CN 5, 6, 7; DAM MULT; DLB 33, 278;
   MAL 5; MTCW 2; MTFW 2005; RGAL
   4; SSFS 16
Johnson, Charles S(purgeon)
   1893-1956 .... **HR 1:3**
   See also BW 1, 3; CA 125; CANR 82; DLB
   51, 91
Johnson, Denis 1949- . **CLC 52, 160; SSC 56**
   See also CA 117; 121; CANR 71, 99; CN
   4, 5, 6, 7; DLB 120
Johnson, Diane 1934- .... **CLC 5, 13, 48**
   See also BPFB 2; CA 41-44R; CANR 17,
   40, 62, 95, 155; CN 4, 5, 6, 7; DLBY
   1980; INT CANR-17; MTCW 1
Johnson, E(mily) Pauline 1861-1913 . **NNAL**
   See also CA 150; CCA 1; DAC; DAM
   MULT; DLB 92, 175; TCWW 2
Johnson, Eyvind (Olof Verner)
   1900-1976 .... **CLC 14**
   See also CA 73-76; 69-72; CANR 34, 101;
   DLB 259, 330; EW 12; EWL 3
Johnson, Fenton 1888-1958 .... **BLC 2**
   See also BW 1; CA 118; 124; DAM MULT;
   DLB 45, 50
Johnson, Georgia Douglas (Camp)
   1880-1966 .... **HR 1:3**
   See also BW 1; CA 125; DLB 51, 249; WP
Johnson, Helene 1907-1995 .... **HR 1:3**
   See also CA 181; DLB 51; WP

Johnson, J. R.
   See James, C(yril) L(ionel) R(obert)
Johnson, James Weldon 1871-1938 .. **BLC 2;**
   HR 1:3; PC 24; TCLC 3, 19, 175
   See also AFAW 1, 2; BW 1, 3; CA 104;
   125; CANR 82; CDALB 1917-1929; CLR
   32; DA3; DAM MULT, POET; DLB 51;
   EWL 3; EXPP; LMFS 2; MAL 5; MTCW
   1, 2; MTFW 2005; NFS 22; PFS 1; RGAL
   4; SATA 31; TUS
Johnson, Joyce 1935- .... **CLC 58**
   See also BG 1:3; CA 125; 129; CANR 102
Johnson, Judith (Emlyn) 1936- .... **CLC 7, 15**
   See Sherwin, Judith Johnson
   See also CA 25-28R; 153; CANR 34; CP 6,
   7
Johnson, Lionel (Pigot)
   1867-1902 .... **TCLC 19**
   See also CA 117; 209; DLB 19; RGEL 2
Johnson, Marguerite Annie
   See Angelou, Maya
Johnson, Mel
   See Malzberg, Barry N(athaniel)
Johnson, Pamela Hansford
   1912-1981 .... **CLC 1, 7, 27**
   See also CA 1-4R; 104; CANR 2, 28; CN
   1, 2, 3; DLB 15; MTCW 1, 2; MTFW
   2005; RGEL 2
Johnson, Paul 1928- .... **CLC 147**
   See also BEST 89:4; CA 17-20R; CANR
   34, 62, 100, 155
Johnson, Paul Bede
   See Johnson, Paul
Johnson, Robert .... **CLC 70**
Johnson, Robert 1911(?)-1938 .... **TCLC 69**
   See also BW 3; CA 174
Johnson, Samuel 1709-1784 . **LC 15, 52, 128;**
   WLC 3
   See also BRW 3; BRWR 1; CDBLB 1660-
   1789; DA; DAB; DAC; DAM MST; DLB
   39, 95, 104, 142, 213; LMFS 1; RGEL 2;
   TEA
Johnson, Uwe 1934-1984 .. **CLC 5, 10, 15, 40**
   See also CA 1-4R; 112; CANR 1, 39; CD-
   WLB 2; DLB 75; EWL 3; MTCW 1;
   RGWL 2, 3
Johnston, Basil H. 1929- .... **NNAL**
   See also CA 69-72; CANR 11, 28, 66;
   DAC; DAM MULT; DLB 60
Johnston, George (Benson) 1913- .... **CLC 51**
   See also CA 1-4R; CANR 5, 20; CP 1, 2, 3,
   4, 5, 6, 7; DLB 88
Johnston, Jennifer (Prudence)
   1930- .... **CLC 7, 150, 228**
   See also CA 85-88; CANR 92; CN 4, 5, 6,
   7; DLB 14
Joinville, Jean de 1224(?)-1317 ..... **CMLC 38**
Jolley, (Monica) Elizabeth 1923- ..... **CLC 46;**
   SSC 19
   See also CA 127; CAAS 13; CANR 59; CN
   4, 5, 6, 7; DLB 325; EWL 3; RGSF 2
Jones, Arthur Llewellyn 1863-1947
   See Machen, Arthur
   See also CA 104; 179; HGG
Jones, D(ouglas) G(ordon) 1929- ..... **CLC 10**
   See also CA 29-32R; CANR 13, 90; CP 1,
   2, 3, 4, 5, 6, 7; DLB 53
Jones, David (Michael) 1895-1974 .... **CLC 2,**
   4, 7, 13, 42
   See also BRW 6; BRWS 7; CA 9-12R; 53-
   56; CANR 28; CDBLB 1945-1960; CP 1,
   2; DLB 20, 100; EWL 3; MTCW 1; PAB;
   RGEL 2
Jones, David Robert 1947-
   See Bowie, David
   See also CA 103; CANR 104

Kanin, Garson 1912-1999 .... **CLC 22**
See also AITN 1; CA 5-8R; 177; CAD;
CANR 7, 78; DLB 7; IDFW 3, 4

Kaniuk, Yoram 1930- .... **CLC 19**
See also CA 134; DLB 299; RGHL

Kant, Immanuel 1724-1804 ..... **NCLC 27, 67**
See also DLB 94

Kantor, MacKinlay 1904-1977 .... **CLC 7**
See also CA 61-64; 73-76; CANR 60, 63;
CN 1, 2; DLB 9, 102; MAL 5; MTCW 2;
RHW; TCWW 1, 2

Kanze Motokiyo
See Zeami

Kaplan, David Michael 1946- .... **CLC 50**
See also CA 187

Kaplan, James 1951- .... **CLC 59**
See also CA 135; CANR 121

Karadzic, Vuk Stefanovic
1787-1864 .... **NCLC 115**
See also CDWLB 4; DLB 147

Karageorge, Michael
See Anderson, Poul

Karamzin, Nikolai Mikhailovich
1766-1826 .... **NCLC 3, 173**
See also DLB 150; RGSF 2

Karapanou, Margarita 1946- .... **CLC 13**
See also CA 101

Karinthy, Frigyes 1887-1938 .... **TCLC 47**
See also CA 170; DLB 215; EWL 3

Karl, Frederick R(obert)
1927-2004 .... **CLC 34**
See also CA 5-8R; 226; CANR 3, 44, 143

Karr, Mary 1955- .... **CLC 188**
See also AMWS 11; CA 151; CANR 100;
MTFW 2005; NCFS 5

Kastel, Warren
See Silverberg, Robert

Kataev, Evgeny Petrovich 1903-1942
See Petrov, Evgeny
See also CA 120

Kataphusin
See Ruskin, John

Katz, Steve 1935- .... **CLC 47**
See also CA 25-28R; CAAS 14, 64; CANR
12; CN 4, 5, 6, 7; DLBY 1983

Kauffman, Janet 1945- .... **CLC 42**
See also CA 117; CANR 43, 84; DLB 218;
DLBY 1986

Kaufman, Bob (Garnell)
1925-1986 .... **CLC 49; PC 74**
See also BG 1:3; BW 1; CA 41-44R; 118;
CANR 22; CP 1; DLB 16, 41

Kaufman, George S. 1889-1961 ...... **CLC 38;
DC 17**
See also CA 108; 93-96; DAM DRAM;
DFS 1, 10; DLB 7; INT CA-108; MTCW
2; MTFW 2005; RGAL 4; TUS

Kaufman, Moises 1964- .... **DC 26**
See also CA 211; DFS 22; MTFW 2005

Kaufman, Sue .... **CLC 3, 8**
See Barondess, Sue K(aufman)

Kavafis, Konstantinos Petrou 1863-1933
See Cavafy, C(onstantine) P(eter)
See also CA 104

Kavan, Anna 1901-1968 .... **CLC 5, 13, 82**
See also BRWS 7; CA 5-8R; CANR 6, 57;
DLB 255; MTCW 1; RGEL 2; SFW 4

Kavanagh, Dan
See Barnes, Julian

Kavanagh, Julie 1952- .... **CLC 119**
See also CA 163

Kavanagh, Patrick (Joseph)
1904-1967 .... **CLC 22; PC 33**
See also BRWS 7; CA 123; 25-28R; DLB
15, 20; EWL 3; MTCW 1; RGEL 2

Kawabata, Yasunari 1899-1972 ..... **CLC 2, 5,
9, 18, 107; SSC 17**
See Kawabata Yasunari
See also CA 93-96; 33-36R; CANR 88;
DAM MULT; DLB 330; MJW; MTCW 2;
MTFW 2005; RGSF 2; RGWL 2, 3

Kawabata Yasunari
See Kawabata, Yasunari
See also DLB 180; EWL 3

Kaye, M.M. 1908-2004 .... **CLC 28**
See also CA 89-92; 223; CANR 24, 60, 102,
142; MTCW 1, 2; MTFW 2005; RHW;
SATA 62; SATA-Obit 152

Kaye, Mollie
See Kaye, M.M.

Kaye-Smith, Sheila 1887-1956 .... **TCLC 20**
See also CA 118; 203; DLB 36

Kaymor, Patrice Maguilene
See Senghor, Leopold Sedar

Kazakov, Iurii Pavlovich
See Kazakov, Yuri Pavlovich
See also DLB 302

Kazakov, Yuri Pavlovich 1927-1982 . **SSC 43**
See Kazakov, Iurii Pavlovich; Kazakov,
Yury
See also CA 5-8R; CANR 36; MTCW 1;
RGSF 2

Kazakov, Yury
See Kazakov, Yuri Pavlovich
See also EWL 3

Kazan, Elia 1909-2003 .... **CLC 6, 16, 63**
See also CA 21-24R; 220; CANR 32, 78

Kazantzakis, Nikos 1883(?)-1957 .... **TCLC 2,
5, 33, 181**
See also BPFB 2; CA 105; 132; DA3; EW
9; EWL 3; MTCW 1, 2; MTFW 2005;
RGWL 2, 3

Kazin, Alfred 1915-1998 ..... **CLC 34, 38, 119**
See also AMWS 8; CA 1-4R; CAAS 7;
CANR 1, 45, 79; DLB 67; EWL 3

Keane, Mary Nesta (Skrine) 1904-1996
See Keane, Molly
See also CA 108; 114; 151; RHW

Keane, Molly .... **CLC 31**
See Keane, Mary Nesta (Skrine)
See also CN 5, 6; INT CA-114; TCLE 1:1

Keates, Jonathan 1946(?)- .... **CLC 34**
See also CA 163; CANR 126

Keaton, Buster 1895-1966 .... **CLC 20**
See also CA 194

Keats, John 1795-1821 ...... **NCLC 8, 73, 121;
PC 1; WLC 3**
See also AAYA 58; BRW 4; BRWR 1; CD-
BLB 1789-1832; DA; DA3; DAB; DAC;
DAM MST, POET; DLB 96, 110; EXPP;
LMFS 1; PAB; PFS 1, 2, 3, 9, 17; RGEL
2; TEA; WLIT 3; WP

Keble, John 1792-1866 .... **NCLC 87**
See also DLB 32, 55; RGEL 2

Keene, Donald 1922- .... **CLC 34**
See also CA 1-4R; CANR 5, 119

Keillor, Garrison 1942- ..... **CLC 40, 115, 222**
See also AAYA 2, 62; AMWS 16; BEST
89:3; BPFB 2; CA 111; 117; CANR 36,
59, 124; CPW; DA3; DAM POP; DLBY
1987; EWL 3; MTCW 1, 2; MTFW 2005;
SATA 58; TUS

Keith, Carlos
See Lewton, Val

Keith, Michael
See Hubbard, L. Ron

Keller, Gottfried 1819-1890 .... **NCLC 2; SSC
26**
See also CDWLB 2; DLB 129; EW; RGSF
2; RGWL 2, 3

Keller, Nora Okja 1965- .... **CLC 109**
See also CA 187

Kellerman, Jonathan 1949- .... **CLC 44**
See also AAYA 35; BEST 90:1; CA 106;
CANR 29, 51, 150; CMW 4; CPW; DA3;
DAM POP; INT CANR-29

Kelley, William Melvin 1937- .... **CLC 22**
See also BW 1; CA 77-80; CANR 27, 83;
CN 1, 2, 3, 4, 5, 6, 7; DLB 33; EWL 3

Kellogg, Marjorie 1922-2005 .... **CLC 2**
See also CA 81-84; 246

Kellow, Kathleen
See Hibbert, Eleanor Alice Burford

Kelly, Lauren
See Oates, Joyce Carol

Kelly, M(ilton) T(errence) 1947- ...... **CLC 55**
See also CA 97-100; CAAS 22; CANR 19,
43, 84; CN 6

Kelly, Robert 1935- .... **SSC 50**
See also CA 17-20R; CAAS 19; CANR 47;
CP 1, 2, 3, 4, 5, 6, 7; DLB 5, 130, 165

Kelman, James 1946- .... **CLC 58, 86**
See also BRWS 5; CA 148; CANR 85, 130;
CN 5, 6, 7; DLB 194, 319, 326; RGSF 2;
WLIT 4

Kemal, Yasar
See Kemal, Yashar
See also CWW 2; EWL 3; WLIT 6

Kemal, Yashar 1923(?)- .... **CLC 14, 29**
See also CA 89-92; CANR 44

Kemble, Fanny 1809-1893 .... **NCLC 18**
See also DLB 32

Kemelman, Harry 1908-1996 .... **CLC 2**
See also AITN 1; BPFB 2; CA 9-12R; 155;
CANR 6, 71; CMW 4; DLB 28

Kempe, Margery 1373(?)-1440(?) ... **LC 6, 56**
See also BRWS 12; DLB 146; FL 1:1;
RGEL 2

Kempis, Thomas a 1380-1471 .... **LC 11**

Kendall, Henry 1839-1882 .... **NCLC 12**
See also DLB 230

Keneally, Thomas 1935- .... **CLC 5, 8, 10, 14,
19, 27, 43, 117**
See also BRWS 4; CA 85-88; CANR 10,
50, 74, 130; CN 1, 2, 3, 4, 5, 6, 7; CPW;
DA3; DAM NOV; DLB 289, 299, 326;
EWL 3; MTCW 1, 2; MTFW 2005; NFS
17; RGEL 2; RGHL; RHW

Kennedy, A(lison) L(ouise) 1965- ... **CLC 188**
See also CA 168, 213; CAAE 213; CANR
108; CD 5, 6; CN 6, 7; DLB 271; RGSF
2

Kennedy, Adrienne (Lita) 1931- .... **BLC 2;
CLC 66; DC 5**
See also AFAW 2; BW 2, 3; CA 103; CAAS
20; CABS 3; CAD; CANR 26, 53, 82;
CD 5, 6; DAM MULT; DFS 9; DLB 38;
FW; MAL 5

Kennedy, John Pendleton
1795-1870 .... **NCLC 2**
See also DLB 3, 248, 254; RGAL 4

Kennedy, Joseph Charles 1929-
See Kennedy, X. J.
See also CA 1-4R, 201; CAAE 201; CANR
4, 30, 40; CWRI 5; MAICYA 2; MAIC-
YAS 1; SATA 14, 86, 130; SATA-Essay
130

Kennedy, William 1928- ... **CLC 6, 28, 34, 53**
See also AAYA 1; AMWS 7; BPFB 2; CA
85-88; CANR 14, 31, 76, 134; CN 4, 5, 6,
7; DA3; DAM NOV; DLB 143; DLBY
1985; EWL 3; INT CANR-31; MAL 5;
MTCW 1, 2; MTFW 2005; SATA 57

Kennedy, X. J. .... **CLC 8, 42**
See Kennedy, Joseph Charles
See also AMWS 15; CAAS 9; CLR 27; CP
1, 2, 3, 4, 5, 6, 7; DLB 5; SAAS 22

Kenny, Maurice (Francis) 1929- ..... **CLC 87;
NNAL**
See also CA 144; CAAS 22; CANR 143;
DAM MULT; DLB 175

NFS 21; PFS 22; RGEL 2; RGSF 2; SATA 100; SFW 4; SSFS 8, 21, 22; SUFW 1; TEA; WCH; WLIT 4; YABC 2

Kircher, Athanasius 1602-1680 .... **LC 121**
See also DLB 164

Kirk, Russell (Amos) 1918-1994 .. **TCLC 119**
See also AITN 1; CA 1-4R; 145; CAAS 9; CANR 1, 20, 60; HGG; INT CANR-20; MTCW 1, 2

Kirkham, Dinah
See Card, Orson Scott

Kirkland, Caroline M. 1801-1864 . **NCLC 85**
See also DLB 3, 73, 74, 250, 254; DLBD 13

Kirkup, James 1918- .... **CLC 1**
See also CA 1-4R; CAAS 4; CANR 2; CP 1, 2, 3, 4, 5, 6, 7; DLB 27; SATA 12

Kirkwood, James 1930(?)-1989 .... **CLC 9**
See also AITN 2; CA 1-4R; 128; CANR 6, 40; GLL 2

Kirsch, Sarah 1935- .... **CLC 176**
See also CA 178; CWW 2; DLB 75; EWL 3

Kirshner, Sidney
See Kingsley, Sidney

Kis, Danilo 1935-1989 .... **CLC 57**
See also CA 109; 118; 129; CANR 61; CDWLB 4; DLB 181; EWL 3; MTCW 1; RGSF 2; RGWL 2, 3

Kissinger, Henry A(lfred) 1923- ..... **CLC 137**
See also CA 1-4R; CANR 2, 33, 66, 109; MTCW 1

Kittel, Frederick August
See Wilson, August

Kivi, Aleksis 1834-1872 .... **NCLC 30**

Kizer, Carolyn 1925- ..... **CLC 15, 39, 80; PC 66**
See also CA 65-68; CAAS 5; CANR 24, 70, 134; CP 1, 2, 3, 4, 5, 6; CWP; DAM POET; DLB 5, 169; EWL 3; MAL 5; MTCW 2; MTFW 2005; PFS 18; TCLE 1:1

Klabund 1890-1928 .... **TCLC 44**
See also CA 162; DLB 66

Klappert, Peter 1942- .... **CLC 57**
See also CA 33-36R; CSW; DLB 5

Klein, A(braham) M(oses)
1909-1972 .... **CLC 19**
See also CA 101; 37-40R; CP 1; DAB; DAC; DAM MST; DLB 68; EWL 3; RGEL 2; RGHL

Klein, Joe
See Klein, Joseph

Klein, Joseph 1946- .... **CLC 154**
See also CA 85-88; CANR 55

Klein, Norma 1938-1989 .... **CLC 30**
See also AAYA 2, 35; BPFB 2; BYA 6, 7, 8; CA 41-44R; 128; CANR 15, 37; CLR 2, 19; INT CANR-15; JRDA; MAICYA 1, 2; SAAS 1; SATA 7, 57; WYA; YAW

Klein, T(heodore) E(ibon) D(onald)
1947- .... **CLC 34**
See also CA 119; CANR 44, 75; HGG

Kleist, Heinrich von 1777-1811 ...... **NCLC 2, 37; SSC 22**
See also CDWLB 2; DAM DRAM; DLB 90; EW 5; RGSF 2; RGWL 2, 3

Klima, Ivan 1931- .... **CLC 56, 172**
See also CA 25-28R; CANR 17, 50, 91; CDWLB 4; CWW 2; DAM NOV; DLB 232; EWL 3; RGWL 3

Klimentev, Andrei Platonovich
See Klimentov, Andrei Platonovich

Klimentov, Andrei Platonovich
1899-1951 .... **SSC 42; TCLC 14**
See Platonov, Andrei Platonovich; Platonov, Andrey Platonovich
See also CA 108; 232

Klinger, Friedrich Maximilian von
1752-1831 .... **NCLC 1**
See also DLB 94

Klingsor the Magician
See Hartmann, Sadakichi

Klopstock, Friedrich Gottlieb
1724-1803 .... **NCLC 11**
See also DLB 97; EW 4; RGWL 2, 3

Kluge, Alexander 1932- .... **SSC 61**
See also CA 81-84; DLB 75

Knapp, Caroline 1959-2002 .... **CLC 99**
See also CA 154; 207

Knebel, Fletcher 1911-1993 .... **CLC 14**
See also AITN 1; CA 1-4R; 140; CAAS 3; CANR 1, 36; CN 1, 2, 3, 4, 5; SATA 36; SATA-Obit 75

Knickerbocker, Diedrich
See Irving, Washington

Knight, Etheridge 1931-1991 ... **BLC 2; CLC 40; PC 14**
See also BW 1, 3; CA 21-24R; 133; CANR 23, 82; CP 1, 2, 3, 4, 5; DAM POET; DLB 41; MTCW 2; MTFW 2005; RGAL 4; TCLE 1:1

Knight, Sarah Kemble 1666-1727 .... **LC 7**
See also DLB 24, 200

Knister, Raymond 1899-1932 .... **TCLC 56**
See also CA 186; DLB 68; RGEL 2

Knowles, John 1926-2001 ... **CLC 1, 4, 10, 26**
See also AAYA 10; AMWS 12; BPFB 2; BYA 3; CA 17-20R; 203; CANR 40, 74, 76, 132; CDALB 1968-1988; CLR 98; CN 1, 2, 3, 4, 5, 6, 7; DA; DAC; DAM MST, NOV; DLB 6; EXPN; MTCW 1, 2; MTFW 2005; NFS 2; RGAL 4; SATA 8, 89; SATA-Obit 134; YAW

Knox, Calvin M.
See Silverberg, Robert

Knox, John c. 1505-1572 .... **LC 37**
See also DLB 132

Knye, Cassandra
See Disch, Thomas M.

Koch, C(hristopher) J(ohn) 1932- .... **CLC 42**
See also CA 127, CANR 84; CN 3, 4, 5, 6, 7; DLB 289

Koch, Christopher
See Koch, C(hristopher) J(ohn)

Koch, Kenneth 1925-2002 .... **CLC 5, 8, 44**
See also AMWS 15; CA 1-4R; 207; CAD; CANR 6, 36, 57, 97, 131; CD 5, 6; CP 1, 2, 3, 4, 5, 6, 7; DAM POET; DLB 5; INT CANR-36; MAL 5; MTCW 2; MTFW 2005; PFS 20; SATA 65; WP

Kochanowski, Jan 1530-1584 .... **LC 10**
See also RGWL 2, 3

Kock, Charles Paul de 1794-1871 . **NCLC 16**

Koda Rohan
See Koda Shigeyuki

Koda Rohan
See Koda Shigeyuki
See also DLB 180

Koda Shigeyuki 1867-1947 .... **TCLC 22**
See Koda Rohan
See also CA 121; 183

Koestler, Arthur 1905-1983 ... **CLC 1, 3, 6, 8, 15, 33**
See also BRWS 1; CA 1-4R; 109; CANR 1, 33; CDBLB 1945-1960; CN 1, 2, 3; DLBY 1983; EWL 3; MTCW 1, 2; MTFW 2005; NFS 19; RGEL 2

Kogawa, Joy Nozomi 1935- ...... **CLC 78, 129**
See also AAYA 47; CA 101; CANR 19, 62, 126; CN 6, 7; CP 1; CWP; DAC; DAM MST, MULT; FW; MTCW 2; MTFW 2005; NFS 3; SATA 99

Kohout, Pavel 1928- .... **CLC 13**
See also CA 45-48; CANR 3

Koizumi, Yakumo
See Hearn, (Patricio) Lafcadio (Tessima Carlos)

Kolmar, Gertrud 1894-1943 .... **TCLC 40**
See also CA 167; EWL 3; RGHL

Komunyakaa, Yusef 1947- .. **BLCS; CLC 86, 94, 207; PC 51**
See also AFAW 2; AMWS 13; CA 147; CANR 83; CP 6, 7; CSW; DLB 120; EWL 3; PFS 5, 20; RGAL 4

Konrad, George
See Konrad, Gyorgy

Konrad, Gyorgy 1933- .... **CLC 4, 10, 73**
See also CA 85-88; CANR 97; CDWLB 4; CWW 2; DLB 232; EWL 3

Konwicki, Tadeusz 1926- .... **CLC 8, 28, 54, 117**
See also CA 101; CAAS 9; CANR 39, 59; CWW 2; DLB 232; EWL 3; IDFW 3; MTCW 1

Koontz, Dean R. 1945- .... **CLC 78, 206**
See also AAYA 9, 31; BEST 89:3, 90:2; CA 108; CANR 19, 36, 52, 95, 138; CMW 4; CPW; DA3; DAM NOV, POP; DLB 292; HGG; MTCW 1; MTFW 2005; SATA 92, 165; SFW 4; SUFW 2; YAW

Koontz, Dean Ray
See Koontz, Dean R.

Kopernik, Mikolaj
See Copernicus, Nicolaus

Kopit, Arthur (Lee) 1937- ...... **CLC 1, 18, 33**
See also AITN 1; CA 81-84; CABS 3; CAD; CD 5, 6; DAM DRAM; DFS 7, 14; DLB 7; MAL 5; MTCW 1; RGAL 4

Kopitar, Jernej (Bartholomaus)
1780-1844 .... **NCLC 117**

Kops, Bernard 1926- .... **CLC 4**
See also CA 5-8R; CANR 84; CBD; CN 1, 2, 3, 4, 5, 6, 7; CP 1, 2, 3, 4, 5, 6, 7; DLB 13; RGHL

Kornbluth, C(yril) M. 1923-1958 .... **TCLC 8**
See also CA 105; 160; DLB 8; SCFW 1, 2; SFW 4

Korolenko, V.G.
See Korolenko, Vladimir G.

Korolenko, Vladimir
See Korolenko, Vladimir G

Korolenko, Vladimir G.
1853-1921 .... **TCLC 22**
See also CA 121; DLB 277

Korolenko, Vladimir Galaktionovich
See Korolenko, Vladimir G.

Korzybski, Alfred (Habdank Skarbek)
1879-1950 .... **TCLC 61**
See also CA 123; 160

Kosinski, Jerzy 1933-1991 ..... **CLC 1, 2, 3, 6, 10, 15, 53, 70**
See also AMWS 7; BPFB 2; CA 17-20R; 134; CANR 9, 46; CN 1, 2, 3, 4; DA3; DAM NOV; DLB 2, 299; DLBY 1982; EWL 3; HGG; MAL 5; MTCW 1, 2; MTFW 2005; NFS 12; RGAL 4; RGHL; TUS

Kostelanetz, Richard (Cory) 1940- .. **CLC 28**
See also CA 13-16R; CAAS 8; CANR 38, 77; CN 4, 5, 6; CP 2, 3, 4, 5, 6, 7

Kostrowitzki, Wilhelm Apollinaris de
1880-1918
See Apollinaire, Guillaume
See also CA 104

Kotlowitz, Robert 1924- .... **CLC 4**
See also CA 33-36R; CANR 36

Kotzebue, August (Friedrich Ferdinand) von
1761-1819 .... **NCLC 25**
See also DLB 94

Lagerlof, Selma (Ottiliana Lovisa)
　　1858-1940
　　See Lagerloef, Selma (Ottiliana Lovisa)
　　See also CA 188; CLR 7; DLB 259; RGWL
　　2, 3; SATA 15; SSFS 18

La Guma, Alex 1925-1985 .. **BLCS; CLC 19;**
　　TCLC 140
　　See also AFW; BW 1, 3; CA 49-52; 118;
　　CANR 25, 81; CDWLB 3; CN 1, 2, 3;
　　CP 1; DAM NOV; DLB 117, 225; EWL
　　3; MTCW 1, 2; MTFW 2005; WLIT 2;
　　WWE 1

Lahiri, Jhumpa 1967- .... **SSC 96**
　　See also DLB 323

Laidlaw, A. K.
　　See Grieve, C(hristopher) M(urray)

Lainez, Manuel Mujica
　　See Mujica Lainez, Manuel
　　See also HW 1

Laing, R(onald) D(avid) 1927-1989 . **CLC 95**
　　See also CA 107; 129; CANR 34; MTCW 1

Laishley, Alex
　　See Booth, Martin

Lamartine, Alphonse (Marie Louis Prat) de
　　1790-1869 .... **NCLC 11; PC 16**
　　See also DAM POET; DLB 217; GFL 1789
　　to the Present; RGWL 2, 3

Lamb, Charles 1775-1834 ..... **NCLC 10, 113;**
　　WLC 3
　　See also BRW 4; CDBLB 1789-1832; DA;
　　DAB; DAC; DAM MST; DLB 93, 107,
　　163; RGEL 2; SATA 17; TEA

Lamb, Lady Caroline 1785-1828 ... **NCLC 38**
　　See also DLB 116

Lamb, Mary Ann 1764-1847 .... **NCLC 125**
　　See also DLB 163; SATA 17

Lame Deer 1903(?)-1976 .... **NNAL**
　　See also CA 69-72

Lamming, George (William) 1927- ... **BLC 2;**
　　CLC 2, 4, 66, 144
　　See also BW 2, 3; CA 85-88; CANR 26,
　　76; CDWLB 3; CN 1, 2, 3, 4, 5, 6, 7; CP
　　1; DAM MULT; DLB 125; EWL 3;
　　MTCW 1, 2; MTFW 2005; NFS 15;
　　RGEL 2

L'Amour, Louis 1908-1988 .... **CLC 25, 55**
　　See also AAYA 16; AITN 2; BEST 89:2;
　　BPFB 2; CA 1-4R; 125; CANR 3, 25, 40;
　　CPW; DA3; DAM NOV, POP; DLB 206;
　　DLBY 1980; MTCW 1, 2; MTFW 2005;
　　RGAL 4; TCWW 1, 2

Lampedusa, Giuseppe (Tomasi) di
　　....................... **TCLC 13**
　　See Tomasi di Lampedusa, Giuseppe
　　See also CA 164; EW 11; MTCW 2; MTFW
　　2005; RGWL 2, 3

Lampman, Archibald 1861-1899 ... **NCLC 25**
　　See also DLB 92; RGEL 2; TWA

Lancaster, Bruce 1896-1963 .... **CLC 36**
　　See also CA 9-10; CANR 70; CAP 1; SATA
　　9

Lanchester, John 1962- .... **CLC 99**
　　See also CA 194; DLB 267

Landau, Mark Alexandrovich
　　See Aldanov, Mark (Alexandrovich)

Landau-Aldanov, Mark Alexandrovich
　　See Aldanov, Mark (Alexandrovich)

Landis, Jerry
　　See Simon, Paul

Landis, John 1950- .... **CLC 26**
　　See also CA 112; 122; CANR 128

Landolfi, Tommaso 1908-1979 .... **CLC 11, 49**
　　See also CA 127; 117; DLB 177; EWL 3

Landon, Letitia Elizabeth
　　1802-1838 .... **NCLC 15**
　　See also DLB 96

Landor, Walter Savage
　　1775-1864 .... **NCLC 14**
　　See also BRW 4; DLB 93, 107; RGEL 2

Landwirth, Heinz 1927-
　　See Lind, Jakov
　　See also CA 9-12R; CANR 7

Lane, Patrick 1939- .... **CLC 25**
　　See also CA 97-100; CANR 54; CP 3, 4, 5,
　　6, 7; DAM POET; DLB 53; INT CA-97-
　　100

Lane, Rose Wilder 1887-1968 ...... **TCLC 177**
　　See also CA 102; CANR 63; SATA 29;
　　SATA-Brief 28; TCWW 2

Lang, Andrew 1844-1912 .... **TCLC 16**
　　See also CA 114; 137; CANR 85; CLR 101;
　　DLB 98, 141, 184; FANT; MAICYA 1, 2;
　　RGEL 2; SATA 16; WCH

Lang, Fritz 1890-1976 .... **CLC 20, 103**
　　See also AAYA 65; CA 77-80; 69-72;
　　CANR 30

Lange, John
　　See Crichton, Michael

Langer, Elinor 1939- .... **CLC 34**
　　See also CA 121

Langland, William 1332(?)-1400(?) .... **LC 19,**
　　120
　　See also BRW 1; DA; DAB; DAC; DAM
　　MST, POET; DLB 146; RGEL 2; TEA;
　　WLIT 3

Langstaff, Launcelot
　　See Irving, Washington

Lanier, Sidney 1842-1881 . **NCLC 6, 118; PC**
　　50
　　See also AMWS 1; DAM POET; DLB 64;
　　DLBD 13; EXPP; MAICYA 1; PFS 14;
　　RGAL 4; SATA 18

Lanyer, Aemilia 1569-1645 .... **LC 10, 30, 83;**
　　PC 60
　　See also DLB 121

Lao Tzu c. 6th cent. B.C.-3rd cent.
　　B.C. .... **CMLC 7**

Lao-Tzu
　　See Lao Tzu

Lapine, James (Elliot) 1949- .... **CLC 39**
　　See also CA 123; 130; CANR 54, 128; INT
　　CA-130

Larbaud, Valery (Nicolas)
　　1881-1957 .... **TCLC 9**
　　See also CA 106; 152; EWL 3; GFL 1789
　　to the Present

Larcom, Lucy 1824-1893 .... **NCLC 179**
　　See also AMWS 13; DLB 221, 243

Lardner, Ring
　　See Lardner, Ring(gold) W(ilmer)
　　See also BPFB 2; CDALB 1917-1929; DLB
　　11, 25, 86, 171; DLBD 16; MAL 5;
　　RGAL 4; RGSF 2

Lardner, Ring W., Jr.
　　See Lardner, Ring(gold) W(ilmer)

Lardner, Ring(gold) W(ilmer)
　　1885-1933 .... **SSC 32; TCLC 2, 14**
　　See Lardner, Ring
　　See also AMW; CA 104; 131; MTCW 1, 2;
　　MTFW 2005; TUS

Laredo, Betty
　　See Codrescu, Andrei

Larkin, Maia
　　See Wojciechowska, Maia (Teresa)

Larkin, Philip (Arthur) 1922-1985 ... **CLC 3,**
　　5, 8, 9, 13, 18, 33, 39, 64; PC 21
　　See also BRWS 1; CA 5-8R; 117; CANR
　　24, 62; CDBLB 1960 to Present; CP 1, 2,
　　3, 4; DA3; DAB; DAM MST, POET;
　　DLB 27; EWL 3; MTCW 1, 2; MTFW
　　2005; PFS 3, 4, 12; RGEL 2

La Roche, Sophie von
　　1730-1807 .... **NCLC 121**
　　See also DLB 94

La Rochefoucauld, Francois
　　1613-1680 .... **LC 108**

Larra (y Sanchez de Castro), Mariano Jose
　　de 1809-1837 .... **NCLC 17, 130**

Larsen, Eric 1941- .... **CLC 55**
　　See also CA 132

Larsen, Nella 1893(?)-1963 .... **BLC 2; CLC**
　　37; HR 1:3
　　See also AFAW 1, 2; BW 1; CA 125; CANR
　　83; DAM MULT; DLB 51; FW; LATS
　　1:1; LMFS 2

Larson, Charles R(aymond) 1938- ... **CLC 31**
　　See also CA 53-56; CANR 4, 121

Larson, Jonathan 1960-1996 .... **CLC 99**
　　See also AAYA 28; CA 156; DFS 23;
　　MTFW 2005

La Sale, Antoine de c. 1386-1460(?) . **LC 104**
　　See also DLB 208

Las Casas, Bartolome de
　　1474-1566 .... **HLCS; LC 31**
　　See Casas, Bartolome de las
　　See also DLB 318; LAW

Lasch, Christopher 1932-1994 .... **CLC 102**
　　See also CA 73-76; 144; CANR 25, 118;
　　DLB 246; MTCW 1, 2; MTFW 2005

Lasker-Schueler, Else 1869-1945 ... **TCLC 57**
　　See Lasker-Schuler, Else
　　See also CA 183; DLB 66, 124

Lasker-Schuler, Else
　　See Lasker-Schueler, Else
　　See also EWL 3

Laski, Harold J(oseph) 1893-1950 . **TCLC 79**
　　See also CA 188

Latham, Jean Lee 1902-1995 .... **CLC 12**
　　See also AITN 1; BYA 1; CA 5-8R; CANR
　　7, 84; CLR 50; MAICYA 1, 2; SATA 2,
　　68; YAW

Latham, Mavis
　　See Clark, Mavis Thorpe

Lathen, Emma .... **CLC 2**
　　See Hennissart, Martha; Latsis, Mary J(ane)
　　See also BPFB 2; CMW 4; DLB 306

Lathrop, Francis
　　See Leiber, Fritz (Reuter, Jr.)

Latsis, Mary J(ane) 1927-1997
　　See Lathen, Emma
　　See also CA 85-88; 162; CMW 4

Lattany, Kristin
　　See Lattany, Kristin (Elaine Eggleston)
　　Hunter

Lattany, Kristin (Elaine Eggleston) Hunter
　　1931- .... **CLC 35**
　　See Hunter, Kristin
　　See also AITN 1; BW 1; BYA 3; CA 13-
　　16R; CANR 13, 108; CLR 3; CN 7; DLB
　　33; INT CANR-13; MAICYA 1, 2; SAAS
　　10; SATA 12, 132; YAW

Lattimore, Richmond (Alexander)
　　1906-1984 .... **CLC 3**
　　See also CA 1-4R; 112; CANR 1; CP 1, 2,
　　3; MAL 5

Laughlin, James 1914-1997 .... **CLC 49**
　　See also CA 21-24R; 162; CAAS 22; CANR
　　9, 47; CP 1, 2, 3, 4, 5, 6; DLB 48; DLBY
　　1996, 1997

Laurence, Margaret 1926-1987 ..... **CLC 3, 6,**
　　13, 50, 62; SSC 7
　　See also BYA 13; CA 5-8R; 121; CANR
　　33; CN 1, 2, 3, 4; DAC; DAM MST; DLB
　　53; EWL 3; FW; MTCW 1, 2; MTFW
　　2005; NFS 11; RGEL 2; RGSF 2; SATA-
　　Obit 50; TCWW 2

Laurent, Antoine 1952- .... **CLC 50**

Lauscher, Hermann
　　See Hesse, Hermann

Lautreamont 1846-1870 .. **NCLC 12; SSC 14**
　　See Lautreamont, Isidore Lucien Ducasse
　　See also GFL 1789 to the Present; RGWL
　　2, 3

Lautreamont, Isidore Lucien Ducasse
See Lautreamont
See also DLB 217
Lavater, Johann Kaspar
1741-1801 .... **NCLC 142**
See also DLB 97
Laverty, Donald
See Blish, James (Benjamin)
Lavin, Mary 1912-1996 . **CLC 4, 18, 99; SSC
4, 67**
See also CA 9-12R; 151; CANR 33; CN 1,
2, 3, 4, 5, 6; DLB 15, 319; FW; MTCW
1; RGEL 2; RGSF 2; SSFS 23
Lavond, Paul Dennis
See Kornbluth, C(yril) M.; Pohl, Frederik
Lawes, Henry 1596-1662 .... **LC 113**
See also DLB 126
Lawler, Ray
See Lawler, Raymond Evenor
See also DLB 289
Lawler, Raymond Evenor 1922- .... **CLC 58**
See Lawler, Ray
See also CA 103; CD 5, 6; RGEL 2
Lawrence, D(avid) H(erbert Richards)
1885-1930 .... **PC 54; SSC 4, 19, 73;
TCLC 2, 9, 16, 33, 48, 61, 93; WLC 3**
See Chambers, Jessie
See also BPFB 2; BRW 7; BRWR 2; CA
104; 121; CANR 131; CDBLB 1914-
1945; DA; DA3; DAB; DAC; DAM MST,
NOV, POET; DLB 10, 19, 36, 98, 162,
195; EWL 3; EXPP; EXPS; LAIT 2, 3;
MTCW 1, 2; MTFW 2005; NFS 18; PFS
6; RGEL 2; RGSF 2; SSFS 2, 6; TEA;
WLIT 4; WP
Lawrence, T(homas) E(dward)
1888-1935 .... **TCLC 18**
See Dale, Colin
See also BRWS 2; CA 115; 167; DLB 195
Lawrence of Arabia
See Lawrence, T(homas) E(dward)
Lawson, Henry (Archibald Hertzberg)
1867-1922 .... **SSC 18; TCLC 27**
See also CA 120; 181; DLB 230; RGEL 2;
RGSF 2
Lawton, Dennis
See Faust, Frederick (Schiller)
Layamon fl. c. 1200- .... **CMLC 10**
See Laȝamon
See also DLB 146; RGEL 2
Laye, Camara 1928-1980 ..... **BLC 2; CLC 4,
38**
See Camara Laye
See also AFW; BW 1; CA 85-88; 97-100;
CANR 25; DAM MULT; MTCW 1, 2;
WLIT 2
Layton, Irving 1912-2006 ..... **CLC 2, 15, 164**
See also CA 1-4R; 247; CANR 2, 33, 43,
66, 129; CP 1, 2, 3, 4, 5, 6, 7; DAC; DAM
MST, POET; DLB 88; EWL 3; MTCW 1,
2; PFS 12; RGEL 2
Layton, Irving Peter
See Layton, Irving
Lazarus, Emma 1849-1887 ...... **NCLC 8, 109**
Lazarus, Felix
See Cable, George Washington
Lazarus, Henry
See Slavitt, David R(ytman)
Lea, Joan
See Neufeld, John (Arthur)
Leacock, Stephen (Butler)
1869-1944 .... **SSC 39; TCLC 2**
See also CA 104; 141; CANR 80; DAC;
DAM MST; DLB 92; EWL 3; MTCW 2;
MTFW 2005; RGEL 2; RGSF 2
Lead, Jane Ward 1623-1704 .... **LC 72**
See also DLB 131
Leapor, Mary 1722-1746 .... **LC 80**
See also DLB 109

Lear, Edward 1812-1888 ..... **NCLC 3; PC 65**
See also AAYA 48; BRW 5; CLR 1, 75;
DLB 32, 163, 166; MAICYA 1, 2; RGEL
2; SATA 18, 100; WCH; WP
Lear, Norman (Milton) 1922- .... **CLC 12**
See also CA 73-76
Leautaud, Paul 1872-1956 .... **TCLC 83**
See also CA 203; DLB 65; GFL 1789 to the
Present
Leavis, F(rank) R(aymond)
1895-1978 .... **CLC 24**
See also BRW 7; CA 21-24R; 77-80; CANR
44; DLB 242; EWL 3; MTCW 1, 2;
RGEL 2
Leavitt, David 1961- .... **CLC 34**
See also CA 116; 122; CANR 50, 62, 101,
134; CPW; DA3; DAM POP; DLB 130;
GLL 1; INT CA-122; MAL 5; MTCW 2;
MTFW 2005
Leblanc, Maurice (Marie Emile)
1864-1941 .... **TCLC 49**
See also CA 110; CMW 4
Lebowitz, Fran(ces Ann) 1951(?)- ... **CLC 11,
36**
See also CA 81-84; CANR 14, 60, 70; INT
CANR-14; MTCW 1
Lebrecht, Peter
See Tieck, (Johann) Ludwig
le Carre, John 1931- .... **CLC 9, 15**
See also AAYA 42; BEST 89:4; BPFB 2;
BRWS 2; CA 5-8R; CANR 13, 33, 59,
107, 132; CDBLB 1960 to Present; CMW
4; CN 1, 2, 3, 4, 5, 6, 7; CPW; DA3;
DAM POP; DLB 87; EWL 3; MSW;
MTCW 1, 2; MTFW 2005; RGEL 2; TEA
Le Clezio, J. M.G. 1940- .... **CLC 31, 155**
See also CA 116; 128; CANR 147; CWW
2; DLB 83; EWL 3; GFL 1789 to the
Present; RGSF 2
Le Clezio, Jean Marie Gustave
See Le Clezio, J. M.G.
Leconte de Lisle, Charles-Marie-Rene
1818-1894 .... **NCLC 29**
See also DLB 217; EW 6; GFL 1789 to the
Present
Le Coq, Monsieur
See Simenon, Georges (Jacques Christian)
Leduc, Violette 1907-1972 .... **CLC 22**
See also CA 13-14; 33-36R; CANR 69;
CAP 1; EWL 3; GFL 1789 to the Present;
GLL 1
Ledwidge, Francis 1887(?)-1917 .... **TCLC 23**
See also CA 123; 203; DLB 20
Lee, Andrea 1953- .... **BLC 2; CLC 36**
See also BW 1, 3; CA 125; CANR 82;
DAM MULT
Lee, Andrew
See Auchincloss, Louis
Lee, Chang-rae 1965- .... **CLC 91**
See also CA 148; CANR 89; CN 7; DLB
312; LATS 1:2
Lee, Don L. .... **CLC 2**
See Madhubuti, Haki R.
See also CP 2, 3, 4, 5
Lee, George W(ashington)
1894-1976 .... **BLC 2; CLC 52**
See also BW 1; CA 125; CANR 83; DAM
MULT; DLB 51
Lee, Harper 1926- ... **CLC 12, 60, 194; WLC
4**
See also AAYA 13; AMWS 8; BPFB 2;
BYA 3; CA 13-16R; CANR 51, 128;
CDALB 1941-1968; CSW; DA; DA3;
DAB; DAC; DAM MST, NOV; DLB 6;
EXPN; LAIT 3; MAL 5; MTCW 1, 2;
MTFW 2005; NFS 2; SATA 11; WYA;
YAW
Lee, Helen Elaine 1959(?)- .... **CLC 86**
See also CA 148

Lee, John .... **CLC 70**
Lee, Julian
See Latham, Jean Lee
Lee, Larry
See Lee, Lawrence
Lee, Laurie 1914-1997 .... **CLC 90**
See also CA 77-80; 158; CANR 33, 73; CP
1, 2, 3, 4, 5, 6; CPW; DAB; DAM POP;
DLB 27; MTCW 1; RGEL 2
Lee, Lawrence 1941-1990 .... **CLC 34**
See also CA 131; CANR 43
Lee, Li-Young 1957- .... **CLC 164; PC 24**
See also AMWS 15; CA 153; CANR 118;
CP 6, 7; DLB 165, 312; LMFS 2; PFS 11,
15, 17
Lee, Manfred B. 1905-1971 .... **CLC 11**
See Queen, Ellery
See also CA 1-4R; 29-32R; CANR 2, 150;
CMW 4; DLB 137
Lee, Manfred Bennington
See Lee, Manfred B.
Lee, Nathaniel 1645(?)-1692 .... **LC 103**
See also DLB 80; RGEL 2
Lee, Shelton Jackson
See Lee, Spike
See also AAYA 4, 29
Lee, Spike 1957(?)- .... **BLCS; CLC 105**
See Lee, Shelton Jackson
See also BW 2, 3; CA 125; CANR 42;
DAM MULT
Lee, Stan 1922- .... **CLC 17**
See also AAYA 5, 49; CA 108; 111; CANR
129; INT CA-111; MTFW 2005
Lee, Tanith 1947- .... **CLC 46**
See also AAYA 15; CA 37-40R; CANR 53,
102, 145; DLB 261; FANT; SATA 8, 88,
134; SFW 4; SUFW 1, 2; YAW
Lee, Vernon .... **SSC 33; TCLC 5**
See Paget, Violet
See also DLB 57, 153, 156, 174, 178; GLL
1; SUFW 1
Lee, William
See Burroughs, William S.
See also GLL 1
Lee, Willy
See Burroughs, William S.
See also GLL 1
Lee-Hamilton, Eugene (Jacob)
1845-1907 .... **TCLC 22**
See also CA 117; 234
Leet, Judith 1935- .... **CLC 11**
See also CA 187
Le Fanu, Joseph Sheridan
1814-1873 .... **NCLC 9, 58; SSC 14, 84**
See also CMW 4; DA3; DAM POP; DLB
21, 70, 159, 178; GL 3; HGG; RGEL 2;
RGSF 2; SUFW 1
Leffland, Ella 1931- .... **CLC 19**
See also CA 29-32R; CANR 35, 78, 82;
DLBY 1984; INT CANR-35; SATA 65;
SSFS 24
Leger, Alexis
See Leger, (Marie-Rene Auguste) Alexis
Saint-Leger
**Leger, (Marie-Rene Auguste) Alexis
Saint-Leger** 1887-1975 .. **CLC 4, 11, 46;
PC 23**
See Perse, Saint-John; Saint-John Perse
See also CA 13-16R; 61-64; CANR 43;
DAM POET; MTCW 1
Leger, Saintleger
See Leger, (Marie-Rene Auguste) Alexis
Saint-Leger
Le Guin, Ursula K. 1929- ...... **CLC 8, 13, 22,
45, 71, 136; SSC 12, 69**
See also AAYA 9, 27; AITN 1; BPFB 2;
BYA 5, 8, 11, 14; CA 21-24R; CANR 9,
32, 52, 74, 132; CDALB 1968-1988; CLR
3, 28, 91; CN 2, 3, 4, 5, 6, 7; CPW; DA3;

Lehmann, Rosamond (Nina)
  1901-1990 .... **CLC 5**
  See also CA 77-80; 131; CANR 8, 73; CN
    1, 2, 3, 4; DLB 15; MTCW 2; RGEL 2;
    RHW

Leiber, Fritz (Reuter, Jr.)
  1910-1992 .... **CLC 25**
  See also AAYA 65; BPFB 2; CA 45-48; 139;
    CANR 2, 40, 86; CN 2, 3, 4, 5; DLB 8;
    FANT; HGG; MTCW 1, 2; MTFW 2005;
    SATA 45; SATA-Obit 73; SCFW 1, 2;
    SFW 4; SUFW 1, 2

Leibniz, Gottfried Wilhelm von
  1646-1716 .... **LC 35**
  See also DLB 168

Leimbach, Martha 1963-
  See Leimbach, Marti
  See also CA 130

Leimbach, Marti .... **CLC 65**
  See Leimbach, Martha

Leino, Eino .... **TCLC 24**
  See Lönnbohm, Armas Eino Leopold
  See also EWL 3

Leiris, Michel (Julien) 1901-1990 ..... **CLC 61**
  See also CA 119; 128; 132; EWL 3; GFL
    1789 to the Present

Leithauser, Brad 1953- .... **CLC 27**
  See also CA 107; CANR 27, 81; CP 5, 6, 7;
    DLB 120, 282

le Jars de Gournay, Marie
  See de Gournay, Marie le Jars

Lelchuk, Alan 1938- .... **CLC 5**
  See also CA 45-48; CAAS 20; CANR 1,
    70, 152; CN 3, 4, 5, 6, 7

Lem, Stanislaw 1921-2006 ..... **CLC 8, 15, 40,
    149**
  See also CA 105; 249; CAAS 1; CANR 32;
    CWW 2; MTCW 1; SCFW 1, 2; SFW 4

Lemann, Nancy (Elise) 1956- .... **CLC 39**
  See also CA 118; 136; CANR 121

Lemonnier, (Antoine Louis) Camille
  1844-1913 .... **TCLC 22**
  See also CA 121

Lenau, Nikolaus 1802-1850 .... **NCLC 16**

L'Engle, Madeleine 1918- .... **CLC 12**
  See also AAYA 28; AITN 2; BPFB 2; BYA
    2, 4, 5, 7; CA 1-4R; CANR 3, 21, 39, 66,
    107; CLR 1, 14, 57; CPW; CWRI 5; DA3;
    DAM POP; DLB 52; JRDA; MAICYA 1,
    2; MTCW 1, 2; MTFW 2005; SAAS 15;
    SATA 1, 27, 75, 128; SFW 4; WYA; YAW

Lengyel, Jozsef 1896-1975 .... **CLC 7**
  See also CA 85-88; 57-60; CANR 71;
    RGSF 2

Lenin 1870-1924
  See Lenin, V. I.
  See also CA 121; 168

Lenin, V. I. .... **TCLC 67**
  See Lenin

Lennon, John (Ono) 1940-1980 .. **CLC 12, 35**
  See also CA 102; SATA 114

Lennox, Charlotte Ramsay
  1729(?)-1804 .... **NCLC 23, 134**
  See also DLB 39; RGEL 2

Lentricchia, Frank, Jr.
  See Lentricchia, Frank

Lentricchia, Frank 1940- .... **CLC 34**
  See also CA 25-28R; CANR 19, 106, 148;
    DLB 246

Lenz, Gunter .... **CLC 65**

Lenz, Jakob Michael Reinhold
  1751-1792 .... **LC 100**
  See also DLB 94; RGWL 2, 3

Lenz, Siegfried 1926- .... **CLC 27; SSC 33**
  See also CA 89-92; CANR 80, 149; CWW
    2; DLB 75; EWL 3; RGSF 2; RGWL 2, 3

Leon, David
  See Jacob, (Cyprien-)Max

Leonard, Elmore 1925- .... **CLC 28, 34, 71,
    120, 222**
  See also AAYA 22, 59; AITN 1; BEST 89:1,
    90:4; BPFB 2; CA 81-84; CANR 12, 28,
    53, 76, 96, 133; CMW 4; CN 5, 6, 7;
    CPW; DA3; DAM POP; DLB 173, 226;
    INT CANR-28; MSW; MTCW 1, 2;
    MTFW 2005; RGAL 4; SATA 163;
    TCWW 1, 2

Leonard, Hugh .... **CLC 19**
  See Byrne, John Keyes
  See also CBD; CD 5, 6; DFS 13; DLB 13

Leonov, Leonid (Maximovich)
  1899-1994 .... **CLC 92**
  See Leonov, Leonid Maksimovich
  See also CA 129; CANR 76; DAM NOV;
    EWL 3; MTCW 1, 2; MTFW 2005

Leonov, Leonid Maksimovich
  See Leonov, Leonid (Maximovich)
  See also DLB 272

Leopardi, (Conte) Giacomo
  1798-1837 .... **NCLC 22, 129; PC 37**
  See also EW 5; RGWL 2, 3; WLIT 7; WP

Le Reveler
  See Artaud, Antonin (Marie Joseph)

Lerman, Eleanor 1952- .... **CLC 9**
  See also CA 85-88; CANR 69, 124

Lerman, Rhoda 1936- .... **CLC 56**
  See also CA 49-52; CANR 70

Lermontov, Mikhail Iur'evich
  See Lermontov, Mikhail Yuryevich
  See also DLB 205

Lermontov, Mikhail Yuryevich
  1814-1841 .... **NCLC 5, 47, 126; PC 18**
  See Lermontov, Mikhail Iur'evich
  See also EW 6; RGWL 2, 3; TWA

Leroux, Gaston 1868-1927 .... **TCLC 25**
  See also CA 108; 136; CANR 69; CMW 4;
    MTFW 2005; NFS 20; SATA 65

Lesage, Alain-Rene 1668-1747 .... **LC 2, 28**
  See also DLB 313; EW 3; GFL Beginnings
    to 1789; RGWL 2, 3

Leskov, N(ikolai) S(emenovich)
  See Leskov, Nikolai (Semyonovich)

Leskov, Nikolai (Semyonovich)
  1831-1895 ... **NCLC 25, 174; SSC 34, 96**
  See Leskov, Nikolai Semenovich

Leskov, Nikolai Semenovich
  See Leskov, Nikolai (Semyonovich)
  See also DLB 238

Lesser, Milton
  See Marlowe, Stephen

Lessing, Doris 1919- .. **CLC 1, 2, 3, 6, 10, 15,
    22, 40, 94, 170; SSC 6, 61; WLCS**
  See also AAYA 57; AFW; BRWS 1; CA
    9-12R; CAAS 14; CANR 33, 54, 76, 122;
    CBD; CD 5, 6; CDBLB 1960 to Present;
    CN 1, 2, 3, 4, 5, 6, 7; CWD; DA; DA3;
    DAB; DAC; DAM MST, NOV; DFS 20;
    DLB 15, 139; DLBY 1985; EWL 3;
    EXPS; FL 1:6; FW; LAIT 4; MTCW 1, 2;
    MTFW 2005; RGEL 2; RGSF 2; SFW 4;
    SSFS 1, 12, 20; TEA; WLIT 2, 4

Lessing, Gotthold Ephraim
  1729-1781 .... **DC 26; LC 8, 124**
  See also CDWLB 2; DLB 97; EW 4; RGWL
    2, 3

Lester, Richard 1932- .... **CLC 20**

Levenson, Jay .... **CLC 70**

Lever, Charles (James)
  1806-1872 .... **NCLC 23**
  See also DLB 21; RGEL 2

Leverson, Ada Esther
  1862(?)-1933(?) .... **TCLC 18**
  See Elaine
  See also CA 117; 202; DLB 153; RGEL 2

Levertov, Denise 1923-1997 .. **CLC 1, 2, 3, 5,
    8, 15, 28, 66; PC 11**
  See also AMWS 3; CA 1-4R; 178; 163;
    CAAE 178; CAAS 19; CANR 3, 29, 50,
    108; CDALBS; CP 1, 2, 3, 4, 5, 6; CWP;
    DAM POET; DLB 5, 165; EWL 3; EXPP;
    FW; INT CANR-29; MAL 5; MTCW 1,
    2; PAB; PFS 7, 17; RGAL 4; RGHL;
    TUS; WP

Levi, Carlo 1902-1975 .... **TCLC 125**
  See also CA 65-68; 53-56; CANR 10; EWL
    3; RGWL 2, 3

Levi, Jonathan .... **CLC 76**
  See also CA 197

Levi, Peter (Chad Tigar)
  1931-2000 .... **CLC 41**
  See also CA 5-8R; 187; CANR 34, 80; CP
    1, 2, 3, 4, 5, 6, 7; DLB 40

Levi, Primo 1919-1987 ...... **CLC 37, 50; SSC
    12; TCLC 109**
  See also CA 13-16R; 122; CANR 12, 33,
    61, 70, 132; DLB 177, 299; EWL 3;
    MTCW 1, 2; MTFW 2005; RGHL;
    RGWL 2, 3; WLIT 7

Levin, Ira 1929- .... **CLC 3, 6**
  See also CA 21-24R; CANR 17, 44, 74,
    139; CMW 4; CN 1, 2, 3, 4, 5, 6, 7; CPW;
    DA3; DAM POP; HGG; MTCW 1, 2;
    MTFW 2005; SATA 66; SFW 4

Levin, Meyer 1905-1981 .... **CLC 7**
  See also AITN 1; CA 9-12R; 104; CANR
    15; CN 1, 2, 3; DAM POP; DLB 9, 28;
    DLBY 1981; MAL 5; RGHL; SATA 21;
    SATA-Obit 27

Levine, Albert Norman 1923-2005
  See Levine, Norman
  See also CN 7

Levine, Norman 1923-2005 .... **CLC 54**
  See also CA 73-76; 240; CAAS 23; CANR
    14, 70; CN 1, 2, 3, 4, 5, 6; CP 1; DLB 88

Levine, Norman Albert
  See Levine, Norman

Levine, Philip 1928- .. **CLC 2, 4, 5, 9, 14, 33,
    118; PC 22**
  See also AMWS 5; CA 9-12R; CANR 9,
    37, 52, 116, 156; CP 1, 2, 3, 4, 5, 6, 7;
    DAM POET; DLB 5; EWL 3; MAL 5;
    PFS 8

Levinson, Deirdre 1931- .... **CLC 49**
  See also CA 73-76; CANR 70

Levi-Strauss, Claude 1908- .... **CLC 38**
  See also CA 1-4R; CANR 6, 32, 57; DLB
    242; EWL 3; GFL 1789 to the Present;
    MTCW 1, 2; TWA

Levitin, Sonia (Wolff) 1934- .... **CLC 17**
  See also AAYA 13, 48; CA 29-32R; CANR
    14, 32, 79; CLR 53; JRDA; MAICYA 1,
    2; SAAS 2; SATA 4, 68, 119, 131; SATA-
    Essay 131; YAW

Levon, O. U.
  See Kesey, Ken

Levy, Amy 1861-1889 .... **NCLC 59**
  See also DLB 156, 240

Lewes, George Henry 1817-1878 ... **NCLC 25**
  See also DLB 55, 144

Lewis, Alun 1915-1944 .... **SSC 40; TCLC 3**
  See also BRW 7; CA 104; 188; DLB 20,
    162; PAB; RGEL 2

Ludlum, Robert 1927-2001 .... **CLC 22, 43**
　　See also AAYA 10, 59; BEST 89:1, 90:3;
　　BPFB 2; CA 33-36R; 195; CANR 25, 41,
　　68, 105, 131; CMW 4; CPW; DA3; DAM
　　NOV, POP; DLBY 1982; MSW; MTCW
　　1, 2; MTFW 2005

Ludwig, Ken 1950- .... **CLC 60**
　　See also CA 195; CAD; CD 6

Ludwig, Otto 1813-1865 .... **NCLC 4**
　　See also DLB 129

Lugones, Leopoldo 1874-1938 .... **HLCS 2;
　　TCLC 15**
　　See also CA 116; 131; CANR 104; DLB
　　283; EWL 3; HW 1; LAW

Lu Hsun .... **SSC 20; TCLC 3**
　　See Shu-Jen, Chou
　　See also EWL 3

Lukacs, George .... **CLC 24**
　　See Lukacs, Gyorgy (Szegeny von)

Lukacs, Gyorgy (Szegeny von) 1885-1971
　　See Lukacs, George
　　See also CA 101; 29-32R; CANR 62; CD-
　　WLB 4; DLB 215, 242; EW 10; EWL 3;
　　MTCW 1, 2

Luke, Peter (Ambrose Cyprian)
　　1919-1995 .... **CLC 38**
　　See also CA 81-84; 147; CANR 72; CBD;
　　CD 5, 6; DLB 13

Lunar, Dennis
　　See Mungo, Raymond

Lurie, Alison 1926- ..... **CLC 4, 5, 18, 39, 175**
　　See also BPFB 2; CA 1-4R; CANR 2, 17,
　　50, 88; CN 1, 2, 3, 4, 5, 6, 7; DLB 2;
　　MAL 5; MTCW 1; NFS 24; SATA 46,
　　112; TCLE 1:1

Lustig, Arnost 1926- .... **CLC 56**
　　See also AAYA 3; CA 69-72; CANR 47,
　　102; CWW 2; DLB 232, 299; EWL 3;
　　RGHL; SATA 56

Luther, Martin 1483-1546 .... **LC 9, 37**
　　See also CDWLB 2; DLB 179; EW 2;
　　RGWL 2, 3

Luxemburg, Rosa 1870(?)-1919 ..... **TCLC 63**
　　See also CA 118

Luzi, Mario (Egidio Vincenzo)
　　1914-2005 .... **CLC 13**
　　See also CA 61-64; 236; CANR 9, 70;
　　CWW 2; DLB 128; EWL 3

L'vov, Arkady .... **CLC 59**

Lydgate, John c. 1370-1450(?) .... **LC 81**
　　See also BRW 1; DLB 146; RGEL 2

Lyly, John 1554(?)-1606 .... **DC 7; LC 41**
　　See also BRW 1; DAM DRAM; DLB 62,
　　167; RGEL 2

L'Ymagier
　　See Gourmont, Remy(-Marie-Charles) de

Lynch, B. Suarez
　　See Borges, Jorge Luis

Lynch, David 1946- .... **CLC 66, 162**
　　See also AAYA 55; CA 124; 129; CANR
　　111

Lynch, David Keith
　　See Lynch, David

Lynch, James
　　See Andreyev, Leonid (Nikolaevich)

Lyndsay, Sir David 1485-1555 .... **LC 20**
　　See also RGEL 2

Lynn, Kenneth S(chuyler)
　　1923-2001 .... **CLC 50**
　　See also CA 1-4R; 196; CANR 3, 27, 65

Lynx
　　See West, Rebecca

Lyons, Marcus
　　See Blish, James (Benjamin)

Lyotard, Jean-Francois
　　1924-1998 .... **TCLC 103**
　　See also DLB 242; EWL 3

Lyre, Pinchbeck
　　See Sassoon, Siegfried (Lorraine)

Lytle, Andrew (Nelson) 1902-1995 ... **CLC 22**
　　See also CA 9-12R; 150; CANR 70; CN 1,
　　2, 3, 4, 5, 6; CSW; DLB 6; DLBY 1995;
　　RGAL 4; RHW

Lyttelton, George 1709-1773 .... **LC 10**
　　See also RGEL 2

Lytton of Knebworth, Baron
　　See Bulwer-Lytton, Edward (George Earle
　　Lytton)

Maas, Peter 1929-2001 .... **CLC 29**
　　See also CA 93-96; 201; INT CA-93-96;
　　MTCW 2; MTFW 2005

Mac A'Ghobhainn, Iain
　　See Smith, Iain Crichton

Macaulay, Catherine 1731-1791 .... **LC 64**
　　See also DLB 104

Macaulay, (Emilie) Rose
　　1881(?)-1958 .... **TCLC 7, 44**
　　See also CA 104; DLB 36; EWL 3; RGEL
　　2; RHW

Macaulay, Thomas Babington
　　1800-1859 .... **NCLC 42**
　　See also BRW 4; CDBLB 1832-1890; DLB
　　32, 55; RGEL 2

MacBeth, George (Mann)
　　1932-1992 .... **CLC 2, 5, 9**
　　See also CA 25-28R; 136; CANR 61, 66;
　　CP 1, 2, 3, 4, 5; DLB 40; MTCW 1; PFS
　　8; SATA 4; SATA-Obit 70

MacCaig, Norman (Alexander)
　　1910-1996 .... **CLC 36**
　　See also BRWS 6; CA 9-12R; CANR 3, 34;
　　CP 1, 2, 3, 4, 5, 6; DAB; DAM POET;
　　DLB 27; EWL 3; RGEL 2

MacCarthy, Sir (Charles Otto) Desmond
　　1877-1952 .... **TCLC 36**
　　See also CA 167

MacDiarmid, Hugh .... **CLC 2, 4, 11, 19, 63;
　　PC 9**
　　See Grieve, C(hristopher) M(urray)
　　See also BRWS 12; CDBLB 1945-1960;
　　CP 1, 2; DLB 20; EWL 3; RGEL 2

MacDonald, Anson
　　See Heinlein, Robert A.

Macdonald, Cynthia 1928- .... **CLC 13, 19**
　　See also CA 49-52; CANR 4, 44, 146; DLB
　　105

MacDonald, George 1824-1905 .... **TCLC 9,
　　113**
　　See also AAYA 57; BYA 5; CA 106; 137;
　　CANR 80; CLR 67; DLB 18, 163, 178;
　　FANT; MAICYA 1, 2; RGEL 2; SATA 33,
　　100; SFW 4; SUFW; WCH

Macdonald, John
　　See Millar, Kenneth

MacDonald, John D. 1916-1986 .. **CLC 3, 27,
　　44**
　　See also BPFB 2; CA 1-4R; 121; CANR 1,
　　19, 60; CMW 4; CPW; DAM NOV, POP;
　　DLB 8, 306; DLBY 1986; MSW; MTCW
　　1, 2; MTFW 2005; SFW 4

Macdonald, John Ross
　　See Millar, Kenneth

Macdonald, Ross ..... **CLC 1, 2, 3, 14, 34, 41**
　　See Millar, Kenneth
　　See also AMWS 4; BPFB 2; CN 1, 2, 3;
　　DLBD 6; MAL 5; MSW; RGAL 4

MacDougal, John
　　See Blish, James (Benjamin)

MacDougal, John
　　See Blish, James (Benjamin)

MacDowell, John
　　See Parks, Tim(othy Harold)

MacEwen, Gwendolyn (Margaret)
　　1941-1987 .... **CLC 13, 55**
　　See also CA 9-12R; 124; CANR 7, 22; CP
　　1, 2, 3, 4; DLB 53, 251; SATA 50; SATA-
　　Obit 55

Macha, Karel Hynek 1810-1846 .... **NCLC 46**

Machado (y Ruiz), Antonio
　　1875-1939 .... **TCLC 3**
　　See also CA 104; 174; DLB 108; EW 9;
　　EWL 3; HW 2; PFS 23; RGWL 2, 3

Machado de Assis, Joaquim Maria
　　1839-1908 .... **BLC 2; HLCS 2; SSC 24;
　　TCLC 10**
　　See also CA 107; 153; CANR 91; DLB 307;
　　LAW; RGSF 2; RGWL 2, 3; TWA; WLIT
　　1

Machaut, Guillaume de c.
　　1300-1377 .... **CMLC 64**
　　See also DLB 208

Machen, Arthur .... **SSC 20; TCLC 4**
　　See Jones, Arthur Llewellyn
　　See also CA 179; DLB 156, 178; RGEL 2;
　　SUFW 1

Machiavelli, Niccolo 1469-1527 ... **DC 16; LC
　　8, 36; WLCS**
　　See also AAYA 58; DA; DAB; DAC; DAM
　　MST; EW 2; LAIT 1; LMFS 1; NFS 9;
　　RGWL 2, 3; TWA; WLIT 7

MacInnes, Colin 1914-1976 .... **CLC 4, 23**
　　See also CA 69-72; 65-68; CANR 21; CN
　　1, 2; DLB 14; MTCW 1, 2; RGEL 2;
　　RHW

MacInnes, Helen (Clark)
　　1907-1985 .... **CLC 27, 39**
　　See also BPFB 2; CA 1-4R; 117; CANR 1,
　　28, 58; CMW 4; CN 1, 2; CPW; DAM
　　POP; DLB 87; MSW; MTCW 1, 2;
　　MTFW 2005; SATA 22; SATA-Obit 44

Mackay, Mary 1855-1924
　　See Corelli, Marie
　　See also CA 118; 177; FANT; RHW

Mackay, Shena 1944- .... **CLC 195**
　　See also CA 104; CANR 88, 139; DLB 231,
　　319; MTFW 2005

Mackenzie, Compton (Edward Montague)
　　1883-1972 .... **CLC 18; TCLC 116**
　　See also CA 21-22; 37-40R; CAP 2; CN 1;
　　DLB 34, 100; RGEL 2

Mackenzie, Henry 1745-1831 .... **NCLC 41**
　　See also DLB 39; RGEL 2

Mackey, Nathaniel 1947- .... **PC 49**
　　See also CA 153; CANR 114; CP 6, 7; DLB
　　169

Mackey, Nathaniel Ernest
　　See Mackey, Nathaniel

MacKinnon, Catharine A. 1946- .... **CLC 181**
　　See also CA 128; 132; CANR 73, 140; FW;
　　MTCW 2; MTFW 2005

Mackintosh, Elizabeth 1896(?)-1952
　　See Tey, Josephine
　　See also CA 110; CMW 4

Macklin, Charles 1699-1797 .... **LC 132**
　　See also DLB 89; RGEL 2

MacLaren, James
　　See Grieve, C(hristopher) M(urray)

MacLaverty, Bernard 1942- .... **CLC 31**
　　See also CA 116; 118; CANR 43, 88; CN
　　5, 6, 7; DLB 267; INT CA-118; RGSF 2

MacLean, Alistair (Stuart)
　　1922(?)-1987 .... **CLC 3, 13, 50, 63**
　　See also CA 57-60; 121; CANR 28, 61;
　　CMW 4; CP 2, 3, 4, 5, 6, 7; CPW; DAM
　　POP; DLB 276; MTCW 1; SATA 23;
　　SATA-Obit 50; TCWW 2

Maclean, Norman (Fitzroy)
　　1902-1990 .... **CLC 78; SSC 13**
　　See also AMWS 14; CA 102; 132; CANR
　　49; CPW; DAM POP; DLB 206; TCWW
　　2

MacLeish, Archibald 1892-1982 ... **CLC 3, 8,
　　14, 68; PC 47**
　　See also AMW; CA 9-12R; 106; CAD;
　　CANR 33, 63; CDALBS; CP 1, 2; DAM
　　POET; DFS 15; DLB 4, 7, 45; DLBY

Martin, Ken
See Hubbard, L. Ron
Martin, Richard
See Creasey, John
Martin, Steve 1945- .... **CLC 30, 217**
See also AAYA 53; CA 97-100; CANR 30, 100, 140; DFS 19; MTCW 1; MTFW 2005
Martin, Valerie 1948- .... **CLC 89**
See also BEST 90:2; CA 85-88; CANR 49, 89
Martin, Violet Florence 1862-1915 .. **SSC 56; TCLC 51**
Martin, Webber
See Silverberg, Robert
Martindale, Patrick Victor
See White, Patrick (Victor Martindale)
Martin du Gard, Roger
1881-1958 .... **TCLC 24**
See also CA 118; CANR 94; DLB 65; EWL 3; GFL 1789 to the Present; RGWL 2, 3
Martineau, Harriet 1802-1876 ...... **NCLC 26, 137**
See also DLB 21, 55, 159, 163, 166, 190; FW; RGEL 2; YABC 2
Martines, Julia
See O'Faolain, Julia
Martinez, Enrique Gonzalez
See Gonzalez Martinez, Enrique
Martinez, Jacinto Benavente y
See Benavente (y Martinez), Jacinto
Martinez de la Rosa, Francisco de Paula
1787-1862 .... **NCLC 102**
See also TWA
Martinez Ruiz, Jose 1873-1967
See Azorin; Ruiz, Jose Martinez
See also CA 93-96; HW 1
Martinez Sierra, Gregorio
See Martinez Sierra, Maria
Martinez Sierra, Gregorio
1881-1947 .... **TCLC 6**
See also CA 115; EWL 3
Martinez Sierra, Maria 1874-1974 .. **TCLC 6**
See also CA 250; 115; EWL 3
Martinsen, Martin
See Follett, Ken
Martinson, Harry (Edmund)
1904-1978 .... **CLC 14**
See also CA 77-80; CANR 34, 130; DLB 259; EWL 3
Martyn, Edward 1859-1923 .... **TCLC 131**
See also CA 179; DLB 10; RGEL 2
Marut, Ret
See Traven, B.
Marut, Robert
See Traven, B.
Marvell, Andrew 1621-1678 .... **LC 4, 43; PC 10; WLC 4**
See also BRW 2; BRWR 2; CDBLB 1660-1789; DA; DAB; DAC; DAM MST, POET; DLB 131; EXPP; PFS 5; RGEL 2; TEA; WP
Marx, Karl (Heinrich)
1818-1883 .... **NCLC 17, 114**
See also DLB 129; LATS 1:1; TWA
Masaoka, Shiki -1902 .... **TCLC 18**
See Masaoka, Tsunenori
See also RGWL 3
Masaoka, Tsunenori 1867-1902
See Masaoka, Shiki
See also CA 117; 191; TWA
Masefield, John (Edward)
1878-1967 .... **CLC 11, 47**
See also CA 19-20; 25-28R; CANR 33; CAP 2; CDBLB 1890-1914; DAM POET; DLB 10, 19, 153, 160; EWL 3; EXPP; FANT; MTCW 1, 2; PFS 5; RGEL 2; SATA 19

Maso, Carole 1955(?)- .... **CLC 44**
See also CA 170; CANR 148; CN 7; GLL 2; RGAL 4
Mason, Bobbie Ann 1940- ... **CLC 28, 43, 82, 154; SSC 4**
See also AAYA 5, 42; AMWS 8; BPFB 2; CA 53-56; CANR 11, 31, 58, 83, 125; CDALBS; CN 5, 6, 7; CSW; DA3; DLB 173; DLBY 1987; EWL 3; EXPS; INT CANR-31; MAL 5; MTCW 1, 2; MTFW 2005; NFS 4; RGAL 4; RGSF 2; SSFS 3, 8, 20; TCLE 1:2; YAW
Mason, Ernst
See Pohl, Frederik
Mason, Hunni B.
See Sternheim, (William Adolf) Carl
Mason, Lee W.
See Malzberg, Barry N(athaniel)
Mason, Nick 1945- .... **CLC 35**
Mason, Tally
See Derleth, August (William)
Mass, Anna .... **CLC 59**
Mass, William
See Gibson, William
Massinger, Philip 1583-1640 .... **LC 70**
See also BRWS 11; DLB 58; RGEL 2
Master Lao
See Lao Tzu
Masters, Edgar Lee 1868-1950 ...... **PC 1, 36; TCLC 2, 25; WLCS**
See also AMWS 1; CA 104; 133; CDALB 1865-1917; DA; DAC; DAM MST, POET; DLB 54; EWL 3; EXPP; MAL 5; MTCW 1, 2; MTFW 2005; RGAL 4; TUS; WP
Masters, Hilary 1928- .... **CLC 48**
See also CA 25-28R, 217; CAAE 217; CANR 13, 47, 97; CN 6, 7; DLB 244
Mastrosimone, William 1947- .... **CLC 36**
See also CA 186; CAD; CD 5, 6
Mathe, Albert
See Camus, Albert
Mather, Cotton 1663-1728 .... **LC 38**
See also AMWS 2; CDALB 1640-1865; DLB 24, 30, 140; RGAL 4; TUS
Mather, Increase 1639-1723 .... **LC 38**
See also DLB 24
Mathers, Marshall
See Eminem
Mathers, Marshall Bruce
See Eminem
Matheson, Richard (Burton) 1926- .. **CLC 37**
See also AAYA 31; CA 97-100; CANR 88, 99; DLB 8, 44; HGG; INT CA-97-100; SCFW 1, 2; SFW 4; SUFW 2
Mathews, Harry (Burchell) 1930- ..... **CLC 6, 52**
See also CA 21-24R; CAAS 6; CANR 18, 40, 98; CN 5, 6, 7
Mathews, John Joseph 1894-1979 .. **CLC 84; NNAL**
See also CA 19-20; 142; CANR 45; CAP 2; DAM MULT; DLB 175; TCWW 1, 2
Mathias, Roland (Glyn) 1915- .... **CLC 45**
See also CA 97-100; CANR 19, 41; CP 1, 2, 3, 4, 5, 6, 7; DLB 27
Matsuo Basho 1644(?)-1694 ...... **LC 62; PC 3**
See Basho, Matsuo
See also DAM POET; PFS 2, 7, 18
Mattheson, Rodney
See Creasey, John
Matthews, (James) Brander
1852-1929 .... **TCLC 95**
See also CA 181; DLB 71, 78; DLBD 13
Matthews, Greg 1949- .... **CLC 45**
See also CA 135

Matthews, William (Procter III)
1942-1997 .... **CLC 40**
See also AMWS 9; CA 29-32R; 162; CAAS 18; CANR 12, 57; CP 2, 3, 4, 5, 6; DLB 5
Matthias, John (Edward) 1941- .... **CLC 9**
See also CA 33-36R; CANR 56; CP 4, 5, 6, 7
Matthiessen, F(rancis) O(tto)
1902-1950 .... **TCLC 100**
See also CA 185; DLB 63; MAL 5
Matthiessen, Peter 1927- ... **CLC 5, 7, 11, 32, 64**
See also AAYA 6, 40; AMWS 5; ANW; BEST 90:4; BPFB 2; CA 9-12R; CANR 21, 50, 73, 100, 138; CN 1, 2, 3, 4, 5, 6, 7; DA3; DAM NOV; DLB 6, 173, 275; MAL 5; MTCW 1, 2; MTFW 2005; SATA 27
Maturin, Charles Robert
1780(?)-1824 .... **NCLC 6, 169**
See also BRWS 8; DLB 178; GL 3; HGG; LMFS 1; RGEL 2; SUFW
Matute (Ausejo), Ana Maria 1925- .. **CLC 11**
See also CA 89-92; CANR 129; CWW 2; DLB 322; EWL 3; MTCW 1; RGSF 2
Maugham, W. S.
See Maugham, W(illiam) Somerset
Maugham, W(illiam) Somerset
1874-1965 .. **CLC 1, 11, 15, 67, 93; SSC 8, 94; WLC 4**
See also AAYA 55; BPFB 2; BRW 6; CA 5-8R; 25-28R; CANR 40, 127; CDBLB 1914-1945; CMW 4; DA; DA3; DAB; DAC; DAM DRAM, MST, NOV; DFS 22; DLB 10, 36, 77, 100, 162, 195; EWL 3; LAIT 3; MTCW 1, 2; MTFW 2005; NFS 23; RGEL 2; RGSF 2; SATA 54; SSFS 17
Maugham, William Somerset
See Maugham, W(illiam) Somerset
Maupassant, (Henri Rene Albert) Guy de
1850-1893 . **NCLC 1, 42, 83; SSC 1, 64; WLC 4**
See also BYA 14; DA; DA3; DAB; DAC; DAM MST; DLB 123; EW 7; EXPS; GFL 1789 to the Present; LAIT 2; LMFS 1; RGSF 2; RGWL 2, 3; SSFS 4, 21; SUFW; TWA
Maupin, Armistead 1944- .... **CLC 95**
See also CA 125; 130; CANR 58, 101; CPW; DA3; DAM POP; DLB 278; GLL 1; INT CA-130; MTCW 2; MTFW 2005
Maupin, Armistead Jones, Jr.
See Maupin, Armistead
Maurhut, Richard
See Traven, B.
Mauriac, Claude 1914-1996 .... **CLC 9**
See also CA 89-92; 152; CWW 2; DLB 83; EWL 3; GFL 1789 to the Present
Mauriac, Francois (Charles)
1885-1970 .... **CLC 4, 9, 56; SSC 24**
See also CA 25-28; CAP 2; DLB 65; EW 10; EWL 3; GFL 1789 to the Present; MTCW 1, 2; MTFW 2005; RGWL 2, 3; TWA
Mavor, Osborne Henry 1888-1951
See Bridie, James
See also CA 104
Maxwell, William (Keepers, Jr.)
1908-2000 .... **CLC 19**
See also AMWS 8; CA 93-96; 189; CANR 54, 95; CN 1, 2, 3, 4, 5, 6, 7; DLB 218, 278; DLBY 1980; INT CA-93-96; MAL 5; SATA-Obit 128
May, Elaine 1932- .... **CLC 16**
See also CA 124; 142; CAD; CWD; DLB 44

Mitchell, Margaret (Munnerlyn)
1900-1949 .... **TCLC 11, 170**
See also AAYA 23; BPFB 2; BYA 1; CA 109; 125; CANR 55, 94; CDALBS; DA3; DAM NOV, POP; DLB 9; LAIT 2; MAL 5; MTCW 1, 2; MTFW 2005; NFS 9; RGAL 4; RHW; TUS; WYAS 1; YAW

Mitchell, Peggy
See Mitchell, Margaret (Munnerlyn)

Mitchell, S(ilas) Weir 1829-1914 .... **TCLC 36**
See also CA 165; DLB 202; RGAL 4

Mitchell, W(illiam) O(rmond)
1914-1998 .... **CLC 25**
See also CA 77-80; 165; CANR 15, 43; CN 1, 2, 3, 4, 5, 6; DAC; DAM MST; DLB 88; TCLE 1:2

Mitchell, William (Lendrum)
1879-1936 .... **TCLC 81**
See also CA 213

Mitford, Mary Russell 1787-1855 ... **NCLC 4**
See also DLB 110, 116; RGEL 2

Mitford, Nancy 1904-1973 .... **CLC 44**
See also BRWS 10; CA 9-12R; CN 1; DLB 191; RGEL 2

Miyamoto, (Chujo) Yuriko
1899-1951 .... **TCLC 37**
See Miyamoto Yuriko
See also CA 170, 174

Miyamoto Yuriko
See Miyamoto, (Chujo) Yuriko
See also DLB 180

Miyazawa, Kenji 1896-1933 .... **TCLC 76**
See Miyazawa Kenji
See also CA 157; RGWL 3

Miyazawa Kenji
See Miyazawa, Kenji
See also EWL 3

Mizoguchi, Kenji 1898-1956 .... **TCLC 72**
See also CA 167

Mo, Timothy (Peter) 1950- .... **CLC 46, 134**
See also CA 117; CANR 128; CN 5, 6, 7; DLB 194; MTCW 1; WLIT 4; WWE 1

Modarressi, Taghi (M.) 1931-1997 ... **CLC 44**
See also CA 121; 134; INT CA-134

Modiano, Patrick (Jean) 1945- .... **CLC 18, 218**
See also CA 85-88; CANR 17, 40, 115; CWW 2; DLB 83, 299; EWL 3; RGHL

Mofolo, Thomas (Mokopu)
1875(?)-1948 .... **BLC 3; TCLC 22**
See also AFW; CA 121; 153; CANR 83; DAM MULT; DLB 225; EWL 3; MTCW 2; MTFW 2005; WLIT 2

Mohr, Nicholasa 1938- .... **CLC 12; HLC 2**
See also AAYA 8, 46; CA 49-52; CANR 1, 32, 64; CLR 22; DAM MULT; DLB 145; HW 1, 2; JRDA; LAIT 5; LLW; MAICYA 2; MAICYAS 1; RGAL 4; SAAS 8; SATA 8, 97; SATA-Essay 113; WYA; YAW

Moi, Toril 1953- .... **CLC 172**
See also CA 154; CANR 102; FW

Mojtabai, A(nn) G(race) 1938- ..... **CLC 5, 9, 15, 29**
See also CA 85-88; CANR 88

Moliere 1622-1673 ..... **DC 13; LC 10, 28, 64, 125, 127; WLC 4**
See also DA; DA3; DAB; DAC; DAM DRAM, MST; DFS 13, 18, 20; DLB 268; EW 3; GFL Beginnings to 1789; LATS 1:1; RGWL 2, 3; TWA

Molin, Charles
See Mayne, William (James Carter)

Molnar, Ferenc 1878-1952 .... **TCLC 20**
See also CA 109; 153; CANR 83; CDWLB 4; DAM DRAM; DLB 215; EWL 3; RGWL 2, 3

Momaday, N. Scott 1934- ...... **CLC 2, 19, 85, 95, 160; NNAL; PC 25; WLCS**
See also AAYA 11, 64; AMWS 4; ANW; BPFB 2; BYA 12; CA 25-28R; CANR 14, 34, 68, 134; CDALBS; CN 2, 3, 4, 5, 6, 7; CPW; DA; DA3; DAB; DAC; DAM MST, MULT, NOV, POP; DLB 143, 175, 256; EWL 3; EXPP; INT CANR-14; LAIT 4; LATS 1:2; MAL 5; MTCW 1, 2; MTFW 2005; NFS 10; PFS 2, 11; RGAL 4; SATA 48; SATA-Brief 30; TCWW 1, 2; WP; YAW

Monette, Paul 1945-1995 .... **CLC 82**
See also AMWS 10; CA 139; 147; CN 6; GLL 1

Monroe, Harriet 1860-1936 .... **TCLC 12**
See also CA 109; 204; DLB 54, 91

Monroe, Lyle
See Heinlein, Robert A.

Montagu, Elizabeth 1720-1800 .... **NCLC 7, 117**
See also FW

Montagu, Mary (Pierrepont) Wortley
1689-1762 .... **LC 9, 57; PC 16**
See also DLB 95, 101; FL 1:1; RGEL 2

Montagu, W. H.
See Coleridge, Samuel Taylor

Montague, John (Patrick) 1929- ..... **CLC 13, 46**
See also CA 9-12R; CANR 9, 69, 121; CP 1, 2, 3, 4, 5, 6, 7; DLB 40; EWL 3; MTCW 1; PFS 12; RGEL 2; TCLE 1:2

Montaigne, Michel (Eyquem) de
1533-1592 .... **LC 8, 105; WLC 4**
See also DA; DAB; DAC; DAM MST; DLB 327; EW 2; GFL Beginnings to 1789; LMFS 1; RGWL 2, 3; TWA

Montale, Eugenio 1896-1981 ... **CLC 7, 9, 18; PC 13**
See also CA 17-20R; 104; CANR 30; DLB 114; EW 11; EWL 3; MTCW 1; PFS 22; RGWL 2, 3; TWA; WLIT 7

Montesquieu, Charles-Louis de Secondat
1689-1755 .... **LC 7, 69**
See also DLB 314; EW 3; GFL Beginnings to 1789; TWA

Montessori, Maria 1870-1952 ...... **TCLC 103**
See also CA 115; 147

Montgomery, (Robert) Bruce 1921(?)-1978
See Crispin, Edmund
See also CA 179; 104; CMW 4

Montgomery, L(ucy) M(aud)
1874-1942 .... **TCLC 51, 140**
See also AAYA 12; BYA 1; CA 108; 137; CLR 8, 91; DA3; DAC; DAM MST; DLB 92; DLBD 14; JRDA; MAICYA 1, 2; MTCW 2; MTFW 2005; RGEL 2; SATA 100; TWA; WCH; WYA; YABC 1

Montgomery, Marion H., Jr. 1925- .... **CLC 7**
See also AITN 1; CA 1-4R; CANR 3, 48; CSW; DLB 6

Montgomery, Max
See Davenport, Guy (Mattison, Jr.)

Montherlant, Henry (Milon) de
1896-1972 .... **CLC 8, 19**
See also CA 85-88; 37-40R; DAM DRAM; DLB 72, 321; EW 11; EWL 3; GFL 1789 to the Present; MTCW 1

Monty Python
See Chapman, Graham; Cleese, John (Marwood); Gilliam, Terry; Idle, Eric; Jones, Terence Graham Parry; Palin, Michael (Edward)
See also AAYA 7

Moodie, Susanna (Strickland)
1803-1885 .... **NCLC 14, 113**
See also DLB 99

Moody, Hiram 1961-
See Moody, Rick
See also CA 138; CANR 64, 112; MTFW 2005

Moody, Minerva
See Alcott, Louisa May

Moody, Rick .... **CLC 147**
See Moody, Hiram

Moody, William Vaughan
1869-1910 .... **TCLC 105**
See also CA 110; 178; DLB 7, 54; MAL 5; RGAL 4

Mooney, Edward 1951-
See Mooney, Ted
See also CA 130

Mooney, Ted .... **CLC 25**
See Mooney, Edward

Moorcock, Michael 1939- .... **CLC 5, 27, 58**
See Bradbury, Edward P.
See also AAYA 26; CA 45-48; CAAS 5; CANR 2, 17, 38, 64, 122; CN 5, 6, 7; DLB 14, 231, 261, 319; FANT; MTCW 1, 2; MTFW 2005; SATA 93, 166; SCFW 1, 2; SFW 4; SUFW 1, 2

Moorcock, Michael John
See Moorcock, Michael

Moore, Alan 1953- .... **CLC 230**
See also AAYA 51; CA 204; CANR 138; DLB 261; MTFW 2005; SFW 4

Moore, Brian 1921-1999 ... **CLC 1, 3, 5, 7, 8, 19, 32, 90**
See Bryan, Michael
See also BRWS 9; CA 1-4R; 174; CANR 1, 25, 42, 63; CCA 1; CN 1, 2, 3, 4, 5, 6; DAB; DAC; DAM MST; DLB 251; EWL 3; FANT; MTCW 1, 2; MTFW 2005; RGEL 2

Moore, Edward
See Muir, Edwin
See also RGEL 2

Moore, G. E. 1873-1958 .... **TCLC 89**
See also DLB 262

Moore, George Augustus
1852-1933 .... **SSC 19; TCLC 7**
See also BRW 6; CA 104; 177; DLB 10, 18, 57, 135; EWL 3; RGEL 2; RGSF 2

Moore, Lorrie .... **CLC 39, 45, 68**
See Moore, Marie Lorena
See also AMWS 10; CN 5, 6, 7; DLB 234; SSFS 19

Moore, Marianne (Craig)
1887-1972 .... **CLC 1, 2, 4, 8, 10, 13, 19, 47; PC 4, 49; WLCS**
See also AMW; CA 1-4R; 33-36R; CANR 3, 61; CDALB 1929-1941; CP 1; DA; DA3; DAB; DAC; DAM MST, POET; DLB 45; DLBD 7; EWL 3; EXPP; FL 1:6; MAL 5; MBL; MTCW 1, 2; MTFW 2005; PAB; PFS 14, 17; RGAL 4; SATA 20; TUS; WP

Moore, Marie Lorena 1957- .... **CLC 165**
See Moore, Lorrie
See also CA 116; CANR 39, 83, 139; DLB 234; MTFW 2005

Moore, Michael 1954- .... **CLC 218**
See also AAYA 53; CA 166; CANR 150

Moore, Thomas 1779-1852 .... **NCLC 6, 110**
See also DLB 96, 144; RGEL 2

Moorhouse, Frank 1938- .... **SSC 40**
See also CA 118; CANR 92; CN 3, 4, 5, 6, 7; DLB 289; RGSF 2

Mora, Pat 1942- .... **HLC 2**
See also AMWS 13; CA 129; CANR 57, 81, 112; CLR 58; DAM MULT; DLB 209; HW 1, 2; LLW; MAICYA 2; MTFW 2005; SATA 92, 134

Moraga, Cherrie 1952- ...... **CLC 126; DC 22**
See also CA 131; CANR 66, 154; DAM MULT; DLB 82, 249; FW; GLL 1; HW 1, 2; LLW

Norris, (Benjamin) Frank(lin, Jr.)
1870-1902 .... **SSC 28; TCLC 24, 155**
See also AAYA 57; AMW; AMWC 2; BPFB 2; CA 110; 160; CDALB 1865-1917; DLB 12, 71, 186; LMFS 2; MAL 5; NFS 12; RGAL 4; TCWW 1, 2; TUS

Norris, Leslie 1921-2006 .... **CLC 14**
See also CA 11-12; 251; CANR 14, 117; CAP 1; CP 1, 2, 3, 4, 5, 6, 7; DLB 27, 256

North, Andrew
See Norton, Andre

North, Anthony
See Koontz, Dean R.

North, Captain George
See Stevenson, Robert Louis (Balfour)

North, Captain George
See Stevenson, Robert Louis (Balfour)

North, Milou
See Erdrich, Louise

Northrup, B. A.
See Hubbard, L. Ron

North Staffs
See Hulme, T(homas) E(rnest)

Northup, Solomon 1808-1863 ...... **NCLC 105**

Norton, Alice Mary
See Norton, Andre
See also MAICYA 1; SATA 1, 43

Norton, Andre 1912-2005 .... **CLC 12**
See Norton, Alice Mary
See also AAYA 14; BPFB 2; BYA 4, 10, 12; CA 1-4R; 237; CANR 2, 31, 68, 108, 149; CLR 50; DLB 8, 52; JRDA; MAICYA 2; MTCW 1; SATA 91; SUFW 1, 2; YAW

Norton, Caroline 1808-1877 .... **NCLC 47**
See also DLB 21, 159, 199

Norway, Nevil Shute 1899-1960
See Shute, Nevil
See also CA 102; 93-96; CANR 85; MTCW 2

Norwid, Cyprian Kamil
1821-1883 .... **NCLC 17**
See also RGWL 3

Nosille, Nabrah
See Ellison, Harlan

Nossack, Hans Erich 1901-1977 .... **CLC 6**
See also CA 93-96; 85-88; CANR 156; DLB 69; EWL 3

Nostradamus 1503-1566 .... **LC 27**

Nosu, Chuji
See Ozu, Yasujiro

Notenburg, Eleanora (Genrikhovna) von
See Guro, Elena (Genrikhovna)

Nova, Craig 1945- .... **CLC 7, 31**
See also CA 45-48; CANR 2, 53, 127

Novak, Joseph
See Kosinski, Jerzy

Novalis 1772-1801 .... **NCLC 13, 178**
See also CDWLB 2; DLB 90; EW 5; RGWL 2, 3

Novick, Peter 1934- .... **CLC 164**
See also CA 188

Novis, Emile
See Weil, Simone (Adolphine)

Nowlan, Alden (Albert) 1933-1983 ... **CLC 15**
See also CA 9-12R; CANR 5; CP 1, 2, 3; DAC; DAM MST; DLB 53; PFS 12

Noyes, Alfred 1880-1958 ...... **PC 27; TCLC 7**
See also CA 104; 188; DLB 20; EXPP; FANT; PFS 4; RGEL 2

Nugent, Richard Bruce
1906(?)-1987 .... **HR 1:3**
See also BW 1; CA 125; DLB 51; GLL 2

Nunn, Kem .... **CLC 34**
See also CA 159

Nussbaum, Martha Craven 1947- .. **CLC 203**
See also CA 134; CANR 102

Nwapa, Flora (Nwanzuruaha)
1931-1993 .... **BLCS; CLC 133**
See also BW 2; CA 143; CANR 83; CDWLB 3; CWRI 5; DLB 125; EWL 3; WLIT 2

Nye, Robert 1939- .... **CLC 13, 42**
See also BRWS 10; CA 33-36R; CANR 29, 67, 107; CN 1, 2, 3, 4, 5, 6, 7; CP 1, 2, 3, 4, 5, 6, 7; CWRI 5; DAM NOV; DLB 14, 271; FANT; HGG; MTCW 1; RHW; SATA 6

Nyro, Laura 1947-1997 .... **CLC 17**
See also CA 194

Oates, Joyce Carol 1938- .. **CLC 1, 2, 3, 6, 9, 11, 15, 19, 33, 52, 108, 134; SSC 6, 70; WLC 4**
See also AAYA 15, 52; AITN 1; AMWS 2; BEST 89:2; BPFB 2; BYA 11; CA 5-8R; CANR 25, 45, 74, 113, 129, 228; CDALB 1968-1988; CN 1, 2, 3, 4, 5, 6, 7; CP 5, 6, 7; CPW; CWP; DA; DA3; DAB; DAC; DAM MST, NOV, POP; DLB 2, 5, 130; DLBY 1981; EWL 3; EXPS; FL 1:6; FW; GL 3; HGG; INT CANR-25; LAIT 4; MAL 5; MBL; MTCW 1, 2; MTFW 2005; NFS 8, 24; RGAL 4; RGSF 2; SATA 159; SSFS 1, 8, 17; SUFW 2; TUS

O'Brian, E. G.
See Clarke, Arthur C.

O'Brian, Patrick 1914-2000 .... **CLC 152**
See also AAYA 55; BRWS 12; CA 144; 187; CANR 74; CPW; MTCW 2; MTFW 2005; RHW

O'Brien, Darcy 1939-1998 .... **CLC 11**
See also CA 21-24R; 167; CANR 8, 59

O'Brien, Edna 1932- ..... **CLC 3, 5, 8, 13, 36, 65, 116; SSC 10, 77**
See also BRWS 5; CA 1-4R; CANR 6, 41, 65, 102; CDBLB 1960 to Present; CN 1, 2, 3, 4, 5, 6, 7; DA3; DAM NOV; DLB 14, 231, 319; EWL 3; FW; MTCW 1, 2; MTFW 2005; RGSF 2; WLIT 4

O'Brien, Fitz-James 1828-1862 ..... **NCLC 21**
See also DLB 74; RGAL 4; SUFW

O'Brien, Flann .... **CLC 1, 4, 5, 7, 10, 47**
See O Nuallain, Brian
See also BRWS 2; DLB 231; EWL 3; RGEL 2

O'Brien, Richard 1942- .... **CLC 17**
See also CA 124

O'Brien, Tim 1946- .... **CLC 7, 19, 40, 103, 211; SSC 74**
See also AAYA 16; AMWS 5; CA 85-88; CANR 40, 58, 133; CDALBS; CN 5, 6, 7; CPW; DA3; DAM POP; DLB 152; DLBD 9; DLBY 1980; LATS 1:2; MAL 5; MTCW 2; MTFW 2005; RGAL 4; SSFS 5, 15; TCLE 1:2

Obstfelder, Sigbjoern 1866-1900 .... **TCLC 23**
See also CA 123

O'Casey, Sean 1880-1964 .... **CLC 1, 5, 9, 11, 15, 88; DC 12; WLCS**
See also BRW 7; CA 89-92; CANR 62; CBD; CDBLB 1914-1945; DA3; DAB; DAC; DAM DRAM, MST; DFS 19; DLB 10; EWL 3; MTCW 1, 2; MTFW 2005; RGEL 2; TEA; WLIT 4

O'Cathasaigh, Sean
See O'Casey, Sean

Occom, Samson 1723-1792 .... **LC 60; NNAL**
See also DLB 175

Occomy, Marita (Odette) Bonner
1899(?)-1971
See Bonner, Marita
See also BW 2; CA 142; DFS 13; DLB 51, 228

Ochs, Phil(ip David) 1940-1976 .... **CLC 17**
See also CA 185; 65-68

O'Connor, Edwin (Greene)
1918-1968 .... **CLC 14**
See also CA 93-96; 25-28R; MAL 5

O'Connor, (Mary) Flannery
1925-1964 ..... **CLC 1, 2, 3, 6, 10, 13, 15, 21, 66, 104; SSC 1, 23, 61, 82; TCLC 132; WLC 4**
See also AAYA 7; AMW; AMWR 2; BPFB 3; BYA 16; CA 1-4R; CANR 3, 41; CDALB 1941-1968; DA; DA3; DAB; DAC; DAM MST, NOV; DLB 2, 152; DLBD 12; DLBY 1980; EWL 3; EXPS; LAIT 5; MAL 5; MBL; MTCW 1, 2; MTFW 2005; NFS 3, 21; RGAL 4; RGSF 2; SSFS 2, 7, 10, 19; TUS

O'Connor, Frank .... **CLC 23; SSC 5**
See O'Donovan, Michael Francis
See also DLB 162; EWL 3; RGSF 2; SSFS 5

O'Dell, Scott 1898-1989 .... **CLC 30**
See also AAYA 3, 44; BPFB 3; BYA 1, 2, 3, 5; CA 61-64; 129; CANR 12, 30, 112; CLR 1, 16; DLB 52; JRDA; MAICYA 1, 2; SATA 12, 60, 134; WYA; YAW

Odets, Clifford 1906-1963 ..... **CLC 2, 28, 98; DC 6**
See also AMWS 2; CA 85-88; CAD; CANR 62; CDALB 1941-1968; DA3; DAM DRAM; DFS 3, 17, 20; DLB 7, 26; EWL 3; MAL 5; MTCW 1, 2; MTFW 2005; RGAL 4; TUS

O'Doherty, Brian 1928- .... **CLC 76**
See also CA 105; CANR 108

O'Donnell, K. M.
See Malzberg, Barry N(athaniel)

O'Donnell, Lawrence
See Kuttner, Henry

O'Donovan, Michael Francis
1903-1966 .... **CLC 14**
See O'Connor, Frank
See also CA 93-96; CANR 84

Oe, Kenzaburo 1935- .. **CLC 10, 36, 86, 187; SSC 20**
See Oe Kenzaburo
See also CA 97-100; CANR 36, 50, 74, 126; DA3; DAM NOV; DLB 182; DLBY 1994; LATS 1:2; MJW; MTCW 1, 2; MTFW 2005; RGSF 2; RGWL 2, 3

Oe Kenzaburo
See Oe, Kenzaburo
See also CWW 2; EWL 3

O'Faolain, Julia 1932- ... **CLC 6, 19, 47, 108**
See also CA 81-84; CAAS 2; CANR 12, 61; CN 2, 3, 4, 5, 6, 7; DLB 14, 231, 319; FW; MTCW 1; RHW

O'Faolain, Sean 1900-1991 ...... **CLC 1, 7, 14, 32, 70; SSC 13; TCLC 143**
See also CA 61-64; 134; CANR 12, 66; CN 1, 2, 3, 4; DLB 15, 162; MTCW 1, 2; MTFW 2005; RGEL 2; RGSF 2

O'Flaherty, Liam 1896-1984 .... **CLC 5, 34; SSC 6**
See also CA 101; 113; CANR 35; CN 1, 2, 3; DLB 36, 162; DLBY 1984; MTCW 1, 2; MTFW 2005; RGEL 2; RGSF 2; SSFS 5, 20

Ogai
See Mori Ogai
See also MJW

Ogilvy, Gavin
See Barrie, J(ames) M(atthew)

O'Grady, Standish (James)
1846-1928 .... **TCLC 5**
See also CA 104; 157

O'Grady, Timothy 1951- .... **CLC 59**
See also CA 138

O'Hara, Frank 1926-1966 .... **CLC 2, 5, 13, 78; PC 45**
See also CA 9-12R; 25-28R; CANR 33; DA3; DAM POET; DLB 5, 16, 193; EWL 3; MAL 5; MTCW 1, 2; MTFW 2005; PFS 8, 12; RGAL 4; WP

O'Hara, John (Henry) 1905-1970 . **CLC 1, 2, 3, 6, 11, 42; SSC 15**
See also AMW; BPFB 3; CA 5-8R; 25-28R; CANR 31, 60; CDALB 1929-1941; DAM NOV; DLB 9, 86, 324; DLBD 2; EWL 3; MAL 5; MTCW 1, 2; MTFW 2005; NFS 11; RGAL 4; RGSF 2

O'Hehir, Diana 1929- .... **CLC 41**
See also CA 245

Ohiyesa
See Eastman, Charles A(lexander)

Okada, John 1923-1971 .... **AAL**
See also BYA 14; CA 212; DLB 312

Okigbo, Christopher 1930-1967 .... **BLC 3; CLC 25, 84; PC 7; TCLC 171**
See also AFW; BW 1, 3; CA 77-80; CANR 74; CDWLB 3; DAM MULT, POET; DLB 125; EWL 3; MTCW 1, 2; MTFW 2005; RGEL 2

Okigbo, Christopher Ifenayichukwu
See Okigbo, Christopher

Okri, Ben 1959- .... **CLC 87, 223**
See also AFW; BRWS 5; BW 2, 3; CA 130; 138; CANR 65, 128; CN 5, 6, 7; DLB 157, 231, 319, 326; EWL 3; INT CA-138; MTCW 2; MTFW 2005; RGSF 2; SSFS 20; WLIT 2; WWE 1

Olds, Sharon 1942- .. **CLC 32, 39, 85; PC 22**
See also AMWS 10; CA 101; CANR 18, 41, 66, 98, 135; CP 5, 6, 7; CPW; CWP; DAM POET; DLB 120; MAL 5; MTCW 2; MTFW 2005; PFS 17

Oldstyle, Jonathan
See Irving, Washington

Olesha, Iurii
See Olesha, Yuri (Karlovich)
See also RGWL 2

Olesha, Iurii Karlovich
See Olesha, Yuri (Karlovich)
See also DLB 272

Olesha, Yuri (Karlovich) 1899-1960 . **CLC 8; SSC 69; TCLC 136**
See Olesha, Iurii; Olesha, Iurii Karlovich; Olesha, Yury Karlovich
See also CA 85-88; EW 11; RGWL 3

Olesha, Yury Karlovich
See Olesha, Yuri (Karlovich)
See also EWL 3

Oliphant, Mrs.
See Oliphant, Margaret (Oliphant Wilson)
See also SUFW

Oliphant, Laurence 1829(?)-1888 .. **NCLC 47**
See also DLB 18, 166

Oliphant, Margaret (Oliphant Wilson) 1828-1897 .... **NCLC 11, 61; SSC 25**
See Oliphant, Mrs.
See also BRWS 10; DLB 18, 159, 190; HGG; RGEL 2; RGSF 2

Oliver, Mary 1935- ... **CLC 19, 34, 98; PC 75**
See also AMWS 7; CA 21-24R; CANR 9, 43, 84, 92, 138; CP 4, 5, 6, 7; CWP; DLB 5, 193; EWL 3; MTFW 2005; PFS 15

Olivier, Laurence (Kerr) 1907-1989 . **CLC 20**
See also CA 111; 150; 129

Olsen, Tillie 1912- ... **CLC 4, 13, 114; SSC 11**
See also AAYA 51; AMWS 13; BYA 11; CA 1-4R; CANR 1, 43, 74, 132; CDALBS; CN 2, 3, 4, 5, 6, 7; DA; DA3; DAB; DAC; DAM MST; DLB 28, 206; DLBY 1980; EWL 3; EXPS; FW; MAL 5; MTCW 1, 2; MTFW 2005; RGAL 4; RGSF 2; SSFS 1; TCLE 1:2; TCWW 2; TUS

Olson, Charles (John) 1910-1970 .. **CLC 1, 2, 5, 6, 9, 11, 29; PC 19**
See also AMWS 2; CA 13-16; 25-28R; CABS 2; CANR 35, 61; CAP 1; CP 1; DAM POET; DLB 5, 16, 193; EWL 3; MAL 5; MTCW 1, 2; RGAL 4; WP

Olson, Toby 1937- .... **CLC 28**
See also CA 65-68; CANR 9, 31, 84; CP 3, 4, 5, 6, 7

Olyesha, Yuri
See Olesha, Yuri (Karlovich)

Olympiodorus of Thebes c. 375-c. 430 .... **CMLC 59**

Omar Khayyam
See Khayyam, Omar
See also RGWL 2, 3

Ondaatje, Michael 1943- ..... **CLC 14, 29, 51, 76, 180; PC 28**
See also AAYA 66; CA 77-80; CANR 42, 74, 109, 133; CN 5, 6, 7; CP 1, 2, 3, 4, 5, 6, 7; DA3; DAB; DAC; DAM MST; DLB 60, 323, 326; EWL 3; LATS 1:2; LMFS 2; MTCW 2; MTFW 2005; NFS 23; PFS 8, 19; TCLE 1:2; TWA; WWE 1

Ondaatje, Philip Michael
See Ondaatje, Michael

Oneal, Elizabeth 1934-
See Oneal, Zibby
See also CA 106; CANR 28, 84; MAICYA 1, 2; SATA 30, 82; YAW

Oneal, Zibby .... **CLC 30**
See Oneal, Elizabeth
See also AAYA 5, 41; BYA 13; CLR 13; JRDA; WYA

O'Neill, Eugene (Gladstone) 1888-1953 ... **DC 20; TCLC 1, 6, 27, 49; WLC 4**
See also AAYA 54; AITN 1; AMW; AMWC 1; CA 110; 132; CAD; CANR 131; CDALB 1929-1941; DA; DA3; DAB; DAC; DAM DRAM, MST; DFS 2, 4, 5, 6, 9, 11, 12, 16, 20; DLB 7; EWL 3; LAIT 3; LMFS 2; MAL 5; MTCW 1, 2; MTFW 2005; RGAL 4; TUS

Onetti, Juan Carlos 1909-1994 ... **CLC 7, 10; HLCS 2; SSC 23; TCLC 131**
See also CA 85-88; 145; CANR 32, 63; CD-WLB 3; CWW 2; DAM MULT, NOV; DLB 113; EWL 3; HW 1, 2; LAW; MTCW 1, 2; MTFW 2005; RGSF 2

O Nuallain, Brian 1911-1966
See O'Brien, Flann
See also CA 21-22; 25-28R; CAP 2; DLB 231; FANT; TEA

Ophuls, Max
See Ophuls, Max

Ophuls, Max 1902-1957 .... **TCLC 79**
See also CA 113

Opie, Amelia 1769-1853 .... **NCLC 65**
See also DLB 116, 159; RGEL 2

Oppen, George 1908-1984 ..... **CLC 7, 13, 34; PC 35; TCLC 107**
See also CA 13-16R; 113; CANR 8, 82; CP 1, 2, 3; DLB 5, 165

Oppenheim, E(dward) Phillips 1866-1946 .... **TCLC 45**
See also CA 111; 202; CMW 4; DLB 70

Oppenheimer, Max
See Ophuls, Max

Opuls, Max
See Ophuls, Max

Orage, A(lfred) R(ichard) 1873-1934 .... **TCLC 157**
See also CA 122

Origen c. 185-c. 254 .... **CMLC 19**

Orlovitz, Gil 1918-1973 .... **CLC 22**
See also CA 77-80; 45-48; CN 1; CP 1, 2; DLB 2, 5

O'Rourke, Patrick Jake
See O'Rourke, P.J.

O'Rourke, P.J. 1947- .... **CLC 209**
See also CA 77-80; CANR 13, 41, 67, 111, 155; CPW; DAM POP; DLB 185

Orris
See Ingelow, Jean

Ortega y Gasset, Jose 1883-1955 ...... **HLC 2; TCLC 9**
See also CA 106; 130; DAM MULT; EW 9; EWL 3; HW 1, 2; MTCW 1, 2; MTFW 2005

Ortese, Anna Maria 1914-1998 .... **CLC 89**
See also DLB 177; EWL 3

Ortiz, Simon J(oseph) 1941- ... **CLC 45, 208; NNAL; PC 17**
See also AMWS 4; CA 134; CANR 69, 118; CP 3, 4, 5, 6, 7; DAM MULT, POET; DLB 120, 175, 256; EXPP; MAL 5; PFS 4, 16; RGAL 4; SSFS 22; TCWW 2

Orton, Joe ...... **CLC 4, 13, 43; DC 3; TCLC 157**
See Orton, John Kingsley
See also BRWS 5; CBD; CDBLB 1960 to Present; DFS 3, 6; DLB 13, 310; GLL 1; RGEL 2; TEA; WLIT 4

Orton, John Kingsley 1933-1967
See Orton, Joe
See also CA 85-88; CANR 35, 66; DAM DRAM; MTCW 1, 2; MTFW 2005

Orwell, George ...... **SSC 68; TCLC 2, 6, 15, 31, 51, 128, 129; WLC 4**
See Blair, Eric (Arthur)
See also BPFB 3; BRW 7; BYA 5; CDBLB 1945-1960; CLR 68; DAB; DLB 15, 98, 195, 255; EWL 3; EXPN; LAIT 4, 5; LATS 1:1; NFS 3, 7; RGEL 2; SCFW 1, 2; SFW 4; SSFS 4; TEA; WLIT 4; YAW

Osborne, David
See Silverberg, Robert

Osborne, George
See Silverberg, Robert

Osborne, John 1929-1994 .... **CLC 1, 2, 5, 11, 45; TCLC 153; WLC 4**
See also BRWS 1; CA 13-16R; 147; CANR 21, 56; CBD; CDBLB 1945-1960; DA; DAB; DAC; DAM DRAM, MST; DFS 4, 19; DLB 13; EWL 3; MTCW 1, 2; MTFW 2005; RGEL 2

Osborne, Lawrence 1958- .... **CLC 50**
See also CA 189; CANR 152

Osbourne, Lloyd 1868-1947 .... **TCLC 93**

Osgood, Frances Sargent 1811-1850 .... **NCLC 141**
See also DLB 250

Oshima, Nagisa 1932- .... **CLC 20**
See also CA 116; 121; CANR 78

Oskison, John Milton 1874-1947 .... **NNAL; TCLC 35**
See also CA 144; CANR 84; DAM MULT; DLB 175

Ossian c. 3rd cent. - .... **CMLC 28**
See Macpherson, James

Ossoli, Sarah Margaret (Fuller) 1810-1850 .... **NCLC 5, 50**
See Fuller, Margaret; Fuller, Sarah Margaret
See also CDALB 1640-1865; FW; LMFS 1; SATA 25

Ostriker, Alicia (Suskin) 1937- .... **CLC 132**
See also CA 25-28R; CAAS 24; CANR 10, 30, 62, 99; CWP; DLB 120; EXPP; PFS 19

Ostrovsky, Aleksandr Nikolaevich
See Ostrovsky, Alexander
See also DLB 277

Ostrovsky, Alexander 1823-1886 .. **NCLC 30, 57**
See Ostrovsky, Aleksandr Nikolaevich

Otero, Blas de 1916-1979 .... **CLC 11**
See also CA 89-92; DLB 134; EWL 3

O'Trigger, Sir Lucius
See Horne, Richard Henry Hengist

Otto, Rudolf 1869-1937 .... **TCLC 85**

Otto, Whitney 1955- .... **CLC 70**
See also CA 140; CANR 120

Otway, Thomas 1652-1685 ... **DC 24; LC 106**
  See also DAM DRAM; DLB 80; RGEL 2
Ouida .... **TCLC 43**
  See De la Ramee, Marie Louise (Ouida)
  See also DLB 18, 156; RGEL 2
Ouologuem, Yambo 1940- .... **CLC 146**
  See also CA 111; 176
Ousmane, Sembene 1923- ... **BLC 3; CLC 66**
  See Sembene, Ousmane
  See also BW 1, 3; CA 117; 125; CANR 81;
    CWW 2; MTCW 1
Ovid 43B.C.-17 .... **CMLC 7; PC 2**
  See also AW 2; CDWLB 1; DA3; DAM
    POET; DLB 211; PFS 22; RGWL 2, 3;
    WLIT 8; WP
Owen, Hugh
  See Faust, Frederick (Schiller)
Owen, Wilfred (Edward Salter)
    1893-1918 ... **PC 19; TCLC 5, 27; WLC
    4**
  See also BRW 6; CA 104; 141; CDBLB
    1914-1945; DA; DAB; DAC; DAM MST,
    POET; DLB 20; EWL 3; EXPP; MTCW
    2; MTFW 2005; PFS 10; RGEL 2; WLIT
    4
Owens, Louis (Dean) 1948-2002 .... **NNAL**
  See also CA 137; 179; 207; CAAE 179;
    CAAS 24; CANR 71
Owens, Rochelle 1936 .... **CLC 8**
  See also CA 17-20R; CAAS 2; CAD;
    CANR 39; CD 5, 6; CP 1, 2, 3, 4, 5, 6, 7;
    CWD; CWP
Oz, Amos 1939- ...... **CLC 5, 8, 11, 27, 33, 54;
    SSC 66**
  See also CA 53-56; CANR 27, 47, 65, 113,
    138; CWW 2; DAM NOV; EWL 3;
    MTCW 1, 2; MTFW 2005; RGHL; RGSF
    2; RGWL 3; WLIT 6
Ozick, Cynthia 1928- .... **CLC 3, 7, 28, 62,
    155; SSC 15, 60**
  See also AMWS 5; BEST 90:1; CA 17-20R;
    CANR 23, 58, 116; CN 3, 4, 5, 6, 7;
    CPW; DA3; DAM NOV, POP; DLB 28,
    152, 299; DLBY 1982; EWL 3; EXPS;
    INT CANR-23; MAL 5; MTCW 1, 2;
    MTFW 2005; RGAL 4; RGHL; RGSF 2;
    SSFS 3, 12, 22
Ozu, Yasujiro 1903-1963 .... **CLC 16**
  See also CA 112
Pabst, G. W. 1885-1967 .... **TCLC 127**
Pacheco, C.
  See Pessoa, Fernando (Antonio Nogueira)
Pacheco, Jose Emilio 1939- .... **HLC 2**
  See also CA 111; 131; CANR 65; CWW 2;
    DAM MULT; DLB 290; EWL 3; HW 1,
    2; RGSF 2
Pa Chin .... **CLC 18**
  See Jin, Ba
  See also EWL 3
Pack, Robert 1929- .... **CLC 13**
  See also CA 1-4R; CANR 3, 44, 82; CP 1,
    2, 3, 4, 5, 6, 7; DLB 5; SATA 118
Padgett, Lewis
  See Kuttner, Henry
Padilla (Lorenzo), Heberto
    1932-2000 .... **CLC 38**
  See also AITN 1; CA 123; 131; 189; CWW
    2; EWL 3; HW 1
Page, James Patrick 1944-
  See Page, Jimmy
  See also CA 204
Page, Jimmy 1944- .... **CLC 12**
  See Page, James Patrick
Page, Louise 1955- .... **CLC 40**
  See also CA 140; CANR 76; CBD; CD 5,
    6; CWD; DLB 233

Page, P(atricia) K(athleen) 1916- ...... **CLC 7,
    18; PC 12**
  See Cape, Judith
  See also CA 53-56; CANR 4, 22, 65; CP 1,
    2, 3, 4, 5, 6, 7; DAC; DAM MST; DLB
    68; MTCW 1; RGEL 2
Page, Stanton
  See Fuller, Henry Blake
Page, Stanton
  See Fuller, Henry Blake
Page, Thomas Nelson 1853-1922 .... **SSC 23**
  See also CA 118; 177; DLB 12, 78; DLBD
    13; RGAL 4
Pagels, Elaine
  See Pagels, Elaine Hiesey
Pagels, Elaine Hiesey 1943- .... **CLC 104**
  See also CA 45-48; CANR 2, 24, 51, 151;
    FW; NCFS 4
Paget, Violet 1856-1935
  See Lee, Vernon
  See also CA 104; 166; GLL 1; HGG
Paget-Lowe, Henry
  See Lovecraft, H. P.
Paglia, Camille 1947- .... **CLC 68**
  See also CA 140; CANR 72, 139; CPW;
    FW; GLL 2; MTCW 2; MTFW 2005
Paige, Richard
  See Koontz, Dean R.
Paine, Thomas 1737-1809 .... **NCLC 62**
  See also AMWS 1; CDALB 1640-1865;
    DLB 31, 43, 73, 158; LAIT 1; RGAL 4;
    RGEL 2; TUS
Pakenham, Antonia
  See Fraser, Antonia
Palamas, Costis
  See Palamas, Kostes
Palamas, Kostes 1859-1943 .... **TCLC 5**
  See Palamas, Kostis
  See also CA 105; 190; RGWL 2, 3
Palamas, Kostis
  See Palamas, Kostes
  See also EWL 3
Palazzeschi, Aldo 1885-1974 .... **CLC 11**
  See also CA 89-92; 53-56; DLB 114, 264;
    EWL 3
Pales Matos, Luis 1898-1959 .... **HLCS 2**
  See Pales Matos, Luis
  See also DLB 290; HW 1; LAW
Paley, Grace 1922- .. **CLC 4, 6, 37, 140; SSC
    8**
  See also AMWS 6; CA 25-28R; CANR 13,
    46, 74, 118; CN 2, 3, 4, 5, 6, 7; CPW;
    DA3; DAM POP; DLB 28, 218; EWL 3;
    EXPS; FW; INT CANR-13; MAL 5;
    MBL; MTCW 1, 2; MTFW 2005; RGAL
    4; RGSF 2; SSFS 3, 20
Palin, Michael (Edward) 1943- .... **CLC 21**
  See Monty Python
  See also CA 107; CANR 35, 109; SATA 67
Palliser, Charles 1947- .... **CLC 65**
  See also CA 136; CANR 76; CN 5, 6, 7
Palma, Ricardo 1833-1919 .... **TCLC 29**
  See also CA 168; LAW
Pamuk, Orhan 1952- .... **CLC 185**
  See also CA 142; CANR 75, 127; CWW 2;
    WLIT 6
Pancake, Breece Dexter 1952-1979
  See Pancake, Breece D'J
  See also CA 123; 109
Pancake, Breece D'J .... **CLC 29; SSC 61**
  See Pancake, Breece Dexter
  See also DLB 130
Panchenko, Nikolai .... **CLC 59**
Pankhurst, Emmeline (Goulden)
    1858-1928 .... **TCLC 100**
  See also CA 116; FW
Panko, Rudy
  See Gogol, Nikolai (Vasilyevich)

Papadiamantis, Alexandros
    1851-1911 .... **TCLC 29**
  See also CA 168; EWL 3
Papadiamantopoulos, Johannes 1856-1910
  See Moreas, Jean
  See also CA 117; 242
Papini, Giovanni 1881-1956 .... **TCLC 22**
  See also CA 121; 180; DLB 264
Paracelsus 1493-1541 .... **LC 14**
  See also DLB 179
Parasol, Peter
  See Stevens, Wallace
Pardo Bazan, Emilia 1851-1921 .... **SSC 30**
  See also EWL 3; FW; RGSF 2; RGWL 2, 3
Pareto, Vilfredo 1848-1923 .... **TCLC 69**
  See also CA 175
Paretsky, Sara 1947- .... **CLC 135**
  See also AAYA 30; BEST 90:3; CA 125;
    129; CANR 59, 95; CMW 4; CPW; DA3;
    DAM POP; DLB 306; INT CA-129;
    MSW; RGAL 4
Parfenie, Maria
  See Codrescu, Andrei
Parini, Jay (Lee) 1948- .... **CLC 54, 133**
  See also CA 97-100, 229; CAAE 229;
    CAAS 16; CANR 32, 87
Park, Jordan
  See Kornbluth, C(yril) M.; Pohl, Frederik
Park, Robert E(zra) 1864-1944 ..... **TCLC 73**
  See also CA 122; 165
Parker, Bert
  See Ellison, Harlan
Parker, Dorothy (Rothschild)
    1893-1967 . **CLC 15, 68; PC 28; SSC 2;
    TCLC 143**
  See also AMWS 9; CA 19-20; 25-28R; CAP
    2; DA3; DAM POET; DLB 11, 45, 86;
    EXPP; FW; MAL 5; MBL; MTCW 1, 2;
    MTFW 2005; PFS 18; RGAL 4; RGSF 2;
    TUS
Parker, Robert B. 1932- .... **CLC 27**
  See also AAYA 28; BEST 89:4; BPFB 3;
    CA 49-52; CANR 1, 26, 52, 89, 128;
    CMW 4; CPW; DAM NOV, POP; DLB
    306; INT CANR-26; MSW; MTCW 1;
    MTFW 2005
Parker, Robert Brown
  See Parker, Robert B.
Parkin, Frank 1940- .... **CLC 43**
  See also CA 147
Parkman, Francis, Jr. 1823-1893 .. **NCLC 12**
  See also AMWS 2; DLB 1, 30, 183, 186,
    235; RGAL 4
Parks, Gordon 1912-2006 .... **BLC 3; CLC 1,
    16**
  See also AAYA 36; AITN 2; BW 2, 3; CA
    41-44R; 249; CANR 26, 66, 145; DA3;
    DAM MULT; DLB 33; MTCW 2; MTFW
    2005; SATA 8, 108
Parks, Gordon Alexander Buchanan
  See Parks, Gordon
Parks, Suzan-Lori 1964(?)- .... **DC 23**
  See also AAYA 55; CA 201; CAD; CD 5,
    6; CWD; DFS 22; RGAL 4
Parks, Tim(othy Harold) 1954- ...... **CLC 147**
  See also CA 126; 131; CANR 77, 144; CN
    7; DLB 231; INT CA-131
Parmenides c. 515B.C.-c.
    450B.C. .... **CMLC 22**
  See also DLB 176
Parnell, Thomas 1679-1718 .... **LC 3**
  See also DLB 95; RGEL 2
Parr, Catherine c. 1513(?)-1548 .... **LC 86**
  See also DLB 136
Parra, Nicanor 1914- ... **CLC 2, 102; HLC 2;
    PC 39**
  See also CA 85-88; CANR 32; CWW 2;
    DAM MULT; DLB 283; EWL 3; HW 1;
    LAW; MTCW 1

Percy, William Alexander
    1885-1942 .... **TCLC 84**
    See also CA 163; MTCW 2
Perec, Georges 1936-1982 .... **CLC 56, 116**
    See also CA 141; DLB 83, 299; EWL 3;
    GFL 1789 to the Present; RGHL; RGWL
    3
**Pereda (y Sanchez de Porrua), Jose Maria
    de** 1833-1906 .... **TCLC 16**
    See also CA 117
Pereda y Porrua, Jose Maria de
    See Pereda (y Sanchez de Porrua), Jose
    Maria de
Peregoy, George Weems
    See Mencken, H(enry) L(ouis)
Perelman, S(idney) J(oseph)
    1904-1979 .. **CLC 3, 5, 9, 15, 23, 44, 49;
    SSC 32**
    See also AITN 1, 2; BPFB 3; CA 73-76;
    89-92; CANR 18; DAM DRAM; DLB 11,
    44; MTCW 1, 2; MTFW 2005; RGAL 4
Peret, Benjamin 1899-1959 .... **PC 33; TCLC
    20**
    See also CA 117; 186; GFL 1789 to the
    Present
Peretz, Isaac Leib
    See Peretz, Isaac Loeb
    See also CA 201
Peretz, Isaac Loeb 1851(?)-1915 ...... **SSC 26;
    TCLC 16**
    See Peretz, Isaac Leib
    See also CA 109
Peretz, Yitzhok Leibush
    See Peretz, Isaac Loeb
Perez Galdos, Benito 1843-1920 ..... **HLCS 2;
    TCLC 27**
    See Galdos, Benito Perez
    See also CA 125; 153; EWL 3; HW 1;
    RGWL 2, 3
Peri Rossi, Cristina 1941- .. **CLC 156; HLCS
    2**
    See also CA 131; CANR 59, 81; CWW 2;
    DLB 145, 290; EWL 3; HW 1, 2
Perlata
    See Peret, Benjamin
Perloff, Marjorie G(abrielle)
    1931- .... **CLC 137**
    See also CA 57-60; CANR 7, 22, 49, 104
Perrault, Charles 1628-1703 .... **LC 2, 56**
    See also BYA 4; CLR 79; DLB 268; GFL
    Beginnings to 1789; MAICYA 1, 2;
    RGWL 2, 3; SATA 25; WCH
Perry, Anne 1938- .... **CLC 126**
    See also CA 101; CANR 22, 50, 84, 150;
    CMW 4; CN 6, 7; CPW; DLB 276
Perry, Brighton
    See Sherwood, Robert E(mmet)
Perse, St.-John
    See Leger, (Marie-Rene Auguste) Alexis
    Saint-Leger
Perse, Saint-John
    See Leger, (Marie-Rene Auguste) Alexis
    Saint-Leger
    See also DLB 258; RGWL 3
Persius 34-62 .... **CMLC 74**
    See also AW 2; DLB 211; RGWL 2, 3
Perutz, Leo(pold) 1882-1957 .... **TCLC 60**
    See also CA 147; DLB 81
Peseenz, Tulio F.
    See Lopez y Fuentes, Gregorio
Pesetsky, Bette 1932- .... **CLC 28**
    See also CA 133; DLB 130
Peshkov, Alexei Maximovich 1868-1936
    See Gorky, Maxim
    See also CA 105; 141; CANR 83; DA;
    DAC; DAM DRAM, MST, NOV; MTCW
    2; MTFW 2005

Pessoa, Fernando (Antonio Nogueira)
    1888-1935 ..... **HLC 2; PC 20; TCLC 27**
    See also CA 125; 183; DAM MULT; DLB
    287; EW 10; EWL 3; RGWL 2, 3; WP
Peterkin, Julia Mood 1880-1961 ...... **CLC 31**
    See also CA 102; DLB 9
Peters, Joan K(aren) 1945- .... **CLC 39**
    See also CA 158; CANR 109
Peters, Robert L(ouis) 1924- .... **CLC 7**
    See also CA 13-16R; CAAS 8; CP 1, 5, 6,
    7; DLB 105
Petofi, Sandor 1823-1849 .... **NCLC 21**
    See also RGWL 2, 3
Petrakis, Harry Mark 1923- .... **CLC 3**
    See also CA 9-12R; CANR 4, 30, 85, 155;
    CN 1, 2, 3, 4, 5, 6, 7
Petrarch 1304-1374 .... **CMLC 20; PC 8**
    See also DA3; DAM POET; EW 2; LMFS
    1; RGWL 2, 3; WLIT 7
Petronius c. 20-66 .... **CMLC 34**
    See also AW 2; CDWLB 1; DLB 211;
    RGWL 2, 3; WLIT 8
Petrov, Evgeny .... **TCLC 21**
    See Kataev, Evgeny Petrovich
Petry, Ann (Lane) 1908-1997 .. **CLC 1, 7, 18;
    TCLC 112**
    See also AFAW 1, 2; BPFB 3; BW 1, 3;
    BYA 2; CA 5-8R; 157; CAAS 6; CANR
    4, 46; CLR 12; CN 1, 2, 3, 4, 5, 6; DLB
    76; EWL 3; JRDA; LAIT 1; MAICYA 1,
    2; MAICYAS 1; MTCW 1; RGAL 4;
    SATA 5; SATA-Obit 94; TUS
Petursson, Halligrimur 1614-1674 .... **LC 8**
Peychinovich
    See Vazov, Ivan (Minchov)
Phaedrus c. 15B.C.-c. 50 .... **CMLC 25**
    See also DLB 211
Phelps (Ward), Elizabeth Stuart
    See Phelps, Elizabeth Stuart
    See also FW
Phelps, Elizabeth Stuart
    1844-1911 .... **TCLC 113**
    See Phelps (Ward), Elizabeth Stuart
    See also CA 242; DLB 74
Philips, Katherine 1632-1664 . **LC 30; PC 40**
    See also DLB 131; RGEL 2
Philipson, Morris H. 1926- .... **CLC 53**
    See also CA 1-4R; CANR 4
Phillips, Caryl 1958- ..... **BLCS; CLC 96, 224**
    See also BRWS 5; BW 2; CA 141; CANR
    63, 104, 140; CBD; CD 5, 6; CN 5, 6, 7;
    DA3; DAM MULT; DLB 157; EWL 3;
    MTCW 2; MTFW 2005; WLIT 4; WWE
    1
Phillips, David Graham
    1867-1911 .... **TCLC 44**
    See also CA 108; 176; DLB 9, 12, 303;
    RGAL 4
Phillips, Jack
    See Sandburg, Carl (August)
Phillips, Jayne Anne 1952- .... **CLC 15, 33,
    139; SSC 16**
    See also AAYA 57; BPFB 3; CA 101;
    CANR 24, 50, 96; CN 4, 5, 6, 7; CSW;
    DLBY 1980; INT CANR-24; MTCW 1,
    2; MTFW 2005; RGAL 4; RGSF 2; SSFS
    4
Phillips, Richard
    See Dick, Philip K.
Phillips, Robert (Schaeffer) 1938- .... **CLC 28**
    See also CA 17-20R; CAAS 13; CANR 8;
    DLB 105
Phillips, Ward
    See Lovecraft, H. P.
Philostratus, Flavius c. 179-c.
    244 .... **CMLC 62**
Piccolo, Lucio 1901-1969 .... **CLC 13**
    See also CA 97-100; DLB 114; EWL 3

Pickthall, Marjorie L(owry) C(hristie)
    1883-1922 .... **TCLC 21**
    See also CA 107; DLB 92
Pico della Mirandola, Giovanni
    1463-1494 .... **LC 15**
    See also LMFS 1
Piercy, Marge 1936- .... **CLC 3, 6, 14, 18, 27,
    62, 128; PC 29**
    See also BPFB 3; CA 21-24R, 187; CAAE
    187; CAAS 1; CANR 13, 43, 66, 111; CN
    3, 4, 5, 6, 7; CP 1, 2, 3, 4, 5, 6, 7; CWP;
    DLB 120, 227; EXPP; FW; MAL 5;
    MTCW 1, 2; MTFW 2005; PFS 9, 22;
    SFW 4
Piers, Robert
    See Anthony, Piers
Pieyre de Mandiargues, Andre 1909-1991
    See Mandiargues, Andre Pieyre de
    See also CA 103; 136; CANR 22, 82; EWL
    3; GFL 1789 to the Present
Pilnyak, Boris 1894-1938 . **SSC 48; TCLC 23**
    See Vogau, Boris Andreyevich
    See also EWL 3
Pinchback, Eugene
    See Toomer, Jean
Pincherle, Alberto 1907-1990 ...... **CLC 11, 18**
    See Moravia, Alberto
    See also CA 25-28R; 132; CANR 33, 63,
    142; DAM NOV; MTCW 1; MTFW 2005
Pinckney, Darryl 1953- .... **CLC 76**
    See also BW 2, 3; CA 143; CANR 79
Pindar 518(?)B.C.-438(?)B.C. .... **CMLC 12;
    PC 19**
    See also AW 1; CDWLB 1; DLB 176;
    RGWL 2
Pineda, Cecile 1942- .... **CLC 39**
    See also CA 118; DLB 209
Pinero, Arthur Wing 1855-1934 .... **TCLC 32**
    See also CA 110; 153; DAM DRAM; DLB
    10; RGEL 2
Pinero, Miguel (Antonio Gomez)
    1946-1988 .... **CLC 4, 55**
    See also CA 61-64; 125; CAD; CANR 29,
    90; DLB 266; HW 1; LLW
Pinget, Robert 1919-1997 .... **CLC 7, 13, 37**
    See also CA 85-88; 160; CWW 2; DLB 83;
    EWL 3; GFL 1789 to the Present
Pink Floyd
    See Barrett, (Roger) Syd; Gilmour, David;
    Mason, Nick; Waters, Roger; Wright, Rick
Pinkney, Edward 1802-1828 .... **NCLC 31**
    See also DLB 248
Pinkwater, D. Manus
    See Pinkwater, Daniel Manus
Pinkwater, Daniel
    See Pinkwater, Daniel Manus
Pinkwater, Daniel M.
    See Pinkwater, Daniel Manus
Pinkwater, Daniel Manus 1941- .... **CLC 35**
    See also AAYA 1, 46; BYA 9; CA 29-32R;
    CANR 12, 38, 89, 143; CLR 4; CSW;
    FANT; JRDA; MAICYA 1, 2; SAAS 3;
    SATA 8, 46, 76, 114, 158; SFW 4; YAW
Pinkwater, Manus
    See Pinkwater, Daniel Manus
Pinsky, Robert 1940- .... **CLC 9, 19, 38, 94,
    121, 216; PC 27**
    See also AMWS 6; CA 29-32R; CAAS 4;
    CANR 58, 97, 138; CP 3, 4, 5, 6, 7; DA3;
    DAM POET; DLBY 1982, 1998; MAL 5;
    MTCW 2; MTFW 2005; PFS 18; RGAL
    4; TCLE 1:2
Pinta, Harold
    See Pinter, Harold
Pinter, Harold 1930- .. **CLC 1, 3, 6, 9, 11, 15,
    27, 58, 73, 199; DC 15; WLC 4**
    See also BRWR 1; BRWS 1; CA 5-8R;
    CANR 33, 65, 112, 145; CBD; CD 5, 6;
    CDBLB 1960 to Present; CP 1; DA; DA3;

Porter, William Sydney 1862-1910
See Henry, O.
See also CA 104; 131; CDALB 1865-1917;
DA; DA3; DAB; DAC; DAM MST; DLB
12, 78, 79; MTCW 1, 2; MTFW 2005;
TUS; YABC 2

Portillo (y Pacheco), Jose Lopez
See Lopez Portillo (y Pacheco), Jose

Portillo Trambley, Estela 1927-1998 .. **HLC 2**
See Trambley, Estela Portillo
See also CANR 32; DAM MULT; DLB
209; HW 1

Posey, Alexander (Lawrence)
1873-1908 .... **NNAL**
See also CA 144; CANR 80; DAM MULT;
DLB 175

Posse, Abel .... **CLC 70**

Post, Melville Davisson
1869-1930 .... **TCLC 39**
See also CA 110; 202; CMW 4

Potok, Chaim 1929-2002 ... **CLC 2, 7, 14, 26,
112**
See also AAYA 15, 50; AITN 1, 2; BPFB 3;
BYA 1; CA 17-20R; 208; CANR 19, 35,
64, 98; CLR 92; CN 4, 5, 6; DA3; DAM
NOV; DLB 28, 152; EXPN; INT CANR-
19; LAIT 4; MTCW 1, 2; MTFW 2005;
NFS 4; RGHL; SATA 33, 106; SATA-Obit
134; TUS; YAW

Potok, Herbert Harold -2002
See Potok, Chaim

Potok, Herman Harold
See Potok, Chaim

Potter, Dennis (Christopher George)
1935-1994 .... **CLC 58, 86, 123**
See also BRWS 10; CA 107; 145; CANR
33, 61; CBD; DLB 233; MTCW 1

Pound, Ezra (Weston Loomis)
1885-1972 .. **CLC 1, 2, 3, 4, 5, 7, 10, 13,
18, 34, 48, 50, 112; PC 4; WLC 5**
See also AAYA 47; AMW; AMWR 1; CA
5-8R; 37-40R; CANR 40; CDALB 1917-
1929; CP 1; DA; DA3; DAB; DAC; DAM
MST, POET; DLB 4, 45, 63; DLBD 15;
EFS 2; EWL 3; EXPP; LMFS 2; MAL 5;
MTCW 1, 2; MTFW 2005; PAB; PFS 2,
8, 16; RGAL 4; TUS; WP

Povod, Reinaldo 1959-1994 .... **CLC 44**
See also CA 136; 146; CANR 83

Powell, Adam Clayton, Jr.
1908-1972 .... **BLC 3; CLC 89**
See also BW 1, 3; CA 102; 33-36R; CANR
86; DAM MULT

Powell, Anthony 1905-2000 ... **CLC 1, 3, 7, 9,
10, 31**
See also BRW 7; CA 1-4R; 189; CANR 1,
32, 62, 107; CDBLB 1945-1960; CN 1, 2,
3, 4, 5, 6; DLB 15; EWL 3; MTCW 1, 2;
MTFW 2005; RGEL 2; TEA

Powell, Dawn 1896(?)-1965 .... **CLC 66**
See also CA 5-8R; CANR 121; DLBY 1997

Powell, Padgett 1952- .... **CLC 34**
See also CA 126; CANR 63, 101; CSW;
DLB 234; DLBY 01

Powell, (Oval) Talmage 1920-2000
See Queen, Ellery
See also CA 5-8R; CANR 2, 80

Power, Susan 1961- .... **CLC 91**
See also BYA 14; CA 160; CANR 135; NFS
11

Powers, J(ames) F(arl) 1917-1999 ..... **CLC 1,
4, 8, 57; SSC 4**
See also CA 1-4R; 181; CANR 2, 61; CN
1, 2, 3, 4, 5, 6; DLB 130; MTCW 1;
RGAL 4; RGSF 2

Powers, John J(ames) 1945-
See Powers, John R.
See also CA 69-72

Powers, John R. .... **CLC 66**
See Powers, John J(ames)

Powers, Richard 1957- .... **CLC 93**
See also AMWS 9; BPFB 3; CA 148;
CANR 80; CN 6, 7; MTFW 2005; TCLE
1:2

Pownall, David 1938- .... **CLC 10**
See also CA 89-92, 180; CAAS 18; CANR
49, 101; CBD; CD 5, 6; CN 4, 5, 6, 7;
DLB 14

Powys, John Cowper 1872-1963 ... **CLC 7, 9,
15, 46, 125**
See also CA 85-88; CANR 106; DLB 15,
255; EWL 3; FANT; MTCW 1, 2; MTFW
2005; RGEL 2; SUFW

Powys, T(heodore) F(rancis)
1875-1953 .... **TCLC 9**
See also BRWS 8; CA 106; 189; DLB 36,
162; EWL 3; FANT; RGEL 2; SUFW

Pozzo, Modesta
See Fonte, Moderata

Prado (Calvo), Pedro 1886-1952 ... **TCLC 75**
See also CA 131; DLB 283; HW 1; LAW

Prager, Emily 1952- .... **CLC 56**
See also CA 204

Pratchett, Terry 1948- .... **CLC 197**
See also AAYA 19, 54; BPFB 3; CA 143;
CANR 87, 126; CLR 64; CN 6, 7; CPW;
CWRI 5; FANT; MTFW 2005; SATA 82,
139; SFW 4; SUFW 2

Pratolini, Vasco 1913-1991 .... **TCLC 124**
See also CA 211; DLB 177; EWL 3; RGWL
2, 3

Pratt, E(dwin) J(ohn) 1883(?)-1964 . **CLC 19**
See also CA 141; 93-96; CANR 77; DAC;
DAM POET; DLB 92; EWL 3; RGEL 2;
TWA

Premchand .... **TCLC 21**
See Srivastava, Dhanpat Rai
See also EWL 3

Prescott, William Hickling
1796-1859 .... **NCLC 163**
See also DLB 1, 30, 59, 235

Preseren, France 1800-1849 .... **NCLC 127**
See also CDWLB 4; DLB 147

Preussler, Otfried 1923- .... **CLC 17**
See also CA 77-80; SATA 24

Prevert, Jacques (Henri Marie)
1900-1977 .... **CLC 15**
See also CA 77-80; 69-72; CANR 29, 61;
DLB 258; EWL 3; GFL 1789 to the
Present; IDFW 3, 4; MTCW 1; RGWL 2,
3; SATA-Obit 30

Prevost, (Antoine Francois)
1697-1763 .... **LC 1**
See also DLB 314; EW 4; GFL Beginnings
to 1789; RGWL 2, 3

Price, Reynolds 1933- .. **CLC 3, 6, 13, 43, 50,
63, 212; SSC 22**
See also AMWS 6; CA 1-4R; CANR 1, 37,
57, 87, 128; CN 1, 2, 3, 4, 5, 6, 7; CSW;
DAM NOV; DLB 2, 218, 278; EWL 3;
INT CANR-37; MAL 5; MTFW 2005;
NFS 18

Price, Richard 1949- .... **CLC 6, 12**
See also CA 49-52; CANR 3, 147; CN 7;
DLBY 1981

Prichard, Katharine Susannah
1883-1969 .... **CLC 46**
See also CA 11-12; CANR 33; CAP 1; DLB
260; MTCW 1; RGEL 2; RGSF 2; SATA
66

Priestley, J(ohn) B(oynton)
1894-1984 .... **CLC 2, 5, 9, 34**
See also BRW 7; CA 9-12R; 113; CANR
33; CDBLB 1914-1945; CN 1, 2, 3; DA3;
DAM DRAM, NOV; DLB 10, 34, 77,
100, 139; DLBY 1984; EWL 3; MTCW
1, 2; MTFW 2005; RGEL 2; SFW 4

Prince 1958- .... **CLC 35**
See also CA 213

Prince, F(rank) T(empleton)
1912-2003 .... **CLC 22**
See also CA 101; 219; CANR 43, 79; CP 1,
2, 3, 4, 5, 6, 7; DLB 20

Prince Kropotkin
See Kropotkin, Peter (Aleksieevich)

Prior, Matthew 1664-1721 .... **LC 4**
See also DLB 95; RGEL 2

Prishvin, Mikhail 1873-1954 .... **TCLC 75**
See Prishvin, Mikhail Mikhailovich

Prishvin, Mikhail Mikhailovich
See Prishvin, Mikhail
See also DLB 272; EWL 3

Pritchard, William H(arrison)
1932- .... **CLC 34**
See also CA 65-68; CANR 23, 95; DLB
111

Pritchett, V(ictor) S(awdon)
1900-1997 ... **CLC 5, 13, 15, 41; SSC 14**
See also BPFB 3; BRWS 3; CA 61-64; 157;
CANR 31, 63; CN 1, 2, 3, 4, 5, 6; DA3;
DAM NOV; DLB 15, 139; EWL 3;
MTCW 1, 2; MTFW 2005; RGEL 2;
RGSF 2; TEA

Private 19022
See Manning, Frederic

Probst, Mark 1925- .... **CLC 59**
See also CA 130

Procaccino, Michael
See Cristofer, Michael

Proclus c. 412-c. 485 .... **CMLC 81**

Prokosch, Frederic 1908-1989 ...... **CLC 4, 48**
See also CA 73-76; 128; CANR 82; CN 1,
2, 3, 4; CP 1, 2, 3, 4; DLB 48; MTCW 2

Propertius, Sextus c. 50B.C.-c.
16B.C. .... **CMLC 32**
See also AW 2; CDWLB 1; DLB 211;
RGWL 2, 3; WLIT 8

Prophet, The
See Dreiser, Theodore

Prose, Francine 1947- .... **CLC 45, 231**
See also AMWS 16; CA 109; 112; CANR
46, 95, 132; DLB 234; MTFW 2005;
SATA 101, 149

Protagoras c. 490B.C.-420B.C. ...... **CMLC 85**
See also DLB 176

Proudhon
See Cunha, Euclides (Rodrigues Pimenta)
da

Proulx, Annie
See Proulx, E. Annie

Proulx, E. Annie 1935- .... **CLC 81, 158**
See also AMWS 7; BPFB 3; CA 145;
CANR 65, 110; CN 6, 7; CPW 1; DA3;
DAM POP; MAL 5; MTCW 2; MTFW
2005; SSFS 18, 23

Proulx, Edna Annie
See Proulx, E. Annie

**Proust, (Valentin-Louis-George-Eugene)
Marcel** 1871-1922 ..... **SSC 75; TCLC 7,
13, 33; WLC 5**
See also AAYA 58; BPFB 3; CA 104; 120;
CANR 110; DA; DA3; DAB; DAC; DAM
MST, NOV; DLB 65; EW 8; EWL 3; GFL
1789 to the Present; MTCW 1, 2; MTFW
2005; RGWL 2, 3; TWA

Prowler, Harley
See Masters, Edgar Lee

Prudentius, Aurelius Clemens 348-c.
405 .... **CMLC 78**
See also EW 1; RGWL 2, 3

Prus, Boleslaw 1845-1912 .... **TCLC 48**
See also RGWL 2, 3

Pryor, Aaron Richard
See Pryor, Richard

Pryor, Richard 1940-2005 .... **CLC 26**
See also CA 122; 152; 246

Pryor, Richard Franklin Lenox Thomas
See Pryor, Richard

Przybyszewski, Stanislaw
    1868-1927 .... **TCLC 36**
    See also CA 160; DLB 66; EWL 3
Pteleon
    See Grieve, C(hristopher) M(urray)
    See also DAM POET
Puckett, Lute
    See Masters, Edgar Lee
Puig, Manuel 1932-1990 .... **CLC 3, 5, 10, 28, 65, 133; HLC 2**
    See also BPFB 3; CA 45-48; CANR 2, 32, 63; CDWLB 3; DA3; DAM MULT; DLB 113; DNFS 1; EWL 3; GLL 1; HW 1, 2; LAW; MTCW 1, 2; MTFW 2005; RGWL 2, 3; TWA; WLIT 1
Pulitzer, Joseph 1847-1911 .... **TCLC 76**
    See also CA 114; DLB 23
Purchas, Samuel 1577(?)-1626 .... **LC 70**
    See also DLB 151
Purdy, A(lfred) W(ellington)
    1918-2000 .... **CLC 3, 6, 14, 50**
    See also CA 81-84; 189; CAAS 17; CANR 42, 66; CP 1, 2, 3, 4, 5, 6, 7; DAC; DAM MST, POET; DLB 88; PFS 5; RGEL 2
Purdy, James (Amos) 1923- .... **CLC 2, 4, 10, 28, 52**
    See also AMWS 7; CA 33-36R; CAAS 1; CANR 19, 51, 132; CN 1, 2, 3, 4, 5, 6, 7; DLB 2, 218; EWL 3; INT CANR-19; MAL 5; MTCW 1; RGAL 4
Pure, Simon
    See Swinnerton, Frank Arthur
Pushkin, Aleksandr Sergeevich
    See Pushkin, Alexander (Sergeyevich)
    See also DLB 205
Pushkin, Alexander (Sergeyevich)
    1799-1837 .... **NCLC 3, 27, 83; PC 10; SSC 27, 55; WLC 5**
    See Pushkin, Aleksandr Sergeevich
    See also DA; DA3; DAB; DAC; DAM DRAM, MST, POET; EW 5; EXPS; RGSF 2; RGWL 2, 3; SATA 61; SSFS 9; TWA
P'u Sung-ling 1640-1715 .... **LC 49; SSC 31**
Putnam, Arthur Lee
    See Alger, Horatio, Jr.
Puttenham, George 1529(?)-1590 ...... **LC 116**
    See also DLB 281
Puzo, Mario 1920-1999 .... **CLC 1, 2, 6, 36, 107**
    See also BPFB 3; CA 65-68; 185; CANR 4, 42, 65, 99, 131; CN 1, 2, 3, 4, 5, 6; CPW; DA3; DAM NOV, POP; DLB 6; MTCW 1, 2; MTFW 2005; NFS 16; RGAL 4
Pygge, Edward
    See Barnes, Julian
Pyle, Ernest Taylor 1900-1945
    See Pyle, Ernie
    See also CA 115; 160
Pyle, Ernie .... **TCLC 75**
    See Pyle, Ernest Taylor
    See also DLB 29; MTCW 2
Pyle, Howard 1853-1911 .... **TCLC 81**
    See also AAYA 57; BYA 2, 4; CA 109; 137; CLR 22, 117; DLB 42, 188; DLBD 13; LAIT 1; MAICYA 1, 2; SATA 16, 100; WCH; YAW
Pym, Barbara (Mary Crampton)
    1913-1980 .... **CLC 13, 19, 37, 111**
    See also BPFB 3; BRWS 2; CA 13-14; 97-100; CANR 13, 34; CAP 1; DLB 14, 207; DLBY 1987; EWL 3; MTCW 1, 2; MTFW 2005; RGEL 2; TEA
Pynchon, Thomas 1937- .. **CLC 2, 3, 6, 9, 11, 18, 33, 62, 72, 123, 192, 213; SSC 14, 84; WLC 5**
    See also AMWS 2; BEST 90:2; BPFB 3; CA 17-20R; CANR 22, 46, 73, 142; CN 1, 2, 3, 4, 5, 6, 7; CPW 1; DA; DA3;

DAB; DAC; DAM MST, NOV, POP; DLB 2, 173; EWL 3; MAL 5; MTCW 1, 2; MTFW 2005; NFS 23; RGAL 4; SFW 4; TCLE 1:2; TUS
Pythagoras c. 582B.C.-c. 507B.C. . **CMLC 22**
    See also DLB 176
Q
    See Quiller-Couch, Sir Arthur (Thomas)
Qian, Chongzhu
    See Ch'ien, Chung-shu
Qian, Sima 145B.C.-c. 89B.C. .... **CMLC 72**
Qian Zhongshu
    See Ch'ien, Chung-shu
    See also CWW 2; DLB 328
Qroll
    See Dagerman, Stig (Halvard)
Quarles, Francis 1592-1644 .... **LC 117**
    See also DLB 126; RGEL 2
Quarrington, Paul (Lewis) 1953- ..... **CLC 65**
    See also CA 129; CANR 62, 95
Quasimodo, Salvatore 1901-1968 .... **CLC 10; PC 47**
    See also CA 13-16; 25-28R; CAP 1; DLB 114; EW 12; EWL 3; MTCW 1; RGWL 2, 3
Quatermass, Martin
    See Carpenter, John (Howard)
Quay, Stephen 1947- .... **CLC 95**
    See also CA 189
Quay, Timothy 1947- .... **CLC 95**
    See also CA 189
Queen, Ellery .... **CLC 3, 11**
    See Dannay, Frederic; Davidson, Avram (James); Deming, Richard; Fairman, Paul W.; Flora, Fletcher; Hoch, Edward D(entinger); Kane, Henry; Lee, Manfred B.; Marlowe, Stephen; Powell, (Oval) Talmage; Sheldon, Walter J(ames); Sturgeon, Theodore (Hamilton); Tracy, Don(ald Fiske); Vance, Jack
    See also BPFB 3; CMW 4; MSW; RGAL 4
Queen, Ellery, Jr.
    See Dannay, Frederic; Lee, Manfred B.
Queneau, Raymond 1903-1976 ..... **CLC 2, 5, 10, 42**
    See also CA 77-80; 69-72; CANR 32; DLB 72, 258; EW 12; EWL 3; GFL 1789 to the Present; MTCW 1, 2; RGWL 2, 3
Quevedo, Francisco de 1580-1645 .... **LC 23**
Quiller-Couch, Sir Arthur (Thomas)
    1863-1944 .... **TCLC 53**
    See also CA 118; 166; DLB 135, 153, 190; HGG; RGEL 2; SUFW 1
Quin, Ann 1936-1973 .... **CLC 6**
    See also CA 9-12R; 45-48; CANR 148; CN 1; DLB 14, 231
Quin, Ann Marie
    See Quin, Ann
Quincey, Thomas de
    See De Quincey, Thomas
Quindlen, Anna 1953- .... **CLC 191**
    See also AAYA 35; CA 138; CANR 73, 126; DA3; DLB 292; MTCW 2; MTFW 2005
Quinn, Martin
    See Smith, Martin Cruz
Quinn, Peter 1947- .... **CLC 91**
    See also CA 197; CANR 147
Quinn, Peter A.
    See Quinn, Peter
Quinn, Simon
    See Smith, Martin Cruz
Quintana, Leroy V. 1944- ...... **HLC 2; PC 36**
    See also CA 131; CANR 65, 139; DAM MULT; DLB 82; HW 1, 2
Quintilian c. 40-c. 100 .... **CMLC 77**
    See also AW 2; DLB 211; RGWL 2, 3

Quintillian 0035-0100 .... **CMLC 77**
Quiroga, Horacio (Sylvestre)
    1878-1937 ... **HLC 2; SSC 89; TCLC 20**
    See also CA 117; 131; DAM MULT; EWL 3; HW 1; LAW; MTCW 1; RGSF 2; WLIT 1
Quoirez, Francoise 1935-2004 .... **CLC 9**
    See Sagan, Francoise
    See also CA 49-52; 231; CANR 6, 39, 73; MTCW 1, 2; MTFW 2005; TWA
Raabe, Wilhelm (Karl) 1831-1910 . **TCLC 45**
    See also CA 167; DLB 129
Rabe, David (William) 1940- .. **CLC 4, 8, 33, 200; DC 16**
    See also CA 85-88; CABS 3; CAD; CANR 59, 129; CD 5, 6; DAM DRAM; DFS 3, 8, 13; DLB 7, 228; EWL 3; MAL 5
Rabelais, Francois 1494-1553 .... **LC 5, 60; WLC 5**
    See also DA; DAB; DAC; DAM MST; DLB 327; EW 2; GFL Beginnings to 1789; LMFS 1; RGWL 2, 3; TWA
Rabi'a al-'Adawiyya c. 717-c.
    801 .... **CMLC 83**
    See also DLB 311
Rabinovitch, Sholem 1859-1916
    See Aleichem, Sholom
    See also CA 104
Rabinyan, Dorit 1972- .... **CLC 119**
    See also CA 170; CANR 147
Rachilde
    See Vallette, Marguerite Eymery; Vallette, Marguerite Eymery
    See also EWL 3
Racine, Jean 1639-1699 .... **LC 28, 113**
    See also DA3; DAB; DAM MST; DLB 268; EW 3; GFL Beginnings to 1789; LMFS 1; RGWL 2, 3; TWA
Radcliffe, Ann (Ward) 1764-1823 ... **NCLC 6, 55, 106**
    See also DLB 39, 178; GL 3; HGG; LMFS 1; RGEL 2; SUFW; WLIT 3
Radclyffe-Hall, Marguerite
    See Hall, Radclyffe
Radiguet, Raymond 1903-1923 ...... **TCLC 29**
    See also CA 162; DLB 65; EWL 3; GFL 1789 to the Present; RGWL 2, 3
Radnoti, Miklos 1909-1944 .... **TCLC 16**
    See also CA 118; 212; CDWLB 4; DLB 215; EWL 3; RGHL; RGWL 2, 3
Rado, James 1939- .... **CLC 17**
    See also CA 105
Radvanyi, Netty 1900-1983
    See Seghers, Anna
    See also CA 85-88; 110; CANR 82
Rae, Ben
    See Griffiths, Trevor
Raeburn, John (Hay) 1941- .... **CLC 34**
    See also CA 57-60
Ragni, Gerome 1942-1991 .... **CLC 17**
    See also CA 105; 134
Rahv, Philip .... **CLC 24**
    See Greenberg, Ivan
    See also DLB 137; MAL 5
Raimund, Ferdinand Jakob
    1790-1836 .... **NCLC 69**
    See also DLB 90
Raine, Craig (Anthony) 1944- .. **CLC 32, 103**
    See also CA 108; CANR 29, 51, 103; CP 3, 4, 5, 6, 7; DLB 40; PFS 7
Raine, Kathleen (Jessie) 1908-2003 .. **CLC 7, 45**
    See also CA 85-88; 218; CANR 46, 109; CP 1, 2, 3, 4, 5, 6, 7; DLB 20; EWL 3; MTCW 1; RGEL 2
Rainis, Janis 1865-1929 .... **TCLC 29**
    See also CA 170; CDWLB 4; DLB 220; EWL 3

Rakosi, Carl .... **CLC 47**
 See Rawley, Callman
 See also CA 228; CAAS 5; CP 1, 2, 3, 4, 5,
 6, 7; DLB 193
Ralegh, Sir Walter
 See Raleigh, Sir Walter
 See also BRW 1; RGEL 2; WP
Raleigh, Richard
 See Lovecraft, H. P.
Raleigh, Sir Walter 1554(?)-1618 .... **LC 31,**
 39; PC 31
 See Ralegh, Sir Walter
 See also CDBLB Before 1660; DLB 172;
 EXPP; PFS 14; TEA
Rallentando, H. P.
 See Sayers, Dorothy L(eigh)
Ramal, Walter
 See de la Mare, Walter (John)
Ramana Maharshi 1879-1950 .... **TCLC 84**
Ramoacn y Cajal, Santiago
 1852-1934 .... **TCLC 93**
Ramon, Juan
 See Jimenez (Mantecon), Juan Ramon
Ramos, Graciliano 1892-1953 .... **TCLC 32**
 See also CA 167; DLB 307; EWL 3; HW 2;
 LAW; WLIT 1
Rampersad, Arnold 1941- .... **CLC 44**
 See also BW 2, 3; CA 127; 133; CANR 81;
 DLB 111; INT CA-133
Rampling, Anne
 See Rice, Anne
 See also GLL 2
Ramsay, Allan 1686(?)-1758 .... **LC 29**
 See also DLB 95; RGEL 2
Ramsay, Jay
 See Campbell, (John) Ramsey
Ramuz, Charles-Ferdinand
 1878-1947 .... **TCLC 33**
 See also CA 165; EWL 3
Rand, Ayn 1905-1982 ...... **CLC 3, 30, 44, 79;**
 WLC 5
 See also AAYA 10; AMWS 4; BPFB 3;
 BYA 12; CA 13-16R; 105; CANR 27, 73;
 CDALBS; CN 1, 2, 3; CPW; DA; DA3;
 DAC; DAM MST, NOV, POP; DLB 227,
 279; MTCW 1, 2; MTFW 2005; NFS 10,
 16; RGAL 4; SFW 4; TUS; YAW
Randall, Dudley (Felker) 1914-2000 . **BLC 3;**
 CLC 1, 135
 See also BW 1, 3; CA 25-28R; 189; CANR
 23, 82; CP 1, 2, 3, 4, 5; DAM MULT;
 DLB 41; PFS 5
Randall, Robert
 See Silverberg, Robert
Ranger, Ken
 See Creasey, John
Rank, Otto 1884-1939 .... **TCLC 115**
Ransom, John Crowe 1888-1974 .. **CLC 2, 4,**
 5, 11, 24; PC 61
 See also AMW; CA 5-8R; 49-52; CANR 6,
 34; CDALBS; CP 1, 2; DA3; DAM POET;
 DLB 45, 63; EWL 3; EXPP; MAL 5;
 MTCW 1, 2; MTFW 2005; RGAL 4; TUS
Rao, Raja 1908-2006 .... **CLC 25, 56**
 See also CA 73-76; CANR 51; CN 1, 2, 3,
 4, 5, 6; DAM NOV; DLB 323; EWL 3;
 MTCW 1, 2; MTFW 2005; RGEL 2;
 RGSF 2
Raphael, Frederic (Michael) 1931- ... **CLC 2,**
 14
 See also CA 1-4R; CANR 1, 86; CN 1, 2,
 3, 4, 5, 6, 7; DLB 14, 319; TCLE 1:2
Raphael, Lev 1954- .... **CLC 232**
 See also CA 134; CANR 72, 145; GLL 1
Ratcliffe, James P.
 See Mencken, H(enry) L(ouis)
Rathbone, Julian 1935- .... **CLC 41**
 See also CA 101; CANR 34, 73, 152

Rattigan, Terence (Mervyn)
 1911-1977 .... **CLC 7; DC 18**
 See also BRWS 7; CA 85-88; 73-76; CBD;
 CDBLB 1945-1960; DAM DRAM; DFS
 8; DLB 13; IDFW 3, 4; MTCW 1, 2;
 MTFW 2005; RGEL 2
Ratushinskaya, Irina 1954- .... **CLC 54**
 See also CA 129; CANR 68; CWW 2
Raven, Simon (Arthur Noel)
 1927-2001 .... **CLC 14**
 See also CA 81-84; 197; CANR 86; CN 1,
 2, 3, 4, 5, 6; DLB 271
Ravenna, Michael
 See Welty, Eudora
Rawley, Callman 1903-2004
 See Rakosi, Carl
 See also CA 21-24R; 228; CANR 12, 32,
 91
Rawlings, Marjorie Kinnan
 1896-1953 .... **TCLC 4**
 See also AAYA 20; AMWS 10; ANW;
 BPFB 3; BYA 3; CA 104; 137; CANR 74;
 CLR 63; DLB 9, 22, 102; DLBD 17;
 JRDA; MAICYA 1, 2; MAL 5; MTCW 2;
 MTFW 2005; RGAL 4; SATA 100; WCH;
 YABC 1; YAW
Ray, Satyajit 1921-1992 .... **CLC 16, 76**
 See also CA 114; 137; DAM MULT
Read, Herbert Edward 1893-1968 ..... **CLC 4**
 See also BRW 6; CA 85-88; 25-28R; DLB
 20, 149; EWL 3; PAB; RGEL 2
Read, Piers Paul 1941- .... **CLC 4, 10, 25**
 See also CA 21-24R; CANR 38, 86, 150;
 CN 2, 3, 4, 5, 6, 7; DLB 14; SATA 21
Reade, Charles 1814-1884 .... **NCLC 2, 74**
 See also DLB 21; RGEL 2
Reade, Hamish
 See Gray, Simon (James Holliday)
Reading, Peter 1946- .... **CLC 47**
 See also BRWS 8; CA 103; CANR 46, 96;
 CP 5, 6, 7; DLB 40
Reaney, James 1926- .... **CLC 13**
 See also CA 41-44R; CAAS 15; CANR 42;
 CD 5, 6; CP 1, 2, 3, 4, 5, 6, 7; DAC;
 DAM MST; DLB 68; RGEL 2; SATA 43
Rebreanu, Liviu 1885-1944 .... **TCLC 28**
 See also CA 165; DLB 220; EWL 3
Rechy, John 1934- ..... **CLC 1, 7, 14, 18, 107;**
 HLC 2
 See also CA 5-8R; 195; CAAE 195; CAAS
 4; CANR 6, 32, 64, 152; CN 1, 2, 3, 4, 5,
 6, 7; DAM MULT; DLB 122, 278; DLBY
 1982; HW 1, 2; INT CANR-6; LLW;
 MAL 5; RGAL 4
Rechy, John Francisco
 See Rechy, John
Redcam, Tom 1870-1933 .... **TCLC 25**
Reddin, Keith 1956- .... **CLC 67**
 See also CAD; CD 6
Redgrove, Peter (William)
 1932-2003 .... **CLC 6, 41**
 See also BRWS 6; CA 1-4R; 217; CANR 3,
 39, 77; CP 1, 2, 3, 4, 5, 6, 7; DLB 40;
 TCLE 1:2
Redmon, Anne .... **CLC 22**
 See Nightingale, Anne Redmon
 See also DLBY 1986
Reed, Eliot
 See Ambler, Eric
Reed, Ishmael 1938- ..... **BLC 3; CLC 2, 3, 5,**
 6, 13, 32, 60, 174; PC 68
 See also AFAW 1, 2; AMWS 10; BPFB 3;
 BW 2, 3; CA 21-24R; CANR 25, 48, 74,
 128; CN 1, 2, 3, 4, 5, 6, 7; CP 1, 2, 3, 4,
 5, 6, 7; CSW; DA3; DAM MULT; DLB
 2, 5, 33, 169, 227; DLBD 8; EWL 3;
 LMFS 2; MAL 5; MSW; MTCW 1, 2;
 MTFW 2005; PFS 6; RGAL 4; TCWW 2

Reed, John (Silas) 1887-1920 .... **TCLC 9**
 See also CA 106; 195; MAL 5; TUS
Reed, Lou .... **CLC 21**
 See Firbank, Louis
Reese, Lizette Woodworth
 1856-1935 .... **PC 29; TCLC 181**
 See also CA 180; DLB 54
Reeve, Clara 1729-1807 .... **NCLC 19**
 See also DLB 39; RGEL 2
Reich, Wilhelm 1897-1957 .... **TCLC 57**
 See also CA 199
Reid, Christopher (John) 1949- .... **CLC 33**
 See also CA 140; CANR 89; CP 4, 5, 6, 7;
 DLB 40; EWL 3
Reid, Desmond
 See Moorcock, Michael
Reid Banks, Lynne 1929-
 See Banks, Lynne Reid
 See also AAYA 49; CA 1-4R; CANR 6, 22,
 38, 87; CLR 24; CN 1, 2, 3, 7; JRDA;
 MAICYA 1, 2; SATA 22, 75, 111, 165;
 YAW
Reilly, William K.
 See Creasey, John
Reiner, Max
 See Caldwell, (Janet Miriam) Taylor
 (Holland)
Reis, Ricardo
 See Pessoa, Fernando (Antonio Nogueira)
Reizenstein, Elmer Leopold
 See Rice, Elmer (Leopold)
 See also EWL 3
Remarque, Erich Maria 1898-1970 . **CLC 21**
 See also AAYA 27; BPFB 3; CA 77-80; 29-
 32R; CDWLB 2; DA; DA3; DAB; DAC;
 DAM MST, NOV; DLB 56; EWL 3;
 EXPN; LAIT 3; MTCW 1, 2; MTFW
 2005; NFS 4; RGHL; RGWL 2, 3
Remington, Frederic S(ackrider)
 1861-1909 .... **TCLC 89**
 See also CA 108; 169; DLB 12, 186, 188;
 SATA 41; TCWW 2
Remizov, A.
 See Remizov, Aleksei (Mikhailovich)
Remizov, A. M.
 See Remizov, Aleksei (Mikhailovich)
Remizov, Aleksei (Mikhailovich)
 1877-1957 .... **TCLC 27**
 See Remizov, Alexey Mikhaylovich
 See also CA 125; 133; DLB 295
Remizov, Alexey Mikhaylovich
 See Remizov, Aleksei (Mikhailovich)
 See also EWL 3
Renan, Joseph Ernest 1823-1892 . **NCLC 26,**
 145
 See also GFL 1789 to the Present
Renard, Jules(-Pierre) 1864-1910 .. **TCLC 17**
 See also CA 117; 202; GFL 1789 to the
 Present
Renart, Jean fl. 13th cent. - .... **CMLC 83**
Renault, Mary .... **CLC 3, 11, 17**
 See Challans, Mary
 See also BPFB 3; BYA 2; CN 1, 2, 3;
 DLBY 1983; EWL 3; GLL 1; LAIT 1;
 RGEL 2; RHW
Rendell, Ruth 1930- .... **CLC 28, 48**
 See Vine, Barbara
 See also BPFB 3; BRWS 9; CA 109; CANR
 32, 52, 74, 127; CN 5, 6, 7; CPW; DAM
 POP; DLB 87, 276; INT CANR-32;
 MSW; MTCW 1, 2; MTFW 2005
Rendell, Ruth Barbara
 See Rendell, Ruth
Renoir, Jean 1894-1979 .... **CLC 20**
 See also CA 129; 85-88
Resnais, Alain 1922- .... **CLC 16**
 Revard, Carter 1931- .... **NNAL**
 See also CA 144; CANR 81, 153; PFS 5

Roa Bastos, Augusto Jose Antonio
See Roa Bastos, Augusto
Robbe-Grillet, Alain 1922- .... **CLC 1, 2, 4, 6, 8, 10, 14, 43, 128**
See also BPFB 3; CA 9-12R; CANR 33, 65, 115; CWW 2; DLB 83; EW 13; EWL 3; GFL 1789 to the Present; IDFW 3, 4; MTCW 1, 2; MTFW 2005; RGWL 2, 3; SSFS 15
Robbins, Harold 1916-1997 .... **CLC 5**
See also BPFB 3; CA 73-76; 162; CANR 26, 54, 112, 156; DA3; DAM NOV; MTCW 1, 2
Robbins, Thomas Eugene 1936-
See Robbins, Tom
See also CA 81-84; CANR 29, 59, 95, 139; CN 7; CPW; CSW; DA3; DAM NOV, POP; MTCW 1, 2; MTFW 2005
Robbins, Tom .... **CLC 9, 32, 64**
See Robbins, Thomas Eugene
See also AAYA 32; AMWS 10; BEST 90:3; BPFB 3; CN 3, 4, 5, 6, 7; DLBY 1980
Robbins, Trina 1938- .... **CLC 21**
See also AAYA 61; CA 128; CANR 152
Roberts, Charles G(eorge) D(ouglas)
1860-1943 .... **SSC 91; TCLC 8**
See also CA 105; 188; CLR 33; CWRI 5; DLB 92; RGEL 2; RGSF 2; SATA 88; SATA-Brief 29
Roberts, Elizabeth Madox
1886-1941 .... **TCLC 68**
See also CA 111; 166; CLR 100; CWRI 5; DLB 9, 54, 102; RGAL 4; RHW; SATA 33; SATA-Brief 27; TCWW 2; WCH
Roberts, Kate 1891-1985 .... **CLC 15**
See also CA 107; 116; DLB 319
Roberts, Keith (John Kingston)
1935-2000 .... **CLC 14**
See also BRWS 10; CA 25-28R; CANR 46; DLB 261; SFW 4
Roberts, Kenneth (Lewis)
1885-1957 .... **TCLC 23**
See also CA 109; 199; DLB 9; MAL 5; RGAL 4; RHW
Roberts, Michele (Brigitte) 1949- .... **CLC 48, 178**
See also CA 115; CANR 58, 120; CN 6, 7; DLB 231; FW
Robertson, Ellis
See Ellison, Harlan; Silverberg, Robert
Robertson, Thomas William
1829-1871 .... **NCLC 35**
See Robertson, Tom
See also DAM DRAM
Robertson, Tom
See Robertson, Thomas William
See also RGEL 2
Robeson, Kenneth
See Dent, Lester
Robinson, Edwin Arlington
1869-1935 .... **PC 1, 35; TCLC 5, 101**
See also AMW; CA 104; 133; CDALB 1865-1917; DA; DAC; DAM MST, POET; DLB 54; EWL 3; EXPP; MAL 5; MTCW 1, 2; MTFW 2005; PAB; PFS 4; RGAL 4; WP
Robinson, Henry Crabb
1775-1867 .... **NCLC 15**
See also DLB 107
Robinson, Jill 1936- .... **CLC 10**
See also CA 102; CANR 120; INT CA-102
Robinson, Kim Stanley 1952- .... **CLC 34**
See also AAYA 26; CA 126; CANR 113, 139; CN 6, 7; MTFW 2005; SATA 109; SCFW 4; SFW 4
Robinson, Lloyd
See Silverberg, Robert

Robinson, Marilynne 1944- ...... **CLC 25, 180**
See also AAYA 69; CA 116; CANR 80, 140; CN 4, 5, 6, 7; DLB 206; MTFW 2005; NFS 24
Robinson, Mary 1758-1800 .... **NCLC 142**
See also DLB 158; FW
Robinson, Smokey .... **CLC 21**
See Robinson, William, Jr.
Robinson, William, Jr. 1940-
See Robinson, Smokey
See also CA 116
Robison, Mary 1949- .... **CLC 42, 98**
See also CA 113; 116; CANR 87; CN 4, 5, 6, 7; DLB 130; INT CA-116; RGSF 2
Roches, Catherine des 1542-1587 ...... **LC 117**
See also DLB 327
Rochester
See Wilmot, John
See also RGEL 2
Rod, Edouard 1857-1910 .... **TCLC 52**
Roddenberry, Eugene Wesley 1921-1991
See Roddenberry, Gene
See also CA 110; 135; CANR 37; SATA 45; SATA-Obit 69
Roddenberry, Gene .... **CLC 17**
See Roddenberry, Eugene Wesley
See also AAYA 5; SATA-Obit 69
Rodgers, Mary 1931- .... **CLC 12**
See also BYA 5; CA 49-52; CANR 8, 55, 90; CLR 20; CWRI 5; INT CANR-8; JRDA; MAICYA 1, 2; SATA 8, 130
Rodgers, W(illiam) R(obert)
1909-1969 .... **CLC 7**
See also CA 85-88; DLB 20; RGEL 2
Rodman, Eric
See Silverberg, Robert
Rodman, Howard 1920(?)-1985 .... **CLC 65**
See also CA 118
Rodman, Maia
See Wojciechowska, Maia (Teresa)
Rodo, Jose Enrique 1871(?)-1917 .... **HLCS 2**
See also CA 178; EWL 3; HW 2; LAW
Rodolph, Utto
See Ouologuem, Yambo
Rodriguez, Claudio 1934-1999 .... **CLC 10**
See also CA 188; DLB 134
Rodriguez, Richard 1944- .... **CLC 155; HLC 2**
See also AMWS 14; CA 110; CANR 66, 116; DAM MULT; DLB 82, 256; IIW 1, 2; LAIT 5; LLW; MTFW 2005; NCFS 3; WLIT 1
Roelvaag, O(le) E(dvart) 1876-1931
See Rolvaag, O(le) E(dvart)
See also CA 117; 171
Roethke, Theodore (Huebner)
1908-1963 .... **CLC 1, 3, 8, 11, 19, 46, 101; PC 15**
See also AMW; CA 81-84; CABS 2; CDALB 1941-1968; DA3; DAM POET; DLB 5, 206; EWL 3; EXPP; MAL 5; MTCW 1, 2; PAB; PFS 3; RGAL 4; WP
Rogers, Carl R(ansom)
1902-1987 .... **TCLC 125**
See also CA 1-4R; 121; CANR 1, 18; MTCW 1
Rogers, Samuel 1763-1855 .... **NCLC 69**
See also DLB 93; RGEL 2
Rogers, Thomas Hunton 1927- .... **CLC 57**
See also CA 89-92; INT CA-89-92
Rogers, Will(iam Penn Adair)
1879-1935 .... **NNAL; TCLC 8, 71**
See also CA 105; 144; DA3; DAM MULT; DLB 11; MTCW 2
Rogin, Gilbert 1929- .... **CLC 18**
See also CA 65-68; CANR 15
Rohan, Koda
See Koda Shigeyuki

Rohlfs, Anna Katharine Green
See Green, Anna Katharine
Rohmer, Eric .... **CLC 16**
See Scherer, Jean-Marie Maurice
Rohmer, Sax .... **TCLC 28**
See Ward, Arthur Henry Sarsfield
See also DLB 70; MSW; SUFW
Roiphe, Anne 1935- .... **CLC 3, 9**
See also CA 89-92; CANR 45, 73, 138; DLBY 1980; INT CA-89-92
Roiphe, Anne Richardson
See Roiphe, Anne
Rojas, Fernando de 1475-1541 ... **HLCS 1, 2; LC 23**
See also DLB 286; RGWL 2, 3
Rojas, Gonzalo 1917- .... **HLCS 2**
See also CA 178; HW 2; LAWS 1
Roland (de la Platiere), Marie-Jeanne
1754-1793 .... **LC 98**
See also DLB 314
Rolfe, Frederick (William Serafino Austin Lewis Mary) 1860-1913 .... **TCLC 12**
See Al Siddik
See also CA 107; 210; DLB 34, 156; RGEL 2
Rolland, Romain 1866-1944 .... **TCLC 23**
See also CA 118; 197; DLB 65, 284; EWL 3; GFL 1789 to the Present; RGWL 2, 3
Rolle, Richard c. 1300-c. 1349 ...... **CMLC 21**
See also DLB 146; LMFS 1; RGEL 2
Rolvaag, O(le) E(dvart) .... **TCLC 17**
See Roelvaag, O(le) E(dvart)
See also DLB 9, 212; MAL 5; NFS 5; RGAL 4
Romain Arnaud, Saint
See Aragon, Louis
Romains, Jules 1885-1972 .... **CLC 7**
See also CA 85-88; CANR 34; DLB 65, 321; EWL 3; GFL 1789 to the Present; MTCW 1
Romero, Jose Ruben 1890-1952 .... **TCLC 14**
See also CA 114; 131; EWL 3; HW 1; LAW
Ronsard, Pierre de 1524-1585 . **LC 6, 54; PC 11**
See also DLB 327; EW 2; GFL Beginnings to 1789; RGWL 2, 3; TWA
Rooke, Leon 1934- .... **CLC 25, 34**
See also CA 25-28R; CANR 23, 53; CCA 1; CPW; DAM POP
Roosevelt, Franklin Delano
1882-1945 .... **TCLC 93**
See also CA 116; 173; LAIT 3
Roosevelt, Theodore 1858-1919 .... **TCLC 69**
See also CA 115; 170; DLB 47, 186, 275
Roper, William 1498-1578 .... **LC 10**
Roquelaure, A. N.
See Rice, Anne
Rosa, Joao Guimaraes 1908-1967 ... **CLC 23; HLCS 1**
See Guimaraes Rosa, Joao
See also CA 89-92; DLB 113, 307; EWL 3; WLIT 1
Rose, Wendy 1948- . **CLC 85; NNAL; PC 13**
See also CA 53-56; CANR 5, 51; CWP; DAM MULT; DLB 175; PFS 13; RGAL 4; SATA 12
Rosen, R. D.
See Rosen, Richard (Dean)
Rosen, Richard (Dean) 1949- .... **CLC 39**
See also CA 77-80; CANR 62, 120; CMW 4; INT CANR-30
Rosenberg, Isaac 1890-1918 .... **TCLC 12**
See also BRW 6; CA 107; 188; DLB 20, 216; EWL 3; PAB; RGEL 2
Rosenblatt, Joe .... **CLC 15**
See Rosenblatt, Joseph
See also CP 3, 4, 5, 6, 7

Rosenblatt, Joseph 1933-
  See Rosenblatt, Joe
  See also CA 89-92; CP 1, 2; INT CA-89-92
Rosenfeld, Samuel
  See Tzara, Tristan
Rosenstock, Sami
  See Tzara, Tristan
Rosenstock, Samuel
  See Tzara, Tristan
Rosenthal, M(acha) L(ouis)
  1917-1996 .... **CLC 28**
  See also CA 1-4R; 152; CAAS 6; CANR 4,
  51; CP 1, 2, 3, 4, 5, 6; DLB 5; SATA 59
Ross, Barnaby
  See Dannay, Frederic; Lee, Manfred B.
Ross, Bernard L.
  See Follett, Ken
Ross, J. H.
  See Lawrence, T(homas) E(dward)
Ross, John Hume
  See Lawrence, T(homas) E(dward)
Ross, Martin 1862-1915
  See Martin, Violet Florence
  Scc also DLB 135; GLL 2; RGEL 2; RGSF
  2
Ross, (James) Sinclair 1908-1996 ... **CLC 13;
  SSC 24**
  See also CA 73-76; CANR 81; CN 1, 2, 3,
  4, 5, 6; DAC; DAM MST; DLB 88;
  RGEL 2; RGSF 2; TCWW 1, 2
Rossetti, Christina 1830-1894 ... **NCLC 2, 50,
  66; PC 7; WLC 5**
  See also AAYA 51; BRW 5; BYA 4; CLR
  115; DA; DA3; DAB; DAC; DAM MST,
  POET; DLB 35, 163, 240; EXPP; FL 1:3;
  LATS 1:1; MAICYA 1, 2; PFS 10, 14;
  RGEL 2; SATA 20; TEA; WCH
Rossetti, Christina Georgina
  See Rossetti, Christina
Rossetti, Dante Gabriel 1828-1882 . **NCLC 4,
  77; PC 44; WLC 5**
  See also AAYA 51; BRW 5; CDBLB 1832-
  1890; DA; DAB; DAC; DAM MST,
  POET; DLB 35; EXPP; RGEL 2; TEA
Rossi, Cristina Peri
  See Peri Rossi, Cristina
Rossi, Jean-Baptiste 1931-2003
  See Japrisot, Sebastien
  See also CA 201; 215
Rossner, Judith 1935-2005 .... **CLC 6, 9, 29**
  See also AITN 2; BEST 90:3; BPFB 3; CA
  17-20R; 242; CANR 18, 51, 73; CN 4, 5,
  6, 7; DLB 6; INT CANR-18; MAL 5;
  MTCW 1, 2; MTFW 2005
Rossner, Judith Perelman
  See Rossner, Judith
Rostand, Edmond (Eugene Alexis)
  1868-1918 .... **DC 10; TCLC 6, 37**
  See also CA 104; 126; DA; DA3; DAB;
  DAC; DAM DRAM, MST; DFS 1; DLB
  192; LAIT 1; MTCW 1; RGWL 2, 3;
  TWA
Roth, Henry 1906-1995 ..... **CLC 2, 6, 11, 104**
  See also AMWS 9; CA 11-12; 149; CANR
  38, 63; CAP 1; CN 1, 2, 3, 4, 5, 6; DA3;
  DLB 28; EWL 3; MAL 5; MTCW 1, 2;
  MTFW 2005; RGAL 4
Roth, (Moses) Joseph 1894-1939 ... **TCLC 33**
  See also CA 160; DLB 85; EWL 3; RGWL
  2, 3
Roth, Philip 1933- ... **CLC 1, 2, 3, 4, 6, 9, 15,
  22, 31, 47, 66, 86, 119, 201; SSC 26;
  WLC 5**
  See also AAYA 67; AMWR 2; AMWS 3;
  BEST 90:3; BPFB 3; CA 1-4R; CANR 1,
  22, 36, 55, 89, 132; CDALB 1968-1988;
  CN 3, 4, 5, 6, 7; CPW 1; DA; DA3; DAB;
  DAC; DAM MST, NOV, POP; DLB 2,

28, 173; DLBY 1982; EWL 3; MAL 5;
  MTCW 1, 2; MTFW 2005; RGAL 4;
  RGHL; RGSF 2; SSFS 12, 18; TUS
Roth, Philip Milton
  See Roth, Philip
Rothenberg, Jerome 1931- .... **CLC 6, 57**
  See also CA 45-48; CANR 1, 106; CP 1, 2,
  3, 4, 5, 6, 7; DLB 5, 193
Rotter, Pat ed. .... **CLC 65**
Roumain, Jacques (Jean Baptiste)
  1907-1944 .... **BLC 3; TCLC 19**
  See also BW 1; CA 117; 125; DAM MULT;
  EWL 3
Rourke, Constance Mayfield
  1885-1941 .... **TCLC 12**
  See also CA 107; 200; MAL 5; YABC 1
Rousseau, Jean-Baptiste 1671-1741 ...... **LC 9**
Rousseau, Jean-Jacques 1712-1778 .... **LC 14,
  36, 122; WLC 5**
  See also DA; DA3; DAB; DAC; DAM
  MST; DLB 314; EW 4; GFL Beginnings
  to 1789; LMFS 1; RGWL 2, 3; TWA
Roussel, Raymond 1877-1933 .... **TCLC 20**
  See also CA 117; 201; EWL 3; GFL 1789
  to the Present
Rovit, Earl (Herbert) 1927- .... **CLC 7**
  See also CA 5-8R; CANR 12
Rowe, Elizabeth Singer 1674-1737 ..... **LC 44**
  See also DLB 39, 95
Rowe, Nicholas 1674-1718 .... **LC 8**
  See also DLB 84; RGEL 2
Rowlandson, Mary 1637(?)-1678 .... **LC 66**
  See also DLB 24, 200; RGAL 4
Rowley, Ames Dorrance
  See Lovecraft, H. P.
Rowley, William 1585(?)-1626 ... **LC 100, 123**
  See also DFS 22; DLB 58; RGEL 2
Rowling, J.K. 1965- .... **CLC 137, 217**
  See also AAYA 34; BYA 11, 13, 14; CA
  173; CANR 128, 157; CLR 66, 80, 112;
  MAICYA 2; MTFW 2005; SATA 109;
  SUFW 2
Rowling, Joanne Kathleen
  See Rowling, J.K.
Rowson, Susanna Haswell
  1762(?)-1824 .... **NCLC 5, 69**
  See also AMWS 15; DLB 37, 200; RGAL 4
Roy, Arundhati 1960(?)- .... **CLC 109, 210**
  See also CA 163; CANR 90, 126; CN 7;
  DLB 323, 326; DLBY 1997; EWL 3;
  LATS 1:2; MTFW 2005; NFS 22; WWE
  1
Roy, Gabrielle 1909-1983 .... **CLC 10, 14**
  See also CA 53-56; 110; CANR 5, 61; CCA
  1; DAB; DAC; DAM MST; DLB 68;
  EWL 3; MTCW 1; RGWL 2, 3; SATA
  104; TCLE 1:2
Royko, Mike 1932-1997 .... **CLC 109**
  See also CA 89-92; 157; CANR 26, 111;
  CPW
Rozanov, Vasilii Vasil'evich
  See Rozanov, Vassili
  See also DLB 295
Rozanov, Vasily Vasilyevich
  See Rozanov, Vassili
  See also EWL 3
Rozanov, Vassili 1856-1919 .... **TCLC 104**
  See Rozanov, Vasilii Vasil'evich; Rozanov,
  Vasily Vasilyevich
Rozewicz, Tadeusz 1921- ...... **CLC 9, 23, 139**
  See also CA 108; CANR 36, 66; CWW 2;
  DA3; DAM POET; DLB 232; EWL 3;
  MTCW 1, 2; MTFW 2005; RGHL;
  RGWL 3
Ruark, Gibbons 1941- .... **CLC 3**
  See also CA 33-36R; CAAS 23; CANR 14,
  31, 57; DLB 120

Rubens, Bernice (Ruth) 1923-2004 . **CLC 19,
  31**
  See also CA 25-28R; 232; CANR 33, 65,
  128; CN 1, 2, 3, 4, 5, 6, 7; DLB 14, 207,
  326; MTCW 1
Rubin, Harold
  See Robbins, Harold
Rudkin, (James) David 1936- .... **CLC 14**
  See also CA 89-92; CBD; CD 5, 6; DLB 13
Rudnik, Raphael 1933- .... **CLC 7**
  See also CA 29-32R
Ruffian, M.
  See Hasek, Jaroslav (Matej Frantisek)
Ruiz, Jose Martinez .... **CLC 11**
  See Martinez Ruiz, Jose
Ruiz, Juan c. 1283-c. 1350 .... **CMLC 66**
Rukeyser, Muriel 1913-1980 . **CLC 6, 10, 15,
  27; PC 12**
  See also AMWS 6; CA 5-8R; 93-96; CANR
  26, 60; CP 1, 2, 3; DA3; DAM POET;
  DLB 48; EWL 3; FW; GLL 2; MAL 5;
  MTCW 1, 2; PFS 10; RGAL 4; SATA-
  Obit 22
Rule, Jane (Vance) 1931- .... **CLC 27**
  See also CA 25-28R; CAAS 18; CANR 12,
  87; CN 4, 5, 6, 7; DLB 60; FW
Rulfo, Juan 1918-1986 .. **CLC 8, 80; HLC 2;
  SSC 25**
  See also CA 85-88; 118; CANR 26; CD-
  WLB 3; DAM MULT; DLB 113; EWL 3;
  HW 1, 2; LAW; MTCW 1, 2; RGSF 2;
  RGWL 2, 3; WLIT 1
Rumi, Jalal al-Din 1207-1273 ...... **CMLC 20;
  PC 45**
  See also AAYA 64; RGWL 2, 3; WLIT 6;
  WP
Runeberg, Johan 1804-1877 .... **NCLC 41**
Runyon, (Alfred) Damon
  1884(?)-1946 .... **TCLC 10**
  See also CA 107; 165; DLB 11, 86, 171;
  MAL 5; MTCW 2; RGAL 4
Rush, Norman 1933- .... **CLC 44**
  See also CA 121; 126; CANR 130; INT CA-
  126
Rushdie, Salman 1947- .... **CLC 23, 31, 55,
  100, 191; SSC 83; WLCS**
  See also AAYA 65; BEST 89:3; BPFB 3;
  BRWS 4; CA 108; 111; CANR 33, 56,
  108, 133; CN 4, 5, 6, 7; CPW 1; DA3;
  DAB; DAC; DAM MST, NOV, POP;
  DLB 194, 323, 326; EWL 3; FANT; INT
  CA-111; LATS 1:2; LMFS 2; MTCW 1,
  2; MTFW 2005; NFS 22, 23; RGEL 2;
  RGSF 2; TEA; WLIT 4
Rushforth, Peter 1945-2005 .... **CLC 19**
  See also CA 101; 243
Rushforth, Peter Scott
  See Rushforth, Peter
Ruskin, John 1819-1900 .... **TCLC 63**
  See also BRW 5; BYA 5; CA 114; 129; CD-
  BLB 1832-1890; DLB 55, 163, 190;
  RGEL 2; SATA 24; TEA; WCH
Russ, Joanna 1937- .... **CLC 15**
  See also BPFB 3; CA 25-28; CANR 11, 31,
  65; CN 4, 5, 6, 7; DLB 8; FW; GLL 1;
  MTCW 1; SCFW 1, 2; SFW 4
Russ, Richard Patrick
  See O'Brian, Patrick
Russell, George William 1867-1935
  See A.E.; Baker, Jean H.
  See also BRWS 8; CA 104; 153; CDBLB
  1890-1914; DAM POET; EWL 3; RGEL
  2
Russell, Jeffrey Burton 1934- .... **CLC 70**
  See also CA 25-28R; CANR 11, 28, 52
Russell, (Henry) Ken(neth Alfred)
  1927- .... **CLC 16**
  See also CA 105

Schlee, Ann 1934- .... **CLC 35**
See also CA 101; CANR 29, 88; SATA 44;
SATA-Brief 36

Schlegel, August Wilhelm von
1767-1845 .... **NCLC 15, 142**
See also DLB 94; RGWL 2, 3

Schlegel, Friedrich 1772-1829 .... **NCLC 45**
See also DLB 90; EW 5; RGWL 2, 3; TWA

Schlegel, Johann Elias (von)
1719(?)-1749 .... **LC 5**

Schleiermacher, Friedrich
1768-1834 .... **NCLC 107**
See also DLB 90

Schlesinger, Arthur M(eier), Jr.
1917- .... **CLC 84**
See also AITN 1; CA 1-4R; CANR 1, 28,
58, 105; DLB 17; INT CANR-28; MTCW
1, 2; SATA 61

Schlink, Bernhard 1944- .... **CLC 174**
See also CA 163; CANR 116; RGHL

Schmidt, Arno (Otto) 1914-1979 ...... **CLC 56**
See also CA 128; 109; DLB 69; EWL 3

Schmitz, Aron Hector 1861-1928
See Svevo, Italo
See also CA 104; 122; MTCW 1

Schnackenberg, Gjertrud 1953- ...... **CLC 40;
PC 45**
See also AMWS 15; CA 116; CANR 100;
CP 5, 6, 7; CWP; DLB 120, 282; PFS 13

Schnackenberg, Gjertrud Cecelia
See Schnackenberg, Gjertrud

Schneider, Leonard Alfred 1925-1966
See Bruce, Lenny
See also CA 89-92

Schnitzler, Arthur 1862-1931 ..... **DC 17; SSC
15, 61; TCLC 4**
See also CA 104; CDWLB 2; DLB 81, 118;
EW 8; EWL 3; RGSF 2; RGWL 2, 3

Schoenberg, Arnold Franz Walter
1874-1951 .... **TCLC 75**
See also CA 109; 188

Schonberg, Arnold
See Schoenberg, Arnold Franz Walter

Schopenhauer, Arthur 1788-1860 . **NCLC 51,
157**
See also DLB 90; EW 5

Schor, Sandra (M.) 1932(?)-1990 ..... **CLC 65**
See also CA 132

Schorer, Mark 1908-1977 .... **CLC 9**
See also CA 5-8R; 73-76; CANR 7; CN 1,
2; DLB 103

Schrader, Paul (Joseph) 1946- . **CLC 26, 212**
See also CA 37-40R; CANR 41; DLB 44

Schreber, Daniel 1842-1911 .... **TCLC 123**

Schreiner, Olive (Emilie Albertina)
1855-1920 .... **TCLC 9**
See also AFW; BRWS 2; CA 105; 154;
DLB 18, 156, 190, 225; EWL 3; FW;
RGEL 2; TWA; WLIT 2; WWE 1

Schulberg, Budd (Wilson) 1914- .. **CLC 7, 48**
See also BPFB 3; CA 25-28R; CANR 19,
87; CN 1, 2, 3, 4, 5, 6, 7; DLB 6, 26, 28;
DLBY 1981, 2001; MAL 5

Schulman, Arnold
See Trumbo, Dalton

Schulz, Bruno 1892-1942 .. **SSC 13; TCLC 5,
51**
See also CA 115; 123; CANR 86; CDWLB
4; DLB 215; EWL 3; MTCW 2; MTFW
2005; RGSF 2; RGWL 2, 3

Schulz, Charles M. 1922-2000 .... **CLC 12**
See also AAYA 39; CA 9-12R; 187; CANR
6, 132; INT CANR-6; MTFW 2005;
SATA 10; SATA-Obit 118

Schulz, Charles Monroe
See Schulz, Charles M.

Schumacher, E(rnst) F(riedrich)
1911-1977 .... **CLC 80**
See also CA 81-84; 73-76; CANR 34, 85

Schumann, Robert 1810-1856 ...... **NCLC 143**

Schuyler, George Samuel 1895-1977 . **HR 1:3**
See also BW 2; CA 81-84; 73-76; CANR
42; DLB 29, 51

Schuyler, James Marcus 1923-1991 .. **CLC 5,
23**
See also CA 101; 134; CP 1, 2, 3, 4, 5;
DAM POET; DLB 5, 169; EWL 3; INT
CA-101; MAL 5; WP

Schwartz, Delmore (David)
1913-1966 ... **CLC 2, 4, 10, 45, 87; PC 8**
See also AMWS 2; CA 17-18; 25-28R;
CANR 35; CAP 2; DLB 28, 48; EWL 3;
MAL 5; MTCW 1, 2; MTFW 2005; PAB;
RGAL 4; TUS

Schwartz, Ernst
See Ozu, Yasujiro

Schwartz, John Burnham 1965- .... **CLC 59**
See also CA 132; CANR 116

Schwartz, Lynne Sharon 1939- .... **CLC 31**
See also CA 103; CANR 44, 89; DLB 218;
MTCW 2; MTFW 2005

Schwartz, Muriel A.
See Eliot, T(homas) S(tearns)

Schwarz-Bart, Andre 1928-2006 .... **CLC 2, 4**
See also CA 89-92; CANR 109; DLB 299;
RGHL

Schwarz-Bart, Simone 1938- . **BLCS; CLC 7**
See also BW 2; CA 97-100; CANR 117;
EWL 3

Schwerner, Armand 1927-1999 .... **PC 42**
See also CA 9-12R; 179; CANR 50, 85; CP
2, 3, 4, 5, 6; DLB 165

**Schwitters, Kurt (Hermann Edward Karl
Julius)** 1887-1948 .... **TCLC 95**
See also CA 158

Schwob, Marcel (Mayer Andre)
1867-1905 .... **TCLC 20**
See also CA 117; 168; DLB 123; GFL 1789
to the Present

Sciascia, Leonardo 1921-1989 .. **CLC 8, 9, 41**
See also CA 85-88; 130; CANR 35; DLB
177; EWL 3; MTCW 1; RGWL 2, 3

Scoppettone, Sandra 1936- .... **CLC 26**
See Early, Jack
See also AAYA 11, 65; BYA 8; CA 5-8R;
CANR 41, 73, 157; GLL 1; MAICYA 2;
MAICYAS 1; SATA 9, 92; WYA; YAW

Scorsese, Martin 1942- .... **CLC 20, 89, 207**
See also AAYA 38; CA 110; 114; CANR
46, 85

Scotland, Jay
See Jakes, John

Scott, Duncan Campbell
1862-1947 .... **TCLC 6**
See also CA 104; 153; DAC; DLB 92;
RGEL 2

Scott, Evelyn 1893-1963 .... **CLC 43**
See also CA 104; 112; CANR 64; DLB 9,
48; RHW

Scott, F(rancis) R(eginald)
1899-1985 .... **CLC 22**
See also CA 101; 114; CANR 87; CP 1, 2,
3, 4; DLB 88; INT CA-101; RGEL 2

Scott, Frank
See Scott, F(rancis) R(eginald)

Scott, Joan .... **CLC 65**

Scott, Joanna 1960- .... **CLC 50**
See also CA 126; CANR 53, 92

Scott, Paul (Mark) 1920-1978 ...... **CLC 9, 60**
See also BRWS 1; CA 81-84; 77-80; CANR
33; CN 1, 2; DLB 14, 207, 326; EWL 3;
MTCW 1; RGEL 2; RHW; WWE 1

Scott, Ridley 1937- .... **CLC 183**
See also AAYA 13, 43

Scott, Sarah 1723-1795 .... **LC 44**
See also DLB 39

Scott, Sir Walter 1771-1832 .... **NCLC 15, 69,
110; PC 13; SSC 32; WLC 5**
See also AAYA 22; BRW 4; BYA 2; CD-
BLB 1789-1832; DA; DAB; DAC; DAM
MST, NOV, POET; DLB 93, 107, 116,
144, 159; GL 3; HGG; LAIT 1; RGEL 2;
RGSF 2; SSFS 10; SUFW 1; TEA; WLIT
3; YABC 2

Scribe, (Augustin) Eugene 1791-1861 . **DC 5;
NCLC 16**
See also DAM DRAM; DLB 192; GFL
1789 to the Present; RGWL 2, 3

Scrum, R.
See Crumb, R.

Scudery, Georges de 1601-1667 .... **LC 75**
See also GFL Beginnings to 1789

Scudery, Madeleine de 1607-1701 .. **LC 2, 58**
See also DLB 268; GFL Beginnings to 1789

Scum
See Crumb, R.

Scumbag, Little Bobby
See Crumb, R.

Seabrook, John
See Hubbard, L. Ron

Seacole, Mary Jane Grant
1805-1881 .... **NCLC 147**
See also DLB 166

Sealy, I(rwin) Allan 1951- .... **CLC 55**
See also CA 136; CN 6, 7

Search, Alexander
See Pessoa, Fernando (Antonio Nogueira)

Sebald, W(infried) G(eorg)
1944-2001 .... **CLC 194**
See also BRWS 8; CA 159; 202; CANR 98;
MTFW 2005; RGHL

Sebastian, Lee
See Silverberg, Robert

Sebastian Owl
See Thompson, Hunter S.

Sebestyen, Igen
See Sebestyen, Ouida

Sebestyen, Ouida 1924- .... **CLC 30**
See also AAYA 8; BYA 7; CA 107; CANR
40, 114; CLR 17; JRDA; MAICYA 1, 2;
SAAS 10; SATA 39, 140; WYA; YAW

Sebold, Alice 1963(?)- .... **CLC 193**
See also AAYA 56; CA 203; MTFW 2005

Second Duke of Buckingham
See Villiers, George

Secundus, H. Scriblerus
See Fielding, Henry

Sedges, John
See Buck, Pearl S(ydenstricker)

Sedgwick, Catharine Maria
1789-1867 .... **NCLC 19, 98**
See also DLB 1, 74, 183, 239, 243, 254; FL
1:3; RGAL 4

Sedulius Scottus 9th cent. -c. 874 .. **CMLC 86**

Seelye, John (Douglas) 1931- .... **CLC 7**
See also CA 97-100; CANR 70; INT CA-
97-100; TCWW 1, 2

Seferiades, Giorgos Stylianou 1900-1971
See Seferis, George
See also CA 5-8R; 33-36R; CANR 5, 36;
MTCW 1

Seferis, George .... **CLC 5, 11; PC 66**
See Seferiades, Giorgos Stylianou
See also EW 12; EWL 3; RGWL 2, 3

Segal, Erich (Wolf) 1937- .... **CLC 3, 10**
See also BEST 89:1; BPFB 3; CA 25-28R;
CANR 20, 36, 65, 113; CPW; DAM POP;
DLBY 1986; INT CANR-20; MTCW 1

Seger, Bob 1945- .... **CLC 35**

Seghers, Anna .... **CLC 7**
See Radvanyi, Netty
See also CDWLB 2; DLB 69; EWL 3

Seidel, Frederick (Lewis) 1936- .... **CLC 18**
See also CA 13-16R; CANR 8, 99; CP 1, 2,
3, 4, 5, 6, 7; DLBY 1984

Sheldon, Alice Hastings Bradley
1915(?)-1987
See Tiptree, James, Jr.
See also CA 108; 122; CANR 34; INT CA-108; MTCW 1

Sheldon, John
See Bloch, Robert (Albert)

Sheldon, Walter J(ames) 1917-1996
See Queen, Ellery
See also AITN 1; CA 25-28R; CANR 10

Shelley, Mary Wollstonecraft (Godwin)
1797-1851 .... **NCLC 14, 59, 103, 170; SSC 92; WLC 5**
See also AAYA 20; BPFB 3; BRW 3; BRWC 2; BRWS 3; BYA 5; CDBLB 1789-1832; DA; DA3; DAB; DAC; DAM MST, NOV; DLB 110, 116, 159, 178; EXPN; FL 1:3; GL 3; HGG; LAIT 1; LMFS 1, 2; NFS 1; RGEL 2; SATA 29; SCFW 1, 2; SFW 4; TEA; WLIT 3

Shelley, Percy Bysshe 1792-1822 .. **NCLC 18, 93, 143, 175; PC 14, 67; WLC 5**
See also AAYA 61; BRW 4; BRWR 1; CDBLB 1789-1832; DA; DA3; DAB; DAC; DAM MST, POET; DLB 96, 110, 158; EXPP; LMFS 1; PAB; PFS 2; RGEL 2; TEA; WLIT 3; WP

Shepard, James R. .... **CLC 36**
See also CA 137; CANR 59, 104; SATA 90, 164

Shepard, Jim
See Shepard, James R.

Shepard, Lucius 1947- .... **CLC 34**
See also CA 128; 141; CANR 81, 124; HGG; SCFW 2; SFW 4; SUFW 2

Shepard, Sam 1943- .... **CLC 4, 6, 17, 34, 41, 44, 169; DC 5**
See also AAYA 1, 58; AMWS 3; CA 69-72; CABS 3; CAD; CANR 22, 120, 140; CD 5, 6; DA3; DAM DRAM; DFS 3, 6, 7, 14; DLB 7, 212; EWL 3; IDFW 3, 4; MAL 5; MTCW 1, 2; MTFW 2005; RGAL 4

Shepherd, Jean (Parker)
1921-1999 .... **TCLC 177**
See also AAYA 69; AITN 2; CA 77-80; 187

Shepherd, Michael
See Ludlum, Robert

Sherburne, Zoa (Lillian Morin)
1912-1995 .... **CLC 30**
See also AAYA 13; CA 1-4R; 176; CANR 3, 37; MAICYA 1, 2; SAAS 18; SATA 3; YAW

Sheridan, Frances 1724-1766 .... **LC 7**
See also DLB 39, 84

Sheridan, Richard Brinsley
1751-1816 . **DC 1; NCLC 5, 91; WLC 5**
See also BRW 3; CDBLB 1660-1789; DA; DAB; DAC; DAM DRAM, MST; DFS 15; DLB 89; WLIT 3

Sherman, Jonathan Marc 1968- .... **CLC 55**
See also CA 230

Sherman, Martin 1941(?)- .... **CLC 19**
See also CA 116; 123; CAD; CANR 86; CD 5, 6; DFS 20; DLB 228; GLL 1; IDTP; RGHL

Sherwin, Judith Johnson
See Johnson, Judith (Emlyn)
See also CANR 85; CP 2, 3, 4, 5; CWP

Sherwood, Frances 1940- .... **CLC 81**
See also CA 146, 220; CAAE 220

Sherwood, Robert E(mmet)
1896-1955 .... **TCLC 3**
See also CA 104; 153; CANR 86; DAM DRAM; DFS 11, 15, 17; DLB 7, 26, 249; IDFW 3, 4; MAL 5; RGAL 4

Shestov, Lev 1866-1938 .... **TCLC 56**

Shevchenko, Taras 1814-1861 .... **NCLC 54**

Shiel, M(atthew) P(hipps)
1865-1947 .... **TCLC 8**
See Holmes, Gordon
See also CA 106; 160; DLB 153; HGG; MTCW 2; MTFW 2005; SCFW 1, 2; SFW 4; SUFW

Shields, Carol 1935-2003 .. **CLC 91, 113, 193**
See also AMWS 7; CA 81-84; 218; CANR 51, 74, 98, 133; CCA 1; CN 6, 7; CPW; DA3; DAC; MTCW 2; MTFW 2005; NFS 23

Shields, David 1956- .... **CLC 97**
See also CA 124; CANR 48, 99, 112, 157

Shiga, Naoya 1883-1971 .... **CLC 33; SSC 23; TCLC 172**
See Shiga Naoya
See also CA 101; 33-36R; MJW; RGWL 3

Shiga Naoya
See Shiga, Naoya
See also DLB 180; EWL 3; RGWL 3

Shilts, Randy 1951-1994 .... **CLC 85**
See also AAYA 19; CA 115; 127; 144; CANR 45; DA3; GLL 1; INT CA 127; MTCW 2; MTFW 2005

Shimazaki, Haruki 1872-1943
See Shimazaki Toson
See also CA 105; 134; CANR 84; RGWL 3

Shimazaki Toson .... **TCLC 5**
See Shimazaki, Haruki
See also DLB 180; EWL 3

Shirley, James 1596-1666 ...... **DC 25; LC 96**
See also DLB 58; RGEL 2

Sholokhov, Mikhail (Aleksandrovich)
1905-1984 .... **CLC 7, 15**
See also CA 101; 112; DLB 272; EWL 3; MTCW 1, 2; MTFW 2005; RGWL 2, 3; SATA-Obit 36

Shone, Patric
See Hanley, James

Showalter, Elaine 1941- .... **CLC 169**
See also CA 57-60; CANR 58, 106; DLB 67; FW; GLL 2

Shreve, Susan
See Shreve, Susan Richards

Shreve, Susan Richards 1939- .... **CLC 23**
See also CA 49-52; CAAS 5; CANR 5, 38, 69, 100; MAICYA 1, 2; SATA 46, 95, 152; SATA-Brief 41

Shue, Larry 1946-1985 .... **CLC 52**
See also CA 145; 117; DAM DRAM; DFS 7

Shu-Jen, Chou 1881-1936
See Lu Hsun
See also CA 104

Shulman, Alix Kates 1932- .... **CLC 2, 10**
See also CA 29-32R; CANR 43; FW; SATA 7

Shuster, Joe 1914-1992 .... **CLC 21**
See also AAYA 50

Shute, Nevil .... **CLC 30**
See Norway, Nevil Shute
See also BPFB 3; DLB 255; NFS 9; RHW; SFW 4

Shuttle, Penelope (Diane) 1947- .... **CLC 7**
See also CA 93-96; CANR 39, 84, 92, 108; CP 3, 4, 5, 6, 7; CWP; DLB 14, 40

Shvarts, Elena 1948- .... **PC 50**
See also CA 147

Sidhwa, Bapsi 1939-
See Sidhwa, Bapsy (N.)
See also CN 6, 7; DLB 323

Sidhwa, Bapsy (N.) 1938- .... **CLC 168**
See Sidhwa, Bapsi
See also CA 108; CANR 25, 57; FW

Sidney, Mary 1561-1621 .... **LC 19, 39**
See Sidney Herbert, Mary

Sidney, Sir Philip 1554-1586 .... **LC 19, 39, 131; PC 32**
See also BRW 1; BRWR 2; CDBLB Before 1660; DA; DA3; DAB; DAC; DAM MST, POET; DLB 167; EXPP; PAB; RGEL 2; TEA; WP

Sidney Herbert, Mary
See Sidney, Mary
See also DLB 167

Siegel, Jerome 1914-1996 .... **CLC 21**
See Siegel, Jerry
See also CA 116; 169; 151

Siegel, Jerry
See Siegel, Jerome
See also AAYA 50

Sienkiewicz, Henryk (Adam Alexander Pius)
1846-1916 .... **TCLC 3**
See also CA 104; 134; CANR 84; EWL 3; RGSF 2; RGWL 2, 3

Sierra, Gregorio Martinez
See Martinez Sierra, Gregorio

Sierra, Maria de la O'LeJarraga Martinez
See Martinez Sierra, Maria

Sigal, Clancy 1926- .... **CLC 7**
See also CA 1-4R; CANR 85; CN 1, 2, 3, 4, 5, 6, 7

Siger of Brabant 1240(?)-1284(?) . **CMLC 69**
See also DLB 115

Sigourney, Lydia H.
See Sigourney, Lydia Howard (Huntley)
See also DLB 73, 183

Sigourney, Lydia Howard (Huntley)
1791-1865 .... **NCLC 21, 87**
See Sigourney, Lydia H.; Sigourney, Lydia Huntley
See also DLB 1

Sigourney, Lydia Huntley
See Sigourney, Lydia Howard (Huntley)
See also DLB 42, 239, 243

Siguenza y Gongora, Carlos de
1645-1700 .... **HLCS 2; LC 8**
See also LAW

Sigurjonsson, Johann
See Sigurjonsson, Johann

Sigurjonsson, Johann 1880-1919 ... **TCLC 27**
See also CA 170; DLB 293; EWL 3

Sikelianos, Angelos 1884-1951 .... **PC 29; TCLC 39**
See also EWL 3; RGWL 2, 3

Silkin, Jon 1930-1997 .... **CLC 2, 6, 43**
See also CA 5-8R; CAAS 5; CANR 89; CP 1, 2, 3, 4, 5, 6; DLB 27

Silko, Leslie 1948- ...... **CLC 23, 74, 114, 211; NNAL; SSC 37, 66; WLCS**
See also AAYA 14; AMWS 4; ANW; BYA 12; CA 115; 122; CANR 45, 65, 118; CN 4, 5, 6, 7; CP 4, 5, 6, 7; CPW 1; CWP; DA; DA3; DAC; DAM MST, MULT, POP; DLB 143, 175, 256, 275; EWL 3; EXPP; EXPS; LAIT 4; MAL 5; MTCW 2; MTFW 2005; NFS 4; PFS 9, 16; RGAL 4; RGSF 2; SSFS 4, 8, 10, 11; TCWW 1, 2

Sillanpaa, Frans Eemil 1888-1964 ... **CLC 19**
See also CA 129; 93-96; EWL 3; MTCW 1

Sillitoe, Alan 1928- .. **CLC 1, 3, 6, 10, 19, 57, 148**
See also AITN 1; BRWS 5; CA 9-12R; 191; CAAE 191; CAAS 2; CANR 8, 26, 55, 139; CDBLB 1960 to Present; CN 1, 2, 3, 4, 5, 6; CP 1, 2, 3, 4, 5; DLB 14, 139; EWL 3; MTCW 1, 2; MTFW 2005; RGEL 2; RGSF 2; SATA 61

Silone, Ignazio 1900-1978 .... **CLC 4**
See also CA 25-28; 81-84; CANR 34; CAP 2; DLB 264; EW 12; EWL 3; MTCW 1; RGSF 2; RGWL 2, 3

Silone, Ignazione
See Silone, Ignazio

Slaughter, Frank G(ill) 1908-2001 ... **CLC 29**
See also AITN 2; CA 5-8R; 197; CANR 5,
85; INT CANR-5; RHW
Slavitt, David R(ytman) 1935- ..... **CLC 5, 14**
See also CA 21-24R; CAAS 3; CANR 41,
83; CN 1, 2; CP 1, 2, 3, 4, 5, 6, 7; DLB
5, 6
Slesinger, Tess 1905-1945 .... **TCLC 10**
See also CA 107; 199; DLB 102
Slessor, Kenneth 1901-1971 .... **CLC 14**
See also CA 102; 89-92; DLB 260; RGEL
2
Slowacki, Juliusz 1809-1849 .... **NCLC 15**
See also RGWL 3
Smart, Christopher 1722-1771 .... **LC 3, 134;
PC 13**
See also DAM POET; DLB 109; RGEL 2
Smart, Elizabeth 1913-1986 .... **CLC 54**
See also CA 81-84; 118; CN 4; DLB 88
Smiley, Jane (Graves) 1949- ...... **CLC 53, 76,
144**
See also AAYA 66; AMWS 6; BPFB 3; CA
104; CANR 30, 50, 74, 96; CN 6, 7; CPW
1; DA3; DAM POP; DLB 227, 234; EWL
3; INT CANR-30; MAL 5; MTFW 2005;
SSFS 19
Smith, A(rthur) J(ames) M(arshall)
1902-1980 .... **CLC 15**
See also CA 1-4R; 102; CANR 4; CP 1, 2,
3; DAC; DLB 88; RGEL 2
Smith, Adam 1723(?)-1790 .... **LC 36**
See also DLB 104, 252; RGEL 2
Smith, Alexander 1829-1867 .... **NCLC 59**
See also DLB 32, 55
Smith, Anna Deavere 1950- .... **CLC 86**
See also CA 133; CANR 103; CD 5, 6; DFS
2, 22
Smith, Betty (Wehner) 1904-1972 .... **CLC 19**
See also BPFB 3; BYA 3; CA 5-8R; 33-
36R; DLBY 1982; LAIT 3; RGAL 4;
SATA 6
Smith, Charlotte (Turner)
1749-1806 .... **NCLC 23, 115**
See also DLB 39, 109; RGEL 2; TEA
Smith, Clark Ashton 1893-1961 .... **CLC 43**
See also CA 143; CANR 81; FANT; HGG;
MTCW 2; SCFW 1, 2; SFW 4; SUFW
Smith, Dave .... **CLC 22, 42**
See Smith, David (Jeddie)
See also CAAS 7; CP 3, 4, 5, 6, 7; DLB 5
Smith, David (Jeddie) 1942-
See Smith, Dave
See also CA 49-52; CANR 1, 59, 120;
CSW; DAM POET
Smith, Iain Crichton 1928-1998 .... **CLC 64**
See also BRWS 9; CA 21-24R; 171; CN 1,
2, 3, 4, 5, 6; CP 1, 2, 3, 4, 5, 6; DLB 40,
139, 319; RGSF 2
Smith, John 1580(?)-1631 .... **LC 9**
See also DLB 24, 30; TUS
Smith, Johnston
See Crane, Stephen (Townley)
Smith, Joseph, Jr. 1805-1844 .... **NCLC 53**
Smith, Kevin 1970- .... **CLC 223**
See also AAYA 37; CA 166; CANR 131
Smith, Lee 1944- .... **CLC 25, 73**
See also CA 114; 119; CANR 46, 118; CN
7; CSW; DLB 143; DLBY 1983; EWL 3;
INT CA-119; RGAL 4
Smith, Martin
See Smith, Martin Cruz
Smith, Martin Cruz 1942- .. **CLC 25; NNAL**
See also BEST 89:4; BPFB 3; CA 85-88;
CANR 6, 23, 43, 65, 119; CMW 4; CPW;
DAM MULT, POP; HGG; INT CANR-
23; MTCW 2; MTFW 2005; RGAL 4
Smith, Patti 1946- .... **CLC 12**
See also CA 93-96; CANR 63

Smith, Pauline (Urmson)
1882-1959 .... **TCLC 25**
See also DLB 225; EWL 3
Smith, Rosamond
See Oates, Joyce Carol
Smith, Sheila Kaye
See Kaye-Smith, Sheila
Smith, Stevie 1902-1971 .... **CLC 3, 8, 25, 44;
PC 12**
See also BRWS 2; CA 17-18; 29-32R;
CANR 35; CAP 2; CP 1; DAM POET;
DLB 20; EWL 3; MTCW 1, 2; PAB; PFS
3; RGEL 2; TEA
Smith, Wilbur 1933- .... **CLC 33**
See also CA 13-16R; CANR 7, 46, 66, 134;
CPW; MTCW 1, 2; MTFW 2005
Smith, William Jay 1918- .... **CLC 6**
See also AMWS 13; CA 5-8R; CANR 44,
106; CP 1, 2, 3, 4, 5, 6, 7; CSW; CWRI
5; DLB 5; MAICYA 1, 2; SAAS 22;
SATA 2, 68, 154; SATA-Essay 154; TCLE
1:2
Smith, Woodrow Wilson
See Kuttner, Henry
Smith, Zadie 1975- .... **CLC 158**
See also AAYA 50; CA 193; MTFW 2005
Smolenskin, Peretz 1842-1885 .... **NCLC 30**
Smollett, Tobias (George) 1721-1771 ... **LC 2,
46**
See also BRW 3; CDBLB 1660-1789; DLB
39, 104; RGEL 2; TEA
Snodgrass, W.D. 1926- .... **CLC 2, 6, 10, 18,
68; PC 74**
See also AMWS 6; CA 1-4R; CANR 6, 36,
65, 85; CP 1, 2, 3, 4, 5, 6, 7; DAM POET;
DLB 5; MAL 5; MTCW 1, 2; MTFW
2005; RGAL 4; TCLE 1:2
Snorri Sturluson 1179-1241 .... **CMLC 56**
See also RGWL 2, 3
Snow, C(harles) P(ercy) 1905-1980 ... **CLC 1,
4, 6, 9, 13, 19**
See also BRW 7; CA 5-8R; 101; CANR 28;
CDBLB 1945-1960; CN 1, 2; DAM NOV;
DLB 15, 77; DLBD 17; EWL 3; MTCW
1, 2; MTFW 2005; RGEL 2; TEA
Snow, Frances Compton
See Adams, Henry (Brooks)
Snyder, Gary 1930- . **CLC 1, 2, 5, 9, 32, 120;
PC 21**
See also AMWS 8; ANW; BG 1:3; CA 17-
20R; CANR 30, 60, 125; CP 1, 2, 3, 4, 5,
6, 7; DA3; DAM POET; DLB 5, 16, 165,
212, 237, 275; EWL 3; MAL 5; MTCW
2; MTFW 2005; PFS 9, 19; RGAL 4; WP
Snyder, Zilpha Keatley 1927- .... **CLC 17**
See also AAYA 15; BYA 1; CA 9-12R;
CANR 38; CLR 31; JRDA; MAICYA 1,
2; SAAS 2; SATA 1, 28, 75, 110, 163;
SATA-Essay 112, 163; YAW
Soares, Bernardo
See Pessoa, Fernando (Antonio Nogueira)
Sobh, A.
See Shamlu, Ahmad
Sobh, Alef
See Shamlu, Ahmad
Sobol, Joshua 1939- .... **CLC 60**
See Sobol, Yehoshua
See also CA 200; RGHL
Sobol, Yehoshua 1939-
See Sobol, Joshua
See also CWW 2
Socrates 470B.C.-399B.C. .... **CMLC 27**
Soderberg, Hjalmar 1869-1941 ...... **TCLC 39**
See also DLB 259; EWL 3; RGSF 2
Soderbergh, Steven 1963- .... **CLC 154**
See also AAYA 43; CA 243
Soderbergh, Steven Andrew
See Soderbergh, Steven

Sodergran, Edith (Irene) 1892-1923
See Soedergran, Edith (Irene)
See also CA 202; DLB 259; EW 11; EWL
3; RGWL 2, 3
Soedergran, Edith (Irene)
1892-1923 .... **TCLC 31**
See Sodergran, Edith (Irene)
Softly, Edgar
See Lovecraft, H. P.
Softly, Edward
See Lovecraft, H. P.
Sokolov, Alexander V(sevolodovich) 1943-
See Sokolov, Sasha
See also CA 73-76
Sokolov, Raymond 1941- .... **CLC 7**
See also CA 85-88
Sokolov, Sasha .... **CLC 59**
See Sokolov, Alexander V(sevolodovich)
See also CWW 2; DLB 285; EWL 3; RGWL
2, 3
Solo, Jay
See Ellison, Harlan
Sologub, Fyodor .... **TCLC 9**
See Teternikov, Fyodor Kuzmich
See also EWL 3
Solomons, Ikey Esquir
See Thackeray, William Makepeace
Solomos, Dionysios 1798-1857 .... **NCLC 15**
Solwoska, Mara
See French, Marilyn
Solzhenitsyn, Aleksandr I. 1918- .. **CLC 1, 2,
4, 7, 9, 10, 18, 26, 34, 78, 134; SSC 32;
WLC 5**
See Solzhenitsyn, Aleksandr Isayevich
See also AAYA 49; AITN 1; BPFB 3; CA
69-72; CANR 40, 65, 116; DA; DA3;
DAB; DAC; DAM MST, NOV; DLB 302;
EW 13; EXPS; LAIT 4; MTCW 1, 2;
MTFW 2005; NFS 6; RGSF 2; RGWL 2,
3; SSFS 9; TWA
Solzhenitsyn, Aleksandr Isayevich
See Solzhenitsyn, Aleksandr I.
See also CWW 2; EWL 3
Somers, Jane
See Lessing, Doris
Somerville, Edith Oenone
1858-1949 .... **SSC 56; TCLC 51**
See also CA 196; DLB 135; RGEL 2; RGSF
2
Somerville & Ross
See Martin, Violet Florence; Somerville,
Edith Oenone
Sommer, Scott 1951- .... **CLC 25**
See also CA 106
Sommers, Christina Hoff 1950- ...... **CLC 197**
See also CA 153; CANR 95
Sondheim, Stephen (Joshua) 1930- . **CLC 30,
39, 147; DC 22**
See also AAYA 11, 66; CA 103; CANR 47,
67, 125; DAM DRAM; LAIT 4
Sone, Monica 1919- .... **AAL**
See also DLB 312
Song, Cathy 1955- .... **AAL; PC 21**
See also CA 154; CANR 118; CWP; DLB
169, 312; EXPP; FW; PFS 5
Sontag, Susan 1933-2004 ... **CLC 1, 2, 10, 13,
31, 105, 195**
See also AMWS 3; CA 17-20R; 234; CANR
25, 51, 74, 97; CN 1, 2, 3, 4, 5, 6, 7;
CPW; DA3; DAM POP; DLB 2, 67; EWL
3; MAL 5; MBL; MTCW 1, 2; MTFW
2005; RGAL 4; RHW; SSFS 10
Sophocles 496(?)B.C.-406(?)B.C. .... **CMLC 2,
47, 51, 86; DC 1; WLCS**
See also AW 1; CDWLB 1; DA; DA3;
DAB; DAC; DAM DRAM, MST; DFS 1,
4, 8; DLB 176; LAIT 1; LATS 1:1; LMFS
1; RGWL 2, 3; TWA; WLIT 8

Stanton, Maura 1946- .... **CLC 9**
  See also CA 89-92; CANR 15, 123; DLB 120
Stanton, Schuyler
  See Baum, L(yman) Frank
Stapledon, (William) Olaf
  1886-1950 .... **TCLC 22**
  See also CA 111; 162; DLB 15, 255; SCFW 1, 2; SFW 4
Starbuck, George (Edwin)
  1931-1996 .... **CLC 53**
  See also CA 21-24R; 153; CANR 23; CP 1, 2, 3, 4, 5, 6; DAM POET
Stark, Richard
  See Westlake, Donald E.
Staunton, Schuyler
  See Baum, L(yman) Frank
Stead, Christina (Ellen) 1902-1983 ... **CLC 2, 5, 8, 32, 80**
  See also BRWS 4; CA 13-16R; 109; CANR 33, 40; CN 1, 2, 3; DLB 260; EWL 3; FW; MTCW 1, 2; MTFW 2005; RGEL 2; RGSF 2; WWE 1
Stead, William Thomas
  1849-1912 .... **TCLC 48**
  See also CA 167
Stebnitsky, M.
  See Leskov, Nikolai (Semyonovich)
Steele, Richard 1672-1729 .... **LC 18**
  See also BRW 3; CDBLB 1660-1789; DLB 84, 101; RGEL 2; WLIT 3
Steele, Timothy (Reid) 1948- .... **CLC 45**
  See also CA 93-96; CANR 16, 50, 92; CP 5, 6, 7; DLB 120, 282
Steffens, (Joseph) Lincoln
  1866-1936 .... **TCLC 20**
  See also CA 117; 198; DLB 303; MAL 5
Stegner, Wallace (Earle) 1909-1993 .. **CLC 9, 49, 81; SSC 27**
  See also AITN 1; AMWS 4; ANW; BEST 90:3; BPFB 3; CAAS 9; CA 1-4R; 141; CANR 1, 21, 46; CN 1, 2, 3, 4, 5; DAM NOV; DLB 9, 206, 275; DLBY 1993; EWL 3; MAL 5; MTCW 1, 2; MTFW 2005; RGAL 4; TCWW 1, 2; TUS
Stein, Gertrude 1874-1946 .... **DC 19; PC 18; SSC 42; TCLC 1, 6, 28, 48; WLC 5**
  See also AAYA 64; AMW; AMWC 2; CA 104; 132; CANR 108; CDALB 1917-1929; DA; DA3; DAB; DAC; DAM MST, NOV; POET; DLB 4, 54, 86, 228; DLBD 15; EWL 3; EXPS; FL 1:6; GLL 1; MAL 5; MBL; MTCW 1, 2; MTFW 2005; NCFS 4; RGAL 4; RGSF 2; SSFS 5; TUS; WP
Steinbeck, John (Ernst) 1902-1968 ... **CLC 1, 5, 9, 13, 21, 34, 45, 75, 124; SSC 11, 37, 77; TCLC 135; WLC 5**
  See also AAYA 12; AMW; BPFB 3; BYA 2, 3, 13; CA 1-4R; 25-28R; CANR 1, 35; CDALB 1929-1941; DA; DA3; DAB; DAC; DAM DRAM, MST, NOV; DLB 7, 9, 212, 275, 309; DLBD 2; EWL 3; EXPS; LAIT 3; MAL 5; MTCW 1, 2; MTFW 2005; NFS 1, 5, 7, 17, 19; RGAL 4; RGSF 2; RHW; SATA 9; SSFS 3, 6, 22; TCWW 1, 2; TUS; WYA; YAW
Steinem, Gloria 1934- .... **CLC 63**
  See also CA 53-56; CANR 28, 51, 139; DLB 246; FL 1:1; FW; MTCW 1, 2; MTFW 2005
Steiner, George 1929- .... **CLC 24, 221**
  See also CA 73-76; CANR 31, 67, 108; DAM NOV; DLB 67, 299; EWL 3; MTCW 1, 2; MTFW 2005; RGHL; SATA 62
Steiner, K. Leslie
  See Delany, Samuel R., Jr.
Steiner, Rudolf 1861-1925 .... **TCLC 13**
  See also CA 107

Stendhal 1783-1842 .... **NCLC 23, 46, 178; SSC 27; WLC 5**
  See also DA; DA3; DAB; DAC; DAM MST, NOV; DLB 119; EW 5; GFL 1789 to the Present; RGWL 2, 3; TWA
Stephen, Adeline Virginia
  See Woolf, (Adeline) Virginia
Stephen, Sir Leslie 1832-1904 .... **TCLC 23**
  See also BRW 5; CA 123; DLB 57, 144, 190
Stephen, Sir Leslie
  See Stephen, Sir Leslie
Stephen, Virginia
  See Woolf, (Adeline) Virginia
Stephens, James 1882(?)-1950 .... **SSC 50; TCLC 4**
  See also CA 104; 192; DLB 19, 153, 162; EWL 3; FANT; RGEL 2; SUFW
Stephens, Reed
  See Donaldson, Stephen R(eeder)
Steptoe, Lydia
  See Barnes, Djuna
  See also GLL 1
Sterchi, Beat 1949 .... **CLC 65**
  See also CA 203
Sterling, Brett
  See Bradbury, Ray; Hamilton, Edmond
Sterling, Bruce 1954- .... **CLC 72**
  See also CA 119; CANR 44, 135; CN 7; MTFW 2005; SCFW 2; SFW 4
Sterling, George 1869-1926 .... **TCLC 20**
  See also CA 117; 165; DLB 54
Stern, Gerald 1925- .... **CLC 40, 100**
  See also AMWS 9; CA 81-84; CANR 28, 94; CP 3, 4, 5, 6, 7; DLB 105; RGAL 4
Stern, Richard (Gustave) 1928- ... **CLC 4, 39**
  See also CA 1-4R; CANR 1, 25, 52, 120; CN 1, 2, 3, 4, 5, 6, 7; DLB 218; DLBY 1987; INT CANR-25
Sternberg, Josef von 1894-1969 .... **CLC 20**
  See also CA 81-84
Sterne, Laurence 1713-1768 .... **LC 2, 48; WLC 5**
  See also BRW 3; BRWC 1; CDBLB 1660-1789; DA; DAB; DAC; DAM MST, NOV; DLB 39; RGEL 2; TEA
Sternheim, (William Adolf) Carl
  1878-1942 .... **TCLC 8**
  See also CA 105; 193; DLB 56, 118; EWL 3; IDTP; RGWL 2, 3
Stevens, Margaret Dean
  See Aldrich, Bess Streeter
Stevens, Mark 1951- .... **CLC 34**
  See also CA 122
Stevens, Wallace 1879-1955 . **PC 6; TCLC 3, 12, 45; WLC 5**
  See also AMW; AMWR 1; CA 104; 124; CDALB 1929-1941; DA; DA3; DAB; DAC; DAM MST, POET; DLB 54; EWL 3; EXPP; MAL 5; MTCW 1, 2; PAB; PFS 13, 16; RGAL 4; TUS; WP
Stevenson, Anne (Katharine) 1933- .. **CLC 7, 33**
  See also BRWS 6; CA 17-20R; CAAS 9; CANR 9, 33, 123; CP 3, 4, 5, 6, 7; CWP; DLB 40; MTCW 1; RHW
Stevenson, Robert Louis (Balfour)
  1850-1894 ...... **NCLC 5, 14, 63; SSC 11, 51; WLC 5**
  See also AAYA 24; BPFB 3; BRW 5; BRWC 1; BRWR 1; BYA 1, 2, 4, 13; CDBLB 1890-1914; CLR 10, 11, 107; DA; DA3; DAB; DAC; DAM MST, NOV; DLB 18, 57, 141, 156, 174; DLBD 13; GL 3; HGG; JRDA; LAIT 1, 3; MAICYA 1, 2; NFS 11, 20; RGEL 2; RGSF 2; SATA 100; SUFW; TEA; WCH; WLIT 4; WYA; YABC 2; YAW

Stewart, J(ohn) I(nnes) M(ackintosh)
  1906-1994 .... **CLC 7, 14, 32**
  See Innes, Michael
  See also CA 85-88; 147; CAAS 3; CANR 47; CMW 4; CN 1, 2, 3, 4, 5; MTCW 1, 2
Stewart, Mary (Florence Elinor)
  1916- .... **CLC 7, 35, 117**
  See also AAYA 29; BPFB 3; CA 1-4R; CANR 1, 59, 130; CMW 4; CPW; DAB; FANT; RHW; SATA 12; YAW
Stewart, Mary Rainbow
  See Stewart, Mary (Florence Elinor)
Stifle, June
  See Campbell, Maria
Stifter, Adalbert 1805-1868 .. **NCLC 41; SSC 28**
  See also CDWLB 2; DLB 133; RGSF 2; RGWL 2, 3
Still, James 1906-2001 .... **CLC 49**
  See also CA 65-68; 195; CAAS 17; CANR 10, 26; CSW; DLB 9; DLBY 01; SATA 29; SATA-Obit 127
Sting 1951-
  See Sumner, Gordon Matthew
  See also CA 167
Stirling, Arthur
  See Sinclair, Upton
Stitt, Milan 1941- .... **CLC 29**
  See also CA 69-72
Stockton, Francis Richard 1834-1902
  See Stockton, Frank R.
  See also AAYA 68; CA 108; 137; MAICYA 1, 2; SATA 44; SFW 4
Stockton, Frank R. .... **TCLC 47**
  See Stockton, Francis Richard
  See also BYA 4, 13; DLB 42, 74; DLBD 13; EXPS; SATA-Brief 32; SSFS 3; SUFW; WCH
Stoddard, Charles
  See Kuttner, Henry
Stoker, Abraham 1847-1912
  See Stoker, Bram
  See also CA 105; 150; DA; DA3; DAC; DAM MST, NOV; HGG; MTFW 2005; SATA 29
Stoker, Bram . **SSC 62; TCLC 8, 144; WLC 6**
  See Stoker, Abraham
  See also AAYA 23; BPFB 3; BRWS 3; BYA 5; CDBLB 1890-1914; DAB; DLB 304; GL 3; LATS 1:1; NFS 18; RGEL 2; SUFW; TEA; WLIT 4
Stolz, Mary (Slattery) 1920- .... **CLC 12**
  See also AAYA 8; AITN 1; CA 5-8R; CANR 13, 41, 112; JRDA; MAICYA 1, 2; SAAS 3; SATA 10, 71, 133; YAW
Stone, Irving 1903-1989 .... **CLC 7**
  See also AITN 1; BPFB 3; CA 1-4R; 129; CAAS 3; CANR 1, 23; CN 1, 2, 3, 4; CPW; DA3; DAM POP; INT CANR-23; MTCW 1, 2; MTFW 2005; RHW; SATA 3; SATA-Obit 64
Stone, Oliver 1946- .... **CLC 73**
  See also AAYA 15, 64; CA 110; CANR 55, 125
Stone, Oliver William
  See Stone, Oliver
Stone, Robert 1937- .... **CLC 5, 23, 42, 175**
  See also AMWS 5; BPFB 3; CA 85-88; CANR 23, 66, 95; CN 4, 5, 6, 7; DLB 152; EWL 3; INT CANR-23; MAL 5; MTCW 1; MTFW 2005
Stone, Ruth 1915- .... **PC 53**
  See also CA 45-48; CANR 2, 91; CP 5, 6, 7; CSW; DLB 105; PFS 19
Stone, Zachary
  See Follett, Ken

Suzuki, D. T.
   See Suzuki, Daisetz Teitaro
Suzuki, Daisetz T.
   See Suzuki, Daisetz Teitaro
Suzuki, Daisetz Teitaro
   1870-1966 .... **TCLC 109**
   See also CA 121; 111; MTCW 1, 2; MTFW
   2005
Suzuki, Teitaro
   See Suzuki, Daisetz Teitaro
Svevo, Italo .... **SSC 25; TCLC 2, 35**
   See Schmitz, Aron Hector
   See also DLB 264; EW 8; EWL 3; RGWL
   2, 3; WLIT 7
Swados, Elizabeth (A.) 1951- .... **CLC 12**
   See also CA 97-100; CANR 49; INT CA-
   97-100
Swados, Harvey 1920-1972 .... **CLC 5**
   See also CA 5-8R; 37-40R; CANR 6; CN
   1; DLB 2; MAL 5
Swan, Gladys 1934- .... **CLC 69**
   See also CA 101; CANR 17, 39; TCLE 1:2
Swanson, Logan
   See Matheson, Richard (Burton)
Swarthout, Glendon (Fred)
   1918-1992 .... **CLC 35**
   See also AAYA 55; CA 1-4R; 139; CANR
   1, 47; CN 1, 2, 3, 4, 5; LAIT 5; SATA 26;
   TCWW 1, 2; YAW
Swedenborg, Emanuel 1688-1772 ..... **LC 105**
Sweet, Sarah C.
   See Jewett, (Theodora) Sarah Orne
Swenson, May 1919-1989 ...... **CLC 4, 14, 61,
   106; PC 14**
   See also AMWS 4; CA 5-8R; 130; CANR
   36, 61, 131; CP 1, 2, 3, 4; DA; DAB;
   DAC; DAM MST, POET; DLB 5; EXPP;
   GLL 2; MAL 5; MTCW 1, 2; MTFW
   2005; PFS 16; SATA 15; WP
Swift, Augustus
   See Lovecraft, H. P.
Swift, Graham 1949- .... **CLC 41, 88, 233**
   See also BRWC 2; BRWS 5; CA 117; 122;
   CANR 46, 71, 128; CN 4, 5, 6, 7; DLB
   194, 326; MTCW 2; MTFW 2005; NFS
   18; RGSF 2
Swift, Jonathan 1667-1745 ..... **LC 1, 42, 101;
   PC 9; WLC 6**
   See also AAYA 41; BRW 3; BRWC 1;
   BRWR 1; BYA 5, 14; CDBLB 1660-1789;
   CLR 53; DA; DA3; DAB; DAC; DAM
   MST, NOV, POET; DLB 39, 95, 101;
   EXPN; LAIT 1; NFS 6; RGEL 2; SATA
   19; TEA; WCH; WLIT 3
Swinburne, Algernon Charles
   1837-1909 ... **PC 24; TCLC 8, 36; WLC
   6**
   See also BRW 5; CA 105; 140; CDBLB
   1832-1890; DA; DA3; DAB; DAC; DAM
   MST, POET; DLB 35, 57; PAB; RGEL 2;
   TEA
Swinfen, Ann .... **CLC 34**
   See also CA 202
Swinnerton, Frank (Arthur)
   1884-1982 .... **CLC 31**
   See also CA 202; 108; CN 1, 2, 3; DLB 34
Swinnerton, Frank Arthur
   1884-1982 .... **CLC 31**
   See also CA 108; DLB 34
Swithen, John
   See King, Stephen
Sylvia
   See Ashton-Warner, Sylvia (Constance)
Symmes, Robert Edward
   See Duncan, Robert
Symonds, John Addington
   1840-1893 .... **NCLC 34**
   See also DLB 57, 144

Symons, Arthur 1865-1945 .... **TCLC 11**
   See also CA 107; 189; DLB 19, 57, 149;
   RGEL 2
Symons, Julian (Gustave)
   1912-1994 .... **CLC 2, 14, 32**
   See also CA 49-52; 147; CAAS 3; CANR
   3, 33, 59; CMW 4; CN 1, 2, 3, 4, 5; CP 1,
   3, 4; DLB 87, 155; DLBY 1992; MSW;
   MTCW 1
Synge, (Edmund) J(ohn) M(illington)
   1871-1909 .... **DC 2; TCLC 6, 37**
   See also BRW 6; BRWR 1; CA 104; 141;
   CDBLB 1890-1914; DAM DRAM; DFS
   18; DLB 10, 19; EWL 3; RGEL 2; TEA;
   WLIT 4
Syruc, J.
   See Milosz, Czeslaw
Szirtes, George 1948- .... **CLC 46; PC 51**
   See also CA 109; CANR 27, 61, 117; CP 4,
   5, 6, 7
Szymborska, Wislawa 1923- ... **CLC 99, 190;
   PC 44**
   See also CA 154; CANR 91, 133; CDWLB
   4; CWP; CWW 2; DA3; DLB 232; DLBY
   1996; EWL 3; MTCW 2; MTFW 2005;
   PFS 15; RGHL; RGWL 3
T. O., Nik
   See Annensky, Innokenty (Fyodorovich)
Tabori, George 1914- .... **CLC 19**
   See also CA 49-52; CANR 4, 69; CBD; CD
   5, 6; DLB 245; RGHL
Tacitus c. 55-c. 117 .... **CMLC 56**
   See also AW 2; CDWLB 1; DLB 211;
   RGWL 2, 3; WLIT 8
Tagore, Rabindranath 1861-1941 .... **PC 8;
   SSC 48; TCLC 3, 53**
   See also CA 104; 120; DA3; DAM DRAM,
   POET; DLB 323; EWL 3; MTCW 1, 2;
   MTFW 2005; PFS 18; RGEL 2; RGSF 2;
   RGWL 2, 3; TWA
Taine, Hippolyte Adolphe
   1828-1893 .... **NCLC 15**
   See also EW 7; GFL 1789 to the Present
Talayesva, Don C. 1890-(?) .... **NNAL**
Talese, Gay 1932- .... **CLC 37, 232**
   See also AITN 1; CA 1-4R; CANR 9, 58,
   137; DLB 185; INT CANR-9; MTCW 1,
   2; MTFW 2005
Tallent, Elizabeth 1954- .... **CLC 45**
   See also CA 117; CANR 72; DLB 130
Tallmountain, Mary 1918-1997 .... **NNAL**
   See also CA 146; 161; DLB 193
Tally, Ted 1952- .... **CLC 42**
   See also CA 120; 124; CAD; CANR 125;
   CD 5, 6; INT CA-124
Talvik, Heiti 1904-1947 .... **TCLC 87**
   See also EWL 3
Tamayo y Baus, Manuel
   1829-1898 .... **NCLC 1**
Tammsaare, A(nton) H(ansen)
   1878-1940 .... **TCLC 27**
   See also CA 164; CDWLB 4; DLB 220;
   EWL 3
Tam'si, Tchicaya U
   See Tchicaya, Gerald Felix
Tan, Amy 1952- ...... **AAL; CLC 59, 120, 151**
   See also AAYA 9, 48; AMWS 10; BEST
   89:3; BPFB 3; CA 136; CANR 54, 105,
   132; CDALBS; CN 6, 7; CPW 1; DA3;
   DAM MULT, NOV, POP; DLB 173, 312;
   EXPN; FL 1:6; FW; LAIT 3, 5; MAL 5;
   MTCW 2; MTFW 2005; NFS 1, 13, 16;
   RGAL 4; SATA 75; SSFS 9; YAW
Tandem, Carl Felix
   See Spitteler, Carl
Tandem, Felix
   See Spitteler, Carl

Tanizaki, Jun'ichiro 1886-1965 ... **CLC 8, 14,
   28; SSC 21**
   See also CA 93-96; 25-28R; MJW; MTCW
   2; MTFW 2005; RGSF 2; RGWL 2
Tanizaki Jun'ichiro
   See Tanizaki, Jun'ichiro
   See also DLB 180; EWL 3
Tannen, Deborah 1945- .... **CLC 206**
   See also CA 118; CANR 95
Tannen, Deborah Frances
   See Tannen, Deborah
Tanner, William
   See Amis, Kingsley
Tante, Dilly
   See Kunitz, Stanley
Tao Lao
   See Storni, Alfonsina
Tapahonso, Luci 1953- .... **NNAL; PC 65**
   See also CA 145; CANR 72, 127; DLB 175
Tarantino, Quentin (Jerome)
   1963- .... **CLC 125, 230**
   See also AAYA 58; CA 171; CANR 125
Tarassoff, Lev
   See Troyat, Henri
Tarbell, Ida M(inerva) 1857-1944 . **TCLC 40**
   See also CA 122; 181; DLB 47
Tarkington, (Newton) Booth
   1869-1946 .... **TCLC 9**
   See also BPFB 3; BYA 3; CA 110; 143;
   CWRI 5; DLB 9, 102; MAL 5; MTCW 2;
   RGAL 4; SATA 17
Tarkovskii, Andrei Arsen'evich
   See Tarkovsky, Andrei (Arsenyevich)
Tarkovsky, Andrei (Arsenyevich)
   1932-1986 .... **CLC 75**
   See also CA 127
Tartt, Donna 1964(?)- .... **CLC 76**
   See also AAYA 56; CA 142; CANR 135;
   MTFW 2005
Tasso, Torquato 1544-1595 .... **LC 5, 94**
   See also EFS 2; EW 2; RGWL 2, 3; WLIT
   7
Tate, (John Orley) Allen 1899-1979 .. **CLC 2,
   4, 6, 9, 11, 14, 24; PC 50**
   See also AMW; CA 5-8R; 85-88; CANR
   32, 108; CN 1, 2; CP 1, 2; DLB 4, 45, 63;
   DLBD 17; EWL 3; MAL 5; MTCW 1, 2;
   MTFW 2005; RGAL 4; RHW
Tate, Ellalice
   See Hibbert, Eleanor Alice Burford
Tate, James (Vincent) 1943- ..... **CLC 2, 6, 25**
   See also CA 21-24R; CANR 29, 57, 114;
   CP 1, 2, 3, 4, 5, 6, 7; DLB 5, 169; EWL
   3; PFS 10, 15; RGAL 4; WP
Tate, Nahum 1652(?)-1715 .... **LC 109**
   See also DLB 80; RGEL 2
Tauler, Johannes c. 1300-1361 ...... **CMLC 37**
   See also DLB 179; LMFS 1
Tavel, Ronald 1940- .... **CLC 6**
   See also CA 21-24R; CAD; CANR 33; CD
   5, 6
Taviani, Paolo 1931- .... **CLC 70**
   See also CA 153
Taylor, Bayard 1825-1878 .... **NCLC 89**
   See also DLB 3, 189, 250, 254; RGAL 4
Taylor, C(ecil) P(hilip) 1929-1981 .... **CLC 27**
   See also CA 25-28R; 105; CANR 47; CBD
Taylor, Edward 1642(?)-1729 . **LC 11; PC 63**
   See also AMW; DA; DAB; DAC; DAM
   MST, POET; DLB 24; EXPP; RGAL 4;
   TUS
Taylor, Eleanor Ross 1920- .... **CLC 5**
   See also CA 81-84; CANR 70
Taylor, Elizabeth 1912-1975 ..... **CLC 2, 4, 29**
   See also CA 13-16R; CANR 9, 70; CN 1,
   2; DLB 139; MTCW 1; RGEL 2; SATA
   13

Thomson, James 1700-1748 .... **LC 16, 29, 40**
See also BRWS 3; DAM POET; DLB 95;
RGEL 2

Thomson, James 1834-1882 .... **NCLC 18**
See also DAM POET; DLB 35; RGEL 2

Thoreau, Henry David 1817-1862 .. **NCLC 7,
21, 61, 138; PC 30; WLC 6**
See also AAYA 42; AMW; ANW; BYA 3;
CDALB 1640-1865; DA; DA3; DAB;
DAC; DAM MST; DLB 1, 183, 223, 270,
298; LAIT 2; LMFS 1; NCFS 3; RGAL
4; TUS

Thorndike, E. L.
See Thorndike, Edward L(ee)

Thorndike, Edward L(ee)
1874-1949 .... **TCLC 107**
See also CA 121

Thornton, Hall
See Silverberg, Robert

Thorpe, Adam 1956- .... **CLC 176**
See also CA 129; CANR 92; DLB 231

Thubron, Colin (Gerald Dryden)
1939- .... **CLC 163**
See also CA 25-28R; CANR 12, 29, 59, 95;
CN 5, 6, 7; DLB 204, 231

Thucydides c. 455B.C.-c. 395B.C. . **CMLC 17**
See also AW 1; DLB 176; RGWL 2, 3;
WLIT 8

Thumboo, Edwin Nadason 1933- .... **PC 30**
See also CA 194; CP 1

Thurber, James (Grover)
1894-1961 .. **CLC 5, 11, 25, 125; SSC 1,
47**
See also AAYA 56; AMWS 1; BPFB 3;
BYA 5; CA 73-76; CANR 17, 39; CDALB
1929-1941; CWRI 5; DA; DA3; DAB;
DAC; DAM DRAM, MST, NOV; DLB 4,
11, 22, 102; EWL 3; EXPS; FANT; LAIT
3; MAICYA 1, 2; MAL 5; MTCW 1, 2;
MTFW 2005; RGAL 4; RGSF 2; SATA
13; SSFS 1, 10, 19; SUFW; TUS

Thurman, Wallace (Henry)
1902-1934 ,,,,, **BLC 3; HR 1:3; TCLC 6**
See also BW 1, 3; CA 104; 124; CANR 81;
DAM MULT; DLB 51

Tibullus c. 54B.C.-c. 18B.C. .... **CMLC 36**
See also AW 2; DLB 211; RGWL 2, 3;
WLIT 8

Ticheburn, Cheviot
See Ainsworth, William Harrison

Tieck, (Johann) Ludwig
1773-1853 .... **NCLC 5, 46; SSC 31**
See also CDWLB 2; DLB 90; EW 5; IDTP;
RGSF 2; RGWL 2, 3; SUFW

Tiger, Derry
See Ellison, Harlan

Tilghman, Christopher 1946- .... **CLC 65**
See also CA 159; CANR 135, 151; CSW;
DLB 244

Tillich, Paul (Johannes)
1886-1965 .... **CLC 131**
See also CA 5-8R; 25-28R; CANR 33;
MTCW 1, 2

Tillinghast, Richard (Williford)
1940- .... **CLC 29**
See also CA 29-32R; CAAS 23; CANR 26,
51, 96; CP 2, 3, 4, 5, 6, 7; CSW

Tillman, Lynne ? .... **CLC 231**
See also CA 173; CANR 144

Timrod, Henry 1828-1867 .... **NCLC 25**
See also DLB 3, 248; RGAL 4

Tindall, Gillian (Elizabeth) 1938- ...... **CLC 7**
See also CA 21-24R; CANR 11, 65, 107;
CN 1, 2, 3, 4, 5, 6, 7

Tiptree, James, Jr. .... **CLC 48, 50**
See Sheldon, Alice Hastings Bradley
See also DLB 8; SCFW 1, 2; SFW 4

Tirone Smith, Mary-Ann 1944- .... **CLC 39**
See also CA 118; 136; CANR 113; SATA
143

Tirso de Molina 1580(?)-1648 .... **DC 13;
HLCS 2; LC 73**
See also RGWL 2, 3

Titmarsh, Michael Angelo
See Thackeray, William Makepeace

**Tocqueville, Alexis (Charles Henri Maurice
Clerel Comte) de** 1805-1859 .. **NCLC 7,
63**
See also EW 6; GFL 1789 to the Present;
TWA

Toer, Pramoedya Ananta
1925-2006 .... **CLC 186**
See also CA 197; 251; RGWL 3

Toffler, Alvin 1928- .... **CLC 168**
See also CA 13-16R; CANR 15, 46, 67;
CPW; DAM POP; MTCW 1, 2

Toibin, Colm 1955- .... **CLC 162**
See also CA 142; CANR 81, 149; CN 7;
DLB 271

Tolkien, J(ohn) R(onald) R(euel)
1892-1973 .... **CLC 1, 2, 3, 8, 12, 38;
TCLC 137; WLC 6**
See also AAYA 10; AITN 1; BPFB 3;
BRWC 2; BRWS 2; CA 17-18; 45-48;
CANR 36, 134; CAP 2; CDBLB 1914-
1945; CLR 56; CN 1; CPW 1; CWRI 5;
DA; DA3; DAB; DAC; DAM MST, NOV,
POP; DLB 15, 160, 255; EFS 2; EWL 3;
FANT; JRDA; LAIT 1; LATS 1:2; LMFS
2; MAICYA 1, 2; MTCW 1, 2; MTFW
2005; NFS 8; RGEL 2; SATA 2, 32, 100;
SATA-Obit 24; SFW 4; SUFW; TEA;
WCH; WYA; YAW

Toller, Ernst 1893-1939 .... **TCLC 10**
See also CA 107; 186; DLB 124; EWL 3;
RGWL 2, 3

Tolson, M. B.
See Tolson, Melvin B(eaunorus)

Tolson, Melvin B(eaunorus)
1898(?)-1966 .... **BLC 3; CLC 36, 105**
See also AFAW 1, 2; BW 1, 3; CA 124; 89-
92; CANR 80; DAM MULT, POET; DLB
48, 76; MAL 5; RGAL 4

Tolstoi, Aleksei Nikolaevich
See Tolstoy, Alexey Nikolaevich

Tolstoi, Lev
See Tolstoy, Leo (Nikolaevich)
See also RGSF 2; RGWL 2, 3

Tolstoy, Aleksei Nikolaevich
See Tolstoy, Alexey Nikolaevich
See also DLB 272

Tolstoy, Alexey Nikolaevich
1882-1945 .... **TCLC 18**
See Tolstoy, Aleksei Nikolaevich
See also CA 107; 158; EWL 3; SFW 4

Tolstoy, Leo (Nikolaevich)
1828-1910 . **SSC 9, 30, 45, 54; TCLC 4,
11, 17, 28, 44, 79, 173; WLC 6**
See Tolstoi, Lev
See also AAYA 56; CA 104; 123; DA; DA3;
DAB; DAC; DAM MST, NOV; DLB 238;
EFS 2; EW 7; EXPS; IDTP; LAIT 2;
LATS 1:1; LMFS 1; NFS 10; SATA 26;
SSFS 5; TWA

Tolstoy, Count Leo
See Tolstoy, Leo (Nikolaevich)

Tomalin, Claire 1933- .... **CLC 166**
See also CA 89-92; CANR 52, 88; DLB
155

Tomasi di Lampedusa, Giuseppe 1896-1957
See Lampedusa, Giuseppe (Tomasi) di
See also CA 111; DLB 177; EWL 3; WLIT
7

Tomlin, Lily 1939(?)-
See Tomlin, Mary Jean
See also CA 117

Tomlin, Mary Jean .... **CLC 17**
See Tomlin, Lily

Tomline, F. Latour
See Gilbert, W(illiam) S(chwenck)

Tomlinson, (Alfred) Charles 1927- .... **CLC 2,
4, 6, 13, 45; PC 17**
See also CA 5-8R; CANR 33; CP 1, 2, 3, 4,
5, 6, 7; DAM POET; DLB 40; TCLE 1:2

Tomlinson, H(enry) M(ajor)
1873-1958 .... **TCLC 71**
See also CA 118; 161; DLB 36, 100, 195

Tonna, Charlotte Elizabeth
1790-1846 .... **NCLC 135**
See also DLB 163

Tonson, Jacob fl. 1655(?)-1736 .... **LC 86**
See also DLB 170

Toole, John Kennedy 1937-1969 ..... **CLC 19,
64**
See also BPFB 3; CA 104; DLBY 1981;
MTCW 2; MTFW 2005

Toomer, Eugene
See Toomer, Jean

Toomer, Eugene Pinchback
See Toomer, Jean

Toomer, Jean 1894-1967 .. **BLC 3; CLC 1, 4,
13, 22; HR 1:3; PC 7; SSC 1, 45;
TCLC 172; WLCS**
See also AFAW 1, 2; AMWS 3, 9; BW 1;
CA 85-88; CDALB 1917-1929; DA3;
DAM MULT; DLB 45, 51; EWL 3; EXPP;
EXPS; LMFS 2; MAL 5; MTCW 1, 2;
MTFW 2005; NFS 11; RGAL 4; RGSF 2;
SSFS 5

Toomer, Nathan Jean
See Toomer, Jean

Toomer, Nathan Pinchback
See Toomer, Jean

Torley, Luke
See Blish, James (Benjamin)

Tornimparte, Alessandra
See Ginzburg, Natalia

Torre, Raoul della
See Mencken, H(enry) L(ouis)

Torrence, Ridgely 1874-1950 .... **TCLC 97**
See also DLB 54, 249; MAL 5

Torrey, E(dwin) Fuller 1937- .... **CLC 34**
See also CA 119; CANR 71

Torsvan, Ben Traven
See Traven, B.

Torsvan, Benno Traven
See Traven, B.

Torsvan, Berick Traven
See Traven, B.

Torsvan, Berwick Traven
See Traven, B.

Torsvan, Bruno Traven
See Traven, B.

Torsvan, Traven
See Traven, B.

Tourneur, Cyril 1575(?)-1626 .... **LC 66**
See also BRW 2; DAM DRAM; DLB 58;
RGEL 2

Tournier, Michel 1924- .... **CLC 6, 23, 36, 95;
SSC 88**
See also CA 49-52; CANR 3, 36, 74, 149;
CWW 2; DLB 83; EWL 3; GFL 1789 to
the Present; MTCW 1, 2; SATA 23

Tournier, Michel Edouard
See Tournier, Michel

Tournimparte, Alessandra
See Ginzburg, Natalia

Towers, Ivar
See Kornbluth, C(yril) M.

Towne, Robert (Burton) 1936(?)- ..... **CLC 87**
See also CA 108; DLB 44; IDFW 3, 4

Tyndale, William c. 1484-1536 .... **LC 103**
  See also DLB 132
Tyutchev, Fyodor 1803-1873 .... **NCLC 34**
Tzara, Tristan 1896-1963 .... **CLC 47; PC 27;**
  TCLC 168
  See also CA 153; 89-92; DAM POET; EWL
  3; MTCW 2
Uchida, Yoshiko 1921-1992 .... **AAL**
  See also AAYA 16; BYA 2, 3; CA 13-16R;
  139; CANR 6, 22, 47, 61; CDALBS; CLR
  6, 56; CWRI 5; DLB 312; JRDA; MAI-
  CYA 1, 2; MTCW 1, 2; MTFW 2005;
  SAAS 1; SATA 1, 53; SATA-Obit 72
Udall, Nicholas 1504-1556 .... **LC 84**
  See also DLB 62; RGEL 2
Ueda Akinari 1734-1809 .... **NCLC 131**
Uhry, Alfred 1936- .... **CLC 55**
  See also CA 127; 133; CAD; CANR 112;
  CD 5, 6; CSW; DA3; DAM DRAM, POP;
  DFS 11, 15; INT CA-133; MTFW 2005
Ulf, Haerved
  See Strindberg, (Johan) August
Ulf, Harved
  See Strindberg, (Johan) August
Ulibarri, Sabine R(eyes)
  1919-2003 .... **CLC 83; HLCS 2**
  See also CA 131; 214; CANR 81; DAM
  MULT; DLB 82; HW 1, 2; RGSF 2
Unamuno (y Jugo), Miguel de
  1864-1936 .. **HLC 2; SSC 11, 69; TCLC**
  2, 9, 148
  See also CA 104; 131; CANR 81; DAM
  MULT, NOV; DLB 108, 322; EW 8; EWL
  3; HW 1, 2; MTCW 1, 2; MTFW 2005;
  RGSF 2; RGWL 2, 3; SSFS 20; TWA
Uncle Shelby
  See Silverstein, Shel
Undercliffe, Errol
  See Campbell, (John) Ramsey
Underwood, Miles
  See Glassco, John
Undset, Sigrid 1882-1949 .. **TCLC 3; WLC 6**
  See also CA 104; 129; DA; DA3; DAB;
  DAC; DAM MST, NOV; DLB 293; EW
  9; EWL 3; FW; MTCW 1, 2; MTFW
  2005; RGWL 2, 3
Ungaretti, Giuseppe 1888-1970 ... **CLC 7, 11,**
  15; PC 57
  See also CA 19-20; 25-28R; CAP 2; DLB
  114; EW 10; EWL 3; PFS 20; RGWL 2,
  3; WLIT 7
Unger, Douglas 1952- .... **CLC 34**
  See also CA 130; CANR 94, 155
Unsworth, Barry (Forster) 1930- .... **CLC 76,**
  127
  See also BRWS 7; CA 25-28R; CANR 30,
  54, 125; CN 6, 7; DLB 194, 326
Updike, John 1932- . **CLC 1, 2, 3, 5, 7, 9, 13,**
  15, 23, 34, 43, 70, 139, 214; SSC 13, 27;
  WLC 6
  See also AAYA 36; AMW; AMWC 1;
  AMWR 1; BPFB 3; BYA 12; CA 1-4R;
  CABS 1; CANR 4, 33, 51, 94, 133;
  CDALB 1968-1988; CN 1, 2, 3, 4, 5, 6,
  7; CP 1, 2, 3, 4, 5, 6, 7; CPW 1; DA;
  DA3; DAB; DAC; DAM MST, NOV,
  POET, POP; DLB 2, 5, 143, 218, 227;
  DLBD 3; DLBY 1980, 1982, 1997; EWL
  3; EXPP; HGG; MAL 5; MTCW 1, 2;
  MTFW 2005; NFS 12, 24; RGAL 4;
  RGSF 2; SSFS 3, 19; TUS
Updike, John Hoyer
  See Updike, John
Upshaw, Margaret Mitchell
  See Mitchell, Margaret (Munnerlyn)
Upton, Mark
  See Sanders, Lawrence
Upward, Allen 1863-1926 .... **TCLC 85**
  See also CA 117; 187; DLB 36

Urdang, Constance (Henriette)
  1922-1996 .... **CLC 47**
  See also CA 21-24R; CANR 9, 24; CP 1, 2,
  3, 4, 5, 6; CWP
Urfe, Honore d' 1567(?)-1625 .... **LC 132**
  See also DLB 268; GFL Beginnings to
  1789; RGWL 2, 3
Uriel, Henry
  See Faust, Frederick (Schiller)
Uris, Leon 1924-2003 .... **CLC 7, 32**
  See also AITN 1, 2; BEST 89:2; BPFB 3;
  CA 1-4R; 217; CANR 1, 40, 65, 123; CN
  1, 2, 3, 4, 5, 6; CPW 1; DA3; DAM NOV,
  POP; MTCW 1, 2; MTFW 2005; RGHL;
  SATA 49; SATA-Obit 146
Urista (Heredia), Alberto (Baltazar)
  1947- .... **HLCS 1**
  See Alurista
  See also CA 182; CANR 2, 32; HW 1
Urmuz
  See Codrescu, Andrei
Urquhart, Guy
  See McAlmon, Robert (Menzies)
Urquhart, Jane 1949- .... **CLC 90**
  See also CA 113; CANR 32, 68, 116, 157,
  CCA 1; DAC
Usigli, Rodolfo 1905-1979 .... **HLCS 1**
  See also CA 131; DLB 305; EWL 3; HW 1;
  LAW
Usk, Thomas (?)-1388 .... **CMLC 76**
  See also DLB 146
Ustinov, Peter (Alexander)
  1921-2004 .... **CLC 1**
  See also AITN 1; CA 13-16R; 225; CANR
  25, 51; CBD; CD 5, 6; DLB 13; MTCW
  2
U Tam'si, Gerald Felix Tchicaya
  See Tchicaya, Gerald Felix
U Tam'si, Tchicaya
  See Tchicaya, Gerald Felix
Vachss, Andrew 1942- .... **CLC 106**
  See also CA 118; 214; CAAE 214; CANR
  44, 95, 153; CMW 4
Vachss, Andrew H.
  See Vachss, Andrew
Vachss, Andrew Henry
  See Vachss, Andrew
Vaculik, Ludvik 1926- .... **CLC 7**
  See also CA 53-56; CANR 72; CWW 2;
  DLB 232, EWL 3
Vaihinger, Hans 1852 1933 .... **TCLC 71**
  See also CA 116; 166
Valdez, Luis (Miguel) 1940- ..... **CLC 84; DC**
  10; HLC 2
  See also CA 101; CAD; CANR 32, 81; CD
  5, 6; DAM MULT; DFS 5; DLB 122;
  EWL 3; HW 1; LAIT 4; LLW
Valenzuela, Luisa 1938- .... **CLC 31, 104;**
  HLCS 2; SSC 14, 82
  See also CA 101; CANR 32, 65, 123; CD-
  WLB 3; CWW 2; DAM MULT; DLB 113;
  EWL 3; FW; HW 1, 2; LAW; RGSF 2;
  RGWL 3
Valera y Alcala-Galiano, Juan
  1824-1905 .... **TCLC 10**
  See also CA 106
Valerius Maximus fl. 20- .... **CMLC 64**
  See also DLB 211
Valery, (Ambroise) Paul (Toussaint Jules)
  1871-1945 .... **PC 9; TCLC 4, 15**
  See also CA 104; 122; DA3; DAM POET;
  DLB 258; EW 8; EWL 3; GFL 1789 to
  the Present; MTCW 1, 2; MTFW 2005;
  RGWL 2, 3; TWA
Valle-Inclan, Ramon (Maria) del
  1866-1936 .... **HLC 2; TCLC 5**
  See del Valle-Inclan, Ramon (Maria)
  See also CA 106; 153; CANR 80; DAM
  MULT; DLB 134; EW 8; EWL 3; HW 2;
  RGSF 2; RGWL 2, 3

Vallejo, Antonio Buero
  See Buero Vallejo, Antonio
Vallejo, Cesar (Abraham)
  1892-1938 .... **HLC 2; TCLC 3, 56**
  See also CA 105; 153; DAM MULT; DLB
  290; EWL 3; HW 1; LAW; RGWL 2, 3
Valles, Jules 1832-1885 .... **NCLC 71**
  See also DLB 123; GFL 1789 to the Present
Vallette, Marguerite Eymery
  1860-1953 .... **TCLC 67**
  See Rachilde
  See also CA 182; DLB 123, 192
Valle Y Pena, Ramon del
  See Valle-Inclan, Ramon (Maria) del
Van Ash, Cay 1918-1994 .... **CLC 34**
  See also CA 220
Vanbrugh, Sir John 1664-1726 .... **LC 21**
  See also BRW 2; DAM DRAM; DLB 80;
  IDTP; RGEL 2
Van Campen, Karl
  See Campbell, John W(ood, Jr.)
Vance, Gerald
  See Silverberg, Robert
Vance, Jack 1916-
  See Queen, Ellery; Vance, John Holbrook
  See also CA 29-32R; CANR 17, 65, 154;
  CMW 4; MTCW 1
Vance, John Holbrook .... **CLC 35**
  See Vance, Jack
  See also DLB 8; FANT; SCFW 1, 2; SFW
  4; SUFW 1, 2
Van Den Bogarde, Derek Jules Gaspard
  Ulric Niven 1921-1999 .... **CLC 14**
  See Bogarde, Dirk
  See also CA 77-80; 179
Vandenburgh, Jane .... **CLC 59**
  See also CA 168
Vanderhaeghe, Guy 1951- .... **CLC 41**
  See also BPFB 3; CA 113; CANR 72, 145;
  CN 7
van der Post, Laurens (Jan)
  1906-1996 .... **CLC 5**
  See also AFW; CA 5-8R; 155; CANR 35;
  CN 1, 2, 3, 4, 5, 6; DLB 204; RGEL 2
van de Wetering, Janwillem 1931- ... **CLC 47**
  See also CA 49-52; CANR 4, 62, 90; CMW
  4
Van Dine, S. S. .... **TCLC 23**
  See Wright, Willard Huntington
  See also DLB 306; MSW
Van Doren, Carl (Clinton)
  1885-1950 .... **TCLC 18**
  See also CA 111; 168
Van Doren, Mark 1894-1972 .... **CLC 6, 10**
  See also CA 1-4R; 37-40R; CANR 3; CN
  1; CP 1; DLB 45, 284; MAL 5; MTCW
  1, 2; RGAL 4
Van Druten, John (William)
  1901-1957 .... **TCLC 2**
  See also CA 104; 161; DLB 10; MAL 5;
  RGAL 4
Van Duyn, Mona 1921-2004 .... **CLC 3, 7, 63,**
  116
  See also CA 9-12R; 234; CANR 7, 38, 60,
  116; CP 1, 2, 3, 4, 5, 6, 7; CWP; DAM
  POET; DLB 5; MAL 5; MTFW 2005;
  PFS 20
Van Dyne, Edith
  See Baum, L(yman) Frank
van Itallie, Jean-Claude 1936- .... **CLC 3**
  See also CA 45-48; CAAS 2; CAD; CANR
  1, 48; CD 5, 6; DLB 7
Van Loot, Cornelius Obenchain
  See Roberts, Kenneth (Lewis)
van Ostaijen, Paul 1896-1928 .... **TCLC 33**
  See also CA 163
Van Peebles, Melvin 1932- .... **CLC 2, 20**
  See also BW 2, 3; CA 85-88; CANR 27,
  67, 82; DAM MULT

Voinovich, Vladimir 1932- .. **CLC 10, 49, 147**
See also CA 81-84; CAAS 12; CANR 33,
67, 150; CWW 2; DLB 302; MTCW 1

Voinovich, Vladimir Nikolaevich
See Voinovich, Vladimir

Vollmann, William T. 1959- ...... **CLC 89, 227**
See also CA 134; CANR 67, 116; CN 7;
CPW; DA3; DAM NOV, POP; MTCW 2;
MTFW 2005

Voloshinov, V. N.
See Bakhtin, Mikhail Mikhailovich

Voltaire 1694-1778 . **LC 14, 79, 110; SSC 12;
WLC 6**
See also BYA 13; DA; DA3; DAB; DAC;
DAM DRAM, MST; DLB 314; EW 4;
GFL Beginnings to 1789; LATS 1:1;
LMFS 1; NFS 7; RGWL 2, 3; TWA

von Aschendrof, Baron Ignatz
See Ford, Ford Madox

von Chamisso, Adelbert
See Chamisso, Adelbert von

von Daeniken, Erich 1935- .... **CLC 30**
See also AITN 1; CA 37-40R; CANR 17,
44

von Daniken, Erich
See von Daeniken, Erich

von Eschenbach, Wolfram c. 1170-c.
1220 .... **CMLC 5**
See Eschenbach, Wolfram von
See also CDWLB 2; DLB 138; EW 1;
RGWL 2

von Hartmann, Eduard
1842-1906 .... **TCLC 96**

von Hayek, Friedrich August
See Hayek, F(riedrich) A(ugust von)

von Heidenstam, (Carl Gustaf) Verner
See Heidenstam, (Carl Gustaf) Verner von

von Heyse, Paul (Johann Ludwig)
See Heyse, Paul (Johann Ludwig von)

von Hofmannsthal, Hugo
See Hofmannsthal, Hugo von

von Horvath, Odon
See von Horvath, Odon

von Horvath, Odon
See von Horvath, Odon

von Horvath, Odon 1901-1938 .... **TCLC 45**
See von Horvath, Oedoen
See also CA 118; 194; DLB 85, 124; RGWL
2, 3

von Horvath, Oedoen
See von Horvath, Odon
See also CA 184

von Kleist, Heinrich
See Kleist, Heinrich von

Vonnegut, Kurt, Jr.
See Vonnegut, Kurt

Vonnegut, Kurt 1922- ... **CLC 1, 2, 3, 4, 5, 8,
12, 22, 40, 60, 111, 212; SSC 8; WLC 6**
See also AAYA 6, 44; AITN 1; AMWS 2;
BEST 90:4; BPFB 3; BYA 3, 14; CA
1-4R; CANR 1, 25, 49, 75, 92; CDALB
1968-1988; CN 1, 2, 3, 4, 5, 6, 7; CPW 1;
DA; DA3; DAB; DAC; DAM MST, NOV,
POP; DLB 2, 8, 152; DLBD 3; DLBY
1980; EWL 3; EXPN; EXPS; LAIT 4;
LMFS 2; MAL 5; MTCW 1, 2; MTFW
2005; NFS 3; RGAL 4; SCFW; SFW 4;
SSFS 5; TUS; YAW

Von Rachen, Kurt
See Hubbard, L. Ron

von Sternberg, Josef
See Sternberg, Josef von

Vorster, Gordon 1924- .... **CLC 34**
See also CA 133

Vosce, Trudie
See Ozick, Cynthia

Voznesensky, Andrei (Andreievich)
1933- .... **CLC 1, 15, 57**
See Voznesensky, Andrey
See also CA 89-92; CANR 37; CWW 2;
DAM POET; MTCW 1

Voznesensky, Andrey
See Voznesensky, Andrei (Andreievich)
See also EWL 3

Wace, Robert c. 1100-c. 1175 .... **CMLC 55**
See also DLB 146

Waddington, Miriam 1917-2004 .... **CLC 28**
See also CA 21-24R; 225; CANR 12, 30;
CCA 1; CP 1, 2, 3, 4, 5, 6, 7; DLB 68

Wagman, Fredrica 1937- .... **CLC 7**
See also CA 97-100; INT CA-97-100

Wagner, Linda W.
See Wagner-Martin, Linda (C.)

Wagner, Linda Welshimer
See Wagner-Martin, Linda (C.)

Wagner, Richard 1813-1883 ..... **NCLC 9, 119**
See also DLB 129; EW 6

Wagner-Martin, Linda (C.) 1936- .... **CLC 50**
See also CA 159; CANR 135

Wagoner, David (Russell) 1926- .... **CLC 3, 5,
15; PC 33**
See also AMWS 9; CA 1-4R; CAAS 3;
CANR 2, 71; CN 1, 2, 3, 4, 5, 6, 7; CP 1,
2, 3, 4, 5, 6, 7; DLB 5, 256; SATA 14;
TCWW 1, 2

Wah, Fred(erick James) 1939- .... **CLC 44**
See also CA 107; 141; CP 1, 6, 7; DLB 60

Wahloo, Per 1926-1975 .... **CLC 7**
See also BPFB 3; CA 61-64; CANR 73;
CMW 4; MSW

Wahloo, Peter
See Wahloo, Per

Wain, John (Barrington) 1925-1994 . **CLC 2,
11, 15, 46**
See also CA 5-8R; 145; CAAS 4; CANR
23, 54; CDBLB 1960 to Present; CN 1, 2,
3, 4, 5; CP 1, 2, 3, 4, 5; DLB 15, 27, 139,
155; EWL 3; MTCW 1, 2; MTFW 2005

Wajda, Andrzej 1926- .... **CLC 16, 219**
See also CA 102

Wakefield, Dan 1932- .... **CLC 7**
See also CA 21-24R; 211; CAAE 211;
CAAS 7; CN 4, 5, 6, 7

Wakefield, Herbert Russell
1888-1965 .... **TCLC 120**
See also CA 5-8R; CANR 77; HGG; SUFW

Wakoski, Diane 1937- ...... **CLC 2, 4, 7, 9, 11,
40; PC 15**
See also CA 13-16R, 216; CAAE 216;
CAAS 1; CANR 9, 60, 106; CP 1, 2, 3, 4,
5, 6, 7; CWP; DAM POET; DLB 5; INT
CANR-9; MAL 5; MTCW 2; MTFW
2005

Wakoski-Sherbell, Diane
See Wakoski, Diane

Walcott, Derek 1930- ... **BLC 3; CLC 2, 4, 9,
14, 25, 42, 67, 76, 160; DC 7; PC 46**
See also BW 2; CA 89-92; CANR 26, 47,
75, 80, 130; CBD; CD 5, 6; CDWLB 3;
CP 1, 2, 3, 4, 5, 6, 7; DA3; DAB; DAC;
DAM MST, MULT, POET; DLB 117;
DLBY 1981; DNFS 1; EFS 1; EWL 3;
LMFS 2; MTCW 1, 2; MTFW 2005; PFS
6; RGEL 2; TWA; WWE 1

Waldman, Anne (Lesley) 1945- .... **CLC 7**
See also BG 1:3; CA 37-40R; CAAS 17;
CANR 34, 69, 116; CP 1, 2, 3, 4, 5, 6, 7;
CWP; DLB 16

Waldo, E. Hunter
See Sturgeon, Theodore (Hamilton)

Waldo, Edward Hamilton
See Sturgeon, Theodore (Hamilton)

Walker, Alice 1944- ...... **BLC 3; CLC 5, 6, 9,
19, 27, 46, 58, 103, 167; PC 30; SSC 5,
97; WLCS**
See also AAYA 3, 33; AFAW 1, 2; AMWS
3; BEST 89:4; BPFB 3; BW 2, 3; CA 37-
40R; CANR 9, 27, 49, 66, 82, 131;
CDALB 1968-1988; CN 4, 5, 6, 7; CPW;
CSW; DA; DA3; DAB; DAC; DAM MST,
MULT, NOV, POET, POP; DLB 6, 33,
143; EWL 3; EXPN; EXPS; FL 1:6; FW;
INT CANR-27; LAIT 3; MAL 5; MBL;
MTCW 1, 2; MTFW 2005; NFS 5; RGAL
4; RGSF 2; SATA 31; SSFS 2, 11; TUS;
YAW

Walker, Alice Malsenior
See Walker, Alice

Walker, David Harry 1911-1992 ...... **CLC 14**
See also CA 1-4R; 137; CANR 1; CN 1, 2;
CWRI 5; SATA 8; SATA-Obit 71

Walker, Edward Joseph 1934-2004
See Walker, Ted
See also CA 21-24R; 226; CANR 12, 28,
53

Walker, George F(rederick) 1947- .. **CLC 44,
61**
See also CA 103; CANR 21, 43, 59; CD 5,
6; DAB; DAC; DAM MST; DLB 60

Walker, Joseph A. 1935-2003 .... **CLC 19**
See also BW 1, 3; CA 89-92; CAD; CANR
26, 143; CD 5, 6; DAM DRAM, MST;
DFS 12; DLB 38

Walker, Margaret 1915-1998 .. **BLC; CLC 1,
6; PC 20; TCLC 129**
See also AFAW 1, 2; BW 2, 3; CA 73-76;
172; CANR 26, 54, 76, 136; CN 1, 2, 3,
4, 5, 6; CP 1, 2, 3, 4, 5, 6; CSW; DAM
MULT; DLB 76, 152; EXPP; FW; MAL
5; MTCW 1, 2; MTFW 2005; RGAL 4;
RHW

Walker, Ted .... **CLC 13**
See Walker, Edward Joseph
See also CP 1, 2, 3, 4, 5, 6, 7; DLB 40

Wallace, David Foster 1962- ... **CLC 50, 114;
SSC 68**
See also AAYA 50; AMWS 10; CA 132;
CANR 59, 133; CN 7; DA3; MTCW 2;
MTFW 2005

Wallace, Dexter
See Masters, Edgar Lee

Wallace, (Richard Horatio) Edgar
1875-1932 ...., **TCLC 57**
See also CA 115; 218; CMW 4; DLB 70;
MSW; RGEL 2

Wallace, Irving 1916-1990 .... **CLC 7, 13**
See also AITN 1; BPFB 3; CA 1-4R; 132;
CAAS 1; CANR 1, 27; CPW; DAM NOV,
POP; INT CANR-27; MTCW 1, 2

Wallant, Edward Lewis 1926-1962 ... **CLC 5,
10**
See also CA 1-4R; CANR 22; DLB 2, 28,
143, 299; EWL 3; MAL 5; MTCW 1, 2;
RGAL 4; RGHL

Wallas, Graham 1858-1932 .... **TCLC 91**

Waller, Edmund 1606-1687 .... **LC 86; PC 72**
See also BRW 2; DAM POET; DLB 126;
PAB; RGEL 2

Walley, Byron
See Card, Orson Scott

Walpole, Horace 1717-1797 .... **LC 2, 49**
See also BRW 3; DLB 39, 104, 213; GL 3;
HGG; LMFS 1; RGEL 2; SUFW 1; TEA

Walpole, Hugh (Seymour)
1884-1941 .... **TCLC 5**
See also CA 104; 165; DLB 34; HGG;
MTCW 2; RGEL 2; RHW

Walrond, Eric (Derwent) 1898-1966 . **HR 1:3**
See also BW 1; CA 125; DLB 51

Walser, Martin 1927- .... **CLC 27, 183**
See also CA 57-60; CANR 8, 46, 145;
CWW 2; DLB 75, 124; EWL 3

Weiss, Peter (Ulrich) 1916-1982 .. **CLC 3, 15, 51; TCLC 152**
See also CA 45-48; 106; CANR 3; DAM DRAM; DFS 3; DLB 69, 124; EWL 3; RGHL; RGWL 2, 3

Weiss, Theodore (Russell)
1916-2003 .... **CLC 3, 8, 14**
See also CA 9-12R, 189; 216; CAAE 189; CAAS 2; CANR 46, 94; CP 1, 2, 3, 4, 5, 6, 7; DLB 5; TCLE 1:2

Welch, (Maurice) Denton
1915-1948 .... **TCLC 22**
See also BRWS 8, 9; CA 121; 148; RGEL 2

Welch, James (Phillip) 1940-2003 ..... **CLC 6, 14, 52; NNAL; PC 62**
See also CA 85-88; 219; CANR 42, 66, 107; CN 5, 6, 7; CP 2, 3, 4, 5, 6, 7; CPW; DAM MULT, POP; DLB 175, 256; LATS 1:1; NFS 23; RGAL 4; TCWW 1, 2

Weldon, Fay 1931- . **CLC 6, 9, 11, 19, 36, 59, 122**
See also BRWS 4; CA 21-24R; CANR 16, 46, 63, 97, 137; CDBLB 1960 to Present; CN 3, 4, 5, 6, 7; CPW; DAM POP, DLB 14, 194, 319; EWL 3; FW; HGG; INT CANR-16; MTCW 1, 2; MTFW 2005; RGEL 2; RGSF 2

Wellek, Rene 1903-1995 .... **CLC 28**
See also CA 5-8R; 150; CAAS 7; CANR 8; DLB 63; EWL 3; INT CANR-8

Weller, Michael 1942- .... **CLC 10, 53**
See also CA 85-88; CAD; CD 5, 6

Weller, Paul 1958- .... **CLC 26**

Wellershoff, Dieter 1925- .... **CLC 46**
See also CA 89-92; CANR 16, 37

Welles, (George) Orson 1915-1985 .. **CLC 20, 80**
See also AAYA 40; CA 93-96; 117

Wellman, John McDowell 1945-
See also Wellman, Mac
See also CA 166; CD 5

Wellman, Mac .... **CLC 65**
See also Wellman, John McDowell; Wellman, John McDowell
See also CAD; CD 6; RGAL 4

Wellman, Manly Wade 1903-1986 ... **CLC 49**
See also CA 1-4R; 118; CANR 6, 16, 44; FANT; SATA 6; SATA-Obit 47; SFW 4; SUFW

Wells, Carolyn 1869(?)-1942 .... **TCLC 35**
See also CA 113; 185; CMW 4; DLB 11

Wells, H(erbert) G(eorge) 1866-1946 . **SSC 6, 70; TCLC 6, 12, 19, 133; WLC 6**
See also AAYA 18; BPFB 3; BRW 6; CA 110; 121; CDBLB 1914-1945; CLR 64; DA; DA3; DAB; DAC; DAM MST, NOV; DLB 34, 70, 156, 178; EWL 3; EXPS; HGG; LAIT 3; LMFS 2; MTCW 1, 2; MTFW 2005; NFS 17, 20; RGEL 2; RGSF 2; SATA 20; SCFW 1, 2; SFW 4; SSFS 3; SUFW; TEA; WCH; WLIT 4; YAW

Wells, Rosemary 1943- .... **CLC 12**
See also AAYA 13; BYA 7, 8; CA 85-88; CANR 48, 120; CLR 16, 69; CWRI 5; MAICYA 1, 2; SAAS 1; SATA 18, 69, 114, 156; YAW

Wells-Barnett, Ida B(ell)
1862-1931 .... **TCLC 125**
See also CA 182; DLB 23, 221

Welsh, Irvine 1958- .... **CLC 144**
See also CA 173; CANR 146; CN 7; DLB 271

Welty, Eudora 1909-2001 .... **CLC 1, 2, 5, 14, 22, 33, 105, 220; SSC 1, 27, 51; WLC 6**
See also AAYA 48; AMW; AMWR 1; BPFB 3; CA 9-12R; 199; CABS 1; CANR 32, 65, 128; CDALB 1941-1968; CN 1, 2, 3, 4, 5, 6, 7; CSW; DA; DA3; DAB; DAC; DAM MST, NOV; DLB 2, 102, 143; DLBD 12; DLBY 1987, 2001; EWL 3; EXPS; HGG; LAIT 3; MAL 5; MBL; MTCW 1, 2; MTFW 2005; NFS 13, 15; RGAL 4; RGSF 2; RHW; SSFS 2, 10; TUS

Welty, Eudora Alice
See Welty, Eudora

Wen I-to 1899-1946 .... **TCLC 28**
See also EWL 3

Wentworth, Robert
See Hamilton, Edmond

Werfel, Franz (Viktor) 1890-1945 ... **TCLC 8**
See also CA 104; 161; DLB 81, 124; EWL 3; RGWL 2, 3

Wergeland, Henrik Arnold
1808-1845 .... **NCLC 5**

Wersba, Barbara 1932- .... **CLC 30**
See also AAYA 2, 30; BYA 6, 12, 13; CA 29-32R, 182; CAAE 182; CANR 16, 38; CLR 3, 78; DLB 52; JRDA; MAICYA 1, 2; SAAS 2; SATA 1, 58; SATA-Essay 103; WYA; YAW

Wertmueller, Lina 1928- .... **CLC 16**
See also CA 97-100; CANR 39, 78

Wescott, Glenway 1901-1987 .. **CLC 13; SSC 35**
See also CA 13-16R; 121; CANR 23, 70; CN 1, 2, 3, 4; DLB 4, 9, 102; MAL 5; RGAL 4

Wesker, Arnold 1932- .... **CLC 3, 5, 42**
See also CA 1-4R; CAAS 7; CANR 1, 33; CBD; CD 5, 6; CDBLB 1960 to Present; DAB; DAM DRAM; DLB 13, 310, 319; EWL 3; MTCW 1; RGEL 2; TEA

Wesley, Charles 1707-1788 .... **LC 128**
See also DLB 95; RGEL 2

Wesley, John 1703-1791 .... **LC 88**
See also DLB 104

Wesley, Richard (Errol) 1945- .... **CLC 7**
See also BW 1; CA 57-60; CAD; CANR 27; CD 5, 6; DLB 38

Wessel, Johan Herman 1742-1785 .... **LC 7**
See also DLB 300

West, Anthony (Panther)
1914-1987 .... **CLC 50**
See also CA 45-48; 124; CANR 3, 19; CN 1, 2, 3, 4; DLB 15

West, C. P.
See Wodehouse, P(elham) G(renville)

West, Cornel (Ronald) 1953- .... **BLCS; CLC 134**
See also CA 144; CANR 91; DLB 246

West, Delno C(loyde), Jr. 1936- .... **CLC 70**
See also CA 57-60

West, Dorothy 1907-1998 ...... **HR 1:3; TCLC 108**
See also BW 2; CA 143; 169; DLB 76

West, (Mary) Jessamyn 1902-1984 ... **CLC 7, 17**
See also CA 9-12R; 112; CANR 27; CN 1, 2, 3; DLB 6; DLBY 1984; MTCW 1, 2; RGAL 4; RHW; SATA-Obit 37; TCWW 2; TUS; YAW

West, Morris L(anglo) 1916-1999 ..... **CLC 6, 33**
See also BPFB 3; CA 5-8R; 187; CANR 24, 49, 64; CN 1, 2, 3, 4, 5, 6; CPW; DLB 289; MTCW 1, 2; MTFW 2005

West, Nathanael 1903-1940 .. **SSC 16; TCLC 1, 14, 44**
See also AMW; AMWR 2; BPFB 3; CA 104; 125; CDALB 1929-1941; DA3; DLB 4, 9, 28; EWL 3; MAL 5; MTCW 1, 2; MTFW 2005; NFS 16; RGAL 4; TUS

West, Owen
See Koontz, Dean R.

West, Paul 1930- .... **CLC 7, 14, 96, 226**
See also CA 13-16R; CAAS 7; CANR 22, 53, 76, 89, 136; CN 1, 2, 3, 4, 5, 6, 7; DLB 14; INT CANR-22; MTCW 2; MTFW 2005

West, Rebecca 1892-1983 ... **CLC 7, 9, 31, 50**
See also BPFB 3; BRWS 3; CA 5-8R; 109; CANR 19; CN 1, 2, 3; DLB 36; DLBY 1983; EWL 3; FW; MTCW 1, 2; MTFW 2005; NCFS 4; RGEL 2; TEA

Westall, Robert (Atkinson)
1929-1993 .... **CLC 17**
See also AAYA 12; BYA 2, 6, 7, 8, 9, 15; CA 69-72; 141; CANR 18, 68; CLR 13; FANT; JRDA; MAICYA 1, 2; MAICYAS 1; SAAS 2; SATA 23, 69; SATA-Obit 75; WYA; YAW

Westermarck, Edward 1862-1939 . **TCLC 87**

Westlake, Donald E. 1933- .... **CLC 7, 33**
See also BPFB 3; CA 17-20R; CAAS 13; CANR 16, 44, 65, 94, 137; CMW 4; CPW; DAM POP; INT CANR-16; MSW; MTCW 2; MTFW 2005

Westmacott, Mary
See Christie, Agatha (Mary Clarissa)

Weston, Allen
See Norton, Andre

Wetcheek, J. L.
See Feuchtwanger, Lion

Wetering, Janwillem van de
See van de Wetering, Janwillem

Wetherald, Agnes Ethelwyn
1857-1940 .... **TCLC 81**
See also CA 202; DLB 99

Wetherell, Elizabeth
See Warner, Susan (Bogert)

Whale, James 1889-1957 .... **TCLC 63**

Whalen, Philip (Glenn) 1923-2002 .... **CLC 6, 29**
See also BG 1:3; CA 9-12R; 209; CANR 5, 39; CP 1, 2, 3, 4, 5, 6, 7; DLB 16; WP

Wharton, Edith (Newbold Jones)
1862-1937 ... **SSC 6, 84; TCLC 3, 9, 27, 53, 129, 149; WLC 6**
See also AAYA 25; AMW; AMWC 2; AMWR 1; BPFB 3; CA 104; 132; CDALB 1865-1917; DA; DA3; DAB; DAC; DAM MST, NOV; DLB 4, 9, 12, 78, 189; DLBD 13; EWL 3; EXPS; FL 1:6; GL 3; HGG; LAIT 2, 3; LATS 1:1; MAL 5; MBL; MTCW 1, 2; MTFW 2005; NFS 5, 11, 15, 20; RGAL 4; RGSF 2; RHW; SSFS 6, 7; SUFW; TUS

Wharton, James
See Mencken, H(enry) L(ouis)

Wharton, William (a pseudonym)
1925- .... **CLC 18, 37**
See also CA 93-96; CN 4, 5, 6, 7; DLBY 1980; INT CA-93-96

Wheatley (Peters), Phillis
1753(?)-1784 ... **BLC 3; LC 3, 50; PC 3; WLC 6**
See also AFAW 1, 2; CDALB 1640-1865; DA; DA3; DAC; DAM MST, MULT, POET; DLB 31, 50; EXPP; FL 1:1; PFS 13; RGAL 4

Wheelock, John Hall 1886-1978 .... **CLC 14**
See also CA 13-16R; 77-80; CANR 14; CP 1, 2; DLB 45; MAL 5

Whim-Wham
See Curnow, (Thomas) Allen (Monro)

Whitaker, Rod 1931-2005
See Trevanian
See also CA 29-32R; 246; CANR 45, 153; CMW 4

White, Babington
See Braddon, Mary Elizabeth

Williams, Hiram Hank
 See Williams, Hank
Williams, Hiram King
 See Williams, Hank
 See also CA 188
Williams, Hugo (Mordaunt) 1942- ... CLC 42
 See also CA 17-20R; CANR 45, 119; CP 1,
 2, 3, 4, 5, 6, 7; DLB 40
Williams, J. Walker
 See Wodehouse, P(elham) G(renville)
Williams, John A(lfred) 1925- . BLC 3; CLC
 5, 13
 See also AFAW 2; BW 2, 3; CA 53-56, 195;
 CAAE 195; CAAS 3; CANR 6, 26, 51,
 118; CN 1, 2, 3, 4, 5, 6, 7; CSW; DAM
 MULT; DLB 2, 33; EWL 3; INT CANR-6;
 MAL 5; RGAL 4; SFW 4
Williams, Jonathan (Chamberlain)
 1929- .... CLC 13
 See also CA 9-12R; CAAS 12; CANR 8,
 108; CP 1, 2, 3, 4, 5, 6, 7; DLB 5
Williams, Joy 1944- .... CLC 31
 See also CA 41-44R; CANR 22, 48, 97
Williams, Norman 1952- .... CLC 39
 See also CA 118
Williams, Roger 1603(?)-1683 .... LC 129
 See also DLB 24
Williams, Sherley Anne 1944-1999 ... BLC 3;
 CLC 89
 See also AFAW 2; BW 2, 3; CA 73-76; 185;
 CANR 25, 82; DAM MULT, POET; DLB
 41; INT CANR-25; SATA 78; SATA-Obit
 116
Williams, Shirley
 See Williams, Sherley Anne
Williams, Tennessee 1911-1983 . CLC 1, 2, 5,
 7, 8, 11, 15, 19, 30, 39, 45, 71, 111; DC
 4; SSC 81; WLC 6
 See also AAYA 31; AITN 1, 2; AMW;
 AMWC 1; CA 5-8R; 108; CABS 3; CAD;
 CANR 31, 132; CDALB 1941-1968; CN
 1, 2, 3; DA; DA3; DAB; DAC; DAM
 DRAM, MST; DFS 17; DLB 7; DLBD 4;
 DLBY 1983; EWL 3; GLL 1; LAIT 4;
 LATS 1:2; MAL 5; MTCW 1, 2; MTFW
 2005; RGAL 4; TUS
Williams, Thomas (Alonzo)
 1926-1990 .... CLC 14
 See also CA 1-4R; 132; CANR 2
Williams, William C.
 See Williams, William Carlos
Williams, William Carlos
 1883-1963 .... CLC 1, 2, 5, 9, 13, 22, 42,
 67; PC 7; SSC 31; WLC 6
 See also AAYA 46; AMW; AMWR 1; CA
 89-92; CANR 34; CDALB 1917-1929;
 DA; DA3; DAB; DAC; DAM MST,
 POET; DLB 4, 16, 54, 86; EWL 3; EXPP;
 MAL 5; MTCW 1, 2; MTFW 2005; NCFS
 4; PAB; PFS 1, 6, 11; RGAL 4; RGSF 2;
 TUS; WP
Williamson, David (Keith) 1942- ..... CLC 56
 See also CA 103; CANR 41; CD 5, 6; DLB
 289
Williamson, Ellen Douglas 1905-1984
 See Douglas, Ellen
 See also CA 17-20R; 114; CANR 39
Williamson, Jack .... CLC 29
 See Williamson, John Stewart
 See also CAAS 8; DLB 8; SCFW 1, 2
Williamson, John Stewart 1908-2006
 See Williamson, Jack
 See also CA 17-20R; CANR 23, 70, 153;
 SFW 4
Willie, Frederick
 See Lovecraft, H. P.

Willingham, Calder (Baynard, Jr.)
 1922-1995 .... CLC 5, 51
 See also CA 5-8R; 147; CANR 3; CN 1, 2,
 3, 4, 5; CSW; DLB 2, 44; IDFW 3, 4;
 MTCW 1
Willis, Charles
 See Clarke, Arthur C.
Willy
 See Colette, (Sidonie-Gabrielle)
Willy, Colette
 See Colette, (Sidonie-Gabrielle)
 See also GLL 1
Wilmot, John 1647-1680 .... LC 75; PC 66
 See Rochester
 See also BRW 2; DLB 131; PAB
Wilson, A.N. 1950- .... CLC 33
 See also BRWS 6; CA 112; 122; CANR
 155; CN 4, 5, 6, 7; DLB 14, 155, 194;
 MTCW 2
Wilson, Andrew Norman
 See Wilson, A.N.
Wilson, Angus (Frank Johnstone)
 1913-1991 . CLC 2, 3, 5, 25, 34; SSC 21
 See also BRWS 1; CA 5-8R; 134; CANR
 21; CN 1, 2, 3, 4; DLB 15, 139, 155;
 EWL 3; MTCW 1, 2; MTFW 2005; RGEL
 2; RGSF 2
Wilson, August 1945-2005 .. BLC 3; CLC 39,
 50, 63, 118, 222; DC 2; WLCS
 See also AAYA 16; AFAW 2; AMWS 8; BW
 2, 3; CA 115; 122; 244; CAD; CANR 42,
 54, 76, 128; CD 5, 6; DA; DA3; DAB;
 DAC; DAM DRAM, MST, MULT; DFS
 3, 7, 15, 17; DLB 228; EWL 3; LAIT 4;
 LATS 1:2; MAL 5; MTCW 1, 2, MTFW
 2005; RGAL 4
Wilson, Brian 1942- .... CLC 12
Wilson, Colin (Henry) 1931- .... CLC 3, 14
 See also CA 1-4R; CAAS 5; CANR 1, 22,
 33, 77; CMW 4; CN 1, 2, 3, 4, 5, 6; DLB
 14, 194; HGG; MTCW 1; SFW 4
Wilson, Dirk
 See Pohl, Frederik
Wilson, Edmund 1895-1972 .. CLC 1, 2, 3, 8,
 24
 See also AMW; CA 1-4R; 37-40R; CANR
 1, 46, 110; CN 1; DLB 63; EWL 3; MAL
 5; MTCW 1, 2; MTFW 2005; RGAL 4;
 TUS
Wilson, Ethel Davis (Bryant)
 1888(?)-1980 .... CLC 13
 See also CA 102; CN 1, 2; DAC; DAM
 POET; DLB 68; MTCW 1; RGEL 2
Wilson, Harriet
 See Wilson, Harriet E. Adams
 See also DLB 239
Wilson, Harriet E.
 See Wilson, Harriet E. Adams
 See also DLB 243
Wilson, Harriet E. Adams
 1827(?)-1863(?) .... BLC 3; NCLC 78
 See Wilson, Harriet; Wilson, Harriet E.
 See also DAM MULT; DLB 50
Wilson, John 1785-1854 .... NCLC 5
Wilson, John (Anthony) Burgess 1917-1993
 See Burgess, Anthony
 See also CA 1-4R; 143; CANR 2, 46; DA3;
 DAC; DAM NOV; MTCW 1, 2; MTFW
 2005; NFS 15; TEA
Wilson, Lanford 1937- .. CLC 7, 14, 36, 197;
 DC 19
 See also CA 17-20R; CABS 3; CAD; CANR
 45, 96; CD 5, 6; DAM DRAM; DFS 4, 9,
 12, 16, 20; DLB 7; EWL 3; MAL 5; TUS
Wilson, Robert M. 1941- .... CLC 7, 9
 See also CA 49-52; CAD; CANR 2, 41; CD
 5, 6; MTCW 1
Wilson, Robert McLiam 1964- .... CLC 59
 See also CA 132; DLB 267

Wilson, Sloan 1920-2003 .... CLC 32
 See also CA 1-4R; 216; CANR 1, 44; CN
 1, 2, 3, 4, 5, 6
Wilson, Snoo 1948- .... CLC 33
 See also CA 69-72; CBD; CD 5, 6
Wilson, William S(mith) 1932- .... CLC 49
 See also CA 81-84
Wilson, (Thomas) Woodrow
 1856-1924 .... TCLC 79
 See also CA 166; DLB 47
Wilson and Warnke eds. .... CLC 65
Winchilsea, Anne (Kingsmill) Finch
 1661-1720
 See Finch, Anne
 See also RGEL 2
Winckelmann, Johann Joachim
 1717-1768 .... LC 129
 See also DLB 97
Windham, Basil
 See Wodehouse, P(elham) G(renville)
Wingrove, David 1954- .... CLC 68
 See also CA 133; SFW 4
Winnemucca, Sarah 1844-1891 .... NCLC 79;
 NNAL
 See also DAM MULT; DLB 175; RGAL 4
Winstanley, Gerrard 1609-1676 .... LC 52
Wintergreen, Jane
 See Duncan, Sara Jeannette
Winters, Arthur Yvor
 See Winters, Yvor
Winters, Janet Lewis .... CLC 41
 See Lewis, Janet
 See also DLBY 1987
Winters, Yvor 1900-1968 .... CLC 4, 8, 32
 See also AMWS 2; CA 11-12; 25-28R; CAP
 1; DLB 48; EWL 3; MAL 5; MTCW 1;
 RGAL 4
Winterson, Jeanette 1959- .... CLC 64, 158
 See also BRWS 4; CA 136; CANR 58, 116;
 CN 5, 6, 7; CPW; DA3; DAM POP; DLB
 207, 261; FANT; FW; GLL 1; MTCW 2;
 MTFW 2005; RHW
Winthrop, John 1588-1649 .... LC 31, 107
 See also DLB 24, 30
Wirth, Louis 1897-1952 .... TCLC 92
 See also CA 210
Wiseman, Frederick 1930- .... CLC 20
 See also CA 159
Wister, Owen 1860-1938 .... TCLC 21
 See also BPFB 3; CA 108; 162; DLB 9, 78,
 186; RGAL 4; SATA 62; TCWW 1, 2
Wither, George 1588-1667 .... LC 96
 See also DLB 121; RGEL 2
Witkacy
 See Witkiewicz, Stanislaw Ignacy
Witkiewicz, Stanislaw Ignacy
 1885-1939 .... TCLC 8
 See also CA 105; 162; CDWLB 4; DLB
 215; EW 10; EWL 3; RGWL 2, 3; SFW 4
Wittgenstein, Ludwig (Josef Johann)
 1889-1951 .... TCLC 59
 See also CA 113; 164; DLB 262; MTCW 2
Wittig, Monique 1935-2003 .... CLC 22
 See also CA 116; 135; 212; CANR 143;
 CWW 2; DLB 83; EWL 3; FW; GLL 1
Wittlin, Jozef 1896-1976 .... CLC 25
 See also CA 49-52; 65-68; CANR 3; EWL
 3
Wodehouse, P(elham) G(renville)
 1881-1975 . CLC 1, 2, 5, 10, 22; SSC 2;
 TCLC 108
 See also AAYA 65; AITN 2; BRWS 3; CA
 45-48; 57-60; CANR 3, 33; CDBLB
 1914-1945; CN 1, 2; CPW 1; DA3; DAB;
 DAC; DAM NOV; DLB 34, 162; EWL 3;
 MTCW 1, 2; MTFW 2005; RGEL 2;
 RGSF 2; SATA 22; SSFS 10
Woiwode, L.
 See Woiwode, Larry (Alfred)

Literary Criticism Series
Cumulative Topic Index

This index lists all topic entries in Thompson Gale's *Children's Literature Review* (CLR), *Classical and Medieval Literature Criticism* (CMLC), *Contemporary Literary Criticism* (CLC), *Drama Criticism* (DC), *Literature Criticism from 1400 to 1800* (LC), *Nineteenth Century Literature Criticism* (NCLC), *Short Story Criticism* (SSC), and *Twentieth-Century Literary Criticism* (TCLC). The index also lists topic entries in the Gale Critical Companion Collection, which includes the following publications: *The Beat Generation* (BG), *Feminism in Literature* (FL), *Gothic Literature* (GL), and *Harlem Renaissance* (HR).

Topic Index

TCLC Cumulative Nationality Index

Hasek, Jaroslav (Matej Frantisek) **4**
Hrabal, Bohumil **155**
Kafka, Franz **2, 6, 13, 29, 47, 53, 112**
Nezval, Vitezslav **44**

DANISH

Brandes, Georg (Morris Cohen) **10**
Hansen, Martin A(lfred) **32**
Jensen, Johannes V. **41**
Nexo, Martin Andersen **43**
Pontoppidan, Henrik **29**

DUTCH

Bok, Edward W. **101**
Couperus, Louis (Marie Anne) **15**
Heijermans, Herman **24**
Hillesum, Etty **49**
van Schendel, Arthur(-Francois-Émile) **56**

ENGLISH

Abbott, Edwin **139**
Abercrombie, Lascelles **141**
Alexander, Samuel **77**
Barbellion, W. N. P. **24**
Daring, Maurice **8**
Baring-Gould, Sabine **88**
Beerbohm, (Henry) Max(imilian) **1, 24**
Bell, Gertrude (Margaret Lowthian) **67**
Belloc, (Joseph) Hilaire (Pierre Sebastien
   Rene Swanton) **7, 18**
Bennett, (Enoch) Arnold **5, 20**
Benson, A.C. **123**
Benson, E(dward) F(rederic) **27**
Benson, Stella **17**
Bentley, E(dmund) C(lerihew) **12**
Beresford, J(ohn) D(avys) **81**
Besant, Annie (Wood) **9**
Blackmore, R(ichard) D(oddridge) **27**
Blackwood, Algernon (Henry) **5**
Bolt, Robert **175**
Bottomley, Gordon **107**
Bowen, Elizabeth **148**
Braddon, Mary Elizabeth **111**
Bramah, Ernest **72**
Bridges, Robert (Seymour) **1**
Brooke, Rupert (Chawner) **2, 7**
Buchanan, Robert **107**
Burke, Thomas **63**
Butler, Samuel **1, 33**
Butts, Mary **77**
Byron, Robert **67**
Caine, Hall **97**
Carpenter, Edward **88**
Carter, Angela **139**
Chesterton, G(ilbert) K(eith) **1, 6, 64**
Childers, (Robert) Erskine **65**
Churchill, Winston (Leonard Spencer) **113**
Clark, Kenneth Mackenzie **147**
Coleridge, Mary E(lizabeth) **73**
Collier, John **127**
Collingwood, R(obin) G(eorge) **67**
Compton-Burnett, Ivy **180**
Conrad, Joseph **1, 6, 13, 25, 43, 57**
Coppard, A(lfred) E(dgar) **5**
Corelli, Marie **51**
Crofts, Freeman Wills **55**
Crowley, Aleister **7**
Dahl, Roald **173**
Dale, Colin **18**
Davies, William Henry **5**
Delafield, E. M. **61**
de la Mare, Walter (John) **4, 53**
Dobson, Austin **79**
Doughty, Charles M(ontagu) **27**
Douglas, Keith (Castellain) **40**
Dowson, Ernest (Christopher) **4**
Doyle, Arthur Conan **7**
Drinkwater, John **57**
Dunsany **2, 59**
Eddison, E(ric) R(ucker) **15**
Elaine **18**

Elizabeth **41**
Ellis, (Henry) Havelock **14**
Firbank, (Arthur Annesley) Ronald **1**
Flecker, (Herman) James Elroy **43**
Ford, Ford Madox **1, 15, 39, 57, 172**
Forester, C(ecil) S(cott) **152**
Forster, E(dward) M(organ) **125**
Freeman, R(ichard) Austin **21**
Galsworthy, John **1, 45**
Gilbert, W(illiam) S(chwenck) **3**
Gill, Eric **85**
Gissing, George (Robert) **3, 24, 47**
Glyn, Elinor **72**
Gosse, Edmund (William) **28**
Grahame, Kenneth **64, 136**
Granville-Barker, Harley **2**
Gray, John (Henry) **19**
Gurney, Ivor (Bertie) **33**
Haggard, H(enry) Rider **11**
Hall, (Marguerite) Radclyffe **12**
Hardy, Thomas **4, 10, 18, 32, 48, 53, 72,
   143, 153**
Henley, William Ernest **8**
Hilton, James **21**
Hodgson, William Hope **13**
Hope, Anthony **83**
Housman, A(lfred) E(dward) **1, 10**
Housman, Laurence **7**
Hudson, W(illiam) H(enry) **29**
Hulme, T(homas) E(rnest) **21**
Hunt, Violet **53**
Jacobs, W(illiam) W(ymark) **22**
James, Montague (Rhodes) **6**
Jerome, Jerome K(lapka) **23**
Johnson, Lionel (Pigot) **19**
Kaye-Smith, Sheila **20**
Keynes, John Maynard **64**
Kipling, (Joseph) Rudyard **8, 17, 167**
Laski, Harold J(oseph) **79**
Lawrence, D(avid) H(erbert Richards) **2, 9,
   16, 33, 48, 61, 93**
Lawrence, T(homas) E(dward) **18**
Lee, Vernon **5**
Lee-Hamilton, Eugene (Jacob) **22**
Leverson, Ada **18**
Lindsay, David **15**
Lowndes, Marie Adelaide (Belloc) **12**
Lowry, (Clarence) Malcolm **6, 40**
Lucas, E(dward) V(errall) **73**
Macaulay, (Emilie) Rose **7, 44**
MacCarthy, (Charles Otto) Desmond **36**
Mackenzie, Compton (Edward Montague)
   116
Maitland, Frederic William **65**
Manning, Frederic **25**
Marsh, Edward **99**
McTaggart, John McTaggart Ellis **105**
Meredith, George **17, 43**
Mew, Charlotte (Mary) **8**
Meynell, Alice (Christina Gertrude
   Thompson) **6**
Middleton, Richard (Barham) **56**
Milne, A(lan) A(lexander) **6, 88**
Moore, G. E. **89**
Morrison, Arthur **72**
Muggeridge, Thomas (Malcolm) **120**
Murdoch, Iris **171**
Murry, John Middleton **16**
Myers, L(eopold) H(amilton) **59**
Nightingale, Florence **85**
Naipaul, Shiva(dhar) (Srinivasa) **153**
Noyes, Alfred **7**
Oppenheim, E(dward) Phillips **45**
Orage, Alfred Richard **157**
Orton, Joe **157**
Orwell, George **2, 6, 15, 31, 51, 128, 129**
Osborne, John **153**
Owen, Wilfred (Edward Salter) **5, 27**
Pankhurst, Emmeline (Goulden) **100**
Pinero, Arthur Wing **32**
Powys, T(heodore) F(rancis) **9**
Quiller-Couch, Arthur (Thomas) **53**

Richardson, Dorothy Miller **3**
Rolfe, Frederick (William Serafino Austin
   Lewis Mary) **12**
Rosenberg, Isaac **12**
Ruskin, John **20**
Sabatini, Rafael **47**
Saintsbury, George (Edward Bateman) **31**
Sapper **44**
Sayers, Dorothy L(eigh) **2, 15**
Shiel, M(atthew) P(hipps) **8**
Sinclair, May **3, 11**
Stapledon, (William) Olaf **22**
Stead, William Thomas **48**
Stephen, Leslie **23**
Strachey, (Giles) Lytton **12**
Summers, (Alphonsus Joseph-Mary
   Augustus) Montague **16**
Sutro, Alfred **6**
Swinburne, Algernon Charles **8, 36**
Symons, Arthur **11**
Thomas, (Philip) Edward **10**
Thompson, Francis (Joseph) **4**
Tolkien, J. R. R. **137**
Tomlinson, H(enry) M(ajor) **71**
Trotter, Wilfred **97**
Upward, Allen **85**
Van Druten, John (William) **2**
Wakefield, Herbert (Russell) **120**
Wallace, (Richard Horatio) Edgar **57**
Wallas, Graham **91**
Walpole, Hugh (Seymour) **5**
Ward, Mary Augusta **55**
Warner, Sylvia Townsend **131**
Warung, Price **45**
Webb, Mary Gladys (Meredith) **24**
Webb, Sidney (James) **22**
Welch, (Maurice) Denton **22**
Wells, H(erbert) G(eorge) **6, 12, 19, 133**
Whitehead, Alfred North **97**
Williams, Charles (Walter Stansby) **1, 11**
Wodehouse, P(elham) G(renville) **108**
Woolf, (Adeline) Virginia **1, 5, 20, 43, 56,
   101, 128**
Yonge, Charlotte (Mary) **48**
Zangwill, Israel **16**

ESTONIAN

Talvik, Heiti **87**
Tammsaare, A(nton) H(ansen) **27**

FILIPINO

Villa, José García **176**

FINNISH

Leino, Eino **24**
Soedergran, Edith (Irene) **31**
Westermarck, Edward **87**

FRENCH

Alain **41**
Apollinaire, Guillaume **3, 8, 51**
Arp, Jean **115**
Artaud, Antonin (Marie Joseph) **3, 36**
Bachelard, Gaston **128**
Barbusse, Henri **5**
Barrès, (Auguste-)Maurice **47**
Barthes, Roland **135**
Bataille, Georges **155**
Benda, Julien **60**
Bergson, Henri(-Louis) **32**
Bernanos, (Paul Louis) Georges **3**
Bernhardt, Sarah (Henriette Rosine) **75**
Bloy, Léon **22**
Bourget, Paul (Charles Joseph) **12**
Claudel, Paul (Louis Charles Marie) **2, 10**
Cocteau, Jean (Maurice Eugene Clement)
   119
Colette, (Sidonie-Gabrielle) **1, 5, 16**
Coppee, Francois **25**
Crevel, Rene **112**
Daumal, Rene **14**

Redcam, Tom **25**

JAPANESE

Abé, Kōbō **131**
Akutagawa Ryunosuke **16**
Dazai Osamu **11**
Endō, Shūsaku **152**
Futabatei, Shimei **44**
Hagiwara, Sakutaro **60**
Hayashi, Fumiko **27**
Ishikawa, Takuboku **15**
Kunikida, Doppo **99**
Masaoka, Shiki **18**
Mishima, Yukio **161**
Miyamoto, (Chujo) Yuriko **37**
Miyazawa, Kenji **76**
Mizoguchi, Kenji **72**
Mori Ogai **14**
Nagai, Kafu **51**
Nishida, Kitaro **83**
Noguchi, Yone **80**
Santoka, Taneda **72**
Shiga, Naoya **172**
Shimazaki Toson **5**
Suzuki, Daisetz Teitaro **109**
Yokomitsu, Riichi **47**
Yosano Akiko **59**

LATVIAN

Berlin, Isaiah **105**
Rainis, Jānis **29**

LEBANESE

Gibran, Kahlil **1, 9**

LESOTHAN

Mofolo, Thomas (Mokopu) **22**

LITHUANIAN

Kreve (Mickevicius), Vincas **27**

MEXICAN

Azuela, Mariano **3**
Gamboa, Federico **36**
Garro, Elena **153**
Gonzalez Martinez, Enrique **72**
Ibargüengoitia, Jorge **148**
Nervo, (Jose) Amado (Ruiz de) **11**
Reyes, Alfonso **33**
Romero, José Rubén **14**
Villaurrutia, Xavier **80**

NEPALI

Devkota, Laxmiprasad **23**

NEW ZEALANDER

Mander, (Mary) Jane **31**
Mansfield, Katherine **2, 8, 39, 164**

NICARAGUAN

Darío, Rubén **4**

NIGERIAN

Okigbo, Christopher **171**

NORWEGIAN

Bjoernson, Bjoernstjerne (Martinius) **7, 37**
Bojer, Johan **64**
Grieg, (Johan) Nordahl (Brun) **10**
Hamsun, Knut **151**
Ibsen, Henrik (Johan) **2, 8, 16, 37, 52**
Kielland, Alexander Lange **5**
Lie, Jonas (Lauritz Idemil) **5**
Obstfelder, Sigbjoern **23**
Skram, Amalie (Bertha) **25**
Undset, Sigrid **3**

PAKISTANI

Iqbal, Muhammad **28**

PERUVIAN

Arguedas, José María **147**
Palma, Ricardo **29**
Vallejo, César (Abraham) **3, 56**

POLISH

Asch, Sholem **3**
Borowski, Tadeusz **9**
Conrad, Joseph **1, 6, 13, 25, 43, 57**
Herbert, Zbigniew **168**
Peretz, Isaac Loeb **16**
Prus, Boleslaw **48**
Przybyszewski, Stanislaw **36**
Reymont, Wladyslaw (Stanislaw) **5**
Schulz, Bruno **5, 51**
Sienkiewicz, Henryk (Adam Alexander Pius) **3**
Singer, Israel Joshua **33**
Witkiewicz, Stanislaw Ignacy **8**

PORTUGUESE

Pessoa, Fernando (António Nogueira) **27**
Sa-Carniero, Mario de **83**

PUERTO RICAN

Hostos (y Bonilla), Eugenio Maria de **24**

ROMANIAN

Bacovia, George **24**
Caragiale, Ion Luca **76**
Rebreanu, Liviu **28**

RUSSIAN

Aldanov, Mark (Alexandrovich) **23**
Andreyev, Leonid (Nikolaevich) **3**
Annensky, Innokenty (Fyodorovich) **14**
Artsybashev, Mikhail (Petrovich) **31**
Babel, Isaak (Emmanuilovich) **2, 13, 171**
Bagritsky, Eduard **60**
Bakhtin, Mikhail **160**
Balmont, Konstantin (Dmitriyevich) **11**
Bely, Andrey **7**
Berdyaev, Nikolai (Aleksandrovich) **67**
Bergelson, David **81**
Blok, Alexander (Alexandrovich) **5**
Bryusov, Valery Yakovlevich **10**
Bulgakov, Mikhail (Afanas'evich) **2, 16, 159**
Bulgya, Alexander Alexandrovich **53**
Bunin, Ivan Alexeyevich **6**
Chekhov, Anton (Pavlovich) **3, 10, 31, 55, 96, 163**
Der Nister **56**
Eisenstein, Sergei (Mikhailovich) **57**
Esenin, Sergei (Alexandrovich) **4**
Fadeyev, Alexander **53**
Gladkov, Fyodor (Vasilyevich) **27**
Gumilev, Nikolai (Stepanovich) **60**
Gurdjieff, G(eorgei) I(vanovich) **71**
Guro, Elena **56**
Hippius, Zinaida **9**
Ilf, Ilya **21**
Ivanov, Vyacheslav Ivanovich **33**
Kandinsky, Wassily **92**
Khlebnikov, Velimir **20**
Khodasevich, Vladislav (Felitsianovich) **15**
Klimentov, Andrei Platonovich **14**
Korolenko, Vladimir Galaktionovich **22**
Kropotkin, Peter (Aleksieevich) **36**
Kuprin, Aleksander Ivanovich **5**
Kuzmin, Mikhail **40**
Lenin, V. I. **67**
Mandelstam, Osip (Emilievich) **2, 6**
Mayakovski, Vladimir (Vladimirovich) **4, 18**
Merezhkovsky, Dmitry Sergeyevich **29**
Nabokov, Vladimir (Vladimirovich) **108**
Olesha, Yuri **136**

Pavlov, Ivan Petrovich **91**
Petrov, Evgeny **21**
Pilnyak, Boris **23**
Prishvin, Mikhail **75**
Remizov, Aleksei (Mikhailovich) **27**
Rozanov, Vassili **104**
Shestov, Lev **56**
Sologub, Fyodor **9**
Stalin, Joseph **92**
Stanislavsky, Konstantin **167**
Tolstoy, Alexey Nikolaevich **18**
Tolstoy, Leo (Nikolaevich) **4, 11, 17, 28, 44, 79, 173**
Trotsky, Leon **22**
Tsvetaeva (Efron), Marina (Ivanovna) **7, 35**
Zabolotsky, Nikolai Alekseevich **52**
Zamyatin, Evgeny Ivanovich **8, 37**
Zhdanov, Andrei Alexandrovich **18**
Zoshchenko, Mikhail (Mikhailovich) **15**

SCOTTISH

Barrie, J(ames) M(atthew) **2, 164**
Brown, George Douglas **28**
Buchan, John **41**
Cunninghame Graham, Robert (Gallnigad) Bontine **19**
Davidson, John **24**
Doyle, Arthur Conan **7**
Frazer, J(ames) G(eorge) **32**
Lang, Andrew **16**
MacDonald, George **9, 113**
Muir, Edwin **2, 87**
Murray, James Augustus Henry **117**
Sharp, William **39**
Tey, Josephine **14**

SLOVENIAN

Cankar, Ivan **105**

SOUTH AFRICAN

Bosman, Herman Charles **49**
Campbell, (Ignatius) Roy (Dunnachie) **5**
La Guma, Alex **140**
Mqhayi, S(amuel) E(dward) K(rune Loliwe) **25**
Paton, Alan **165**
Plaatje, Sol(omon) T(shekisho) **73**
Schreiner, Olive (Emllle Albertina) **9**
Smith, Pauline (Urmson) **25**
Vilakazi, Benedict Wallet **37**

SPANISH

Alas (y Urena), Leopoldo (Enrique Garcia) **29**
Aleixandre, Vicente **113**
Barea, Arturo **14**
Baroja (y Nessi), Pio **8**
Benavente (y Martinez), Jacinto **3**
Blasco Ibáñez, Vicente **12**
Echegaray (y Eizaguirre), Jose (Maria Waldo) **4**
García Lorca, Federico **1, 7, 49, 181**
Jiménez (Mantecón), Juan Ramón **4, 183**
Machado (y Ruiz), Antonio **3**
Martinez Sierra, Gregorio **6**
Martinez Sierra, Maria (de la O'LeJarraga) **6**
Miro (Ferrer), Gabriel (Francisco Victor) **5**
Onetti, Juan Carlos **131**
Ortega y Gasset, José **9**
Pereda (y Sanchez de Porrua), Jose Maria de **16**
Pérez Galdós, Benito **27**
Ramoacn y Cajal, Santiago **93**
Salinas (y Serrano), Pedro **17**
Sender, Ramón **136**
Unamuno (y Jugo), Miguel de **2, 9, 148**
Valera y Alcala-Galiano, Juan **10**
Valle-Inclán, Ramón (Maria) del **5**

TCLC-187 Title Index

ISBN-13: 978-0-7876-8941-4
ISBN-10: 0-7876-8941-6

90000